James Payn

The Wheel and Cycling Trade Review

Vol. III - No. I

James Payn

The Wheel and Cycling Trade Review
Vol. III - No. I

ISBN/EAN: 9783744762588

Printed in Europe, USA, Canada, Australia, Japan

Cover: Foto ©Andreas Hilbeck / pixelio.de

More available books at **www.hansebooks.com**

The Wheel
and Cycling Trade Review

P. O. Box 444 N. Y.

3 Pub Row N. Y.

Vol. III.—No. 1.]   NEW YORK, MARCH 1, 1889.   [Whole Number, 53.

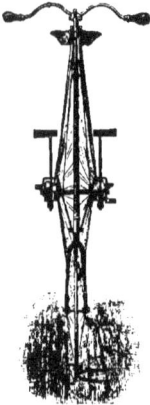

Warwick Perfections

READY TO FILL ORDERS.

BOYS' WHEELS,
YOUTHS' WHEELS,
MEN'S WHEELS,
LADIES' WHEELS.

The Warwick Perfection Ordinary is equal to the highest grade bicycles in material, construction and finish, and has a dozen points which make it the King of Ordinaries.

The Warwick Perfection Safety is suitable for either a lady or gentleman. It has a strong, light double-tube frame, anti-vibration spring-forks, *and is not sensitive.*

WILLIAM HALPIN & CO.,

No. 13 MURRAY STREET,

P. O. Box 2225.   NEW YORK.

Full Line of "Warwicks."   Full Line of "Clubs."

Large Stock of American Cycles.

SECOND-HAND WHEELS.

THE WHEEL

— AND —

CYCLING TRADE REVIEW.

Published every Friday morning.

Entered at the Post Office at second class rates.

Subscription Price, - - - $1.00 a year.
Foreign Subscriptions, - - - 6s. a year.
Single Copies, - - - - 5 Cents

Newsdealers may order through AM. NEWS CO.

All copy should be received by Monday.
Telegraphic news received till Wednesday noon.

Advertising rates on Application.

F. P. PRIAL, Editor and Proprietor
23 Park Row.

P. O. Box 444, **New York.**

Persons receiving sample copies of this paper are respectfully requested to examine its contents and give us their patronage, and as far as is convenient, aid in circulating the journal, and extend its influence in the cause which it so faithfully serves. Subscription price, $1 per year.

THE *Ironmonger*, the leading organ of the English hardware world, has a leader on the extent of the cycle trade, and advocates closer relations between hardware men and the manufacturers, on the ground that retail hardware stores are excellent distributing points for agents. The *Ironmonger's* comment suggests a theme productive of much interesting speculation. In this country we find wheels sold by perhaps two thousand agents, of which a very large proportion devote themselves solely to the sale of cycles, and as their territory is generally very small and their discounts not so large as are given on other articles of luxury, a fair proportion of these agents are financially irresponsible; they seldom increase their capital, being rarely able to make more than a good living. We also find—at least it is the opinion of the manufacturers whom we have consulted—that large sporting houses, which make their bicycle business a department, have not been so successful as those agents who make a specialty of the cycle business. To sum up, it may be safely stated that at the present time, the elements of friendship, sociability and popularity are really valuable capital, and that purchasing cyclists are more liable to be influenced by those considerations than are buyers in other markets. It is a question which time and the increase of the trade will solve, whether the retail cycle trade will be handled by large houses, as distributing agents, such as sporting goods and hardware houses, or whether the elements that at present influence sales will always remain.

AMERICAN cyclists have recently been astonished by the news that the Rudge Triplet had been driven one mile on the road in 2m. 18 1-5s., and that S. G. Whittaker had ridden a Rudge Safety one-half mile on the road in 1m. 9 2-5s. These performances were chronicled in the English cycling press and, as the more influential English cycling papers accepted and published them as records, we likewise accepted them as such. From a private letter, signed by a gentleman who is an authority on English sports, we learn that both the records alluded to above may not be *bona fide*. We

would endorse them as fakes were there not a possibility that perhaps our correspondent has been misinformed. At least our informant will not object to giving the English cycling press the benefit of the doubt, and the privilege of substantiating these two remarkable performances and clearing themselves of the charge of accepting as records performances made under circumstances which should prevent their acceptance as such. We quote from our correspondent's letter:

"You would doubtless like to know something about the 2:18 1-5 mile and other startling road feats—more than you are likely to receive from the British wheel press, which is bound, soul and body, to the advertisers. The 2:18 1-5 was accomplished like this: The start was flying, the course a selected road, straight-away, and for a considerable part down hill [Our correspondent indicates the grade by a line which would give an incline as steep as a hill road.] On a dead level, straight road, with smooth surface and the machine geared to 80 or 90, I believe the trotting record could be equaled. Whittaker's 1:09 2-5 half-mile was accomplished down hill."

AT the Nautilus Boat Club games, held at the Palace Rink, Brooklyn, February 21, the board track was fourteen laps to the mile, and the short straights were seven feet wide. Two facts are to be noted about this track, and they may be applied to any racing circuit of like description. It is not only dangerous to ride, but the limit man can always win, unless he is fouled and brought to grass by some of his competitors. In the race held on the Palace Rink track several men fell, bruising themselves more or less; those who did not fall rode so cautiously that they dropped to the rear and never had a chance of winning. We should advise racing cyclists not to compete on these small tracks; but if they will insist on doing so, they should also insist on the tracks being wide and the race of the "scratch" variety, that the nerviest man may win.

EDITORIAL VIEWS ON NEW JERSEY'S ROAD LAW.

There are only two papers in the State of New Jersey, thus far heard from, that oppose the proposed county road law. One is the Sussex *Herald*, which argues that the farmers have now such heavy taxes that they can't pay them, that there is really no such necessity for good roads as there used to be when it was a long ways to market, and that the demand for better roads is made chiefly by those who drive for pleasure. The other is the Plainfield *Times*, which argues that Plainfield has built up a national bank and secured a number of other valuable improvements in its town and throughout Somerset County, says of this bill:

"We sincerely trust the bill may become a law and that the movement may spread."

And the Warren *Republican*, which represents a very large agricultural district that is quite interested in roads, says:

The interest in the improvement of county roads is spreading. If we can judge from our exchanges; and as agitation in the local press is the first step toward better methods, the present sign is encouraging. But while these papers unite in deploring the existing condition of the only means of communication and agitating for some change. We all know real improvement can be hoped for until the lawmakers of each State unite with experienced engineers, and together formulate a law that will compel a change. We all know the roads are bad; that waste is wanted is the mind is clear; the method of making them better, and the means of totally abolishing the present stupdard system of not doing it. The opposition to improvement assessments will come from the

parties who will in the end be most benefited—that is, the farmer—and any new laws must be carefully framed, so as to be both just and firm with this element of our population. First of all, law is wanted to properly appropriate the cost of new work; enforce a well digested system of highways, and provide for the faithful execution of plans, with this power in hand. The legislative bodies must take the first step.

The only objection to this is that it is a little behind the date. The farmers of Union County have formally approved of Senator Miller's bill, which covers every point raised by the *Republican*. The State Board of Agriculture has endorsed it for the farmers of the State, and the Senate Committee on Agriculture has reported it favorably. The era of better roads is practically inaugurated, and the farmers of Union County are among the very first to see the advantages they will derive from them.—*Elizabeth Daily Journal.*

THE NEW JERSEY ROADS IMPROVEMENT BILL BECOMES A LAW.

TRENTON, N. J., Feb. 26.—The County Road bill has passed the Senate.

HARLEM WHEELMEN'S RECEPTION AND ENTERTAINMENT.

The Harlem Wheelmen's Entertainment Committee, composed of Messrs. Newcome, Rairbeck and Emanuel, have arranged an entertainment and reception for Wednesday evening, March 13, at West End Hall, 125th Street near Eighth Avenue. The entertainment will commence at 8 o'clock. Tickets will be sold at $1.

A CYCLIST RUNS INTO A JUDGE.

INDIANAPOLIS, Feb. 21.—As Supreme Court Judges Coffee and Berkshire came out of the Capitol grounds at noon to-day a careless wheelman ran into them. Judge Coffee was struck by the bicycle in his side and fell heavily to the pavement. His wrist was badly sprained and he was perhaps seriously injured. He was assisted to the Dennison House. Judge Berkshire also received slight injuries. The wheelman was not arrested.

N. A. A. A. BICYCLE HANDICAP.

The N. A. A. A. mammoth games will be held at Madison Square Garden on Saturday evening, commencing at eight o'clock. A very large number of entries have been received and the games will be more than usually interesting. Over fifty entries have been received for the 1½-mile bicycle handicap, the principal entries being as follows: Davis and Kingsland, scratch; Hanker, 15; Coningsby, 90; King, 75; Beazley, 80; T. J. Hall, Jr., 100; W. F. Murphy, 90; C. M. Murphy, 110; Wise, 75; Marshall, 65; Burhaus, 90; Hanson, 90; Kellum, 100; Zimmerman, 105; Class, 85; Schoefer, 65; Borland, 90; Matthews, 110; Jones, 100; Ostermayer, 105; Powers, 95; Waters, 100; Mellor, 120.

NEW YORK STATE BOARD OF OFFICERS MEET.

NEW YORK, February 23, 1889.

An adjourned meeting of the Board of Officers of this Division will be held at the New York Bicycle Club house, 146 West End Avenue, near Seventy-second Street, New York, at 8:30 o'clock, Monday evening, March 4. As certain amendments to our by-laws will be presented at this meeting, as well as other business demanding our attention, I earnestly request the attendance of every member.

Yours truly,

GEO. R. BIDWELL, *Chief Consul*

DECISION AGAINST SIDEWALK BICYCLING.

INDIANAPOLIS, February 25.

A novel case was decided Saturday by the Supreme Court, Chief-Justice Elliott delivering the opinion, wherein it was held that a person who "rudely and recklessly" rode a bicycle against a man standing on a sidewalk, was responsible in damages for an assault and battery. The Court, in its opinion, declares that inasmuch as bicycles are vehicles, and as sidewalks are exclusively for the use of footmen, no one has a right to ride a bicycle on the sidewalk. Coincident with this case is the singular fact that Judge Coffee, of the Supreme Court Bench, is now confined to his bed suffering seriously from a blow received from a bicycle only a few days ago.

SCRANTON WHEELMEN'S RECEPTION.

BRILLIANT OPENING OF THE NEW CLUB HOUSE ON WASHINGTON AVENUE.

On last Monday evening the Scranton Bicycle Club gave its first grand reception in its new home. Their club house is situated on Washington Avenue and is a model bicycle club building. The entire building, from basement to roof, is beautifully furnished, and as the guests scattered themselves through the house on Monday evening exclamations of surprise and appreciation were heard on every hand.

Upon entering the building one is surprised at the completeness of arrangement in every detail. The basement, which is entered from Olive Street, contains a large wheel room, a locker room, toilet rooms, shower bath, furnace room, janitor's cellar, etc. The first floor is divided into a large hall, parlor, reception room and dining room. The doors are so constructed that these rooms can be thrown into one apartment. The building is finished in light wood. The handsome mantel that adorns the main parlor is a gift from Architect Duckworth, who designed the club house. In the parlor and other rooms the skill of an expert house decorator is manifested in the handsome portieres and other hangings, which have been arranged in such a manner as to produce the most artistic effect.

Ascending the staircase that leads to the main hallway on the second floor, two cozy little card rooms greet the eye at the left. At the end of the hall, in the lower over the main entrance, is situated the President's room. This is a little gem, exquisitely furnished, and connected by portieres with the club living, lounging and smoking room, which are also finely furnished. Adjoining the President's room is the reading room, with its comfortable leather chairs, and beyond this is the billiard room.

Upon the third floor are the kitchen and a number of bed-rooms. The windows in the hallways are fitted with stained glass, and the building is lighted by numerous incandescent lights and gas burners, which are fixed upon the beautiful chandeliers about the building.

The invited guests began to arrive at 7 o'clock, and in a short time the house was all life and gaiety. Mrs. J. A. Scranton, Mrs. S. P. Hull, Mrs. G. A. Jessup and Mrs. Dr. Frey, in company with President Jessup, received the guests with a cordiality that made all feel at home. The orchestra filled the house with sweet strains during the evening. The refreshment tables were spread on the third floor and were invitingly arranged. The collation was all that the most fastidious taste could desire. All the boys were in a supremely happy mood and were assiduous in their attentions to the guests. Each guest was conducted to the register of the club, and the autographs of all were secured as mementoes of the happy occasion. The number of people present was very large, approximating a thousand, a large number of whom were ladies.

The following were among the guests from out of town: Miss Jennie Hull, Miss Agnes Hull, Mrs. G. Hull, Mr. and Mrs. J. S. Luce, Grace C. Hull, of Olyphant; Albert Beardsley, Springville; Mary T. Goucher, Miss B. Harrington, Miss Agnes L. Black, of Philadelphia; D. J. Whitford, Taylorville; Percy H. French, W. S. Northup, Wilson M. Berry, Maude Phillips, John H. Blackman, Gertrude Shifler, Belle Green, Belle Collins, of Pittston; Mrs. M. E. Berry, of Washington, D. C.; Henry Lizz, Rochester, N. Y.; Mrs. A. A. Snyder, New York City; Mr. and Mrs. A. L. Ring, Passaic, N. J.; Miss May Kulp, Wilkesbarre; Miss Minnie Weiss, Honesdale; Miss Annie Fenner, South Bethlehem; Mrs. Alonzo Potter Kennedy, Pittsburg; Miss S. Dunning, Addison; Francis A. Powell, Boston, Mass.; Mr. and Mrs. W. J. Mulford, of Montrose.

Frank H. Clemons,	F. W. Edwards,
F. K. Killam,	S. J. Billings,
Jno. P. Fowler,	J. P. Baumeister,
T. A. Simpson,	F. Q. Hartman,
Col. H. A. Coursen,	J. B. Woolsey,
Chas. C. Conrad,	R. E. Prendergast,
J. T. Jenkins,	Ed. Barnard,

C. B. Pratt.

HONORARY MEMBERS.

E. B. Sturges.	Dr. J. B. O'Brien.
	Dr. C. P. Knapp, Wyoming.
	Mr. S. B. Vaughn, Kingston.
	Mr. T. L. Newell, Kingston.

THE ELEVENTH ANNIVERSARY OF THE BOSTON BICYCLE CLUB.

The eleventh annual dinner of the Boston Bicycle Club was held at Parker's last Saturday evening. There was a goodly attendance, and all were in a jolly mood. The entire absence of formality and freedom from constraint which marked the occasion contributed much to the general merriment.

President Hodges, in opening the after-dinner exercises, expressed his pleasure at the large attendance, which, he said, had been secured without any particular effort or the offering of special inducements. He described all present as "stayers," and expressed his belief that they, having withstood the shocks of eleven Boston Club dinners, would be able to stand many more. He then, after a short reference to the Town Club, retired in favor of the recently elected President of that organization, W. B. Everett, who presided during the remainder of the evening.

After the cheers had subsided, President Everett arose and made a short speech in which he eulogized the Town Club. He then called upon F. W. Weston, who bears the honorary title of the "Father of the Club."

Mr. Weston made a few happy remarks, in which he expressed his gratification at being with so many old friends, and predicted a long era of prosperity for both the Town and Boston Clubs.

J. S. Dean was the next speaker, and was greeted with unrestrained enthusiasm. He spoke of the hearty co-operation of the two clubs, and expressed his confidence in their ultimate success.

Ex-Commodore Savage, of the Dorchester, was next introduced. He expressed his appreciation of the honor of being called upon to speak for his club, but modestly withdrew in favor of his friend, Jesse Wiley. That gentleman was then called for with cheers, and responded in a short and eloquent speech.

Charles W. Reed sang a song, which was enthusiastically received.

"The Wheel" was the next toast, and was responded to by Captain Kendall. His remarks were greeted with applause.

J. Fred. Brown made a short and brilliant speech, which was well received.

Geo. A. Doane responded to the toast of the Boston Athletic Club, and Richard Toombs, an ex-captain of the club, made a response for the natatory element which created the wildest enthusiasm.

Captain Robinson, of the Revere Cycling Club, spoke to "Our Neighboring Cycling Clubs." He stated that while the interest in cycling club life had been on the wane in Boston it had flourished in the suburbs. He congratulated the club upon its success, and expressed his wish for its future prosperity.

John R. Chadwick sustained his reputation as the Chauncey Depew of the Boston Club by making an excellent humorous address.

Treasurer Geo. B. Woodward read an interesting poem, and Mr. Myers delivered an interesting address. Many more witty speeches and bright stories kept up the festivities until

NEW LIFE IN THE HARLEM WHEELMEN.

It was through the efforts of Messrs. Newcome, Ralsbeck, Emanuel and Robus, assisted by Mrs. Newcome and Miss Raisbeck, that the members and friends of the Harlem Wheelmen enjoyed the Progressive Euchre party given at their club house Saturday evening, 23d inst. A party of sixteen sat at the small tables playing the interesting game for an hour or so, during which time selections were rendered upon the piano. The prizes were both elegant and elaborate, and were won by Miss T. Wood, Mr. F. Phillips, Miss Sadie Field and Captain E. C. Parker. After the game dancing was indulged in until midnight, interrupted only long enough for the ladies of the club to serve a fine collation. Among those present were: Mr. and Mrs. Judge Newcome, Mr. and Mrs. L. B. Haber, Mr. and Mrs. H. Cochrane, Mr. F. Phillips and Miss Wood, Mr. Frank Ridabock and Miss Sadie Field, Mr. Dean R. Robus and Miss L. B. Bland, the latter adding much to the pleasure of the evening by rendering selections on the piano; Mr. T. A. Raisbeck and daughter, and Mr. C. F. Frazer and Miss C. Bidwell. There were also present Messrs. W. H. V. Hoffman, W. W. Braden and Mr. Otto Emanuel, who, by special request, gave the new cry which he would like adopted by the club, but which can never be, as Otto is the only one who can get around it. The affair broke up just as Sunday was at hand, and was voted a grand success, much to the credit of the committee.

In glancing around, a list of candidates for office caught our eye—viz.: For President, T. A. Raisbeck; Vice-President, L. A. Newcome; Secretary, W. W. Braden; Treasurer, W. H. DeGraaf; Trustees, Messrs. L. B. Haber and J. B. Halsey; Captain, C. E. Parker; First Lieutenant, W. W. Braden; Second Lieutenant, Frank Lord; Color Bearer, Frank Ridabock; Bugler, George Schrader.

The pool tables have been moved from the front room and one placed in the back, using the front for sitting and meeting room, which has been very prettily decorated by the ladies. Hereafter the Harlems will hold a smoker every Wednesday evening, which will put renewed vigor in the old and famous Harlem Club, who have much to be proud of.

A grand reception is to be held at West End Hall March 13. THE EYE.

CYCLING AT ST. AUGUSTINE, FLA.

Cycling matters are beginning to take practical shape at St. Augustine. Some of the more energetic cyclists have succeeded in bringing about the formation of a club. It is called the "Alcazar Bicycle Club," and is composed of the following members: President, L. Brinkerhoffe; Captain, E. K. Knowlton; Secretary-Treasurer, J. J. Howatt; B. W. Spiller, W. Henry, H. Snow, E. Howatt, E. N. Wilson, C. Hernandez, S. Genovas. E. G. Capo, S. Rolliston, W. House, W. P. Eichbaum, W. E. Hinch and Fred. de C. Davies.

The club gave its first dinner on Tuesday, the 19th inst., at which all the members were present. The menu was elaborate, and a very enjoyable time was spent. The members are all active and feel confident about the future success of their club.

TENTH ANNUAL BANQUET OF THE BUFFALO BICYCLE CLUB.

On last Friday evening the Buffalo Bicycle Club cele-

WHEEL GOSSIP.

We have letters for S. G. Whitaker.

Lehr, the German champion, trains to spurt two laps, one-half mile.

It is rumored that Bob Cripps will be seen on the Irish racing path this season.

The *American Athlete*, of Philadelphia, will shortly become a weekly publication.

The Harlem Wheelmen enjoyed a "smoker" at their club house on Wednesday evening.

The New York *Herald's* English Sunday edition is distributed with the aid of carrier tricycles.

William Halpin & Co. are showing the new Warwick wheels at 13 Murray Street, New York.

The Harlem Wheelmen had a progressive euchre party at their club house last Saturday night.

J. Purvis-Bruce, "Jack," alias "Gentleman John," arrived in New York from England on Monday.

The business of H. M. White, of Trenton, N. J., has been reorganized under the firm name of The White Cycle Co.

Mr. Ed. Loane, formerly with the Victor people at Baltimore, will probably be connected with their Washington store.

S. G. Whittaker is expected in this country in a few days. It is rumored that he will apply for reinstatement in the amateur ranks.

Chief Justice Elliott, of Indiana, has decided, and very justly, that the bicycle, being a vehicle, should not be ridden on a sidewalk.

N. H. Van Sicklen will be seen upon the path this year. His terrible fall at Buffalo has evidently not dampened his enthusiasm.

ONE OF THE 13,000.—We have received an electrotype from a dealer, which was carefully wrapped in a copy of the *Bicycling World*.

The basis on which a successful club is built is youth and enthusiasm—not too much of the former and just enough of the latter.—*Bicycling News.*

The family of ex-President Hayes own a tandem tricycle, which Miss Fannie Hayes and one of her brothers pedal about the streets of Fremont, Ohio.

Among the patents filed this week are A. H. Overman's, for a velocipede; H. S. Owen's, for a bicycle, and the H. B. Smith Machine Co.'s, for a steam tricycle.

Wheeling hears that George Hendee has struck a bright idea in connection with a spring-fork. George is of a peaceful nature; he must have had strong provocation.

"The Coaster," of Jersey City, N. J., is becoming famous. The *Bi. News* reproduces his "Woo-Wah-Whoo!" smoker call and his comic description of that event.

The Boston *Herald*, of Sunday last, published a "speaking portrait" of "Doc" Kendall, Captain of the Boston Bicycle Club, and a genial and hospitable Boston cyclist.

A meeting of the Bowling League will be held at the New York Club house on Tuesday night. The dispute over the Atalanta-Harlem Wheelmen game will be investigated and decided.

An interesting object at the New York Club house is the bottle of champagne won by Messrs. Nisbett and Pendleton on New Year's morning. The bottle, which yet contains the champagne, is framed in an artistic case.

Mr. A. L. Cline, of Cline Bros., 304 West Baltimore Street, was in New York on Thursday. Mr. Cline has been in Springfield and Boston, and has made arrangements to handle Victors and Warwicks in Baltimore.

The Capital Cycle Co. ask us to state that they are sole United States agents for the Psycho wheels. We have been informed that the Pope Mfg. Co. were importing ladies' Psychos, so that there would seem to be a clash of interests.

The Lincoln Cycling Club, of Chicago, formally opened its gymnasium on Saturday last. The programme, a pretty specimen of the printer's skill, consisted of a first-class athletic exhibition. We are indebted to President F. W. Gerould for a copy of the invitation.

We took the initiative in condemning the six-day female bicycle race recently held in New York. We find our exchanges for this week taking precisely the same stand and drawing largely on the dictionary for terms of disapproval.

The Scranton boys are quite proud of their new club house, and their representative at the National Assembly meet, Mr. J. J. Van Nort, invited the members to drop into the Scranton's headquarters and partake of Pennsylvania hospitality.

Chief Consul Harry Hodgson sends us an invitation to the New Orleans Carnival, which is to be held March 5. The invite is a triumph of the artist and the printer, and quite beyond our powers of description—"simply magnificent," as Harry himself would say.

The *Sporting Life*, 148 Fleet Street, London, E. C., has issued its sporting almanac for 1889. The almanac is a ninety-six page pamphlet containing historical and record information of all kinds of sport, and will be a valuable edition to a sportsman's collection of data.

W. E. Findley, N. Y. B. C., who broke his collar-bone at the Twelfth Regiment games, December 12, was out on the road on Washington's Birthday for the first time since his accident. The New York Club held a run to Yonkers on that day, seven men being out.

M. Constant, an observant Frenchman, gave his views on America in the *Herald* of Sunday last. As they were deemed of enough importance to be cabled over, his opinion on the "vile pavements of New York City, which would disgrace a French provincial town," will have an eye-opening effect.

The Western Arms and Cartridge Co., of 49 State Street, Chicago, have an extensive cycle department. This firm occupies a double building, which gives them ample room to display their large stock of safeties, ordinaries and sundries. The manager of the business is Mr. Oniel, who is assisted by Messrs. Temple and Roe.

About twenty-five members of the Waltham Bicycle Club traveled to Boston from the "City of Watches," and partook of their annual banquet at the Revere House last Thursday evening. The affair was made the more enjoyable by its informality, although speeches were made by President Davis, F. A. Clarke and E. DeBarthe.

Cycling is at top notch in Chicago. Messrs. "Ned" Oliver and "Bob" Gardner have done much to boom the sport. Messrs. Gardner and Stokes intend to combine forces and open a very large and fine riding hall, something that will dwarf all other halls, as Chicago's growth has dwarfed all other growths, except possibly that of St. Louis.

In our exuberance of good feeling we came near putting our foot in it when we were about to ask Harry, "How is your circulation old fellow?" As it was only our intention to ask the condition of his health, it would have been awkward under the circumstances if we had put it *that* way, wouldn't it it?—*Bicycling World.* [Yaas, very.—ED.]

The New York Bicycle Club Board of Management have called a special meeting for March 5. At this meeting important business will be transacted. A successor will be elected in place of J. B. Roy, resigned; the Entertainment Committee will be asked to report, and steps will be taken to revive a strong interest in club work.

Chief Consul George R. Hidwell will tender his resignation at the meeting of the New York State Division Board, and will transfer all the effects of the Division to Vice-Consul Bull. Mr. Bull, with the assistance of Secretary-Treasurer Nisbett, will at once proceed on the policy pursued by Mr. Hidwell, and which has made the Division the strongest in the League.

The *Cyclist* is decidedly of the opinion that the "Rational" ordinary is *the* tall machine of the future, that it will drive out the present type of ordinary, much as the Rover type has retired the Kangaroo type. It thinks the present "Rational" type would be improved if foot rests were attached to the forks for use in coasting, and if there was more room between

the top of the tire and the bottom of the crown of the fork, so that the wheel would not be clogged up with mud.

At the Stanley Show 132 firms showed 1,201 cycles, composed of 826 bicycles and 375 tricycles. Of the bicycles, 644, or over half of the total machines shown, were dwarf safeties, 87 ordinaries, 52 rationals, 33 tandem safeties and 10 high safeties. Of the 375 tricycles, 234 were direct steerers, 64 tandems, 21 carriers, 13 crippers and 11 sociables. The Show has been held every year since 1878. The total number of wheels shown progressed as follows: 74, 112, 146, 250, 433, 522, 365, 287, 620, 633, 750, 1,201.

The Capital Cycle Company's announcement for 1889 will be found on another page. This firm is in the field with as fine a line of safeties as we have ever seen, with many good points to recommend them, and magnificently finished. The firm writes us: "Our catalogue bids fair to be the finest the trade has ever seen, and, we think, will be sought after by every wheelman. We mean business this year, and intend to have a front seat before 1890. We come in with honest intentions and good principles, firmly believing we are benefiting the cause."

We want to be chivalrous, but when Miss Pauline Hall causes a "split" in a cycling club, it is time to call a halt in this blind worship of this fair singer on wheels. The New York *Herald* recently headed its amusement gossip with the statement that the fair Pauline was making a big "ad" out of her cycle riding, and no doubt we shall soon have all the theatrical world on wheels. It is a ripe time to dissipate the idea that cycling has received a sort of divine sanction because the leading lady of the Casino Company has taken to the bicycle.

The Gormully & Jeffery Mfg. Co.'s catalogue for 1889 is a well printed pamphlet of 80 pages, and somewhat of an advance in appearance and scope over their previous catalogues. Thirty-six pages are devoted to illustrations and descriptions of the 1889 wheels, of which the following is a list: American Champion, American Light Champion, American Challenge bicycle, American safety, American Light safety, American Rambler, American Ideal Rambler, American Ideal bicycle, American Ideal tricycle, American Ideal tandem, American Challenge tandem. The remainder of the catalogue is devoted to a large assortment of sundries.

Among the visitors to the Stanley Show was George M. Hendee, the well-known American flyer, in company with Messrs C. E. Pratt and Belden. A short chat with the erstwhile hero of Springfield, over whose women wept and men had hysterics, showed that Hendee, like most of the American cracks, had suffered from the knack their journals have of writing their men up to the skies. Quiet and modest, without a bit of "gas," the American flyer made a most excellent impression. He will have for the States in about a week. One of his first visits was to the C. P. track, of which he spoke highly.—*Bicycling News.*

Yes, Hendee is "quiet and modest," but *Bicycling News'* ravings to the contrary, the women did weep when the strong man of Lynn defeated the Springfield pet on the famous Springfield path. It may all seem very silly to George, now that he is a solid, sensible benedict, but we ourselves saw the weepings and we want to preserve this page of cycle racing history at all hazards. The real lesson to the cracks of the present day is that they should cultivate the same modest manly ways which made the boy Hendee Springfield's idol.

The recent female bicycle race (?) at New York proved to be what was suspected before the start—a fake of the boldest type; eight of the contestants were under contract to a single individual and were putting in the time under salary, while the public were led to believe that the affair was a genuine contest for supremacy and gate receipts. These fakirs proposed to extend their tricks to other cities, but the expose of the New York fraud will doubtless cause them to change their plans. Should they, however, visit this and other cities they should receive scant welcome. Even if honestly conducted, there is no sport in a contest of endurance between women. Such a spectacle is not only hurtful to the sport of cycling, but degrading in its tendencies alike to the unfortunate women who are compelled to resort to such means of livelihood, and to the lookers-on at this sorry spectacle. Woman has no legitimate place in athletic contests save as a spectator or patron.—*Sporting Life.*

ST. LOUIS.

"We looks towards you, and we likewise bows." It has been a long time since this section of the country has been represented by correspondence in the WHEEL, and I am sure that your enterprise in locating a correspondent here will be fully appreciated by the wheelmen of the South-west. Since "Phoenix" laid down his pen and moved to the village at the other end of the bridge, to accept a position with President Pullman, of the Palace Car Company, St. Louis has had no correspondent worthy of the high reputation which he earned, and she is not likely to have one for a good while to come.

Those who have been so fortunate as to meet "Phœnix" lately, report him as looking sleek and prosperous, and his many friends are all rejoiced to hear of his success.

The reports that come to us from all sections of the country of the mild, open winter, are equally applicable to this vicinity. Just at present we are wrestling with an old-time blizzard, but it is actually the first one of the season and causes the first interruption to riding that we have experienced. Even now the roads are in good condition, but the temperature is not calculated to make riding an unmixed pleasure. Notwithstanding the kick made by a local scribbler, the result of the election of League officers gives general satisfaction here. Missouri has fared exceedingly well, and in return for this recognition it is hoped that she will show a big increase in membership next year. We are fortunate in having Mr. A. Moore Berry at the head of the Rights and Privileges Committee, for we are likely to need his services sooner than we expected. Late last fall, one of our St. Louis riders was run down on "Soloman's Hill" by a farmer living near the county line. The matter was placed in the hands of Attorney A. C. Stewart, and the farmer was forced to pay for the broken wheel, the attorney's fees and other legal expenses, and a good round sum for damages to the rider's feelings. The farmer threatened to get even, and his threat has taken shape in the introduction of a bill in the Legislature, compelling wheelmen to dismount one hundred yards before meeting any vehicle hauled by a horse or mule, and to remain dismounted until such vehicle has passed twenty-five yards beyond. The penalty for violation of the law is a fine of not less than $10, nor more than $100. In addition to the fine, riders are to be held responsible for any damage that may arise in consequence of horses or mules becoming frightened at the wheels. This is the first attempt at hostile legislation that has ever been started in Missouri, and it will be fought vigorously. I understand that the Chief Consul has consulted with Messrs. Stewart and Berry, and the course to be pursued has been fully determined upon. There are a large number of riders in the State who are not members of the League, and it is the duty of those who are members to call the attention of the outsiders to this threatened invasion of their rights, and induce them to join with us in defeating the bill. The Division has plenty of money in hand for all present necessities, but if the fight should prove a long one, more funds will be needed, and there is no better way of raising the money than by increasing the membership. In addition to fighting this vexatious bit of "hayseed" legislation, we have a bill for the improvement of the roads and highways pending in the Legislature which we want to pass. In this matter we have been greatly aided by the numerous excellent articles on the subject of better roads that have appeared in the WHEEL from time to time. We recognize that paper as the pioneer in the campaign for better roads, and we hope that you will "keep a hammerin'."

I understand that the details of the Stone-Lumsden series of races have all been agreed upon by Messrs. Garden and Brewster, for their respective principals. The forfeits are up and the races are a sure thing. I will give you the details in my next letter.

The annual election of the Missouri Bicycle Club will be held on the night of the first Tuesday in March. Mr. Berry can have the presidency if he wants it, notwithstanding the fact that Chauvenet and others of the so-called "silk-stocking" element are pressing Will Brown. Brown is a clever fellow, but he is training with the wrong crowd if he really desires election.

ST. LOUIS, February 23, 1889. ITHURIEL.

CYCLING IN TENNESSEE.

Our sister city of Murfreesboro is decidedly the best wheeling town of its size in the South. A recent trip to that beautiful town of beautiful girls and genial young men convinced the writer that Murfreesboro and its environments is, indeed, a wheelman's paradise. The streets about the city are all wide and well paved, while the pikes which centre there are as fine as any in the State. The general lay of the country for some miles around is well adapted to good riding, being generally smooth and level. Quite a large number of young men of the town ride wheels, and a more whole-souled lot would be hard to find.

Probably the foremost in cycling matters is Jesse Sparks, Jr., son of the Senator. Young Sparks has always taken the initiative in his town and county, not only in those things which would tend to build up cycling as a health-giving sport, but also in matters of general interest to the community. He is Secretary of the Rutherford County Fair Association, and it is needless to say the work which comes within the province of his office is ably and well attended to. He has been a wheelman four or five years and is a dangerous rival in the State of Herndon, the Clarksville crack.

As stated some time ago, a trip awheel to Washington has been planned. There will probably be three or four in the party, two of whom will be Mr. Sparks, of Murfreesboro, and Mr. Tom Petri, of this city. We have not yet learned the details of the proposed trip, but it will likely be made in the early part of June.

Before the summer is over Nashville cyclists will no doubt be favored by the acquisition to their ranks of riders of the feminine persuasion. Mr. Jo Combs, the well known wheelman, yesterday showed the *American* man a new American safety of the Gormully & Jeffery pattern, which he had just received from the factory. It is a beauty and is designed for either lady or gentleman. Mr. Combs stated that his purpose in getting it was to attempt to create an interest in riding among the ladies, and that he will teach his wife to ride, which he thinks will be easier than is popularly supposed. If he finds it practicable he will next year get a tandem, a machine arranged for both lady and gentleman.—*Nashville American.*

TROY NOTES.

Looking over my "Notes" in a late issue of THE WHEEL, I was a little amused to find the following paragraph: "In fact she told me that she once rode with a severe headache for nearly ten miles into the country, and that she never felt better than she did on dismounting at the end of the trip." Now, it would seem that because the lady *had* the headache she never felt better at the end of the trip. It should have read: "For nearly ten miles *of a 50-mile run* into the country."

Friday, the 15th, the Troy Bicycle Club's seventh social was given at the popular Bicycle Hall, and the 18th the club's bowling team (composed of Clarence R. Wilson, Charles Biermeister, Frank Perkins, Alfred Hogben and John Van Arnam) played a team from Coon & Co.'s collar shop (composed of Robert Lang, C. Tuttle, Fred Schuth, A. Hogben and William Theissen), and were defeated by a score of 1,635 to 1,841.

The large hall of the T. B. C. is so convenient for fairs, etc., that the club is doing quite a business letting it for such purposes.

So C. H. Luscomb is our new President. He ought to make a good one, for he has the ability, and I hope the League will reach the coveted 15,000 under his administration. I am sorry Pennsylvania is not represented, as such a large membership as she has in the League ought to be represented in the chief board.

Where is the "Owly" Egan nowadays? His articles in the wheel papers used to be so interesting that many of the older wheelmen must miss his bright and witty sayings.

I have been looking over the *Bulletin*, and I must say it was a much better paper, as edited by Aaron, than we get now in the place of it. If it was not for THE WHEEL I would be lost for *news* at the present time. A short time ago I was looking for an account of an important meeting in the *official organ*, and it was impossible to find the data I was in search of. I turned to my file of THE WHEEL and found the *complete* account of the meeting at once, and saved myself a long trip in consequence. I only wish your paper would reach me on Saturday instead of Monday, as it now comes.

The Trojan Wheelmen gave a private social at Harmony Hall last Wednesday evening, and it was as select as the affairs of this *social* club generally are.

On Thursday the eighth social of the Troy Bicycle Club was given in their large hall. The boys *meant* to have a good time this winter, and they *are* having it.

Saturday a bowling contest at the Troy Bicycle Club's room, between the Bachelors and Benedicts, resulted in the defeat of the latter by a score of 1,853 to 1,841.

I have lately heard that the reason the T. B. C. left the League was because they could not secure one of the national championship races last year, and, with the Albany Wheelmen, give a large race meet between Albany and Troy. It seems very funny that such should be the case unless they wanted some particular race.

ONNH QBA.

February 25, 1889.

PHILADELPHIA.

The month of March is not the most auspicious time to make your debut as a cycle correspondent, since good "wheel" news is not abundant; but with the advent of more seasonable weather I hope to furnish a more readable and interesting letter chronicling the doings of wheelmen in the "City of Brotherly Love" and "cobble-stones."

The tandem "goat" fever seems to be contagious, especially among the "Century Wheelmen," the latest additions being the Allen brothers. This club now has four tandem teams and several more are likely to materialize before long.

All of the clubs had runs called for George's Birthday, but the weather man put a dampener on the riding in the form of snow and rain. We have no cause to complain, however, as the riding has been excellent all winter.

There will be several improvements in Fairmount Park this year which will greatly interest wheelmen. One will be a broad road or avenue from the river drive to Germantown direct, and the other will be placing electric lights along the banks of the Schuylkill River. A more romantic and picturesque ride than the one along this river at twilight cannot well be imagined. The placid basin of the river, unruffled save by the wash of a small steamboat or the oars of one of the racing shells, on one side, and on the other high butting crags casting huge shadows which in the half light look like gigantic monsters, a pall of silence covering all as though even nature was awed by the sublime grandeur of herself. It is truly a magnificent road, which Philadelphia wheelmen don't half appreciate.

The alterations to the "Century's" new brown-stone mansion are being rapidly pushed. The reason it was bought so cheap ($17,000) is that it has the reputation of being haunted. The other night, after rehearsal, the "Glee Club" thought they would go over to the new house and see what effect music (?) would have on his ghostship. Kirk Brown was requested to come along with his flute. Upon their arrival at the scene the "Centurians" entered the dimly lighted room (a couple of bicycle lamps furnished the illumination) and filled the air with their melodies, but no ghost made its appearance. Then Carter—he of the Prince of Wales whiskers—started to warble "Don't Leave Your Mother, Tom," with flute obligato. When he was about to paralyze high C, and Brown was trilling his sweetest trill on the flute, a long-drawn wail was heard, the lamps flickered (so did the boys), and MacGlathery swore he saw a ghostly form float out of the window. That last song did the business. The supposition is that when on the earth its name was Tom, and the way that Carter sang the song so played on its feelings that it went to hunt its "mama." The reason that it is called a glee club is not quite plain, unless it be because of the fiendish glee with which they bounce the members from the best room in the house when they want to practice; or, perhaps, on account of the gleeful way in which they sing those funereal songs which they spring on their unsuspecting club-mates.

ARGUS.

LONG ISLAND.

The Long Island Wheelmen officially opened the season of 1889 on Washington's Birthday by a club run to Coney Island by way of the Park and Boulevard and return, twenty-two miles in all. The L. I.'s turned out twenty-eight strong, under command of Captain Teller, and as the roads were in very fair condition considering the time of year the run was made in good time and without incident or mishap. Some trifling insubordination among the "goat" contingent furnished amusement for the others and work for the Third Lieutenant in his efforts to bring them back to line. A short drill was taken on the concourse, during which the First Lieutenant took occasion to perform a new but striking manœuvre not recommended by authorities on such matters.

The electioneering epidemic has drifted along Bedford Avenue from the L. I. W. to the K. C. W., preparatory to the annual election of officers in the latter club to be held next month. Comparatively no opposition has appeared to the caucus nominations of Bridgman for President and Marion for Captain, and these gentlemen will doubtless be elected. The most hotly contested office is that of First Lieutenant, and the result of the fight between Crichton and Tom Hall is very doubtful.

After passing through a very unusually close and exciting election of officers for 1889, the Long Islands have settled down to comparative peace and quiet. With the presidency of the L. A. W. vested in him, Mr. Luscomb may easily look with resignation upon the fact that by a narrow margin Mr. Mabie was the successful candidate for the presidency of the club.

Last Thursday night, the 21st, the L. I. W. gave a ladies' reception and dance at their club house, at which there were about sixty couples. The preliminary entertainment consisted of feats of sleight-of-hand by Mr. Howard J. Knudson, of Brooklyn, which were very cleverly done and apparently were thoroughly enjoyed. At 11 o'clock dancing was commenced and continued, with an intermission for refreshments, until nearly 2:30. The refreshments aforesaid on this occasion were of such a pleasing and bounteous nature that your correspondent was, perforce, obliged to blush at a previous slighting reference made on a similar subject, and to "wish he hadn't."

The Committee of Arrangements are booming the combined theatre party to the "Pearl of Pekin," to be given March 29 at the Park. Notices are posted up at each club house advising members to hand in their names at once, and the committee expect to dispose of at least 250 seats for that night. Arrangements are also contemplated for a joint supper as a proper winding-up of the evening, if some suitable place can be found. Nothing definite, however, has been done in this direction, though it seems as if a social spread would add a great deal to the success of the affair and go far toward preserving the present intimate relations between the different clubs.

The total mileage of the L. I. W. for January was 1,884, seventy-four men reporting. Considering the season this is a very fair showing, and the Road Committee look upon it as an indication that for 1889 the club will report a mileage much larger than was ever before attained and that will compare favorably with any club in the country.

NYX.

At the National Assembly meet, Mr. George R. Bidwell, of the Uniform Committee, gave very clear and satisfactory reasons why the League uniform contract was transferred to Browning, King & Co., of New York. Both John Wanamaker and Wanamaker & Brown were making the League uniforms at a loss, and neither gave satisfaction. The Uniform Committee had given Wanamaker & Brown ample notice of their dissatisfaction, and, no improvement being shown, they had transferred the contract to Browning, King & Co. as the best firm to handle the business.

Messrs. Brewster Bros., owners of large roller mills at Unadilla, N. Y., write: "Please find enclosed check for $1 for THE WHEEL AND CYCLING TRADE REVIEW, as we think it is the best paper for wheelmen, and we therefore wish to try it for one year."

PSYCHO WHEELS FOR 1889.

IMPORTERS: CAPITAL CYCLE CO., WASHINGTON, D. C.

The Psycho cycles are imported by the Capital Cycle Company, of Washington, D. C. This firm were the first to recognize the merits of all forms of rear-driving safeties, and in 1885 imported the first one ever brought into this country. They also designed and introduced the first tandem safety in 1888. They designed and manufactured in 1887 the first rear-driving ladies' safety bicycle, and credit should be given them for their efforts in this direction. They have accomplished as much for the weaker sex by reducing friction, weight, and by giving increased pleasure, as did the inventor of the spider wheel for the stronger sex by improving the boneshaker.

PSYCHO LIGHT ROADSTER.

PSYCHO LADIES' ROADSTER.

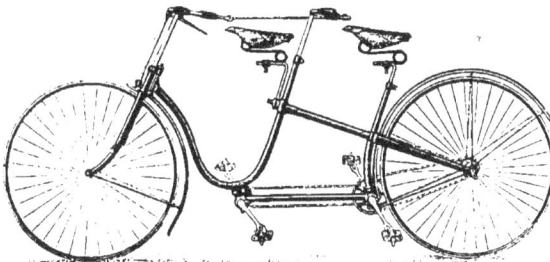

PSYCHO TANDEM SAFETY.

They handle only one form of three-wheeled machines, and that a hand lever tricycle for cripples, which is remarkably light and can be steered and driven by the hands. The Psycho cycles imported by this firm are made from designs by Mr. H. S. Owen. The wheels are remarkable for their lightness, strength, harmonious and uniform construction, simplicity, fewness of parts, and general gracefulness of design.

They are made of weldless steel tubing (not credenda) throughout, including frame, rear forks, saddle post, handle-bar and upright. They have ball bearings to all parts except head, butt-ended direct spokes, more to rear wheel than front, done to proportion the machines for strains.

Psycho cycles do not have hollow rims, tangent spokes, ball head or spring forks. No change will be made in Psychos over the 1888 pattern. The Fish hammock saddle will be used on all Psychos. The plunger brake will be used, as it is the simplest and very powerful. This firm have hoped for years past, and now claim, that the wheel of the future will be a rear-driving safety which has dropped frame, suitable for both sexes. They anticipate some prejudice at first, but show their faith in their belief by introducing four styles of dropped-frame safeties suitable for either lady or gentleman, having detachable brace rods; and although they import two forms of straight-frame safeties, suitable only for men, they advise intending purchasers to give the preference to the dropped-frame, not only on account of its adaptability to use by all members of the family, but also for its grace and strength. The Capital Cycle Company claim to give the best guarantee in the trade, as they guarantee not only against defects in workmanship and material, as do other firms, but also against construction, which is more important. A machine may break not only on account of a flaw, but from bad proportioning. The Capital Cycle Company introduce seven forms of safety or rear-driving bicycles for both sexes for this season, varying in weight, construction and price. They are as follows:

1. "Men's Straight Frame Psycho Safety," as per cut, 30 inch wheels, ⅞ and ⅞ inch tires, geared to 57 inches, weight 47 lbs. Price, $140.

2. "Men's Light Roadster Psycho Safety," 30-inch wheels, ⅞-inch tires, made for gentlemen riders and scorchers on good roads, geared to 60 inches, weight 38 lbs. Price, $140.

3. "Men's Dropped Frame Psycho Safety" is designed like ladies' safety (see cut), 30-inch wheels, ⅞ and ⅞ inch tires, weight 50 lbs. Will stand any weight on any road. Detachable brace rod makes it suitable for ladies and a general family machine. Price, $140. Geared to 57 inches.

4. "Ladies' Roadster Psycho Safety," ⅞-inch tires, 29-inch wheels. Detachable brace rod suitable for short or medium height gentlemen. Will stand any weight. Weight, 44 lbs. See cut. Geared to 50 inches.

5. "Ladies' Light Roadster Psycho Safety," 29-inch wheels, ⅞ and ⅞ inch tires, weight 38 lbs. Superb finish, very light and easy running, intended for light weight ladies, but will carry 175 lbs. Geared to 50 inches.

6. "Psycho Tandem Safety," intended for lady and gentleman or two gentlemen, ⅞-inch tires to both wheels, very strong, light and simple. Will carry any weight. Price, with two separate brakes, $200. Geared to 57 inches.

7. "Psycho No. 2" is intended as a cheaper safety, suitable for both sexes. It will equal in strength and design any of the above, and having ball bearings to both wheels and crank shaft, weldless steel tubing frame and steel forks, it will be as durable as the higher grade Psychos, but of cheaper construction and finish. 30-inch wheel, ⅞-inch tires, geared to 54 inches. Price, $100.

All of the above machines are guaranteed to the fullest extent. The Capital Cycle Company have prepared for their share of the trade this year, relying upon the merits of their wheels. They only handle two-wheeled safeties; no ordinaries or tricycles.

PREMIER SAFETY AND TANDEM SAFETY.

We shall publish in next week's paper cuts of the "Special Premier safety" and "Premier tandem safety" imported by L. H. Johnson, of Orange, N. J. From photographs shown us we should say that both will be popular with American riders. The safety has 30-28 wheels, non-slipping tires, butt-ended spokes, weldless steel tube forks and frame, detachable stay, ball-bearings to wheels, crank shaft and pedals, non-stretching steel chain, mud guards, chain guard, reversible saddle-post, Lamplugh & Brown's combined saddle and spring. The safety weighs 48 pounds.

The tandem has 30-inch wheels, 3⁄4 and 1 inch non-slipping tires, all the features of the single, and weighs 90 pounds; price, $200.

HAYSEED LEGISLATION IN THE WEST.

A bill has been introduced into the Missouri Legislature, and it will be favored and very probably passed by the influence of hayseed legislators, which will seriously affect cycle riders in the State. The provisions of the bill are, that it shall hereafter be unlawful for any person or persons to run or engage in any race mounted on any vehicle usually called velocipede or bicycle on any highway or public road in any of the counties outside of any city limits in this State; and all persons traveling by the use of such vehicles upon any such highways or roads, on meeting any person or persons on horses or mules, or in vehicles of any kind, shall come to a halt at a distance of 100 yards from the place on such highways or road where said person or persons on horses or mules, or in vehicles drawn by horses or mules, are met; and the bicycle rider shall dismount from the velocipede or bicycle and remain so until the persons met shall have passed a distance of twenty-five yards. For a violation of the provisions of this law the rider shall, on conviction, be deemed guilty of a misdemeanor and be fined not less than $10 and not more than $100. In addition to the fine he shall also be liable to civil action for any damage to persons or property by reason of any horses or mules becoming frightened at the bicycle.

A SELECTED LIST OF PATENTS.

{Reported especially for THE WHEEL AND CYCLING TRADE REVIEW by C. A. Snow & Co., patent attorneys, Washington, D. C.}

Albert H. Overman, Newton, Mass. Velocipede.

Herbert S. Owen, Washington, D. C. Bicycle.

Gustav A. Schubert, Berlin, Germany. Driving mechanism for velocipedes.

Hezekiah B. Smith, Smithville, N. J. Steam tricycle.

Chas. Sprake, Detroit, Mich. Ice velocipede.

All bearing date of February 26.

CYCLING.

Cashiers and Bookkeepers, you should have one of those "Daily Cash Balance Books." It is the most handy, neat and labor-saving book made to keep your cash straight. Circul rs on application. W. L. Surprise, 55 Madison St. Memphis, Tenn.

THE BOWLING LEAGUE

GAMES TO BE PLAYED.

New York vs. Hudson County, New York, March 1.
Kings County vs. Harlem. Brooklyn, March 5.
Hudson County vs. Atalanta, Jersey City, March 6.
Atalanta vs. New York, Newark, March 14.
Harlem vs. Hudson County, Harlem, March 15.
Atalanta vs. Hudson County, Newark, March 22.

GAMES PLAYED.

January 4 Harlem, 1,429; New York, 1,342.
January 5—Hudson County, 1,408; Kings County, 1,488.
January 10—Harlem, 1,346; Atalanta, 1,343. Draw.
January 11—Kings County, 1,535; New York, 1,347.
January 14—Kings County, 1,437; Atalanta, 1,338.
January 18—Hudson County, 1,350; New York, 1,130.
January 25—Harlem, 1,369; Kings County, 1,260.
February 1—Hudson County, 1,405; Harlem, 1,154.
February 2—Atalanta, 1,456; New York, 1,357.
February 5—Kings County, 1,465; New York, 1,167.
February 15—Hudson County, 1,513; Kings County, 1,283.
February 16—New York, 1,273; Harlem, 1,705.

LADIES' BICYCLES.

"PONY" FAVORS THEM.

NEW YORK, February 23. 1889.

EDITOR OF THE WHEEL:

Dear Sir—Referring to W. W. Stall's letter in this week's issue of THE WHEEL regarding the use of the "bike" by ladies, I know a great many who have discarded the tricycle for the light and easy running "bike," and I am satisfied they are all well pleased with the change that they would not care to again take the backward step. For myself, I had no trouble in learning to ride a ladies' wheel—a little difficulty at first in mounting, but it is all very easy. Our roads are not of the best in and around New York City, but in Boston and the suburban towns, where they have such excellent roads, I wonder the ladies' wheel is not accepted at once as the proper thing, and the tricycle laid aside. From what I can learn there will be a great increase in lady riders this coming spring, and there are many new riders who have taken the bicycle. Oh, the "bike" has come to stay, and after the manufacturers of tricycles realize this fact, as they will be compelled to do in a short time, they will direct their attention to manufacturing ladies' wheels. Mrs. "S," I think, should learn to ride and thereby encourage other women to do the same. She will never regret it if she once commences. As to the tandem "bike"—what I have seen of them on difficult roads—I agree fully with Mr. Stall in preferring the three-wheeled tricycle.

Yours,

PONY.

"I tested one of your (Brooks) cyclometers on the fifty-mile course used by S. G. Whittaker in his road races, and found it to be exactly correct. I think it is the best cyclometer for the money made."

J. A. PETERSON, Potato Creek, Ind.

Only $5. Brooks Odometer Co., Lowell, Mass.

THE SPRINGFIELD ROADSTER BICYCLES

Hold the World's Records

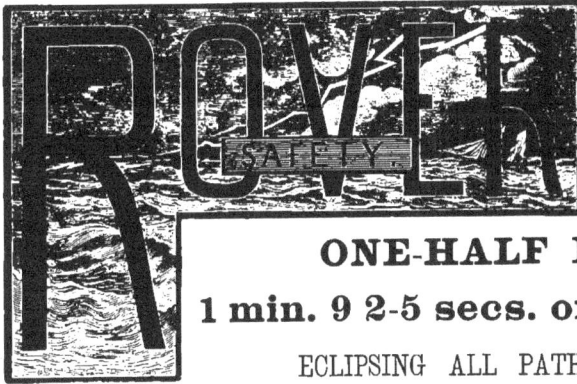

For twelve years the Columbia cycles have been upon the market *For* twelve years they have occupied a front rank position. Twelve years of statistics show that there are more Columbias in use in the United States than all other makes of high grade machines combined. *For* twelve years the Columbias have stood the test of the road and the path. *For* twelve years the best mechanical experts in America have been unanimous in their unsolicited statements that the Columbia machines are the best made of cycles, and reach as close to the mechanical perfection line as modern mechanical skill has been able to go. It is easy to make claims, and printed claims may be as thin as the ink which covers the paper. The broad claim made for the Columbia cycles is that they are in every respect the finest made, and the most durable machines which modern mechanical skill has produced, and this claim is backed by twelve years of experience and by the opinion of unprejudiced mechanical experts and the majority vote of American wheelmen. The Columbia Catalogue should be in the hands of every wheelman. It is free to everybody. POPE MFG. CO., Boston, New York, Chicago.

Press of F. V. Strauss, 110-116 Walker St., New York.

THE WHEEL

—AND—

CYCLING TRADE REVIEW,

Published every Friday morning.

Entered at the Post Office at second class rates

Subscription Price, - - - $1.00 a year.
Foreign Subscriptions, - - - 6s. a year.
Single Copies, - - - - - 5 Cents.

Newsdealers may order through AM. NEWS Co.

All copy should be received by Monday.
Telegraphic news received till Wednesday noon.

Advertising rates on Application.

F. P. PRIAL, Editor and Proprietor
23 Park Row,
P. O. Box 444, New York.

Persons receiving sample copies of this paper are respectfully requested to examine its contents and give us their patronage, and as far as is convenient, aid in circulating the journal, and extend its influence in the cause which it so faithfully serves. Subscription price, $1 per year.

THE very quiet way in which the Chief Consul of New York State is permitted to retire to private life is a lasting reproach to the members of the New York State Board of Officers.

WE have worked hard on our paper for two years. At last we begin to feel that success is within our grasp. Why? Because all the cycling papers are attacking us. Sure sign of success, this thing they call jealousy.

WE are assured that President Luscomb will give us an active administration. But there are pitfalls, and an active administration will introduce antagonistic influences which will call forth all the tact and diplomacy which the newly elect possesses.

VICE-CONSUL BULL is now, to all intents and purposes, chief officer of the New York State Division. He enters upon his duties filled with a determination to advance the cause of cycling in the Empire State, through the influence of the League. He will make mistakes, as all men do, be their position high or low ; but the cyclists of this State, especially those who are fitted by nature with qualities of leadership, should remember that the office which comes to Mr. Bull is one demanding self-sacrifice on his part, and that while his actions may be open to criticism, his motives are not to be questioned. The renewal season will be here shortly, and we hope all League members in the State will not fail to send in their renewals of membership and use every effort to induce cyclists who are not members to join. The New York State Division can accomplish much. It has yet to present and engineer its roads improvement bill through the Legislature. The privileges New York State cyclists enjoy on the New York Central and West Shore roads—obtained through League influence and endeavor—are simply invaluable. To lose these privileges would entail a vast amount of discomfort and monetary loss. Therefore, support the Division which secured these favors and will insure them as long as it remains an influence and a factor.

CYCLISTS and intending purchasers of wheels will now find in our columns the announcements of all the leading dealers and importers in this country. In the files of our paper from January 1 to the present day they will find a deal of valuable information. By a perusal of THE WHEEL they will be au courant with the cycling news of the day. THE WHEEL is the only subscription cycling weekly published in this country.

PROMINENT members in some of the clubs are talking up the advisability of having a cycling division in the parade to be held in New York on April 30. It is suggested that a number of wheelmen would turn out and that they would make a fair show on the pavement of Fifth Avenue. The movement has as yet taken no shape. We have been asked to call for suggestions, but we would ourselves suggest that the men who favor the project should work up private interest, and, if the results are favorable, call an informal meeting for discussion.

CHIEF CONSUL BIDWELL has discovered that he cannot resign to the Board of Officers of the New York State Division. He can only shift the mantle of office to the Vice-Consul at the will of the members, so he will shortly issue his third resignation. As no meeting of the members will be held until the meet at Buffalo next September, Mr. Bidwell will be compelled to wear his title, even though he may vest all his rights in Vice-Consul Bull. How very much legislated we League members are ! Another case of the least governed being the happiest.

WE have been trying to ascertain the extent of the demand or the wish for ladies' bicycles. We have not merely noted that which came across us, but have endeavored to obtain the opinions of ladies in various parts of the country, who are prominent among the lady riders of their sections, and may be presumed, in slight degree, to set the fashion. This week, "Marguerite" favors us with her views on the subject. They will be found exhaustive, comprehensive and commanding. They may be read with pleasure and profit. We have published many reasons why ladies should prefer the two to the three-wheeler; we are anxious to present the other side of the question. If there are any practical reasons why ladies should stand by the tricycle in preference to the bicycle, our readers would be glad to hear them. All the present stage of the game, it would seem that those who have made ready for a heavy trade in ladies' bicycles will not be disappointed.

AT the League meet, speaking of the necessity of assessing the State Divisions, one of the officers stated that the League would be unable to do any roads improvement work within the next two years, owing to the lack of funds. It may be stated, with a fair degree of safety, that in two years there will be but little or nothing for the League to do in the direction of roads improvement. Even now, public-spirited men are calling conventions and are privately and publicly urging roads improvement. The League should have been a leader in this matter. To have inaugurated a national roads improvement agitation would have forever redounded to the credit of the League, even in future years when it will have ceased to exist. But it has always seemed fated, this powerful organization, capable of doing so much, to be always handicapped by some petty form of mis-

management just at a time when some important work was on the card. Its present condition may be traced to its experiment as a publishing concern.

THE *Bicycling World* accepts the mile triplet record of 2m. 18 1-5s., because Messrs. Rudge & Co. have written a letter to that paper; a letter which contains no further information than did the meagre announcements of the trial in the English papers. Without stopping to exclaim over this glaring example of gullibility, we wish to protest against the acceptance of this record by the American sporting authorities. We furnish affidavits with records in this country, and even with these the English hem and haw before they give our records a grudging acceptance. We don't expect the English to furnish affidavits with all claims for records; we are not quibblers; but we are privately informed that the remarkable record which Rudge & Co. claim was accomplished on a down-hill bit of road. It is better for Rudge & Co. to have not the slightest suspicion rest on this record, and we shall refuse to accept it until we have read a surveyor's opinion of the road, and are informed how the timers clocked the *straightaway* mile. By the way, the editor of our esteemed contemporary calls Rudge & Co.'s letter of mere assertion a "mass of evidence."

THE anti-liberty bill recently introduced into the Missouri Legislature is exasperating, also somewhat amusing. The bill provides, among many things, that a rider shall dismount one hundred yards before meeting "a horse or mule," and "to remain dismounted until the "horse or vehicle drawn by horse or mule" shall have passed twenty yards beyond the point where the cyclist stands. It should be noted that the cyclist must dismount only upon the appearance of a horse or mule; nothing is said of jack-asses; no doubt the framer of the bill wished to appear disinterested. Our Missouri correspondent says the bill is "narrow, unreasonable, and obviously unconstitutional," all of which is true, but many of our readers will prefer to express their opinions of it in "cuss" language. The cyclists of Missouri should band together and have the bill amended as follows : " Each cyclist shall be armed with a blunderbuss, and when within one hundred yards of a mule, horse, or any other kind of four-legged beast, shall place his right hand on said blunderbuss; and should such mule, horse, or any other kind of four-legged beast evince any symptoms of antagonism, the cyclist shall draw said blunderbuss and shall blow out the brains of said mule, horse, etc."

CHIEF CONSUL BIDWELL has many excellent ideas on cycling, as a man of his long experience in the trade should have. Here are some of his ideas on teaching men to ride. They must be taught as quickly as possible, while the fever is at its height. They must not be discouraged and driven away by a long series of lessons ; once disgusted, always disgusted. Every cycling establishment should have a competent teacher. As soon as a man learns to ride he becomes a purchaser, and is not satisfied with a bicycle either, but wants a lamp, cyclometer and all the rest of the trimmings. Every time you teach a man to ride you have made a cyclist. In New York there is but one teacher. If there were six teachers there would be as many more riders as there are, for the view is taken that there is plenty of material to work

on and that a man has but to be guided through the a, b, c of cycling when he will become an enthusiast. A small, narrow hall is not the proper place to teach the art of riding. It is difficult, not to say unpleasant, to learn in such a place. Here in New York the best place is the public road, because no suitable building is obtainable. The moral of all this is that sellers of cycles should use every effort to teach men to ride.

FROM time to time we are in receipt of criticisms on wheels, which we are compelled to reject, and our refusal to publish is generally made the basis of a charge that we are bound to the trade, and "are afraid to publish anything against dealers." We have thought very seriously whether such communications are or are not entitled to publication, and we have decided that they are not, and for several reasons. The first reason is that we do not conceive it to be our duty to tell Jones that Robinson's wheels are no good, any more than the New York World has a right to inform its readers that Brown's goods are a deception and a snare In fact, we believe that any direct statement in a public print to the effect that a merchant's goods are unreliable would be sufficient grounds for an action for damages. We should be willing, however, to publish a careful criticism of any wheel, pointing out its good qualities and recommending improvement in defective points. But such criticisms are rarely received. The critic usually picks out some bad feature—and all wheels have weak points—and harps on it until the general public might readily believe that the wheel was fit only for the scrap heap.

A "CEAD MILLE FAILTHE" TO THE AMERICAN TOURING PARTY.

SIR: You are no doubt already aware that a party of about twenty-five cyclists, under the guidance of Mr. F. A. Elwell, of Maine, will leave America toward the end of May on a pleasure trip to Europe of about three months' duration, reaching our shores about the beginning of June, when they purpose riding from Queenstown to Dublin; but as their time in Ireland will be rather limited, they will unfortunately not be able to turn aside to visit Glenga. riffe and Killarney, but have decided to travel via Cork, Youghal, Waterford, Enniscorthy, Vale of Ovoca, Glendalough, on to Dublin. As many of our prominent wheelmen have expressed a desire to give our American cousins a hearty reception when they come among us, I think that this reception should be as representative of Dublin cyclists as possible ; so I propose, when the time for the arrival of Mr. Elwell's party approaches, to ask the captains and secretaries of the various metropolitan clubs to meet for consultation with the view of giving the visitors a *cead mille failthe*. Trusting to receive your co-operation and support, I remain,
Faithfully yours,
J. WHITE,
Chief Consul, C. T. C., Dublin.
97 Donore-terrace, South Circular-road.
Dublin, February 18, 1889.
—Irish Cycling and Athletic News.

A SELECTED LIST OF PATENTS.

[Reported especially for THE WHEEL AND CYCLING TRADE REVIEW by C. A. Snow & Co., patent attorneys, Washington, D. C.]

Henry S. Credlebough, New Carlisle, Ohio. Luggage carrier for bicycles.
W. C. Foster and W. H. Merritt, Somerville, Mass. Tricycle.
Charles E. Bentley, New York, N. Y. Velocipede.
All bearing date of March 5, 1889.

THE BOWLING LEAGUE

GAMES TO BE PLAYED.

Hudson County vs Atalanta, Jersey City, March 8.
Atalanta vs. New York, Newark, March 14
Harlem vs. Hudson County, Harlem, March 15.
Atalanta vs. Hudson County, Newark, March 21.

GAMES PLAYED.

January 4—Harlem, 1,490; New York, 1,342.
January 5—Hudson County, 1,408; Kings County, 1,488.
January 10—Harlem, 1,346; Atalanta, 1,343. Draw.
January 11—Kings County, 1,525; New York, 1,357.
January 15—Kings County, 1,432; Atalanta, 1,398.
January 18—Hudson County, 1,350; New York, 1,350.
January 25—Harlem, 1,669; Kings County, 1,360.
February 1—Hudson County, 1,203; Harlem, 1,154.
February 2—Atalanta, 1,456; New York, 1,357.
February 3—Kings County, 1,263; New York, 1,167.
February 15—Hudson County, 1,303; Kings County, 1,283.
February 16—New York, 1,393; Harlem, 1,205.
March 1—Hudson County, 1,494; New York, 1,335.

HUDSON COUNTY vs. NEW YORK.

The game between these two clubs was bowled at New York March 1, and resulted in a victory for the Hudson County Wheelmen. Following is the score :

HUDSON COUNTY.		NEW YORK.	
Grant	190	Nisbett	173
Stenken	133	Paynter	151
Keer	130	Guicouria	121
Korth	176	Moses	105
Shone	162	Daniels	151
W. Robertson	132	Leydecker	151
Whitman	128	Sutphen	153
Soper	179	Blake	178
Earl	132	Findley	109
Eldridge	132	Stott	137
Total	1,494	Total	1,355

Umpire, T. C. Crichton, K. C. W.
Scorers : E. H. Allaire, H. C. W. ; J. M. McFadden, N. Y. Bi. C.

MASSACHUSETTS DIVISION BOARD OF OFFICERS MEET.

The regular monthly meeting of the Board of Officers of the Massachusetts Division of the L. A. W. was held at the Colonade Hotel, Boston, on the evening of March 2. Chief Consul W. H. Emery presided. The members present were : Vice Consul A. W. Robinson, of Charlestown ; Secretary Sanford Lawton, Springfield ; J. Fred. Adams, F. I. Gorton, North Attleboro; I. E. Maeltrop, Roxbury ; J. B. Seward, Chelsea ; W. A. Moseman, Jamaica Plain ; C. S. Howard, Boston.

Following the reading of the Secretary's report by Mr. Lawton, a detailed report of the expenditures of the Division since January 1, 1888, was read. This showed that at the time of the annual meeting, last September, there was a balance of $199.27 on hand. Since then but $39 had been received. All of that money, with the exception of $16.07, has been spent. There was an animated discussion over various matters connected with the expenditures, which ended by all being approved. Various matters of routine business were transacted, and the meeting adjourned until the first Saturday in April.

Frank Brown, K. C. W., will be a member of the N. J. A. C. team this season. The team will consist of Caldwell, Bowman, Baggot, Pendleton and Brown.

SO VERY WELL INFORMED, YOU KNOW.
In consequence of the change of the female cyclists (troupe management, Philadelphia will be spared the delight of a six-days race (?) Shake, Quaker, my boy.—*Bicycling World*.

The female bicycle race at the Columbia Rink, Philadelphia, was brought to a successful conclusion on March 2 in the presence of a large number of apparently highly gratified spectators. At 10:30 P. M., when the race ended, the score stood as follows : Woods, 307 miles 6 laps; Lewis, 307 miles 6 laps; Baldwin, 197 miles 5 laps; Brown, 286 miles 5 laps. Louise Armainde rode an exhibition five miles in 18 minutes 45 seconds. She has further lowered the record she made on Friday night at this distance by 18 seconds.

Perhaps we shall be let alone after a time. We believe in and will follow the advice which Polonius gave to his son.

WHY LADIES SHOULD RIDE BI-CYCLES.

EDITOR OF THE WHEEL :
In response to your editorial invitation of February 15 relative to ladies using the safety bicycle in 1889, I wish to state a few reasons why we should use the two-wheeled machine, which it is my intention this season to ride.
"Many cyclists object to their wives or sisters riding bicycles on the score of impropriety." Where this comes in I fail to see. It may be in the word bicycle, which is ignorantly connected with the ordinary machine, and which only a gentleman can decorously ride. I find that the people who object are those who have no knowledge whatever of the machine to which they refer and deride so unmercifully. The cyclists are, as a rule, more charitable to the newcomer, for they doubtless suspect the advantages the two-wheeler holds over the tricycle. They also know (what the general run of people don't) that the mount and position is in every way similar to that of the "trike," only more graceful.

Because over-zealous circus managers, etc., have introduced certain unbecoming and questionable elements in the first stages of legitimate feminine bicycling, there is no reason why we should be deprived of the benefits accruing from the use of the new wheel. I admit that the result of the recent New York fiasco will be felt for a time, though mostly in the case of half-hearted converts and the fickle outside public.

It has always been an anomaly to me, as well as others, that the so-called weaker sex should, in cycling, have to make use of the heaviest and most ungainly machine. By no means the smallest advantage gained in the new departure is the great reduction of weight—the difference between thirty-six to forty-five pounds and sixty to eighty. This item in itself is enough to make one seriously consider discarding the old machine, not to mention the good riding we shall secure owing to our wheel being but single-track. Also, take into consideration the extra places (though few, they still count) which to visit on a tricycle is almost an impossibility. The bicycle will thus extend our riding circuit. Last season one trip in particular I was desirous of making, but was told, time and time again, by more experienced friends who had "been there before," and knew whereof they spoke, that it would be folly to attempt to ride there on a three-track wheel. So if I don't visit Portsmouth, N. H., and kindred places, this season it certainly will be because a break-down or some equally serious calamity prevents.

The bicycle will also afford the ladies who ride tandems exclusively an excellent opportunity for finding out, in reality, how much they are dependent on the gentleman rider for that most necessary cycling commodity, the "motive power." I feel certain that many a lady in the end of a day's ride imagines that she has most effectually done her share of the work, the mistake occurring not through a desire to shirk, or through inability to pedal, but because it is impossible to tell or judge how much effort is needed. It will also secure independence for the lady, since she at any time can take a ride, and not, as is the case if she rides tandem, lose many opportunities, having to wait until her brother, husband or friend is at hand, not in spirit but material force. Another most important and favorable advantage is the ease with which they can be stowed away. They require no house or shed to store them ; and, if away touring and weather prevents riding, can easily be expressed home with but little trouble. Many active bicyclists have before now been able to appreciate the latter blessing.

The only drawbacks which I see clearly as yet are the more sensitive steering and the inability to stand still without dismounting. These are certainly slight in comparison to the many advantages. The mount and dismount are so easy after one is familiar with the machine that very little objection can be based on the latter ground. But there is always two sides to a question, and it is best to consider both. The sensitive steering is also a fault remedied by continued use of the wheel.

I have not heard many ladies in and around Boston signify their intention of riding the safety this year, but I, nevertheless, consider that they are the best innovation in the interest of cycling for ladies.

Of course my views must be looked upon as partly theoretical, since my experience is limited to riding a tandem safety; but think there is little doubt but the concession will be granted that the progress of the past shows that a suitable bicycle for ladies means the introduction of a machine which will give the maximum of pleasure with the minimum of work.

MARGUERITE.

MAPLEWOOD, MASS., March 2, 1889.

FOR LADIES.

As the weather is now it renders riding quite impossible. I would impress upon ladies who possess a cycle the importance of closely studying the mechanism of their mounts. It is most important if anything goes amiss when out riding, that the rider should be capable of seeing at a glance the cause, for it open happens that what at first looks like a serious mishap may be only some small matter which can be put right in a few minutes. It is possible that a cycle repairer may not be near at hand, but there generally is a blacksmith or some mechanic close by who could put things right if pointed out in an intelligent manner. Such a case occurred to me a short time ago, and if I had not known what was the matter I should have had to walk my machine for about ten miles. A few extra nuts and screws with a complete set of tools, such as a spanner, screw-hammer, screw-driver, a bit of copper wire, etc. which will weigh but a trifle, should be carried. It is also very important to closely inspect every nut, bolt and bearing before starting on a ride. It is so easy to tighten up anything that has worked loose, and the result of having a loose nut or bolt causes other parts to also work loose if neglected and throws the machine considerably out of order. I am quite aware that this advice has been often tendered before, but it cannot be too often impressed upon riders.

Ladies purchasing a safety should be most particular in choosing a machine that has plenty of room between the back and front part of the frame above the crank arrangement, as the dismount can only be gracefully accomplished by drawing the right foot over to the left or near side and then alighting on the left foot. Care should be taken to do this when the left pedal is at the lowest point, then when the foot touches the ground the pedal will be farthest from the leg. I noticed some of the ladies' safeties at the Show that were much too closely built. So far as my experience goes it would be very awkward to dismount from them, and the same applies to mounting.

I noticed in one or two cycle papers that a small driving-wheel is deprecated. I have tried both sorts—a 30-inch and a 26-inch—and for convenience of mounting and dismounting, in my opinion, there is no comparison, the 26-inch being preferable of the two. Intending purchasers will certainly be wise in trying both sorts before deciding.

I also noticed that one writer advocated that the seat should be placed as near between the driving and steering wheel as possible; upon inquiry, and closely inspecting the position of the saddle of a large number of prominent riders, I found the saddle put as far back as possible. Having found this to be the case, I have adopted this position and am most pleased with the result.—*Wildflower, in Wheeling.*

PAULINE HALL AND THE CHICAGO CLUBS.

EDITOR OF THE WHEEL:

We are getting weary, oh! so weary, of all this rot about Pauline Hall causing a split between the cycling clubs of Chicago. Practically the fight is simply between the captains of the Chicago and Illinois clubs, and if it were not for the bull-headedness of only one member of the Illinois the whole matter would have been patched up long ago.

In the first place the theatre party that caused all the trouble was not a club affair. It was gotten up by Tom Roe and paid for *in full* by him. The Chicago Club, with the exception of his invited guests, knew nothing of the matter until it was all over and war had been declared. Mr. Roe has all along accepted all the blame, and does not see why the Chicago Club should be held at fault for his private acts.

The party was simply given as a joke, and would have been taken as such by any club not composed of *boys*.

By giving my little kick an inch or so you will greatly oblige,

BLUE AND GOLD.

CHICAGO, March 4, 1889.

THE FIFTH ANNUAL BALL OF THE NORTHAMPTON WHEEL CLUB.

The Northampton Bicycle Club held its fifth annual ball on last Monday evening. The opening exercises consisted of musical selections by the Opera House orchestra and fancy riding on the wheel by Mrs. Elliott, of Newton, and W. S. Maltby. Mrs Elliott gave a very pretty and graceful exhibition on a ladies' bicycle, and showed to good advantage the working of those machines. Mr. Maltby performed his wondrous feats on the wheel with his accustomed expertness and gracefulness. He introduced several new features, such as the backward riding movement and riding over a plank placed upon a box, tipping the plank as his machine went over it from one end to the other. His plucky and successful efforts in the execution of this act called forth rounds of applause.

At the close of this exercise the grand march was formed, in which sixty-six couples, led by President Campbell, participated. Refreshments were served and dancing continued till a late hour.

Among those present from out of town were: Miss Wilson, J. W. Drown, Harry Shipman, Mr. Hosmer, F. W. Dewey, Albert Hart, of Springfield; Charles Creigh, Miss Pike and Miss Hunt, of Boston; Miss Thayer, of Williamsburg, and F. O. Smith, of Holyoke. There was also present a large delegation from the Florence Cycle Club. The entertainment was financially and socially a success, and "the boys" feel much pleased with the result of their efforts.

THE SIZES OF WHEELS FOR SAFETIES.

Since the introduction of the rear-driver the wheels, both driving and steering, have pretty well by one consent been of a uniform size—namely, 30-inch diameter. During the past few months, however, some changes have been made, chiefly by those whose desire is for novelty, and much eulogium has been applied to the different systems suggested. Considering the steering-wheel first, we have had both small and large wheels advocated. Indeed, two of the earliest rear-drivers were the "Humber" and "B.S.A.," both of which were provided with very small steering-wheels. These, however, have disappeared, having given place to wheels of larger diameter. Some have recently advocated an advance in the other direction as far as 36-inch, the lessening of vibration being the main advantage claimed. As to whether this is or is not an advantage to the safety we are not yet prepared to pass a definite opinion, seeing that we have not had the opportunity of testing a machine on these lines sensibly constructed. True, we have tried a machine with 36-inch steering-wheel, but it had an abnormally small back-wheel, and we are inclined to think that perhaps this great difference between the sizes was the cause of our dissatisfaction with it, rather than the fault of the large steering-wheel alone, so that until we have tried, and put to a thorough test, a machine such as some persons, in their enthusiasm, are designating a Rational, we would prefer to pass no opinion. The fact remains, however, that the smaller the steering-wheel the quicker the steering, and *vice versa*. A rider on a machine with a small steering-wheel can turn very sharply, while as the size increases the movement becomes slower, and more like that of an ordinary. The excessive quickness of the steering with a very small wheel, has, indeed, as much as anything else, been the cause of its falling out of favor. It was so quick in action as to be at times unreliable. On the point of driving wheels the size of 30-inch, which has been until the beginning of this season an almost universal one, it was adopted as one that could readily be stridden over by the rider of average height. Several very painful accidents occurred, in one or two instances to riders who had been accustomed to the front-driving type of safety, which was an universal favorite before the introduction of the "Rover," but these were caused mainly through the method of dismounting adopted—namely, that of springing backward from the saddle and alighting upon both feet simultaneously, a method which though general with riders of the "Kangaroo" has never found favor with riders of the rear-driver. The change proposed with regard to the driving-wheel is in a downward direction, and machines with 28, 26, or even 24-inch drivers have been constructed. So far as the racing path is concerned, we see no reason to object to a small wheel—unless for exceptionally tall riders—as it will be rolling upon an entirely smooth surface. Our experience, however, with a machine having 26-inch driving-wheel has certainly not been satisfactory, and we are inclined to doubt very much if for road work these machines will meet with any amount of popular favor. The vibration is excessive, and as another fad in connection with the small driving-wheel is the placing of the rider immediately over it, this is rendered ten times worse. One of the strong points in the position of the rider on a safety as usually built, is the placing of the body between the wheels, whereby the amount of rise each wheel has to make to surmount an object is halved or thereabouts, by the time it reaches the rider. The placing, however, of the rider on the top of the wheel makes it a certainty that every inch the wheel rises over a stone or drops into a hollow, just so much must the rider rise or fall, and in practice we found the theory most fully carried out. For the use of ladies, who may possibly be supposed, to ride only on selected roads, the small driving-wheel may perchance have an advantage, insomuch that it is more easily covered with a dress-guard, and the mounting from the front, which a lady is compelled to do, is rendered somewhat more feasible, but even this we are not at all inclined to consider as a foregone conclusion. Our own opinion on the driving-wheel question is, that so far as male riders are concerned at least, a very tall rider will be a gainer with a 32-inch driving-wheel, and that for no one but very short riders, to whom the possibility of alighting on the mud-guard in dismounting may be present, should any reduction from 30-inch be made. On the point of undue smallness of driving wheel and excessive size of steerer there can be no two opinions to one who has practically tried such a machine. Not only is it ugly in the extreme, but its frame is necessarily long and awkwardly arranged, and the vibration from the back wheel is excessive, every jolt and jar of the machine being felt by the rider, while the steering is slow and awkward. For a tall rider, too, the seat pillar is unnecessarily dangerously long. In the machine which was submitted to us for experiment we found the longest seat pillar made by the company was not sufficient to give us our full reach upon it, and an extra one had to be made, with the result that it always felt to us dangerously weak. So far as we can see, there can be little gained in a departure from the 30-inch so far as the driving-wheel is concerned, and in the matter of steering a 32-inch wheel will give entirely satisfactory results; and until, as we said before, we have experimented with a properly constructed 36-inch steerer, we cannot conscientiously advocate any serious departure from ordinary sizes. —*The Cyclist.*

VICTOR CATALOGUE, 1889.

While the general run of catalogues this year has been of high grade and artistic in conception, the Victor, the latest to come to our notice, is by far the prettiest of the lot, the cover being of a singularly bold and beautiful design.

The introductory states that the Overman Wheel Co. have been in business for seven years; that every move has been based on the desire to secure permanent success by making such changes and turning out such work as would recommend itself; that the firm has ever been reaching upward and ahead; that careful watching of the development of the art, combined with "that keen Yankee wit, which, never satisfied, strives ever for something better," has produced the Victor of to-day. The introductory is as crisp and as clear as the catchy advertisements which have made the Victor people famous. Several paragraphs are devoted to descriptions of the materials used, illustrated descriptions of the Bown ball-bearing, hollow rims, method of inserting tire, etc., etc.

All the wheels turned out by the Overman Wheel Co. are fully illustrated and described. The mounts described are the Victor Light Roadster, with cuts of the hub, cranks and arrangement of the spokes, description of forks, hubs, handle-bars, handles and spokes; also cuts of the head, pedals, saddles and step. The Light Roadster, 50-inch, sells at $125.

The Victor safety is carefully dissected, illustrated in whole and in part and described. The remarkable popularity of this wheel, the result of its thorough construction and the anti-vibration spring fork with which it is fitted, is too well known to need comment. The stock wheel is geared to 54, but will be geared to 51, 57 or 60 inches upon order; price, $135.

The other wheels described are the Victor tricycle, a bicycle steerer, with the front forks fitted with an anti-vibration spring, similar to that used in the safety; price, $160; and the Victor Junior bicycle, a high grade boys' and youths' wheel, made from 38 to 50 inches, and selling from $40 to $55. Ten pages of the catalogue are devoted to a list of sundries. Overman Wheel Co., Boston; special agents, A. G. Spalding & Bros., New York and Chicago.

NORTHAMPTON NOTES.

Though winter's reign in this part of Massachusetts can scarcely be said to be over, yet there are faint signs of an awakening interest in cycling matters, and those early birds, the new patterns of '89 wheels, are alighting among us. Samples of the Star safety, Columbia Light Roadster safety and the Eagle have been received, and much interest is shown by those thinking of a new mount for the coming season. The Eagle, of which so much is expected, is the latest comer, and even old riders show a becoming timidity in attempting to guide its flight. Barring a little seeming "crankiness" in steering and learning to mount by the pedal, there seems to be no reason why any fair rider of the ordinary should not easily learn to manage it. At the annual grand ball of the Northampton Wheel Club, which comes off March 4, a sample will be exhibited, and it is hoped an expert will be present to give an exhibition of the wheel's many good qualities. Mr. and Mrs. Elliott, of Newton, Mass., are to be present and exhibit the "Sterling" quadricycle and ladies' bicycle, and it is announced that any lady interested in the latter mount can be taught to ride, free of charge, in one hour's time, on the afternoon of that day. May the interest thus awakened have a healthy growth!

Posters for the ball are already out, and quite an elaborate programme for the opening concert is being prepared. The matter of decorations for the City Hall is in the Executive Committee's hands, but I doubt if anything elaborate is attempted this year, as former years seem to show that the whole labor falls on a few members, and the increase of attendance does not appear to justify the trouble taken.

At the last business meeting of the Wheel Club six new members were added, two active and the remainder associate. I understand the limit of associate membership—twenty—is nearly reached, and hope the club will not make the mistake so often made by other clubs of allowing associate members the privilege of voting, and so a voice in the conducting of affairs. Debarring them of that privilege is much more apt to induce them later to apply for active membership. Some few disgruntled members complain that too free a use of club privileges is made by associates, but I can hardly see why that should be a cause for complaint. A club is always being reduced in membership from one cause or another, and it is necessary sometimes to recruit the ranks and replenish the club treasury from sources outside of active riders.

Two attempts have lately been made for a club photo, and the latter, on Washington's Birthday, proved very successful, twenty-four members turning out to be "took." The first was rather in the line of experiment with the "flash" light, but the faces looked so drawn and ghastly that the idea of developing was given up. A set of photos of scenes along the side path between this city and Holyoke serve to help ornament the ante-room or small parlor opening into the club rooms, and are the gift of Mr. Farr, of the Holyoke Bicycle Club, one of the most active members and largely instrumental in carrying out the good work of building such a path. Were it not for the enthusiasts among us, little would be accomplished in such ways.

I notice from a late copy of *Wheeling*, that J. Purvis Bruce is on his way back to this country, and the news will especially be received with joy by his many friends in Minneapolis, Minn., and vicinity. He was about the only wide-awake man that had an interest in cycling matters there and a good chance to air his ideas through the daily press. In a recent letter from that city, I learn that Heath & Co. have again removed, this time to a stand in the "Permanent Exhibit" store, on Fourth Street, South, across the street from their former location, and that Colie Bell will ride and represent the Eagle in that city for 1889. Of the two clubs there, but one, the Minneapolis, shows signs of life, and prominent members of the Mercury threaten to leave and apply for membership in the former club if their long-dormant organization does not wake up and "do something." In my humble opinion, nothing but the Judgment Day will ever accomplish that result.

L. B. G.

FENTON'S FANCIES.

That very unwelcome guest, a bad cold, was with me last week, and in consequence I was unable to furnish my usual weekly letter. However, in the shibboleth of the circus, "Here we are again." I hope that my adversaries won't feel badly that I did not give them a chance this last week to pick some more flaws in my rhetoric, criticize my ideas, and form vague verbal caricatures of my personal appearance—absurd enough, it is true, but satisfactory in that at last my windy and would-be critics have the pleasure of seeing their ebullitions in cold type. The joy of the youthful writer is most tremendous and awe-inspiring when he first has the pleasure of seeing some of his writings in print. How I envy Nemo, our juvenile Solon of cycing laws! Just imagine his infantile glee as he perused his own article, and remarked to himself, "I guess I've settled Fenton this time." Oh, Nemo, my infant Socrates! You are young in years and your methods are childish, but you and your friends, Constant Reader, Veritas and Pro Bono Publico, are chestnuts, just the same. Some one ought to gather you next fall, and in the same basket should be put "Old Nestor, whose wit was mouldy ere your grandsires had nails on their toes." And you ask me who Nestor is? That you must find out for yourselves, but I will tell you that he and ex-Mayor Hewitt ran a dead-heat for the world's championship at letter-writing. There's a clue for you!

The smooth running machinery of the League has ground out a nice new president for us, and in consequence we should all be in a perfectly ecstatic state of bliss, I suppose. But are we? What do A and B, ordinary members of the League, have to say about the election of a president for the ensuing year? What value has your opinion, my dear friend C? A little bird whispers to me that the answer can only be algebraically expressed, and that X, representing an unknown quantity, is the correct reply. True enough, such an example can be proved at sight. Let us suppose that the two candidates for the presidency were named Buncomb and Messup. Neither A nor B wished to see either of these gentlemen elected, and yet were unable to help in electing their own candidate, the honest and upright O. K. Everyway, whom everyone likes. But the end of the present system of League politics is approaching. The march of public opinion is slow moving, but, like the Alpine glacier, it gathers resistless force with each inch that it advances. You cannot check it. As well try to stay the progress of an avalanche, or, like King Canute, bid the sea stand still. The Alpine peasant, with that unobtrusive common-sense which is so often to be found among the common people, leaves his house to its fate when he finds the glacier is approaching, knowing that too long delay will force him into an abyss from which there will be no chance of emerging. The ground is slowly opening now beneath the feet of the "League ring." Let us hope that they and their "dog-in-the-manger" politics may be speedily engulfed by the abyss, for their short-sighted wisdom can never equal the stolid perception of the peasant, as far as practical utility goes.

The industrial and civic parade, which occurs during the Washington Centennial celebration, in April, ought to afford a good opportunity for a large turn-out of bicyclists. Here's a fine chance for some energetic club to distinguish itself by organizing a bicycling division for the occasion.

The bowling team of the New York Bicycle Club have at last succeeded in winning a game. By all accounts the Harlem-New York game, on the latter's alleys, was an easy win, the score showing eighty-eight pins difference in the New Yorks' favor. This practically settles the championship in the Hudson County Wheelmen's favor.

FENTON.

From the *Cyclist* we republish an editorial on the size of wheels in safeties. The conclusions of the *Cyclist* on this matter will be at once coincided with by every thoughtful and experienced rider. Those who have had no experience should read this article.

Colonel George A. Jessup is already in the field for 1890.

JERSEY CITY.

In my letter a few weeks ago, I mentioned the fact that several of the wheelmen in this section of the State were in favor of running Mr. Llewellyn H. Johnson for New Jersey's Chief Consul at the next election. The appearance of that paragraph in THE WHEEL has been the cause of several letters being addressed to me, and numerous verbal communications hurled at me, naming other gentlemen than Mr. Johnson for that position. Every really active wheelman in this State feels that something definite must be done, and that quickly, in order to restore the League membership where it was a year or two ago, and the question arises; "Who will be the *best* man to undertake this feat?" Several enthusiasts from the Southern part of the State have been heard from, naming their favorites for this position; I notice, however, that the tide runs in favor of Dr. G. Carlton Brown, of Elizabeth. There is no doubt as to Dr. Brown's ability to properly fill the position. "He's been there before." He has been tried and found O. K. The League membership of this State was at its zenith when he was at the helm. He has been more or less identified in almost continuous service for the L. A. W. for six years past, and is, at the present time, on the L. A. W. Membership Committee and Vice Consul of New Jersey. He has been instrumental to a great extent in furthering the interests of wheelmen, in connection with the New Jersey County Road Bill, which recently passed our Senate. From what I can learn, there is no doubt that if Dr. G. Carlton Brown can be induced to accept the nomination, he will be the next Chief Consul of New Jersey.

A story is told of one of our enthusiastic members, who until recently has been in the habit of taking out his wheel every evening and going to the residence of his "best calico."

His route led him across some vacant lots, on a well-beaten path, probably one hundred yards long, which he took as a means of short cut.

It was but natural that he took advantage of all short cuts when on such a mission.

One day the owner of the lots had a gang of men at work, digging cellars for a row of houses he intended to erect, and the following evening our hero mounted his wheel as usual, and started for *her* home.

The night was dark.

The Jersey City Economical Board had not provided gas lamps in that vicinity.

When he reached the path across the lots, he started on a grand "Willie Windle" spurt. He went a la Windle for about 16 feet. And then—then—he—*felt—that—he—was—soaring—soaring!!* There was a distinct feeling of goneness. The earth had left him. Thousands of thoughts crowded his mind in that fraction of a second. If his life was only spared, he would pay up his back dues and a year's dues in advance to help out the Rent Committee; he would never send potatoes as a substitute for fruit to another smoker; he would nev—bang! He had landed; he had reached what he felt was another world.

* * * * * *

When he became thoroughly separated from his wheel, he found that what he supposed to be Australian soil was the bottom of McGinness's cellars. With the assistance of the numerous small boy, he managed to leave the cellar, take his wheel and walk home. No, he would not call on his Imogene in his then "dynamitic" frame of mind. The incident, however, has had the effect of having Mr. Wheelman call on Miss Girl in citizen's clothes. He naturally feels that night-riding is not conducive to good health.

I am glad to note that Jonah, in the last issue of the *Bicycling World* is in sympathy with my proposition to form "The New Jersey Team Road Racing Association." Captain Day, of the Hudson County Wheelmen, has been working the matter up, and he finds, as stated by Jonah, that there are several cycling clubs in the neighborhood of South Jersey and Monmouth who are willing and anxious to contribute to the support of such an association. The Freehold boys, I am told, have some good stock in the way of racing material, and I thi[illegible], with proper management, there would be no [illegible]oubt as to the success of the N. J. T. R. R. A. [illegible] derstand that each of the races run [illegible] pices of the defunct association [illegible] borhood of $75.00 or $80.00, [illegible] not in the ring, seems rather exorbita[illegible] think that this new bidder for public support could be run on a much more economical basis, and, at the same time, award place medals as was done by the old association. The cost of a suitable first prize for the winning club would be apt to have a bad effect upon the treasury, and I am heartily in accord with the suggestion made by Jonah to the effect that the dealers be requested to put up the trophy.

The captains of all cycling clubs in New Jersey are requested to correspond with Captain Edw. J. Day, of the Hudson County Wheelmen, Jersey City, in order that united action may be secured and speedy organization effected.

The first one-mile struggle for the Benedict medal was run off on the morning of Washington's Birthday. This medal has to be won three times to become the property of a competitor. Only such members of the H. C. W. who have never won first or second place in any race are allowed to compete. The course selected was from the old ro[illegible] racing starting point on Springfield Avenue, toward Irvington. J. L. Robertson, Jr., finished first in 3m. 35s., Captain Day second, and Morse and Cordner third and fourth respectively. The time was good, considering the fact that the men raced in their regular uniforms, and that they did not mount their wheels until after the word "go" was given.

The next competition will probably be held about April 1.

The good luck of the H. C. W. bowling team sticks to them. On Saturday evening last the team, accompanied by their shouters, went over to play their old friends, the New York Bicycle Club. The bowling team yell of "Ki-yippy, ki-yippy, ki-yippy, ki-yah; Hudson County, here we are; who-wah, who-wah, hah, hah, hah!" seemed to encourage the boys, and when it became frequent on the last frame, the fever caught Nisbett, of the New Yorks, who wound up with three strikes. The score is published in another column.

COASTER.

TROY NOTES.

At "Bicycle Hall," Monday evening, February 25, the Troy Bicycle Club's bowling team defeated the team of the Railroad Young Men's Christian Association by a score of 2,056 to 1,792. The bicycling team was composed of the following: J. M. Van Arnam, captain, F. S. Schutt, H. B. Hogben, C. F. Biermeister, W. M. Thiessen; and the R. R. Y. M. C. A.'s team, G. W. Daley, captain, A. H. Seeley, F. Howland, C. Clowser and H. Fisher.

The Troy Bicycle Club is going into baseball, if reports are true, as they have applied for membership in the local baseball league. They might use their wheels to run the bases, if a spot can be found smooth enough around the city to play baseball on.

Chas. H. Wilson, of the Trojan Wheelmen, wants to sell his Humber tandem, which he and his brother used to ride before the yachting craze took possession of them. John Drake, of the same club, is not seen out on his wheel he used to ride so *carefully*. He would need a tandem now.

Ex-Representative George A. Spicer thinks of going to Chicago to live. He would take a good sized ordinary, as he measures 6 feet 4 inches in his stocking feet and weighs about 275 pounds. His brother, Le Grand, is talking of getting a safety, but I fear it will have to be one which has a good reach, as *he* measures 6 feet 2 inches and weighs 205 pounds. I think the former one of the largest members of the League.

Representatives Knowlson and Gallien have plenty of work before them if they "boom" the League in this city and Albany this year. I hope they will keep at it, and at the same time not forget the "roads question."

I hear that Representative Reynolds and wife, of Stockport, talk of riding a safety tandem this year.

ORNH QBA.

MARCH 4, 1889.

The *Sewing Machine and Cycle News* steals Mr. L. H. [illegible]rter's admirable translation of "Gedicht," w[illegible]ch recently appeared in this paper.

BALTIMORE.

Ever since bicycle riding began in Baltimore there has been open warfare between the knights of the wheel and the horsemen of the city. The former claim that they have been continually interfered with by horsemen who will not extend to them any of the courtesies of the road, and some trouble of this kind has occurred even within the past year. This state of things has naturally caused some bad feeling. Horsemen, as a rule, look upon the advent of cycling as a public nuisance. They claim that the bicycles scare their horses, and sometimes cause considerable damage. But there is not the same danger there once was, as the presence of wheels on almost every avenue and driveway has accustomed horses in a great measure to them.

The Centaur Club is seeking for new headquarters in the neighborhood, on East Lombard Street. The present club house is not roomy enough to accommodate the members.

The usual weekly dance, held at the Baltimore Club house, brought out many members.

The annual election of officers of the Maryland Club will take place on Monday, March 11. Messrs. Yates Penn[illegible]an, S. T. Clark, Albert Mott, H. E. Brown, I. H. Balderson, Fred. Hutchinson and Ira C. Canfield, the Nominating Committee, are preparing the ticket.

The regular quarterly meeting of the Board will be held March [illegible]. It is proposed to invite the National League to hold the annual meet here.

The Maryland Club will hold a banquet at the club house on Thursday, March 14.

The annual election of officers of the Maryland Club will take place on Monday, March 11.

C. L. Leisen, a member of the Pennsylvania Club, of Philadelphia, spent last Friday evening in this city at the Maryland Club.

Bad weather has arrived and stopped wheeling in this city.

Almost all the Baltimore wheelmen would have most likely attended the inauguration parade if it had not been for the disagreeable weather which was prevailing.

The Baltimore Club presented J. M. Cummings, Secretary of their club, with a handsome silver dinner set at his wedding, which took place at 1743 Park Avenue, the home of the bride, Miss Edith F. Brittain.

BAY RIDGE.

UNIVERSAL CYCLING CLUB NOTES.

Brooklyn Institute was crowded beyond the expectation of the members of the U. C. C. on Friday evening last, it being their second annual reception. The hall was tastefully decorated with wheels and the club's colors.

Following are the names of those noticed among the crowd: Mr. and Mrs. Fred. Miller, Mr. C. Dunham, Miss L. Dunham, Mr. J. Judd, Miss M. Cochrane, Mr. C. Isbell, Miss L. Stein, Mr. W. Finn, Miss M. Meaney, Mr. W. Shannon, Miss N. Southern, Mr. D. Hennessy, Miss L. Hennessy, Mr. A. H. Miles, Miss P. Drewback, Mr. P. Finn, Miss N. Smith, Mr. and Mrs. F. Swift, Mr. C. Denison, Miss P. Francis, Mr. and Mrs. W. Blanchard, Mr. W. Roberts, Miss R. Roberts, Mr. M. Goodstein, Mr. W. Stanton, Mr. W. Masterson, Mr. A. Levy.

W. S. Hannon has been doing considerable riding of late, except when his wheel has been in the repair shop.

The club has decided to award mileage prizes for the members having the largest mileage during 1889.

Lieutenant Fred. has been recruiting during the last few months, but intends to make a break and try to make that "Blarsted Smithtown Run," which did him up last season.

HUSTLER.

March 4, 1889.

George W. Kreger, of the Long Island Wheelmen, has been in the "gym" all winter and will race this spring. Kreger should show form equal to that of Crist and Rich at their best.

ST. LOUIS.

The wheelmen of this city and State are thoroughly aroused over the threatened invasion of their rights by the Warner Bill, referred to in my last letter. This is really the first attempt at hostile legislation in the State, and the results are anxiously awaited. A copy of the bill has been received here, and for absolute absurdity it easily takes the premium. The provision requiring riders to dismount one hundred yards before meeting "a horse or mule or any kind of vehicle drawn by horse or mule," and to remain dismounted until the "horse or mule or vehicle drawn by horse or mule" shall have passed beyond twenty-five yards, is especially brilliant. Possibly through oversight, but more likely through ignorance, the law is not made applicable to tricycles, and if it passes and stands the test of the courts we shall all have to buy trikes or quit riding. In that event this will be a good locality for some of our manufacturers to unload their surplus stock of old trikes. It is very humiliating to the cyclists of this State, that while New York, New Jersey, Massachusetts, Ohio and other enlightened localities are passing laws to protect wheelmen and establish their rights, Missouri is considering the passage of laws that will drive them off the highways and utterly annihilate the sport. However, the bill presented by Warner is so narrow, unreasonable and obviously unconstitutional that we cannot think for a moment that it has a chance of passing. We have a large number of riders in the city, as well as in the interior portions of the State, who, while professing to be enthusiastic lovers of the sport, have steadily resisted all efforts to get them into the League. They could not see any use or advantage in belonging to the organization. Now that their rights are menaced, they are quite willing that the League should take up the cudgel in their behalf and protect their interests. This means that they realize their own helplessness in a dilemma such as now confronts them, and recognize the value of an organization fully equipped to defend and protect their interests. To me it seems incredible that there should be so many riders who persistently refuse to join the League and yet are quite content to enjoy the privileges which that organization has and can secure for them. If this sort of thing is not selfish and parsimonious to the last degree I do not know what is. It will be, perhaps, in the nature of a gratifying surprise to your readers to know that Brother Page has seen the error of his ways and has sent in his application. There are others quite as much in need of repentance as he was, and if they all come in this Warner Bill may prove a blessing in disguise.

The arrangements for the Stone-Lumsden races are as follows: The first, a track race, distance one mile, to take place at Chicago Saturday, May 18; the second, also on the track, distance three miles, to be ridden at St. Louis Saturday, May 25; and the final contest, twenty miles on the road, to be run off at Crawfordsville, Indiana, Monday, May 27. The prizes are medals valued at $50 on each event, and one valued at $100 to go to the one winning the series. The story comes down here from Chicago that St. Louis had to be shamed into making the match, and unless this story is contradicted from the Chicago end, the entire correspondence that passed between Garden and Brewster will be given out for publication. That will effectually settle the question as to who was shamed into making the match.

There is nothing new to report concerning the approaching election of the Missouri Club. It is possible that there is a still hunt being indulged in, but if so it is being kept very quiet. The committee appointed to consider ways and means to increase the interest in cycling in the city has been hard at work, and it is understood that they will have an interesting report to make at the next meeting of the club. The committee consists of Professor Stone, Geo. K. Andrews and William Brown.

Since the foregoing was written, the report comes down from Jefferson City that the Warner Bill, at the urgent request of its author, has been reported favorably by the Committee on Roads and Highways, and is now on the House calendar. Remonstrances against its passage have been prepared and mailed to all the local Consuls throughout the State, with the request that they [illegible]ned and sent to their respective rep[illegible] the Legislature. There will be a [illegible] sent from here.—ITHURIEL.

BUFFALO.

The Buffalo Bicycle Club celebrated their tenth anniversary by a banquet at the Genesee on Washington's Birthday. Covers were laid for fifty. The club was organized ten years ago in the office of Dr. H. T. Appleby, on West Eagle Street, with three charter members. The present membership is about 150, and their club house is one of the finest in the country, being equipped with every requisite of a model wheel home.

Bicycle news appears to be unworthy of attention on the sporting page of some of our city dailies, and whenever an item does appear it is generally old and incorrect. The other day a morning paper announced that S. G. Whittaker had made a mile in 2m. 18 2-5s.

A new sporting paper, *The Whip*, will make its appearance about April 1. It is to be devoted to sports in general, and will include bicycling as one of its specialties. "Pendragon," a well-known sporting writer, both in this country and in England, is at its head. The Buffalo and Rochester Clubs, and several other wheeling and sporting organizations in this part of the State, have adopted the paper for their official organ.

The asphalt pavements are in good shape for riding, the recent rains having melted and washed the snow away. There is some talk of club runs, but in all probability ere this goes to print a snow-storm will unawares swoop down upon us and our hopes of an early season.

The Ramblers have lost three, and perhaps four, members by their departure to other parts of the country. Wirtner and Hughson started for California after the theatre party of last Wednesday night; Graham is now employed in New York City by the Erie Railroad Company, and may remove there permanently; Schmidt has gone to Boston, and with him the club dog, "Rambler," who made the 100-mile run from Erie with the boys last summer, when they lowered the time made by the Buffalos a few weeks previous to their attempt.

Vice Consul W. S. Bull is about to begin the preparation of a State Division hand-book. It will contain a list of League hotels and local Consuls in the State, and also several articles by local wheelmen.

H. E. Ducker will not leave until autumn to take charge of the Boston enterprise.

Pauline Hall may not have the kindest of feelings toward the cyclists of the Queen City of the Lakes, but then it was not our fault, and it happened thusly: Several months ago when it was announced that the Casino Opera Company would visit Buffalo, the Buffalos, in the local papers, gave it out that they were going to honor the stately Pauline with a theatre party. The Ramblers also decided to have a theatre party, and it was to occur on the same night as the Buffalo's, but Marie Jansen was selected as the particular one to whom they wished to show favor. At a meeting of the Buffalos the theatre party was brought up, and after a stormy discussion was voted down, much to the chagrin of the younger element. Wednesday night at last arrived. Marie had been notified of the attention which she was to receive, and acknowledged the honor by a very sweet letter to the club. About eight o'clock the Ramblers arrived in their "claw-hammers," took their seats and awaited the rising of the curtain. The Buffalos had not put in an appearance, and the rumor, which had been circulated the day before to the effect that they had given up their party, was soon verified. The curtain arose, and Pauline made her entrance, the club colors of the Ramblers, white and blue, being conspicuously displayed on her person. There was something wrong. Then came Marie dressed in the flimsy garments of *Nadjy*. Up the centre aisle came the boy with the floral tribute for the gauzy *Nadjy*. He performed his work correctly, and the curtain went down. In the next act it was noticed that Pauline had discarded her blue and white, and her face bore not the sweetest smile imaginable. Who made the mistake? is the question that has been troubling the boys. Surely not they.

To.

NOTES FROM THE CITY OF BROTHERLY LOVE.

Friends of Robert L. Shaffer, and he has a legion, will hear with regret that at the last municipal election he ran for the humble but important position of School Director and was defeated. It was rather hard, for his benevolent ways and fatherly smile would have made him an ideal member of the board. But, alas! the ward in which he lives is overwhelmingly Republican while he is a staunch Democrat, and this accounts for his overthrow. However, his political ambition has by no means received its death blow, and some day we hope to hear our friend "Bobby's" name resounding through the halls of fame as—as——but why anticipate? Time will tell.

The South End Wheelmen intend, as a fitting finale to their series of successful hops, to give a grand ball some time after Lent in one of our large halls. This will be the first one of its kind in Philadelphia, and under the skillful management of the same gentlemen who managed the club's private affairs, cannot be otherwise than a success.

The subject of holding a grand inter-club run has at various times been agitated, but with no result. Now I have another scheme which I think is thoroughly practical. Why not hold a mammoth picnic in Fairmount Park, say on Decoration Day? Let every club participate, and wheeling would get a great boom here. In the afternoon they could all ride to the famous Lan-

caster Pike and Montgomery Avenue, only a few miles distant, and hold several road races. I think the idea would take if it were only pushed, and am sure it would do much to promote among the wheelmen of this city a fraternal feeling, which at the present time is sadly lacking.

There is a charming young lady living on Diamond Street, who every Sunday sits at her window to see the Century Wheelmen start on their weekly club runs. When they arrive opposite the house in which she resides a general taking off of hats—or caps, I should say—is in order, a salute which she answers with a pleasant smile. Now, here is where the joke comes in. Each and every heart-breaker in the club, and there ARE a few, fondly imagines that the smile is aimed at him in particular, and congratulates himself that he has such a nice "mash;" but a little bird residing in the neighborhood has told me that there *is* one, and after he has glided by on his steed of steel she leaves her post not to return again till the afternoon, when she watches for his return. I have promised not to tell who it is, and it would not do anyway, for it would shatter the hopes of some of the "boys" and I would be answerable for the consequences. So keep right on, look your prettiest, but still the right man is under the watchful eye of

ARGUS.

PHILADELPHIA, March 3, 1889.

HARLEM WHEELMEN'S ENTERTAINMENT.

The entertainment and reception of the Harlem Wheelmen will be held at West End Hall on Wednesday, March 13. From the interest shown by the members and their friends in this affair, it will undoubtedly be a grand success. The entertainment will consist of music under the direction of Professor Julius Luster. Mrs J. Williams Macy, the contralto, has been engaged, as well as the Perry Brothers, together with J. M. Young, in his imitation of celebrated actors, and F. W. Isenbarth, on the zither. Tickets admitting gentleman and ladies to entertainment and reception, $1. Tickets can be had of club members or at the door.

The progressive euchre party given by the lady members of the Harlem Wheelmen, at the club house, on Wednesday evening, was, as usual, a great success. The prizes were won by Miss Sadie Field, Mrs. L. A. Weaver, Prof D. R. Robus and Mr. Millard Cossit. The party was largely attended. Among the visitors were : Mr. Clark, of the Citizens ; Charles A. Sheehan, of the Manhattans ; Mr. B. Ambroy, of the Detroit Bicycle Club, of Detroit, Mich.; Mr. and Mrs. Cossit, of the Riversides, of this city, and Mr. and Mrs. Henry Cochran. At 10.30 refreshments were served, followed by dancing. These pleasant evenings of the Harlem Wheelmen are a new departure for this club, and the members are beginning to appreciate the change. Their grand entertainment, to be given at West End Hall on Wednesday, March 13, will be the event of their season, and we would advise all wheelmen to attend.

THE WORLD will come to you in *rolls* next week.—*Bicycling World.*

So they are going to feed League members on *Bi. World* sandwiches! This is the "other concessions" referred to by the Executive Committee in its late report.

We saw five *Bicycling Worlds* at the New York Club house on Thursday evening last, *with the wrappers all on.*

A deal of abuse has been heaped upon the head of the New York Club within the past few weeks. This paper has assisted at the heaping. The result is increased activity in the club. The billiard-room is lively ; the game of "hearts" progresses in lively fashion. The kitchen is taxed to its utmost resources to satisfy the epicures of the club. The house no longer suggests the icy habitat of the Esquimaux. The members are riding. The club is doing good work in securing petitioners for the pavement of the Boulevard. Its President will shortly don overalls, roll up his sleeves and direct the minions of the Park Department how to properly pave Seventy-second Street. Altogether it is a very active and happy family, in the New York Club. Long may it wave !

Mr. A. E. Schaaf, of the Gormully & Jeffery Manufacturing Company, was in town on Friday last. He has started on an extended trip " Down East."

The New Bedford (Mass.) Club dined " Doc " Emery on March 6.

The Cambridgeport Cycle Club will hold a fancy dress ball on March 27.

F. A. Elwell's European party will sail on May 18.

The Universal Cycling Club, of Brooklyn, held an enjoyable reception at the Brooklyn Institute on last Friday evening.

MY DEAR PRIAL.

SAN FRANCISCO, Cal., Feb. 14, 1889.
MY DEAR PRIAL:

I think you have the best of the *Bulletin* in the argument as to circulation. I know that not one-third of the wheelmen here read the *Bulletin* or even take it out of its wrapper. The riders here say there is no comparison between the papers—that the *Bulletin* is the poorest apology for a cyclists' paper they have ever seen.

Sincerely yours,
R—— S——.

Thanks, awfully.

" We have examined the (Brooks) Cyclometer, and must say that it is the simplest and must be the most durable, as there is nothing to wear."
LINCOLN HOLLAND & Co.,
Worcester, Mass.
Only Five Dollars. Brooks Odometer Co.,
Lowell, Mass.

THE WHEEL

— AND —

CYCLING TRADE REVIEW,

Published every Friday morning.

Entered at the Post Office at second class rates

Subscription Price,	-	- -	$1.00 a year.
Foreign Subscriptions,	-	-	6s. a year.
Single Copies,	-	- - -	5 Cents.

Newsdealers may order through AM. NEWS Co.

All copy should be received by Monday.
Telegraphic news received till Wednesday noon.

Advertising rates on Application.

F. P. PRIAL, Editor and Proprietor
23 Park Row,

P. O. Box 444,   *New York.*

Persons receiving sample copies of this paper are respectfully requested to examine its contents and give us their patronage, and as far as is convenient, aid in circulating the journal, and extend its influence in the cause which it so faithfully serves. Subscription price, $1 per year.

"BY FAR THE BEST."

CARPENTERSVILLE, ILL., }
February 2, 1889. }

F. P. PRIAL:

Dear Sir—Enclosed find draft for $1, for which please send THE WHEEL for one year, from March 1, 1889. This is by *far the best cycle paper* published. Send me a few extra copies, and I will try and secure names for you.

Yours, etc.,   FRED. E. MCEWEN.

A HIGH-CLASS, HONEST AMERICAN PAPER.

The *Wheel* flatly contradicts Wood'side's statement as to Rowe not being as much to blame as Morgan and Temple in the late swindle, and "shutting down the lid on the garbage can," says all were equally to blame. Though this is not our view, we give it as that of a high-class, honest American paper.—*Wheeling.*

OUR New Orleans correspondent, "Bi," recently commented as follows on the method of electing the officers of the League:

The fight for the League presidency has given me a bit of food for reflection, and the idea has dawned upon me that there is a little too much one-man power vested in our officials. Take Louisiana, with its one vote, for instance. We all know that a fair proportion of our membership takes little or no interest in these matters, but those of us who have nor the slightest voice in the selection of the national officials. Our Chief consul has sent his proxy to a Luscomb man and Loui-iana's vote will go to that gentleman; and yet by actual inquiry I know that Mr. Jesup is the choice of almost every member with whom I have conversed, and, to tell the truth, I believe with Hodgson himself, and his giving his vote to Luscomb is purely from policy, not choice. Now, is this either just or right in the rank and file? I say no. Is one man competent to speak for a hundred in matters of this sort? I dare say Louisiana's case is but a parallel with other States, and for one I claim he is not, and surely the sentiment of the general membership is entitled to some consideration. We are not tied to a vote or some say in these matters. Don't you think so, Mr. Editor? It looks to me as if, so long as the present method is pursued, "rings" and "combines" will continue to "rule the roost" and everything else. I think, if the League is to model after the United States Constitution, that it should be carried out still further and elections be held in each State, and relegate the board of officers into a mere electoral college. That would be something like a fair deal.

"Perseus," cycling editor of the *Sporting Life*, makes " Bi's " comments a text for a sensible homily, the lesson of which is that the " proxy system " is an evil one and that the only fair manner of electing League officers—we refer to national officers, as President, Vice-President and Treasurer—is by the direct vote of the membership at large. "Perseus" wants the Constitution amended, and wants to know what we think of his suggestion.

As a matter of fact, as well as of right, the

League Constitution, which is generally understood to be analagous in its construction to the United States Constitution, should provide for the election of its national officers by popular vote. This much will be granted as a matter of principle, but no man has yet advanced a feasible plan for carrying out an election on such a basis which will give as good results as are accomplished under the present system. We must take things as they are, not as they ought to be. " Perseus " should remember that when the people of the United States rush to the ballot-box to avail themselves of their right to determine who shall govern them, they are urged on by many serious considerations which do not affect the League member. In the great world of American politics there have always been important questions at issue, and every intelligent citizen has been compelled to record himself for or against an idea, according to his light or his prejudices.

In the smaller world of League politics there is absolutely no question at issue. The policy of the League is well defined. It would advance the cause of wheeling by guarding the rights of its members, by securing protective legislation, by obtaining transportation and hotel privileges, by aiding the cause of roads improvement, and by binding together the wheelmen of this country so that they may be a political factor whenever the rights of wheelmen are endangered. There is no room for discussion within the League ranks ; the policy, as outlined above, is accepted by all. The element which enters into the selection of a national officer is personal fitness, and this is merely a question of personal influence.

There being no parties in the League, it is a logical presumption that but a small proportion would record themselves in an election by popular vote, and those who would vote would be largely influenced by sectional feeling. Another phase of the question to be considered is that all popular elections are conducted by an electioneering bureau, which means a heavy outlay of money, and as there is no profitable patronage in League politics there would be no incentive in following the lines laid down in American politics.

We have come to the conclusion that it no longer is worth the time to worry about the League Constitution as its methods of government. Our ideas as to the League's possibilities have settled into well-defined limits. It should have an active, intelligent Executive Board, that its finances may be well regulated, and its national committees supervised. Its Racing Board should constitute itself and be recognized as the arbiter and director of all cycle racing contests on either the path or the road. Its Transportation Committee should extend the work inaugurated by the immortal Burley B. Ayres. Its Rights and Privileges Committee should aid in the enactment of proper and obstruct the passage of obnoxious and discriminating laws. Its Roads Improvement Committee should educate the American people into the necessity of good roads, and an economical policy should be pursued in order to give this committee as strong financial backing. The work of local improvements and local advancement should be undertaken by State Divisions.

The most important thing to be done at the present time is the establishment of a national roads improvement bureau, under the management of the National Roads Improvement Com mittee. With such important work to be accomplished, forms of government and methods

of elections fade into insignificance. We think that the League never can be properly governed. It is a mammoth social club, though without the closer ties that exist in such a club. Its members are allied for their mutual enjoyment and protection, but being scattered over so great a territory, a truly representative popular meeting never can be convened. We express our personal preferences in the representatives we send to our State Boards of Officers, and they express the States' preferences in the delegates they elect to the National Assembly. This seems to us to be as near as we ever can get to popular representation in League national affairs.

IT is some satisfaction to note that the man-who-wants-something-for-nothing is gradually disappearing from cycling. This specimen of the genus homo, while he has been of some use to the sport, should be frowned out of existence by cycle dealers. He is the kind of man who airily and confidently informs A, who has to pay for his mounts, that he never thinks of paying for a machine ; that he has influence with so and so, who will let him have any kind of wheel he wills. He is a source of discontent. He breeds the man who can sell three machines and will place a lump order for a discount off ; he incites the man who has real or fancied speed on either path, road or hill, to make an "offer" to a concern—he calls it an "offer," though it generally is a begging letter—and to eternally "talk down" said concern if said offer is refused ; he excites the cupidity of the man who wants to ride across the continent, if expenses and salary are guaranteed; he is constantly, often unconsciously, recruiting the ranks of the order of genteel beats.

There are tricks in all trades, and the cycle business has its own share. Happily they are fading away before the advance of a more legitimate system of trading. In the pioneer days of the sport it was necessary to force it upon the public, and any more-than-ordinary feat, which invited notices from the general press, accomplished valuable missionary results. The climax of these extraordinary performances was Thomas Stevens' earth-girdling journey. But the sport has grown into the public mind so rapidly that it is no longer necessary to boom it as in the earlier days. As a matter of fact, transcontinental journeys and feats of that ilk no longer have any advertising value.

This train of thought is suggested by a letter received from an ambitious cyclist, an assistant postmaster in a Western town, who offered to ride from San Francisco to New York if we would guarantee his expenses and salary. The benefit to accrue to us from the "remarkable advertisement it would give our paper" is painted in glowing colors; but not being able to see it that way, we courteously declined and advised the youth to stick to his post-office provided the new administration will permit him.

VIBRATION IN CYCLING, was the subject of a paper recently read by Dr. B. W. Richardson, at a meeting of the Society of Cyclists. "I am of the opinion," says the Doctor, "that nothing produces so much injurious fatigue, or so bad an effect on the health in cycling as vibration. It is a shock to the nervous system, causing a continued feeling of vibration through the body, a sense of nausea, and a degree of nervous prostration, accompanied with a reduced power of the lower limbs, which, to say the least of it, is very inconvenient, and which in a feeble person may be attended with actual risk."

The cause of the mischief is what medical men call "spinal shock." It is very much like, and in essence is the same as that kind of shock which is noted in railway accidents, the difference being that in railway accidents the shock is inflicted by one or two violent concussions, while in cycling the shock is produced by a number of minor shocks, which produce the injurious effect from an accumulative action upon the spinal cord, and, through it, to some extent, on the brain. Excessive vibration causes a general fatigue and a painful reduction of muscular power in the lower limbs.

The Doctor concludes that, now that the danger is known, mechanical constructors should strive to produce a machine which shall be almost free from vibration. "This would be a vital advance in the art of cycling. Because in cycling we must work, we need not vibrate. Vibration is so much unperceptible work thrown away."

CYCLING FOR WOMEN.

Undoubtedly the feature of cycling for 1889 is the introduction of bicycles for women. As a *possible* inducement to women to become cyclists, I heartily welcome them. From striking personal experience, I know the immense value of cycling for women, and I have seen with regret the painfully slow advance that has been made in the number of feminine riders. In my own district, one of the best in the country, there has been practically no advance at all.

Large numbers of wheelmen are married men who ride primarily for their health. They are quick enough to recognize the benefits which accrue to themselves; but why do they never think of their wives? There are few instances in which the wives do not need the exercise, air and exhilaration of a ride, as much, if not more, than their husbands. Some men excuse themselves on the ground that wives do not want to ride, when the seeming reluctance is due to an idea that their husbands do not want them to. In other cases, a long ride is taken, the woman exhausted, and led to believe that cycling is all hard work. Lastly, many men are too outrageously selfish to care how their wives feel, or to take the trouble to teach them to ride, or to do the slightly increased amount of work necessary on a tandem with a feminine companion.

With regular, judicious practice, a woman soon ceases to be a burden on the front seat of a tandem. On good roads, ten miles an hour is easily reached, and this is faster than the average wheelman travels. There is no company so pleasant in cycling as your wife, or if unmarried, a good lady rider. As a married man I say to married wheelmen, it is an outrage that every one of you do not teach your wives to ride. There are exceedingly few cases where a woman cannot learn with great advantage to herself. I have seen such successful results from such unfavorable beginnings that nothing could discourage me.

The utility of the tandem safety I am inclined to question. While unquestionably easy and fast on good roads, it needs a skilled rider and cool head to control it; it is awkward to make a full turn with it, and in soft, bad places it must be very difficult to manage, and clearly inferior to a good tandem tricycle. This last view is borne out by the experience of others. It seems to me that the function of this machine is scorching for our racing men.

The rear-driving safety for men ought, of itself, to double the ranks of wheelmen. To one who has not ridden the ordinary, its steering is very easy from the start, and readily mastered. When well ridden it is safe under nearly every possible condition. It is as easy as the ordinary, and more convenient to mount and handle. It makes cycling easy to men of all ages.

I have already noticed here something that is complained of in England—I mean a tendency in safety riders to ride carelessly, without sign of endeavoring to improve. It is so easy to learn to ride the safety that many do not realize that they can go on indefinitely in improving

their form and in perfecting their control of the wheel. One can improve in the management of the safety as much as with the ordinary, and riders ought to look to this point.

5678.

FAVORS LADIES' BICYCLES.

Dear Editor of The Wheel :

When I was in the office of a friend of mine the other day I happened on a copy of your paper, and read "Pony's" letter about ladies' bicycles. I want to lend my voice to swell the chorus of thanks to the man who invented them and the woman who first rode one and proved it was a feasible and very delightful thing to do.

I am a new rider, have in fact only been out on the road three times, but I am so delighted by my experience that I never want to ride a tricycle again.

I have ridden a tricycle for two years, and many a time I have toiled along in the rear of a run on my heavy machine only keeping up by means of a friendly tow once in a while over a particularly stiff bit of the way, while my sister, who isn't nearly as strong as I, just sailed along well up to the front on her Psycho safety.

At last I made up my mind to learn, or die in the attempt, and after four or five lessons I found I could get along with only a semi-occasional tumble, and that a very mild one.

I haven't been on any long runs yet, for the roads are hardly in condition outside the city, but I have been for a short ride on a country road and enjoyed it so much that I am impatient for warmer days that I may do it again and more of it.

I did not see Mr. Stall's letter, so I can't say whether I agree with him or not; but my personal experience of a tandem bicycle has been very pleasant, and think they are far ahead of a double tricycle.

Psyche.

Washington, D C., March 13, 1889.

LONG ISLAND'S STAG.

This popular Brooklyn club held a "stag" at its club house last Saturday night.

A number of the members from the Kings County Wheelmen and Brooklyn Bicycle Club were present, making a sort of happy family, very much in contrast to the days when the three Brooklyn clubs were kept at daggers' points through misunderstandings, misrepresentations and certain pretentions to exclusiveness, which have been swept by the board by the march of events, backed by a well organized and well sustained kick.

Mr. Clark was master of ceremonies. From a platform in the club's front parlor he introduced the "Jolly Six" to the audience of some hundred cyclists who were present. The "Jolly Six" told funny stories—we know that they were funny because Kreger said so. Individual members of the "Jolly Six" also exhibited their specialties. one lum-tumming the banjo, another ringing the changes on "Mrs. Maloney's Cat," "Where did You Get that Hat, Where did You Get that Tile?" and other comic etceteras.

The more solid entertainment of the evening was supplied from among the cyclists. Mr. Fuller, of the Brooklyn Club, played several selections on the violin ; Mr. Howard Sp lman and Mr. Torrey, both members of the Brooklyn Club, were well received in some recitations.

After the programme had been concluded refreshments and smokables made conversation easy, as visitors and members sauntered through the club house.

Altogether the L. I. W. "stag " was a pleasant gathering, giving its members an opportunity to extend their hospitality to their neighboring club members.

THE "CITS'" LADIES' RECEPTION.

The annual ladies' reception of the Citizens' Bicycle Club took place at their club house on the evening of Friday, March 8, 1889. An extensive loan collection of pictures and bronzes had been gotten together and added very materially to the success of the affair. Original examples from the pens or brushes of some of the following artists were on view—viz.: C. C. Curran, Sydney Mortimer Lawrence, J. M. Barnsly, Morgan McIlhenny, G. Coe, G. D. Stearns, E. Iriande, H. Hawley, C. C. Huntington, J. A. S. Monks, H. Fenn, W. H. Shelton,

Geo. Inness, Alfred Parsons, Kenyon Cox, Taber, Volk, Snedley, J. Swain Gifford, F. Lengren, Jo. Pennell, A. L. Brennan, Henry Sandham, E. R. Butler, F. H. Church, J. C. Beard, Mary Hallock Foote, Robt. Blume, and a collection of twenty-one cycling sketches, principally by Jo. Pennell, which were displayed in the supper room.

About one hundred people were present, the number being necessarily limited to the size of the parlors. They were entertained for nearly two hours by Mr. and Mrs. Macy, Mr. Springmeyer and Mr. Dobson and assistant. Supper, by Mazetti, was served in the large wheelroom, after which "dancing occupied the time," etc.

THE STAG.

On Saturday evening the house was thrown open to all the up-town clubs, and a fine programme, similar to the one of the evening before, was served up. The Riversides sent the largest delegation, and representatives were there from the New York, Manhattan and Harlem clubs—about sixty in all—a good-sized crowd for short notice.

It is to be hoped that the ball of sociability thus set rolling will encounter no hill too steep for it.

CITIZENS' CLUB NOMINATIONS.

At the annual meeting, to be held March 18, the following ticket will be voted on : President, John C. Gulick ; Vice-President, Knight L. Clapp ; Secretary, J. T. Francis ; Treasurer, Alfred E. Paillard ; Trustees, Thos. McKee Brown, N. M. Beckwith, William H. Cook, Richard Nelson, Simeon Ford, William C. Frazee and Francis E. Faulkner ; Captain, William H. Krug ; First Lieutenant, Wm. G. Conklin; Second Lieutenant, Henry W. Mooney; Lieutenant of Tricycles, Geo. Martin Huss; Surgeon. J. Scott Aitken, M. D. ; First Color Bearer, George Sloane ; Second Color Bearer, Samuel V. Hoffmar; First Bugler, E. A. Hoffman, Jr.; Second Bugler, Fred. C. Thomas.

IN MEMORIAM.

At a meeting of the members of the Keystone Bicycle Club, held in Pittsburg, March 6, 1889, the following preamble and resolutions were adopted:

Whereas, It has pleased an all-wise Providence to remove from his earthly career our late fellow member, Frank Magill,

Be it resolved, That in this sad bereavement we tender to his family our most respectful feelings of sympathy and regret, and that in his death this club has lost a most useful, attentive and worthy member ;

Resolved, That a copy of these proceedings be sent to the family of the deceased and be placed on the records of the club.

HE SHOULD SUBSCRIBE TO A CYCLING PAPER.

Danville, Va., January 23, 1889.
The Clark Ciccle Co.:

Dear Sirs—I wish you would write me by return mail whether you can furnish me with the stuff already prepared to *renicele a bicicle.*
P. S.—I enclose stamp to pay postage.

FIXTURES.

Mar. 16, 1889.—Harlem vs. Hudson County, at Harlem.
Mar. 21, 1889.—Atalanta vs. Hudson County, at Newark.
Mar. 27, 1889.—New York Bicycle Club's Smoker.
Mar. 28, 1889.—Cambridge Cycle Club's Fancy Dress Ball.
Mar. 29, 1889.—Brooklyn Club's Theatre Party at Park Theatre.
April 1, 1889.—H. C. W. second competition for Benedict Medal.
April 27, 1889.—Manhattan Bicycle Club's Reception at West End Hall, 125th Street.
May 16, 1889.—A. Elwell's European Party sails from New York.
May 18, 1889.—Stone-Lumsden 1-mile Match Race, at Chicago, Ill.
May 25, 1889.—Stone-Lumsden 3-mile Match Race, at St. Louis, Mo.
May 27, 1889.—Stone-Lumsden 25-mile Match Race at Crawfordsville, Ind.

WHEEL GOSSIP.

St. Louis cyclists are working up a project to build a race path.

The Racing Board should adopt a rule separating safety and ordinary riders into classes.

Mr. and Mrs. Kennedy-Childe are at St. Louis, the gentleman in the interest of the Warwick Cycle Co.

"Jonah" is engaged in writing up "Elizabeth as It Is," for a book to be shortly issued by the Board of Trade of Elizabeth, N. J.

"Perseus," commenting in the *Sporting Life* on the late League elections, states that W. M. Brewster had enough proxies to control the election.

The Plainfield (N. J.) Bicycle Club propose giving a grand cycling and athletic tournament at the Crescent Rink on Thursday evening, April 4.

The Boston *Herald* reports that Herbert W. Hayes, C. C. of Massachusetts, sailed from Brazil on March 5, and will arrive in Boston early in May.

The Brooklyn Bicycle Club will move into their new house at 62 Hanson Place, on May 1. Their new quarters will be the biggest cycle club house in Brooklyn.

Philadelphia wants a race track; also, a boulevard from the Public Buildings to Fairmount Park. The Quaker City is not contented with its Postmaster General.

D. B. Burnett, Elizabeth Wheelmen, rode 224 miles in January. At the regular monthly meeting held March 5, the club called in a large block of stock for redemption.

A POINTER TO AGENTS.—W. E. Eldredge, of the Hudson County Wheelmen, uses more wheels than any other cyclist in this vicinity, except, perhaps, De Graaf, of the Harlem Club.

L. P. Thayer, of West Randolph, Vt., will send a copy of his paper, *The Bicycle*, for one year to any person sending him the names and addresses of ten prospective bicycle riders.

Kolb, New York Bicycle Club, is going south for his health. He will visit Philadelphia, Baltimore, Washington and Old Point Comfort. At the Point he will tarry to drive inflammatory rheumatism out of his system.

They have a Vegetarian Cycle Club in London. There are already one hundred members, pledged to strict abstinence from fish, flesh or fowl as food. They recently met at the Apple Tree restaurant in London, and perfected organization.

"Doc" Johnson, of the Hudson County Wheelmen, accompanied by Mrs. Johnson, sailed for the Bermudas on Thursday. He has taken a tandem with him and expects to do considerable riding in the balmy isle. He will be gone about three weeks.

The burning question of the hour in the Manhattan Club is the whereabouts of Shaffner's trousers. These trousers mysteriously disappeared some time since, leaving no word as to their future movements. It is said that Detective Newcome is working on the case.

The St. Louis *Spectator* refers to *Bicycling World* as "The serene and innocuous placidity of that intellectual duckpond, the *Bicycling World*, is again ruffled, and, as usual, I am the innocent cause of it." Poor Page, always putting your foot in it. We can sympathize with you.

A. B. Barkman has the photographic craze, and with a Waterbury camera has caught views of the City Hall Park, opposite Spalding's, views of the Brooklyn Bridge and other local places. Look out for him; he is a dangerous man, stalking about and shooting everything he sees.

The New Jersey men express a decided preference for Dr. G. Carleton Brown for C. C. of the State, and it would be difficult to make a better selection. Dr. Brown's efforts to wake up the State to the necessity of roads improvement should guarantee him a walk-over for the Chief Consulship. For Vice-Consul, T. F. Merseles, of the Hudson County Wheelmen, is spoken of, and he will be elected, even against his inclination. Merseles is good-fellowship itself, and is a "Coaster" from way back. Geo. Pennell, of the Elizabeth Wheelmen, will be run by his friends for Secretary-Treasurer of the Division.

Henry E. Ducker is simply surcharged with schemes. He is going to make the Boston Athletic Park a success, may establish a $100,000 athletic park in the heart of New York City, and wants to take a team of athletes, including the champions at all out-door sports, on a tour around the world.

Flint, Michigan, has a club of thirty members. On March 4 they met and elected the following officers: President, J. B. E. Castue; Vice-President, H. W. Ober; Secretary, B. McDonald; Treasurer, Geo. T. Smith; Captain, H. E. Kellerman; First Lieutenant, R. W. Selleck; Second Lieutenant, Eli S. Jeffers; Color Bearer, Albert Luty.

Fred. Jenkins, well known to cyclists of the earlier days of the sport in New York, has associated with H. F. Fuller, formerly a cyclist of Chicago, Ill., who has purchased "Castle Inn," a palatial estate at New Rochelle, N. Y., and will fit it up as a first-class summer hotel. The mansion is being refitted in modern taste, and when completed will afford a most luxurious home.

President Charles H. Luscomb of New York, First Vice-President James R. Dunn of Massillon, O., Second Vice-President Sanford Lawton of Springfield, Chief Consul Emery, Vice-Consul Robinson, C. W. Fourdrinier, Charles E. Pratt, E. W. Pope and Abbot Bassett were entertained at dinner at the Algonquin Club, at Boston, by Col. A. A. Pope, last Saturday evening.

Mr. C. R. Zacharias, of Asbury Park, N. J., cycling and good roads enthusiast, sends us a copy of the *Seaside Enterprise*, which contains an exhaustive editorial on better roads. "There is no reason," says the writer, "why the finished highways which form one of the attractions of the Old World to the American tourist should not be found everywhere in the better settled parts of our own country."

Willie Windle will make his appearance as a fancy rider March 15, at the Worcester Bicycle Club's entertainment. Willie has been taking fancy riding lessons from Maltby during the winter and is claimed to be very expert. He has fattened up considerably during the "off" season and weighs over 160 pounds. He has a strong desire to go to Europe as a member of the Manhattan or New York Athletic Club team.

The third annual meeting of the Atalanta Wheelmen was held last Wednesday in the club rooms, No. 443 Broad Street, Newark, and the following officers were elected for the ensuing year: President, George H. Miller; Vice-President, Allen N. Terbell; Secretary-Treasurer, Clint. G. Halsey; Captain, Will A. Drabble; First Lieutenant, Lewis A. Edwards; Second Lieutenant, Alfred P. Rummell; Color Bearer, John H. Crane.

Mr. H. H. Hodgson, C. C. of Louisiana, has written a letter to the New Orleans *Picayune* advocating that a convention be held to consider the subject of improved roads, and to discuss the following queries:

What is the condition of the roads in your parish?

What are you doing to improve them?

What amount of work and money is expended each year?

What material is most available?

What will we do to improve our roads?

We think that Master Eddy Mohrig, of San Francisco, Cal., is the youngest rider of a bicycle in the world. He is only three years old. The effete East cannot produce so young a bicycle rider.—*Bicycling World*.

The effete East can. Schwalbach to the rescue! Mr. Schwalbach, of Brooklyn, is papa to the youngest bicycle rider the world ever saw. Schwalbach, Junior, rode a bike when but eighteen months old. He was even skillful enough at that age to circle his little wheel on top of a dining table.

Very few men are aware that Secretary Bassett's salary was raised from $1,500 to $2,000 a year. The change appeared in the by-laws, and elicited no comment when they were submitted at the National Assembly meet. While it seems strange that the Secretary-Editor's salary should be raised while the League is in such bad financial condition, yet we are assured that the Executive Committee and the Reorganization Committee were unanimous in the opinion that the position and the officer were worth the increased amount.

According to Dr. Kunze, of Halle, cycling is a health stimulating exercise, which ought to be commended by medical men. It is a powerful means of strengthening the human body, and may even be considered an exercise acting as a preventive and curative, of no mean order, of certain bodily ailments. Looked upon in the latter light, cycling is a kind of gymnastic exercise possessing specific effects which are absent in ordinary gymnastics.—*Scientific American*.

The "lady" bicyclists who recently favored our city with a visit are now at Omaha. They were conveyed thither under the protectorate of Mr. Thomas Eck. Their manager, Troy, is with them. There is talk, and it may be nothing else than mere talk, that the "ladies" are to ride in Eastern cities and will then make a foreign tour. They will wear becoming "ladies'" costumes in the future, not the habiliments associated with the go-as-you-can tan-bark track, and will ride ladies' bicycles, which, it is said, are being made by the Gormully & Jeffery Manufacturing Co.

The proposition to pave certain portions of Broad Street, Newark, with asphalt pavement is very likely to be rejected and a belgian block pavement substituted, owing to the ignorance of the authorities who control the matter. The bid was about to be awarded to the Barber Asphalt Co., of New York, who control the Trinidad asphalt, but the opposition of a Newark contractor has been aroused, and he has supplied the Newark press with the alleged opinions of alleged residents of Washington and Buffalo, who condemn asphalt. An effort should be made by the League's official representative in Newark to have the street paved with asphalt.

While walking into Central Park last Sunday afternoon we saw a most painful spectacle. The background of the spectacle was the Grand Circle, named "Grand" by some waggish Park Commissioner, no doubt. On the curb surrounding a part of the Grand Circle were several urchins and urchinesses, of assorted sizes. They possessed one mark in common—an expansive and expressive grin. We sought the cause of this universal grin, and beheld a wheelman circling about on the smooth pavement. He had a bright nickeled wheel and a beard. He threw his legs over the handle-bar; he sat sidewise on the saddle; he cavorted hither and thither in many a sinuous curve, his face mantled all the while with a minute-metal-deity-on-wheels smile. We pursued our way sadly. We had seen a specimen of the —— fool wheelman.

I am sorry to have stepped on the most excruciatingly tender corn of the *Bi-World* in my remarks on rings, small politicians, etc. But unless I do it, how will it be done? The *Bi-World* dare no longer claim its own soul, all on account of being the League organ and having 13,000 circulation. Time was when it was somewhat independent and enterprising, but the day when it could do that is gone, and "anything to get on smoothly" is apparently its motto; and the circulation which it had before becoming the official organ has melted away to 844, including free list and exchanges, which shows how much wheelmen feel inclined to support a dishwater policy. Even Brer Prial, who started out to annihilate rings, seems to have weakened under some invisible pressure, and sings small. The *Spectator* can afford to be independent and is going to remain so. It is willing to give all just credit for any good work the League may do, but has nothing to withdraw in the way of criticism. The *Bi-World* and the *Wheel* know the facts in the case and are afraid to tell them; the *Spectator* also knows the facts in the case and is not afraid to tell them. This is the difference.—*St. Louis Spectator*.

Now, now, Brer Page, play fair! What "case" is it? We want to know all about it.

REASONS FOR IMPROVED STREETS.

The suggestions as to the need of improving the dirt streets, which are published elsewhere, come from a correspondent whose judgment and capacity could not be questioned. The necessity for the improvement is universally acknowledged, and the Street Committee has taken some action in the direction desired; but the Street Commissioner has neither sympathy with the movement nor has he shown the ability to handle such work. There are three phases of this question. First, the public health is endangered by the present system of neglecting the dirt streets; second, that property adjoining is seriously injured; and, third, that every grocer, coal dealer, butcher, etc., etc., is required to pay more for horse-flesh and wagons by reason of the bad condition of the streets, and, of course, taxes back his extra expenditure upon the consumer.—*Newark Call*.

SAN FRANCISCO.

The fine weather of the past few weeks has had the effect of drawing many of the old riders on the road again, and also a host of new men. It is really astonishing the number of riders one meets ten or fifteen miles from the city, mounted on all kinds of wheels and clothed quite frequently in the ordinary apparel of the day, including heavy shoes and hard hats.

We have had the Vice-Consul of this Division, Mr. J. P. Percival, in our midst for the past week. He came up from Los Angeles to present the claims of that city for the League meet this year. He succeeeded in his efforts, and the League meet will be held there on May 30. He enjoyed his visit very much, and seemed to have a season ticket for all kinds of entertainments.

A Mr. Toie, of, I believe, the Louisville, Ky., Club, has also been here on a visit, and has enjoyed a number of pleasant runs with our boys. He thinks this a wheelman's paradise.

Mr. Sharkley, at one time Second Lieutenant of the Massachusetts Bicycle Club, is now a resident of this city. He rides a safety, and has joined the Bay City Wheelmen. This club has at present a membership of ninety-five, with three applications to be acted upon, and is financially and otherwise in splendid condition.

CALIFORNIA DIVISION BOARD MEET.

At the meeting of the California Division of the L. A. W., on Monday evening, February 18, the following officers were present: Chief Consul Mohrig, of San Francisco; Vice-Consul Percival, of Los Angeles; Secretary-Treasurer Ireland, of Oakland; Representatives Moore, of Stockton, Hill and Sanford, of San Francisco; Club Representatives Bliss and Moore, of the Bay City Wheelmen, and Curragh, of the San Francisco Bicycle Club.

With reference to the Cherokee Lane affair, it was unanimously decided that if any suit was brought against Mr. Wright, the League would defend the same. It was also decided that if the County Commissioners of San Joaquin County placed any restriction on the use of the highway by bicycles, that a test case should at once be made, and the matter carried to the Supreme Court of the United States if necessary.

The Secretary-Treasurer and Mr. Bliss, of the committee, submitted samples of a road book. It was decided that the committee report again, after receipt of sample road books from other Eastern Divisions.

Mr. Bliss submitted a suggestion for a circular, detailing the advantages of the League to wheelmen, which was unanimously adopted, and 5,000 copies were ordered printed for distribution.

The Chief Consul reported that the National Association had called upon him for assistance from the Division, to the extent of twenty-five cents per capita. It was decided to bring this matter before the general meeting of the Division members.

MEETING OF DIVISION MEMBERS.

The annual meeting of the Division members was held at the San Francisco Bicycle Club rooms, on the evening of the 19th inst., Chief Consul Mohrig presiding.

The Secretary-Treasurer's report showed a balance of $752.75 on hand, and no outstanding debts, and a membership of 407.

The Chairman of the Racing Board submitted his report, in which he stated that certain time standards had been established for the current year, and each contestant beating those standards would receive a time medal.

It was unanimously decided to hold the next meet at Los Angeles on May 30.

A resolution was passed heartily indorsing the action of the League Board on the preceding evening, relative to the Cherokee Lane affair.

It was decided that no funds would be appropriated from the Division treasury for the assistance of the National Association, but that a voluntary contribution would be called for from members of this Division.

At the games of the Olympic Athletic Club, held on Washington's Birthday, a half-mile bicycle race was decided.

The starters were: C. W. Hammer, B. C. W., scratch, first, 1m. 32 2-5s.; F. W. Pierson, B. C. W., 30 yards, second; C. N. Langton, B. C. W., 50 yards, third.

Langton, on a roadster safety, cut out such a hot pace that the other men did not seem to reduce his lead in the first lap, but at the commencement of the last lap Pierson went to the front, followed by Hammer; the latter made a great effort in the last 100 yards, and when twenty-five yards from home was even with Pierson. From this point they fought every foot to the tape, Hammer winning by a yard. Coming up to the tape the wind was heavy against the riders, and it was here that Hammer's strength told. The race was handicapped by Chief Consul Mohrig, and could not have been done better. All three rode roadster wheels. The time was fast.

On the same day the Oakland riders had a small meeting. The racing was excellent, but the attendance was very small. The first announcement of the races was made on the 11th inst.

One of the curiosities of the day was a well-built young man named H. C. Leslie, "of Indianapolis," who turned up with a 57-inch racer that had apparently seen some use. He won the *novice* race, was beaten by an Oakland rider in a two-mile scratch race, and then won what was advertised to be a professional race, but was changed to an *amateur* by the promoters of the meeting withdrawing the money prizes and giving instead a set of medals.

This is the third out-door bicycle race meet we have had this year. What country can beat that record? CALIFORNIA.

SAN FRANCISCO, February 24, 1889.

MACON, GA.

I do not know whether Macon, a little town of only 40,000 inhabitants, has attained sufficient dignity to warrant its mention in the valuable columns of THE WHEEL; nevertheless, I shall make the attempt, and possibly enclose some news items.

A delegation of the Central City Wheelmen, composed of the Captain and "Honorable General Secretary," as the English write it, held a conference with the Entertainment Committee of the Georgia State Agricultural Society, and as a result they have offered us a sufficient amount to enable us to get up a four-days tournament, to take place next fall while the annual State Fair is in progress here. Among the features will be fancy riding, slow races, the one and two mile State championships, and a number of handicaps and open races. One of the main attractions is that there will be no "professional distractions" allowed.

Under the auspices of the Macon Public Library, the Central City Wheelmen expect to have about half a dozen races on the Fourth of July. Amateur participants from Atlanta, Augusta, Columbus and Savannah are looked for then, as well as at the State Fair.

Hal H. Beatty, the Pope Company's agent here, says he expects to be able to get out a display of wheels from his house, and if it is as nice a one as they had over at the Augusta Exposition, it will be excelled by none. It is also quite probable that the Clark Cycle Company will also have out some safeties and trikes, as well as a racer or two on our track, which has not an equal in the State.

The most conspicuous movement in the South, as regards roads improvement, is at present taking place in Georgia. A call for a "Road Congress," to meet in Atlanta in May, has been made by the Legislature, when a representative of each county will be present. The matter of building new gravel roads and rebuilding the old ones, and ways and means of accomplishing same, will be discussed and acted upon.

There are over a dozen young men here now who are just on the eve of becoming full-fledged wheelmen, and it is hoped that our ranks will soon be increased by the addition of their numbers.

The Dixie Wheelmen, of Atlanta, propose giving a three-days race meet in May, and, everything considered, there is the brightest outlook for the most prosperous year in the South for the sport that is the grandest and greatest on the face of the earth.

CHAS. ALEX. PERSONS.

ST. LOUIS.

The annual meeting of the Missouri Club was held on the evening of the 5th inst. and was a quiet affair. Neither Mr. Brown nor Mr. Berry would consent to run, and George Andrews was elected President. It is no discredit to Mr. Andrews to say that he would not have been chosen had Mr. Berry consented to the use of his name. There seems to be a general impression that Andrews will make a good officer if he will only curb his propensity for making speeches. The announcement of a speech from George is generally equivalent to a motion to adjourn. The objection is not so much to what he has to say as to the time he takes to say it in. The office of Secretary went begging. The duties of that office are so onerous and the retiring officer, George Boswell, has set such a high standard of efficiency, that no one felt inclined to step into his shoes. The choice finally fell on S. C. Newman, who was not present to decline the honor. Kidson, the Treasurer, was the only one of last year's officers who would consent to a re-election, and he was chosen without opposition. His annual report on the finances of the club was simply no report at all, and he was somewhat sharply criticised, both in the meeting and out of it, for his neglect of duty. He receives a fair salary for his services and should be required to attend to the work properly. The club declined to accept the report he offered and instructed him to prepare a complete report for submission at the next meeting. The club was particularly happy in the choice of a librarian. His name is J. H. Taylor. Some of his envious critics say he knows too much; others go even further and confidently assert that he knows it all, but of course that is no disqualification for the office of librarian. His review of Socrates' commentary on the Bible is more than instructive—it is edifying.

Mr. Andrews, from the committee appointed to devise plans to create more interest in cycling in the city, made an interesting report. There were three schemes submitted. The first two referred to the Missouri Club exclusively, and were, first, the offering of medals to every rider making 1 000 miles or over on the road during the season, and, second, the arranging of a handicap road-race, open to all members, to be run on the Manchester road in April, and for which suitable prizes were to be awarded. Neither of these propositions received, nor deserved, any serious consideration. The third was a proposition for the formation of a track association, and accompanying the report was a paper for stock subscriptions. This was numerously signed. The idea is to confine the membership in the association to the Missouri and Cycle Clubs; to raise the sum of $1,500, and to lease the old Red Stocking ball grounds for an athletic park. The grounds are now controlled by the St. Louis Gun Club, and they offer the use of them to the association at a very reasonable figure, the only stipulation being that the Gun Club shall have exclusive use on Saturday afternoons and on the Fourth of July. The park is fully inclosed and contains dressing rooms and a good grand stand. The location is convenient, and there is ample room for tennis courts, ball grounds and a quarter-mile track. The scheme looks well, and if carried to a successful issue the second of the Stone-Lumsden series of races will be run off on the new track.

There is nothing new to report in relation to the Warner "anti-liberty" bill. The remonstrances continue to pour in and we are gaining friends all the time. It is rumored that Mr. Warner is willing to amend the bill, and wants the wheelmen to make suggestions. The only suggestion that we have to make is that the bill be withdrawn. The *Republic* had an editorial a few days since condemning the measure, and the *Post-Dispatch* had a long article in its local columns the same day, giving interviews with the more prominent wheelmen on the subject.

A. Kennedy-Child arrived in the city Thursday morning, accompanied by his brand new bride. There is no "fake" about it this time. He has her with him, and a very pretty, interesting little woman she appears to be. Kennedy immediately established his base of supplies at "Anheuser's," and announces his determination to stop here for a week or two.

The light roadster raffled for at the Cycle Club last week was won by John Stockight, of the Missouri Club.

The *Spectator* man has his usual bilious attack this week, and your correspondent comes in for a bit of his venom. He says Brown was not elected because he would not run. Perhaps he is like the man who "would not live always;" he was not urged sufficiently. [THURREL.

PHILADELPHIA.

If anyone wishes to see the two extremes in roads they should come to Philadelphia. Broad Street, one of our noblest thoroughfares, from Columbia Avenue up to Cumberland Street, a distance of about a mile and a quarter, is paved with sheet asphaltum, making as fine a surface as could be desired; but from that point it is literally a sea of mud, making it almost impossible for a team to pull through, let alone a bicycle. It is a disgrace that such a state of affairs should exist in so large a city as this, and if the members of the Associated Cycling Clubs of Philadelphia would exert some of their energies to at least trying to remedy some of these evils they would show that they meet for some other purpose than to elect officers and think what they might do some day.

At the last meeting of the Century Wheelmen, eight candidates for membership were admitted. Among them were Frank Bechtold, a once prominent racing man, and Mr. Brown, father of Kirk Brown, the cycle dealer. Mr. Brown, although sixty-five years of age, was admitted as an active member, and in this case the word active is no misnomer, as Mr. Brown scarcely misses a day during the riding season, and this year intends going on the club runs with the boys on the shorter trips. By the way, it is rumored that the Centurions intend raising the initiation fee as soon as they get in their new house, which will not be very long, as the alterations were begun this week. The wheel room, when completed, will be 65x25 feet, and so arranged that for suppers, hops etc., the wheels can be removed and leave quite a large hall.

Nothing killed racing more effectually in this city last year than Mr. "Irv" Halsted. Very few riders cared to compete with him, and preferred to stay out rather than court sure defeat. His past few things are looking brighter. Mr. H. has gone west, the Tiogas have an excellent track, and several new fast men loomed up at the end of last season that gave promise of making "good ones." · So a list made up of "Manny" and Charley Kolb, Diamond, Wilson and Bradley, of the South Ends; Scott and a "dark horse," from the Mount Vernons; Frank Bechtold, Bailey, Garrigus and Spier, of the Centurys; Draper, Leisen and Louis Hill, of the Pennsylvanias, and several more from the Tiogas, ought to make some pretty good sport this spring, especially with the new tandem "bikes."

As was predicted, the ladies' (?) bicycle fake was a failure, financially and otherwise. The attendance was fair, but the expenses were heavy, so the total loss amounted to about one hundred dollars. One evening the great and only "Armaindo" was guyed beyond even her endurance, so she jumped off her wheel and kindly invited someone to step up so that she could mop up the floor with him, and the request was not couched in the most polite language, either. Unnecessary to say, her invitation was not accepted, so the wrathy "Louise" vented her spite in a few choice cuss words and continued on her record-breaking performance. Delightful!

The Century Wheelmen's "Annex" was completely destroyed by fire on the morning of March 5. This annex is, or was, situated in a large building not far from the club house, and all the wheels that could not be stored in the main building were kept in there. But for the presence of mind of the McGlathery boys all these wheels would no doubt be destroyed. When they found out where the fire was they hastened to the scene, and it was a sight for the gods to see the way Mac wrestled with those tandem tricycles (almost as big as himself), and for the time being actually forgot to laud the praises of a well-known typewriter which he peddles; but it comes from good authority that after everything was safe he busied himself by sticking those infernal stickers, which he always carries a store on, everything he could, from the blackened and ruined walls down to a fireman's hat, so that they looked like advertis-

ing signs for his machines. But, all joking aside, had it not been for the two Macs and some others, all the wheels, including four new tandem bikes, would have been destroyed, entailing a loss of at least $2,500. There was one man, however, who was sorry his wheel was saved—it was a chestnut, but INSURED.

ARGUS.

PHILADELPHIA, March 11, 1889.

NEW ORLEANS.

The female bicyclist has made her appearance in the South in somewhat of a new rôle. The thirteen-year-old son of a prominent resident of Albany, Ga., became enamored of the "beauty on wheels" connected with a traveling ten-cent show which recently stopped over in that little Georgia city; and, appropriating a pistol, a silver watch, and a Bland dollar from among the paternal possessions, the youngster hied himself after his ignis fatuus, only to have his youthful dream rudely dispelled a day or two later by being overtaken and shipped—boy, pistol and all—back to the "bosom of his family," where the dust of travel was effectually removed from the bosom of his trousers.

Six successive days of sunshine, and our spirits bubble! But will it last?

Geo. G. Clarke, Chief Consul of Mississippi, with two or three fellow wheelmen from Greenville, that State, were among our carnival visitors. They brought their wheels with them, and carry home pleasant recollections of New Orleans asphalt and shell roads.

The ennui which has pervaded the cycling atmosphere of this neighborhood for the past three months promises to be dispelled somewhat on the 20th inst. On that day W. M. Hathorn and H. C. Christy, two shining lights of the Louisiana Cycling Club, have a friendly "go" at each other of one mile and a quarter, the result of a challenge from Christy. Hathorn is the club champion, but Christy—who, by the way, was not in the championship race—has developed quite a finishing spurt, and it is an open question as to whether the former is still the "best man." Hence the "breeze." Jeff Frederic, too, is to challenge the winner, and that will further serve to keep things humming for a while.

R. W. Slusser, an erstwhile Memphis "flyer," is in the city and will probably locate here. By way of variety he will link with one of the clubs and help to make the Batson medal winner hump himself.

And now that the weather appears to have settled and the roads are commencing to dry, interest in those long delayed races is reviving, and with another week of sunshine we will probably set the ball rolling Sunday week.

BI.

CONNECTICUTINGS.

Owing to the frosty macadam so much of the time during the winter, our cyclers have been favored with considerable riding, and now that March is here we begin to realize that most of our discontent is over.

Ex-Captain Hurlbutt threatens to go to Bermuda.

Editor Jessup and some others are moving in the matter of forming an athletic club. Better late in the season than never, but wheeling will soon be here, and that discounts all other forms of manly exercise.

Several of our big wheelers are down with the safety fever, and well they may be, at least until our roads are made more ridable the year round.

Instead of doing something for the street surfaces, that are in such a wretched condition, our Selectmen voted to double the salary of the head one, who now has $2,000 to see the people wade in mud and misery, for we who pay the taxes do not see what else he does!

The Solitary Club, our veteran winter rider, has missed but six days, up to this writing; he averages eight miles daily, except Sundays, during the winter.

Traveler's two and a half columns in this paper of February 22 was a delightful bit of reading, and was a vivid reminder of our own

experience over that same glorious road, and among those charming old English towns.

That ride from Wolverhampton to Stratford-on-Avon repays one for the voyage to and from England, even if he had no more; but think of thirty-five days of cycling joy of the sort "Mr Traveler" writes of! It is like living over again the grand saunterings awheel we had in 1887, to read anything on the subject from Traveler, and his tour will be something to remember during life.

His criticism of the way some of the English cyclers ride is well merited, for in addition to back-pedaling down hill, we saw them with brakeless wheels.

The writer is too tired to work down, as well as up hills, when a good brake will save so much needless exertion.

Success to Traveler, and may we read more from his pen.

STAMSON.

BROOKLYN BICYCLE CLUB'S NEW HOUSE.

When the Brooklyn and Ilderan Bicycle Clubs consolidated last spring, it was their ultimate intention to build a fine club house to represent and bind into one those sections of Brooklyn which each had previously represented as individual clubs. But the first efforts toward the consummation of the idea were confronted by a very serious obstacle. The most desirable sites were either already built upon or the few lots suitable were held at figures which precluded their purchase. It was soon realized that the alternative of hiring a suitable house must be accepted. But the ordinary dwelling house was inadequate to the wants of the Brooklyn Bicycle Club, and the committee on building have worked steadily for some time to procure the proper accommodations. They have just reported at the regular monthly meeting of the club, held on the 12th inst., the final negotiations, pending for several months, resulting in a five years' lease of the house standing on the southwest corner of Hanson Place and South Elliot Place.

The future home of the Brooklyn Bicycle Club is a three-story brick house, 20x15 feet, with a 25-foot extension, including the basement and parlor floors. To meet the necessity for large wheel room and billiard room, this extension will be continued at the basement floor to cover the entire lot, and will be raised to include the second story. This will give a ground floor of 90 feet depth, two floors of 70 feet depth and one floor of 45 feet depth.

While of a more unpretentious exterior than her stylish neighbors across-town, the Brooklyn's new club house will not lack those comforts which a solid treasury and the rekindled enthusiasm of a large membership will surely guarantee.

When, three years ago, the Brooklyns held high their heads, because they were the only club in the city occupying a club HOUSE, they did not realize how soon their title would be disputed. But their latest move has rescued them from the shadow which the fine houses of the Kings County and the Long Island Wheelmen had cast upon their modest abode in St. Felix Street, and bidding adieu to the rooms hallowed by those memories which are so familiar to him who has grown up with a club from its early days, they will hereafter enjoy the distinction of occupying the largest bicycle club house in Brooklyn.

The new house will be occupied on May 1, and the superb location will enable its members who appreciate the advantages of a roomy house with comfortable furnishings and modern conveniences. The friends who have been wont to drop in and see "the boys in blue" will be assured that same hospitality, if after May 1 their footsteps will occasionally guide them to No. 62 Hanson Place.

ALBERT.

Aleck S. Hill, representing the Coventry Machinists' Company, Limited, was in New York a few days this week. He will make an extended trip in the interest of the "Club" wheel. The business of the Coventry Company has increased during the past two years, under the management of Mr. George W. Stevens and Mr. Hill. This year new agents are being appointed, and a larger business is expected than that of any previous year.

"THE M. A."

[Scene from the new Comic Opera, as recently played by the N. C. U. Executive.]

PETITIONING SUSPEND—
    I have a song to sing, O!
EXECUTIVE—Sing us your song, O!
PETITIONING SUSPEND—
    It is sung with a sigh and a tear in the eye,
    For it tells of a grievous wrong, O!
    It's the song of a cyclist, moping, mum,
    Whose soul is sad and whose glance is glum,
    And whose amateur status they say is a " hum,"
    For they reckoned his conduct shady,
    Heighdy! Heighdy!
    Misery me! Luckaday dee!
    Whose amateur status they say is a " hum,"
    For they reckoned his conduct shady.
PETITIONING SUSPEND—
    I have a song to sing, O!
EXECUTIVE—Sing us your song, O!
PETITIONING SUSPEND—
    It is a song in the chant of a regular " plant,"
    Which was played by a traitorous friend, O!
    It's the song of a racer bravely fired,
    Who many a time his field has led,
    And races has won on the post " by a head."
    As an amateur scorcher I held my own,
    Till they said that the taint of professional tone
    Was on me; so now I leave racing alone,
    And outside the amateur ranks I moan;
    While the Union says I shall not race
    Unless as a pro. I force the pace;
    But the cyclist sits a moping mum,
    For his soul is sad and his glance is glum,
    While his amateur status is reckoned a " hum,"
    And his conduct considered shady—
    Heighdy! Heighdy!
    Misery me! Luckaday dee!
    Whose amateur status they say is a " hum,"
    For they reckon his conduct shady.
—*Sport and Play.*

GLITTERING GENERALITIES.

We American cyclists are at a great disadvantage as compared with our English brethren. The same cause which makes cycle racing a failure here operates to make the spread of cycling slow. I mean the area of the country, the distances which separate wheelmen, and the heavy expense incurred in attending meets of every kind.

Put all the wheelmen in the United States into New England, increase their number tenfold, and you would have a dense cycling population that would themselves attend race meets, and from sheer force of numbers interest others to do likewise. Cycle racing would flourish as a natural growth. Make all the roads equal to those around Boston, establish a dozen new manufactories, reduce prices by competition, and every one in New England would ride.

Under existing conditions, I do not believe that the Racing Board, or any other body, can popularize path racing. (I make one reservation to be explained later.) The status of cycling here is not such as to make path racing easy, convenient or profitable to its promoters. Professional racing is not likely to be looked upon with much favor for some time to come. Now for my reservation. First, negatively, I do not think that path racing can possibly become a real success until cycling itself is much more popular than at present, and the cycling population becomes a larger portion of the community. But, one thing can be accomplished now in many centres. Wherever there is an athletic club there are lots of wheelmen as members. These clubs have open meets and minor home competitions. The cycling members should see to it that there are always two or three wheel events, and that the grounds of the club contain a suitable track. This seems to me about the only way to keep amateur path racing alive.

Cycling is undoubtedly on the increase in this country, but is spread over so great an area that it is not always easy to tell where the growth is taking place. In some of the old centres there appears to be no change, or even, perhaps, a falling off. The early enthusiastic spirit has departed, clubs have lost their activity, some have disbanded, and those that are left remain in many cases as mere names.

It is somewhat curious that American cycle clubs should be already decaying, while the English clubs, as would appear from the English wheel papers, are on the increase and flourishing. Wheelmen here do not care for runs except in parties of two or three, and they do not wish to meet at a given time to ride over a given route. Clubs, indeed, have other functions than taking runs, but I fear that they are generally not much more successfully carried out.
5678.

SHURMAN ON HILL CLIMBING.

Shurman was born at Amherst, N. S., October 30, 1859. He is by trade a shoemaker, and his home is in Lynn. He weighs when in condition 140 pounds, and his height is about 5 feet 8 inches. Shurman has been riding a wheel ever since 1882. His mount was then a Star, and he retained this until he began hill climbing in 1887. He was always regarded as a very sturdy and strong rider, one of the best in Lynn, and it was no easy matter to run him down. He gave some attention to the track and showed considerable speed. All of his racing has been done on the Lynn track. In his five races he won three prizes. His best time on the track has been a mile in 3m. 2s., and while in practice he has gone a mile in 2m. 47s. His first hill climbing was on October 30, 1887, when he attempted to beat Hal. Greenwood's record up and down Corey Hill, in Longwood. He failed in this on the second trip, but in the subsequent attempt on November 5, he climbed the hill four and a half times, stopping on account of the breaking of the handle-bar of his wheel.

Mr. Shurman says: "Stickney Hill, in Lynn, is the hardest hill that I ever tried. It was very taxing. Next in point of difficulty I would place Corey, and afterward Eagle Rock, Spurwick Hill, in Maine, and Park Street Hill, in Portland."

"How does the ascent of these hills tell upon you?"

"It is of the hardest possible nature. There is a strain all over your frame. When I climbed Corey Hill for the first time I could not see. I felt a great loss of strength, and the blood all rushed to my legs and loins, and not to any extent elsewhere. I do not use my arms at all in hill climbing, but lift my body out of the saddle and use the levers. The hardest work for me is on the third trip. After I have got as far as that I feel as if I could keep along all day. The feeling when you have finished your climb is of extreme weariness all over. As soon as I am done I am rubbed down and put to bed, where I take a long rest. This brings me around all right, and I do not generally feel the least trouble afterward."

"What is your method of going at a hill?"

"I go at it straight in all cases, never swerving from the line more than I can help. The middle of the hill is where it seems to tell the most. It makes you very tired indeed to think that you have got to go so much farther. The pain begins just as the hill begins, and increases as the hill does. I come down very swiftly, faster than any one else, I suppose, because I am considered so reckless a rider. I speeded down Eagle Rock at the rate of a mile in about 2m. 5s. I doubled my own record there and stopped. I could have gone on if it were necessary. It was very cold on the day I rode there and I was astonished that the spectators stayed as long as was the case. I stood as long as they kept me company."

"What about training? Do you make any preparations for these efforts?"

"Most certainly I do. I partake of the diet generally prescribed for athletes. I take plenty of road exercise and indulge in a great deal of hill climbing. I think that there is not a hill that cannot be ascended awheel. If there is, I would like to hear of it and you can count upon me to make the attempt."—*Lynn Bee.*

AN OLD VET. IN SEARCH OF A SAFETY.

I've looked them all o'er, from the East to the West,
In search of a Safety—the one I'd like best ;
And when I had seen them I said with a smile,
The *Light Roadster's* the dandy to rake in my pile.

For comfort, light running, for elegance, strength,
And every good quality summed up at length,
I need n't look farther—it is not worth while ;
The *Light Roadster's* the dandy to rake in *that* pile.

In seeking for pleasure, or health, day by day,
O'er mountain and valley I'll up and away ;
There's nothing to hinder, and naught to beguile,
The *Light Roadster's* the dandy to rake in the pile.

And night-riding, too, will become a delight,
I can ride just as safely in day time or night ;
I'll push up my read-record mile upon mile ;
The *Light Roadster's* the dandy to rake in the pile.
                        'KATOONE.

[The above verses were sent to the Pope Mfg. Co. by a Columbia crank.—ED.]

THE DORCHESTER BICYCLE CLUB ANNUAL MEETING.

A CYCLIST CAUSES A RUNAWAY.

On Sunday last, Mr. E. W. Ward, of Elizabeth, N. J., while out driving on the Boulevard, met a cyclist, who caused his horse to take fright and run off, throwing Mr. Ward from his wagon. Mr. Ward was not seriously injured. The cyclist made profuse apologies and appeared to feel very badly over the mishap. The Elizabeth *Daily Journal* comments on the accident as follows: "The machine was a full nickeled wheel. An informant says that several other wheelmen passed, but the horse did not notice them, as their wheels were enameled dark and therefore did not present the glittering appearance which so often frightens horses."

This is very amusing. The horse meets several cyclists and exhibits no symptoms of fear; yet on the appearance of a "glittering nickeled" wheel, he takes fright. Perhaps the nickel was worn off in spots and the esthetic spirit of the horse rebelled. Perhaps the horse objected to nickel on general principles. Here is a golden opportunity to add to our knowledge. We should advise the *Journal* reporter to interview the horse and find out why he objected to the appearance of that particular wheel.

THE TANDEM SAFETY ON BAD ROADS.

EDITOR OF THE WHEEL :

I do not agree with W. W. Stall and " Pony " that the tandem tricycle is preferable to the tandem safety on difficult roads. It certainly is not reasonable that a two or three tracked machine would run easier over such surfaces than a single-tracked one, and my experience with the tricycle, which dates back to 1880, and with the tandem " bike," which commenced with the first introduction of them in this country, has demonstrated the superiority of the latter for any and every kind of riding. Last September a friend of mine, with his wife, started on a 100-mile straightaway run over the rough roads of Western Pennsylvania and New York ; with them started two good riders on a three-wheeler, who were out-distanced and turned back disgusted after half a day's struggle to keep up with the tandem bike. My friends kept on, overtaking and passing several riders of ordinary bicycles, and reached their journey's end without accident and in good shape. My experience is that wherever there is a rut, strip of turf or foot-track, the tandem safety will run with ease and steadiness ; of course deep sand with a tricycle ; but who can ride deep sand with a tricycle? I have often swung off the tandem bike on running into such a spot and pushed it through at a smart dog-trot, my companion remaining on and pedaling. This saves time and labor of pushing a lumbering tricycle through it. Don't try to steer a tandem safety from the front seat ; put the heaviest rider behind when practicable. And don't imagine that you have the slightest conception of the enjoyment of riding a " double" until you have tried a good tandem safety.

March 6, 1889.   IXION.

JERSEY CITY.

There was sadness in the camp of the Hudson County Wheelmen last Friday evening. Our team was defeated for the first time by the crack team of the Atalanta Wheelmen, of Newark The alleys were crowded with friends of both clubs. It was a decidedly noisy gathering. A dozen musical instruments played by the Newarkers helped to make things lively, but each of the Jersey City boys, not to be outdone, brought both of their lungs with them and used them to their fullest extent. The home club opened with a lead of nine points, but on the second frame the visitors tied the score and steadily forged ahead, winning by 109 pins. The battle now lies between the H. C. W. and the A. W. for first place, each club having won five and lost one game. The Newark club have the advantage, however, in that their two remaining games are to be played on their own alleys, while our two final games are on opponents' alleys. Following is the score :

H. C. W.		ATALANTA.	
Grant	135	Drabel, S	142
Stenken	119	Halsey, E	120
Whitman	133	Snow	102
Korth	135	Terbell	123
Shone	129	Drabel, W	144
Robertson	106	Muchmore	99
Eldridge	124	Throme	135
Tuthill	154	Muller	190
Soper	135	Halsey, C	146
Earl	112	Edwards	190
Total	1,282	Total	1,391

Referee, Dr. H. E. Benedict. Scorer for H.C.W., J. Curran; for Atalanta, A. F. Runnell.

Below is given a record of the Wheelmen's League to date :

	Won.	Lost.	Played.	To Play.
Hudson Co	5	1	6	2
Kings Co	4	4	8	0
Harlem	2	5	7	1
N. Y. B. C	1	6	7	1
Atalanta	5	1	6	2

It seems to me that publishers of cycling papers, as well as advertisers, should exercise more care as to the appearance of advertisements in their papers. Every subscriber to the League organ has noticed a certain advertisement of a Boston house, accompanied by a cut, which tends to shock their animals. I do not pose as a Comstock, or any other crusader, against "bare piano legs," but we should take into consideration that not only is that paper sent to the lady members of the L. A. W., but it is also brought into the *homes* (no pun) of the gentlemen, where their wives, mothers and sisters see them. Be careful, gentlemen ; remember the ladies.

I notice that the latest comer into the cycling world is "Bown's Velocipede," a cut and description of which appears in the *Scientific American* of March 2. The wheels of this machine are constructed "sociable style." There are but two wheels. The saddle, pedals, etc., are between the wheels, of course, and below the axle, as is most of the mechanism, presumably to keep them rider upright by having the machine weighted. Judging from the cut the wheels appear to be about seven feet diameter. A peculiar feature of this velocipede is a device by which the wheels may be inclined V-shap d, the lower part of the wheels being moved inward to run on a narrow path. The machine is steered by raising what is called a friction wheel out of contact with its companion wheel on one side, thus propelling the machine with one side.

Two of the lady members of the H. C. W. appeared on our streets this week on ladies' bicycles.

COASTER.

Willie Windle is about to join the New York Athletic Club, and will represent that club in England this season.

F. A. Elwell, manager of the European tour, writes that owing to the large number of applications from cyclists who wish to join the party, he h is increased the limit to thirty.

No quorum was present at the New York State Board of Officers' meeting, called Tuesday evening, March 5, at the New York Club house. Among those present were : C. C. Bidwell, B. J. Shriver, C. A. Sheehan, J. T. Warwick and Joshua Reynolds Mr. Reynolds was the only out-of-town member present. Chief Consul Bidwell has discovered that he must resign to the membership of the Division.

THE TRADE.

A SELECTED LIST OF PATENTS.

(Reported especially for THE WHEEL AND CYCLING TRADE REVIEW by C. A. SNOW & CO., patent attorneys, Washington, D. C.)

Aaron G. Rose, Greencastle, Ind. Bicycle.
Geo. T. Warwick, Springfield, Mass. Bicycle and safety bicycle and ball-bearing for Velocipedes.

All bearing date of March 12. Copy of any one of these patents will be sent on receipt of 25 cents.

The Pope Manufacturing Company get up a neat advertisement in the form of a baseball scorer.

The New York Bicycle Co. are handling the Coventry Machinists' Co.'s wheels and the Star wheels for New York City. They have a "Swift" safety at their Warren Street store.

The Pope Mfg. Co. have imported a number of the best foreign ladies' bicycles, which they offer for sale at $115 and $120, respectively. These machines are thoroughly made and of the best of foreign manufacture, but the Pope Co. have offered them at this very low price because they think that the ladies should be given the concession of a material reduction. These machines can be seen at the Pope Co.'s offices in Boston, New York and Chicago.

Very few wheelmen know that the house of Wm. Read & Sons, which they only know from its connection with the bicycle trade, has quite a history. The business was established in 1822, opposite Faneuil Hall, Boston, which then had a population of 60,000 people. The house is one of the oldest in the gun and shooting-tackle trade. Mr. William Read, Sr., died in 1884, being at that time eighty-four years of age, and actively engaged in business. The present members of the firm are William, John and Edward Read.

THE NEW MAIL IN NEW YORK.

The New York City agents for New Mails are Messrs. Schoverling, Daly & Gales, of 302 Broadway, a house which has long occupied an established position in the fire-arms and sporting goods world. The firm have an elegant store on Broadway, and the New Mails show to advantage in their windows, attracting much attention. The bicycle department is on the first floor, and is in charge of L. B. Whymper. A large stock of 1889 New Mails is already in this department, as well as a line of American cycles and boys' and girls' bicycles, tricycles and velocipedes.

H. B. SMITH MACHINE CO.'S CATALOGUE.

The 1889 catalogue of this firm are now ready for distribution. Their '89 catalogue is a thirty-four-page pamphlet. The novelty for this year is the "39x24"—a special Star bicycle with 24-inch front and 39-inch driving wheel. The wheels described and illustrated are the American Star, built from 42 to 54 inch large wheel, and ranging in price from $75 to $105 ; the semi-racing Star, weight 45 to 50 pounds, sizes 48 to 54, price $102 to $122; the Special Star bicycle, sizes 48 to 54 price $107 to $127; the Special Pony Star bicycle, 42 to 45, price $107 to $117; the new "39x24" Star, selling from $107 to $117. The catalogue contains a complete illustrated list of safeties.

WM. READ & SONS' CATALOGUE.

The "New Mail" catalogue for 1889 is the most complete Messrs. Wm. Read & Sons have published. The New Mail Light Roadster is illustrated and described in whole and in part, and the mechanism of the wheel is explained with clearness and minuteness. The leading points of the wheel are its perfection back-bone, ball-bearing head, detachable handle-bar and tangent spokes. The wheel is made in sizes from 48 inch to 60 inch, and is driven by wheels from $125 to $140. The New Mail safety, the firm's rear-driver for 1889, has the following special features : Spring fork, rear-wheel band-brake, straight-front forks, tangent spokes, strengthened base rim, ball-bearing head and special safety saddle. The New Mail safety is retailed at $135. The firm are also making a boys' safety, price $40, in higher grade $65 to $75, and also handle the American Ideal bicycles and tricycles.

ODDS AND ENDS.

A bicycle club has been formed at Pamrapo, N. J.

H. Wimmel, of *Puck*, and wife are devotees of the tandem tricycle.

The Riverside Weeelmen will move into a new house on 104th Street on May 1.

The riding spirit in the Citizens' Club is active. The club will present 1,000-mileage bars this year.

Mr. Thomas Whitaker, a prominent wheelman of Millville, N. J., was elected Mayor of that town on Tuesday, March 12.

The Manhattan Bicycle Club will hold a reception at West End Hall, 125th Street, New York City, on Friday evening, April 27.

The Columbia safety tandem, the first tandem bicycle ever manufactured in America, is now ready for delivery, and can be seen at the Pope Co.'s offices in Boston, New York and Chicago.

The Twelfth Regiment games will be held at the armory on May 10. The cycle events are 2-mile handicap, half-mile novices and 1-mile novices. Entries close May 4, with C. J. Leach, P. O. Box 3201.

"This (the Brooks) is the only cyclometer on the market, sold at a reasonable figure, which has given entire satisfaction."
W. C. BOAK, Le Roy, N. Y.

Only $5. Brooks Odometer Co., Lowell, Mass.

Among the cycle visitors in town this week was Mr. W. Frank Pierce, of Oakland, Cal. Mr. Pierce is about six feet five inches tall, splendidly proportioned, and weighs 275 pounds. He rides a Veloce, which has carried his enormous weight without accident.

The annual election of the Manhattan Bicycle Club will be held March 18. There will be three tickets in the field. The club held its regular monthly reception on Friday, March 6, at the club house. About thirty couples were present and enjoyed dancing and ref eshments.

The card of Messrs. Collins & Nuttall will be found in our advertising columns. This firm have an extensive repairing and nickeling shop in West Twenty-seventh Street. They have repaired and nickeled for the trade for some years, and are favorably known by the work they have turned out. They are now prepared to do repairing and nickeling for individuals as well as for dealers.

The members of the New York State Board of Officers will vote, by mail, on an amendment to reduce the League dues from $1.50 to $1 ; also, on the appointment of a nominating committee, as provided by the constitution, to name candidates for the offices of Chief Consul, Vice Consul and Secretary-Treasurer. The names suggested for the nominating committee are W. H. De Graaf, New York; George S. Dakin, Buffalo, and H. C. Spalding, Elmira.

The Newton (Mass.) Bicycle Club met at the office of W. W. Stall, 509 Tremont Street, Boston, Tuesday evening, and elected the following officers : President, Freelon Morris ; Vice-President, Herbert A. Fuller; Secretary, William W. Stall; Treasurer, Edwin T. Martin; Captain, F. Stedman Wilson; First Lieutenant, H. Albert Henderson; Second Lieutenant, E. P. Marsh ; Club Committee, Walter H. Barker, Eben H. Ellison, Louis A. Hall and George H. Hastings. A supper and speaking followed.

The Citizens' Bicycle Club held a ladies' reception last Friday night at their club house in Sixtieth Street. It was a perfect success, as all the Citizens' affairs of the kind are. The rooms were hung with rare tapestries, loaned by Messrs. Johnson, Faulkner & Co., Sixth Avenue. In addition a number of the club's very fine paintings were loaned by the club members, and these, with some original sketches sent by the *Century* and *Outing* companies, made an enjoyable art display. The programme of entertainment was music, dancing and a supper. On Saturday evening a large number of members of the New York Club visited the Citizens' house by general invitation and inspected the paintings and sketches.

THE ORIGINAL BICYCLE.

At the late Stanley Show was exhibited the machine which is now generally conceded to be the original bicycle. We present a cut of the machine reproduced from the *Scottish Cyclist*, also a representation of the features of the inventor, one Gavin Dalzell, a merchant of Lesmahgon, Lanarkshire, Scotland. Dalzell was born August 29, 1811, and died June 14, 1863. He possessed decided talent for mechanical inventions. From the written testimony of a letter, and the testimony of J. B. Dalzell, son of the inventor and present owner of the machine, it is proven that it was in use previous to 1846, and there are eye-witnesses who recollect the inventor riding his bicycle over the roads of Lanarkshire.

In construction the Dalzell Bicycle is the exact prototype of the now popular rear-driving safety.

It is constructed chiefly of wood, which, though worm-eaten, is still wonderfully strong, especially in the wheels, these seeming to have stood the ravages of time and rough usage much better than the frame-work. The rear wheel—the driver—is of wood, shod with iron, about forty inches in diameter, and has twelve spokes, each about an inch in diameter. The front wheel is of similar construction, but only of about thirty inches in diameter. From the front wheel hub the fork—straight, and with a rake which some of our modern makers could copy with profit—passes up, when joined together, through the fore-part of the wooden frame-work. A pair of handles are then attached and bent backward into a V shape to suit the rider, who sits about two feet behind the front wheel hub. These were commonly termed the "reins." The main frame is somewhat like that which is now termed the "dip" pattern, the design of which is applied in an extended form to ladies' safeties.

A wooden mud-guard rises from this frame, covering about one-fourth of the circumference of the hind wheel; from this to the back forks, which are horizontal, and of wood, vertical flat stays run down, forming a dress-guard after the manner of those on the latest cycling development—the ladies' safety. From the front curved portion of the frame to this mud-guard a horizontal bar runs, on which is placed the seat—we cannot call it a saddle. This is immovable and made of leather, with slight padding underneath. The driving mechanism is by means of cranks fitted to the rear wheel hub, connected by rods to long levers hinged to the wooden frame close to the head; the connecting rods being joined to the levers at about one-third of their whole length from the pedals, which are merely projecting bolts affixed to the lever ends. The action thus obtained is not rotary, being a downward and forward thrust with return, the feet describing a small segment of a circle. That the gearing, which constitutes the chief wonder to the critical and historical reader, was actually on the machine while being ridden by Mr. Dalzell is proved by the receipted accounts of the blacksmith, John Leslie, who made all the iron work used in its construction.

Thomas Stevens sends his first letter to the *New York World* of Sunday last. It is dated at Aden, Arabia, February 4.

Editor Prial is off his base when he remarks that Van Sicklen will race this season. That gentleman has not decided to do so.—*Referee.*

The information was received direct from Mr. Van Sicklen's brother, who is a reporter on the *New York World.*

The Century Run Committee will hold a meeting at Newark to-morrow evening.

At the annual meeting of the Plainfield Bicycle Club, held Monday evening, March 11, the following officers were elected for the ensuing year: President, Townsend Rushmore; Vice-President, Thos. S. Burr; Treasurer, Robinson Pound; Treasurer, Harold Serrell; Trustees, J. H. Cooley, M. D., J. H. Hallock, J. A. Worth, H. J Runyon and John M. Crane; Captain, Frank L. C. Martin; First Lieutenant, M. S. Ackerman; Second Lieutenant, David H. Lenox; Color Bearer, Geo. S. Martin; Bugler, E. Sidney Dorman.

The Twelfth Regiment will shortly hold their annual spring games. The bicycle events will be a two-mile handicap and a one-mile for novices.

The New York Club will have a "clam smoker" at their house, Seventy-second Street and West End Avenue, on Friday evening, March 22.

The annual meeting of the Manhattan Bicycle Club will be held at its club house on March 18. The contract for the club uniform has been awarded to E. O. Thompson, 345 Broadway, New York.

Two Murfreesboro (Tenn.) wheelmen, T. Petri and Jesse Sparks, Jr., will start July 1 for a trip to Washington.

A thirteen-year-old Georgia boy became enamored of a woman cyclist who was a member of a company of barn-stormers. Boy stole pistol, silver watch and a dollar, and pursued his Juliet. Boy, pistol and watch discovered in two days, expressed home, thoroughly dusted off, and laid in a cool place.

AMATEUR PHOTOGRAPHY.

The greater part of those improvements that the professional and amateur are enjoying to-day originated with the latter. There is no doubt that the experiments tried by amateurs in every branch of the science of photography has greatly simplified the process, and the credit of making it a popular recreation should be ascribed to them.

There is no recreation that combines so much of pleasure and instruction at the same time as photography. There is always something new to be discovered in its practice which makes it doubly interesting, and to a person that is mechanical there is something fascinating about it.

It can be practised by young and old alike with equal profit. This fact has been noted, and to-day the amateur is counted by the thousands where only a few years ago they were only in the hundreds. The architect makes it a part of his business, the physician finds it of the greatest importance, the traveler preserves likenesses of places he has visited, and it is of the greatest assistance to the lecturer. In England these practising photography outnumber those in the United States, but in both countries there are nearly as many females as males among the amateurs. The recreation is one of refinement, and, as it deals more with nature than with anything else, it leads man to seek those places most pleasing to the eye and elevates his mind. Unlike the old wet-plate process there is nothing disagreeable in the practice of the present system. The introduction of the gelatino-bromide process has so entirely revolutionized photography that it requires but little preliminary knowledge of its principles to accomplish good results. The chemicals required are so few and inexpensive that a person with only the average intelligence can by exercising a little judgment and taste accomplish results that will be truly surprising. Its great simplicity has caused many to engage in its practice.

The rapidly increasing demand for amateur outfits has unfortunately led persons to engage in the manufacture of apparatus and materials wholly inadequate for the attainment of satisfactory results. This being the case, the safest rule for a prospective amateur to pursue is to purchase of houses only of known reputation, and, where it is possible, with the manufacturer direct. This rule applies equally well to all merchandise. It is always safest to let others try the experiment where any doubt exists.

The house of E. & H. T. Anthony, of New York, with an experience of over sixty years to their credit, present a line of goods that for excellence in every particular make them articles made or sold by this concern is assured that he owns the best that can be obtained for the money. It is with these goods that we shall deal. When selecting an outfit, the following points should be well considered. First, the size of the camera, and second, the style or kind desired. The larger the camera, the greater the bulk and weight, while in a small camera both bulk and weight are economized; a large picture cannot be taken with it, while with the large one a small one is obtainable. The kind of apparatus to be purchased depends greatly upon the amount of money one may wish to expend. The policy best pursued in every case is, get the best that your means will allow. An outfit costing $40 will give good results, but one costing $40 will be far more satisfactory. Purchase at the outset only the best; money and time are saved by doing so. As the amateur advances, he feels the necessity of an outfit superior to the cheap one he has, and it is either sold at a sacrifice or laid aside, not to be used again except on rare occasions, and the original is replaced by a better and more satisfactory apparatus, thus making a double outlay, which might have been saved at the beginning, and the results have been more satisfactory. However, this can be said of the cheaper outfits, that some of the best landscape photographs in a recent exhibition in London were made on an outfit costing only about $15, and it is safe to say that an apparatus of American manufacture is in every particular as good as those made in England.

England, France and Germany have enjoyed the reputation of making the finest lenses, but the American makers, realizing the great future in them, have steadily improved in the manufacture, so that now they have attained an excellence almost equal to any foreign maker, both for grinding and mounting. A lens may be perfectly ground and yet spoiled in the mounting.

NOTES ON CAMERAS.

The American camera is pre-eminently the superior of all foreign makes, in workmanship, simplicity, elegance of finish and portability. The same grade of apparatus costs less here than it does in England or France, and is much better finished. Anthony's Amateur Equipments, varying in price from $9 to $15, are marvels of cheapness. The $9 equipment consists of a mahogany camera, made of well-seasoned wood, nicely polished and finished.

Pictures 4 x 5 inches can be made with it. It has a folding bed, and is furnished with a good achromatic lens. The ground glass or focussing screen is hinged at the bottom, and can be folded back when the plate holder is placed in position. The lens is made especially for these outfits, and for landscape work will give satisfactory results. The plate holders are well made, and are light and strong. A light and portable tripod completes the equipment. When the camera is not in use the lens board is removed and the lens reversed, so that when placed in the carrying case the camera occupies but little space. The case is intended to hold camera, plate holder, and top of tripod, and is furnished with either a brass or leather handle.

THE WHEEL

— AND —

CYCLING TRADE REVIEW,

Published every Friday morning.

Entered at the Post Office at second class rates.

Subscription Price,   -   -   - $1.00 a year.
Foreign Subscriptions, -   -   6s. a year.
Single Copies,   -   -   -   -   5 Cents.

Newsdealers may order through AM. NEWS Co.

) All copy should be received by Monday.
Telegraphic news received till Wednesday noon.

Advertising rates on Application.

F. P. PRIAL, Editor and Proprietor
23 Park Row,
P. O. Box 444,   *New York.*

Persons receiving sample copies of this paper are respectfully requested to examine its contents and give us their patronage, and as far as is convenient, aid in circulating the journal, and extend its influence in the cause which it so faithfully serves. Subscription price, $1 per year.

MR. E. J. SHRIVER, whose utterances and writings always command close attention, sends a letter commenting on an editorial in last week's WHEEL, in which we stated our views on present and possible methods of electing League officials. Mr. Shriver is mistaken in supposing that we have changed our "front." We have threshed out the League Constitution according to our lights, and, while Mr. Shriver has the right and the ability to object to any conclusions we may have come to, we are of the opinion that a further sifting of the League Constitution will yield nothing newer or more valuable than the conclusions already arrived at.

Having determined to our own satisfaction that the League never can be perfectly governed, and having obtained a general verdict that the Constitution, as at present constructed, was imperfect and unsatisfactory, we turn to fields and pastures fresh and green to prosecute and emphasize the important work of roads improvement.

For detailed objections to the method of popular vote suggested by Mr. Shriver, we refer to our views as expressed in last week's WHEEL. Perhaps a trial of Mr. Shriver's system of election would prove our objections totally unfounded, and we refer it to the members of the National Assembly, who are the proper people to determine whether such trial shall or shall not be made.

THE Centennial celebration to be held in New York on April 30 and May 1 promises to be the biggest event of the kind ever held in Gotham. On the first day three parades will be held, and many cyclists believe that cycling should be represented in one of these parades. It has been suggested that a cyclists' division be formed, and that the members of the clubs should parade in uniform, if it should be found inadvisable or inconvenient to ride. An informal meeting will shortly be held to consider the matter.

On the second day of the celebration an industrial parade will be held, showing the progress in manufactures within the past hundred years. We think this would afford a golden opportunity to have the cycle trade represented in the procession. If no general exhibit of cycling will be made, we hope that some of our largest makers and importers will show their wheels, mounted on floats. A full line of modern wheels contrasted with a selection of antiquities would make an imposing show.

NOW that her County Roads Improvement bill has become a law, New Jersey must be credited with the first general legislation enacted for roads improvement. Among the cyclists who have aided in the good work is G. Carleton Brown, who believes that a macadamized road will yet connect New York and Philadelphia.

THOUGH the New York and New Jersey Road Racing Association has been buried, the spirit of road competition is not dead, merely smouldering. A number of New Jersey clubmen are anxious to form a local road racing association, and the formation of a like organization is being agitated in Brooklyn We suggest that the Hudson County Wheelmen's captain call a meeting of delegates from New Jersey clubs and consider the formation of a local road racing club. We suggest that the Captain of the Long Island Wheelmen call a meeting for a discussion of the same object.

THE announcements recently issued by the Pope Manufacturing Company and the Overman Wheel Company, to the effect that certain firms were infringing on their patents, also that they were selling certain makes of wheels below regular prices, will bring forth controversial statements, and, besides, might, if unexplained, hurt the interests of any or all of the parties interested. The facts are that the Pope Manufacturing Company and Overman Wheel Company, after repeated notices of infringement of patents, have issued a circular stating that the following firms were infringing their patents : Warwick Cycle Manufacturing Company, Springfield, Mass. ; Clark Cycle Company, Baltimore, Md.; Capital Cycle Company, Washington, D. C.; Smith National Cycle Company, Washington, D. C.; L. H. Johnson, Orange, N. J.; Strong & Green Cycle Company, Philadelphia. Messrs. Pope & Overman also state that they are selling ladies' safeties of the Psycho, Rover and Premium patterns at $120, $115 and $115 respectively. Of the firms mentioned above the Warwick Cycle Manufacturing Company have issued a circular advising their agents that they will assume all suits brought against them. These details are made public because the matter is being discussed by cyclists, many of whom do not understand the real import of the questions at issue, and who have been misled by untruthful and magnified rumors and misstatements. It is justice to all parties to state the facts as they are. The question of infringement will doubtless be determined by the courts. We will publish any accurate statement of facts which any of the parties mentioned may send us, and, furthermore, we are open to correction in any of the statements made above.

MR. GEORGE R. BIDWELL does not confine himself to the theory that the more men taught to ride properly the greater will be the gain to the sport, but he will put his ideas to the test by opening a riding school in New York on April 1. There will be competent instructors, the lessons will be strictly private, only two persons being on the floor at the same time, and no spectators will be permitted to witness the pupils' efforts to master the rudiments of cycle riding. We feel that Mr. Bidwell's school will be a success, and should advise agents in all large cities to make an attempt to establish riding schools. If an agent cannot manage it, he could combine with his neighbors in trade to their mutual advantage, as have Messrs. Stokes & Gardener, of Chicago. May the riding school flourish!

NEW JERSEY WILL HAVE GOOD ROADS.

The County Roads Improvement bill, introduced in the Senate by Senator Miller, was passed in that body by a vote of 15 to 3. On Monday night, the house passed the bill by a vote of 34 to 10. On Tuesday morning, Governor Green signed the bill and it became a law. New Jersey will at last have an improved system of roads. The people in cities may drive into the country at all times of the year : the people in the country can drive into the cities, for pleasure or business, at all times of the year. The condition of public roads is an evidence of the civilization and progress of a community, and increased prosperity in New Jersey may be anticipated. The *Elizabeth Daily Journal* deserves much credit for the masterful perseverance it exhibited in its efforts to shape public opinion toward improved roads.

CHIEF CONSUL BULL WANTS INFORMATION.

Chief Consul Bull is anxious to have a record of every club in the State Division, and will thank club secretaries if they will send him the following information : Name of c ub, city or town, club-house or rooms, street and number, monthly meeting nights, number of members, L. A. W. club or not, club officers, Secretary's name and address. Information should be sent to W. S. Bull, 754 Main Street, Buffalo, N. Y.

OFFICIAL HANDICAPPER OF NEW YORK AND NEW JERSEY.

Mr. C. S. Davol, Chairman of the Racing Board, has appointed Mr. F. P. Prial, Official Handicapper of New York and New Jersey, which States comprise the second United States Racing District.

MR. SHRIVER ON POPULAR VOTING.

234 PEARL STREET,
NEW YORK, March 18, 1889.

EDITOR OF THE WHEEL :

Your change of front on the League constitution question, as indicated in this week's leading article, is somewhat startling, and, to me, inexplicable. You still hold that the constitution "should provide for the election of its national officers by popular vote, as a matter of principle," but say that "no man has yet advanced a feasible plan for carrying out an election on such a basis which will give as good results as are accomplished under the present system," and that this system (of electing State Boards, which elect a National Board, which elects executive officers) is "as near as we ever can get to popular representation in League national affairs." All this is not only strangely in contrast with your former utterances, but even more strangely oblivious of the possibilities.

At the last election, in July, 1888, we who belong to the New York Division voted a ballot like this : For Chief Consul, George R. Bidwell; for Vice-Consul, W. S. Bull; for Secretary-Treasurer, E. M. Nisbett; for Representatives from the—District, John David Roe, John Smith. Now, what was there to have prevented printing that ballot on a larger sheet of paper and having it begin: For President, Charles H. Luscomb (or George A. Jessup); for First Vice-President, James R. Dunn ; for Second Vice-President, Sanford Lawton; for Treasurer, W. M. Brewster, and have it continue with the State ballot as above? No new machinery of election would be needed. The same officers

who count the votes for Chief Consul can without great menial strain count the vote on same ballots for President and return the result to League headquarters.

Nor is there any dangerous novelty in such a scheme. Every two years, on the Tuesday after the first Monday in November, each of us goes to the polls and votes for local and State officers and for representatives to Congress all on one ballot, or in one bunch of ballots, and every fourth year we do the same thing, and for President and Vice-President of the United States besides, except that in place of naming these officers specifically we name a lot of dummies that we call electors, whose only real duty is to automatically record the verdict given by popular suffrage. The only thing in political elections corresponding to our fearfully and wonderfully made League constitution is the manner of choosing United States Senators, which has resulted in more corruption than any other one thing in our politics and produced a legislative body that in many respects is worse even than the British House of Lords. The League system may not be as bad as that, but it is certainly peculiarly calculated to cement rings and foster wire-pulling, in which is wasted much of the real strength of the League.   Yours truly, -
                                        E. J. SHRIVER.

BROOKLYN.

It is with a certain amount of fear and trembling that I launch myself forth into the trials and pleasures of a journalistic career. For I realize in its entirety the fact that I am destined to pass many sleepless nights in consequence of the scathing and merciless criticisms of the many scribes of the cycling press throughout the bit of earth which has lately indulged in the festive pleasures of an inauguration.

However, I arm myself with the thought that I am writing Brooklyn news as much as possible, and feel that each item will be appreciated by some one who pedals around the Belgian-block streets of the City of Churches.

There is a rumor now in circulation to the effect that the Coney Island Boulevard is to have one of its side bridle-paths macadamized its entire length by the residents of that thoroughfare and vicinity, in co-operation with the Cyclists' Union of Long Island. Let us hope that the scheme may be carried through without opposition or delay, for it would certainly be a great big blessing to Brooklyn wheelmen.

I have it on good authority that the C. U. of L. I. will commence work on a certain bit of side-path leading to Bath which was made unridable at times last year by a certain gentleman (?) with a sweet and lovely temper and a large idea of his own rights and privileges.

The Union is also exerting its influence in the direction of Cobblestone Hill, which, in its time, has caused such a limited (or otherwise) amount of profanity that, were it all lumped together, it might be used to pave the said hill in very good shape.

The big theatre party is booming very favorably. There is to be a supper at the Clarendon Hotel after the performance, for which joyful event intending participants should "see" the committee at once. Mr. Marion, of the K. C. W., who is one of the committee, has developed quite an artistic bump, having executed two large notices of the theatre party, which may be seen posted on the walls of the respective club-houses of the K. C. W. and the B. B. C.

The annual election of officers for the B. B. C. takes place at their April meeting, and the regular nominations have just reached my desk. They are: For President, Jas. Fox; Vice-President, Herman H. Koop; Secretary, Bert M. Cole; Treasurer, H. E. Raymond; Captain, W. H. H. Meeteer; First Lieutenant, H. G. Fay; Second Lieutenant, F. L. Hebert; Buglers, P. Seixas and W. E. Fuller; Color-bearer, J. F. Borland. There are various whisperings of opposition tickets, but none have as yet been made public. The Brooklyns are very enthusiastic on the subject of roller skating, and one evening last week they had all its beauties and fine points illustrated to them by means of a stereopticon, manipulated by Messrs. Greenman and Robertson, who are two of the camera fiends of the club.
                                        ATOL.

NOTES FROM THE CITY OF BROTHERLY LOVE.

The Century Wheelmen, I understand, are getting ready to take immediate possession of their new club-house, having succeeded in leasing their present quarters to the Columbia Club, a social organization. The alterations in their new house are being pushed rapidly toward completion, and their wheel annex, it is hoped, will be finished this week. The club are considering the advisability of taking in lady members, and, with Mr. P. S. Collins advocating the move, it seems more than likely that the necessary changes in their by-laws will be made before long.

On Friday evening, February 15, the Pennsylvania Bicycle Club held their last stag entertainment. The committee in charge surprised the members with a handsomely engraved invitation requesting the presence of themselves and friends. This promised a good entertainment, and every one of the 300 or more present granted the promise well kept. Mr. Alf Bracher deserves especial commendation for the varied and entertaining programme, consisting of several choruses, solos by Mr. J. S. Bretz and Mr. Jno. Braun, sleight-of-hand performance by Mr. G. M. Sperry, of New York, with an exhibition of fancy billiards by the same gentleman; several boxing-matches and musical selections on the piano by different talented members. It was, without doubt, the finest stag entertainment ever given by any city club, and the members reluctantly left the refreshment and music room to catch the last car home.

The Tuesday evening dances held by the Pennsylvania Bicycle Club are a great success. At the last one some eighty odd persons were present. This desirable result is due largely to the welcome assistance of our lady members, who, in co-operation with Mr. Fred. Brown, are doing their utmost to make each gathering specially attractive. The best proof of their success is that a member attending one of these social gatherings generally assures his presence at the succeeding one.

The Philadelphia Bicycle Club, the last one in the city to maintain allegiance as a League club to the League, have decided to drop from their by-laws, at the expiration of the present year, the clause compelling all members to be League members. And thus one by one the leaves do fall.

Mr. S. C. Levy, of the Pennsylvania Bicycle Club, has presented a handsome split-second stop watch for competition in either mileage, number of days out or attendance at club runs, the watch to be placed in the hands of the road officers to be disposed of as they deem fit. Some hard-hearted wretch made a motion at the club meeting that the road officers be debarred from competition, but, thanks to the generosity of the members of the club, the motion was lost, much to the gratification of Charles L. Leisen. A handsome gold medal has also been presented by a member of the club, whose modesty deters him from revealing his identity. This is also to be placed in the hands of the road officers, to be awarded according to their judgment.

What safety are you going to ride this year? is the interrogation you meet everywhere. The poor ordinary is not even mentioned, and I fear, as far as new wheels for 1889 are concerned. It is doomed, as I do not know of a man who intends purchasing one. The Hart Cycle Co., representing the Columbia; Edward K. Tryon, Jr., & Co., representing the New Mail, and Philadelphia Cycle Co., representing the Victor people, have all had their new safeties out at the different clubs for trial. I have tried them all and pronounce decidedly in favor of — never mind, I won't say, as I have an 1888 safety and think mine A1.

On Tuesday evening, March 19, the associated cycling clubs met at the South End Wheelmen's rooms. Several matters of importance were discussed. A committee, consisting of Messrs. Burt, Zook and Evans, was appointed to draw up a petition to endeavor to secure free transportation of wheels on the Pennsylvania and Philadelphia and Reading roads. A committee, consisting of Messrs. Supp'ee, Hare and Edwards, was also appointed to consider the advisability of an inter-club run on Decoration Day. A good scheme if you chain the scorchers.

The Pennsylvania Bicycle Club, elated with the great success of their recent full-dress dances, have decided to end the season with a grand ball on Thursday evening, April 25, and have already secured enough names to insure success.

Have you tried the new Eagle bicycle? No, thanks, not insured; although I had the offer of one if I could mount it first trial. Excuse yours truly. I will resign my chances in some one else's favor.

I had the pleasure of receiving a very interesting and lengthy epistle from E. Irving Hallsted some days since. He is situated at present at Tacoma, W. T. We all envy the inhabitants of that place his good company, but warn them if he starts any riding out there to beware, or they will find out that the Harlem-Pennsylvania man is a goer from 'way back.

On Sunday last the Century Wheelmen had about a score of riders out from 9 o'clock until 12, while the Pennsylvania Bicycle Club had eleven representatives to dinner at Fort Washington. A good run that of thirty-six miles over hilly roads, for this time of year. But, as the present quarters, having leased a spacious building on Clarke Street for a term of years.
                                        WESTFIELD.

ATALANTA WHEELMEN, NEWARK, N. J.

At the third annual meeting of the Atalanta Wheelmen, held March 6, the following officers were elected for the ensuing year: President, George H. Miller; Vice-President, A. N. Terbell; Secretary-Treasurer, C. G. Halsey; Captain, W. A. Drabble; First Lieutenant, L. A. Edwards; Second Lieutenant, A. T. Rummell; Color-bearer, J. H. Crane.

The present membership numbers thirty, with a bright outlook for a large increase the coming season. On May 1 the club will vacate their present quarters, having leased a spacious building on Clarke Street for a term of years.

About twenty-five members sat down to the club's annual dinner on March 11, and a general good time was indulged in until long after midnight. -
                                        HAL.

CHICAGO.

The Aeolus Cycling Club, of Chicago, will move to their new club-house April 1. They have the finest club-house in this city, having a frontage of 150 feet. They have adopted a new uniform, it being of gray cloth with black binding. Their election took place on March 4 with the following result: George F. Koester, President; G. E. Lawson, Vice-President; John A. Erickson, Recording Secretary; Paul A. Dragorius, Corresponding Secretary; Carl L. Steen, Treasurer; Thomas Bray, Captain; Frank Raabe, First Lieutenant; Fred Wittenberg, Second Lieutenant; Walter Bray, Color-bearer; Henry J. Freeman, Bugler; Rudolph Beygeh, Quartermaster. Executive Committee—William I. Herns, Martin Bowbeer, A. C. Huehling, Charles Wittenberg. The Aeolus boys will give their next reception at the Columbia Skating Academy on March 29.   OBSERVER.

FIXTURES.

SOME RUNS ABOUT WASHINGTON TO PLACES OF HISTORICAL INTEREST.

I believe the cyclists of any locality might learn of many interesting places they would like to visit by devoting an evening occasionally to local history. The history of every State, county and hamlet has certainly been published in some form or other.

A record of about 2,000 miles in the vicinity of Washington last season carried me to many places of historical interest, and I will venture to write up a few of them for THE WHEEL, hoping that they may be of some service to the cycling public.

Washington cyclists are particularly favored with historical localities near by. Access to many of them is over country roads which are the terror of novices and the delight of expert wheelmen.

There are the familiar runs through the Soldiers' Home and to Arlington, and the famous run to Cabin John Bridge (the largest single span in the world). Great Falls on the Potomac, and thence along the tow-path of the Chesapeake and Ohio Canal to Harper's Ferry, sixty-three miles distant.

The run to Marlboro, Md., is a fine one. It is twenty miles East, over an excellent pike. These runs, and the one to Sandy Springs and Ashton, Quaker settlements lying twenty miles to the north, can be taken immediately after a wet season. The old residents in the latter places have many interesting relics of Colonial times.

There is an excellent road out to Hyattsville, near which lies the Lord Baltimore estate, over which you can roam at will, and admission to the old mansion can be obtained by permission from the agent. There is no one living on the estate except the keeper of the lodge.

On the way to Hyattsville you pass the historic dueling ground where Commodore Decatur met his death from a pistol in the hands of Commodore Barron. Many duels were fought at this place during and prior to the late war. You next pass through the little village of Bladensburg, where ships used to land on the Eastern Branch in 1876, now a shallow stream that would not float a mud scow.

There are the roads following the devious and beautiful windings of Rock Creek, where the Zoological Park is to be laid out.

Occoquan, Va., one of the old Colonial settlements, at one time the largest tobacco-shipping port in the South, with its picturesque ruins and romantic scenery, is only twenty-eight miles distant. The route is via Alexandria, Acotink and J'ohick Church (one of the churches where Washington used to attend service; built, in the last century, of bricks imported from England). This side of Acotink one can turn off to Mt. Vernon, which is sixteen miles from Washington.

Another interesting run is to the battle-fields of Bull Run and Manassas, only thirty miles distant, by way of Falls Church, Fairfax Court-House and Centerville. You can return from Occoquan or Manassas Junction by rail.

There is also an interesting run to Brandy-wine, through Silver Hill P. O. and Surratville, where Mrs. Surrat, one of the conspirators against the life of President Lincoln, lived for many years. One of the old residents told me that this woman used to attend church in Washington, sixteen miles distant, regularly, and always walked both ways, rain or shine. The gloomy old homestead of the Surrats is still standing, but is occupied by another family.

"TOURIST."

ROXBURY CYCLISTS AT DINNER.

The Roxbury Bicycle Club observed the third anniversary of its formation by a dinner at Young's Hotel, Boston, last Saturday night. There was a goodly gathering of jolly fellows, and from 7 o'clock until midnight no restraint was placed upon the merriment. The Roxbury club is among the best and most widely known cycling aggregations of the city's suburbs. Among its number are those who have attained eminence in social and business circles, and as a club it has always been noted for enthusiastic devotion to the sport.

The affair on Saturday night was as enjoyable as it was informal. President W. H. Emery, who is also Chief Consul of the Massachusetts division of the League of American Wheelmen, presided with becoming grace over the festivities. The guests were: Abbott Bassett, secretary of the L. A. W.; George A. Perkins, J. C. Kerrison and Charles S. Howard. Among the others present were: I. E. Wardtrop, Louis Heintz, Jr., A. H. Draper, E. T. Titlow, C. S. Merrill, George E. Marsters, G. Alfred Titcomb, F. F. Scholl, J. Dolph, Charles W. Eaton, John Graham, Frank Howard, Frank E. Peterson, James E. Silver, Walter F. Emery and Captain John S. Lovell.

When President Emery arose to begin the after-dinner exercises, he was greeted with much enthusiasm. He referred briefly to the many successes of the club during the past year, and introduced as the first speaker Abbott Bassett. This gentleman read an entertaining poem.

In introducing the next speaker, President Emery said that there was one wheelman, Geo. A. Perkins, in Massachusetts, to whom insufficient credit had been given. He was one who had always been faithful to the interests of the wheel, and as a representative to the General Court had done much for the cause of cycling.

Mr. Perkins was greeted with hearty applause. He referred at considerable length to the road-improvement bill, and expressed confidence of success in its passage. He told how, although engineered by cyclists, the bill for improvement of roads was a matter in which every resident of the State was personally interested.

Charles S Howard responded for the Boston Bicycle Club, and short addresses were made by many of the Roxbury Club members.—*Boston Herald.*

WHEELS—THEIR SIZES AND GEARS.

A table showing, and rules to ascertain, the circumference of different-sized wheels, and the number of revolutions each makes in a mile; also the most ready method to determine if a driving wheel is geared level, or how much up or down:

Diameter of wheel in inches.	Circumference in inches and 7ths.	No. of revolutions per mile.
30	94.2	672.00
32	100.4	630.00
34	106.6	592.95
36	113.1	560.00
38	119.3	530.52
40	125.5	504.00
42	132.0	480.00
44	138.2	458.18
46	144.4	438.25
48	150.6	420.00
50	157.1	403.20
52	163.3	387.69
54	169.5	373.33
56	176.0	360.00
58	182.2	347.68
60	188.4	336.00

To find the circumference of a circle, multiply the diameter by 3.1416, or 3 1-7. Example, a driving wheel 48 in. diameter:

48
3 1-7

141
6.6

150.6. Answer: 150 6-7, say 151 inches.

To find the number of revolutions a wheel makes in a mile, reduce the mile to sevenths of an inch, thus: 1,760 yards = 5,280 feet = 63,360 inches = 443,520 sevenths of an inch. Divide this by the circumference (150 6-7) of the wheel as above reduced to sevenths of an inch. Example:

150 6-7
7

1056)443520(420. Answer: 420 revolutions in a mile.
4224
———
3112
3112

A driving wheel of tricycle or safety bicycle is geared level when the number of cogs is the same on both chain wheels. If geared up, the cogs of chain wheel on driving axle are *less* in number than chain wheel on crank axle. If geared down, the cogs of chain wheel on driving axle are *more* in number than chain wheel on crank axle. To find how much a driving wheel is geared up or down, multiply the diameter of wheel by the number of cogs on crank axle, and divide the product by the number of cogs on driving axle. Example: Driving wheel, 30 in. diameter; chain wheel of ditto, 10 cogs; crank chain wheel, 16 cogs.

$$\frac{3^0}{16}$$

10), 80(geared up to 48 inches.

The number of revolutions made by the crank, which is the actual number of times the foot has to move round in going a mile, must be taken on the size the wheel is geared to: thus, a 30-in. wheel makes 672 revolutions of the crank in a mile, but if geared to 48 in. the crank only makes 420 revolutions to propel the machine the same distance as the 672 revolutions would if geared level.—*Wheeling.*

A ROADS IMPROVEMENT CONVENTION AT NEW ORLEANS.

Some weeks ago we printed a communication urging the importance of a general policy of improving country roads in the State, and suggesting the holding of a State convention to consider the subject in this city some time in April or May next. The interests at stake are of such general importance that the idea of a convention has been largely approved by the press throughout the State.

In order, then, that there may be some concert of action in the matter, we would suggest to the Board of Trade and the commercial exchanges of the city to adopt resolutions favoring the holding of such a convention, the delegates to be appointed by the police juries of parishes and the mayors of cities, the State engineers and State Commissioner of Agriculture to be also specially invited.

The whole question of the economic considerations of the construction and maintenance of country roads, so necessary to the commercial development of the State, should be treated fully and the best methods adopted.

The subject is one of such public and commercial importance that it is fully within the purview of our commercial bodies. Doubtless the Governor would give official sanction to the undertaking, upon assurance that a convention will meet a popular demand.—*New Orleans Item.*

STEVENS LEAVES ZANZIBAR.

[Special Cable Despatch to the New York *World.*]

ZANZIBAR, March 16.—I am just leaving for Mombasa, which is the principal seaport of the territory of the British East African Trading Company, and the starting point for the most important caravan routes to the great lake regions of Central Africa.

Mombasa, one of the most important cities and fortresses on the East African coast, and situated to the south of Zanzibar, is perched on an island in the middle of an inlet of the sea forking off into two branches and running deep into the land. The island, which is about three miles in length, is low-lying and covered with splendid mango, guava and cocoa palms, and is inhabited by about three thousand Wasuaheli and by about five hundred Arabs. The city consists of the ancient fort built by the Portuguese in the year 1594 and the ruins of the Portuguese town of Gavana and what is known as the black town.

It is the basis from whence the United Methodist missions and the Church Missionary Society dispatch their caravans and supplies to their stations on the shores of Lake Victoria Nyanza.

It is also the starting point of a number of important caravan routes to the eastern portion of the lake region of the Nile, and carries on an important traffic in ivory, copal gum, corn, rhinoceros hides, etc.

A SELECTED LIST OF PATENTS.

[Reported especially for THE WHEEL AND CYCLING TRADE REVIEW by C. A. Snow & Co., patent attorneys, Washington, D. C.]

Thos. O'Brien, New York. N. Y.—Bicycle. This patent consists in the combination with two equal-sized wheels of a frame composed of two tubes, one receiving the other, spring bars, an arm and bracing rods, the whole forming a bridge free from vibration.

Dated March 19.

PHILADELPHIA.

It seems as if the weather man must have a spite against Philadelphia wheelmen, as the weather of the last four Sundays made wheeling decidedly uncomfortable. But last Sunday, notwithstanding the lowering clouds, a number of club men braved the mud and a chance of a ducking and indulged in club runs. Captain Supplee took nineteen Pennsylvania men to Fort Washington, gladdening the hearts of the sons of Erin by the green ribbons they sported in honor of St. Patrick. The Centurions, under Captain Carter, took a run to Bryn Mawr with twenty-two in the ranks, the orange ribbon of their colors calling forth some uncomplimentary remarks from the celebrating Irishmen. Every one is wishing for good weather, so as to get a long ride. The state of the roads at present renders it impossible to go off the macadam, and around these parts there are mighty few of that kind.

Am sorry to state that the next "smoker" of the Century Wheelmen, which was to have taken place March 28, has for some unexplained reason been declared off. This is a disappointment to many members, as they had anticipated a good time. Both Brown and Dietsch have been in active training for their bout with the gloves, and each was sure he could knock the other out. It would have been a great exhibition, a contest, as some paper had it, of "red hair" vs. "pink whiskers." And then what is to become of the fellows who were to wrestle; and, alas! (a tear) what of the Glee Club?

About every other member of the Century Club you meet has an idea that he is a runner, and that idea broadens itself that he can beat anyone he knows of. I hope that some time this spring the opportunity will offer itself to try these wonders and to see who is really the best man.

The members of the Pennsylvania Bicycle Club are in the main a jolly and whole-souled lot of fellows, ever ready to lend a helping hand to wheelmen or exchange greetings on the road, and are known far and near for their generosity and hospitable conduct; but there are a few who are associated with them who, by their snobbish behavior, their apish stiffness and general disagreeableness, make themselves ridiculous to their friends and an object of disgust to all they come in contact with. As usual with people of this sort, they should be the last to act in this manner. Blood will tell, and shoddiness is sure to crop out some time.

The alterations to the Century's new house are progressing very rapidly. It is expected by the end of this week that their splendid wheel room will be ready for occupancy. In a month's time we are assured that it will be furnished from top to bottom in the latest and most approved fashion. Then for the "house warming" of one of the largest and most commodious bicycle club-houses in the country.

How about that little game of cards on the train going to Washington, in which even Deacon Hare took a hand? The question now going the rounds is, "Who scooped the jack pot?" And echo answers, "Who?"

March 19, 1889.　　　　ARGUS.

NEW ORLEANS.

Spring, gentle spring, has landed both of her dainty tootsy-wootsies right here, and in consequence we are reveling in the most glorious weather imaginable. The effect is plainly visible in the cycling ranks, and quite the largest crowd that have been together since the September meet turned out Sunday last (10th) to take a sniff of the g. w. and to witness the Christy-Hathorn race; but they were somewhat disappointed.

Hathorn was out of trim and failed to make the fight expected. For half a mile the race was nip and tuck, but after that Hathorn commenced to fag and Christy to draw away, and at three-quarters there was no question as to who would win. Christy crossed the line with a lead of well over a hundred yards, doing the distance (1½ miles) in 4m. 51s R. G. Betts, starter, and C. M. Fairchild, E. M. Graham and C. H. Fenner, at the finish, officered the event.

Immediately after the race L. J. Frederic, of the Louisiana Club, challenged the winner, who has accepted, the course to be the same and March 17 the day.

Mr. A. M. Hill has presented a handsome silver cup to the New Orleans Bicycle Club for a series of races to be contested during the summer months. A committee has been appointed to arrange the details.

The Louisiana Cycling Club's races for the Patson medal will be inaugurated Sunday next (24th). This club also holds its annual election April 1.

Bi.

ST. LOUIS.

The Warner bill received its first test vote in the House on the 15th inst. It was called up by the author, who asked that it be engrossed. It has been amended since it was first presented, and now only applies to racing on the highways. The penalty for violation of the law is a fine of not to exceed $100, and lays the offender liable for any damages that may be caused by horses frightening. The objectionable dismounting feature is entirely eliminated, and the bill in its present shape is quite harmless, except so far as it opens the way for special legislation. The bill was argued at some length by representatives Warner and Pollard in its favor, and Clark and Dempsey against it. On the vote it was ordered to engrossment, but the opinion prevails that it will be defeated when it comes up for passage. The League has made an excellent fight against the bill and will surely win. Nevertheless, I suppose there are still a good many "mossback" wheelmen who see no use in belonging to the organization. The *Republic* and *Post-Dispatch* of this city, and the *Times* and *Journal* of Kansas City, have worked hard for us all through this agitation, and the wheelmen, I hope and believe, are truly grateful. The *Republic*, in an editorial printed in its issue of the 12th, says: "As long as Missouri is a free State, the people in it can ride what they please on the highways, whether it be bicycles or hobbies, just as long as they give other people room to pass and leave the highway as free and open to others as it is to them. The bicycle has come to stay, and we trust Hon. Ira B. Warner will succeed in making up his mind that it is really no more frightful than the New Mexican *burros*, imported by his St. Louis county constituents to make the Manchester road hideous with their alarming voices, etc." I noticed in the Legislative proceedings printed in the same issue the following: "Mr. Pollard read a letter from one of his constituents, in which it was stated that the wheelmen were hiring men to solicit subscriptions to the remonstrances, and were paying five cents per name."

There could be nothing more absurd, and yet I have no doubt that many of the country members will believe it. The necessary steps were at once taken to place the League in its proper light on this point before the Legislature.

The Missouris are to have another European traveler in the person of C. C. Hildebrand. He leaves here on the 18th inst. for Boston and Springfield, at which points he will make short visits with Dr. Emery and his old chum, E. C. Klipstein, and on the 27th inst. he will sail from New York on the "Saale" for Bremen. I fear he will leave an aching void at Kirkwood.

The Missouris' new captain is trying the experiment of short runs this year, thus enabling his men to get back to town for dinner. The runs for March are to Bartold's, eight miles, on the 17th; Point Breeze, ten miles, on the 24th; and Webster, twelve miles, on the 31st. This does not look much like business, and I do not think the idea will meet with much favor, except with a very few. The next thing we may look for is a called run to the "pump" and return for dinner.

The proposed track association is making good progress, and the indications point to a successful consummation of the enterprise. The only drawback to it is the fact that the grounds cannot be had for Saturday afternoons. At the price asked it would pay to rent the grounds if only for the base-ball and foot-ball privileges.

ITHURIEL.

BROOKLYN.

The roads in Prospect Park and the Boulevard have made gigantic strides toward reaching the condition of excellence they attain during the summer and fall. In view of the season of the year the Park riding is unprecedented, and any Brooklyn rider who still permits his wheel to rust undisturbed in the cellar because the season is not yet sufficiently advanced makes a large mistake, and is losing nearly as good riding as he can ever have in this vicinity.

A ride around the Park circuit on Sunday morning means as certain a meeting with a baker's dozen of well-known Brooklyn wheelmen as a visit to the country church reveals the presence of the usual contingent of deacons. Before you complete the two miles you will have met the omnipresent Wise, the twin scorchers Beasley and Tom Hall; Murphy, the long-distance "fiend;" the hard-working Schumacher, and such well-known club men as Fuller, Spelman, Halsey, Steves, Barkman, Bell, Healey, Bogert Munne and Morehouse. From passing observation, there seems to be at present quite a predominance of the "greys" on pleasant Sundays. Perhaps this merely signifies that the "fossils" naturally stand the winter best, or are more susceptible to early thaws, rather than that a majority of the other clubs are seeking spiritual consolation elsewhere at that time.

F. G. Brown, of the K. C. W., is reported very publicly to have become a member of the New Jersey Athletic Club team, with Baggott, Caldwell, Bowman and Pendleton. Brown will undoubtedly add a good deal of strength to the team; in fact, it is an open question whether he will not be the strongest man in it. Brown's development as a racing man during the latter part of the season was tremendously rapid; from an inferior man in '87 and the fore-part of '88, his work last fall has raised him to a high rank among the New York and Brooklyn cracks. If he continues to improve this year as he did last year there will be very few men in this vicinity who can touch him.

Mailler, of the L. I. W., has returned from a two months' stay in Buffalo. Few wheelmen in Brooklyn are as well known to other club men and to the unattached in general as Mailler, and his absence from the road for any continued period affects Brooklyn riders much as the removal of an old and respected landmark.

Club hospitality in this section of the country is markedly improving. Perhaps it is due to the Cyclists' Union and the common interests resulting therefrom; perhaps it is due to the forgetting or living down of the ancient traditions of petty rivalries and jealousies; or perhaps it is due to the mutual discovery that one's own club does not necessarily contain all the good fellows who ride the wheel. The L. I. W. stag on the 9th has furnished a rattling precedent for the other clubs, and one which we hope will be followed.

The boys are eagerly anticipating the theatre party of the 20th, and indications point to its being the greatest affair of the kind ever given entirely by wheelmen. They say the committee are desperately at work evolving new gags and clothing anew others of very respectable age. In this respect the committee have an abundance of material on which to work, and a great amount of additional fun is expected as the result of their efforts.

NYX.

MARYLAND.

Cycling is booming in Baltimore, and it seems highly probable that the sport will be more popular this season than ever before. Many new recruits have joined the ranks of whirling wheelmen during the past winter, and crowds of fresh faces will be seen on the roads and highways in the vicinity of Baltimore when the season is fairly opened.

At the annual election of officers of the Rambler Club for the ensuing year the following gentlemen were unanimously elected: F. L. Brauns, President; E. J. Sultan, Vice-President; C. M. Pitt, Treasurer; Lew Warrington, Secretary; W. H. Thomas, Captain; H. Jones, First Lieutenant; E. M. Cole, Second Lieutenant; C. E. Wingo, E. B. Jones, S. R. Boyd, H. R. Barrington and W. Jackson, Executive Committee.

The Potomac Wheelmen, of Western Maryland, were organized, March 11, at Cumberland, Md. Sixteen applications for membership were received. Mr. A. C. Willison was made temporary chairman and James D. Wineow temporary secretary. This club expects to join the League. A meeting will be held March 25, when permanent officers will be elected, etc.

The roads and pikes leading from the city are in good condition, and almost every day crowds of wheelmen can be seen making long-distance trips.

The Hagerstown, Md., Bicycle Club will hold a meet and races on July 2, 3 and 4. The first two days will be devoted to tours through their delightful valley and on the five splendid pikes out of town, where many historic points can be visited, as the battle-fields of Antietam and South Mountain, Pen-Mar, Cumberland Valley and many others that are not to be overlooked by the tourist and pleasure-seeker.

The third day there will be a parade and some entertainment at night. It is probable that clubs from all parts of the country will participate. The cyclers of this city will attend in large numbers, and there will be many visitors from other parts of the State. The Scranton, Pa., and Chambersburg, Pa., clubs have already signified their intention of participating, and also several clubs of the adjoining States. The hotel accommodations, an important consideration, are ample and good.

The meet will not be under the auspices of the L. A. W., nor the Maryland Division, but is the enterprise of the Hagerstown Club, which is a flourishing organization. This meet is expected to surpass the one held on July 4 last. Many lady cyclists will attend and add grace and beauty to the occasion. Although the invitations have not yet been sent out, the meet promises to be a success.

The Maryland Club held their seventh annual banquet at their club-house, on Mt. Royal Avenue, on Thursday, March 14. A large T-shaped table was set in the gymnasium on the third floor, where seventy-five men in full-dress suits sat down to a sumptuous repast. The following toasts were responded to: By President Moses Norris, "The Maryland Bicycle Club;" Captain E. F. Le Cato, "On Road and Path;" Chief Consul Albert Mott, "Cycling with a Purpose;" of the Maryland Division, Joseph Thompson, "The Corporation;" Robert Unduch, "The Big 19;" P. S. Brown, "The Fraternity of Cyclists." The committee in charge of the banquet were, George H. Miller, Howard Williams, E. F. Le Cato, W. H. Beatty and C. F. Hutchinson. Emerich's orchestra was in attendance.

The annual meeting of the stockholders of the Maryland Club was held at their club-house on Mt. Royal Avenue. The report of the Board of Trustees was read, showing the club's financial condition to be satisfactory. The revenue for the past year was over $1,800 in excess of all actual expenses during the same period. The 530 shares of stock remaining in the treasury unsold were subscribed for, thus completing the entire capital stock of 2,000 shares. The old Board of Trustees, consisting of Moses Norris, Yates Penniman, James D. Mason, E. F. Le Cato, S. T. Clark, H. E. Brown, were re-elected.

BAY RIDGE.

MANHATTAN BICYCLE CLUB.

The annual meeting of the Manhattan Bicycle Club was held at their club-house, in West Seventieth Street, last Monday evening. The principal business was the election of officers. Three tickets materialized during the evening, and as every one was buttonholing every one else the result was chaos. Later in the evening the supporters of one of the tickets performed a *coup d'état* by appearing with a mammoth poster on which were painted the names of the candidates. This work of art completely dwarfed the poster of the opposition, a "wee sma' thing," and won over many who were undecided. The race for the Captaincy was a nip-and-tuck affair between "Billy" Sheehan

and "Johnny" Post, Billy winning by a nose—we mean by two votes. The chief officer this year will be John M. Warwick, re-elected, a gentleman who fills his post with dignity and has also done a deal of hard work for the Manhattan Club. Charles A. Sheehan, a downright hustler, who has been tireless in his efforts to advance the club, has been re-elected Secretary. D. H. Thistle will again retain the purse-strings; he has been a valuable man in an important office. The Vice-President is a new man, Mr. J. A. Clairmonte, better known as the "Colonel," the man who almost "headered" in the Niagara Whirlpool—a man of foresight and of kindly and gentlemanly instincts. The list of officers is as follows: President, John M. Warwick; Vice-President,

J. A. Clairmonte; Secretary, Charles A. Sheehan; Treasurer, D. H. Thistle; Trustees, D. C. Newton and Dr. G. R. Hird; Captain, J. W. Sheehan; First Lieutenant, P. G. Keane; Second Lieutenant, V. F. Pelin; Surgeon, J. I. Metzger, M. D.; Color-bearer, Ethan Allen; Bugler, C. E. Clemens.

The boxing, fencing and wrestling championships of the A. A. U. will be held this Saturday evening at the Metropolitan Opera-House, New York. The programme will be the most attractive, athletically, that has ever been held in this country.

"Has bicycling anything to do with consumption?" is a query addressed to the *Bicycling News*. Yes: it develops consumption—of large quantities of food, ice cream and liquid refreshments.

THE VICTOR.

KING OF THE SAFETIES.

A. G. Spalding & Bros.,
SPECIAL AGENTS,

NEW YORK AND CHICAGO.

FOR YOUR SAFETY.

The Buffalo Safety

BICYCLE STAND

Firm, Strong, Portable.

Price, $1.00.

A. G. SPALDING & BROS.,
Sole Agents,

NEW YORK AND CHICAGO.

The Trade Supplied.

A. G. Spalding & Bros.,

Makers of the Official L. A. W. Sundries.

Caps. League Regulation	$1.25
Shirts. League Regulation	2.00
No. XX Fine Cheviot for hot-weather wear	1.00
Stockings. Our celebrated Linen Sole Stocking, League color	1.00
Belts. No. X Silk, Edge's League color, white centre, Snake Buckle	.50
No. XX Worsted Solid, League color, Snake Buckle	.40
Shoes. Our new L. A. W. Kangaroo Shoe, hand-made, light, strong, elastic	6.00
No. 1, Canvas, leather trimmings	8.50

Sent post-paid on receipt of price.
Send for Catalogue Knit Racing and Training Suits

A. G. Spalding & Bros.,

241 Broadway, New York;

108 Madison St., Chicago.

NEW YORK BICYCLE CO.,

No. 8 WARREN STREET,   No. 4 EAST 60th STREET,

DEALERS IN NEW AND SECOND-HAND WHEELS.

FULL LINE CYCLING ACCESSORIES.

WHEELS BOUGHT, SOLD and EXCHANGED.

Renting, Repairing, Nickeling.

DIFFICULT REPAIRING A SPECIALTY.

Prices Reasonable.   Satisfaction Guaranteed.

Wheels to Rent by the Hour, Day, Week or Month.

UP TOWN AGENTS FOR

MESSRS. A. G. SPALDING & BROS.

Sporting and Tennis Goods.

City Agents SPECIAL PONY STAR (39x24)

AND STAR SAFETY.

Examine our Bargain List in another Column.

THE SPRINGFIELD ROADSTER BICYCLES

Hold the World's Records

No. 1 Wheel, plain and cone-bearing, 50-inch	$75
" 2 " ball-bearing, 50-inch	100
" 3 " plain and cone-bearing, 46-inch	75
" 4 " ball-bearing 46-inch	100
" 5 " ball-bearing, 50-inch	110

This wheel has tangent spokes and hollow rim.

No. 6 Wheel, ball-bearing, 46-inch	110

This wheel has tangent spokes and hollow rim.

No. 7 Volant Safety, 31 and 30 inch diameter wheels, ball-bearing 115

For Speed,

Safety

1889

Catalogue Now Ready.

Sent Free.

Beauty

Durability.

SPRINGFIELD BICYCLE MFG. CO.,

178 Columbus Avenue, BOSTON, MASS.

HEADERS IMPOSSIBLE.   BEST HILL-CLIMBERS.

WHEEL GOSSIP.

The New York *Press* of Sunday last had some interesting wheel notes.

Miss Redding, editor of the *Art Journal*, rides a Psycho ladies' bicycle.

The intercollegiate games will be held May 25, place not yet decided. The bicycle event will be a race of two miles

A number of wheelmen attended the New Orleans Carnival, and were well taken care of by the New Orleans boys.

The Capital Cycle Co. are sole U. S. agents for the "Monarch" lanterns made by Miller & Co., of Birmingham, Eng.

The Humber tandem drawn for at Fair Haven, Conn., on March 15 was won by Geo. W. Frutichey, of New York City.

W. I. Harris, Clarence L. Smith and W. E. Smith have been unanimously elected to membership in the Citizens' Bicycle Club.

Dr. Emery, C. C. of Massachusetts, has issued an eloquent circular letter to the members of the division appealing for renewals.

A meeting of cyclists attached to Boston papers was held yesterday at the *Herald* building, the object being to organize a bicycle club.

Some members of the Huntington, L. I., Bicycle Club have offered a bottle of wine for the first wheelman of the city of Brooklyn who arrives in their town this season.

"The above letter from Messrs. Rudge and the like from *Wheeling* seem to put a more reasonable light on the record, and so down it goes as a wonderful road performance."

Messrs. Garden & Stokes, respectively representing the Columbia and Warwick and Springfield Roadster wheels in Chicago, have secured a large hall and will establish a riding school.

At the Crystal Palace, Leipzig, a cycle show was held from February 13 to March 3. There were 146 exhibitors, many of whom were agents for English houses and showed English wheels.

A Roads Improvement Convention will be held at New Orleans this spring, Chief Consul Hodgson, who was instrumental in having the convention called, will represent the League.

Senator Jacob Cantor, who introduced New York's Liberty bill into the Assembly, has been very ill at Albany. It is expected that he will shortly leave for Old Point Comfort for the benefit of his health.

THE WHEEL is one of the liveliest and best cycle papers published. Current cycling events and general news of interest to wheelmen are chronicled by it every week —*Daily American*, Nashville, Tenn.

The Warner "anti-liberty" bill, introduced some time since in the Missouri Legislature, has been so modified that, even if it should become a law in its present shape, it would be perfectly harmless.

The Brooklyn *Citizen* of March 17 devotes a column article and an illustration to Charlie Schwalbach and the efforts he has made to advance the sport in Brooklyn. Charlie is a Prince at working the lay press.

The New York Club, always on the alert to advance wheeling, has sent out 1,250 blank petitions, advocating the passage of the Boulevard pavement bill. A large number of petitions have been returned signed.

The English amateur championships for 1889 will be run in July, on the Paddington track. The dates are: July 20, 1-mile bicycle; 25-mile bicycle; 5-mile tricycle; July 27, 1-mile tricycle, 25-mile tricycle, 5-mile bicycle.

The Atlanta Wheelmen, who now have their own rooms over the North ward Bank, have obtained possession of the Trinity Church Chapel, on Clark Street, near Belleville Avenue, Newark, and propose to fit up a fine clubhouse.

Three Australian riders, Messrs. Betteridge, Bloxham and Hitchcock, recently made a bicycle trip of 710 miles through the very watery Australian bush. The journey occupied eleven days. The wheels used were two New Rapid ordinaries and one safety.

Considerable opposition to the Roads Improvement bill has developed in the New Jersey Assembly. The strongest point raised by the opponents of the bill is that the freeholders in some counties may be too extravagant; all of which is puerile, it is needless to say.

The Brooklyn Cycle Club's continuous pool tournament, commenced February 28, was won by Charles S. Spaulding. George W. Cooper and Charles Coe tied for second place. C. A. Harrington won the leather medal for having lost the largest number of games.

The Brooklyn clubs are looking forward to the theatre party to be held at the Park Theatre on March 20. It is expected that over two men will be present. Tickets may be obtained by addressing Bert Cole, 111 St. Felix Street, Brooklyn. After the theatre a dinner will be served at the Clarendon.

The anti-bicycle bill recently introduced into the Missouri Legislature by Mr. Warner has been amended so that it now only prohibits racing on the public highways. The Missouri members of the League have fought the bill expected that over two men will be present, will be in passage in any form.

The Twelfth Regiment games will be held at the armory. Sixty-second Street and Ninth Avenue, New York City, on Friday evening, May 10. The bicycle events are a 2-mile handicap, 15-mile novices and 1-mile novices. Entrance fee fifty cents for each event. Close May 4 with C. J. Leach, P. O. Box 3301, New York City.

The *Bicycling World* has not accepted the 3.18 1-3 Triplet mile as a record, merely as a wonderful road performance. We presumed that the *World* accepted this remarkable trial as a record, basing our presumption on the sentence quoted below, which the *World* used in reference to the trial. We are glad to correct ourselves.

Messrs. William Read & Sons announce the good points of the New Mail ordinary and New Mail safety on another page. The ordinary was in good demand last year, and numbers of letters from prominent wheelmen attest its popularity. The New Mail safety is a high-grade rear-driver, and already orders have been booked for it.

THE CENTURY RUN OF 1889.

At a meeting of the Century Run Committee, held at Newark last Saturday evening, it was decided to hold the run on Saturday, June 8, unless this date conflicts with the date of the League meet. The rendezvous will be made at Orange, N. J., on the previous evening, where good accommodations will be provided. The route will include Newark, Elizabeth, Plainfield, New Brunswick, Princeton, Trenton and Philadelphia. The run is open to all wheelmen. Further particulars will be furnished by L. A. Clarke, 23 Broad Street, New York.

ON SAFETIES.

Mr. C. Levi, an English cyclist who has had forty years' experience as a mechanic, writes an interesting letter to *Wheeling* about safeties. About 2,000 safety riders pass his house every day on Sunday. He favors large steering wheels, from 30 to 36 inch, to secure steadiness of running and reduce vibration. The most advantageous position for the seat on a rear-driver is as far back over the driving-wheel as possible. The handle bars should be brought well backward, so that it may not be necessary to constantly lean forward to grip them.

The Pope Mfg Co. have sent out the following price list: Ladies' Rover, made by Starley & Co., $115; Ladies' Premier safety, made by Hillman, Herbert & Co-per, $115; Ladies' Psycho safety, made by Starley Bros., $100. These prices are lower than the regular retail prices if the same wheels imported by agents. The Pope Mfg Co. have also issued a circular to agents stating that the following firms are selling wheels infringing on its patents: The Clark Cycle Co., of Baltimore; Warwick Cycle Co. Springfield; H. S. Owen, Washington; L. H Johnson, Orange, N. J.; Strong & Green, Philadelphia, and the Smith National Cycle Co., Washington.

The Thompson Electric Welding Co., with offices at Boston, recently held an exhibition at their factory, at which was shown their new process of welding metal by electricity. These machines of different sizes are used for welding. The first has a capacity for welding from a quarter of an inch to an inch bar of iron. It will also weld copper from one-eighth to one-half inch. The next larger machine welds two-inch iron pipe as well as smaller sizes. The third machine will weld a two-inch bar of iron, from a welding a pipe, the weld is stronger than the metal itself, and the pipe will break sooner at any other point than at the weld. It is expected that the electric system of welding will come into general use.

N. A. A. A. A. BICYCLE HANDICAP.—The 1¼-mile handicap decided at the N. A. A. A. A. games held Saturday evening, March 2, at Madison Square Garden, New York, proved a frost on account of the bad track, which caused almost every competitor to fall. The two trial heats decided in the afternoon let the following men—all winners of heats—into the final: R. W. Steves, K. C. W., 10 yards; J. W. Scheeler, B. B. C., 65 yards, second; J. H. Hinman, N. Y. B. C., 90 yards; Fred. Coningsby, B B C., 90 yards; E. A. Powers, M. W., 95 yards; H. A. Kellum, Thirteenth Regiment A. A., 100 yards; J. Hinds, M. A. C. The 1¼-mile handicap was won by Steves; Scheeler, second; Powers, third. Time — 3m. 37s. All the contestants, except the three placed men, fell either one or more times. Scheeler gained a round of applause by riding over three of the fallen men up on to the board floor and back again on the track; some six inches below the floor. Charley Schwalbach's men did good service with his wagons, carrying the wheels of the Brooklyn men over to the "Garden" and home again.

In accordance with a resolution adopted at a special meeting, February 16, the New York Bicycle Club met on Friday and Monday evenings and voted on the adjourned amendments with the following result:

	YEAS	NAYS
AMENDMENT A.—To provide for election of committee chairmen by the club, each chairman to appoint his committee and the captain his lieutenants	69	6
AMENDMENT B.—To establish monthly meetings of the club	56	11
AMENDMENT C.—To give election of new members to the club instead of to the trustees	56	22
AMENDMENT D.—Prohibiting proposal of rejected candidates within six months	63	6
AMENDMENT E.—Changing mode of electing officers	56	7
AMENDMENT F.—Prohibiting the holder of two or more offices by any member	57	10
AMENDMENT G.—Establishing an entertainment committee and prescribing duties of the several committees	64	4

Amendment C, not having the required three-fourths affirmative vote, was rejected.

HARLEM WHEELMEN'S RECEPTION.

A very jolly, nice crowd of people attended the Harlem Wheelmen's reception, held at West End Hall, 125th Street, on Wednesday evening, March 15. The reception was preceded by an entertainment, the feature of which was the singing of Miss Macey.

Dancing was commenced shortly after 10 o'clock and was continued until 4 A. M., with an intermission for supper at 1 o'clock.

Among those present were the "Deacon," the "Judge," the "Hustler" and the "Shoutist;" also Mr. and Mrs. L. A. Newcome, Mr. T. A. Halpin, members of the Manhattan Bicycle Club; Mr. Herne and Mr. Moore, Riverside Wheelmen; Mr. W. H. P. Veysey, Citizens Bicycle Club, and Mr. F. P. Prial, New York Bicycle Club.

The committee having the reception in charge, Messrs. Newcome, Emanuel, Raisbeck and Robus, were entitled to much credit for the success that attended the reception.

CYCLING FOR WOMEN.

DEAR EDITOR OF THE WHEEL :

Of late I have been hearing so much of the destruction of dresses on the wheel that I want to give you some of my experience on the subject.

Of course, every woman wants to look well on the wheel, as she does everywhere else, and that is certainly not accomplished when the wheelwoman comes to the fray with draperies, reeds and too narrow skirts. Bustles have been inveighed against for so long that if any one still wears one it would seem to be a waste of words to say anything more, and yet I often see those riders who have willingly sacrificed reeds and draperies still cling to the ungraceful, unnatural and unhealthy wad.

I have at last seen a dress which is pretty, comfortable (its owner says) and utterly uncatchable by wheel or chain. It is made of corduroy; the skirt is gored in front slightly, all the fullness is in the back; the skirt measures two yards. It opens far back on the side so that it cannot catch on the saddle in mounting and yet does not show. The waist is a coat, shaped something like a riding-habit's body ; and for warm weather a waist, made in the same style, of light flannel. With this skirt the rider wears knickerbockers and stockings of the same color and no underskirts. In warm weather the knickerbockers are made of silesia or light cambric. The whole get-up is the prettiest I have seen.

Corduroy was adopted by the rider after two years' experience of flannel, etc., and it (corduroy) seems to have many advantages. It outwears any other material, is heavy enough not to fly back from the ankles on windy days or when coasting rapidly, still enough to utterly refuse to be caught in wheel or chain, pretty, and reasonable in price. It is no warmer than flannel for summer.

I want to disagree with two of your correspondents, if you do not mind. First, with "Marguerite," about the small steering wheel ; then with "Wildflower" when she says the saddle ought to be as far back as possible.

As to the small steering wheel, I never rode any but the Psycho Ladies' Safety myself, which has the two wheels alike, twenty-nine inches; but my two sisters learned to ride on a wheel which has a 24-inch steering wheel and a 30 inch driving wheel, and they have both given it up for the Psycho, which they find easier to mount, dismount from and ride generally. Indeed, among the half dozen wheelwomen that I know the sentiment is unanimously in favor of the two wheels of like size, though some of them still ride the machine with small steering wheels, having bought them before trying the Psycho. Wildflower says she likes the saddle as far back as she can get it. Here again I disagree, for I find it much more comfortable and, I think, very much more sightly to have the saddle as nearly over the pedals as possible. Of course it depends a good deal on the build of the rider as to the amount of space which must be allowed, but I think as little as possible should be left.

PSYCHE.

"WILDFLOWER" FAVORS THE TWO-WHEELER.

. Cycle makers, as a rule, appear not to favor ladies riding safeties, as the class of machines ladies ride is not of much consequence to them, providing they do ride. The tricycle, as a rule, is mostly recommended, and the questions of weight, ease of propulsion and safety are not taken into account. My assertion that the safety is safer than a tricycle will no doubt be questioned, and in a crowded thoroughfare the tricycle may have an advantage, that of stopping without dismounting ; but for the country riding the safety has many advantages, and not the least is its safety In riding down hills. I speak from experience and I am not an over-courageous rider, and should have very much questioned this assertion if made before I learned to ride the safety if anyone had advanced it. Ask safety riders who have ridden tricycles the question as to the relative safety of machines, and I believe the universal answer will be in favor of the safety.

I very much doubt if 100 ladies who now ride the three-wheeler were to learn to ride the safety whether one out of the number would return to the old love. Do any of our readers know a gentleman who after learning the safety has returned to the tricycle ? This should be some criterion to go by, and I am confident in my own mind that the lady cyclist of the future will ride a safety.— *Wildflower in Wheeling.*

AMATEUR PHOTOGRAPHY.

An outfit costing $12.00, for making pictures 5 x 8 inches, is next in order. The camera is of mahogany, seasoned several months before using, and is finely finished. The folding-bed is made rigid by means of two clamp-hooks, one on each side of the frame. It is an exceedingly simple contrivance, but one that insures perfect rigidity. An E A single achromatic lens, with two stops or diaphragms, accompany each outfit. The stops are made so as to fit snugly in the lens tube, so that when they are not in use both are inserted in the tube, and there is little or no danger of them being in any but the right place when needed for use. The dry-plate holder is one of the lightest and strongest in the market. The construction of the Patent Perfect Double Holder is such that several sizes of plates can be used without the aid of inside kits ; for instance, any plate measuring five inches one way and not over eight inches the other can be used. This is a most convenient arrangement where experiments regarding time are being made and narrow strips instead of an entire plate are being used. Kits for holding smaller sizes of plates still can be used in the holder. It is also a very easy holder to handle in the dark-room.

The camera, lens, plate holder and top of tripod are packed in a neat carrying case. The tripod legs are strapped together.

The outfit just described can be fitted with an instantaneous shutter at a small additional cost. The shutter will be found very useful, as there are occasions without number where it will be found necessary to make an instantaneous picture to gain the best effects.

With this equipment an extra lens board is supplied, to which a pair of single achromatic lenses, like those shown in the cut, for making stereoscopic views, 4 x 5 inches, can be obtained at a small additional outlay.

The camera is fitted with a dividing screen, which is easily removed when a picture covering the entire plate is desired.

We come now to a mahogany camera for making pictures, 4 x 5 inches, of a slightly higher grade than those just described.

The focusing on this camera is done by a rack and pinion, which enables the operator to obtain a better image on the focusing screen, and there is less liability of the focus being changed by a jar while placing the plate holder in position. A movement of the camera after the focus has once been obtained will many times cause a complete failure. It is also a most convenient attachment. It also has, in addition to the other cameras, a rising front. This consists in making that part of the camera to which the lens is attached movable, so that it may be raised, and thus admit of bringing portions of a view into focus without changing the position of the camera. It is also of the greatest advantage in photographing architectural subjects. Oftentimes it is impossible to get the entire subject on the plate without placing the camera a long distance from it, and this is not always convenient. By slightly raising the front of the camera this difficulty is overcome and greater detail is obtained. The bellows are of rubber. A single achromatic lens is furnished with the outfit.

The N. P. A. cameras have, in addition to the rising front, what is known as the swing back. This is just as important an adjunct as the former, but, used in connection with it, it is doubly valuable. It is made in its simplest form by attaching that part of the camera which holds the focusing screen in such a manner that it may be inclined from a vertical position either forward or backward. Its use is to bring objects at varying distances from the camera into focus. In other respects the outfit is the same as that last described.

This camera is altogether the neatest and most compact of its kind ever made. When folded it can be carried in an ordinary grip, it measuring only 5 x 5 x 3½ inches, and weighs only 14½ ounces. The holders are correspondingly light and compact.

It has sliding front, hinged ground glass, and folding-bed. It is made rigid by a most novel arrangement which can be adjusted in a few seconds. It is made of mahogany, handsomely finished, and fitted with brass mountings. For tourists this is a most invaluable instrument, as it occupies little space and is exceedingly light. It was this camera that the now famous Thomas Stevens carried on his journey around the world on a Columbia bicycle. The plates used—3½ x 4½—are the same size as those used in making magic-lantern slides.

The Warwick Cycle Manufacturing Company having what it believes to be reliable information that the Pope Manufacturing Company of Boston, Mass., and the Overman Wheel Company are attempting, by means of threats of litigation, to intimidate the customers of the Warwick Cycle Manufacturing Company and prevent as far as they can, by such proceedings, the sale and use of the said manufacturing company's machines, hereby informs its customers and all others interested that the said company will defend them in any suits that the Pope Manufacturing Company, the Overman Com-

pany or any one else may attempt to bring against them, based upon the alleged infringement by said Warwick Cycle Manufacturing Company of any existing bicycle patents; and the Warwick Cycle Manufacturing Company hereby requests all of its customers and correspondents to communicate to it at once any threats, verbal or otherwise, that they may receive as to legal proceedings in the matter of said alleged infringement, or any other papers having relation thereto, in order that it may at once take upon itself the duty of protecting its customers from such annoyance.

Further, the Warwick Cycle Manufacturing Company hereby informs the public that the

rumors which it has reason to believe are circulated by the Pope Manufacturing Company and the Overman Wheel Company or their agents, to the effect that legal proceedings have been commenced against the Warwick Company for infringement of patents, and that an injunction has been obtained against the said Warwick Company by the Overman Wheel Company, or by any one else, are utterly without foundation in fact, and that the Warwick Company is pursuing its manufacturing and selling business now as heretofore, and will continue so to do.

THE WARWICK CYCLE MFG. CO.
Geo. T. Warwick, Pres.
Springfield, Mass., March 22, 1889.

FENTON'S FANCIES.

I had quite a long talk with Captain McFadden, of the New Yorks, the other evening, and, in the course of conversation, the subject of the parade in April came up, and I remarked that wheelmen did not seem to be taking up the idea of a bicycling division with very much enthusiasm. The location of the line of march, " Mac " suggested, might have a good deal to do with the lukewarm spirit displayed in regard to the matter. The success for riding of a street railroad rail involves a vast expenditure of that " man' strength " by which the proverbial Hibernian vigorist was enabled to extract harmony from his instrument, and the Captain remarked that a ride from the Battery to Fifty-ninth Street over the track-covered surface of the adway might be a bit to trying to a good many of us. Nevertheless, I hope that the bicyclists will be represented in goodly numbers when the time comes.

I am in receipt of an invitation from the New York Bicycle Club to attend a " smoker " to be held on the evening of the 2nd. On the strict q. t. I am informed that a roaring farce, entitled " The Baremasted Dudes," will be performed by Messrs. Reese, Sbultas and Ingraham. Val Muller will probably charm us with the sweet tones of his zither, and the " great and only " De Gricour a will oblige with some flowers of melody recently p'ucked on the sunny shores of Cuba. Messrs. W. F Pendleton and W. C. Heydecker are in charge of the affair, which, without doubt, will be a great success. The significant little word " collation," which I find on one corner of the invitation, insures a large attendance.

With all due respect to " Ithuriel," it strikes me that the amount of talk expended upon the Lumsden-Stone races has almost reached its limit, and that it should be dammed up, as it has already been, in another sense, by a good many wheelmen in this locality.

I noticed in a recent number of THE WHEEL that the name of Mr. Charles E. Bentley appeared as the patentee of a velocipede. Mr. Bentl y is a member of the New York Bicycle Club and an enthusiastic believer in touring. He invented some time ago an appliance by means of which, when tired of the forward motion of the wheel, it is possible to work backward without altering the advance of the wheel Mr. Bentley is not the only inventive member of the club. Mr. Carkie, one of the older members has an appliance fitted on one of his wheels by means of which the hands and arms can be used to assist the often weary legs and feet in toiling up a long stretch of hill.

Two comic-opera stars, well known to the New York theatre-goer, seem to be able to create more disturbance in some of the Western cities than a hotly contested election, or the tinkering which is apparently an absolute essential preliminary to an inter-city race, in that section of the country. When such unpleasant events occur the New York wheelman chuckles to himself and murmurs gleefully, " We're uninterrupting ; we've only got racin' clubs; we haven't any good racing men; but, thank Heaven, we haven't caught the comic-opera fever, or the man-against-man inter-city racing delirium, and we're not going to either." I met a couple of wheelmen from New York last fall at Buffalo, and all the charges against New York cyclists that are given above were showered upon me as one of the representatives of bicycling in the Empire City. I did not refuse any of them then and took it pretty good-naturedly, and now that it is our turn let us hope that they will do the same.

FENTON.

At the annual meeting of the Citizens' Bicycle Club of New York, held Monday evening, March 18, the following officers were elected for the ensuing year : President, John C. Gulick ; Vice-President, Knight L. Clapp ; Secretary, J. T Francis ; Treasurer, A. B. Paillard ; Trustees, Geo. T. Wilson, N. M. Beckwith, William H. Book, Richard Sulson, Sim-on Ford, William C. Frazee, Francis B. Faulkner ; Captain, Wm. B. Krug ; First Lieutenant, Wm. G. Conklin ; Second Lieutenant, Henry W. M-oney ; Lieutenant of Tri-cycle , Geo. Martin Huss ; Sur.eon, J. Scott Aiken, M. D. ; First Color-bearer, Geo. Sloane ; Second Color-bearer, Samuel V. Hoffman ; First Bugler, E. A Hoffman, Jr ; Second Bugler, Fred. C. Thomas The Treasurer's report showed the club to be in excellent financial condition.

" I have completed a most satisfactory test of your (Brooks) Cyclometer."

A. B. BARKMAN,
Chairman L. A. W. Board of Information.
Only $5   Brooks Odometer Co , Lowell, Mass.

The Cycler and Tourist,

An illustrated Monthly Magazine, devoted to out-door recreation adventure and travel. Only $1 a year Address The Cycler and Tourist Pub. Co., Stamford, Conn.

WANTED!

The name of every Wheelman in America for THE WHEELMEN'S DIRECTORY. Send 10c. in silver or 15c. in stamps to cover cost of mailing, etc., and your name and address will be printed in the Directory, and one mailed you when completed. The Directory will be printed in book form, and will not sell for less than $1, but will be mailed free to all who answer this advertisement.
Send 10c extra and we will send the " Cycler and Tour-ist " illustrated) three months on trial.
Address The Cycler and Tourist Pub. Co., Stamford, Conn.

FOR SALE, EXCHANGE, WANTS.

NEW MAIL, 52-inch; 1888 pattern ; not ridden 50 miles ; balls all over ; condition A1 ; will sell at gre-t sacrifice. Address R. D. Boniface, 141 Clinton Street, Brooklyn.

4-22

FOR SALE.—A 53 inch Columbia Light Roadster, in excellent condition, '87 pattern wheels and '88 pattern handle-bar and backbone, Brooks Ideal Cyclometer to be same. Nothing broken or worn out about it. What offers?
B. H. Graves, Northampton, Mass.

FOR SALE.

BICYCLE FOR SALE. Expert Columbia, 46-inch ; all nickeled ; almost new ; used part of one season only ; cheap. Ryall, 103 Broadway, New York.

THE BUFFALO SAFETY BICYCLE STAND.

Holds any rear-driving Safety by either wheel. Price, $1.

E. N. BOWEN,
585 Main St.,   Buffalo, N. Y.

THE WHEEL

—AND—

CYCLING TRADE REVIEW,

Published every Friday morning.

Entered at the Post Office at second class rates.

Subscription Price,   -   -   - $1.00 a year.
Foreign Subscriptions,   -   -   -   6s. a year.
Single Copies,   -   -   -   -   -   5 Cents.

Newsdealers may order through AM. NEWS Co.

All copy should be received by Monday.
Telegraphic news received till Wednesday noon.

Advertising rates on Application.

F. P. PRIAL, *Editor and Proprietor*
23 Park Row,

P. O. Box 444,   New York.

Persons receiving sample copies of this paper are respectfully requested to examine its contents and give us their patronage, and as far as in convenient, aid in circulating the journal, and extend its influence in the cause which it so faithfully serves. Subscription price, $1 per year.

THE Editor of this paper has been on an extended trip down East, and any shortcomings in last week's WHEEL or in this number are due to his absence. He has visited a number of the most influential people in the trade, dealers as well as manufacturers. He reports a marked increase in business up to date, with every outlook that this will be the most prosperous year cycling has ever known. An extended report of his trip will be published in next week's paper.

NOTES FROM THE CITY OF BROTHERLY LOVE.

HALT!

Hold on, Brother "Argus." Let me beg of you, as a brother wheelman. to refrain from making any further such remarks as are contained in your last letter to the members of the Pennsylvania Bicycle Club. I am Pennsy from the top of my head to the soles of my feet, and any such remarks cut to the quick. Let me say, in response to your unkind words, only this: You do not know the members of the Quaker Club, or you would hesitate to make the remarks you did. But let me ask of you, please do not make such personal and cutting remarks, as they will only cause bad feeling; and, at present, the members of the club to which I have the honor to belong hold the Century Club and her members in high esteem and have been proud of the good fellowship existing between the two organizations. Of course, we all meet men whom we do not fancy and very often our feelings cause us to form wrong opinions of them, but in what writing I have done for our worthy paper, THE WHEEL, I have endeavored at all times to refrain from caustic remarks. If, however, I have at any time offended, I crave pardon; and I must assuredly hope there will be no further chance for the remarks of any club to take offense at your notes.

Chas. L. Leiser, First Lieutenant of the Pennsylvania Bicycle Club, has been off on a business trip. When returning home he visited the Hudson County Wheelmen, who entertained him most hospitably, as is their wont, furnishing him with a wheel and a suit, as well as a crowd of jolly good fellows for company on a ride through the Oranges. By the way, he succeeded in climbing Eagle Rock Hill, although he did not find the medal he won at the hill-climbing contest last fall.

I stopped in, a few days ago, at Strong & Green Cycle Co.'s headquarters and was greeted by a most welcome sight. Everybody busy, and busy as bees. This company has gone into business in earnest, and I am happy to state is meeting with success. My wish is, may it continue.

Ex-President Elwell, of the Pennsylvania Bicycle Club, has a fine young wheelman in his family. At last reports both mother and child were doing nicely, and "Dad"—well, about as proud a man as ever walked the streets.

Sunday last was a day of days for wheelmen. I think it was. without exception, one of the finest days I have ever been out, and from the crowds I met I judge others thought likewise. The Century wheelmen, on account of the torn-up condition of their quarters, did not have any regular club run. The Mt. Vernon wheelmen, under Captain Scott, had about ten men on a run out to Bryn Mawr in the afternoon, while I saw the Pennsylvania Bicycle Club riding down through the Park, in double file, with forty-two men in line. Twenty of them had braved the country roads to Norristown for dinner, and were met on their return by the party swelling the number up into the forties. Of the number out, at least two-thirds were on safeties. So who can say that club runs are losing their interest and that the safety craze is only for a short period? Nix ; it is the wheel of the day.

Ex-Captain Flemming, of the Century Club, is expected home shortly from his trip to Florida. Soon after his return he will start out on his tour through the States to California.

The Century wheelmen are already located in their new club-house, having been obliged to vacate their old quarters at 1807 N. Broad Street. At present their club-house is badly torn up. The workmen have promised that everything will be in apple-pie order within thirty days. Then the house-warming !

WESTFIELD.

MARYLAND.

Signs of a building boom among the cycle clubs of this city are in the air. Three clubs are considering the advisability of erecting houses of their own instead of occupying rented structures. The Maryland Club were the only club that took any action in the matter ; they built a handsome club-house, fitted with all modern conveniences, on Mr. Royal Terrace. It is located on the side of the reservoir at Druid Hill Park. The Baltimore Club have been discussing the advisibility of purchasing their own property and building a club-house. Friday, March 22, Mr. Stansbury, President of the club, called a special meeting of the Baltimore Club to consider the matter of erecting a club-house, and brilliant results are promised for the scheme. The proposition is to spend $25,000 on the house and grounds, which will be located within the city limits. Although the meeting held was not a very large one, $7,000 was at once subscribed. One of the plans under consideration is modeled after the home of the King's County Wheelmen, of New York State, and the purpose is to make the house distinctly a bicycle club-house, where anything of service to riders will be supplied in the most convenient and satisfactory way. An eight-lap track for training is one of the possibilities connected with the new house, which would not cost very much to get into condition. The Centaur Club also has a building committee out, and it is understood that the Crescent Club is likewise considering a similar scheme, though in the latter case nothing of a definite nature has been done.

The Crescent Club was incorporated Wednesday, the 20th, by Chas. F. Hanson, Dr. Jacob J. Bowersox, Robert J. Aiken, Wm. S. Callaghan and Wm. G. Ostendorf.

The Baltimore Club will have monthly races, for which gold medals will be offered as prizes, for the members only. The distance is to be ten miles and hand cap two miles. The first race will probably be run about the first of April.

The death on Monday, March 18, of Charles C. Gaskins is a subject of deep regret to the members of the Centaur Club. Mr. Gaskins was the first President of this club, and was a favorite with all whom he came in contact with. Among the many floral designs at the funeral on Thursday was one, a handsome cross about

three feet high, made of ivy leaves and lilies of the valley, which was sent by the club. Resolutions appropriate to the occasion were also passed at the meeting.

The prowess of the Maryland Club in winning cup races is exceeded only by its record on the road. The total mileage of the club for the past twelve months, in tour runs, excursions, etc., amounted to over 100,000 miles. There are 106 machines owned by the members. The most popular machines in the Maryland Club are New Rapids and Quadrants.

The regular quarterly meeting of the State Board of Officers was held on the 16th inst., at the residence of Albert Mott. A large attendance was present. The principal matter considered was the road-book which Mr. Kirkwood is getting up. It being stated that it will contain twenty five pages of advertisements in the volume. Consideration of the matter also showed that, the copyright remaining with him the division would be at the publisher's mercy at the expiration of the year's contract. Mr. Kirkwood said he would sell his information and copyright to the division, so that the division could become the publisher. He named $400, which a special meeting of the Board of Officers, held Monday night, at the Maryland Club-house, decided was too much.

The committee in charge of the matter was then instructed to propose to Mr. Kirkwood that the division take 500 or more copies of the book, which should not contain so much advertising matter ; that the division be given the privilege of making stereotyped plates. said plates to be the property of the division, which should also own the copyright after January 1, 1891. The proposition was declined by Mr. Kirkwood and it is now probable that he will publish the book for general sale. At any rate, it seems that negotiations for Kirkwood's book as the official road-book of the division are at an end. The book which is being prepared by the Pennsylvania Division. which is to include the States of Pennsylvania. Maryland, Delaware, New Jersey and New York, will soon be examined, and if it is found to be an improvement on the old League road-book for this State it will probably be adopted as the official guide of the Maryland Division. If not, it has been proposed that the division itself will prepare a map of the State on which the roads shall be marked in various ways to indicate the character thereof, which will, it is thought by some, serve the purpose intended better than a road-book would. At any rate, members of the division are promised some form of road information which will be the best possible to obtain.

BAY RIDGE.

BUFFALO.

The riding season has opened with a rush. A score of safeties have been sold, and there has been a good demand for ordinaries, both new and second-hand. The ranks of the fair devotees of the wheel have also been increased. This year promises to be a notable one in the annals of Buffalo cycledom. Business men are beginning to realize the utility of the bicycle as a means of transportation to and from their work. The army of riders to be seen on Main Street before and after business hours shows the general use to which the wheel is being put.

The Buffalos are rapidly nearing their limit of 150 members, 133 being the present number. The gymnasium is nightly filled by those who are anxious to get in condition for some early "scorches." Another too-mile ride from Erie is among the possibilities to take place on Decoration Day.

The Zig-Zags will take possession of their new club-house on Porter Avenue, near the Circle, on May 1. No better location could have been selected. All runs of the three clubs start from the Circle, and the Zig-Zags' new quarters are within a couple of blocks of the Buffalos' club-house.

The Ramblers are to have a new club uniform. Seven new applications for membership are to be acted upon at the next meeting. which will make the number an even 100.

The chances for the International Fair Association holding a fall tournament are very favorable, but nothing definite has as yet been decided upon.

Zo.

JERSEY CITY.

I notice that the New York *Sun* is paying some attention to the wheelmen by occasionally mentioning the sport and inserting some wheel news. This is a good idea, as in this way notes of the sport reach persons who do not receive cycling papers, and is apt to make converts to the wheel.

I am more than happy to report that our mutual friend Strugnell has recovered from his long illness and is again looking after the wheelmen's interest at Devlin's.

We received a call from Charlie Leisen, of the Pennsylvania Bicycle Club, on Sunday last. He was on his way home from the East and stopped here long enough to take a run out to the Oranges with some of our boys, "do" Eagle Rock and skip on toward Quakerville.

Your suggestion in last week's WHEEL that the Captain of the Hudson County Wheelmen call a meeting of delegates from the cycling clubs in New Jersey to form the proposed N. J. T. R. R. A. was acted upon before it was made, or rather before it appeared. Capt. Day had already prepared a circular letter, which he intends to send to all New Jersey cycling clubs, and he hopes to have the organization meeting held at an early date in order that a race may take place on Decoration Day. It is hoped that captains of clubs receiving the letter will give the matter very prompt attention.

And Hudson! Poor Hudson! "Ring the bell softly; there's crape on the door." Second place again. You see, we're so used to getting second place that we throw away first. However, we succumbed to the good bowling, superior luck and supreme inhuman lungs of the Atalantas at the match bowled at Newark March 21. The following score will tell the sad tale :

ATALANTA.	s.	HUDSON CO.	s.
S. Drable.......	149	Grant...........	116
S. Halsey.......	183	Stelsen.........	136
Snow...........	162	Kerr...........	171
Terbell.........	165	Korth..........	166
Gregory........	163	Shone..........	100
W. Drable......	159	Robertson......	164
Throme.........	110	Tuthill.........	128
Miller.........	135	Demmert.......	149
C. Halsey.......	160	Eldridge.......	141
Edwards........	163	Earl..........	114
Total.......	**1,549**	**Total.......**	**1,454**

FRAMES.
Atalanta—121, 301, 454, 615, 785, 932, 1,096, 1,252, 1,400, 1,549.
Hudson Co—142, 302, 468, 611, 760, 893, 1,043, 1,183, 1,325, 1,454.
Scorers—For Atalanta, A. J. Rummell ; for Hudson Co., H. G. Hornfeck.
Umpire—G. M. Nesbit, of New York.

The H. C. W. Glee Club and Orchestra has been formed. On all the residences in the neighborhood may be seen the sign "To Let." This is due to the nightly rehearsals. The music would sound better if Morse would refrain from eating cheese at the same time he blows the bugle.

There are more cycle agents in the H. C. W. than there are spokes to a wheel, but it is unnecessary to add that they do not depend entirely on their agencies for a livelihood. It takes two years for a Jersey City agent to sell a wheel—the first year to impress upon the mind of the should-be cyclist that the streets of Jersey City are glass-like in their "smoothness," and the other year to get him on the wheel.

THINGS WE WOULD ALL LIKE TO SEE :
The Hudson Counties in a new club-house.
A road race under the auspices of the N. J. T. R. R. A.
Two uniforms alike in the H. C. W.
An old-time three-day tournament on the Roseville track.
The "New Jersey Road Book" make its appearance.
COASTER.

The New Orleans *Times-Democrat* of March 25 has a long editorial on the necessity of better public roads in Louisiana. It urges the holding of a road convention.

NEW ORLEANS.

The match race Sunday, March 17, between L. J. Frederic and H. C. Christy, of the Louisiana Cycling Club, resulted in a win for the latter by some four or five yards, after a hot race. Time, 4m. 41s.; d'stance, 1½ miles.

Our papers still keep up the road-improvement agitation, and it looks as if something would result. One of the Parish Police Juries has petitioned the Governor to call a convention to treat on the subject. An up-country agricultural club has also adopted resolutions commending the agitation, and recommending its notice to the State organization.

Though at this writing a gentle rain is falling, and the elements seem against it, weather permitting, the Louisiana Cycling Club's long-delayed race for the Batson medal will be inaugurated Sunday, 25th inst. The course will be from the toll-gate to West End (three miles) and the start be made about 9:30 A. M. The entries and handicaps are as follows : Hathorn, Christy; M. S. Graham, scratch ; Bern Angamar, Betts, Frederic, 45s.; Bogel, Renaud, E. M. Graham, 1m. 30s.; Nathan, DeBuys, Grivot, Hobson, Harris, 2m. 15s.

Hodgson has presented the New Orleans Bicycle Club with a complete tennis outfit, and the boys expect to do considerable in that line during the summer months.

The Louisiana Cycling Club's regular Wednesday night runs have commenced for the season.

This is one that a local wheelman tells on his employer : The I. w.'s bike was in the office hallway, and the handle bar extending out pretty far made it something of a nuisance. Quoth the employer : "I say, Charlie, can't you take the arms off of your velocipede and get them out of the way."

How's that, coming from a cultured and intelligent man?

The Louisiana Cycling Club elects officers April 1.
Bt.

CHICAGO CYCLE TOURNAMENT AND EXHIBITION.

At last the great Chicago Cycling Exhibit and Tournament is a positive fixture. This was originally announced six weeks ago, but, just when everything appeared to be settled, difficulties arose which made it uncertain whether the immense Exposition Building could be secured, and until Saturday last no positive information on the subject was forthcoming. All difficulties have at last been removed, however, and the good work will go on rapidly. The only departure from the original plan will be a change of date from May 6 to 11, to 13 to 18, on account of delay.

All the clubs, dealers and manufacturers having promised assistance, the former in forming committees on reception, parades, tours and a hundred other things, and the latter by placing exhibits. An attendance of wheelmen from other cities equal in number to that of any other tournament is expected, and to that end applications have been made to the various passenger associations for cheap rates. Particulars on this subject will be announced later.

The programme is to be discussed at a general meeting this week. There will be a professional race of six days, eight hours per day, for which $1,000 will be given, divided (provided there are eight or more starters) into five prizes, as follows : $500, $250, $125, $75 and $50. Entries for this event close May 1. The amateur events will include races for all sorts and conditions of men. Everyone who can ride at all will be given a chance. The principal event will be a 1-mile handicap, in which every starter who fails to secure one of the nine prizes will receive a souvenir. Particulars as to the number of operating this event will be given after the meeting.

Parades, tours, receptions and the many other events which assist to make affairs of this kind enjoyable will be held daily, and headquarters for visitors will be provided close to the building, to which mail matter may be addressed. The Club will have the supervision of Mr. S. A. Miles, 199 S. Clark Street, Chicago.

W. H. Caldwell, of the Elizabeth Wheelmen and the N. J. A. C., has decided to give up racing for a few years at least, if not forever.

ST. LOUIS.

It appears that I was mistaken, after all, in saying that Bro. Page had finally realized the error of his ways and had sent in his application for membership in the League. His name was sent in by Bob Holm, who says that Page authorized him to do so, but the latter denies that he gave any such authority. He says that he agreed to contribute to the Missouri Division an amount equal to the League subscription, *i. e.,* $1.25, to help carry on the fight against the Warner bill, but declined to lend the organization the moral support of his name and the weight of his influence. I do not know whether the money has been proffered or not, but I think not, and I do not believe that the Div'sion would accept it under the circumstances if it were proffered. The Warner bill has been shorn of its terrors and practically defeated already, without the aid of Mr. Page, and it looks as if he would have to continue to occupy the position of "riding on roads that are kept open for him by the *charity of other wheelmen.*" He seems to have a grievance, but what that grievance is no one has ever been able to find out. I am glad to note that you have called on him for specifications. As you say, "we want to know all about it."

The Cycle and Missouri Clubs started the season's runs last Sunday, the former going to Clayton and the latter to the Sulphur Spring on the Manchester road. Both runs were largely attended. Kennedy-Child went out with the Missouris, and in his own peculiar way gave them some examples of fancy riding. He says, however, that hereafter he will not be so rash as to attempt to ride gutters that the St. Louis riders shirk. He did not appear to like either the roads or the spring water. Concerning the latter, he says that when he drinks water he wants the kind that can be drank without a clothes-pin on the nose.

I see by THE WHEEL that Mr. Jessup is already in the field for the presidency in 1890. He might have secured the prize this year if he had come out as a candidate before certain of his friends had pledged themselves elsewhere. He evidently is not going to repeat that mistake.

L. S. C. Ladish, of Kansas City, dropped in on his many St. Louis friends last week. He reports good work on the part of the Kansas City wheelmen in defeating the Warner bill. He "hustles" any enterprise in which he is engaged and we miss him hereabouts.

The Cycle Club has issued notices calling for a meeting next Sunday afternoon to inquire into the feasibility of consolidating the different athletic and bicycle clubs in the city for the purpose of having a good race-track built. The plan will not work There are too many interests to be harmonized, and the rivalry between the principal athletic clubs is too bitter to make any joint action possible. Besides, the Missouri and Pastime Athletic Clubs have already made arrangements for grounds for the season, the former at Sportsmen's Park and the latter at the Fair Grounds, and it is not at all likely that they would change their plans at this late date even if the consolidation scheme could be worked.
ITHURIEL.

FIXTURES.

April 1, 1889.—H. C. W. second competition for Benedict Medal.
April 2, 1889.—Annual Dinner of the Cambridge Bicycle Club, at Young's Hotel, Boston.
April 25, 1889.—Cambridge Bicycle Club's last Ladies' Night of the season.
April 26, 1889.—Manhattan Bicycle Club's Reception, at West 22nd Hall, 119th Street.
May 10, 1889.—Twelfth Regiment Games. Entries close May 4 with C. J. Leach, P. O. Box 3,001.
May 11, 1889.—Spring race meet of the Harvard Bicycle Club.
May 13-18, 1889.—Chicago Cycling Exhibit and Tournament. Exposition Building.
May 18, 1889.—B. Elwell's European Party sails from New York.
May 18, 1889.—Stone-Lumsden 1-mile Match Race, at Chicago.
May 25, 1889.—Stone-Lumsden 3-mile Match Race, at St. Louis, Mo.
May 27, 1889.—Stone-Lumsden 10-mile Match Race at Crawfordsville, Ind.
May 30, 1889.—Maine Division Meet, at Biddeford, Me.
June 6, 1889.—Century Run, Orange, N. J., to Philadelphia. Consult A. L. Clarke, 25 Broad Street, New York.

"FORGOTTEN."

A REVERIE.

Upon a road one summer's night,
O'er surface smooth and fair,
Faint shadows casting subdued light,
Balmy the languid air ;
A tricycle—a snatch of girlish song -
The moon springs up to view—
A scene, of riders side by side ;
For I was there- and you.

The evening cool, with grateful shade,
Is warm with summer's kiss ;
'Twas on that "trike"—a man and maid
Ride on in idle bliss.
The word you spoke to me still rings
In ears which could forget—I wish they could ;
I saw your eyes alight with things
Unsaid—but understood

How sweet that balmy, blissful day
To mem'ry's fancy seems !
The snow-bound winter fades away,
Replaced by these dear dreams.
Again I fancy your voice seems near
Once more in tender tone ;
However, thou art far away—I here,
Forgotten and—alone.   G.

CYCLING FOR WOMEN.

In regard to the advantage of bicycles for
ladies, I think it is what the ladies want, and
I think you are doing good work in publishing
letters like those from "Marguerite" and
"Psyche." I hope you will publish more on
the subject.

Mr. 5,678 I am glad to see in print again, as
his many articles have added much to what is
interesting in cycling literature. He certainly
tells the truth in regard to the wives of many
of our wheelmen, for I think, and have said
before, that the ladies *need* out-door exercise
more than the gentlemen, and yet are neglected,
or are discouraged in the thought if express'd.
Why ? One great reason is because the ladies
have to go too slow to suit their husbands or
brothers, on account of having to ride a heavy
tricycle. But how would it be if the lady should
ride a ladies' bicycle and make her husband
ride the tricycle ? How would that work for a
while ?

If the wheelman will give up scorching, etc.,
and ride as he ought, to *enjoy* cycling, he will
then take pleasure in riding with the ladies.

The tandem tricycle as the *only* wheel in the
family is often inconvenient, I will admit ; but
now that the safeties have proved so good there
is no excuse.   ORNH QBA.

THE BICYCLE FOR LADIES.

EDITOR OF THE WHEEL :

"Marguerite's" interesting letter impels me
to add "my word" in favor of the "ladies'
bicycle." Though I have never ridden one, yet
I am sure that it would be much more convenient to tour upon than the tricycle, for my
experience with the latter, over rough roads,
and often under trying circumstances, has qualified me to judge. The arguments of "Marguerite" call to mind the trouble my husband
and I had with my tricycle on a trip to Poughkeepsie late in the fall.

After a pleasant ride thither of fifty miles, and
just as we reached the hotel, it began to rain,
compelling us to "put up" for the remainder
of the day. As it was still raining the next
morning, we had to get a boy to push the tricycle to the boat, which we were obliged to
take as the only available means to progress
homeward. It still poured as the boat reached
her landing, and, being yet somefive miles from
home, we had to leave my wheel at the freight
house, but with my husband's *bicycle* we readily
found passage on the train to our own station.
Had to send a *wagon* for the tricycle. If my
mount had been a ladies' bicycle, the train
could have taken us directly home from Poughkeepsie.

On a trip to Troy, the doorways were too
narrow and no club house was convenient for
my bulky machine, and it therefore remained
out-of-doors all night, and we had to detach the
saddle and take it in-doors to keep it dry. The
rain continuing next day, it cost us *only* $2 50
for expressage on my "trike" thirty miles
home.

Another time eight miles riding of muddy
roads was the penalty for using a tricycle, being
obliged to take the boat instead of a train which
would have landed us near home.

Living as we do near the Hudson, we have
always had to travel by boat in stormy weather,
and in planning for trips had first to consider
this necessity before starting. Many pleasant
trips have thus been abandoned, the tricycle
being inconvenient for a baggage car.

I shall not soon forget a jaunt we took *via*
Troy boat to Brooklyn, because of the trouble
that my poor old "trike" gave us. The transfer
by way of the ferry and Annex boats was an experience to make one old before her time, as
you may infer without a recital of details. I
would not undertake it again for anything.

For *visiting*, as "Marguerite" says, the ladies'
bicycle is far superior to the tricycle, and, unless the roads are soft, I should think it preferable under most circumstances. I know that
rapid coasting where the road is narrow is un-
safe upon the latter, and my husband avers
that the ladies' bicycle is much the safer, because one can pick her way better in the centre
of the track.

I want to try this safety the coming season,
and if my wish is gratified you shall learn my
opinion as to how it compares with the tricycle,
which has borne me thousands of miles, over all
kinds of country roads, since 1884.

It is unnecessary for me to refer to the difference in weight between the two machines, as
the advantage of that is obvious ; and as to the
tricycle's argument in case of soft or sandy
roads, *I* think it is not so much of an argument,
after all, because there are many soft, sandy
and dusty roads which it is "horrid" to ride
over on a tricycle, while the ladies' bicycle
could easily seek and follow the almost invariably accompanying hard and ridable side-path.

For a lady to use in shopping around town,
where the streets are not well paved and dismounts are often made, the tricycle is probably
best ; but for "touring" and country riding I
think (so far as I can yet judge) that the ladies'
bicycle is the coming wheel. Some argue that
one cannot stop and talk on it. For answer to
this I will quote what my husband says. When
warm from riding, and stopped for a chat, he
will say, in a tone of reproof, "I wish you had
to get off every time you stop, for then you
would not take cold sitting still in the wind"
Or, "I *do* wish you would *ride* instead of sitting
there talking "

As to its not being *ladylike* to ride a ladies'
bicycle, I do not consider the assertion worth
answering.

I think that some of the ladies who ride the
new wheel, and who have had experience on
ordinary roads, will give us the benefit of their
views. It would be greatly appreciated by
Yours truly,
March 21, 1889.   MRS. 4,386.

MAPLEWOOD, Mass., March 28, 1889.

EDITOR THE WHEEL :

Will "Psyche" be kind enough to show which
part of my letter the criticism contained in your
issue of March 22 applies to ? My communication of March 2 was in favor of what I considered the advantages of bicycles for ladies, and
was not an effort in favor of any particular-
styled machine.   MARGUERITE.

FENTON'S FANCIES.

The "smoker" given by the New Yorks on
the evening of the 22d was the biggest kind of
a success in every way, and the Entertainment
Committee deserve the highest praise for their
painstaking efforts in behalf of the club. During
the early part of the evening, the house was
inspected by the visitors, of whom there were a
large number present, and by some of the older
members of the club, who are not often seen at
the "cycling palace," as I heard it called the
other day. Later on, the following gentlemen
rendered a choice and interesting programme :
Mr. Anson Carroll, S. I. A. C.; Mr. William
Neuman, N. J. A. C.; Mr. Frank Fullerton, Mr.
Frank Hayden, Mr. Val Muller, Mr. C. F.
Shultas, Mr. W. A. de Gouria and Mr. Dudley,
of the N. Y. B. C. Encores were plenty, and
the amiability so much talent it is impossible to par-
ticularize. Among those present during the
evening were : Messrs. J. A. Clairmonte, C. A.
Sheehan and J. W. Sheehan, of the Manhattans;

Palmer, of the Bloomfield cyclers ; Sanford, of
the M. A. C. and N. Y. B. C., and F. C. Miller,
one of the New York non-residents, and a
member of the S. I. A. C. "Doc" Griffin
represented the unattached, and lots of wheelmen of the "79t" period were on hand to swap
reminiscences with Frank Egan and Pitman,
who were both of them very much present. By
the way, speaking of Pitman, I heard the other
day that his "trike" is out of order more days
than he has ever ridden miles on it, which accounts perhaps for the small mileage the "Vet"
has put in thus far. Somewhere around three
o'clock the party broke up, and, full—if praise of
the "smoker," the participants wended their
way homeward.

His omnipotent highness "Jack," *alias*
"Gentleman John," may be a very amusing and
interesting writer, but his choice of English is a
considerable distance above my head, and, in a
number of cases, anybody else's. If I am not
too inquisitive, will the gentleman please tell
me what a "way cycle" is? By Jove, what a
beautiful sight Geo. Lacy Hillier must have
been when he was riding with "rythmetical " (?)
movement his 58-inch ordinary! Such a spectacle would almost tempt one to leave for England
at once, provided that "Jack" would promise to
exhibit some "rythmet cal movements on the
wai cycle." Perhaps, at the same time, Mr. St.
Clair-Granville would oblige with some "babonic " actions, in order to insure our getting
our money's worth. I have admired a good
many of your writings, friend Jack ; but when
you stick any such nonsense on us as is contained in your last letter to the *Bicycling World*,
I am obliged to quote those familiar lines from
"Hudibras :"

He that has but impudence,
To all things has a fair pretence ;
Yet as 'tis counterfeit and brass,
You must not think 'twill always pass.

Last Sunday was a most beautiful day for
riding. All of the local clubs were well represented on the road, more particularly the
Citizens, who turned out an unusually large
number. What a "hustler" L. A. Clarke, one
of their recent acquisitions and formerly of the
Mercurys of Flushing, is! He can be safely
counted on to rouse them out of their comfortable state of rest, or I miss my guess.

"Star," the *World* correspondent from Cincinnati, describes at some length a new street-
cleaning apparatus. now on trial in this city.
Merely for purposes of information I hied me to
the office of the D. S. C. to discover where this
wonderful machine was exhibited. None of the
employees knew anything about it, and the chief
seemed equally ignorant of its existence, so that
I had to disconsolately give up the search.
Perhaps this is another case of "so very well
informed, you know !" *Quien sabe?*

Semi-official word comes to me that the Harlem
Wheelmen refuse to bowl at any time the game
with the H. C. W., which was scheduled for
March 15. This seems rather strange conduct,
but there may be the method in their madness. At
any rate, the Atalanta Wheelmen get the championship, and I imagine the result is a surprise
to the other clubs in the League.
FENTON.

Howard A. Smith & Co., Newark, N. J., are
handling almost every known make of machine.
They have been appointed New Jersey agents
for A. G. Spalding & Bros., and will push the
Spalding goods as hard as they can be pushed.

"The Brooks is the only cyclometer we can
afford to handle. It *must* work. We are pleased
with its simplicity."
CAPITAL CYCLE CO., Washington, D. C.
Only $5.   Brooks Odometer Co., Lowell,
Mass.

A SELECTED LIST OF PATENTS.

[Reported especially for THE WHEEL AND CYCLING TRADE
REVIEW by L. A. Snow & Co., patent attorneys,
Washington, D. C.]

Peter Gendron, Toledo, Ohio.—Velocipede.
Wm. Goulden, Clapton, Middlesex Co.,
England.—Velocipede.
Wm. Goulden, Clapton, Middlesex Co.,
England.—Velocipede.
Frederick E. Kohler, Canton, Ohio.—Tricycle.
Joseph Knapp, Buffalo, N. Y.—Velocipede.
John M. Marlin, New Haven, Ct.—Velocipede
brake.
Thos. B. Jeffery, Ravenswood, Ill.—Velocipede
brake.
All bearing date of March 26.

BROOKLYN.

Sunday was an ideal day for the sport of cycling. During the morning Prospect Park was alive with wheelmen, and even a few ladies could not resist the temptation of taking their first ride of the season. All the scorchers and all the novices were there, and the number of wheelmen out seemed the larger because the majority of them remained in the park, although a few riders reached Coney Island and brought back great tales of the recent wash-outs at the beach. Among the scorchers were Schumacher and Kreger, L. I. W., who seemed to be regaining some lost laps of the circuit.

I also noticed Lewis, of the Brooklyns, on a new safety. Quite a come-down for a Baltimorean.

The B. B. C. seemed to hang together, and an observer might readily have thought it their first club run, when about thirty of them passed by in double file, making a tour of the park under the leadership of Meeteer and Cole.

The much-talked-of election of the K. C. W. took place last Tuesday, and the officers for the ensuing year are: President, M. L. Bridgman; Vice-President, T. Snyder; Secretary, W. C. Nellis; Corresponding Secretary, Geo. Courtney; Treasurer, J. H. Long; Assistant Treasurer, A. P. Stevens; Captain, W. C. Marion, Jr.; First Lieutenant, T. C. Crichton; Second Lieutenant, R. W. Staves; Color-bearers, J. F. Storm and D. Morehouse; Buglers, C. Hartman and H. S. Weigand. The K. C. W. are to be congratulated on their new Board of Officers. A handsome medal was presented to W. F. Murphy for the largest mileage of the past year, having covered ground to the extent of 8,177 miles; T. J. Hall and C. Murphy also received mileage medals.

I saw the committee on the big theatre party hard at work on their gags last Monday night, and the chances are that, by the time this goes to press, some of the boys will have been hit pretty hard. So tremble, all ye prominent men.

The camera craze appears to have gained a strong hold on cyclists this spring. Especially is it noticeable in the B. B. C., where about one-third of the club are deeply interested in the pursuit. Among the more prominent devotees are H. Greenman, D. W. Barker, J. F. Horland, A. B. Barkman, W. E. Sheffield, H. S. Stallknecht, W. F. Miller and N. A. Robertson.

Fuller and Class had a collision in the park on Saturday, which resulted in a sprained hand for Mr. Fuller, but he expects to be on his wheel again at no very distant date. He holds the largest mileage record of the past year in the B. B. C., I believe.

Preliminary arrangements are already being made for another Century run to Philadelphia this summer. It will probably take place on Saturday, June 8, and a large number of the Brooklyns intend to participate. I trust that "Larry" will have a better understanding with the weather clerk than he did last year, as the boys, who were novices in the art of swimming, did not get any further than Trenton on the 1888 "Century."

ATOL.

Brooklyn, March 26, 1889.

KINGS COUNTY WHEELMEN'S ANNUAL MEETING.

The annual meeting and election of officers of the Kings County Wheelmen was held at their club-house on Thursday, March 21. The meeting was an unusually lively one, but perfect harmony and good feeling prevailed throughout.

After the transaction of the regular routine business, the reports of the outgoing officers were read. Secretary M. H. Leighton's report showed a membership of 183. Treasurer Theodore Snyder's report showed the club to be in a prosperous financial condition, its assets being about $3,700. Captain M. L. Bridgman's report included the names of the club winners of mileage and other medals, and the records made by the most active riders during the past year. The handsomest and by far the most noteworthy of these medals was the elaborate gold souvenir offered by Charles Schwalbach to the wheelman covering the greatest number of miles during the year. The prize was secured by W. F. Murphy, champion long-distance rider, who placed to his credit last season a total of 8,177 miles. The top bar of this medal bears the name of the donor, Charles Schwalbach. On a second bar are engraved the words "Long-distance medal," and a raised crescent has on it the name of the winner, "William F. Murphy." The body of the medal consists of the club design—a wheel, in the centre of which are the club initials, "K. C. W., 1888," and the letter "S" is inscribed on another bar; and suspended from this are twelve gold bangles bearing the recipient's monthly record from March, 1888, to March, 1889, inclusive, as follows: 150, 566½, 831, 971, 1,218½, 511½, 1,440½, 1,700, 306, 151½, 200, 130. The total, 8,177½, is engraved on the last bar in large enameled letters, above which is a miniature representation of a cyclometer. The whole is appropriately mounted on a silk ribbon of cardinal and brown, the club colors. Murphy also secured the first prize medal for the two-mile race run at Queens, L. I., last September, and a mileage medal with one gold and two silver bars. T. J. Hall, Jr., also received a gold bar, indicating that he had covered 5,000 miles or more during the season. C. F. Murphy secured the medal for the 25-mile club handicap road race ridden on November 6 last, and a mileage medal. J. Bensinger was awarded second prize for this race. Other record medals were awarded J. Bensinger, Walter Bonner, Robert F. Hibson, R. L. Jones, C. Koch, David Morehouse, A. L. Ward, F. G. Brown, H. J. Hall, Jr., J. H. Long and R. W. Steves. The five highest club records were attained by W. F. Murphy, 8,177; T. J. Hall, Jr., 4,957; C. F. Murphy, 3,178; David Morehouse, 2,794; R. F. Hibson, 2,754. Twenty members of the club rode an aggregate of 50,000 miles. The recipients of the medals above mentioned came in for rounds of applause, and were warmly congratulated.

The election of officers then took place, and the following were elected for the ensuing year: President, Malcolm L. Bridgman; Vice-President, Theodore Snyder; Recording Secretary, W. C. Nellis; Corresponding Secretary, Geo. L. Courtenay; Treasurer, John H. Long; Assistant Treasurer, John P. Stevens; Captain, W. C. Marion; First Lieutenant, T. C. Crichton; Second Lieutenant, R. W. Steves; First Color-bearer, F. F. Storms; Second Color-bearer, David Morehouse; First Bugler, C. F. Hartman; Second Bugler, H. S. Wiegand; Trustees, M. H. Leighton and F. M. Loucks.

ELWELL'S EUROPEAN TOUR.

The great European tour projected by Mr. F. A. Elwell, of Portland, Me., is now, barring accidents, an assured success. The touring party, consisting of twenty-five American cyclists, intend to leave East Boston on May 18 for a tour through the principal places of interest in England, Ireland and Scotland. Mr. Elwell has corresponded with most of the prominent cyclists on the other side of the "wet," and has received encouraging replies.

The programme as outlined by Mr. Elwell pays a tribute to his clever management. To quote his own words: "The idea is that this is a vacation for the participants, a period of enjoyment and rest with the pleasures of wheeling over good roads, sight-seeing and good fellowship thrown in. With this idea in view the distances laid out for the day's runs are somewhat under what could be accomplished by the average wheelman. The majority of the 'runs' can be done in half a day, leaving the rest of the time for sight-seeing. Each one can choose his own gait, can stop by the way as fancy inclines, or scorch to the day's objective point and so secure a longer stay in that place. Only on one or two occasions will any long run be attempted, one between Chester and Birmingham (74 miles), where the country between is unattractive. But even here those who do not care to undertake it can stop over in Stafford (half way) and join us the next night in Coventry, where time saved in the long run will be spent in visiting the cycling works. In a long tour like this we shall, of course, have all kinds of weather, and a prolonged wet spell would throw any exact calculations as to where we should be on such and such days out of gear. Consequently, we shall only attempt to carry out the printed programme so far as can be done with comfort, and adapt ourselves to circumstances."

Great preparations are already advancing in Ireland for the reception of the tourists. Mr. Allport, manager of Rudge & Co.'s cycling depot in Cork, is to engineer a big dinner for the visitors. On their way to Dublin they will be met by a large body of Dublin cyclists, headed by Mr. White, of the Cyclists' Touring Club, who will escort them to the capital, where they will be entertained by a public banquet.

The original tour through Ireland has been slightly altered and is now as follows: On arriving at Queenstown, the party will proceed to "Cork's own town," then visit Youghal, Wexford and County Wicklow, taking in such places as "The Vale of Avoca," "The Meeting of the Waters" and "Seven Churches," which Tom Moore has ma deso famous. Their time being limited prevents them from visiting the Lakes of Killarney and Glengariff.

PHILADELPHIA.

PHILADELPHIA, March 25, 1889.

There is a club of young men in this city known as the Knickerbocker Assembly whose members pledge themselves to wear on all appropriate occasions the reform evening dress—*i.e.*, short breeches, silk hose, etc.; and at all the balls, hops etc., that they give they make a splendid showing with their seemingly strange but tasty costume. At one of our swell balls, given not long ago, about a dozen of the members appeared in them, and created quite a furore.

We have not heard much lately of the proposed Pennsylvania Division L. A. W. meet, to be held at Reading. If it were held there, it would insure a large delegation from Philadelphia, as they could easily ride up on their wheels in a day. For the Reading boys, I would say that it would be a hard matter to find a more jolly and sociable lot of fellows anywhere, as anyone who has once enjoyed their hospitality can testify. By all means, let it be Reading.

The South End Wheelmen's ball, to be given on April 25, promises to be an elaborate affair. It is called a *bicycle* and full-dress ball, the novel feature of which will be members of the various clubs in their respective uniforms. The demand for tickets has been so great that they have been compelled to limit the number so as to avoid overcrowding the ball, thus insuring a pleasant time to all who are fortunate enough to go.

Anyone who went to the "Century's" new house on Friday night witnessed a veritable chaos. They had moved from the old house that day, and you never saw such a mixture in your life. It was awful! In a back room (the new wheel-room not being finished) all the wheels were jumbled together—a hopeless mess. The large reception room was the very personification of a first-class junk shop, everything being mixed up in the worst fashion. However, toward the latter part of the evening, after the boys had worked like beavers, order was pretty much restored; but, of course, the place is nothing like it will be when it is finished. Later on, I intend giving a complete description of the place.

A road (?) sculler race was in progress during last week, and as usual with affairs of this kind in this city, proved a tremendous failure. How anyone could for a moment compare these ungainly things with a bicycle seems absurd. As a road machine they are perfectly useless, it being totally impossible to ascend any kind of a hill on one; and another thing, just imagine yourself toiling with your arms, back, legs—in fact, every part of your body—on a hot summer day along a dusty country road! *No, thanks!*

A more perfect day than last Sunday one could not imagine, and you bet the wheelmen took advantage of it with a vengeance. Every kind of a machine was to be seen, from the kind that Noah used to ride on the deck of his ark to the latest improved safety. Wheelmen in long pants, cutaway coats and derby hats, coming cyclers, were never so numerous. We even saw (what is now a *rara avis*) a wheelman in fiery red stockings. Ye gods!

The Pennsylvania Club took twenty men to Norristown, where also went three Centurions, who left the club run at General Wayne Hotel. They reported the roads in fine condition, and on the return trip five Pennsy boys and one Century man succeeded in climbing Conshohocken Hill, a pretty good feat for so early in the season.

What has become of that long-talked-of road book of Pennsylvania, New Jersey and Maryland? We are asked to have a little patience, and if we do not get it this spring or summer, we are *sure* to get it by New Year's, so as to pass away the long winter nights in looking over the roads tabulated therein. Of course no one is to blame, of course not. How can anyone dare to say somebody's to blame?

Mr. Theodore Schaffer, Pennsylvania's ex-champion, was seen on the road the other day for the first time since last October. It is hinted that he will go on the path again this spring. The more the merrier.

That Decoration Day picnic scheme mentioned in THE WHEEL several weeks ago has taken root, and has already caused some discussion in the clubs. "Keep it a-moving."

Since moving into the new house, some fellows with big ideas have already formulated a scheme for raising the dues. This, I think, will be a big mistake, as they will find out to their sorrow. Go slow, gentlemen; go slow!

ARGUS.

The regular nominations of the Brooklyn Bicycle Club for 1889 are as follows: President, James Fox; Vice-President, H. H. Koop; Secretary, B. M. Cole; Treasurer, H. E. Raymond; Captain, W. H. Meeteer; First Lieutenant, H. G. Fay; Second Lieutenant, F. L. Hebert; Surgeon, A. C. Brush, M. D.; Color-bearer, J. F. Borland; Buglers, P. Seixas, W. E. Fuller; Trustees, W. E. Fuller, C. M. Dutcher, W. R. Snedeker.

AMATEUR PHOTOGRAPHY.

There is nothing that appeals to man's sense of what is beautiful like a handsome camera. To the uninitiated there is an air of mystery surrounding a camera which he feels impelled to solve ; the desire increases according to the beauty of the equipment. In none but the handsomest and most graceful cameras are found these adjuncts which, when combined, make the perfect instrument ; and to obtain the best results these are necessary. To one unaccustomed to the uses of a camera these additions appear to make the instrument exceedingly complex and difficult, but in reality they greatly simplify the working of it. Without them the operator would frequently meet with difficulties that would cause him considerable trouble to surmount in order to obtain a much-coveted picture ; and there are instances where, without their aid, the picture could not be taken.

NOVELETTE VIEW CAMERA.

Anthony's Novelette View and Fairy Cameras combine all that is necessary for the make-up of a perfect camera.
The Novelette View Cameras are made in the best possible manner, of the finest mahogany, highly polished. They are furnished with the sliding front and double or single swingback. The bellows are coned, and of extra length. The folding bed is compact and rigid. The two sections of the bed are made firm by the assistance of hooks, which is a more preferable arrangement than screws.
A most novel feature in this camera is that the back part is not made stationary to the bed, but is held in position by means of key slots which are fastened to two keys on the bed. This arrangement is for the purpose of allowing the operator to take a picture either vertically or horizontally, as he may wish. The change is effected by simply moving the back to one side, and by raising it slightly, revolving it to the position desired.
The front end of the bellows is arranged in a frame-work which runs on two hollow brass rods, so that when the rear end of the camera is separated from the bed, the whole revolves at one time. This is a great time-saving improvement. The ground glass is hinged to the back of the camera. It is a back focus, and worked by a rack and pinion.
It is a very compact and light camera, one that can be recommended to the amateur desiring a low-priced but good instrument.

THE FAIRY CAMERAS.

The Fairy Cameras are of a higher grade than the Novelette. In point of workmanship they are equal to any made. Having all the adjuncts of a perfect camera, the very essential points of portability, strength and compactness have also been well considered.
It has long been our desire to place before the public a camera that would at once em-
brace these most necessary requirements— portability, compactness and strength, combined with beauty and accuracy of working.
Hitherto, the nearest approach to this has been the " Novel " Camera, which for a time seemed to be everything that could be desired. But urgent calls for something still better were frequently made, and we therefore devised the Fairy Camera, by far the most attractive and elegant piece of apparatus of its kind ever offered. In presenting it we invite attention to the following advantages it possesses over all others :
They are put together as rigidly as wood and metal will admit of, and occupy less space than any other view cameras of the same capacity ; the plate holders are made of hard wood, with metal carriers for the plates, and fitted with all the later improvements.
The small columns to which they may be reduced renders them in this respect superior to any other. They are packed in canvas-covered wooden cases, and each double plate holder has its own compartment. The cover of the case telescopes over its body.
Several new features have been availed of in the construction of this camera :
The bed may be instantly rendered rigid, without the use of screws, by means of a brace of hooks that hold the two sections of the bed with great firmness.
The rabbet commonly found on the plate holder is dispensed with, and instead it is placed on the camera, thus saving the otherwise additional weight rendered necessary for twelve such rabbets when made on the plate holders (two on each of the six usually carried).

The camera is focused with a long, continuous metallic rack, cogwheel and pinion, the latter being firmly held in position by a binding screw.
The ground glass springs backward in its frame, like that in the regular Novel Camera, and is held tightly in position by metallic spring corners. When windy this is a decided advantage.
The Fairy Camera is made of finely polished mahogany, the metal-work being nickel - plated, thus making it a most elegant and perfect camera.
In outward appearance, and to the ordinary observer, this latest modification of the Detective Camera looks exactly like an alligator hand-satchel that is carried by a shoulder-strap at the side of the pedestrian. Upon closer observation, one sees that it consists of an artfully concealed Detective Camera, in which all the various movements to secure a picture are situated upon the under side. For use, the camera is held so that the base of the satchel rests against the body of the operator. By means of a brass pull at the side the shutter is set. A plate is placed in the regular holder in position at the back of the

camera, and the slide is drawn ready for exposure. The release of a short catch exposes the front of the shutter ready for action, and by raising a small leather-covered lid the little camera obscura called the finder, on the (now) upper side of the camera, shows the position that the object will occupy on the plate. The slightest touch upon a small brass button releases the shutter, and the exposure is made. Replacing the slide in the plate holder, reversing the holder and setting the shutter again leaves the apparatus in readiness for another shot, when the plate-holder slide is withdrawn as before.
By releasing a spring bolt on the under side of the case the camera proper can be removed from its cover, and a tripod screw serves to attach the camera to a tripod for ordinary use.

This last form of the Detective Camera allows the operator to carry with him twelve plates in the interior of the apparatus, and so carefully packed away that no light can strike them. It is also furnished with an ingenious attachment by which the speed of the shutter can be regulated to suit the speed of the object, moving with greater or less velocity ; while, by simply releasing a catch, time exposures can be made at the will of the operator. In fact, the whole affair is the latest achievement in ingenious and compact light photographic apparatus.

WHEEL GOSSIP.

Mr. and Mrs. Cosutt, of the Riverside wheelmen, are talking of joining the great Century run to Philadelphia.

Captain J. W. Sheehan and Secretary C. A. Sheehan, of the Manhattan Bicycle Club, will shortly be seen on a Columbia single track tandem.

The ladies' bicycle is becoming very popular in New York among the fair sex. There will be over fifty ladies riding this season.

The members of the Manhattan Bicycle Club rode over 50,000 miles in 1888. Messrs. W. H. Putney, Captain J. W. Sheehan and J. R. Post, Jr., having ridden the greatest number of miles.

The ladies' receptions given at the Harlem Wheelmen's rooms have put new life and vigor in the members. By the way, they are a happy family. Think of having three generations in the club (in name only). Miss Sadie Field has been dubbed "Mother." Otto Emanuel is called "Hubby," while Frank Ridabock answers to "Sonny." "Pop" De Graaf looks on with pleasure, while "Grandpop" Vesey is proud of his happy family. All are spiritually cared for by "Deacon" Raisbeck, and all disputes decided by "Judge" Newcome and wife. The Harlem Wheelmen can hold their own for nicknames.

A gay party of ladies and gentlemen, consisting of members of the Harlem, Manhattan and Riverside clubs, assemble every Tuesday night at West Side Hall, 116th Street, and bowl under the name of "Acme Bowling Club." The party are always full of life and fun. Bowling is indulged in for hours, and prizes given for best score. Mrs. L. A. Newcome captured a prize on several occasions. Miss M. E. Sheehan scored 186 points the first time she tried the art. A collation is generally served, and dancing in the hall and songs help to make the evening pleasant, while all this brings the three clubs closer together.

At a meeting of the Baltimore Bicycle Club there was $7,000 subscribed toward building a club-house.

The Centaur Club, of Baltimore, Md., are considering a scheme to build a club-house.

Chas. Schwalbach and William F. Murphy, of the Kings County Wheelmen, have been appointed a committee to make arrangements for a two days' race meet to be held in the latter part of June, probably at Washington Park, Brooklyn.

L. W. Beasley and W. F. Murphy, of the K. C. W., will ride a Columbia tandem safety this year.

The Hyde Park (Mass.) Bicycle Club has thirty-one members.

The Boston Bicycle Club members dine together for the last time, at Vieth's, on Saturday night. These dinners have been very enjoyable and have afforded much consolation to the members in the absence of a club-house.

On the evening of April 6, the members of the L. I. W. and male friends only will be entertained at the club-house by Col. John Oakey, who will deliver a humorous address on "Cycling and Cyclists of Brooklyn." Other interesting features also will characterize the event.

SNOWHILL, MD., March 23, 1889.

MR. F. P. PRIAL:

Dear Sir—Inclosed find check for $1 to renew my subscription to THE WHEEL. Cannot do without THE WHEEL; it is far superior to any cycling paper that I have seen.

Respectfully yours,
J. W. VINCENT.

At a meeting of the Troy Bicycle Club, held Monday evening, March 18, the following officers were elected for the ensuing year:
President, R. D. Cork; Vice-President, W. B. Seeley; Treasurer, A. R. Mulliken; Financial Secretary, C. E. Wilson; Recording Secretary, C. E. Salisbury; Corresponding Secretary, G. H. Fales; Trustees, B. Herman, W. M. Hogbee, J. G. Zimmerman, Jr., J. M. Van Arnam, T. W. Hislop; Captain, P. F. Hawley; First Lieutenant, E. S. Homer; Second Lieutenant, H. M. Hudson; Color-bearer, A. C. Frings; First Bugler, G. W. Allen; Second Bugler, F. A. Uldrich; Surgeon, E. L. Grandall.

The close of the social season of the Manhattan Bicycle Club will be celebrated by a spring reception, to be held at West End Hall, Friday, April 26, 1889. The members will appear in their new uniform of black, with white vest and four-in-hand tie. Admission by ticket only, which can be had of any member. The number has been limited, in order that the rooms will not be over-crowded. Wheelmen attending are reques ed to appear in uniform. The affair promises to be, as usual, a grand success. The chairmen of the committees are as follows: C. A. Sheehan, Reception Committee; Washington Ritter, Floor Committee; D. C. Newton. Arrangement Committee.

"Judge" L. A. Newcome, of the Harlem Wheelmen, is one of New York's shrewdest detectives; but, alas! he has once failed. It happened in this way:

The "Judge" and wife have given up the old and heavy tandem, and purchased two safety bicycles. He took a spin the other afternoon, and, on turning into 110th Street, noticed an object quickly pass him. The "Judge," with his usual curiosity, commenced pedaling until at last he was up to the quickly moving machine. He held his head down, and looked over his eyeglasses in his usual comical way. The object proved to be Mrs. Cosett, of the Riverside Club, but what she was trying to say was a mystery to the "Judge," who began to think that the wee glass he had taken was beginning to work on his brain. The fair lady was crying in vain to be heard, and was moving her mouth in all sorts of shapes and positions to make the "Judge" understand her. The "Judge" thought her mind wandering, and was alarmed for her safety upon the safety bicycle, fearing she would be run down. At last the "Judge" succeeded in adjusting his glasses, and after recovering himself from the shock he had received, discovered that Mrs. Cosett was suffering from a severe cold and could not speak, but endeavored to be pleasant by the moving of her lips.

Secretary-Treasurer Carr will very shortly forward renewal blanks to all League members of the Maryland Division who are not members of League clubs. The Chief Consul requests that all receiving these will fill them out and return them at once to Abbott Bassett, 12 Pearl Street, Boston, with the renewal fee.

It is probable that the Crescent Bicycle Club will shortly join the League. Nearly all of its members are already members of the League. The club is to give a house-warming after this summer.

Mr. Geo. W. Baker, of Easton, Md., who has been threatened with a lawsuit by a man whose horse became frightened by Mr. Baker's machine, has been notified by the Chief Consul that, in the event of suit being brought, the attorney of the division will defend him free of charge. Mr. Baker promises a large increase in League membership from his locality.

The Baltimore wheelmen have pretty definitely decided not to ask the League to meet there this summer.

The wheelmen of Atlanta, Ga., will hold a three-day meeting in May.

HARVARD-TECH ROAD RACE.

The Harvard Bicycle Club has accepted the challenge of the Tech men for a road race. They have accepted the challenge for April 13, and have appointed a committee composed of Brown '91; Davis, '91, and Greenleaf, '92, to meet a similar committee from the Tech Club to arrange the details of the race. The Harvard men would like to make the race an annual fixture and make the prize a perpetual challenge cup.

The New England Chief Consuls and Secretaries are as follows: Maine—Chief Consul, Dr. G. E. Dow, 507½ Congress Street, Portland; Secretary, A. L. T. Cummings, Biddeford. New Hampshire—Chief Consul, H. M. Bennett, Manchester; Secretary, Geo. F. Hill, Great Falls. Vermont—Chief Consul, H. A. Webster, Montpelier; Secretary, F. E. Doubis, West Randolph. Massachusetts—Chief Consul, Dr. W. H. Emery, 1177 Tremont Street, Boston; Secretary, Sanford Lawton, Springfield. Rhode Island—Chief Consul, C. S. Davol, Warren; Secretary: N. H. Gibbs, 218 Westminster Street, Providence. Connecticut—Chief Consul, C. E. Larom, 386 State Street, New Haven; Secretary, E. De Blois, Weathersfield.

The annual election of officers of the Harlem Wheelmen was held on Friday, March 15. The following are the officers elected to serve for the ensuing year:
President, L. I. Haben; Vice-President, Judge L. A. Newsome; Secretary, C. E. Fraser; Treasurer, W. H. De Graaf; Captain, F. Lord; First Lieutenant, W. W. Braden; Second Lieutenant, O. N. Emanuel; Color-bearer, F. A. Ridabock; Bugler, G. Schrader; Executive Committee, T. H. Raisbeck, Jos. B. Halsey.

CAMBRIDGEPORT CYCLE CLUB'S FANCY-DRESS BALL. A largely attended fancy-dress ball was given Wednesday evening in Armory Hall, Central Square building, Cambridgeport, under the auspices of the Cambridgeport Cycle Club. There were about 200 couples in attendance, and dancing was enjoyed till a late hour to the music of Edmands' orchestra. Mr. James W. Bean officiated efficiently as floor director, and was assisted in his duties by a number of aids. At midnight a Lenten collation was served.

All manner of fancy and grotesque costumes were worn, and much fun was created by the capital manner in which the characters were assumed and sustained.

Mr. H. H. Hodgson, of the New Orleans Bicycle Club has written the following letter to the Secretary-Treasurer Louisiana Division L. A. W.:

Dear Sir—As the New Orleans Bicycle Club and the Louisiana Cycling Club have both started a series of races, in which the members of those clubs only are allowed to contest; as there are a number of wheelmen who are League members and unattached to either club, and as I desire to promote racing in this division during the present year as a means of increasing our membership and to bring all the Louisiana riders together in friendly contest; I hereby donate gold and silver medals to be contested for by the members of the Louisiana Division L. A. W., and its first and second prizes. All races to be time handicaps. Six races to be run, one each month, commencing the latter part of April, the last race to take place in September, at the annual Division races. The handicappers to be appointed two each from the N. O. B. C., L. C. C. and the unattached wheelmen, six in all, who will make handicaps, select dates and distances and other arrangements. Points to count. First prize, gold medal; second prize, silver medal.

Fraternally yours,
H. H. HODGSON, C. C.

THE B. & O. THROUGH TO NEW YORK.

A complete service of Fast Express Trains is now in full operation between New York, Philadelphia, Baltimore and Washington via the Baltimore and Ohio Railroad. The New York outlet is furnished by the Central R. R. of New Jersey, and passengers are landed at the station of the latter company at the foot of Liberty Street, New York, two blocks from the Elevated Railroad. All the trains are composed of handsome coaches and Pullman's Parlor and Sleeping Cars. Two of the trains are composed exclusively of Vestibuled Cars, but, in accordance with its long-avowed policy, the B. & O. exacts no extra fare for improved service. Passengers occupying Parlor or Sleeping Cars must, of course, pay the ordinary Pullman charges, but no extra charge for Limited Express service is imposed by the B. & O.

The B. & O. still continues to operate the fastest trains ever placed in service between Philadelphia, Baltimore and Washington, and the remarkable record for punctuality achieved by these trains indicates what the public may expect of their New York schedule.

It is a fact, now generally known, that the fastest trains in America are run on the B. & O. R. R. between Baltimore and Washington. There are eight trains, in the schedule of twenty-four each way, that cover the distance of forty miles in 45 minutes, or at the rate of fifty-three miles per hour. Faster time has been made in spurts, but the B. & O. trains do it every day, and have done it every day for several years.

The line between New York and Washington is double-tracked and laid with heavy steel rails on oak ties, ballasted with broken stone. There is not a better constructed, better maintained, better equipped or better operated road in the world, and with these conditions the new line is prepared to render efficient service and thereby aims to secure public approval and patronage.

⁂

HARRISBURG WHEEL CLUB'S RE-CEPTION.

One of the most delightful affairs of the sea-son was the "musicale and reception" given by the Harrisburg Wheel Club to their friends on Wednesday evening, March 20, in the club's handsomely furnished quarters at Third and Market streets.

As early as 8 o'clock the guests began to arrive, and at 9 o'clock the rooms were filled with handsomely attired ladies and their es-corts. Immediately upon their arrival they were shown to the cloak-room, where wraps, bonnets, etc., were taken charge of by attend-ants. Mr. T. S. Peters escorted the guests to the reception committee, composed of the fol-lowing ladies: Mrs. Wm. H. Lyter, Miss Sara Chayne and Miss Mame Oves, by whom they were cordially welcomed. The committee also presented each visitor with a knot of ribbons composed of the club colors—red, yellow and black. The rooms were tastily decorated with pictures, lamps, rugs, curtains and flags, and on the tables were several fine floral offerings from friends. A very delightful musical pro-gramme had been arranged, and at 9 o'clock Mr. J. C. Duke opened the exercises with a bril-liant piano solo, which was followed by an ad-dress by Mr. Harry W. Stone, President of the club, who, in a few happy remarks, again ex-tended welcome to the guests.

The remainder of the programme was as fol-lows :

Vocal Duet.....................	The Misses Hahn
Vocal Solo....................	Mr. S. D. Sansom
Piano Duet.....................	The Misses Knoche

Vocal Solo, with Flute Obligato.
Miss Chayne and Mr. C. H. Chayne

Vocal Solo	Miss Worley
Cornet Duet........	Messrs. Hoffman and Cook
Vocal Solo.......................	Miss Hahn
Vocal Solo..................	Mr. H. A Chayne
Piano Solo....................	Mr. J. C. Duke

At the conclusion of the programme an elab-orate repast was served. When the repast was finished, R. F. Cromulin, stenographer of the Executive Department, and a member of the club, gave an exhibition of the graphophone. Several of the ladies sang into the instrument, and, with perfect silence in the room, Mr. Cromulin turned the crank and every note was wafted back, being distinctly audible twenty feet from the table. After this interesting per-formance the billiard room was cleared, and dancing was indulged in for several hours. For those who did not dance there were cards, checkers, pool and other games.

Time passed swiftly, and at 1 o'clock the "Good-night Chorus" from "Erminie" was sung by the entire party. The wheelmen and their friends separated, well pleased with the evening's entertainment.

LANCASTER, PA.

What beautiful weather we are having! Al-ready the buds are beginning to swell ; the brown lawns to look green, and the blackbirds to stalk through the grass by the dozen, looking for the early worm. The voice of a solitary robin is heard in the distance, and all things betoken that spring is at hand.

And what a winter we did have, especially for the cycler ! My wheel was never once laid up, and to this time my rides number more than the days of the year. My friend Charley G. and I started in for '89 on New Year's Day. The weather was fine, but the roads had a gen-erous top dressing of mud. But we had our run, and really enjoyed it, as we had previously made up our minds to do ; and we have kept it up, weather permitting, ever since.

Some of the best riding I ever had was during the colder weather of the winter. I remember a night-ride in particular (February 14) as one of the most enjoyable rides. The surface of the ground had been frozen and worn down smooth and was almost like a floor. The moon was quite full and the weather just cold enough to require brisk exercise to keep warm. We rode out to the Lancaster Pike ; but not the famous East End, where "Centurions" and other scorchers from the City of Brotherly Love con-gregate, and where said congregations blow their sanctimonious (?) heads over the handle-bars and "git." Our ride was at the other end of the line, toward the setting sun, on

what is known to us as the Philadelphia Pike, where we do not have so much to boast of. Nevertheless, we had a glorious run.

As we passed the County Prison we thought of the unhappy wretches hidden behind its walls, among whom are several condemned murderers ; and we could not help comparing their sad condition with our own, which we, drawing the long full breath of freedom, real-ized to be a condition of ideal happiness.

Riding by the city reservoir, the sound of the water falling from the top of the stand-pipe almost caused a shudder, and I could not but think how differently the music of the falling water would sound some time in July or August, when the lads and lasses in couples will make haste slowly along the pebbly walks beneath the leafy branches of the overhanging trees. To the right we pass the magnificent County Poorhouse and Hospital, where the unfortunate enjoy the hospitality of the garden spot of Pennsylvania, and I take a hasty glance at the inclosure set apart for the convenience of our cosmopolitan friend, the tramp, into which he is willing to force an entrance to obtain a good square meal, and out of which he will fight his way when shown the slowly increasing stone pile.

We do not ride eastward much beyond the terminal of the street railway, on account of the hill beyond. This hill is a snare and a delusion to the unwary cycler, on account of the numer-ous "breaks" for the benefit of heavily loaded teams. If the wheelman is not aware of the existence of these breaks, or goes recklessly down, legs over, he is apt to perform the flying-trapeze act when not just prepared to do so. Some serious accidents have occurred in this way.

We were not traveling by that route, so we re-versed, and after riding about an hour and a half were loath to give up, we felt so much in-vigorated, and were fresher when done riding than when we started. This, I take it, constitutes the true inwardness of the benefits of cycling :

A cycle's a delight when properly used,
But, like other good things, it must not be abused.,
It will do its work well on the hillside or level ;
If imposed on, be sure it will kick like the—mischief.

TE*TOONE.

Lancaster, Pa., March 20, 1889.

TROY NOTES.

The annual meeting of the Troy Bicycle Club was held at the club-house the 18th, and Frank G. Snyder was defeated by Ensign S. Homer on the ballot for first lieutenant by 17 to 21 votes.

The reports of the retiring trustees and officers were read and accepted, and the club's finances were found to be in good condition.

The monthly meeting was held right after the annual meeting, and George A. Ruth and Henry Kinney were elected members.

Mr. Hislop reported that all the indebtedness

of the bowling-alleys was paid, and Mr. Hawley asked that the matter of a club tournament be taken from the committee to whom it had been referred.

Mr. Perkins explained that the subject was receiving attention from the committee, and that sub-committees had been appointed on printing, "talent" and music. The committee was discharged.

President Cook appointed the following to arrange for the club's annual tournament: Messrs. Hogben, Wilson, Thiessen, Zahn, Per-kins, Fales, Hawley, Snyder and Van Arnam.

Captain P. J. Hawley was chosen chairman of the committee and the meeting adjourned.

The Congress Street Bridge Co. have always charged wheelmen *five* cents toll to *ride* over their bridge, but only the regular two-cent toll to *walk*. If they do it on account of wear, walking wears the planking more than riding the wheel ; and I should think our clubs would take this matter up and *push* it, so as to get this out-rageous charge reduced to the regular toll.

As many "Trojans" live in West Troy and use this bridge every day, it would make it very convenient to mount at your residence and ride all of the way to your business. To pay three cents *extra* for the privilege of riding amounts to a great deal in a year, and to dismount and walk over the nice surface of the bridge is a nuisance. Here is work for our Consul.

ORNH QBA.

Troy, March 22, 1889.

ODDS AND ENDS.

Mr. C. R. Overman was in town on Tuesday. He has been on quite an extended business trip.

Col. Albert A. Pope gave a dinner on last Monday night to a number of Boston gentlemen who are interested in roads improvement.

Mr. John Read was in New York and Brook-lyn on Monday and Tuesday. He is pushing the New Mail quite extensively this season.

Burley U. Ayres, the well-known Chicago wheelman, has removed to Milwaukee, Wis., where he has taken a position on the Milwaukee and St. Paul Railroad.

Messrs. A. G. Spalding Bros. will add pho-tography to their many other branches of sport-ing goods after April 1, and will keep a full line of photographic outfittings.

The members of the Brooklyn Baseball team are learning to ride the wheel, under the tutor-ship of Charles Schwalbach. Ten out of four-teen of them are riding safeties.

Among a number of the New York Po-lice force, is 6 feet 6 inches in height. He finds his 60-inch bicycle uncomfortably small for him and is having a 64-inch machine made.

Messrs. Spalding Bros. cycle catalogue is now ready, and will be mailed free on application. They have enlarged this department in anticipa-tion of doing a very heavy business this season.

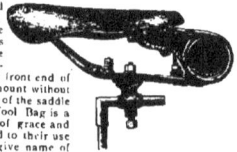

Twenty of the most congenial spirits of the Dorchester Bicycle Club sat down to the annual "feed" of the club at the United States Hotel on Tuesday evening. President Schallenbach presided, and speeches were made by him, Ex-President Forbes, who responded to the toast of the L. A. W., and Captain Benson, who spoke of the Eastern Road Club, and by many of the others.

Howard A. Smith & Co., Newark, N. J., are making the greatest preparation to supply the cycle trade with sundries this coming season. Our representative comes home from a visit to Oraton Hall, and reports that the above concern have the best facilities for supplying riders with sundries and machines that he has ever seen outside of the manufacturers.

The annual dinner of the Cambridge Bicycle Club will be held at Young's Hotel on April 3. The last ladies' night of the season is booked for April 25, on which occasion the Governor, the Lieutenant-Governor and the Mayor of Cambridge will be present as guests.

The new General Passenger Agent of the N.Y., C. & H. R. R. R., appointed to succeed Mr. Henry Monett, deceased, is Mr. George H. Daniels, at present Vice-President of the Central Traffic Association, and Chairman of the Chicago East-bound Passenger Comm ttee, with headquarters at Chicago. The late Mr. Monett was friendly to wheelmen, and made every reasonable concession that could be expected. We trust that Mr. Daniels will be as considerate as his predecessor.

The Keystone Club, of Philadelphia, has contributed twenty-five dollars to defray the debts of the L. A. W.

At the eighth annual meeting of the Kings County Wheelmen, held at the club-house Thursday evening, March 21, the following officers were elected for the ensuing year: President, M. L. Bridgman; Vice-President, Theo. Snyder; Recording Secretary, W. C. Nellis; Corresponding Secretary, G. L. Courtenay; Treasurer, J. H. Long; Assistant Treasurer, J. P. Stevens; Captain, W. C. Marion, Jr.; First Lieutenant, T. C. Critchton; Second Lieutenant, R. W. Steves; First Color-bearer, F. F. Storm, Jr.; Second Color-bearer, David Morehouse; First Bugler, Chas. F. Hartm an; Second Bugler, H. S. Wiegand.

THE VICTOR.

KING OF THE SAFETIES.

A. G. Spalding & Bros.,

SPECIAL AGENTS,

NEW YORK AND CHICAGO.

FOR YOUR SAFETY.

The Buffalo Safety

BICYCLE STAND

Firm, Strong, Portable.

Price, $1.00.

A. G. SPALDING & BROS.,

Sole Agents,

NEW YORK AND CHICAGO.

The Trade Supplied.

A. G. Spalding & Bros.,

Makers of the Official L. A. W. Sundries.

Caps. League Regulation.................$1.25

Shirts. League Regulation.................2.00
No. XX Fine Cheviot for hot-weather wear.................1.00

Stockings. Our celebrated Linen Sole Stocking, League color.................1.00

Belts. No. X Silk, Edge's League color, white centre, Snake Buckle.................
No. XX Worsted Solid, League color, Snake Buckle.................50
.40

Shoes. Our new L. A. W. Kangaroo Shoe, hand-made, light, strong, elastic.................5.00
No. 1, Canvas, leather trimmings.................8.50

Sent post-paid on receipt of price.
Send for Catalogue Knit Racing and Training Suits.

A. G. Spalding & Bros.,

241 Broadway, New York;

108 Madison St., Chicago.

NEW YORK BICYCLE CO.,

No. 8 WARREN STREET,   No. 4 EAST 60th STREET,

DEALERS IN NEW AND SECOND-HAND WHEELS.

FULL LINE CYCLING ACCESSORIES.

WHEELS BOUGHT, SOLD and EXCHANGED.

Renting, Repairing, Nickeling.

DIFFICULT REPAIRING A SPECIALTY.

Prices Reasonable.   Satisfaction Guaranteed.

Wheels to Rent by the Hour, Day, Week or Month.

UP TOWN AGENTS FOR

MESSRS. A. G. SPALDING & BROS.

Sporting and Tennis Goods.

City Agents SPECIAL PONY STAR (39x24)

AND STAR SAFETY.

Examine our Bargain List in another Column.

THE SPRINGFIELD ROADSTER BICYCLES

Hold the World's Records

No. 1 Wheel, plain and cone-bearing, 50-inch....	$75
" 2 " ball-bearing, 50-inch..............	100
" 3 " plain and cone-bearing, 46-inch......	75
" 4 " ball-bearing, 46-inch........	100
" 5 " ball-bearing, 50-inch...	110

This wheel has tangent spokes and hollow rim.

No. 6 Wheel, ball-bearing, 46-inch.............. 110

This wheel has tangent spokes and hollow rim.

No. 7 Volant Safety, 31 and 30 inch diameter wheels, ball-bearing............... 115

For Speed,
Safety
1889
Catalogue Now Ready.
Sent Free.
Beauty
Durability.

SPRINGFIELD BICYCLE MFG. CO.,

178 Columbus Avenue, BOSTON, MASS.

HEADERS IMPOSSIBLE.   BEST HILL-CLIMBERS.

🖈︎🄷︎🄴︎ 🅆🄷︎🄴︎🄴︎🄻︎

—AND—

CYCLING TRADE REVIEW,

Published every Friday morning.

Entered at the Post Office at second class rates.

Subscription Price, - - - $1.00 a year.
Foreign Subscriptions, - - - 6s. a year.
Single Copies, - - - - 5 Cents.

Newsdealers may order through AM. NEWS CO.

All copy should be received by Monday.
Telegraphic news received till Wednesday noon.

Advertising rates on Application.

F. P. PRIAL, Editor and Proprietor
23 Park Row,
P. O. Box 444,   New York.

Persons receiving sample copies of this paper are respectfully requested to examine its contents and give us their patronage, and as far as is convenient, aid in circulating the journal, and extend its influence in the cause which it so faithfully serves. Subscription price, $1 per year.

ON the cycling scroll of fame—and cycling should have its heroes—let us add McCormick to Dalziell, Lallement, Pope, Stevens and Kron. McCormick lives on the road leading from Brooklyn to Bath. He, like many of his neighbors, has been much annoyed by the efforts of one of the residents to annoy wheelmen; a road hog of low degree, a man who once tied a rope across the sidepath to drive wheelmen out on to the muddy road. McCormick has bethought himself of a noble revenge. He will accord the wheelmen gracious hospitality. No thirsty wheelman will ever be denied at the McCormick villa, and, best of all, the thirst-destroyer will be dispensed by one of the Miss McCormicks. Long live the clan McCormick!

WE would call to the attention of the Racing Board the necessity of at once considering the advisability of barring safeties from bicycle races, that is, making them a class. As most racing men commence to compete before they have properly mastered the art of steering safety riders, that class of bicycles, being so sensitive, would cause many accidents. We trust the Board will legislate in favor of classing the rear-drivers. In England the leading amateurs have discussed the matter, and many racing men have agreed not to use safeties in ordinary bicycle races. The N. C. U. Council has decided to establish safety championships, and the English press urges the Union to class safeties as suggested above.

A DEAL of interesting matter is crowded out of this week's paper, including our Down. East tour and the Brooklyn Club's theatre party and dinner.

THE last number of the *Bicycling World* is a fine specimen of enterprise, intelligence and the typographer's art. It may rank as the finest number of any cycling paper ever produced in this country. We congratulate Messrs. Fourdrinier and Neumann on their success.

PSYCHE ON LADIES' BICYCLING.

EDITOR OF THE WHEEL:
I have an apology to offer "Marguerite." I read her letter and "Wildflower's" at the same time, and made the mistake of thinking that "Marguerite" was the one who made the statement about the small steering wheel being preferable. I have read her note in your issue of March 29, and on referring to the number for March 2 I see how very careless I have been. "Wildflower" was the maker of both of the remarks with which I disagree, and I apologize for the mistake, and hope "Marguerite" will shake hands over the bloody chasm.

I frankly admit that I am a partisan of the Psyche. but I don't mean to question anyone else's taste who differs from me. I think it the prettiest, lightest and strongest ladies' wheel made. Mine weighs thirty-nine pounds complete, and has been ridden steadily for a year, with a reasonable amount of rough riding thrown in, and shows not the slightest sign of giving out yet. I shouldn't have chosen it for my own riding if I had not thought it the best wheel going.

I see that Mrs. 4386, in speaking of the bicycle as compared with the tricycle, says she has no practical experience of the former in shopping or visiting, and doesn't know how it stands the comparison under those circumstances. I have tried both machines, for both shopping and visiting, and find the bicycle far and away the most convenient. It is immensely easier to mount and dismount from (when once you know how), it takes so little room, and is so light that it can easily be led up on the sidewalk and put entirely out of the way of annoyance to passers-by or of damage to itself. I have used a Cripper tricycle and always found it disagreeable to mount before an audience, and have never seen anyone mount one with any degree of grace; while the bicycle mount is, in nine cases out of ten, very graceful and always easy. I think everyone will agree with me that I am not overstating the case when I say that one can mount and dismount from a bicycle in a quarter of the time it takes on a tricycle, and with only a fraction, and that a very small one, of the exertion. As to the impossibility of sitting on your machine while you stop, that seems to me a blessing very thinly disguised, for it is a change of posture which unconsciously rests one.

I think the difficulty of learning to mount is a good deal overrated. It seems desperately hard at the first trial, but I caught the idea at my second lesson, and after a little practice I was all right.

What we call here the "curb-stone" mount is the easiest and a pretty one, though I always feel as if I were shirking when I use it.

For this I bring my wheel up close to the curb, with the further pedal half way up in front; I arrange my dress, sit down on the saddle, push down the pedal and I am mounted. This I learned from imitation; I saw some one else do it and tried it, to succeed at the first trial.

The second mount is harder and not so graceful, I think, but very useful, for you are independent with this and can use it at any time—in the country, for instance, where no friendly curb-stones are in reach. For this I stand on the left side of my wheel, with the further pedal half to two-thirds of the way up, incline the wheel a little toward me, put my right foot through to the pedal, arrange my dress over the saddle, then step upon the pedal and rise to the saddle as it (the pedal) goes down. I would suggest that it makes it easier if you lean a little forward against the handle bar, and your dress is less likely to catch on the saddle.

The third mount is a good deal more difficult to get hold of, though once it is yours you will probably use it more than either of the others, for it is far the prettiest.

Stand on the left side of your wheel, with the pedal nearest to you half way up, lean the machine a little from you, put your left foot on the left pedal, and as you rise swing your right foot over the frame on to the right pedal, ride on the pedals until your dress falls into place. This was the hardest mount for me to learn, but I have managed to conquer it, and am fully paid for my efforts and bruises.   PSYCHE.

Pendleton, of the New Yorks, seems to be a good deal of a "star" man as regards euchre as well as riding. He won first prize at an invitation euchre party given by the Manhattans the other evening.

NEW YORK STATE DIVISION L. A. W
—OFFICIAL NOTICES.

*To the Members of the New York State Division
L. A. W.:*

In accordance with the by-laws of this Division, I hereby assume the duties of Chief Consul *vice* Mr. George R. Bidwell, resigned.

Closely associated with Mr. Bidwell as I have been for the past three years in the capacity of Vice-Consul, I have had abundant opportunity to know of his unselfish labors in the cause of wheeling, rendered oftentimes at the expense of his own private business affairs. The wise judgment and unrivaled executive ability displayed by Mr. Bidwell, and by which he has made the Division of the Empire State the Empire Division of the League, deserves grateful acknowledgment. I desire, therefore, to express the thanks of the New York State Division to Mr. George R. Bidwell for his great labors and untiring zeal in behalf of our organization. Hoping to receive from the officers and members of the Division the same hearty support they have accorded my predecessor, I desire to call attention to the necessity of promptly renewing membership and of recruiting new members. All the energies and resources of the Division are being devoted to securing an improvement in our highways. In order to secure the necessary legislation, we need a largely increased membership.

As improved roads and the right to use them, which has been secured to all wheelmen by our organization, appeal to every cyclist, there should be no trouble in adding to our strength if each member will only bear in mind that the privilege of membership in the League of American Wheelmen is not without its accompanying duties. The most important of these *should be the endeavor on the part of every member to increase the numerical strength of the organization,* thereby advancing its interests and extending its influence.

Trusting that it will only be necessary to call attention to the urgency of an earnest and immediate effort on the part of every member, and anticipating a largely increased membership, I am,

Yours fraternally,
W. S. BULL, Chief Consul.

EXECUTIVE COMMITTEE APPOINTMENT.

To the Members of the New York State Division:
I hereby appoint Dr. George E. Blackham, of Dunkirk, N. Y., third member of the Executive Committee, vice Mr. John C. Gulick, resigned.   W. S. BULL,
                                                    Chief Consul.
BUFFALO, N. Y., March 20, 1889.

THE ADAMS MEDALS FOR HIGHEST MONTH'S MILEAGE.

Messrs. Adams & Sons, the manufacturers of Adams "Tutti-Frutti" Chewing Gums, so extensively used in this country and abroad, are unique advertisers. Their latest form of advertising is an enterprising step, which will be appreciated by all road fiends.

Messrs. Adams & Sons have offered two gold medals, valued at $100 and $50, the first of which will be presented to the American wheelman who makes the highest one month's record between the first day of May, 1889, and the first day of November, 1889. The fifty-dollar medal will be presented to the wheelman making the second highest record. The first medal will be more costly and valuable than the first prize presented at the Pullman Road Race of last May. The conditions are as follows: All records must be submitted to C. W. Fourdrinier, of the *Bicycling World*, or F. P. Prial, of THE WHEEL. Records must be accompanied by sworn affidavits of the rider and Captain of club to which he belongs. The affidavit must state distance ridden each day and cyclometer must be inspected before and after the ride. The cyclometer used must be tested before final awards are made. The records will be published from time to time.

J. R. Blake, of the New York Bicycle Club, while riding through the Park, Sunday, March 17, was run over by a horse and carriage. He is now able to be around again, but his bicyclette is a total wreck.

FENTON'S FANCIES.

The enterprise displayed by the wheelmen of Brooklyn ought to, and I hope will, set their brethren of New York to thinking, and perhaps rouse them out of the comfortable state of inanition in which they have been resting for so long. In an old black-letter manuscript in the possession of a book collector of my acquaintance, I read the history of a saint whose life, I am sure, deserves to be better known; as an account of it may perhaps serve as a warning to some of us here in the metropolis. Tiring of the gay delights of the ancient court of which he was an ornament, a certain gay young nobleman, whose name I omit for fear of giving offense to his descendants, decided to go into the recluse business. He purchased the good-will, gas fixtures and stock in trade, together with the residence, of an estimable hermit who was retiring from active business on account of ill-health, and immediately began trade on his own account, "at the old stand," as his business cards announced. But our friend had no *musca domestica* on him! Casting aside all the hackneyed ways of ordinary reclusi, he resolved to enter upon a new line for himself. Flagellation was a good deal of a chestnut; starvation was not yet *ton*; what course should he adopt in order to make a striking success in his chosen career? Damfino! he exclaimed, in the mystic language of his race, many times, before, like the rush of the "puller-in" upon the unsuspecting wanderer through Chatham Street, an idea forced itself upon him, which he immediately proceeded to carry out. Rising at the pleasing hour of ten, he sat down to a frugal breakfast of some sixteen courses, served by a neighboring restaurant. Having completed this, he affixed a neat sign on the front door, conveying the information that the hermitage was open to visitors, who on the payment of a shekel could witness the edifying sight of the hermit engaged in devising plans for the good of the human race. He then seated himself in an arm-chair and cast his eyes upon the ground, from which he never removed them until the close of business hours, which was usually about four in the afternoon. The result may easily be guessed. The people flocked to see him, the pile of shekels rapidly increased and the simple life of the hermit now presented more charms to him than all the gay frivolity of the court, particularly as he came to be regarded as a philanthropist and a sage by the majority of the populace. It is true he never revealed any of his plans for the amelioration of the human race; but let critics be silent—many a philanthropist of our time has made reputation in the same manner! He died at the early age of ninety-six, leaving his scanty savings to an executor for the purpose of founding a faro bank, in which the hard-earned gold of the prudent laborer might be deposited. Canonized by popular vote, his name and actions were cherished for many years by a grateful nation. I have given you a long sermon, my brethren; but there is a warning in it. The wheelmen of New York have had their eyes on the ground too long. Let us hope that they will soon get up and put their shoulders to the wheel. Brooklyn has set the ball rolling and now New York should step in. In plain language, what is the matter with a theatre party and dinner for the wheelmen of this city? A slight exercise of enterprise would make it a success.

I hear something every now and then about a Baseball League of the clubs and hope it will go through. The success of the Bowling League shows that the scheme is feasible, and I'm sure would be a source of even more enjoyment to the men taking part. President Bridgman, of the K. C. W., is a good deal of a baseball "fiend," they tell me. Here's his opportunity to help on the national game!

The election of the New Yorks occurs in May, and a preliminary meeting for the reception of nominations was called for Wednesday. One of the slates, and a good one too, runs about as follows: Shriver, for President; Terry, for Vice-President; Findley, for Secretary, and Shaw, for Treasurer. Chairmen of Committees—House, Lansing; Auditing, R. W. Weir; Entertainment, Heydecker; Membership, Roy. Last, but not least, McFadden, for Captain. This ticket is a good one throughout, and, provided all the gentlemen named consent to run, stands a good chance of being elected.

FENTON.

BROOKLYN.

The big theatre party is now but a memory, but in many respects a pleasant one. Mayor Chapin presented himself to us, both at the theatre and afterward at the supper, and seemed impressed with the abundance of manly beauty upon which he gazed at the latter place. The boys witnessed the performance in rather a cold-blooded state of mind, and, until the curtain dropped on the finale, each one anxiously and impatiently awaited the arrival of a really deserving moment in the opera. It is but charity to think that a premature dropping of the curtain prevented the arrival of such a moment; for certainly, as presented to us, "The Pearl of Pekin" proved a disappointment. The dialogue was expected to be replete with gags and pointed personalities, but every one escaped without damage; no, not every one, as Wise was favored twice, and the Murphy medal for the long-distance championship adorned the manly breast of the star, while the flags of the different clubs were tumbled promiscuously about the stage. The committee desires it known that many hits of different men were prepared, and sent to the High Muck-a-muck, Harrison, but were there suppressed. Harrison's conduct in reproducing so few of the expected hits, and his jealous refusal to let any other member of the company gain the good-will of the boys in that way, hardly made him deserve the consideration and attention he received during the course of the dinner. The spread produced a fuller and more amiable feeling in general; very happy speeches were made by Mayor Chapin and others, including "ye Editor," who was in attendance in body and in spirit, and his description of the festivities should sparkle, e'en as the limpid ice-water he imbibed. The feasters hung together for about three hours, with few deserters, but many slipped away on the castor-oil story, and thereafter the break-up was rapid.

In striking contrast to the conduct of a near neighbor, Mr E. C. McCormick, through the medium of THE WHEEL, extends a cordial invitation to all passing wheelmen to stop at his house and indulge themselves in a few moments' rest. Mr. McCormick resides at Mapleton Villa, on Eighteenth Avenue, the usual route to Bath, on the north side of the Sea Beach Railroad—a point at which many men feel inclined to stretch themselves for a few minutes, and to whom a glass of cool water, or perchance a glass of milk from one of Mr. McCormick's Alderney cows, would be most acceptable. We strongly advise club men on their way to Bath to take advantage of Mr. McCormick's gracious hospitality, and to thereby show their appreciation of the spirit that has prompted the invitation. Between Mr. McCormick and the Boulevard resides also the most marked species of human hog in this vicinity, who shows that it takes all kinds of people to make a world, and under which axiom lies his only excuse for living.

On Saturday night the Brooklyns will visit the L. I. W. Club House, the occasion being another of the L. I.'s celebrated stags. Col. John Oakey has been announced to speak upon cycling in general and Brooklyn in particular; in addition, Captain Marion, K. C. W., will hold the floor for an uncertain period; Mr. Nickolds will sing, and probably Chairman Clark, of the Entertainment Committee, may be induced to give us one of his much-prized recitations. The Brooklyn survivors of the Clarendon wine cellar are expected to turn out in force. NYX.

"Muck-a-hiah!"
"Does it go?"
"It goes, it permeates!"

The prevailing expressions at the theatre party are still ringing in my ears. It is my first pleasant duty to heartily congratulate the Committee of Arrangements on the successful manner with which the entire affair was conducted.

They have, in a measure, put their collective foot in the consommé, though, for the wheelmen of Brooklyn will hereafter want at least one such an affair each year, and they will undoubtedly press the same efficient committee into service again.

The colors of each club were conspicuously worn in various parts of the theatre by the many feminine admirers of the boys, who had secured seats in advantageous locations where they might obtain the best view of the fun. Club colors also abounded on the stage, where each performer wore the colors of at least one of the clubs.

Mayor Chapin was entertained by Bert Cole and George Bancroft in their private box, where his entrance was the signal for prolonged applause from the boys in the orchestra.

The souvenir programmes were "things of beauty, etc.," and I venture to assert that each person who received one will treasure it for a long time to come as a memento of a most enjoyable occasion.

The enthusiastic road-riders of the different clubs had various plans laid to get their wheels out of town on Sunday, but probably the only men who succeeded in putting in a ride were A. C. Banker and W. E. Fuller, B. B. C., who started at 6 A. M. for Patchogue. They, however, changed their route and came back to Brooklyn by train from Jamaica, where they met the unexpected in the shape of a snow storm.

The 1889 Century run is now assuming a definite shape, and particulars in full are to be seen on the bulletin boards of the K. C. W., L. I. W. and B. B. C. In the latter club Messrs. Meeteer, Warner, Fay, Rogers, Banker, Barkman, Borland, Fuller and Weed have signified their intention to participate. The K. C. W. will also send several men.

J. F. Borland, B. B. C., will take charge of the new "Photographers' Supplies" department, which A. G. Spalding & Bros. are about to open in their store.

The Long Islands are making preparations for an elaborate stag racket, at their club house next Saturday night, and those who are so fortunate as to attend may be assured of a royal good time. ATOL.

Brooklyn, April 2, 1889.

JERSEY CITY.

The N. J. T. R. R. A. will doubtless be organized in the near future. Answers to Capt. Day's circular-letter are coming in rapidly, and every reply received to date gives promise that assistance will be rendered by clubs in every part of the State. Capt. Day hopes to have race No. 1 run on Decoration Day.

There is a story afloat among the cycling and daily papers to the effect that C. E. Kluge is in active training with the intention of practically "living" on the path this year. I was speaking to Kluge last night and he denies that there is any truth in the rumor whatever. His business demands his entire attention, and he cannot, therefore, spare the time necessary to devote to path racing this season. It is therefore doubtful if Roseville sees him this year, except, perhaps, as a spectator.

The following is a copy of the postal received by the members of the H. C. W. a few days ago:

HEADQUARTERS OF THE
HUDSON COUNTY WHEELMEN,
555 Communipaw Avenue.

JERSEY CITY, March 28, 1889.

Ki-Yippy, Ki-Yippy, Ki-Yippy, Ki-Yah, Hudson County, Here We Are, Who-Wah, Who-Wah, Hah, Hah, Hah!

We are not dead, but sleepeth, and have just awoketh.

On Tuesday evening, April 2, 1889, a GRAND SMOKER will be smoked. The Committee have been at work for the past two months in securing the best talent from the Bowery; Tony Pastor's Banjo Quartette (Messrs. Wood, Wolford, Eldridge and Damitt); our old friend Levy, the tear-extractor, will again paralyze us; the Bjingstein Bjorston Brothers, in their chilly six-act drama entitled "Seven Quarts of Blood, or The White Man's Revenge."

A Dime Museum will be connected with the entertainment, including "The Ossified Man on the Bicycle," "Walt Whitman, the Man with the Pink Whiskers." Samson Morse will break a dollar bill into four quarters.

Every Eldridge. Body Benedict. May Merseles. Work the Whitman. Growler. Griffiths.
SMOKER COMMITTEE.

The result of this spirited invitation was that the H. C. W. rooms were very much crowded on Tuesday evening. A great deal of fun was caused by the appearance of the committee in ballet burlesque costumes *à la décolleté*. A topical song, entitled "I Think So," was sung by Messrs. Merseles and Eldridge. Recitations and vocal solos were rendered by the club talent, after which refreshments were served. The Bicycola was again brought into use, Mr. C. W. Higgins securing first prize, in the shape of a very handsome silver-mounted cane, and Mr. Griffiths second prize, a bronze clock. Messrs. Demmert, Shone and Post also secured prizes. Mr. J. L. Robertson won the special prize (I do not recollect what it was) for making highest score with eyes shut. A sample of fancy needle-work was presented to two of the members by Mrs. Earl and Miss Rich, members of the ladies' division of the club.

COASTER.

PSYCHO WHEELS FOR 1889.

Sole Importers: Capital Cycle Co., Washington, D. C.

The Pyscho cycles are imported by the Capital Cycle Company, of Washington, D. C. This firm were the first to recognize the merits of all forms of rear-driving safeties, and in 1885 imported the first one ever brought into this country. They also designed and introduced the first tandem safety in 1889. They designed and manufactured in 1887 the first rear-driving ladies' safety bicycle, and credit should be given them for their efforts in this direction. They have accomplished as much for the weaker sex by reducing friction, weight, and by giving increased pleasure, as did the inventor of the spider wheel for the stronger sex by improving the boneshaker,—*Wheel*.

Psycho Cycles do not have hollow rims, tangent spokes, ball head or spring forks. No change will be made in Psychos over the 1888 pattern. The Fish hammock saddle will be used on all Pyschos.

Psycho Cycles are remarkable for their lightness, strength, harmonious and uniform construction, simplicity (fewness of parts) and general gracefulness of design. **Beautifully finished.**

PYSCHO LIGHT ROADSTER.

PYSCHO LADIES' ROADSTER.

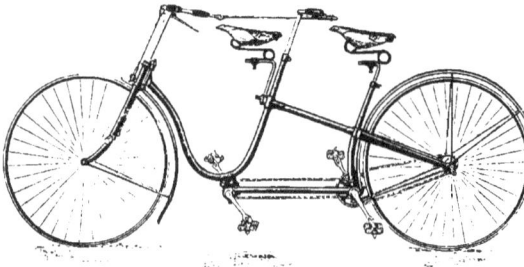

PYSCHO TANDEM SAFETY.

SEVEN FORMS

OF

PSYCHO SAFETIES,

Varying in Weight and Design.

1. "**Men's Straight Frame Psycho Safety,**" 30-inch wheels. ⅞ and ⅝ inch tires, geared to 57 inches, weight 47 lbs. Price $140.

2. "**Men's Light Roadster Psycho Safety,**" 30-inch wheels, ⅝-inch tires, made for gentlemen riders and scorchers on good roads, geared to 60 inches (see cut), weight 38 lbs. Price, $140.

3. "**Men's Dropped Frame Psycho Safety**" is designed like ladies' safety (see cut), 30-inch wheels, ⅞ and ⅝ inch tires, weight 50 lbs. Will stand any weight on any road. Detachable brace rod makes it suitable for ladies and a general family machine. Price, $140. Geared to 57 inches.

4. "**Ladies' Roadster Psycho Safety,**" ⅝-inch tires, 29-inch wheels. Detachable brace rod, suitable for short or medium-height gentlemen. Will stand any weight. Weight, 44 lbs. See cut. Geared to 50 inches.

5. "**Ladies' Light Roadster Psycho Safety,**" 29-inch wheels, ⅝ and ⅞ inch tires, weight 38 lbs. Superb finish, very light and easy-running, intended for light-weight ladies, but will carry 175 lbs. Geared to 50 inches.

6. "**Ladies' Extra Light Psycho,**" same design as "Ladies' Psycho," with rear forks like "Men's Light Roadster Psycho," 28-inch wheels. Weight 34 lbs. Price, $140. We cannot deliver this much under thirty days.

7. "**Psycho Tandem Safety,**" intended for lady and gentleman or two gentlemen, ⅞-inch tires to both wheels, very strong, light and simple. Will carry any weight. Now in its second season. Price, with two separate brakes, $200. Geared to 57 inches.

All of the above Machines are guaranteed to the fullest extent.

A CORRECTION.—The Pope Mfg. Co. desire us to say that they did not issue announcements or circulars stating that certain firms and companies were infringing on their patents. The Pope Mfg. Co. does not deny that it claims that some concerns are infringing on its patents, and that it has so informed its own agents by private communication. The Pope Mfg. Co. further states that it does not intend to do business, or prevent other people from doing business, by threats or intimidation. We are pleased to give the above statement publicity. In an original reference to the alleged infringements, we stated that in matters of fact we were open to correction. We supposed that the letter sent by the Pope Mfg. Co. to its agents was a public circular-letter.

"BY FAR THE BEST."

BOSTON, MASS., March 13, 1889.

Bicycling World Co., 12 Pearl Street, City:

GENTLEMEN—It may be of value to you to know the following facts in regard to your paper as an advertising medium. We have tried two of the leading cycling papers besides your own in advertising second hand wheels. The replies received from the advertisements in the two papers were exactly one each, while we take pleasure in stating that we can trace directly the sale of over thirty machines to the advertisement which we placed in your valuable medium. You are at liberty to use this as you see fit.

Very truly yours,

SINGER & Co.,
Per Wm. L. Ross, Mgr.

[We won't so far abuse confidence as to give the names of the other two papers, but we don't think our advertisers will have to work their imagination very hard to guess correctly.—ED.]

[The above notice appeared in the *Bicycling World* of March 22. In the March 29 edition of THE WHEEL, and in future editions, our readers will find the advertisement of Messrs. Singer & Co., so we pass the Boston innuendo over to our Western brethren of the cycling press.—ED.]

ELWELL'S EUROPEAN TEAM IN IRELAND.

The scorcher, a correspondent of the Irish *Cyclist*, sends the following letter to Mr. F. A. Elwell, from which it will be judged that the American tourists will receive a taste of that hospitality which one always associates with the Emerald Isle:

"If you have only one week in Ireland you will have to keep going all your time. Lose no time on the road, and you will have two or three days in Dublin, which is famous for several things. The route you have now decided on is not half bad—tons in front of your original scheme. White tells me that he will look after you carefully with regard to all such matters. My dear, boy don't apologize. The Dublin cyclers will only be too pleased to have some excuse for staying out late, and all that sort of thing. White will let you know the interesting details concerning your route—he lives only for work of the kind. You will pass through the Vale of Avoca, unless you go some miles out of your way especially to avoid it. Some Dublin fellows will probably meet you at Queenstown and ride up to Dublin with you. There is no direct steam communication between Dublin and Birkenhead (which latter place is a horrible invention—the worst I ever was in), but you can get direct by steamer from Dublin to Liverpool. The sail is twelve hours, and the vessels very poor. There are no state-rooms, and the accommodation generally is better adapted for the lower animals than anything else. You have only to cross a ferry from Liverpool to Birkenhead, the two towns being separated by the River Mersey. A better route is from Dublin to Holyhead steamer (fairly comfortable), thence by rail to Liverpool, and cross the ferry. By both routes the vessels leave Dublin about 7 P.M., but the second is some three hours shorter than the first."

The East side bicyclists of Rochester met on Tuesday evening, March 26, and formed an organization which they have called the "Flower City Wheelmen." The following officers were elected: President, F. B. Weeks; Vice-President, F. W. Maxson; Secretary-Treasurer, J. H. Brown.

CARRIAGES WITH CYCLE WHEELS.

The idea of rubber-tired wheels for carriages seems about to be practiced by an American firm, from whose prospectus we publish the following paragraphs:

"About five years ago, however, Mr. William Carmont, of Manchester, Eng., patented a means of applying rubber tires to vehicles which has since been extensively used in Great Britain and Continental Europe, thereby demonstrating the practicability of the use of rubber in this connection. The London Noiseless Tire Company was incorporated to work Mr. Carmont's patents, and has been eminently successful, having now running in London alone some 12 000 sets of their tires, while the whole number of rubber tires now in use in Europe on all sizes and kinds of vehicle wheels is estimated at 70,000 sets. The Earl of Shrewsbury, whose interests in cab property are among the largest in the world, recognizing the merit and growing demand for these tires, has bought up the entire capital stock of the Noiseless Tire Company, and he is said to have paid the stockholders six times the par value of their shares. The Earl, in addition to his large interests in London cab property, has introduced into Paris during the past six months several hundreds of hansom cabs with rubber tires.

"Mr. Howard M. Dubois, a resident of Philadelphia, visited Europe twice, each time making a careful study of the problem of adopting rubber tires on American vehicles. With the information thus gained, he therefore set to work to overcome the objections pointed out, and finally succeeded in solving the problem of securing a durable cushion of rubber between the carriage wheel and the roadbed. Patents have been granted to him on a number of applications, and others are pending covering the whole field, and the wheels are now being manufactured by the American Cushion Tire and Wheel Co., 18 South Broad Street, Philadelphia.

CYCLING AS A YOUTH-RESTORER.

Cycling is not a patent medicine, as the above title would seem to imply, but it certainly is equal to the Floridian spring, the fount of youth which old Ponce de Leon hunted for. Listen to what "Perseus" writes to the *Sporting Life*:

"The bicyle is the modern alchemist's oven; you shove in an old man, shut the door; there is a sizzling sound for a few moments, the door flies open and out steps a youth. I know an old man who was shoved in and sizzled and his cheek is now colored with the ruddy glow of health, his step is as elastic as a boy's and he does not look a day older than forty, though he is over sixty.

"I will not tell you his name, but he lives not a thousand miles from Kingston, Pa., and the members of the Pennsylvania Division who attended the meet at Scranton will remember his hospitality on the run down to Wyoming, and one rider in particular remembers his kindness and deftness with the needle in repairing damages to his unmentionables. He can do almost anything now without astonishing his friends, but I certainly was surprised the other day when he walked in and told me that he had come to town to take lessons in waltzing. Sixty-five and learning to dance!"

PROSPECT WHEELMEN ELECT OFFICERS.

At a meeting of the Prospect Wheelmen, of Brooklyn, held at the residence of Mr. Chas. Newbourg, 637 President Street, on Thursday, March 27, the following officers were elected to serve for the year 1889: President, Fred. J. Bosse; Captain, Harry Newman; Lieutenant, Wm. Shannon; Secretary, Chas. Newbourg.

Captain Newman wore the new uniform of the club, which is of blue cheviot cloth—sack coat, handsomely braided; standing collar, with gilt Old English letters "P. W." It is evident the Prospects intend to make a good showing this season, in appearance as well as in numbers. Although a young club, they have been very prosperous.

Mr. S. C. Devy, of the Pennsylvania Bicycle Club, has presented for competition a stop-watch, to be given either for mileage or the greatest number of times out on club runs. Captain Supplee is to name the winner.

DO BICYCLES RUN EASIEST AT NIGHT?

Some American engineering papers are discussing the greater ease with which it is alleged machinery runs during the night. Many engineers of considerable standing have expressed the opinion that there is undoubtedly an increase of speed and ease of motion, whatever the cause may be. One writer states:

"For a number of years I have been the rider of a bicycle, and, during that time, have had occasion to take many night rides. I have found in nearly every instance that the wheel is propelled with about one-half of the power required during daylight. I have started out for a ride by daylight and let darkness overtake me on the road while still in the saddle, and I never failed to note that, as the shadows deepened, my speed increased under less exertion. Where before I had found a hill hard plodding, I now rode easily over it. Another peculiar fact was, the darker the night became the less power I required. I have at such times, even during heavy mists, ridden with but a small proportion of exertion, when in the daytime it required my best efforts. The feeling I experienced at such times was as if all friction or weight had been suddenly removed, and all that was required in riding was to keep the legs in motion. Other riders who have been my companions at such times have often spoken of this subject and wondered at the cause. In the bicycle, the cause can lie only in one or two mediums, and the less density of the atmosphere during the night would probably be the one favored by the majority, although there are those who claim that the peculiar electrical conditions during the night-time have more to do with it than is generally supposed."

Our own experience entirely agrees with the above, and those of our readers who "fly by night" as well as by day may be able to bear us out in this. The question has not been discussed in our columns, and it would be interesting to have an expression of opinion from some of our more observant friends.

THE WINSLOW SKATE COMPANY'S NEW WHEEL.

The Samuel Winslow Skate Manufacturing Company, one of the largest manufacturing concerns at Worcester, Mass., have established as fine a bicycle plant at their skate factory as we have seen, and are turning out a high-grade wheel which they have named the "Vineyard," after a skate of their make which had as high a reputation in the skate-manufacturing world as "Columbia" has in the cycling world.

The "Vineyard" is made in sizes of 38, 42, 44, 46, 48 and 50 inch. The first three sizes named have $\frac{3}{4}$ tires to front, $\frac{5}{8}$-inch tires to rear wheel. The last three sizes named have $\frac{7}{8}$ tires to front and $\frac{3}{4}$ to rear wheel. The weight varies from 31 to 41 pounds, and the price from $35 to $60. A cut of the wheel will be found in the company's advertisement. The following are the specifications of the "Vineyard:"

SPECIFICATIONS OF 50-INCH.—Red rubber tires, $\frac{7}{8}$-inch to front and $\frac{3}{4}$-inch to rear wheel. Crescent felloes. 52 and 18 direct spokes. 16-inch rear wheel. 4-inch hub flanges. Detachable cranks, 4 to 5 inch throw. Parallel pedals, with corrugated rubbers. Adjustable parallel bearings to front, cone to rear wheel. Solid front and rear forks. Adjustable step. Suspension saddle. Cowhorn handle-bars. Spade or pear handles. Leg guard. Tool-bag and tools.

The materials used in the "Vineyard" are the best that can be obtained; the finish is in much better style than that found in wheels of this grade; the wheel is fitted with cowhorn bars, spade or pear handle, adjustable step and suspension saddle. The wheels are strongly made; the hubs are of the best cast steel. The backbone is of high-quality drawn steel, carefully tapered and curved; the tires are of Para rubber. The bearings are of a special patent, and will be found most satisfactory. The company wish agents in every city.

The prowess of the Maryland Bicycle Club in winning cup races is exceeded only by its record on the road. The total mileage of this club for the past twelve months in club runs and individual excursions and tours on the wheel foots up over 100,000 miles.

London racing men have started to train on the Crystal Palace track.

WHEEL GOSSIP.

The German champion, Lehr, with a party of European racing men, will visit England in July. The fame of England will be upheld by Synder, Osmond, Mayes, Morris, Langley and Illston. Windle, the American champion, may also be there. Osmond, the bicycle crack, and Mills, the road demon, are reported as having fared very badly this winter, both suffering from cold and not looking in good form.

The Scotch championship will be held June 15.

The *Phonetic Journal* says, with regard to the system it advocates : "If the lerner iz a selklist he wil feind that fonograpi iz to longhand whot the safeti bei or the trusti trei is to stumping it on foot. The wun iz fleet and ful ov plexhur, the uther iz toilsum and ful ov trubel."

An English firm, Joseph Lucas & Son, call cycling sundries "Cyclealities," and have coined "Cyclorn" to describe an automatic horn, the horn being blown by pressing an India-rubber ball attached to a tube.

At the Leipsic cycle show, 140 firms exhibited, the principal English firms being represented through their Continental agents. The King of Saxony visited the show. During the show the German makers organized a union. The machines of German manufacture did not compare with the English product, being clumsier and poorly finished. The principal German exhibitors are : Durkopp & Co., Bielefeld ; Siedel & Naumann, Dresden ; Heinrich Kleyer, Frankfort ; Marsch & Kertzschmar, Dresden ; Winkhofer & Iaenicke, Chemnitz ; F. E. Trinks, Dresden ; C. Bescherer, Zeitz ; Haase & Stamm, Berlin ; Paul Focke & Co., Leipsic ; Carl Marschutz, Nuremberg ; Goldschmidt Bros., Neumarkt ; Frankenburger & Ottenstein, Nuremberg ; Dissel & Proll, Dortmund ; Lenzau & Scharbau, Hamburg (this firm make a copy of the American "Star" bicycle) ; Adam Opel, Russelskeim, Frankfort, and Pinzen Bros., Munich.

The American "Star" bicycle is being copied by Messrs. Lenzau & Scharbau, of Hamburg, Germany, who make and market the wheel.

THE N. C. U. CHAMPIONSHIPS.

The following are the dates of the N. C. U. championships for this year, all of which will be held at the Paddington track : July 20, 1-mile bicycle ; July 20, 25-mile bicycle ; July 20, 5-mile tricycle ; July 27, 1-mile tricycle ; July 27, 25-mile tricycle ; July 27, 5-mile bicycle.

Chief Consul Emery addressed a meeting held last Wednesday evening at Worcester, Mass., for the purpose of stimulating improved roads and interest in the L. A. W.

"I am fully convinced that it (The Brooks) is the most simple and the best idea for a Cyclometer I have seen."

J. WILKINSON, Bridgeport, Conn.
Only $5.　Brooks Odometer Co., Lowell, Mass.

A PNEUMATIC TIRE.

The *Irish Cyclist* says that Messrs. Edlin & Co., of Belfast, are introducing a "Pneumatic" safety, of which it remarks : "The principal features of these machines is a hollow tire filled with air, which absorbs nearly all vibration, and renders the going as easy over square setts as on a cinder path. We examined a tire that had been some months in use, and there was not a single cut in it, the sharp stones seeming to produce no effect, as they sink into the yielding surface. Messrs. Edlin & Co. are making the machines themselves."

An English firm, Burroughs, Welcome & Co., of London, sell a "cyclist's pocket medicine case." One of the preparations contained in the box is a "saccharin" tablet, which is several times as sweet as sugar. One tabloid of the size of half a pea will sweeten a cup of tea or coffee.

It is rumored in England that the authorities will make an effort to suppress road races.

The "Star" bicycle has received first prize in the Melbourne (Australia) Exhibition.

On Tuesday evening, March 26, a half-dozen wheelmen of Rochester were arrested for violating the ordinance which forbids cycling on the sidewalks in the business part of the city between the hours of 6 A. M. and 9 P. M.　Supt. Cleary has instructed the patrolmen to strictly enforce this ordinance.

Howard A. Smith & Co., Newark, N. J., are probably teaching more persons to ride than any previous year. The ladies seem to be taking to the ladies' safeties. Oraton Hall seems to suit them to learn to ride in, owing to its immense space without posts and the fact that it is easy of access.

The New York Bicycle Company's season opens with a rush. They report business booming at both their houses. The company handle all makes of crank machines this season, and are New York agents for the Smith Machine Company's "Star" safety, Special, Pony (39x24), etc. A specialty is made by the Irvings of taking old mounts in part payment for new ones of any standard make. At the company's uptown branch, No. 4 East Sixtieth Street, difficult repairing is attended to promptly, and is all done under their personal supervision. As uptown agents for Messrs. A. G. Spalding & Bros., the company carry a fine assortment of this firm's celebrated brands of sporting and tennis goods. This will be a great convenience to buyers in the upper districts. The New York Bicycle Company's bargain list should be perused by all intending purchasers. Their stock of slightly used wheels is unexcelled in point of variety and excellence, and their prices are very reasonable.

At the National Cross-Country Association games, to be held at the Gentlemen's Driving Park on Saturday, April 27, a three-mile bicycle handicap will be decided. The grounds may be reached from the Grand Central road to Morrisania station, or via Jerome Avenue, the road leading to them branching off Jerome Avenue to the left about half a mile above Macomb's Dam Bridge.

CYCLING AT TACOMA, W. T.

Prince Wells has just opened a Gormully & Jeffery agency at Tacoma. Among the visiting wheelmen are E. I. Halsted, of the Harlem Wheelmen, and Dr. Aitken, of the Citizens' Bicycle Club, who is taking an extensive trip for the benefit of his health. The roads in the city and vicinity are level, and present a good surface for cycling. The Indians are quite friendly, and occasionally afford much amusement to wheelmen. The weather has been beautiful during the past week, and already there is a stir among the wheelmen which betokens great activity during the coming season.

The Harlem Bicycle Company will remove May 1 to their new double store at 310 Lenox Avenue, near 126th Street. Their new headquarters will be much larger than their present store, and will give them more room for repairs and renting and storing wheels.

The Elastic Tip Company of Boston are patentees, manufacturers and dealers in rubber goods of every description. One of their specialties is bicycle handles, made in various styles, which they sell largely to the cycle trade.

At the meeting of the New York Club, held Wednesday night, the following gentlemen were nominated by the club members (the ballots will be received on May 6, from 8 to 11 P. M.): For President, J. J. Shriver, F. W. Kitching and E. S. Terry, of whom Mr. Shriver will probably be elected ; Vice-President, E. S. Terry—will probably be elected ; Secretary W. E. Findlay, unanimously ; Treasurer, Irving Shaw—will probably be elected ; Captain, Mr. Shaw and Jos. McFadden, of whom the latter stands the best chance. House Committee, Mr. Lansing, Chairman ; Auditing Committee, Messrs. Shaw and F. I. Stott ; Entertainment, W. C. Heydecker. Membership, Messrs. Heydecker and John R. Blake.

Chief Consul Bull will arrive in New York on Sunday morning. On Monday he will attend the "Spalding" banquet at Delmonico's as representing cycling.

Messrs. A. G. Spalding & Bros., U. S. special agents for Victor wheels have just published a sixty-four page catalogue of Victor wheels and cycle sundries ; Messrs. Spalding & Bros. are supplying the L. A. W. official caps, shirts, stockings, belts and badges. The L. A. W. shoe, price $5.00, is hand-made and from specially selected kangaroo stock ; it is light, strong and elastic, and, being laced more open at the toe, can be made to give a snug fit. A bicycle shoe at $3.50 is attracting brisk demand.

The annual meeting of the Massachusetts Bicycle Club was held at Young's Hotel last evening, about twenty-five members being present. In the absence of the President, Mr. A. S. Parsons was chosen Chairman. The Treasurer's report showed the club to be in a sound financial condition, and the Membership Committee reported that twenty-five gentlemen had been admitted into the club during the past year. After some minor business had been transacted, these officers were elected : R. G. Amory, President ; W. H. Minot, Treasurer ; C. C. Ryder, Secretary ; R. G. Amory, A. D. Salkeld and E. B. Pillsbury, Executive Committee ; A. D. Peck, Jr., C. D. V. Graves, C. C. Ryder, H. B. Salkeld and H. M. Sabin, Membership Committee ; A. D. Peck, Jr., Captain, and J. M. Sprague, Lieutenant.

Plainfield, N. J., will have five newly macadamized streets, an ordinance having just been passed to that effect.

I do not know anything about the respective circulations of THE WHEEL and the *Bicycling World*, but I do know that I read THE WHEEL and don't—.—*Perseus in Sporting Life.*

Griff Glover, a St. Louis wheelman, strongly opposed the Warner Bill, and employed a skillful lobbyist to help defeat it.

Mr. Page, in St. Louis *Spectator*, says : "I am inclined to think that 'Ithuriel's' plain, every-day-business name is Wm. Brewster." Mr. Page is unwise to publish mere "inclined thinks." "Ithuriel's" plain every-day name is not Wm. Brewster.

The Plainfield, N. J., B. C. held an athletic meet at the Crescent Rink on Thursday evening. The Elizabeth Wheelmen sent a strong delegation.

Elizabeth wheelmen are eagerly inspecting the new "Eagle" just received by N. H. White. Messrs. L. D. and D. B. Bonnett will push a "Columbia" tandem this season. They have already received the wheel, which attracts much attention.

The Boston *Herald* of March 31 publishes almost two columns of Stanley Show notes, based on information furnished by Mr. Charles E. Pratt, of the Pope Mfg. Co. The article is an exhaustive and intelligent review of the Show, the *Herald* man having made the most of the authentic and extensive information furnished by Mr. Pratt. The *Herald* man could have made a sensation had he interviewed Mr. Pratt on his return from the Show.

Louis Harrison, who was one of the choice spirits of the Boston Club in its palmiest, punchiest days, has joined the New York Bicycle Club. Mr. Harrison is a magazine writer, a specialist on theoretical naval architecture, and moves in one of those metropolitan literary-artistic eddies which are a part of the shadowy gas-lit world called "Bohemia."

"Tommy" Finlay, the Star rider, will be seen on the racing path this year.

The *Sewing Machine and Cycling News*, English, publishes a weekly column of American notes captioned "Stars and Stripes," which is stolen bodily from this paper.

CYCLING AS A DYSPEPSIA CURE.

The real benefits of cycling as a health-giving sport cannot be fully appreciated by the uninitiated. One is so accustomed to hearing this form of exercise spoken of as a stimulant to muscular development and a panacea for the ills of the flesh that these general assertions lose their effect until specific cases are cited to impress forcibly their truth upon the average mind. It may be that it is not so much the form of exercise as the exercise itself that produces such good physical results, but certain it is that the devotees of cycling, as a rule, are blessed with good digestion and robust health. Bicycling, after one has passed the initiatory stage of discouragement and oftentimes disgust, is so fascinating that one is loath to abandon it, and it is this every-day devotion that keeps the limbs supple, the muscles hard, the appetite good, the digestion unimpaired and the mind vigorous.—*Nashville American.*

It will be interesting to many wheelmen to learn that a book entitled "The Bicycle : Its Use and Action," by Charles Spencer, was published in London in 1870.

NEW ORLEANS.

Rain knocked out the Louisiana Cycling Club's Batson medal race again last Sunday. The next attempt will be made on March 31.

May 18, June 22, July 20, August 17 and September 21 are the dates set for the New Orleans Bicycle Club's races for the A. M. Hill cup.

The spirit of progress is abroad in our midst, and it looks as if this is to be about as lively and prosperous a year as cycling has yet enjoyed in "these diggings." The Louisiana Club is maturing a building scheme, and, after incorporation, which will probably be the order of next week, the scheme will be brought to head. The idea is feasible, and, with the enthusiasm that has met its inception, there seems little doubt but that favorable action on the part of the club will follow. It is about time anyway that we New Orleans boys were doing something to place "the cause" in a big city like this on a permanent foundation.

The New Orleans Bicycle Club has adopted a bottle-green, black-trimmed uniform and placed the contract with Wanamaker & Brown, Philadelphia.

The Hill cup is to remain a perpetual club trophy and be raced for annually, each year's winner to have his name inscribed thereon and to be awarded a medal as a personal testimonial. President Shields has generously donated the 1889 medal. BI.

"NO DYSPEPTIC CLERGYMEN, IF YOU PLEASE."

This is the title of a three-inch square advertising pamphlet, published by the Overman Wheel Company. It is so unique that we describe it. The cover is of the brightest red. The second page bears only these two lines:

See what Mr. Harris says about it. It would do as much for you as it has for him.

Then follows the Rev. Mr. Harris's letter:

FAR ROCKAWAY, L. I.,
13th Feb'y, 1889.

OVERMAN WHEEL CO.:

Gentlemen—My "Safety" wears like an old coat, more comfortable every day, save that it doesn't wear out. For the mere purpose of making pastoral calls I find it worth its price; it is better than a horse as to expense, care, risk (to machine), danger (to me) and cleanliness. It saves me much time every day, and I get also immense pleasure while fulfilling my engagements.

I feel grateful for a machine that has done so much for my health, my spirits, and consequently my work, and for this reason should like to have you show this note to any young pastor who wonders whether it pays to have a "Safety." If his elders or deacons object that such a conveyance is unsuitable for a minister, let him take his Bible and his bicycle and go where people demand healthy sermons, no dyspeptic ministers for me, if you please, and hence my appreciation of the Victor Safety.

Yours sincerely,
THEO. W. HARRIS.

The last page contains a cut of the Victor Safety, underlined as follows: "Here it is; it is made by the Overman Wheel Co."

RACING IN INDIA.

At the recent sports of the Parsee Gymkhama at Bombay there were two cycle races, of which the following are particulars:

Two-Mile Bicycle Race.—K. M. Satin (1); R. M. Satin (2). The contest lay only between the Satin brothers. K. M. Satin was as good a rider as his elder brother, and he did not let go the advantage of a good start which he had gained over his brother. Time, 10m. 5s.

One-Mile Tricycle Race.—P. M. Dalal (1); D. D. Dubash (2). There were originally six entries for this race, but only three appeared on the field. The race was, however very interesting, although the contest was by no means very keen. Dalal led off at the start, and maintained his position to the end. Dubash, who was encumbered by a rather heavy machine, was, in spite of his best endeavors, a bad second. Time, 5m. 5s.—*The Cyclist*.

THE "EAGLE" ON EAGLE ROCK.

Weather and the condition permitting, B. Gaylor, of the Eagle Bicycle Company, and Wm. A. Clark, of Stamford, Conn., will be at Eagle Rock at 2.45 P. M. on Saturday, April 6. Mr. Clark will attempt to mount the Rock on a 50-inch "Eagle" with 5½ inch cranks.

CYCLING FOR WOMEN.

AN EXPERIENCE OF THE LADIES' SAFETY.

Having perused the article entitled "Shall we Ride Tricycles?" in a recent issue of *The Lady*, and finding that the writer, whoever she may be, seems to have written upon a subject with which she is not very familiar, I trust I may be allowed to give my opinion and experience of the "ladies' safety," and that the editor will find room for it. Truly "the wonders of the age are many, but the wonders of the age are not ahead of the impudence of some of those who live in it," to quote our unknown friend's—or, rather, enemy's—own words. How very applicable they are! I, too, was present at the Stanley show, and was greatly pleased to see the number of firms which exhibited "safeties" made expressly for the gentler sex, and at their elegant appearance and finish. This undoubtedly indicates that at no distant period we may hope to see very many of them in active service. I was especially struck with one, made and exhibited by Mr. Leni, of Hammersmith, which contains several important improvements, chief of which is that the saddle is made on a hinge, and falls down when the rider mounts, thus enabling her to do so with

MUCH GREATER EASE,

and rendering the catching of the dress on the peak an impossibility. The fore wheel is considerably enlarged, being 36-inch, while the driver is only 26-inch. This is quite an innovation, and it remains to be seen whether it will be a success. Up till now the usual style has been equal to 28-inch or 30 inch, or the front wheel two inches less. I hope to try this machine when next in town, and to report as to its merits. "Unknown" says: "It is, from its nature, utterly unsuited to the purpose for which it is designed." How so? Will she write and explain, or ask the makers why they have designed a thing that is useless and unsuitable? I should like some competent replies to the above to remove the prejudice which may be spread by this most unwarranted assertion. With regard to learning to ride, I cannot do better than record my own experience. I advertised in the *Bicycling News* last autumn, and soon had plenty of replies. I selected a dainty little "Psycho," by Starley Bros., and was much pleased with the machine when it arrived. Unfortunately, the weather was most unpropitious, and my patience was sorely tried; but at last, in a day or two, it cleared up enough for me to make my first attempt, and I sallied forth with my page to meet some friends who were

WELL UP IN CYCLING,

and to receive my first lesson. With the help of a little support, I got on capitally, and was soon able to go alone. I found mounting a little difficult by myself; but, being determined to overcome it, I tried a good many times one day, until I was completely master of it, and then my happiness was complete. I have been used to a tricycle for some years, but I can safely say I much prefer my little two-wheel, and mean to keep it, too, in spite of the long faces of my relations and others. I have not had one fall, though the machine slipped once or twice through my being a little over-hasty, and I have ridden twice down a very steep hill. If the "tyro" does go out to practice "when the milkman is delivering his cans, and the paper-boy crying the news," she will find priceless treasures and renewed health and strength by inhaling the pure, sweet-smelling morning air, and the exquisite scent of the flowers and grass in the spring and summer, and she will return home with a healthy appetite to enjoy her breakfast, and not be too particular as to what it consists of, putting to shame those of her sex who spend most of their nights in the stuffy ball-room or theatre, and finish up by either breakfasting (or trying to breakfast) in bed or else making their appearance so late that, by the time they have taken their first meal, it is nearly time for the next. Need we wonder at their digestions being bad, and at their having no appetites? The knack of mounting is learned in a very short time. The rider takes her machine by the handle, standing on the left, or near side, and wheels it a few paces, until the right pedal is just past the highest point; then, standing well forward, she places her right foot on the said pedal, and springs lightly into her seat, at the same time letting the machine go, which the weight of the rider on the pedal will move; the left foot will soon find its pedal, and she is started before she knows where she is. As to gracefulness, the two machines cannot be compared. It is to the fact of always having to keep your balance on a safety that it owes its gracefulness, as the body must always incline slightly, to whichever side you are steering. It is impossible for any but a good rider to become a proficient; by this I mean one who is naturally good at balancing, for without this capability she will find it almost useless to persist, as it is in this that the secret lies. Any woman can ride a tricycle (or thinks she can); but if "Unknown" had seen the frights that I have seen on them, the doubled-up forms, pounding away in a series of jerks at the pedals, with their shoulders up to their ears, and then stopping to gasp for breath and wipe their perspiring faces, I am sure she could not do otherwise than agree with me as to which was the more graceful of the two. You must have your wits about you when on a safety, or you will soon kiss Mother Earth, whether you will or no. Of course, if people will

RIDE LIKE MANIACS,

they must expect to come to grief; and I, for one, would never sanction tearing down hill, feet up, either for man or woman, especially with only a spoon-brake, which is the only thing I am not satisfied with, and I sincerely hope that band brakes may be fitted as satisfactorily to safeties as they are to tricycles—they will then be perfect. Are women to give up hunting, boating, tennis, riding, etc., because of the terrible accidents which so frequently occur, and which could have been prevented by the use of a little care and prudence? I know which are the true ladies, and I would rather have for my friends those who find innocent pleasure in their outdoor pursuits (though they may be a little rough and uncouth in their manners) than those finicking, small-waisted, deformed little minxes of society who think of nothing but balls, parties, and theatres, and last, but not least, of young men, and who cannot converse upon any subject of ordinary interest. I conclude my remarks with this advice to my sisters—that they should not think so much of what their neighbors say and think about their doings, or their dear but very artificial "Mrs. Grundy," but take their own line in life, studying to be useful, and taking their recreation as a reward for their work, in whatever way they may see fit, as long as it is not wrong in God's sight. I know that propriety must be studied to a certain extent, but be careful you do not make yourself a slave in free England to conventionality."—*Bicycling News*.

THE LADIES' BICYCLE AT POUGHKEEPSIE.

Mr. Theodore W. Roberts, of Poughkeepsie, N. Y., writes us that a number of ladies are interested in cycling, and particularly in the ladies' bicycle. Mr. Roberts testifies that the ladies' bicycle can be ridden without assistance after a very few lessons, Mr. Roberts succeeding in teaching a young lady to ride in the Casino Rink after three lessons, which occupied a total of two hours. The wheel used was a Rambler.

Mr. Roberts remarks that having become accustomed to mounting and dismounting the wheel "lady fashion," he really prefers that way to ordinary mounts and dismounts.

Mr. Roberts tells us that the ladies of Vassar College were quite interested in the sport of cycling last fall, and that the abatement of their interest in the sport is due in no small part to the awkwardness of the tricycle, which they were compelled to use.

Mr. Roberts incloses us the following names of ladies who are interested in cycling: Misses M. Carbutt, M. T. Christie, M. E. Chester, E. H. Griggs, Frances E. Litch and the Misses Van Vliet.

I am told that an arrangement is at present being perfected by which a lady can mount a safety in a quiescent state, and, when she is in the saddle and ready to start, dispense with her support by simply touching a spring. It will be introduced by a firm renowned for its practical novelties, so that, however much I may have scoffed at the idea of standing still on a one-tracker, I cannot express my disbelief in this. I shall hope to announce further particulars in a later issue.—*Violet Lorne in Bicycling News*.

ST. LOUIS.

St. Louis is going to have a big boom in cycling this year—a regular League meet year—from present indications. There are more riders than ever, and more wheels for them to ride. The dealers have nearly all got their cards out and their stock displayed. The St. Louis Wheel Co., handling the Victor line, have moved to larger quarters, on Fourteenth Street, right at the beginning of the Locust Street asphaltum, and are much more snugly fixed up than ever before. The repair shop is located in a separate building, and they have established a stable for wheels, where riders who do not care to ride down town on the granite streets can leave their machines during the day, for a nominal charge. The Warwick Co. have made St. Louis one of their distributing points, with D. Snitjer, No. 1012 Olive Street, as agent, and J. H. Child to look after the details. They will have a local agency besides, with A. A. Knight in charge. This firm will also handle the Springfield roadsters. Wilder & Laing are out at No. 1724 Olive Street with a well-equipped repair shop and a full line of the Gormully & Jeffery wheels. Their location is somewhat inconvenient, but they are enterprising young men and will take pains to let people know where they are and what they have to sell. George Tivy has the "Eagle," and Stars can still be purchased at Meacham's, where Hal Greenwood may be found, as usual, always ready to descant on the merits of that particular style of wheel. There seems to be some uncertainty as to who will handle the Columbia line this year, it being rumored that the Simmons Hardware Co. are going out of the cycle business. However, it is reasonably certain that the Pope Co. will not allow this market to go by default, and when the season opens they will be on hand, as usual. None of the English wheels are regularly represented.

As predicted in my last letter, the consolidation meeting called by the Cycle Club was a failure, none of the clubs taking enough interest in the matter to send representatives. It is true that the cycling clubs are not strong enough financially to stand the expense of a first-class track, and if a combination could be effected with the athletic organizations it would be an excellent idea; but it is obviously impossible, and the only chance that is offered to get any track at all is to join the proposed track association. If a sufficiently large list of subscribers can be secured a good temporary track can be laid, and, with what can be made out of a few economically managed race meetings, a good track could be built next year. So far only about fifty shares have been taken, while at least two hundred are needed. These shares would not go begging if we only had a bit of the enthusiasm of two or three years ago, when the rivalry between the Ramblers and Missouris was so sharp; but, alas! those stirring times have gone, and it takes considerably more than a race-meeting to stir up any enthusiasm nowadays.

I have heard it rumored that Hildebrand tried Corey hill during his recent visit to Boston and failed to get up, but the rumor comes to me in a roundabout way and lacks confirmation. If the rumor should prove to be a fact, I don't believe that Klip will feel heart-broken over it. He had something of an experience on Corey himself.

"Fenton" seems to be an amiable sort of a fellow, albeit a trifle unreasonable in demanding that matters which do not happen to interest him and the wheelmen in his locality shall be summarily "dammed up;" but if it is true, as he states, that he listened "good-naturedly" to the conversation of two Chicago men, at Buffalo, I think we may safely indulge the hope that he will not find his good nature seriously strained if we should happen to give him a little more of the Stone-Lumsden matter occasionally. If he could stand the one, and do it "good-naturedly," the other ought not to trouble him. The fact is, Western wheelmen are intensely interested in these races, and their anxiety for the latest information concerning them ought to be gratified, even at the expense of boring our Eastern friends a little. Don't you think so?

ITHURIEL.

The Pope Manufacturing Company, of Boston, gave a reception and entertainment to wheelmen at their magnificent building, 79 Franklin Street, on last Saturday evening. The entertainment was given both as a dedication of the recent enlargement of its quarters and a celebration of the opening of the riding season. There was a large attendance, and all had a jolly time.

PHILADELPHIA.

The South End wheelmen, with their accustomed activity, are preparing to entertain the Camden wheelmen in their usual royal fashion. This club has always made it a custom to keep up a social intercourse with the other clubs, notably with the Mount Vernons and their Camden neighbors. Anyone who has ever been fortunate enough to attend one of these delightful affairs can never think of it except with pleasure. Although informal, they possess features which would be lacking in a more official reception, making each one sorry when the time comes to leave and everyone wish an early repetition.

The Tioga Athletic Club have a scheme with which they hope to enlist wheelmen in their ranks, and I think it a good one. It is this: The initiation fee of every wheelman who joins will be devoted to building a bicycle track; and, of course, the more wheelmen the better track. Everyone who has a taste for athletics should subscribe, as it is a worthy object. A good track is something that has been sadly lacking in Philadelphia.

Some members of the Century Wheelmen have formed a boxing class, to meet twice a week, one evening for practice, the other for taking lessons, for which they have engaged a prominent professor of the manly art, so that when the time for "smoker" comes again, the boys can present more evenly matched pairs than heretofore.

It is strange what ideas an over-enthusiastic man gets into his head. When the alterations to the Century's new house were being discussed, a member (who was prominently connected with the improvements) thought it would be an excellent plan to start a restaurant in connection with the club. Another member has in view an increase in membership to 350 (when?), and proposes to tear down the back part of the house to accommodate that number of wheels.

It is often said that truth is stranger than fiction, and this was demonstrated not long ago. A new member of one of the prominent clubs is the possessor of a fine new safety wheel. Not long ago while out riding he noticed that one of the pedals worked rather hard (the reason was it was bent). Not knowing anything about the ball bearings, he unscrewed the milled nut, and when he saw the row of balls, just guess what he did. He took them out and threw them away with the remark that some funny "bloke" had put a lot of *shot* in his wheel; he then had the pleasure of walking some distance back to the club-house. That puts me in mind of another member who owns a number of wheels, from a tricycle to a tandem "bike." The other Sunday he was entertaining a number of fellow-clubmen with soul-harrowing stories about hill climbing, and dwelt on one exploit in particular. It was about a certain "stiff" hill in the Park. After he had told how easily he had pushed his wheel up the grade, the quietest man in the room broke him all up by saying, "Were you on the wheel when you went up?" The silence was awful! No one had the heart to laugh except the club kid, and then *the* club liar got a chance to work his little gag. Talk about a madman. Ye gods!

ARGUS.

Philadelphia, April 1, 1889.

RICHFIELD SPRINGS, N. Y.

The members of the Waiontha Bicycle Club, of this village, assisted by local talent, will present, some time during the latter part of April, the well-known drama, "Our American Cousin." Peculiar interest is attached to this play, as it was being presented at Ford's Theatre the evening Lincoln was assassinated.

A twelve-mile run around Lake Canadarago is a very popular one with local wheelmen, who look forward with much expectancy to the first run of the season. On April 27, 1888, Captain August Kinne and Dr. D. P. Bailey, of the local club, made the first trip.

At present the roads are in a terrible condition, quite discouraging to early runs. Snowstorms occasionally prevail, and the probabilities are that it will not be good wheeling until May.

The annual election of officers of the Waiontha Club will occur Wednesday evening, April 24. The efficiency of the present incumbents will doubtless recommend them for re-election.

The safety type of wheels, popularly known as "goats," has become quite popular here. Several business men of the place ride them. Our wheel agents are quite partial to them, and from present indications Richfield will have a large number of safety riders ere the season closes.

Several prominent wheelmen of this vicinity suggest that a fifty-mile road race be added to the programme of the 1889 tournament of the Waiontha Club. The course to be around Lake Canadarago, finishing on a half-mile race-track, where the meet will be held. The proposed course is twelve miles in length, and is usually in prime condition in July or August, during which months the race will occur. The more enthusiastic have strongly favored the project, and doubtless will make the race a certainty. The prizes will be worthy the presence of the best men, who may rest assured of fair treatment in all respects. "BUZZ."

March 30, 1889.

MARYLAND.

It is stated in last week's WHEEL that the Maryland Club was the only one that owned its club-house. Since then it has been learned that the Crescent Club also owns its club-house, which is situated on North Avenue. The house is handsomely furnished, and shortly after Easter will be formally opened. The club has at present thirty-two members, among whom are some of the best riders in the city. This club will enter the races for the cup in Druid Hill Park in the autumn.

The Maryland Club are thinking about having their club-house enlarged and further improvements made. This club is in a prosperous condition. It now has ninety-four active members and about eighty additional members. Its limit to both lists is 100.

A bicycle club will be organized in a few weeks at Easton, Talbot County, Md. There are twenty-five riders there and the number will increase as the season advances. Comparatively few of the riders are members of the League now, as they say they cannot see what benefits would accrue to them from joining it. The roads in Talbot County are in pretty good condition for cycling, and a 100-mile spin can be easily had. Every year a number of Baltimore cyclists go there for a few days, and generally have a good time. The County Commissioners will be petitioned to have the roads thoroughly scraped about twice a year, and when that is done they will be in excellent condition for cycling.

The Maryland Club had a dance on Thursday, March 28, at their club house on Mount Royal Avenue. About a dozen couples were present and all had an enjoyable time.

At a meeting of the Baltimore Club the advisability of changing the color of their uniform was discussed. The uniform, which at present is blue, will very likely be changed to steel-gray, of regulation cut, and will be trimmed with wide black braid.

Application has been made to the Mayor to have the officers patrolling Eutaw Place instructed to arrest all wheelmen riding there at a speed of more than ten miles an hour. There is a temptation to travel fast on the asphalt block pavement and racing speed is not uncommon. It was to break up this practice that the application was made.

About fifteen members of the Maryland Club spent last Sunday at Middle River.

There is a general demand for the safety bicycle in this city.

Isaac Hinds, one of the fastest riders of the Baltimore Club, met with a serious accident not long since. He was returning from the park, where he was training, and while coasting down Eutaw Place took a header, striking on the asphalt blocks with such force as to render him unconscious. One of his teeth was knocked out, his chin split open and his head and body terribly bruised. He has been confined to his bed for a week and his physician says it will be some time before he can get out.

BAY RIDGE.

The Louisville Cycle Club held its twelfth regular meeting last week, at the residence of Mr. C. G. Lucas. Three new members—Edward Hergel, E. H. Vernon and Chas. Grunwald, Jr.—were added to the roll. The club decided on a blue yacht cloth, with blue stockings and cap, as a club suit.

SINGER & CO.'S AMERICAN HOUSE.

One of the finest cycle depots in Boston is Singer & Co.'s branch house, on Berkeley Street. Their store, being on a corner, is especially well lighted. It is fitted up as a handsome salesroom; the wheels, as well as everything about the place, are scrupulously clean. The floors are covered with a bright pattern of linoleum. A portion of the store is fitted up as a counting room.

Messrs. Singer & Co.'s wheels have long been imported into this country, formerly by Mr. W. B. Everett, and at present by the company, their resident manager and American representative being Mr. W. L. Ross. Mr. Ross reported that the business of last year was large enough to more than gratify the parent house, and this year the wheels are shipped off as fast as they are taken out of the Custom-house.

A very complete line of cycles is manufactured by this concern. The leader this year is the Safety, a rear-driver of the highest quality, with a strong weldless steel tube frame and combined saddle and spring. The other dwarf types made by Singer & Co. are the Royal Singer and the Ladies' Safety. The firm's Safety Tandem, which has a loop frame, so that either a lady or gentleman may occupy the front seat, is a combination of the Royal Safety and the Ladies' Safety; price, $220

The high-grade Ordinary of this firm is the Apollo, a light roadster of the highest grade, containing all the features of a highest-grade wheel. Singer's Challenge bicycle is a strong roadster bicycle at the moderate price of $100. Singer's Challenge bicycle is a thoroughly good Ordinary, of lower grade than the Challenge, and sells for $75. One of the most successful wheels ever turned out by Singer & Co. is its Boys' Safety, a high-grade miniature wheel; price, $60.

Singer & Co.'s tricycles have long been in high favor with riders and with the trade. A really good tricycle for young riders is Singer's miniature tricycle; price, $70. The leading full-grown single three-wheeler is Singer's "SSS," which may be called celebrated, so popular is it. The weight is 90 lbs., and the price is $175. A modified form of this wheel admits of the tricycle being reduced from 36 inches to 22 inches in width, for purposes of storage. The reducible wheel is sold at $185. The special "SSS" tricycle is convertible; price, $165. A cheaper form of the "SSS" tricycle, a strong and reliable wheel, is put on the market at $60. The Singer tandem tricycle has as great a reputation as the single. It is strong, safe, comfortable and convertible; price, $250.

The firm handles an extensive line of sundries, among them the "Invincible" head lamp for safeties and tricycles; price, $6. At their Boston headquarters is a completely equipped repair shop, with skillful machinists.

HOLMES & COMPANY'S CATALOGUE.

Messrs. Holmes & Co.'s 1889 catalogue is a neatly printed illustrated pamphlet of sixteen pages. This firm has recently removed to a handsome building on Kingston Street, Boston, where they occupy a large floor. The head of the firm, Mr. Holmes, has made a close study of hygienic clothing, and is constantly inventing new designs in Jersey-fitting and athletic garments. The firm have nearly fifty different styles of garments described in their catalogue, of which a few of the leading styles are mentioned.

Jersey-fitting shirt, long sleeves, standing collar, $3 to $4. Same quality, with long sleeves, turn-over collar and laced front, $3 to $4. Shirt with long sleeves, no collar and low neck, $2.50 to $3.50. Low-neck shirt, short sleeves, $2.25 to $3. Sleeveless and collarless gymnasium shirt, $1.50 to $2.50. Full Jersey-fitting tights, $2 to $3.50; heavy rib, double seat and pocket. Knee tights, $1.50 to $3. Racing tights, light, medium or heavy weight, $2 to $2.50. Holmes' thigh stockings, improved over styles of previous years, $2.50. Jersey-fitting supporter, $1. Jersey-fitting stocking, assorted colors, $1 to $1.50. The garments are knit, fit close to the body, and their weight is equally distributed.

PLEASED WITH THE IMPROVEMENT.

MR. F. P. PRIAL:

Dear Sir—I am pleased to note the steady improvement in your paper, and would not be without it for three times its cost. Wishing you continued success,

I remain,
Very truly yours,
ART. W. COWDIN,
Delphos, Ohio.

THE LATE H. L. CORTIS, ENGLISH AMATEUR CHAMPION.

FIXTURES.

April 25, 1889.—Cambridge Bicycle Club's last Ladies' Night of the season.

April 26, 1889.—Manhattan Bicycle Club's Reception, at West End Hall, 125th Street.

May 10, 1889.—Twelfth Regiment Games. Entries close May 4 with C. J. Leach, P. O. Box 3,201.

May 11, 1889.—Harvard Bicycle Club Open Amateur Race Meet at Cambridge, Mass. Entries close May 4 Address R. H. Davis, Cambridge, Mass.

May 13-18, 1889.—Chicago Cycling Exhibit and Tournament, Exposition Building.

May 18, 1889—F. A. Elwell's European Party sails from New York.

May 18, 1889.—Stone-Lumsden 1-mile Match Race, at Chicago, Ill.

May 25, 1889.—Stone-Lumsden 3-mile Match Race, at St. Louis, Mo

May 27, 1889.—Stone-Lumsden 25-mile Match Race at Crawfordsville, Ind.

May 30, 1889.—Maine Division Meet, at Biddeford, Me.

June 8, 1889.—Century Run, Orange, N. J., to Philadelphia. Chairman, L. A. Clarke, 25 Broad Street, New York.

July 2, 3, 4, 1889.—Hagerstown, Md., Meet.

WHEEL GOSSIP.

Several very gratifying bits of intelligence come to us from the Emerald Isle, which will be of interest to English lady riders. I am told that the spectacle of ladies doing their shopping awheel in Dublin has become too common to excite remark; that the ladies' club has already settled its list of meets for the coming season, and that the number of ladies making inquiries about machines at the various depots has been so particularly large as to raise high hopes as to the amount of feminine recruits in this year of grace. When I remember the holy horror with which—not so many years ago, either—an Irish lady, to whom I ventured to enlarge on the fascinating subject of cycling, threw up her hands and exclaimed, in accents of consternation, "Thank goodness, *Irishwomen* haven't taken to that style of thing, at all events!" I can only congratulate my sisters across the Channel upon the happy change.—*Violet Lorne in Bicycling News.*

Master Slaughter, a 3½-year-old boy, of Coventry, England, is the proud owner of a 12½-pound tricycle.

Entries for the Pullman road race this year will close May 10. The handicaps will be allotted May 12, add will be published after the Chicago Tournament.

The Missouri Bicycle Club has extended to all Chicago wheelmen, through N. I. Miles, an invitation to attend the Stone-Lumsden race on May 25, and remain over the next day as guests of the club. Quite a number will accept.

J. W. Schoefer, Brooklyn Bicycle Club, has joined the Berkeley Athletic Club, and has started to train on the club track at Berkeley Oval. Schoefer will ride a Columbia racer.

A. E. Schaaf, representing the Gormully & Jeffery Manufacturing Company, was in New York on Wednesday.

W. H. Schumacher, L. I. W., who has removed from Brooklyn to Hempstead, L. I., will train on the Queens' track this season. He will ride a Columbia racing wheel.

Wm. Fish, long connected with his uncle, Warren L. Fish, in the manufacture of saddles, has taken his degree and established himself as a dentist at Roseville, N. J.

Messrs. A. G. Spalding & Bros. have just opened a photographic department at their New York house. The firm will carry a full line of cameras, lenses, amateur outfits and photographic apparatus, materials and supplies of all kinds. The department will be under the charge of A. B. Harkman and Frank Horland, the latter of the Brooklyn Bicycle Club, and well known as the Armory fiend on account of his scientific method of getting around indoor tracks. The growth of photography and the resources of Messrs Spalding & Bros. insure success to the photographic department.

"Senator" Morgan was in Gotham on Wednesday. He returned to Chicago in the evening. He will remain at Omaha for at least a month, and will then go to Chicago until the tournament is over. After that he may go to Europe, but that is only a probability. He reports that the women who engage in the six-day races now wear skirts, so that the managers of the girls were not jumped upon without good results. Mr. Morgan says that the "best people" of Omaha attended the races. This is rather hard on the "best people," or else the show has become respectable, which it was not when held in New York.

Charles Richards Dodge sailed for Europe on Saturday.

Frank Egan is writing cycling notes for the New York *Press.*

The theatre party of the Harlem Wheelmen at the Grand Opera House, on Saturday night, was a grand success. The boys went stag. They were much surprised, however, on their arrival to see in one of the boxes, seated and smiling, the lady members of the club. One by one the boys, headed by Emanuel "Don't-you-see," left their seats in the orchestra and joined the fair ones. The ladies will be invited to the next party given by the club.

The Harvard Bicycle Club will give an open race meet on May 11. Six hundred dollars in prizes will be distributed among seven events. The prizes are the most appropriate and valuable ever offered outside of Springfield or Buffalo.

The Holmes Field track, at Harvard College, Cambridge, Mass., is one of the best in the country. It is a quarter-mile, oval-shaped, with easy corners and a very hard, springy surface. The Harvard cycling team commenced training on it Thursday, March 28.

Van Sicklen denies that he will race this year. His business occupies all his time.

Trade is very brisk in Chicago Big stories are being told as to the number of wheels sold.

F. E. Armitage, of Kingston, N. Y., has been appointed agent by Messrs. Merwin, Hulbut & Co.

On last Friday afternoon a number of prominent newspaper men of Boston met in the *Herald* office and organized a cycle club. Mr. Chas. W. Fourdrinier, of the *Bicycling World*, was chosen temporary Chairman, and Mr. J. C. Morse temporary Secretary. Messrs. S. A. Wetmore and J. C. Kerrison, of the *Herald*, and E. R Tilton, of the *Post*, were appointed a nominating committee, and Messrs. Drake, of the *Journal*; Howard, of the *Globe*, and Draper, of the *Herald*, were appointed a committee to draft a constitution and by-laws. The meeting then adjourned to Monday, April 8. Applicants for membership are requested to send their names and addresses to the temporary Secretary, Mr. Morse, of the *Herald*.

Lumsden, the noted Chicago rider, has been sick and is now recovering. His illness will not prevent him from getting into trim for the coming season.

Burley B. Ayres, the well-known Chicago wheelman, has taken a position on the Milwaukee and St. Paul Railroad. He will hereafter reside at Milwaukee.

Wheelmen all over the country should use their utmost endeavors to secure the passage of the many road bills and liberty bills that are now being drawn up and introduced to the legislatures of the several States.

The Potomac Wheel Club has been organized at Cumberland, Md. M. A. C. Wilson is temporary Chairman and Jas. D. Winslow temporary Secretary.

The Kingston Knitting Company's line of athletic, gymnasium, bicycle and general out-door goods is more complete than their line of last year, so well and favorably known to the trade. The company has a line of bicycle jerseys in every variety of shade, long-sleeved, sleeveless, with single or double collars or low-necked. The company also manufactures a line of high-grade jerseys, knee-tights, full-body tights and pants.

We call attention to the Butcher Cyclometer Co.'s announcement, which will be found in our advertising pages. The mile measure marketed by this firm is second to none in reputation and has been repeatedly tested and used with good results when accuracy was the desideratum.

CENTURY WHEELMEN'S NEW CLUB-HOUSE.

The Century Wheelmen, on Saturday last, moved into their magnificent new quarters at No. 1605 North Broad Street, Philadelphia, which the club purchased a few weeks ago, and have since been engaged in altering so as to conform to the requirements of a wheeling club. Owing to the burning of the Columbia Avenue Market House the Century Club were enabled to dispose of the lease of their old house, located on Broad Street, above Montgomery Avenue, to the Columbia Social Club, who had occupied rooms in the market house, and they were therefore enabled to take possession of their new home much earlier than they had expected to, and before the carpenters were out of the building.

The house is just above Oxford Street, convenient to the asphalt, which begins at Columbia Avenue, and has a frontage of twenty-five feet, with a lot 150 feet running back to Carlisle Street. The lower story is of brown stone, set back from the street, with the second, third and fourth stories of brick, with brown stone trimmings. On the right of the wide hallway are the spacious parlors, which are to be furnished in a style second to none in the city and which will be used for the reception of the club's visitors. Back of these come the ladies' reception rooms, and in what was the kitchen will be the boiler for heating the water for the bath-rooms, there being several in the building, the principal one of which is located on the second floor, immediately back of the locker and dressing room. Adjoining the house proper an addition to the building is now in course of erection, 65 by 25 feet, which will be used as the wheel room of the members, with an outlet on Carlisle Street. It will be completed in a week or two, and meanwhile the machines are stored in the reception rooms. Above the wheel house a gymnasium will be built within a year, which will be completely equipped for its purpose, forming a strong inducement for the associate membership.

On the second story is the meeting room, 17 by 34 feet, with the secretary's office adjoining, and locker, dressing and bath rooms in the back building, all of which are being fitted up with the latest conveniences. A billiard and pool room large enough to accommodate three tables is on the third story, front, with the living apartments of the janitor's family in the rear, while the rooms on the fourth floor are to be used for athletic purposes, one being devoted to fencing, another to boxing and a third to wrestling. Ample room for storage is on this floor, the house containing seventeen rooms and the club not utilizing all of them at present.

It will probably be a month before the alterations are all made, and it is the intention of the wheelmen to give a house-warming that will be a memorable event in the annals of the club.

The Century Wheelmen have been in existence about three years and now number one hundred and thirty men. The officers are as follows : President, Thomas Hare ; Vice-President, C. A. Snyder ; Secretary, R. C. Swayse ; Treasurer, Dr. Fruhe ; Captain, Mr. Carter.

FOR SALE, EXCHANGE, WANTS.

THE CHICAGO CYCLING EXHIBIT AND TOURNAMENT.

The Chicago Cycling Exhibit and Tournament, which is to be held from May 13 to 18 inclusive, promises to be a success. Preparations for the great event are going on rapidly. The Western wheelmen are strongly interested, and are exerting themselves with more than their usual activity.

During the past week a general meeting was held, at which the greatest enthusiasm was manifested. A Business Committee, consisting of Messrs. J. M. Erwin, Lincoln C. C.; Frank Riggs, Illinois C. C.; N. H. Van Sicklen, Chicago C. C.; E. T. M'Pike, Oakland W. C.; Thomas Bray, Aeolus C. C.; H. J. Gottheil, Douglas C. C., and Geo. Dennison, Englewood C. C., has been appointed to assist W. I. Niles in electing committees for various duties. The president of each club was also requested to appoint two of the members of his club to serve as a reception committee. It was considered impossible to arrange to meet all trains, but large parties, notifying the committee in advance of their intended visit, will be met and cared for upon their arrival. For those who arrive in small parties, headquarters will be established at which some one will always be in attendance.

The Racing Committee will meet this week and arrange the programme, which, among other events, will contain the following : Scratch events, 1 and 3 mile novices ; 1 mile for men who have never raced ; 2 miles for members of suburban clubs only ; quarter mile dash, open ; 1 mile, 3 minute class ; 2 miles, 4 minute class ; 3 miles, 6.20 class ; 1 mile safety Rover type, open ; 1 mile flying start, open ; 5 miles, open ; half mile unicycle, open ; 2 miles tandem, open ; 10 miles, open. Handicaps, 1 mile safety, Rover type, 1, 2, 3 and 10 miles, open ; 1 mile, local, Lamsden, Van Sicklen, Roe and Winship ; 1 mile lap under 16 ; 1 mile lap under 17 ; 2 miles. L. A. W. members only. Special events, 3 mile team race, open or teams of three from any club in the world ; club drill and fancy riding.

Two thousand cycling photographs will be on exhibition. They will include the champions of America, England, Ireland, Scotland, France, Germany and Australia, besides celebrated newspaper men, manufacturers and officers of various institutions.

The exhibit of wheels is expected to be the largest ever seen in America ; but as there are over 30,000 feet of available space, there will be no crowding, and each exhibitor will be able to secure a desirable location.

Letters are received daily from all directions, which indicate that in the matter of attendance the Chicago tournament will compare favorably with any that has gone before.

DR. W. G. KENDALL,

Captain Boston Bicycle Club.

"IRVY" HALSTED AT TACOMA, W. T.

Another gentleman, well known in athletic circles in the East, is Mr. E. I. Halsted, the bicyclist, who is interested in the Adamant Manufacturing Company, soon to begin operations here. Mr. Halsted is a member of the Harlem Wheelmen and New York Athletic Club, and has a brilliant record of victories in hotly contested races in New York and New Jersey. His business will require most of his attention, but his lively interest in bicycling is attested by the fact that he has now on the road, somewhere between this city and New York, two of his "machines," one of them being a light bicycle on which he will doubtless show some of the Tacoma wheelmen what fast riding really means. Mr. Halsted is also much interested in the plan for an athletic park, and so far as his business will permit, will aid in its establishment.—*Tacoma Globe.*

On Saturday, March 23, Wm. A. Clark, of Stamford, Conn., mounted on his "Eagle" machine, rode over to Greenwich and succeeded in climbing the steep grade which is known as "Put's Hill." The grade is one foot in nine, increasing to one in seven or eight at the top, and is a hundred yards or more in length. The surface is one mass of imbedded cobbles, with a generous sprinkling of loose ones.

Read and Remember

That Ladies can learn to ride the Ladies' Safety Bicycle at

ADELPHI HALL,

52d Street and Broadway,

NEW YORK.

Only a few lessons necessary to become proficient.

Competent and experienced instructors in charge.

Lessons private; only two pupils on the floor at one time.

Floor 80x100, affording ample space for satisfactory instructions and practice.

Gentlemen also instructed in the use of the Safety or regular bicycle.

Classes now forming.

Engagements for *lessons* may be entered in advance, and special hours reserved.

Applications for lessons should be made at my office.

Send for further particulars and terms.

GEO. R. BIDWELL,

313 W. 58th St.,

NEW YORK.

The New "FISH" SAFETY SADDLE

FOR 1889.

AT LAST! AT LAST!

A Cycle Saddle which cannot be improved.

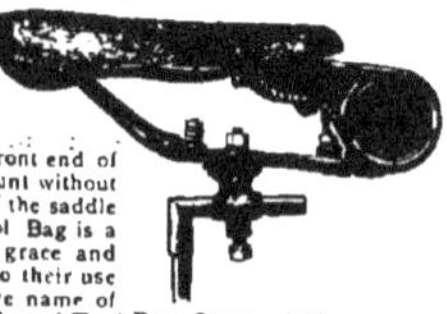

The accompanying cut represents *this* saddle and speaks for itself. It is perfectly adapted to either sex. The frame is jointed, and this, in combination with the springs in the front and rear of saddle, entirely removes vibration, and gives a soft, settling motion, without the usual sagging. It is adjustable to any angle by a simple contrivance underneath the stretcher plate. The front end of top is rounded so as to allow a lady to mount or dismount without danger of catching her skirts. Every desirable action of the saddle to suit the most fastidious rider is obtained. The Tool Bag is a special novelty, and all combined presents a form of grace and beauty. Ladies will find these saddles better adapted to their use than any other now on the market. In ordering give name of machine, also whether for lady or gent. Price of Saddle and Tool-Bag, $7.00. Address,

WARREN L. FISH, 69 Roseville Ave., Newark, N. J.

SINGER CYCLES.

Valuable Novelties for 1889.

The "Singer" Safety made during 1888 gave entire satisfaction to the thousands who used it.

To the new pattern several valuable improvements have been added, the frame being of improved shape and great strength, and a perfect ball steering included. Also a direct plunger brake of increased power.

We can most strongly and confidently recommend this cycle.

Specification.—30 inch wheels speeded to 57 in. (or 54 in.), patent spring wired tires (⅞ in. to back wheel, ¾ in. to front wheel), SINGER BALL STEERING, ball bearings to all running parts, including pedals, weldless steel tube frame, handle-bar and forks, guard to both wheels and to chain, brake, foot-rests, lamp-holder, best combined saddle and spring, spanner, "Singer" ball pedals, etc., etc. Enameled, and with parts plated.

Price $135.00.

A full line of SINGER CYCLES now in stock.

MERWIN, HULBERT & CO.

26 West 23d Street, New York.

THE SAMUEL WINSLOW SKATE MFG. CO.,

WORCESTER, MASS.

Manufacturers of Ice and Roller Skates and

THE "VINEYARD" BICYCLE.

STRONG, DURABLE AND CHEAP.

As good as the best for road and business purposes.

FOR BOYS AND MEN.

Diameter Front Wheel	Front Tire.	Diameter Rear Wheel.	Rear Tire.	Weight all on.	Length of leg inside to sole of foot.	Price.
38 inch	¾ inch	14 inch	⅝ inch	31 lbs.	27 inch	$35.00
42 inch	¾ inch	14 inch	⅝ inch	33 lbs.	29 inch	40.00
44 inch	¾ inch	16 inch	⅝ inch	35½ lbs.	30 inch	45.00
46 inch	⅞ inch	16 inch	¾ inch	38 lbs.	31 inch	50.00
48 inch	⅞ inch	16 inch	¾ inch	39½ lbs.	32 inch	55.00
50 inch	⅞ inch	16 inch	¾ inch	41 lbs.	33 inch	60.00

Orders solicited from dealers. Descriptive Catalogue and discounts sent on application.

| Vol. III.—No. 7.] | NEW YORK, APRIL 12, 1889. | [Whole Number, 59. |

Albany, N. Y., March 27, 1889.

Messrs. GORMULLY & JEFFERY:

Gentlemen—I feel great pleasure in communicating to you the appreciation I feel for your American Rambler. .When I purchased the Rambler, I did so believing it the best cycle to be had, but since using it it has so far outstripped my best anticipations that I feel it a duty as well as a pleasure to inform you that to my mind it stands **unrivaled**. I have used it on all sorts of roads and have given it every conceivable test, and have found it, not alone the lightest and easiest-running, but the most elastic and thoroughly reliable cycle I have ever ridden. It is certainly the culmination of mechanical art. I shall be very glad to recommend it in every instance to those of my friends who anticipate a purchase.

Very truly yours,

J. L. ADRIAN,

Albany, N. Y.

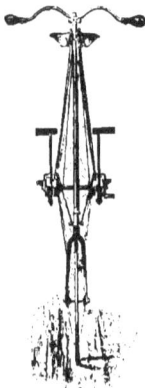

THE NATIONAL SAFETY.

Price, with Ball Bearings to Wheels, **$75**
"   "   "   all round,   **90**

A First-Class Safety at a Reasonable Price. Rear wheel, 30 inches, geared to 54 ; 30 inch steering wheel ; ⅞-inch crescent steel rims and ⅞ inch best quality rubber tires ; direct spokes, of special drawn steel wire of best quality ; cranks adjustable from 5½ to 6½ inch throw ; chains of special patent ; vulcanite handle-grips ; wheels fitted with ball bearings ; adjustable suspension saddle, with coiled rear and front springs. Spade handle, if desired.

The National Ladies' Safety.

Price, with Ball Bearings to both Wheels, **$75**
"   "   "   all over,   **90**

This Wheel is of the same general style as the men's wheel, except for the loop frame.

WILLIAM HALPIN & CO.,

No. 13 MURRAY STREET,

P. O. Box 2225.   NEW YORK.

Full Line of "Warwicks."   Full Line of "Clubs."
Large Stock of "American" Cycles.

AGENTS WANTED IN EVERY CITY AND TOWN IN NEW YORK STATE.

SECOND-HAND WHEELS.

THE WHEEL

—AND—

CYCLING TRADE REVIEW,

Published every Friday morning.

Entered at the Post Office at second class rates.

Subscription Price, - - - $1.00 a year.
Foreign Subscriptions, - - - 6s. a year.
Single Copies, - - - - - 5 Cents.

Newsdealers may order through AM. NEWS Co.

All copy should be received by Monday.
Telegraphic news received till Wednesday noon.

Advertising rates on Application.

F. P. PRIAL, Editor and Proprietor
23 Park Row,

P. O. Box 444, *New York.*

Persons receiving sample copies of this paper are respectfully requested to examine its contents and give us their patronage, and as far as is convenient, aid in circulating the journal, and extend its influence in the cause which it so faithfully serves. Subscription price, $1 per year.

Why Not Employ Convict Labor on Public Roads?

On the second day of August, 1888, the fifteen hundred men confined in the New York State Prison at Sing Sing were cast into legalized idleness, paralyzed by law, as it were, and from that time until the present day no hum of industry has been heard within the prison walls. The law which caused this sinful waste of manpower was conceived and coddled through the Legislature by a combination of whimpering manufacturers who found themselves unable to compete with convict labor, and who claimed that their interests suffered, which, translated from the jargon of corporate monopoly, means that these convicts worked out a small proportion of contracts which otherwise might fall to them, and they wanted that small proportion.

It seems somewhat incomprehensible, leaving out all considerations of lobby and boodle, that no strong objections were raised against this bill, for many objections there are. It was an unnatural and therefore unconstitutional waste of force, out of harmony with the economy of nature. It created 1,500 self-supporting profit-makers into 1,500 miserable paupers, charges on the people they had disgraced or plundered.

The object of a properly operated judiciary department, according to latter-day opinion, is to remove from society the human birds of prey who sin against it—who jeopardize its harmony, its safety and its property. The process of sifting the chaff of vice and dishonesty from the wheat of respectability and honesty is an expensive enough process. Why, therefore, should society, which is compelled to pay for the process, be further mulcted to maintain the impurities it has cast off? This consideration, reinforced by a contemplation of the effect of idleness on closely confined men, should have been enough to defeat the bill. It does not weaken the argument to admit that certain manufacturing interests suffered in competition with contract labor. Trade is largely speculative and should be self-protective. A tradesman must be

prepared to encounter scores of ever-varying conditions, over some of which he has no control, and must be prepared to employ his capital in more profitable fields when conditions master him.

The unhealthy effect of casting 1,500 illy fed caged men into complete stagnation cannot be over-estimated. The sum total of misery endured by these men is incalculable. We consider our selves badly off should we pass a sleepless, restless night, yet these men retire to their cells, night after night, to toss about on their cots in utter misery until the morning. It is scarcely in accord with modern humane ideas to maintain that these law-breakers are treated no worse than they deserve. Before deciding on such a harsh conclusion, we must recollect that few of them are naturally bad, that the majority are where they are by reason of conditions outside of themselves; that birth, inheritance, circumstances and the natural gravitation toward depravity, which is our common lot, have driven them to the felon's cell. They are entitled to mercy as well as to justice.

A number of plans have been suggested to mitigate the evils of this idle prison life. The Governor of the State has given some considerable thought to the subject, but the plan of employing the convicts on the roads of the State, a phase of the question quite familiar to roads-improvement enthusiasts, seems never to have been seriously discussed by the State Legislature. Surely this plan must commend itself to our law-makers at Albany. The convicts, instead of being penned up in our great institutions, could be sent to small prisons in different parts of the State, from which they could readily and safely be conveyed to their work of building and maintaining the roads. They could be much better handled in smaller prisons. Their health, both of mind and body, would be much improved, and they would be of some use to the people, rather than a charge on them, as they are at present. From the New York *Sun* we republish some statements recently made by the principal keeper of Sing Sing, Mr. Connaughton:

"Is insanity on the increase among the prisoners? Yes, it is, and it is increasing very rapidly. What can you expect when the men have no work? It is worse for them to be confined in idleness than to be at hard labor. The present system is inhuman, and out of mere regard for society, and without considering the feelings of the convicts, we ought to have a change and have something for the 1,500 prisoners to do, so that they won't go crazy on our hands."

Out in the prison yards ten files of prisoners were shuffling over the ground walks. Each of the ten files numbered 100 men. The leader of each line of convicts seemed to be the only man who had anything with which to busy his mind. The man behind held his hands on the leader's sides under the armpits, and so on to the one-hundredth fellow; but all the ninety-nine who followed the leader walked mechanically, held their eyes mechanically to the right, each of the ninety-nine pairs being fixed at just such an angle and all being as devoid of expression as the eyes of an old-fashioned wooden Indian on a cigar store's steps. Their faces are dull and listless, and when their eyes meet yours it is only in a vacant stare.

And yet these men, while thus walking about their eyes mechanically to the right, each of the ten, are supposed to take exercise, themselves. This walking is their only work, their only recreation. They are at it hour after hour during the day. It is all they have to do. Some of them know that they will have nothing more to do for five, ten, twenty years, some for life, and all know that they will have to keep up this walking as long as they are under the banishment of Sing Sing. It is the knowledge that they must walk, walk, walk, and do nothing else but walk, that is making insanity increase among the convicts.

Mr. Connaughton says that in the fiscal year ending last October there were four men who

had to be sent to asylums because they had become insane. In the first five months of this fiscal year there have been eight more sent away for insanity. At this rate there would be seventeen or eighteen cases of insanity developed this year among the prisoners, or more than four times as many as last year. Night after night the corridors ring with the noise of men whose minds are breaking down. They throw themselves about their cells and rap on their barred doors, and the prison apothecary has to be on duty all night long to administer opiates when other means of quieting the unfortunates have failed.

"I do not go to my rooms any evening," said Mr. Connaughton, "but that I expect surely to be called time after time during all the night to attend to some prisoner who is losing his head because he hasn't work. I tell you it is a fearful condition of affairs. Here are 1,500 men in absolute idleness. Almost all of them are accustomed to manual labor. They don't get it, and naturally at the end of each day they don't find themselves tired enough to go to sleep. The walking doesn't tire them enough. It is the best we can do for them, but it is only exercise for the legs, for in the lock step they can't swing their arms. Then, you see, too, that walking in files is nothing that requires them to use their minds. It is simply to follow the leader, and in the lock step the walking is all mechanical. The result is that the poor fellows can't sleep. They toss on their cots, and night after night lie awake until morning. Sickness comes, then they get to worrying; they beg for work and it doesn't come; their worry increases, and the first thing we know this man or that man breaks down and is half insane. We can't do much in these cases. Sometimes we put a sick man with a well man, and have to depend upon the well man to quiet the other fellow in case he breaks out. When the men had work we used to have from ten to fifteen cases in the hospital every day, but nearly all of them were there because of feet burned in the foundries or because of accidents that happened to them while they were at work. Now, when there is nothing to do, there are from twenty-two to twenty-eight cases in the hospital every day. None of these are due to accidents or burned feet. Some, of course, are cases of natural sickness, but almost all are due to the worry caused by lack of work."

The following editorial from the New York *Tribune* is a true summing up of the question:

The State Legislature should be put under the strongest pressure of public opinion until it provides work for the convicts in the State prisons and penitentiaries. Just now there are several bills pending with this object in view, but a strong opposition to each one of them has been shown, and between apathy on one side and reluctance on the other there is danger that the session may come to an end before action is taken in the matter. That would be worse than a misfortune. It would subject the Legislature to a responsibility little, if at all, short of being criminal, and it would entail lasting evil and discredit upon the State of New York. To have to repeat the fundamental principles which teach the cruelty, folly and barbarism of keeping hundreds of prisoners without any employment is indeed humiliating, for it seems to involve a distinct retrogression in the intelligence which governs the Legislature. It is certainly a sharp and caustic commentary. But the situation is too grave to justify neglect of any opportunity to stimulate our sluggish and backward representatives to do their plain duty, and therefore it must again be insisted upon that society has no warrant in ethics for inflicting its criminals such penalties as are involved in enforced idleness during the service of a penal sentence.

Idle convicts, if secluded, suffer in their intelligence. Solitary confinement without occupation will overthrow the strongest mind. Confinement which is not solitary tends always to the debauching of the convicts without work. To herd together the vicious trained and inclined and deprive them of engrossing work is to subject all who graduate with the highest distinction those who entered the prison types and neophytes. Lawmakers too obtuse to realize the extent of the wrong done the convicts in exposing them to these debasing influences may be acute enough to perceive that if our prisons

are so managed as to make criminals worse instead of better the public will have to pay a high price for this experiment in the steady growth and intensification of crime. For we cannot convert State prisons into schools of vice without paying for the support of the scholars and finding exercise for their talents when they return to the world. Heavier taxation, therefore, is what the present situation signifies, and a demand for more prisons and police and courts and all the appendices of criminal administration. If the rascals are to be maintained in idleness, in other words, the honest men will have to do extra work to provide for them, and thus New York will present the singular spectacle of a State with an aristocracy of criminals served and supported by a commonalty of upright citizens.

The objection to convict labor based on theories about the competing capacity of its products is chimerical. It has been proved repeatedly that the fancied competition has no actual existence, and is really nothing but a delusion, imposed upon unthinking people for ulterior purposes. But the consequences of indulging this fantastic hypothesis have already been grave, and threaten to be still more so. Society has quite as much ground of complaint, moreover, as the convicts have. It is the taxpayers of New York who are put under the harrow in all such cases. They are the purse-bearers, and all bills for damages are handed to them. If crime increases, if prison expenses are left without offset in remunerative work done, if new outlays are made necessary, it is the taxpayers who must bear the burden. Some of these times the memory of the principal victims may acquire more vigorous tone, and then the representatives who act as if public opinion were a matter of complete indifference to them will experience a disagreeable surprise. At present there is but one course, and that is to insist upon the absolute necessity of agreement upon some one of the pending laws providing work for the convicts. Surround the law with as many precautions as may be thought desirable; but see that the convicts are enabled to return to wholesome and steady work; and remember that picking oakum and breaking stones are not wholesome occupations, though they may be continuous.

WE have received a number of inquiries as to the location of the 1889 League meet, which will be especially significant as the tenth anniversary of the League's existence. The first definite step taken in the matter is in the nature of an intimation to the Baltimore Division that an invitation to Baltimore would be accepted by the League. No action has as yet been taken on the letter.

At the National Assembly meet Mr. George S. Atwater, Chief Consul District of Columbia, informally stated that he would request the District Board of Officers to consider the practicability of entertaining the League in Washington this year. As yet nothing has been done.

It seems that it is asking too much of the Maryland Division to entertain the League two years in succession. From the very commencement of these annual meetings each city has endeavored to out-entertain the other, until St. Louis climaxed with the most unique and well-sustained entertainment a reception it would be difficult to equal. This striving after the intense has made the entertainment of the national body something to be carefully considered—a mammoth entertainment, requiring heavy expenditure of money, time and talent. Entertainment committees have been proverbially worked to death.

We hope that Washington will entertain the League this year. It is a slow city, and there would be no difficulty in getting a representative crowd of League members. The features of the meet might be a general meeting of the character of the annual general meetings—a parade, a race meet, a theatre party and a number of runs. The success of the Baltimore meet rested as much with the men as with the Entertainment Committee, admirably as their work was performed, because of the spirit of good-fellowship and the intention to enjoy which were everywhere apparent. If the meet were held in Washington we feel certain that Baltimore would furnish dessert in the form of a day's entertainment. It is getting late in the season, and the date of the annual meet should be fixed at once.

WE call the attention of club Boards of Officers to the method of electing officers recently adopted by the New York Bicycle Club. This system, which was formulated by one of the clearest parliamentarians in cycling, might be profitably adopted in many clubs, especially in large organizations.

THROUGH the combined efforts of Messrs. Prince Wells and Mr. E. I. Halsted, late of New York City, THE WHEEL will be represented and pushed in the new State of Washington, where wheeling is rapidly developing.

WHEELMEN are vitally interested in securing the passage of the New York State Roads Improvement Bill. The success of the bill depends on the numerical and financial strength of the New York State Division. Every cyclist in the State should join the Division at once. Inclose $2 to Secretary Abbot Bassett, 12 Pearl Street, Boston.

"PERSEUS" ON ELECTING NATIONAL LEAGUE OFFICERS BY POPULAR VOTE.

We desire to give "Perseus'" reply to our recent editorial on the above subject as much publicity as we gave our objections to "Perseus'" views on election by popular vote. "Perseus'" reply, published in the *Sporting Life*, is here reproduced. "Perseus" complains that we erect a wall and then complain that it cannot be scaled. The wall is merely the popular-vote theory, erected by "Perseus," "Bi," Mr. E. J. Shriver and others. The wall represen s what "Perseus" and others think ought to be done. We have simply climbed the wall, looked on one side to see what might be done, looked on the other to see what could not be done, and drew conclusions. "Perseus" is wrong in stating that we have concluded that a national popular vote is impossible. We simply ask, Is it better than the present method of electing; would it give better results, and is it not better to turn the matter over to the National Assembly for extended discussion than to give it incomplete consideration in newspapers which might better devote their time, energy and talent to prosecuting more practical work, as roads improvement, etc.?

We do not believe in always "taking things as they are, not as they ought to be," though we have followed that course on the present occasion. The question has been fully ventilated. Now let "Perseus" and Mr. Shriver, both of whom are members of the National Assembly, present their views at the next meeting of that body. We have not sat down, folded our hands, shaken the head of doubt and sighed the song of the doleful. We have written all we knew for and against popular voting; we have published Messrs. Shriver's and "Perseus'" views, which differed from ours, and then we pass on to the enlargement of our roads-improvement work. Perhaps "Perseus" wants us to devote a weekly column to the popular-vote question from now until next spring, when the National Assembly will meet:

Mr. Prial, of THE WHEEL, answers my inquiry of a short time since, as to why the League officers should not be elected by the membership at large, and while his article is well written and shows careful thought and a thorough knowledge of the subject, I cannot help separating it into three sections, which I shall head, "How to do it," "It cannot be done" and "I give it up," which is about the pith of the argument.

In the first place, he takes for granted that the vote would have to be taken in the same manner as the vote for President in the United States, and, of course, sees all kinds of difficulties in the way. He erects a wall and complains that it cannot be scaled. The vote for national officers could be taken in each State at the same time as the election of State officers is held, thus entailing no extra expense or trouble; each State could be entitled to a certain number of electoral votes in proportion to its League population, and this electoral ticket (an abstract thing, remember) should be elected by a plurality vote. Each State could attend to the appointing of tellers, judges, etc., and the vote could be forwarded by the secretaries to the national secretary, to be in turn counted by another body of tellers and judges appointed by the national board. This is very similar to the scheme for our government elections and could be made to work as well. The first meeting of the national board before the election would be the proper time for the nominations. This would be similar and less cumbersome than the political conventions that meet every four years. The State elections and the national tellers parallel our November elections and the Senate; but the electoral college would exist only in the abstract, and there would be no necessity for a gathering of actual electors at considerable expense. Is not such a plan practicable and simple?

Of course, this can never be done if we follow Mr. Prial's advice to "take things as they are and not as they ought to be." To sit down and fold your hands in your lap, shake your head and dolefully sigh that things are as they are, is not the way to better them; such a course is not consistent with Mr. Prial's professions and his past record.

Of course, there would be a large number who would not take the trouble to cast a vote, but that is not the least reason why the larger number, who would cast their votes, should be disfranchised; and as to sectional feeling being displayed, there is more room for that, and there is more of it, in the board than there would be in the membership at large.

Mr. Prial has certainly failed to present any argument against the scheme of popular enfranchisement, and, in fact, I doubt if he or any one else can.

AN OUTING IN NORTHERN CALIFORNIA.

Six of our local wheelmen made the first run of the season on Sunday, March 31. Leaving Eureka on the 6:30 A. M. train, we reached Singleys Station at 7:15, and were obliged to cross Eel River on the ferry, a somewhat old-fashioned affair, hitched to a wire rope stretched across the river, and propelled by the action of the current. Arriving at the other side, a beautiful scene lay stretched before us; the swift, winding river crept in and out amongst the farms and patches of green like a huge serpent, and everywhere the dew glistened like diamonds. The roads were something grand, being perfectly level and as hard as a board.

We visited several small towns and rode into Ferndale, a town of 1,000 inhabitants, for breakfast, at 9:10, having travelled at the rate of about eight miles an hour. And that breakfast! Verily, it makes my mouth water to think of it. We were off again at 10:30, and, having reached the brow of a small hill, a little east of the town, a sight greeted our eyes that we are not likely to forget. There before us, stretching away as far as the eye could reach, and resembling a large white chalk line drawn on a green background, lay ten miles of the hardest and most level road on the Pacific Coast. Some of you Eastern wheelmen who revel in what you call fine roads and beautiful weather should have been with us that morning.

Well, we scorched those 10 miles in 55 minutes. Here we found another ferry; then 2½ miles of up-hill work against the wind, and then the town of Fortuna. We rested here about two hours, leaving at 2:30 o'clock and arriving at Singleys again (five miles distant) at 2.45. There being two hours yet before train time, we wandered off to a dairy near by and our little (?) half-dozen punished two gallons of rich milk, but, verily, the way of the transgressor is hard. One of the boys remarked an hour later, "Oh! I am so sick."

Our party was composed of Captain Tom Cutler, the Victor agent for our county, riding an 89-in. Victor safety; Mr. Ernest Sevier, one of our leading attorneys, on the same style of machine; Mr. E. H. Burnett, agent for the Springfield Roadster, on one of his own machines; Mr. Ambrose Foster, riding a Champion Light Roadster; Mr. James McNamara, riding a 54-in. Expert Columbia, and your humble servant propelling a 48-in. Challenge (ball-bearing)—"little, but oh my!" We are thinking seriously of forming a club and joining the League. Could you give us some advice and oblige

Yours, etc., STUMP.

Eureka, Cal., April 3.

IT IS NOW

The season when riders are looking over the wheels in the market with critical eyes, and selecting for their use during the season just coming on the wheels that have the most of what are

ACKNOWLEDGED BY ALL

To be the best features in wheel construction. The Victors for '89 are, as ever, at the very front of the market in such respects. They are stronger, handsomer and lighter-running than any others, and you may be sure

THAT THE

Victor devices are the best from the fact that lots of people copy them. The Victor Safety is the only successful spring fork machine. It is finer than anything else of the kind in the market.

VICTORS BEAT THE WORLD!

OVERMAN WHEEL CO., MAKERS,

BOSTON, MASS.

Special Agents,

A. G. SPALDING & BROS.,

NEW YORK AND CHICAGO

PSYCHO WHEELS FOR 1889.

Sole Importers: Capital Cycle Co., Washington, D. C.

The Psycho cycles are imported by the Capital Cycle Company, of Washington, D. C. This firm were the first to recognize the merits of all forms of rear-driving safeties, and in 1885 imported the first one ever brought into this country. They also designed and introduced the first tandem safety in 1886. They designed and manufactured in 1887 the first rear-driving ladies' safety bicycle, and credit should be given them for their efforts in this direction. They have accomplished as much for the weaker sex by reducing friction, weight, and by giving increased pleasure, as did the inventor of the spider wheel for the stronger sex by improving the boneshaker.—*Wheel*.

Psycho Cycles do not have hollow rims, tangent spokes, ball head or spring forks. No change will be made in Psychos over the 1888 pattern. The Fish hammock saddle will be used on all Psychos.

Psycho Cycles are remarkable for their lightness, strength, harmonious and uniform construction, simplicity (fewness of parts) and general gracefulness of design. **Beautifully finished.**

SEVEN FORMS

OF

PSYCHO SAFETIES,

Varying in Weight and Design.

1. **"Men's Straight Frame Psycho Safety,"** 30-inch wheels, ⅞ and ¾ inch tires, geared to 57 inches, weight 47 lbs. Price $140.

2. **"Men's Light Roadster Psycho Safety,"** 30-inch wheels, ⅞-inch tires, made for gentlemen riders and scorchers on good roads, geared to 60 inches (see cut), weight 38 lbs. Price, $140.

3. **"Men's Dropped Frame Psycho Safety"** is designed like ladies' safety (see cut), 30-inch wheels, ⅞ and ¾ inch tires, weight 50 lbs. Will stand any weight on any road. Detachable brace rod makes it suitable for ladies and a general family machine. Price, $140. Geared to 57 inches.

4. **"Ladies' Roadster Psycho Safe-ty,"** ⅞-inch tires, 29-inch wheels. Detachable brace rod, suitable for short or medium-height gentlemen. Will stand any weight. Weight, 44 lbs. See cut. Geared to 50 inches.

5. **"Ladies' Light Roadster Psycho Safety,"** 29-inch wheels, ¾ and ⅞ inch tires, weight 38 lbs. Superb finish, very light and easy-running, intended for light-weight ladies, but will carry 175 lbs. Geared to 50 inches.

6. **"Ladies' Extra Light Psycho,"** same design as "Ladies' Psycho," with rear forks like "Men's Light Roadster Psycho," 28-inch wheels. Weight 34 lbs. Price, $140. We cannot deliver this much under thirty days.

7. **"Psycho Tandem Safety,"** intended for lady and gentleman or two gentlemen, ⅞-inch tires to both wheels, very strong, light and simple. Will carry any weight. Now in its second season. Price, with two separate brakes, $200. Geared to 57 inches.

All of the above Machines are guaranteed to the fullest extent.

PSYCHO LIGHT ROADSTER.

PSYCHO LADIES' ROADSTER.

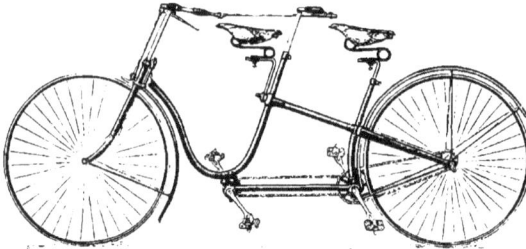

PSYCHO TANDEM SAFETY.

The Pilgrimage of W. S. Bull.

I have never met a man more earnestly devoted to the advancement of League and wheeling interests than Mr. W. S. Bull, of Buffalo, Chief Consul of the State Division—"Billy Bull," as the "gang" call him.

Mr. Bull arrived in Gotham on Sunday morning. I had intended to meet the train that dumped him into Hoboken, but, alas, I had tarried too late the night before at the New York Club-house with Fenton, Mac, The Coaster, Halsey, Edwards of Newark, Semple and other good men and true. We dallied with fire-water, Yuengling brand, and lingered over the wee sma' chop at Burns', where we fell in with Willie Wall and Lengthy Lansing. That is why I slumbered past service hour on Sunday, so that the Bull arrived without being met. I afterward ran across him at Bidwell's, and it was my pleasant lot to take him over to Brooklyn to introduce him to the boys. At the Kew Club-house we met President Bridgman, now Vice-Consul Bridgman, if you please. In the president's pleasant bachelor apartment at the top of the club-house we had a long chat, in which Mr. Bull developed some ideas that will meet with hearty accord all over the State, and especially in Brooklyn.

Mr. Bull wants to raise the Division membership to 3,000. He will devote all the energy and money of the Division to securing the passage of the Roads Improvement Bill, now being prepared by Mr. Isaac B. Potter. He will pursue a policy independent of all cliques, gangs and rings, will lop off much of the dead wood which has sapped the energies of the Leagueal tree, and in the appointment of committees and consuls will recognize the new people who have come up within the past few years. He recognizes the fact that local improvement must be accomplished largely by local organizations, and he advises the formation of the same. He is heartily in sympathy with the objects of the Long Island Cyclists' Union. Every cyclist in the Division will have any opinion advanced by him carefully considered. In fact, Mr. Bull seems in a fair way to make the Division a large and happy family, of much use to wheeling and to themselves.

At the K. C. W. parlors Mr. Bull was introduced to Messrs. Crichton, Long, Marion, C. and W. Murphy, Beazley, T. J. Hall, and a number of others.

After a short, informal talk, I took him to the Long Island Wheelmen's club-house, but alas! the members had all gone. I was given to understand that Sunday night in Brooklyn is a very girly-girly time, and that in the front, dimly-lit parlors of the churchly city more soft, meaningless nothings are said than there are sands in Sahara's beerless desert.

I forgot to mention that the picturesque old mansion opposite the L. I. W. and K. C. W. club-houses has been torn down, and the pretty foreground furnished by the Brevoort estate is likely to succumb to the cellar-digger, the mason and the plumber, which we call the march of civilization—rather the deadly advance of brick and mortar. I almost failed to note that K. C. W. will increase its locker-room; that it will establish a circulating library for club members, H. J. Hall, Jr., librarian; that it will hold a two days' meet at Washington Park this summer; that Wicks and Isbell, two new members, raptured the bottles of wine offered by the Huntington Bicycle Club to the first two Brooklyn wheelmen who reached their town this spring; that I saw Alden and Wise escorting one of the fair sex across Bedford Avenue. On Monday the Chief Consul met John A. Blake, New York B. C.; Wm. Halpin, Manhattan B. C.; John C. Gulick, Citizen B. C.; W. F. Miller, Brooklyn B. C.; L. A. Newcome, Harlem wheelmen, and F. P. Prial, New York B.C., all of whom were satisfying the inner man at "Mouquin's" restaurant.

On Monday evening I parted with Mr. Bull, who was due at the "Base Ball" dinner. I did not see each other. The dinner was probably too much for him, but I learn that he met C. A. Sheehan, Manhattan B. C., President of the L. A. W., C. H. Luscomb, and Isaac H. Potter, Brooklyn B. C. One of the pleasantest incidents of his tour was a conversational lunch with Lord Chesterfield Furst and Baron "Ollie" Harris. Mr. Bull will publish a complete list of his State committees in THE WHEEL of April 19. Through the kindness of the cycle trade Mr.

Bull will shortly publish, without cost to the State Division, a hand-book which will be sent to every cyclist in the State whose name and address Mr. Bull can obtain. This hand-book will contain L. A. W. Constitution and By-laws, State Constitution and By-laws, national officers and committees, State officers and committees, State League clubs, State League hotels, papers on roads improvement, the law as affecting cycles, training, temporary repairs, methods to be pursued in case of accidents and other valuable information.

The chief consul will attempt to perfect the League Hotel System. The proprietor will be required to sign a legal contract fixing rates for meals and lodging, which may be obtained only upon presenting League tickets. He must also keep in a prominent place a record book furnished by the Division. In this book touring wheelmen will be asked to note such information as will aid other tourists.

I wish the Chief Consul success in his work this year. He is so disinterested, personally, that every wheelman in the State should help him.   TITNAM.

MASSACHUSETTS BOARD MEET.

The regular monthly meeting of the Massachusetts Board of Officers of the L. A. W. was held at the Clarendon Hotel last Saturday night. Chief Consul Emery presided, and C. S. Howard served as secretary. Among those present were W. H. Emery, Roxbury; Mr. Forbes, Dorchester; W. A. Moulton, Jamaica Plain; G. A. Perkins, Cambridge; W. G. Kendall and C. S. Howard, Boston; I. W. Drown, Springfield; L. A. Campbell, Northampton.

On motion of Mr. Howard it was voted to give a copy of the Massachusetts and Rode Island Road-book to all who join the L. A. W. in this State. A communication was read from the President of the League asking if Massachusetts desired the honor of entertaining the L. A. W. at its annual summer meeting. It was voted that the division was not in a position to extend such an invitation. Mr. Forbes reported progress for the committee on preparing a map of the State roads.

On motion of Dr. Kendall a committee of three was appointed to consider the advisability of holding a meet of Massachusetts wheelmen in Boston early in the spring. The committee appointed was as follows: W. G. Kendall, G. A. Perkins and C. S. Howard. This committee is to act with the chief and vice-consuls.

Dr. Emery reported what he had done as chief consul since the last meeting. He had addressed gatherings of wheelmen in many cities of the State. Good results had already come in the form of a largely increased number of applications for League membership. He said that the meeting of Boston wheelmen at America Hall to-morrow evening was likely to prove of much importance. Addresses will be made by the Chief Consul, C. E. Pratt, Colonel A. A. Pope and G. A. Perkins. Everything possible is being done to further the passage of the bill for the improvement of highways, which is to be voted upon by the Legislature, April 17.

BOSTON WHEELMEN MEET TO AID ROADS IMPROVEMENT.

A large number of the most prominent wheelmen of Boston and vicinity assembled in America Hall last Monday evening, in answer to the call issued by Chief Consul Emery and others, who desired to make some organized movement to help the passage of the road improvement bill now before the Legislature. The meeting was called to order by Dr. W. H. Emery, who made a thorough statement of the object of the meeting. Mr. C. E. Pratt, the First-president of the L.A.W., Vice-Consul A. W. Robinson and President Chedwood of the Jamaica Plain Cycle Club made interesting remarks. Captain A. W. Robinson of the Charlestown Rovers, Capt. A. P. Henson of the Dorchester Bicycle Club and Capt. Carle Cubberly of the Somerville Cycle Club were appointed a committee to take into consideration the advisability of calling club runs to a central point on one Sunday of each month.

"Must say it [the Brooks Cyclometer] is the best instrument we ever saw for the price."
MYER & VAN HORN, Denver Col.

Price, $5.   The Brooks Odometer Co., Lowell, Mass.

Twenty-five Mile Handicap Road Race.

IRVINGTON-MILBURN COURSE, May 30.—The many road-racing enthusiasts who have been in the habit of assembling semi-annually on the Irvington-Milburn course to witness the contests of the now defunct New York and New Jersey T. R. R. A., will be glad to know that on Decoration Day next a twenty-five mile handicap road race will be held on the same course, the scheme of which will probably eclipse in interest any similar event ever held in this vicinity.

The race is being gotten up by Mr. A. B. Barkman, of the Brooklyn Bicycle Club, with the idea of promoting the local interest in cycling and at the same time bringing together the cracks from all parts of the country in one grand contest. The race will be entirely free from all trade interests, although the local dealers will be requested to co-operate and make the event a success, and to contribute prizes if they so desire. A Light Roadster bicycle will be offered for first prize, a gold watch for second, and it is the intention that another gold watch be offered as a special prize to the competitor making the best time over the course, regardless of handicap. The total number of prizes will probably be twelve, ranging from $25 to $135. The race will be open to all amateur wheelmen who have never been professionals or promateurs. The entrance fee will be $1, same to be sent to A. B. Barkman, 251 Broadway, New York City, on or before May 10, and must in every case accompany the application, or no notice of same will be taken.

Each contestant must furnish with his application specific data as to his riding in any road race or trial of speed in which he has competed during the past year, same to be endorsed by two officers of the club of which he may be a member, or by two responsible wheelmen. The handicapping to be done by a committee of three and the general arrangements will be managed by a committee selected from the principal clubs in New York City and vicinity. Everything possible will be done to have the race fair and honest, and to have the arrangements as near perfection as the publicity of the course will allow. This event will be one not to be missed, and we, therefore advise all interested to send in their applications as early as possible. The number of entries will be limited to one hundred. We sincerely hope that this event will be the means of bringing together, if not all, of the noted Western fliers of which we h ar so much, in competition with their brothers of the East, and we guarantee them if they come they will receive a royal welcome.

FIXTURES.

Mr. George T. Warwick, President of the Warwick Cycle Co., was recently granted twenty patents on improvements on bicycles.

MARYLAND.

The following letter was received last week by the Chief Consul:

New York, April 2, 1889.

Dear Sir,—The place for the annual League meet of 1889, has not yet been settled, but it is now the proper time to determine what shall receive it and where it shall be held. As it is very important that the executive committee shall know at the earliest date the place to be selected, and that the many injquiries from our members may be answered, I would ask you to confer with your division officers at the earliest practicable moment and advise me if your division desires the annual meet of 1889, and the sentiment of your members upon this subject. The importance of these annual gatherings cannot be over estimated, and the cause of wheeling, particularly in the locality where the meet is held, is benefitted thereby to a very considerable degree. There should also be held at the same time a race meet, at which the national championships should be run off.

I would suggest, in considering the advisability of your division undertaking the meet of 1889, that extensive and expensive entertainment be dispensed with; that the assembling of the League be upon simple principles for the general advancement of wheeling interests, the promotion of the welfare of the League and the interchange of opinions and ideas upon all matters connected with wheeling and our organization. The object should be to bring our members together for mutual acquaintance, discussion and enjoyment from the wheelman's standpoint.

Please write me as soon as practicable and in as much detail as possible.

Yours fraternally,
Charles H. Luscomb,
President L. A. W.

The meet held here last year was so successful, that it reads as an invitation to the Maryland Division to invite the League here again this year. The entertainment of the 1,500 or more wheelmen, is looked upon as a big job, and the Maryland wheelmen do not take very kindly to it. President Luscomb's letter intimates, however, that very much less entertaining than last year would be perfectly satisfactory. The Chief Consul will consult the Hagerstown, Md. Club on the matter before answering the President's letter. The Hagerstown Club are to hold a meet and races in the first part of July, which could easily be turned into the annual L. A. W. meet. The hotel accommodations are ample and good, and the several fine pikes and roads leading to historic points, etc., would beyond doubt be acceptable.

Harry Kingsland, the Baltimore crack bicycle rider, will be one of the contestants in the races at the Chicago Cycling Tournament, on May 13.

Cline Bros., had several new machines in front of their store, on W. Baltimore Street, last week, when some one cut with a knife in a number of places two Victor Safeties, and the two saddles of a tandem. The perpetrators have not been caught.

The Chesapeake Club proposes to buy a club-house and fix it in handsome style. The club-house is at present located on Fulton Avenue, $5,000 will be subscribed. This club is in flourishing condition. It has forty active members.

Charles Ludwig, an ex-member of the Baltimore Club, arrived in Baltimore from his present home in Ashtabula, O., Friday, the 5th, at 3 P. M., was married at 4 P. M., and left with his bride, formerly Miss Josie Nehr, at 5 P. M., for his home. This is rather quick work.

Isaac Hinds, who recently came to grief on Eutaw Place, knocking two teeth from his mouth and receiving other injuries, has improved and is about.

The Centaur Club will celebrate Arbor Day quite appropriately. A tree will be planted at Patteman Park, and probably several addresses and speeches will be delivered.

An enjoyable dance was given by the wives of several of the members at the Maryland Club, at their club-house on Mt. Royal Avenue, on Thursday, April 4. A large number of invited guests were present.

Mr. Victor Emerson climbed the celebrated elevation at Mt. Washington last week. Mr. Emerson also broke the record from Reisterstown last week, making the trip through mud and against a head wind, in an hour and ten minutes, including eight minutes stoppage.

Among the members in the race from Baltimore Club-house were, W. G. Hill, "Lew" Warrington, Fred Townsend, Victor Emerson, Walter Lowery, Arthur Emery and Joseph Greigan.

Bay Ridge.

TACOMA, W. T.

A year ago the City of Tacoma boasted of one bicycle and *two* riders, Messrs. Ulman and Harlow. About this time Mr. Prince Wells stopped at Tacoma to give a two week's exhibition of fancy riding. His daring feats upon his bicycle and wagon wheel created no little enthusiasm among the young men of this city, and having become thoroughly acclimated to the place, and not slow to see the interest shown in cycling, Mr. Wells decided to open an agency. Nor did he make a mistake in so doing, for between April 1 and July 10 forty wheels were sold here and twenty-five in Seattle (thirty miles north of Tacoma by water, but about seventy by road).

On March 23, 1888, the boys organized "The Tacoma Wheelmen," which soon had a membership of about eighty, composed of twenty riders and about sixty non-riders. The new riders made rapid headway in the art of riding, and could be seen every Sunday starting out for all-day runs. On July 4 and 5 the Seattle club entertained our boys, the programme being composed of parade, racing and banquet. We reciprocated this favor in August, and everybody seemed to be well pleased.

Since this time new riders have come to town, and all have been surprised to find such good roads in the vicinity and to the lakes. But recently the club has seemed to lose its grip, and, like many similar organizations, we were badly in need of new life. On Saturday evening, March 30, the old club was disbanded and on the following Monday a new club was organized under the name of "The Tacoma Bicycle Club.

Everything tends to point to a bright future for the new club, and we hope it will now be run on a new basis. The association now has many good riders, among whom may be mentioned Messrs. Barlow, Culver, Baker and Keene, all of whom are enthusiastic Wheelmen.

The latest topic at the evening gatherings of the cyclers is the proposed 25-mile road race for the championship of Washington. Rumor has it that Keene—who so far this year has proved himself the best long-distance rider of Tacoma—will have to do some tall riding to get first medal, for Barlow and Culver mean business this time. Then we hear that Clark (of the Seattle Club and former champion of Canada) will make or boys hustle. Prince Wells, of Denver, and Halsted, of New York, will also make some of the contestants move pretty fast.

Snohomish.

CHICAGO MEET.

Three meetings were held in Chicago last week in connection with the Chicago Cycling Exhibit and Tournament. At a meeting of the Business Committee, Messrs. J. M. Erwin, Lincoln C. C.; H. J. Gotthelf, Douglas C. C., and F. T. Harmon, Chicago C. C., were appointed to assist Mr. Miles with the racing programme, selection of officers, etc., and a committee composed of Messrs. E. J. Roberts, T. T. Roe, Chas. Sieg, Otto Maas, Harvey Angle, E. F. McPike, A. W. Harris, Fred. Smith, T. Bray, F. M. Reynolds, H. A. Stoddard and H. J. Gotthelf were appointed to take charge of the parades.

The Racing Committee met on Wednesday and produced the following list of events as the fruit of their labors:

PROGRAMME OF RACES.

1. One-mile handicap. Nine prizes.
2. One-mile scratch. Three prizes.
3. One-mile novices. Two prizes.
4. One-mile scratch, for men who have never raced prior to this tournament. Two prizes.
5. One-mile scratch, 3-minute class. Three prizes.
6. One-mile scratch, flying start. Three prizes.
7. One-mile handicap, Rover type safeties. Three prizes.
8. One-mile handicap, local, Lumsden, Van Sicklen, Roe, Ehlert, Winship and Hammel barred. Three prizes.
9. One-mile handicap, boys under 16. Two prizes.
10. One-mile handicap, Rover type safeties, boys under 17. Two prizes.
11. One-mile scratch, tandem, lady and gentleman. Four prizes.
12. One-mile scratch, ride and run, Rover type safeties. Two prizes.
13. Two-mile handicap. Three prizes.
14. Two-mile handicap, L. A. W. members only. Three prizes.
15. Two-mile scratch, members of suburban clubs only. Two prizes.
16. Two-mile scratch, 6:20 class. Three prizes.
17. Two-mile scratch, Rover type safeties. Three prizes.
18. Two-mile scratch, tandem. Two prizes.
19. Three-mile handicap. Four prizes.
20. Five-mile handicap. Four prizes.
21. Ten-mile scratch. Four prizes.
22. Quarter-mile scratch. Two prizes.
23. Half-mile bicycle scratch. Two prizes.
24. Three-mile club teams of three. Three prizes and club trophy.
25. Club drill, teams limited to fifteen men. One prize.
26. One-mile consolation. Two prizes.

The mile handicap is to be the event of the meeting, and will, in reality, include three events in one. It will be run in this way: Imagining, for example, that there are forty entries, they will be divided into five heats, the winners of which will run in the final, the first three men taking the first series of three prizes. The thirty-five men beaten in the first round will then run again in a second race of five heats, the winners of which will run for the second series of three prizes. And so on with the thirty men beaten in the second round. Every man who fails to win one of the nine prizes will receive a silver souvenir of the event.

The 1-mile flying-start race will be another novelty, and has been introduced solely to test the practicability of such contests. The committee endeavored to give every one, from the best to the poorest rider, a chance to win something, and they seem to have succeeded.

A greatly reduced rate has been secured over all roads in the Central Traffic Association, the other organizations not having been heard from yet. Full particulars on this head will be duly announced.

Two parades will be arranged, one on the opening night, when every rider in the procession will be admitted to the building without charge, and one later in the week. The start will probably be from the front of the building, which stands on Michigan Avenue, one of the finest stretches of road in the world.

Entry blanks and all other particulars are obtainable of S. A. Miles, 199 South Clark Street, Chicago.

The Wheel improves every week. Allow me to congratulate you on its fine appearance. I want no better paper.

August Kinne.

Richfield Springs, New York.

The building occupied by Henry C. Squire at 178 Broadway, New York, was partially destroyed by fire on Thursday morning. Mr. Squire's stock was damaged to the extent of several thousand dollars.

SCHEDULE OF THE CENTURY RUN.

Orange to Philadelphia, June 8, 1889.

Rendezvous Friday evening, June 7, at Mountain House, South Orange (Mountain Station, D., L. and W. R. R., Barclay and Christopher Street ferries, New York City; wheels free). Dinner, lodging and breakfast, $2.00; lodging and breakfast, $1.25. The schedule of the run is as follows:

Road	M.	Total		Time A.M.	Rate per hour	
			Orange...Le.	4:00		
Fine....	5	5	Newark.....	4:30	9	
Fine.....	6	11	Elizabeth....	5:5	8	
Good....	7	18	Westfield.....	6:15	7	
Fine.....	5	23	Plainfield.....	7:30	6½	Rest and photo.
Fine if dry..	12	35	N. Brunswick	9:00	8	
Good....	14	49	Kingston....	10:30	6½	
Good....	3	52	Princeton....	11:30	3	Rest. See College, perhaps photo.
				P.M.		
Fair to good...	6	58	Lawrenceville	12:30	6	Photo.
	7	65	Trenton Arr. / Le.	1:30 / 2:30	7	Dinner, Trenton House, 75c.
Various, but generally good to fine.	35	100	Philadelphia..	7:00	8	Via Bristol and and Frankford or Camden L. A. W. Hotel. The Colonnade

Wheelmen who wish to participate in the run should notify the secretary, L. A. Clarke, 25 Broad Street, New York, as soon as possible after June 1. Club members should put their names on the cards posted on club bulletin boards. The run will not be a road race and the pace stated in the schedule will be closely adhered to. At Philadelphia, the party will dine at the Colonnade Hotel, and then take train for home; fare $2.50, which may be reduced.

THE "EAGLE" ON EAGLE ROCK.

On Saturday last, about 3 P. M., a score or more wheelmen from Orange, Newark and Elizabeth gathered at Eagle Rock Hill to witness a trial of the hill-climbing qualities of the new "Eagle" bicycle. As various adverse opinions have been expressed regarding the efficiency of the "Eagle" machine in this respect, it may be of interest to many to know just what it will do.

The climbing was done by Wm. A. Clark, of Stamford, Conn., and the wheel used was a regular 50-inch "Eagle," weight 44½ lbs., cranks 5¼ inches throw. As Mr. Clark had never seen the hill before, he made two preliminary trials, and then, coasting at a terrific pace from the top to the extreme bottom, he turned and rode straight to the summit again without a waiver or hardly slacking his pace. No time was taken, as the object of the trial was to test the climbing qualities of the machine and not the endurance or speed of the rider.

Among those present were: E. S. Walsh, L. B. Gaylor, I. F. Wardwell, C. S. Wardwell and C. E. Gaylor, from Stamford; A. P. Folk, of Brooklyn; Mr. Pierson, from Howard. A. Smith, of Newark, and several other representatives of neighboring cycle dealers.

At the National Cross-Country Association games, to be held at the Gentlemen's Driving Park, on Saturday, April 27, a three mile bicycle handicap will be decided. The grounds may be reached by the Grand Central road to Morrisania station, or *via* Jerome Avenue, the road leading to them branching off Jerome Avenue to the left about half a mile above Macomb's Dam Bridge. The prizes will be sterling silver cups. The entrance fee is $1; close April 17 with Will Frank, P.O. Box, 3102, New York. Prizes will be on exhibition at Spalding's. Games commence at 4 P.M. Handicapper, F. P. Prial. Track is one mile circuit, in good condition.

Mr. Robert McClure, Secretary of the Riverside Wheelmen, sailed last week for England, where he will stay for six months. Mr. McClure still remains a member of the R.W.

About a dozen members of the Riverside Wheelmen have signed to go in the Century run. Mr. Cossett, on a lady's safety, will go with the Riversides.

The Riverside wheelmen will give a house-warming on May 18, at their new club-house.

Warwick Perfection Wheels.

Warwick Perfection Safety.   Price, $135.00.   Weight, 48 lbs.

Warwick Perfection Ordinary.   Price, $125.00   Neck, Head, Brake, etc.

No More Fractured Handle-Bars.   No More Rattling Joints.

PERFECTION STEP.   ADJUSTABLE BALL BEARINGS.   SECTION OF RIM.

We show cut of our new Safety. Its points over all other wheels are: Absolute freedom from sensitiveness; freedom from vibration, the spring forks saving machine as well as rider by absorbing all jars; direct action plunger brake; it is not necessary to remove the hand from the handle to work the brake; the pedals are perfectly adjustable and dust-proof; the spokes may be quickly replaced (see cut of section of rim); the rubber tire covers the edges of the rim and is warranted never to come out; the saddle is instantly detachable and will not stretch from wet or perspiration; it can be adjusted to any wheel; the spade handles are of a new form, and conform to the angle of the rider's body; the enamel is of a high grade and polish, and cannot be broken with ordinary use; the frame is of strong double tubing; the dress guard is of flexible wire, which may be quickly attached or detached—it is the best dress guard ever invented.

We show a cut of our Perfection Ordinary, which has many of the features which make the Safety superior to all other dwarf wheels. The step (see illustration) is the only step that will not slip, that is so fashioned that the finish of the backbone is not destroyed in mounting.

WARWICK CYCLE MFG. CO., Factory and Offices, Springfield, Mass.

WM. HALPIN & CO., New York State Agents, New York.

D. SNITJER, South-Western Agent, St. Louis.

H. A. LOZIER & CO., Western Agents, Cleveland.

CHAS. F. STOKES, North-Western Agent, Chicago.   [Adv.]

WHEEL GOSSIP.

Phil Hammel will ride in the Pullman road race.

The Melrose, Mass., Cycle Club will hold its annual reception April 24.

Lumsden, the Chicago crack, will shortly commence training at Cheltenham.

The Manhattan Club took a run to Yonkers on Sunday last, twenty men turning out.

The Intercollegiate games will be held at Berkeley Oval on May 25. Yale will be represented in the bicycle event by Weare, Clark and Koutz.

We regret to announce that Mr. Page published a pun in the last issue of the *Spectator*. We sincerely pray that the attack may be of short duration.

A thief recently broke into Humber & Co.'s offices at Coventry, England, and stole £400 which had been drawn from the bank to pay the men's wages.

Entries for the Pullman road race, to be run from Chicago to Pullman on May 30, close May 24 with R. D. Garden, 291 Wabash Avenue, Chicago.

Australian racing cyclists are compelled by the racing rules to wear an absurd and gaudy costume, consisting of loose satin jackets and jockey caps with six inch-peaks.

In the King's County Wheelmen's club-house (active membership about 160) there are but four safeties, and one of them is for sale. Mr. Marion is the proud possessor of an "Eagle."

The Camden Wheelmen's Association have secured the rooms formerly occupied by the Camden Republican Club, which they will extensively alter and fit up as club-rooms.

Messrs. Singer & Co. have cleared out almost their entire stock of second-hand wheels. They yet have on hand a few second-hand ordinaries and safeties, which they are selling at cut prices.

The Kingsbridge Road House will be opened April 15 as a cafe and restaurant by Bernard, who has a place at 123d Street and Seventh Avenue. Cyclists will find this a good stopping place.

The Missouri Bicycle Club has invited Chicago wheelmen to make their headquarters at their club-house on the day of the Lumsden-Stone race, which will be held May 25. A run will be held May 26 for the entertainment of the visitors.

Mr. Samuel T. Clark sailed on Wednesday morning for London. He goes abroad in the interests of the New Rapid, for which wheel, in its rear-driving form, there is an enormous demand this season. Mr. Clark will remain away about one month.

Howard A. Smith & Co., Oraton Hall, Newark, N.J., have about two hundred second-hand machines for sale, ranging in price from $20 to $100 each, besides their very large stock of new machines. Intending purchasers should give them a call at once.

The *Sewing Machine and Cycle News* after publishing an extended editorial on the propriety of giving credit, "culls" "Old Hanki-Panki," a bright bit of verse which recently appeared in this paper. We should say that the editor of the *Sewing Machine and Cycle News* is a hypocrite as well as a literary thief.

Mr. C. E. Leach, who is about to go into business in New York, has resigned the captaincy of the Cambridgeport, Mass., Bicycle Club. At a meeting of the club held Tuesday, April 2, Mr. Leach was elected an honorary member. Mr. W. T. Koop was elected to fill the vacant office. The club took a run to Echo bridge on Thursday afternoon, April 4.

Mr. J. K. Boyden, of the Illinois Club, while out riding on March 28, ran into a safety rider, which threw him against the curbstone, fracturing his skull and forcing a portion of the bone into the brain. Mr. Boyden died on Tuesday, April 2. He was a careful rider and recently told a friend that he neither intended to race or scorch this year.

It is rumored in America that *S. G.* Whittaker, who has just returned to the States, will apply for reinstatement as an amateur. We offer up a gentle smile.—*Wheeling.*

We ran across this paragraph on April 8, at which time Whittaker had not yet been "sighted." Please let Mr. Whittaker land, at least, gentlemen; then pen your stupid pars

The Twelfth Regiment games will be held at the armory, Sixty-second Street and Ninth Avenue, on Friday evening, May 10. The bicycle events are a two-mile handicap and a one-mile novice scratch. Entries close May 4 with Chas. J. Leach, P. O. Box 3,201, New York City. Wheelmen may obtain the privilege of practicing at the armory on certain evenings. Full information may be obtained from the secretary. The bicycle event will be handicapped by F. P. Prial.

The Cambridge Bicycle Club has called the following runs for this month: April 6, Lexington, start at 10 A. M.; 13th, forenoon run over the new extension, and in the afternoon through Medford, Arlington and Belmont, starting morning at 10 and afternoon at 2; 20th, Dedham, via Forest Hills and Roslindale, dining at Hyde Park; 27th, South Natick, dining at Bailey's.

The Portland Wheel Club has elected the following officers: President, John Calvin Stevens; Vice-President and Captain, Lyle B. Chase; Secretary and Treasurer, Charles D. Alexander; First Lieutenant, W. T. King; Second Lieutenant, J. H. Hannaford; Bugler, George T. Barnes; Club Committee, F. H. Sawyer, George B. Morrill. The club has fifty-two members and is in splendid condition. At the annual meeting of the club, Mr. E. B. Pillsbury, of the Massachusetts Bicycle Club, was elected an honorary member.

At the annual meeting of the Roxbury Bicycle Club the following officers were elected: President, W. H. Emery; Vice-President, John S. Lowell; Secretary, Charles W. Eaton; Treasurer, W. T. Johnson; Captain, Irving E. Moultrop; First Lieutenant, James Keltie; Second Lieutenant, John Graham; Bugler, V. Dreiling. The following runs have been called for April: 7th, reservoir; 14th, Waltham; 21st, Milton; 22d, Roxbury suburbs; 28th, Medford; 30th, Great Sign Boards. The club is in a very prosperous condition, and expects to receive many accessions to its membership during the riding season.

The annual dinner of the Cambridge Bicycle Club, which took place at Young's Hotel last Monday evening, was a great success. There were forty members present, and President George A. Perkins was in the chair. Secretary Editor Bassett, of the League of American Wheelmen, Vice-Consul Robinson and Chief Consul Emery were the guests of the club. Among those present were Charles S. Clark, James H. Grimes, H. C. Getchell, W. J. Newman, Dr. W. G. Kendall, Will S. Atwell, A. S. Kendall and George A. Perkins. The after-dinner speeches, though informal, were very entertaining. Chief Consul Emery made a stirring address, in which he pictured the advantages of L. A. W. membership. He was followed by Vice-Consul Robinson, Dr. Kendall, A. N. Oliver, H. H. Burns, Joshua Winson, J. C. Kerrison, W. C. Curtis, Charles S. Clark and Henry Ward.

In accordance with the powers recently vested in them, the Elizabeth, N. J., Board of Freeholders have appointed committees to consider and recommend a plan to locate and improve the highways. Speaking on the subject of improved roads, Freeholder West said:

One essential thing for the prosperity of the county, and to hold its own and keep up to the spirit of the nineteenth century, is good county roads. The one way to build it up is to make it desirable for home sites for the people of the overcrowded cities of Brooklyn, New York, etc. If a good road system is established the county will double its population in five or ten years, the property will be enhanced in value, and inaccessible property will be opened up to settlement. Farm property in the Eastern States is depreciating in value, and will depreciate until it can be utilized into home sites. What is necessary is to inaugurate and adopt a practical road system, and it will return 100 cents for every dollar expended, and the county will make rapid strides toward prosperity. This should be done everywhere until there is a grand highway from the wave-washed shores of the Atlantic to the golden gate of the Pacific. This is not a fine-spun theory, a wild scheme, but it is a practical and businesslike undertaking, and when every one realizes it and acts on it the time will not be distant when the British lion, the American eagle and the pet bird of New Jersey will occupy the same tree and hatch birds from the same nest.

NOTES FROM THE CITY OF BROTHERLY LOVE.

Mince pie, did you say? Do I like the article? Ask George Gideon if any of the members of the Pennsylvania Bicycle Club like mince pie, and I will wager he will drop into a fit before you. Nor would you wonder if you could have seen seventeen members from the above-mentioned club in the great feat of each man to a pie, or rather one pie for each man. The reason whereof, 'twas as follows: Mr. Gideon has often asked the club to come up some Sunday on their regular club run, and he would provide mince pie enough to satisfy the appetite of a Dr. Tanner after a forty-day fast, or a wheelman after a twenty-mile ride, which is one and the same thing. Well, on Sunday, the 7th, the road officers made arrangements for a run to Fort Washington, and promised the genial George that they would stop on their way, and warned him to be ready. So, about 10:30 on Sunday morning, the crowd drew up in front of mine host's house, dismounted, and, after a few minutes, were busily engaged in devouring mince pies that were worthy the name they bore. Poor George was all in a glow before he was through helping. Nor do I wonder, as I was watching one man and saw him eat four good-sized pieces, and they tell me that the man who was watching did likewise.

After washing down the pastry with a few cups of coffee, the party withdrew to the parlors and listened to some banjo selections by our host, and then started for Fort Washington, each man feeling very grateful to our worthy host, and with a stomach full of pie to remind him of the pleasant hour he had passed. Strange to say, there was no desire to scorch for an hour or more, and, stranger still, no one was heard to kick when arrived at Fort Washington, where they found the landlord in a very bad humor and dinner not to be ready for an hour. But the kicking came with the dinner. Dinner, did I say? Never mind, I won't complain; but I hope the captain takes us in another direction next Sunday.

Messrs. Merrihew, McDaniels and Elliott, of Wilmington, were in the city on Sunday last, and accompanied the Pennsylvania Bicycle Club on their run, McDaniels and Elliott riding a Premier Tandem Safety.

Who is "Pennsy?" is the question that has agitated wheelmen in this vicinity of late. He has been writing for the *Athlete*, and, having the faculty of "getting on to the boys," has given several of them away. They all promise sweet revenge when they catch him. So far, however, he has concealed his identity, and, I judge, will be sharp enough to do so in the future. But if he should trip, let him beware.

The petition blanks furnished by the associated cycling clubs to petition the Pennsylvania and Philadelphia and Reading R. R. are being rapidly filled up. Question: Will it do any good? The boys are giving it a trial, at any rate.

The Century Club are gradually getting into good shape, and ere long promise us an invitation to view their headquarters. This club, under Captain Carter's leadership, are starting out with largely increased attendance on their Sunday club runs, and promise to push "Pennsy" this coming season

Messrs. William H. Kirk and Carl Herring, of the Pennsylvania Bicycle Club, will start on the European tour in May.

The Mount Vernon Wheelmen have changed their mind regarding their club uniform, having discarded the proposed gray and adopted the more dressy blue.

Trips to Ardmore have already commenced, although the boys were much worried last week, when rumor had it that mine host Moos was to be sold out by the sheriff. But he has undoubtedly made satisfactory arrangements with his creditors, as the notice of sale has disappeared, and on Sunday last he was dispensing cream to the riders who ventured out.

A member of the Pennsylvania Bicycle Club, whose modesty prevents his allowing his name to be known, has presented a handsome medal for competition among the members of the club. It is left in the hands of the road officers for disposal. They have offered it to the man who makes the greatest number of days out, no ride of less than ten miles to count.

WESTFIELD.

NEW ORLEANS.

That "everything comes to him who waits" has been aptly illustrated in the case of the Louisiana Cycling Club and the Batson medal, and at last, after a long wait and many disappointments, the clerk of the weather finally smiled upon a particular date set for the inauguration of the long-delayed series for that trophy, and on last Sunday (March 31) the races were fairly opened with a three-mile contest.

Of sixteen entries, twelve started. The handicaps were over-generous, and the back-start men stood little show; consequently a limit man romped across the line a winner, with a lead of some twenty yards.

The following shows the result in full:

	Handicap.	Actual time.
Foster De Buys	2 min. 15 sec.	12:38
E. M. Graham	1 min. [illegible] sec.	11:49
W. C. Grivot	1 min. [illegible] sec.	13:10
W. H. Renaud	1 min. 30 sec.	13:15
M. S. Graham	25 sec.	12:16
L. J. Frederic	45 sec.	12:40
W. M. Hathorn	25 sec.	12:44
A. M. Hill	Scratch	12:30
G. C. Angamar	45 sec.	—
H. W. Nathan	2 min. 15 sec.	—
C. W. Bogel	1 min. 30 sec.	—
A. B. Harris	2 min. 15 sec.	—

Messrs. C. H. Fenner, at the start, and C. M. Fairchild, R. G. Betts and M. B. Sprigg, at the finish officered the event.

The next race is fixed for April 14, distance 6½ miles.

This has been a big week for the Louisiana Cycling Clubmen. On Monday, the 1st, the annual meeting occurred, when the following officers were elected:

President, W. H. Renaud, Jr. re-elected third term; Vice-President, F. B. Born; Secretary-Treasurer, E. M. Graham, re-elected; Captain, R. G. Betts, re-elected third term; Lieutenant, L. J. Frederic, re-elected; Executive Committee, President, Vice-President, Captain and Messrs. C. M. Fairchild and H. H. Hodgson.

The reports showed the club in a prosperous condition, a strong membership, no debts, and a nice little nest egg in the treasury. After adjournment, a spread occupied the rest of the evening, and now if you would have the boys smile, just ask them if they have ever tasted *becassine fesandé*. Perhaps you, Mr. Editor, have partaken of this French delicacy and can appreciate the smile.

Thursday (4th) the regular meeting took place, and the knowledge that the club building movement would be introduced brought together the backbone of the organization, and as a result, barring of course, the unforeseen, I believe that within the next six or eight months the club will be in a house of its own. At the meeting, sixteen members alone pledged $1,375, and there are still twenty-five to be seen. The matter of incorporation is now in the hands of an attorney, and so soon as the charter is received the site is to be selected. Large grounds and a $2,000 house, capable of enlargement, is the idea.

At this same meeting, a challenge to the N. O. Bi. Club for a team race was authorized and the application record broken; ten new members being admitted and three delinquents dropped. This brings the roll up to forty-one. Two years ago at the organization it was nine.

A meeting of the League State Division is fixed for April 8. The fall tournament and a constitution and by-laws are some of the matters to be wrestled with.

A word or two in regard to the popular election system in the L. A. W. Like others who have expressed their sentiments, I too am somewhat surprised and chagrined at THE WHEEL's change of policy *in re* the League Constitution. Principle is worth fighting for at any time, and this appears to be not only one of principle but of right; and while it may be true that the League has no two differing policies at stake, and that it is purely a matter of men, now that there appears some active competition for League offices, that alters the case but little. Measures without the men, or men without the measures, doesn't go for much, and it is only natural that folks should differ in their ideas of both, and care to have a say in that respect. To my mind, it seems to me that one way toward securing the desired end would be for the delegates (chief consuls, representatives, etc.) of the different districts to call a meeting for an expression of opinion from their constituents, and vote accordingly; or, failing to do this, what is to prevent the circulation for a called meeting, at which these delegates who directly cast the all-important vote be INSTRUCTED to cast his ballot or proxy for this candidate or for that one? Those who take an interest in the affairs of the L. A. W. would then be present; those who do not wouldn't, that's all. It is true that when we elect our State officers we indirectly vote for the higher officers, but do these State officials always speak the minds of their people on such important matters? Not much.

BI.

TROY NOTES.

Mr. Le Grand Spicer has taken the agency for the popular Columbia wheels, and will ride a Light Roadster Safety, which is anxiously expected every day. He will make a strong road rider, as he has ridden considerably on a tricycle and always managed to keep up with the crowd. Anybody wishing Columbia repairs will find Mr. Spicer at Howe & Co.'s.

Wednesday evening, the 3d, the annual election of the Trojan Wheelmen was held in the club parlor, over the Troy City Bank, and the result was as follows: President, C. E. Betts; Vice-President, G. W. Stowe; Secretary, T. T. Chase; Financial Secretary, George B. Friday; Treasurer, James W. Hislop; Trustees, Geo. S. Coutie and Harry Snyder. G. W. Stowe was appointed chairman of a committee to make arrangements for a reception to be given at the club's rooms very soon. Two applications for membership were received.

Mr. Joshua Reynolds has ordered a Rover ladies' bicycle for his daughter, and expects Mrs. R. will also ride it. He says *he* will stick to his old Columbia Light Roadster, which has carried him nearly 6,500 miles. I believe his son will ride a Junior Safety this season.

So the editors of the *Bi. World and Bulletin* have come to the conclusion that the ladies need a little space in their paper, eh? I should not wonder if THE WHEEL had stirred them up to it.

The League ought to do more for the *ladies* (as suggested by a correspondent of THE WHEEL and seconded by Secretary Bassett), but I suppose it will not come so long as politics absorb everything else. Riding, routes, roads, rights, racing and rates "R" good words for the League to bear in mind, but the greatest of all is *roads*.

Who is the League Consul for Troy now?

April 6, 1889. ORNH QBA.

FENTON'S FANCIES.

WHEELMEN'S BOWLING LEAGUE MEET.

A meeting of the Wheelmen's Bowling League was held at the New York Bicycle Club on Saturday, April 6. Delegates from all the clubs of the organization were present, with the exception of the King's County Wheelmen, whom a previous engagement prevented from attending. John R. Blake, New York Bicycle Club, was re-elected President, and L. S. Edwards, Atalanta Wheelmen, Secretary. The resignation of the Harlem Wheelmen was tendered by E. C. Parker. The championship for 1889 was awarded to the Atalanta Wheelmen, and the second prize to the Hudson County Wheelmen. The President appointed the following committees: Schedule, Eldridge, Semple and Halsey; Rules, Nisbett, Bridgeman and Earl. The meeting then adjourned to the billiard room, where a quiet time was enjoyed by those present. The delegates to the meeting were Messrs. Merseles and Tuthill, of the H. C. W.; Parker, H. W.; Edwards and Halsey, A. W., and Semple, N. Y. B. C.

Mr James B. Roy, one of the pioneers of the New York Club, has decided to enter the ranks of the noble army of Benedicts. The invitations are out for his marriage on Tuesday, the 23d, to Miss Libbie A. Wood, at the Church of the Heavenly Rest. Mr. Roy has the best wishes of the entire New York Bicycle Club, for whom he acted as Treasurer for some years.

The Seventh Regiment has a very large contingent of wheelmen in its ranks, and some of the best racing men to be found around the city. To mention just a few, N. M. Beckwith, S. V. Hoffman and Arthur Taylor, of the Citizens; I. M. Shaw, W. F. Wall, J. H. and T. E. Tripler, of the New Yorks, and A. B. and S. H. Rich, of the Staten Island Athletic Club. C. F. Burhaus, of "B," has such a happy knack of skimming round the corners of the track that he has so far been undefeated. Former racing men in the regiment count E. T. Weber and J. N. Stearns among their ranks. There are lots of others, but I have mentioned enough to show that this branch of athletics is well represented in the regiment, in spite of "The Owl's" tirade against the militia in the columns of *The Cycle* (R. I. P.) a few years ago.

I had the pleasure of meeting our new Chief Consul on Monday. I am sure that the members of the New York State Division will find him a good and enthusiastic champion of their cause, and in return should give him their best support. One of the largest districts of the Division gave a foolish exhibition of petty spite and obstructionist policy toward Chief Consul Bidwell during the past year, with the result that he quietly proceeded on his course, and the District was named the "kicker," a title which seems likely to stick. It is to be hoped that such a course will not be pursued toward Mr. Bull, who deserves it just as little as Mr. Bidwell ever did. Besides, obstruction is a very weak policy to pursue. Mr. Parnell admits that the system of obstruction carried on by the Irish members of the House of Commons some five years ago gave their cause a blow from the effects of which they are barely recovering now. *Verb. sap.!*

The different New York City clubs will be represented by the following men on the track during the coming season: Riverside, E. A. Powers; New York, Hanson, Findley, Pendleton, Nisbett and Heydecker; Citizens', S. V. Hoffman. The New Yorks will probably hold a series of races for the championship of the club some time during June.

FENTON.

BROOKLYN NEWS.

The Long Island Wheelmen entertained the Brooklyns at their club-house on Saturday last, but were very unfortunate in having their principal attraction desert them at the last moment. The delinquent guest was Col. Oakey, who was expected to give the boys a very interesting talk. However, the committee were equal to the occasion and produced a number of entertaining men, who talked to the large audience in a most desultory and yet most effective way. Mr. Clarke deserves great praise for his good management under such trying circumstances. Schumacher, K. C. W., was there, but remained in the cool hall nursing a slight headache occasioned by a header taken that afternoon while *en route* from Hempstead, where he has taken up his residence.

The three best mileages of the Long Islands to March 1 are Schmid, 463; Wise, 360; Beecher, 230.

I saw the following item of news in the red-letter edition of the *Bicycling World* of last week: "Hurrah for the effete East! Schwalbach, of Brooklyn, has a son who rides a bicycle younger than Mohrig, Jr., of San Francisco." "Charley" asserts that he has made no claim upon the possession of any extraordinarily young bicycle. Can the *Bicycling World* be in error?

Last Sunday was a *windy* day. It was a wind without rebate or discount off, and yet C. M. Isbell and another member of the K. C. W. reached Huntingdon, L. I., and captured some wine which awaited the first comer. Messrs. Harkman, Borland and Banker, B. H. C., were also down on the Island as far as Bay Shore, and Mead, Brown, Lewis and Cole were out in the Oranges counting miles for the same club.

Each man paid for his pleasure (?) the following day in the most approved style of fatigue. It is even stated that they "haven't done anything since." The annual election of the Brooklyns was held last night, and the entire ticket of regular nominations was elected. There was no opposition ticket, so the election was most harmoniously conducted. The officers' names were published in a previous letter. The Brooklyn club-house has assumed an entirely domestic appearance. Some new walls have been put in place to r place their counterparts, which the club removed on taking possession of the house. They cannot commence improvements on their new house until the latter part of April, but no time will be lost by the vigilant Building Committee when they do at last get possession of it.

Brooklyn, April 10, 1889. ATOL.

PHILADELPHIA.

Mr. J. R. F. Edwards, of the South End Wheelmen, who came pretty nearly capturing the long-distance record last year, has already covered over 1,300 miles up to date since the first of January. Any one who does not know what kind of roads Mr. Edwards has to contend with cannot realize what a stupendous job it is to roll up the mileage he did last year. The roads in the southern part of the city are of the poorest kind, and yet Mr. Edwards seldom misses a night that is tolerably fit for riding. What to others would seem like a monotonous job is to this intrepid rider a source of pleasure, and we predict that this year he will beat any record that has been made. In person Mr. Edwards is rather tall, seemingly of not so very strong a build, a perfect gentleman and the last one in the world one would pick out for a long distance rider.

So "Ariel" mentions something about the associated cycling clubs arranging for a combined club run on Decoration Day, *if possible*. Let "Ariel" listen. To start with, I would say a club run to any of the towns adjacent to Philadelphia is *not* possible, for the simple reason that they are all too far away for every one to ride there, and, even if they were near enough, what would be done, as "Ariel" truthfully remarks, for dinner? Norristown is the only available place we could go to, and that is nearly forty-five miles for the round trip. Added to this, no hotel would feed us, because the town would be filled with country folks who would have come to see the ceremony of decorating General Hancock's grave. This brings us to the original scheme proposed in THE WHEEL several weeks ago—a run to the Pike in the morning, dinner at Belmont Mansion and races in the afternoon. The accommodations at the Mansion are excellent. They have a large banquet hall, large enough to hold several hundred, and I am sure that arrangements could be made with the proprietor by which the wheelmen could be furnished with a dinner for a reasonable sum, say fifty cents. "Ariel" is very non-committal about the matter, but I think, or hope, he will give this his full attention, and, if he thinks favorably of it, boom it up in the the papers he writes for—literally put his shoulder to the wheel (no pun)—and help to make the first inter-club run a success.

Mr. W. T. Fleming, ex-Captain of the Century Wheelmen, has arrived home from Florida, where he has been spending the winter months. He reports that he has had a glorious time, and some of the fish and alligator stories he is telling are making the C. L. seriously think of handing in his resignation. The Centurions played a rather rough joke on the genial Fleming. The former tenant in the new house had left a large sign with the following painted in large letters: "Headquarters Executive Prohibition Committee." This they hung in the wheel-room in a conspicuous place, and it was the first thing that caught the ex-Captain's eye. As William is a decided Anti-Prohibitionist, as might have been expected, his nerves got quite a shock from which he soon recovered under the soothing influence of a couple of "Carl's" schooners.

It seems that a statement of mine which appeared in THE WHEEL several weeks ago concerning the Pennsylvania Bicycle Club has raised quite a whirlwind. Perhaps it is not strange that in a club of 180 members there are a few black sheep; therefore I deem it my duty to apologize to the Pennsylvania Bicycle Club, *as a club*, for any wrong I may have seemingly done them, but still stick to my former assertion about those "few," an assertion backed up by every member of the club. As to those beautiful eyes somebody was to kindly present me with, I am very sorry that I cannot accept them, but, rather than have them go to waste, he could give them to the "few." Perhaps they then could see the errors of their ways as well as

ARGUS.

Philadelphia, April 8.

ST. LOUIS.

At the meeting of the Missouri Club, held last Tuesday evening, a large number of applications were favorably acted upon and steps were taken to secure a larger and more regular attendance on club runs. The new road officers are of opinion that club runs are not "played out," and they intend to work that feature of club life for all that it is worth. The card for the month of April is a happy combination of long and short runs, and the so-called "tough" and "tenderfoot" element are both catered to. In Hildebrand, Lewis, Peckham, Woestman and Lynch the club has a most efficient corps of road officers, and their efforts to awaken an interest in road riding should be given the encouragement they deserve. Mr. S. C. Newman, the winner of the mileage record for last season, was presented with the medal. Mr. Brown made the annual presentation speech, and it was a model of forensic eloquence and scintillating wit. Here it is: "I having ridden three miles last season, and Mr. Newman having ridden 5,003 miles, he is clearly entitled to the medal, which I now have the pleasure of presenting to him."

Mr. Newman is about to remove to Chicago, much to the regret of his many friends here. St. Louis thus loses and Chicago gains a most valuable man. Although Mr. Newman seldom took an active part in the affairs of the club, he could always be depended on to do his full share when called upon, and his quiet and gentlemanly demeanor at all times made him many friends. His associates in the Missouri Club heartily commend him to the good offices of the Chicago wheelmen.

Speaking of the Chicago wheelmen reminds me that they have been invited to visit St. Louis on the occasion of the second of the match races between Stone and Lumsden (patience, Brother Fenton), and to remain over the following day as the guests of the Missouri Club. The invitation appears to have been sent through Mr. Miles, of the *Referee*, as the most direct way of getting it before all the Chicago wheelmen. According to the *Spectator*, Mr. Miles has replied accepting the invitation, and assuring us that we may expect a large delegation. I understand that it is the intention to give them a cordial reception and to make the day as agreeable as may be. If I might offer a hint in that connection, I would suggest that the road with the fewest hills be selected for the run. Our Chicago friends, not being used to hills, cannot reasonably be expected to favor that kind of a road, and as it is our desire that they enjoy themselves while here, the road presenting the fewest difficulties should be chosen. However, that part of the programme can be safely left with Aleck Lewis.

The Missouri Club has repealed the house rule forbidding the playing of games on the club premises on Sunday, and the billiard and card rooms are now as freely open on that day as any other of the week. To a large number of the members, whether a majority or not it is, of course, impossible to say, this action will be viewed with regret. They think that a change in the rules of so sweeping a character should not have been made without a full and free discussion of the matter before a representative meeting of the club. There were less than twenty members present when the resolution was adopted. The argument used in support of the change was that it would increase the revenue of the club. It would seem as if there might be better ways of accomplishing this object, if, indeed, it is necessary, than the one adopted.

The visitors in town this week were Messrs. Bode and Ambler, of Chicago, and Hill, of the Coventry Machinists Co., Boston.

ITHURIEL.

SAN FRANCISCO.

The local riders are all enjoying the fine weather of the present time and getting ready for a splendid season's riding.

The Bay City Wheelmen are appropriately closing the pleasantest winter season of their existence by a theatre party, held on Thursday evening, at which most of the members were on view. On next Saturday they will have one of of their popular "smokers"—a Bay City smoker, by the way, is an entertainment long to be remembered—and invitations for them are most eagerly sought by all riders, irrespective of club membership. On April 26 the closing dance of the season will be given.

Captain Fred. Russ Cook has called a club run for tomorrow to Belmont, twenty-five miles from the city, over a fine road and through a picturesque country. It is expected a large number of riders will attend.

The Bay City Wheelmen have now one hundred members, having elected the one hundredth man at the last meeting. Few cycle clubs in any country have done more for the sport than the Bay City Wheelmen. It has never made a failure of any of its undertakings, and stands to-day among the foremost clubs of the world. Its race meets, carnivals, ladies' night runs and all entertainments peculiar to bicycling clubs have always been successful. It takes the initiative in promoting any scheme beneficial to cycling in this city and State.

The local runners and athletes are complaining about the hardness of our new track. They forget that it was built solely through the efforts of local bicycle riders and principally for bicycle riders. The track is in excellent condition and a number of men will soon begin training for the races on May 30. The California Division Meet has obtained the three-mile national championship, and it will be run at Los Angeles, May 30. If Mr. E. I. Halstead comes down from Washington Territory and decides to enter he may make it interesting for some of our best men, although if F. D. Elwell rides Mr. Halstead will find a most worthy competitor.

I would suggest to the gentlemen organizing the monster Century run in the East that they select the route they intend to ride and go over it several times and arrange a schedule so that they will not go over the first part too slow and have to make up the time on the return journey. Our plan is to arrange this schedule regulating the speed according to the nature and state of the road. On the day of the run one man has this paper and another carries a watch, and the men are not allowed to fall behind the schedule. This plan will bring through many riders who could not otherwise make the run. If a strong rider were allowed to lead at his own pace, he would soon break up the weaker ones. We have also found that a steady pace without unnecessary stoppages gives the best results.

CALIFORNIA.

March 30, 1889.

Irving Halsted has already worked up a road-race fever at Tacoma, Washington. "The boys are chock full of it," he writes.

THE BROOKLYN WHEELMEN'S THEATRE AND DINNER PARTY.

"Oh, call back yesterday, bid time return!"

Rather late in the day to resurrect the fizzling reminiscences of this delightful incident.

It was a red-letter night, and from the metaphorical as well as the artistic standpoint, for much quiet painting was done, and

"Those did drink who never drank before,
And those who *always* drink now drank the more."

When the curtain rose Louis Harrison was confronted by 275 immaculate shirt fronts, topped by 275 ready-to-be-amused faces. Louis worked off some local hits, which were received with the

"Shrill, sudden shout,
The cry of an applauding multitude."

He had been thoroughly posted by the committee, but forgot many of the gags intrusted to him. The colors of the various clubs and the Schwalbach medal added local cycling color to the performance.

After the theatre party about two hundred of the wheelmen adjourned to the Clarendon, where dinner was served at long tables. Mr. Luscomb and party, who occupied a private box at the theatre, did not attend the dinner.

At the centre of the principal table sat Toast-master Michael Furst.

"Soft-tongued and golden-toned,
He swayed the cycling mass as if he were its soul."

At his right, as the honored guest of the evening, sat Mayor Chapin.

"A man in all the world's new fashions planted,
That hath a host of phrases in his brain."

On the left I noted Mr. F. P. Prial, of THE WHEEL, the guest of the Long Island Wheelmen

"Why did I write? What sin, to me unknown,
Dipped me in ink—my parents' or my own?"

After the first few courses had been served, Toast-master Furst called on Mr. James Fox, President of the Brooklyn B. C.—

"Bid me discourse,
I will enchant thine ear,"—

who made a sound, practical speech, to be followed by Mayor Chapin, who made the longest speech of the evening, speaking enthusiastically of the favorable impression he had received of cycling from the gathering before him, and promising to resurface "Cobblestone Hill."

Mr. M. L. Bridgman, Kings County Wheelmen, responded to the toast of "Racing;" after which the Toast-master introduced the toast of "The Cycling Press" with these lines:

"Here shall the Press the Wheelmen's rights maintain,
Unaided by influence and unbribed by gain."

Ye editor evidently believed that

"Therefore since brevity is the soul of wit
I will be brief.

Or else we could not withstand the attraction of his *frizzle* water, for his talk was short and sweet.

Mr. E. A. Bradford, L.I.W., responded to "The Ladies."

"They are pretty to walk with,
They are witty to talk with
And pleasant, too, to think on."

Mr. Bradford, who was well up in his subject, discussed learnedly on the beauty and goodness of the fair sex.

After the regular list of toasts, several gentlemen informally entertained the company. Mr. Louis Harrison told stories and sang.

"And I did laugh sans intermission,
An hour by the clock."

Mr. Torrey and Mr. Spelman, of the Brooklyon Club, informally spoke and recited. In the excitement of the moment, Mr. Torrey dropped into poetry.

"He was full of joke and jest,
All things talked thoughts to him."

Mr. George B. Bancroft, of the Brooklyn Club, was called upon but was too full—of emotion for utterance. He had been toasting

"Bacchus ever fair and young,
Drinking joys did first ordain,
Bacchus' blessings are a treasure
Drinking is the cyclists' pleasure,
Rich the treasure,
Sweet the pleasure,
Sweet is pleasure after pain."

About four o'clock the party broke up. It was broke up long before that hour, but did not realize it at once. The last view I had of the supper-room was ye editor, who is fitted with ball-bearing jaws, talking 345 words a minute to Walter Sinn and Louis Harrison. I felt relieved next day when I learned that Mr. Harrison was able to complete his Brooklyn engagement.

"Not Heaven itself upon the past has power,
And what has been has been,
And we have had our hour."

TITNAM.

PLAINFIELD BICYCLE CLUB'S TOURNAMENT.

The annual tournament of the Plainfield Bicycle Club was held on April 4. There was an unusually large attendance, and everything passed off without a hitch. The prizes were costly and valuable and well worthy the best efforts of the competitors. Following, in regular order, are the list of events and the names of the winners: First event, Plainfield Bicycle Club parade, led by Capt. F. L. C. Martin and Acting Lieutenant Geo. C. Martin, Jr.; second event, 70-yard dash, won by E. S. Walz, Jr., and Jos. W. Sandford, Jr.; third event, sack race, won by F. P. Van Buren and F. L. C. Martin; fourth event, quarter-mile run, open, won by D. Watts; fifth event, slow bicycle race, won by F. P. Van Buren and Geo. W. Morrison; sixth event, hurdle race, won by L. J. Kron and H. D. Morrison; seventh event, fancy riding on the "star" by T. R. Finley, whose wonderful performance elicited tremendous applause; eighth event, half-mile run, won by L. J. Kron and H. W. Beebe; ninth event, tug of war between the teams of the Plainfield Bicycle Club and the Elizabeth Wheelmen, won by the Plainfield Bicycle Club team; tenth event, three-legged race, won by F. L. C. Martin and Geo. C. Martin, Jr., and H. W. Beebe and E. S. Walz, Jr.

The winners were showered with congratulations, and the large assemblage dispersed well pleased with the day's entertainment.

CYCLING AS A PROMOTER OF HEALTH.

"A man who has followed a sedentary occupation begins to experience increasing disinclination to exertion, chronic constipation, with sometimes stiffness and, it may be, flying pains in the joints; for such a man a tricycle is capable of accomplishing a great deal; exercise ceases to be a trouble, the bowels become more regular, and the joint-troubles, which may be at first a little aggravated, disappear. Dr. Jennings believes that chronic gout and rheumatic gout may thus be cured, or, at least, kept at bay, even when the patient has been seriously crippled by several attacks. He also speaks very confidently as to the cure of obesity, if the patient will refrain from gratifying the thirst, which is at first very trying. He even finds some reason to believe that his favorite exercise may be a useful adjuvant in the treatment of early phthisis. There are certain warnings, continues the writer, which ought to be given when recommending cycling. In the first place, the cyclist ought to be suitably dressed in all-wool clothing from head to foot, special directions being given to the tailor to make no use of cotton linings, stiffening or padding; secondly, his motto should be *festina lente*, he should not attempt long journeys or fast journeys until he has thoroughly gauged his own strength; thirdly, he should not force himself to ride up long hills; fourthly, he must, as far as possible, abstain from alcoholic beverages while on a journey."—*Health*.

A SELECTED LIST OF PATENTS.

[Reported especially for THE WHEEL AND CYCLING TRADE REVIEW by C. A. Snow & Co., patent attorneys, Washington, D. C.]

Leon Baudreau, Chicopee Falls, Mass. Spring fork for bicycles.

D. A. Babe, Paris, France. Bicycle.

John B. Brooks, Birmingham, England. Bicycle saddle.

Malcolm A. Norton, Hartford, Conn. Velocipede.

Charles E. W. Woodward, Chicopee Falls, Mass. Velocipede.

"Stump," writing from Eureka, Northern California, hits off one of our ideas when he writes: "Knowing that you like to hear from all parts of the globe once in a while, I send you a sketch of our first club run of the season." The sketch appears in another column.

FRAGMENT OF LETTER FOUND IN STREET.

HEAP SWEET AH LEE, Phillee:

Lettee you lite cum click;
Heap nice.
Diam solly you no cum see
Great Centiy Lun cum Phillee
June. See? Heap big clowd.
All clowd sweetee shirtee.
You ketch um, washee! See!
Makee the mon so heap much!
Big bistickel lide, too!
Look out don't ketch pigtail.
Me heap laff you do.

Displectly,

AH THERE.

A NOVEL PLAN FOR ELECTIONS.

The new system of voting at the New York Club, under which the coming election is to be held on May 6, is quite an innovation on the methods generally prevailing in cycle and other clubs. At the annual meeting April 3, held on the first Wednesday in April, nearly a month prior to the election, after the reports of officers for the year just closed had been submitted, a ballot was taken for nominations. The candidates were not presented in the usual manner, by some member rising and proposing a name; but each member had to write his individual choice for every office. The vote being counted, the two names which stood highest for each office were posted as candidates; any five members having the further privilege of proposing in uniting additional candidates for any or all of the officers, which privilege expires on April 26, ten days before the election. The Secretary will then have printed an official ballot containing all the names which have been thus proposed, and only this ballot will be accepted by the tellers. Unless further names are added the ballot will read as follows:

For President,
O. G. Moses.
B. J. Shriver.
E. S. Terry.

For Vice-President,
F. W. Kitching.
J. H. Tripler.

For Secretary,
W. E. Findley.
G. M. Nisbett.

For Treasurer,
Irving M. Shaw.
Ross W. Weir.

For Captain,
J. M. McFadden.
Irving W. Shaw.

For Chairman of the House Committee,
W. E. Lansing.
Frank I. Stott.

For Chairman of the Membership Committee,
John R. Blake.
W. C. Heydecker.
James B. Roy.
E. S. Terry.

For Chairman of the Auditing Committee,
Frank I. Stott.
J. H. Tripler.

For Chairman of the Entertainment Committee,
W. C. Heydecker.
E. S. Terry.

As will be readily seen, every member must exercise some individual discretion in voting, as the ticket cannot be voted as a whole but must be *marked to indicate the choice* in each instance. It is claimed that this will stimulate independent voting, and that the system of nominations ensures a full field of candidates from which to make a selection. The chairmen of the several committees with the executive officers form the Boord of Trustees; each chairman having the appointment and removal of his committee, for which he is then held personally responsible.

As other clubs may be favorably impressed by the New York's new system of government, we append those portions of the by-laws under which it is established, together with the amendment clause, also a product of the recent revision.

ARTICLE IV.

SEC. 1. At the annual election there shall be chosen (in the manner set forth in Art. XI., Sec. 3) a President, Vice-President, Secretary, Treasurer, Captain, Chairman of the House Committee, Chairman of the Membership Committee, Chairman of the Auditing Committee and a Chairman of the Entertainment Committee. These nine officers shall constitute the Board of Trustees.

SEC. 2. Each chairman of a committee shall appoint and remove at pleasure the members of his committee, for whose conduct in office he shall be responsible to the club.

ARTICLE V.

SEC. 5. The captain shall be the chief road officer and shall command the club at all runs, meets or excursions. He shall appoint first and second lieutenants, whom he may remove at pleasure and for whose official conduct he shall be responsible to the club.

The lieutenants shall assist the captain in his duties and in his absence shall assume command in the order of their rank.

SEC. 6. The standing committees shall be composed as follows:
House: Chairman and four other members.
Membership: Chairman and two other members.
Auditing: Chairman and two other members.
Entertainment: Chairman and two other members.

ARTICLE XI.

SEC. 2. The annual meeting shall be held on the first Wednesday in April, when the reports of the several officers shall be read and a secret ballot taken for nomination to the various offices. The candidates receiving the highest and next highest vote for each office shall be deemed regularly in nomination for such office, as shall also any candidate certified to the secretary at least ten days before election by five or more members, no member being allowed to sign more than one nomination paper for each office; and the names of all candidates nominated as aforesaid shall be posted upon the bulletin as soon as nominated.

SEC. 3. The annual election of officers specified in Sec. 1 of Art. IV., shall be held on the first Monday in May, the polls to be open during such hours and under the inspection of such officers as may have been ordered by the annual meeting. The secretary shall cause to be printed ballots bearing the names of all candidates nominated as provided in the foregoing section, with a blank space for the writing of additional names, and each member, in voting, may designate his choice either by putting a mark opposite the name for which he wishes to vote or by scratching out all other names. A majority vote shall elect and the officers elected shall hold office until the day after the next annual election. No proxy voting shall be allowed.

ARTICLE XVI.

All proxy amendments to these by-laws must be moved at a club meeting, which may thereupon order a ballot to be taken at least two weeks later, appointing inspectors for such ballot and fixing the hours for the polls to be open, which may be upon one or more days but shall not be less than three hours in all. Every member shall be entited to vote in person or by a signed mailed vote, addressed to the secretary, who shall deposit such vote in the ballot box. At least twenty-five per cent. of the club's active membership must vote to result in any action and unless a majority of the entire club shall vote in favor of the proposed amendment, it shall require a three-fourths affirmative vote of those cast for adoption. Notice shall be sent by the secretary to every member, at least three days in advance, that such a ballot is to be taken, stating the general nature of the proposed amendment, and he shall also post upon the bulletin a copy of the amendment in full immediately upon adjournment of the meeting at which it has been moved.

L. H. JOHNSON'S 1889 CATALOGUE.

Mr. L. H. Johnson, Orange, N. J., imports Premier Safeties, Sparkbrook bicycles, Humber tricycles and tandems, all of which wheels are illustrated and described in his new catalogue.

The Special Premier Safety, $135, may be used by lady or gentleman. It is a light wheel, with strong tubing and strong diamond frame; 28-inch driver geared to 53 inches; 30-inch steering wheel; weight, 46 lbs.

The Popular Premier is a full roadster safety; price, $105.

The Premier Tandem Safety, for lady and gentleman or two gentlemen, is the type of wheel used by Mr. Johnson last season, and highly commended by all who rode it. The wheel has 30-inch wheels, driver geared to 55 or 60 inches. The power is applied to both sides of the driving hub, equalizing the strain. Weight, 90 lbs.; price, $200.

The Special Sparkbrook Bicycle, pin 50 inches, $125. This is a product of the Sparkbrook Manufacturing Company, Limited, a firm favorably known on the other side. The material is best weldless steel tubing, steel drop forgings, Para rubber. Runs are hollow Warwick, which do not project over the tire, and are therefore not dented and cracked by stones. Single ball bearings to wheels and pedals. Saddle, a special patent of the Hammoch style, made on specifications by Lampleigh & Brown. Weight of 50-inch, 38 lbs.

Youth's Premier Safety, $65. This is a highest-grade boy's safety and small adult's wheel.

The Humber Cripper Tricycle, price $160, and the Humber Cripper Tandem Tricycle, price $250, are too well known to need extensive notice. Both wheels are equal to the best ever put on the market, and the tandem has many excellent features found in no other wheel of the kind.

In Lanterns, Mr. Johnson handles the Unique Safety, $5; the Arlington Safety, $4.50; the Boss Safety, $4; the Cyclops Hub Lamp, $4, and the Guide Hub Lamp, $2.

GEORGE R. BIDWELL'S 1889 CATALOGUE.

Mr. George R. Bidwell has just issued his 1889 catalogue, a pocket-size pamphlet containing a deal of information on the wheels handled by Mr. Bidwell, as well as full information of his renting, repairing, storage and instruction departments.

Mr. Bidwell's main office and headquarters are at 313 West Fifty-eighth Street. They have recently been redecorated, and present a fine appearance. Full directions are given for reaching the store from various parts of the city. There is a short essay on learning to ride. Mr. Bidwell teaches both outdoors and at Adelphi Hall, Fifty-second Street and Broadway, where ladies and gentlemen are given private lessons without the discomfort of having their elemental efforts afford amusement to the spectators.

Complete details of the renting department are given. Mr. Bidwell is a firm believer that rented wheels should always be first-class, that the novice may get as much pleasure as possible out of the sport. In accordance with this principle the list of wheels rented by him are all 1889 brand-new wheels, and give as much satisfaction as if owned by the riders. Mr. Bidwell puts in a word on the danger of coasting and speeding in the parks, and advises all wheelmen to turn corners and pass cross drives with their wheels under perfect control.

Mr. Bidwell stores wheels and provides lockrooms at reasonable rates. There are ample dressing accommodation and bathing facilities.

The catalogue contains an illustrated description of every pattern of Columbia wheel, as well as of the Psycho ladies' safety bicycle; also a full list of sundries. Mr. Bidwell carries an excellent line of second-hand wheels, and has a well-equipped repair shop.

The Reading Bicycle Club should settle the difficulty which has caused so much discussion in the club without publishing the details of the case, which will put both the club and cycling in bad odor with the public. As we understand the case, the silver cup now held by one of the members of the club was won principally through the efforts of that member. He not only raced and scored points for the club, but also paid the entrance fees and expenses of the team who won the cup. If he paid said expenses in his official capacity he should be reimbursed by the club and the cup should become its property, that is, if the team who won it agree that they will present it to the club. The cup was won at the Lancaster meet last June. The members who are opposed to giving the cup to the club have withdrawn and have formed the Penn. Wheelmen. They have four nicely furnished rooms. The formation of an opposition club will spur club life in Reading. For the sake of his reputation we should advise the gentleman who holds the cup to have an impartial committee appointed, submit the facts to them and abide by their decision. The Reading Club may obtain redress and a fair hearing by submitting the entire case to their State Racing Board.

On April 29 the Long Island Wheelmen will hold a ladies' reception. Clara Rionda, the child elocutionist, will be the feature of the evening's entertainment.

The Brooklyn Club expect to move into their new house, at 62 Hanson Place, about May 1.

The "Inseparables" of the Harlem Wheelmen were out on the road on Sunday. The "Inseparable" family is composed of Judge and Mrs. Newcome, Otto, Frank, Professor, Maud and Sadie. The Deacon and the Deacon's daughter are also members of the family, but he was probably at service. On the return home, Maud lost her brake on a down grade in the park and veered into the bushes. The bushes were unhurt; not so Maud, who nurseth a many-colored eye.

The people of Hempstead, L. I., have voted to build a macadam road, thirty-five miles in length, from Flushing to Newtown, Roslyn and Little Neck.

The suggestion that safeties be classed separately from ordinaries, made in the last issue of this paper, was incorporated in the amended racing rules of the Board and published in the *Bicycling World* of March 22. We were not aware that this distinction had been made by the Racing Board, because the copy of *The World* received at this office did not contain the separate sheet on which the amended rules were printed.

The "sweet girl graduates" of Vassar received copies of last week's WHEEL, which contained much of interest on cycling for ladies.

Chief Consul Bull represented the League at the Spalding dinner given at Delmonico's on Monday evening.

The Minneapolis Bicycle Club opened the season April 7 with a formal run, in which forty men took part.

The Long Island Wheelmen entertained the Brooklyn Club at their home on last Saturday evening. The chief entertainer of the evening, Col. John Oakey, had been compelled to break his engagement on account of the Tracy reception; but Chairman Clarke, cool-headed Clarke, secured enough talent to entertain the boys until midnight.

The Capital Cycle Co. publish a page of details of their beautiful Pycho wheels. The Capital Company are U.S. agents for these wheels.

The following clever pen picture of E. R. Shipton, Secretary of the N. C. U., is contributed by Junius Junior to the Irish *Cyclist*:

"It is suggested in some quarters that the C. T. C. is going to take action against road racing. I should have thought E. R. Shipton had enough enemies without interfering in this question. I think he is too clever to do so. For E. R. S. is clever, not as a journalist, but as a secretary and organizer of the thousands who contribute to his support. One cannot help an amused feeling of admiration for the man who has worked up this Touring Club to its enormous dimensions, chiefly by inspiring a lot of idle or weak-minded individuals with the idea that their duty to their fellow-man demanded the absorption of their leisure hours in unpaid labors for the Cyclists' Touring Club. Among these fanatics is a frantic desire to work for the C. T. C. ranks next to godliness, if not before it, and, with a staff of unfortunate clerks who are reminded by announcements on the walls that they must never cease to work, Sir Bumptious Ragman (O rare 'Faed,' for those words much thanks !) sits at his ease and compiles his *Gazette*, or jaundiced man's best companion. The most humorous thing in connection with the C. T. C. is the intense dignity of Shipton, whose speeches, when he so favors the sound waves and paralyzes a respectful audience, are redolent of self-satisfaction, and suggestive to a degree of the caste of Vere de Vere, with which, however, I fancy the victim of Justice Wills' withering satire has actually very little in common."

The ever-popular New Rapid Wheels, made by the St. George's Engineering Co., are being manufactured as rapidly as of yore, yea, even more so. One firm in the United States takes thirty-six machines per week, and the firm's books are teeming with orders from all parts of the world. The genial C. A. P. regards his order and day books with loving looks, and likewise bestows a glance of approval upon the admirable finish of the machines as they are conveyed to the packing-room.—*Sport and Play.*

Samuel B. Sterling, of Trumbull, Conn., would like to have a companion for a transcontinental trip, which he expects to start on in May. We believe that Mr. Fleming is looking for a companion for a like trip.

A NEW BRAKE.

To thoroughly enjoy the sport of cycling, it is essential that, whatever kind of machine is ridden, the brake power should be adequate to meet all contingencies. The muscular power required to obtain full benefit from those at present in use is too great to be maintained for any length of time, so that, on steep or long gradients, the rider is under the necessity of dismounting to obtain relief, or else suffer great inconvenience. To obviate this many remedies have been tried, but far and away the best, in our opinion, is the one above depicted—the invention of Mr. James Boyd, Cycle Depot, Galashiels. In applying a brake of the spoon description to a machine in motion, the wheel, responding to the motive power, exerts a force which would counteract the power of the hand if the brake-rod was not secured by means of a collar, or the spoon hinged to the arch of the forks. It is this force Mr. Boyd has utilized. Doing away with the collar or hinge supporting the original brake, a connection is carried to the back of the forks to another spoon working by means of a double hinge, from a fixture which also accommodates the mud-guard, and springs to draw up the brake when pressure on the lever is removed. On applying the brake, the wheel, endeavoring to carry forward the front spoon, draws on its auxiliary and produces a combination, the full strength of which will hold the proverbial horse with very little expenditure of muscular power. A glance at the above engraving reveals its lightness, simplicity and adaptability to all machines, and these, combined with cheapness, should command a large demand for what is undoubtedly the beau-ideal of an effective brake.—*The Scottish Cyclist.*

Cycling is making advances in the Island of Ceylon. Two publications, "Bicycling, Its Theory and Practice" and "Health Upon Wheels," have also been published on the island.

All the Accepted Road Records

PATENTED FEB. 15, 1887.

were measured with, and thousands of the best wheelmen use only, the

Butcher Spoke Cyclometer

FOR

ORDINARY BICYCLES.

Not suitable for Safeties.

Sent free by mail on receipt of

Ordinary Bicycle, - $10.00
Safety Bicycle, - - 11.00

PRICE, - - - - $5.00

Butcher Cyclometer.

SEND FOR CIRCULAR TO THE

BUTCHER CYCLOMETER CO.,
338 Washington Street,
BOSTON, MASS

Mention this paper.

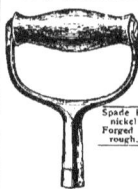

COLUMBIA RECAPITULATION.

COLUMBIA LIGHT ROADSTER SAFETY.

$135. Tangent Spokes, Cold-Drawn Seamless-Steel Hollow Fellors, Columbia Tubular Steel Frame with anti-vibrating Spring Fork, Ball-Bearings all around, Ball-Bearing Socket Steering-Head, One-Piece Hollow Handle-Bar, Improved Ewart Chain. Readily adjustable to meet the requirements of any rider. We have put more money into its construction than any other bicycle ever built. The machine for business and professional men. Furnished with continuous Front Fork if desired.

COLUMBIA LIGHT ROADSTER.

$125. The handsomest, strongest, most extensively used, and most generally satisfactory Light Roadster ever made. The lightest road machine. The nearest to perfection of anything yet attained in wheel construction.

EXPERT COLUMBIA.

$120. Best-known bicycle in the world. The established favorite for long-distance touring, and all other uses where the highest possible qualities are requisite, with durability pre-eminent. Note this point—as light as most Light Roadsters. All our latest improvements.

COLUMBIA TANDEM SAFETY.

$200. Tangent Spokes, One-Piece Hollow Handle-Bars, Columbia Tubular Steel Frame, Ball-Bearings all around, Ball-Bearing Socket Steering-Head, Improved Ewart Chain, Columbia "Double-Grip" Ball-Pedals. Connected steering, and separate brakes. A light, graceful, and easy-running machine for two riders, suitable for anybody. Readily adaptable for a lady on the front seat by removing one brace.

COLUMBIA TANDEM.

$250. A front-wheel handle-bar steerer, which two ladies can ride if desirable, capable of being steered and controlled by brake from either seat, and readily convertible into a handle-bar steering "single"; in appearance graceful and well-proportioned, in construction as nearly perfect as long experience in cycle building can make it, and, withal, as light as a roadster Tandem can reasonably be expected to be.

SURPRISE COLUMBIA TRICYCLE.

$150. A very desirable Tricycle. Safe, easy, and convenient. Practically a rear-driving Safety, with two front wheels. The running track variable in width from 34 inches down to about 30, and then folding to a width over all of 29 inches, enabling it to go through almost any door. Easiest running tricycle. An excellent hill climber. Needs fewest repairs.

COLUMBIA SEMI-ROADSTER.

$75. The most durable, easiest running, and best equipped boys' bicycle yet built.

VOLUNTEER COLUMBIA.

$100. The best wheel for the money. Made to ride and guaranteed to wear. All steel and no castings. The general construction of the Expert, with some of its least essential advantages modified.

VELOCE COLUMBIA.

$125. A thoroughly well-made first-class safety bicycle. The leading safety of last season.

STANDARD COLUMBIA.

$75. "The old reliable Standard."

IMPORTED.

RUDGE.

Rudge Light Roadster, $100; Rudge Bicyclette, $135; Rudge Crescent Tricycle, $140; Rudge Crescent Tandem, $200; Rudge Humber Tandem, $175.

PSYCHO LADIES' BICYCLE.

$120. 2-20 inch wheel with ¼-inch tire. Weight, 46¾ lbs. with pedals and saddle.

ROVER LADIES' BICYCLE.

$115. Front wheel 30 inches, with ¼-inch tire; rear wheel 28 inches, with ¼-inch tire. Weight, 45¾ lbs. with pedals and saddle.

❋   ❋

THE FINEST LINE EVER PRESENTED.

CRANKS vs. SAFETIES. Both have advantages, both have exclusive admirers. For young and active riders we advise the crank machines, for older riders the Safety.

LARGE ILLUSTRATED CATALOGUE FREE.

POPE MFG. CO., Boston, New York, Chicago.

PRESS OF F. V. STRAUSS, 100-104 WALKER ST., NEW YORK.

𝕿𝕳𝕰 𝖂𝕳𝕰𝕰𝕷

—AND—

CYCLING TRADE REVIEW,

Published every Friday morning.

Entered at the Post Office at second class rates

Subscription Price,　-　-　-　$1.00 a year.
Foreign Subscriptions,　-　-　-　6s. a year.
Single Copies,　-　-　-　-　-　5 Cents.

Newsdealers may order through Am. News Co.

All copy should be received by Monday.
Telegraphic news received till Wednesday noon.

Advertising rates on Application.

F. P. PRIAL, Editor and Proprietor
23 Park Row.

P. O. Box 444,　　　　　　　New York.

Persons receiving sample copies of this paper are respectfully requested to examine its contents and give us their patronage, and as far as is convenient, aid in circulating the journal, and extend its influence in the cause which it so faithfully serves. Subscription price, $1 per year.

The Remedy Found.

In our editorial last week on convict labor we were more prophetic than we set out to be. We described the disease and pointed out the only practicable remedy—the employment of convicts on the public highways. And behold ! as we went to press a narrow majority of the Assembly voted to progress Judge Yates' bill to accomplish this very end. Modesty bars us from claiming credit for this result, but we nevertheless take great pleasure in falling in with the procession and urging our readers to exert all their influence in behalf of the Yates Prison bill, which has yet to pass the gauntlet upon its actual adoption.

Briefly described, this bill accepts the situation that a large part of the population of this State will not consent to the employment of convicts either on the contract or the State account system, in competition with free labor, and proposes just what we advocated : that they should be distributed among the smaller prisons and put to work at the much-needed building and maintenance of good roads. A section of the press has been led by prejudice and ignorance of the subject to violently condemn the plan, but without giving any reasons for their opposition. As a rule, it will be found that such newspapers have no better reason than that they hate trades-unions and all their works ; and because the unions blindly fight against convict labor in the penitentiaries without offering any substitute, these papers just as blindly insist that the convicts shall be kept at work on the old plan. On the same side are arrayed certain sentimentalists with a fad for maintaining Prison Reform Associations, for the conversion of convicts into Sunday-school scholars, which can only make a show when the convicts are massed together in large numbers.

As a matter of fact, such convicts as are not degraded beyond all possible hope of reformation stand a much better chance of being improved in a small prison than in a large one ; but this is the least important part of the problem. Our civilization has reached a point where

men have to bid against each other for the opportunity to work, and the rates of wages depend on the number of men whose services are at the disposal of those who have work to give. Whether or not it is right that this should be so or could be prevented, it is an existing fact ; and it does make a difference to the wage-earner if in selling his labor he has to meet with competition of any sort, and, most of all, with such competition as convict labor affords. On the other hand, it is unwholesome in the extreme that convicts should remain idle, and unfair that the community should have to support them in idleness ; although it is also true that the increase of taxation for this purpose, falling upon the laboring classes, is smaller than the effect upon wages which convict labor has.

Road improvement gives the solution ; for here is a branch of work which ought to be done, but will not be done in most cases if it is left to the spontaneous action of rural localities. Accordingly there is no free labor to be displaced, and the State can, without disturbing the industrial situation, get a most beneficial return for the money spent in maintaining the convicts. The 10,000 wheelmen of New York State can bring much influence to bear in support of this measure, not only by their personal efforts, but by awakening local sentiment in its favor ; and there is no step which they can take that will lead to better results in the betterment of our roads.

IT is a remarkable fact that while Judge Yates' bill, providing for the employment of convicts on the public roads, raised a strong feeling of dissent, a bill introduced by Gen. Husted, and providing for the removal of Sing Sing Prison to some other county than Westchester, was passed by the New York Assembly with only two dissenting votes. The reasons for the removal, as given by the supporters of the bill, are that it destroys the value of the property on the Hudson at Sing Sing ; that the residents of the county don't want it any longer, and that the view from Gen. Husted's residence includes the prison. Gen. Husted's bill provides for the appointment of a committee of five to consider the project and report at the next session of the Legislature.

It is a further remarkable fact that while Judge Yates was delivering his three hours' speech on his bill the members of the Assembly should amuse themselves in directing "spit-balls" at each other. The fact that the lives of 1,500 men were affected by Judge Yates' bill did not prevent them from having their little time and converting the law-making chamber into a bear-pit. It cannot be argued that the dullness of Judge Yates' bill was directly responsible for their behavior, for they allowed him to speak two hours over the regular time, and nearly every member remained in his seat until the little Judge had concluded.

THERE is something both amusing and yet emulative in the incident which happened on the Brooklyn-Bath road on Sunday last, as told by our Brooklyn correspondent. It seems that four members of the Brooklyn Club, while riding on the side-path toward Bath, met four posts, which had been planted across the path by a cyclophobian, and which for some time have compelled wheelmen to make a skillful and annoying detour. The posts were obstinate and refused to budge, so that one of the Brooklyn men bit the dust. With a determination almost satanic, they dismounted, proceeded to a neighboring inn and resurrected a hatchet.

Armed with this weapon of destruction, they returned to the obstinate posts, and plying their blows right merrily, the posts were razed to the ground amid war-whoops. The men afterward proceeded on their journey, wearing chips of the posts in their caps. When the road-hog becomes bumptious, wheelmen should not be too scrumptious, but, recollecting that patience at times is no virtue, they should apply the hatchet of annihilation to the point of obstruction.

WE are happy ! Just read Psyche's rejoinder to Helen Grey, the lady who has just taken charge of the *Bicycling World's* ladies' department. The little tiffs between Faudry and ourselves are nothing ; we are mere featherweights, and not in it with Psyche and Helen Grey. It is all very sad, Helen, just at the outset of your career, too ; but we think Psyche is right.

ASSEMBLYMAN YATES' BILL NOW PROGRESSING THROUGH THE NEW YORK ASSEMBLY.

Mr. Yates' bill provides that no motive power or machinery for manufacturing purposes shall be placed or used in any of the State or county prisons, penitentiaries, etc.; and no person confined in any such institution shall be required or allowed to work at any trade or industry where his labor, or the profit of his labor, is farmed out, contracted, etc.

Only such articles as are commonly needed or used in such institutions may be manufactured by the inmates thereof, and all such articles not required for use shall be furnished to the several alms-houses, asylums, etc., supported either wholly or in part by the State.

Sec. 4.—*The sheriffs of the several counties of the State are hereby required and directed to cause all prisoners who may be sentenced by the judgment of any of the courts of this State to confinement to the county jail at hard labor, to be put at work in cultivating and improving the county and town lands, highways, roads and bridges, breaking stone therefor, and such other public work, and at such time and at such locality within their several counties, as the board of supervisors thereof may direct.*

PRISON LABOR.

There has been considerable legislation at Albany within the last few days in reference to the management of prisons and convict labor. Mr. Yates has succeeded in placing a bill before the Assembly which authorizes the employment of convicts in outdoor labor, such as road-making, bridge-building, etc. He returns to the degrading chaingang system. Mr. Husted has secured the passage of a bill looking to the suppression of Sing Sing Prison and providing for the employment of convicts in the erection of a new prison.

Referring to the Yates Bill, the *Commercial Advertiser* holds that there is too much sentimentality in the discussion of the prison question. It says that the inmates of our prisons are enemies of society who have committed crimes of every known variety, and that any consideration of their claims to congenial employment is a waste of generous sentiment, etc. It says : "These people have been sent to prison to be punished for their crimes in order that criminal impulses may be restrained, and in the choice of work for them it is absurd to rule out employments merely because they are less agreeable than others." It is quite evident that this writer is not informed as to the true theory of our State prisons. They are held to be reformatory as well as punitive. The theory is that more than half the men who reach State prison are the victims of misfortune and circumstances over which they have no control, and are bad, in any sense, vicious or natural enemies of society. More one man goes to prison ten thousand men who have technically violated laws, and cunning scoundrels who know how to evade laws, remain outside. Subjecting prisoners to degrading servitude and treating them with the brutality which prevailed in olden times when slavery was recognized and debt was considered a crime, would have the effect of making these men professional enemies of society. The theory, very properly, is that men are restrained of liberty as a means of punishment for violated laws, and are treated humanely in order that they may become convinced of the error of their ways and adopt honest methods of livelihood. To teach a man, not wholly vile, a good trade while in prison is to prepare him for better citizenship ; and all the statistics of our prisons prove that brutality toward convicts yields a very poor return.

What we need in our prisons is a system of labor carried on under the auspices of the State rather than contractors, which will not bring prison products into unjust competition with legitimate business, but will teach skilled men habits of industry and good trades, instead of resentful, vicious and brutalized enemies of every established system. There is no union to-day before our law-makers which has been so bedogged with the logic of political clap-trap as this matter of convict labor. It is a question that should be treated honestly and intelligently and with reference solely to the best interests of society.—*New York World.*

BILL TO EMPLOY CONVICTS ON PUBLIC ROADS.

The Assembly discussed the Prison Labor bills for several hours in Committee of the Whole on April 11. Judge Yates substituted his bill for the Savery bill, and the substitute was ordered to a third reading. The Yates bill provides for the employment of the convicts on the roads, at public works, at manufacturing articles needed by the State, and at hand labor. It does not interfere with the workings of the Departments of Charities and Correction in New York City and Brooklyn. The Fassett substitute will come up as an amendment on third reading. A provision was inserted in the Yates bill by Judge Greene that every prisoner should be allowed ten cents a day out of the proceeds of his labor, and that at the end of his term this money should be paid him to start out with.

Judge Yates said that his bill, which was passed last year, had been amended against his wish, and that it had not had a fair trial by the prison authorities. The prison authorities were opposed to his plan, and would not comply with the law and carry it out. "I am the target of philanthropists and women," he said. "No sooner was my bill passed than the prison ring locked the convicts up in their cells, and did not work them as provided by my bill. These philanthropists describe the misery and punishment of the prisoner. Why do they not go to the home of the poor workingman and describe his misery and suffering? They send through the land the story of every prisoner who goes insane through lack of work, which my bill directs the prison authorities to keep him employed at, and which the prison ring do not do. Why do they not describe in terms of equal pity the insanity and the suicide that come in the workingman's home from lack of employment? A keynote of this clamor is the music of the money of the prison ring."

Judge Yates spoke over two hours and made one of the most interesting speeches of the session. He charged the prison officials with being a ring that profited by the State account system, and were unwilling to try any other system because it did not give them the same opportunities for personal profit. He said that they did not comply with the law, and that they locked their prisoners in cells and blamed it on him and his bill, whereas his bill required the employment of the prisoners as much as they are now employed on Blackwell's Island and in the King's County Penitentiary.

ROADS IMPROVEMENT IN MASSACHUSETTS.

The legislative committee has reported favorably upon the recommendation in Governor Ames' message of the creation of the office of commissioner of roads and bridges for Massachusetts, and the bill is expected to come up for consideration to-morrow. It is a step toward the improvement of the roads of the State, in which so much has been done with advantage of late years. This work has been much confined to the larger towns and to particular portions of the State, but at the present session of the legislature a bill has already passed authorizing the appointment of a superintendent of streets in each town, which will be another step in advance in this matter. It is intended that the State Superintendent of Roads and Bridges shall be an advisory officer to co-operate with town superintendents. The advantage he is likely to be to them is easily apparent. The State officer will doubtless be a skilled engineer, fully informed in scientific road-building. He will be at the call of the town superintendents, who will many of them need the kind of information that he is fitted to furnish.

The expense of this office will be small. Including the travel that will attend it, and other incidental outlay, it will probably not exceed $5,000. While the expense of towns is, therefore, not increased beyond the infinitesimal portion of the State tax to meet this sum, every town has at its call, under this arrangement, a skilled officer to advise as to its roadways in case any improvement is in contemplation. The people are becoming awake to the fact of how great the advantage is in acting intelligently on this subject. Under the old methods much road mending has been so conducted as to be worse than wasted. In the country towns gravel is dumped on roads often without regard to its adaptability or the method of applying it. Here is to be an officer who has made the subject a scientific study. If the people of the State are desirous of seeing what can be done under the best methods in road-building, there are abundant examples of it in the vicinity of Boston. It is hardly expected that all the country towns will equal this, but they can approximate to it, and under competent direction it can be done in the end at less expense than is now involved in the old-fashioned inferior methods.

If the building of bridges is something likely to be less frequent in the towns of the State, the aid furnished by the officer in it will be yet more important, in cases where it is applied. He will be a man of the fullest information upon the subject, and entirely disinterested in the conveying of it. When, as has often occurred in the past, there shall be differences of opinion as to the proper course to be pursued in towns in bridge building, the advice of such an authority will be invaluable. It will be really like referring the case to an authoritative umpire.

Every one wants the best roads to be obtained, for they are something that every one more or less uses. Every taxpayer feels the mistake in his pocket if they are not constructed or kept in repair as they should be. This bill is one of enlightened progress, therefore in the public interest. It is not reasonable to anticipate any opposition to it, for it is hard to see how even the most inveterate conservatism can object to the creation of an office which involves so slight expense, and is purely advisory in character. This, aside from the strong, positive advantages it offers which we have pointed out above.—*Editorial in Boston Herald, Tuesday, April 16.*

THE POET WHITTIER ON IDLENESS IN PRISONS.

A letter from John G. Whittier, protesting against the enforced idleness of convicts in penitentiaries, has been received by Mr. M. F. Round, and was read at the meeting of the Prison Association at Steinway Hall last Monday. It is as follows:

DANVERS, Mass., April 5, 1889.

MY DEAR MR. ROUND—I am glad to hear that a public meeting is to be held in your city to protest in the name of Christianity and humanity against the enforced idleness in prisons, perilous alike to body and mind, which can only result in filling your prisons with maniacs. My sympathies are with the laboring class in all their just demands, and I would favor every legitimate measure which promises to benefit them. But the suppression of labor in the prisons is too small a gain for them to be purchased by the transformation of prisons into madhouses. I trust further reflection and the knowledge of the dreadful consequences of the slow torture of brooding idleness will ere long induce them to forego what must be a very trifling benefit at the best. With my best wishes for the success of your philanthropic endeavors, I am very truly thy friend,

JOHN G. WHITTIER.

LONG ISLAND WHEELMEN ON THE ROAD.

The following are the ten highest records for March and April, compiled by Captain Teller:

HIGHEST FOR MARCH.		HIGHEST TO APRIL 1.	
L. H. Wise	618	L. H. Wise	953
Wm. Schmid	353	Wm. Schmid	816
W. J. Gilfillan	266	W. J. Gilfillan	786
F. E. Bogert	278	A. P. Topping	433
A. P. Topping	242	E. F. Beecher	369
E. L. Blake	204	G. G. Teller	356
Robt. Evans	178	Wm. Hawxhurst	300
A. S. Willdig	178	F. E. Bogert	292
G. G. Teller	165	C. L. Healey	257
C. L. Healey	152	A. S. Willdig	250
Total	2,654	Total	4,812

NEW YORK STATE DIVISION, L. A. W. OFFICIAL NOTICES.

A STATE OFFICIAL ORGAN.

BUFFALO, April 10, 1889.

To the Members of the New York State Division:

I have this day appointed THE WHEEL AND CYCLING TRADE REVIEW the official organ of this division.

W. S. BULL,
Chief Consul.

* * *

VICE-CONSUL APPOINTMENT.

To the Members of the New York State Division:

Mr. M. L. Bridgman, of Brooklyn, is hereby appointed Vice-Consul of this Division, and will assume the duties of the office from this date.

W. S. BULL,
Chief Consul.

BUFFALO, N. Y., March 10, 1889.

ESSEX BICYCLE CLUB MEET, NEWARK, N. J.

The tenth annual meeting of the Essex Bicycle Club was held at Davis' parlors last Thursday evening. The reports of the several officers were most satisfactory, excepting that part of the Captain's "log" which showed a falling off in attendance upon club runs. Action, however, was taken looking toward improvement in this direction. The Secretary reported a marked increase in membership since the last annual meeting. After transacting necessary business, which provoked some lively discussions, the club adjourned to the dining-room to partake of the annual dinner.

The toasts, although impromptu, were responded to with vivacity and wit, Elwood C. Harris responding to "The Old Guard," Wm. S. Righter to "Headers," E. Eugene Sargeant to "Individual Idiosyncrasies," Madison Alling to "Wheeling Sketches," F. W. Keer to "The Ladies," S. N. Atwater to "Our New Members." A humorous poem by Herbert W. Knight was received with much favor, eliciting unbounded applause, followed by a general interchange of views on cycling and the experience of several tourist members on the admirable roads in Bermuda.

The officers of the club for the present year are: John B. Lunger, President; Herbert W. Knight, Vice-President; William S. Righter, Secretary and Treasurer. The Executive Committee consists of Samuel N. Atwater, Cecil H. MacMahon, Frederick E. Nichols, and the officers above named *ex officio*. E. Eugene Sargeant, Captain; Andrew Kirkpatrick, Jr., First Lieutenent; A. J. Hedges, Jr., Second Lieutenant.

THE CENTURY RUN.

EDITOR WHEEL:

It isn't often I "get into the papers," but I am generous enough to desire some of your other readers to enjoy with me two particularly rich tid-bits in your issue of 12th inst.

Your correspondent from Eureka, Cal., after painting in large, luscious words an account of a ten-mile stretch of road which resembled a "large, white chalk-line drawn on a green background," proceeds to astonish us "Eastern wheelmen" with the statement that they "*scorched* those ten miles in *35 minutes*." Great Scott!

And from "California," of San Francisco, comes some very kind, brotherly advice concerning the management of a "monster Century run" which he understands us as intending to organize. For fear that it may be imagined that there is a chance for failure through lack of care in making the arrangements, I would like to detail some few of the various little items which have to be looked after.

There are about twenty-two clubs in the metropolitan district, ranging from five to a hundred and sixty members, which have a say in the make-up of the committee to organize the run. The committee decides on date and route, and the rest is left mainly to the chairman, who arranges the schedule, canvasses the clubs, visits hotels, corresponds with railroads, photographers, distant wheelmen, hotel managers, wheeling papers, newspapers and various others.

Then the enlistment-cards and badge-schedules have to be gotten up. The former includes distance, total distance, places, time and such other concise information as can be given two months in advance, and the entire route is gone over a few days before the run and reported on to the committee.

The most difficult task remains in persuading would-be starters that it is not a road race, but merely an extraordinary exemplification of the practicability of the wheel for long distances.

Thus our friend in effete California will realize, I hope, that we are doing everything in our humble, if obsolete, way to make the G. C. R. '89 a success. Judging from all indications, barring very bad weather, I estimate the starters at not less than one hundred.

L. A. CLARKE.

The long, lank countryman who dashes up and down the Broadway and Fourth Street pavement on a full-nickeled Star is now a member of the club.

There is a certain long-nosed individual who seems to think that Third Street was built especially for his own benefit. He is out nearly every afternoon in a buggy, and never loses an opportunity to crowd wheelmen into the curbing. The boys will have to watch him.

—*Nashville American.*

IT IS NOW

The season when riders are looking over the wheels in the market with critical eyes, and selecting for their use during the season just coming on the wheels that have the most of what are

ACKNOWLEDGED BY ALL

To be the best features in wheel construction. The Victors for '89 are, as ever, at the very front of the market in such respects. They are stronger, handsomer and lighter-running than any others, and you may be sure

THAT THE

Victor devices are the best from the fact that lots of people copy them. The Victor Safety is the only successful spring fork machine. It is finer than anything else of the kind in the market.

VICTORS BEAT THE WORLD!

OVERMAN WHEEL CO., MAKERS,

BOSTON, MASS.

Special Agents,

A. G. SPALDING & BROS.,

NEW YORK AND CHICAGO.

The Premier Tandem Safety.

FOR LADY AND GENTLEMAN, OR TWO GENTLEMEN.

Victor Cycles.

Singer Cycles.

Tandem Safeties are coming into general use (for two people), as they make one track only, thus requiring less power to propel, and go where the Tricycle Tandem cannot.

Eastern Agency for GORMULLY & JEFFERY'S Full Line of American Cycles and Sundries.

Eastern Agency for INDIANA BICYCLE MFG. CO.'S "DANDY" SAFETY.

Eastern Agency for GEM TRICYCLE MFG. CO. Send for Bicycle Catalogue, FREE.

MERWIN, HULBERT & CO.,

Agents wanted in all unoccupied territory. 26 WEST 23d STREET, NEW YORK.

═══NEW MAIL═══

From F. D. ELWELL.

Champion of Pacific Coast.

SAN FRANCISCO, CAL.,
February 19, 1889.

DEAR SIRS:

I desire to express my appreciation of the 56-inch New Mail bicycle purchased four months ago.

The great rigidity and easy steering of the Trigwell Ball Head is a pleasant relief after years of experience with the ordinary cone.

Since receiving the New Mail I have won from scratch all races in which I have competed, and am more than pleased with its easy running qualities. I truly believe it is the best all-round bicycle manufactured.

F. D. ELWELL,

Champion Cal. Div. L. A. W., 1888.

SEND FOR CATALOGUE.

SPECIALTIES.

WITH TRIGWELL BALL HEAD.

The advantages of Trigwell's Ball Head to the Ordinary is even surpassed in its application to a Safety (in fact it seems specially Designed for a Safety), for by its rigid bearing, and not needing adjustment, it keeps the front wheel steady, and obviates sensitive steering, which fault all Safeties have had.

SPRING FRONT FORK, preventing vibration—very easy and out of sight.

REAR AXLE BAND BRAKE the place for a brake—not fouled with mud as when near the tire.

Has PERFECTLY STRAIGHT FRONT FORK, giving steadiness of running to front wheel.

Has TANGENT SPOKES, half-nickeled to intersections, giving a very handsome appearance.

Has STRENGTHENED BASE HOLLOW RIM.

Has KEYSTONE SADDLE, very easy, and specially fitted for a Safety, as it has no side or rocking motion, which is fatal to steadiness on a Safety.

Approved by R. H. Davis, the Champion Safety rider, and others, as the Best.

STEEL FORGINGS throughout.

DON'T buy a Safety or Ordinary until sending for our Catalogue.

SEND FOR CATALOGUE.

SEE THESE WHEELS.

MANUFACTURERS.

WILLIAM READ & SONS,

107 Washington St., Boston.

PSYCHO WHEELS FOR 1889.

Sole Importers: Capital Cycle Co., Washington, D. C.

The Psycho cycles are imported by the Capital Cycle Company, of Washington, D. C. This firm were the first to recognize the merits of all forms of rear-driving safeties, and in 1885 imported the first one ever brought into this country. They also designed and introduced the first tandem safety in 1888. They designed and manufactured in 1887 the first rear-driving ladies' safety bicycle, and credit should be given them for their efforts in this direction. They have accomplished as much for the weaker sex by reducing friction, weight, and by giving increased pleasure, as did the inventor of the spider wheel for the stronger sex by improving the boneshaker.—*Wheel.*

Psycho Cycles do not have hollow rims, tangent spokes, ball head or spring forks. No change will be made in Psychos over the 1888 pattern. The Fish hammock saddle will be used on all Psychos.

Psycho Cycles are remarkable for their lightness, strength, harmonious and uniform construction, simplicity (fewness of parts) and general gracefulness of design. **Beautifully finished.**

PSYCHO LIGHT ROADSTER.

PSYCHO LADIES' ROADSTER.

PSYCHO TANDEM SAFETY.

SEVEN FORMS

OF

PSYCHO SAFETIES,

Varying in Weight and Design.

1. **"Men's Straight Frame Psycho Safety,"** 30-inch wheels, ⅞ and ⅞ inch tires, geared to 57 inches, weight 47 lbs. Price $140.

2. **"Men's Light Roadster Psycho Safety,"** 30-inch wheels, ⅞-inch tires, made for gentlemen riders and scorchers on good roads, geared to 60 inches (see cut), weight 38 lbs. Price, $140.

3. **"Men's Dropped Frame Psycho Safety"** is designed like ladies' safety (see cut), 30-inch wheels, ⅞ and ⅞ inch tires, weight 50 lbs. Will stand any weight on any road. Detachable brace rod makes it suitable for ladies and a general family machine. Price, $140. Geared to 57 inches.

4. **"Ladies' Roadster Psycho Safety,"** ⅞-inch tires, 29-inch wheels. Detachable brace rod, suitable for short or medium-height gentlemen. Will stand any weight. Weight, 44 lbs. See cut. Geared to 50 inches.

5. **"Ladies' Light Roadster Psycho Safety,"** 29-inch wheels, ⅞ and ⅞ inch tires, weight 38 lbs. Superb finish, very light and easy-running, intended for light-weight ladies, but will carry 175 lbs. Geared to 50 inches.

6. **"Ladies' Extra Light Psycho,"** same design as "Ladies' Psycho," with rear forks like "Men's Light Roadster Psycho," 28-inch wheels. Weight 34 lbs. Price, $140. We cannot deliver this much under thirty days.

7. **"Psycho Tandem Safety,"** intended for lady and gentleman or two gentlemen, ⅞-inch tires to both wheels, very strong, light and simple. Will carry any weight. Now in its second season. Price, with two separate brakes, $200. Geared to 57 inches.

All of the above Machines are guaranteed to the fullest extent.

CYCLING CENTRES.

BROOKLYN NEWS.

The West Side Boulevard in Prospect Park has been repaired to the extent of a few loads of gravel dumped upon it and raked over, and then rolled with a steam roller. This will fill up some of those water-shed ruts, and I trust that the carriages will pack the gravel sufficiently to make the West Side Drive a little less bumpy than it was.

The Park Commissioners will spread themselves on an imposing entrance to be built at the Ocean Parkway gate. I am told by parties holding the contracts that the new entrance will present a very handsome appearance.

The Brooklyns held their first Saturday afternoon run on the 13th. Captain Meeteer and Lieutenant Hebert led the party, consisting of Messrs. Skinner, Blood, Adams, Bradley, Moore, Fuller, Lang and others down the road to a favorite hostelry, where a pleasant time was passed, after which they returned to do the Park circuit.

Tandem bikes are to be very popular this season, and each of the clubs will have its tandem fiends. There will undoubtedly be some fast time made, and perhaps some records broken. Several club members are buying tandem safeties to ride with their lady relatives and friends, and the new mount will probably inveigle some ladies into riding who otherwise might not have taken up the sport.

Mr. Smith, of the Long Island Wheelmen, took a fall on Sunday, which resulted in a broken arm. The fall was taken through an ambitious desire of the rider to ride over a curbing where riders generally dismount. I hope that the fracture will not prove serious, and that Mr. Smith may soon be on his wheel again.

How very gorgeous all the new road officers of the various clubs appear at this season of the year! They all wear brand-new shoulder straps and other insignia, and, as a rule, new uniforms to complete the *tout ensemble*, and, taken on the road, they form a most beautiful sight to behold, and fill the souls of the ordinary high-private with a large and unwieldy lump of envy.

Captain Meeteer, of the Brooklyns, is planning a Canadian tour for the latter part of August, on which he expects to take some thirty men. A specially good time is anticipated at Toronto, as there has always been a strong fraternal feeling between the Toronto wheelmen and the B. B. C., which has been cemented by sundry visits back and forth of individual members of the two clubs.

Previous to last Sunday there were two posts which were most cunningly placed in the side-path leading to Bath. They were so placed (by that inveterate enemy of cyclists who lives at that spot) that it was necessary to make a most careful and skillful turn to successfully ride by them. The posts are now *non est*. It seems that four members of the B. B. C. rode that way on Sunday, and one of their number took a fall in consequence. So they turned around and rode back to Nungesser's, where they left their wheels, and, borrowing an ax, walked back to the place of torture, and proceeded without further delay to chop down the bugbears of safe riding. After carefully depositing the posts in some neighboring fields, they rode on to the Island, each wearing a chip from the posts in his cap. The largest of these chips found its way to the B. B. C. bulletin board with the following verses inscribed by the club poet:

This is a part of the post
  That obstructed the path
To "do" the wheelmen
  On their way to Bath.
But the following wheelmen,
  With grim intent
And an ax so keen,
  It to Hades sent.
Bow to the following:
B. M. Cole,
G. Bancroft,
C. L. B. Snedeker,
H. E. Raymond.

Well done, boys! You got ahead of the Cyclists' Union on that bit of work, but the Union may claim half of the honor, as two of its leading lights were in the party. ATOL.

Brooklyn, April 16, 1889.

TACOMA, WASHINGTON.

The first week of April has given us perfect weather, and most of the boys have availed themselves of the opportunity to commence scorching, as preliminary practice for the 25-mile road race. Subscriptions are coming in from all points, and already the amount subscribed foots up $125.00. There will be little or no trouble in securing the balance ($75.00), as Prince Wells has a happy faculty for "striking" people for subscriptions, and he doesn't often get left. Ed. Barlow and W. H. H. Keen are still the favorites for this race, although McCoy, Rainey and Will Brackett are working hard to make a good fight for first place.

On Sunday, April 7, twenty-one of the Tacoma wheelmen attended the first regular club run, and Captain Wells must be congratulated for the manner in which he superintended the arrangements. The run was to Steilacoom and American Lake, full mileage being 35. Pretty good for most of the boys, it being their first long ride this season.

The prairie roads were in excellent shape, and all returned well pleased with the day's sport. On Monday McCoy and Rainey rode out to Puyallup, 10 miles, to report on the condition of the roads, which were found sufficiently good to warrant a club run in that direction for next Sunday. Upon the return trip from Puyallup Monday afternoon, McCoy enlightened a Swede, and forcibly explained to him the definition of the word "header." The Swede saw the cyclers approaching and took a firm position in the middle of the road, which left a rut on one side of him and a tree root on t'other. In dismounting (*over the bars*) Mac's foot planted itself in the foreigner's stomach, to the great amusement of Rainey. But, strange to relate, neither Mac nor "Swedey" saw the joke—they are both wiser and sadder. But speaking of the ride to Puyallup, oh, how you Eastern boys would like to spend an afternoon on this road!

For several miles the road winds through the Indian Reservation, and the many sights of grandeur beggar description. We frequently meet "bucks" and squaws coming to market, the latter riding straddlewise and carrying pappooses on their backs, tied up in blankets. They are generally friendly, and grant a salutation to passers-by. Emerging from the Reservation, Mt. Tacoma looms up in the distance, and there is nothing so refreshing, on a summer's day, as the sight of this snow-covered mount, the altitude of which is 14,444 feet. Although 65 miles southeast of Tacoma, Mt. Tacoma is plainly seen from the city. Strangers here invariably guess the distance to be from 10 to 20 miles, and are inclined to present a "liar" card when informed of the correct distance. On clear days we can also see the Olympian Range, 75 to 100 miles north of Tacoma, which is also snow-capped throughout the year. Such sights as these greatly surprise our Eastern friends, and all agree that it is worth a trip to the Pacific Coast to view them, not through telescopes and strong glasses, but with the naked eye.

I hear from Mr. R. Agassy that the Seattle Club will reorganize next week, and on a much more solid basis. Social members need not apply. The new club wants *bona-fide* cyclers only, and we congratulate Mr. Agassy on this turn of affairs. Good luck to the reorganized club! May they live long and prosper! The Seattle Club members regret the loss they have sustained through the removal of Mr. Clark (ex-champion of Canada) to Whatcom, in which place he will interest himself in the wholesale drug business. We wish him success. We hear that Clark will not have time to train for the coming 25-mile road race, but we hope he will be able to reverse his decision. What a fine race would be insured with Clark, Keen, Halsted, Wells and Barlow to buck against each other!

It will not be many weeks before a hill-climbing contest is on the tapis. Although these contests are of the "chestnut" order in the East, we have not yet experienced the delights and comforts (?) of a pull up a "one foot in four" hill. But we will live and learn, and, from my past experience on Tacoma hills, I will wager that there will be many wars of words as to the accomplishments of Tacoma's hill-climbing fiends. May the best man win.

'Tis noised around that Culver's safety is *not always* guided by his steady hand unless it is guided with his hand on the saddle while he gently instructs the fair rider to do thus and so. Keep it up, my dear boy, and may you have many pleasant rides later in the season, when your pupil has gained full mastery of the goat. SNOHOMISH.

April 11, 1889.

BUFFALO.

The Ramblers had the first club run of the season on Wednesday last, and thirty-six members responded to the call. The weekly runs of the Buffalos will commence April 26.

By the first of May the Buffalo Ladies' Bicycle Club will be a reality, as a dozen or more of the enterprising women of this city have decided to form a club. A pretty uniform of dark blue-gray corduroy has been designed by Wanamaker of Philadelphia. The organization will belong to the League of American Wheelmen. Our claim to the second ladies' wheel club in the United States is put forth.

Preparations are being made by the Buffalos for their second annual run of 100 miles from Erie on Decoration Day. The run of last year was made by twenty-three riders out of twenty-eight starters. The gymnasium has been a scene of activity during the winter months, and fifty is the estimated number who will attempt the ride this year.

The asphalt on Delaware Avenue is being extended from Virginia Street to Niagara Square. But we must have more. On Supper, from Delaware to Main Street; on Chippewa, from Ellicott to Delaware; on Huron, from Ellicott to Prospect, and then out Prospect to Porter Avenue. This is all we ask, and then our claim for Buffalo as the wheelman's paradise *par excellence* could not be disputed.

Safeties are still the rage, and heavy sales are reported by the dealers.

The Eagle has not yet made its appearance, but one is expected daily. F. W. Brinker will be the first to introduce the new wheel. Brinker took a nasty header in the city championship race at last year's tournament. On the same day, Van Sicklen, of Chicago, was badly injured, and for a time his life was despaired of. Brinker tries the Eagle this year, while "Van" has retired from the path.

ZO.

Greenville has a lively cycling club with eighteen members. It is known as the Pamrapo Athletic Club Wheelmen, and the members wear a dark-blue uniform. C. R. Vogel is Captain, E. Altaire Lieutenant, and H. Burke Secretary.

WILMINGTON.

The Wilmington Wheel Club is talking of giving a race meet during midsummer or the early fall.

The Wilmington Wheel Club is refitting its new room up very neatly, including a pool table and other features to promote social enjoyment and club life.

Nothing has yet been heard from Dampman as to whether he will race this season or not. He has picked up considerable fat during the winter, and he would require some training to get into racing trim

Charles C. Kurtz, at one time the champion local rider, has removed to Pittsburg, where he has accepted a position with the wholesale lumber firm of H. B. Nease, Son & Co. He will continue to ride, and expects to join one of the Smoky City wheeling clubs.

Our neighboring little town of Middletown has the honor of having produced the first Delaware lady who has been seen in public astride of "one of them" bicycles. She sat in front of J. B. Maxwell on a tandem, and rode up and down the main street totally unconscious of the sensation which she created.

Frank Slothower, one of our most popular wheelmen, has removed to Philadelphia, where he has accepted a very responsible position with a large wholesale house. Mr. Slothower is an enthusiastic wheelman as well as dancer, and is quite a favorite among the ladies.

The Pennsylvania Bicycle Club will shortly be the guests of the Wilmington Wheel Club in a joint run to Middletown or some other neighboring town. These friendly visits between these two clubs have become annual features, and have engendered a good feeling between the two organizations, which is one of the most pleasant features of the club life in cycling.

A party of about fifteen wheelmen will make a trip to Washington on Saturday next, April 20, to see the sights at the National capital. They will be taken care of by the Capital Bicycle Club during their stay of two days.

About fifty new wheels have been sold here this spring, and all the agents report numerous inquiries and prospective purchasers denoting a healthy interest in this king of sports. Several of our business men have taken to the wheel, and the cycle is seen daily in use as a means of locomotion for transacting business as well as a casual pastime. The different makes of wheels are almost as numerous as the riders. Among the latest acquisitions to our local ranks are a lady cycler on a bicycle, a tandem tricycle and several tandem bicycles. The popular tendency, however, is toward safeties, and they are selling like the proverbial hot cakes. The club is feeling the increase in the number of riders by a healthy addition to its membership.

Merrihew, McDaniel, Elliott, Gregg, Lofland and other would-be champions of the Wilmington Wheel Club expect to enter for the big handicap race over the Irvington-Milburn course on May 30. The last three are novices, and, together with several others, expect to show their mettle this season in order to ascertain whether any more latent champion material is lying around the club loose.

The question of improving the public roads is agitating the public mind at the present time, and the Legislature has been asked to pass a law requiring the prisoners of our various county jails to work on the roads. Common humanity would urge this project as at once useful as well as reformatory in its effects, and it hardly seems possible that we will get any better roads except by some such method. A very sensible law is now pending to abolish our old and antiquated levy court, which never had much to show for its large expenditures, and substitute three County Commissioners, of whom much more would be expected.

"JACK'S JOTTINGS."

Probably no wheelman in the United States has access to as fine a piece of roadway as has the man who presses the pedal in New York City. A system of roadway is found in Central Park which compares very favorably with any English park in existence, not excepting the famous Hyde or St. James' Park, or Richmond or Bushy Park, a little distance from the great city of cities, and in the same county. Not even is the surface of the famous Indian Gardens in the far Occident superior to New York's Central Park, which for the last year has been open to wheelmen. Charming, too, to leave the glare of the hot stone or brick pavement of the city and glide noiselessly among the trees of the Park, set out in the highest style of the landscape gardener's art. Transported at once from the bustle of the city, where elevated trains rush in such a thoroughly American haste past one another, utterly unable to meet the growing want of the city for an adequate rapid-transit system, we find ourselves in a perfect garden of cool greens of every shade—from the deepest ebony sage to the most delicate of lettuce-greens. Sparrows twitter among the branches or flutter on the roadways men in heavy box-cloth overcoats, three sizes too big for them, with the inevitable "horsy" red geranium or carmine pink showing against their almost cream-colored coats, guide more or less valuable or well-bred trotters up the grand avenues of the Park, which only need time to give their trees the luxurious foliage of a South of England oak or elm. Here we may see all kinds of people, all kinds of babies in perambulators, all kinds of scrawny or sleek horses; bicycles of all nationalities and every imaginable vintage, from the old short-handled high-headed "kicker" of 1884 to the new spring-forked Victor or the round-the-world "Columbia." Little boys on safeties with twenty-two inch wheels glide along among the stream of seemingly impatient drivers of trotters and horsemen, with a sense of security which was unknown in the days when the straight-forked ordinary was "all the go."

Staid-looking business men, with beards and spectacles and trim gray suits, wheel quietly along on their season' choice, and study the human nature that in "buggy" or ultra-English-looking dog-cart are bent on but one thing—to *get past* those in front of them. The day's work is over for the masses, and here they are enjoying themselves after their own peculiar individual fashion.

Gray-coated policemen stand at the crossings to preserve order in the stream of machines, the most of these "custodians" of a far superior-looking type to the general run of regular street policemen. And this is Central Park, a lasting monument to the progress of a great city.

"JACK."

MARYLAND.

A meeting of the Hagerstown, Md., Club was held Monday, April 8, at which the question of holding the annual League meet in that city was freely discussed. President V. M. Cushwa and Capt. George Updegraff were appointed a committee to confer with Chief Consul Mott and the Executive Committee of the L. A. W. in Baltimore, and, if satisfactory arrangements can be made, to begin preparations at once for the coming meet. The Hagerstown boys who are a very enterprising and energetic set of fellows will doubtless make it a success if they undertake it. The Hagerstown wheelmen promise, if that place is selected, to show how well they can dispense Maryland hospitality in entertaining the several thousand visitors who will attend.

No further action has been taken with reference to the proposed building of a new club-house by the Baltimore club, but it is expected that in the near future the plans of the members will be laid before the public.

The Baltimore Club (it is said) received about thirteen members from the disbanded Rambler Club, which breathed its last a few weeks ago.

The principal feature of the meet to be held at Hagerstown in July will be an an excursion to Pen-Mar, designed for the pleasure and entertainment of the many visitors. It was proposed to make it a moonlight excursion, but there was considerable opposition among the members of the local club to this arrangement.

The Chesapeake Wheelmen Stock Company, of Baltimore, were incorporated with the following men as incorporators: C. F. Abbott, J. C. Robinson, J. D. Wheeler, Jas. B. Reed and Wm. G. Speed. The capital stock is $5,000. The directors are those named as incorporators and James C. Stansbury, Chas. R. Eisenbrandt, Philip Kratz, Jr., and Wm. Holland. The company has organized for pleasure, social and beneficial purposes.

The white oak tree "Centaur" planted by the Centaur Club gives promise of thriving.

H. G. Priest, of the Quadrant Bicycle Company, Birmingham, England, spent a week in this city. Mr. Priest is making a tour of the United States, dividing his time between pleasure and business.

Harry Taylor, late a member of the Baltimore Club, visited this city. Mr. Taylor's name is being engraved on the Baltimore Club Championship cup, which was won by him last season, and the medal testifying to the fact, also his property, is being made.

The Centaur Club planted a white oak tree in the new extension of Patterson Park on Arbor Day, in the presence of Superintendent Anderson, the uniformed members of the club and a large gathering of people. The tree was decorated with the club colors, blue and white. An appropriate address was made by C. Henry Eisenbrandt, President of the club.

Bay Ridge.

MACON, GA.

Spring days are here and the wheelmen are out touring—riding along the shaded, quiet country roads and lanes to the music of the mocking-bird, robin and thrush, or perhaps out under the stars, with the great white moon shedding upon them its silvery light, and the mellow notes of the whippoorwill floating in from the distance.

The first results of the new season are now being felt among the wheelmen here, and six new riders have mounted their wheels, which is merely the preface of the book of riders which we expect and hope will follow.

There is no State in the Union which is at present getting into such great shape for road work as Georgia. A "Road Congress" is to be held in Atlanta next month, and representatives from each county will form the body. All the leading dailies of the State are advocating the work, and some are in favor of employing the State convicts upon them. The amount laid aside for the street improvements in the State this year amounts to some millions of dollars. Of this Macon will use $150,000; Chattanooga, $700,000; Jacksonville, $750,000; Anniston, $200,000; West Knoxville, $100,000, and various other cities will expend like amounts. With the State looking after the roads, and the cities the streets, the chances are that this section will soon become a perfect wheelman's paradise.

A good thing for a wheelman to occupy his time with is to take all his old cycling papers and cut the advertising pictures out of them and paste them on board. Some quite handsome ornaments can be fixed up in this way, and when well grouped will set off a wall to advantage. I counted twenty-nine in my room to-day, and with a new lot from my last batch of English and American papers the number will be greatly increased. They are set off by a colored sketch, from life, of Thomas Stevens, a wheel, and a frontispiece from *Outing*, while on either side are the "Star Against Time," and the Singers' hanger of the "Coat of Arms Bridge near Coventry;" surrounding the whole are the Pope's people on their different wheels. It takes but little trouble to get up a collection of this kind, and is well worth the time expended upon it.

Yesterday I ran across one of the victims of "the big wheel craze" of some seasons back. I was riding downtown and saw a wheelman whom I judged to be a new rider, but whom, upon closer investigation, I found to be a stranger. He was mounted on a 58, with short cranks, a hard saddle and short handle-bars. We went out for a little run, and after riding for about two hours he had received, all told, fourteen falls, seven of which were headers. Our roads are wide, but I always found it safest to stay either in front of or behind him. Sometimes he would be riding on one side, when, suddenly, and without warning, he would cut across to the other, and then when he would jerk his wheel into line again, oh, how the little one would protest, cut figures, and rise, like a buzz-saw, up in the air! We swapped wheels once, and he got along on my 54 much better. I had only one fall, and that was off his 58. But oh! didn't it seem as if I were coming down out of a balloon, though, when the descent did begin!

Chas. Alex. Persons.

S. G. Whittaker has not "mysteriously disappeared," as reported. He is training on a Rover safety at Coventry, with the ultimate intention of having a try at the road records.

ST. LOUIS.

I presume New York thinks she is going to have something of a celebration on the 30th inst., and she probably will do the best she knows how in that direction, but *the* celebration of that date is to be held right here in St. Louis. It becoming apparent that we could not all get away to join in with the New Yorkers in properly observing the centennial anniversary of Washington's inauguration, it was determined to get up an affair on our own hook. Accordingly a meeting was held on 'Change, appropriate committees on programme, finance, etc., were appointed, and, to make sure of the success of the undertaking, the wheelmen were invited to participate in the parade. The acceptance of this invitation presents rather a troublesome dilemma. As the wheelmen will, of course, ride their machines, while the remainder of the paraders walk, it will be a difficult problem to keep the component parts of the procession together. Either the wheelmen will have to be sent along to finish the journey on their own account, or else be held back until the rest of the paraders have had their innings. In either event the dignity of the procession, as a whole, will be more or less violated. I have not learned how the matter is to be arranged, but it appears that Secretary Newman has accepted the invitation for the Missouri Club.

The many friends of Ed. Sells are welcoming him back to St. Louis after an absence of five months in the South. He is as brown as a berry and looks the picture of health. Visitors to the St. Louis meet will remember Mr. Sells as the chairman of the reception committee, and they will testify to his watchful care over them during their stay. His sub-committees were models of efficiency in their respective capacities, more especially the committee on "Terminal Facilities," over which Fred Beckers, better known in some quarters as "Blondy," presided with such signal ability. What with photography and horses, Sells has almost entirely dropped out of cycling, and this is to be deplored, for he was one of the most enthusiastic workers we ever had.

I do not think that we have heard the last of the Sunday law in the Missouri Club. The repeal of the house rule was conducted so quietly that not a third of the members knew anything about it until many days after it was an accomplished fact. The opponents of the repeal do not think they have been treated fairly in the matter, and they contend that they should have had an opportunity to at least put themselves on record on the question. On the other hand, the fact remains that they received the usual notice of the meeting, and if they had taken a proper interest in the affairs of the club they would have been present. They probably realize now that "eternal vigilance" is the price of other things besides liberty, and the effect of this will doubtless show itself in a larger attendance at future club meetings.

Captain Lewis evidently believes that

"The best of all ways
To lengthen our days
Is to steal a few hours from the night," etc.,

for he has called the Sunday run of this week to commence on Saturday night. He is to take the boys out to Ballwin at 8:30 P. M., and continue on to the county line the following day. The dividing of this county line run into two days illustrates most forcibly the degeneracy into which the riders of the present day have fallen. It is not a decline in ability, for the riders of to-day (St. Louis riders I mean) are as fine as they ever were, but there seems to be a lack of ambition and an indisposition to uphold the fair fame St. Louis has always had for excellent road riders. Ithuriel.

TROY NOTES.

The "Trojan Wheelmen" will give the last of their enjoyable socials at Harmony Hall the first Wednesday after Easter.

There seems to be a "little boom" in anticipation, for the Troy Bicycle Club members will purchase a number of new machines this spring.

Le Grand Spicer's new Columbia Light Roadster Safety is attracting quite a crowd at Howe & Co.'s store. I ran in to see it, and must say it is the finest machine I ever saw. Quite a number were talking with "Don" while I was there, who never rode a wheel, and I predict some sales in the near future.

At the meeting of the Troy Bi. Club last Monday evening, the consideration of important changes to the constitution was taken up and the number of trustees was increased to six instead of five. The Tournament Committee has prepared an interesting programme for the entertainment at the club-house. There will be dumb-bell exercises, club-swinging, fencing; performances on the horizontal bars, rings and trapeze; boxing, leaping, balancing, contortions, fancy bicycle riding, and a fine club drill.

The Rensselaer Polytechnic Institute Banjo Club will furnish music, and athletes will be present from Albany, Schenectady and the Railroad Young Men's Christian Association.

I hope a "tug of war" with the Albany Wheelmen will not be omitted, for I think Troy ought to do better than she did at the Albany tournament.

I would like to suggest a race meet, to be given by the Troy and Albany clubs, at Island Park. I think it would pay and increase the interest in cycling, if properly worked up by the combined efforts of *all* the clubs.

Hold the meet at a time when it will be convenient for the State Division and in connection with it, if the matter can be arranged. If some of our "flyers" could be induced to come, and the fact advertised, it would make success certain.

Come, gentlemen, if we are to have better roads we must have more wheelmen, and to have more wheelmen we must keep up the interest in cycling.

The New York Division of the League needs your help in the cause for good roads. It has already done well by passing the "Liberty Bill," and if it is supported by *all* interested in cycling, a bill for the improvement of the present system of road-making will become a law, and we will have *decent* roads to tour on. We want the membership of our division increased this year to 3,000, and it ought to be. It only costs *two* dollars to join, and *one* dollar to renew if already a member. If it were not for the League of American Wheelmen, touring would not be the pleasure it is, and any wheelman *not* a member is receiving benefits—derived from the League—at some one else's expense.

April 13, 1889. Ornk Qba.

"Fenton vs. Jack."—We are betting on "Jack," who is a more skillful pen-jabber, more expert at parry and thrust, than young "Fenton."

NEW ORLEANS.

At a meeting of the Louisiana Cycling Club, held on Thursday evening, April 4, sixteen members subscribed $1,400 for the purpose of building a new club-house. There are twenty-five other members still to be heard from. Ten new members were admitted and three delinquents dropped. The club has issued a challenge to the New Orleans Bicycle Club for a 2½-mile team race, teams to consist of eight men each.

The Louisiana State Division, L. A. W., met at the rooms of the New Orleans Bicycle Club on April 8. A new constitution was adopted.

The Secretary-Treasurer's report showed $87 on hand and a decrease in membership of fifteen. The Chief Consul, in making his report, suggested that a tour during the summer through the "Arcadia" country, or a short encampment somewhere along the Gulf coast, might be of considerable advantage to the Division, besides making an enjoyable outing. The suggestion was well received, and on motion placed in the hands of the following committee of five—Messrs. Christy, O'Reardon, Graham, Fenner and Gore—for further investigation and report.

In compliance with the new by-laws the Chief Consul also made the following committee appointments: Racing—Randall, Shields, Renaud, Gore and C. H. Fenner; Roads Improvement—Hill, Fairchild, Russ, Betts and Graham; Rights and Privileges—Zeigler, Rea, Crane, Christy, and Walters of Shreveport.

The arrangements for the series of races for the Chief Consul's medals was placed in the hands of a committee composed of Messrs. Betts, Rea, Gore, Frederick and Russ, who will meet on Saturday evening and arrange a programme.

The Chair then called for suggestions for the position of official handicapper for the Southern Division. Suggestions were plentiful, but no one seemed disposed to accept the position. Mr. A. M. Hill was finally prevailed upon to accept.

The following resolutions were then unanimously adopted, ordered spread upon the minutes, and a copy transmitted to the Board of Trade:

Whereas, The impassable condition of the public highways throughout the State during a goodly portion of each year is such as to seriously hamper the interests, both public and private, of its people; and,

Whereas, The agricultural element and parish authorities have commended the agitation and the calling of a road convention, as witnessed by the action of the Hammond Agricultural Relief Association and the Pointe Coupee police jury; therefore,

Be it resolved, That this organization, representing a class deeply interested in the improvement of the public roads, along with other branches of the government, views with pleasure the present agitation of the subject, and pledges as far as possible its assistance and support, both moral and material, to any movement that looks toward a betterment of existing conditions; and

Be it further resolved, That the attention of the officials of the Board of Trade be respectfully directed to the suggestion that they are the proper body to take the matter in hand and outline a course of action.

The Louisiana Club's second race for the Batson medal will take place on Sunday, April 14. The course will be from the corner of Canal and Claiborne, via Broad, to Schadwell's, on Gentilly Road. Distance, 5.69 miles. Start to be made at 8 o'clock A. M. The following are the entries and handicaps: A. B. Harris, 4m. 30s.; C. W. Bogel and H. W. Nathan, 3m. 30s.; F. De Buys and W. C. Grivot, 2m. 15s.; W. H. Renaud and H. C. Christy, 2m. 10s.; G. C. Angamar and E. M. Graham, 1m. 40s.; L. J. Frederic, F. B. Born and R. G. Betts, 1m. 20s.; M. S. Graham and W. M. Hathorn, 40s.; A. M. Hill, scratch.

New Orleans, April 12, 1889.

LANCASTER, PA.

The Lancaster, Pa., Bicycle Club expects on the coming 4th of July to outdo its efforts of last season, and arrangements are already being made and everything at this early day points to success.

Last year we held a race meet in June at our driving park. The track, which is one-half mile, is exceptionally fine, and all of the racing men spoke highly of the condition in which we had put it, and were all well pleased with the generous prizes offered.

Well, it was "our first offense," but, considering everything, was very successful.

This year we intend to improve, and the annoyance to racing men of last season of a crowd of wheelmen and citizens on the track, which resulted from a misunderstanding all around, will be absent. Races will be run in the morning and afternoon of the 4th. At the last monthly meeting an amendment to the by-laws was passed, making the Lancaster Bicycle Club again a League club.

We are all live and active wheelmen, and wheeling was never up to such "high-water mark" as now, and we hope any wheelmen coming through Lancaster will give us an opportunity to show our hospitality and interest in cycling affairs.

D. F. Grove, President Lancaster Bicycle Club.

The Staten Island Athletic Club Games will be held at West New Brighton, S. I., May 18. A two-mile tricycle handicap is on the programme. Entries close May 11 with F. W. Janssen, West New Brighton, S. I.

W. E. Haskell, editor of the Minneapolis *Tribune* is an enthusiastic safety rider.

Thomas Stevens, writing from Zanzibar, February 24, sends a several-column letter to the New York *World* of Sunday, April 14. The principal portion of Stevens' letter is devoted to a description of Germany's attempts at colonization on the East Coast of Africa.

The Racing Board, L. A. W., will shortly issue printed copies of the new racing rules.

SAN FRANCISCO.

If there is not a big boom in wheeling in this city and vicinity, my eyes deceive me, as new riders are to be seen in all directions. In passing through the small towns between here and San José, one sees all sizes and conditions of riders who apparently reside in the neighborhood and do their errands on their wheels. The genus cads-in-castors have also put in an appearance, but they have not as yet caused any adverse criticism from the press or people.

On April 30, the Bay City Wheelmen will have another race meet at the Haight Street Park. Valuable prizes will be provided for each event, and it is expected a liberal entry will be secured. This is outdoor race meet number four since January 1; no wonder wheeling is booming. It has become necessary for the Bay City Wheelmen to extend their membership limit. Membership under the constitution of the club was restricted to 100, and, this number having been reached, it was decided at the last meeting to extend the limit to 125. Some of the older and more conservative members were not in favor of increasing the limit, believing that, with a full membership and the impossibility of admitting new members except as vacancies occurred, the privilege of being a Bay City Wheelman would be the more eagerly sought for by outsiders and the more highly valued by those already admitted. A two-third vote, however, decided upon the increase to 125; and as this limit will probably be reached within a few months, the question of further increase will have to be shortly considered.

The club smoker last Saturday evening was the most enjoyable they ever held. The foundation, so to speak, of these smokers is a concoction named "Uncle Robert's Punch," so called after the maker, a gentleman whom the riders in this city and State should never forget, not because of this punch, however, but because of more enduring work. As very welcome guests for the evening, the club had W. S. Maltby and his cousin, Mr. Smith. Mr. Smith said that wheelmen in the East never had such a jolly time; they were too conservative, he said. Maltby enjoyed himself immensely, and was placed in the front of a number of groups of the members when photographs were being taken by flash light. If these photos come out well, they will certainly be worth seeing. The usual programme of songs, recitations and music was given.

Late in the evening a loud noise was heard at the door, which was then thrown violently open and two persons staggered in and proceeded to hammer one another in a merry fashion on the floor. It was all over in a few minutes, and those present saw it was our Irrepressible Secretary Pierson with a stuffed man. It was a most comical sight and was so well done that it "brought down the house."

A person who saw the figure from a distance being taken from Pierson's store to a buggy remarked to him afterward: "Your friend seemed quite sick!" "Yes," said Frank, "he was." He sent it to a friend near the club-house, with a note requesting him to "keep the stiff till to-night." When the messenger took the blanket off the "stiff," the friend says, his first thought was to run, until he saw what it was. He stood it up in a corner, and his hired girl nearly fainted when she saw it. Altogether, that "stiff" caused much commotion before it was finally disposed of.

Maltby was surprised to see how close some of the members had followed his movements in the papers.

On the last day of March the club had a run to Redwood City, about thirty miles and return, over almost perfect roads. The day was perfect, and the run was much enjoyed by the twenty-five members who participated. On the return trip a stop was made at San Mateo for a swim. The water was warm, the beach all that could be desired. What Eastern city could make such a showing at this time of the year? On Monday night a large party of riders attended the theatre where Maltby commenced a short engagement. The boys all sat in one part of the theatre, and had their voices with them. Maltby seldom had a more appreciative audience or a more demonstrative one.

Yours, CALIFORNIA.

April 10, 1889.

The Bay City Wheelmen have renewed their membership as a League club. *Every* member of the club is a member of the League. One hundred renewals were forwarded to Secretary-Editor Bassett last week. Can several other clubs in this city who claim to be League clubs prove that all their members belong to the National organization? I think not.

"Hurrah for the effete East! Schwalbach, of Brooklyn, has a son who rides a bicycle younger than Mohrig, Jr., of San Francisco."—*Bicycling World*.

Mr. S. may have a son who rides a "younger bicycle" than Mohrig, Jr., but how about the son being younger?

Mr. Editor, I wish you could be with us next Sunday. Why? Well, the Bay City Wheelmen are to have a "picnic" run to San Mateo Beach. The programme is: A fine ride to San Mateo, including a stop to dispose of some milk kindly furnished by Mr. Donnelly; a delightful swim, and then, to top that off, a regular "picnic lunch" spread under the trees. These runs are one of the most familiar ways that this enterprising club have of enjoying themselves, and you can depend upon it that they *do* enjoy themselves. If we are so fortunate as to have our "camera fiend" along, I will send you a picture of as jolly a crowd of wheelmen as can be found. Sorry you can't be with us.

W. L. Hughson and J. J. Wirtner, of the Buffalo Ramblers, are in town, and are seriously thinking of locating here permanently. Mr. A. L. C. Marsh, of Plainfield, N. J., is also here on a visit.

Several members of a certain club here, whose boast is that they are the "second oldest," either not knowing how or having the inclination to ride a wheel, amuse themselves by telling Eastern visitors that the Bay City Wheelmen are a lot of "kids" and "small boys." I think if the members of this certain club would do less riding on paper, and tackle some of the "kids" on the road or path, that they would soon find out that the "kids" are not so childish as they fondly think.

The Bay Citys pride themselves on being composed of "young blood," no "fossils" in their ranks.

"HEADERS."

L. S. C. Ladish, formerly editor of the *American Wheelman*, deceased, has been appointed official handicapper for Missouri and Kansas.

The Harvard Bicycle Club held a hare and hounds chase Tuesday afternoon. The hares were Rogers, '90, and Spencer, '90.

PHILADELPHIA.

The weather man smiled on us once more last Sunday. It was a splendid day, and the wheelmen were not at all backward in taking advantage of it. The Pennsylvanias had their usual large turnout, with Norristown as their destination, while the Centurions, with sixteen men in line, took a spin to Fort Washington, where they had dinner. On the return trip six of the party climbed Chestnut Hill, which, to say the least, is no mean feat. By the way, Captain Carter, of this club, has invented a new way of getting the boys out on the club runs. In order that all can go, he sends the fast men ahead by a longer route, under the captaincy of one of his lieutenants, while he himself takes the new riders under his wing by some shorter way, of course, all coming home together. So far the scheme has worked first-rate, and men have been induced to go who would otherwise have remained home, on account of the pace being too fast or the distance too great.

Next week will be a week of gayety among the cycling folk of Philadelphia. The South End wheelmen hold their grand ball on Thursday, the 25th. The Philadelphia and Pennsylvania clubs hold dances in their respective club-houses, while the Century wheelmen have their annual dinner on the 24th, at the Colonnade Hotel. What more could one desire?

At last! The quondam champion of Philadelphia, M. J. Baily, alias "Maggie," has at last bought himself a racing wheel. It seems that various items in the papers have been reflecting on the riding of the aforesaid ex-champion, so one day he got right mad and hied himself to a well-known dealer, where he quickly swapped some of his lucre for a beautiful twenty-four-pound racer, and now he vows that he will mop up the track with everything around here, or—or—well, never mind, it will be something horrible.

At the last meeting of the Century Wheelmen, when the question of ladies' membership was brought up, Mr. Kirk Brown made the statement that *eight* ladies were already clamoring for admission. A very promising start, indeed, but on account of some alterations having to be made, it was impossible to take them in at present, and the club gallantly tendered them the privilege of using the wheel-room for the storage of their wheels until the necessary repairs are finished. It is now a common sight to see a lady on a "bike." Mr. Charlie Sulzner, he of the Star wheel with dog attachment, was seen out riding with his better half last Sunday, both mounted on safeties. And then there is Will Allen, who quite frequently takes a very pretty young lady out on his new tandem bicycle. I tell you, boys, if you want to do the elegant with the girls, buy (as one of our fellows puts it) a "double-barreled goat."

Several Sundays ago Mr. Louis Geyler, of the Century, to the edification of a crowd of people, performed the difficult, not to say embarrassing, feat of taking a header off the "Star," and, just think, he is one of the worst "Star fiends" in the club. The way he jumped up and rode away was a caution; but, all the same, he was not quick enough for the watchful eye of ARGUS.

Philadelphia, April 16.

JERSEY CITY.

The bugbear that occasionally agitates every cycling club is now harassing the H. C. W. At the last meeting of the club the old, threadbare subject of uniform was brought up and the ideas expressed were so varied and lengthy, positive and comical that it was necessary to adjourn the meeting in order to let the members get home in time for breakfast. A special meeting was held last Thursday evening to consider the uniform business. It required the combined efforts of three stenographers and two phonographs to do the work of the Secretary in order that the motions could be recorded. It was finally decided to adopt a dark shade of Oxford gray cloth to be trimmed with three-quarter-inch black braid; narrow ribbed black stockings and low black shoes. There was no material change made in the style of cap and shirt we wear with our present uniform. Bids were received from several first-class firms, and after a deal of sparring it was decided to place the contract with Devlin & Co.

The next race for the Benedict medal will take place on the 30th inst., on the Bull's Head Road, S. I. There will be about seven starters. The boys feel confident that Nick Feury will be the first to cross the line—at the start.

Moonlight runs of the H. C. W. were taken on the 13th and 15th inst—the former to Orange and return, and the second to Elizabeth. The latter run was not very well attended, but those who stayed back and played pool missed the sport. Our "esteemed contemporaries," the Elizabeth Wheelmen, met us at the Newark end of the Elizabeth Boulevard and refreshed us. Thanks, E. W.

In last Sunday's *Wurrald* an article appeared on the amateur theatricals given by the Jersey City Athletic Club, and had drawings (?) or would-be photographs of several of the principal actors. Among them was one sad-eyed individual with flowing mustache, dishevelled hair and prominent nose above the name "E. W. Johnson." Then followed a personal sketch of the well-known Doctor, stating that he *is* the Chief Consul of the L. A. W., and *is* the Captain of the H. C. W. I don't know, but it is probable the Doctor has already instituted a libel suit against that newspaper on account of this cartoon. Oh! these newspaper schemers! Probably the same cut will be used in connection with descriptive articles on the coming Centennial celebration, as a picture of George Washington or Mike Mahaha. Any one who has ever met Dr. Johnson would smile at that picture.

COASTER.

THE ORANGE WANDERERS.

The following schedule of runs has been arranged by the Orange Wanderers for April, May and June:

Morning runs—Saturdays, commencing May 4, at 5:30 o'clock.

Long runs—Tuesday, April 30, 9 A. M., Pompton; Thursday, May 30, 7:30 A. M., Pine Brook and Morristown, returning in time for road races, if held; Saturday, June 8, century run; Monday, May 27, 5 P. M., 5-mile club handicap race.

Afternoon runs—Wednesdays, at 4 o'clock, as follows: April 24, at Rutherford Park; May 1, Caldwell and Roseland; May 8, Central Park and Riverside Drive, N. Y., to start at 1 P. M.; May 15, Llewellyn Park, Eagle Rock and St. Cloud; May 22, Little Falls, Paterson and Passaic, to start at 3 P. M.; June 5, Milburn and Springfield; June 12, Bloomfield and Montclair; June 19, Verona and Pleasant Valley; June 25, Elizabeth and Rahway, returning from Elizabeth after supper.

Evening runs—Mondays, at 7 o'clock, as follows: Vailsburg and Roseville; May 13, Franklin Park and Brighton; May 20, around town and return for club meeting; May 27, Newark and Watsessing; June 3, Tory Corner and Llewellyn Park; June 10, Maplewood; June 17, East Orange and return for club meeting; June 24, Montrose.

The question as to whether the Orange Wanderers will continue as a separate organization or be merged with the Orange Athletic Club has been finally decided. The club will not only retain its name and organization, but is to have a "local habitation." For some time past subscription lists have been quietly circulated among the members, with the gratifying result that enough money has been secured to purchase a lot and erect a substantial and commodious club-house. The location is to be a central one, contiguous to Main Street, and in every way desirable. The club-house will be a frame building, neatly furnished, and of some architectural pretensions. It will contain two sixty-foot bowling-alleys, a billiard-room large enough for three standard tables, a parlor, general meeting room and probably a gymnasium. It is the intention to admit non-cycling members, and an effort will be made to increase the membership to 200 or 250.

FIRST UNION RUN OF BOSTON WHEELMEN.

The wheelmen of Boston and vicinity are to have an enjoyable outing next Sunday. At a meeting held April 8 there was a hearty expression in favor of a union run once each month of all the local cycling clubs. A committee was appointed to make proper arrangements, and a circular has just been issued requesting the captains of clubs to call a run to Salem on Sunday, April 21.

A party will start from the Somerville Club rooms, corner of Marshall Street and Broadway, at 9:15 A. M., and ride at a pace of not more than eight miles per hour. Others will join en route or report at the Essex House on arrival. Some will return home on Sunday afternoon, while others will wheel to Gloucester, stopping over night at the Pavilion Hotel, and returning to Boston on Monday, a legal holiday.

The committee is as follows: Chairman, Captain Arthur Robinson, of the Charlestown Rovers (address, 33 Winter Street, Boston); Captain Carl Cubberly, Somerville Bicycle Club; Captain A. P. Benson, Dorchester Bicycle Club. Unattached wheelmen are invited to attend, and the chairman of the committee requests that all notify him as soon as possible if they intend to participate.

The Milwaukee Wheelmen have gotten out one of the prettiest invitation cards for their first grand reception and May ball, to be held April 27. The Committee of Arrangements are Messrs. A. H. Thompson, H. R. Miller, C. A. Erdman, V. J. Schoencker, Jr., and E. Phillips.

FIXTURES.

April 21, 1889.—First Union Run of Boston Wheelmen.

April 25, 1889. Cambridge Bicycle Club's last Ladies' Night of the season.

April 26, 1889.—Manhattan Bicycle Club's Reception, at West End Hall, 125th Street.

May 4, 1889.—Titan Athletic Club Games. Two-mile Bicycle Handicap. Entries close April 27, with A. Surcott, 361 Broadway, New York.

May 10, 1889.—Twelfth Regiment Games. Entries close May 4 with C. J. Leach, P. O. Box 3,201.

May 11, 1889.—Harvard Bicycle Club Open Amateur Race Meet at Cambridge, Mass. Entries close May 4. Address R. H. Davis, Cambridge, Mass.

May 13-18, 1889.—Chicago Cycling Exhibit and Tournament, Exposition Building.

May 18, 1889.—F. A. Elwell's European Party sails from New York.

May 18, 1889.—Stone-Lumsden 1-mile Match Race, at Chicago, Ill.

May 18, 1889.—Staten Island Athletic Club's Games at New Brighton, S. I. Two-mile Bicycle Race.

May 22, 1889.—N. J. A. C. Games at Bergen Point, N. J. Three-mile Bicycle Handicap. Entries close May 22, with A. M. Stout, Box 262, Bergen Point, N. J.

May 25, 1889.—Stone-Lumsden 3-mile Match Race, at St. Louis, Mo.

May 27, 1889.—Stone-Lumsden 25-mile Match Race at Crawfordsville, Ind.

May 30, 1889.—Maine Division Meet, at Biddeford, Me.

May 30, 1889.—Bicycle and Athletic Tournament and 2-mile L. A. W. Championship Race at Narragansett Park.

June 8, 1889.—Century Run, Orange, N. J., to Philadelphia. Chairman, L. A. Clarke, 25 Broad Street, New York.

July 2, 3, 4, 1889.—Hagerstown, Md., Meet.

July 20, 1889.—One-mile and 25-mile Bicycle and 5-mile Tricycle N. C. U. championships at Paddington, Eng., race track.

July 27, 1889.—One-mile and 25-mile Tricycle and 5-mile Bicycle N. C. U. Championships at Paddington, Eng., track.

HARVARD'S RACE MEET.

The last year has been marked by the great increase in the interest taken in bicycling at Harvard. The bicycle club has held two road races and a hare and hounds chase, besides a team road race with Tech. This spring the interest is still on the increase. Saturday, the 20th, the second road race with Tech. comes off, and from all appearances Harvard will have to work to win. Tech., last fall, would have won the race but for an accident to Bradley, one of her best men, and this was doubtless the reason for her challenge this spring. Harvard's team will consist of Greenleaf, '92; Davis, '91; Bailey, '91; Barron, '91; Wirts, '92; Rogers, '90; Holmes, '92; Cromwell, '92, and Kelley, L. S.; Brown, '91, has given up road riding and will not race.

The most important event in bicycling, however, is doubtless the race meet, which will be held on Holmes Field Saturday, May 11. It is expected that all the principal riders of New England and the adjacent States will compete. Already entries have been received from New York. Following are the events and prizes: One-mile safety handicap (open), one hundred yards limit. First prize, Kodak camera; second prize, Columbia cup, given by the Pope Manufacturing Company; third prize, Flobert rifle. Quarter-mile bicycle scratch (open). First prize, Anthony's Lilliput detective camera, given by Barker & Starbird, 56 Bromfield Street, Boston; second prize, Smith & Wesson Hammerless revolver; third prize, "Pettitt" tennis racket. One-mile inter-scholastic scratch, open to all preparatory schools in Massachusetts. First prize, sole-leather traveling-bag; second prize, "Sears Special" racket; third prize, silver cup. One-mile bicycle handicap, 120 yards limit (open). First prize, Meyrowitz Bros. yachting glass, given by the Coventry Machinists' Company; second prize, traveling-bag; third prize, engraved silver cup. One-mile bicycle, 3.20 class, scratch, open to members of H. B. C. First prize, United States signal glass, given by William Read & Sons; second prize, "Sears Special" racket, given by Wright & Ditson; third prize, engraved silver cup. Two-mile tandem safety scratch (open). First prize, two brass standing lamps; second prize, two stop watches; third prize, two engraved silver cups. Two-mile bicycle handicap, 250 yards limit. First prize, Eagle bicycle, value $130, given by Eagle Bicycle Company; second prize, Kodak camera; third prize, Winchester repeating rifle; fourth prize, old silver cup. Entrance fee, $1 for each event, except interscholastic. One-mile interscholastic, fifty cents. Entries close Saturday, May 4, at 12 P. M., with R. H. Davis, 153 Brattle Street, Cambridge, Mass. There is a special rule made, allowing safety bicycles to compete in the bicycle events. The track is hard, and perhaps the fastest quarter-mile track in the country. Besides Davis, '91; Brown, '91; Bailey, '91, and Greenleaf, '92, the following Harvard men intend to train for this race meet: Cromwell, '92; Wirts, '92; Barron, '91; Spencer, '90, and several others.

The first open cycle race of the English season took place April 13.

The English are very much upset over the question of separating safeties from ordinaries in path races. The difference between English and American temperaments and methods is shown by the promptness with which our Racing Board classed the wheels, while the English have, as yet, only arrived at the boiling-point of discussion.

The Kansas Division race meet on June 4, 5 and 6. First-class track, and $600 worth of prizes. They want Missouri Division to co-operate.

The Harvard Bicycle Club will hold an open race meet at Holmes' Field on May 11. A number of events are on the programme, and we hope amateur racing men will support the meet. Entries close May 4 with H. Davis, Cambridge, Mass.

A 2-mile bicycle handicap will be held at the New York Athletic Club games, to be held at Travers Island, June 15. Entrance fee, $1.00; close June 5 with F. D. Sturgis, 104 West Fifty-fifth Street, New York City.

MEETING OF THE LOUISIANA DIVISION OF THE L. A. W.

The Louisiana Division of the League of American Wheelmen met April 7, with Chief Consul H. H. Hodgson in the chair. A new constitution was adopted.

Chief Consul Hodgson suggested that a summer tour or encampment be organized and put into the hands of a committee of five.

Mr. Betts then made the same proposition in the form of a motion, which was seconded and carried, and the following committee were appointed: Messrs. Christy, O'Reardon, E. M. Graham, Gore and Fenner.

Messrs. Randall, Shields, Renaud, Gore and Fenner were appointed to constitute the new racing board.

The chair appointed Messrs. Hill, Fairchild, Russ, Betts and Graham as a committee on improvements of highways.

On rights and privileges were appointed Messrs. Ziegler, Rea, Christy, Crane and Walters.

Chief Consul Hodgson stated that he has offered a gold medal for the winner and a silver one for second place, to be contested for by the members of the L. A. W., in six handicap races to be run in June, July, August and September, respectively. The following committee were appointed to select the time and road: Messrs. Betts, Rea, Graham, Gore, Fredericks and Russ.

Mr. A. M. Hill was appointed official handicapper for the States of Mississippi, Arkansas, Texas and Louisiana.

Mr. Betts then offered the following resolution, which was accepted and ordered placed on the minutes, and that a copy be sent to the Board of Trade:

Whereas, The impassable condition of the public highways throughout the State during a goodly portion of the year is such as to seriously hamper the interests, both public and private, of its people; and

Whereas, The agricultural element and parish authorities have commended the agitation and the calling of a road convention, as witnessed by the action of the Hammond Agricultural Relief Association and the Pointe Coupee police jury;

Be it resolved, That this organization, representing a class deeply interested in the improvement of the public roads, along with other branches of the Government, views with pleasure the present agitation of the subject, and pledges as far as possible its assistance and support, both moral and material, to any movement that looks toward a betterment of existing conditions; and

Be it further resolved, That the attention of the officials of the Board of Trade be respectfully directed to the suggestion that they are the proper body to take the matter in hand and outline a course of action.

The meeting then adjourned.

The Louisiana Division members have adopted a sensible resolution, expressing their sympathy with, and support of, any movement having a system of better roads for its object. They believe in agitating, assisting and supporting, both morally and practically, any method of roads improvement. Every Division in the League should adopt similar resolutions.

The English are estimating the number of American cycle agents at 2,000. We think there are more than this number, and we have been unable to obtain lists of agents from any of the larger firms.

CYCLISTS' UNION OF LONG ISLAND.

At a meeting of the Executive Committee of the union, held April 8, 1889, the following *new* members were elected:

NO.	NAME.	ADDRESS.	CLUB.
230	M. L. Allen,	765 Carroll St., Bkn.	Bkn Bi. Club.
231	F. W. Bradner,	206 Washington Av., Bkn.	" "
232	O. C. Belding,	79 Leonard St., N. Y.	" "
233	A. C. Banker,	76 West 23d St., N. Y.	" "
234	H. L. Bradley,	47 3d St., Bkn.	" "
235	H. R. Brown,	36 Sterling Place, Bkn.	" "
236	R. W. Candler,	11 Monroe St., Bkn.	" "
237	S. V. Carman,	Hempstead, L. I.	" "
238	W. K. Cleverly,	349 20th St., Bkn.	" "
239	H. G. Fay,	480 Broadway, N. Y.	" "
240	F. C. Farnsworth,	725 President St., Bkn.	" "
241	T. B. Hegeman,	561 Lafayette Av., Bkn.	" "
242	J. E. Hayes, Jr.,	134 Park Place, Bkn.	" "
243	H. Hornbostel,	39 Second Place, Bkn.	" "
244	E. Hornbostel,	39 Second Place, Bkn.	" "
245	A. S. Haviland,	436 Grand Av., Bkn.	" "
246	W. F. Homan,	407 Clermont Av., Bkn.	" "
247	W. M. Kenyon,	216 Berkeley Place, Bkn.	" "
248	W. J. Kenmore, Jr.	93 St. Felix St., Bkn.	" "
249	T. F. Mulqueen,	49 Willoughby St., Bkn.	" "
250	W. E. Mayor,	195 South Oxford St., Bkn.	" "
251	G. B. Owen, Jr.,	18 Willoughby Av., Bkn.	" "
252	F. H. Pough,	146 Hicks St., Bkn.	" "
253	F. Powell,	Hempstead, L. I.	" "
254	E. L. Ropkins,	84 North 2d St., Bkn.	" "
255	N. Rogers,	218 Dean St., Bkn.	" "
256	E. C. Smith,	219 Washington Av., Bkn.	" "
257	B. C. Smith,	210 Washington Av., Bkn.	" "
258	C. L. B. Snedeker,	109 Park Place, Bkn.	" "
259	F. B. Stewart,	470 Broome St., N. Y.	" "
260	T. C. Snedeker,	141 Adelphi St., Bkn.	" "
261	E. Skinner,	227 Cumberland St., Bkn.	" "
262	W. E. Sheffield, Jr.	362 1st St., Bkn.	" "
263	A. L. Tinker,	528 Clinton Av., Bkn.	" "
264	N. H. Weed,	120 Broadway, N. Y.	" "
265	G. L. Warner,	175 Atlantic Av., Bkn.	" "
266	E. Williams,	189 St. John's Place, Bkn.	" "
267	J. H. Mellor,	In care of	Prospect Harriers.
268	J. W. Bate,	In care of	" "
269	H. Filmer,	481 Macon St, Bkn.	Unattached.
270	W. T. Zugalla,	390 Carlton Av., Bkn.	"

The Road Improvement Committee reported that communications had been held with Mayor Chapin in reference to Cobblestone Hill, and that he had informed them that the proper authorities would give the hill their immediate attention.

The following letter was received from Mr. Charles Schwalbach and accepted by the committee:

"E. K. AUSTIN, President
"Cyclists' Union of Long Island.

"*Dear Sir*—I have the pleasure of submitting to you the following offer: I will present, on or before the first of May, 1890, to the member of the Cyclists' Union of Long Island making the greatest mileage during the year, commencing April 1, 1889, and ending April 1, 1890, a valuable and suitable gold medal, to be competed for on the following conditions;

"All distances to be made on the road, it being understood that this offer is made in promotion of touring. Reports of each month's mileage to be handed the President of the Cyclists' Union on or about the first of each succeeding month, after being duly checked and authenticated by officers of the club to which the member may belong, and total mileage for the season to be sworn to before a notary. Reports from members not of any regularly organized club to be duly authenticated to the satisfaction of the Executive Committee of the Union, and total mileage sworn to before a notary. In no case is any person's mileage at any time during the twelve months to be made known by you to others competing or not competing. In the case of regularly organized clubs, your Executive Committee may waive the condition requiring a member to confirm his total mileage before a notary.

"Yours fraternally,
"CHARLES SCHWALBACH."

Members of the union intending to compete for the above medal should send mileage reports as stated to E. K. Austin, President, 82 Front Street, New York City.

It was decided by the committee to drop from the membership roll the names of all original members who shall fail to renew their membership by May 1, 1889. Renewals should be sent in at once to the Secretary.

Signed BERT M. COLE, Secretary,
126 South Elliott Place,
Brooklyn, L. I.

Brooklyn, April 12, 1889.

Says the Nashville *American*: "THE WHEEL, the leading cycling paper in this country," etc.

We have received a neat invitation for the Bay City Wheelmen's reception, which will be held Friday, April 26, at Odd Fellows' Hall, San Francisco.

THE LEAGUE MEET.

EDITOR OF THE WHEEL:

In the current issue of your entertaining journal—which, parenthetically, I wish to add is the most interesting of them all—I notice a communication to the Chief Consul of Maryland, from the President of the L. A. W., in which it is broadly hinted that the Maryland Division again invite the Executive Committee to hold the meet in their section; Baltimore presumably being the place intended for the honor(?). And, further, it is suggested that a repetition of the liberal and hospitable entertainment of last year might be curtailed, though at the same time a programme is outlined which would require much hard work as well as hard cash.

Now, for truly monumental "gall" I rather think the communication quite lays over anything that the League has been treated to during its existence, and I am glad to see that your correspondent, "Bay Ridge," graciously but decidedly turns it down. As "Bay Ridge" truly says, the meet held there last year was a great success, and, as far as the efforts of the Baltimore wheelmen could make it, was all that could be desired, and was characteristic of that generous hospitality for which Baltimore is so noted, and which I, with many others, was sorry to see so grossly outraged by the rough conduct and "horse-play" of many, at both the smoker at the Opera House and the supper at Bay Ridge.

And, for all that was done, how much has Baltimore been benefited? Did the League, as is customary with other bodies when in convention, bestow any of the places of official honor on the Maryland Division? If so, which one? Did they contribute in any way to the great expense of the occasion, and if so, how much? Did they even pay for the hire of the hall in which they held their meetings, and which is really not generally considered as a part of the "entertainment?" I doubt it. Did they at the time, or have they in any way since done anything officially to recognize the time, labor and expense bestowed upon them? I am much inclined to doubt that also. In fact, I am very much inclined to doubt that they even so much as returned the customary and inexpensive vote of thanks.

And now, having had a good time last year, and wanting to enjoy at small cost to themselves a repetition of it, and failing to find in his daily mail an avalanche of invitations from other places, the President casts his eyes around the arena and finally decides that once more Baltimore should be privileged, and hence his letter to the C. C.

But why not New York? It is now several years since they entertained the League, and they have both numbers and wealth. Or Brooklyn? which is a good-sized town with wide streets and a fine park. Wheelmen are plentiful there, too, I believe, and they have not yet been favored with a League meet. Besides, the President himself, being near by, could very materially assist.

Philadelphia, also, is a town of no small dimensions, and enjoys a grand park and many wheelmen. Then out West there is Chicago, and Cincinnati, and Cleveland, and Columbus, and many others, all equally as eligible as Baltimore and having the one advantage of novelty, as I do not recall that either of those mentioned has been favored. Possibly, though, the President wisely concludes with Shakespeare, slightly altered, however, that

> 'Tis better to enjoy the pleasures we have had,
> Than fly to others that we know not of.

Baltimore, no doubt, appreciates the great honor Mr. Luscomb would do it, and the C. C. will no doubt make full express on of it in his reply; but if it is true, as I have heard, that one of their best clubs, the "Ramblers," have since "given up the ghost," he may be unable to agree with him that "the cause of wheeling in the locality where the meet is held is benefited thereby to a very considerable degree."

Possibly it is none of my business, as I am not a member of the Maryland Division, and I may be meddling in something which does not concern me, but I am much inclined to think I express the feelings of a large number who are interested, but who, with true Maryland gallantry, would sooner die or "bust" than admit it.

In an editorial article, THE WHEEL comes to the rescue and suggests Washington as the place. Thanks, awfully, but, having already been once favored, we do not crave any more. We are not exactly like the lamented Oliver Twist because we *do* know when we have had enough, and, speaking as one of the workers in 1884, we have had a "genteel sufficiency," and are not hoggish. I recall now the days and nights of hard and generous work done by that little handful of enthusiastic workers on that occasion, the various ways and means devised to entertain the strangers within our gates, the personal responsibility so frequently pledged to obdurate and unsympathetic tradesmen, hotel keepers, decorators, printers and others; the numberless dimes and quarters paid out here and there which could not be accounted for, but which made up a very respectable total that came out of the individual pocket. Then, too, the magnificent races which gave the League something over $600 to take away with them, and for which we did all the work, without so much as a penny to our advantage, and were even compelled to pay our own admission fee. And for all this we got—well, if my memory serves me right, we did get the usual perfunctory vote of thanks, in a "let's-get-it-off-our-minds" sort of way. And was "the cause of wheeling benefited in this locality?" Well, not to any "considerable degree," as far as the League club was concerned, for very shortly thereafter it was in such a state of "innocuous desuetude," to quote a phrase of the late administrator, that it was only by the application of heroic treatment that it pulled through alive, and to-day but two of the two dozen members of that time still remain with it, and all, or nearly all, the others have given up the wheel.

NO; Washington does NOT hanker after the honor. One dose is sufficient to cure the desire, and we do not wish to deprive other places of the glory and—work. Signed. F. P.

A FEW WORDS TO "FENTON," WHO FANCIES SOMETIMES.

I am pained beyond expression that "Fenton," in one of his "fancies" in a recent number of THE WHEEL, should agitate his poll about my unfortunate "choice of English," which he asserts is occasionally "above" his, "and, in a number of cases, anybody else's head." Bemoaning my deplorable but characteristic ignorance of the language of my fathers (which, by the way, has been greatly improved and enriched by such mannikins as "Fenton"), I apologize for my paucity of suitable language with which to express the ideas which at rare intervals occupy my noddle. The compound word "wai-cycle," to which he takes such exception, was written "war-cycle"—a cycle *intended* for military purposes; and when Fenton writes a little more, and grows, in consequence, more modest and charitable in his demeanor to a fellow-scribe, he will be forced to acknowledge that compositors, proofreaders, writers of letters and the men who "edit" them (being human) are not invested with Fentonian infallibility.

I humbly crave Fenton's permission to use the word "rythmetical," which I suggest *might* be applied to an even or regular pedal action. Thomas Carlyle (a man who, especially since his death, has been awarded an acknowledged position in the world of letters) uses the word "rythmetical" in his "Hero-Worship." He doubtless had his own quaint reason for so doing. According to a dictionary, I find the word permissible, although "*rhythmetical*" and "*rhythmical*" are in more frequent use. I am sorry that I have lived to annoy Fenton, but hope he won't grasp his *tere* Thor's hammer "until his knuckles grow white," as it would be labor lost to sling impotent ink at one so hardened as I have become (through the unaccountable attention of an army of "those who are of weaker capacity") to adverse criticism. I am painfully aware that my English is faulty and graceless, that "my fingers are all thumbs, and my hands all feet;" that I use words too big for a man of my size (and which I can neither understand nor spell); that my writings are full of untruths, "bulls," provincialisms and technical errors, but my intentions are good—very good; "and my opinion on politics, religion, baseball and the amateur cycle question unchangeable," as is also my respect for and admiration of "Fenton" and his "fancies."

The lines from "Hudibras" have been selected with great care, and describe my utter worthlessness to a nicety, and show that Fenton has his eyes open to the faults and failings of *other people*, whom he sees with remarkably accurate impartiality.

His remarks also show him to be charitably inclined to his fellow-scribe whom he never saw. And, dear Fenton, if you will but make a chart of the way in which you "fancy" I should see, write and walk in this lachrymose valley, I shall endeavor to walk worthy of even your esteemed approval. No, dearest Fenton, you are not at all inquisitive; you are retiring and modest to a fault, and show remarkable taste. Only, my boy, be a little more *practical* in future and *fancy* less, and you shall meet with the good-will and esteem of "JACK."

MR. SHRIVER ON DIRECT REPRESENTATION.

NEW YORK, April 15, 1889.

EDITOR OF THE WHEEL:

Dear Sir—Not really being invested with the honor to which your latest issue assigns me—of membership in the National Assembly—and not even being allowed by the League Constitution to vote for my representatives in the Assembly, such part as I may take in discussing League government must necessarily be through the press; so perhaps you will give me a chance to say another word on what seems to be growing into one of our burning issues again—the manner of electing our cycling legislators and executive officials. You ask do we who want direct representation believe that it would be better than the present method. The answer is that we do; and not only because every organization is better managed when it has direct responsibility, or because it is an inherent right of the men who support the League by payment of dues to have a voice in its control; but even more, because the chances for wire-pulling and consequent bad selection of officers and waste of energy are infinitely greater in a small than in a large electorate.

We think, therefore, that it would give better results if the whole membership of the League had the power of voting directly for its officials, and that such a system would more certainly bring about the choice of the men who would do most good work, rather than the men who are most skillful in making combinations to swing the delegates from this or that Division. And as no legislative body can act intelligently on a question which its members have not previously considered, we think it eminently proper to agitate the subject in advance of the Assembly's meeting.

The burden of proof in such a discussion should lie upon the advocates of our present system, which is utterly artificial and unnatural; but inasmuch as it is established, our side has to take the aggressive and propose a substitute. This I did in my last letter to you on this subject, and would like very much to know from yourself or some one else who opposes a return to a natural system, what are their objections to voting at League elections a ballot which records directly the voter's choice for each office to be filled—from President down to District Representative. Yours truly, E. J. SHRIVER.

NEW YORK, April 15, 1889.

MR. PRIAL, EDITOR WHEEL:

Dear Sir—I wish to dispel one of Fenton's "fancies," as appeared in THE WHEEL March 29.

Mr. F. has evidently been misinformed, and the article mentioned is apt to create a wrong impression as regards the H. W. bowling team.

The first of the season, when the Bowling League was formed, we had an understanding with the proprietor of the alleys we bowled on to have the use of the alleys *any* Friday night we wanted. Before the season was over the alleys were rented to another club, they using them every Friday night. This left the H. W.'s out.

Our Captain, Mr. P., wrote the H. C. W.'s requesting that the game be rolled any Tuesday night that suited their convenience. This they refused to do. It was that date or not at all, and we were compelled to let the game go by default. We wanted then, and still want, to bowl the H. C. W. team, and, although not together as a team, we can scrape up bowling members enough to make any of the teams hustle.

By giving the above space in your paper you will oblige Yours,

C. E. FRASER, Sec'y H. W.

LADIES BICYCLING.

DEAR EDITOR OF THE WHEEL:

In the issue of the *Bicycling World and Bulletin* for April 5, 1889, there is a letter from "Helen Grey," taking charge of the ladies' department. She has never ridden a bicycle, and seems not over enthusiastic to do so.

I register a protest right here.

It certainly does seem as if the editor might prevail in the choice of having some knowledge whereof she speaks to take upon herself the office.

Bicycling needs no discouragement, we all know, and any little hit tells against it.

If there were no bicyclists in Boston it might do to make a tricyclist "guide, philosopher and friend," but to have one in the guise of counselor make unfounded statements of facts of which she has no practical knowledge—well, I think it is time for a protest.

I have been amused by the crude views advanced by *future* bicyclists. If they yearn to help their fellows to a proper enjoyment of wheeling, why don't they learn a little something about it personally before doing harm instead of good? A practical bicyclist laughs over the ignorance displayed, but a would-be rider is frightened from her intention by some sibylline utterance which has no foundation in fact.

Miss Grey thinks that there must be no little expenditure of nervous force in maintaining the balance of the bicycle. Of course there is while you are learning to ride, as there would be if you were learning to ride a horse, or learning to skate or swim; but when once you know how, it becomes second nature and no drain on the nervous system whatever. I do assure all readers,

Miss Grey thinks a tricycle should rank high as a protection against dogs. I never had the luck, good or bad, to be chased by a dog, so I am much in the same situation with regard to dogs as Miss Grey is in regard to bicycles; but my theory would be that a bicycle would be less easier to keep between one and the ravening dog, being more easily moved and light enough to be shifted according to the exigencies of the situation, whereas a tricycle leaves the rider exposed in the rear, if a handle-bar steerer, and front and rear if a side steerer, and most dogs that I know under such circumstances would probably be mean enough not to content themselves with a side attack.

By the way, I think it is on record that a bicyclist sustained an attack from a dog armed only with a simple upright, and defied the animal from behind his machine with such success that he fled ignominiously.

It is wonderful with what calm confidence absurdities are put in print about ladies bicycling, notably in the same issue in which is the letter with which I have just finished quarreling.

The statement is made that some ladies of Newton went down to try one of the new machines and in the course of the evening mastered it. Those who were persistent became good riders before the evening was over. Positively, after reading two or three of the wheeling papers, I come to the conclusion that none of the writers know anything of what they are writing; even the men seem to have temporarily lost their knowledge of the kindergarten facts of bicycling.

There are over 150 of us in Washington, and I have yet to hear of one who rode well under two or three weeks.

I am afraid I shall get the reputation of a "scrapper." I am not, but it does vex me to have women as bicyclists put in such a false and ridiculous light. There must be any number of wheelwomen who read these papers who know what they are reading is perfect trash. Why don't they come forward and help their sisters by their personal experience to a new, delightful and healthful sensation?

PSYCHE.

LADIES BICYCLING IN THE SOUTH.

The Wheel, the leading cycling paper in this country, recognizing the growing importance of the subject, has been devoting much of its space of late to lady riders who have ridden both kinds of wheels. The subject has been discussed in all its bearings, but every

lady who has ridden the two-wheeler is loud in its praises, and the preponderance of evidence is on the side of the "pony," and would seem to indicate that it is only a question of time when the tricycle will be, in a measure, superseded by the later machine. One of these correspondents, who signs herself "Psyche," gives the relative merits of the wheels after this style: "I see that one correspondent, in speaking of the bicycle as compared with the tricycle, says she has no practical experience of the former in shopping or visiting, and doesn't know how it stands the comparison under those circumstances. I have tried both machines for both shopping and visiting, and find the bicycle far and away the most convenient. It is immensely easier to mount and dismount from (when once you know how), it takes so little room, and is so light that it can easily be led up on the sidewalk and put entirely out of the way of annoyance to passersby or of damage to itself. I have used a Cripper tricycle, and always found it disagreeable to mount before an audience, and have never seen any one mount one with any degree of grace, while the bicycle mount is, in nine cases out of ten, very graceful and always easy. One can mount and dismount from a bicycle in a quarter of the time it takes on a tricycle, and with only a fraction, and 'that a very small one, of the exertion. As to the impossibility of sitting on your machine while you stop, that seems to me a blessing very thinly disguised, for it is a change of posture which unconsciously rests one. I think the difficulty of learning to mount is a good deal overrated. It seems desperately hard at first trial, but I caught the idea at my second lesson, and after a little practice I was all right." "Psyche" here gives in detail a description of three mounts, which, she says, can be learned in an hour. They are simple and graceful, and can be taught by any ordinary wheelman.—*Nashville American.*

A NEW BICYCLE LANTERN.

The Bowers pedal lamp is the result of investigations made with the idea of producing a bicycle lantern that shall do away with the many objections raised against other lamps. The experiments were so satisfactory that an application for a patent was forwarded and granted. It is safe to say that so far as practicability and convenience are concerned it cannot be duplicated. It is fastened on either pedal by means of a neat, stiff steel spring, which grips the pedal pin in such a way that the use of tools, screws, etc., is entirely done away with. The absolute absence of play or rattle is a marked feature. Freedom from occupancy of the hub of the wheel allows the use of a hub cyclometer, while the annoying difficulty of having the shadow of the wheel rim directly in

your path is completely obviated by having the lantern under the pedal, which consequently casts that shadow to the rear.

There is no uncontrollable forward and back swinging motion, but, on the contrary, the light is under perfect command of the rider, so that in going down hill, by a slight pressure of the toe, the light is thrown forward and down, just where you want it. At other times the bull's eye is nearly perpendicular.

It can be set at any angle on the pedal pin. Necessity does not require but one lantern, but by carrying two a double brilliancy is obtained. Every wheelman who has examined and tried the patent is satisfied that it will supersede all other lighting appliances.

To drivers and pedestrians the brilliancy of a revolving light is very attractive. The weight of the lamp is such that a rider would never mistrust its presence, and the steadiness of the light on the ground has a tendency to annihilate the idea that the lantern is continually revolving in a circle with the pedal.

Work is being pushed as fast as possible, and it is expected they will be ready for the trade in a very short time.

The above description is written by the inventor of the lamp, W. T. Bowers, Saco, Me.

DO CYCLES RUN EASIEST AT NIGHT?

Our cycler had an experience last Wednesday night, April 10, which tends to show that riding by night appears to be easier than riding by day. With two friends, our cycler took a run, starting at 7.30 P. M., through Malden (one of Boston's prettiest suburbs), where Mr. G. took a bad "header." He was taken to a drug store, and in about thirty minutes came out with his wrist bound up, saying that it had been sprained. When in Everett—half-way home—he said that he felt no pain, and was for carrying out the original programme. They turned back and rode to Maplewood, Linden, Revere, Cliftondale to Saugus. The roads were very good, and they seemed to glide rather than ride over them. On their right they could see the lighthouse on Egg Rock, and everything appeared to be in a drowsy state; yet the party was making ten miles an hour.

When we parted (9.50 P. M.) each said it had been a fine run—eighteen miles. Our cycler "took in" a very steep but short hill, and it was mounted with a rush. You can imagine our cycler's surprise next morning to hear that our friend's wristbone had been cracked, and that he would be unable to use it for three weeks; and yet, strange as it may seem, he had ridden eighteen miles in one hour and fifty minutes. It is our cycler's opinion that the dense quiet that pervades everything and the faint light assist in seeming to make our wheels run much easier than in the strong light of day.

CONSUL.

AN IMPROVED TRICYCLE.

A tricycle designed to be easily operated and guided is illustrated herewith, and has been patented by Mr. Patrick Gallagher, of No. 145 East Forty-second Street, New York City. It has a light but strong iron frame-work, and is propelled by means of a crank-handle mounted in arms adjustably pivoted to uprights on the frame, one of the ends of the crank-handle having a sprocket wheel connected by an endless chain with a sprocket wheel on the axle of the driving wheels, while the other end of the crank-handle has two fly-wheels to steady the motion of the machine, and so that but little exertion will be required to run it after a high degree of momentum has been obtained. By removing or adding links in the chain, and the adjustment of the arms of the crank-handle in the uprights, the machine is readily made easy of operation by persons with long or short arms. The guide wheel has its bearings in a fork having a post extending

through bracket arms, and is adapted to be readily turned by a convenient located foot-board. The lever of a suitable braking mechanism extending up at one side of the seat, whereby the operator can readily regulate the speed of the vehicle without changing his or her position on the seat.

The machine is especially adapted for ladies, and can be used for invalids. It has a motion which will exercise the chest. It is very easily operated, and can be stopped instantly.

CYCLING: ITS ADVANTAGES TO CLERGYMEN.

To the Editor of the Church Record:

I want to speak a word to my brother clergymen and call their attention to the great advantages which many of them are losing in not becoming riders of the bicycle. Do you realize, ye plodding pastors who tramp many weary miles in your parishes or who work in your studies till "much learning doth make you mad," that this is an age of steam, electricity, telegraps, telephones and bicycles? All are additions to the facilities for business, communication and locomotion. You cannot neglect them without being behind the times. How any active man under fifty years of age can be content to see others ride the bicycle while he does not I cannot comprehend.

Clergymen, I know, in many cases have the financial obstacle against them. With the needs of family, books and charity, they do not feel at liberty to put their money into a bicycle. If they did but know it, they would find this a better investment than any railroad stock. I estimate that my wheel earns over 30 per cent. on its cost every year in saving of car-fare, horse hire, etc., not to speak of increased health and enjoyment.

Some, perhaps, are deterred by timidity, but there need be no trouble on that, or on their heads, either, for the excellent rear-driver safety machines can be ridden by any one after a few lessons without a single accident.

Some, perhaps, are afraid of their dignity, but this fear is quite unnecessary. There are several ministers in our neighborhood, and some hundreds throughout the country, who ride constantly without any damage to the respect in which they are held.

The fact is, a bicycle is a great addition to a clergyman's usefulness, especially if he cannot afford to keep a horse. He can visit distant parishioners more easily, hasten to the relief of the sick and poor, ride to outlying missions and save much time for his study, besides keeping up a vigorous health, which will show itself in all parts of his work.

Here, then, is a suggestion for vestries, church committees, or, perhaps, still better, members of wheel clubs. Go around your neighborhood, to the heathen as well as the Christians, and collect money enough to make your pastor a present of a bicycle. Or let the wheel be the property of the congregation, like the parsonage, for the use of the minister for the time being, as it is adjustable easily for different sizes. If any ministers to whom the gift is made are doubtful about learning to ride, I shall be happy to offer my assistance to persuade them.

As to the kind of machine, use your own judgment. I have ridden an "Expert" for several years, and have had no desire to change until lately, when I tried the new "Columbia Light Roadster Safety," which is certainly an admirable machine. However, any wheel is far better than none.

You might adopt an expedient like that of a Western church fair for a donation. Have a collection book or box labeled: "Put a dollar in the slot and see the minister ride a bicycle; see him doubling his activity in the parish; see dyspepsia, dullness and weariness left behind him; see his sermons growing more full of life and power; see the church sleepers waxing fewer and the whole parish moving on more vigorously on the minister's wheels."

You can easily raise the money if you try. I know of two parishes where this evidence of good sense was shown in making a useful present to their minister. In one, the pastor had a bicycle, which was stolen from him. The people, finding that their loss was as great as his, wisely and generously gave him another steed of steel. Yours truly,

J. H. WATSON.

Hartford, Conn., March, 1889.

—*Church Record.*

"Elm City" writes to *Bicycling World*: "What has become of the Le Feur Brothers, who started up the Amazon River? I have been awaiting news of them for some time." To which [Ed.] parenthetically remarks that Para must have proved too attractive for them. This will not do! *Bi. World* sends out two innocent young men for a bicycle ride up the Amazon. The young men have not since been heard from. What has become of them? Were they murdered? or did they read one of those 1,471½ circulation editorials and die? Produce them, *Bi. World!*

TEA-DRINKING.

A QUESTION FOR CHEMISTS AND MEDICAL MEN.

It is generally conceded that tea is a very beneficial form of refreshment for cyclists. Personally, I never feel so "fit" for a fast spin as after having a good cup of tea; and, considering the prominent place which this beverage occupies in the Saturday fixtures of the clubs, tea must be granted a foremost place in the cyclist's commissariat. As an habitual drinker of tea, both at breakfast and in the afternoon, I have sometimes tried the experiment of taking no other form of stimulant, and scarcely any other beverage, when on a long ride; but I have found it to be the case with me, as I believe it is traditionally with others, that excessive tea-drinking is injurious, although the precise point at which this mild stimulant ceases to benefit and commences to be deleterious I am unable to determine. However, there can be no doubt as to tea being an excellent refresher for quite a number of hours when a cyclist is engaged upon a long and fast ride; and what I wish to find out is whether any of

OUR EXPERIENCED CYCLING MEDICOS

can formulate any rule as to the quantity or frequency of tea-drinking which may be considered innocuous and beneficial. I also have a suggestion which I should like to put before any of your readers skilled in the chemistry of the subject. In the "National Encyclopedia" article "Stimulants," I find the following remarks: "Tea, used moderately, seems to be wholly beneficial to the system—a great contrast to the class of alcoholic stimulants, whose pleasure is purchased at the cost of vital energy, even when they are sparingly used. Tea is found to quicken and deepen the respiration, and to make it easy, at the same time to act but slightly on the pulse, and to act more powerfully on the skin, inducing free perspiration, and hence a refreshing coolness (an effect very remarkable on hot summer afternoons). This is not due to the effect of the hot water, for it occurs also when cold tea is drunk. Tea thus promotes the transformation of food without supplying nourishment, and, consequently, should not be taken pure without food, but the common practice of adding milk and sugar to it somewhat modifies this remark, since that addition certainly brings tea within the rank of foods of a certain small value. Tea has an excellent effect upon the mind, brightening and wakening it; and occasional doses of tea will usually keep a watcher awake during a whole night quite easily. At the same time it increases muscular activity, so that Professor Tyndall has recorded that cold tea was found by him to be

THE BEST POSSIBLE LIQUID

upon which to accomplish his arduous Alpine investigations. In both these particulars the action of tea presents a remarkable and favorable contrast to the stupefying and enervating effects of alcoholic liquors." Elsewhere in the same article it is stated that the deleterious effect of excessive tea-drinking is occasioned by the quantity of alkaloids contained in the tea; and it therefore occurs to me to ask whether this excessively alkaline beverage might not be safely taken in greater quantities if its consumption is alternated by some acid drink, or even the sucking of lemons, grapes, or oranges, so that the acid of the fruit would counteract the alkali of the tea. Should this supposition of mine be correct, the knowledge will be of great value to long-distance riders, to whom both tea and acid fruits are grateful merely by reason of their taste. On behalf of this class, I express a hope that some of the medical or chemical readers of *B. N.* will give us a few hints on the subject, with especial regard to the quantity of tea which may safely be drunk during a day's ride, the nature and quantity of acid fruits useful in counteracting the deleterious effects of the tea, and any modifications in such rules necessitated by peculiarities of food eaten during the day.—*Bicycling News.*

Chas. Schwalbach, Prospect Park Plaza, Brooklyn, has just published one of the neatest catalogues of the season. Mr. Schwalbach, as fully detailed and illustrated in the catalogue, handles the New Mail, New Mail Safety, Columbia L. R., Expert, Volunteer, Columbia Safety, Columbia Semi-Roadster, Columbia tandem, Ideal Bicycle, Pet, Juno and Crescent safeties, Central Gear tricycle, Lever tricycle, Surprise tricycle, adjustable iron velocipede; also a line of sundries, a complete stock of bicycle and tennis garments, such as caps, mitts, tights, blazers, belts, shirts, etc. Mr. Schwalbach also repairs, rents and stores wheels, and has competent riding instructors.

DELAY IN PROCURING PARTS.

PHILADELPHIA, April 16, 1889.

EDITOR OF THE WHEEL:

Dear Sir—"Interchangeable parts" is a feature in most high-grade cycle catalogues to which the attention of intending purchasers is particularly called.

This is very commendable and extremely useful when you can get those parts *promptly*; but, when as your subscriber and some of his friends and others have had to wait from two to three months (the extreme case), it is very mortifying and praise of "interchangeable parts" lose their effect.

I know of one person (not the subscriber) who was so unfortunate as to break an important part of his machine and has been deprived of its use for over two months owing to the manufacturers not sending the parts promptly. In my own case it was not so bad, as I have been able to make use of my "bike," but wished the parts for my own convenience.

Of course in the busy season this may be excused, as the manufacturers seem to prefer to sell a machine instead of taking care of an old customer, but the cases cited were in the *dull* season.

Perhaps our cases have been unfortunate, but if others have met with the same treatment it will be well to have the manufacturers' attention called to it in your valuable paper.

KLERCY.

A SELECTED LIST OF PATENTS.

[Reported especially for THE WHEEL AND CYCLING TRADE REVIEW by C. A. Snow & Co., patent attorneys, Washington, D. C.]

Richard H. Fletcher, Socorro, N. Mex. Ter. Bicycle.

Wm. J. Fitzpatrick, South Boston, Mass. Gearing for bicycles.

Samuel A. Burns, Bridgeport, Ct. Brake.

Bearing date of April 16.

"*The Sewing-Machine and Cycling News*, English, publishes a weekly column of American notes, captioned 'Stars and Stripes,' which is stolen bodily from this paper." So says THE WHEEL; but hold on there, friend WHEEL: not altogether stolen from thee. We notice various peculations from the *American Athlete* also, but our friend across the water is welcome to the same. Don't you think, friend WHEEL, that his judgment is good, if his method of showing such to be the case is bad?—*American Athlete.* [Very good. Very good.]

The funny paragraphists call W. C. Murphy, of the Kings County Wheelmen, "Bars" Murphy. No, gentlemen, "Miles" it is, though we doubt not he is as clever at bars as he is at miles.

The Manhattan Bicycle Club, at its regular monthly meeting, held last Monday, admitted five riders to membership—E. N. Burnett, G. A. Litchhult, W. H. Pederson, F. W. Ruhl and W. H. Liebs.

Mr. J. F. Marsters, a sporting-goods dealer on Court St., Brooklyn, near the City Hall, is starting a bicycling department. Mr. Marsters' store is not near the riding district, but is in the heart of the shopping district, and he should do well.

Messrs. Schoverling, Daly & Gales report a large business in new Mails. The firm has just issued a new catalogue descriptive of the following wheels, for which they are agents: New Mail Light Roadster, New Mail Safety, American Ideal bicycle, American Ideal Rambler, "Vineyard" bicycle, the "Pet" boys' and girls' Safety, the "Junior" boys' Safety, the "Gem" tricycle and a line of sundries.

The Gormully & Jeffery Manufacturing Company publish twelve pages of their new catalogue in the advertising pages of this number.

William Halpin & Co., who are general Eastern agents for the St. Nicholas Manufacturing Company's goods, report large sales of their National safeties. These safeties are good machines, and are sold at a reasonable price. They are made in two styles, one for gentlemen and one for ladies. Agents are wanted in every city in the East to sell these wheels.

THE arrangements for the 25-mile handicap road race, to be held May 30, on the Irvington-Milburn course, are being rapidly completed. Many members of the trade have responded to the appeal for prizes, and the success of the race is now assured. A meeting of representatives of various clubs will be held next week, and sub-committees will be appointed. The conditions of the race and an entry blank will be published in next week's WHEEL.

Warwick Perfection Wheels.

Warwick Perfection Safety. Price, $135.00. Weight, 48 lbs.

Warwick Perfection Ordinary. Price, $125.00.

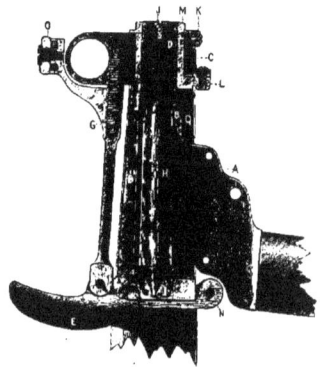

Neck, Head, Brake, etc. [Advt.]

WHEEL GOSSIP.

The Bay City wheelmen will hold a race meet on April 30.

Messrs. Lucas & Sons, manufacturers of the "King of the Road" lamps, will shortly enlarge their premises.

The Rhode Island wheelmen will give a grand bicycle and athletic tournament at Narragansett Park on Decoration Day, May 30. A special feature of the event will be the two-mile L. A. W. championship race. Entries close May 25.

The Coventry Machinists' Co., Limited, have four branch offices—at Boston, London, Manchester and Paris. Their London offices, at Holborn Viaduct, were established in 1880. The "Swift No. 3" has been the best seller so far this year. The demand for Ladies' Safeties abroad has been very small. In England a lady must have a guarantee that she will be taught to ride without cost before she will purchase a bicycle.

W. J. Corcoran, who is at present training Yale's racing men for the Intercollegiate Games, will locate in New York about June 1. Mr. Corcoran has trained Crist, Hendee, and many crack racing men, and will make a specialty of preparing men for the path. We have no trainer in New York who makes a specialty of training cyclists, and if Mr. Corcoran locates at a good track our racing men could vastly improve their form by placing themselves under his mentorship.

The Brooklyn *Standard* awards high praise to Mrs. Grace Clark, who impersonated Mrs. Nettletop in the sketch, "How She Loved Him," presented April 10 at the Brooklyn Academy of Music by the Gilbert Amateur Dramatic Society. Mrs. Clark is prominently identified with wheeling in Brooklyn. She is the wife of Mr. W. J. Clark, Chairman of the Entertainment Committee of the Long Island Wheelmen, whose members and guests have often been entertained by Mrs. Clark's readings.

We alluded some time back to the new "Keen" ball pedal, which was invented by the "old hoss" and manufactured by William Bown. It has since been tried by a number of practical riders, and our original opinion that it was to the veteran's designs by W. Bown. The pedal, we are told, is already "going" well, and amongst others Ernest Mayes, Harry Osborne, and May, of the Surrey, have expressed themselves entirely satisfied with its action, and pronounce it the best thing of the kind they have ridden with yet. Let us hope there may be "millions in it," for Happy Jack's sake.—*The Cyclist.*

HAPPY JACK'S LATEST. We understand that Mr. Sydney Lee has been appointed the London representative for the new "John Keen" ball pedal, which is being manufactured

CHICAGO EXPOSITION BUILDING.

The Chicago Exposition Building, in which the coming exhibit and tournament in that city are to be held, is by all means the finest structure for the purpose in the world. It is the largest roofed area in the world without interior supports, even the mighty Agricultural Hall in London being almost insignificant in comparison. In length it is 1,000 feet; in width, 230 feet, and in height, to the base of the flag-staff, 160 feet. The location of this leviathan is one of its principal charms. It stands on the lake front, 100 yards from the starting-point of the great Pullman road-race. To the south lies Michigan Avenue, a magnificent boulevard for upward of a dozen miles directly south; to the north lie the approaches to Dearborn Avenue, an asphalt road three miles in length, and the Lake Shore Drive, another famous boulevard, connecting the city with Lincoln Park; to the west is Jackson Street, the most popular of West Side routes, running to Garfield, Humboldt and Douglas parks. The City Hall, all principal hotels, theatres and railroad depots are within ten minutes' walk of the building, which, in addition to being the largest, is doubtless the most centrally located in America.

Around the inside runs a gallery, varying from 12 to 30 feet in width. It is over 500 yards in circumference, and on it several records were made four or five years ago. Several riders, including Phil Hammel, who was reinstated by the L. A. W. Racing Board, and Senator Morgan, are now training there. The tracks, of course, will be laid on the main floor—one for amateurs and one for professionals.

Percy Furnivall has entered for the English heavy weight boxing championships, as a member of the St. Bartholomew's Hospital Athletic Club.

The Brooklyn Club admitted eleven new members at their annual meeting, among them Walter Sinn, of the Brooklyn Park Theatre.

THE WHEEL

—AND—

CYCLING TRADE REVIEW,

Published every Friday morning.

Entered at the Post Office at second class rates.

Subscription Price,   -   -   - $1.00 a year.
Foreign Subscriptions,   -   -   -   8s. a year.
Single Copies,   -   -   -   -   5 Cents.

Newsdealers may order through AM. NEWS Co.

All copy should be received by Monday.
Telegraphic news received till Wednesday noon.

Advertising rates on Application.

F. P. PRIAL, *Editor and Proprietor*
23 Park Row,
P. O. Box 444,   New York.

Persons receiving sample copies of this paper are respectfully requested to examine its contents and give us their patronage, and as far as is convenient, aid in circulating the journal, and extend its influence in the cause which it so faithfully serves. Subscription price, $1 per year.

League Meet, 1889.

It is more than probable that the 1889 meet will be held at Hagerstown, Md., on July 2, 3 and 4, although the date may be changed to earlier in the year. A Baltimore cyclist, who is as well informed on current cycling news as any man in Maryland, and who is in a position to know how the cat will jump, writes us a personal letter, which we take the liberty of publishing. The letter explains why Baltimore men do not think kindly of holding the meet in their city, and why the selection of some other place would insure greater interest and success. He tells us that the Maryland Division has already forwarded an invitation to the Executive Committee, L. A. W., to hold the meet at Hagerstown, summarizes some of the advantages of this southern city and assures us that there are men of ability who will take hold and make the meet a success. The only drawback we can see is that the weather would be most uncomfortably hot at that time of the year.

"Your note received, and I reply at once. I am thoroughly satisfied that there would be no possible chance of an invitation going from Baltimore for the League meet this year, for, while it is generally conceded that it has helped the cause here, no one would be found willing to do the work again this year. Besides, it could not be made so successful as last year for various reasons. The number of visitors would be less, because few men would care to go to the same place two years in succession. When the average rider spends much money for a trip or vacation he either wants to see something new or go through some section that offers better riding than his home district. Our roads are only fair, hence Baltimore would offer neither of these attractions to those who came last year.

"Less work would also be done by our local wheelmen, because the lack of novelty of a second meet would naturally mean lack of enthusiasm. After all, it is enthusiasm, more than anything else, that induces men to go in

for a lot of hard work and worry when they have nothing to gain personally. This roughly and hastily expresses my ideas so far as Balto is concerned.

"But there has recently developed a new factor in the case which has altered everything, and the Maryland Division, L. A. W., has already forwarded an invitation to the Executive Committee of the League to hold the annual meet on July 2, 3 and 4 at Hagerstown.

"A decided change of front, you will doubtless think, but the Hagerstown Club were getting up quite an elaborate three-days' meet, and are very anxious for this Division to give them a chance at managing a League meet, so our board of officers has sent the invitation as above. There is plenty of local talent, energy and enthusiasm in Hagerstown to make a success of it if the League wants to go there, ample hotel accommodations and one of the finest riding districts in this country. Within a radius of twenty-five miles there are several hundred miles of perfect pikes over beautiful rolling country. Close by are the Potomac river, Blue Ridge mountains, several battle-fields ot the late war and many places of general interest. In fact, a meet of an entirely different character can be arranged that should please wheelmen generally.

"If the invitation is accepted the Hagerstown boys will shoulder the work at once, and at the same time receive considerable assistance and advice from those here who have had experience and who have the time to help.

"BALTIMORE, April 22."

Important to Racing Cyclists.

An important clause in the new L. A. W. Racing Rules reads as follows:

Any *cycle* club will be allowed, under the special sanction of this board, to pay the entrance fees and reasonable travelling expenses of a member whom they may desire to represent them upon the path; but without this special sanction no competitor in amateur events shall accept from his own club, or from a club promoting sports at which he competes, any payment for his expenses under penalty of suspension from the track for a time at the discretion of the board.

The old rule—the famous Rule H—prohibited payment of expenses, and the new rule, as quoted above, was substituted in a liberal spirit. The restricting clause, compelling clubs desiring to pay competing members' expenses, to apply to the board for special sanction, was introduced as a safeguard, largely to prevent manufacturers—so we are officially told—from forming clubs among their employees and maintaining representatives on the path.

The new rule is excellent, but seems to have caused some commotion among racing men whose expenses are paid by athletic clubs. Here is an example. Jones belongs to the Elizabeth Wheelmen, but is also a member of the New Jersey Athletic Club, which he represents on the race path, and which pays his entrance fees and, perhaps, his expenses. His friends claim that as the rule does not permit athletic clubs to apply for permission to pay expenses, that when he competes in a cycling event for the club, and accepts his entrance fees and travelling expenses, that he not only loses his standing, but also forfeits his membership in his bicycle club. As we understand it, such a claim is absurd. Jones represents an athletic club. According to the rules governing athletics, which are recognized by the Racing Board, Jones may compete for an athletic club and may have his expenses paid without losing his amateur status, and he must be considered

an amateur both by the athletic and cycling path legislators.

The rule should be amended as follows: "Cyclists representing athletic clubs on the path may accept such expenses as are allowed by the athletic rules without the club they represent obtaining the special sanction of the Racing Board."

A LADIES' TOUR ALONG THE HUDSON.

We have been asked time and again, "Why not boom a ladies' tour along the Hudson?" We thought the scheme a good one, and last year made some private inquiry to discover how much interest would be taken in such a tour. We have every reason to believe that such a tour, properly planned and projected, would give pleasure to a large number of cyclists. The only bad stretch of road on the route could be avoided by training from Tarrytown to Garrisons.

The New York *Press* is responsible for the following: "There are rumors of an approaching consolidation of ten of the most prominent city wheel clubs, which, if accomplished, will result in an extremely powerful wheel organization appearing in club circles."—*Bicycling World*.

We can't trace the rumors to anything very substantial. It is true that some wheelmen think that the cyclists of New York should combine forces and locate in a central and convenient part of the city a magnificently appointed club house, which should be in the wheeling world what the New York Athletic Club house is in the athletic world. The idea has been seriously considered. The Citizens have a nice house, are neither dead nor dying and just come out occasionally to show the world that they still retain their grip and have not lost the knack of giving perfect entertainments. The New Yorks have a splendid house on West End Avenue, and their revenue equals their expenditure, while their membership steadily increases. The New York Club is not dead, but very much alive, both on the road and at home. The Manhattan Club, which has grown faster than any club ever established in New York, have a fine club house, second only to the New Yorks, and are easily able to pay their way. They are very active, almost every member of the club taking a personal interest in its welfare. The Riverside Wheelmen have just rented larger quarters and seem in clover. The Harlem Wheelmen's club life is at a low ebb, but it is kept alive principally through the exertions of a few of the members. It is the only club which might consolidate with advantage to the members, but it is doubtful if they have ever seriously considered the question.

M R. E. K. AUSTIN has resigned all active work in cycling organizations. Mr. Austin has long been identified with cycling in Brooklyn. He was one of the pioneer members of the Kings County Wheelmen, and devoted his club. He was also identified with the League and the Long Island Cyclists' Union. As Secretary-Treasurer of the New York State Division he was eminently satisfactory, his office being conducted on sound business principles. Mr. Austin was capable of a deal of hard work, and this quality, combined with good reasoning power, made him a valuable committeeman. His retirement will be regretted by a large number of cyclists. But matrimony, business and the rest of it—they all get there and then good-bye cycling.

We recorded, with gusto, in last week's Wheel, the removal of the three posts which a crusty cyclophobian bad planted on the side-path of the road leading from Brooklyn to Bath and which largely interfered with the pleasure of Brooklyn wheelmen, with whom this route is a favorite. We are now pained to note that three *iron* posts have been planted on the path. The determination of this aged couple is masterful—it is Napoleonic. We say aged couple because we feel that they are a soured couple; so many people sour with age. Fate is often unkind to them and they are left old, childless and churlish. They are not to be blamed. The wheelmen should leave this old couple severely alone. The Cyclists' Union should have the authorities remove the posts and instruct the aged couple as to the right and wrong of the thing.

The Massachusetts roads improvement bill has been defeated. The State Division, led on by the invincible and eloquent "Doc" Emery, made every effort to have the bill passed. Had the bill been carefully considered its merits would have helped it through, but a strong feeling prevailed that the new street-superintendent system ought to be given at least a year's trial, which killed the bill for the present. The latter system is a great concession, however. The roads of each township are now under the care of a superintendent, which is much better than the old system of highway surveyors. Had the Highway Commissioners' bill been passed Massachusetts would have had an almost perfect system of roads. The wheelmen are still fighting for the good cause, and a new bill will be introduced next year.

The suggestion that wheelmen take part in one of the Centennial parades has not been received with much favor among New York wheelmen. To be sure, there are a few who are anxious to parade, but the large majority know that riding is impossible, and they see the absurdity of a walking delegation of wheelmen. We feel certain that no cyclist will ride in the parade, and it is very probable that none will walk.

'RAH FOR MOTT AND MARYLAND.

Editor of The Wheel:

Baltimore, Md., April 24, 1889.

Dear Sir—It was a very graceful act in President Luscomb to suggest to the Maryland Division, in connection with the question of the Annual League Meet, "that extensive and expensive entertainment be done away with." It is noticed, however, that it has furnished a text for a few writers from this division, to preach a sermon on economy, and it is feared the false impression may get abroad that the Maryland Division, while inviting the fraternity to partake of its hospitality, really has not much, if any, hospitality to offer. Economy is an excellent thing in its place, but it has no place now, nor never had, at Maryland's hospitable table. Maryland's guests never yet felt a sense of being unwelcome, or of grudging hospitality in the host, and they never will. Any wheelman who takes a seat at our board July 2, 3 and 4, will experience the good old lang syne with no modern innovations.

To the few members of the Maryland Division who are discussing in public the question of economy in Annual League Meets, and who in the main are right enough in their deductions, it is suggested that this is not the proper time, and they are urged to desist for the present for reasons that will be apparent on reflection. The State Board of Officers will see that the division finances do not suffer; there shall be no unwilling strain on the pockets of the cyclists of the division, and the personal service of any cyclist who assists in preparing to entertain our guests shall be only those who volunteer to do so, and that cheerfully. In view of all this, members are asked not to embarass the workers by putting in "cold print" personal opinions, however worthy, which have a tendency to give our guests the impression that our hospitality will not be bountiful or that it is grudgingly offered. To entertain the League is a privilege, not a task.

To the members of the L. A. W. it may be said simply, "this is the same old Maryland that had you for guests in eighty-eight," and they will know what that implies for eighty-nine.

Respectfully and truly yours,

Albert Mott,

C. C. Md. Div. L. A. W.

[This letter has the right ring. When hospitality comes in at the door, economy flies out at the window.—Ed.]

NEW YORK CLUB NOTES.

Geo. M. Nisbett, and W. E. Findley, New York Bicycle Club, will start from the Franklin House, Tarrytown, next Monday, April 28, at 2 P. M., to make a tandem bicycle record from Tarrytown to Fifty-ninth Street and Boulevard, New York; route, Kingsbridge Road. The bicycle record is 2h. 50m., held by Philip Fontaine, Citizen B. C. Messrs. Nisbett & Findley will be grateful for any assistance rendered them in the way of pace-making. They will ride a Psycho Tandem.

H. E. Cleveland, N. Y. Bi. C., is in San Francisco. A. L. Smith, N. Y. Bi. C., started for Frisco last week. Mr. C. E. Bentley and Chas. Von Dorp sailed for England last Wednesday.

The New York Club are organizing a baseball nine. B. G. Sandford (Manhattan A. C.) will probably pitch for them.

The mileage medals for 1888 will be awarded at the annual meeting, May 6, 1889.

E. J. Shriver has been appointed chairman of the Rules and Regulation Committee, L. A. W.

The President has at last purchased a new wheel—a Sparkbrook. The scorchers had better look to their laurels now.

Mrs. E. J. Shriver is a convert to the bicycle, and is practising daily.

At the monthly meeting of the club to be held on May 1 a fifty-three-inch New Mail Bicycle will be raffled for. Chances, $1.25

The club will probably enter G. M. Nisbett in the 25-mile race at Irvington on Decoration Day.

W. E. Findley has entered for the 3-mile race at Fleetwood on Saturday, 27.

W. C. Heydecker will appear on the track this season. If he rides as well as he bowls no one in New York will be able to approach him.

PHILADELPHIA.

Glorious weather! What more could a wheelman desire? Judging from the number that were met on Good Friday, Easter Sunday and Monday, the wheelmen of this vicinity could wish for nothing better. Particularly noticeable on Good Friday was the large number of ladies who were cycling. They were mounted, for the most part, on tricycles, but quite a number have already mastered the neat and trim-looking two-wheeler. It is really astonishing what a large number of Philadelphia ladies find exercise and pleasure in wheeling, yet I venture to predict that by the end of the year the number will be doubled. Those who have an idea that a lady mounted on a bicycle looks vulgar and ungraceful need only one glance to satisfy themselves that such is not the case—indeed, quite the contrary.

A petition is being extensively circulated among the wheelmen for signatures praying the Philadelphia and Reading Railroad to abolish the charge for the transportation of wheels. Of course it is impossible to tell what the outcome will be, but it seems to me that the formidable array of signatures that is being obtained should carry some weight, even with a grasping monopoly.

Another Philadelphia record taken! Not a road record nor a mileage record, not even a record for making the fastest mile, but a record for the largest number of membership propositions in one month. Thirty-two is the number. Thirty-two propositions have been received by the Century Wheelmen during April. The boom has struck them at last, and if it continues it won't be long before the roll will foot up to the much-desired 200. It seems as though its new house was a tremendous success.

A fifty-mile road race between teams made up of city clubs is on the tapis. There is some excellent road-racing material in Philadelphia, which needs only a little development, and a race of this sort is just the thing to show who are the best men.

The Century Wheelmen have followed the example of the Pennsylvanias by paying toll on the Montgomery Avenue by the year. This is an excellent arrangement, saving a great deal, financially and otherwise—otherwise in this case meaning getting off your wheel and fishing for loose change, while the scorchers whirl past shouting back that they will wait you about five miles further on, while you have the pleasure of footing the hill.

What has become of the Decoration Day scheme? Hope it has not fallen through.

The "Great New York Century Run" is receiving generous support at this end, a great many names having already been signed to the official slips and posted in the club houses.

Some fellows are wondering and guessing who "Argus" can be. Well, I may as well tell you: He is Argus.

Philadelphia, April 23.

BROOKLYN NEWS.

Easter Sunday was a most delightful day overhead, but a trifle muddy for riding. However, as Brooklyn wheelmen are noted for their indifference to the condition of the roads while there is a clear sky overhead, the most enthusiastic riders of the three clubs were out on the road and in the park, while the majority of the clubmen dressed themselves in their new spring outfits, and hied them to their respective churches. I am told that the park looked almost deserted by the wheelmen that morning, which, to say the least, was little short of a miracle for such a beautiful morning.

I spoke in last week's letter of a party of wheelmen who removed some posts which were planted on the sidepath leading to Bath. The path is now obstructed by three *iron* posts, which are anchored and almost immoveable.

The Cyclists' Union of Long Island will now take the matter in hand and ask the authorities of that township to decide the rights of the wheelmen. We all sincerely hope that the rights of the case may be proved on our side, for the double purpose of safety and comfort while riding that way, and for the satisfaction of obtaining a victory over the narrow-minded couple who live there, for of all the unpleasant and disagreeable people it has been my misfortune to meet during life these two are, without exception, the worst.

The Cyclists' Union have issued their membership tickets, which bear the *fac-simile* of the union badge. It is a design quite odd and appropriate, and although I have not seen one of the badges I should imagine they might present quite a unique appearance. The secretary published in last week's Wheel a list of forty-one new members, of which thirty-seven were from the B. B. C. What is the matter with the K. C. W. and L. I. W.?

Schoefer and Class, B. B. C., will ride in several of the events at the Harvard race meet, which is to be held at Holmes' Fields, Cambridge, on May 11. They appear to be confident of bringing to Brooklyn some of the numerous prizes offered by the managers of the meet.

In a letter from Macon, Ga., of last week I notice that the people and authorities of that part of the Sunny South are certainly up to the times on the road improvement question. The outlook as pictured by the Macon correspondent is specially fine, and we congratulate our Macon friends on their good luck.

The new road officers of the Brooklyn Bicycle Club have changed the usual mode of awarding mileage medals in that club for the coming year by offering a bronze medal for 1,000 miles and an extra bar attached for each additional 1,000 miles. They will also give a gold medal to the member making the highest mileage for the year, and a silver medal to the member holding the next highest record. They are to have a one-mile novice and a one-mile handicap (championship) race, and a five-mile handicap road race (time limit). In each race a gold medal is offered to first and a silver medal to second. Atol.

Brooklyn, April 23.

CONNECTICUTTINGS.

Stamford begins to feel the usual spring awakening in cycling lines, and some new mounts have have been bought, among them a Facile, by Mr G. W. Southwick, who will be a Leaguer and subscriber to the leading "Wheel-ing" paper as well. Let the good work go on. *Vive la yecycle!*

Nettled somewhat by the eagle's scream of late, cycler Thos. Cumming, of the prettiest Sound View Point in this section, repeatedly climbed Put's Hill, near Greenwich, and is ready for other fields to win. He rides Colonel Pope's Light Roadster Safety, and is very satisfactorily mounted.

The New Canaan *Messenger* has lately established a cycling column, as might have been expected since Editor Kirk and son both became wheel devotees. The quiet old town has about twenty cyclers now, and is pushing right along at a good pace.

The "marksman" of the *Cycler and Tourist* staff, recently shot five times at a big and ferocious dog, making a clean miss each time, owing to the small size of the pistol and to excitement. He threatens to carry a revolving shot-gun after this, for where such beasts abound human life is very insecure.

During the winter Adams' Express Co. lost a saddle from one of our wheels in transit from Newark, and have been trying for two months to avoid paying for it. That is the usual way with big concerns, who should set us lesser lights examples.

About twenty of the New Canaan cyclers ran down here last Saturday, and in their club run enthusiasm put to shame many of our Stamford clubites of years ago, and their visit was a reminder of our "palmy" days, when the tyro, on taking his frequent "drop," either landed on his head, back, or "palms"—hence "palmy days!" But the safeties have done away with all of that, and we who still ride enjoy it more than in the old times, for there are those among us who do not believe that the whole of cycling is to be up in the air and make a display.

The fair, late April days are bringing out the flowers and verdure, the birds and bees, and the roads, so long rough, are getting into fine order. Some of ours about Stamford and Sound Beach have been graveled, and we shall have delight on them this season more than ever. Tourists will find the old post road much improved in many places, and we hope road-bettering throughout the country will progress as never before.

Touring cyclers are fraternally invited to call at the *Cycler and Tourist* rooms, 175 Main Street, Stamford, where we shall be glad to assist them in any way possible. The latch string protrudes. Stamson.

Mr. W. L. Yost, late of the Springfield Bicycle Mfg. Co., and known by all who have had dealings with him as a courteous, painstaking gentleman, has returned from Los Angeles in greatly improved health. He will wind up all his Eastern business relations and make Southern California his permanent home.

JACK'S JOTTINGS.

Some occasional correspondents to this, our unique cycling press, are continually criticizing the descriptive cycling writer, preferring the "Tommy's oil-can" scribe. To some prosaic individuals, whose love of bare, statistical productions has rendered them incapable of appreciating even the efforts of a "prosaic Poet Laureate of the fools," there is no doubt that a leisurely system of handling cycling subjects must be unendurable. To the man who, old-coated, old-piped and old-slippered, sits in his easy-chair after the labors of the day, the descriptive rambler will have more attraction. There is to him more restfulness in his style of expression, fewer monotonous or wearisome passages, fewer angles and corners, fewer abrupt places. The git-there-Eli journalist (?)—this latter word is *cruelly* misapplied nowadays—has little sympathy with our susceptibilities.

In the *Morning Journal* of the 19th he begins his paragraph "Poe, Poverty and Fame," and then goes on to say that the little cottage where Edgar Allen Poe lived during the years 1846 and 1847, in Fordham, was sold to William Fearing Gill, of Madison Avenue, for a very small sum. The paragraph states that in this little frame cottage Poe wrote his "Raven," "The Bells" and others of his famous poems. The reporter then goes on to include in the paragraph the sale of other *real estate transfers* than the cottage at sums of from $1,700 to $25,000. In this little cottage it was that Poe wrote his name into everlasting fame, while he and the woman he loved were in actual necessity of their daily bread. Have we no care in life for the men whose memories we cherish so proudly after death? Must we insult them after death (though denying them the cup of cold water and the crust while they are among us) by erecting expensive though perhaps vulgar stone and bronze monuments to their "memory" on our thoroughfares, in our parks or in the sanctities of Westminster? There is something to me very pathetic about this. Poe, Poverty and Fame! Bah! even the prosaic real estate reporter was aware of the injustice and *neglect* from which poor, sad, delirious Poe suffered. Only a madman could have written "The Raven." During his life-time, when his fond wife and golden haired little ones were clinging to their father through all the vicissitudes of misfortune, inappreciation or actual poverty, where was the Saurwein or the O'Shaunessy who would give half that amount to save that deserving, gentle family from actual starvation? None; there might have been no printed notice of the act of charity and no personal good accrue from it, and some slight pecuniary loss would be sustained by our monument subscribing parvenus, our Saurwein-O'Shaunessy. Yes. Poe, poverty and fame Fame, but at such a terrible cost! A loving wife being denied the food which the world *owed* her husband. Bah, you sicken me!

And now, to keep you in mind that this is from the pen of a *cycling scribe*, I must tell you that Tommy has got *another* new oil-can and Jimmy is going to get one just like Tommy's first one. I shall keep my ears wide open for any rumor (true or otherwise) about the introduction of any newly-arrived oil-cans into our community at Bumbletown.

Well, to-day I had the pleasure of meeting the "Coaster" of Jersey City, and had quite a chat with him and "Harry" Strugnell, in the office of The Wheel. The talk here is of the 25-mile Milburn-Irvington race, which is going to be a good one, and which I would not miss seeing for a good deal. Barkman reports a great many entries, though half the number of 100 entries have not yet been received. But if you are going to enter do so at once. Above all things send in accurate times made in races or speed trials during the past year, that you may win (or take a place in) the race upon merits alone. One race honestly won is worth more in the eyes of a gentleman sportsman than any number of *crooked* winnings. And the public find these things out "in the long run," and then! On this Milburn-Irvington course (which I have not seen) the twenty-five miles have been made in something like 1:32, so the road must be a good one. It is a macadam surface without loose stones, but has two "clipping" hills of the gradual type. Ordinaries and safeties should have about equal show on this course, if all I hear is correct.

The safety rider, like the poet, abusive critic and book-agent, *nascitur, non fit*, is born, not made. So is the rider of the ordinary.

As a rule a long, slim, clean-cut man will ride an ordinary with better satisfaction than a safety. To ride a safety well you want to be of the Whittaker build—thick of chest, strong of hip and thigh and pony-made or short-jointed. Old tricyclists, of course, make grand safety riders, as the hard training on some of the obsolete hook-and-ladder affairs has put a muscle into these men which nothing but toil can give, and which "counts" when applied to the light-running safety. W. A. Rhodes would make a regular monkey of himself on a safety, as all his fine, long leverage of limb would be thrown away. Thomas Stevens would make a grand safety rider, and could ride with a gear sufficiently high to make up for fast pedalling on account of his muscular power, but the average rider, who rides once a week, wants a gear not more than an inch or two inches higher than the diameter of the ordinary and he can ride comfortably.

The safety will suit a class of men whom the ordinary never would have tempted, and *vice versa*. They are both good. Choose the one you like, and which suits you best.

Diogenes, when he emerged nightly from his tub-dwelling, turned the searching rays of his Lucas' bullseye into all the likely places where he expected to find honest men—the Treasury Department, Tammany Hall, the Board of Aldermen, the excise and customs departments, etc.—and, finding nothing approaching that which he sought, he swapped his lamp for a bottle of Scotch whiskey, some loaf-sugar and a kettle full of boiling water, and sat down in his tub with his bare feet dangling over the sides, and drowned his sorrow in the flowing bowl. We are told there were no flies on the exterior of Diogenes. Have we not the text in French?—*Il n' y a pas desmouches sur Diogenes* (There are *no* flies on Diogenes). But history hath not in its wondrous store evidence which proved that the old methodical madman had not them about him. And now our latter-day hunter after the good and pure and beautiful, our "Coaster," has discovered that man is not to be purified by word of mouth or word of pen, that advertisements sufficiently plain on account of their nature to call immediate attention to them are not thought by the advertisers to be sufficiently plainly delineated to rivet the eye of the casual or innocent reader, and so they have caused their merchandise to be *labeled* so that the reader, whether of the Adam or Eve type of humanity, may make no possible mistakes, and can have accurate knowledge of the appearance of these wondrous structures from every vantage point except a side "view," and, perhaps, that is at this moment in the hands of the engravers. Let us have this last by all means. Shades of Comstock! but, egad, we can dispense with such "higher education." "Coaster," when I saw him yesterday, was in tears and broken in spirit. His body was bent with grief, his collar was unbuttoned and his neckwear was awry. "Be not so moved, friend Coaster," said I, as, taking advantage of the momentary burst of grief, I removed from his vest pocket a twenty-five-cent cigar, which seemed to take the gilt-edge off a purity hunter, and calmly bit the end off. "Be not so moved; the time will come when even the sombre pantaloon will encase each leg of the pirouetting compass, when even our friends of the ballet will wear Glen Urquhart check trousers with side pocket, and so drive away the bald-headed contingent from the orchestra stalls." At the words "our friends of the ballet" "Coaster" dried his tears, and smiled as he went out of the room with his hat on the back of his head, his thumbs in the arm-holes in his vest, and crooning softly, "O, we've all been there before, many a time, many a time." That is the last I saw of him, but I heard he had gone down to see the newspapers to persuade them to put the "*births*" and "hotel *arrivals*" in separate columns.

Apropos of your editorials on prison labor, and John G. Whittier's letter, which says "idleness in (and out) of prison is perilous alike to mind and body," I suggest that a committee be appointed to round up all the defunct Coventry rotaries and other obsolete cycles, and to present them to the prison authorities. There are also latter-day bicycles which, on account of their impracticability, hideousness and worthlessness, might be removed from the world of public cycling to the seclusion of prison life with appreciable benefit to "us boys."

There need be no lack of idleness, and it is certain that the men would sleep soundly at night, and records might be broken (backs and hearts also). It would be a case of the survival of the fittest. But speaking seriously, something should be done for these poor fellows, *some* of whom are, no doubt, suffering unjust sentences—sentences where circumstantial evidence has been pitted against their liberty, and where c. e. won. O, for a day when convicts can be "transported," as in the good old days of "Botany Bay," to some out-of-the-way region to form a colony by themselves, and have at least the freedom of sea and sky, of earth, and the green field and tree. These latter *will* influence a man for good—the Chubb or Yale lock, the fetter and prison fare and confinement between walls of plaster and stone and iron—never.

Siberia, with its wilderness, is preferable to such a life, hermetically sealed (in some instances) from the world, which has forgotten their existence.

L. A. Clarke calls the attention of the public to the fact that a correspondent from Eureka, Cal., "*scorched those 10 miles in 55 minutes.*" Eureka! what would he have the Californian do—ride faster? Ten miles in 55 minutes from a truthful man is better than 35 (on paper) any way, and faster than the *doings* of the paper-flyer, too. I think that 10 miles in 55 minutes is p. d. quick. But wait till the Officially-Handicapped Scratch Liar, L. A. W., gets a chance at those 10 miles against time (and reason), and poor Eureka's record will go the way of all honest records when the fully-evolved liar gets his work in. Jack.

BUFFALO.

Gray, black or brown, for a uniform is the question which is still bothering the Ramblers. At the next meeting the matter will come to a focus, and black will probably be selected. It took the Buffalos just one year to decide upon their present uniform, and now a movement for another change has made its appearance. But the women's wheel club, composed of twenty-two members, is having the most interesting discussion on this momentous question. There are just twenty-two preferences, and the outlook for a choice is too far distant to be thought of. There appears to be a majority in favor of dark green as second choice, but each one still holds to her first preference.

One dealer reports having sold fifty-four safeties to five ordinaries. The dwarfs are selling with a rapidity that is surprising. While I was in a down town store the other day the agent sold three safeties to middle aged men in less than fifteen minutes. This will show how active the trade is, and especially illustrates how the bicycling ranks are being increased by the addition of men well along in life.

Buffalo can boast of at least twelve lady bicycle riders, and six of them own wheels of their own. Miss Mabel, daughter of Henry E. Ducker, was the first Buffalo girl to mount a safety, though she has been a tricycle rider for five years. Last September she commenced riding the dwarf. Her sister, Miss Eva L. Ducker, is also an expert on the two wheeler. Mrs. A. H. Stevenson, of Linwood Avenue, can well lay claim to being the best long distance lady tricycle rider in the city, as she has accomplished 100 miles in one day.

The Zig-Zags are doing some great hustling this season. The club has had three out of town runs thus far this season, while the other clubs have not ventured out of the city limits.

Many wheelmen are anxiously waiting for the Warwick to make its appearance. Many orders have been given, but no wheels have arrived. Unless the Warwick company fills the orders within a few days, many of them will be countermanded.

The Ramblers are considering the advisability of holding an annual tournament, commencing with this year. The matter is being actively agitated, and the indications are that commencing with the one proposed to be held this fall, the Ramblers will yearly give a race meet that will equal those of Springfield and Lynn in their palmiest days. The membership of the club is now 107, and the end of the year will see at least 150. The Ramblers have shown a progressive and active spirit which will ere long, unless the other wheel organizations bestir themselves, make the club the foremost one of the city.

The *Whip*, the new athletic paper, has made its appearance, and for a first number makes a very creditable showing. It is ably edited by "Pendragon," and the bicycle department is newsy and interesting.

Where, oh where, will the L. A. W. meet for 1889 be held? It has been suggested by local men that the Ramblers entertain the League this year, but nothing has been definitely decided upon by the club in regard to the invitation.

Zo.

ST. LOUIS.

A meeting in the interest of the new track association was held at the Missouri club house last Monday night. Both clubs were well represented and there was no lack of enthusiasm, although a disposition to carefully weigh both sides of the question was manifested early in the proceedings. The temporary organization was effected by the selection of President Lucas of the cycle club as chairman, and Mr. Brewster as secretary. Mr. Andrews gave a resume of the negotiations up to the time of the meeting, and after the scheme had been thoroughly discussed in all its bearings, the conclusion was reached that the number of subscriptions already pledged rendered the project a feasible one, and the permanent organization was then proceeded with. It is to be called the St. Louis Bicycle Track Association, and will have a capital stock of $2,000, divided into 200 shares of $10 each, half paid up. The following named officers were chosen: President, Geo. K. Andrews; Vice-President, B. N. Sanders; Secretary-Treasurer, W. M. Brewster; Board of Directors, E. A. Smith, Will. Brown, B. L. Mockler, W. A. Todd and the President, *ex-officio*. The hardest kind of an effort is going to be made to get the track built in time for the Stone-Lumsden race. To persons familiar with the building and management of bicycle tracks, the amount of money which this association has seems ridiculously small, and it *would* be if the intention was to build a permanent track and equip grounds, but these grounds are already equipped with everything excepting the track, and owing to the uncertain tenure of our lease it would be folly to spend any great amount of money in building a track which we may not be able to use longer than this summer.

Concerning the parade of the 30th inst., the committee has decided that the bicycles would be out of place in the day procession with the pedestrians, and have made overtures to the wheelmen for an illuminated parade at night. They propose to contribute $400 towards paying the necessary expenses, provided a sufficiently large turn out is guaranteed. It is doubtful, however, if the matter can be arranged at this late date, especially as we have no workers to take the places of the indefatigable Stettinius and the mercurial Hicks. The latter is abroad, or was when last heard from, and the former has other matters, more important than illuminated parades to engage his attention. The bulk of the work would necessarily fall on Presidents Andrews and Lucas, and while both of them are qualified in every way to carry the scheme through, it is doubtful if either of them could devote the time required without detriment to his business affairs. It is a pity that the matter was not brought up sooner, for a parade such as was given three years ago would help our cause with the business community immensely.

Captain Lewis had thirteen men out for his moonlight run last Saturday, and eight of them went through to the county line the next day. The cycle club went to Belleville and report the roads bad.

The *Spectator* announces that Sam Miles, manager of the Chicago Cycling Exhibit and Tournament, will be here next Sunday and Monday in the interest of that enterprise. He is to meet the racing men at the Missouri's club house Sunday afternoon. Hodgen, Stone and perhaps two or three others will enter. Lewis, Smith and Barnard will be in Garden's Pullman road race.

The two clubs have organized base ball nines, and the first contest will take place next Sunday morning. The Cycle boys got the better of the Missouris in the foot ball games last winter, and the latter now propose to get even.

Ithuriel.

FENTON'S FANCIES.

The axe has fallen after a delay of weeks, and Jack the executioner is proudly standing with the gory weapon in his hand, upon the body of his latest victim. But the vital spark still feebly scintillates and the trembling hand can still move the pen. When I ventured to criticize Jack, I wrote in good faith and without the slightest intention of personal rudeness. But our friend is by no means so kind to me. Being super-sensitive to criticism, as he has often proved himself to be in the past, he makes a very weak attempt to explain the use of some words to which I took exception, and then takes up invective as a sure means of demolishing me.

According to Jack it is a crime to be young. So be it. But for that reason, should I refrain from writing a criticism of what I don't like, because the author happens to be my senior in point of age? Hardly! He, in a very gentlemanly way calls me a "mannikin." The conclusion which must be drawn is that in the literary "dime-museum" Jack would pose among the freaks as the "*babonic* giant," while I would appear as the "Fentonian mannikin." There is no danger of his assuming the latter role, for he is too well qualified for the former position. Jack evidently would make a fine Falstaff, for some of the lines allotted to that character are eminently fitting for his utterance as the aged and sapient cycling writer. Changing the names of the characters let us take the following from King Henry IV.

Jack.—I am old, I am old.

The Reading Public.—I love thee better than I love e'er a scurvy young boy of them all.

I see the Sheehan boys flying round the park on a tandem safety every now and then, and their mileage should be piling up in proportion. But take it all in all the tandem safety seems to be but little ridden in this city. I have had but one ride on this type of machine and found the swinging motion which it possesses somewhat trying. Perhaps a second trial may induce me to change my opinion, but for the present I am rather sceptical in regard to its success.

The new uniform of the Manhattans is a great success. It is neat and handsome and the color, though a trifle sombre, is well fitted for the purpose. At the last meeting of the New Yorks, an endeavor was made to make a slight change in the bill of dress, but was voted down by a large majority.

An informal association of members of the New Yorks meet at the club-house on Sunday evenings. They bear the striking title of "The Brannigan Club," and have a very select attendance at their gatherings at the round table. Captain McFadden is senior warden and chaplain of the organization, and among the members are Messrs. Cambreleng, Reese, Shultas, Blake, Pitman and de Goicouria. Mr. J. N. Glass and Mr. C. H. Nicholls have recently become members.

Fenton.

CYCLING AS A THERAPEUTIC AGENT.

There can be little doubt that the ingenious Frenchman who first popularised the use of the bicycle in this country conferred a great benefit upon the men of moderate means. Not that the invention of the modern "cycle" can be attributed to the genius of one man alone; the "Draisienne" in France, and the hobby-horse and velocipede in England, date back fully a century, and the use of wheeled vehicles propelled by the passenger had never fallen altogether out of use. Twenty years ago, however, the velocipede of the day, now irreverently dubbed a "bone-shaker," was a cumbrous toy, from which schoolboys and a few enthusiasts could alone extract any pleasure or amusement. The new era is not more than ten, or, at most, fifteen, years old, but within that period the bicycle and the tricycle have been brought to a state of perfection which almost appears to approach finality. The manufacture of these machines has grown to be an industry of vast proportion, employing thousands of skilled hands, and involving a large amount of capital. There is not a town, hardly a village, throughout the length and breadth of Great Britain which does not contain at least a few inhabitants who possess a "cycle." It carries the mechanic to his work, the tourist through his summer holiday, and the doctor on his daily round; tradesmen use it for delivering their goods, and newspaper proprietors for the distribution of their wares.

It is above all as a recreation that cycling has become known, but the influence which this form of exercise has upon health has not escaped the attention of medical writers. Of these the most recent is Dr. Oscar Jennings, of Paris, who, in a brightly-written pamphlet, has brought together from the writings of other medical authors, and from the pages of the newspapers and magazines devoted to cycling topics, a considerable mass of evidence. Dr. Jennings is an enthusiast, and claims not only that cycling is free from objection, but that it is curative, and in itself a perfect form of exercise. The truth probably is that as an exercise it is inferior to rowing and riding on horseback, but superior to most others. The lucky man who—to parody Swift's picture of happiness—has a river at his garden end, an extra horse to mount a friend, need not trouble himself about cycles; but to that large class who are less fortunately placed they are a great boon.

It is perhaps inevitable that persons who have no personal experience should accuse the exercise, on theoretical grounds, of producing various evils; in this way it has been said to cause varicose veins, hernia, hæmorrhoids, urethral stricture and various forms of cardiac and nervous disease. No definite evidence, however, has ever been advanced to prove those theoretical assertions. As to varicose veins, it seems to be clearly established that in those cases in which this condition is due to chronic local causes, to constipation and a sedentary life, actual benefit is derived from cycling, and that even in those cases which are due to organic visceral disease no harm is done. Dr. Jennings can find no evidence that hernia, hæmorrhoids or urethral stricture have ever been produced or aggravated. As to cardiac and nervous disease, the case is different. Race meetings and the silly craze to "break the record"—to cover a mile, or twenty miles, or the whole distance from Land's End to John o'Groats in so many seconds or minutes or hours less than the last "record-breaker"—have much to answer for. It is not difficult to understand how such exercises may cause permanent injury to the heart, neurasthenia or even organic nervous disease. No rule can be laid down, for each man's possibilities vary, and the symptoms which over-exertion will produce vary also. The commonest, probably, are some disturbance of cardiac rhythm (usually intermittence), insomnia and loss of appetite. If the cyclist persists in performing journeys which produce such symptoms he must expect to suffer, and cannot fairly blame the form of exercise because he has chosen to indulge in it.

Cycling as a therapeutic agent has a considerable future; it ought not to be taken up at too early an age; the so-called "bicycle back"—round, stooping shoulders—is particularly liable to be produced in a growing lad who uses the bicycle too much; a convenient rule is to avoid recommending it till a lad has passed the age when the chief growth in height takes place. Dr. Jennings' book confirms the impression formed from observation and perusal of scattered notices in fugitive literature, that cycling is a form of exercise specially useful to men who are growing to be a little more than middle-aged. A man who has followed a sedentary occupation begins to experience increasing disinclination to exertion, chronic constipation, with some stiffness, and it may be flying pains in the joints; for such a man a tricycle is capable of accomplishing a great deal; exercise ceases to be a trouble, the bowels become more regular, and the joint troubles which may be at first a little aggravated, disappear. Dr. Jennings believes that chronic gout and rheumatic gout may thus be cured, or at least kept at bay, even when the patient has been seriously crippled by several attacks; he also speaks very confidently as to the cure of obesity, if the patient will refrain from gratifying the thirst, which is at first very trying; he even finds some reason to believe that his favorite exercise may be a useful adjuvant in the treatment of early phthisis.

There are certain warnings which ought to be given when recommending cycling. In the first place, the cyclist ought to be suitably dressed in all-wool clothing, from head to foot, special directions being given to the tailor to make no use of cotton linings, stiffening, or padding; secondly, his motto should be *festina lente*, he should not attempt long journeys or fast journeys, until he has thoroughly gauged his own strength; thirdly, he should not force himself to ride up long hills; fourthly, he must as far as possible abstain from alcoholic beverages while on a journey.

With regard to the choice of a machine, the first question is whether a bicycle or tricycle is preferable. The man who intends to use his machine for exercise alone will choose the former, selecting a "safety;" this new pattern presents many advantages, it is easy to mount, carries the rider nearer the ground than the old pattern, and is cheaper than a tricycle; a good deal of patience and practice, however, are required in order to become proficient in its use. The tricycle is more comfortable, carries a change of clothes more conveniently, is more easily learnt and managed, requires less constant attention while riding, and is on the whole safer. In either case it is wise to purchase of one of the best makers; a good modern tricycle or bicycle is a marvellous combination of ingenuity and first-rate workmanship, and cannot be had at a cheap price.—*British Medical Journal.*

To the members of the New York State Division:

It is the sad duty of the Chief Consul to announce to the Division the death of H. C. Spaulding, Jr., of Elmira, who died in that city April 12.

Mr. Spaulding was a member of the Division Board of officers and also of the Nominating Committee.

He always gave the Division his best work and most judicious advice, and brought with these an enthusiasm which helped to brighten and lighten the duties of his confreres.

He was soon to depart for Europe, to do the old world on his wheel, proving that he was a practical wheelman, who believed in the use as well as the pleasure of cycling.

The Division will mourn his loss as that of one it could ill spare.

Yours fraternally,
W. S. BULL,
Chief Consul.

PENNSYLVANIA'S LIBERTY BILL PASSED.

The following bill has been passed by the Senate. If signed by the Governor it will become a law.

AN ACT

Defining the rights and regulating the use of bicycles and tricycles.

SECTION 1. *Be it enacted by the Senate and House of Representatives of the Commonwealth of Pennsylvania in General Assembly met, and it is hereby enacted by the authority of the same.* That bicycles, tricycles and all vehicles propelled by hand or foot, and all persons by whom bicycles, tricycles and such other vehicles are used, ridden or propelled upon the public highways of this state, shall be entitled to the same rights and subject to the same restrictions in the use thereof as are prescribed by law in the cases of persons using carriages drawn by horses.

TACOMA, WASHINGTON TERRITORY.

The long-looked for Sunday run to Puyallup (for April 14) had to be postponed until next Sunday in consequence of a heavy shower of rain Saturday evening. However, Captain Wells and McCoy took a ten or twelve mile run in the forenoon and reported side paths in excellent condition. The other boys could not be found at the time appointed for the rendezvous but appeared in the afternoon.

Prince Wells reports a good trade in wheeling during the past ten days, and if cycling keeps on booming as it has for the past month Tacoma will soon be fully able to uphold her own as a cycling town. Those who never mounted a wheel before late last fall or early this year are making rapid strides toward attaining sufficient proficient speed to enable them to go out with the "old hands."

As proof of the above statement, I might mention the fact that on Tuesday afternoon two of the "beginners," the Thompson brothers, went out to the Insane Asylum (merely for a ride, you know) accompanied by Halsted and McCoy. To the surprise of the latter twain the kids did 'em in great style, and 'twas pitiful to observe the puzzled expression on Halsted's face. It betokened a wonder-when-they-are-going-to-slow-up expression; but it appears that the Tacoma wheelman makes it a practice to "do up" any novices or new acquisitions the first few runs they take with the crowd. While Halsted is by no means a novice, as some of our Eastern brothers can probably testify, still he came under the head of "new acquisitions" and the boys lost no time in getting under way, and, if ever they succeded in making a stranger tired, success surely crowned their efforts on this occasion. Later in the evening, after their return, Halsted was seen at the *lunch counter* standing up like a little man. His regular waiter told some of the boys that Hal. tried to sit down but he claimed the seat of the chair felt red hot and he thought he would try standing. Strange! It was his first road ride since last fall, which may explain.

But "he laughs best who laughs last." The afternoon of Wednesday McCoy, Thompson brothers, Hayes, Manning and Halsted took a ride over to "Old Town" and afterward rode to the western limits of the city. A game of "follow the leader" was suggested and agreed upon and the "man from New York" commenced to think the others were trying to kill him outright. But here is is where the "last laugh" comes in. After several of the leaders bit the dust in trying to do some outlandish "stunts" Halsted finally got up to the head of the line and then the circus commenced. He went up and down gutters (of hard turf and dirt), rode over heavy pieces of lumber and seemed to thoroughly enjoy hearing the wheels tumble in a heap as the followers struck the obstructions. Then, to the surprise of all, the leader jumped his bike off the sidewalk and started off on one of the footpaths for the ungraded streets, jumping roots, riding between huge rocks and otherwise tempting Providence. Headers were numerous, although no serious hurts or strains were recorded. The boys now want to know if all Eastern roads are full of roots and boulders, for Hal. seemed to be more at home on the "corduroy" roads than on the boulevards.

Since vacating the hall formerly occupied by the now defunct Tacoma Bicycle Club the committee have been looking around for convenient headquarters, and report a successful find. In future the Tacoma Wheelmen will boast of commodious rooms on St. Helen's Avenue. This location could not be improved upon, for it is central, and members can mount at the door and ride without dismounting to any part of the city. We congratulate the committee.

Several new members will be added to the charter list, and by May 1 the club will surely boast of thirty members, and *all riders*. Pretty good showing for a town that never saw a bicycle before last year.

The safety craze has finally struck Tacoma, and half a dozen "Goats" were telegraphed for by Prince Wells early this week. Ed. Barlow will be seen on a safety, although he will do much of his mileage on his trusty little 50-inch. Mr. Thompson, father to the Thompson Bros., has not only fully succeeded in gaining mastery over his safety, but also three-quarters persuaded Dr. McCoy to join the ranks. We trust Ed. McCoy will be able to attend to the other quarter, and that the doctor will soon be the possessor of a wheel. What a sight his six feet two inches would make on an ordinary!

The course of the twenty-mile road race has not finally been decided upon, but I have it from good authority that Wells, Halstead and Brackett (the Racing Com.) have decided to have the race on a five-mile stretch, so that the spectators can see how the contestants are riding at the half-way post. This is an excellent plan, and, it is hoped, will not be changed. Carl Thompson is practising assidiously for this event, and deserves a front place at the finish. There will be seven or eight prizes, and all of the competitors who work for a place are sure of a trophy.

The boys are all very much pleased with THE WHEEL, and are glad to see that you spare a little space for items from "The City of Destiny," in order that the Eastern and Southern riders may see that the vast North-Western point of the United States is not dead.

SNOHOMISH.

Tea-drinking is, in the last number of *Bicycling News*, again favorably commented upon as good for cyclists. "White Rose" (who with "any other name would" write with as much authority) says that the deleterious effects of excessive tea-drinking may be easily counteracted by the use of some acid to counteract the effects of the alkaloids contained in tea, and recommends "a slice or two of lemon in place of milk being put in the tea-cup." This is good advice, and, as he says, counteracts the effects of cake, preserves and other trash which cyclists often consume in quantities at the tea-table. Still, I never liked the name of tea, though I liked the taste of it. My mind always wanders back to the saying, "beer and baccy; tea and tracts." There's fun in the one and innocence in the other—if *both* are *taken* in *moderation*.

NEW SAFETY BICYCLE.

PATENTED BY HERBERT S. OWEN, WASHINGTON, D. C.

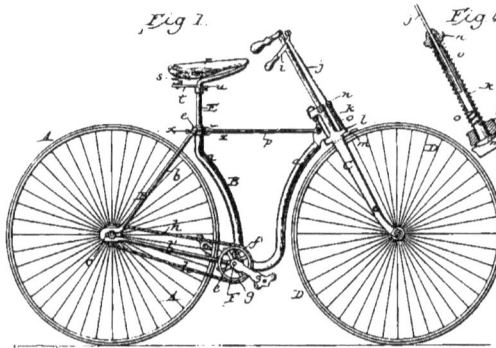

To all whom it may concern:

This invention relates particularly to the construction of the frame-work, having in view the adaptation of the bicycle for the use of ladies and children and a reduction in the cost of its manufacture. In the accompanying drawings, Figure 1 is a side elevation of the complete machine. Fig. 2 is a side elevation of the main frame. Fig. 4 is a vertical central section through the brake mechanism. Fig. 5 is a longitudinal vertical section through the lower part of the frame.

Referring to the drawings, A represents the rear wheel; B, the frame or reach, divided at the lower end to receive said wheel; C, the front steering-fork provided with a steering-bar, and swiveled, as usual, to the front end of the frame that it may turn horizontally, and D the front steering-wheel. The frame consists, essentially, of a tubular bar, *a*, provided at its forward end with steering-centers, as usual, and curved thence downward between the two wheels to or about the level of the pedal-shaft and carried thence upward in front of the rear wheel, its rear end terminating in a vertical position, so that it is adapted to receive and support the seat-standard, E.

The rear wheel is carried on each side by two arms, *b b'*, one connected to the lower and the other to the upper portion of the rear part of the reach. These arms, which are preferably formed in one piece, meet at the centre of the wheel, being bent, as shown particularly in Fig. 2, in such manner as to leave between them a horizontal slot, *c*, for the reception of the axle. The arms are preferably formed of drawn or rolled steel rods or tubes, and are attached at their ends to the frame or reach B by brazing or welding them thereto, or, through the means of suitable clips, *e*, welded or otherwise fastened to the reach.

F represents a shaft provided with the usual crank and pedals and lying transversely beneath the frame in front of the rear wheel, being supported by a suitable bearing plate or plates, *f*, brazed or otherwise secured to the reach. The lower arms, *b'*, may be connected to the same plate, as shown in Fig. 2. The shaft is provided with a sprocket-pulley, *g*, connected in the usual manner by a sprocket-chain, *h*, with a pulley on the driving-wheel.

The brake-lever, *i*, is pivoted to the steering handle or bar, as usual, and jointed to the upper end of a rod, *j*. At its lower extremity this rod enters the upper split end of a tube, *k*, passing through a suitable guide, *l*, on the front of the steering-fork, attached at its lower extremity to the brake-shoe, *m*. The tube *k* is tapered externally at the upper end and threaded to receive a nut, *n*, by which it may be contracted firmly upon the rod *j*. This nut also serves as a collar or bearing for the upper end of a spiral spring, *o*, which encircles the tube and bears upon the guide *l*, as shown in Fig. 4, for the purpose of holding the brake normally out of action.

Owing to the downward curvature of the frame between the wheels, the machine may be used by ladies without interference with their skirts and without the necessity of sitting astride of the frame, as in other machines.

In order to strengthen the frame for the use of heavy persons, a detachable brace, *p*, may be applied between the two extremities of the reach, as shown in the drawings. This brace *p* is not claimed as part of the present invention.

The saddle is preferably constructed, as shown, by carrying the upper end of the standard E forward to support the front extremity of the flexible seat, *r*, which is sustained at its rear end by springs, *s*, attached to a plate thereon and supported in their turn by a vertically-adjustable arm, *t*, encircling the standard E and confined by a set-screw, *u*.

If necessary, the main frame may be stiffened by the insertion of a filling before it is bent, as shown in Fig. 5.

The claims made are:

In a bicycle-frame, and in combination with the U-shaped bar, *a*, the two carrying-arms for the rear wheel, each arm consisting of a continuous rod bent to an angular form, its two extremities rigidly attached to the bar *a* and its central or angular portion adapted to receive the axle of the wheel.

In a bicycle-frame, the wheel-carrying arms *b b'*, formed in a single piece and bent to form the axle-receiving slot *c*.

In combination with the brake-shoe, its tubular standard, the operating rod *j* and nut *n*.

In a brake for bicycles and the like, the brake-shoe having the tubular standard, in combination with the operating-rod adjustably secured thereto.

In a bicycle or tricycle, the seat consisting of the standard E, bent laterally at its upper end, the arm *t*, springs *s*, and flexible seat *r*.

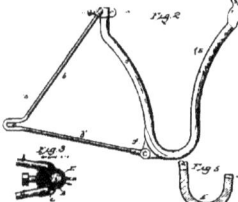

CURIOUS FACTS AS TO WHEELS.

The product of the cycle manufacturers for 1889 exhibits little departure in types of bicycles, tricycles and safeties, but a number of quite noticeable improvements in details in the direction of strength and lightness, simplicity and ease of use. As usual, the old New England makers have the lead in the finer machines.

The cycling industry is still comparatively young on both sides of the metropolis. It began at Hartford about eleven years ago and took root in other places two or three years later. From the first the New England bicycles were built for men's use, first-class mechanically and first-class in price.

Whether it is impossible or inconsistent to make both high and low grades of bicycles in the same factory, or whether there is some other local or trade reason for it, the fact is the costlier and finer grades never appear from the same factory with the cheaper and inferior grades.

It may be worth observing, in connection with the fact that the high grade bicycles continue to be made by the two or three leading makers of the East, that there is a difference in the average grades of workmen, often quite apparent. Talent and skill are not only cumulative in the same factory by years of practice, but also go somewhat from generation to generation. Skill, ingenuity and steady industry, which contribute so much to the productive power represented on any pay-roll, are found at a higher average in our older manufacturing centres. Articles and machinery of accuracy or delicacy, or complexity or difficulty of construction, like bicycles, guns and watches, require in their production just this sort of superior skilled labor and steadiness of force, especially in the finer grades. Manufacturers of experience take this into account in locating.

The difference in grade and construction of machines made has no necessary relation to the character of the machines that are used in the different sections; the sale of fine grades in all sections is very large and increasing. While the East may not lose its excellence or prestige in cycle making, it is quite likely that the West will gain until its marks may be as good as a Boston, Hartford, or Chicopee Falls mark. It took Birmingham some time to equal Sheffield, and then some time longer to overcome the "Brummagem" reputation; but it got there, and, as every one knows, is now a center for really fine manufactures.

Of course, not all that is made in the East in this line is best, since wherever a successful business is founded imitators spring up; but generally speaking, in design of machines, in material used, in workmanship and finish, in substantial improvements over last year's productions, in all that goes to make up the best bicycle, tricycle, or safety, the old New England makers still hold the lead.—*Scientific American.*

Dan Canary arrived in New York on Thursday morning, bringing with him his wife and two children. Canary, who has been very successful abroad, will sail May 11 to fill an engagement at Southampton, England, commencing May 20. Canary has been away almost four years.

Mr. W. L. Ross, manager of the Singer Cycle Co.'s American business was in New York on Thursday, leaving for Boston Thursday night.

The Æolus Cycling Club have removed to their new club house. The building is a handsome one and is beautifully situated. The grounds are inclosed by large trees and dotted here and there with beautiful flowers. First Lieutenant Bray, who last season carried away several trophies of the race track, has just recovered from a severe cold and states that he will not race in the Chicago tournament; in fact, he will do no more racing this season, as his physician forbids it. Kohler will race in the Chicago tournament.

The safety lever is speading like a prairie fire. The Capitol Cycle Co. has begun to clear out stock by disposing of fifteen uprights at fifty per cent. discount.

The demand for Psychos is so great that the weekly shipments by the Capital Cycle Co. is barely adequate to the demand.

M. G. Peoli, New York Club, is with George R. Bidwell.

J. B. Roy, Treasurer of the New York Club, was married Tuesday evening at the Church of the Heavenly Rest. A number of the boys went down to the church to see the wedding.

G. A. Litchholt, has rented a large store at 351 Lenox Avenue, near 128th st. He will handle new and second-hand bicycles, rent, repair, store, etc.

TWENTY-FIVE MILE HANDICAP ROAD RACE.

Letters have been sent out to all the local clubs and it is expected that a representative gathering of cycling men will be at the Knickerbocker Cottage—Jacquin's—Twenty-eighth Street and Sixth Avenue, New York City, Thursday evening, April 25, at 8:30.

The trade has responded liberally, and a complete list of prizes will be published in next week's WHEEL. There will be several hundred dollars' worth of prizes, including high-grade bicycles, gold stop-watch, gold medal, cyclometer and a handsome gilt and ivory handled revolver.

A number of entries have already been received. No entries will be received after May 15.

TO A. B. BARKMAN,
241 Broadway, New York City.

Dear Sir—I herewith inclose $1.00 as entrance fee for the Twenty-five Mile Handicap Road Race to be held May 30, 1889; and I hereby certify that I have never been a professional or a promateur, and that my best time in any open event or private trial of speed is as follows, viz.:

5 miles.......................... Date........................ Place.......................
10 " .... " .... " ....
15 " .... " .... " ....
20 " .... " .... " ....
25 " .... " .... " ....
Name.................................... Club....................................
Address..

We hereby certify that the above statement is correct:
Name.................................... Address....................................
Name.................................... Address....................................
Dated...1889.
....

The right to reject any entry is reserved.

HARVARD-TECH. ROAD RACE.

In spite of the rain of last Saturday, Harvard and Tech. held their semi-annual road race. The course, which was gone over twice, began at the new Beacon Street extension, to Englewood Avenue, round both Chestnut Hill reservoirs and back to the starting point. Shortly before the start it began to rain, and the men were sent off in the midst of a hard shower, which made the roads very heavy and greasy. This, together with the twenty hills in the course, made the time—57 min 31 3-5 sec.—for fifteen miles, very fast.

Greenleaf, Bailey and Brown, all of Harvard, went to the front, and soon had a lead of several hundred feet. "We've left them already," said Bailey. A few minutes later Norton, of Tech., passed the Harvard men like a steam engine, and for the remainder of the way set a pace that strongly discouraged further conversation.

When turning into Englewood Avenue Bailey's wheel slipped, and he fell almost in front of Brown. It is noteworthy that the only two men who were thrown through inequalities in the road, rode safeties: Roots, who fell while coming down Englewood Avenue, caused Barron to fall over him.

Kirk Corey had started out with the riders, and when Bailey fell Corey gave him his machine. At the end of the first lap Bailey changed to Davis' wheel. At this time the points stood 28 to 27 in favor of Tech., and her men entertained great hopes of winning. Norton, at various times during the race, made desperate efforts to shake off the Harvard men, sometimes gaining several hundred feet, but they always caught him again on the hills.

A mile from the finish Bailey, coached by his brother on a tandem, spurted ahead, followed closely by Norton, Greenleaf and Brown fell behind, but the former caught them again half a mile from home, and despite the great exertions of the other two, won by a yard, amidst the cheers of a large body of wheelmen. Norton was close to Greenleaf, and Bailey, who was considerably handicapped by his fall and two changes of wheels, a second behind. Brown, who came in fourteen seconds later, had not trained for this race at all, and only went in at the last moment because Wirts, one of Harvard's best men, was disabled by a severe accident.

The men came in as follows, Harvard winning by 29 points to Tech.'s 26:

		Points.		Time.	
		Harvard.	Tech.	M.	S.
1.	W. B. Greenleaf, '92	10	..	57	31 3-5
2.	Norton	..	9	57	31 4-5
3.	E. A. Bailey, '91	8	..	57	32 3-5
4.	Kenneth Brown, '91	7	..	57	47
5.	Edwards	..	6	..	..
6.	Warner	..	5	..	..
7.	Hadley	..	4	..	..
8.	T. Barron, '91	3	..	..	..
9.	Roots	..	2	..	..
10.	Wasson	..	.	..	.
11.	Webster	..	..	..	..
12.	Holmes	1	..	..	..
	Total	29	26		

Each college entered as many men as they pleased, but only the first five on each side counted.

FIXTURES.

May 4, 1889.—Titan Athletic Club Games. Two-mile Bicycle Handicap. Entries close April 27, with A. Surcott, 361 Broadway, New York.

May 10, 1889.—Twelfth Regiment Games. Entries close May 4 with C. J. Leach, P. O. Box 3,201.

May 11, 1889.—Harvard Bicycle Club Open Amateur Race Meet at Cambridge, Mass. Entries close May 4. Address R. H. Davis, Cambridge, Mass.

May 13–18, 1889.—Chicago Cycling Exhibit and Tournament, Exposition Building.

May 18, 1889.—F. A. Elwell's European Party sails from New York.

May 18, 1889.—Stone-Lumsden 1-mile Match Race, at Chicago, Ill.

May 18, 1889.—Staten Island Athletic Club's Games at New Brighton, S. I. Two-mile Bicycle Race.

May 22, 1889.—N. J. A. C. Games at Bergen Point, N. J. Three-mile Bicycle Handicap. Entries close May 22, with A. M. Stout, Box 262, Bergen Point, N. J.

May 25, 1889.—Stone-Lumsden 3-mile Match Race, at St. Louis, Mo.

May 27, 1889.—Stone-Lumsden 25-mile Match Race at Crawfordsville, Ind.

May 30, 1889.—Maine Division Meet, at Biddeford, Me.

May 30, 1889.—Bicycle and Athletic Tournament and 2-mile L. A. W. Championship Race at Narragansett Park.

May 30, 1889.—Pullman Road Race, Chicago to Pullman.

May 30, 1889.—Twenty-five-mile Handicap Road Race, Irvington, Milburn course. Entrees close May 15th with A. B. Barkman, 241 Broadway, New York.

May 30, 1889.—Rhode Island Wheelman's Race Meet at Narragansett Park, Providence, R. I. Entrees close with C. E. Campbell, Providence, R. I.

June 8, 1889.—Century Run, Orange, N. J., to Philadelphia. Chairman, L. A. Clarke, 25 Broad Street, New York.

June 15, 1889.—L. A. W. Race Meet at Brooklyn Athletic Club Grounds.

June 15, 1889.—Two-mile Bicycle Handicap at New York Athletic Club Grounds, Travers Island.

July 2, 3, 4, 1889.—Hagerstown, Md., Meet.

July 20, 1889.—One-mile and 25-mile Bicycle and 5-mile Tricycle N. C. U. championships at Paddington, Eng., race track.

July 27, 1889.—One-mile and 25-mile Tricycle and 5-mile Bicycle N. C. U. Championships at Paddington, Eng., track.

RHODE ISLAND WHEELMEN'S RACE MEET, PROVIDENCE, R. I., MAY 30.

The committees on the athletic exhibition to be given under the auspices of the Rhode Island Wheelmen, on Memorial Day, at Narragansett Park, are getting down to work. About every sport that has devotees in this city is expected to be represented, and the bicycle events will be especially interesting. The 2-mile national championship race will attract the Eastern racing men and a large representation of prominent flyers is looked for. The H. B. Smith Machine Company, manufacturers of the Star Bicycle, have requested Messrs. Campbell & Co., their agents in this city, to present a race medal to the Rhode Island Wheelmen, to be contested for at these races. The medal is to be given in any race that the tournament committee may suggest.

For the cycle events the committee have endeavored to give a list of races that will in a moment show that they intend to have the races closely contested, and that will show up the best racing qualities of the competitors. And to keep up the interest and give a snap and life, they work in between races such attractions as foot races, tug-of-wars, horsemanship, football, etc. The full list of cycling events is as follows:

Two-mile L. A. W. national championship; 5-mile State championship, open; 1-mile team race, three men; 1-mile novice race; 1-mile tandem safety, open; 2-mile tandem safety, handicap; 1-mile bicycle, handicap; 1-mile safety, handicap; 2-mile safety, open; 1-mile safety L. A. W. State championship; 1-mile bicycle, open.

Chief Consul Davol feels that he has a good corps of assistants in the division's executive board and staff of local consuls, but he wishes some of the latter would answer the occasional official letters that he sends them a little more promptly than they do.

CHICAGO TOURNAMENT.

It is probably not generally known that the Exposition Building, in which the races are to be run, is the largest structure in the world without interior supports. It is 1,000 feet in length, 240 feet in width, and 160 feet in height to the base of the flagstaff. The gallery, around which many a fast mile has been run, is over 500 yards in circumference, and around it several long distance records were made by Woodside five years ago. In the Agricultural Hall, London, the track is but six laps to a mile, taking in the whole building, while a track that size can be laid in one-half of the Exposition. The exhibits will be placed on the west side of the building, in the north addition, and in the east wing adjoining the art gallery. Spaces varying from 500 to 2,000 feet have been secured by the cycling houses, and the value of the exhibit will not be less than $75,000.

At a meeting of the Tournament Racing Committee last week it was decided to run the events as nearly as possible according to the following schedule, though possibly some small changes may be made for the accommodation of out-of-town riders:

Monday, May 13.—One mile, novice; 1 mile, boys under 16; 2-mile safety, preliminary heats; 2-mile, 6:20 class, preliminary heats; 1-mile handicap, first series, preliminary heats.

Tuesday, May 14.—One-mile handicap, second series, heats; 3-mile handicap; 1-mile flying start, heats; 1-mile, men who never have raced prior to this tournament, heats; 2-mile, 6:20 class, final; 2-mile safety, final.

Wednesday, May 15.—One mile handicap, third series, heats; 1-mile flying start, final; 1-mile safety heats; 1-mile, for men who have never raced prior to this tournament, final; 1 mile safety, for boys under 14; club drill.

Thursday, May 16.—Two-mile suburban clubs only; 1-mile safety, final; 1-mile, 8-minute class, 2-mile tandem; 2-mile handicap.

Friday, May 17.—One-half-mile unicycle; 1-mile scratch; 1-mile, local, heats; quarter-mile dash; 1-mile ride and run; 5-mile handicap; 3-mile team, heats.

Saturday, May 18.—One-mile local, final; 3-mile team, final; 1-mile handicap, finals of first, second and third series; 10-mile scratch; 2-mile, L. A. W. members; 1-mile safety handicap, road wheels, 1-mile consolation.

The 1-mile handicap for road wheels has been added to the regular programme, and will be No. 26. Three prizes will be given, and the entry fee will be 50 cents.

The managers of the coming tournament have decided not to give a 24-hour race, but to have a race of 100 miles on Thursday, May 16. This will be open to all amateurs and all descriptions of machines weighing 35 pounds or over.

KANSAS DIVISION MEET.

The next annual meet of the Kansas Division will be held at Forest Park, Ottawa, Kansas, June 4th, 5th and 6th. The managers are making every effort to have it the largest and most successful meeting of the wheelmen ever held west of the Mississippi, not excepting the national meet at St. Louis, in '87. The race programme consists of twenty events, to be run on the 5th and 6th, and includes two State championships, and the half mile and ten mile National L. A. championships. $500 will be given in prizes. The Ottawa wheelmen have secured the exclusive control of the park for the meet, and the track for the ten days' preceding. The track, which has always been one of the best in the West, has been recently improved at a large expense, and will be in the finest condition for racing. It is hoped that eastern wheelmen will not be deterred by distance from attending. The prizes will be of a character to repay the expense and trouble of a long trip. A guarantee fund has been raised sufficient to pay all expense and for all prizes, and everyone can rest assured that all promises will be faithfully carried out.

TO "FENTON."

Dear Fenton! (Most amusing of thy sort),
Why "fancy" you can write about our sport;
For many weekly errors do we see
In Fenton's weakly meditations ("fancy free")!

Fancy too free, for one day while out roaming,
He thought "Jack's" 'Glencoe-latin' was not Roman;
And with much verbiage (of which he's short),
He pads his notes with 'Hudibras'—("when common sense ran short").

And this same Fenton, failing to distinguish
'Twixt dictionary words and Carlyle English,
Rushed into print—with air severe and solemn,
(To get two correspondents snubs in one short column).

Why make us idly spend a *mauvais quart d'heure*,
As o'er your wondrous manuscript we pore,
For each succeeding week—as we expected—
You've had your fearful flagrancies corrected.

But hide not thou thy autocratic head,
Again "rush in where angels fear to tread;"
(The less one knows about a cycling matter,
The easier 'tis to write a lot of senseless blatter).

O, ever thus, since first we donned the breeches,
We've noticed lion's skins and asses' speeches;
If we have crossed the erstwhile friendly pen,
I'll wipe mine clean and shake your hand again.

"JACK."

MERWIN, HULBERT & CO.'S 1889 CATALOGUE.

Messrs. Merwin, Hulbert & Co., whose sporting goods building is the best appointed and best arranged of any similar house in New York, being handsomely finished and furnished from cellar to roof, have just issued a catalogue for their cycling department, which is in charge of A. C. Banker, the well-known racing man. An entire floor is devoted to the cycle department, and a stock of the various wheels handled by the concern is always kept on hand so that orders may be filled at once.

The firm are special agents for New York and vicinity for the Gormully & Jeffrey wheels and allow dealers regular discounts on all G. & J. goods. The leading strings of the G. & J. product are the American Rambler, the American Ideal Rambler, and the Girls Junior Rambler, also the Dandy Safety, the G. & J. American Challenge Tandem, the American Champion Ordinary, the Light Champion, American Challenge, the Ideal bicycle, Ideal tricycle and the Challenge tricycle.

Among other wheels handled by Messrs. Merwin, Hulbert & Co. are the Victor Safety, Singer Safety for gentlemen, Singer Safety for ladies, Singer's Straight-stem Tricycle, Singer's Special "S. S. S." Tricycle, Singer's "Traveler Tandem" and "S. S. S." Tandem Tricycles, Victor Light Roadster B'cycle, Victor Junior Bicycle, Springfield Roadster Bicycle, and the Volant Safety.

The firm also carry a complete line of sundries and cyclists' outfittings. Catalogue sent on application.

E. I. HORSMAN'S 1889 CATALOGUE.

This firm, for many years established on Nassau and William Streets, New York City, and well known in the sporting goods world, have just issued their spring catalogue. The firm handle a line of bicycle, tennis, gymnasium and photographic goods besides games, toys, velocipedes, carriages, etc.

The bicycle department is in charge of Mr. Chapman. The wheels carried in stock are as follows:

The Horsman bicycle, a good roadster for boys, youths and small-sized men; has steel spokes, hollow backbone, solid, malleable iron front forks, solid steel axle and rubber treadles; all bearings adjustable and all parts interchangeable; sizes, 28 to 52 inches; weight, 16 to 47 lbs; price, $12.50 to $68.

American Ideal, American Light Champion, American Rambler, American Ideal Rambler, Ideal tricycle and American Challenge tricycle, all of which are made by the Gormully & Jeffery Mfg Co., and are well known in the cycling world.

Horsman Safety, a boy's safety, in two sizes, 20 and 24-inch wheels, and priced from $18 to $35.

The cycle trade includes lines of children's bicycles, tricycles and velocipedes, also a line of the principal sundry articles found in all cycle dealers' places.

The New York Bicycle Company are handling Ryan's Eagles, Swift Safeties and Ladies English Rovers among their other machines this season. They are also putting up enamel and lubricating and signal oils, which they confidently recommend in every particular. Also we note their line of second-hand machines is very complete. A list of these wheels may be found in another column.

Two hundred second-hand machines for sale at Howard A. Smith & Co.'s, Oraton Hall, Newark, N. J. "Send for list, or better still, call prepared to take one home with you."

At Spalding's, Dan Ivel's "Ivel" Tandems attract the notice of every rider who visits their cycling department. The ladies' tandem is a thing of beauty, lightness and strength.

Two bargains offered in our Sale and Exchange column this week are a brand-new safety, which owner must sell, and a tandem tricycle.

L. H. Johnson has a novel method of showing his wheels. Any cyclist may call at his Orange store and take a trial spin on the Premier single and tandem safeties. A cyclist recently tried a Premier tandem, and at once bought one for the use of himself and his wife. A cyclist says of the Premier Safeties: They are up to the high water mark of modern invention."

Thomas Maber, of Orange. N. J., will shortly locate at Washington, D. C., from which city he will introduce the Pegasus, or Flying Horse Safety. He will also do local business and repairing. Mr. Maber's brother manufactures this safety in England.

The Western Toy Company will not be able to fill boys' safety orders for six weeks, their stock having been sold out.

ELWELL'S EUROPEAN TOUR.
A.J. Wilson, "Faed," will accompany the tourists through England and Ireland. The last man to enroll his name on the list is C. B. Shannon, Los Angeles, Cal. The ages of the tourists range from sixteen to forty-nine. The party has received an invitation from the Birchfield Club, of Birmingham. Eng., to dine with them on their arrival in that city. The tourists will meet at the Tremont House, Boston, the night before starting. The majority of the party reside West of the Great Lakes.

A number of gentlemen, who are very fond of walking and who call themselves the "Outdoor Club," will walk from Newark to Philadelphia some time during May. They will take two days for the journey.

A portion of Broad Street, Newark, will be asphalted. This is but the opening wedge of the street committee, who expect to pave many of Newark's principal streets with asphalt.

J. K. STARLEY & CO.'S WHEELS.

The firm of J. K. Starley & Co. recently succeeded Messrs. Starley & Sutton, the original manufacturers of rear-driving dwarf bicycles. The firm have factories at Coventry, England, are in high repute in England and are making a strong bid for American trade. Among their largest agents here are the Pope Mfg. Co., Boston; Overman Wheel Co., Boston, and John Wilkinson Co., Chicago. The principal types manufactured by Messrs. Starley & Co. are illustrated below:

"NEW LIGHT ROVER."

This machine is twelve pounds lighter than the regular road wheel. Wheels—30 front; 28 rear; geared to 56, unless otherwise ordered. Adjustable ball-bearings to both wheels; crank axle and pedals; tires ⅞, front, for American roads; direct or tangent spokes, as preferred; vertical adjustment to seat pillar; spoon brake; finished in black enamel or painted and lined in two colors; £20.

"POPULAR ROVER."

Has 30-inch wheels, geared to 54-inch; adjustable ball-bearings to both wheels and crank-axle; tires, ⅞-inch and ⅞-inch to front and back wheels respectively; adjustable handles; vertical seat pillar adjustment; spoon brake on front wheel; mud guards; Starley's patent detachable cranks; best saddle and spring; lamp-bracket, foot-rests, valise, spanner and oil-can; finished in plain black enamel or painted and lined in two colors; all bright parts plated; price, £18.

"UNIVERSAL ROVER."

This is a cheap, sound and serviceable machine. Specification.—30-inch front and 28-inch back wheels, geared to 54-inch; curved front-forks; ball-bearings to both wheels and crank-axle; tires, ⅞-inch; adjustable handles; vertical seat adjustment; mud guards to both wheels; lamp-bracket and foot-rests; saddle, spanner and oil-can; finished plain black enamel; bright parts plated; price, £14.

"LADIES' ROVER."

Specification.—28-inch and 26-inch wheels, geared to 51-inch unless otherwise ordered; adjustable ball bearings to both wheels crank axle and pedals; tires, ⅝-inch and ¾-inch; adjustable handles and seat; spoon brake to front wheel; chain and wheel guards; best saddle and spring; lamp-bracket, foot-rests, valise, spanner and oil-can, etc.; finished in best black enamel or painted and lined in two colors; all bright parts plated; price, £20.

In addition to the wheels described, the firm manufacture the "Socket-Steerer Rover," with ball-bearing head; £21; the "spring frame Rover," price, £21 10s.; and the "Rational Rover," price, £20. Catalogue, containing specifications of above wheels, as well as cuts and descriptions of the firm's "Ordinaries," will be sent upon application to the firm—or to any of its agents—J. K. Starley & Co., Meteor Works, West Orchard, Coventry, England.

FROM MARGUERITE.

The Middlesex Cycle Club held a most enjoyable meeting Friday evening, March 29. I do not think an account of it would be out of place. A special invitation was extended by Mr. F. L. Washburne, through the Melrose members of the club, to hold the meeting at his elegant new residence, in Wyoming. Initiation of the '89 riding season and alteration of the yearly dues were the objects of the gathering; and, while the latter caused no delay or dissension, the former was, doubtless, the more pleasant feature. Greetings and handshakings were frequent; also introductions of new members, while numberless wishes were exchanged relative to meeting often on the wheel during the coming season. The club was started only last August, and runs were limited in number on account of miserable weather giving but slight opportunity to the members for mutual acquaintance. This year we start out differently—on a much more social basis.

President Gorrie opened the meeting by stating the business on hand. Thanks were tendered Mr. and Mrs. Washburne for their kindness; and Secretary Jones was kept fully occupied for a short time reading the minutes of previous meetings. The club dues were changed to the satisfaction "of all parties concerned."

The meeting over, a musical and literary programme, arranged through the efforts of Mr. J. M. Gorrie and Mrs. J. Hilbourne, was presented, which, judging from the applause, was very favorably received. Those contributing were: Piano solo, Miss E. White; vocal duett, Messrs. Crafts and Phillips; trio, banjos and guitar, Mr. and the Misses Kirkwood; reading, Miss Barrett; vocal selection, Mrs. Chas. Atkinson; song, Mr. J. M. Gorrie; vocal selection, with violin obligato, the Misses Newhall.

Refreshments were served, after which the home members indulged in dancing; their less fortunate fellow-members departing on the last train. Those present were: Mr. and Mrs. F. L. Washburne, Mr. and Mrs. J. Hilbourne, Mr. and Mrs. J. Hilbourne, Mr. and Mrs. F. K. M. Jones, Mr. and Mrs. J. M. Gorrie, Trowbridge, Mr. Sands, Miss Marsden, Mr. and Mrs. F. K. M. Jones, Mr. and Mrs. J. M. Gorrie, Misses Newhall,* Messrs. Crafts and Phillips,* Mr. A. M. Beers, Miss M. C. Beers, Miss Nichols, Miss White,* Mr. Menns, Mr. Dearborn.* Miss Bicknell, Mr. Coggeshall, Mr. and Mrs. G. J. McArthur, Mr. and Mrs. S. P. Brock, Mr. and Mrs. Jas. Butcher, Mr. and Mrs. W. A. Carey, Miss Brown,* Col. Hesseltine, Miss Barrett, Mr. Bailey, Mr. W. Kirkwood and the Misses Kirkwood. (Those marked * are non-members.)

Long life to the Middlesex Cycle Club! as it has certainly done much in the interest of cycling for ladies around Boston, though so recently organized.

RAINY REMINISCENCES.

Reading "Mrs. 4386's" reminiscences of rainy cycling trips, brings to mind two similar occurrences in my experience which were anything but delightful. The first was a return trip from Gloucester—my sister and I, in company with our brother and a friend, having ridden down the previous afternoon. The morning looked very doubtful, but it was deemed best to start for home. We were then riding a much heavier tandem than now, but for all that we enjoyed many rides with its assistance—the one I am now describing by no means being on the favored list. When about five miles out it commenced to rain, but nearing Manchester-by-the-Sea, where we stopped for soda, it seemed as if the weather was clearing. We found no such good luck awaiting us, however, after partaking of the above-mentioned soda, which was not remarkable for its delicious flavor. Water is preferable when riding, but I have yet to find the obliging druggist or store-keeper who has such, in conjunction with a soda-fountain. Two miles from Manchester it poured so hard that we sought shelter under a large tree, but, alas! trees are not waterproof for any length of time and we were obliged to ask permission to wait on a small (very small) wayside veranda while the storm abated. What tugging and twisting to get that tandem deposited on the piazza, which, when the two bicycles and ourselves were safe out of the rain, was more than comfortably filled. Here we waited three-quarters of an hour, hoping against hope that it would clear up. My brother and friend could easily have taken the train for home at Manchester, but what could possibly be done with a tricycle tandem? Nothing but "scoot" (excuse the expression, since it was really nothing more or less) for home, which we decided to do in short order.

More tugging, twisting and scraping and we were off. It raining very steady, we were soon drenched, and the roads were one vast sheet of mud. The hills dragged considerable, but it was "do or die," and we "did," Through Pride's Crossing, Beverly and Salem to Lynn, pedestrians staring at us in open-mouthed astonishment. Here our friend left us for the R. R. depot, as we would not hear of h m riding any further when he could train it so easy. Fast riding was necessary to prevent taking cold, we now being literally soaked. Six miles more in the splashy wet and we reached home. Glad the word did not half express our feelings, and it took almost a week to clean the machines.

Our second predicament was on the last Ladies' North Shore Tour, the rain commencing on Saturday, the third day. From Magnolia, where we had dinner, to Salem was a go-as-you-please race, accomplished in a cold drizzle. Everybody got drenched—those longest on the road suffering

TOURING.

BY FRED J. SHEPARD, BUFFALO BICYCLE CLUB.

The chief pleasure which a bicycle affords is to be got in touring in congenial company over good roads, through an unfamiliar country abounding in fine scenery or interesting historical associations. The ideal number for a touring party is perhaps four, though two is generally to be preferred to three. In the case of three there is likely to be an odd man; in the case of more than four a lack of harmony may develop, and delays made to gratify one may be irksome to others. It will be found convenient for one member of the party to act as the paymaster, while to another is delegated the care of the baggage. A trip of eight or ten days will satisfy most riders, and if there is a spare day sandwiched in the middle, on which a rest is taken, the enjoyment of the tour will gain zest. Forty or fifty miles a day should be the maximum distance even over the best roads, and if the tourist is to get the most satisfaction from his outing and mount every morning full of ardor for the day's ride, he will content himself with considerably less. The comment of an old tourist who sees a party of wheelmen devoting one day out of their trip to an attempt to make a century run and the next one to recuperating from the effort is: "It is magnificent, but it is not touring." Two or three days after finishing a tour—if ever—is the time for feats of this sort. That the baggage to be carried on the wheel must be reduced to the smallest possible amount will be impressed upon the novice during his first day's run. A change of underclothing, four or five handkerchiefs and a toothbrush rolled up in a yard of rubber cloth will make as big a bundle as he will enjoy carrying when his coat is added to it. If he think them indispensable a pair of stockings may also go into the roll, and if he wear the "Jersey fitting garments" he must carry slung over his back a small bag containing what he would otherwise place in his pockets. All his remaining baggage he should express ahead in his valise. He can generally so arrange that he can get at this every night if he chooses, but once in every three or four days will answer the requirements of most men. Upon arriving at his hotel at night the rider, after enjoying a cold bath and a hard rub, and putting on his dry underclothing, should see to it that the garments which he has just taken off are thoroughly dried over night by a fire. If he does not take special pains to impress upon the hotel people the necessity of absolute dryness, the clothing may come back to him in the morning still damp, in which case he will have to finish the drying process when he stops that day for his noonday meal. Unless he establishes communications every night with his valise, he will have to sleep sometimes in his underclothing—not altogether a disadvantage, for the sheets of country inns are sometimes damp. It is hardly worth while to carry any rubber clothing, even in the valise, for if it rains, and the tourist is unwilling to remain under cover, he can procure overshoes when he happens to be. Riding in rubber garments of any kind is intolerable. The coat and shirt pockets of a wheelman ought to be so arranged as to permit them to be buttoned up, but in the absence of buttons safety pins will be found convenient. This remark applies especially to the coat, because it is carried most of the time on the handle-bar. A serious objection to luggage carriers attached to the backbone is the difficulty of climbing over them.

While on the road the writer has followed without ill effects Karl Kron's rule of drinking whatever was to be had and as often as he was thirsty. Milk is about as satisfactory as anything to most stomachs, and a lemonade with an egg broken into it proves a very gratifying form of refreshment. Beer is decidedly heating, and if a wheelman drinks spirits at any time it should be only at the end of his day's run, after his bath and before his evening meal. Some tourists think highly of the practice of carrying a lozenge in the mouth to allay thirst. The writer has always had in his pocket a drinking cup, but very likely Karl Kron's plan of carrying a small piece of rubber tubing is preferable.

League hotels should be patronized in every case, not only on account of the reduced rates which they usually offer, but also because they are more likely to recognize the peculiar wants

the most. At the hotel, fires were lighted, and by supper-time the riders were tolerably comfortable. We kept our spirits up, trusting that Sunday would bring fair weather. We were doomed to disappointment, since the morning brought a steady down-pour. Many of the party trained home, either sending their machines in the barge (which, unfortunately, would hold but few) or leaving them at the hotel, to be ridden home at some future time. A few tarried at the hotel to wait for good riding. Now, I didn't see the fun in training it unless bag, baggage and wheel trained it, too. "Mac" and his wife, of whom I have previously written, were of the same opinion; so we decided to ride home, a distance of thirteen miles, rain or no rain. The loss of a week's riding—to us a terrible calamity—hastened our decision, as we probably would not be at liberty to secure our wheels before the succeeding Sunday. Some considered us rash and foolish, but we said good-bye to all, and, taking our opportunity when the rain had considerably lightened, we started, a large (?) party of two tandems. It was all right for about four miles ; in fact we were congratulating ourselves on our nice escape, when we felt the drops thicken, and "Mac" made haste to secure his wife's rubber-cloak and over-shoes. This was the first time I had seen these articles carried on a wheel and used, but they were certainly useful on this occasion. Oh! how it did pour as we rode through Lynn and along Ocean Street—the water-side. It came in blinding sheets! No need to describe the roads ; I will leave that to your imagination. How we did laugh at out condition! but all things must end, and this trip shared the common fate. We parted at the most handy crossing, leaving our friends with two or three miles more to ride, which did not rouse our envy in the slightest.

Our friend "Mac's" experience in the future will be more favorable, since he and his wife are now mounted on a Columbia Tandem Safety.

In conclusion, will only remark how different the results of these trips had we been riding ladies' safeties. I notice that your pleasant coorespondent, "Mrs. 4386," likewise confirms the advantages of ladies' bicycles in regard to easy handling.

MAPLEWOOD, MASS., April 10, 1889.   MARGUERITE.

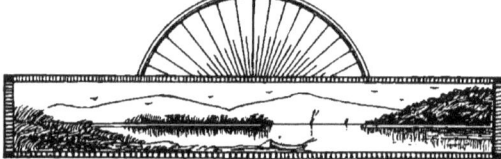

of wheelmen than are other inns. They will prove more trustworthy sources of information in regard to the roads, and will offer fewer obstacles to the demand for bathing facilities than will houses at which wheeling tourists are less frequent guests. Early starts in the morning are a feature rather of speculative than actual touring. People who really have tried one speak enthusiastically of the joys of a day-break ride, but it is to be hoped that no tenderfoot will be beguiled by these siren voices into ever getting off without his breakfast. The advisability of a rest in the middle of the day of at least two hours is admitted by most if not all tourists.

The writer has been requested to add some remarks as to touring by women. His own experience has been that, when mounted upon tandem tricycles, they were able to stand as long a day's jaunt as their companions felt disposed to take. The great obstacle to their admission to the delights of touring has been, of course, the difficulty of finding roads over which a tricycle could be driven with much pleasure. The writer knows of but two districts containing such roads—the North Shore of Massachusetts and the Shenandoah Valley. The trouble in securing transportation for tricycles over some railroads aggravates matters. But the introduction of the woman's bicycle and especially of the tandem bike seems to promise that in the future many a pleasant bit of country may be traversed in the company of wife or sister, and that the wheelman may spend his brief summer vacation touring, without leaving the women of his household.

A real want of tourists is a hand-book, or, better, a series of hand-books, that will describe the different touring regions of the country, pointing out the objects of interest in each town. The strange wheelman finds a little work like the "Hand-book of Essex County (Mass.) Wheelmen" vastly more useful than the orthodox road-book. As ι is, he who intends to take the Lake George tour must content himself with a careful preliminary perusal of Lossing's "Field Book of the Revolution," and the Shenandoah Valley tourist may with advantage study the volume in the "Campaigns of the Civil War" series relating to the region. Even so small a book as the latter proves something of a burden if carried on the wheel, though the maps ought really to be taken. The separate chapters of Karl Kron's book, which he sells for a quarter apiece, if carried in the pocket will prove interesting to a tourist going over the same ground. The bother of taking along a road-book may be avoided by copying off the pages which will be needed. The writer ventures to hope that the wheelmen of touring regions will take into consideration the necessity of providing small hand-books that will tell the tourist what there is to see in their districts.—From the New York State Hand-Book.

GEARING AND PACE.

Sir—Many riders are fond of estimating their pace when riding, and I have made a few simple calculations in order to arrive at a fairly accurate method of obtaining a ready determination. It so happens that the case of a wheel geared to 56 inches gives the simplest rule, which is as follows : Count the number of revolutions made by the crank-axle in ten seconds, and this will be the number of miles per hour at which the machine is traveling. Other guides for other gears can easily be found, of which I may give a couple of examples : For a 60-inch gear, 12 revolutions of the crank-axle in ten seconds correspond to a speed of 15 miles an hour ; for a 52-inch gear, 14 revolutions of the crank-axle in ten seconds correspond to a speed of 15 miles an hour. Quite generally, if a machine is geared to x inches and the speed is m miles an hour, then the number of crank revolutions per second will be $\frac{m}{x} \times 5 \cdot 6$. From this formula a person can deduce a rule applicable to his own particular machine, whether geared or ordinary, the ordinary being, of course, regarded as geared level. Two factors that might be considered occur to me in making such an estimate as I have suggested—one is the slip of the driving-wheel ; the other the reduction of its effective diameter due to the pressure on the tire. Both these sources of error, however, negligible, for scarcely any appreciable slip takes place save under exceptional circumstances; and, in the other case, if, say, a ¾-inch tire were compressed by the load upon it to the extent of ⅜-inch, the consequent difference in the distance covered would only amount to a yard in every 34 revolutions of the wheel. Returning to the formula given above, let us compare a 50-inch gear at, say, 10 and 18 miles an hour with a 60-inch gear at the same speeds. We shall find that the distance of pedaling rate at the lower speed is less than a fifth of a revolution in a second, or 11 per minute ; while at the higher speed the difference amounts to a third of a revolution in a second, or 20 per minute. It is this increase in the difference, when the pace increases, that makes a low gear tiring to drive at a high speed ; but, in all-round riding, one is oftener traveling at 10 miles an hour —thereabout—than at the higher speeds, consequently low gears, when used for other purposes than racing, are not open to this, the only objection against them.—F. T. R. in Bicycling News.

THE BAR SINISTER.

Oh' weep for the dwarf that is blocked,
On account of the tall 'un it mocked,
    And often would pass
    On the cinder and grass
In a style which was dreadful—and shocked
Oh! wait for the slackness of nerve,
That kicks at a lurch or a swerve,
    Or a staggering tack
    On a narrow-made track,
With a smash at the end of a curve.

It is merely a matter of spill,
Not much you will murmur—but still
    'Tis an excellent plan
    For a bold racing man
To bring his backbone to no ill.

Oh! groan at the manifest,
That's preparing to Synyer & Co.,
    To hurl in the face
    Of the brave pigmy race,
And queer the best fun of the show.
How shameful to ruffle and vex
Such a lot for the sake of the necks
    And limbs of a few
    Or a window or two—
While teeth can be purchased by pecks.

Some say it's a question of skill,
Which the clever can practise at will,
    But doubts will arise
    When the loss is two eyes,
And the medico sends in his bill.

Oh! yell at the wheels that are high
And cracks that are speedy and spry,
    Who holler ' No mix,'
    And their signatures fix
To a document subtle and sly.
Farewell to the spokes in a pile,
To the handle-bar "all of a spile,"
    To cripples and gore,
    And repairings galore,
And a flopping of six in a mile!

But really the danger is nil,
For seldom you hear of a kill;
    While beetians flout
    At the wreckage and shout,
"Yah! bar and be blowed if you will!"
    —F. F. S., in Bicycle News.

New York State Division L.A.W.

OFFICERS FOR 1889.

CHIEF CONSUL,
W. S. BULL, 734 Main Street, Buffalo, N. Y.

VICE-CONSUL,
M. L. BRIDGMAN, 1255 Bedford Avenue, Brooklyn, N. Y.

SECRETARY-TREASURER,
GEO. M. NISBETT, 50 Wall Street, New York City.

EXECUTIVE AND FINANCE COMMITTEE.
W. S. BULL,
M. H. BRIDGMAN,
DR. GEORGE E. BLACKHAM, Dunkirk, N. Y.

TO THE MEMBERS OF THE N. Y. STATE DIVISION:
New York State Division Committees for the year 1889 are hereby appointed and announced as follows :

EXECUTIVE AND FINANCIAL.—W. S. Bull, M. L. Bridgman, Dr. Geo. E. Blackham, Dunkirk, N. Y.

RIGHTS AND PRIVILEGES.—Walter S. Jenkins, 18 East Eagle Street, Buffalo, N. V.; Michael Furst, 16 Court Street, Brooklyn, N. Y.; L. A. Newcome, 169 Broadway, New York City.

RULES AND REGULATIONS.—E. J. Shriver, N. Y. Metal Exchange, New York City ; A. B. Gardner, 11 Broad Street, Utica, N. Y.; J. M. Warwick 30 Broad Street, New York City.

IMPROVEMENT AND HIGHWAYS.—I. B. Potter, 38 Park Row, New York City ; C. E. Wilbur, U. Tel. Co., Albany, N. Y.; A. M. Dickinson, 125 East Seventy-sixth Street, New York City.

ROAD BOOK.—A. B. Barkman, 608 Fourth Avenue, Brooklyn, N. Y.; John S. Kellner, 197 Pearl Street, Buffalo, N. Y.; W. H. De Graaf, 47 West Fourteenth Street, New York City.

Yours fraternally,
W. S. BULL,
Chief Consul.

BUFFALO, N. Y., April 20, 1889.

CYCLING AROUND THE HUB.

Muddy roads and threatening weather greeted the wheelmen of this vicinity when they took a look outdoors Sunday morning, and, although most of them attired themselves in bicycling suits and started for the rendezvous of the day, more than one returned home, being afraid of the dubious weather and sticky roads. The streets around the Somerville Cycle Club house presented an animated appearance early, when cyclists could be seen coming from all directions to participate in the formal opening of the riding season. At 10 o'clock Capt. Cubberly of the Somerville club had a dozen men on the ground, Capt. Newman of Cambridge had 10, while Capt. Robinson had eight of his Rovers, all mounted on Safeties, and after waiting some time for any derelict wheelmen, Capt. Robinson took command of the party and ordered the march to Salem. The route lay over the Malden turnpike, which was plentifully sprinkled with mud, and thence through Maplewood and Hopedale. At the latter place the party was increased by a number of the Malden Bicycle Club under command of Capt. Jacobs, and he turned his men over to the command of Tourmaster Robinson. From this point the run was past Sunnyside through Lynn, and several towns, to the Essex House at Salem, and here were met several members of these clubs : Maverick Wheel Club, Wakefield Bicycle Club, Chelsea Cycle Club, and Medford Cycle Club, the latter organization parading 15 men. The Dorchester Bicycle Club was represented by Capt. Benson, the Chelsea Ramblers by Capt. Pratt, the Press Cycling Club by Capt. Kerrison and 1st Lieut E. A. Wilkins. After everybody had taken a rest the saddle-tired wheelmen marched into the dining room, and after dinner were photographed. About one-half of the party made the return trip to Boston Sunday afternoon, and the others continued the journey to Gloucester, where they remained over night, and on Monday took a trip around the Cape, returning to Boston in the afternoon. After leaving Salem the Boston-bound party commenced to break up, some desiring to "scorch," while others, who were taking their first ride of the season, preferred to "lay back." Just before the party reached Lynn, and while going over a piece of bad road, Worden, the hill climber, accepted an invitation to race a horse, and, just to amuse the party, he began to put on all speed, and very soon the horse was some distance behind, but when the equine "got his second breath," it begun to lessen the distance, and after a short time the noted hill climber was given a tow.—*Boston Herald.*

John C. Wetmore, good old "Jonah," is writing a history of Elizabeth, N. J., for the Board of Trade o that city. The club house of the Elizabeth wheelmen will be illustrated and described in the book.

The Board of Chosen Freeholders of Elizabeth County, N. J., met at Elizabeth on April 18th, and, in accordance with the law recently passed by the New Jersey Legislature, they have gone to work to issue bonds, map out the roads, etc. They propose to connect Elizabeth in direct lines with Linden, Rahway, Roselle, Crawford, Westfield, Fanwood, Netherwood, Plainfield, Springfield, Summit and New Providence. This, with the connections it will open, will be the largest system of macadamized roads in the United States. The new roads, in connection with the Orange system, will cover an area of 100 square miles.

The Lancaster Club will hold a race meet at the Driving Park on July 4.

MEETING OF THE CYCLISTS' UNION OF LONG ISLAND.

At a meeting of the Union held Wednesday night the resignation of E. K. Austin from the presidency was accepted, and M. L. Bridgman, President K. C. W. was elected to the vacancy. The Union instructed the Roads Improvement Committee to employ men to clear Cobble-stone Hill of the loose stones which now cover its surface. The Rights and Privileges Committee were instructed to discover whether the proper authorities could not prevent the posts being erected on the Booklyn-Bath road. The Union is doing practical work.

The invitation of the Maryland Division has been accepted and the League meet will be held at Hagerstown, Md., July 1, 3 and 4.

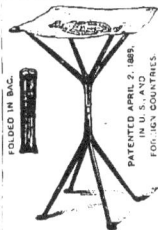

THE REVOLVING FOLDING STOOL.

Messrs. Ira Perego & Co., 126 Fulton Street, New York, have a novelty in the revolving folding stool. The stool is of neat design and nicely finished. It may be easily carried when folded ; it weighs but twenty-five ounces. The stool will be found very convenient for sketching on the baseball, athletic and tennis fields, for camping, fishing, etc. Price, $1.

A SELECTED LIST OF PATENTS.

[Reported especially for THE WHEEL AND CYCLING TRADE REVIEW by C. A. Snow & Co., patent attorneys, Washington, D. C.]

April 23.—H. Kunath, Dresden, Germany ; ball bearing.

April 23.—S. Curlin, Union City, Tenn.; marine velocipede.

HOWARD A. SMITH & CO.,
ORATON HALL, NEWARK, N. J.

Everything in the Cycle Line,

And Catalogue ready for mailing. Send for one.

SECOND-HAND MACHINES
OF ALL MAKES AND SIZES.

Call and Inspect at once or send for list.

HARLEM BICYCLE CO.,
284 Lenox Ave., near 125th Street,

AGENTS FOR

VICTOR CYCLES
AND ALL THE

BEST AMERICAN AND ENGLISH WHEELS,

Boys' and Girls' Bicycles, Velocipedes
and Tricycles.

Renting, Storing, Lockers, etc.

REPAIRING A SPECIALTY.

Bicycle and Athletic Goods.

THE KINGSTON KNITTING CO.,
OF BOSTON, MASS.,
Manufacturer for the Trade and Clubs.

The most beautiful line of ATHLETIC GOODS made, and in the latest colors, in Plain, Striped and Mixed Cloths, in WORSTED, WOOL and Jersey spun COTTON, for Bicycle Riders; Gymnasium, Baseball, Football and Lawn Tennis Suits; Rowing and Yachting Outfits, Hosiery, Caps, etc.—all from our special weaving, and for styles, elasticity and durability cannot be excelled.

Our JERSEYS, KNEE TIGHTS, KNICKERBOCKERS, FULL BODY TIGHTS, TRUNKS and SUPPORTERS are unsurpassed for good taste, comfort and easy fitting. Many novelties in PLAIN and RIBBED suits and sweaters.

Our prices are very reasonable. Address

KINGSTON KNITTING CO.,
27 KINGSTON ST., BOSTON.
CORRESPONDENCE SOLICITED.

HOLMES & CO.

We call special attention to our New Circular for the coming season. We have added several new things to our list, which we trust the trade will appreciate.

Jersey-Fitting Garments
FOR
Bicycle Riders, Lawn Tennis Players, Yachting and Rowing, Base-Ball and Foot-Ball, Gymnasium.

League Color, Gray Mixed, Black, Navy or any Color, Plain or Stripe.

This Supporter is in use by Bicycle Riders, Base Ball Players, Athletes, Bathers and Gymnasts, and we are told that it is the

Best and most satisfactory Supporter made.

Let every Sportsman try it.

Price, $1.00.

Will send by mail on receipt of price.

Send size of Waist and Hip.

Holmes' Thigh Stocking.

The attention of the Wheelmen and the trade is kindly called to our new Thigh Stocking. The enclosed cut gives a correct description of this stocking and its design, and needs no argument to show that it is the best thing that has been made for holding the stocking in position. They are Ribbed, Jersey-Fitting and very elastic, regular made, double heel and toes. The form and proportions of the foot, heel, toe, ankle, calf and leg are perfect, as represented in the cut, and there is no better made or better fitting stocking in the market. The part above the stocking for holding it in position is made of cotton, and comes up and fastens around the waist same as around the waist same as where they belong.

Price, $2.50; without Supporter, $1.50.

Send us your order for either of these, with color, size of foot and inside length from bottom of foot to crotch, and post-office order for amount, and we will send same by mail or express to any part of the country; and if you do not find them satisfactory, return them and we will refund amount paid for them. Address,

HOLMES & CO.,
109 Kingston St.   BOSTON, MASS.

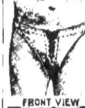

T̞H̞E̞ W̞H̞E̞E̞L̞

—AND—

CYCLING TRADE REVIEW,

Published every Friday morning.

Entered at the Post Office at second class rates.

Subscription Price, - - - $1.00 a year.
Foreign Subscriptions, - - - 6s. a year.
Single Copies, - - - - - 5 Cents.

Newsdealers may order through AM. NEWS Co.

All copy should be received by Monday.
Telegraphic news received till Wednesday noon.

Advertising rates on Application.

F. P. PRIAL, Editor and Proprietor
23 Park Row,
P. O. Box 444,   *New York.*

Persons receiving sample copies of this paper are respectfully requested to examine its contents and give us their patronage, and as far as is convenient, aid in circulating the journal, and extend its influence in the cause which it so faithfully serves. Subscription price, $1 per year.

BETTER THAN ALL OTHERS.

I am a subscriber to all other Cycling Papers published in this country, and will say that I think more of yours than any other. It gives the best news.
    J. B. CAMPBELL, Akron, Ohio.

NEW YORK'S JUBILATION.

The first half of the business week of Gotham was given over to Centennial Celebration, the wheels of business being entirely clogged. The grand central fact was the nation's hundredth birthday ; the grand central figure was George Washington, the Hero of War, the Nestor of Peace, and the Father of His Country. The celebration was inaugurated with a very stagey reception to President Harrison, who, instead of being swept into Jersey City on a Pennsylvania Palace Car, was lugged down through out-of-the-way Elizabethport, and theatrically landed at the Battery, just like the first President, " don't yer know." The other features of the celebration were receptions at the Equitable Building and the City Hall on Monday afternoon and a ball in the evening, at which the wine flowed so freely, that McAllister's " four hundred" acted just like McSweeny's or anybody else's " four hundred," when they have tipped the ruby too often. The features of Tuesday were a military parade, at which a million and a half of people witnessed fifty-two thousand paraders, and a grand banquet in the evening, to which eight hundred " representative men "— just a few not representative, however—did justice to the inner man and listened to a feast of reason renowned for quality rather than for quantity. The great Industrial parade, a more pleasing, though not so imposing a spectacle as the military parade, attracted the attention of the million and a half on Wednesday. On both Tuesday and Wednesday evenings, both residents and visitors attempted to impart a tinge of luridity to the town, with more or less success.

The Centennial demonstration afforded a limited number of nobodies an opportunity to parade their descent, their wealth and their dearth of executive ability, almost everything going wrong in which they had a hand. It also afforded the multitude to gaze on some of our little-great men, on our Chief Ruler and our Ex-Chiefs, on an imposing array of Governors, and on a vast outpouring of the military and industrial strength of the country. On the other hand, it revived the glory of Washington, who was brought forth out of the dim hatchet-and-cherry-tree atmosphere, with which a grateful country had surrounded him. The pages of history were searched and the pens of the moderns enlisted so that a clear conception of the really great character of Washington was projected, and he was placed in that niche to which only thorough students of his character had assigned him.

Aside from the patriotism and loyalty aroused by the great demonstration, the only other valuable incident was the sermon of Bishop Potter, delivered at St. Paul's Church, of historic memories, in the presence of the President and Vice-President. The Bishop, aware that his words would be published throughout the American continent, sent out a great plea for the preservation of that exalted spirit which is Washington's chief consideration to greatness. The Bishop's peroration is here reproduced :

" And, again, another enormous difference between this day and that of which it is the anniversary is seen in the enormous difference in the nature and influence of the forces that determine our National and political destiny. Then, ideas ruled the hour. To-day, there are indeed ideas that rule our hour, but they must be merchantable ideas. The growth of wealth, the prevalence of luxury, the missing of large material forces, which by their very existence are a standing menace to the freedom and integrity of the individual, the infinite swagger of our American speech and manners, mistaking bigness for greatness, and sadly confounding gain and Godliness—all this is a contrast to the austere simplicity, the unpurchasable integrity of the first days and the first men of our Republic, which makes it impossible to reproduce to-day either the temper or the conduct of our fathers. As we turn the pages backward, and come up on the story of that 30th of April, in the year of Lord 1789, there is a certain stateliness in the air, a certain ceremoniousness in the manners, which we have banished long ago. We have exchanged the Washingtonian dignity for the Jeffersonian simplicity, which was, in truth, only another name for the Jacksonian vulgarity. And what have we got in exchange for it? In the Elder States and Dynasties they had the trappings of Royalty and the pomp and splendor of the King's person to fill men's hearts with loyalty. Well, we have dispensed with the old titular dignities. Let us take care that we do not part with that tremendous hope for which they stood ! If there be not titular royalty, all the more need is there for personal royalty. If there is to be no nobility of descent, all the more indispensable is it that there should be nobility of ascent—a character in them that bear rule, so fine and high and pure, that as men come within the circle of its influence they involuntarily pay homage to that which is the one pre-eminent distinction, the royalty of virtue !"

THE LEAGUE MEET.

From a personal letter to us, we learn that there is every prospect of the Hagerstown meet being as successful as any of the previous meets. Chief Consul Mott has taken a deal of interest in it, and will give the Hagerstown men in-valuable assistance.

The whole towns-people are filling up with enthusiasm on the subject, and by July they will be " red hot." Owing to the elevation of the city, the climate is cooler than might be expected in July, and the nights are refreshing and pleasant.

WE deeply regret the death of Stephen Terry, of Hartford, Conn. Mr. Terry was a man of solid physique, of genial countenance and well-balanced intellect—a man who appeared too broad to be worried by trifles and too bright to misinform his constitution by overwork. He played his public part in cycling life in an intelligent and dignified manner, and his death will be deplored by a large number of cyclists, not only in Connecticut, but throughout the United States.

Important to Racing Cyclists,

In last week's WHEEL we discussed the assertion that racing cyclists who are members of athletic clubs as well as cycling clubs, and who accept the payment of entrance fees and traveling expenses, forfeit their cycling club membership. We drew the following conclusions :

Jones represents an athletic club. According to the rules governing athletics, which are recognized by the Racing Board, Jones may compete for an athletic club and may have his expenses paid without losing his amateur status, and he must be considered an amateur both by the athletic and cycling path legislators.

The rule should be amended as follows: "Cyclist representing athletic clubs on the path may accept such expenses as are allowed by the athletic rules without the club they represent obtaining the special sanction of the Racing Board."

We are informed by the Chairman of the Racing Board that our interpretation of the spirit of the racing rules is correct; also that the Board will recognize the athletic rules of the A. A. U. and N. A. A. A. A., thus avoiding all complications.

T̞HE three holidays of this week and preparations for a special edition next week rather curtailed our work on this week's WHEEL. Yet a deal of interesting matter is to be found in its several pages of solid nonpareil.

T̞HE man who don't read the advertisements deprives himself of a treat. The perusal of an advertisement will give as much pleasure as an interesting article. Our patrons are constantly sending us new matter for their advertising space, and a study of the matter and style of their " ads " is amusing and instructive.

TRAINING.

It is the height of folly in an athlete to commence the work of training, in its strictest sense, when completely out of condition. But it is our firm belief that for a man to do his very best in the racing season, he should take only a moderate amount of athletic exercise during the winter months. Cross-country running once a week keeps the wind in splendid order, and prevents excess of adipose tissue. At the same time it has been our experience that a course of training for cross-country championship honors, has, by developing the muscles used in running, at the expense of those used in cycling, retarded our getting anything like " fit " until near the end of the racing season. Football, gymnastics, and walking in the winter time, indulged in moderately, maintain the tone of a man : indulged in to excess, the muscles used in cycling suffer.

There are a few good all-round athletes. That is men who can swim well, run well, ride well, and who are perhaps good gymnasts, and so on. But these are the exception. With the great generality it is a physical impossibility to excel at once in several forms of athletic exercise which bring into play different, and, as it were, antagonistic sets of muscles. Thus when the bicyclist is riding at his best, he will make a poor show in a foot race, and that although when trained for foot running he may be a first-class pedestrian. To reduce this general principle to a narrower basis. It is a rarity to find a man capable of shining at about the same time on road and path. The heavy road work slows him down, but gives him plenty of muscle.

Many Englishmen, distinguished path riders, seldom mount a roadster, but commence their training with path work. But nearly all our Scottish cracks believe in a preliminary working up of the muscle by two or three weeks road riding, and this is always a safe plan.

Presuming that our novice has taken the russiness off by a few weeks road riding, he must next decide at what hour of the day he will do his track riding. Regularity in all things is of primary importance. He should, if at all possible, eat his meals and do his riding at the same hours every day. Usually the evening, when business is over, is the most convenient time to train. Training in the earlier part of the day takes so much out of one that he is unable to give due attention to his daily work ; and in no instance should business be made subservient to pleasure.

At the commencement of his training, unless the rider is very spare, and cannot afford to lose much flesh, he should wear plenty of clothes. At first, too, the work should be light. Coming off his road work he will have plenty of stay, but no speed. His endeavor must be to cultivate fast pedalling. He should ride a few laps at half speed, then spurt for two or three hundred yards at his best pace ; ride quietly round for a lap or two, and repeat the spurting ; a short rest, and a half-mile burst to finish with is quite enough for the first day. Seldom in the earlier stage of training should any long distance at full speed be attempted. Spurts of from one hundred yards to a quarter, and occasionally half a mile, engaged in for a week, will improve one's pace more than months of hard grinding at longer distances. The novice must try to finish these spurts "all out." In his earlier racing he will probably find that the experienced rider will beat him, but finish the more exhausted of the two. This is on account of the old hand's experience, which enables him to run himself almost to a standstill at the finish of a race, while the less experienced rider may have enough left in him for another mile, but lacks the ability to use it up.

There will probably be disappointment felt at the progress made at first. It is often the case that at the end of the first week there is no perceptible improvement, perhaps even a slight falling off ; but shortly there commences a real improvement, and the rider has a feeling that he is making progress. A friend should be asked to time quarter and half-miles occasionally. But there is no need for feeling put out if the time is sometimes slower than it was at the previous trial. It is quite possible to be going on nicely with the training, and yet happen at an odd time to be a little below par.

In three or four weeks it will be safe to experiment a little, and do time trials for longer distances, but the novice should always keep in view that he is more liable to err on the score of doing too much work than too little. He will find it of great advantage to train along with other, and, if possible, better men.— *The Scottish Cyclist.*

[TO BE CONCLUDED NEXT WEEK.]

SPRING-FORK FOR BICYCLES.

LEON BAUDREAU, OF CHICOPEE FALLS, MASS.

Be it known that I, Leon Baudreau, residing at Chicopee Falls, Mass., have invented new and useful improvements in spring-fork devices for bicycles, of which the following is a specification.

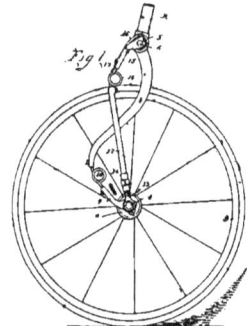

Fig. 1.

This invention relates to bicycles and similar vehicles, the object being to provide improved spring-fork connections between the wheel-axle and the fork-head, whereby an easy vertical spring motion of the parts of the machine whose weight is carried by said axle is obtained, and the wheel is supported by and between the fork-legs in its proper plane of rotation; and the invention consists in the peculiar construction and arrangement of said spring-fork con-

nections, all as hereinafter fully described and pointed out in the claims.

In the drawings forming part of this specification Fig. 1 is a side and Fig. 2 a front elevation of a vehicle-wheel and spring-fork devices applied thereto constructed according to my invention. Fig. 3 illustrates a modified construction of portions of said devices.

The supporting devices for the fork-head, including the spring features thereof, which are interposed between said head and the axle 4, are constructed and operate as fo lows: Two curved forked legs, 8, are hung by their upper ends on said shaft 6 at opposite ends of the head part 5, and have a degree of vibratory motion thereon. Said legs 8, as shown, extend downward, first in a curved line toward the rear of the wheel 3, and then in a reverse direction, whereby the lower ends thereof are brought to a position above and considerably forward of the wheel-axle 4. The lower end of each of said fork-legs 8 is connected with the wheel-axle 4 through the intermediary of an arm, 9, whose lower end is rigidly clamped to said axle, and to the upper end of which is rigidly attached one end of a coil spring, 10, and the opposite end of said spring is rigidly attached to the lower end of said leg. The upper ends of said legs 8 have a connection with other coil-springs, 16, as below described, the last-named springs and said springs to constituting the spring-resistance connected with said legs between said fork-head part 5 and the axle 4.

An arm, 15, is rigidly clamped on each end of the shaft 6, and extends toward the forward edge of the wheel 3 in a downwardly inclined direction, and a coil-spring, 16, has one end thereof attached, as shown, to the inner side of said arm, and the opposite end of said fork-leg 8 by inserting the end of said spring in a suitable perforation in the end of said leg, and there rigidly securing it, or by other suitable means. To the lower end of each of said arms 15 is rigidly secured one end of a coil-spring, 18, a cap, 17, being secured on the upper side of said arm 15, having its lower end extending partially over said spring 18 to form a suitable finish at the junction of said spring and the arm 15, and to more or less strengthen the connection of said spring with said arm. A post, 12, has its upper end rigidly connected to the lower end of each of said springs 18, and the lower end of each of said posts 12 is connected by a tubular nut, 14, with the end of an arm, 13, which is hung on the outer end of the axle 4 in such a way that it may have a certain degree of vibratory motion thereon. A circular nut, 7, (see Fig. 3), is screwed onto each end of the shaft 6, outside of the upper ends of the fork-legs 8, to hold the latter in position against the ends of the head-part 5, and the said coil-springs 16 encircle said nuts. A washer, 19, is placed on the axle 4 between each end of the wheel-hub a and the adjoining ends of the arms 9, and a washer, 20, is placed on said axle, between the latter named arms and the arms 13.

The above described spring-fork connections or fork-head-supporting devices are so constructed and applied between said head and the axle 4 that the spring elements thereof—18 and 10, especially—are mainly in positions forward of said axle, and the application of weight on the fork-head causes said springs 18 and 10 to be thrown still farther forward, the consequence of which is that when the vehicle is moving rapidly and the wheel encounters some obstacle upon the road, whereby it is suddenly thrown upward, the ends of the arms, the posts, and the legs 8, which are connected with the springs 10 and 18, together with the latter, are thrown still farther forward beyond the axle 4, thereby producing such an action of the said supporting devices between the axle and the fork-head as obviates in an important degree the constantly present danger which exists in bicycles that the rider may be thrown headlong over his wheel.

In addition to the foregoing advantages arising from the use of the above described construction, the interposition of the springs 10, 18 and 10 between the fork-head and the axle 4, together with the peculiar arrangement of the fork-legs 8, the posts 12, and their connecting-arms, as described, constitute spring-supporting devices possessing peculiar features, which

conduce essentially to ease in riding a vehicle fitted with said devices, and obviate entirely the inconvenience pertaining to such vehicles, in which the rider is constantly subjected to the shaking and trembling motion of vehicles as ordinarily constructed. The said springs 16, connected each between the arm 15 and the upper end of the leg 8, offer resistance to the upward motion of the arm 15 and to the vibratory motion of the leg 8 when weight is applied to the fork-head, said springs 16 thus supplementing the resistance which the springs 10 and 18 offer to said weight, and serving to maintain the parts normally in the positions shown.

The above-described construction of fork-head and axle connections embodies therein the said shaft 6, substantially parallel with the axle 4, which shaft is so nearly of the same length as said axle that it constitutes such a lever-connection between said devices and the fork-head as gives the wheel to have what is termed a "twisting" motion or movement when the rider attempts quickly to change the direction of movement of the vehicle.

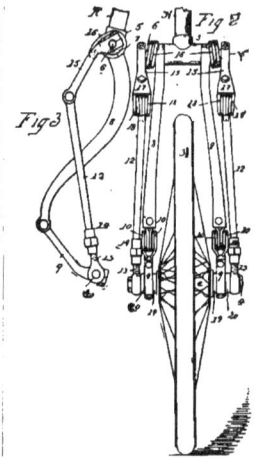

Fig. 2.

Fig. 3.

The above referred to modification of construction (illustrated in Fig. 3) consists in dispensing with the springs 10 and 18, and making, by suitable pivot or hinge connections, the ends of the arms 15 and posts 12, and the arms 9 and the legs 8, whereby said arms, posts and legs are permitted to have substantially the same action, as described, as they are capable of when said springs are employed, and the springs 16, under such conditions of construction, are made proportionately heavier to provide for the weight they must alone resist. The said leg 8, arm 9 and spring 10, and the post 12, the arm 15 and spring 18, constitute two sets of curved or angular arms (identical on each side of the wheel), each intermediately jointed, whether by springs or pivot connections, and so arranged in relation to each other, and to said axle 4 and shaft 6, as to form substantially a figure 8.

The nuts 14, connecting the lower ends of the posts 12 with the ends of the arms 13, provide means for adjusting said posts longitudinally and the springs 18. Aside from said adjusting feature, the post 12 and arm 13 may be made in one piece.

The above described spring-fork devices may be advantageously applied to both the front and the rear wheel of a bicycle, and when applied to the said rear wheel the rear end of the backbone is rigidly connected to the said part 5, in substantially the position of the broken-off post K.

TROY NOTES.

Last week I called on that "cyclist of cyclists," Will Gardner, a wheelman through and through, and owner and rider of twenty different wheels since he commenced to ride. Though only weighing about 100 lbs., yet he is one of the best road riders and hill climbers in the city. He rides a great deal, and is well posted in regard to the roads for miles around. A better league consul could not be found, and it seems queer he has not been chosen before this. I enjoyed a ride on his Premier Tandem Safety with him through Waterford, Cohoes and Lansingburg last Monday, but whether *he* enjoyed it or not I will not say, as it was my first attempt. The safety ran very nicely, both up and down hill and over the rough pavements, but when "Will" wanted to go one way and I the other, I felt as though I was going to get left. He did the steering and most of the work, I think, but he did not eat as much as I did when we sat down to the very enjoyable supper presided over by his kind wife. Mrs. Gardner was one of the first ladies to ride the tricycle in this section, and, I think, would make a good rider of the safety. After supper I was shown around their beautiful home, which contained electrical conveniences—some of them original—which were new to me. Sitting in the parlor or drawing-room, the push of a button or the pull of a cord commands light, heat and sound, and it will be a wonder if Will does not put an electric lamp and motor on his Columbia Light Roadster.

I dropped in the new rooms of the Trojan Wheelmen, over the Troy City Bank, and found them all one could wish for for social purposes. The four large rooms are well and nicely furnished—one of them containing billiard and pool tables—and are very pleasant, but the wheel is *minus*. Only about half a dozen wheels are owned by members and only two or three of those are ridden.

The Troy Bicycle Club is really the only wheel club here now, and the members seem more enthusiastic this year than last. Hope they will ride more this season, and try and induce the ladies to try the wheel too.

Since writing about the exorbitant charge for riding a wheel over Congress Street Bridge, I hear that a petition has been circulated among wheelmen to have the charge reduced to two cents, the regular toll. It is to be hoped that it will succeed, as it will pay the bridge company and greatly benefit the wheelmen.

It is a Col(c)d day when Herbert P. Cole gets left, for on Wednesday last he was married to the very pretty Miss Minnie Stewart, at her pleasant new home on Sixth Avenue. Rev. Dr. Maxey, of Christ Church, officiated, in the presence of about forty invited guests. The presents were many and useful, especially the patent oil stove, with illustrated instructions.

The only startling thing about the ceremony was the sound of a pistol shot when "Little" G. A. S. congratulated the bride.

After refreshments the bridal pair hurried to the 5:30 p. m. train for New York, carrying the usual amount of rice away with them.

Mr. and Mrs. H. P. Cole are both good riders of the wheel, and living some distance from the centre of the city, on a very ridable street, they ought to be able to profit by the use of a cycle.

The same evening Mr. Cole was married the Trojan Wheelmen held the last dance of the season at Harmony Hall, some sixty-five couples being present to enjoy an order of eighteen dances to the music of the Troy Orchestra.

I regret very much that a previous engagement made it impossible for me to accept the kind invitation offered by one of their members, but from all accounts everything passed off very nicely without me.

Among those present were Miss Hotchkins, Miss Anthony, Mrs. Lynd, Mrs. Zeph Magill, Mrs. Wm. L. Gardner, Miss Spencer, Miss Simpson, Miss Louise Crowley, Miss Mattie Townsend, Miss Carrie Johnson, Miss Bessie Clansing, Miss Van Alstyne, Miss Proctor, Miss Morris, Miss Mamie Connell, Miss Vandenburgh, Misses Lucy and Gertie Stande, Misses Grace and Mabel Priest, Miss Hattie French, Miss Mary Ball and Mrs. Harry Snyder.

Of the gentlemen, Wm. L. Gardner, Charles E. Wilson, F. E. Outhout, E. W. Wood, D. B. Boutecon, John McArthur, J. A. Hislop, E. R. Stephens, R. H. Van Alstyne, Zeph Magill, George Hallett, Thomas White, George Cavanaugh, Walter Lynd, Lewis Crowley, Samuel Magill, F. E. Lape, James Hyatt and Samuel Fowler.

The committees were: General—G. B. Friday, Harry Snyder and T. T. Chase. Floor—W. R. Curry, J. W. Stowe, R. Vandenburgh and T. T. Chase.

Chas. E. Wilson has again taken to the wheel and now rides a Safety.

Thursday evening last the Troy Bicycle Club gave their annual tournament at Bicycle Hall, and the room was crowded, the larger portion being of the fair sex—pretty girls (we have lots of them here) enjoying the daring feats of the athletes.

The R. P. I. Banjo Club rendered some fine music, which was loudly applauded, and the little son of George Buffington pleased the audience by a fine exhibition of club swinging. The bicycle drill, under Capt. Hanley, was very pretty; the horizontal bar and rings by Profs. Zahn and Rousseau were fine, and the contortions by Mr. Kennedy showed that he was flexible as a "busted" football. Messrs. Magill and Smith fought three rounds; Prof. Vandervere and J. E. Ryan gave a beautiful exhibition on the trapeze, and Mr. Starkweather "*foiled*" Mr. B. Herman.

Mr. L. Herman gave an excellent exhibition of club swinging; Prof. Secor balanced on a trapeze with a chair and ladder, and Capt. Hanley had a bout with Mr. Ginebra, of the R. P. I., ending in a draw after three rounds. Eddie Ellenwood's fancy riding elicited hearty applause, and he deserved it, for he is a very pretty rider. Profs. Zahn, Bose and Perkins pleased the large audience with their fine exhibition of strength and skill, and the tournament ended with a tug-of-war between the R. P. I. and the Bicycle, Club, the former winning in two successive pulls with ease their weight being 630 pounds for four persons.

It was a fine entertainment and might be repeated with success and pleasure.

Rev. Dr. Maxey, of Christ Church, is talking Safety, and it will do him good should he indulge.

Mrs. Joshua Reynolds is visiting her sister, Mrs. H. R. Mann, with her daughter and younger son. Miss Mary I. Reynolds has just received a Rover Ladies' Safety, which she is very anxious to learn to ride on, but cannot until she returns home.

Now is a good time to ride, as the country looks beautiful, the roads are very good and it is cool.

Get out your wheel instead of your spring medicine, and be happy.

Ornh Qba.

April 29, 1889.

ST. LOUIS.

We St. Louisians are enjoying the talk that is going on in the cycling world just now concerning the League Meet for this year, though, with all the invitations that President Luscomb is supposed to have sent out, we wonder why St. Louis has been slighted.

I cannot learn that any overtures have been made to our city to entertain the League this year. There has been a good deal said about the burdens that have been imposed on the different localities that have entertained the national meetings, in consequence of the lavish entertainments provided, and, if we are to believe all we hear, there is a loud call for more modest programs, so that, as the *Bi. World* has it, it would be "a pleasure to entertain and not a burden." When wheelmen conduct themselves as they did at the St. Louis meet, it could be nothing else than a pleasure to entertain them, but, I presume that the case might present itself in a different light if we had been treated with the shameless abuse of hospitality which characterized the behavior of some of the visitors at Baltimore last year. From a pecuniary point of view, I think this talk about "burdens" is just the least bit unreasonable. With the exception of St. Louis, which you were kind enough to say recently, "Climaxed with the most unique and well sustained entertainment, a reception it would be difficult to equal;" the meets for the last four years, at least, have not been money-losing affairs for the entertainers. Boston, Buffalo and Baltimore all made money. St. Louis had a surplus of $500.00 after all the bills were paid, and every dollar of it was turned over to the League, an example for which they had no precedent, and which we regret to say was not followed a year later at Baltimore. If President Luscomb desires to call the annual meeting here we will guarantee to furnish a hall, in which to transact the necessary business, and will pay the rent. We make this generous offer in spite of the slight shown us, and thus do we heap coals of fire on the heads of the Executive Committee.

The Citizen's Committee, at their meeting, Monday afternoon, appropriated $400.00 towards defraying the expenses of an illuminated parade on the night of the 30th inst., and in consequence of this tardy action we find ourselves face to face with a big undertaking, and less than a week to accomplish it in. Nevertheless, the boys have pitched in with characteristic vigor, and at a largely attended meeting, held Tuesday night, the preliminaries were arranged. President Lucas, of the Cycle Club, will be marshall, and the difficult duties of that office could not have fallen in better hands. Bob Holm is the Secretary, and the committee on arrangements comprises such workers as J. A. Lewis, A. L. Jordan and J. S. Keuhn. The difficulties in the way seem well nigh insurmountable—the time is so brief—but there is a determination to do the best we can under the circumstances, and if the parade is not the success that our citizens seem to anticipate, the blame must rest with their committee, which delayed the appropriation until so late a date, and not with the wheelmen.

The rumor comes to me that our crack racing man, Percy Stone, will join the ranks of the benedicts some time in June. The placing of the date after the races with Lumsden gives color to the additional rumor that the young lady in the case has made the winning of her hand conditional on his winning the series from Lumsden. If this be true, Lumsden will have to hump himself, for Percy has a larger prize at stake than the mere glory that his victory would bring him, or the medals that Bob Garden expects to pay for.

H. A. Lienhard, of the Pope Co., has been in the city for the past week, and will probably remain until an agency for the Columbia machines is established. He is interesting himself in the illuminated parade, and promises to turn out with something entirely novel.

Ithuriel.

THE SOUTH END WHEELMEN'S PUBLIC RECEPTION.

What was certainly the most elaborate affair that has yet taken place in cycling circles in this city occurred on Thursday evening, April 25, the occasion being the first bicycle and full dress reception of the South End Wheelmen. Unnecessary to say it was a glorious success in every particular, and too much credit cannot be given to the gentlemen who so faithfully served on the different committees and who worked so hard and unremittingly to make the ball a success. But if the sight of so many of their friends enjoying themselves to their hearts' content was any pleasure to them whatever, then they surely did not go wholly unrewarded, for not a person was there who could say they did not have a good time.

On entering St. George's Hall, where the reception was held, the eye was greeted by a profusion of flowers tastefully arranged and liberally entwined with the club colors, which are blue and white, large streamers of which hung from the chandeliers and walls in graceful folds, while over the stage hung the beautiful banner which was presented to the club last fall by their lady friends.

At precisely 9 o'clock the orchestra struck up the grand march (which, by the way, was composed especially for this occasion by Prof. D. C. Ferrazzi, introducing the club call, also bugle calls, &c.), and sixty couples, led by President S. J. Jackson, Jr., and wife, went through many intricate yet pleasing manœuvres, finally bringing up all facing the music, when the march suddenly melted into the strains of the soul stirring waltz from "Don Cæsar," and 100 lads and lasses tripped the light fantastic, formally opening the only public cyclists' ball ever given in Philadelphia.

About midnight T. R. Finley gave an exhibition of fancy riding on the "Star," beginning his performance by riding down a flight of stairs from the upper hall, much to the terror of the ladies. Then followed a number of feats which, to those who never saw "Tommy" ride, seemed an utter impossibility. When he was through he was presented with a beautiful gold badge, consisting of a wheel pierced by an arrow, the emblem of the S. E. W. Mr. F. gracefully acknowledged the gift and retired amid tremendous applause, the ladies present voting him too nice for anything and his riding just lovely.

Towards midnight there were fully 150 couples present, including representatives from all the clubs in this city, Camden, Wilmington, &c., a considerable number in their cycling costumes making a very pretty effect. Dancing was kept up until a late hour, but as everything must have an end, finally the last waltz, lights out, cab called—home.

For once the Blue and White owned the town.

Philadelphia, April 29, 1889. Argus.

NOTES FROM THE CITY OF BROTHERLY LOVE.

The wheelmen of Lansdowne—one of the pretty suburbs of our Quaker City—have organized a new bicycle club, which they call the Lansdowne Wheelmen. They have elected the following officers to serve for the ensuing year: President, W. C. Biddle; secretary and treasurer; R. Manley Miller; Captain, Frank Maris. They are all active men and strong riders. Mr. Biddle has hitherto confined his riding to the Star, but this year he expects to do considerable riding on a Tandem Safety, with Robert Biddle as mate. If you meet them look out, for in a scorch they will make a hard team to leave or to even hold on to.

John G. Fuller is entered for the Harvard races of May 11. He has done no riding at all up to present time, but promises to start in and work from now on. As he will evidently meet Brown, of Harvard, he has got to work or take a back seat.

Messrs. Draper and Taxis have started the century-run ball rolling, having covered 107 miles a few days since. They happened to pick out a good, warm day, which showed itself by presenting the riders with a good coat of tan—a regular sea-shore hue.

The Pennsylvania Bicycle Club has, through the kindness of George D. Gideon, been presented with a very handsome crayon portrait of their late member, Samuel Gideon. The picture represents our former friend and club-mate standing in riding costume. It is a very good likeness.

On Sunday last both the South End Wheelmen and the Pennsylvania Bicycle Club had arranged to go to Norristown. Fortunately Old Probabilities forbid. I say fortunately, as there would most certainly have been a scorch between the two clubs on their ride home, and I must confess that, with a good many others, I am not particularly stuck on Sunday impromptu road races. They certainly do the sport no good, and hurt the clubs more or less. I think, for my part, that it would be better to have this club rivalry settled some other way than as first proposed.

On Thursday evening, April 25, the Pennsylvania Bicycle Club and South End Wheelmen both wound up their social season, the former with a ball at their spacious club house, the latter with a ball at St. George's Hall. I had the pleasure of attending the Pennsy dance, and most assuredly had a delightful time, as every one present seemed to, and the only complaint that was made was when those present found that it was time to go home. Then the fleet-footed time was bitterly complained of.

By the way Pensy has been found out. Well, poor fellow, he did get his foot into the mire once or twice, without intention, of course, as I believe he had no intention of causing any bad feeling by any of his remarks; but I likewise hope that he intends to adopt new tactics, and I believe that his notes will then be read with interest by all.

On Friday evening, May 3, the Philadelphia Bicycle Club will give a full-dress sociable at their club house, Twenty-third and Perot. As this is the last of a very pleasant series, an enjoyable evening is sure to be passed by all who attend.

On Tuesday, April 30, a tandem party from the Pennsylvania Bicycle Club, under charge of First Lieut. Charles L. Leisen will ride to Wayne. The party, consisting of fifteen couple, will leave the club house not later than 10 A. M., go to the Bellevue at Wayne for dinner, and riding home late in the afternoon.

Westfield.

BIRMINGHAM, ALABAMA.

Bicycling here is growing steadily but slowly. Our roads and streets are yearly being improved, and in a few years they will compare favorably with the streets of much older cities. The assessable property of Jefferson County (the county in which Birmingham is situated), is $35,000,000. A special tax of ten per cent. is levied on this for road improvement within the county only. That gives $35,000 a year. In addition to this, the labor of the county convicts is devoted exclusively to the improvement of the roads. There are already between forty and fifty miles of macadam in this county. In each of the thirty-eight Precincts in the county, there are three road supervisors, whose business it is to see that each male between the ages of eighteen and forty-five works six days during the year on the road, or pays in lieu thereof $3. Your correspondent is indebted to Judge M. T. Porter, one of the County Commissioners, for the foregoing information. The city engineer tells me that about $50,000 will be expended in the city this year for paving the streets, and about $25,000 for macadam.

Your Macon, Ga., correspondent was considerably "off" in including Chattanooga, Jacksonville and Anniston among the Georgia cities which had raised large amounts for street improvement. Nearly every one knows where Chattanooga is, while Jacksonville and Anniston are in Alabama.

A party of wheelmen from Columbus, Ga., with Mr. T. L. Ingram as their Koko, are arranging for a tour from Columbus to this city, from here to Anniston (60 miles), thence to Gadsden, to Guntersville, to Decatur, Athens, Huntsville, and winding up at Chattanooga. The trip will occupy about two weeks, and the greater part of it will be through the Northern or mountainous part of Alabama.

It is bad enough, Mr. Editor, to have the South misrepresented by partisan political papers, and misrepresentations of that kind are certainly not within the province of a bicycle paper. Yet a party, calling himself "Jack," in the *Bicycling World*, and once hailing from a Southern State, in order possibly to gain a cheap kind of popularity, has a mean fling at the State of Mississippi, about its shootings and hangings. He winds up his attempt at wit about "necktie parties," "dances at the end of a short rope," etc., by referring to the South as "dear old Dixie." If "dear old Dixie" could transport all of his ilk, it would tend to a much better understanding between the different sections of the country. This is the same party who writes such newsy, brilliant letters, according to the *Bicycling World*, that they had an editorial congratulating their readers on having secured his facile pen and ready wit.

The first of the dwarf safeties that has made its appearance here is an American Rambler, which attracts a good deal of attention, where only the ordinary has been seen heretofore. Stars, Columbias and Victors predominate in this region; but it is a matter of time only before the little safety will be in general use, except among small boys.

Lytate.

MARYLAND.

THE LEAGUE MEET.

The following is a copy of a letter from President Luscomb to Mr. Albert Mott, Chief Consul Maryland Division, L. A. W., which will explain itself:

OFFICE EXECUTIVE COMMITTEE,
280 Broadway, New York,
April 23, 1889.

DEAR MR. MOTT.—The Executive Committee, after careful consideration of your cordial invitation to hold the League Meet of 1889 at Hagerstown, under the auspices of the Maryland Division, has decided to accept the invitation, and names Hagerstown and July 2d, 3d and 4th as the time and place of the meet.

In full appreciation of the fraternal warmth of your response to my inquiry as to the desire of your members for the annual gathering of the L. A. W. two years in succession, I beg you will consider most carefully the departure from the line of previous meetings, intimated in my letter of inquiry, upon the matters of expense and costly entertainment.

In the judgment of the present administration, it is a mistaken principle that the national meeting should be a financial burden and drain upon resident members, who give in addition, their time and attention to the reception and care of the visitors.

Wheeling independence dictates that every man should pay his own way, and I am most solicitous that you should have this idea as firmly imbedded in the minds of your members as I shall endeavor to impress it upon the minds of the membership at large, in the general notice to the League of the acceptance of your invitation and the announcement of the meet of 1889.

I am very desirous of full conference with you upon the new departure in the method and character of our annual meets, and hope to have frequent discussion with you upon the possibility of making this meet a pleasure without a burden, and a gathering which shall be of substantial advantage to our members from which they shall derive material benefit.

Expressing to you and the Division, the pleasure of the Executive Committee, at your loyal and immediate recognition of the interests of the L. A. W., and your desire to assist it, I am yours fraternally,

CHARLES H. LUSCOMB,
President L. A. W.

ALBERT MOTT, Esq.,
Chief Consul Maryland Div. L. A. W.

The Hagerstown Club were jubilant when they received the notice that the fifth annual League Meet had been ordered for Hagerstown, to take place on the 2d, 3d and 4th of July. The first meet was held in Boston, and subsequently and in rotation in St. Louis, Washington and Baltimore. Hagerstown is next, and comes near to the front, for two reasons: First, because of its admirable facilities for the accommodation of such a gathering, and secondly for the purpose of establishing a precedent for the control of future meets. Heretofore it has cost the local wheelmen thousands of dollars to entertain their guests at these meets. The custom became burdensome to such an extent—each community endeavoring to outrival the preceding host—that everybody fought shy of the honor of securing the next annual gathering, and nobody could be found, willing to try the new rule of inviting the distinguished guests to pay for what they got, until the Hagerstown Club stepped forward.

It was thought by many that Washington, D. C., would be the place of the League meet this year. There are several reasons for their not undertaking it this year. In the first place the Capital Club, which is the largest club there, is not a member of the League, which has such a small following in the District that the members could not bear the expense of the meet. It is certain that the reception in July will be creditable to both community and club. Daylight and night parades, moonlight excursions to Pen-Mar, way up in the altitudes of the picturesque Blue Ride Mountains, races, entertainments at night, tours on the many elegant pikes surrounding Hagerstown, where many historic and picturesque points can be reached without any exertion whatever. The programme is in course of preparation, and will certainly be novel and entertaining. The Hagerstown meet will in no case be the least in importance, satisfaction and magnitude of the several that have preceded it.

The past week very little cycling was done, owing to the rainy weather which was prevailing and the bad condition the roads were in.

The Crescent Club gave an enjoyable hop and reception, Friday, April 26, at their club-house situated on North avenue, it being the opening of their cozy club-house. About eighty odd guests were present. The building is new and of ample size for the present needs of the club. The elaborate supper and dancing, which continued nearly all night, was very much enjoyed by all who were present. The president of the club, C. F. Hanson, was presented with a handsome diamond ring by Mr. Lloyd, on behalf of the club.

H. L. Kingsland left for Chicago on Wednesday, May 1. He is entered in fourteen events. Mr. S. T. Clark, who will return from England shortly, will bring with him Kingsland's New Rapid Safety and ordinary racers. Kingsland will ride under the colors of the Manhattan Athletic Club. From Chicago he will go to Woodstock, Ont., for the races of May 24, and will spend a week at that place.

BAY RIDGE.

AROUND THE HUB.

The annual dinner of the Chelsea Cycle Club will be held at Young's Hotel this Friday evening.

At the annual meeting of the Chelsea Cycle Club, held April 26, these officers were elected: Charles E. Walker, president; C. M. Gibbs, vice-president; W. S. Fracker, secretary and treasurer; A. E. Bailey, captain, and J. R. Barrie.

Capt. Benson of Dorchester Club will try and lower the 25-mile Safety record made by him during one of the Eastern Road Club races.

A large and brilliant audience gathered in Association Hall, Charlestown, last Thursday evening, on the occasion of the annual minstrel show of the Rovers' Cycle Club, and liberally applauded the efforts of the charcoaled riders. The programme was gotten up in unique style. The entertainment opened with the regulation semi-circle, and the four end men kept the assemblage in a continual roar of laughter by their many local "gags," while some fine songs were contributed by the graver members of the company. E. H. Glose was just about to spring his best "gag" when a bouquet of flowers, around which were fastened black and orange ribbon, was handed over the footlights to Interlocuter Tom Hall, and he received them in behalf of the club, to which it was presented by a delegation from the Cambridge Bicycle Club. The second part of the programme consisted of humorous humorosities by Mr. F. G. Reynolds; a few minutes with Mr. Walter E. Stone; burlesque magic by Mr. E. W. Emerson; Messrs. Reynolds and Emerson in their "living pictures." After the show the members of the club, together with their invited guests, adjourned to the Waverley House, where a collation was served to the tired minstrel cyclists.

BROOKLYN NEWS.

The closing ladies' reception of the season was given last night by the Long Islands. It was a fitting event to close the festivities of the winter season, as it was perfectly managed and successfully carried through. The entire club-house was beautifully decorated with flags, bunting, fancy and artistic lanterns, and a profusion of flowers and plants most beautifully arranged in all available places. The house was thronged with members and their fair friends, and the ladies could scarcely find sufficient words to express their appreciation of the social side of cycling, as demonstrated by the L. I. W.

The Kings Countys will have their final stag racket on Wednesday, May 8. It is in the hands of a most competent committee, and will undoubtedly go through with a rush.

The K. C. W. will send some fifteen men to Philadelphia on the great century run of 1889. The number will include Murphy and Beasley and the two Halls on tandem safeties. The L. I. W. expect to send about twelve men on the run.

Wise and Schumacher, L. I. W., are expected to enter in the 25-mile road race to be held on the Irvington-Milburn course on Decoration Day.

Speaking of racing calls to mind the new racer of "Miles" Murphy. The wheel in question has the most extraordinary handle-bars I have yet seen, and I am at a loss to give a name to the shape which they assume. The boys have dubbed him "Bars" Murphy since the advent of said wheel.

The K. C. W. had a meeting on Monday, April 22, to form a couple of base ball nines from the enthusiasts on the game who are members of the club. The two nines will informally do each other up during the coming summer season.

Regular Saturday afternoon short runs are bulletined for the L. I. W. and the B. B. C. until further notice is given the two clubs.

The Brooklyns moved into their new house last Saturday, and their house committee are working the superfluous flesh off their bones in getting the house to rights. Builders will commence work immediately on the additions which the club will build, and everything is expected to be in shipshape order by the middle of June.

ATOL.

Brooklyn, April 30, 1889.

PROVIDENCE.

The spring all-day run Bostonwards of the Rhode Island Wheelmen is fixed for Monday, May 20. A straight course has been laid out, twenty-one miles from Sharon into Boston. Dinner will be had at the Clarendon at 1, and thereafter the party is at liberty to break up, although the main body will probably take an excursion over the new boulevard to Chestnut Hill Reservoir.

Will Windle's father, who runs down to this city several times a week, is authority for the statement that the wonder of last season will race again this year. Windle is in splendid condition and proposes to enter the R. I. W. races at Narragansett Park, Memorial Day.

Things are progressing for the R. I. Wheelmen's big cycle and athletic tournament at Narragansett Park, Memorial Day, as rapidly as possible at this early day, and the various committees are actively laying their wires. The tournament will be opened at one o'clock in the afternoon by a foot ball game between the British Hosiery team and the Providence F. B. Club's eleven, matched for elegant silver medals, one for each member of the winning team. For all classes of out-of-door athletics that have representatives in Rhode Island and vicinity the tournament will offer an opportunity that has never before been afforded in the State. The cycle events will be sandwiched in the usual tedious waiting places by foot races, horsemanship exhibitions and other sports, and the day promises to be memorable in the annals of field sports in this State. Especial arrangements will be made for adequate steam and horse car service to the grounds.

BUFFALO.

Sunday's rain spoiled many contemplated tours to surrounding towns. The Ramblers were to have gone to Hamburg, the Zig-Zags to Batavia and other parties for the Falls of Niagara and adjoining places had to be abandoned.

The Buffalos will take their first out-of-town run to Alden on the 30th. Games of baseball and football will be indulged in, and the return will be by way of Bomansville.

The old drill corps of the Buffalos is to be revived, and some fancy drilling may be expected before long. The "old eight" had no superiors and but few equals in this part of the State.

Chief Consul Bull is doing good work for the L. A. W. Many recruits to the League attest to his faithfulness and energy.

The Buffalos propose to make the run of 100 miles from Erie an annual event. Out of twenty-eight starters last Decoration Day twenty-three made the run. This is a feat that has not been equalled by any club in the country.

Gus C. Miller has taken to the wheel and joined the Zig-Zags. He holds the ninety-pound boxing championship of the city, and pitched for the Athletic Baseball Club last year.

All wheelmen of Buffalo and vicinity who send their names to Consul W. S. Bull, 754 Main Street, will receive a neat little volume containing the L. A. W. by-laws and other valuable information to wheelmen. Mr. Bull has in hand the revision of the New York State Road Book. A record-book will be placed in every League Hotel, and wheelmen who stop at such are earnestly requested to enter therein any information which they may be able to give.

ZO.

JACK'S JOTTINGS.

FROM THE HUB.

The writer had the pleasure of meeting at "Ye Towne Clubbe" (Yclept The Boston Bicycle Club), Mr. H. G. Priest, of the Quadrant Cycle Co., of Birmingham, England. Mr. Priest reports "good business" in both safeties and tricycles. He is somewhere on the way to Assiniboine in Western Canada and will take steamer for England about May 18. Mr. Priest is a member of the Speedwell Bicycle Club. He is now Member of Parliament for the district of Manhattan, having been carried by a large majority. The writer hopes to meet this gentleman again, either on this American continent or at next year's Stanley Sho'.

"Gold Seal" and "Pommery" were circulating freely when first I clapped my eyes on "Papa" Weston—Mr. Frank W. Weston.

The musicianly voices of the trained-impromptu choir of "Ye Towne Clubbe" were singing their evening hymn, and a dim religious light pervaded the cycling-sanctuary. With hands aloft and eyes heavenward, the chant is repeated (to "hoodoo" microbes and molecular imperfections perhaps). "God bless you, my children!" said "Papa," the father of all, to the bearded ones gathered lovingly around him. "The same to you," said Editor Fourdrinier, as he remarked that it was "fruity;" but this I could not understand (as I was always averse to potations). And so I was tendered the privileges of "Ye Towne Clubbe" by "Papa" who said he'd add me to his family and keep an eye on me.

Editor Fourdrinier is a gentleman whose quality makes up for his quantity. Not unlike Tommy Moore of the *Cycle News*, England, in appearance, with fine silken hair that is tinged with silvery touches—the result of sleeplessness occasioned by the worries of the Amateur rule. A meandering dark-brown mustache, that twitches by the agency of a sensitive but firm mouth when he laughs, gives a French piquancy to his dark face, but the 'tache has not the overwhelming proportions which gives Tommy Moore such a top-heavy appearance. A pair of merry brown eyes that twinkle, and a finely cut nose with perceptive nostrils of the Thomas Bailey Aldrich type, completes the impression.

Put an impertinent communication from some impudent Western lout in this little man's hand and you'll be likely to hear some sarcasm dictated to the stenographer that will have its effect if its subtle meanings are completely understood by the fat-headed recipient. (When a man has a roll of fat on his brain he does not shine, as a rule.)

Bert Owen, of the Capital Cycle Co., of Washington, D. C., has got an excellent looking safety frame, as per the cut in last week's WHEEL. It has many good points. The gentleman roomed next door to me at "Brown's" in Dover Street, Piccadilly, but I did not see him much.

Charles M. Richards, of the Warren Street, New York, branch of the Pope Mfg. Co., is the best natured man in the cycle trade. A perpetual smile wreaths his upper lip and mingles with the hirsute adornment thereon displayed, which is going to make its presence felt some day.

Of course, I called and saw Col. Pope, in Boston, and had lunch with him. Ever full of business, he has the interests of the riders at heart. A good place for a cycle scribe is their headquarters in Boston and much news may be picked up. Charles S. Howard, of the *Globe*, is a regular visitor, and Kerrison, or "Kerry," of the *Herald*, drops in also. I met such notables as Mr. E. W. Pope, the Secretary; Mr. Chas. E. Pratt, the counsellor; Mr. Lester E. Hickok, well-known to the boys on the road; Mr. N. C. Fowler, Jr., who looks after the "ads," and others.

I took a trip a few days ago to Westboro, Mass., and saw the new White Cycle safety, which, mark me, shall be heard from yet. The Company have a very perfect factory, where interchangeable parts can be made with absolute accuracy. The machines will soon be on the market. The roads around Westboro are fairly good, but a trifle sandy.

C. R. Overman is believed to be in Washington, D. C., on business, so he was out when I called. Theodore Rothe and W. C. Overman were holding the fort.

Next door to them the Springfield Bicycle Co. have hung out their shingle, and Mr. J Ruggles Weld, Jr.; Herbert Barrows and F. S. Hodgman are busy talking about their machine.

Had a good chat with Wm. L. Ross, Singer & Co.'s American Manager. This gentleman took me down and showed me the enameling furnace where he so narrowly escaped being atomized. This place is a dangerous place anyway, for not long ago some boys, in an adjoining store, were shooting a big-bore pistol, and the lath and plaster intervening did not stop the bullet which crashed right through the workshop and stuck in the opposite wall. Had it not been dinner time some of the workmen would have had a close shave, as the line of the bullet's flight was only a foot or so from their work-bench in front of which they would have been working. So there's an uncanny air about the place. Still Mr. Ross says he has much to be thankful for, that he might have been riding a hand-pump "Velociman," or wearing glass eyes to see to write with. Some people are always contented, others would grumble if they were going to be hung.

"JACK."

TACOMA, WASHINGTON.

Cycling is still on the boom. Several wheels have been sold the past week, and the novices are all doing well.

Mr. Ed. Adams, of the Bay City Wheelman, San Francisco, is in town. Mr. Adams is the champion amateur fancy rider of the Pacific coast.

Last week was very favorable for cycling, and the boys availed themselves of the opportunity to commence preparations for the coming road race.

It has not yet been fully decided whether the bicycle race shall be held prior to the grand sculling race, May 18th, or afterwards. The month of May will be full of excitement in this part of the new State of Washington. The city election, May 9th. The boat race the 18th. The celebration of the Queen's (of England) birthday on the 24th at Victoria, British Columbia, when there will be bicycle races, &c. And last, but not least, the 20-mile champi nship road race upon a day yet to be named. Who says we are asleep?

Up to the present time we have had little or no trouble with "Road Hogs," until Saturday last, when a "fly" coachman tried to run over Halsted and Adams. The driver was going to make short work of the crowd of "Dudes," but suddenly changed his mind. Any action on the part of "Road Hogs" to abuse or intimidate cyclers will be taken note of, and the offenders dealt with according to law, or otherwise.

On Saturday seven of the boys rode out to Steilacoom. The party was composed of Thompson, Barlow, Adams, of San Francisco, McCoy, Halsted, Hayes and Rainey. When they reached the Prairie roads, a regular "Scorch" was commenced and kept up to the asylum, resulting in a win for Halsted and Thompson, with Barlow a close third. 'Tis rumored that the road race, however, will see some changes in this order.

One of the most comical occurrences that have been recorded in the annals of Tacoma cycling, was witnessed during this run, just before the party reached their destination. Ed. Barlow started down a hilly road, on one side of which was a deep ditch, and the other side a high fence. He had gotten a good "move on him," and was midway down the hill, when a mellow-eyed cow started in hot pursuit of the 1st Lieut., brave and indomitable as he is. A shout from his companions warned Barlow of the impending calamity, and when he saw his predicament, he put on more steam to get out of harm's way. The others followed up the bovine, which only tended to frighten the animal the more. It was surely a race for life, and fortunately our worthy officer reached a level road in time to speed away, but not until the ferociously poised horns of bossy were within a few inches of Barlow's spinal column. 'Twas Ed.'s treat, sure, and all drank his health.

To emphasize my assertion that cycling is now enjoying a healthful boom, I might also state that the kids of Tacoma are procuring wheels, and they make very apt scholars. The boys of the club take a fatherly interest in most of the kids, and take pleasure in teaching the youngsters the numerous mounts and other tricks.

An invitation has just been received by the Tacoma Bicycle Club from the young ladies of Lakeview to attend a May party next week. They boys are wanted early in the afternoon to take part in the lawn exercises. And they are to participate in the dancing and collation in the evening. Full club uniforms are to be worn. But what show will we unfortunate ones have with the fair girls, if Brackett, Howell, Stiers and Manning are there? O, that I had comeliness instead of riches!

We expect to have a goodly number of the Seattle Club members visit us the day of the 20-mile road race. And probably several of the Seattleites will enter the contest.

The proposed bicycle and athletic track bids fair to be a certainty. If final arrangements can be made in due season, and the track put in shape, Prince Wells will attempt to eclipse all records on unicycle for one hour. He holds the first and only record for this style of riding without a dismount.

We are glad to hear that Manning received no serious injuries when he took his header a few days ago. He looks "all broke up," but the bright smiles of his many young lady visitors has had a great deal to do with his steady recuperation. We hope soon to see his bright face on the road.

SNOHOMISH.

Entries for Twelfth Regiment bicycle races close May 4, to-morrow, with C. J. Leach, P. O. Box 3201, N. Y. City.

NEW HAVEN.

The New Haven Club enjoyed a parade and a club run on Fast Day. The parade was held in the morning, and the run in the afternoon. The boys rode to Branford Point, where they dined and played a game of ball, two nines picked from among the club members played a match game.

Messrs. Backus, Picket and Verhoff wheeled to Boston last week. They spent three days wheeling about the Hub, and report a very pleasant trip.

The riding season has opened promisingly here, with so big a demand for Safeties that orders cannot be filled on some makes. One of the newest things in town is a Columbia Tandem Trike, ridden by Messrs. Sperry & Welton. Backus rides an "Eagle," which he claims gives him more speed and hill-climbing power than any previous mount. Mr. Clarke, of the Eagle Co., was here several days ago, and climbed several of our steepest hills to show the hill-climbing qualities of the Eagle.

Palmer Freleck, one of our most daring riders, rode half way up a toboggan slide on a 54 inch Expert, dismounted, and coasted down. The coast was about 100 feet. We expect to hold a grand tournament here next Fall.

"ELM CITY."

FIXTURES.

May 4, 1889.—Titan Athletic Club Games. Two-mile Bicycle Handicap. Entries close April 27, with A. Surcott, 361 Broadway, New York.

May 10, 1889.—Twelfth Regiment Games. Entries close May 4 with C. J. Leach, P. O. Box 3,201.

May 11, 1889.—Harvard Bicycle Club Open Amateur Race Meet at Cambridge, Mass. Entries close May 4. Address R. H. Davis, Cambridge, Mass.

May 13-18, 1889.—Chicago Cycling Exhibit and Tournament, Exposition Building.

May 18, 1889.—F. A. Elwell's European Party sails from New York.

May 18, 1889.—Stone-Lumsden 1-mile Match Race, at Chicago, Ill.

May 18, 1889.—Staten Island Athletic Club's Games at New Brighton, S. I. Two-mile Bicycle Race.

May 22, 1889.—N. J. A. C. Games at Bergen Point, N. J. Three-mile Bicycle Handicap. Entries close May 22, with A. M. Stout, Box 262, Bergen Point, N. J.

May 25, 1889.—Stone-Lumsden 3-mile Match Race, at St. Louis, Mo.

May 27, 1889.—Stone-Lumsden 25-mile Match Race at Crawfordsville, Ind.

May 30, 1889.—N J. A. C. 1½ mile handicap. Entries close May 22, with A. M. Sweet, P. O. Box 262, Bergen Point, N. J.

May 30, 1889.—Maine Division Meet at Biddeford, Me

May 30, 1889.—Bicycle and Athletic Tournament and 2-mile L. A. W. Championship Race at Narragansett Park.

May 30, 1889.—Pullman Road Race, Chicago to Pullman.

May 30, 1889.—Twenty-five-mile Handicap Road Race, Irvington, Milburn course Entrees close May 15th with A. B. Barkman, 241 Broadway, New York.

May 30, 1889.—Rhode Island Wheelman's Race Meet at Narragansett Park, Providence, R. I. Entrees close with C. E. Campbell, Providence, R. I.

June 4, 5, 6, 1889.—Kansas Division Meet at Forest Park, Ottawa, Kansas.

June 8, 1889.—Century Run, Orange, N. J., to Philadelphia. Chairman, L. A. Clarke, 23 Broad Street, New York.

June 15, 1889.—L. A. W. Race Meet at Brooklyn Athletic Club Grounds.

June 15, 1889.—Two-mile Bicycle Handicap at New York Athletic Club Grounds, Travers Island.

July 2, 3, 4, 1889.—League Meet at Hagerstown, Md.

July 4, 1889.—Race Meet at Brownsville, Pa.

July 20, 1889.—One-mile and 25-mile Bicycle and 5-mile Tricycle N. C. C. championships at Paddington, Eng., race track.

July 27, 1889.—One-mile and 25-mile Tricycle and 5-mile Bicycle N. C. U. Championships at Paddington, Eng., track.

THE CHICAGO TOURNAMENT.

A 100-mile race has been added to the programme already announced, for which ten entries are assured. These will include Bert Myers, of Peoria, Alec Lewis, of St. Louis, two Omaha men, and Mason, Riggs, Hammel, Spooner and Van Sicklen of Chicago.

This event will occur on Thursday, May 16, starting at 2:30 P. M. It is open to both safety and ordinary wheels weighing thirty-five pounds or over. Entries will be received up to May 14, the fee being $1.

The short amateur races will commence at 8 o'clock each evening.

Arrangements have been made hy the Reception Committee to have two representatives at headquarters (Palmer House) during the entire week. Visitors desiring information on any subject can obtain it there. The club room at the hotel will always be open for the exclusive use of wheelmen, and mail matter addressed there will receive careful attention. A large store-room has been set apart for wheels.

Parties coming from a distance who notify the management in advance will be met at depot.

The most desirable hotels, with their special rates for the occasion are: Palmer House, $2.50 per day; Grand Pacific, $2.50 to $3.50; Tremont, $2.50 to $4; Briggs, $2; Continental, $1.50 to $2; Commercial, $1.50 to $2. European plan: Palmer House, 75 cents per day; Windsor Hotel, 75 cents per day; Kuhn's 75 cents per day.

All of these houses are within easy distance of the building and the boulevards. There are scores of others within easy reach, and this list is given as being the houses most frequented by wheelmen.

At headquarters a list of desirable boarding-houses and furnished rooms, with prices, will be found.

It is estimated that at least 1,500 visitors will be in attendance. Address communications, S. A. Miles, 199 S. Clark st.

DRAMATIC SITUATIONS AT A SIX-DAY BICYCLE RACE FOR FEMALES.

We take no notice of these contests deeming them hurtful to Cycling, but the following is not only rich, but it justifies our policy of contemptuous silence.

Two thousand men were craning their necks and shouting at the female bicyclists as they sped like the wind around the track in Battery "D" last night. It was the last night of the race. Interest was beginning to run high, though it was only 8:30 o'clock and the riders had two hours before them.

Suddenly an excited man dived under the railing which separated the spectators from the track. He thrust his cane between the spokes of Miss Jessie Oaks' wheel. It was going at the rate of 15 miles an hour. A gasp went up from those who saw her danger.

Click, click, click, b-u-r-r-r went the cane on the spokes, and Miss Oaks was spinning safely on.

Then the spectators raised a cry of indignation at the man who had attempted to stop the rider. Thomas W. Eck, manager of the tournament, snatched the man from the track, knocked him over the head, then as many men as could get at him fell upon him and cuffed and kicked him from the hall. When he picked himself up on the sidewalk, bruised, broke and bloody, he was heard to say:

"In all my 22 years experience as a constable this is the first time I've been treated this way."

But it was the first time also that Constable Scanlon had ever tried to stop a female bicyclist in the presence of her admirers. He had chosen this novel way to levy on the box receipts of the show to satisfy a writ for $600 from the John Wilkinson Bicycling Company.

The humorous side of the incident was that while Mr. Eck was leading his gallant hosts in the assault on Scanlon, Mrs. Eck, divining the object of the constable's visit, had raked the receipts into her hand-satchel and gone to her hotel. Constable Scanlon eventually secured $3 from late comers, along with the arrest of Lew Munger, supposed by the constable to be one of his assailants.—*Tribune.*

S. G. Whittaker arrived in New York, by the Aurania, on Tuesday morning. He left in the evening for Boston where he will remain until Friday, when he will return to New York. He will very likely go on the road for the Gormully & Jeffery Mfg. Co.

Howell, the English professional champion and Synyer, the English amateur champion, competed at North Shields on April 6. Howell was not placed in the two mile professional handicap, but Synyer won the mile handicap from scratch, doing 2m. 58 4-5s.

At the N. J. A. C. games to be held at Bergen Point, May 30, at 2 P. M., a 1½-mile bicycle handicap, open to amateurs, will be decided. Entrance fee 50 cents. Entries close May 22 with A. M. Sweet, P. O. Box 262, Bergen Point, N. J.

The cross-country championship contest will be held at Fleetwood Park to-morrow, Saturday afternoon at 4 o'clock. Train leaves 42d St. depot at 3:27. The entries and handicaps for the three mile bicycle handicap are as follows: Klugs, scratch; Schoefer, 50 yards; F. G. Brown, 90; Baggott, 100; Hanson, 175; Steves, 225; Muller, 225; Preyer, 225; Powers, 250; Findley, 250.

The games of the Twelfth Regiment Athletic Association will be held Friday evening, May 10, at their Armory, Sixty-second street and Ninth avenue. There are two bicycle events on the programme, a 2-mile handicap and a mile scratch for novices.

Dan Canary arrived in Gotham on Thursday last. Mr. Canary is a pleasant-faced, intelligent man, of about twenty-four years. He was a telegraph operator at Meriden, Conn., but developed ability as a fancy rider when about eighteen years of age. His first attempts were made on a home-made wheel, but so clever did he become that the public discovered him and he became a professional trick rider, originating that school of riding. He was a feature at Springfield and Hartford, and after the Hartford meet of '85 he invaded England and the Continent, and was a distinct success. Canary's performances were regarded as marvels of grace and skill. His weight, 130, permitted him to be peculiarly cat-like in his movements, and his forte is rapidity, lightness and grace. He appeared only at the best theatres abroad, and invariably received his own price for his services. Canary will sail on May 11, as he opens on May 20 at Southampton, Eng. He will be at Paris during the summer. He is accompanied by his wife and his two children.

Miss Hodgman, of Boston Highlands, is one of the most enthusiastic bicycle riders. She rides a Singer's Ladies' Safety.

TWENTY-FIVE MILE ROAD RACE.

In response to a letter sent by A. B. Barkman to representatives of the various local clubs a number of cyclists met at the Knickerbocker Cottage on Thursday evening last to discuss the details of the road race. The men present were: A. B. Barkman and W. E. Fuller, Brooklyn Club; M. L. Bridgman and T. C. Critchton, Kings County Wheelmen; William Halpin and Chas. A. Sheehan, Manhattan Club, and Jos. McFadden and F. P. Prial, New York Club.

Mr. A. B. Barkman was elected chairman and F. P. Prial secretary of the meeting. On motion, it was decided to place the management of the race in the hands of a committee of seven, composed of Messrs. Barkman, Bridgman, DeGraaf, Fuller, McFadden, Halpin and Prial, who constitute a permanent committee of arrangements. The permanent committee will meet at the office of THE WHEEL this evening and appoint sub-committees, the chairman of each sub-committee being a member of the permanent committee.

Chairman Barkman reported that a number of valuable prizes had already been contributed and that other prizes had been promised. The evening was spent in discussing the arrangements, and suggestions were made and noted down by the secretary for the benefit of the permanent committee. A summary of these rules is as follows:

The race will be a 25-mile handicap, open to all amateur wheelmen, ex-professionals and expromateurs being barred.

The officers of the race will be a referee, seven judges, five time-keepers, a starter, a clerk of course and assistants, and as many scorers and umpires as may be found necessary. All protests made before the race will be referred to the permanent committee. All protests during the race and immediately after its conclusion will be decided by the referee. There will be three judges at the finish and two at each turn. The umpires will be placed at convenient points along the course and will report to the referee any violation of the rules.

Competitors must be at the tape and ready to start promptly at the appointed time. No man will be allowed to compete without a number. The start will be stand-still, from a push-off. Under no circumstances will there be a recall after the first man has started. Men who are too late to start with their class may start with the first group that is sent off. **The race will be started at 11 a.m., sharp.**

The law of the road shall be strictly observed, and any contestant causing a foul shall be disqualified. No side paths shall be taken. Contestants may change machines, but may not make any progress except on a wheel. Any rider who consents to have the pace made for him will be disqualified.

The race will be handicapped by John C. Wetmore, A. B. Barkman and F. P. Prial.

PSYCHE ON LADIES' CYCLING.

EDITOR OF THE WHEEL:

I see that the *Nashville American* was so kind as to copy part of one of my letters to you, but in so doing has made a mistake.

It says that I assert the three mounts of which I give a description can be learned in an hour. Far from this, I am quite sure that it is next to impossible to become mistress of these three mounts in as many days. I don't see the object of misrepresenting the difficulties of cycling. If a neophyte comes to the struggle expecting to accomplish the feat without any particular effort it is very discouraging to find that days and weeks stretch out before her before she can step on her wheel and glide off as the older rider does. She is apt to think herself a monument of stupidity, and the tendency is to discourage the would-be rider to the extent of giving up in despair. Bicycling needs perseverance, patience and good sense, and when at last the art is mastered it will repay the toiler a hundred times for the, after all, insignificant time and trouble expended.

Sterling Elliott, in the *Bicycling World*, seems to be another Easterner persecuted by dogs. What is the matter with the New England dogs any way? Is it bicycles that they so rootedly object to, or are the New England wheelmen and women more tempting to the canine taste? Fresher, perhaps. I have been making inquiries among my different friends hereabouts, and no one seems to have been bothered at all. Mr. Elliott might try a tricycle. Miss Grey finds it works on her section of dogs.

Miss Grey has evidently a weakness for tricycles. She brings forward another argument in support of them in this last issue of the *Bi. World*. They are going to be cheap. Superseded articles generally are. The great American public knows a good thing when it sees it, and the demand for ladies' bicycles, though small at present, has a growing feature about it that the wide-awake dealer recognizes and in consequence he begins to unload as rapidly as possible.

Miss Grey thinks the manufacturer has not done all that he can for feminine humanity's comfort in the way of tricycles. She should recognize the ladies' bicycle as the logical outcome of their efforts for femininity's comfort. As for the hope she expresses that the weight of tricycles may be reduced to 30 pounds, she may be happy for that is already of the past; Mrs. W. W. Stall, who weighs between 130 and 150 pounds, rides and has ridden for two years a tricycle weighing not over 35 pounds.

Undoubtedly "a great many adhere to the three-wheeler," Miss Grey says. In the first days of our great grandmothers' daring to ride on saddles of their own, and publicly proving their ability to guide and control a horse for themselves, *their* grandmothers undoubtedly clung to the pillion and thought the younger generation going to destruction because of their wild defiance of tradition; the pillion is a relic now, and the tricycle will be in the near future.

PSYCHE.

P.S.—Helen Grey's letter in the last issue of the *Bi-World* is such that I feel that I really must answer it, or tacitly acknowledge that she has some right on her side.

I am glad Miss Grey expected some one to take her to task, and doubly glad that there was some one to take that duty in hand.

Miss Grey says that I did not attempt to reply to her arguments, except in one instance. I will go further, and say that I saw no *argument* at all, merely some statements, two—to be more exact—in favor of the tricycle, one as to dogs, which I have said quite enough about, and the other to the effect that one could carry more baggage on the tricycle than on the bicycle. I have seen a man carry his two children, one three and the other five, on a safety, and that is about all a tricycle can accommodate, I think. The luggage-carrier of the safety can and does carry fully as much as can be stowed on a tricycle, always excepting the tricycle used for delivery wagons.

P.

HOW QUICKLY THE LADIES LEARN TO RIDE BICYCLES.

EDITOR OF THE WHEEL:

In your issue of the 19th inst., "Psyche" expresses herself on the universal ignorance "of even the men" about ladies' bicycles. She refers to some ladies who came to Newton to try the two-wheeler, "and in the course of the evening mastered it," this latter statement she quotes from the *Bi. World* of April 5, and adds, "I come to the conclusion that none of the writers know anything of what they are writing." As I was wholly responsible for the coming of the ladies to try the "new machines" I wish to make a statement, not for the benefit of "Psyche," but for the cause which seems to be near her heart, and for which she is evidently working in good faith.

I have in many cases known ladies to ride a bicycle with less than one hour of practice, in fact I have never known a person of *either* sex to persistently try for *half* an hour without being able to balance the machine and ride for a few rods. In one instance a twelve mile ride was made on the road with a previous practice of less than two hours.

Of course no lady should attempt to ride a bicycle who has not already become familiar with pedaling, by the use of a quadricycle or tricycle.

I have seen a man ride a bicycle fairly well within five minutes of the start, and the only reason a lady should have more trouble is on account of the abominable custom of wearing skirts The 150 ladies refered to by "Psyche," can, if they will, make fashionable at once, some style of dress which would spread like an epidemic (the present costume spreads like an umbrella). All ladies feel the same and declare skirts are a nuisance. One or a few are powerless to start the reform; if 100 could unite in one place it would be an easy matter.

I don't know just what "Psyche" means by riding "well." W. S. Maltby rides well, but we can't all do that. We know that Washington ladies are as smart as anybody, and we presume they have good wheels, but I should say that a lady who had to work two weeks before she could mount, ride and dismount, in reasonably good form, either had a very poor machine or was not properly instructed.

STERLING ELLIOTT.

Newton, Mass., April 24.

WHEEL GOSSIP.

Kilkelly, the fastest man in Ireland, is already going great guns. After him, the five brothers, Du Cros, show good form.

The Fostoria Bicycle Club's invitations to its annual ball, held May 30, are beyond ordinary in artistic conception and execution.

The English papers, *Cyclist*, *Wheeling* and *Bi-News* seem to have fallen into ruts. There is no life about them; everything is noticed, reported and written up in a worked-out sort of fashion.

Col. George A. Jessup, C. C. of Pennsy, is in town. We saw him on Sunday last darting across upper Broadway, one of a half million others who had come to Gotham to see the high old Centennial jinks.

Chief Consul Hodgson is booming the Louisiana Division. Last year the division numbered 56 members; of these 45 have renewed, and a new membership of 25 totals 65 members. The Chief Consul is aiming for the century mark.

The New York Bicycle Club held a meeting Wednesday night and awarded mileage medals to G. M. Nisbett, H. M. Farr, J. M. Andreini, E. Del Genovese, J. R. Blake, I. M. Shaw and W. F. Pendleton, for having ridden over 2,000 miles in 1888.

F. A. Elwell, Manager of the European Team, discovered that all the hotels in Ireland, with which he communicated, were, with one exception, owned by one man, who named exorbitant prices. An Irish cyclist of influence saw this hotel monopolist, and the charges were reduced to reasonable proportions.

A HEARTY ENGLISH WELCOME.

The Cyclist bespeaks a hearty English welcome for the Elwell party. Says *The Cyclist* editorially:

"The tourists may be expected to spend the middle of June with us, and if the clubs whose districts will be touched will keep their dates a little open about the time they may be expected to visit them they can show the courtesies of the wheel by meeting the party at different points and escorting them through their territories, if even hospitality extends no further. When Frank Weston's party paid us a visit we believe they did not ride a mile alone, but were 'handed on' from one club to another through the country, and thus provided with enthusiastic guides who could point out the beauties of the country *en route*, and show the strangers to the best advantage the beauties of our lovely country. Now the cyclists in England number four or five times as many—or even more—as they did in those days, so there should be no difficulty in finding during the 'leafy month of June' many willing volunteers to show our Yankee cousins the best side of English cycling."

I notice in the last week's *Wheel* an article urging cyclists to join the League. The *Wheel* has usually claimed that there was no advantage in League membership, and so I was pleased to see this evidence of a change of heart.—*Elm City in Bicycling World.*

We have never claimed that there was *no* advantage in League membership. For three years we have been claiming that the League was capable of much, but accomplished little, through misdirection of energy. We have simply tried, according to our lights, to point out how that energy might be directed into proper channels. We have always claimed that the National Organization could serve as little more than a powerful factor, but that the real work of advancing cycling must be accomplished by the Divisions. "Elm City," and other interested parties will please note that the National Body is weakening each day, and that the Divisions are becoming stronger; that more money is now given to the Divisions than hitherto; that the League was a failure as a publishing house; that it is just commencing to devote its attention to roads improvement. We were the first to advocate the above reforms, and it was our enthusiastic perseverance that finally drove this into the head of the legislative body of the League. We predicted the League's failure as a publishing concern. Our present League enthusiasm is due entirely to the fact that the New York State Division will introduce its roads improvement bill into the Legislature next Fall. Other State Divisions are also taking up the work of improving the roads, and by increasing League membership and interests, we are indirectly advancing an object which is dear to us, the establishment of better roads, without which cycling will never attain its fullest possible growth in this country.

CAPITAL CYCLE CO.'S CATALOGUE FOR 1889.

By far the finest catalogue of the year is just issued by the Capital Cycle Co., and it will prove a valuable addition to the collector and a handsome club-room ornament. It is in the form of a calendar, composed of twelve sheets, 7x7, of greenish-tinted heavy bristol board. These are perforated and tied with silk ribbon.

On the face of each card is an illustrated calendar for one month. The illustrations are the work of Francois Noije, and the engraving bears the imprint of the Moss Engraving Co., of New York. The subjects, which are appropriate to the season, are six inches square. In plain fact the finest calendar we have seen.

The back of each sheet is devoted to advertising, the matter being put together in light type and in harmony with the general style of the catalogue.

One cannot but be struck by the original manner in which the Capital Cycle Co. gets up its advertisements. Here are some selections :

"We confine ourselves to simple statements of facts."

" Absolute perfection will never be reached, nor will statements made by interested parties be fully believed."

"We advise intending purchasers to hear all the arguments, *pro and con,* relating to the different makes of cycles, and to follow their own inclination in the matter of selection, choosing from among the first-class makes, and keeping up with the improvements. The best are not too perfect considering the valuable burden they have to carry."

"We recommend the drum-frame, rear-driving safety to all, on account of safety, ease of mounting and dismounting, comfort, speed, hillclimbing qualities, its adaptability as a family machine, and the double demand it will meet when necessary to sell."

"We were the first to introduce the safety bicycle into America (1885), the first to design and introduce the tandem safety bicycle (1888), and the first to design, import and manufacture the ladies' safety bicycle (1887)."

The following is the list of Psycho cycles :

" Psycho " Straight Frame Safety, 47 lbs., $140 ;
Men's Drop Frame " Psycho " Safety, 50 lbs., $140 ; " Psycho " Light Roadster Safety, 38 lbs., $140, the lightest safety in the market ; Ladies' " Psycho " Roadster Safety, 44 lbs., $140 ; Ladies' " Psycho " Light Roadster, 32 lbs., $140 ; Psycho Tandem Safety, for two gentlemen or a lady and a gentleman, 78 lbs., $200. The Capital Company are United States agents for the Bell Rock Lanterns for ordinaries and safeties.

Mr. G. A. Litchhult has opened a new agency in Harlem, at 118th Street and Lenox Avenue. Mr. Litchhult will make a leader of Singer's line of wheels, will sell other prominent makes, and carry a general line of new goods. He will also repair, rent and store wheels.

The Capital Cycle Co., judging from the number of drop-frame Psychos they sell for gentlemen's use, claim that it will be as difficult to sell straight frame Safeties in the near future as it now is to sell ordinaries. They also claim that the drop-frame Psycho is stronger than the straight-frame, even without the detached brace-rod.

The Acme Special 5-inch Pocket and Bicycle Wrench is expressly designed and constructed for the above named purposes. It combines lightness (6½) with strength, and on account of its shape can be nicely carried in the pocket. The very best material is used only in all goods, and a special finish it given this little tool, making it not only serviceable, but also attractive. They are made in all nickeled and bright finish, with black handle, as referred to in price list. If desired, each one is put in a paper box.

NEW YORK BICYCLE CO. REMOVE UPTOWN.

We would call the attention of wheelmen to the change of address of the New York Bicycle Co. From their Warren Street Rooms they have moved to No. 4 East Sixtieth Street, Fifth Avenue entrance to Central Park, where they will be happy to receive all their old friends and as many new ones as shall be pleased to call upon them. The company have been contemplating this step for some time, and now that they have made up their minds to concentrate their energies upon the one " stand," we believe the step now taken is most wise. They have facilities at the new store that they never could have downtown. Their present salesroom is larger than their old one. They have right off this one of the best-equipped Repair Shops in the county. They rent and store wheels, are uptown agents for Messrs. A. G. Spalding & Bros., a full line of whose baseball, tennis and general sporting goods they carry, and in time, should their business still warrant further enlargement, they will add a Riding Hall and another story or two to their present apartments. We are glad to note this evidence of prosperity on the part of one of the younger firms in the bicycle line, and trust further success will wait upon their energy and progressiveness.

WESTERN ARMS & CARTRIDGE CO.'S CATALOGUE.

This enterprising Western concern handles New Rapids, Quadrant, Coventry Singer and Star Wheels, all of which are minutely described and illustrated in a 48-page catalogue, just issued. The catalogue also describes one of the most carefully arranged list of sundries we have seen.

NOTICE TO THE CYCLING PUBLIC.

The public is hereby notified that the English manufacturers have appointed the Capital Cycle Co., of Washington, D. C., their sole and exclusive agents in the United States for the sale of " Psycho " machines. Any and all " Psychos " purchased from or through the said Capital Cycle Co. are guaranteed in every respect.

The public is cautioned against purchasing the so-called " Psychos " through other American dealers who sell machines which are not guaranteed.

The public is also notified that the use or sale of any " Psycho " bicycle in the United States, unless sold by said Capital Cycle Co., is an infringement of letters patent covering said machines, and that purchasers, agents and others will be held responsible therefor.

CAPITAL CYCLE Co.*₊*

" We are satisfied it (The Brooks Cyclometer) is a good and cheap instrument."

CLARK CYCLE CO., Baltimore, Md.

Brooks' Odometer Co., Lowell, Mass. Price, $5.

A SELECTED LIST OF PATENTS.

[Reported especially for THE WHEEL AND CYCLING TRADE REVIEW by C. A. Snow & Co., patent attorneys, Washington, D. C.]

J. Kibbe, Amsterdam, N. Y. Bicycle.
H. P. Chapin, Chicopee, Mass. Bicycle step.
C. J. Colling, Cincinnati, Ohio. Handle-bar for bicycles.
C. G. Duryea, Washington, D. C. Velocipede.

All bearing date of April 30.

New York State Division L.A.W.

OFFICERS FOR 1889.

Chief Consul, W. S. BULL, 75¼ Main Street, Buffalo, N. Y. Vice-Consul, M. L. BRIDGMAN, 1155 Bedford Avenue, Brooklyn, N. Y. Secretary-Treasurer, GEO. M. NISBETT, 50 Wall Street, New York City. Executive and Finance Committee, W. S. BULL, M. L. BRIDGMAN, Dr. GEORGE E. BLACKMAN, Dunkirk, N. Y.

The builders of the Lynn Cycle track failed, and were sold out, and now the latest lessee has been compelled to vacate for non-payment of the lease money. Isaiah Graves, owner of the land on which the track is built, has taken possession of the property, which he will put into good shape and let for $400 per year to responsible parties. We well remember the day on which the track was opened. Bright, sunny, with hundreds of wheelmen gliding towards the grounds; the Boscobel Inn, crowded with hungry wheelmen ; the Houton Club, with its tally-ho, and its private punch lever at the Boscobel ; later a crowded grand stand and lots of enthusiasm. And now the grounds go a-begging at $400 a year ; the promise of that opening day has never been fulfilled.

An attempt was made by G. M. Nisbett and W. E. Findley, New York Club, on Wednesday, to establish a tandem safety record between Tarrytown and Fifty-ninth Street and the Grand Boulevard. The roads being in a poor condition, fast time was not made. The trip occupied 2h. 19m. The bicycle record is 1h. 59m.

Mr. S. T. Bennett, the new proprietor of the Franklin House, Tarrytown, took possession Wednesday, May 1, and gave a dinner to eighteen wheelmen who happened to call there. He proposes to cater to wheelmen, to give the usual bottle of champagne—in fact, to live up to all the old traditions of the house.

The committee having charge of the Brooklyn Centennial Banquet sent invitations to the Presidents of the L. I. Wheel men, Brooklyn Bicycle Club, and the K. C. Wheelmen. The banquet was held at the Brooklyn Academy on Tuesday evening, the auditorium having been floored over, and tables were set for about 500. Wheeling was represented by Mayor Chapin and Messrs. Michael Furst, G. W. Mabie and W. R. Smith.

The League year ended on Tuesday, April 30. Members are carried on the list until July 1, and may renew any time in May or June.

The Manhattan Bicycle Club will have a run to Coney Island on Sunday.

The National Cyclists Union has at last established a racing board. It is hoped under the management of the new racing board that each meeting in England will be more wisely conducted in the future than it has been in the past.

On strike—A cyclist taking a header.

W. C. Boak, of Le Roy, N. Y., was in town on business and to see the Centennial.

L. I. W. Club runs : May 4, 4 P. M., Bath, 18 miles : May 11, 4 P. M., Coney Island, 12 miles ; May 18, 4 P. M., 18 miles ; May 25, 4 P. M., Fort Hamilton, 22 miles ; May 30, 8.30 A. M., Orange and Milburn, 45 miles.

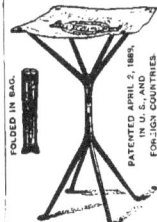

THE WHEEL

—AND—

CYCLING TRADE REVIEW,

Published every Friday morning.

Entered at the Post Office at second class rates.

Subscription Price, - - - - $1.00 a year.
Foreign Subscriptions, - - - - 6s. a year.
Single Copies, - - - - - - 5 Cents.

Newsdealers may order through AM. NEWS CO.

All copy should be received by Monday.
Telegraphic news received till Wednesday noon.

Advertising rates on Application.

F. P. PRIAL, Editor and Proprietor
23 Park Row,
P. O. Box 444, New York.

Persons receiving sample copies of this paper are respectfully requested to examine its contents and give us their patronage, and as far as is convenient, aid in circulating the journal, and extend its influence in the cause which it so faithfully serves. Subscription price, $1 per year.

FAR AHEAD OF ITS E.C's.

The cyclists of Tacoma were pleased to note that *The Wheel*, published in New York City, has devoted a long account to the cycling fraternity of Tacoma and Seattle. The boys pronounce the paper far ahead of its e. c's. It is full of "facts and fancies" pertaining to the sport, and also contains news from all the cities where cycling is indulged in. In the last issue Tacoma held a prominent place among the larger cities, and was congratulated on the rapid increase of her riders.—*Tacoma Herald.*

NOW FOR KNEE-BREECHES.

We have a correspondent in New Orleans whose hobby is the introduction of knee-breeches to take the place of the trousers which at present obtain in polite society. This man with a hobby will rejoice when he reads the following editorial from the New York *Herald*:

"What we sigh for just now is a change in the fashion of men's clothing. Our coats, hats and trousers need revision. They are neither becoming nor comfortable.

"The stovepipe hat is simply an abomination; likewise the stiff felt hat. They bind the head, and when worn for any length of time leave a broad red band on the forehead, nature's protest against a device of the enemy.

"Just look at the pictures of Washington, Hamilton, Franklin and Adams in the galleries of the Metropolitan Opera House. Imagine them in those twin meal sacks miscalled pantaloons, or in a nobby cutaway coat and a shiny hat! It takes our breath away.

"The next dress reform for men will undoubtedly include knee-breeches. They cover up those physical deformities known as bow legs, give one a sense of freedom which creates the desire for a long walk, and are altogether the most picturesque covering for the nether extremities of that 'forked radish' known as man.

"Who will be the pioneer?"

OUR Maryland correspondent, "Bay Ridge," sends us some notes of the League meet. The programme, as at present sketched, is as follows:

July 2.—Business meeting of the League. Excursion to Pen Mar, by wheel and rail. Supper.

July 3.—Run to battle-fields of South Mountain, Boonsboro, Antietam; visit to battle-fields and National Cemetery. Return to Hagerstown over a different route. Supper. In the evening, run to Williamsport, on the Potomac. Swim. Illumination.

July 4.—Parade, with lunch in a grove. Afternoon, races. Night, open air smoker, in a grove, with grand military band concert.

IN our edition of April 26 we published an editorial letter from a prominent Baltimore cyclist giving "inside" information on the prospects of Maryland entertaining the League this year. In the same issue we announced that the meet would be held at Hagerstown, as the Executive Committee of the League had accepted the Maryland Division's invitation. One week later the *Bicycling World* announced that the meet would be held at Hagerstown. Comment is needless.

IN this issue of THE WHEEL we reproduce the Capital Cycle Co.'s art calendar, forming perhaps the most attractive advertisement ever published in a cycling paper. The Capital Co. do business in fair and square man-fashion style. They resort to no pretense, and make no effort to deceive the public. Their Psycho wheels are built on special lines to order by an English firm of repute for work unsurpassed in durability, in design and in finish.

IN the ladies' column, "Pioneer" tells us of her experiences while learning to ride the bicycle. "Pioneer" is the "First Lady in the Land"—that is, the first to master a bicycle. Her experiences will become historical.

STRONG PLEA FOR BETTER ROADS.

There is one particular sign among the other signs of the times, upon which we wish to congratulate our readers, and that is, the dimensions to which the public agitation, all over the country, in the matter of good roads is growing. We hear from every direction of grumbling and growling over the state of the public highways, and the greater the grumbling and the longer it is kept up and the louder it becomes the better for cyclers, carriage drivers and "cattle." Owing to the "magnificent distances" of this great country, and owing to the fact that, contemporary with the great development of our resources, railroads started into existence and obtained a monopoly of our transportation, our public roads have been, in the majority of cases, what might be called, with perfect propriety, merely necessary public nuisances. Now, however, wealth and luxury all over this immense land of ours are taking the places of poverty and simplicity, we are approximating, more and more, toward the condition of life in England, and our rising generation, instead of having to work early and late to keep body and soul together or to reclaim a wilderness, find professions and callings of all kinds ready to their hand, and also find abundant leisure to cultivate the higher attributes of the body and mind. Immense centres of civilation are springing up, and as the public taste becomes educated, and public desires and needs multiply, the amending of existing disabilities under which our civilization, like a young giant, has irresistibly grown up, is certain to come about. As before remarked, railroads have up to the present done, and will continue to do, the work which in older countries was done by magnificent public highways, but that does not constitute a reason for this country remaining possessed of the most execrable roads on the face of the earth. Round our large cities, and connecting them one with another we should have a net-work of good public roads. Let us have a system of main public highways, carefully looked after and kept in condition by public officials, and then leave to private enterprise the filling in of the net-work, which as a necessary result will come. An example of what is meant will be found out Lancaster Pike, from which main road now branch out numerous excellent macadamized highways that some five years ago only existed in the imagination or upon paper. Philadelphia is not alone in the present awakening on the matter of the necessity for good public roads. New York, Buffalo, Chicago and many other cities and towns are commencing to systematically extend and improve their streets and suburban roads, and when these improvements extend and join hands, then, and not till then, should agitation relax, and then only partially.—*American Athlete.*

WHEEL GOSSIP.

The fellow who skips the long articles will miss a treat if he fails to read "An Idyl," published in another column.

The *American Athlete*, under the editorial management of Chris Wheeler, is doing good work in spreading the idea of roads improvement.

Philadelphia has developed a new scorcher in Fred Whiteside, of the Century Wheelmen. He rides a Starr and recently hung on to Dampman, McDaniels and Merribew's coat-tails on a ten-mile scorch over the Lancaste, Pike.

"Jake" Morse, for several seasons the cycling representative of the Boston *Herald*, is baseball correspondent for the *Sporting Times*. A cut of Mr. Morse's intellectual, bespectacled and incisive face is published in the latest issue of the *Times*.

The Pope Manufacturing Co. had a speaking "ad" in the Centennial number of *Harper's Weekly*. We would suggest that in mediums of that class the figure mounted on the safety should represent a middle-aged man instead of a young man. The use of the wheel must be developed among the older classes.

The Louisiana Division L. A. W. will be represented at the League meet by C. C. Harry Hodgson and his confreres. Last year they came to Baltimore in immaculate white flannel and were the observed of all observers. This year they will be clothed in bottle green, with silk braid, cut naval style, and will be fastened with hooks, not with buttons.

WHAT THEY ARE TALKING ABOUT.

St. Louis—A new track.

Providence—The May 30 meet.

Hagerstown—The League Meet.

Tacoma—The 20-mile road race.

Philadelphia—A 50-mile inter-club race.

New York—The Decoration Day road race.

Boston—The Harvard meet and Fast Day Runs.

San Francisco—Their successful race meet just held.

Brooklyn—Cobblestone Hill, those Iron Posts, the Brooklyn's new house, the Long Island and K. C. W. race meets.

Chicago—The grand cycle exhibit and tournament, the late beauty six day race and the number of wheels the dealers have sold, and the Stone-Lumsden races.

W. I. Wilhelm, of Reading, was in New York on Wednesday.

Howard A. Smith & Co. are teaching more beginners how to ride than they have ever before in the history of Oraton Hall.

The track at Washington Park, Brooklyn, is four laps to the mile, with raised corners. The K. C. W. meet should attract a large entry list.

A. E. Schaaf, representing the Gormully & Jeffrey Co., and C. C. Candy, representing the Overman Wheel Co., have been in Minneapolis, drumming up trade.

The English pressmen almost always have a big fight on. G. Lacy Hillier is alleged to have stated that *Wheeling* was for sale. The *Wheeling* people deny the rumor.

The Manhattan Bicycle Club should interest some men in the 25-mile road race. They give perfect entertainments, hold famous club runs, are often represented on the racing path, but have never shown us their scorchers.

Captain Meeteer, of the Brooklyn Club, has instituted a one-mile club handicap championship. There can be no such thing, Cap., since "championship" implies a scratch race. To call a man a "Handicap Champion" is absurd.

Frank White, of Spalding's, is always jubilant. He is just now rejoicing over a big sale of sporting goods to John Wanamaker, over the result of the famous baseball dinner recently held at "Del.'s," and wondering whether Chief Consul Bull didn't rather enjoy himself as the representative of the L. A. W.

The Long Island Cycle Co. is the latest addition to the list of local agents. The company is situated at 1150 Fulton Street, Brooklyn, the business manager being John Derry, a practical repairer and well known to Brooklyn cyclists. The company handle Warwick, Victor and Club cycles, repair and rent wheels and let locker room.

One of the most popular wheelmen in Jersey City, is Frank Eveland, of the Hudson County Wheelmen. Mr. Eveland is proprietor of a prosperous and well-appointed drug store, well stocked with that which kills and that which cures. Incidentaly Mr. Eveland is agent for the Columbia wheels, which are kept in that little back room which is so popular with the boys.

THE WHEEL is at present devoting a great deal of space to the subject of the feasibility and advisability of the Government, or rather the State Governments, employing prison labor in the work of keeping our public highways in proper repair. The matter under notice in the columns of our New York contemporary is one that will bear the closest investigation, and very little can be said against this plan of putting to good use criminal labor. The best thing that our contemporary can do, now that it has started on this subject, is to keep up talking on it, and the best thing the other cycling journals can do is to step in and lend a hand.—*American Athlete.*

RIVERSIDE WHEELMEN'S NOTES.

The R. W.'s had a club run to Dobb's Ferry on May 5, and found the roads in good condition, although somewhat dusty. The next regular club run of the R. W. will be to Coney Island, on Sunday, May 12, starting from club-house, 118 West 104th Street, at 8.30 A. M. Messrs. Fred. Menger, F. R. Miller and E. A. Powers have the largest mileage so far for the club record.

We admitted twenty-five new members at our last regular meeting, and we now have nearly seventy members. "What's the matter with the Riversides?" [No Soup in theirs.—ED.]

Mr. F. R. Miller will appear on the track this season, and the R. W.'s expect him to show good form. SEC.

DELIGHTFUL TRIP IN THE WALLKILL VALLEY ON A MACHINE.

TWO ENTHUSIASTIC WHEELMEN MAKE A HEALTHFUL AND PLEASANT JOURNEY—SIGHTS BY THE WAY—BEAUTIFUL SCENERY MET WITH ON EVERY HAND.

On the principle that "two's company, more's a crowd," our party was composed of but two persons, a star rider of the L. I. W., and the writer, a L. A. W. Columbia "Expert" rider. The former, my friend Peter, is a well-known "anti-scorcher," and a popular member of the fraternity in the City of Churches, and it was through his knowledge and brilliant description of the roads and abiding places in the Hudson River and Walkill Valley district that the narrator was induced to make the tour.

Preceded by about a week by my friend, who took a preliminary run through Orange, Ulster and Dutchess Counties, the writer on the last Saturday in July left New York City by the afternoon steamboat Mary Powell, bound for Cornwall-on-the-Hudson (fifty-five miles from New York), and as this, the fastest boat on the river, glided through the water, his anticipations were of a most agreeable kind, the day itself being sunny, yet not too warm, and a pleasant harbinger of the weather to follow. A three hours' sail up the river, through lovely rolling country, brought "Mary" in view of the welcome figure of "Peter" on the Cornwall landing, and during the stiff climb which followed up the mountain side on which this picturesque town on the Hudson is situated, plans were discussed and something of a schedule arranged for future reference, though under such circumstances there can be little doubt that the best plan is to make no hard and fast rule as to dates, number of miles to be covered each day, etc., but to leave it, to some extent at least, to one's inclination as the days go by.

The roads around Cornwall are invariably good, and, in the town itself, of the finest character. On the following morning, accompanied by two native cyclers, we took a run through Canterbury and Mountainville and found the roads rather hilly, the grades being such as to somewhat surprise one not accustomed to their variety, though the surface on the whole was fair. At Mountainville a dismount was made near a smartly running brook and again after riding a little, at the request of Peter (who is a fond lover of the weed), we lingered for a time nearby Houghton's Model Farm enjoying the rugged, mountainous scenery which surrounds the locality. We returned to Cornwall over the hills by a slightly different route, thoroughly in trim after our twenty mile ride to do full justice to our noontide repast. In the afternoon we wheeled, via Canterbury and New Windsor, to Newburg. From this point the little trip across the river to Fishkill was one of the most enjoyable features of our whole excursion. The Sabbath afternoon was a lovely one; all nature seemed to smile on us and bid us welcome and godspeed. The ferryboat itself was a charming picture and one not beneath the brush of an artist; its upper deck, made cool and pleasant by gentle zephyrs, was filled by the good people of the adjacent towns, who, for a small extra fare, are permitted to remain on the boat at their own sweet will, many of them, we were told, spending half the day in this pleasant and practical way of communing with nature.

Almost all our energies were required to ascend the steep hill at the Fishkill landing, at the summit of which we turned left to Wappinger's Falls, where a delightful coast was enjoyed. Thence on to Poughkeepsie, over exceedingly good roads. Here we again crossed the river, to Highlands, which was reached about dusk, and where we spent the night at Terwilliger's Hotel.

On Monday, mounting our wheels, we proceeded along splendid roads to New Paltz for breakfast, after which we rode the short distance between the village and the foot of the Shawangunk Mountains, on whose summit, 1,200 feet above the level of the Hudson, Lake Mohonk is situated. Our wheels, by the courtesy of a farmer, being stored in an outhouse at the foot of the hills, we advanced on foot up the mountain side to the lake, a stiff climb of two and a half miles. As time, however, was no object, we enjoyed the walk without hurrying, and resting, now by a cool spring, where we quenched our thirst, and again, in the summer houses, which are built by the wayside for the comfort of travelers, and that they may the more fully enjoy the magnificent views on all sides, some of the finest in this beautiful section of the country. Lake Mohonk was reached at last, and we felt amply repaid in the grandeur of the scenery, for the physical exertion needed to reach the summit. From the crest of Sky Top, 500 feet above the lake and 1,700 feet above the Hudson, portions of six States may be seen on clear days, while the number of mountain peaks or ranges of mountains seemed to us, almost countless. Altogether, we were much charmed by the lovely reach of sight obtained, beside being interested and amused by the perfect echo heard from the mountain sides, and which was repeated back to us, apparently, from the depths of the lake.

Returning to New Paltz for the night, Tuesday morning saw us wheeling through Ireland Corners, New Hurley and St. Andrews en route for Walden, the grades at times being rather steep, though the surface was invariably fair, and as we approached Walden excellent. We dined at Walden, and as the town was a favorite abiding place of my friend, he having numerous cycling and other acquaintances in the neighborhood, we concluded to stay over night. We passed the afternoon in a visit to Gail Borden's milk condensery at Walkill, a short distance out, and where, through the courtesy of Mr. Smith, the Superintendent, and under the efficient guidance of his assistant, Mr. Jansen (a cyclist of local fame), we were shown through the establishment. We were much impressed with the cleanliness in all departments, from the glass bottles in which the milk is sent to New York, to the immense copper cylinders in which the milk is stored previous to being tested as to its purity, as is every drop taken in. The condensery is charmingly situated near the Walkill River, and a short distance from the village of Walkill, to which place we rode by a path along the river bank, afterwards taking a run up to Mr. Borden's private park, through the enormous cattle barn and round the estate generally. On our return to Walkill from the park we encountered a pretty steep and lengthy hill down which we partly pedaled and partly coasted. About half way down the hill we met a carryall in which was seated an aged countrywoman, who, on account of her horse, seemed greatly exercised at the sight of us and beseeched us to "git hoff." Our persuasive powers were brought into full play to convince her that this was almost impossible to accomplish on such a grade, and finally to our (and, presumably, also her) gratification, we passed her in safety, though the risk was immeasurably increased on account of the narrowness of the road, the evident balkiness of her animal and the great speed at which we were coasting. During the night a steady fall of rain descended, our spirits were accordingly sent down to zero, and the lookout for the morrow was rendered dismal in the extreme.

On Wednesday, as may be supposed, the roads were not at their best, but as we wished to make Port Jervis that night we wheeled on through Middletown, Otisville and Cuddebackville, arriving at Port Jervis in time for supper at the Delaware House, where we stayed overnight. To any one, however, whose destination is, as was ours, Delaware Water Gap, Pa., we would strongly recommend going right through without stopping over at Port Jervis, as this town has little to invite one to abide within its walls. The Delaware House, on account of its close proximity to the depot and tracks of the Erie Railroad, is not the pleasantest and most peaceful hotel in the world, there being an almost continual clanging of engine bells to be heard, whilst the traffic during the night (as we found to our cost) seemed almost interminable, disturbing our repose not a little. Better, therefore, to push on the nine additional miles to Milford, especially as the roads are A1 the whole distance, and when that primitive village is reached the choice between the one and the other is so apparent and in favor of the latter that the little additional exertion required is not worth taking into account.

Not having given these points the previous consideration they deserved, we made the best of things as we found them, and on Thursday (of necessity) awoke with the lark, and what was more to the point, got up also, being on the way to Milford by the time the cock was crowing, and eating our breakfast there with the appetite and zest which expectation and hunger combined always give. It would be hard to choose a prettier spot than Milford, or one around on which finer roads abound. We were particularly delighted with its fresh and pure air and with the charming surroundings of the village. Its pine woods form an attractive feature, being pleasantly shaded by overhanging trees, having a cool atmosphere at all times and a pretty babbling brook to keep one company. We also viewed the Sawkill Falls, a favorite retreat for visitors located in the woods at the other end of the village.

On Friday, the last day of our jaunt, accompanied by another Brooklyn cycler, we took in the famous run to the Delaware Water Gap, a round trip of sixty-four miles, passing en route Conashaw, Dingman's Ferry and Bushkill. This ride surpassed anything in our whole touring experience, and we are greatly delighted that it bore out the impressions given us by friends who had previously made the trip. With the exception of a few short strips under repair (as there will be in all roads, even the best), the surface the whole distance was of the finest nature, "fine as silk" being thoroughly applicable to its condition. The views along the route were extremely interesting. On one side of the road the Delaware River meandered along through the woods and cultivated fields, while on the other hand were mountainous cliffs, covered with noble trees, whose foliage afforded a most welcome shade, and, though the weather was very warm, we hardly felt the heat at all.

ASHTON NICHOLS, L. A. W.

[CONCLUDED NEXT WEEK.]

THE GREAT CENTURY RUN.

While in Philadelphia the run will stop at the Continental Hotel, the best general hotel in the city, at a special rate of $2.50 per day, or $2 for supper, lodging and breakfast.

Parties will be made up to run to several different points for dinner on Sunday, the 6th.

In response to many inquiries, I would like to reiterate that the G. C. R., '89, is not a road race, and that ladies and all other riders of single-track wheels are welcome, but that the committee does not advise ladies to attempt the whole distance in one day. Plainfield and New Brunswick make good half-way stopping places. Mrs. L. A. Newcomb, Harlem Wheelmen, is arranging for a party of ladies to leave New York on one of the noon trains on the day of the run, Saturday, June 8, to meet the run that evening and to spend the next day with the party. All ladies are referred to Mrs. Newcomb, H. W., Sixth Avenue and 124th Street, New York City.

A large party of wheelmen are coming from Philadelphia to ride homewards, including Kirk Brown and two "survivors of '88"—Messrs. Bromley and Speier.

L. A. CLARKE,
Chairman Com. of Arr.

THE NEW WARWICK SAFETY IN NEW YORK.

After many promises and weeks of delay, the new Warwick Perfection Safety is "out." We saw one of the new wheels at Messrs. Halpin & Co.'s Murray Street store. The new Perfection is certainly a very handsome wheel, and if it "stands the racket" it will be a great go. The safety has a number of innovations Its makers claim for it "non-sensitiveness" and a number of improvements. It is a very handsome looking mount.

A SELECTED LIST OF PATENTS.

[Reported especially for THE WHEEL AND CYCLING TRADE REVIEW by C. A. Snow & Co., patent attorneys. Washington, D. C.]

T. W. Moore, Plainfield, N. J.; bicycle.

G. Hayes, Jr., Hingham, Mass.; treadle for bicycles.

F. Barbig, New York, N. Y.; lantern.

C. A. Frayer, Keithsburg, Ill.; oil can.

C. F. Sweet, Auburn, Me.; saddle for velocipedes.

All bearing date of May 7, 1889.

The members of the St. Louis Cycle Club and the cycle trade made a rare turnout for the illuminated bicycle parade. Ithuriel sketches the scence graphically; the unique designs; the sorry attempts of hoodlums to be obnoxiously funny, and the vain effort of a dissatisfied swell youth of the pa's-rich-couldn't-earn-a-dollar-if-he-tried species, who attempted to drive through the lines, and who was held up.

The Brooklyn Club will house-warm their new club building on June 1st.

At the Harvard College Spring meet, held Tuesday afternoon, May 7th, a two mile bicycle race was contested, in which K. Brown, '91, E. A. Bailey, '91, H. H. Davis, '91, W. R. Greenleaf '92, E. F. Rogers, '90, and R. W. Holmes, '90, were the starters. This race was a bit of a surprise to most, for Davis is usually a sure winner in this event, but Bailey was too much for him in this case, beating him by considerable distance, and covering the course in 6m. 15s., breaking the Harvard record, which was established by Davis last year. Bailey rode a Safety, and as he has only begun riding this machine this Spring, more good time may be expected of him in future, especially as he has always been rather handicapped by the smallness of his wheel.

THE POSTS MUST GO.—The authorities of New Lots have decided that those iron posts must be removed.

NOTES FROM THE CITY OF BROTHERLY LOVE.

On Tuesday, April 30, the Pennsylvania Bicycle Club, under command of First Lieutenant Leisen, took their first ladies' run, which was such a success that one or two more are already being arranged for at some later dates. About 9 o'clock the party assembled at the club headquarters, but it was about 10 before the thirteen couple on hand succeeded in starting with the handsome lieutenant in the lead. The party rode leisurely to Wayne, where dinner was enjoyed at the Hotel Dellema. After spending some little time here the start was made for home. The only thing to mar the pleasure was an accident, one young lady being thrown from her machine. At first it was feared that she was seriously hurt, but I hear that she is now as well as ever.

Messrs. McDaniels and Merrihew, members of both the Wilmington Wheel Club and Pennsylvania Bicycle Club, are entered in the 25-mile road race for Decoration Day. I fear that at present neither of them are in the pink of condition, but two weeks may change this, and I think, with proper handicapping, that both of them will come in with the first batch. Draper, also of the Pennsylvania Club, talks of entering.

By the way, L. J. Kolb, of the South End Wheelmen, proposes to meet B. Frank McDaniels on Sunday next for a ride from Fifty-second Street to the foot of Devon Hill. A year ago Mr. Kolb challenged a member of the Pennsylvania Bicycle Club, and then made a most ungraceful backdown. I trust for his sake that he will not fail to put in an appearance this time, as I think defeat (which I feel he will meet with) is better than another such backdown. If they ride I hope to be there to see the fun.

How about the Century house warming? The boys have been waiting for some kind of an invite before making their appearance on North Broad Street, but threaten to go some time soon, bid or no bid. On Sunday last some twenty-one men from the Pennsylvania Bicycle Club and ten members of the Century club rode to West Chester. The day was a scorcher, and taking a country road for about the first time proved too much for some of them, and one of the boys made a hasty trip home, via train; poor devil, he is not in the habit of ending trips in such a manner, and it galled him considerably.

What club in our city has adopted the keystone for a badge? This emblem has been to date acknowledged Pennsylvania and Pensy only, and you can imagine their surprise on seeing a party of wheelmen out on Sunday last with large silver keystones in their caps. I think their desire should have been to have some individuality about their badge, however, if such were not the case, I should judge that courtesy would have led them to have adopted some other emblem.

W. T. Flemming expects to start the latter part of this month on his Western tour. He hopes to have J. E. Gould accompany him. Neddy will, I fear, have a hard tussle for a few days as he has done no riding the past year, and when he starts with a man who yearly rolls up from 6,000 to 8,000 miles it means go ahead.

The Pennsylvania Club announce the following club runs for balance of May: Sunday, May 12, Duffryn Mawr; Thursday evening, May 16, moonlight run to Tioga; Sunday, May 19, Willow Grove; Sunday, May 26, Bristol.

WESTFIELD.

PHILADELPHIA.

It has been a long time since the good people of the town of West Chester saw such a number of wheelmen as were congregated about the Mansion House at noon on Sunday, May 5. There were twenty-one members of the Pennsylvania Club, six members of the Century Wheelmen and nine members of the Wilmington Bicycle Club, making a grand total of thirty-six, not such a bad showing when one takes into consideration the eighteen miles of bad road from Paoli to West Chester and back.

On the return trip, after leaving the dirt road the scorching began. The great Wilmington team, Dampman, McDaniels and Merrihew and Draper, of the Pennsylvanias, started off at a rattling pace, closely followed by Whitesides, Geyler, Degn and Spier of the Centurions. This order was kept up for some miles, the speed at times being something terrific (for the famed Lancaster Pike was in splendid condition), and the rest of the crowd was soon left in the rear; then Whitesides on his new wheel made himself felt. To the utter astonishment of the famous trio, this little rider stuck to the big guns like a leech, answering spurt after spurt in a way that commanded the admiration of the Wilmington boys, winding up the ten miles at Ardmore in a bunch, with Geyler a few hundred yards behind, and Degn and Spier following closely after. The pace for the last three miles was killing, neither of the first five having any decided advantage at the finish. Without a doubt Fred. Whitesides is now the best star road rider in Philadelphia, and a member of whom the Century Wheelmen are justly proud.

"Ariel," the Pennsylvania correspondent of the *Bulletin*, was seen on the road last Sunday looking lovely in a brand new Pennsylvania uniform, airing his "phenomena," who, by the way, sported his papa's old league cap, quite an acquisition to the aforesaid "phenomena."

Decoration Day is now only a few weeks off, and the associated cycling clubs have thus far publicly decided on—nothing.

Rather a sad accident that occurred to George Caryl, the well known member of the South Ends. While scorching on the "pike" he took an awful header which rendered him unconscious for some time. He was removed to the Presbyterian Hospital, and at last accounts was doing splendidly.

The other night I had a funny dream. I dreamt that a lot of wheelmen, in fact a young army of them, were following a will-o'-the-wisp, but the faster they rode the faster *it* seemed to go. Presently the light grew stronger and stronger, and gradually evolved into some letters; with a groan I read, *Pennsylvania road book*. It was the first of May.

At the last meeting of the Century Wheelmen it was decided by a vote of 27 to 22 *not* to admit lady members at present. There was weeping and gnashing of teeth.

ARGUS.

Philadelphia, May 6, 1889.

MARYLAND.

The Hagerstown Club is hard at work changing their local meet into the L. A. W. meet, which has been ordered at Hagerstown, Md., the dates being July 2, 3, 4. Chief Consul Mott was in Hagerstown helping to arrange the programme, which includes the schedule of entertainments. On the morning of July 2 the business meeting will be held, and which will be followed by an excursion to Pen-Mar by wheel and by rail, where supper will be served. On July 3 there will be a run, skirting the battlefield of South Mountain, following the line of the Confederate retreat through Boonsboro to Antietam. Here guides will be waiting to show the party over the battlefield and through the national cemetery. The return to Hagerstown will be over a different route. After supper a line will be formed, and each man furnished with a towel and a supply of fireworks. A six-mile run will bring the party to Williamsport, on the Potomac river. At this point big bonfires will be lit along the river banks, and the boys will enjoy a swim and return to Hagerstown, after having had their stock of fireworks renewed for display on the return trip. The morning of the Fourth will be devoted to a parade about the city, over streets superior to those of Washington. This will be dismissed in a grove which is abundantly supplied with limestone springs, and here refreshments will be served. The races will follow in the afternoon. They will include a one-mile L. A. W. bicycle, one-mile tricycle and one-mile safety. At night there will be a grand national open-air smoker in a beautiful grove, one of the attractions to which will be a grand concert by a military band. This programme will be supplemented by a number of smaller events, which will be bulletined at the hotels, as will also a thoroughly unique entertainment for a fourth day.

LEAGUE MEET NOTES.

At a special meeting of the committees on the Bicycle Meet, held recently, the members of the club exchanged congratulations upon their success in securing the annual League Meet. Additional work was assigned and the committees reported progress.

A Baltimore club expect to camp out at Hagerstown from June 29 to July 4.

The Hamilton House at Hagerstown will be the League headquarters. The Maryland Club has made engagements for a parlor and fifty rooms at the same hotel.

A number of members of the Capital Club of Washington, D. C., prefer going by train to Martinsburg and wheeling the remaining twenty-five miles to Hagerstown. The road is one of the finest in this locality, and no doubt will be the favorite route from this city and Baltimore. Others talk of going on their wheels the entire road from here, but they are only the seasoned veterans.

At a meeting of the Potomac Wheelmen at Cumberland, held recently in the Y. M. C. A., the following officers were elected to serve for one year from May 1, 1889: President, Dr. H. V. Porter; Vice-President, Hervey Laney; Captain, A. C. Willison; Secretary-Treasurer, J. D. Wineow; Lieutenant, D. A. Smith; Bugler, H. C. Walker; Executive Committee, Dr. H. V. Porter, A. C. Willison, J. D. Wineow, L. C. Rossler, J. R. Sinouse.

Rev. Wayland D. Ball, of the Associated Reformed Church, lectured to a full audience at the Y. M. C. A. Hall on bicycling. He gave his personal experience, saying that for six years he had been an enthusiastic bicyclist. He read Will Carleton's rural poem, "On a Wheel," which gives an amusing account of how the city bicyclist captured a rural belle in spite of the rural affianced Josh, and the father of the girl. The lecture was praised by all cyclers present.

The medal for the championship of the Baltimore Club for last year is about ready for delivery to the winner, Harry G. Tyler. It is a pretty design, in gold, of wheels, wings, scroll and shield, appropriately engraved.

The Chesapeake Club will soon have a housewarming upon the opening of their fine new clubhouse at Fulton and Lafayette Avenues. This house was recently purchased at $5,000. It is three-story high, and has been handsomely fitted up with modern conveniences. The expenditures on the house amounted to $1,500.

BAY RIDGE.

SAN FRANCISCO.

In reading the last issue of your excellent paper I was forcibly reminded of a remark made by a local rider that "sooner or later the person who writes on cycling topics will get into hot water." In that issue "Jack" calls Fenton to account, the ladies have their differences and Mr. Clark directs his subtle sarcasm in this direction. It was hardly fair to quote the words of "Eureka" where he tells of "*scorching* ten miles in 55m.," and by inference applying it to my information. Up to the time I wrote I had seen no reference to his schedule, and as we have had a number of these runs I thought a little *practical* information would not be out of place. I am surprised to see that he estimates the number of starters at "not less than 100." With the splendid arrangements he and his colleagues have made and the fact that the attendance will be drawn from twenty-two clubs I should think he could count on a much larger number. From a personal experience of such runs I say to all riders, "try the experiment," you will be surprised how easy it is to cover the required distance, and it will give you pleasure to think over it afterward.

The riders in the East must understand that we have, in this State, hundreds of miles of roads almost as fine as those in the vicinity of Boston, that our wheels are generally the best makes of Pope and the Coventry firms, and that our riders can hold their own with the riders of any State in the Union.

The hop of the Bay City Wheelmen last night was a success in every particular, the music was the best obtainable, the floor perfect—what more could be desired? All the arrangements were in the hands of F. W. Pierson, who received the highest praise on all sides for the excellence of his arrangements. The race meet on Tuesday next gives promise of being a notable one, the entry list is large and some of the Coast records will surely go down.

W. S. Maltby left for Australia on the steamer Umatilla, yesterday. The evening previous he gave a fine exhibition at the skating rink, his work on the Eagle bicycle was excellent considering the fact that he has had but little practice on it.

Fred Russ Cook, the ex-champion of the Coast, has been recommended for the position of official handicapper for this district.

Yours,

April 27, 1889. CALIFORNIA.

ST. LOUIS.

The wheelmen of St. Louis were right on their metal last Tuesday night, and the illuminated parade was an unqualified success. It fully equalled, and some think it surpassed, the display of two years ago. The day parade was an immense affair, being upwards of ten miles long, and, from a numerical point of view, left nothing to be desired, but it lacked point and distinctiveness, and after it had passed a stranger could scarcely have told what it was all about. The bicycle parade, on the other hand, though only one mile long, was replete with novel features, appropriate designs, beautiful as well as startling effects, and a general effect that was at once weird and charming. I have yet to see the first person who is not enthusiastic over the pretty display made by the cyclers. The scene at the starting point was one of indescribable confusion, and for a while it looked as if it would be impossible to bring order out of the existing chaos, but after a start had been made the different paraders fell into line, and, though badly mixed up as to their alloted places, made the best of the bargain and rode it out where they were. Of course, this spoiled to some extent the symmetry of the line. The Missouri Club led off under command of Alex Lewis, and through his and his brother Ab's efforts, everyone in this division was properly placed, and there was no confusion or disorder at any time. The Cycle Club, under Captain Sanders, and the unattached wheelmen, under Captain Stone, did not fare so well, and these two divisions got wofully mixed up. It is only fair to state, in justice to the respective captains, that the fault of this condition of affairs did not lie with them, but was probably due to a lack of understanding among some of the aids. Some of the noteworthy features of the parade were: A monster ship, navigated by the Hurck Bros.; Hal Greenwood in a balloon, probably intended to call attention to the resemblance his Star has to a balloon for getting up in the world; Alex Lewis and the Lawnin Bros., on bicycle, handsomely and tastefully trimmed; little Eddie Snitjer, representing the youthful George, with the inevitable hatchet, and a great many other novel and pretty designs. One of the prettiest machines was the tandem ridden by H. A. Lienhard and J. H. Child. The wheel was appropriately decorated with the national colors, and in the centre of it rose the proverbial cherry tree, with lanterns suspended for cherries. The riders were costumed as George and Martha Washington. Mr. Child was the Martha, and his "make up" was simply immense, though the taking of this character involved the sacrifice of his luxuriant mustache. I will state *en passant*, that it was just such self-denying acts as this that made the demonstration such a success. H. B. Pogus, as George Washington's body servant, "aged 127 years, 4 months and 8 days," made a great hit. He fell in alongside the George and Martha trike, and his trite remarks, clothed in the richest negro dialect, kept the spectators in the best of humor all along the line.

One of the most pleasing features of the affair was the splendid *esprit de corps* which the preliminary work developed. Missouris, Cycles and unattached worked fraternally together with a singleness of purpose and an absence of all envy or jealousy that was most commendable. The good effects of this united effort are bound to be felt for some time to come. Though the streets were crowded all along the line of march, and no police protection worth speaking of, there were few attempts at hoodlumism, and, with two or three exceptions, they were prompted more by mischievousness than viciousness. At no point was the procession marred or interfered with. One tough tried to commit suicide by hitting Alex Lewis in the mouth with a piece of mud, but he escaped scot free, for Alex was so encumbered with his elaborately decorated wheel that he could not leave it, but he got even with another, who tried to snatch one of his lanterns, by giving him a swinging kick square in the mouth. Some dentist got a job as a result of that incident. Another fellow threw a billet of wood at Ab Lewis. In picking out a victim he could not have made a worse selection. Ab caught him after a chase of about a block and proceeded to administer condign punishment. He had not quite finished when an officer appeared and stopped the performance. A kid seated on the curb was amusing himself by seeing how near he could put a stick to the wheels without getting it in the spokes. He was espied by one of the demon squad, who cut his enjoyment short by by dropping a hat full of red fire in his lap. The smell of burning cloth accelerated the pace slightly at this point, but otherwise the incident was unnoticed, and there was plenty of red fire left. Two young men about town tried to drive through the line at Locust and Garrison Avenues, and were only prevented from doing so by the determined action of a few of the spectators, who held the horses and prevented the young men from going either forward or back. The parties are well known to many of the wheelmen, and their conduct was the result of too much "Buck." One of them is a heavy swell, in his own opinion, and prides himself on his good looks. He would have felt terribly mortified had his ivories been stove in and his nose set around under his ear, and yet that is about what would have happened had he succeeded in breaking into the line.

The participants are to hold a congratulatory meeting and banquet at the Calumet Club on Saturday night.

ITHURIEL.

NEWARK.

Only nine members of the Atalanta Wheelmen turned in mileage for April, the total of which was 1,375 miles. This month the club total of miles ridden will reach at least 5,000 miles.

At the last regular meeting five new members were elected, swelling the membership to thirty-three. It was decided to have an informal opening of the club-house with a "smoker," on Tuesday, May 14. Representatives from all the neighboring cycling clubs are expected, and those who come know how to enjoy themselves, and will have a good time. All come and help Eichorn drink his "milk."

On Tuesday last a party of Atalanta Wheelmen started for Morristown by way of Eagle Rock. They turned off to the left on the other side of the mountain, and struck a road half under water. They were compelled to walk at least five miles, part of that distance through water up to their knees. What fun it must have been to see President Miller wade!

The club runs of the Atalantas for May are as follows: Friday, May 10, 5 P. M.; route, Orange. Thursday, May 16 (moonlight), 7:30 P. M.; route, South Orange. Saturday, May 18, 5 P. M.; route, Rutherford. Friday, May 24, 5:30 P. M.; route, Montclair. Thursday, May 30, to the races, Irvington, and to Coney Island.

Visitors are always made welcome on club runs, and the boys always say the more the merrier.

SPARK.

JACK'S JOTTINGS.

A. M. Gooch, of Newton Centre, Mass., was a visitor to Westboro on Sunday. He showed the writer an ordinary bicycle of his own construction, which certainly was a staunch one, though light, carrying the 200 pounds which are the physical representation of Mr. Gooch here in the flesh, in first-class order. About 4:30 P.M. he started out for home, expecting to "do" the twenty-eight miles in something like three hours. He rides a 50-inch, and seems to have "power" to shift a wheel.

Westboro, Mass., is a clean little model village of some 6,000 inhabitants. The main industry is the manufacture of straw goods, such as ladies' bonnets, etc. "Men of straw" are not made here, as the employees are (nearly to a man) girls, and this branch of the straw trade has not yet been attempted. The town is strictly a prohibition town, so whiskey-drinking is *sub rosa*, and the "express" business from Boston especially good. Instead of men buying a single drink at a time, they buy a keg or a bottle or a demijohn, and the prohibitionists hug themselves about their fancied victory over the whiskey-drinker, whose appetite is only augmented by the fact that intoxicants are hard to get, and therefore more desirable.

The White Cycle Co. have the neatest, cleanest, most perfect factory I ever saw, and already employ fifty men. This number will be increased to seventy when the season advances.

According to the Boston *Herald*, President Foudrinier, of the Press Cycling Club, and editor of the *Bicycling World*, has been spending all his leisure time during last week in entertaining J. Purvis Bruce and H. C. Priest, of the Quadrant Cycle Company, who are stopping in Boston for a few days. Canoe-sailing from the Puritan Canoe Club in South Boston Bay, pool-playing at the Boston Town Club and London Gaiety Co. distractions helped to keep the hours from hanging heavy. Mr. C. W. Foudrinier, who is Member of Parliament for the district of South Boston Bay and City Point, H. C. Priest, M. P. for Manhattan; and J. Purvis-Bruce, M. P. for Ripley, whiled away the hours on Centennial day by congratulating each other and H. G. Priest, of the Quadrant Cycle Co., England, insisted on singing:

"Rule, rule Britannia,
God save the queen,
Good old Manhattan,
The best that e'er was seen,"

and the strains of his mellow voice came near breaking the windows of the Town Club.

The absurd nonsense which was talked some time ago about men covering the knee in *races* on road or path, *as bare knees were indecent* has gradually disappeared before the more sensible attention which it received from men who knew what was what.

Bare knees can never be indecent in a road or path race. Tights worn on the under body *are* indecent and always will be, and it is a most caddish thing to wear them for ordinary riding purposes. *The* thing for road *racing* is fairly loose flannel trousers, cut off about two inches above the knee, the rest of the leg to the ankle *bare* and a black or blue sock worn turned down to the shoe, though some riders prefer a tight fitting sock pulled up on the limb. For ordinary road racing, touring, etc., respectable garments (and not tights) should always be worn. You are supposed to be a gentleman, not an acrobat or tramp, clad in black underclothing, and the sooner you make up your mind *to put some clothes on* the better you will look, the better you will be treated by horsemen on the road, and the more rights you will have to the considerate respect of fellow creatures who break none of the rules of *decency* in regard to clothing.

But if you are a fat-headed lout, "keep on" riding in tights, but do not wonder if respectable wheelmen walk around you as if you were a white crow. Tights resemble a certain article of masculine apparel too closely to be decent. But what's the use of talking to the ——n fool wheelman?

The howl against bare knees in racing recalls the following lines from the New York *Tribune*, a peculiarly cleanly paper:

"The naked hills lie wanton to the breeze;
The fields are nude, the groves unfrocked.
Bare are the shivering limbs of shameless trees;
What wonder is it that the corn is shocked!"

With tights there is no protection from draughts, the dust flies through the open material, and I have overheard the feminine criticism that they are just too hor-rid for anything—and they are.

I have often noticed that *cycles* as well as boats run easiest at night. Not long ago in Scotland, I rode from Melrose to Peebles in less than two hours. I left Melrose Abbey Inn at ten o'clock and reached Peebles at ten minutes to twelve. It is over twenty-four miles, and I had some bad hills to ride in the dark on a twenty-eight pound safety without lamp or brake. I had also to ride through part of Melrose, Galashiels, Clovenfords, Walkerburn and Innerleithen. I could not without great exertion have ridden the distance over these roads, bad and hilly, in the same time in daylight. When I got to Peebles I was quite fresh and remarked the time on the luminous old town clock. What the reason for this is I do not know, but I think it is nevertheless true. Hills which I did not care about in the day time I have ridden at night. I remember riding some hills behind G. T. Langridge, of the North Road Club, one night when we were chased by a policeman in Kingston (Surrey), for being lampless. We dashed past him and up some lanes behind a dog cart, whose light helped us greatly on our way over the rough and hilly road to London. The hills were all ridden without fatigue, while in the day time they *feel* bad. The *sight* of a hill has something to do with it, just as they say beauty is alle samee in the dark. Who knows?

Tea, well diluted with water (without "cinders" of a *spiritual* nature) and luke warm, will be found to be a first class drink for cyclers. Milk and soda (the washy stuff) is good, as is oat-meal and water, or the flour from rice in a little water. Lime juice, despite all statements to the contrary, is wash of the vilest kind, and ruinous to the gastric juices of the stomach. That is, the ordinary lime-juice with the turpentine smell to which *we* have been accustomed. Such as is found in the average road-house or tavern. There are other drinks which are more toothsome and taken in *proper quantities* are I think beneficial before a long ride. Bass' Ale and Dublin Stout are very strengthening. Tanglefoot is hurtful to cyclers and should be avoided, except a glass of pure stuff, well diluted with cold water (not iced) after a billing race or ride. After a ride, but not to ride on.

"Happy the man, where'er he be,
Who loves a cup of fragrant tea,
But d——n the sanctimonious ass
Who scorns or dreads the name of 'Bass.'"

The man who conducts ("edits," as he says on the front page) the theatrical, pugilistic and dog-fighting *Whip* of Buffalo, a paper of the theatre-advertising programme type, has a cheek which Boulanger might envy. He calls himself "Pendragon," the world-renowned *nom de plume* of the English sporting authority who, in consort with "*Dagonet*"—George R. Sims (the second edition of the Prince of Wales)—edits the *Referee*, of London. This self-appointed American "Pendragon" had better leave his *nom de plume* on a peg in his office if ever he sets foot in England, or he may have some English "whip" laid athwart his shoulders.

This is a theft of the boldest and most contemptible sort. There is plenty of room at the top, and if this small-bored American counterfeit of a "Pendragon" wants to get there he should boom himself by his own and fair means, not by stealing the *nom de plume* of a writer who has written himself by gradual and honest stages to a foremost place in the English sporting press. JACK.

BROOKLYN NEWS.

The Kings County Wheelmen have taken the initiative step toward forming a baseball league among the cycling clubs of this vicinity. A preliminary meeting was held at their rooms on April 22, and the matter was discussed in all its pros and cons, and the Secretary of the K. C. W. Baseball Club was instructed to notify the other clubs of their purpose. A second meeting will be held in the K. C. W. parlors on May 11, when each club desiring to participate in the proposed scheme is requested to send two delegates to represent them. Any communications should be sent to J. R. Bedford, Secretary K. C. W. B. B. C. The idea is the result of sundry discussions held last season, when the boys of the K. C. W. and B. B. C. occasionally rode out to the Parade Grounds with their bats strapped on their handle-bars and a pocket or so distended with a ball, and there practised batting out or played a stuff game. There are a great many baseball enthusiasts among the Brooklyn wheelmen, and they should all fall in line with the K. C. W. and form a league whereby they might have an interesting series of games.

The Cyclists' Union has hired some men to remove the loose stones from Cobblestone Hill, which will materially lessen the discomforts of the wheelmen who are obliged to ride over it to reach the Park and other good riding grounds. It is a disgrace to Brooklyn that some of our principal thoroughfares are allowed to remain in such a disreputable condition. The Cyclists' Union cannot, with its present membership, undertake the expense of repaving a road or street, and their action in this case is about all they can do with the exception of "working" the authorities, which, I understand, they are doing. Another "rocky" street is Sixth Avenue. It was at one time macadamized, but all the foundation stones have worked up through the surface with holes at intervals along its entire length, so that it is now a dangerous surface to ride over at night. And this is one of Brooklyn's best residential streets! The Park Commissioners are repairing the West Side Drive between the Flatbush Avenue entrance and Third Street. Wheelmen may avoid the repairs and yet retain the best part of the West Side Drive by riding along the outside of the Park and going in at the Third Street entrance. The L. I. W and K. C. W. have a fine course for pleasant little evening rides, in the ride along Bedford Avenue to the fountain, and any pleasant night one can observe some of the boys out for a little exercise. It is also a favorite ride for the ladies who live in that part of the city.

The Murphy Brothers, K. C. W., captured first and second place in the Titan A. C. games held at the M. A. C. grounds Saturday afternoon. Schoefer, B. B. C., came in third, and while returning to the city jumped from a car and renewed a sprain which he got while riding last winter.

Bancroft and Seixas, B. B. C., were seen *driving* down the road and in the Park several times lately, and I believe they have purchased a very nobby rig, and will use it more during the summer than their wheels. Two good men gone wrong.

Capt. Meeteer, accompanied by First Lieut. Fay and E. Williams, all of the Brooklyns, enjoyed a run to Babylon last Sunday, and report that the roads are in good shape.

Brooklyn, May 7, 1889. ATOL.

NEW ORLEANS.

The second day of the entertainment for the benefit of the Home for Homeless Women, attracted a large number of visitors to Audubon Park on May 2. It was a day of excellent sport, deserving liberal patronage on its merits not to mention the worthiness of the cause. The affair proved successfully financially, which is the best reward to the noble ladies who unselfishly devoted their efforts to the charity.

The first part of the afternoon was devoted to bicycle races. Messrs. Harry Hodgson and B. C. Rea and R. Sherhouse were the judges, Mr. E. A. Shields the starter, and Messrs. C. E. Fenner and Harry Fairfax the timers.

The first race was for boys under 16 years, half-mile dash for a silver medal. The entries were:

	Age	Size of wheel inches.
H. Shaw	11	38
E. Dupre	13	42
Tony Golding	11	42
H. M. Hardie	14	46

Golding set the pace, Hardie passed him and led down the backstretch, and Dupre closed gradually, caught Hardie in the last turn and led easily in the stretch. Dupre won in 2:01¾, Hardie second, Golding third.

The second race was a mile handicap for a gold medal. The following were the starters and handicaps:

A. M. Hill, N. O. B. C., scratch; B. M. Sprigg, 71 feet; Harold Christy, L. C. C., 129 feet; Jeff Frederick, 129 feet, W. M. Hathorne, L. C. C., 129 feet; E. M. Graham, 156 feet; Frank Born, 207 feet; Jack Dodge, 234 feet; W. C. Grevot, 234 feet; W. H. Renaud, 245 feet; Charles Shute; 300 feet.

Capt. Hill, the scratch man, was never in the race. Shute led for a quarter of a mile, with Hathorn spurting through the bunch a second, but in the stretch, in the first round, Christy went by all of them and was never beaten. Hathorn held on to second place until the last turn, where Sprigg caught and passed him and made a good finish. Christy won in 3:23 1-5; Sprigg second, 3:24; Hathorn third, 3:30; Dodge, Frederick, Hill and Born following in that order; the others straggling in.

These races were so well contested that an extra half-mile dash, for a silver medal, was gotten up. The entries were I. Mehlig, of St. Louis and B. M. Sprigg, L. C. C. N. O. B. C.; W. C. Grevot, Chas. Shute, Jack Dodge, W. M. Hathorn and Jeff Frederick. Little Dupre ran for sport, but could not beat the big fellows. Frederick set the pace for a little, but Sprigg went out and rode a good race, winning in 1:37 1-5, Hathorn a good second, Frederick Dodge, Grevot and Shute following, the St. Louis man not finishing.

SAN FRANCISCO.

The bicycle races held under the auspices of the Bay City Wheelmen, at the Haight Street Athletic Grounds, yesterday afternoon, furnished a rare day's sport. The morning was dull and threatened rain. An early visit to the grounds showed the track—a quarter mile—in fine order, but a stiff wind was blowing. The track was measured and found to be six feet eight inches over in the lap. Owing to the procession in honor of the Washington Inauguration starting late, it was nearly 3 o'clock before the grounds presented a lively appearance. The first race was called soon after that hour. The wind was blowing down the finish very strong and interfered greatly with the riders.

As representatives of all the principal bicycle clubs in the State participated in the events the following table will explain the meaning of the different initials which appear in the subjoined report: B. C. W., Bay City Wheelmen; S. F. Bi C., San Francisco Bicycle Club; G. C. W., Gadren City Wheelmen; S. J. Un., San José Unattached; O. L. W., Oak Leaf Wheelmen; Un., Unattached; U. W., University Wheelmen. The following are the names of the officials: Fred Russ Cook, referee; Edwin Mohrig, L. Devany and Frank F. Osborn, judges; George H. Strong, Richard Thompson and C. P. Fonda, timers; Sanford Plummer, starter; L. M. Hall, J. E. Bauer, C. B. Wheaton and Al Merigot, umpires; F. W. Pierson and W. E. Thompson, clerks, C. A. Angell and C. E. Elliott, scorers.

The starters in the first heat of the novice race were W. A. Shockley, B C W.; E. P. Hilborn U. W.; E. F. Haas, U. W.; R. L. Ingram, S. F. Bi. C.; Thomas H. Doane, B. C. W.

Hilborn and Haas alternated in leading until the last lap, when Haas spurted and crossed the tape with a good lead; Doane second; Shockley a good third. Time, 3m. 14 3-5s.

The starters in the second heat were C. A. Howard, B. C. W.; T. W. Durrant, Un; Henry Smith, G. C. W.; Joseph Desimone, G. C. W.; Paul Stockton, Un. The finish, between Smith and Desimone, was very exciting, Smith winning in the last spurt by a yard; Desimone second. Time, 3m. 14 2-5s.

The final heat was watched with interest, as a close race was looked for between Haas, Smith, Doane and Desimone. Doane cut out the pace and the clip was a very brisk one until half the distance was completed, when the riders began to open up gaps on each other. Haas, toward the finish, went to the front with a splendid spurt, and, although Smith made a great effort to remain in company with him, he failed in the last lap and Haas rode over the line an easy victor. Result—Haas first; Smith second. Time, 3m. 13⅗s.

In the half-mile handicap the starters were J. E. Hickinbottom, O. L. W., scratch; R. L. Ingham, S. F. Bi. C., 30 yards; R. W. Turner, B. C. W., scratch; George T. Balch, S. F. Bi. C., 30 yards; F. E. Southworth, O. L. W., 20 yards; T. W. Gilmour, B. C. W., 40 yards; Alphonse Col, G. C. W., 25 yards. At the crack of the pistol Gilmour, from the limit mark, rode as hard as he could, with Hickinbottom, scratch, gaining gradually. At the lower corner Ingham and Southworth both went over and nearly brought Hickinbottom with them; he had to do some skillful riding to avoid them, and then went in pursuit of Gilmour, whom he caught 100 yards from the tape, and then followed as pretty a finish as was ever seen. Gilmour finished "all out," and the decision of the three judges was that he won by inches in 1m. 26⅘s. Hickinbottom's time was phenomenal considering the heavy wind up the straight to the finish and the fact of the men falling in front of him in the first lap. Had the day been calm he could have beaten the coast record of 1m. 22s. for the distance.

The third event on the programme was a 3-mile handicap for which were entered Julius Smith, G. C. W., scratch; J. Desimone, G. C. W., 150 yards; J. E. Hickinbottom, O. L. W., scratch; Clive Weathers, G. C. W., 175 yards; F. E. Southworth, O. L. W., 120 yards; Thomas H. Doane, B. C. W., 175 yards; F. E. Richardson, B. C. W., 120 yards. Richardson got away sluggishly but soon overtook the limit men and had a good chance to win, but he was nervous about the "hospital corner," and the consequence was he back-pedaled each time he passed the corner, and in the last mile Smith easily overtook and passed him and going in won as he pleased in [illegible] second.

Two riders started in the 1-mile university championship, namely E. P. Hillborn and C. E. Townsend. The race was the only "waiting" race of the day and was won by Townsend. Time, 3m. 44 1-5s.

The 2-mile safety handicap brought out the following starters and resulted in a very interesting race: L. R. Cole, S. J. Un., scratch; C. B. Lakenau, U. W., scratch; W. A. Shockley, B. C. W., scratch; C. F. English, B. C. W. scratch; George T. Balch, S. F. Bi. C., 75 yards; C. N. Langton, B. C. W., 100 yards; George H. Siebe, B. C. W., 125 yards, Paul Stockton, S. J. Un., 125 yards. In the final mile the slow ones dropped out gradually until the field of battle was left to Lakenau and English. The former put on some excellent bursts of speed and held the winning position for a couple of laps. English, who was riding like a veteran, took premier position two laps from home and, responding to every spurt of Lakenau's, won a splendid race in the fast time of 6m. 11 4-5s., Lakenau second.

The ½-mile juvenile race was very amusing. Six youngsters started but three pushers-off did not get out of the way in time and in consequence three of them "croppered." They were by no means discouraged and started after the leaders, but they could not overtake Harry Button, who won looking around in 2m. 3s., fairly good time for the distance.

The 1-mile handicap brought out the following contestants: J. E. Hickinbottom, O. L. W., scratch; F. F. Southworth, O. L. C., 40 yards; H. Smith, G. C. W., 60 yards; L. G. Hodgkins, B. C. W., 40 yards; Alphonse Col, G. C. W.,

60 yards; W. Needham, G. C. W., 60 yards. Hickinbottom rode the first lap very fast and had just got up with the field when Hodgkins went over torough touching handle-bars with Southworth. This rattled Hickinbottom and he quit on the next lap. Southworth and Smith riding very strongly, had a lively "dust-up" at the finish, resulting in a win for Southworth, Smith second. Time, 3m 2 1-4s.

The contestants for the two-mile university championship were C. E. Townsend and E. F. Haas. It was thought that Townsend would be a sure winner, but Haas, who was in splendid condition, cut out a lively pace in the last half of the race, and won a comparatively easy victory in 6 minutes 52 3-5 seconds.

Townsend could not hold his pedals in the last lap, but Haas proved a splendid rider and will be heard from again.

The final event of the day was a five-mile handicap, for which were entered: Julius Smith, G. C. W., scratch; R. W. Turner, B. C. W., scratch, and J. E. Richardson, B. C. W., 100 yards.

Richardson had recovered from his nervousness about the bad corner, and took it much better and rode generally in better form than in the three miles. Smith on the contrary did not come up to his three-mile form, possibly because Turner rode lapping him for the five miles, something he was not accustomed to. Richardson held his handicap the entire distance, and won easily in 17:00 2-5. Smith and Turner had a determined spurt for second place, which resulted in favor of Smith by two feet.

The long programme was run off without a hitch, and although some bad-looking headers were taken no one was injured. The prizes were valuable and attracted all the crack riders within 100 miles of this city. The handicapping was excellent, especially as fifteen of the twenty-eight entrants had never previously ridden in a race, and consequently were without records for the handicap committee to work on.

A number of Eastern riders were in the audience, among them Messrs. Wirtner and Hughson, of Buffalo, Toie, of Louisville, and D. Wood, of the Manhattan Athletic Club, of New York. CALIFORNIA.

May 1, 1889.

PROVIDENCE.

Mr. Howard L. Perkins, whose connection with cycling in this city and State has been long and active, and who is one of the most prominent members in the State Division and the R. I. W., has sent in his resignation to be released from all offices and committees with which his name is associated. Mr. Perkins is Vice Consul of the Division and *ex-officio* member of the finance committee, and is the special committee of the executive board selected to get up the league hand-book. He holds the office of Captain in the Rhode Island Wheelmen and is also Treasurer of that club. His resignation from all the various offices has been sent in to the Chief Consul of the Division and the President of the club respectively. By Mr. Perkin's retirement from official position in the Division and in the club both organizations are losers. His wide knowledge of and large experience in cycling matters made him especially valuable in official capacity, aside from the qualities of energy and sound sense on all matters pertaining to the interests of the organizations, that he possessed in high degree. Mr. Perkins has long been looked up to as one of the seers in things wheeling in this State, and he maintained an active appreciation of affairs that remains with too few cyclers when they have become "veterans." Mr. Perkins' business and his private affairs engage him so much that he feels obliged to relinquish his official connection with concerns outside.

The route of the spring club and ladies' run of the Rhode Island Wheelmen Monday, May 20, is as follows: Sharon to Boston, via Canton, Ponkapoag and Milton Lower Falls, with an afternoon run to Chestnut Hill Reservoir and return. A circular will be issued by the committee shortly giving all details of the trip.

Three members of the Pawtucket Fire Department respond to alarms on safeties.

North Attleboro is practically without hotel accommodations, the famous league hotel, the Wamsutta, having made an assignment, and being closed up pending action by the creditors. The wheelmen most will hope for its early reopening, and for the quick recovery of mine host Davenport from his financial trouble.

Rev. B. B. Haskell, of the Baptist Church, Hope Valley, is the latest addition to the clerical cyclers in the State.

The committee of the Rhode Island Wheelmen on the Memorial Day tournament are laboring industriously and things are getting into shape. The Chairmen of the various sub-committees meet every Saturday night and hold special meetings occasionally beside.—*Providence Journal.*

TROY NOTES.

The bowling alley committee of the Troy Bicycle Club awarded the gold badge to John M Van Arnam on the evening of May 1 for the best average in five games played during the Winter and Spring. The badge is of unique design and consists of pins and balls neatly arranged. Mr. Van Arnam's scores were 260, 288, 248, 277 and 275, an average of 270 nearly. There has been a lively competition among members of the club for this honor and the result has been greater proficiency in the art of bowling.

The *Telegram*, of Monday last, says: "A large number of the Troy Bicycle Club's riding members went on a run to Mechanicville yesterday morning. Raymond S. Coon, of Boston, was one of the party."

This is recorded as the *first* run of the season. It seems to me rather a late *first* run as the roads have been in condition some weeks.

I do not believe in regularly organized runs on Sunday. There may be no harm in riding quietly along out into the country to enjoy the beauties of nature, but publicly called runs and races held on Sunday do cycling and the persons who participate no good.

I ride on Sunday and enjoy a short tour in the afternoon, but a large party scorching along, racing with horses, etc., I hardly think is just the thing. It is no worse riding a wheel than riding behind a horse or walking on Sunday, but either one is wrong if improperly indulged in. The rector of our church uses his wheel on Sunday and thinks it a good thing, but what would we think should he race with every horse he overtook and scorched along with members of his church or others? There is no harm in *riding* a wheel on Sunday but (draw your own conclusions.)

May 7, 1889. ORBIT CITY.

Twenty-five Mile Road Race.

The Twenty-five Mile Road Race to be run over the Irvington-Milburn course May 30 has excited great local interest, and from the present outlook it bids fair to be the greatest road contest ever held in this vicinity.

The committee having charge of the details of the race held a long session at the office of THE WHEEL on Friday evening last. The rules adopted for the management of the race will be found in another column.

The entries close May 15, with A. B. Barkman, 241 Broadway. No entries received after that date will be considered.

The race will start at 11 o'clock sharp, and contestants who calculate for the usual hour's delay will "get left."

The handicapping committee, composed of Messrs. Wetmore, Barkman and Prial, will do their utmost to give every competitor a fair chance.

The following prizes have already been contributed:

Overman Wheel Co., a bicycle, ordinary or safety, valued at $130; Mr. J. W. Spalding, a gold watch, valued at $80; Mr. George R. Bidwell, a French marble clock, valued at $50; Mr. F. P. Prial, a heavy-plate silver cup, fourteen inches high, lined with gold, valued at $40; Messrs. Merwin, Hulbert & Co., an M. & H. double action revolver, gold plated barrel and pearl handle, value, $25; Eastman Dry Plate and Film Co., a "Kodak" camera; William Halpin & Co., a "Waterbury" camera; Messrs. Holmes & Co., a Centennial jersey; The Butcher Cyclometer Co., a cyclometer; Mr. H. J. Hall, Jr., of Highland Mills, N. Y., a superb trout fishing outfit; Messrs. Ira Perego & Co., a wristlet, with silver watch; New York Bicycle Co., a sterling silver handled umbrella; Messrs. Singer & Co., prize not yet selected; Messrs. H. A. Smith & Co., prize not yet selected; Mr. Chas. Schwalbach, prize not yet selected.

The entries received to date are: Wilmington Wheel Club will enter nine men, names not yet given; Quotropp, Q. C. W.; Beazley, K. C. W.; T. J. Hall, K. C. W.; Wilson, K. C. W.; W. H. and C. M. Murphy, K. C. W.; Steves, K. C. W.; F. B. Hesse, K. C. W.; Bensinger, K. C. W.; H. J. Hall, Jr., K. C. W.; Purvis-Bruce, Ripley Road Club; Schumacher, L. I. W.; Nisbett, N. Y. B. C.; Class, B. B. C.; Williams, B. B. C.; Waters, B. B. C.; Putney, Manhattan B. C.; A. C. Banker, New York; W. D. Banker, Pittsburg, and L. H. Wise, L. I. W.

The headquarters of the competitors and officials will be at the Hilton Hotel. A large room has been hired at the hotel, which will be placed at the disposal of competitors and attendants.

RULES OF THE DECORATION DAY ROAD RACE.

TWENTY-FIVE MILE HANDICAP ROAD RACE.

To be held May 30, 1889, on the Irvington-Milburn course, Open to all amateur wheelmen who have never been professionals or promateurs. Entrance fee $1, to be sent to A. B. Barkman, 241 Broadway, New York, on or before May 15.

Special entry blanks must be filled out. Same can be had on application as above. The right to reject any entry is reserved.

GENERAL RULES TO GOVERN CONTEST.

The officers of the race shall be a referee, seven judges, five timekeepers, one starter, one clerk of the course and assistants, one scorer and nine assistants, two umpires and assistants, and two marshals and assistants.

REFEREE.

The referee shall have general supervision of the race during its progress, and shall give judgment on protests received by him; shall decide all questions or protests respecting foul riding, etc., of which he may be personally cognizant, or which may be brought to his notice by any other official. He shall decide all questions whose settlement is not provided for in these rules. His decision shall be final.

JUDGES.

There shall be seven judges at the finish. In case of a disagreement, a majority shall decide. Their decision as to the order in which the men finish shall be final.

CLERK OF THE COURSE.

The clerk of the course shall arrange the men in groups according to handicap ready for the start. Competitors must report to him promptly as their numbers are called.

UMPIRES.

It shall be the duty of each umpire to oversee that part of the course to which he is assigned by the chief umpire, and to watch closely the riding, and immediately after the race to report to the referee any competitor or competitors whose riding may be considered unfair.

COMPETITORS.

Each competitor must be at the tape and in position according to handicap, and ready to start promptly at the time appointed. Each man competing shall be distinctly numbered. The start shall be made from a standstill by push-off, and no call-back will be allowed under any circumstances after the leading men have started. Any competitor who is not on his mark and ready to start promptly on time will be placed with the first group starting after his arrival. Any competitor failing to finish race within two hours after the start shall not be entitled to a position. Competitors must be properly attired.

RULE OF THE ROAD.

The law of the road shall be strictly observed. All contestants must keep to the right, and when passing in the same direction must go to the left. Any violation of this rule shall be to the violator's peril, and in case of a foul be shall be ruled out.

The contestant reaching the turning point first shall have the right of way. No side paths shall be taken. Violation of this rule shall be judged a foul.

CHANGE OF MACHINES.

Contestants may change machines during the race, but they must at all times be with a wheel, and make no progress unaccompanied by a wheel.

PROTESTS.

All protests in regard to foul riding may be submitted to any judge or umpire, and shall be decided by the referee.

PACE-MAKING.

If clearly proven that any contestant submits by consent to pace-making he shall be liable to disqualification.

TIME OF EVENT.

The race shall start at 11 o'clock A. M. sharp, rain or shine.

L. I. W. RACE MEET.

The Long Island Wheelmen's second annual meeting will be held at the Brooklyn Athletic Club's grounds, corner De Kalb and Classon Avenues, Saturday June 15, 1889, at 3 P. M. Events, under L. A. W. rules:

1 Mile Novice, open.
1 and 3-Mile Handicap, open.
1 Mile Ride and Run, open.
1 4-5 Miles Relay Club Race (three men each club).
1 Mile Safety Race, open and handicap.
1 Mile Novice, B. B. C.
1 Mile Consolation.
½ Mile Run, open, A. A. U. rules.
2 Mile L. I. W. Club Handicap.

Entries close Saturday, June 8, 1889, with L. H. Wise, 1281 Bedford Avenue, Brooklyn. Entrance fee 50 cents, to accompany entry or not received. Relay race $2 per club. Admission 25 cents. Reserved and numbered seats, 50 cents. Procurable at L. I. W. clubhouse, 1281 Bedford Avenue. Handicapper, F. P. Prial, WHEEL. Gold and silver medals to first and second on all events. Banner to winning club in relay race.

Distances on Long Island from Prospect Park, Plaza entrance.

South Gate via West Drive	2
" " " Circuit	2½
Olmsteds " West Drive	3½
Howes " " "	4½
Bath " " "	6½
" " Kings Highway	7½
Coney Island	7½
Sheepshead Bay	7½
Canarsie Beach	7½
Bay Ridge (Shore)	6
Fort Hamilton via Parkville	8½
" " " Kings Highway	9½
East New York " Atlantic Avenue	4½
Jamaica (Pettits)	7½
Queens	10½
Hyde Park	14½
Garden City	17½
Hempstead	19½
Roslyn	[illegible]
Amityville	32½
Babylon	35
Islip	[illegible]
Patchogue	[illegible]
Far Rockaway via Hempstead	[illegible]
Fountain to Fountain (Bedford Avenue)	[illegible]

THE CAMBRIDGE CLUB MINSTRELS GIVE THEIR ANNUAL SHOW.

The Cambridge Bicycle Club gave its annual minstrel show last Thursday evening in Union Hall, Cambridgeport, before a good-sized audience. Some of the local hits of the end men were capital, and the audience was quick to "catch on." The topical song, "What Would Be Left in It Then?" sung by the author and composer, Mr. A. H. Davenport, was well received. The remainder of the programme was given by Walter E. Stone, "Meet a Coon To-Night;" F. L. Torrey, "Farewell, Marguerite;" H. H. Burns, "Whistling Coon;" A. R. Torrey, "Little Fisher Maiden;" W. C. Curtis, "Up Dar in de Sky;" J. J. Coleman, "Marriage Bells;" selections by the orchestra, glee club and Cambridge Banjo, Mandolin and Guitar Club. Mr. John Amee acted as interlocutor, Henry J. Ballou as musical director, and the following as end men: Walter E. Stone and W. C. Curtis, bones; A. H. Davenport and H. H. Burns, tambos.

During the performance several of the talent were presented with floral designs. The programme was in the form of a souvenir, and was a very handsome affair.

K. C. W.'s RACKET

I had to go over to Brooklyn on Wednesday night; I didn't want to go, but the managing editor said that the K. C. W.'s racket must be reported. The affair was stag, and was tendered to the L. I. W., many of whose members were present.

A stage had been erected at one end of the K. C. W.'s ample front parlor, or rather in a room connecting the front and back parlors, and from this eminence the talent was let off. About one hundred men were present, and the gathering included all the "good people," by whom I mean the men who run Brooklyn's Clubs. Among those present I ran across President Bridgman, T. C. Crichton, George Courtenay, "Charl." and "Miles" Murphy, the road fiends; "Tom" Hall and "Tom" Beazley, scorchers from way back; G. D. Neppert, Harry Hall, Jr., who wants to be at scratch in the road race—laudable ambition; R. W. Steves, future champion; J. P. Stevens, of the race meet committee; "Cap." Marion, Hagnall, scribe of the *Times*; Riefschneider, scribe of the *Press*; Roberts, scribe of the *Citizen*. The Long Island braves were out in force. I saw President L. A. W. Luscomb, with his attendant luminaries "Doc." Gilfillan and Frank Shaw; Michael Furst, Lieut. Wise, "Cap." Mabie, President L. I. W. Mabie, Clarke, Isaacson, Harris, and a host of others.

The most exciting sport of the evening was the boxing. Mr. William Robertson, Brooklyn A. C. acted as master of ceremonies. The first pair were two Brooklyn men, Messrs. Lutz and Schuster, both heavy men, who furnished good sport in three rounds and a wind-up. Lutz, being the cleanest hitter and delighting in quick work, Schuster relying on rushes and strength.

The next pair were two Pastime men, Messrs. Steffins and Donoghue. Donoghue was quick as a cat, and worked his arms nervously, getting in some telling blows. Steffins presented a good front and gave as good as he received. This was the liveliest bout of the evening. The other pairs were Messrs. Fenton and Finn, and Bensinger and Pettitt, the latter pair giving a good show.

Mr. Clarke cleverly recited a parody on Poe's "Raven," in which it appeared that a stupid "donk," of Celtic extraction, wandered into the cabin of a native Hibernian. "Donk" stupidly reiterated the name of Mary Moore, name of girl worshipped by native. Patrick got "hunk" on the "donk" with the aid of a blackthorn. Mr. Whymper, K. C. W., gave an excellent violin solo, Dr. Plympton gave a better than ordinary seance of magic and spiritualistic manifestations, and told the boys how it was done; Mr. F. W. Knight gave negro imitations. After the entertainment the boys adjourned to the wheel-room, cleared for the occasion, where refreshments were serv. d.

"Doc" Gilfillan has ridden 1300 miles this year; splendid record for a man of his age and physique. The "Doc" is after a medal.

Charley Schwalbach has been riding a "goat," not a rear-driver, but that mysterious animal which it is generally supposed a newly-initiated Mason rides.

Twenty-five per cent. of the L. I. W. are Masons. Frank Shaw has reached the 32d degree, and is now a Prince of the R. S. and Master of the G. S.

There is lots of big scorching being done in the Park. It is said that the handicapping committee have touts out in the Park who hold watches on every man around the circuit. This is untrue, however; it is merely a rumor. T. L. Wilson was going like snakes, but took a bad header a few days ago. Tom Hall is riding very fast; so is Beazley. Miles Murphy is piling up miles, but the number is a dead secret. The Murphy brothers are the greatest pot hunters and mile hunters on wheels.

TITNAM.

The Wheel is still pegging away at the road improvement question, and from the pertinacity and knowledge of the subject displayed by the editor, much good can be expected. After all, this matter of road improvement is the most important function of the League, and if the subject were given the attention it deserves, much good would result. The agitation of the subject will do more to bring the L. A. W. into prominence, and aid it in proselytizing than all the race meets and junketing tours, to which some of its leading officers seem so partial. *The Wheel* can be relied upon, let the other cycle papers fall into line. In the language of a shrewd, but rather illiterate merchant of this city, "A good copy is better as a bad original!" *Pittsburg Bulletin.*

CURSORY TRAINING.

With the opening of the racing season there will be many hundreds of young men who, while having neither opportunity, time nor inclination to indulge in that systematic course of path training to which our champions and other fliers of note resort, still have the desire to undergo some sort of rough preparation for the fray which they anticipate in the local or other sports, or in their club championship, and to these a few words may not be out of place. In the first place, we take it for granted that if there is a track handy there the tyro will go, but as tracks are a rarity, we deal with the road. Beyond everything must be remembered the old adage, "Practice makes perfect," and, indeed, for such cursory training as we refer to practice is the main thing. The distance for which the novice desires to prepare himself should be ridden over daily, not at top speed, but at a good swinging pace nearly equal to it, and this should be continued until the rider can easily get over the distance without "blowing," and feel he can raise a 200 yards sprint at any time to the finish. This sort of practice will consolidate his staying powers, and then he may turn his attention to speed, and, selecting some straight road with good surface and free from traffic, he can indulge in short bursts at the highest speed he is capable of, putting every ounce in, setting himself first a distance of about 100 yards, and gradually increasing this distance up to, say, 250 yards, or a bit more if he feels himself able. Two or three of these speed bursts a day will be quite sufficient, and when he can go the distance he has set himself without feeling the strain on his lungs, he can try the full distance again as before, and see if he can carry his sprint throught at the end of it, and practice it until he can. To the average individual, whose mornings and evenings only are at his disposal for training, we would advise no sprinting before breakfast—let all this work be kept for the evening. If, after his practice, a bath or good rub down and a change into dry garments can be had, so much the better; and we would here advise no one to do any hard riding on the road in other than woolen underclothing, and to be careful to put a neck-wrap on and button up the coat closely when dismounted or ceasing to ride fast. In regard to diet much nonsense has been written in the past, and our novice, beyond refraining from over-indulgence in either food or drink, and eschewing those things which his own experience teaches him do not agree with his internal economy, need not trouble himself. He should, in fact, live "well and wisely." For the man who rides either safety or tricycle, and while occasionally racing on path or good grass courses, has to do what training he does upon the road, we can here give a tip from our own experience in years gone by, which is to use the same machine—a semi-racer—but *have two gearings fitted.* All that will, with most machines, be required for this will be a spare crank-bracket, wheel and chain. Let him then use the lower gear upon the road, and shift his gear for the higher one for path or good grass work. For a rough grass course, naturally, he would use his road gearing. The reason for this is—and everyone who rides on a track for the first time will find it out—that the running is so much easier that the machine runs away from the rider practically—*i. e.*, using the same exertion.

Before and after his training he should rub himself well down with a coarse bath towel, and may follow this up by an application of flesh gloves. By this means the perspiration is all removed, and there remains no unpleasant feeling of stickiness for the rest of the day. A bath, when the training is over, is most enjoyable, but does not agree with everybody, and unfortunately, the proprietors of most tracks in Scotland look upon bathing accommodation as quite an unnecessary luxury.

The old ideas of having to eat half-raw beef-steak and eschewing everything in the way of vegetables, and getting up at five o'clock in the morning when in training for any kind of athletic exercise, have fortunately exploded. And for cycle-racing, it is not of so much importance to diet oneself with care, as, for instance, for foot-racing. To our mind the less that the cyclist, in training, deviates from his ordinary feeding the better. It is always well to avoid pastry, plum puddings and anything very indigestible, but vegetables and fruit taken in moderation are anything but harmful. For breakfast, porridge, and some fish, eggs, steak, or chops; for dinner, almost anything, except what is mentioned above; for tea, omitting the porridge, the same dishes as mentioned for breakfast, may safely be recommended. A little beer or stout may be taken to dinner.

The adage of "six hours' sleep for a man, seven for a woman and eight for a fool," does not apply to the man who is training. He wants plenty of sleep, and should have eight hours at least in bed every night if he can manage it. A short walk, or five minutes with a pair of light dumb bells and a cold bath should precede breakfast. But any very violent exertion on an empty stomach is very bad for one, whereas a few minutes of exhilarating exercise will sharpen one's appetite wonderfully, and assist digestion. As we have already observed, a cold bath does not agree with everybody, and if there is the least feeling of chill or discomfort of any kind after it, it should be stopped.

In the course of a few months, it may be weeks only, the rider may become "stale." He will first have reached a certain stage of perfection, and then commenced to go backward. There is a feeling of weariness, of lassitude, and usually very little flesh on his bones. A week's road riding, and fairly liberal potations of beer and stout, unless the subject is a rabid teetotaller, will often have a wonderful effect. But if it is near the end of the season when the "staleness" comes on, it will be as well to give up path work and enjoy the few riding weeks remaining with road work.

While we do not recommend much road-riding when in training for laurels on the path, a club run once or twice a week will do little, if any harm.

We have, of necessity, made our remarks of a very general nature. This is not a treatise on training, but a few unambitious hints; and the idiosyncrasies even of athletes are so varied that the course of training suitable for one man might, in a fortnight, hopelessly ruin another's chance of success for a whole season. The novice will, in course of time, find out for himself how best to make the most of his athletic talents, but to one thing he may as well make up his mind at once—if he hasn't got the right stuff in him, if he train until Doomsday he will always make a poor show.

RIDING A BICYCLE UNDER WATER.

BOSTON, May 5 (Special). - *The Globe* is responsible for the following story: The recent sinking of the little steamer Carlotta in the Merrimac River, just below Mitchell's Falls, was marked by a wonderful feat of a bicyclist. James Webb and several other wheelmen were on the deck of the steamer. Webb was mounted on his bicycle doing the "standstill" act. The Carlotta, under full head of steam, made a rush to ascend the rapids, but before reaching them a little rope broke and the boat was thrown out of her course. Going at a high rate of speed, she struck on the smooth ledge which rises out of the water at the foot of the falls with such a force that the boat was carried half her length on the slippery surface. The propeller then broke on the rock, and the Carlotta sank like a bar of lead. Webb's friends all managed to swim ashore with no more damage than a thorough wetting. But Webb and his bicycle were thrown over the side of the vessel and sank immediately. Webb is thoroughly at home in the water, and when he went overboard he did not think of letting go of his bicycle. It was too valuable to lose. The wheel must have slid down between two stones, for when the machine struck the bottom it remained upright. Instinctly Webb's feet sought the pedals, and, putting forth all his muscle, he actually propelled the bicycle over the hard, sandy bottom, and up the ledge for a distance of sixty feet. It can be easily imagined what a cheer greeted the appearance of his head above the water. There have been some people skeptical enough to doubt this performance, but when shown through a water-glass the wheel's track in the sand they have been promptly convinced. Webb has become enthusiastic over submarine cycling, and says that as soon as he can devise some way of keeping up the supply of air he will try for a one-mile bicycle record under water. He is prepared to receive challenges.—*New York Tribune, May 6, 1889.*

FIXTURES.

May 10, 1889.—Twelfth Regiment Games. Entries close May 4 with C. J. Leach, P. O. Box 3,201.
May 11, 1889.—Harvard Bicycle Club Open Amateur Race Meet at Cambridge, Mass. Entries close May 4. Address H. H. Davis, Cambridge, Mass.
May 13-18, 1889.—Chicago Cycling Exhibit and Tournament, Exposition Building.
May 18, 1889.—A. Elwell's European Party sails from New York.
May 16, 1889.—Stone-Lumsden 1-mile Match Race, at Chicago, Ill.
May 18, 1889.—S. I. A. C. games at West New Brighton, S. I. Two miles bicycle handicap. Entries close May 11, with F. W. Janssen, P. O. Box 125, N. Y. City.
May 25, 1889.—Stone-Lumsden 3-mile Match Race, at St. Louis, Mo.
May 27, 1889.—Stone-Lumsden 15-mile Match Race at Crawfordsville, Ind.
May 30, 1889.—N. J. A. C. 1½ mile and 3-mile handicaps. Entries close May 27, with A. M. Sweet, P. O. Box 160, Bergen Point, N. J.
May 30, 1889.—Maine Division Meet. at Biddeford, Me.
May 30, 1889.—Bicycle and Athletic Tournament and 5-mile L. A. W. Championship Race at Narragansett Park.
May 30, 1889.—Pullman Road Race, Chicago to Pullman.
May 30, 1889.—Twenty-five-mile Handicap Road Race, Irvington—Milburn course. Entries close May 25th with A. B. Barkman, 121 Broadway, New York.
May 30. 1889.—Rhode Island Wheelman's Race Meet at Narragansett Park, Providence, R. I. Entries close with C. E. Campbell, Providence, R. I.
June 4, 5, 6, 1889.—Kansas Division Meet at Forest Park. Ottawa, Kansas.
June 8, 1889.—Century Run, Orange, N. J., to Philadelphia. Chairman, L. A. Clarke, 25 Broad Street, New York.
June 13, 1889.—L. A. W. Race Meet at Brooklyn Athletic Grounds. Entries close June 8 with L. N. Wise, 1,281 Bedford Ave. Brooklyn.
June 15, 1889.—Two-mile Bicycle Handicap at New York Athletic Club Grounds, Travers Island.
June 28, 29, 1889.—Kings County Wheelmen's Annual Meet at Washington Park, Brooklyn. Address W. C. Nellis, 1,835 Bedford Avenue.
July 2, 3, 1889.—League Meet at Hagerstown, Md.
July 4, 1889.—Race Meet at Brownsville. Pa
July 20, 1889.—One-mile and 5-mile Bicycle and 5-mile Tricycle N. C. U. championships at Paddington, Eng., race track.
July 27, 1889.—One-mile and 25-mile Tricycle and 5-mile Bicycle N. C. U. Championships at Paddington, Eng., track.

CHICAGO TOURNAMENT ENTRIES.

ONE-MILE, SCRATCH.—Percy Stone, St. Louis; George Beard, Lew Fleshey, Frank Seifken, Omaha; H. L. Kingsland, Baltimore; Bryson Burroughs, Cincinnati; W. D. Sherriff, California, Mo.; T. T. Roe and A. M. Luce, Chicago.

ONE-MILE, NOVICES. — F. H. Tuttle, H. F. Beckman, W. H. Arthur, L. M. Cope, W. S. Farrant, H. E. Loveday, Albert Kuehuel, H. A. Kohler, A. L. A. Wallace, F. L. Chase, Jr., and R. G. Goodrich.

ONE-MILE (men who have never raced).—F. H. Tuttle, H. F. Beckman, R. H. Goodrich, W. H. Arthur, L. M. Cope, W. S. Farrant, H. E. Loveday, P. K. Tyng, C. J. Guthrie, J. R. Black, A. Kuehuel, A. L. A. Wallace and F. L. Chase, Jr.

FIVE-MILE HANDICAP.—Same as 3-mile, except Bodach, Loveday and Thorne.

TEN-MILE, SCRATCH.—A. E. Lumsden, T. T. Roe, F. E. Spooner, Chicago; C. C. Peabody, Geo. Beard and Lew Flesher, Omaha; H. L. Kingsland, Baltimore; Bryson Burroughs, Cincinnati; Bert Myers, Peoria; Percy Stone, St. Louis; F. Seifken, Omaha.

QUARTER-MILE, SCRATCH.—O. Wimmerstedt, F. E. Spooner, Geo. P. Washburn, H. F. Beckman, T. T. Roe, H. E. Loveday, Frank Riggs, H. A. Kohler, Chicago; Alfred Barrett, Birmingham, England; Percy Stone, St. Louis; Geo. Heard, Frank Seifken and Lew Flesher, Omaha; W. D. Sherriff, California, Mo.; H. L. Kingsland, Baltimore; Bryson Burroughs, Cincinnati.

THREE-MILE TEAM RACE.—Chicago, Illinois, Lincoln and Douglas clubs, Chicago, and Omaha B. C.

CLUB DRILL.—Illinois C. C., Douglas C. C.

ONE-MILE ROAD, SAFETIES. — Bryson Burroughs, Cincinnati; Bert Myers, Peoria; H. L. Kingsland, Baltimore; John Mason, A. L. A. Wallace, Chicago; Geo. Beard, Frank Seifken and Lew Flesher, Omaha.

THREE-MILE HANDICAP. — Percy Stone, St. Louis; Alfred Barrett, Birmingham, England; Lew Flesher, Geo. Beard, Frank Seifken and Will Pixley, Omaha; H. L. Kingsland, Baltimore; W. D. Sherriff, California, Mo.; Bryson Burroughs, Cincinnati; Bert Myers, Peoria; C. C. Peabody, Omaha; O. Wimmerstedt, A. M. Luce, F. E. Spooner, F. Bodach, F. H. Tuttle, H. S. Evans, T. T. Roe, H. E. Loveday, Geo. A. Thorne, J. R. Black, A. Kuehuel, A. L. Wallace, Chicago.

TWO-MILE, SAFETY.—John Mason. G. P. Wintermute, E. L. Thornton, Chicago; Percy Stone, St. Louis; Frank Seifken, Lew Flesher and George Beard, Omaha; H. L. Kingsland, Baltimore; W. D. Sherriff, California, Mo.

TWO-MILE, L. A. W. MEMBERS.—F. E. Spooner, A. M. Luce, F. Bodach, O. Wimmerstedt, F. H. Tuttle, H. S. Evans, T. T. Roe, H. E. Loveday, H. A. Kohler, F. L. Chase, Jr., Chicago; Percy Stone, St. Louis; Bryson Burroughs, Cincinnati; H. L. Kingsland, Baltimore; W. D. Sherriff, California, Mo.; George Beard, Lew Flesher and Frank Seifken, Omaha.

TWO-MILE, TANDEM.—H. L. Kingsland, T. T. Roe, Frank Riggs and A. E. Lumsden.

ONE-MILE RIDE AND RUN.—Bert Myers, Peoria; H. L. Kingsland, Baltimore; Lew Flesher and Frank Seifken, Omaha; Percy Stone, St. Louis; T. T. Roe, Frank Riggs, E. L. Thornton, Chicago.

ONE-MILE, HANDICAP.—Bryson Burroughs, Cincinnati; W. D. Sherriff, California, Mo.; Will Pixley, George Beard, Lew Flesher and Frank Seifken, Omaha; Alfred Barrett, Birmingham, England; A. M. Luce, O. Wimmerstedt, F. H. Tuttle, H. S. Evans, T. T. Roe, H. E. Loveday, George Thorne, J. R. Black, A. Kuehuel, Chicago; H. L. Kingsland, Baltimore.

ONE-MILE, SAFETY.—Percy Stone, St. Louis; H. L. Kingsland, Baltimore; George Beard, Lew Flesher and Frank Seifken, Omaha; F. E. Spooner, John Mason, O. D. Richardson, T. T. Roe, G. P. Wintermute, John Thiele, E. L. Thornton, A. M. Harris, Chicago.

ONE-MILE, LOCAL.—O. Wimmerstedt, A. M. Luce, F. E. Spooner, Frank Bodach, F. H. Tuttle, O. D. Richardson, H. E. Loveday, F. Riggs, George A. Thorne, J. M. Crennan, C. J. Guthrie, Albert Kuehuel, H. A. Kohler, A. L. A. Wallace, H. S. Evans, T. T. Roe, F. E. Spooner.

ONE-MILE, BOYS UNDER 16.—Will Pixley, Omaha; R. Richardson and James Levy, Chicago.

ONE-MILE, 3 MINUTE CLASS.—W. D. Sherriff, California, Mo.; George Beard, Lew Flesher, Omaha; Percy Stone, St. Louis; Alfred Barrett, Frank Riggs, F. E. Spooner, T. H. Tuttle, O. Wimmerstedt, H. F. Beckman, H. E. Loveday.

ONE-MILE, FLYING START.—H. L. Kingsland, Baltimore; Bryson Burroughs, Cincinnati; George Beard, Lew Flesher, Omaha; Frank Seifken, Omaha; Percy Stone, St. Louis; A. L. A. Wallace, H. E. Loveday, T. T. Roe, F. E. Spooner.

THE ENGLISH RACE PATH.

The "Big Four" this year will be Synyer, Osmond, Illston and Furnivall, all of whom, Illston excepted, will ride Humbers. Illston will mount a Rudge. Synyer, Osmond and Illston are big men; Furnivall has not grown much since his visit here. Synyer will probably show improved form over last year, and is capable of great things. Osmond is probably a 2.30 man, and Furnivall has done as square a 3.30 trial as ever was clocked, and he should improve for the rest he has had. Illston has been off the path for a year, having been suspended on a charge of makers-amateurism. Great things are expected of him.

Rowe's 2.29 4-5 is likely to go by the board this year. If the English makers covet the record, they can hire amateurs who can beat 2.29 even. More value is attached to an amateur than to a professional record. It is much better "ad."

Many of the crack English amateurs and English pros. are employed by makers. Their salaries range from 25 "bob" to £2, which they consider quite a good salary.

The racing season at Leicester opened April 20. F. W. Allard, 35 yards start, won the professional mile handicap in 2m. 48 4-58.

Osmond, scratch, won the mile handicap at Coventry on Easter Monday; time, 2m. 46 4-58. The quarter mile scratch bicycle race brought Illston and Osmond together. Illston won his heat in 38 4-58; Osmond had a walk over in his preliminary. In the final Osmond won inside position on a toss, and getting away first won by a foot; time, 38 3-58.

Howell, the professional champion, defeated English, Lee and other fast men in a two mile handicap, run at North Shields on Easter Saturday; time, 6m. 33 4-58.

Arthur Du Cross Synyer and Kilkelly competed at Ball's Bridge, Dublin, on April 27. Du Cross, with 140 yards start, won the mile bicycle handicap. In the four-mile handicap Synyer was giving Kilkelly 75 yards start, but lost by more than his handicap, the latter winning in 15m. 03 4-58. Arthur Du Cross showed splendid form in the mile tricycle handicap for scratch in 2m. 57 4-58. Synyer and Kilkelly, the fastest men in England and Ireland respectively, met on the three mile scratch race. The pace was waiting. Turning into the home stretch, Kilkelly had a lead of several yards, but the tire of his wheel came off and he most badly cut to remount and the English champion won the challenge cup. Synyer showed a splendid performance in the mile handicap, riding eight yards behind 2m. 39 1-58.

S. G. WHITTAKER RETURNS TO AMERICA.

Stillman G. Whittaker arrived from England on Tuesday, April 30. Whittaker had not heard of our centennial high jinks and he was much bothered at the crowds, the parading and general bustle of celebration. He at once hurried to a small town near the Hub, where he remained until Friday, reaching New York Saturday and leaving for Chicago on Saturday evening.

Whittaker sailed on March 17 with the "real" American team, called the "Yankee" team by the English, composed of Whittaker, Crocker and Knapp, managed, promoted and manipulated by the "only" Eck. The team arrived in England after the bogus American team had skimmed all the cream, so that prosperity was a stranger to them for many moons. In fact, the team just about managed to get their passage money for home.

But Whittaker did not return with them. He had broken his collar bone and was unable to ride. Crocker, whose acquisitive talent is developed to miserliness, objected to Whittaker burdening the team and he was left to shift for himself. He found a good friend in Mr. J. K. Starley, of Rudge Co., the original makers of dwarf safeties. Whittaker went into training and made some remarkable road and path safety records, lived well, made friends and returned home, the richest of any of the combination, to the "Yankee" team. In conversation, Whittaker made many interesting observations on cycling abroad.

"I have had my eyes opened to cycling; we have no real cycling in this country. The English roads are the finest in the world, far as good, as many of Indiana's roads. The French roads are very fine. Cycling is almost as popular in France as it is in England.

"The safety is king pin in England; but few ordinaries are ridden, fewest sold and hardly any made. The largest English makers do a large domestic trade. Almost the entire product of Rudge & Co., is sold in France, through De Civry, their agent at Paris. It is rumored that several large English firms will be directly represented in the United States next year.

"Mr. J. K. Starley, a very fine gentleman, will come over this summer. He is the head of

J. K. Starley & Co., who have agents over here now. Mr. S. Golder, of the *Cyclist*, will also be over during the riding season. He will tour among the mountains, probably in the far West. He makes a similar trip every year, spending last summer in Norway.

"I found the English people very kind. Their crack amateurs are big men and put up wonderfully compared with our American amateurs. With such men as Synyer, Osmond and Illston, Crist and Windle have very little chance on account of their small size. A good big man is better than a good little man every time, you know.

"My principal work was done on the safety. My greatest performances were a half mile on the path in 1m. 9 2-5s.; 21 miles 126 yards in the hour, made in France August 15, and my 21 miles 380 yards at Long Eaton, in which trial I was seven seconds ahead of Rowe's record at eleven miles. I regard Rowe as the fastest man in the world on an ordinary, but Howell is the greater rider—has more heart and more head than "Billy." You can't do anything on the English professional path unless you are in with the gang. They are up to all sorts of games and it is hard to beat the combination unless you are in good favor with them. Temple I regard as Rowe's inferior.

"I have brought over eight machines with me, including a 22lb. racing safety, a J. K. Starley 32lb. lady's roadster, a 22lb. ordinary racer and a Rudge lady's safety. Many English ladies ride the trike; few ladies ride bicycles in England. The tandem safety is a go and is very popular with scorchers. The triplet is just making an impression. This is the fastest type yet invented. With two others up I have made a mile in 2m. 27s., and two miles in 5m. on the road from a stand-still start. We won the road race from Buckden to Peterborough, 21 miles, in 1h. 7m., and have ridden 20 miles on a hilly road course in 1h. 6m.

The English do not buy new mounts every year as American do. They prize their old wheels—"old crocks" they call them—and the older they are the more highly they value them. They haven't enough money to buy as often as the Americans do. Besides, the dealers do no exchanging business.

"I am entirely done with professional racing, at least for the present. I shall make an attempt to be reinstated. I understand that it will be a difficult job, but I hope to succeed. I was first suspended on an unjust accusation. I have always ridden straight as a professional. My connection with the McCurdy-Chicago fiasco can be explained away. Circumstances made it impossible for me to tell my side of the story. It will now come out. I am entirely done with teams. I shall not clique with Eck, Morgan or any of that party. I was taught a good lesson and will now ride for myself. I hope to represent Messrs. Gormully & Jeffery on the road this season. I expect to appear on the path and road, but I want to ride as an amateur. Professionals have a bad name in this country; a professional has no status here and perhaps they are somewhat to blame for it."

PRESENTATION TO S. G. WHITTAKER.

On Tuesday evening, April 17, a select meeting was held at the Hare and Hounds Hotel, Keresley, for the purpose of presenting a gold medal to Mr. S. G. Whittaker, the American safety champion of the world, in commemoration of his record ride last year at Bordeaux, and for the half-mile record at Buckden, on a "Rover" safety cycle. Mr. J. K. Starley, of the well-known firm of J. K. Starley & Co., presided at an excellent spread given previous to the presentation. After the cloth was cleared and the usual formalities gone through, the chairman, briefly referring to the object of the gathering, said that it would be remembered last year Mr. Whittaker did a tremendous performance on a "Rover" safety, at Bordeaux, and also at Buckden, early in this year, which so pleased him (the chairman) that he resolved to present their friend with the medal to commemorate the event, as they were now on the eve of Whittaker's departure for America, where he hoped good fortune awaited him. The chairman went on to say: You will readily understand that these safety records are more interesting to me than to most manufacturers, as I have identified myself more particularly with this machine than any other, excepting perhaps the old "Meteor" now extinct. I may mention I was so much impressed with the points of advantage that could be introduced into the "Rover" and lead me to make this machine, that the old firm were at one time on the point of calling the machine "The Future Cycle." Time has, however, proved that the name "Rover" is a far more taking one. We have had Americans over here reputed to be very fast men, but very few records have been wrested from English riders except the safety records which have been established by S. G. Whittaker on the "Rover." An Englishman always admired pluck and endurance, from whatever country it came, and he was sure they were only too pleased to give all honor to Mr. Whittaker for what he had done since he came to this country, and he believed he was the best rider of a safety in the world, and his success was greatly due to his pluck and endurance.

He then presented Mr. Whittaker with a handsome gold medal specially designed, on which is the following inscription: "Presented by J. K. Starley & Co., Coventry, to S. G. Whittaker, of Chicago, for riding 21 miles 126 yards within one hour, on a 'Rover' safety, at Bordeaux, April 15, 1888, and for the half-mile at Buckden in 1m. 9 2-5s. on the road."

Mr. Whittaker suitably replied, and said he was pleased that the work he had done on the "Rover" had been appreciated so highly. He assured them that one of the reasons of his visit was to show that he could do as well here as he had done in his own country, and he wished to thank the English people for the reception he had received since he had been here.

The evening was pleasantly spent by the company, which separated with cordial wishes for Mr. Whittaker's safe return to his native country.—*The Cyclist.*

An international race meet will be held May 30 at Schwenniger, near the Hague, in Holland.

A two-mile bicycle handicap will be held at the Staten Island A. C. games, to be held at West New Brighton, May 18. Entrance fee 50 cents, closing May 11 with F. W. Janssen, P. O. Box 125, New York City.

Two races will be held at the N. J. A. C. Grounds on May 30, at 1 P. M., 1½-mile and 3-mile handicaps. Entries close May 23 with A. M. Sweet, Bergen Point, N. J. The grounds are at Bergen Point and the track is a quarter-mile cinder path.

The Kings County Wheelmen will hold a race meet at Washington Park, Brooklyn, Friday and Saturday, June 28 and 29. The committee in charge of the meet are: Charles Schwalbach, J. P. Stevens, W. C. Nellis, C. J. Long and W. F. Murphy, Chairman.

At the Titan Athletic Club games, held at the Manhattan A. C. grounds, New York, on Saturday last, C. M. Murphy, K. C. W., 80 yards, won the 2-mile handicap, time, 6m. 41 4-5s.; W. J. Murphy, K. C. W., 70 yards start, second. J. W. Schoefer, B. B. C., scratch, should have won, but could not get through on the home-stretch.

T. R. Finlay will be seen on the race path this year. There is considerable rivalry between Lamb and Weber, two other Smithville riders. Weber has generally beaten Lamb, but through the latter's bad luck. Lamb has challenged Weber to a 5-mile race in which he will allow Weber a quarter mile start. It is probable that the race will fall through.

Wheeling Round the World.—Two members of the Melbourne, B. C., Messrs. Bourston & Stokes, have reached Constantinople from Egypt, after traveling 4,000 miles on bicycles on their way to England. They will now proceed to Italy, and thence continue their wheeling tour to the Channel. After visiting England they will return homewards overland by a new route. They hope to complete the trip by the autumn of next year."

During a 3-mile scratch race between Synyer and Kilkelly, the English and the Irish champions, Kilkelly fell, and Synyer dismounted, as a matter of fair play. Before Synyer had time to dismount, however, one of the mob hurled an umbrella through the railings at the spokes of Synyer's mount. The idea of exalted old-country fair play is a myth. We don't have that kind of thing in this country, yet we never advanced a special claim to sportsmanship. The European sportsman may be all right, but the European mob certainly is not.

Cyclists should demand that the official handicapper or some other well posted cyclist should handicap the cycle events held at local athletic games. At the Titan athletic games, held last Saturday at the Manhattan A. C. grounds, it was announced that F. P. Prial had handicapped the bicycle race. This was untrue. The post of official athletic handicapper has been vacated by Walter Hegeman, and E. C. Carter, N. Y. A. C., has succeeded him. Mr. Carter, however, knows nothing of cycling, and it is unfair to cyclists to permit him to allot the starts in bicycle races.

The starters in the cross country 3-mile bicycle handicap, run at Fleetwood Park, on Saturday afternoon, finished as follows: R. W. Steves, K. C. W., 225 yards, 9m. 32 1-5s.; E. A. Powers, Riverside Wheelmen, 250 yards, second by several lengths; F. R. Miller, R. W., 225 yards, third, close up; F. G. Brown, K. C. W., 90 yards, 0; C. E. Kluge, H. C. W., scratch, 0. Kluge was out of form and did not show to advantage; Steves developed an excellent home-stretch spurt; Muller showed excellent form for a novice; Brown rode with bad judgment and showed still worse judgment in publicly blaming the handicapper, giving the bystanders a childish exhibition of temper.

FOR THE LADIES' COLUMN.

Please allow me to say a few words in your valuable column

"To the promoters of the wheel."

I, like the little birds, cannot resist rejoicing with the beautiful balmy air of spring time. Spring! Spring! Oh, glorious spring! How we do welcome thee. With all thy delightful pleasures, midst birds, trees and flowers. You may ask: Why do I rejoice? Because the beautiful days have once more returned when I with my brothers and sisters of the wheel can resume our long runs through the parks and meadows which always make one so happy. I have just come in after a long and delightful run, and, so delighted am I, that I feel I must say a few words in favor of bicycling.

Every pleasant morning I have my hour's run, starting about 7 A. M., my husband being my escort; and I must not forget my little companion, "Jack," the dog. I know he loves the bicycle as much as I do, and if left at home he seems to feel as though his best friend had forsaken him. I am sure if a wheel could be built so that dogs could ride he would be the pioneer.

But to-day we, with all our fraternal citizens of the United States, rejoice on this great national centennial holiday. All work is set aside to honor and commemorate the anniversary of the founder of the constitution of our country, the author of our national civilization, George Washington.

So, after spending an hour or so in devotion, held in memory of him who was so brave and so noble, we take our recreation. Off to the woods are we, through the hills and valleys, for a distance of eight miles, when we reach a pretty little village called Cabin John's Bridge. This place is noted for having the largest and highest stone span bridge in the world.

For nearly two years my husband has been trying to persuade me to ride a bicycle, and promised me if I would ride that he would build me one. My continual cry was: Oh, these heavy tricycles! Shall I ever see the day that I can glide along as swiftly and silently as gentlemen do? And still I could never realize that I would be able to mount a two-wheeler. So, finally, I concluded that I would attempt it, and, on November 13, 1887, he invited me down to his riding school. I was amazed when he showed me the wheel. Handing it to me he said, with a smile, "This is what I have wished you would ride for so long; take it and, with courage and confidence, you will become a fine rider." Well, reader, really I was so confused that I did not know whether to believe him or not. I could not realize it at first. What, ride a bicycle?

Well, I soon made up my mind to commence following the instructions given me by my husband and his brother, for he, too, was as anxious to see me ride, and they both left me in my glory.

I had a few good laughs at myself, but, of course, I mustn't tell tales out of school. But, what do you think was the reward of my two hours' struggling, all by myself? Why, the capital of the United States possessed "the first lady bicyclist," much to the surprise of my many friends and myself. When the tidings were announced my friends could hardly believe it. I then invited them down to the riding school. Many evenings had not passed when, one evening, unexpectedly, there were fully fifty people present to see the manifestation of that which seemed to them impossible. Not only I, but the public at large already appreciated the advantage of the bicycle over the cumbersome tricycle. Several of these demonstrations were given. On the 22d of February, 1888, by request of many of our local wheelmen, I volunteered to show at our E Street Rink the merits of the wheel and how nicely it could be ridden. By this time it had become known to the world, and mostly every lady seemed to have the bicycle craze. I was so attached to my wheel and enjoyed the pleasures of the cycling world so much, that on March 5 I was in New York, at which time I imparted the knowledge to several of the League officials, one of which was our esteemed friend Mr. Kirkpatrick, who was then President of the League. Words of appreciation were heard from every direction.

My next trip was to the Baltimore meet, held June 18. Many thanks to the gentlemen for the courtesy shown me. I wonder if the gentleman who represented the Messrs. Gormully & Jeffery

Mfg. Co., the one who stole my photograph, thought that he was extending his courtesies.

Finally, I being a native of Buffalo, I thought I would close my tours for the season by going to the World's International Exhibition, held in that city September 5th to the 14th. September 6 the W. W. C. held a reception, which I attended. The ladies, on seeing my wheel, soon became enthusiastic, and all expressed themselves as being delighted, and I was amused to see how many resolved that they would abandon their tricycles as soon as possible and take to the two-wheeler. Will the ladies please accept my appreciation for the particular attention they displayed while showing them the curbstone mount on the cobblestoned street, on which occasion some strange wheelman offered to take my wheel to a smooth street to master it, but, thanking him pleasantly, I took the wheel from him and said I preferred the rough street on this occasion.

I now have been riding eighteen months, and I am very sorry that I can't say years, for, really, when I look back to the days when I used to take long strolls with my companions, I cannot see how I lived so long without a wheel. My bicycle is and always will be my bosom friend.

I would rather part with my diamonds than with my wheel, and you know that all ladies are fond of diamonds, and those who do not possess any coax their husbands for them. Take my advice and beg for a wheel for the improvement of your health and beauty and then you will be investing in a valuable treasure, for health and happiness is the making of one's lifetime, and there is nothing to compare to the bicycle for nature's helpmeet, both for health and pleasure. If the ladies will only make up their minds that they can ride, and will ride, accompanied with the two leading features, "courage and confidence," spoken of heretofore by the inventor "of the first ladies' bicycle," I am sure that they, too, like me, will think the two-wheeler perfection itself. Fraternally yours,

PIONEER.

WASHINGTON, D. C., April 30, 1889.

STEPHEN TERRY, OBIT. APRIL 23, 1889.

The funeral of Stephen Terry took place last Saturday from Christ Church, Hartford. A large number of cyclists were present. A close personal friend writes of him as follows:

"I can scarcely believe that he is no more. Few people either understood or appreciated the real man, as we knew him to be beneath a somewhat cold exterior. Mr. Terry was forty-seven years of age at the time of his death. He was interested in cycling from the time it was introduced into this country until the last. He commenced riding in 1883. During that year he was appointed first Chief Consul of Connecticut by Dr. N. M. Beckwith, the then President of the League. He served as President of the Connecticut Bicycle Club from 1884 to 1887; was Treasurer of the L. A. W. in 1885, and Vice-President of the L. A. W. in 1886–7. He was a prominent member of the League Board of Officers, made an excellent presiding officer and was keen and incisive in debate; was a man of very decided opinions and stubbornly fought for his ideas, and always from sincerest motives.

"Mr. Terry was very prominent throughout Connecticut. He was a prominent feature at all the big race meets and League gatherings, and acted as legal counsellor in all matters affecting his State Division. He graduated at Hamilton College and was associated in the law with Hon. Elisha Johnson, of Hartford. In professional circles, his reputation extended beyond Hartford. He was an esteemed member of Christ Church, was a man of considerable means and took life easily.

"While on an excursion through Mexico and California, he took cold at Los Angelos. This developed into typhoid pneumonia before he reached San Francisco and he died soon after his arrival at the Palace hotel, April 23. The news of his death has occasioned surprise and deep regret among hundreds of wheelmen who knew him."

When the mental and visual mind becomes thoroughly saturated with the immensity, the indescribability of an event, one falls back on some trite phrase such as, "It must be seen to be appreciated." This is very applicable to Messrs. Merwin, Hulbert & Co.'s sporting goods catalogue. It is an immense volume of 500 pages, 9 by 11½ inches, the type being close and small. Every department of sport is covered, the paraphernalia of each described, illustrated and priced; besides this, game laws of the various states, laws of tennis, athletics, etc., are published in the book.

H. B. SMITH MACHINE CO.'S STEAM-TRICYCLE.

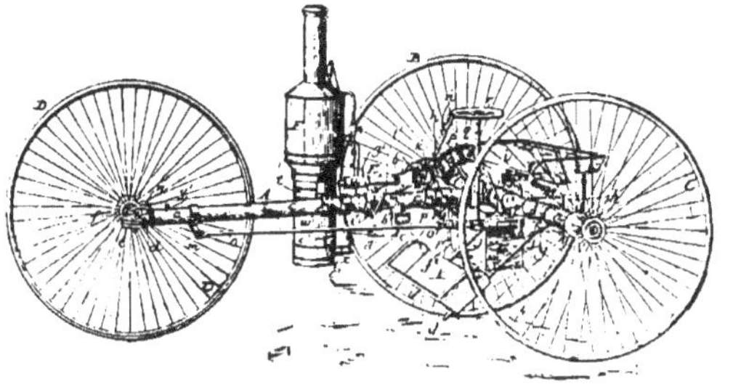

Be it known that I, Hezekiah B. Smith, of Smithville, in the county of Burlington and State of New Jersey, have invented certain improvements in Steam-Tricycles, of which the following is a specification;

The aim of the invention is to provide a light, simple, and easily-managed vehicle, which may be safely placed under the control of unskilled persons, and which shall be adapted to travel at high speeds over ordinary roads, carrying a supply of fuel and water sufficient for journeys of considerable length.

In the accompanying drawings, Figure 1 represent a perspective view of my improved vehicle.

Referring to the drawings, A represents the main frame of a substantially L form, and B, C, and D its supporting-wheels. The frame is composed of iron pipe or other tubular material, and consists in the present instance of the axle a, joined near one end by the T-shaped coupling b to the reach c. At its two ends the axle is closed and provided with solid journals to receive the wheels B and C. At its forward end the reach is closed and provided with a forked arm, d, supporting the ends of a vertical pivot or journal, e, which in turn supports the outwardly-extending arm f, having its extremity fashioned into a journal or axle for the steering-wheel D, this wheel being arranged in line with the rear driving-wheel, B, the machine being of the ordinary two-track type.

The wheels may be of any suitable construction, but are preferably of the ordinary suspension type, with rubber tires now employed in bicycles and tricycles. They may be of any appropriate size; but I prefer to make the three wheels of equal size and of a diameter of from forty to fifty inches.

Around the axle I place clips or collars g, in which I secure by set-screws vertically-adjustable rods h, the upper ends of which are bent forward horizontally and passed through clips provided with set-screws on the under side of a seat i, the seat being thus supported upon and directly over the axle and adapted for both horizontal and vertical adjustment, as required. To the collars g, I also secure downwardly-extending arms j, which pass through sockets or clips on the under side of a foot-rest, k, the sockets being provided with set-screws in order that the rest may be raised or lowered, as required.

In order that the operator occupying the seat may readily steer the machine, I pivot to a collar around the forward end of the reach a lever, m, connecting one end of the same by a link, n, to the arm which carries the steering-wheel and connecting its opposite end to a rod o, which is extended rearward and provided at its rear end with a rack engaging a pinion, p, on a vertical shaft, q, which is mounted in a bracket fixed to the axle and provided on the upper end with a hand-wheel or other operating device, r, by which the attendant is enabled to change the position of the steering-wheel at will. These devices may, however, be replaced by any suitable connections which will enable the operator to control the front wheel, various contrivances adapted for this purpose being known in the art in connection with tricycles.

For the purpose of propelling the machine, I clasp around the reach near its rear end one or more collars, t, which give support to an engine, E, of the ordinary reciprocating type, which is connected through intermediate gearing with the driving-wheel B in the manner which will now be explained.

The engine-cylinder a' lies horizontally and its piston is connected by the usual pitman, b' to a crank, c' on a cross-shaft, d', this shaft-bearing being preferably formed, as usual, in an arm forming a continuation of the cylinder-head and supported at its rear end by a collar encircling the reach. The shaft d' carries a pinion, f', engaging a spur-gear, h', on a second cross-shaft i', which receives its support from a collar clasping the reach. The shaft i' carries loosely two spur-gears, k' and l' of different diameters, and an intermediate clutch, m', splined thereto, so that it may be thrown into engagement with one or the other of the gears at will by means of a hand-lever, n', provided for the purpose.

To the side of the driving-wheel I permanently connected, by devices to be presently explained, two spur-gears, o' and p', which engage constantly with k' and l', respectively. By throwing the clutch into engagement with one or the other of the gears l' and k' motion will be transmitted from the engine to the driving-wheel, which will receive a high or a low speed according as the larger or the smaller of the driving-pinions is called into action. This duplex system of gearing admits of the machine being adjusted to travel at high speeds on level ground, or of its being adjusted for hill-climbing and other work requiring a greater expenditure of power. If desired, the additional gears may be omitted and a single train of gear employed between the engine and the driving-wheel.

The engine proper is of the ordinary type, with a reciprocating piston and a slide-valve, which latter is actuated by an eccentric, t', on the shaft d', as shown in Fig. 2.

In order to relieve the gearing from violent shocks and strains in traveling over rough ground when the driving parts are thrown suddenly in and out of gear, I interpose between the wheels o' and p' and the main wheel yielding connections. I prefer the construction shown in Figs. 2 and 3, in which the two wheels o' and p' are mounted on a sleeve revolving loosely around the main axle, the sleeve having at one end a series of fingers which enter between corresponding fingers on the hub of the wheel, with rubber or other elastic material, u, inserted between them, as shown. This allows the wheel a slight rotation independently of the sleeve and driving-gear.

For the purpose of supplying steam to actuate the engine, I provide a steam-boiler, F, preferably of the upright tubular type, and support the same from the reach c. I recommend, as the most simple means of sustaining the boiler, an encircling ring, w', the inner end of which is clipped to or around the reach, as shown.

I provide the boiler near its base with an oil-burner, x', preferably of the familiar atomizing type—such as are commonly used in the well-known Shipman engines of the present day—in which a steam-jet is directed across the mouth of an oil-delivery tube, the jet acting to induce the flow of the oil through the tube and to shatter and atomize the oil and deliver it in a fine mist or spray into the fire-box, where it is burned. This burner in itself is not claimed of my invention.

The tubular frame of the machine already described serves as a reservoir for the oil used as fuel. The frame is provided with a top opening, y', closed by a cock or otherwise, to permit the introduction of the oil, and is provided at any convenient point, as shown in Fig. 4, with an outlet-opening, a^2, through which the oil is delivered into an underlying chamber, b^2, filled with sponge or other fibrous or granular material to serve as a filter and to prevent the impurities which may be contained in the oil from passing to the burner. From the bottom of this filter a pipe, c^2, leads, as shown in Fig 4, to a small chamber, d^2, in which the pipes lead to the two burners. A pipe, e^2, conducts steam from the boiler, and at its lower end is forked or branched, and its two ends lead to the respective burners, as shown.

For the purpose of carrying the proper supply of water, I suspend from the axle a tank or resevoir, G, which may be of any appropriate form, and from this resevoir a pipe, f^2, is led, as shown in Fig. 5, to a feed-pump, g^2, and thence to the boiler. The feed-pump, which may be of ordinary piston-type, may be supported by the plate which sustains the engine, and its piston is connected with and actuated by an eccentric, h^2, on the gear-shaft i'. The feed-pipe will be provided with the usual check-valves and a stop-valve, if desired.

In order that the operator may control the advance of the machine independently of the engine, I provide a brake consisting of a rock-shaft, i^2, provided at one end with a brake-shoe, j^2, and at the opposite end with a crank-arm, l^2, in position to be readily operated by the foot of the rider. This brake-shaft is sustained, as shown in Fig. 6, by plate or arm, m^2, clipped at one end to the reach.

While I prefer to employ the frame as an oil-reservoir and the tank as a water-reservoir, it is manifest that the water may be carried in the frame and the oil carried in the tank, the arrangement of pipes being changed to correspond.

It will be observed that under my organization or arrangement of the parts the weight of the engine-boiler and gearing and the principal part of the rider's weight are carried at the driving side of the machine, whereby the driving and steering wheels are caused to take the required hold upon the ground; that the tubular frame is utilized as a reservoir for the fuel; that the brake is in position to be conveniently operated by the foot of the rider, and that the steering and engine-controlling devices are brought in such relation to the rider's seat that they may be quickly and conveniently operated.

The location of the boiler and of the gearing on the outer side of the reach, which is in turn located near the driving wheel, admits of the rider being seated close to the inner side of the reach and protects his person from contact with the operative parts of the mechanism, the reach being in effect employed as a guard or fender between the rider and the mechanism. The location of the boiler on the opposite side of the reach is also advantageous, not only in that the weight is brought more directly in line with the driving and steering wheels, but also in that the rider being carried out of line with the boiler, is free from the annoyance which would otherwise be experienced from the heat and products of combustion. The feed-water and steam-pipes may also be carried through the boiler-frame.

AN IDYL?

Some time ago, while suffering from a fit of temporary aberration of the mind, I sold out my interest in a trust company and invested the proceeds in a bicycle. At this late day it is perhaps unnecessary to tell you what a bicycle is, but for the benefit of some yap from some remote senatorial district I will state that a bicycle is a combination of wheels, springs (falls) and general cussedness, such as is seldom seen in one entire aggregation.

There are two kinds of bicycles, the male and female bicycle. The female species, more generally known as the tricycle, is harmless enough when taken moderately, but the full-blown, nickel-plated male bicycle is a corker, and in his wild state is often the cause of more sorrow and disaster in an erstwhile happy family than a toy pistol or a promissory note. However, when captured and laid away on a top shelf in the wood-shed it is harmless enough, and can be approached with ease by the veriest novice.

Not having my natural history with me just at present, I am unable to state with certainty just who first discovered the bicycle, but that a boon was conferred upon suffering humanity by the discovery is a matter of considerable doubt in my mind. I think that science sometimes overreaches itself, as witness the case of Frankenstein, the high-browed student, who manufactured a man out of various materials, endowed him with life, and then was kept pretty busy settling damage suits for a considerable while after. However, it is too late now to enter a demurrer, and we will have to grin and bear it.

As mentioned above, I disposed of my interest in a "sure thing" game and purchased a bike. It was a highly polished, nickel-plated affair, and as it rested against the corner of the house, reflecting back the sun's bright rays on its glistening surface, it looked a thing of beauty and a joy for ever. It seemed a gentle, retiring little thing, and had the most guileless countenance imaginable. My wife said it seemed a pity to ride the dear little creature, and so I thought myself, but I have since learned not to put any faith in guileless countenances. I would rather loan money to a poor relation any day than trust even an A1 Timken spring, side-bar guileless countenance again.

One bright morning in spring, when the buds were budding and the roses rosing, I betook myself to the rear extremity of my stately demesnes, betooking with me at the same time my beautiful little bike. It was a lovely day, and all Nature seemed to smile. I guess all Nature was "on to me with both feet," as the players have it, and was joyously anticipating the coming "picnic." Half an hour's brisk walk brought me to the desired locality, and when I arrived on the grounds there were several small boys chucking dornicks at a cat up in one of my trees. They were apparently enjoying themselves hugely, but when they saw preparations being made for an attraction on a scale hitherto undreamed of they left off, and came over and offered numerous suggestions as to the best method of subduing my fiery, untamed steed.

Now I do not like small boys. They know too much. How on earth such mines of wisdom, such vast, inexhaustible stores of knowledge, such profound penetration, can be concentrated within about four feet of small boy is a clincher for me. "The child is father to the man." I never composed a truer proverb in my life, and I have been in the proverb business for years, but at the same time one cannot help but ask himself why is it these precocious small boys do not become men of superhuman erudition, or intellectual giants of supernatural growth. I knew a P. S. B. once that for pure smartness and genuine originality taked the cook, and we all predicted that some day he would fill a position requiring more unadulterated intellect than a grand jury. He is now running a hay press up in the San Juan country, and apparently as happy as a clam. But to get back to this confounded bicycle business.

I had seen several long-legged, hungry-looking experts mount their machines in this way. They would grasp the handles, place the left foot on a small step on the lower left-hand side of the crupper, hop several times with the right and then vault lightly and gracefully into the saddle. This looked simple enough, and I thought I would try it. With the easy grace which characterizes my every action I placed my foot on the step, took a good, drowning-sailor grip of the handles, started her forward and then jumped. I did not land lightly and gracefully in the saddle. I did not land in the saddle at all. My foot slipped, or the thing must have kicked—but we will pass over this painful episode. I am not easily discouraged, and have always on hand a large store of cheering proverbs and wise old saws, and can at any time readily call to mind the exact number of times the historical spider endeavored to build his web in the historical cave where Robert Bruce was hidden. This is very comforting, and has helped to make me the bloated millionaire that I am. I give this secret to the world freely, trusting to receive my reward—but there I go trusting again. I will be dead broke soon if I don't quit this bad habit.

Once more I grasped the handles and went through the other preliminary movements. This time I landed all right, but could not get my feet in the stirrups. Consequently when he bucked I had to go. And I went; and the confounded thing went with me, and I will do it the justice to say that it stayed with me. I couldn't get away from it, and must have spent ten golden minutes in getting my feet out of the spokes and pulling the running gear out of my abdomen. By this time there were several thousand small boys there, and a person over in the next county would have thought that a game of ball was being played and Nick Smith had made a home run the way they cheered. I never did see the way that small boys can congregate. Ours is a quiet, peaceful neighborhood, far from the city's crowded marts, and you wouldn't think that over five, or say, five and a half, small boys could be scared up in the entire congressional precinct, but here were fully three thousand. They remind me of turkey-buzzards. A casual glance into the blue dome of heaven will fail to discover the faintest speck of anything, but let your horse give out and drop by the wayside. Then watch. Carefully inspect the great vault above you. Nothing, absolutely nothing. Then look again. Yes, away up in the mighty space above you is a speck. It grows larger. It is a buzzard. Look again; another. In ten minutes there are fifty of them, coming from God knows where, and then it's all day and part of the next with the poor animal below. This is the way these small boys congregated.

Now I am a self-made man, and naturally I am very self-possessed in company. I am perfectly at home in the midst of excitement and danger. I fairly revel in a piece of cold mince pie just before going to bed, and a feminine hair-pulling match does not disconcert me in the least; still, one does not like to make a holy show of himself for the edification and delectation of about six thousand (they are increasing) dirty little boys, and I hope the gentle reader will not blame me too much if I said a bad word or two. However, I picked myself up, ignoring the tumultuous applause from the gallery, and endeavoring to conduct myself in such a manner as to create the impression that that was my customary way of getting off a bicycle. This did not deceive them, though, and that is why I say that I do not like small boys.

Just then my wife arrived. Now my wife is one of the most lovable characters imaginable, and as an humble sharer of my joys and sorrows ranks second to none; still, just at this particular moment I would rather she had remained in the house and stood off my creditors. Her face wore such a look of mingled alarm and concern that my heart smote me two or three hard smotes, and, but for my dad-binged determination, or, to put it more aptly, stubbornness, I would have quit then and there.

With a Duke-of-Wellington-at-Waterloo's taciturnity I said nothing, but, motioning to two of the boys to hold the bike, I looked around for an axe. Seeing none, however, I concluded to go her once more for the cigars. Getting two sturdy youths to steady it, I used another for a step and succeeded in getting safely into the seat. They then walked it off for a few yards, and all was well. I then said, "Let go her head, boys," and they let go. For exactly three feet my meteor-like course was smooth and uninterrupted, and then there was trouble. The brake in some way became entangled with the walking beam, causing the fly-wheel to slip a cog or two and revolve in mid-air in a most startling manner. I instantly applied the automatic and "chawed gravel" for all I was worth, but just then the drum-head busted and the anchors commenced to drag. There was a shout, a wild, piercing scream from a woman's lips, a horrible, sickening thud, and all was still. When I came to I was a sight to behold, and slowly and sadly my wife led me into the house and applied the proper restoratives. And the sun went down upon my wrath. HEADERS.

THE SAMUEL WINSLOW SKATE MFG. CO.,

WORCESTER, MASS.

Manufacturers of Ice and Roller Skates and

THE "VINEYARD" BICYCLE.

STRONG, DURABLE AND CHEAP.

As good as the best for road and business purposes.

FOR BOYS AND MEN.

Diameter Front Wheel	Front Tire.	Diameter Rear Wheel.	Rear Tire.	Weight all on.	Length of leg inside to sole of foot.	Price.
38 inch	3/4 inch	14 inch	5/8 inch	31 lbs.	27 inch	$35.00
42 inch	3/4 inch	14 inch	5/8 inch	33 lbs.	29 inch	40.00
44 inch	3/4 inch	16 inch	5/8 inch	35½ lbs.	30 inch	45.00
46 inch	7/8 inch	16 inch	3/4 inch	38 lbs.	31 inch	50.00
48 inch	7/8 inch	16 inch	3/4 inch	39½ lbs.	32 inch	55.00
50 inch	7/8 inch	16 inch	3/4 inch	41 lbs.	33 inch	60.00

Orders solicited from dealers. Descriptive Catalogue and discounts sent on application.

CYCLING IN STRANGE LANDS.

It appears from the narrative of Mr. G. W. Burston of his travels on a bicycle all round the world, that there are yet portions of this planet where a wheelman on his machine is an object of wonderment and curiosity. From Alexandria Mr. Burston and his party went to Jaffa and "cycled to Jerusalem " and back, finding themselves the centre of attraction in every town they visited. The mountains of Lebanon were rather more in the way of laborious climbing than the cyclers ' had bargained for." From the summit, after gazing their fill at the vast landscape, they "ran down some two thousand feet " to Shtora, and then, after ascending the anti-Lebanon, sailed merrily along on the down grade for twenty miles to Damascus, where the authorities—who, like Mr. Rider Haggard's mystic Princess, "must be obeyed " —requested them to ride for the gratification and amusement of the people. This they did with an excited rabble at their heels. At Baalbec they were treated "like victorious generals," but were constrained to give another exhibition for the amusement of 4,000 or 5,000 spectators. "Riding back," says the writer, "was quite impossible owing to the narrow road and immense crowd ; hundreds of people waited round the hotel till midnight, and all the villages on the plains posted watchmen to signal our approach." Those who would follow this example are warned that traveling through countries where a European is rarely seen has its disadvantages and discomforts, but in India they were everywhere treated with kindness. It speaks well for the Indian roads that in eighteen days the cyclists were able to cover 1,641 miles, when, owing to an attack of cholera, the trip was brought for a while to an abrupt stand. Their best day's work in India is recorded as 137 miles in 11½ hours, including stoppages. Mr. Burston's letter is dated Beyrout, March 27. It informs us that the party were then going round the coasts of Asia Minor to Constantinople, intending thence to visit Greece before landing in Italy, and sojourning awhile in Rome, all which is deemed consistent with a hope to be in London by the end of May. It is not every one, or even every cyclist, who could find a pleasure in a spin of 137 miles in one day upon the roads of India ; but it is impossible to read Mr. Burston's exhilarating narrative without feeling what a valuable means the horse that wants neither corn nor stable has provided for remedying that most miserably limited powers of locomotion.—*London Daily News.*

Frank L. Wing, Captain of the New Bedford Wheelmen, has been appointed L. A. W. Consul for New Bedford, Mass.

The contest for the Adams medals commenced May 1.

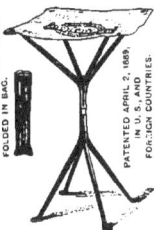

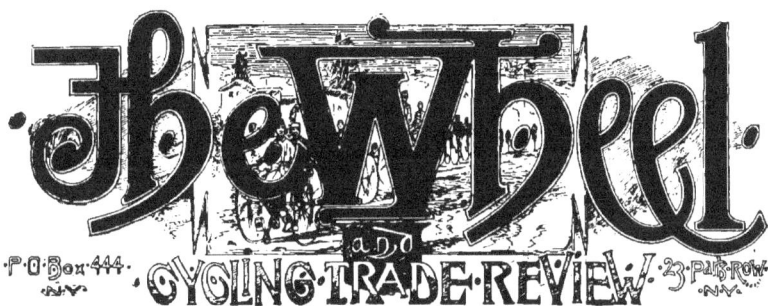

The Wheel and Cycling Trade Review

·P·O·Box·444· N.Y. 23 Park Row N.Y.

VOL. III.—No. 12.]   NEW YORK, MAY 17, 1889.   [WHOLE NUMBER, 64.

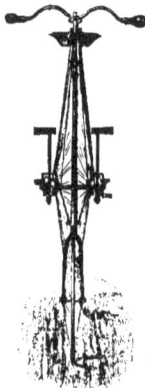

THE WHEEL

—AND—

CYCLING TRADE REVIEW.

Published every Friday morning.

Entered at the Post Office at second class rates.

Subscription Price, - - - $1.00 a year.
Foreign Subscriptions. - - - 6s. a year.
Single Copies, - - - - 5 Cents.

Newsdealers may order through AM. NEWS CO.

All copy should be received by Monday.
Telegraphic news received till Wednesday noon.

Advertising rates on Application.

F. P. PRIAL, Editor and Proprietor
23 Park Row,

P. O. Box 444, *New York.*

Persons receiving sample copies of this paper are respectfully requested to examine its contents and give us their patronage, and as far as is convenient, aid in circulating the journal, and extend its influence in the cause which it so faithfully serves. Subscription price, $1 per year.

FROM the *Cyclist* we reproduce portions of a letter, accompanied by running comments of our own, credited to "Uncle Sam," of New York. "Uncle Sam" is a specimen of that tribe of American scribblers who serve up distorted facts and fancies for the benefit of the English people. Their lucubrations are so skilfully interlarded with flattery that the English press men temporarily forget the use of the pruning blue pencil; on the other hand, it may be possible that they conceive it to be their duty, as Englishmen, to aid the renegade American scribes in belittling cycling in their own country. We have a logical suspicion that "Uncle Sam" of New York is not of New York, but—well, never mind.

The discussion in the *Cyclist* over the Bown patent ball bearing is attracting widespread attention among the trade in this country, though but one paper, the *Sporting Life*, has had the independence to comment on it.

The *Sporting Life* is a base-ball paper, published in Philadelphia, containing a column of sharp and intelligent cycling comments by "Perseus." The policy of any paper, from the *London Times* and the *New York Herald* down the scale, is dictated from the counting-room, and the high-salaried editor or the millionaristic proprietor of a great daily is not more independent than the editor of a struggling trade paper.

The *Sporting Life* is not a trade paper. Its greatest principal is derived from sales and not from advertising. Its editor has, very probably, no definite policy in conducting the special departments. The policy of the cycling column is left entirely to "Perseus," and as "Perseus'" identity is not made public, we are at liberty to assume that he is writing in his own interests, that the *Sporting Life* is his mill-stone, and that he is grinding his own little hatchet.

In regard to the Bown patents it requires no independence to discuss them. The case may be fairly stated in few words, which will cover the columns of matter which "Perseus" has reproduced from the *Cyclist* and other English papers. It appears from letters written to the *Cyclist* that certain English makers have been making ball bearings; that they deny the validity of the Bown patents; that they deny any infringement; that they are not manufactur-

ing under licenses, as Bown claims. They challenge him to prove the validity of his patents. This petty epistolary warfare carries but little weight with it. We are not certain that it is not a game of "bluff." No doubt it pays the English firms who are manufacturing ball bearings, to deny infringement and the validity of Bown's patents, to fight him in the courts, and should the Bown patents be declared valid after a tedious and complicated patent case, they can well afford to pay royalties out of the profits on the business they have done. We believe this is a profitable and favorite game.

In our opinion the letters written to the *Cyclist* are of no value in determining the real issue. It is a question whether the writers of them would stand by them in the courts. They raise a number of fine points. If an American manufacturer secured the American patents on Bown's bearings in good faith, would not the patents hold good in this country, no matter what their status may be abroad, provided of course, that they are not antedated by similar patents? We are told that the expense of patent litigation runs up into the thousands. We should very much like to obtain decisions on the above question, but we really could not afford to pay the five hundred dollars per column fee which we are certain the high mightics of patent law would charge us.

A great many dealers who have heretofore been acting only as agents for the manufacturers are now importing wheels from England, and running the risk of a suit for infringement. The feeling is generally that the combination has lost its grip on the trade, and that tribute will no longer have to be paid to owners of alleged patents. The immediate effect of this is an immense increase in the number and makes of imported wheels that are to be found on the market. All kinds and all qualities are to be seen, and I have noticed the announcement of some "high grade imported wheels," whose names are new and whose makers are kept in the background.

The above is the poorest kind of journalistic work. Who is "Uncle Sam" that he should decide whether the patents are "alleged" or *bona fide?* It would cost thousands of dollars and years of persistent inquiry and examination to determine the validity of these patents, yet "Uncle Sam," with superb impudence, decides that they are "alleged," and the *Cyclist* publishes his statements.

It will elucidate " Uncle Sam's " statement that, " the combination is loosing its grip," if he will interpret "the combination," resolve it into its component parts. The increased number of new makes, both imported and domestic, is due to the unusual trade activity this spring. We know of no "announcements of high-grade wheels," in which the names of the makers are kept in the back-ground. Name them, "Uncle Sam."

A great many cheap wheels are also being marketed, and the result is a general lowering of prices and a feeling of uncertainty. No doubt, if the validity of the Bown patent is disproved, there will be a big business done in importing wheels, and that will continue till American manufacturers lower their prices below the point where it will pay to sell a foreign made wheel, as they undoubtedly can do.

We can unearth no lowering of prices on high grade wheels. The prices stand as firm as a rock at $125 to $140. The great number of cheap wheels now being marketed is due to the foresight of the makers. They act on the same principle as the retail butter dealer, who will supply "cream dairy" at 40 and "boarding house" at 28, and make a profit on both.

It is surprising in this connection, as I hinted before, how silent the cycle press of the country is on the subject; not one of the distinctively cycling papers has had a single word to say either one way or the other. The reason is very evident, though, they are afraid of losing the patronage of the wheels, and that will continue till American manufacturers dubbed " the ring." Their fears, I think, are unfounded for, even if they were disposed to take such a high-handed course, the makers could not afford to go on record before the wheelmen of America as blackmailers; but then I do not believe that Pope or Overman, whether they do or do not believe in the validity of the Bown patent, would so strongly object to a fair discussion of a question of such wide-spread interest.

The reason of the silence of the cycling press is an excellent one. To start with, there are few

cyclists in this country who understand the details of any of the suits now pending. The parties who bring the suits are, of course, wise enough to save their ammunition for the courts. This ammunition consists of letters patent, and even these are valuless until the courts decide otherwise. The only real valuable light that the plaintiffs could throw on their case, is to publish the expert opinions of their patent lawyers, and, of course, it is ridiculous to expect that.

On the other hand, the parties being sued object to publicity. They claim, *imprimis,* that it is none of the public's business; secondly, that a statement of suit being brought hurts their credit, and in the case of a weak house, might irretrievably impair it. They also rightly claim that, as defendants, they bear the heaviest burden, that they bear a certain amount of public disapproval, owing to the charge that they are infringing on other people's rights. They want to work on in the dark until the courts set the seal of approval or disapproval. Thus, by silence, the cycling press protects the rights of both parties.

And the public do not suffer. They are interested in results only, and if "Uncle Sam" will take the trouble to hunt through "back numbers" he will find all final decisions on patent litigations carefully recorded. If "Uncle Sam" occupied the editorial chair of the New York *Herald* he would very likely state that the late Mrs. Stewart was insane, decide the case against Mr. Henry Hilton, and precipitate a five million dollar suit for damages on the paper.

We can safely claim then, that the editors of the cycling press have a truer journalistic insight and a higher regard for justice than has "Uncle Sam" or the editors and proprietors of the papers who publish his opinions, his allegations and his unproven statements.

His fling at the "dependence" of the cycling press might as well be disposed of at once and forever. There are but two American cycling papers now published which have any claim to financial and journalistic respectability. We speak for ourselves as a matter of fact and for our Boston contemporary as a matter of belief. The day has passed when the cycling publisher is a feeder on the trade, a cringing suppliant for business, a pleading beggar for subsidies. In the early days of the sport, when the trade was indeed narrower in its limits, papers were subsidized, and they richly deserved the subsidy. It is useless to deny that, outside of the intrinsic merits of cycling as a pleasure and a benefit, the sentiment inspired by the press and manifested in race meets, clubs, tours, organization and that sort of thing, has rapidly extended cycling, and the publisher who was subsidized that he might make both ends meet had but little obligation to answer for.

At the present time brains count, and the man who has the brains and the enterprise to publish a respectable paper of the sport will find himself supported, while the experimentalist who depends on favors and subsidies will live a brief hand-to-mouth existence. As we find it, the trade is friendly to the publisher according to his worth, and appreciates him according to his work.

There are rumors in the air that "the ring" is about to break up. We don't know much about the matter, but with what truth there is in it I cannot say, but certain it is that a good many dealers are having cold chills down the back, as if they already felt the rush of air from the flap of the hawk's wings.

We can't explain the cold chills, for has not old "Nunc Sam" told us that the combine is losing its grip, and that the good feeling is spreading. Then, why cold chills?

The fight, though, has another phase to it. Gormully and Jeffery are making threats, and it looks as if there would be another big suit between that firm and Pope. Gormully says before he is through with the business he will make Pope pay him a royalty for every bicycle he has ever made, and the Westerner (who, by the way, is an Englishman) has plenty of money with which to back up his threats. His Smith patent on ball bearings antedates the Bown in this country by about three years, though no one thinks it is worth the paper it is written on.

We doubt if Mr. Gormully ever made a confidant of "Uncle Sam." The shrewdness which aided him to his present condition of prosperity would naturally prevent him from confiding his plans on so important a matter to "Uncle Sam," or to any one outside his firm.

To show the folly of discussing these patent questions, let us take a case out of "Uncle Sam's" paragraph. He states that Mr. Gormully's Smith patent antedates the Bown in this country by three years. Now, how can a newspaper intelligently discuss such a point? We do not know the technicalities of the Smith patent, and if we did we could not distinguish between the validity of the claims of the Smith and the claims of the Bown. All we can do is to wait until the point is decided and publish the decision. This is what the public wants. Any previous discussion of the question is generally erroneous, possibly impertinent and probably criminal. This conception of our "business" is what "Uncle Sam" calls "dependence." If so 'tis a sweet dependence, and we shall endeavor to maintain it.

GIVE US BETTER PAVEMENTS.

In our efforts to advance road improvements, care should be taken that we do not scatter our energies too much, and make them ineffective for want of concentration. The best plan is, undoubtedly, to take up one small point after another—short sections of road, for example—and perfect these, when each step will be found to make the next one easier. Such a step is suggested in our correspondent's letter in another column, on "the Orange route." An even more important direction in which wheelmen of New York City might exert some influence would be in inducing the New Public Works Department to perform the repairing which it will shortly take in hand more rationally than has been done by former administrations. Mayor Grant has already belied the cavillers against his election, and proved that Tammany control of the city government can be interpreted to mean the most careful and energetic guarding of the public interests; and Commissioner Gilroy's reputation is a guarantee that he will also strive for a record in his new office that will redound to his credit. The following from the *Evening Post* of recent date, is a suggestion of the course that should be followed; and wheelmen who may belong to Tammany Hall cannot do better than urge upon the leaders a fair trial of the improved styles of pavement which are here mentioned:

Now that the Legislature has begun the serious business of passing important bills, it is more than probable that our Department of Public Works will shortly be granted a large sum, anywhere from one to three millions, with which to repair the down-town streets, and the question becomes an interesting one, what use will be made of the money?. Are we to be afflicted with a perpetuation of the granite-block abomination that disgraces the streets of the American metropolis? Or will some attempt be made to find a material that is not filthy, noisy, and unbearably rough?

It will not do to say that no such material has been discovered, for New York has never given an adequate trial to any of the manifold substitutes for stone, although the latter, as we have seen it laid, has certainly given no such proof of durability as entitles it to any special preference. It is doubtful, indeed, whether even asphalt, which is generally assumed to be fit only for light wear, would not stand as well under heavy traffic as have our block pavements. But we are not confined to asphalt. In Baltimore,

an asphalt block pavement has been tried with even better results than the plain asphalt. In a number of Western cities, they have introduced a fire-brick pavement which has worn excellently and is rather smooth and noiseless, without the glassy surface of asphalt. Of course, the traffic in none of these cities compares with that of the avenues and principal business streets of New York; but there is no reason why any or all of the substances mentioned should not be used on the cross-town residence streets; and it would certainly be useful to try at least some of them on enough blocks of each of the avenues to determine really whether or not there is anything that wears worse than the Belgian pavement, which seems impossible.

One thing certainly should be insisted upon by the press; that if stone blocks are to be used at all in the new pavements, they should be hewn with smooth edges, not broken roughly into shape; and that they should be laid in cement.

CONVICT LABOR ON THE PUBLIC ROADS OF NEW YORK STATE.

With their accustomed faculty for doing things wrong, the New York State Legislature have mangled the Yates Prison bill all out of shape. So far as can be judged from the somewhat imperfect press reports, its most valuable feature—that which required the employment of convicts upon the improvement of public highways—has been eliminated; and the Albany Solons have arrived at a half-baked compromise between the trades-unions and the conservative newspapers, by which the convicts will be put to work in such a way as will be most expensive to the State without removing the evil of their competition with free labor.

The principal argument against using their labor on the roads, where it would be most productive and in an economical way, appears to have been that of the sickly sentimentalist which insists on sacrificing society to its outcasts. One grain of comfort is to be derived from this solution of the problem, that it can never be a final one.

THAT Chief Consul Bull is working with a will to perfect League work in the State, is patent from the work he has already accomplished. He has placed the League hotel system on a new and improved basis, using much care in selection, and making it certain that only League members get the benefit of a rebate. A complete list of the League hotels of New York State and a list of Consuls are published in the Division's official department.

A TARIFF FOR CARRYING WHEELS.

At a meeting of the Eastern Trunk Line Association, held in New York, May 7, the following resolution was adopted:

Resolved : That bicycles shall be charged for at the rate of twenty-five cents for every 100 miles or part thereof.

The members of the Eastern Traffic Association are the West Shore, N. Y. Central, D. L. and W., Erie, Pennsylvania and other large Eastern systems. The news of the new rates on the transportation of cycles will be read with regret all over the country. It means a vast expenditure to cyclists and the planning of tours without that reliance on the railroads as an adjunct, as was the case when cycles were carried free of charge.

At a meeting of the committee, held on Wednesday, letters were read from prominent cyclists, and Mr. Geo. R. Bidwell appeared before the committee. Mr. Charles A. Sheehan also made every effort to see the members of the association and explain the case to them. The association was firm, and showed no inclination to rescind the rule or even modify it.

The free transportation represented seven years of work on the part of the League's

transportation committee. Mr. Wm. Brewster, St. Louis, is chairman of the committee, and Mr. Geo. R. Bidwell, who had only a few days ago declined appointment on this committee, gallantly comes to the rescue. It is certain that nothing will be done within sixty days, but the committee will get to work and do all in their power. General-Passenger Agent Lambert warmly supported us on the debate on the resolution. Under the new rule cyclists must pay 25 cents for having their wheels carried even the shortest distance.

PROSPECT PARK RIDING RULES.

After conferring with representatives of leading bicycle clubs in Brooklyn, the Executive Committee, Department of Parks, Brooklyn, have adopted the following rules regulating bicycle and tricycle riding in Prospect Park :

RULES FOR THE REGULATION OF BICYCLE AND TRICYCLE RIDING IN PROSPECT PARK, BROOKLYN.

I.—Riding at a greater speed than eight (8) miles an hour, is prohibited, except that speeding will be permitted on the Nethermead Circuit and the Past and West Drives completing the Circuit, in the morning before seven o'clock.
II.—Riding will be permitted only on the roads, except that the paths may be used in the morning before nine o'clock and wheelmen, dismounted, may bring the wheels upon the paths, short distances, when necessary.
III.—Blowing of whistles will not be permitted, and wheels will not be allowed in the Park at night, except when carrying lighted lamps.
IV.—Upon down grades, riders of ordinary or crank bicycles, must keep the feet on the pedals; riders of Star bicycles need not keep the levers in motion, riders of Safety bicycles and of tricycles and tandems, may rest the feet upon the coasting bars; but the brake must be kept on and in no case shall the speed be increased beyond eight (8) miles an hour.
V.—Wheelmen will be required to keep upon the right side of the road, and in passing vehicles going in the same direction, pass to the left whenever practicable.

SENSIBLE VIEWS HEARTILY INDORSED.

We are glad to see the WHEEL advocating the employment of convict labor on the highways. The Vermont Division was, we believe, the first body to start the discussion of this subject and by unanimous vote placed itself on record as in favor of this idea, at the annual meet in Montpelier in June 1886. It is difficult to see how any good argument can be made against the employment of such labor on the highways. In the first place the roads certainly need all the work expended upon them that the state can afford to expend. They are, in general, exceedingly poor and the present system of repairing gives no promise of anything better in the future. On the other hand the labor question has caused the convicts to be kept in idleness in many states, that they may not compete with free, paid labor to the injury of the latter. This is the case in New York where 1500 men are idle. These men, for their own good, for the good of the state and the people ought to labor, but where, so as not to take the bread out of the mouths of some honest laboring man's family? In no place excepting on the highways, and then, such labor should be employed only in making permanent roads. Success to you in this crusade, Brother Prial.—*Bicycle* for May.

ROAD LITERATURE WORTH HAVING.

Long ago as March 16, 1889, a meeting of property owners living in the suburbs of Philadelphia was called to protest against the improper and unsatisfactory way the resurfacing of the Kensington and Oxford Turnpike was being carried out in, even after earnest and repeated protests by Mr. Wm. H. Rhawo had been laid before the proper authorities.

At this meeting which was largely attended, a well written paper was read by Mr. Rhawn, entitled "A Plea for Better Roads," which we regret space at our disposal does not permit of reproducing. A complete report of the proceedings, including Mr. Rhawn's paper and the various protests made by him, has recently been published, and city or town authorities that contemplate macadamizing streets can not do better than send for it. We have no doubt that copies can easily be obtained either of Mr Rhawn, or the Franklin Printing Company at Philadelphia.

IT IS NOW

The season when riders are looking over the wheels in the market with critical eyes, and selecting for their use during the season just coming on the wheels that have the most of what are

ACKNOWLEDGED BY ALL

To be the best features in wheel construction. The Victors for '89 are, as ever, at the very front of the market in such respects. They are stronger, handsomer and lighter-running than any others, and you may be sure

THAT THE

Victor devices are the best from the fact that lots of people copy them. The Victor Safety is the only successful spring fork machine. It is finer than anything else of the kind in the market.

VICTORS BEAT THE WORLD!

OVERMAN WHEEL CO., MAKERS,

BOSTON, MASS.

Special Agents,

A. G. SPALDING & BROS.,

NEW YORK AND CHICAGO.

Do You Want to Ride a Safety?

We have the Finest Line of Safety Bicycles and Tandems, for all riders and uses, on the American market. Safeties for Ladies, Light Men, Heavy Men, Youths, Boys. Safeties for Touring. Safeties for Scorching. 32 to 49 pounds for Road Machines, complete with Saddle, Brake and Pedals. We have the Finest Tandem Safety built, and the *only* one made on correct mechanical principles It will pay you to run out and try these machines on the "Orange Macadams." Thirty minutes from New York. Trains leave Christopher or Barclay Streets, at 6.30, 7.00, 7.20, 7.30, 8.00, 8.30, 9.10, 9.20, 10.10, 11.10, 12.10, 12.40, 1.30, 2.30, 3.10, 3.30, 4.00, 4.30, 4.50, 5.00, 5.20, 5.40, 5.50, 6.00, 6.10, 6.30, 7.00, 8.00. Store open until 9 P.M.

NEW ILLUSTRATED CATALOGUE ON APPLICATION.

L. H. JOHNSON,
SOLE IMPORTER,
401 & 403 Main St., Orange, N. J.

THEN BUY A PREMIER.

KING OF THE ROAD LAMPS.

THE BEST AND MOST POPULAR ON THE MARKET.

STILL FURTHER IMPROVED FOR 1889.

Don't Fail to See our New Safety and Tricycle Lamps before Placing your Orders.

HOLDS TEN HOURS' OIL SUPPLY.

IMPROVED

Anti-Vibration Spring.

Instantaneously Detachable Reflectors.

SIDE SLIDE FOR LIGHTING.

Front View, Showing Glass.

Back View, Showing Spring.

ALL PATTERNS OF BOTH HEAD AND HUB LAMPS

FULLY DESCRIBED IN OUR 1889 CATALOGUE.

THE TRADE are cordially invited to send for our Descriptive Discount Sheet, now ready.

THE CLARK CYCLE CO., Baltimore, Md.,

SOLE UNITED STATES AGENTS.

PSYCHO WHEELS FOR 1889.

Sole Importers: Capital Cycle Co., Washington, D. C.

The Psycho cycles are imported by the Capital Cycle Company, of Washington, D. C. This firm were the first to recognize the merits of all forms of rear-driving safeties, and in 1885 imported the first one ever brought into this country. They also designed and introduced the first tandem safety in 1888. They designed and manufactured in 1887 the first rear-driving ladies' safety bicycle, and credit should be given them for their efforts in this direction. They have accomplished as much for the weaker sex by reducing friction, weight, and by giving increased pleasure, as did the inventor of the spider wheel for the stronger sex by improving the boneshaker.— *Wheel.*

Psycho Cycles do not have hollow rims, tangent spokes, ball head or spring forks. No change will be made in Psychos over the 1888 pattern. The Fish hammock saddle will be used on all Pyschos.

Psycho Cycles are remarkable for their lightness, strength, harmonious and uniform construction, simplicity (fewness of parts) and general gracefulness of design. **Beautifully finished.**

PSYCHO LIGHT ROADSTER.

SEVEN FORMS
OF
PSYCHO SAFETIES,
Varying in Weight and Design.

1. **"Men's Straight Frame Psycho Safety,"** 30-inch wheels. ⅞ and ¼ inch tires, geared to 57 inches, weight 47 lbs. Price $140.

2. **"Men's Light Roadster Psycho Safety,"** 30-inch wheels, ¼-inch tires, made for gentlemen riders and scorchers on good roads, geared to 60 inches (see cut), weight 38 lbs. Price, $140.

3. **"Men's Dropped Frame Psycho Safety"** is designed like ladies' safety (see cut), 30-inch wheels, ⅞ and ¼ inch tires, weight 50 lbs. Will stand any weight on any road. Detachable brace rod makes it suitable for ladies and a general family machine. Price, $140. Geared to 57 inches.

4. **"Ladies' Roadster Psycho Safety,"** ¼-inch tires, 29-inch wheels. Detachable brace rod, suitable for short or medium-height gentlemen. Will stand any weight. Weight. 44 lbs. See cut. Geared to 50 inches.

PSYCHO LADIES' ROADSTER.

5. **"Ladies' Light Roadster Psycho Safety,"** 29-inch wheels, ¼ and ⅞ inch tires, weight 38 lbs. Superb finish, very light and easy-running, intended for light-weight ladies, but will carry 175 lbs. Geared to 50 inches.

6. **"Ladies' Extra Light Psycho,"** same design as "Ladies' Psycho," with rear forks like "Men's Light Roadster Psycho," 28-inch wheels. Weight 34 lbs. Price, $140. We cannot deliver this much under thirty days.

7. **"Psycho Tandem Safety,"** intended for lady and gentleman or two gentlemen, ⅞-inch tires to both wheels, very strong, light and simple. Will carry any weight. Now in its second season. Price, with two separate brakes, $200. Geared to 57 inches.

PSYCHO TANDEM SAFETY.

☞ **Art Calendar and Price List,** beautifully illustrated, now ready.

All of the above Machines are guaranteed to the fullest extent.

JACK'S JOTTINGS.

A writer to the "*Cape Argus*" (Cape Town, South Africa), makes a few suggestions which may be of interest to those men who "look upon the wine while it is red" and "unload the schooner," with a frequency which militates against good going on the road or path, or perhaps going at all. It is all well enough to lie on a bamboo lounge in Japan or British Burmah (or other of the places where England sends her "younger sons" or "scape graces" and smoke Trichinopolis with an "esparto-grass" straw in the centre and drink *ad lib* brandy and seltzer, but the American people are a temperate lot, and frown upon a man who is too "good company," and then the pace that they work at in their larger cities, would astonish a man who has had experience of a London "City" life, or an even more leisurely life in the canny Scotch Capital. The American climate is such that the use of any form of spirituous liquor should be taken in very moderate doses, and then only when the system is run down and needs "a bracer." Beer in moderate quantity is good for a road-rider if taken *after* a long ride, or several hours *before* the rider squats himself on the "pig-skin" (this is a 'horsey' term but let her go). This writer whose experience among colonial Englishmen (who as a rule drink their share and sometimes "the other man's"), may be of interest to some.

"He has seen the common forms of drunkenness treated with marked success by nux vomica in combination with rhubarb and carbonate of ammonia. I think it is a great error (Dr. Roberts writes) to speak of the various conditions of the digestive and nervous systems resulting from the excessive or injudicious use of alcohol as a specific disease, as they are similar to those which result from the excessive use of other foods, nervous excitement, and mental and physical excesses of all kinds. The setting apart of the treatment of these diseases as a specialty is one of the greatest evils of the prevailing evil of specialisms, as is obvious by the nonsense which is talked by such specialists as to the hereditary character of the disease, and the incurability of some cases. At present we have no evidence that acquired habits are transmissible from parent to child, and moreover there are no definite and uniform lessons resulting from the use of alcohol to be transmitted, if such transmission were possible. That the child of a drunken mother should have feeble health is likely enough, as its nutrition has been interfered with; and that the children of intemperate parents should acquire their habits from imitation and the facilities for falling into them, is likely enough also. But this is not heredity, even in the very loosest way in which the word is used by medical men. . . . There is great advantage in the treatment of habits of intemperance of all kinds by travelling and intellectual pursuits, and the removal of the patient from all former associations. As a confirmed disease alcoholism is, I think, more nearly related to gout than any other constitutional condition, and in its more chronic states it is most successfully treated by iodide of potassium and bark."

This may seem "snaky" to the fanatic who has never sipped the seductive "cocktail" or the deadly *Absinthe Frappé* of the *Quartier Latin*, or those who are wont to boast that they never had the "heather step" from too liberal use of "Glenlivet" or "Campbelltown" or "J. J. Jamieson," but to those who have had visitations from extinct orders of *reptilia*, and have tried to catch the hall door knob when it came round to them, after having vainly tried to open the front door with a cigarette or a corkscrew (instead of the more effective latch key), the words may not come amiss, and may be pasted in their hat with good effect. The words may be pondered upon by the awkward squad of the "Bally-hooly blue-ribbon Army":

> "Who don't care what they ate,
> So they drink the whiskey nate,
> In the Bally-hooly blue-ribbon army."

There is nothing like letting a young man drink the "cup of pleasure to the bitter lees," and, finding the dregs bitter, he is more likely to turn out a sensible, liberal-minded man than the boy who has been kept tied up to his "mother's apron string," and temptations (created mainly by the stringent methods employed to keep him *virgo-intacta*) have more attraction for the downy-lipped undergraduate, who just wants an opportunity to "make up for lost time," than the boy who has always had a latch-key, and whose parents were liberal enough in their ideas to make allowance for the natural tendencies of warm-blooded youth and the natural law of human gravitation. As the French mother said to her daughter: "Clochette, marry a man who *before marriage* has a knowledge of the world, so that *after marriage* he will not, with trouble to himself and neglect to you, begin finding it out." The warm-hearted, wild boy usually settles down to be the steady husband. He is also the most careful of all men that his wife should be a model of womanliness and sincerity—a *companion* whom he can love and trust with his life and happiness, and he has long since come to the conclusion that union in marriage with a dolly-girl, whose pretty face is her sole qualification, is not worth the trouble. A pretty woman is often the devil's subtlest hiding place, as too many fine fellows have found out to their cost. Rather an intelligent face, beaming with the light of a higher idealism from within, than the bewitching beauty of some Eastern Houri, whose mission is to cater to the baser senses, rather than to afford ennobling companionship to her consort. Better a poor girl with a high sense of honor and duty than the daughter of a Sauerwein O'Shaunessy, whose million ducats are solely responsible for his reception by those of more delicate clay, and who are *really* nothing more or less than a higher order of human organism. Social equality has been tried and found to be a failure. The wealthy pig and the delicate deer cannot breathe the same atmosphere with beneficial result. One man is *not* as good as another unless he *makes himself so*, by reason of his innate attractiveness or personal qualifications. The man who would huddle all classes into one human bouquet would get a contrast of color and perfume that would nauseate the most pronounced socialist. Men, like water (if socialistic or millionaire legislation be not brought to bear upon them), will find their own level. In what is known to the caddish parvenu as "society," there are a great many fine old gentlewomen and sweet girls left out, who would rather sip the more delicate nectar of retirement in the seclusion of their own refined home than rub shoulders with Toms, Dicks and Harrys whom they would not dream of asking to their house; and rather than accept invitations which they would blushingly return, they keep out of "society," and are only known to the few of their own clean-living, unostentatious acquaintanceship. Here endeth the first lesson.

"JACK."

TROY NOTES.

The second run of the Troy Bicycle Club occurred Sunday last, when at about 10 o'clock eighteen members left the club-house for Newtonville, arriving at Capt. Peltier's hotel at 11 o'clock. The First Lieutenant was in charge of the run. The return trip was made at 4 o'clock P.M.

Captain Hanley has ordered two runs a week—Tuesday and Friday mornings, at 5 o'clock. Next Sunday a run will be made to Russell's on the River road; May 26, to Snyder's Lake; Decoration Day to Melrose, and June 2, to Kinderhook Lake, near Niverville. The annual parade will take place Thursday, June 6, though Captain Hanley has not yet issued official orders for it. It will be quite an affair, as a number of out of town wheelmen have been invited to participate.

At the regular monthly meeting of the Troy Bicycle Club, held last Tuesday evening, James R. Knowlson L. A. W. representative; Wm. C. Seaton, Jr., Joseph B. Bittner, James J. Phalen, Charles V. Sullivan, William S. Gunnison and Alfred Wallerstein were elected members.

The resignations of Herbert P. Cole, W. Woodhall, Charles R. Hill, Horan B. Loveland, and J. T. Heister, were presented and accepted.

Mr Cole has found married life and club life too much of a good thing, I suppose, and therefore very wisely resigns the latter. Mr. Heister has removed to Buffalo, and his name will be placed on the honorary list. The President appointed R. Hovee, W C. Simmons, F. S. Heister, F. G. Snyder, and A. R. Hogben, a committee on the pool-table, and Messrs Perkins, Schutt, Stone, Nolan, Sweet, Mead and Biermeister, a gymnasium committee.

Mr George Albert Spicer, ex-representative L. A. W., started for Chicago last Saturday, where he will take charge of the office of his cousin, George Allen Spicer, of the firm of Biermeister & Spicer. He will be known by his 6 ft. 4 inches and glasses, if any wheelman of Chicago meet him. I think Mr. Oliver must have met him when he (Mr. O.) was in Troy, also Mr. Ayers on the "Big 4 Tour" when they stopped at Stockport to lunch at the residence of Joshua Reynolds.

Hope the "little boy" will be taken care of out there, where there is no day of rest.

Last Sunday, while out walking, I met four wheelmen mounted; one on a Star, one on an ordinary and two on safeties. The one on the ordinary seemed about "played out," and could hardly keep along with the others. Does it mean that the safety is the best wheel? I think possibly the rider of the ordinary was a novice, as he looked quite young and did not ride steadily.

I wish some of your lady correspondents would kindly state how the "Ladies' Safety" compares with the tricycle on common country roads, which would be met with on long tours.

(See "Marguerite's" letter, in this issue.—Ed.)

May 14, 1889. Obnh Qba.

MARYLAND.

One thousand wheelmen from Pennsylvania alone will attend the Hagerstown Meet July 2, 3 and 4. It is almost certain that a much larger number of wheelmen from different cities will attend this year's meet than the preceding one, which is due to the selection of Hagerstown as the place for the meet.

Col. Pope's representative has secured three double rooms and a large parlor at the Baldwin House, Hagerstown, such as were desired having been all taken at the Hamilton.

The Western Maryland Railroad is scattering posters broadcast along their line, advertising the races of July 4, which will, it is believed, draw 5,000 people on that day from the country surrounding Hagerstown. The general committee has secured the Opera House, which will be the Division headquarters during the week.

Yesterday a week ago it was announced to Baltimore wheelmen that Mr. Wm. A. Clarke, of the Eagle Bicycle Manufacturing Company, or an expert rider of the Eagle bicycle, would give an exhibition of the hill-climbing qualities of that machine, with an attempt to break the record at Windigate Hill, Mount Washington. This attracted the attention of a number of Baltimore bicyclists, who proceeded toward the celebrated elevation, but upon arrival found only the usual sights—sand, rocks and an elevation of two feet in ten, 1,600 feet in length. Among those present were: Walter Lowry, Joe Geigan, Claude Worthington and V. L. Emerson, from the Baltimore Cycle Club, and Mr. William Harrison, from Washington. After a short halt Mr. Geigan made the attempt on the *hill*, followed by Lowry and Emerson, the latter making five successive trips without a dismount with apparent ease, eclipsing any former attempt by three trips. Mr. McDaniels, of Wilmington, Del., is the only one who ever succeeded in making more than one trip. All those who mounted the hill rode "Star" machines.

The Chesapeake Club has moved into its new club house at Fulton and Lafayette Avenues. The club will have a regular housewarming on Tuesday, the 21st, Mayor Latrobe having promised to attend.

The Maryland Club have adopted and are using a badge which is unique and beautiful. It consists of a gold button with the monogram "M. B. C." set in a red enameled background.

Mr. Geo. F. Updegraff, of the Hagerstown, Md., Club, is in receipt of a letter from H. H. Hodgson, of New Orleans, La., in effect that several wheelmen of that place will attend the L. A. W. Meet at Hagerstown in July. It is said that the New Orleans Bicycle Club are preparing a handsome present for the Hagerstown Club. Mr. Hodgson said that New Orleans will take the League Meet in 1891, say in February, about Mardi Gras time; that is, if they carry out the idea of not expecting a division to do too much. This is but a sample of the many letters of congratulations that are pouring in upon the Hagerstown Club.

Louis J. Ginter has prepared the designs for the new club house of the Centaur Club, which will be located close to Patterson Park. The house will be 20 x 85 feet, pressed brick front, trimmed with brownstone. The wheelroom and bowling alleys will be in the basement of the building, which will only be one foot below the pavement. When finished the club will have one of the handsomest club houses in the city.

A disposition has at last been made of the Division sinking fund, amounting to $1,000, which is the profit on the meet held in Baltimore last year, for which an investment has since been sought. The committee having the matter in charge will deposit the money in the Central Savings Bank in the name of the Division, and subject to the joint order of the Chief Consul and the Secretary-Treasurer.

Several of the Maryland Club members spent last Sunday at Middle River ducking shore. Chairman Chism has recently added to the advantage of the shore by securing from the P. W. and B. Railroad free transportation of wheels to the nearest station, "13-mile-switch," which is only two and a half miles from the shore.

A copy of the official programme of the Hagerstown Meet will be sent to each League member; 14,952 copies will be mailed.

The races at the Hagerstown meet on the third day will be as follows: One-mile bicycle, L. A. W. national championship; 1-mile safety, L. A. W. national championship; 1-mile tricycle, L. A. W. national championship; ½-mile heat race, three heats; 2-mile handicap; 1-mile novice; 100-yards, slow race; 2-mile club championship; 1-mile team race. All open events, L. A. W. rules to govern. The course is a fine half-mile track, and especially prepared for fast time. Handsome gold medals for all first prizes and valuable second prizes. In the team race the prize will be a fine silk banner. Inquiries and applications for entry blanks should be addressed to H. B. Irwin, 34 West Franklin Street, Hagerstown, Md.

Chairman Jos. T. Chism, of the transportation committee, has arranged for one and one-third rate for the round trip from all points, which is the same as that given last year.

Mr. S. T. Clark says that he found the bicycle business in England very active. Our trans-Atlantic neighbors, he noticed, show some disposition to return to straight wheels, built on rational lines, or in other words, upon the model, familiar to all American wheelmen, which has a large rear wheel and plenty of "rake." This is probably due to natural reaction and partly to the fact that the English safety machines were very often too light in construction and too many breakages occurred.

Bay Ridge.

PULLMAN ROAD RACE.

Entries for this great event closed May 10, and if all expected starters make their appearance, over one hundred will contest for prizes said to aggregate over $1,000 in value. Gold medals have been given by Gormully and Jeffery and the John Wilkinson Co., while the Pope Mfg. Co. and Western Toy Co. each contribute Safeties as prizes. Permission has been granted by the Park Commissioners to use Michigan and Grand Boulevards, and the race will start at the Leland Hotel.

BROOKLYN NEWS.

The Brooklyn Club enjoyed an amusing finale to their monthly meeting last night, thanks to the officer in command of the Twenty-third Regiment Cadet Corps, who was drilling the cadets on Hanson Place. About 10 P. M., after the club meeting had adjourned, the bugle of the cadets was heard approaching the club-house, and, word being passed to that effect, the entire club membership then present repaired to the front of the house and saluted the regimental boys with the club bugle calls, cheers, etc., whereupon the officer in command brought his men to a company front at the curbing, and then went through a portion of the manual for the delectation of the B. B. C. It was well executed, and a hearty round of applause was given them as they marched away towards their armory.

The Brooklyns have nearly completed the additions which are being built on their new house and their house committee are rapidly producing order out of chaos. They intend to give a large and elegant house-warming on June 21, which will be the tenth anniversary of the club. Of course, the special features of the affair are as yet in embryo, but I believe there will be an entertainment, a smoker, a collation, and, in fact, all things which are considered good in club life rolled into one big lump of good fellowship.

The Brooklyn Bicycle Club was the only club that responded to the invitation of the Kings County Wheelmen Base Ball Club to send delegates to their meeting. The meeting was quite satisfactory to those present, and indications show that the scheme of a base ball league among the cycling clubs will find followers if it is started well, but *tempus fugit*, you know, boys, and every week counts. The first game will be played between the K. C. W. and B. B. C. nines on May 25, at 4 P. M., at the Prospect Park Parade Grounds.

L. H. Wise, L. I. W., heads the mileage list of the club to May 1, with a total of 1,723 miles. He unfortunately took a fall last week which injured his knee severely, which will prevent him from riding again for two or three weeks.

One of the principal topics of conversation in clubdom now is the big 25-mile road race on Decoration Day, and many are the conjectures as to the winners. The Brooklyn clubs will all turn out in force to witness the event, and there will probably be more spectators at the race than have ever been present at one of the team races, as most of the clubs in New York and New Jersey have also called club runs to witness the race.

A new rule in Prospect Park prohibits riding at a faster pace than eight miles per hour, and some of the K. C. W. boys were called to account for violating it yesterday. The rule is really an old one which has never been rigidly enforced as the park police have always been under the impression that five miles per hour was about the highest possible limit for a bicycle to reach. They are just waking up, that's all.

A goodly-sized party of B. B. C. men will attend the Suburban races on a tally-ho, and I have no doubt they will make themselves known while there.

Schoefer and Class, B. B. C., have returned from the Harvard meet with a good stock of small talk to regale the boys with. There was no "three in the race" but "Warrie" had a good time. Schoefer won an Eagle bicycle there.

The Kings County Wheelmen were out in force to inspect the Irvington-Milburn course last Sunday, and report it in fair condition.

ATOL.

BROOKLYN, May 15, 1889.

K. C. W. NOTES.

If any club, contemplating giving a slow race, will kindly notify the undersigned, they will greatly oblige. We wish to enter our house committee in all such open events.

There will be a large turnout on the 30th for Millburn-Irvington, etc. "Road race—good course—what handicap," etc., is part of all conversations overhead at the club.

Brown was in hard luck at Cambridge. To win a race, and then be protested by a duffer, because one's starter steps over the line, does seem hard. But then starters should obey the rules. Duffers will always protest if they can by so doing win a prize; they want the bauble and have never heard of *sport*.

Accept congratulations, Jno. Shoefer, but what will you do with that *Eagle?*

Sunday evening last the "Robbers' Association" held its regular meeting in the club parlors, President Beazley in the chair.

Three members of the K. C. W. were arrested on Tuesday for fast riding in Prospect Park. The charge was disproved. One of the trio rode a *New Mail*.

For the past week the janitor has done nothing but uncrate new wheels, and all from across the bridge. What has Charles done?

The Universal C. C. held a meeting on Sunday to decide on future plans. To continue as a club or not is the question.

There are ten members of the K. C. W. entered in the road race, and all have declared they will win that "Centennial Jersey," and wear it, too.

WHAT WE ALL WOULD LIKE TO SEE.

That famous needle-bath in condition for use.

The man in the club who does not want to borrow Miles Murphy's safety.

The assistant janitor do a day's work.

Harry Hall ride fast enough to keep warm.

"Tug" Wilson do a little running.

Frank Douglass once more on a scorch.

Our ball team win on Saturday.

The man who does not know

RAM LAL.

Brooklyn, N. Y.

ST. LOUIS.

The lunch—called by courtesy a banquet—last Saturday night, was a most dismal affair. For some reason, not exactly clear, the Lindell Hotel could not accommodate us that evening, and the Calumet Club was selected to furnish the spread. This is where the mistake was made, and if there is any value in the teachings of experience it is entirely safe to say that no more wheelmen's suppers will be given at that place.

The Calumet Club is nothing more nor less than a plain, every day saloon, conducted as a club in order to avoid paying the dram-shop license, and was hardly a fit place to entertain an honored guest such as Mr. Thompson was. The menu was poor, the cooking abominable, the supply utterly inadequate and the service wretched. The blame for the failure should not be laid to the committee. Their intentions were all right, but they were buncoed just as the rest of us were. Mr. Brown was the toast master, and performed his duties as well as the circumstances in the case would permit.

The Missouris had a lively meeting last Tuesday night. Everything passed off smoothly until the order of "new business" was reached, and then everybody drew a long breath and settled back in their chairs for a siege. Mr. Stewart promptly moved that the action taken at the last meeting be rescinded and house rule 3 be restored. This is the rule prohibiting the playing of any games on the club premises on Sunday. Mr. Stewart made a short address in support of the restoration of the rule, and was followed by others for and against. President Andrews took the floor and spoke against the rule. In the course of his remarks he took exception to the articles that have appeared in the WHEEL and the *Spectator*, intimating that the opponents of the rule had taken "snap judgment" on the other fellows, and he warmly denied the charge. With the article in the *Spectator* I have nothing to do; the writer of it is presumably able to take care of himself; and, after a careful examination of my letters to the WHEEL, I fail to find anything reflecting on him in any way, or charging bad faith on his part. I simply stated that the friends of the rule did not think that they had been accorded fair treatment by the other side, in not receiving some notice or intimation that a repeal or change in the rule was contemplated, and the President's virtuous indignation lost much of its force when he admitted, in the course of his remarks, that he had *purposely taken care not to let the information get out that a repeal was contemplated, for fear that the friends of the rule would turn out and defeat the proposed action.* This may not be "snap judgment," but it was certainly taking an unfair advantage. The debate was conducted in an amiable spirit, and, while the lines were sharply drawn, there was nothing said on either side to give offense to the other. The remark of Mr. Brown, that playing a quiet game of billiards or cards on Sunday was more respectable than riding out through the country with a lot of bicyclers, sounded strangely out of place in a meeting of a bicycle club, and it will set a good many of the members to wondering whether the Missouri Club is a bicycle organization, or merely a social club for the encouragement of billiards, cards and tennis. The vote was finally taken on Mr. Stewart's motion, and it prevailed by a majority of two. A motion was afterward carried that no further changes should be made in the house rules without previous notice to all members. With a very few exceptions the result was accepted in the proper spirit, and with a determination to abide by the action of the meeting. One or two disgruntled ones, however, were inclined to be disorderly, and threatened all sorts of vengeance on those who had the temerity to differ with them. One little bow-legged fellow spluttered around at a great rate, declaring, among other foolish things, that he would play billiards next Sunday on the club tables in spite of the rule forbidding it. If he does I presume he is prepared to take the consequences, which, in this case, would be a reduction in the club membership by at least one. Inadvertent or technical infractions of the rules may be overlooked, but deliberate violations don't go in the Missouri Bicycle Club just yet. The position taken by this party, that no house rule can be enacted, amended or repealed, unless first recommended by the house committee, is simply puerile. That it is the duty of the house committee to recommend changes in the rules whenever it may appear necessary or desirable, is not to be denied; but to say that the club cannot make its own rules without first fixing the house committee, is rank nonsense. Such an admission would imply that a very small tail could wag a very large dog, and there is a popular impression abroad that this cannot be done successfully.

Mr. Newman's resignation as Secretary was received and accepted, Mr. J. B. S. Lynch being elected to fill the vacancy. Mr. Newman has gone to Chicago.

ITHURIEL.

ST. AUGUSTINE, FLA.

At the semi-annual meeting of the Alcazar Bicycle Club held recently, the following officers were unanimously elected to serve for six months: President, Frederick de C. Davis; Captain, F. J. Howatt; First Lieutenant, Henry Snow; Secretary-Treasurer, Walter Henry. Three new members were added to the club, and interest in cycling matters seems to be on the increase. Nothing but a visitation from that unwelcome guest "Yellow Jack" can dampen the boys' spirits. At a three-mile race held on Pablo Beach, between Messrs. Howatt and Davis, of the Alcazar Bicycle Club, and a member of the Jacksonville Club, the first two came in in order named, the Jacksonville man being hopelessly left. Time made, 11m. 18s., was not so bad for a sandy track. On the last of May a race will be held at Pablo for the State championship, the principal prize being a beautiful gold and silver cup.

Arrangements for forming a State Division of the L. A. W. are rapidly approaching completion, and if successful it will do much to promote a community of interest among Florida wheelmen and give them one common cause to work in: that of advancing cycling in the semi-tropical State. You may be sure that all in the power of yours truly will be done to advance this most worthy object.

FREDERICK DE C. DAVIS.

May 10, 1889.

The Mount Saint Vincent Restaurant in the Park has been appointed a League hotel by Consul C. A. Sheehan. The Hotel Hamblin, at Chambers and Hudson Streets, convenient to the down-town ferries, has also been appointed a League hotel. The proprietors of both houses readily deduct as per cent. on presentation of the League ticket.

PHILADELPHIA.

The long-drawn-out controversy regarding the relative scorching qualities of the Pennsylvania Bicycle Club and the South-end Wheelmen, finally culminated in a twelve-mile road race between what they considered their champions, namely: McDaniels for the former club and L. J. Kolb for the latter. About 2:25 P. M., May 11, they started at the Fifty-second street toll-gate, and rode out the Lancaster Pike to the foot of Devon Hill. Wallis Merrihew acted as pace-maker for McDaniels, while John Green and C. McCloskey, on a tandem "bike," performed a like service for his opponent.

Over a hundred wheelmen were congregated at the finishing point anxiously awaiting the issue, and when the racers hove in sight it was seen that Kolb held the best position, finally coming in the winner by about twenty feet, in the slow time of 43 minutes, showing that it had been pretty much a loafing race all the way through. Although the pacers had started at the same time as the principals, they actually beat them in, the tandem team being 30 seconds ahead of Kolb and 10 seconds to the front of Merrihew. The result was somewhat anticipated, as it is conceded that McDaniel is a much better rough road rider than pike racer, which is quite the reverse with Kolb. Of course this does not take any of the shine off a victory so justly won. M. J. Bailey, of the "Centurions," kindly acted as referee.

Much bad blood has been stirred up by the outcome of the contest, and it won't be long before these two riders will meet in a race from West Chester to Philadelphia, and if a third race is necessary a 25-mile track race is proposed.

The South-end Wheelmen, with their accustomed energy, are arranging for a mammoth club run to Delaware Water Gap, Dingman's Ferry, etc., to take place some time this coming summer.

What is the matter with the road officers of the Century Wheelmen? They are continually crying for larger attendance on club runs, and then do not show up themselves. Sudgner, the Second Lieutenant, has never attended a club run since he has been appointed. If he can't make it convenient to go, let Capt. Carter appoint another man in his place. In the inter-club team road race that is to take place shortly, it is intended to limit the members of the respective teams to *residents of this city*. This move is intended to bar out the imported talent, which it is sometimes convenient to bring into a club when a race is to be won. About a year ago a sample of this imported talent was elected a member of a city club *between two meetings*, for the purpose of racing under their name, and this is what they call "elevating the sport of cycling."

A quiet tip—the Schaeffer-Bailey race is going to be for blood. Let the band play.

Philadelphia, May 14, 1889. "ANGUS."

MACON, GA.

The great southeastern tour will begin on Sunday morning at 4 o'clock, A. M., June 2. Mention of it was made in THE WHEEL recently by the Birmingham correspondent. The route has been changed somewhat. The party—who will be under the leadership of Mr. Thos. L. Ingram—with about six others, will do the entire trip from Columbus via Byhow, Anniston, Gadsden, Decatur, Athens, Huntsville, and up through Tennessee to Nashville, and then southeast to Chattanooga, Atlanta and Macon.

I have letters before me now from riders along the route who describe the "Pikes" of North Alabama and Tennessee as "simply perfection." Quoting from a letter just received from Mr. Ingram is the following: "If we don't happen to strike a house to stop in (!) away up in the wilds of Alabama, who is going to kick against spending a night in the bushes? If our 'Patent Safety, Anti-dog Device' (44 Bull-dog), does up a farmer's best hound along the way, and he chases us for a few miles with a club, that'll be fun—*a few weeks later*. If we run upon some of those 'wild cat' stills in the mountains, we'll break them up by *drying* them up. And then there'll be exploring unexplored caves; going down in coal mines; a little fishing in the rushing streams up in the mountains, and all that. If you don't come, you'll miss what would otherwise be a chapter in your life-time." The entire distance traveled will be over 800 miles, averaging about forty per day.

Prospects for the race meets in these parts this year look bright. There will be a four-days' meet here in October, conducted by Central City wheelmen. All amateur events. There will be a big meet in Atlanta during the Piedmont Exposition, of three days, and one in Montgomery, Ala., where the prizes will be between $500 and $1,000 value, with numerous small affairs during the summer.

Macon has a young amateur who has jumped on the track at a gait close to three minutes, and has not had a day's training. Recently, on a roadster wheel and in a business suit, he did a mile in 3:10. In training and on a light wheel he should come down to 2:50 or less. Look out for him!

CHAS. ALEX. PERSONS.

FUTURE PLANS OF MINNESOTA WHEELMEN.

Says the *Minneapolis Tribune* of May 12, speaking of the proposed September Division Meet in that city:

If the local wheelmen succeed in getting the September meet of the L. A. W. here it will be a great feather in their caps, and as matters now stand it is likely their efforts will not be in vain. If they are successful the citizens are to be given a treat in the way of bicycle processions and riders, as about 3,000 cyclists from all parts of Minnesota, Iowa and Wisconsin will be present. The matter has gone so far that Chief Consul Slosson, of Minnesota, has written to the consuls of the other two States and feels sure they will consent to his request. The meet will be held during the sessions of the Exposition, and perhaps a bicycle day will be given to the wheelmen by General Manager Byron. In addition to this, there will be a lantern parade with 3,000 wheels in line. The management of the ball team are to put in an excellent cinder track upon which all the races will be run. It will be six laps to the mile, and great pains are to be taken to make it one of the best in the country. During the meet runs to the lakes and banquets will be of frequent occurrence. In other words, while the meet lasts the city will belong to cyclists and the Exposition; regattas, ball games and races will be merely of minor importance.

FIXTURES.

May 13-18, 1889.—Chicago Cycling Exhibit and Tournament, Exposition Building.
May 18, 1889.—New Orleans Bicycle Race for the Hill Cup.
May 18, 1889.—F. A. Elwell's European Party sails from New York.
May 18, 1889.—Stone-Lumsden 1-mile Match Race, at Chicago, Ill.
May 18, 1889.—S. I. A. C. games at West New Brighton, S. I. Two miles bicycle handicap. Entries close May 11, with F. W. Janssen, P. O. Box 125, N. Y. City.
May 20, 1889.—Annual Run of Rhode Island Wheelmen, in charge of George L. Cooke, Box 1101, Providence, R. I.
May 24, 1889.—Ottawa Bicycle Club Meet and Races, Ottawa, Can.
May 25, 1889.—Stone-Lumsden 3-mile Match Race, at St. Louis, Mo.
May 27, 1889.—Stone-Lumsden 25-mile Match Race at Crawfordsville, Ind.
May 30, 1889.—N. J. A. C 1½-mile and 3-mile handicaps Entries close May 22, with A. M. Sweet, P. O. Box 262, Bergen Point, N. J.
May 30, 1889.—Maine Division Meet, at Biddeford, Me.
May 30, 1889.—Bicycle and Athletic Tournament and 2-mile L. A. W. Championship Race at Narragansett Park.
May 30, 1889. Pullman Road Race, Chicago to Pullman.
May 30, 1889.—Twenty-five-mile Handicap Road Race, Irvington—Milburn course Entries close May 15th with A. B. Barkman, 241 Broadway, New York.
May 30, 1889.—Rhode Island Wheelman's Race Meet at Narragansett Park, Providence, R. I. Entries close with C. E. Campbell, Providence, R. I.
May 30, 1889.—Annual 5-mile Handicap Race of New Haven Bicycle Club, at Hamilton Park.
May 30, 1889.—Sixth Annual Meet and Races of Woodstock A. A. A., at Woodstock, Ontario.
May 30, 1889.—North Adams Wheelmen's Races. Entries close May 28, with John B. French, Secretary, North Adams, Mass.
May 30, 1889.—Hill-climbing contest among members of Wheel Club, at Northampton, Mass.
May 30, 1889.—Second Annual Tournament of West End Bicycle Club, Rochester, N. Y. Entries close May 29, with C. J. Iver, 22 Exchange Street.
May 30, 1889.—Winsted Wheel Club's Meet, at Winsted, Conn.
May 30, 1889.—Bay City Wheelmen's Race Meet, at San Francisco.
May 30, 1889.—California L. A. W. Division Meet, at Los Angeles.
June 4, 5, 6, 1889.—Kansas Division Meet at Forest Park, Ottawa, Kansas.
June 8, 1889.—Century Run, Orange, N. J., to Philadelphia. Chairman, L. A. Clarke, 25 Broad Street, New York.
June 15, 1889.—L. I. W. Race Meet at Brooklyn Athletic Grounds. Entries close June 8 with L. H. Wise, 1,281 Bedford Ave., Brooklyn.
June 15, 1889.—Two-mile Bicycle Handicap at New York Athletic Club Grounds, Travers Island.
June 17, 1889.—Annual Meet of Massachusetts Division, L. A. W., at place to be decided later.
June 18, 1889.—Third Annual Meet of Tennessee Division, L. A. W.
June 22, 1889.—New Orleans Bicycle Club's Race for the Hill Cup.
June 28, 29, 1889.—Kings County Wheelmen's Annual Meet at Washington Park, Brooklyn. Address W. C. Nellis, 1,255 Bedford Avenue.
July 2, 3, 4, 1889.—League Meet at Hagerstown, Md.
July 3, 1889.—L. A. W. Race Meet, at Hagerstown, Md. Entries close June 26, with Harry B. Irwin, 34 West Franklin Street, Hagerstown, Md.
July 4, 1889.—Race Meet at Brownsville, Pa.
July 4, 1889.—Illinois Division, L. A. W. Meet, at Ottawa.
July 4, 1889.—Tournament held by Lancaster (Pa.) Bicycle Club.
July 20, 1889.—One-mile and 25-mile Bicycle and 5-mile Tricycle N. C. U. championships at Paddington, Eng., race track.
July 27, 1889.—One-mile and 25-mile Tricycle and 5-mile Bicycle N. C. U. Championships at Paddington, Eng., track.

EUROPEAN CYCLING FIXTURES.

Austro-Hungary.—Graz, May 26 and June 9 and 10. Pilsen, June 9 and 10; Prague (Smichow) June 29 and 30; Germany.—Berlin, May 5, June 16 and 17, July 21, September 15; Hanover, May 12, June 23, September 8; Cologne, May 12, June 2 and 30, August 12; Chemnitz, May 12, September 8; Munich, May 19; Frankfort-on-the-Maine, May 19, September 1; Mannheim, May 19, September 8; Crefeld, May 26, September 8. Hamburg.—Altona, May 26, September 22; Bochum, May 30, August 25; Soram, June 9; Coburg, June 9; Magdeburg, June 30, September 8. Denmark.—Copenhagen International Meeting, August 18.

National Cyclist's Union.—Championship Fixtures—At Paddington, August 24, 50-mile Bicycle and 1-mile Dwarf.

SECOND ANNUAL TOURNAMENT OF WEST END BICYCLE CLUB.

This club, with customary enterprise, has arranged an interesting programme for Memorial Day, including the following events:

Half-mile open handicap, 50 yards limit; one-mile Safety, open, novices; three-mile Monroe County championship; one mile open, novices, for Roadster wheels not under 35 lbs.; one mile open handicap, 100 yards limit; one hundred yard slow race; five mile open handicap, half mile limit; quarter-mile dash, open; two-mile State championship; one and one-half mile, open, handicap, 200 yards limit; one-mile Tandem Bicycle, open; one mile, Bicyclist vs. Horse; one mile, open, for Safeties only; one-mile consolation, handicap, 100 yards limit.

When we add that prizes are handsome and valuable, that the entrance fee is but 50 cents, and that music will be furnished by the Fifty-fourth Regiment Band, enough has been said. Would that Rochester were nearer!

ANNUAL RACE MEET OF HARVARD BICYCLE CLUB—CAMBRIDGE, MAY 11, 1889.

With favorable weather and a large and enthusiastic attendance, the above must be chronicled an entire success. For so early in the season, and at a time when in the nature of things very hot weather can scarcely be counted on, the times made were remarkably good. Owing to a header lately taken by Windle, that much-dreaded phenomenon failed to "bob up serenely" in time for this meet. Two riders, possibly emulous of similar distinction, indulged in the same acrobatic feats, but came off better than Windle. The offer of $500 in prizes brought out a good attendance of fast riders. Following is a summary of races run, in regular order:

One-mile safety scratch race, 5 starters: won by R. H. Davis, in 2m. 53 3-5s., with Bailey, of Harvard Bi. Club, second. Time of others not taken.

Quarter-mile ordinary scratch race, ridden in heats: F. G. Brown, N. Y. A. C., wins first, in 41 2-5s.; Kenneth Brown, Harvard B. C., second, in 45s., and F. A. Delabarre, of Amherst A. C., third, in 46¼s., riding over the course alone.

One-mile inter-scholastic scratch, also ridden in preliminary heats: Philip Davis, of Brown & Nichols, winning first in 3m. 15 1-5s., though closely followed by Atwater, of Roxbury Latin, who took a bad header at end of third lap, and whose pluck in remounting won him much applause from the audience; S. R. Kimball, of Cambridge Latin, rode the second heat alone in 3m. 41 1-5s.

One-mile safety handicap: R. H. Davis and E. A. Bailey were placed at scratch, with G. H. Herriott at 25 yds., and Peter Berlo, W. G. F. Class and Wm. Porter at 75 yds. each. Davis, as might be expected from handicaps like the above, won in 2m. 52 4-5s. by a lead of 3 ft.; Bailey second.

Two-mile handicap, ordinary: J. W. Schaefer won the first heat in 5m. 52 2-5s., after a finely-contested race, with 6 starters; F. A. Delabarre, who would seem to be fated to "go it alone," made the second heat in 7m. 10 3-5s.

One-mile Harvard Bi. C., 3.20 class: This had 3 entries, and was won by T. Barron, '91, in 3m. 9 3-5s., Rogers, of '90, coming in second.

Final heats of the one-mile inter-scholastic: This was won by Davis, of Brown & Nichols, in 3m. 20s., with three men contesting.

In the final heat of the quarter-mile ordinary scratch, F. G. Brown won, but was disqualified because his starter stepped over the line on the send-off; Kenneth Brown, who came in second, was given first prize, and F. A. Delabarre second. Time made by F. G. Brown, 41 1-5s.

Two-mile tandem safety scratch: Three contesting pairs entered for this, prominent among whom were R. H. Davis and Geo. Hendee on one tandem, but their combined good looks and fast riding (for one lap) brought them in only second, and E. A. Bailey and E. W. Bailey won by half a lap in 6m. 46s., the third pair not being in it at all.

In the concluding heats of the two-mile ordinary handicap, J. W. Schaefer (100 yds.) won, with J. P. Clark (125 yds.) second, and F. A. Delabarre (200 yds.) third. Time of winner, 5m. 50 2-5s.

Officers of the meet were: C. W. Fourdrinier, referee; with L. H. Morgan, of '89, J. D. Bradley, of '86, and S. G. Wells, '85, as judges; Messrs. Lothrop and Carpenter, of '88, and Burr, of '89, acted as timers, and Mr. E. C. Wright, of '86, as starter; Mr. G. S. Mandell, of '89, was clerk of the course, with a host of assistants also acting as clerks, scorers, ushers, etc.

Prizes given were rich and varied, ranging from a silver paper-weight to Winchester rifles and silver cups, and all seemed well satisfied.

RHODE ISLAND WHEELMEN'S TOURNAMENT.

The Rhode Island Wheelmen's athletic tournament, at Narragansett Park, Memorial Day, is looming up and the early promises of one of the most notable occasions of the sort are assured of fulfillment. The committee have been working hard, and are now devoting themselves especially to the handsome official programme that is to include a score card. Arrangements have been made with the New York and New England Railroad whereby a 50-cent ticket will carry the bearer from this city into the grounds and return. Wheels and all paraphernalia of the various classes of sports that will be represented in the meet will be carried free of expense. The tournament will open at 1 o'clock in the afternoon with a football game between the Providence and British Hosiery Football Clubs for silver medals. Other athletic contests will comprise a 100-yard dash (professional) for prizes of $15, $7 and $3; one-half mile amateur foot race for a silver cup and pair of running shoes; a match game of tennis and a tug-of-war, the latter probably between teams from the Young Men's Christian Association and Brown University.

The cycle events and the prizes are as follows:

Two-mile National L. A. W. Championship—First prize gold medal; second, silver medal.

Three-mile State Championship—First prize, gold medal, presented by Campbell & Co.; second, World type writer.

One-mile State Safety Championship—First prize, gold medal, presented by Coventry Machinist Co.; second, safety lantern, presented by Clark Cycle Co.

One-mile Team race—Prize, elegant silver cup.

Two-mile Safety (open)—First prize, Kodak camera; second, Victor cyclometer, presented by Overman Wheel Co.; third, pongee silk shirt, presented by William Barton.

One-mile Bicycle (open)—First prize, gold medal, presented by H. B. Smith Machine Co.; second, Butcher cyclometer, presented by Singer & Co.; third, pair Kingston Jersey breeches.

One-mile Handicap—First prize, gold medal; second, entire Jersey suit, presented by Whitten, Godding & Co.; third, billiard cue, presented by Brunswick-Balke Co.

One-mile Safety Handicap—First prize, gold medal; second, Smith & Wesson revolver; third, pair kangaroo bicycle shoes, presented by T. F. Pierce & Co.

One-mile Tandem Safety Handicap—First prize, two leather-cased toilet sets; second, two pairs Lemair opera glasses.

One-mile Tandem Safety—First prize, two fine meerschaum pipes; second, two silver-headed canes.

One-mile Novice—First prize, silver cup, presented by Pope Manufacturing Co.; second, seal ring; third, solid silver charm ("Pigs in Clover"); fourth, Oklahoma house lot (if you can get it).

Entry blanks and all particulars can be had by addressing C. I. Campbell, Box 266, Providence.

In the two-mile bicycle race at Bethlehem, Pa., May 10, under the management of Lehigh University A. A., Riegel, '90, won in 5m. 19 1-5s.

The Yale two-mile bicycle record was reduced from 6m. 24s. to 6m. 21s., at the annual spring games of Yale College A. A., by Clark, of '91, on May 13.

Harriman, of '89, took the 2-mile bicycle race at Worcester Polytechnic A. A.'s spring sports May 11, in 8m. 51 2-5s., with Davis second, in 9m. 4 3-5s.

At the annual spring games of Columbia College, A. A., May 11, the two-mile bicycle race was won by Arthur Jones, of '91, in 6m. 51s, with W. H. Hall second.

Bicycle races, twelve in number, are to be held at Ottawa, Kansas, on June 5 and 6, and many valuable trophies are offered. At least one rider in the Northwest, Colie Bell, will compete, and perhaps others will accompany him.

The open 2-mile bicycle race at Pennsylvania University sports was won by W. Taxis, of the Y. M. C. A., in 6m. 26s., with E. G. Kolb, of the S. E. W., a good second. The 2-mile Pennsylvania University race, scratch, was won by C. H. Kean, of '89, in 6m. 10s., with H. V. Restner, of '92, second.

Two L. A. W. Championship races have been assigned to Ottawa, Kansas, to be run at the Division Meet, June 5th and 6th. In addition, the half-mile, mile and five-mile State championship races will be held there. The Ottawa Wheelmen would seem to be a go-ahead club, and some of our Eastern clubs might profit by their push.

The two-mile bicycle races at the spring sports of Swarthmore College A. A., on May 11, was won by Heulings in 6m. 48s., with Coles, of '92, second. On the same afternoon, at Haverford College A. A. annual field meeting, Nicholson took the half-mile bicycle race in 1m. 45s., with Stokes second and Fox third.

The Intercollegiate Championship games will be held at Berkeley Oval, May 25. The following men have entered the two-mile bicycle race: R. H. Davis, E. S. Bailey, W. B. Greenleaf and R. Browne, Harvard; C. B. Keen, B. Brown and H. V. Regster, U. of P.; W. W. Ware, F. A. Clark and A. J. Kountze, Yale; F. A. Delabarre, Amherst; W. H. Hall, Columbia; Fred Gubelman, Stevens; A. H. Zimmerman C. C. N. Y.; Fred Speakman and W. L. Hurlings, Swarthmore.

RACES RUN AT NATIONAL GUARD ATHLETICS, MAY 10.

One-mile bicycle race, for those who had never won a prize: J. W. Judge, Riverside Wheelmen, first, in 3m. 24 2-5s.; L. A. Schoeler, New York City, second. Two-mile bicycle race: J. F. Borland, Brooklyn Bicycle Club, 50yds. start, first, in 6m. 39 3-5s.; L. A. Schoefer, New York City, 80yds. start, second; E. P. Baggott, New Jersey Athletic Club, 50yds., third. Handicapper for bicycle races, F. P. Prial.

THE HAGERSTOWN RACE MEET.

In connection with the Tenth Annual Meet of the L. A. W. at Hagerstown, Md., the following races will be run on the third day, viz.: July 4, 1889:

1 Mile Bicycle, Ordinary; L. A. W. National Championship.
3 Mile Bicycle, Safety; L. A. W. National Championship.
1 Mile Tricycle; L. A. W. National Championship.
Half-mile Heat Race, three heats.
2 Mile Handicap.
1 Mile Novice.
100 Yards Slow Race.
1 Mile Club Championship.
1 Mile Team Race.

All open events, L. A. W. rules to govern. The course is a fine half mile track and specially prepared for fast time. Handsome gold medals for all first prizes and valuable second prizes. In the team race the prize will be a fine silk banner. Address all inquiries and applications for entry blanks to Harry B. Irvin, 34 W. Franklin Street, Hagerstown, Md.

BALTIMORE, May 11, 1889.

WOODSTOCK, ONTARIO.

At the sixth annual meet and races of the Woodstock A. A. A., to be held May 24, or "Queen's Birthday," this interesting programme is outlined:

Bicycle Club Competition, open. Fine secretary for club rooms and silk banner.
Mile novice race on road machines. Gold medal; gold and silver medal.
One mile, open to all. Solid gold stop watch; fine diamond sleeve buttons. If 1:40 is beaten in this race a solid gold "split second" stop watch, worth $165, will be given for first prize.
Five mile, open to all, handicap. Fine diamond ring; fine diamond pin.
Half mile, open to all, handicap. Amateur photo outfit; split bamboo fish pole.
One mile, open to all, handicap. Silver stop watch; pearl opera glass.
County race. Championship of Oxford County. Two miles, on road machines, W. A. A. A. Cup.
One mile, open to all, handicap; safety machines. Double-barrel breech-loading shot gun; gold-headed cane. One mile consolation. Combination diamond stud and scarf pin; fine athlete's valise.

Roscoe, the coming amateur of Canada, is rapidly getting in trim for the above, and good time on the asphalt track may be looked for. The Toronto Bic. Club also promises to attend in force. For evening entertainment the Woodstock Minstrels may be looked to as completely filling the bill.

THE CARRIER TRICYCLE IN A NEW ROLE.

Probably the only bicycle passenger car in America is used in this city. An old chap, who lives out in M street, about a mile from the business centre, has rigged up a four-wheeled vehicle with seats for six passengers besides himself. He is conductor, driver, proprietor and motive power. A very comfortable vehicle it is, for the seats are good and an awning affords protection against sun and rain. Every night this strange vehicle stands near the door of Albaugh's Theatre as the audience comes out, and the proprietor solicits passengers like a hansom or carriage driver. Usually he does not have long to wait for a load, for his route is well known and novelty counts for much in his favor. He charges 10 cents a passenger, and lands his customers at their doors. Sometimes he takes out small pleasure riding parties, and his vehicle is a favorite among the children of his neighborhood. Already he has earned with his wagon much more than it cost him.—*Washington letter in Philadelphia News.*

A SELECTED LIST OF PATENTS.

[Reported especially for THE WHEEL AND CYCLING TRADE REVIEW by C. A. Snow & Co., patent attorneys, Washington, D. C.]

W. E. Smith, Washington, D. C., Bicycle.
S. Clark, Childs Hill, England, Lamp holder or frame.
M. F. Abbott, Jeffersonville, Ind., Velocipede. All bearing date of May 14.

In the 5-mile bicycle race at University of Pennsylvania, May 11, a new man, Register, '91, was developed, and one who promises in the future to do some good work for the University.

THE WHITE FLIER.

Westboro, Mass., is a little Massachusetts town, some seven or eight miles out of Worcester, Westboro is a prohibition town; it is also the location of the White Cycle Co.'s manufactory. The building is about eight minutes walk from the depot, or two minutes run, if you want to get a train. It is situated in somewhat rural seclusion in Cedar or Oak, or some such shrubbery-named street; opposite it is a cemetery. The company doubtless kills off advertising agents, men who want something for nothing, and men who want to represent the company on the road. God's Acre is already quite well settled.

The White Cycle Co.'s factory is the cleanest, prettiest place one could see. It is a long, low, brick building, splendidly lighted. There are two out-buildings which will contain the blacksmith and enameling shops, and the boilers and motive power engines.

The company was organized by Mr. Frank White, an enthusiastic Boston Cyclist, who has ridden a type of the White Flier for some time. It is capitalized at $100,000, has made every effort to put up a perfectly equipped factory and will make a leading string of a high grade safety, of which we present a cut and the most minute description, the latter from the facile pen of "Jack."

This distinctively American machine is the latest among the already large and prosperous cycle family, and bids fair to hold its own among its older brothers and sisters. The White Flier is the product of the White Cycle Co., of Westboro, Mass., and is a rear-driving safety with equal sized wheels of 30 inch diameter or 6-inch or more.

THE PEDALS are so adjusted that they can be stepped in any position, and by equal pressure of both feet they become foot rests. The length of the stroke can be varied, pushing one pedal down raises the other a corresponding distance. The swing of the spring used to draw the pedals back to the starting point, the weight of the one pedal when it is pressed down raises the other one. A very good point in this machine is that any person affected by a stiff knee, or one whose leg has been injured, so as to make one shorter than the other, can by adjusting the pedal and driving chain suit the peculiar conditions. The swing or guide frame hanging from the backbone, on which the pedals move up and down, can be thrust while the rider is in motion to almost any angle. Thus if he wishes a vertical tread the frame can be swung so that the pedals come well under the saddle. If, on the contrary, the rider wishes to change the position and get more of the thrust stroke which uses the thigh muscles, as in a rotary motion crank safety, this can instantly be done by swinging the frame toward the front wheel. This ability to vary the stroke will rest the rider, who may often weary of the monotony of a never-exchanging motion, and yet by the peculiar construction of his machine he is unable to change it. With the White Flier this is different.

It is claimed that when the driving pedal is on top of the guide frame, and in the beginning of a stroke, the construction is such that the rider has more leverage than at any other point in the whole stroke. The leverage lessens as the pedal moves down and as the legs straighten out, thus equalising the force to be exerted necessary to drive the machine. The stiffness of the machine are rollers and the adjustment of the points is so delicate that the bearings are positively proof. It is claimed that the bearings will without adjustment or touching (except of course occasional oiling) wear as long as the machine itself. Some people may say, "Why do they not put in ball-bearings?" Well, simply my friends, because it is an absolute impossibility to make a perfectly accurate sphere of steel. There is not a ball-bearing in the market that has a roll of balls in its bearing-case with anything like uniformity. Micrometer and sensitive scale tests have proved this, and our ball in a bearing-case, varying the one thousandth part of an inch from its fellows will raise the d—l with the running of the bearing. A roller-bearing are be turned with positive accuracy so that variations of even the four thousandth part of an inch would unsuit it for the bearing cases which are placed on the White Flier.

And why was the old roller bearing discarded? Simply because it was an imperfect absurdity, which twisted and jammed, and was a source of annoyance and mistrust and danger to the rider of machines upon which they were used. As soon as the ball-bearing was invented "the trade" discarded the then imperfect roller bearing and used the ball-bearing instead. But if you are properly hardened steel rollers in a case where there is no room to twist, and they will "out-coast old coaster himself."

The front wheel of the White Flier fitted with their perfected and perfect roller bearing, ran eight minutes—not by computation, but by the watch—and any one of them will do it, as the most perfect system of interchangeability is insisted upon by the White Cycle Co.

The machine must really be seen to be appreciated. Its beautiful finish, the accuracy and perfect interchangeability of the parts, and the easy, frictionless qualities of the bearing surfaces have captivated more than one old sceptic of a rider of many years experience.

There are no dead centres on the "White Flier." Take any crank machine for instance. When the crank and pedal are at twelve o'clock they are on dead centre, when they are at one o'clock the dead centre is being gradually overcome, when they are at three o'clock, or "fifteen minutes past," the rider has attained his maximum power. When the pedal is at six o'clock it is again on dead centre, and all the way from six o'clock, on the revum of the pedal, absolutely no power can be applied to that pedal unless the rider's shoes were fixed to the pedals. Then he will get an upward pull which it very severe on the under thigh muscles. If you have time and inclination drop down and see the factory. It is open to every one.

You can be shown through and see and believe for yourself.

The White Cycle Co. start out handicapped in no way. They have plenty of funds and perhaps the most perfect little factory on the globe for the manufacture of high-grade cycles.

The above cut is a fair representation of the machine. The machin is not awkward or ugly, as in the case of several of the unmechanical abortions which have been a waste of material and a hindrance to enjoyable cycling in this country.

Mr. Frank White is the inventor of this machine, and has spent much time in perfecting it. He is the same gentleman who closed Corey Hill on a tricycle of his own construction in '85, when that hill had been ridden but once that year on a high tricycle. Much could be said for the machine, but the experience of actual riding this season will be better praise than all the newspaper advertising.

Mr. J. Purvis-Bruce is with the company, and will go among the boys with the new "goat." He will meet his many old friends and make new ones. The White Cycle Company's factory is at Westboro, thirty-two miles from Boston, on good roads and make new ones. The White Cycle Company's factory is at Westboro, thirty-two miles from Boston, on good roads by the way of Boston Common, out Beacon Street into Newton Lower Falls, then by Wellesley, Natick and South Framingham. Here you can either take the shortest road by way of Framingham and Ashland to Westboro, or by way of Southboro to Westboro, which is two miles longer but a better road. If you come out some Saturday bring your pipe with you. You will find "Jack" there, unless he is in New Orleans or Montana or some other place. "Look out for the White cycles."

New York State Division L.A.W.

OFFICIAL ORGAN.

OFFICERS FOR 1889.

Chief Consul, W. S. Bull, 754 Main Street, Buffalo, N. Y. Vice-Consul, M. L. Bridgman, 1433 Bedford Avenue, Brooklyn, N. Y. Secretary-Treasurer, Geo. M. Nisbett, 80 Wall Street, New York City. Executive and Finance Committee, W. S. Bull, M. H. Bridgman, Dr. George E. Blackham, Dunkirk, N. Y.

ANNUAL DIVISION MEET.

To the members of the New York State Division:

The annual Division meet must be held in September.

Clubs desiring the meet should communicate with this office at once, as it is very important in order to insure a large aud successful gathering that the time and place be made known to the members at the earliest possible date.

Yours fraternally,
W. S. Bull,
Chief Consul.

ATTENTION, TOURISTS.

Touring wheelmen will please note the following extracts from the hotel agreement now in force in the New York State division, and govern themselves accordingly:

"That will during the continuance of this agreement furnish any member of the L. A. W., *producing his membership ticket for the current year*, accommodations equal in all respects to those furnished to regular guests, at rates to be agreed upon, which are to be found noted in the Record Book."

"That will *not* accord any privileges, reductions, use or inspection of the 'Record Book,' or other benefits derivable under this agreement to any wheelmen, except members of the L. A. W. *who shall produce* their *individual tickets of membership* for the current year."

"That will hang in a conspicuous place in the hotel office the certificate of appointment furnished by the division."

"That will securely keep in the hotel office, at the disposal of L. A. W. members only, a 'Record Book,' which shall be furnished by and remain the property of said division."

The Record Books are placed in such hotels only as sign the above agreement, and in order that they may be used as a means of communication between touring members, who are urged to *fully describe* the best routes, *condition of the roads*, points of interest in the locality, and other information deemed of value to members of the League who may subsequently visit the hotel. All entries should be signed and dated.

At the end of the riding season the information contained in these books will be used to correct and enlarge the Road Book.

Yours fraternally,
W. S. Bull,
Chief Consul.

NEW YORK STATE LEAGUE HOTELS.

To the members of the New York State Division:

There should be a consul in every place where there is a league member; and, as there should be no place in New York where there is not a League member, I want a consul and League hotel in every city, town and hamlet in the Empire State. The vacancies in the following list of consuls and hotels must be filled at once, as the touring season is at hand:

PLACE.	CONSUL.	HOTEL.
Albany		Hotel Kenmore
Alden		Martins
Alfred Centre		Burdick House
Amsterdam	Seeley Conover	Hotel Warner
Angelica	F. W. Warner	Charles Hotel
Angola		Union House
Arena	F. H. McLean	Arena Hotel
Arkville		Commercial
Attica	Hugh Miller	Wyoming
Auburn	Edward Leonard	
Bainbridge	A. M. Welch	Central
Baldwinsville	H. P. Bigelow	
Batavia	L. D. Collins	
Bellmore	Edward Self	
Binghamton	C. E. Titchener	
Blauveltville	C. J. Hogart	Orangeburgh Road House
Blue Stores	R. M. Washburn	Blue Stores Hotel
Brooklyn	W. C. Marion, Jr., K. C. W.; Geo. G. Teller, L. I. W.; W. H. Meeteer, B. Bi. C.	
	Prof. A. C. Richardson, B. Bi. C.	Tifft House
Buffalo	John S. Kellner, R. Bi. C.; Geo. J. Hearne, Z. Bi. C.; H. E. Ducker, R. Bi. C.	The Stafford
Brinkerhoffville	A. S. Ambler	
Campbell		Central
Canajoharie		Hotel Wagner
Canastota	Chas. H. Wolf	Lewis House
Canisteo	F. H. Peck	Canisteo House
Castile	L. H. Jones	
Catskill	Dr. G. C. Gulick	Windsor
Cazenovia	B. S. Stanley	Hotel Finch
Cherry Creek		Central Hotel
Cherry Valley	Chas. W. Drane	Central House
Chester	John P. Bull	Howland House
Cincinnatus	J. W. Osgood	
Clarks Factory	A. E. McLean	
Clifton Springs	H. K. Carpenter	
College Point	G. A. S. Wieners	
Collins Centre	A. C. Bates	
Corona	S. G. Putnam	
Cortland	I. B. Knickerbocker	Messenger House
Croton Falls	Geo. Walton Abrams	Croton House
Cuba	C. O. Osborne	Kinney House
Dansville	Jas. A. Jackson	The Sanitarium
Deposit		Oynaga House
Dawnesville	Geo. W. Holmes	
Dryden	J. Giles Ford	
Dundee		Harpending House
Dunkirk	H. M. Dickinson	Hurlbert House
East Aurora	B. S. Burzette	Globe Hotel
East New York	Jos. C. Van Uril	John Guenther's
East Norwich		Hurrell House
East Springfield	C. F. Gray	Platner House
Ellenville	E. W. Terwilliger	Terwilliger House; Mount Meenahga
Ellington	Geo. E. Haman	Ellington Hotel
Elmira	Chas. F. Stevens	Rathbun House
Flushing	L. A. Clark	
Fort Edward	W. C. Spicer	Eldridge House
Frankfort	L. B. Haynes	Central
Franklinville	Chas. A. Perley	
Fredonia	Dr. A. Wilson Dods	Park Hotel
Friendship	E. G. Latta	American House
Gainsville	E. W. Tiffany	
Garrisons	J. W. Garrison	Highland House
Geneva	John W. Millen	
Glen Cove	R. Frank Bowne	Allen House
Glens Falls	H. W. Knight	Rockwell House
Glen Head	Townsend Scudder	
Gloversville	H. A. Baird	
Greene	A. W. Davidson	Chenango House
Green Haven	J. B. German	
Groton	W. Grant Rhodes	
Havana	Frank G. Hills	Montour House
Herkimer	W. I. Taber	Mansion House
Holley	C. E. Hayden	
Homer	F. B. Carey	
Hoosick Falls	J. C. Haswell	Hotel Fitchburg
Hudson	R. W. Evans	Worth House
Huntingdon	Chas. B. Scudder	Huntington House
Ithaca	G. W. Slocum	Clinton House
Jamaica	Newton F. Walters	Pettit's Hotel
Johnstown	Wm. H. Young, Sr	Wm. Johnson Hotel
Kingston	James V. Bruyn	Eagle Hotel
Lake George	Herbert Morris	
Little Falls	Geo. L. Smith	
Little Genessee	C. L. E. Lewis	
Livingston	F. H. Clancy	
Lockport	Elmer E. Pool	The Grand; The Niagara
Long Island City	J. H. Jacobs	
Lowville	C. E. Pelton	Hotel Windsor
Margaretville		Ackerley House
Mechanicville		Mechanicville House
Medina	A. B. Eddy	Hart House
Middlefield		Phœnix Mills Hotel
Middletown	H. C. Ogden	
Milton	A. E. Bell	
Minetto	E. T. Seymour	River Side Hotel
Newark	A. J. Perkins	
New Berlin	H. J. Halstead	Central
Newburgh	A. J. Barton	
New Rochelle	H. F. Fuller	Huguenot House
New York City	Chas. A. Sheehan, M. Bi.	Grand Union
	L. A. Newcome, H. W.	Hamblin House, Mount St. Vincent
Niagara Falls	Neil Campbell	
Olean	P. D. Spaulding	
Oneida	J. F. Aldrich	Hotel Brunswick
Oswego		Lake Shore Hotel
Painted Post	C. B. Schuyler	Bronson House
Patchogue		Roe's Hotel
Pawling	F. C. Taber	Dutchess House
Pavilion	Geo. R. Henry	
Peekskill	D. C. Hasbrouck	Eagle Hotel
Penn Yan		Benham House
Perry		Walker House
Phœnix Mills	C. A. Ayres	
Pike	W. C. Smith	Powers Hotel
Port Jervis	E. F. Laidley	Delaware House
Poughkeepsie	Chas. F. Cossum	Morgan House
Princes Bay, S. I.	Robert Bishop	
Purdy Station	L. G. Sloat	
Ramapo	M. Prineveau	
Randolph		Palace Cafe
Richfield Springs	E. A. Hinds	Darrow House
Richmond Hill	H. F. Quortrup	
Richmondville	W. H. Reightmyer	Westover House
Rochester	M. F. Shafer	Powers Hotel; New Osburn House
Rome		Arlington Hotel
Roslyn		Mansion House
Round Island	Frank H. Taylor	The Frontenac
(Thousand Islands, St. Lawrence River.)		
Roxbury		Delaware Valley House
Sag Harbor	Frank B. Glover	Nassau House
Schaghticoke		American Hotel
Schuylerville		Schuylerville House
Sherbourne	E. W. Smith	Daniels House
Sidney		Hotel Sidney
Skeneatales		The Packwood
Sloatsburg	A. B. Taylor	Taylor House
Silver Lake		Walker House
Silver Springs		Walker House
Springfield Centre	E. A. Ninger	Central
Stamfordville	Rev. Alva H. Morrill	
Stockport	Joshua Reynolds	
Suffern	D. B. Van Wagener	Eureka House
Suspension Bridge	O. Phillips	Atwood's Western Hotel
Syracuse	H. W. Chapin	Vanderbilt House
Tannersville	B. Howard	Roggens' Mt'n. House
Tarrytown	A. L. Embree	Franklin House
Tonawanda	Frank E. Drulland	
Tottenville, S. I.		West End Hotel
Tremont	D. Hamilton	
Troy	F. S. Hamer	
Tuxedo Park	W. D. Phillips	Tuxedo Boarding House
Unadilla	E. S. Brewster	Unadilla House
Utica	E. H. Crosby	St. James Hotel
Van Beuren Point		Van Beuren Point Hotel
Van Ettenville	Harry Barfield	
Van Weis Point	Frank T. Snyder	
Verplanck	Henry Tate	
Walden	C. W. Sadlier	
Wallkill	J. A. Jansen	Wallkill House
Wappingers Falls	H. H. Brown	Warren House
Watertown	Geo. B. Calder	Woodruff House
Watkins	Jno. M. Thompson	Jefferson House
Waverly	Thos. W. Hawyrth	Tioga
Weedsport	H. E. Rhenbottom	
West Chester	H. M. Randell	
Westfield	Chas. W. Allen	Mintan House
Westhampton Centre		Atlantic House
Westmoreland	N. De Roy Lee	Tobars Hotel
Whitehall	J. D. Culver	
Whitneys Point	L. G. Collins	Beach House
Wilson	W. B. Metzger	American
Wyoming		R. R. Hotel
Yonkers	H. W. Pagan	

Yours fraternally,
W. S. Bull, Chief Consul.
754 Main Street, Buffalo, N. Y.

NEW HOTEL AT GLEN COVE, L. I.—ROAD FROM MINNEOLA TO GLEN COVE.

Editor of the Wheel:

Will you kindly state that there has been a first-class League hotel opened at Glen Cove, known as the Allen House; that I can recommend it to all wheelmen. I would also say that the road from Minneola or Roslyn to Glen Cove was in good riding condition. From Minneola brick tavern to Glen Cove is eleven miles, and it can be ridden in one hour without any trouble.

R. Frank Bowne,
Consul at Glen Cove.

Glen Cove, May 13, 1889.

THE ORANGE ROUTE.

Editor of The Wheel:

About a year ago I sent you an itininary of the little-known route to Orange by way of Bergen Hill, Carlstadt, Rutherford and Avondale, which I would now like to supplement with the discovery that one can avoid nearly a mile of stone pavement in Newark by turning off from Washington Avenue where it is crossed by the Greenwood Lake R. R., and following a very fair series of sidepaths through Watsessing to Grove Street. Part of this route has improved and part deteriorated since last season, but it is, on the whole, much better riding now than then. The macadam on the Paterson plank road from west side of Bergen Hill to Carlstadt is getting badly worn; but, on the other hand, its completion to the latter place makes the whole distance ridable. Some additional macadam has also been laid and the sidepath improved between Rutherford and Avondale, so that no dismount is now necessary from Carlstadt to Newark.

A WHEELMEN'S FERRY ON SEVENTY-SECOND STREET, WEST.

The chief obstacle to making a quick trip from New York to Orange is now the detour which has to be made by either the Forty-second Street or the Fort Lee Ferry to cross the river. Why cannot a wheelmen's ferry be established from the foot of Seventy-second Street, which is a central point for the New York, Citizens, Manhattan and Riverside Clubs? These organizations have at least 300 members in the aggregate, a tax on whom of $2 apiece would buy a naphtha launch, which could then be run at a nominal expense. Yours truly,

L. A. W., 2449.

At the last meeting of the Cycle Club Mr. Chas. G. Lucas was elected to fill the office First Lieutenant C. L. Crush recently resigned from and Mr. W. M. Waters to the office of Second Lieutenant, vice C. G. Lucas, promoted. Resolutions of regret at the departure of Mr. Crush for Chicago were unanimously adopted.

THE LADIES' COLUMN.

EDITOR OF THE WHEEL:

Am now in possession of a ladies' safety, and trusting that my experiences may prove beneficial to other ladies, would relate how I fared when learning to ride absolutely the most beautiful steed now in the market for ladies. Have written previously giving reasons why we should ride the bicycle, and now am pleased I can say that I do ride that style machine. A Swift is my choice, which for symmetry and easy running exceeds my expectations, and is a credit to the makers.

The wheel was received at Boston, my brother riding it home for me. Thus, Wednesday night, May 15, found me on a fairly smooth street in front of our domicile fully engrossed with the two-wheeler. Up and down the short street, my brother holding it up and to the best of his ability "coaching" me; we had what might commonly be called a short "picnic." The first sensible idea I caught hold of was that I must swivel or oscillate the front wheel, and not try to pull the handles by main force from the side it seemed to be leaning toward. Hitherto when I had felt the machine tipping to either side, my frantic efforts to pull that side *up* by strength were alarming. My brother soon noticed the fault, and though generally he is capable of a great deal of sympathy, I know he was laughing horribly at me and thinking how much strength he had had to put forth to prevent both us and the machine from meeting Mother Earth, also inwardly groaning over the waste of his shoe leather. By and by, when I had got into the notion of swinging the front wheel over to the side it more than frequently tipped; I was able to go a short way alone. A possibly new version of part of one of Scott's favorite poems, depicts in the best language my struggles during this interesting battle:

> "We tug, we strain, down, down we go,
> Two wheels above and me below."

My sister now had a try with it, or to be more elegant, commenced her first lesson; doing just as well if not better than I. The first time I tried a small square (one-quarter mile) with its four corners, the combination of a horse in the distance and a large amount of soft sand was too much for me, and I came to grief on the third side.

The result of the night's work was that we could both ride it (after a fashion), but ride it we did around the square several times with no help.

Thursday night we were more expert with it, and finally after practice could mount it. Early Friday morning, before work, I rode four miles in company with my brother, experiencing trouble only on the hills. This was owing to my pulling on the handles as I had been used to do on our tandem tricycle. Friday night it rained, while Saturday morning gave me six miles of easy riding. Sunday, the 12th, I rode forty-one miles, part with the Middlesex Cycle Club, and dismounted on no hills whatever.

Do I need to say anything more but that I consider the bicycle *the* machine for ladies who ride any distance. I do not attempt to say that it is very easy to learn, and can understand how it may come readier to some than others, but when by an exercise of perseverance you have mastered it, the pleasure fully repays all outlay, and makes me confident that the safety bicycle is the best means of transit yet introduced for the benefit of ladies.

The Middlesex Cycle Club's first run of the season is now a thing of the past, having taken place Sunday, May 12. While it was fairly well attended, twenty-three members participating, the number would doubtless have been increased had "Old Sol" shown his face at the proper time. Early (for Sunday morning) risers found the sky looking decidedly doubtful, while between 7 and 7:30 A. M. it clouded up, and a very sharp shower was the result. The roads being dusty it did no harm, but I fear that the remaining clouds suggested more moisture to the fair-weather riders, who deeming "discretion the better part of valor," stayed at home, thereby missing a good deal, since about noon the sun shone warm and bright. Capt. Morton being absent, the run was conducted by Lieut. McArthur for Harvard Square and Chestnut Hill Reservoir. The former-named place for the convenience of the weaker riders, who might not feel able at this stage of the season to go the full distance. The starting point was in Malden, and time 9:30. Members from Melrose, Oak Grove, Malden, Everett, Somerville, Cambridge and Maplewood were on hand, and certainly covered a fair amount of territory, rendering a central meeting-place an absolute necessity.

The line was formed punctually (for cyclists). Three tandem safeties, with a lady on each, one lady bicyclist, the rest on tandem and single trikes, gentlemen's safeties and ordinaries, made up the party. The former machines started at the head to prevent mischief. When other wheels came too close for comfort, practice in dodging to the other side of the road was freely indulged. Am afraid that there will be considerable difficulty in uniting the pace of the safety riders with that of the tricyclers. It is certainly different, and in almost every case the gearing of a tandem safety is much higher than the tandem trike, making it difficult for the former to go slow enough for the latter, or the latter fast enough for the former. Besides, it is a recognized item that the safety is going to have the best of the road question, on account of being single-track. Some slight trouble was experienced in keeping the party undivided, owing to the majority of riders not being in cycling trim. Let us hope that the fault can and will be remedied by judicious management, and by no means give any chance for two sections in the club, *i. e.*, a bicycle and tricycle division.

The route lay through Medford, West Somerville and North Avenue, Cambridge, the latter in a most truly terribly muddy condition. Otherwise the roads were fair, and but two or three of the party left at Harvard Square. However, the Wakefield Bicycle Club, now joining us, more than made up the deficiency, and after a stoppage of fifteen minutes we were off, bound for the Reservoir, where we found some members from the other side of the city awaiting us.

Although the different papers said many clubs had called runs for other places, there seemed to be no falling off in the attendance of wheelmen at the Reservoir. A goodly number will always be found safely ensconced within its space, whether the roads see many cyclists or not. Many more than the usual number of lady cyclists were met, and as "a straw shows which way the wind blows," so similarly do we find that more ladies are finding out the benefits of cycling this year than previously.

A rest was taken, new '89 mounts tried, and slight brushes between the racing-inclined wheelmen were watched with interest. The Lieutenant's call for the homeward start found that a few had deserted the ranks, some in favor of visiting convenient friends (who will blame them? it was now very near the never-forgotten dinner-hour), and some had decided to dine at Brighton, while those who found the pangs of hunger less demonstrative, lost no time in mounting wheels and reaching the Beacon Street surface, where plain sailing is easy for all.

The return trip was made over much better roads, which no one objected to; neither was there a dissenting voice heard when some one whispered "Soda." This was the only dismount made, and now we were near Cambridge and Somerville, afterward Malden; at each place one, two, or three saying good-by, leaving the Melrose and Everett members to halve the finish.

A run on Decoration Day is an expected certainty, of which more anon.

MARGUERITE.

Maplewood, Mass, May 13

SHALL WOMEN RIDE THE SAFETY?

On this topic, a valued correspondent, who gives promise of becoming an adept at writing as well as at cycling, says:

"In regard to cycling for ladies, I have a few words to say. I am comparatively a new rider of the safety, but had previously ridden a tricycle for a couple of years. Having tried both mounts, I think the tricycle cannot be compared to the Safety for feeling at ease and for convenience of control on the road. I am naturally a timid rider, but after learning to manage a Safety, one soon looses that feeling, and enjoys the sport of wheeling in earnest.

I think if some of the young ladies that now ride tricycles could be induced to once try a Safety and see the advantages it possesses, they would at once be convinced that the mount is more enjoyable, and riding much less work. Of course it takes a little perseverance at first to learn the rudiments, but each succeeding time you and a little has been gained. My fourth lesson found me out on the road, and I cannot describe the delight I felt when I found myself gliding along with apparently very little exertion compared to the labor of propelling my tricycle.

As regards suitable dress, I would say that I have tried a number of different styles and find that a corduroy skirt made plain, about two yards in width, with some soft goods for the waist, gives me best satisfaction. E.

IRVINGTON-MILBURN ROAD RACES.

Following is a complete list of entries for the road race on May 30: L. W. Beaseley, Jr., T. J. Hall, Jr., T. L. Wilson, Wm. Murphy, R. W. Steves, F. B. Hesse, Chas. Murphy, John Bensinger and H. J. Hall, Jr., all of K. C. Wheelmen; Clarence A. Elliott and Fred B. Elliott, of Washington W. C.; Frank M. Dampman, Honeybrook, Pa.; S. W. Merrihew, B. F. McDaniel, G. M. Gregg, Albert Jeffries and Z. H. Lapland, all of Wilmington, Del.; J. Purvis Bruce, Ripley Road Club; Wm. Schumacker, L. I. W.; G. M. Nisbett, N. Y. B. C.; J. Frank Borland and W. F. G. Class, B. B. C.; I. M. Williams, Summit, N. J.; N. F. Waters, B. B. C.; W. M. Taxis, Philadelphia; H. Quortropp, Q. C. W.; L. H. Wise, L. I. W.; F. W. Lincoln, Flushing; H. D. Ludwig, Wilmington; F. Coningsby and A. Jelliffe, B. B. C.; H. L. Pyle, Wilmington; John A. Wells, Philadelphia; W. D. Banker, Pittsburg; F. R. Miller, R. W.; W. H. Putney, N. Y. C.; G. W. King, K. C. W.; J. L. Robertson, Jr., H. C. W.; E. Van Wagoner, Bridgeport, Ct.; W. I. Wilbelm, Reading, Pa.; J. H. Mellor and J. W. Bates, Pros. H.; F. Gubelman, S. B. Bowman and E. P. Baggot, all of H. C. W.; David Morehouse, K. C. W. Forty-six in all.

LONG ISLAND WHEELMEN'S MILEAGE.

TEN HIGHEST RECORDS FOR APRIL.

L. H. Wise, 770 miles.	A. P. Topping, 487 miles.
E. L. Blake, 464 miles.	Wm. Schmid, 445 miles.
E. F. Beecher, 431 miles.	F. E. Bogert, 420 miles.
Wm. Schumacker, 400 miles.	U. Palmedo, 331 miles.
W. J. Gilfillen, 314 miles.	G. G. Teller, 305 miles.

TEN HIGHEST RECORDS TO MAY 1.

L. H. Wise, 1,723 miles.	Wm. Schmid, 1,261 miles.
W. J. Gilfillen, 1,100 miles.	A. P. Topping, 920 miles.
E. F. Beecher, 800 miles.	F. E. Bogert, 712 miles.
E. L. Blake, 690 miles	G. G. Teller, 662 miles.
Wm. Schumacker, 644 miles.	Wm. Hawxhurst, 550 miles.

SURREY SPRING MEET.

This important meet was held at Kenington Oval, April 27. The mile bicycle scratch for the Sydney challenge cup brought F. P. Wood and T. J. Osmond together, Wood winning in 3m. 14 2-5s., Osmond going very stale.

The 10-mile race for the challenge cup, which has been won by Cortis, Speechley and Furnivall, in their day, also fell to Wood, Osmond riding second. Wood will undoubtedly be among the foremost of the cracks this season.

The American papers still persist in spelling Synyer's name Snyder.—*The Cyclist.* Which American papers please? Why not be specific, or let it alone?

Four members of the Minneapolis Bi. Club, Messrs. Stockdale, Hale, Grant and Colie Bell, made the trip of ninety-two miles from Minneapolis to Mankato, on May 4, arriving there in fine shape. A start was made with five men, but one had had enough at Le Seuer, and took the train for home. The long ride over sandy and hilly roads reflects great credit on the staying qualities of the plucky participants.

Efforts will be made by the Minneapolis Bi. Club and other interested riders, to have the State L. A. W. meet in September held in that city.

The Lynn Cycle Club has decided not to hold a race meet at Glenmore Park this year, on Memorial Day, but a committee has been appointed to arrange for an entertainment there later on.

On Sunday, May 26, the Lynn Cycle Club will make a run to some point ten or twelve miles out, where a spread will be served and all local wheelmen invited to participate. An invitation of that sort ought to bring out a fair attendance if anything will do it.

All our young readers should read "Jack's Jottings" in this number. "Jack" sermonizes on alcoholism, physical beauty vs ideal mentality, or what we should marry, society and a multitude of things, all in his own mellifluous strain.

GOOD FOR BOYS.

Mr. Thomas Lloyd, of Queens, L. I., having offered a prize for the fastest ½-mile ridden by boys under 13, flying start, up to date, these times are on record: R. W. Kellogg, 57s.; W. A. Kissam, 57s.; C. C. Hendrickson 57 3-4s.; J. R. Lane, 1m.; D. Doughty, 1m. 1 2-5s.; C. B. Hendrickson, 1m. 2 4-5s.; H. Hendrickson, 1m. 3s.; R. P. Hendrickson, 1m. 4s.; W. Demorest, 1m. 4 1-5s. The track is now open to boys for practice. In addition to prize mentioned, a gold medal will be given to any amateur breaking track record of 1m. 50 4-5s.

TACOMA, WASHINGTON.

The 30th of April, 1889, and its festivities are of the past. To be sure, we had no great parades, either upon land or water, nor have we participated in any Centennial Ball. But Tacomans, and those particularly who are members of the Tacoma Bi. Club, will long treasure the memory of the most glorious celebration ever attended in this city.

The day was perfect, and everybody was happy in anticipation of the pleasures before them. Captain Prince Wells had called a club run to American Lake, and after spending a few moments with a photographer, the party of fifteen started for that beautiful sheet of water. It was the jolliest crowd the club had ever gathered together for a run, and, strange to say, no "kicking" was indulged in, excepting when Halsted's Star kicked up its front wheel, sometimes causing its rider to take a back dismount. It was the first time in over a year he had ridden his Star, and consequently the boys started in to have some fun with the coffee mill. Upon reaching the the prairie roads the boys started a scorch, probably to see how every one had trained up for the road race. To the surprise of all, Halsted and his Star proved themselves invincible at the end of the three-mile race, with Prince Wells in the rear 100 feet, and Karl Thompson a good third.

The next excitement occurred at that part of the road which is crossed by a brook. All the boys had signified their intentions to ride across the foot-bridge, which is about thirty-five feet long and only ten inches wide. This bridge has a very bad approach, which adds greatly to the risk attached to crossing it, and although it has been ridden only twice this year (by Thompson and Halsted) still all of the boys have made many attempts, which have always resulted in an impromptu plunge—not even do I except Mr. Prince Wells, the champion unicycle rider of the world, for he also has cooled off in this same gurgling brook. But yesterday Wells rode the narrow plank without a waver, and the spirit of emulation so swelled the manly breasts of the others that half a dozen safely crossed what before had appeared to them an impossibility. But "'tis a poor rule that won't work both ways," which was proved when "Dear Brother" Baker took a fair and square header. As he "bobbed up serenely from below," he heard a most hearty shout from his companions, who urged him to try again. But he was more discreet than some others who followed him, and decided that he had taken enough water for one day. Halsted next tried his luck and twice saved himself a drenching by resorting to that convenient back dismount known only to riders of Stars, but the third time he took a fair and square header, but, by dexterously "spreading" over the handle bar, landed feet first. Like Brother Baker, he was satisfied, especially as he had ridden the bridge twice on his Expert. The final act of this comedy was left to the tender mercy of our worthy and handsome Mr. Brackett, who had fixed up to kill the gentler ones whom he expected meeting at the lake. His first and second attempts were faulty, but his third trial proved to be most excellent, for he succeeded in getting over—well, I should judge about seven-eighths of the bridge, when something happened. We saw a splash, a mighty upheaval of the waters, and our hero had disappeared—excepting his new straw hat, that was seen floating off toward the lake. We next beheld an object similar in appearance to the famous "What is it," of circus renown, which subsequently proved to be him who had so shortly before presented such an immaculate appearance. Mud from crown to heel but faintly tells the story. A desire to spare his feelings precludes my going further into details.

But even the dampened spirits and clothes of those who had coveted the waters of the Babbling Brook were forgotten upon arrival at the picnic grounds.

The committee in charge reserved seats for the bicycle club, and to our utter surprise, tempted us with most delicious viands, including lemonade and—well they wanted us to keep "Mumm." Some of the boys said it was a very wet occasion, but the writer is of the opinion that it was "Extra Dry" (and the best procurable).

After thoroughly satisfying the appetites of our party, a trip on the steam launch was enjoyed, and subsequently the party went off in pairs—some to row, and others to meet friends. Most of the boys took a swim, and afterward spent an hour or two rowing about the lake—darting in and out of the many little bays and inlets that fringe the shore, and also exploring the several islands. Many tete-a-tetes were suddenly interrupted by "those horrible bicycle boys," of course, accidentally. Culver was the most fortunate of the boys, as he successfully captured "three little maids from school" who graced his boat. Ed. Barlow was also noticed flitting hither and thither, and seemed to know everybody. Poor Will Brackett's appearance prevented his mingling in the crowd. But it is said he went off "by his lone" to a quiet nook and with him took a — "Mumm" to drown his troubled mind. Prince Wells and Ed. McCoy were lost to the eye, but their merry laughter attested their proximity. We all regretted Bert Manning's inability to ride his wheel, in consequence of his recent fall, but he was present on horseback, and was able to participate in the ceremonies.

Taking things all in all, the throngs of people who visited the lake during the day expressed themselves as highly pleased with the general entertainment, and many were the congratulations showered upon the committee who had framed the programme. For my part, I wish there were some more Centennials to be celebrated in the near future.

The 11th of May is coming on apace, and all the contestants who have signified their intention to compete in the 20-mile road race are getting into good shape. Thompson, Halsted and Wells are riding in great form, Halsted being the favorite, as is shown by the several wagers that have been made. Wells is thought too light to stand a hard race from start to finish. Thompson is a *strong*, steady rider, but he lacks experience; however, he may surprise some of the older riders. There is a great amount of mystery surrounding Ed. McCoy, especially since he has received his new mount, on which he has shown much better speed. Messrs. Seares, Avery and Clark, (ex-champion of Canada) will compete, and we are in a blissful state of uncertainty as to their chances of success.

May the best man win, and no accidents mar the pleasure of the day, is the wish of

SNOHOMISH.

May 7, 1889.

LATER.

Special telegram to THE WHEEL, May 13, 1889.

"Halsted wins the 20-mile race in 1h. 26m., with Thompson second, and McCoy third.

RHODE ISLAND WHEELMEN'S ANNUAL RUN.

The touring committee of the R. I. W. has arranged for the annual run Monday, May 20, according to the following circular:

Leave Providence Depot for Sharon at 7 A. M., arriving at 8:06. Morning run about 21 miles. Leave Sharon station at 8:15 and through Sharon village northerly to Old Bay road; thence direct through South Canton and Canton Corners to Ponkapoag, from Ponkapoag, via Canton Avenue, skirting Blue Hill, through Milton Centre, to School Street (near Milton Lower mills); School Street and cross Neponset River; River and Washington Streets, through Dorchester, branching off near Blue Hill Avenue for Franklin Park, and to and around the Playstead; Walnut, Warren, Cabot and Tremont Streets, Columbus and Warren Avenues, to Clarendon Hotel, Tremont Street, and dinner at 1 o'clock.

Afternoon run, about 13 miles, leaving hotel at 3 o'clock, and via the new boulevard to Chestnut Hill Reservoir and return. Go-as-you-please supper at J. M. Hill's new restaurant, corner of Boylston and Washington Streets. Train for Providence at 8:30 P. M.

All wheels must be at depot at 6:45 A. M., and must return on the 8:30 train to Providence.

The expense of the run will probably not exceed $4 a person. Other clubs of this State, the Columbia Bicycle Club, of North Attleboro, Mass., and all members of the Rhode Island Division, L. A. W., are cordially invited to j in in the run.

Pers ns intending to participate in the run must notify George L. Cooke, Box 1101, Providence, R. I. on or before Thursday next. If stormy, the run will be indefinitely postponed.

WHEEL GOSSIP.

W. W. Stall, of Boston, wants a good repairer.

George Warwick was in Gotham on Friday last.

Miss Eisinger, of the Harlem Wheelmen, has just purchased a Swift.

C. R. Overman is at the Overman Wheel Co.'s Washington store, making things boom.

Our "Marguerite" received her ladies' safety on Wednesday and was able to put in forty-one miles on the Sunday following.

The Universals, one of Brooklyn's younger cycling clubs, disbanded last Tuesday night. Probably the members will unite with other clubs.

A moonlight steamer excursion by the Cycle Club is to be held the middle of July, and, as theatrical posters say, it will be "the event of the season."

A serious header was indulged in recently by Mr. Ben Shepard, of Mankato, Minn., his right arm being broken in two places and face badly bruised.

The large riding park of the Capital Cycle Co. is now protected from sun and storm by a handsome tent made for them by Boyle & Co., of New York.

An important discovery has been made by L. A. W. number 2,449. He tells how to avoid a mile of stone pavement in Newark, on the route to the Oranges.

The Capital Cycle Co. report that they are entirely out of Ladies' Light Psychos (39 lbs.), the demand has been so great, but they expect to begin shipping this week.

At the last meeting of the Long Island Wheelmen the following gentlemen were elected members: Adolph Birck, Jr., Chas. M. Nichols, Chas. L. Taylor, G. B. Van Wart, J. H. Bagg and F. Schmidt.

On Centennial Day five members of the Atlanta Wheelmen had a run to Morristown and return. The Passaic River was so swollen by recent rains that some 200 feet of wading *sans* shoes and stockings was needed.

Three Nashville riders took a run of ninety-five miles last week, going to Columbia and return. Though several hours were spent at the county's capitol, and a hot head-wind bothered them all the way out, the return to Nashville was accomplished before dark.

The Capital Cycle Co.'s latest importation, the Psycho Light Roadster, is meeting with great favor among experienced wheelmen. It proves to be a very fast, stiff road machine, and its weight recommends it to good riders, who know how to care for and enjoy a light wheel.

The season for long runs is once more with us, and even in the sunny south—popularly supposed to be too warm for "scorching"—wheelmen are trying a foot at it. From Nashville, Tenn., to Murfreesboro, by way of Lebanon, is pronounced a fine run, and can be covered in a day.

A hill-climbing contest will vary the monotony of the annual club run held by the Northampton Wheel Club, May 30. What is known as "Round Hill" will first be essayed, and if that proves too easy a task, the scene of action will be transferred to "Hospital Hill." Safeties are not barred.

The Sunday club run would seem to have come to stay among the clubs in Boston and vicinity. Eight regular runs are reported on last Sunday, besides the tally-ho combination run of the Boston Bicycle Club. This was taken through Dorchester and Milton to Quincy and return, led by Capt. Kendall on his wheel.

Mr. R. P. Gormully, who has been in New York several days, left for Chicago Tuesday evening. He reports excellent business in "G. and J." goods, reports sales of 70 per cent. ordinaries and 30 per cent. safeties, and states that he doesn't know "Uncle Sam." The men at the "G. and J." factory are working thirteen hours a day.

The rules governing bicycle and tricycle riding in Prospect Park, Brooklyn, recently adopted by the Board of Park Commissioners, are so reasonable and sensible, that we recommend them to the consideration of all park officers in other cities. We reproduce them in another column. President Luscombe is one of the Commissioners.

Regular runs are announced for May 19, 26, and 30, by the Cambridgeport Bicycle Club, Cambridge Bicycle Club, Charleston Rovers, Somerville Cycle Club and the Dorchester Club. If all ridable roads are not tested that day it will not be the fault of their well-laid plans. Particularly on Memorial Day will the wheel be a common sight.

The proposed Southeastern tour to be taken in Alabama next month will cover some 800 miles of territory, much of which has never felt a bicycle tire. With caves to explore, whiskey stills to discover and sample, and the curiosities of natives and dogs to gratify, the prospect is at least mildly exciting. A camera will be carried, and our Macon correspondent may be counted on to let us have a detailed account.

A new bicycle club has been organized among the Y. M. Gymnastic Club, at New Orleans, with thirty members, fifteen of whom are active ones. Officers elected are as follows: President, H. R. McLean; Vice-President, R. E. McKnight; Captain, Chas. Fourton; Treasurer, D. H. Marsh; Secretary, A. J. Boissoneau. A wheel room will be built by the gymnasium management as soon as the active membership reaches twenty-five.

ALL TOGETHER, PLEASE.

Roll on, my wheel, roll on!
O'er road and pathway smooth,
Roll on!
It's true I've lots of bills o'erdue;
It's true my prospects all look blue;
But don't let that unsettle you,
Never you mind,
Roll on!

An interesting article from the ready pen of "Verax," going quite fully into historical details and covering six pages in the May number of *Wheelmen's Gazette*, not only gives much good advice to clubs in need of that article, but incidentally throws in a good portrait of the writer. Several illustrations adorn the pages, among them views of the present club offices and cuts of the Lincoln Club House and Gymnasium interiors. The constitution and by-laws, reproduced in full, may serve other clubs to model theirs upon.

On Sunday last Messrs. McFadden, Bogart, Chamberlain and George Daniels rode from the Getty House, Yonkers, to the New York Bicycle Club House in 49m., including a stop for seltzer (?). They made a "loop" on the way. What a "loop" is no one but the "big four" knows. The joke is so good that the record-breakers have been asking the boys to "step up," and "imbibe" ever since they rode that 15 miles in 49m. The four claim that they can break any existing road record if they can only finish up with a "loop."

The Louisville *Commercial* of Sunday last contained a cut of a good-looking phiz labeled Mr. Harry T. Esterle, and described as the oldest rider in that city, formerly secretary-treasurer of the old Louisville Wheel Club, and one of the most prominent members of the Louisville Cycle Club. Mr. Esterle, though father of a family, and with a cycling experience of eight years, has an excellent habit of frequently riding ten or twelve miles before breakfast. As so often the case with old wheelmen, the ordinary is good enough for him.

"Safeties are a craze here, and the manufacturers know it, and no doubt the conservative tone of the cycling press is due to the fact that the manufacturers and dealers wish to 'unload' a heavy stock of ordinaries. Why, there seems to be two to one safeties in Chicago at present, and the rage increasing." Senator Morgan thus writes to the *Cyclist*. The cycling press has printed hundreds of columns of stuff in favor of safety vs. ordinary. The senator calls this conservatism. But never mind, the Senator must get back at us for exposing his little game to swindle the good people of New England.

According to the Newark *Sunday Call*, clubs in that city so favored with good roads in the immediate vicinity, are contemplating admitting to active membership lady riders, and where the by-laws conflict, a change may be made. The Orange Wanderers, with a lady membership of nearly one-third that of the male riders, would seem to be possessed of liberal ideas in the matter. Possibly the fact that several of the members' wives ride tandems with their husbands may have caused this wise move on the part of the Wanderers. A regulation costume is worn of dark flannel (usually navy blue) with full short skirt and blouse. A distinguishing mark is the letters "O. W." marked in white upon collars. The Wanderers would seem to be composed of proficient riders, many making use of their wheels to ride to and from business. One member's hair and beard are whitened by the snows of seventy winters.

Chief Consul Emery's circular letter to the wheelmen of Massachusetts, appointing Messrs. Simmons & Co., of Boston, League tailors to Massachusetts, will probably be a dead letter. The Uniform Committee have selected a League tailor, and the Chief Consul was at once notified that his appointment could not hold good. Secretary Bassett's supply of cloth was at once cut off. Messrs. Simmons & Co. expected to order their cloth through the secretary. Some two years has been spent in getting up a League uniform and obtaining satisfactory service, and now that some degree of success has been achieved it seems unwise to commence undermining the system. If Massachusetts is permitted to appoint her own tailor she will in time desire to select her own cloth. Other States will claim the same privilege, and the League will lose any distinctive uniform. We do not say that this would or would not be a good thing, but so long as there is a League and a League uniform why not stick to it.

GOOD, IF TRUE.

A New Trick Rider.—A really remarkable and clever performance was witnessed on Easter Monday at the Aston Lower Grounds. A new trick rider in the person of A. H. Minting, for the first time accomplished the wonderful feat of riding up a spiral fifty feet high on one wheel. As this was his first attempt in public, fully 20,000 witnessed the attempt. Precisely at the appointed time Minting appeared and was greeted with rounds and rounds of applause. After going through a lot of tricks that would do credit to Canary, Temple, or even Kaufman, the youth prepared to ascend the spiral. It being the first time, he no doubt took longer than he would usually do. All being now ready, Minting, without a second's hesitation, mounted his wheel, and before you would have time to look about you he was at the top. The greatest difficulty, however, was the descending, during this part you could hear a pin drop in the big hall, but Minting again mounted his wheel, and, with the coolness of a judge, descended safely with apparent ease. Minting, we believe, appears at the Paris Exhibition. He is only seventeen years old, and can safely claim the title, Champion of the World.—*Cyclist*.

THE WAY THE LOUISIANA CYCLING CLUB ENJOYS ITSELF.

Last week it was remarked that the Louisiana Cycling Club would "excursh" to Bay St. Louis on Sunday, the 5th.

We went. We are home again.

7:30 A. M.—We are on the train, in the baggage car. Our wheels are also there. The train moves ; so do we.

8 A. M.—The weather is lovely. The scenery ——. Everyone is quiet, even De Buys. He is very much interested in getting on the outside of a sandwich. All the others are occupied, some with their newspapers. Christy has just read that owing to his latest victory he will be classed as a scratch man. He mutters something that sounds very much like "rats."

8:30.—Fun begins. De Buys, Bogel and Frederic are "taking off" the gumbo Frenchman abroad. It is rich ! We laugh, can't help it. Fenner passes round some "blane coffey "} ! !

8:40.—Train stops. Shute gets off.

8.50.—Train stops. Shute's off again.

9.15.—Frederic seats himself on the Brusseled floor and hob-knobs with the writer ; tells me about a red scalp. Says he plucked it on Friday of last week at the Audubon Driving Park ; asks me to make a note of it in my next letter to the SOUTH ; says it will be all right. * * *
Shute's off again.

* * *

We have arrived at the Bay, and are peddling like good boys for "Villars' Villa." Renaud and Walshe are together. They turn a corner. Renaud turns too short and Walshe runs into him, tumbles and tears pants.

We are at Villars, up in our room. Some of the boys are washing up ; some doing the high jump in an effort to touch the ceiling; some lying down. "Ella" Graham and Walshe are off in a corner. Walshe has his back to us, but Graham has his breeches and is sewing. We see !

We lunch ; we feel better ; we ride. De Buys falls in with "fellow-countryman." We hold our sides and grin. De Buys will do. We are under a tree. The gnats are getting in their work. Bogel and Sprigg climb a tree. others stretch out on the grass. We are going to have a race for Batson medal. Fairchild, Fenner and Graham fix handicaps. Read 'em out :

"Sprigg, scratch ; Frederic, 50 seconds ; Christy, 1 minute ; Betts, 1 minute 10 seconds ; De Buys. 1 minute 20 seconds."

Kicking, handicap rotten, more kicking, no go.

Race starts. Frederic and Sprigg pass others in short order. De Buys gets tired, sits down and quits after riding a mile.

Sprigg catches up with Frederic on the return trip and spurts past him half a mile from the finish, and wins by 15 or 20 yards. Time 16:23. Distance 4 miles with a turn. Christy and Betts made dead heat for third place. It was very dead.

We ride some more. We go bathing. That is, all but Renaud and Walshe. Water's too damp for them. Some swim out to a schooner anchored in deep water, some don't—can't. We rest a bit. Ah ! dinner. We eat now. It goes good.

We have finished now ; more rest. We ride again. Frederic and Sprigg have a two-mile brush, and Jeff again gets done up on the spurt.

Getting near train time now. We make for the depot. Get there, a crowd of "yaps," big and little, white and black, are also there. They gather around us and stare and stare until we grow weary and homesick. Can the attraction be Jeff's "siders," Fenner's whiskers, or De Buys' exquisite calves ? Oh ! if we could but turn on the hose. We get uneasy and move. The crowd still stares.

Pay a couple of "coons" to do some high and lofty tumbling. Want them to dance, they want more money. They are still wanting it. Train comes. Charlie Fenner is talking— "All aboard !" Charlie says dammit. Don't blame him.

In the baggage car again. Conductor tells joke, we laugh. Bogel tells Dutch story, we laugh some more. Somebody sings. All join. Some more sing. Boys getting quiet now. Some asleep, some nodding, all tired.

* *

Home again, glad of it. Good-night, now to bed.—"Pitts" in Spirit of the South.

DELIGHTFUL TRIP IN THE WALL-KILL VALLEY ON A MACHINE.

CONCLUDED.

At Conashaw, midway between Milford and Dingman's, we would advise all tourists to sample the pure spring water to be found in the well near the bridge, as its flavor seemed to us particularly appetizing. Nature's vacuum was liberally supplied at Bushkill in the shape of a good dinner, and, though, on account of the lack of time, we did not visit either the Bushkill or Conashaw Falls, they are highly spoken of, and should no doubt be seen by all who have the opportunity. There is only one fault to be found with the road just described, viz, its comparative narrowness, and on this account, on the return trip to Milford, an accident befell two of our party, which, happily, did not have as serious a result as it easily might have had. The narrator was in the lead a short distance and met a two-horse stage. Asking for room to pass he was surlily given it, the ladies in the stage looking as if they liked not the chance of the animals shying. The other two cyclers were about forty yards back, and, though they asked the Jehu for room, he paid not, or seemed not to pay, the slightest attention to their request. The "Star" rider immediately applied his brake, forgetting, in the excitement of the moment, his "Ordinary" friend, who was in the rear, and slackening his pace so suddenly that the rear man ran into him, causing a nasty fall down a (fortunately) dry and grassy ditch, the other rider falling on top of him. Providentially neither the frames of men nor machines were broken, and after the fallen riders had bountifully told the driver what they thought of him we went on. The cycler not in the melee happened to look round just as the accident was taking place, and the sight of the one rider and machine falling plump on the top of the other was too much for his risibilities and he had to laugh both long and loud, thus adding greatly to their chagrin. We heard, the same afternoon, of another accident, to a New York doctor, which took place on this road, he being thrown by a driver who refused to extend to him the courtesies of the road and allow him room enough to pass, the doctor being, consequent ly, seriously bruised. In this case, however, justice was partly meted out, as the man of medicine, to revenge his injured feelings, threw a small-sized rock at the retreating form and "winged his bird."

There is no railroad at Milford, and, therefore, on Saturday morning we wheeled to Port Jervis, and, taking the Erie railroad, returned to New York, with the satisfactory feeling of having enjoyed ourselves immensely, viewed some charming scenery, took some much-needed exercise, and last, but not least, laid in a new store of health. There can be no doubt that the tour described is a very delightful one, and that a cyclist desiring to see something of the country and spend many agreeable hours cannot make any mistake in covering the same ground.

League hotels and rates will be found in the following table, comprising the Hudson River, Wallkill Valley, and Pike Co., Penn., districts : Cornwall, Wiley's, $3 ; Highlands, Higlands', $3 ; New Paltz, Stein's, $2 ; Walden, St. Nicholas', $1.50 ; Port Jervis, Delaware House, $4 ; Milford, Crisaman's, $2 ; Delaware Water Gap, Kittaniny, $3.

ASHTON NICHOLS, L. A. W.

"FOR WE'VE BOTH BEEN THERE BEFORE !"

The new dissipation of tandem practice is becoming very prevalent. Hardly an evening but a score of the double-seated tricycles are rolling more or less erratically over the roads in and near the park. The friendly cover of night is necessary on account of the liability of skirts to tangle up in the wheels, for the seats of a tandem are not comfortable or convenient as an arm-chair.

The tandem is an innocent-looking contrivance, and as it can stand alone and does not rear and plunge like its two-wheeled cousin—the bicycle—it is generally regarded with confidence. This confidence has, however, at least in one instance, been rudely shaken.

Statesman J. J. Kenny, clerk of Police Court No. 1, was out last Wednesday night with his very best holiday girl, when a tandem glided smoothly by, bearing an interesting couple, Mr. Kenny's young lady thought that riding on a tandem must be awful nice.

Mr. Kenny gallantly offered to give her a tandem ride and she accepted the offer.

Mr. Kenny engaged one of the machines and trundled it up

a secluded spot on the road, and there, after some difficulty, they took their seats and started off.

In half an hour Mr. Kenny, all alone, walked into the place where he had rented the tandem, dragging the machine behind him. He was pale and tired and his high collar had melted with perspiration.

"We had a hard time," he said, with an effort at cheerfulness.

"Yes, I saw you on the road," answered the man in charge, carelessly.

"Did you ?" eagerly inquired Mr. Kenny. "What was the matter ? "

"You were both on backwards."

Charley Schwalbach's spring opening was held at his Prospect Park store on Thursday evening last. The wheels had been stored away, many of them overflowing onto the sidewalk, and the salesrooms, repair shop and locker rooms were open to the guests. A large number of wheelmen were present and congratulated Charley on the growth and improvement of his place. A platform has been built in the salesroom, almost doubling its capacity. The repair shop has been enlarged and new apartments, well arranged and well ventilated, have been added. The features of the opening were opening "hard and soft" stuff, and. liq., a speech by the proprietor and a presentation of a basket of flowers to him.

"OUR AMERICAN CORRESPONDENT."

The utter folly of one man's trying to cover and elucidate all the points that the cycling industry in this country fairly bristles with, is clearly shown by the perusal of the last communication to the *Cyclist* from " Uncle Sam." Speaking of the " Eagle " bicycle, one of the most new and original types put on the market this season, he does his little best to spread a foolish surmise that Colonel Pope (thinly disguised as " Colonel What's-his-name "), is backing the manufacture of this wheel, because of a long-standing grudge against the Star, another type the Eagle somewhat resembles in general appearance. It *might* perhaps be a good business policy for a concern that can hardly fill its own orders, to contract with a manufacturing company in another city to secretly build wheels to undermine a rival's popularity, but we hardly think the same concern that already supplies two

other rivals would be selected in that event. The facts in the case, as " Uncle Sam" might easily find for himself, are these : The "Eagle " is built by a regularly organized stock company, with distributing head-quarters at Stamford, Conn., and every wheel turned out is built by contract with the Ames M'f'g. Co. at Chicopee, Mass., no machine being accepted that does not in all ways come up to the high degree of finish called for by the contract. The fact that for a new wheel, the finish of the Eagle is remarkably good in all points, may have led the sapient correspondent into his error, and his surmises have been twisted into would-be facts.

The early closing movement this season promises to be almost universal, hardly a store of any standing in the large cities throughout the country remaining open Saturday afternoons, and the great majority of them closing at 5 o'clock on the other week days. To aid in furthering this movement the Pope Manufacturing Company, of Boston, has issued a handsome lithographic announcement card which gives the hours of closing, and is convenient to hang in window or door. These cards are sent free upon application.

The Cycler and Tourist,

An Illustrated Monthly Magazine, devoted to out-door recreation, adventure and travel. Only $1 a year. Address The Cycler and Tourist Pub. Co., Stamford, Conn.

ENAMEL AND TIRE CEMENT.

Best in the Market.

PUT UP IN BOTTLES AND BOXES FOR THE TRADE.

Write for Prices.
W. L WILHELM, Reading, Pa.

HOLMES & CO.,
BOSTON, MASS.

FULL PANTS.

Are knit with a selvedge edge, in two separate parts from the waist to the feet, and formed while being knit to fit the limbs, so the strain upon the garment is equally divided on every part of the body. The seam being a selvedged edge, is small and flat and will not rip. *Buttoned in Front, some as Pantaloons, without Certain Objections.*

626. H'v'y Rib, c'l'd. seat, straps and puck., $4 50
626. H'v'y Rib, unp'd d'bl. seat, strap & "   4 50
627. Plain Stitch, heavy and pocket,   4 50
    Silk,   "   " $10 00 to $15 00

JERSEY-FITTING STOCKING.

3–3. Full Fashioned, Narrowed at ankle, in black, navy, League brown, grey-mixed and any other color, $1.50

3–1. Black, navy, grey-mixed, $1.25.

1–1. Black, navy, grey-mixed, $1.00.

Send for Illustrated Catalogue and Price List.

Manufactured by

'HOLMES & CO.,
109 Kingston Street, Boston, Mass.

HOWARD A. SMITH & CO.
ORATON HALL, NEWARK, N. J.,

General Agents for all the Safeties.

WHOLESALE AND RETAIL

DEALERS IN CYCLING SUNDRIES.

Send for Illustrated Catalogue.

Store and Riding Hall open evenings.

200 SECOND-HAND MACHINES CHEAP.

Improved 5-inch Acme Steel Wrench.

FOR POCKET AND BICYCLE USE.

THE STRONGEST AND BEST.

Made of Best Quality Steel.

Weight, 6 1-2 oz.

NICKELED AND BRIGHT FINISHED.

EVERY WRENCH WARRANTED.

For sale by all cycle manufacturers and dealers.

CAPITOL MFG. CO.,   *Chicago, Ill.*

Bicycle and Athletic Goods.

THE KINGSTON KNITTING CO.,
OF BOSTON, MASS.,
Manufacturer for the Trade and Clubs.

The most beautiful line of ATHLETIC GOODS made, and in the latest colors, in Plain, Striped and Mixed Cloths, in WORSTED, WOOL and Jersey spun COTTON, for Bicycle Riders ; Gymnasium, Baseball, Football and Lawn Tennis Suits ; Rowing and Yachting Outfits, Hosiery, Caps, etc.—all from our special weaving, and for styles, elasticity and durability cannot be excelled.

Our JERSEYS, KNEE TIGHTS, KNICKERBOCKERS, FULL BODY TIGHTS, TRUNKS and SUPPORTERS are unsurpassed for good taste, comfort and easy fitting. Many novelties in PLAIN and RIBBED suits and sweaters.

Our prices are very reasonable. Address

KINGSTON KNITTING CO.,
27 KINGSTON ST., BOSTON.
CORRESPONDENCE SOLICITED.

Second-Hand
BICYCLES and TRICYCLES.

New York Bicycle Co.,

No. 4. E. 60th St.

☞ We make a specialty of taking old mounts in part payment for New Victors, Stars, Rapids, Eagles, Malls, and for cycles of all other good makes. ☜

KEY TO DESCRIPTION.

FINISH.—" 1 " Full nickeled. " 2 " All nickeled except rims. " 3 " Wheels enameled, balance nickeled. " 4 " Enameled with nickel trimmings. " 5 " Enameled with polished parts. " 6 " Half bright and enameled or painted. " 7 " Spokes nickeled, balance enameled.

BEARINGS.—" 1 " Balls to both wheels and pedals. " 2 " Balls to front, cone to rear, plain pedals. " 3 " Balls to front, cone to rear, plain pedals. " 4 " Plain to front, cone to rear, plain pedals. " 5 " Balls to front, cone to rear, ball pedals.

CONDITION.—" 1 " Very little used, fully as good as a new machine. " 2 " Tires show but very slight wear, finish and bearings as good as new. " 3 " Tires but little worn, finish only slightly marred, bearings A 1. " 4 " Finish, bearings and tires all in condition of uniform excellence. " 5 " Tires slightly worn, finish somewhat marred, bearings A 1. " 6 " Finish and bearings in first-rate shape, tires somewhat worn. " 7 " Has new tires, finish and bearings excellent. " 8 " Tires somewhat cut, finish somewhat marred, bearings in very good order. " 9 " Good, durable machine, considerably used, but in very fair condition.

No.	Size.	Name.	Cost.	Price.	Fin.	Brg'g.	Cndtn.
460	'48	Columbia Semi-Rdstr..	$75 00	$45 00	4	3	2
465	55	Columbia Lt. Rdstr.,	140 00	75 00	2	3	2
469	—	Kangaroo 5fty. (36x25)	135 00	60 00	4	1	2
470	51	Otto Special,	35 00	15 00	5	4	3
475	52	Special Star,	135 00	65 00	3	Ball	2
485	50	British Challenge,	130 00	70 00	2	1	2
485	52	Special Club	135 00	65 00	3	1	2
480	—	Springfield Roadster,	85 00	58 00	3	Plain	3
492	54	English,	135 00	90 00	4	1	2
493	—	Springfield Roadster,	75 00	45 00	2	Plain	2
494	55	Racer,	140 00	30 00	4	1	1
498	48	Columbia Standard,	97 50	50 00	4	4	3
490	48	Singer Lt. Roadster,	130 00	60 00	3	1	2
500	54	British Challenge,	140 00	90 00	2	1	2
508	54	Sanspareil,	115 00	135 00	2	1	2
512	42	Victor Junior,	55 00	40 00	4	1	3
517	—	Humber Tandem,	300 00	140 00	2	1	2
518	48	Columbia Mustang,	85 00	55 00	4	4	4
521	56	American Club,	135 00	90 00	2	1	2
522	54	Victor Roadster,	130 00	75 00	4	1	2
524	52	Dictator,	130 00	65 00	2	1	2
526	56	Special Star,	135 00	100 00	4	Ball	1
533	51	Rudge Lt. Roadster,	138 75	100 00	4	1	2
538	48	Special Star,	137 50	85 00	3	Ball	2
539	51	New Mail,	148 75	75 00	4	1	2
543	51	S. S. S. Tandem,	250 00	180 00	4	1	2
545	—	Victor Safety,	135 00	110 00	1	1	1
550	—	Marlboro Club Tdm.,	250 00	165 00	4	1	1
552	54	Singer Matchless,	170 00	70 00	1	1	2
555	52	Otto Special,	40 00	12 00	6	4	4
556	—	Boy's Rover Safety,	35 00	16 00	4	4	3
558	—	Col. Lt. Rdstr. Tke.,	160 00	115 00	1	1	2
565	50	Columbia Tandem,	350 00	185 00	4	1	2
567	54	Columbia Expert,	130 00	80 00	1	1	2
576	—	Victor Roadster,	130 00	78 00	4	1	2
572	54	Columbia Expert,	115 00	60 00	2	1	2
577	50	N. R. Roadster,	130 00	115 00	4	1	2
586	53	Columbia Lt. Rdstr.,	137 50	88 00	4	1	2
588	55	Victor Lt. Roadster,	137 50	100 00	4	1	2
590	—	New Rapid Safety,	135 00	80 00	4	1	1
303	50	Columbia Expert,	135 00	75 00	1	1	1
507	52	Victor Junior,	50 00	30 00	4	4	3
508	50	Otto Special,	60 00	20 00	6	4	4
598	52	Columbia Expert,	130 50	85 00	1	1	2
601	—	Col. Lt. Rdstr Tricycle,	160 00	90 00	1	1	2
602	54	Columbia Expert,	130 00	75 00	1	Ball	2
603	52	Columbia Expert,	137 50	90 00	1	1	2
605	56	Columbia Expert,	117 50	90 00	1	1	2
606	50	Singer's Matchless,	130 00	37 00	4	1	6
607	50	Special Peny Star,	130 00	85 00	3	Ball	2
608	50	Victor Lt. Roadster,	115 00	90 00	1	1	2
610	51	Columbia Lt. Rdstr.,	135 00	115 00	1	1	1
611	—	Victor Safety,	135 00	105 00	1	1	2
612	54	Premier,	135 00	90 00	1	1	6
613	48	Columbus Expert,	130 00	70 00	3	1	2
614	50	British Challenge,	135 00	95 00	3	1	2
615	54	Special Star,	150 00	85 00	4	Ball	2
616	52	Special Club,	135 00	45 00	4	1	6
617	54	Columbia Standard,	80 00	55 00	4	4	4
618	48	Ideal,	60 00	33 00	5	1	6

Upon receipt of $5 any Bicycle on above list will be sent C. O. D. for balance, with privilege of examination. Correspondence invited.

NEW YORK BICYCLE CO.,
No. 4 East 60th St.,

Dealers in New and Second-hand Machines.

Uptown Agents for Messrs. A. G. Spalding & Bros. Agents for H. B. Smith Machine Co.'s "Star" Wheels.

THE ROVER SAFETY

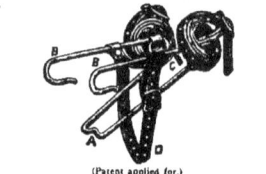

THE WHEEL

—AND—

CYCLING TRADE REVIEW,

Published every Friday morning.

Entered at the Post Office at second class rates.

Subscription Price, - - - $1.00 a year.
Foreign Subscriptions, - - - 6s. a year.
Single Copies, - - - - 5 Cents.

Newsdealers may order through AM. NEWS Co.

All copy should be received by Monday.
Telegraphic news received till Wednesday noon.

Advertising rates on Application.

F. P. PRIAL, Editor and Proprietor
23 Park Row,
P. O. Box 444,   New York.

Persons receiving sample copies of this paper are respectfully requested to examine its contents and give us their patronage, and as far as is convenient, aid in circulating the journal, and extend its influence in the cause which it so faithfully serves. Subscription price, $1 per year.

THE May 17 issue of THE WHEEL covered a vast field and has been much commended on all sides. It was a regular edition of the paper and no special preparation was made. It is interesting to compare THE WHEEL and *Bicycling World* of the same date. THE WHEEL contained 58,320 ems of nonpareil and 33,982 ems of brevier type. The *Bicycling World* contained 32,528 ems of brevier type. In other words THE WHEEL contained 27,943 words and the *Bicycling World* 10,992 words. THE WHEEL had a page editorial on patents, and smaller editorials on pavements, road improvements, League work and on the new tariff adopted by the railroads; besides the new rules for riding in Prospect Park, a review of a bright roads improvement pamphlet, complete details of the Harvard, Rochester, Rhode Island, Hagerstown and Woodstock tournaments ; a complete description of the new White Flier, the most complete column of racing fixtures published in this country, new matter in Orange, two columns of news for women cyclists, wheel gossip, trade notes, letters from Tacoma, Brooklyn, Troy, Westboro, Maryland, Chicago, St. Louis, St. Augustine, Philadelphia, Georgia and Minnesota, and the most complete selection of advertisements ever published in a cycle paper. We almost forgot that page of New York State Division League news.

THE GREAT ROAD RACE.

The greatest road event ever held in this vicinity will be the twenty-five mile contest, to be decided over the Irvington-Milburn course on May 30. The race was projected by A. B. Barkman, who secured the prizes and then turned over the management of the race to a number of representative club men. The trade responded liberally to Mr. Harkman's appeal, and the prizes attracted the unusually large number of fifty-three entries.

The race will be started at 11 o'clock, rain or shine. All the local clubs have called runs to the course, and public interest has been so stimulated by the newspapers that a greater crowd

will probably be present than has ever attended any previous race. The greatest difficulty has been found, during past races, to keep the course clear. The road, being a public highway, could not be cleared of vehicles, but these caused less trouble than the wheelmen. There will be twelve marshals present whose duty it will be to keep the course clear, especially at the finishing point. These men intend to perform their duty at all hazards. It is sincerely hoped that wheelmen spectators will assist them. After the race is started, no wheelman who is not a competitor should be seen riding on the course. We should say that any wheelman who paddles up and down the course is inviting a grave accident to the competitors and should be looked upon with contempt. The only motive we can ascribe to the men who ride up and down the course is that they want to "show off." We should advise the club captains to group their men at various parts along the road and request them not to again mount until the race is finished.

The handicaps, as published below, were the result of four hours' conscientious work. A copy of the list of entries and the records credited to each man was forwarded to each member of the Committee, and three sets of handicaps were made out. When the men met in Committee Meeting, it was discovered that one man had allotted very liberal starts, that another had been very conservative, and that another had struck a happy medium. Each man's case was taken up separately and carefully discussed. The men who gave no records, and who were not personally known to some member of the committee, received two-thirds of the limit.

COMPLETE LIST OF ENTRIES.

The following is a complete list of entries ; containing name, club and handicap. The numbers given are the numbers which each competitor will wear in the contest.

NO.	NAME.	CLUB.	H'CAP MINUTES.	REC'D.
52	Hall, Jr., H. J.	K. C. W	o	1 31 00
51	Baggott, E. P.	H. C. W	o	1 32 00
50	Bradley, H. L.	B. B. C.	o	1 34 00
49	Wilhelm, W.	Wilkesbarre.	o	1 35 00
48	Wilson, T. L.	K. C. W	1	1 31 00
47	Dampman, F. M	Wilmington.	1	1 37 37
46	Van Wagoner,	Newport	1	———
45	Bearsley, L. W	K. C. W	1	1 34 00
44	Hall, Jr., J. J	K. C. W	1	1 34 00
43	Merritew, S	Wilmington.	1	1 55 36
42	McDaniels, B. F	Wilmington	1	1 37 37
41	Risbett, Geo. M	N. Y. C. W	4	———
40	Banker, W. D	Pittsburg	4	———
39	King, N. O.	K. C. W	5	1 36 00
38	Hesse, F. B	K. C. W	6	———
37	Schumacher, W	K. C. W	6	———
36	Moorehouse, David	K. C. W	6	1 37 00
35	Wise, L. H	L. I. W	6	———
34	Wells, John A.	Penn B. C.	6	———
33	Taxis, W. W	Philadelphia	7	———
32	Stern, R. W	K. C. W	7	1 50 00
31	Murphy, Chas	K. C. W	7	1 50 00
30	Bensinger, John	K. C. W	7	1 39 00
29	Murphy, Wm.	K. C. W	7	1 32 00
28	Pyle, Howard J.	Wilmington	8	———
27	Bowman, S. B.	N. C. W	8	1 40 00
26	Borland, E. F	B. B. C.	7	1 39 45
25	Gubelman, F	N. J. A. C.	9	1 39 00
24	Class, W. G	B. B. C.	9	1 40 30
23	Waters, N. F	B. B. C.	9	1 40 30
22	Coningsby, F. W	B. B. C.	9	———
21	Elliott, F. B	Wilmington	10	———
20	Elliott, C. A.	Wilmington	10	———
19	Gregg, G. M.	Wilmington	10	1 53 00
18	Jefferis, Albert	Wilmington	10	———
17	Lofland, Z. H	Wilmington	10	———
16	Bruce, J. Purvis	Westboro	10	———
15	Lincoln, P. W	Flushing	10	———
14	Ludwig, H. D	Wilmington	10	1 53 00
13	Jelliffe, A.	Brooklyn	10	———
12	Kuhney, C. W	Talcottville	10	———
11	Robertson, J. L.	H. C. W	10	———
10	Van Wagoner, E	Newport	10	1 46 45
9	Dauchy, Edwin	West Winsted.	11	———
8	Miller, F. R	R. W	11	———
7	Putney, W. H	R. W	11	———
6	Quortrup, K	R. W	11	———
5	Boegler, O. C	New York	11	———
4	Williams, J. M	Summit	11	———
3	Mellor, J. H	Brooklyn	11	———
2	Hate, J. W	Brooklyn	11	———
1	H. P. Matthews	B. B. C.	12	2 00 00
—	F. I. Herbert	B. B. C.	12	2 00 00

LIST OF PRIZES.

1. Victor Bicycle, Overman Wheel Co.
2. Gold Watch, Mr. Walter Spalding.
3. French Clock, G. R. Bidwell.
4. Waterbury Camera, William Halpin.
5. Pearl-Handled "M. & H." Revolver, Messrs. Merwin, Hulbert & Co.

6. Kodak Camera, Eastman Dry Plate and Camera Co.
7. Watch and Wristlet, Ira Perego & Co.
8. Silver-Handled Umbrella, New York Bicycle Co.
9. Butcher Cyclometer, Butcher Cyclometer Co.
10. Trout-Fishing Outfit, Mr. H. J. Hall, Highland Mills, N. Y., and F. A. Leland, B. B. C.
11. Signal Cyclometer, Strong & Green Cycle Co.
12. King of the Road Lamp, Clark Cycle Co.
13. Invincible Lantern, Singer & Co.
14. Gold League Pin, Howard A. Smith & Co.
15. Tennis Racket, E. I. Horsman.
16. Bicycle Shoes, Charles Schwalbach.
17. Centennial Jersey, Holmes & Co.
18. Bicycle Shoes, Charles Schwalbach.
19. Box of Cigars, C. P. Abbey
    Silver Cup for Best Net Time, F. P. Prial, of THE WHEEL.

COMMITTEE OF ARRANGEMENTS.

A. B. Barkman, B. B. C.   F. P. Prial, N. Y. B. C.
W. H. DeGraaf, H. W.   W. E. Fuller, B. B. C.
Wm. Halpin, M. B. C   M. L. Bridgman, K. C. W
            Jos. McFadden, N. Y. B. C.

OFFICIALS OF RACE.

REFEREE.

George R. Bidwell, Citizens' B. C.

JUDGES.

H. Greenman, B. B. C.   H. E. Raymond, B. B. C.
M. L. Bridgman, K. C. W.   L. H. Johnson, Orange.
Michael Furst, L. I. W.   L. A. Newcome, H. W.
            J. M. Warwick, M. B. C.

TIMEKEEPERS.

Frank White, Orange A. C.   F. K. Austin, K. C. W.
W. H. De Graaf, H. W.   J. F. Pedersen, M. A. C.
F. H. Douglass, K. C. W.   E. W. Johnson, H. C. W.
            Howard A. Smith, Newark.

CLERK OF COURSE.

T. C. Crichton, K. C. W.

ASSISTANT CLERKS OF COURSE.

F. H. Jones, H. B. C.   G. L. Courtenay, K. C. W.
            C. C. Alden, L. I. W.

STARTER.

A. B. Barkman, Brooklyn B. C.

SCORERS.

F. P. Prial, New York Bicycle Club.
(Nine Assistants.)

CHIEF UMPIRES.

Waldo Fuller, B. B. C.   R. F. Hibson, K. C. W.

ASSISTANTS.

W. F. Findley, N. Y. B. C. W. Bonner, K. C. W.
W. Watkins, N. Y. B. C.   Arthur Ward, K. C. W.
A. Bogart, N. Y. B. C.   Edw. Jones, K. C. W.
G. W. Krieger, L. I. W.   L. Q. Long, K. C. W.
Rob. Evans, L. I. W.   Chas. Long, K. C. W.
A. P. Topping, L. I. W.   W. Newman, K. C. W.
A. Clarke, C. B. C.   Frank Brown, K. C. W.
George Sloane, C. B. C.   W. C. Ryan, K. C. W.
L. H. Dutcher, H. B. C.   F. J. Shipsey, N. Y. B. C.
N. H. Weed, B. B. C.   C. Y. Quimby, B. B. C.
L. C. Adams, B. B. C.   J. W. Schlefer, B. B. C.

MARSHALS.

W. C. Marion, K. C. W.   W. Halpin, M. B. C.

ASSISTANTS.

J. A. Clairmonte, M. B. C   D. H. Thistle, M. B. C.
C. A. Sheehan, M. B. C.   Dr. G. B. Bird, M. B. C.
            Paul Keane, M. B. C.

The race will be started at eleven o'clock, rain or shine. The men must respond to their names as they are called by the clerk of course. They will be started in the following order, one line wheeling out on to the road as the line in front of them is sent off.

Start.
1. Hebert, Matthews, Bate, Mellor, Williams.

2. Boegler, Quortrup, Putney, Mellor, Dauchy,

3. E. Van Wagoner, Robertson, Kuhney, Jelliffe.
5. Ludwig, Lincoln, Bruce, Lofland.
5. Jefferis, Gregg, C. A. Elliott, F. B. Elliott.

6. Coningsby, Waters, Class, Gubelman, Borland.

7. Bowman, Pyle, W. Murphy.

8. Bensinger, C. Murphy, Stern, Taxis.

9. Wells, Wise, Moorehouse, Schumacher, Hesse.

10. King.

11. Banker, Misbett, McDaniels, Merritew.
11. T. J. Hall, Jr., Beareley.

13. W. Van Wagoner, Dampman.

14. Wilson.

15. H. J. Hall, Jr., Baggott, Bradley, Wilhelm.

The headquarters of the competitors and their attendants will be at the Hilton Hotel ; admission by ticket only. The nearest station to the course is Maplewood.

TIME TABLES D. L. & W.

	Leaves		Arrives at	
Barclay St.	Christopher St.	Newark	Maplewood.
7:00	7:05	7:44	
7:05	7:15	8:04	8:31
7:20	8:15	8:55	
8:00	8:35	9:00	9:30
9:00	9:05	9:45	
10:00	10:15	10:45	11:10

K. C. W. NOTES.

The K. C. W. membership has increased so much of late that the already large locker accommodation has had to be largely added to. The locker room on the second floor, one of the finest rooms in the house, has been in the past week furnished with a double row of lockers in the centre. This spoils the room for cards, etc., but makes what all must concede to be the finest locker and dressing-room in any *cycle* club-house in the country.

The entries for the great road race have all been received, and the boys will peruse with anxious eyes this week's copy of The Wheel, for the handicappers have decided the fate of all.

Alas! I pity the unfortunate gentlemen who have allotted the starts. Their fate will indeed be a sad one. Think of forty-seven indignant aspirants for a "Victor" calling on Prial in a body. [We shall be "out."—Ed.]

Our Captain is a worker. He has secured quarters and attendants at Hilton for the racing representatives of the club, and can be seen every afternoon out with the training men, always ready to lend a hand or help a tired club-mate at the pace.

The success of the K. C. W. men in the past has been largely due to the good care that has been given them, and on the 30th inst. the boys feel assured all former efforts to look out for the boys in black will be put in the shade.

The Universal Cycle Club is no more. The young clubs cannot become successful in Brooklyn, for the three stronger and older organizations draw most of the riders not too young for membership.

At the meeting of the K. C. W. on Thursday, the 16th, the fact that the U. C. C. had disbanded, and that therefore twenty-two cyclists, good and true, were in want of club comforts, was discussed. Finally a committee was appointed to confer with the members of the aforesaid club relative to their joining the K. C. W. Messrs. Miles, Newman and Marion will no doubt soon have several applications for membership to hand in.

The resignation of Charles Schwalbach from the race committee was accepted, and Mr. Miles appointed to fill the vacancy. Mr. Whymper, who, by the way, is a pusher, was also added. The committee now stands: Nellis, Stevens, C. I. Long, Mills, Whymper and W. F. Murphy, chairman. No drones there, and on June 28 and 29 such a race meet will be held at Washington Park as even the K. C. W. never held before.

Do not forget the date. On June 28 and 29 *all* roads lead to Washington Park.

Among the many other interesting events to be held on the above date, the 3-mile L. A. W. Championship, will, of course, take premier position. The track is four laps, with easy corners, and we intend to have the largest array of cycling talent ever seen in Brooklyn. Our cycling friends are cordially invited and we promise all a regular K. C. W. time.

We all hope that the slight sprain L. W. Beazeley is now troubled with will soon be on the mend. Such a man of stay and pluck as Lester will be greatly missed the 30th.

Tom Hall will be able to ride the race of his life, and those who think they have a "sinch" when youngsters compete had better keep both eyes on Chas. Murphy.

Club runs are more popular than ever before, but the informal runs are the ones that the boys attend. Last Sunday twenty-three and two weeks ago twenty-five for Roslyn and return, and this over forty-four miles of L. I. roads.

The Hudson County men who were out with us on Sunday appear to think our riders better than our roads.

Five new members on Thursday. Still they come. Let the good work go on.

The burning of the grand stand at Washington Park will in no way interfere with the sale of seats for the K. C. W. meet. Come right up and secure seats early, for they are going fast. The Com. are in session every evening at 1355 Bedford Avenue

Brooklyn, May 22. Ram Lal.

BROOKLYN NEWS.

As the time for the big 25-mile road race draws near, it becomes more and more the principal topic of conversation at the cycling club houses in Brooklyn, and if it is causing as much talk, comment and conjecture among the other clubs in the vicinity of New York, it bids fair to go down in the archives of cycling history as one of the most important events ever held.

All the Brooklyn clubs have men entered, with the usual friendly and enthusiastic partisanship, which characterizes the wheelmen of this city. Mr. A. B. Barkman deserves a great deal of praise for the masterly way he has originated and carried through the many details of the undertaking to the present date.

As I said last week, there will be a large attendance from Brooklyn clubs, and with the new regulations of the railroad companies charging twenty-five cents each way for a wheel, the transportation costs on Decoration Day will amount to a very snug little sum. There is a great deal of dissatisfaction over the additional charge for wheels, and a large number of Brooklyn riders who were accustomed to take very frequent rides in the Oranges, now swear they will not go there while such an exorbitant price is put upon their pleasure. The L. A. W. will, no doubt, arrange the matter satisfactorily with the Eastern Traffic Association which controls the rates and charges of the different roads.

The B. B. C., however, will have an informal run in the Oranges next Sunday, with their usual disregard of expenses. A number of the Brooklyn Club boys took a ride across Staten Island last Sunday which was very enjoyable, but marred by a few more or less serious accidents.

Bert Cole started the list by breaking a pedal-pin and was obliged to ride the length of the Island, using a small wrench handle for a pedal. Lieutenant Fay, who rode in the rear of the party, unfortunately frightened a horse driven by an elderly couple, which resulted in the overturning of their carriage and some bad bruises for the inmates. Healy and F. R. Bogart, L. I. W., also accompanied the Brooklyns on the run, the whole party returning from Perth Amboy to Elizabeth, from which point they trained to the city.

I have had inquiries lately from ladies who are learning to ride safeties, as to the proper material and construction of their new uniforms, or riding habits, and as I am ignorant in that respect, could give no satisfactory information. I think if some lady rider with experience would write an article on the subject, it would be appreciated.

Atol.

Brooklyn, May 21, 1889.
[See "Marguerite's" letter in sent issue.—Ed.]

PSYCHE'S NOTES.

It was a mistake for me to say so positively that Mrs. Stall's tricycle weighs only 35 lbs., as I did in my last letter. I knew nothing about it personally, and I wish to amend the statement and say that I *have been told* that the tricycle in question weighs only 35 lbs.

Miss Helen Grey, in the last issue of the *Bicycling World*, says that I am wrong, and that she has seen the machine and that it weighs 15 lbs more than I said. She is probably right, and the owner of the lightest tricycle on record is still more handicapped than I thought.

I see that she is under a misapprehension as to the weight of ladies' bicycles. She inquires why I ride a 45-lb. bicycle? I don't.

I have ridden from the first a 39-lb. Psycho, and in July I am to have a machine of the same make weighing 34 lbs. My weight is 128 lbs.

I believe there is one, perhaps more, of the same make and weight in Boston, and I would advise Miss Grey to look it up and increase her knowledge of bicycles.

I am puzzled to know what I can have said to mislead any reader of my letters to the extent of thinking that I wanted to exalt the tricycle at the expense of the bicycle. On the contrary, I think and say that, given the same weight of machine, the bicycle is still far ahead, out of sight in fact, of the tricycle.

As to my espousing the cause of the bicycle as a defence against dogs, I think Miss Grey's terrors must confuse her vision. If I were choosing a mount with regard to its defensive qualities against dogs I think I should choose a push cart, and perhaps never feel really safe till I was in a hearse (that is if I looked at the subject as Miss Grey does).

I see that my friend congratulates herself on the sympathetic utterances of an English correspondent in favor of tricycles, and at the same time assures the public generally that she is in favor of bicycles. It calls to my mind very forcibly a Scriptural quotation beginning "Thou art neither hot nor cold," etc. I leave my readers to look it out for themselves.

One of your Troy friends wants some opinions of practical wheelwomen as to the comparative merits of bicycles and tricycles on country roads:

I have ridden a good deal on both styles of machines over country roads and find the two-wheeler immensely superior. There is almost always a little hard track where the wagon wheels have beaten the dirt hard and smooth, and this a two-wheeled machine can take advantage of, a narrow bit of grass, a little foot-path, all these can be used by the bicyclist to dodge heavy traveling, and this is out of the question on a tricycle.

I enjoyed "Marguerite's" bright letter in your last issue. We have a good deal of the same sort of fun here, though there is no annex to the men's club and no ladies' club. Still, we go out in parties of from two to a dozen and have great fun. I congratulate her heartily on her new mount. I rode a tricycle for two years and can appreciate her delight in the change.

Psyche.

THE PROPER DRESS FOR LADIES RIDING SAFETIES.

I see no reason why we need a dress in any way different from that suitable for the tricycle, though a slightly shorter length would be no drawback. I find that when I mount, using the right foot first in starting, my dress has sometimes an awkward habit of winding and twisting under my left foot, making it difficult to properly catch the pedal. Perhaps this will disappear when thoroughly accustomed to the machine.

Almost every wheel-woman one meets, entertains a different idea on the dress question. What shows it better than some club-runs, where no two ladies are dressed alike, with a possible exception of two *sisters*.

My sister and I have worn out, to our sorrow, a fair number of cycling suits, and in the two latest we have taken most comfort, the very last being but a "second edition" of the previous dress. A grey tricot, medium shade to hide dust and grease spots, made in the plainest style. A full skirt, with opening at side, no trimming; blouse, with fulled sleeves, tight-fitting wrists and sailor collar. For summer wear we have a white Danish cloth (non-shrinkable) blouse, making a nice change, and also being cooler. Some object to the tricot as being too light and liable to fly too much when out riding in any wind, but this can be remedied by goring and lining the skirts. Ladies' cloth makes a very pretty suit, while I think corduroy too heavy. Although its wearing qualities are lasting, it drags considerably.

Last Sunday's *Boston Herald* contained an interesting article from "R. L. G." relative to Bicycling for Ladies. The part regarding dress is good, and I have taken the liberty of giving it here. "Her dress is in but two sections, as Lord Dundreary would naively put it—a blouse and skirt. The skirt is very full, four yards, and double that allowed by Dame Fashion when she laid down this season's edict of directory and empire gowns narrow and plain. The width gives free action to the feet, it being required that there be no restraint when moving the bicycle. The material chosen should be one that will not readily catch the dust, and the revivified brilliantines are found admirably suited to the needs of the lady rider. The make of the skirt is a kilt, in wide or narrow pleats, from the waist down, except in the back breadths, which are shirred three or four times across. No reeds whatever are called for, and tournures are out of date in the drawing room and in the street, as well as totally uncalled for on a bicycle. Common sense rules where the latter is concerned. The blouse or body waist is very full, notably so in the sleeves, and, as the English blouses are the rage, the bicyclist has great margin here for the becomingness and the 'high lights' of artistic effects. With a bicycle adopted by womankind, the *olloi polloi* associate the Dr. Mary Walker or the divided skirt, but a more absurd impression never existed. Any full skirt will do, provided that in its fullness there be enough to give free action and a concealment of the movements of the knees. The best shoes are those with rubber soles. A hat with a visor that will shield the face from sun and wind is probably better than that adopted by common usage on the tennis field and for tricycle wear, the Tam O'Shanter. For the hands, gloves with two buttons in the fashionable coarse grained kid or the Suxe Biarritz. The fair rider must have a whistle, and when she is attached by direct or honorary membership to a club she wears its c lors and a club pin."

Will not other ladies give their opinion on this vital problem for the benefit of those who may not feel entirely satisfied, and, also for the new riders whom we like to see join us every year.

Maplewood, Mass. Marguerite.

RIVERSIDE WHEELMEN'S HOUSE-WARMING.

The Riverside Wheelmen opened their new house, at 104th Street West, on Friday evening last, with a neat programme of music, refreshments and dancing. The house is a large frame building, a few steps from the "L" road station at 104th Street, only a few rods from the "Drive" and within easy distance of the Park. The building was formerly occupied by Mr. H. Wimmel, of *Puck*, an enthusiastic wheelman, who is about to leave for Europe on an extended trip, and rented his house to the Riversides for three years.

There are front and rear parlors, lunch-rooms, janitor's apartments and a few spare bed-rooms. There is an outbuilding to be used as a wheel-room, and a stable.

The programme rendered during the evening was as follows: Banjo duet, Messrs. Blackman and Brown; song, Miss Driggs; piano solo, Mr. Schwab; recitation, Mr. J. G. Lamb; song, Mr. H. H. Foster; piano duet, Mrs. Block and Miss Schwab; banjo solo, Prof. Dobson.

Between the numbers refreshments were served.

Among those present were: Mr. Terwilliger, Harlem Wheelmen; E. A. Powers and Miss F. Powers, Chas. Stitt and Miss Britton, Mr. and Mrs. Cossitt, H. C. Bryan, Miss Wilson, Mr. and Mrs. J. C. Wilson, Mr. and Mrs. J. W. Miller, L. Johnson and Miss Johnson, R. F. Macey and Miss D. Wright, G. B. Hogan and Miss Macey, J. L. Miller and the Misses Everett, Mr. and Mrs. Whitrell, Mrs. Barry, Mr. and Mrs. Beam, Mr. and Mrs. Odell, Mr. Ducayet and Miss Glassier, Mr. C. M. Driggs and Miss Driggs, Mr. E. Hallet and Miss Newcombe, Mr. S. W. Schwab, Miss Schwab and Miss Stitt, L. A. Clarke and I. C. Wilson, of the Citizens; M. L. Bridgman, Mr. Crichton, of the K. C. W.; Masterson, of the Brooklyns; J. W. Judge, F. R. Miller, A. R. Barry, F. P. Prial, of the N. Y. H. C.; J. G. Lamb, Edwd. de R. Brighton, Wm. Potter, Oscar Schrader.

Entertainment Committee: S. W. Schwab, H. H. Foster, C. H. Taylor, I. F. Hearn, Oscar Schrader.

The West End Bicycle Club, of Rochester, N. Y., recently elected these officers: President, J. A. Huesner; First Vice-President, C. J. Iven; Second Vice-President, Wallace Hanney; Recording Secretary, L. G. Mabbett; Financial Secretary, L. B. Vincent; Treasurer, Frank Chamberlain; Captain, Robert Leadley; First Lieutenant, James Barnes; Second Lieutenant, Nat Roe.

A number of wheelmen witnessed the S. I. A. C. games, held at the club grounds, at Staten Island last Saturday afternoon. The event of the afternoon was the two-mile handicap. Windle and Rich were at scratch, but neither turned out. The race was interesting from start to finish; F. G. Brown, K. C. W., made a splendid break away on the last lap and winning easily. The Yale men rode in splendid form but without dash. Schumacker rode stronger than any man in the race. He very wisely decided to ride safely, and took the turns wide and very slow; otherwise he could have won as he showed a splendid form on the straights. The race resulted as follows: F. G. Brown, K. C. W., 155 yards, 5.46 2-5, the best time ever made on this track; S. B. Bowman, N. J. A. C., 160 yards, second by several lengths; D. Oakes, Bloomfield A. C., 225 yards, close up; F. A. Clarke, Yale College, 100 yards, 0; R. W. Steves, K. C. W., 185 yards, 0; J. H. Hanson, M. A. C., 215 yards, 0; W. Schumacker, L. I. W., 0; W. E. Findlay, N. Y. B. C., 0.

FIXTURES.

May 25, 1889.—Stone-Lumsden 3-mile Match Race, at St. Louis, Mo.

May 27, 1889.—Stone-Lumsden 25-mile Match Race at Crawfordsville, Ind.

May 30, 1889.—N. J. A. C. 1½ mile and 3-mile handicaps. Entries close May 22, with A. M. Sweet, P. O. Box 267, Bergen Point, N. J.

May 30, 1889.—Maine Division Meet, at Biddeford, Me.

May 30, 1889.—Bicycle and Athletic Tournament and 2-mile L. A. W. Championship Race at Narragansett Park.

May 30, 1889.—Pullman Road Race, Chicago to Pullman.

May 30, 1889.—Twenty-five-mile Handicap Road Race, Irvington—Milburn course. Entries close May 15th with A. B. Barkman, 241 Broadway, New York.

May 30, 1889.—Rhode Island Wheelman's Race Meet at Narragansett Park, Providence, R. I. Entries close with C. E. Campbell, Providence, R. I.

May 30, 1889.—Annual 5-mile Handicap Race of New Haven Bicycle Club, at Hamilton Park.

May 30, 1889.—Sixth Annual Meet and Races of Woodstock A. A. A., at Woodstock, Ontario.

May 30, 1889.—North Adams Wheelmen's Races. Entries close May 28, with John B. French, Secretary, North Adams, Mass.

May 30, 1889.—Hill-climbing contest among members of Wheel Club, at Northampton, Mass.

May 30, 1889.—Second Annual Tournament of West End Bicycle Club, Rochester, N. Y. Entries close May 29, with C. J. Iven, 22 Exchange Street.

May 30, 1889.—Winsted Wheel Club's Meet, at Winsted, Conn.

May 30, 1889.—Bay City Wheelmen's Race Meet, at San Francisco.

May 30, 1889.—California L. A. W. Division Meet, at Los Angeles. Entries close May 25, at 10 P. M.

June 1, 1889.—Manhattan Athletic Club 1½-mile Handicap. Entries close May 25, with C. C. Hughes, 524 Fifth Avenue, N. Y. City.

June 4, 5, 6, 1889.—Kansas Division Meet at Forest Park, Ottawa, Kansas.

June 6, 1889.—Five-mile Bicycle Race at Seymour, Ind. Entries to be made to John A. Ross, Seymour, Ind.

June 8, 1889.—Century Run, Orange, N. J., to Philadelphia. Chairman, L. A. Clarke, 23 Broad Street, New York.

June 8, 1889.—Two-mile Bicycle Handicap at Schuylkill Navy A. C., Univ. of Penn. Grounds, Phila. Entries close June 1, with W. T. Wallace, 123 North 7th Street, Phila., Pa.

June 10, 1889.—Regular Annual Meeting of Kentucky Division, L. A. W., at Danville, Kentucky.

June 12, 1889.—Bicycle Race at Huntington, L. I. Entries close with S. C. Ebbetts, Huntington, June 8.

June 13, 1889.—Two-mile Bicycle Race at Berkeley Oval—Eastern championship, A. A. A. Entries close May 25, with W. Janssen, P. O. Box 125, N. Y. City.

June 15, 1889.—L. I. W. Race Meet at Brooklyn Athletic Grounds. Entries close June 8 with L. H. Wise, 1,281 Bedford Ave., Brooklyn.

June 15, 1889.—Two-mile Bicycle Handicap at New York Athletic Club Grounds, Travers Island.

June 17, 1889.—Annual Meet of Massachusetts Division, L. A. W., at Squantum, Mass.

June 18, 1889.—Third Annual Meet of Tennessee Division, L. A. W., at Nashville, Tenn.

June 22, 1889.—New Orleans Bicycle Club's Race for the Hill Cup.

June 28, 29, 1889.—Kings County Wheelmen's Annual Meet at Washington Park, Brooklyn. Address W. C. Nellis, 1,255 Bedford Avenue.

July 2, 3, 4, 1889.—League Meet at Hagerstown, Md.

July 3, 1889.—L. A. W. Race Meet, at Hagerstown, Md. Entries close June 26, with Harry B. Irwin, 34 West Franklin Street, Hagerstown, Md.

July 4, 1889.—Race Meet at Brownsville, Pa.

July 4, 1889.—Illinois Division, L. A. W. Meet, at Ottawa.

July 4, 1889.—Tournament held by Lancaster (Pa.) Bicycle Club.

July 4, 1889.—Fort Schuyler Wheelmen, Utica, N. Y., 50-mile Road Race.

July 20, 1889.—One-mile and 25-mile Bicycle and 5-mile Tricycle N. C. U. championships at Paddington, Eng., track.

July 27, 1889.—One-mile and 25-mile Tricycle and 5-mile Bicycle N. C. U. Championships at Paddington, Eng., track.

EUROPEAN CYCLING FIXTURES.

Austro-Hungary.—Graz, May 26 and June 9 and 10; Pilsen, June 9 and 10; Prague (Smichow) June 29 and 30. Germany.—Berlin, June 16 and 17, July 21, September 15; Hanover, June 23, September 8; Cologne, June 2 and 30, August 12; Chemnitz, September 8; Frankfort-on-the-Maine, September 1; Mannheim, September 8; Crefeld, May 26, September 8. Hamburg.—Altona, May 26, September 22; Bochum, May 30, August 25; Soram, June 9; Coburg, June 9; Magdeburg, June 30, September 8. Denmark.—Copenhagen International Meeting, August 18.

National Cyclists' Union.—Championship Fixtures—At Paddington, August 24, 50-mile Bicycle and 1-mile Dwarf.

RECORD CLAIMED FOR TWO-MILE TANDEM SAFETY.

By a typographical error in THE WHEEL of May 17, the time made by the Bailey brothers in the tandem safety race at Cambridge, May 11, was given as 6m. 46s., instead of 6m. 4-5s., the correct time. This is claimed as record for that type wheel for distance named.

RACES RUN AT CHICAGO MAY 13 TO 18.

FIRST DAY, MAY 13.

ONE-MILE NOVICE SCRATCH.—First heat: H. E. Loveday, Illinois, C. C., first; F. L. Chase, Lincoln C. C., second. Time 3m. 4 1-5s.

Second heat: F. H. Tuttle, Illinois C. C., first; R. H. Goodrich, Braidwood, Ill., second. Time, 3m. 5 4-5s.

TWO-MILE SCRATCH RACE.—First heat: H. L. Kingsland, Manhattan A. C., first; John Mason, Illinois C. C., second. Time, 6m. 9 3-5s.

Second heat: Walk over by E. L. Thornton, Pastime C. A. A. Time not taken.

ONE-MILE HANDICAP.—Run in six heats. First heat: W. Maas, Illinois C. C., handicap 70 yards, first; B. Burroughs, Avondale B. C., Cincinnati, 15 yards, second. Time, 2m. 50 1-5s.

Second heat: R. H. Goodrich, Braidwood, 120 yards, first; W. D. Sheriff, California, Mo., 90 yards, second. Time, 2m. 52 2-5s.

Third heat: Frank Riggs, Illinois C. C., 90 yards, first; A. Guthrie, Alpha C. C., 120 yards, second. Time, 2m. 53s.

Fourth heat: George Thorne, Chicago C. C., 75 yards, first; A. M. Luce, Lincoln C. C., 40 yards, second. Time, 2m. 48 3-5s.

Fifth heat: H. E. Loveday, Illinois C. C., 55 yards, first; F. E. Spooner, Lincoln C. C., 60 yards, second. Time, 2m. 43 1-5s.

Sixth heat: F. H. Tuttle, Illinois C. C., 60 yards, first; O. Wimmerstedt, Lincoln C. C., 60 yards, second. Time, 2m. 44 1-5s.

ONE-MILE RACE (Boys under 16).—W. Pixley, Omaha, first; R. Richardson, Washington, second. Time, 3m. 6s. Prizes, Junior bicycle and silver cup.

TWO-MILE SCRATCH, 6.20 CLASS.—First heat: Won by F. E. Spooner in 5m. 30 1-5s.

Second heat: Won by F. H. Tuttle in 5m. 54 4-5s.

MAY 14.

MILE SCRATCH RACE.—Open only to men that had never raced before—First heat: C. J. Guthrie, Englewood, in 3m. 8 1-5s.

Second heat: A. Guthrie, Alpha C. C., in 3m. 1 2-5s.

Third heat: F. H. Tuttle, I. C. C., in 2m. 54 3-5s.

TWO-MILE SAFETY RACE—Final heat: Won by John Mason, Illinois C. C., in 6m. 31 3-5s.

ONE-MILE HANDICAP, SECOND SERIES.—First heat: F. E. Spooner, L. C. C., in 2m. 56 4-5s.

Second heat: O. Wimmerstedt, L. C. C., in 2m. 48 4-5s.

Third heat: A. Guthrie, A. C. C., in 2m. 49 2-5s.

Fourth heat: Bodach, A. C. C., in 2m. 52s.

Fifth heat: Luce, L. C. C., in 2m. 50s.

Sixth heat: Walkover by A. L. A. Wallace, of Chicago.

TWO-MILE, 6.20 CLASS.—Final heat: Won by Myers, Peoria, Ill., in 5m. 45 2-5s.

ONE-MILE, FLYING START.—Second heat (run first): Kingsland, M. A. C., in 3m. 8 2-5s.

First heat: Burroughs, first, in 3m. 3s.

THREE-MILE HANDICAP.—First heat: Thorne, of C. C. C., in 8m. 50s.

Second heat: Luce, of L. C. C., in 8m. 52s.

Third heat: Myers, of L. C. C., in 8m. 47 3-5s.

MAY 15.

ONE-MILE SCRATCH.—Open to men that had never raced before—Final heat: F. H. Tuttle, I. C. C., first, in 2m. 54 4-5s.

Lovedale a close second.

ONE-MILE SAFETY.—In heats—First heat: O. D. Richardson, W. C. C., in 2m. 52 3-5s.

Second heat: Barrett, by four inches, in 2m. 57s.

ONE-MILE HANDICAP.—In heats—First heat: Pixley, of Omaha, in 2m. 51 1-5s.

Second heat: O. D. Richardson, Chicago, in 2m. 51 4-5s.

Third heat: Burroughs, of Cincinnati, in 2m. 57 1-5s.

Fourth heat: Black, of L. C. C., in 2m. 44 4-5s.

Fifth heat: Richardson, in 2m. 51 1-5s.

ONE-MILE SAFETY.—Boys under 17—Won by Richardson in 3m. 3 3-5s., with five contestants.

ONE-MILE, FLYING START.—Final heat: Won by Burroughs, of Cincinnati, in 2m. 48 3-5s.

MAY 16.

ONE HUNDRED MILE AMATEUR RACE.—Won by Spooner, of Lincoln C. C., in 5h. 59m. 40s., breaking the 100-mile amateur record by 13m. 20s.

Seven starters had entered for this race, among whom Van Sicklen, of Chicago, and Myers, of Peoria, were favorites, and the race thought to be certainly between them. At the finish Spooner was over two miles ahead of Hammel, who finished second, and the supposed winners had drawn out before covering fifty miles. Spooner was carried from the track amid wild enthusiasm and a shower of bouquets.

ONE-MILE, 3M. CLASS.—In heats—First heat: Neilson, of Boston, in 3m. 13 3-5s.

Second heat: Tuttle, of S. C. C., in 2m. 50 4-5s.

TWO-MILE HANDICAP.—In heats—First heat: Black, of L. C. C., in 5m. 37 1-5s.

Second heat: Kohler, of A. C. C., in 5m. 42 3-5s.

ONE-MILE HANDICAP.—Final heat: Won by Richardson of W. C. C., in 2m. 46s., 160 yards.

ONE-MILE, 3M. CLASS.—Final heat: Tuttle, first; Lovedale, second; Time, 2m. 51 4-5s.

HALF-MILE.—Boys under 12—Clarence Simpson, aged 11, won in 1m. 59 2-5s., from thirty yards mark, with Allie Johnson, also 11, second, from scratch.

TWO-MILE HANDICAP.—Final heat: Won by Burroughs of Cincinnati, with a great spurt, in 5m. 42 1-5s.

MAY 17.

THREE-MILE HANDICAP.—Final heat: Won by Myers, of Peoria, in 8m. 34s., with Luce second.

QUARTER-MILE.—In heats—First heat: Washburne, in 40 3-5s.

Second heat: Riggs, in 42 2-5s. (walk-over).

Third heat: Loveday, in 48s. (walk-over).

ONE-MILE SCRATCH RACE.—Won by Burroughs, of Cincinnati, in 2m. 54 1-5s.

ONE-MILE RIDE AND RUN.—(First quarter ridden and the others alternately run and ridden), Myers of Peoria, won easily in 4m. 29s.

ONE-MILE HANDICAP.—First heat: Tuttle, in 2m. 48 3-5s.

Second heat: Bodach, in 2m. 49s.

QUARTER-MILE.—Final heat: Won by Washburne, in 39s. Three starters.

FIVE-MILE HANDICAP, and Final Race of the Evening.—First heat: Myers, of Peoria, first, in 17m. 20s.; Burroughs, of Cincinnati, second. This was practically a scratch race and the prettiest of the evening, as both men started from the 90 yards mark, and Myers won by not more than inches.

Second heat: Riggs won in 14m. 26 1-5s.

MAY 18.

ONE-MILE NOVICE, Final heat.—Won by Tuttle in 3m. 11 4-5.

ONE-MILE SAFETY, Road Wheels.—Won by Mason in 2m. 54 4-5s.

ONE-MILE HANDICAP.—Won by Tuttle in 2m 42 4-5s., in striking constrast to his previous time in the One-Mile Novice.

TWO-MILE, L. A. W., Members Only.—Won by Kohler in 5m. 39 3-5s.

THREE-MILE TEAM RACE.—Illinois Club first in 8m. 57 2-5s.; Chicago second.

TEN-MILE SCRATCH RACE.—Won by Burroughs, of Cincinnati, in 31m. 48 3-5s.

FIVE-MILE HANDICAP.—This was given to Riggs, as the only other contestant, Burroughs, was taken ill, and fell from his wheel.

During the entire tournament a six-day professional race has been contested on another track in the same building, with the usual entries that a long-suffering public is familiar with. One recent addition is Reading, of the Twenty-Second Regiment, stationed at Fort Omaha. Prince, under whose care and training Reading has been, would seem to have had charge of him both morally and physically, for by those two "pocketing" Knapp, the latter was kept from first place, and Reading allowed to win. Chicago papers characterize this piece of business as open fraud, and cries of "Prince is a robber," "Rule him off," etc., were common. By a daring spurt, when three laps were yet to be ridden, Knapp went ahead, and took second money, to the crowd's great satisfaction. Of course, all the above is nothing new to those that have watched the course of these professionals, and we can feel little sympathy for Chicago people that were victimized by such well-worn tactics. Barnum was certainly right when he said the public enjoyed being humbugged.

FOREIGN RACING ITEMS.

In the 1-mile handicap at Paddington, Eng., May 4 (safeties and ordinaries in alternate classes), Shute of the Polytechnic, 160 yards, won first heat easily in 2m. 36 1-5s. Schafer also of Polytechnic, scratch, came second in the fastest mile yet made on a safety, 2m. 37 1-5s.

H. D. Faith, of London, on an ordinary took the second heat in 2m. 43 2-5s. In the final heat Shute won again by 25 yards, the only ordinary rider coming in a bad fourth.

W. H. Langdown, of the Pioneer B. C., New Zealand, who will be remembered as visiting America a few years since, has won the Cyclist's Alliance 5-mile Championship in 18m. 28 4-5s. Reports speak of the finish as a grand one, Langdown winning by but two lengths.

On the 17th of April, while trying a new racing bicycle at the Frankfort track, Lehr, the famous German racing man, was thrown to the ground by the left pedals breaking, and fractured his left arm in three places. Mr. Lehr had been expected to compete in the N. C. U. Championships at Paddington, Eng.

At the cycling races in Plymouth, on Whit-Monday, the leading prize was the Plymouth C. C. Cup, costing over £105 net, or $525 in our currency. That would be considered worth working for even on this side.

The Catford Cycling Club's 20-mile handicap road ride was won by Messrs. Tom Green and F. Adams, from the 6m. 30s. and 6m. marks, who dead-heated for first place in net time 1h., 10m. 12s.

Where safeties and ordinaries compete, as in several recent English events, the only chance the safeties seem to have is to set a sharp pace at start and keep it up all the way through—"Slogging," as our contemporaries term it.

Mr. P. P. Kilkelly, the racing hope of Ireland, and seemingly the only foeman worthy of Synyer's notice, is confined to his bed from inflammation of the left knee and a high fever. This was due to a bad fall received in the race for the Dunboyne Cup. Mr. Kilkelly's father states that his son will certainly not be able to mount a bicycle again this year, though the case is progressing favorably. Mr. Kilkelly will have the regrets of all racing men over this piece of ill-luck.

A 2-mile bicycle handicap will be held at the Athletic Club Schuylkill Navy games, to be held at the University of Pennsylvania grounds June 8. Entries close June 1, with W. T. Wallace, 123 North Seventh Street, Philadelphia, Pa.

MEMORIAL DAY.

PROVIDENCE RACE MEET.

The list of events and prizes is as follows:

One-mile handicap—First prize, gold medal; second prize, entire jersey suit from Whitten & Co.; third prize, billiard cue from Brunswick-Balke Co. One-mile safety handicap—First prize, gold medal; second prize, Smith & Wesson revolver; third prize, pair kangaroo bicycle shoes. One-mile team race—Prize, a fine silver cup. One-mile tandem safety — First prize, two extra fine meerschaum pipes; second prize, two silver-headed canes. One mile State Safety Championship.—First prize, gold medal from Coventry Machinists' Co; second prize, lantern from Clark Cycle Co. Two-mile National L. A. W. championship—First prize, gold medal; second prize, silver medal. Three-mile championship of State—First prize, gold medal from Campbell Co.; second prize, World typewriter. One-mile (open) bicycle—First prize, gold medal from H. B. Smith Machine Co.; second prize, Butcher cyclometer from Singer & Co.; third prize, pair Kingston jersey breeches. Two-mile safety (open)—First prize, Kodak camera; second prize, Victor cyclometer from Overman Wheel Co.; third prize, Pongee silk shirt. One-mile tandem safety handicap—First prize, two leather-cased toilet sets; second prize, two pairs Lemair opera glasses. One-mile novice—First prize, silver cup from Pope Mfg. Co.; second prize, seal ring; third prize, "Pigs in Clover" (solid silver charm); fourth prize, Oklahoma house lot (if you can get it).

TWO-MILE BICYCLE A. A. W. CHAMPIONSHIP.

The Eastern championship of the A. A. W. will be held June 1 at the Berkeley A. C. grounds, on the Harlem River. Among the events is a ten mile handicap. Entries close May 25 with F. W. Janssen, P. O. Box 125, New York City.

AGAIN THE BICYCLE THIEF.

The bicycle thief and swindler has appeared recently in a new form at Lynn, and nearly succeeded in taking with him to London two bicycles, one a single and the other a tandem safety. These had been purchased by one Alfred Nightengale on the instalment plan of Mr. C. E. Whitten, of Lynn, and $50 paid on one wheel. Not content with these two machines, he also tried to work Mr. Whitten for a lantern by the old familiar dodge of representing that a friend of Mr. Whitten's had sent for it by him. The lantern was sent, but meeting the friend and learning that no lantern had been ordered by him, Mr. Whitten suspected that all was not right, and made a visit to Linden, where the thief resided. Finding the house empty, and, learning that Nightengale was about to sail for Europe, Mr. Whitten returned to Lynn and put Detective Shaw on his track. Officer Shaw on reaching Boston fortunately learned that one bicycle was laid up for repairs with the Hope Bicycle Mfg. Co., but that the tandem was packed ready to send to England on the steamer Catalonia. Nightengale was too old a bird to go to the repairer's himself for the bicycle, but sent another man who took it where the tandem was stored, followed by the detective in a Herdic. Here Nightengale, who had taken tickets for himself and wife under fictitious names, was arrested and locked up to await examination. Nightengale's sweet song will doubtless only be heard from the "cage" for some time to come.

LATER.

At the hearing of Nightengale's case, in Police Court at Lynn, testimony was brought forward a little more favorable to him, one witness for the prosecution admitting that he lied to Detective Shaw about the lantern. The prosecution's strongest point was supposedly the stealing of the lantern, so this rather nonplussed them. Other charges were technically disposed of, and Nightengale required to furnish $300 bail. Scores of wheelmen were present, and the streets looked like a meet on a small scale.

On May 14, at Trinity College Sports, R. K. Hubbard, of '92, captured the 2-mile bicycle race in 6m. 43s.

Entries for the two-mile A. A. N. Eastern Championship close to-morrow with F. W. Janssen, P. O. Box 125, New York City.

POINTS ON THE HAGERSTOWN MEET.

EDITOR OF THE WHEEL:

From a curs(e)ory glance at some of the work of a few correspondents of wheel papers, who sign various *nom de plumes* like Jassax and all that sort of thing, it is apparent that for some occult reason, they are attempting to give the Hagerstown Meet a black eye, or else their information is at fault. There is no use—the real wheelmen—the road riders—are coming to the Tenth Annual Meet. They are the men who want a Meet on a wheelman's basis and not on that of a mischievous literary dude's. The everyday entertainments of the stereotyped Meet in a large city can be had at home, but the unique features to be enjoyed at the Meet in the mountain city of Hagerstown "catches" them. The hyper-critics call it a hamlet. It is a city of about 20,000 population, with the enterprise and ambitious edifices of one of half a million; has about thirty miles of roller-made street surfaces, so that you can mount your wheel at the doors of the hotels and enjoy them, and is of no insignificant commercial importance. They call it "hot" up there. It is not so hot in the first part of July as Boston, Chicago, New York, Philadelphia or Baltimore; in fact it is one of the resorts for people of larger cities to escape the heat of their own. The roads are superb, with a variety of choice in grade, from dead level to hilly or mountainous, and with smooth coasts of from a few yards to several miles. These roads radiate in all directions. Wherever you go, whether in the city, into the surrounding country or across the mountains, the road-bed is that same hard, smooth limestone surface, and leads you through scenes of entrancing beauty. Do you want to follow the immortal "Sheridan's ride" with "Winchester twenty miles away?" Well, you can do it over the smoothest, speed-inspiring pike you ever saw, while the grand mountains towering above you, the odors from the blooming locust trees standing sentinel in picket line along the road, and the charming sights that greet the eye on every hand, all combine in creating a variety of pleasant sensations that pen is powerless to describe. Do you want to ride to the battle-fields of Gettysburg, Antietam, South Mountain, Cedar Creek and many more of lesser note? The finest stretch of roads in the country for wheelmen leads you through them. Do you wish to visit the renowned city of Frederick that inspired Whittier to write of grand old Barbara Fretchie when she defied that great chieftain, Stonewall Jackson, and his cohorts with:

> "Shoot, if you will, this old gray head,
> But spare your country's flag," she said.

Well, you can do so over a sand-papered pike that crosses two mountains and valleys, and shows you such sights as will dwell in memory to your last days, and all a-wheel for a four hours' slow ride. But what is the use? The road-books, the tales of tourists, the pens of contributors to magazines and wheel papers, have all united in spreading the fame of the Shenandoah Valley riding district, and the real wheelman thirsts for a taste of its pleasures. The Tenth Annual Meet is to be in this favored spot, and the riders are coming to it. The wisdom of President Luscomb and the executive committee in selecting it will be amply vindicated in a short time by all the lucky participants in the Meet, and then, perhaps, the carping hyper-critics and chronic kickers will crawl in their slimy holes and die while reflecting on the fact that it would have been better to have had some knowledge of the subject they were writing about.

You will soon be furnished with an illustrated article on the Hagerstown Meet that will give more elaborate information.

Respectfully and truly yours,
ALBERT MOTT,
BALTIMORE, Md., May 16. C. C. Md. Div.

THE HAGERSTOWN MEET.

The following circular letter has just been issued by President Luscomb, of the L. A. W.:

"It is suggested that six meetings be held during the coming meet, at convenient hours, and that the subjects to be discussed at the several meetings be as follows:

"1. Rights and privileges of wheelmen in cities and on the road.

"2. Improvement of highways and condition of roads.

"3. Racing and its rules.

"4. Our constitution and by-laws; the scope and development of the L. A. W. and the advantage of League clubs.

"5. Railroads and transportation.

"6. Wheels and their appurtenances from the practical riders' standpoint.

DOUBTS DISPELLED.

If any wheelmen had a secret suspicion that at Hagerstown, Md., the mercury's favorite position was plus 95° in the shade, or that Hagerstown itself was a mere hamlet of 5 000 or so, let them read Chief Consul Mott's letter in another column. If their minds are not set at rest and enthusiasm aroused, they must be indeed classed among the blase "400." Mr. Mott is a man whose statements can be taken without salt, and he knows whereof he writes. With a spirit roused by articles he thinks intended to slur Hagerstown, he "talks right out in meeting." But that feeling is pardonable, and the enthusiastic description of Hagerstown's attractions most commendable. By all means, make your arrangements to go to Hagerstown and spend a week, for no three days will exhaust its resources. Don't be afraid of swooping down on the stricken hamlet and eating the inhabitants out of house and home. Things to eat are grown in that country, and, at the worst, we can go out foraging.

> "Fair as a garden of the Lord,
> To the eyes of the famished wheelmen horde."

CYCLISTS' UNION OF LONG ISLAND.

CYCLISTS' UNION NOTICE.

All members of the Cyclists' Union intending to compete for the Schwalbach Mileage Medal, as per his offer published in THE WHEEL of April 19, should send their mileage at the end of each month to M. L. Bridgman, President C. U. of L. I., 1,255 Bedford Avenue, Brooklyn, instead of Mr. Austin, as previously stated.

[Signed] BERT M. COLE, Secretary.

The above medal is to be of gold, suitably inscribed, and given for the greatest mileage from April 1, 1889 to April 1, 1890. For the benefit of possible readers not receiving THE WHEEL of April 10, we reproduce the conditions upon which the medal must be won, as follows:

"All distances to be made on the road, it being understood that this offer is made in promotion of touring. Reports of each month's mileage to be handed the President of the Cyclists' Union on or about the first of each succeeding month, after being duly checked and authenticated by officers of the club to which the member may belong, and total mileage for the season to be sworn to before a notary. Reports from members not of any regular organized club to be duly authenticated to the satisfaction of the Executive Committee of the Union, and total mileage sworn to before a notary. In no case is any person's mileage at any time during the twelve months to be made known by you to others, competing or not competing. In the case of regularly organized clubs, your Executive Committee may waive the condition requiring a member to confirm his total mileage before a notary."

KARL KRON AND THE WASHINGTON SQUARE ARCH.

In each daily issue of the *Commercial Advertiser* of last week, May 13 to May 18, Karl Kron printed a letter in support of the committee who are engaged in raising a popular subscription of $150,000 for the erection of a Centennial Memorial Arch in his own beloved Washington Square. The series seems likely to be continued through this week also, judging by his seventh letter in Monday's paper. He writes to us as follows: "I want THE WHEEL to freely advertise the fact that the Society of Amateur Photographers are to give an interesting stereopticon exhibition of views of the Centennial parade, at Chickering Hall, May 28, all the profits going to the Arch fund. I shall be glad to have any reader of "X. M. Miles" who feels kindly towards the Square, because of the praises of it which I have printed there, buy a ticket to the show, and thus help build the arch. If he is liberal enough to help it by a dollar or two, the money may be sent to the treasurer, W. R. Stewart, 54 William Street.

New York, May 20. KARL KRON."

In the 1-mile handicap bicycle race at College City of N. Y. Sports, May 11, F. P. Wier, '93, 20 yards, defeated A. H. Zimmermann, '91, scratch, in 3m. 11 3-5s.

Mr. J. W. Bate, a member of the Prospect Harriers, and well known to many Brooklyn wheelmen, will open a cycle agency on June 1, at 465 Flatbush Avenue, Brooklyn, a few minutes walk from the Plaza entrance of Prospect Park. He will handle a general line of wheels, and rent, repair and store. He is also special agent for Graff's seamless bicycle shoes.

ST. LOUIS.

It is sincerely to be regretted that the efforts of Bob Garden to open the Pullman road race to St. Louis riders has failed. The fault is not his; he did all in his power to get our men in and they fully appreciate the enterprise and good feeling he has displayed. The facts in connection with the matter are these: He wrote down here some time ago, inviting the St. Louis men to go in, and in response to that invitation eight entries were sent up last week. On receipt of them, Garden wrote back that he regretted he could not accept so many; that the Chicago riders on scratch only numbered three, and they objected to more than that number starting with them. Indeed, they protested against any outsiders being allowed to enter, but Garden said he would accept four of our men, without further argument, if that would be satisfactory. He said further that the committee in charge of the race had decided that all the St. Louis entries must start from scratch. Of course, that was understood. Any other disposition of the St. Louis riders would be manifestly absurd. The mere idea of St. Louis road riders accepting a handicap from Chicago riders is calculated to cause a broad smile from any one who is posted as to their relative merits on the road. Well, the upshot of it all was that the St. Louis men resented the gratuitous insult conveyed in the refusal of the Chicago men to allow themselves to be outnumbered at the scratch. That protest implied, if it did not express the fear that the St. Louis men might use their surplus to the disadvantage or detriment of the three little Chicago men, and as we could not submit to any such imputation as that and retain our self respect, the entries were all withdrawn. Garden then agreed to let all our men in, but they did not think they could consistently enter in the face of the protests which the Chicago men had made, and the fact that the entries had first been refused. We only know Garden down here by reputation, but he has shown himself to be built on the broad gauge plan, and it is a pity that he cannot be located at St. Louis, where men of that stamp are more thoroughly appreciated than they appear to be in the village on the lake. This is the third attempt the St. Louis men have made to get in the Pullman road race, and it is safe to say it will be the last.

By the time this letter reaches you the first of the Stone-Lumsden races will have been decided. Stone is having hard luck with his training on account of the bad weather and it is doubtful if he will acquire sufficient familiarity with the track to do his best work. Besides he has been disappointed in not getting the wheel he wanted and he will be badly handicapped on that account. Under these circumstances his chances look slim and he will not carry much St. Louis money. A party including Stone, Holm, Brewster, Child, Jordan and others, will go up Friday night to see the race and visit Sam Miles' show.

The grading of the new track is all finished and the surface will be put on at once. If the weather is favorable the track ought to be finished for the three-mile event on the 25th inst. If not, the fair-ground board track will be used.

The cycle club to the number of eighteen went to Ballwin last Saturday night, and were held there all day Sunday by a fierce rain storm which lasted the entire day. They got back about 7 P.M. wet and bedraggled but full of enthusiasm. Captain Sanders is making a record with this club and the men under him are doing great work this season. It is a bicycle club with all that the term implies.

A. L. Jordan, late repairer for Simmon's Hardware Co. and L. H. Frost, at one time Captain of the Chelsea club, have taken the Pope agency and are located at 1320 Washington Avenue. The style of the firm will be A. L. Jordan & Co., and they ought to be able to do their share of business, notwithstanding their late start.

The many St. Louis friends of L. J. Berger will be glad to hear of his continued good fortune. He sailed on the "City of Paris" from New York the 15th inst., for England along with Geo. M. Pullman, Minister Lincoln and other distinguished men. We are compensated for his temporary absence by the return of Captain Hilderbrand, who will probably land on the 24th.

ITHURIEL.

SAN FRANCISCO.

The local riders were surprised and pained to learn of the death of Mr. Stephen Terry in this city. They did not know he was here, or they would have been pleased to render him any assistance in their power.

Eastern riders visiting this coast should come provided with credentials, such as their League card or a letter from their club Secretary.

The members of the Bay City Wheelmen, whose club-rooms are at 230 Van Ness Ave., are also pleased to show visitors points of interest in this vicinity. Intending tourists please note.

Mrs. Mohrig, the wife of our Chief Consul, accompanied the Bay City Wheelmen on their run to San Mateo last Sunday. It was a treat to see how gracefully she rode. Her mount was a forty-five pound "Cyclo" bicycle geared to fifty inches.

R. M. Welch, J. J. Bliss and H. W. Burmester, of the Bay City Wheelmen, made the trip to San Jose and return last Sunday. The distance ridden was about 105 miles, over our regular "century run" course. The start was made at 5 A.M., in a light rain, which interfered very much with the riders. The first stop was at Redwood City, twenty-five miles, for breakfast, or rather for their second breakfast. A wind from the south began to make its presence felt after they left Redwood, and they had to push against it to San Jose, which city was reached at 11:20, ten minutes ahead of the schedule time. After a substantial dinner the return journey was commenced, when it was found that the wind had again shifted and now blew quite strongly from the north. San Francisco was reached at 8 o'clock. The roads were in fine order, and were it not for the rain in the morning and the head winds encountered during the day, the trip would have been quite enjoyable.

On the same day the Bay City Wheelmen had their first picnic run of the season. Thirty members rode to San Mateo, twenty miles from this city. It was raining when the members left the city, which accounts for the small attendance. When the picnic ground was reached the day had cleared up and the boys had a fine swim.

On July 4 Stockton will hold another race meet, and the club hopes to make it as great a success as the one of last July.

Yours, CALIFORNIA.

TACOMA, WASHINGTON.

My telegram of the 12th inst. apprised you of the result of the twenty-mile road race for the championship of Washington Territory. As I predicted, Halsted, formerly of New York City, won, with Thompson a close second. Notwithstanding the fact that cycling is still in its infancy throughout Washington, the interest manifested by the public in the contest was very great. For the past week mystery surrounded the doings of those competing, and finally public favor switched from Halsted and Prince Wells to W. H. H. Kean. Many bets were made, mostly in favor of Kean. But, unfortunately, his hand sustained an ugly bruise several days ago, which troubled him through the race. Saturday could not have been more propitious, and all remarked upon the advantages enjoyed by the competitors. Many of the spectators were disappointed to learn that Prince Wells would not ride. The Seattle boys would not enter for the same reason—lack of practice—so that, instead of ten entries only five appeared. The start was made at 3.47 P.M., the spectators all making suggestions to their respective favorites as to pace, etc.

The quintette dashed off at a lively rate amid the cheers of spectators and waving of handkerchiefs by young ladies. Many of the latter thought Halsted—"dear boy"—had lost the race because he took last place in the procession.

The first mile was ridden in 3m. 12s., with Kean in the lead, closely followed by McCoy, Thompson, Halsted and Wilson. These positions were maintained to the five-mile post. Time, 18m. 5s. The ride to the starting point was against the wind, which retarded progress. At the seven-mile post Wilson's wheel tightened in the bearings and he was forced to quit. McCoy reached the eight-mile post one-quarter mile ahead of the field, which lead he kept to the turning post, ten miles. As he rode over the small hill three-quarters of a mile from the stake, a yell went up, and his friends went wild with excitement. Thompson was next to appear, and although his first race, he showed excellent judgment by not spurting down the homestretch. The coaching of Halsted during the entire race kept Thompson down to a uniform speed and benefited him materially. Some few seconds after Thompson, Kean and Halsted dashed over side by side, fully a quarter of a mile behind McCoy. Again a loud cheer went up, for these two were favorites.

Bets of $100 to $80 on Halsted found no takers. Kean's left hand troubled him considerably, but he made a good showing as he spurted down the stretch, using only his right hand. Halsted followed him closely, and not caring to take undue advantage, he also used but one hand, to the great amusement of the spectators. McCoy finished the 10 miles in 41m., and made a quick turn. Thompson slowed up to take a drink and was again away before Kean and Halsted reached the stake. The former did not stop, thinking it a bad practice to drink while racing. I suppose Halsted has had enough experience on the race-path to realize the danger of drinking ice-cold water. His only excuse is the fact that the water was brought to the turn by two young ladies, who seemed particularly interested in his success. By actual timing he lost just two minutes, making McCoy's lead three minutes. But the inspiration infused in him evidently gave strength, for Kean was soon overtaken and dropped in the rear. Then Thompson was caught, and the two gradually gained on McCoy, not catching him till the fifteen mile turn had been made. From this point to the finish the three kept close together, each watching the other. The pace was hot through the sandy part of the road and up the hill, and the many spectators yelled themselves hoarse. The people at the finishing post became excited as the time drew near for the riders to appear, and one and all eagerly gazed in that direction. They were not long held in suspense, for suddenly McCoy's black cap and black and white suit were recognized, with Thompson close on his little wheel. But "Where is Halsted?" was asked by his friends. Many thought he had taken a header.

As the riders reached the hard road and the dust settled, Halstead was seen immediately behind Thompson. It was anybody's race, and only a half mile from the finish. Clerk of the Course Mr. Bast successfully kept the homestretch clear, and Prince Wells was everywhere yelling and shouting to the people to keep back. At the half-mile post Halsted fooled the boys, for they expected he would not spurt until he reached the quarter pole.

As McCoy and Thompson rode around the *outer* edge of a large puddle, Haldstead dashed *through* the middle of it, got the inside of the road, and commenced his spurt. Thompson was game to the end, and drew up alongside Halsted 300 yards from home and stuck there a few seconds. At this juncture the large crowd went crazy, and with difficulty were kept off the road. Halsted increased his speed and pulled away, winning the race in 1h. 26m.; Thompson second, in 1h. 26m. 15s.; McCoy third, in 1h. 26m. 30s.; Kean fourth, in 1h. 28m.

Many Eastern people were present, and they all said a finer race could not have been run. Halsted and Wells, who have before competed in road races, were surprised when the time was announced, for they thought 1.30 could not be broken. The riders were warmly congratulated, and from appearances, I will guarantee that many hearts were beating more rapidly than usual as the victor rushed from one carriage to another to exchange a few words.

During the interval between the start and finish some impromptu races were run off, on both bicycles and horseback, and in this manner the spectators kept interested.

Some of the boys are dissatisfied with the result, and a competition will probably be on the tapis for July 4. Many of the wheelmen think Thompson purposely slipped his pedal when spurting down the homestretch so he would not beat Halstead, and this fact has strengthened their opinion that the latter cannot ride a short race. It is rumored that Prince Wells will challenge Halsted to compete with him in three races, distances to be one-quarter mile, one mile and two miles.

After the finish a man was heard to say that *his* bet was off, for he had positive proof that Halsted is a professional. In vindication, Halstead referred to the League official handicapper as to his amateur status, and also volunteered the information that if he *were* a professional the bet would not be affected, as the L. A. W. claims no jurisdiction over road races. [Mr. Halsted's amateur standing is A 1 and has never been questioned.—ED.]

On May 24th the boys intend taking a trip to Victoria, B. C., to participate in the celebration of the Queen's Birthday.

SNOHOMISH.

May 13, 1889.

The Manhattan Bicycle Club held an enjoyable reception at its club house last Friday evening. A party of young ladies, friends of the members, decorated the house a few evenings before in a most artistic and admirable manner.

BUFFALO.

The Decoration Day runs of the clubs have been decided upon. The Ramblers will go to Batavia, the Zig-Zags likewise, and the Buffalos will have their "century run" from Erie.

The arrangements of the Buffalos for their "century" are as follows: Leave Buffalo at 7 P.M. on the night of the 29th on the Empire State, of the Lake Superior Transit Line. Breakfast will be taken aboard the boat, and the start made from Erie at 6 A.M. The first stop will be made at Westfield, thirty miles from Erie. Fredonia, twenty miles further on, will be the next resting place, and here a group picture of the riders will be taken. At Angola dinner will be had, and then will commence the "scorching" part of the run to Buffalo. It is not the intention of the club to make this a race, but merely an enjoyable trip, and to see how many riders can be brought through. Thirty-one have thus far signified their intention of making the run.

The uniform question has been disposed of by two of the clubs. The Ramblers have adopted black and the Buffalos will retain their present blue. The Women's Wheel Club has not as yet decided this vexatious question, but at the next meeting a choice will be made.

The Zig-Zags are settled in their club-house at the Circle, and will soon give a reception to local wheelmen.

The Ramblers will be met at Batavia on Decoration Day by the Genesee Club, of Rochester.

The "goat" is not in favor as a road wheel in these parts. A party of Ramblers went to Aurora last week, and among them were four safety riders. Three of them returned to the city by train.

The action of the passenger agents of the trunk lines in New York on May 9 is at present a matter of much concern among local wheelmen, and Chief Consul Bull has issued a circular to the local consuls of the State, urging them to write from their respective districts to the heads of the roads patronized by them, protesting against this action.

At the last regular meeting of the Women's Wheel Club six new members were admitted. The fair sex have got the craze, and ladies' bicycles are a common sight on our streets.

ZO.

NEWARK.

The smoker of the Atalanta Wheelmen on the 14th, was a decided success, owing to the untiring efforts of the committee, Messrs. Drabble and Eichhorn. Many thanks to them.

Among the other prizes for the 25-mile race at Irvington, May 30, is a handsome bicycle lamp, from Howard A. Smith & Co.

On last Saturday afternoon (18th), fifteen members of the Atalanta wheelmen started for Rutherford, leaving the club-house at 5:30. At Avondale they were met by Captain Dean, of the Rutherford Field Club, and taken around town until finally the R. F. C. House was reached. There the boys amused themselves with billiards and pool until 9 o'clock, when supper was served, and at 10 o'clock they started for home. A *walk* of *two* miles (over fences and through ditches) brought us to a comparatively good road. The "dismiss" was blown at 11:30, and the boys started on "Home, Sweet Home."

SPARK.

"JACK" ON AMERICA.

In that part of *Wheeling* devoted to "Scientific Wheeling" (rather a misnomer, is it not?) "Jack," under the caption of "A Few Notes from America," is allowed to air his views as a quondam Englishman. We reproduce parts that we think will be of interest to our readers:

The safety bicycle seems to have taken on the American cyclist's mind about the same kind of hold which it took in England some years ago. For every ordinary bicycle I saw in the Central Park, New York, the other day, I noticed at least two safeties, the majority of them being Victors or Columbias, though the Swift, Ivel, Premier and Demon, of English manufacture, were noticed. The Rational, which is bound to be a popular mount in America in a year or two, is as yet only discussed with, I must say, a good deal of favor. Experienced riders have found that machines with as few screws and parts possible are the only ones which can be expected to stand long usage or give anything like satisfaction on this continent.

The surface of the roads in Central Park are on an average as good as anything to be found in England, though some wofully "hummocky" roads are to be found just outside the park. Nickel-plating is much more in vogue here than in England, where the cycle has gradually become less of a machine for amusement than for practical use. The Citizens' Bicycle Club is reputed to be the best New York club, and certainly contains some gentlemen who are in every way creditable to the sport. The club-house is well appointed at 26 West Sixty Street, in the fashionable quarter of New York, and has every convenience in the way of dressing-rooms, hot or cold shower baths, lockers and wheel rooms, while a colored janitor is at the beck and call of the members of the club. The house is well heated, and one can ride right to the door from the park. In fact, it has every convenience requisite to the enjoyment of the sport around New York (still it does not come up to the Anchor at Ripley). It is the rule in New York to leave all cycling togs, &c., at the club-house and come down on the elevated roads or street cars in a business suit, which is doffed at the club-house and the abbreviated garments of cycling donned. In America knee trousers or knickerbockers are only worn by bicyclists or baseball players, by pedestrians and shooting men very seldom.

The tricycle has gone out of favor very much since the safety has come in, and it is even whispered that ladies are going to ride the safety quite extensively over here. Geo. R. Bidwell has opened a riding school where ladies may learn safety riding in privacy, far from the gaze of the impertinent gamist or the insolent street cad.

J. PURVIS-BRUCE.

The latest form of bore in cycling is the reporter of the lay paper, who calls at the office, informs you he is now going to do the cycling for the *Daily Citizen* or whatever, and wants you to fill him up.

CALIFORNIA'S L. A. W. MEET.

The programme gotten out by the California League Division is at hand, and a remarkably neat-looking piece of work it is, one that would do credit every way to the national organization itself. If any comparison is to be made, in style and shape it reminds us slightly of the programme issued for the League meet at St. Louis. Men and maidens ride various types of ordinaries and safeties on the outside pages, and California's seal and the familiar L. A. W. badge of that State, surmounted by the grizzly bear, are also there.

The meet is held at Los Angeles, May 30, and events, briefly summarized, are as follows:

Parade on Thursday morning at 10 o'clock over the asphaltum streets.

Ten different clubs, besides the Division officers and the "great unattached" will take part.

Races Thursday afternoon at Agricultural Park, called at 2 o'clock sharp.

These events will be run off One-mile novice; 1-mile open, 3:15 class; 1-mile State championship; ½-mile dash, open; ½-mile dash, open; 1-mile dash, boys under 18; 3-mile national championship; 5-miles, open; 1-mile, safety; 1-mile, open.

The prize in the 5-mile is a special star, winner's choice, style and finish.

On Friday, May 31, a run through the famed San Gabriel valley will be made, covering some 25 miles.

Saturday, June 1, includes a hill-climbing contest at 10 a. m. The hills selected are on Olive Street and Second Street At 2 o'clock in the afternoon a run to Cahuenga Pass will be made. The scenery here is said to be magnificent.

Sunday, June 2, and the final day, a visit to "Santa Monica-by-the-Sea" is planned, where all that wish can test the coldness of the Pacific's waters. We predict a large attendance and a thoroughly enjoyable time. The principal officers of the State Division are: C. C. Edwin Mohrig, San Francisco; V. C. J. Phil Percival, Los Angeles; Sec.-Treasurer Alex. S. Ireland, San Francisco.

SPRING MEET OF MASS. DIVISION L. A. W. AT SQUANTUM.

The following circular has been issued by the committee in charge of arrangements:

"The spring meet of the Division will be held on June 17, at Squantum.

Through the courtesy of President Hodges and Paul Butler, of the Boston Bicycle Club, the "old Squantum estate" has been placed at our disposal.

The programme as now contemplated is as follows: Assemble in Copley square at 10 A. M., leaving at 10:30; a run of seven miles to Squantum, where racing, boating, bathing, bowling and ball playing can be indulged in.

Two races will be run and two medals will be given for prizes. Captains of clubs are requested to call runs for the day in accordance with this programme. All wheelmen are invited. Further details will be given prior to June 17."

The K. of P.'s will hold a celebration at Seymour, Ind., June 6, and among the attractions will be a five mile bicycle race for medals to the value of $100. Make entries to Mr John A. Ross, Seymour, Ind., who will furnish any information concerning the race.

The Kentucky Division of the L. A. W. will hold the regular annual meeting of this division at Danville, Ky., June 10. There will be no races, but a short tour will be inaugurated there, taking the route toward High Bridge. All L. A. W. members are earnestly requested to be present.

The Massachusetts L. A. W. Division's summer meet will be held at Cottage City the second week in August.

Col. Pope will own a steam yacht this summer. It is understood that he will give a few outings to members of the Legislature, hoping to secure their votes in favor of the recently defeated bill for the improvement of Massachusetts roads.

MARYLAND.

The Frederick Bicycle Club was recently organized at Frederick, Md., with eighteen active members. Mr. W. Levy Mantz was elected President, and in a neat speech of acceptance outlined the object of the club, which he stated was to advance the interest of cycling in that community, which by reason of its magnificent roads and scenery is so well adapted for riding. John A. Kennedy was elected Secretary and Treasurer. The election of a Captain, etc., was deferred till the next meeting.

At a meeting of the Board of Trade at Hagerstown recently, one hundred and twenty-five dollars was appropriated to advertise the city. Fifty dollars was donated to the bicycle club to be applied to the expenses attending the national meet in July.

BAY RIDGE.

The grand stand at Washington Park, Brooklyn, was destroyed by fire on Sunday night. The fire consumed J. W. Miller's bicycle, which was stored in the structure.

AMERICANS ABROAD.

From a neatly-printed pamphlet just at hand containing the roll-call, itinerary, and a few remarks by the manager of the tour, we glean that twenty-nine wheelmen were to leave Boston on May 18, by steamer Cephalonia, and, beginning May 27, at Cork, Ireland, from that time on do considerable wheeling, finishing up July 30 at Rotterdam, from whence the members of the party can travel homeward or in any direction that inclination moves them. Though we note no Boston or New York riders taking part, yet the representation of this country is pretty widely scattered, ten different States being represented. Pennsylvania claims seven, while Maine follows closely with six; Illinois sends four, Ohio three, New York, New Jersey and Massachusetts, two each, while Connecticut, Michigan and Missouri have but one. On arriving in England the party will be under direction of Mr. Joseph Pennell, the well-known American artist, as regards routes taken. Mr. Pennell's long residence abroad renders him specially fitted for this important position, and a thorough knowledge of two or three European languages will not come amiss. Eight days will be spent in Ireland, mostly between Cork and Dublin. At Dublin train will be taken to Chester, England, and the sixteen days following devoted to that country. Six of these will be spent in London, or just enough to get a very, very faint idea of the immensity of that city. From Newhaven steamer will be taken to Dieppe, and twelve days in France follow. As eight of these all-too-few days are spent in Paris, it is safe to conclude that the wheelmen's impressions of France as a country will be a little vague. Possibly clearer on the subject of the way Paris *cafés* and *cochers* know how to charge the "strangers within their gates." Now come ten days in Switzerland, to our mind the most fascinating part of the whole tour. Ten days more in Germany brings the party to Cologne, where steamer is taken to Rotterdam.

This whole tour has been carefully laid out with a view of getting the most enjoyment possible from the time spent and money expended, and the manager acknowledges much obligation to the C. T. C. for information received. Stops will be made at hotels and inns recommended by that organization, and many courtesies are promised from foreign wheelmen and cycling clubs. A prominent English wheelman, Mr. A. J. Wilson, will join the party at London. Mr. Wilson is well known to all readers of cycling literature under the *nom de plume* of "Faed," and is one of the earliest and most enthusiastic wheelmen in England.

Regarding the makes of machines that will carry the party, it seems the English makers have secured the lead, the "Quadrant" Safety being selected by no less than seventeen out of the thirty. Singer & Co. follow with four, while the Pope Mfg. Co. and Overman Wheel Co. have each two. Four of the party have not yet made choice of a mount. The preponderance of "Quadrants" would seem to be due to their extensive luggage carrying capacity, and the fact that this company contracted to deliver wheels at Cork in ridable shape every way for £19 or $95, nearly. As a first-class Safety will bring about that in this country, even if second-hand, the investment cannot be a losing one. The "Few Remarks," which cover four or five small brevier pages, are the best part of the pamphlet to our mind, and should be cut out and pasted in the hats of all tourists at home or abroad. Space permits of quoting but a sentence or two, but there is food for reflection in those: "We are the largest party of Americans to traverse Europe a-wheel, and, whether we wish it or not, our movements will be noted, and the impression we create will be made public. We claim to be gentlemen. We shall never have a better chance to prove it."

This rather extensive comment will be explained by the fact that THE WHEEL will be represented among the party, and our readers can be sure of correct and interesting accounts of the party's haps and mishaps.

If arrangements for a good time generally, do not fall through, the American tourists have much in store. At Cork, Dungarvan, Waterford and Dublin, in Ireland alone, they are to be entertained by different clubs. In England the Birchfield Club at Birmingham, the Stanley C. C. in London, and the Ripley Road Club, will take a hand at it. A strong effort will be made to unfold the joys of a Ripley Sunday to them, and a cyclist's service will be attended in the afternoon. Dyspepsia would seem to be all the tourists can suffer from, but it will be in a good cause.

THE PROPOSED TENNESSEE TOUR.

For some time past a tour of League members in this State has been talked over, and the plans now begin to assume shape. June 10th, or the day after the Annual Division, L. A. W., Meet at Nashville, is set for the day, and the route outlined as follows: First day, Nashville to Shelbyville, via Nolensville and Eaglesville; Second day, Shelbyville to Lynchburg, via Fayetteville; Third day, Lynchburg to Murfreesboro; Fourth day, Murfreesboro to Nashville, via Lebanon. This gives an average of 50 miles per day, and is intended to suit the capacities of both young riders and veterans. League members only are wished on the tour, and outsiders applying will be respectfully referred to the Membership Committee of that body. The tourists from Columbus, Ga., of whom our Macon correspondent spoke last week, will reach Nashville between June 12th and 20th. It is hoped they will be induced to join the Tennessee boys on their tour. At least, they will be heartily welcomed and entertained by the Nashville boys, and a chance given them to compare Tennessee and Georgia roads.

THE ATALANTA "SMOKER."

The elegant new quarters of the Atalanta Wheelmen, on Clark Street, were formally opened on Tuesday, the 14th, with a smoker. The building was artistically decorated with Japanese lanterns, flags and bunting, lending a gala-like appearance to the scene. The large gymnasium room was used for dancing and lunch, while smaller ones were used as wardrobe and billiard rooms. The house is admirably adapted to the purposes of the club, as the rooms are separated by sliding partitions, and can all be thrown into one large room.

Nearly two hundred guests were present to help the Atalantas "warm" their new house. As the different ones flit past, dancing the polka, waltz, or quadrille, we notice in the crowd of faces, Messrs Brown, Pennell and Bonnett, of the Elizabeth Wheelmen; Capt. Pierson and other Bloomfield Cyclers; Llewellyn Johnson and Amzi Dodd, Orange Wanderers; Atwater, Kirkpatrick and Nichols, Essex Bi. Club; Capt. Dean and others from the Rutherford Field Club, while the H. Co. Wheelmen were represented by Messrs. Earl, Eldridge, Edge, Benedict, Muller, Demmet, Allen, Robertson, Menseles, Tuthill and McLaughlin, commanded by Capt. Day.

The old N. J. Wheelmen were also well represented.

Capt. Wm. A. Drabble and Francis W. Eichhorn, of the Atalantas, acted as a reception committee, and judging from appearances, they did their work well.

Several violin solos were rendered by Mr. Milton H. Gruet, the well-known violinist, of Newark. Banjo music by Messrs. Van Ness, Goldie, Miller and McVicar, is not to be passed by without mention. "Stag" dances of every description were kept up until a late hour, and finally ended by a Rah!-Rah!-Rah! Ata-lan-ta! Sis-Boom-Ah! A-t-a-l-a-n-t-a Zip! and the Atalanta Wheelmen's smoker was a thing of the past.

SPARK.

TOO GOOD TO BE GIVEN UP.

The New York *Herald* again demonstrates in a recent editorial that its support can be safely counted on in behalf of any sensible agitation, even in matters of dress reform for men, as follows:

We are glad to notice that our numerous contemporaries are keenly interested in the subject of dress reform for the masculine gender.

Some of them treat the matter of knee breeches lightly and with good-natured badinage, but it is really one of the most serious topics of the time.

Nothing makes or unmakes a man, so far as appearance is concerned, so much as trousers. Their shape changes every year or two, but it is simply a change from the awful to the horrible. A sensitive artist cannot paint a full length portrait without going into something like delirium tremens over these bifurcated monstrosities.

A few years ago trousers were made to fit like a glove, and the man of fashion had to be melted every morning and poured into them. Of course he looked like a beer barrel with two pump handles for legs. Then again, at the Loan Exhibition, there is a picture of Lafayette which imperils one's mental equilibrium. His trousers are wide at the hips, evidently puffed out by means of some infernal contrivance on the inside. Then they taper rapidly, like an inverted funnel, and when they reach the ankles are only a span wide. Poor Lafayette has a mournful expression of face, as though he really couldn't stand it much longer.

Knee breeches, on the other hand, are the artistic ideal of manly vestments. They give free play to the limbs, are picturesque, needn't be turned up on a muddy day, and add dignity to the wearer.

The moment the human race gets over the busy season and has a chance to view its proportions in a mirror, trousers will be abandoned forever and knee breeches will have their day.

WHERE ARE YOU SAFE?

Some riders say upon the high wheel,
And others say upon the low,
The former do the safest feel.
While the latter do also.
Now which is safest, can you tell?
The question put to any man,
I've ridden both and off both fell,
To me they're similar and no shenanegan.

"OLD HANKEY PANKEY."

THE LEAGUE HOTEL.

In the *American Athlete* of May 10 "Verex" takes a pessimistic view of the League hotel. As an old and enthusiastic wheelman, his remarks are entitled to consideration, and, if not overdrawn, they plainly show that a mistake is being made somewhere. He says:

"Speaking about hotels, is there a chestnut before wheelmen with a hollower interior than the so-called League hotel? I sometimes laugh when I see some unsophisticated youth pull out his membership card to secure a reduction, only to be informed that he must, to get a reduced rate, induce somebody to share his bed with him and take up with the worst accommodations in the house. Well-posted riders have little to say about the League when registering, and generally avoid the hotel that seeks their patronage under the guise of cheapness."

From our own personal experience, we fear there is much truth in the above, and would offer a suggestion. Monopoly of any one class of travelers is a good thing for the hotel having the monopoly, if not for the travelers. Why not let the chief consul of each Division agree, in consideration of a yearly sum—perhaps a small one—paid to the L. A. W. Division, to use all practicable influence for the hotel, recommending all League tourists to stop there and assuring them of good accommodations and courteous treatment at regular rates? In this way each Division member would secure an indirect benefit, and not be subjected to snubs or sent to the top floor back when he asks for League rates. If our patronage as League men is worth having, it is worth paying for in one or the other way.

COULD THIS BE MALTBY?

The champion innocent is a Surrey Hills man, who came along by Moore Park and found a cyclist emulating the famous feat of Boyle; and though he did not stand still on his machine for two hours, he did manage to keep it stationary for several minutes. The passer-by paused a moment and then said, sympathizingly: "Won't she go, Mister?" "No," said the cyclist gravely, "can't get her along!" The sympathizing man said: "Hold on, I'll shove ver," and he did so; but a judicious pressure on the up pedal still kept her fixed. "Oh, she *must* go somehow!" and he shoved real hard. For some seconds the bicycle did not budge, until the rider, unable to stand the strain longer, the whole three went over kerslop. The sympathizing man picked himself up saying, "Ah, that machine'll never go again, Mister. She's clean worn out." And as he brushed his hat and went off, he meditatively remarked: "Well; I *never* seed one so stiff as that!"—*Australian Cyclist.*

PECULIAR IDEAS.

A suit recently brought in the Superior Court, at New Bedford, Mass., is one of peculiar interest to cyclists all over the country. Not so much from the fact that the plaintiff, J. A. Beauvis, brings suit against J. G. Bradford for frightening his horses, so they ran away, by taking a header in front of them, but from the most extraordinary claim of the plaintiff's lawyer that the defendant *had no right* to take a header. Unless the jury is of less than common intelligence, the suit's outcome is easy to foresee. But, what of the attorney that upholds such a stupid idea? If a wheelman, already, he of course knows better. If not, he should proceed to experiment, and we predict an entire change of heart after one afternoon's wrestling with an "Ordinary." Of what use is the noble sport of cycling, deprived of the inalienable right of all wheelmen to take headers? We commend "An Idyl," as published in WHEEL of May 10th, to the plaintiff's lawyer.

LANTERN PARADE, AT FLINT, MICH.

The lantern parade of the Flint Wheelmen last night was a unique spectacle, and participated in by about thirty members and friends of the club, and four lady cyclers. For several days the wheelmen have been at work decorating their machines, which last night were gorgeous with bunting of different colors. Chinese and Japanese lanterns of many colors almost hid from view many of the riders, as they passed along the streets amid a blaze of light.

The paraders formed at the Court-house, proceeding north on Saginaw Street around the park, under command of Captain Ben. Kellerman, and south on the same street to the corner of First and Saginaw Streets, where they were dismissed. The spectacle was a delightful one, and witnessed by large crowds along the street.

R. W. S.

WHEEL GOSSIP.

George R. Bidwell will referee the road race.

The Racing Board have issued copies of the racing rules in neat pamphlet form.

Kingsland, of Baltimore, had an ugly fall in the Chicago races, and was badly injured internally.

Pleasure runs to places near Louisville seem to be popular and well attended, with the usual gustatory accompaniment.

Secretary Hack, of the Minneapolis Baseball Club, is to build a bicycle track in that city, directly in the rear of the West Hotel, and in the heart of the city.

The Hudson Co. Wheelmen were entertained by the Elizabeth Wheelmen May 15, at their Club-house, on East Broad Street, and a "smoker" enjoyed.

Some members of the *Bicycling News* staff have been "trying" the Rudge Triplet—the three seated machine credited with a mile in 2m. 18 1-5s.—and pronounce a most favorable verdict.

The opening of P. A. Bernard's hotel and restaurant at Kingsbridge, 225th Street, takes place on Wednesday, May 22. Mr. Bernard has always been most attentive to the wants of wheelmen.

The Long Island Wheelmen admitted seven new members at its last monthly meeting. The club has kindly given the use of its rooms to the Ladies' Cycling Club to hold their monthly meetings.

The Pennsylvania Club has called runs for May 19, 26 and Decoration Day. Willow Grove and Bristol being destined points on the first two dates mentioned, and route of run on the 30th to be announced later.

The first century run in New York of this year was made by Messrs. Scudder and Gruman, of the Huntington Bicycle Club, on Monday, May 13, leaving Huntington at 4 o'clock A. M. and returning at 7 P. M., after covering 110 miles.

The Hudson County Wheelmen are endeavoring to have the opening 15 miles road race between members of cycling New Jersey clubs on Decoration Day. The Irvington-Millburn course has been selected, if arrangements are completed in time.

The Providence *Sunday Journal* asks: "Where is Karl Kron nowadays?" We commend to the *Journal's* perusal a short paragraph appearing from Karl Kron's typewriter in another column, which shows that he is by no means in a state of coma.

The following officers were elected at the annual meeting of the St. John's (Mich.) Bicycle Club: President, J. C. Hicks; Vice-President, E. C. Whetstone; Secretary-Treasurer, H. H. Fitzgerald; Captain, R. G. Steele; First Lieutenant, H. Coleman.

Messrs. A. C. and W. D. Banker, of Pittsburg, Pa., will shortly go into training, and it is rumored they will try their speed on the tandem safety on English soil against English riders. Mr. A. C. Banker will wear the colors of the Brooklyn and Manhattan Bicycle Clubs.

Fred A. Horn, aged fifteen, and John M. Hamden, aged sixteen, rode from Newburyport to Boston and return a week ago Saturday, a distance of 100 miles in fourteen hours. They are undoubtedly the youngest pair that ever took the trip, and the performance was most creditable.

Some two hundred riders are expected to leave Newark at 4 A. M. June 8, to take part in the century run to Philadelphia. Ordinary club captains that have vainly tried to get even five or ten riders out at that unearthly hour will smile cynically to themselves when they read this statement.

It ill becomes "Hawkshaw" to send up his little sneer about the cycling press. If the cycling press is inaccurate, as "Hawkshaw" states, he has been one of its shining lights for several years, and has romanced as much in his time and under different *nom de plumes* as all the rest of us put together.

Hopkins Street, one of the steepest hills to be found in Eastern Massachusetts, the grade being one foot in six, was successfully climbed Tuesday afternoon by Mr. H. F. Campbell, on a 39-inch Star bicycle. This is the first time any wheelman has ever been able to ride the narrow track on this hill.

C. D. Vesey, at one time very prominent on the English path, has presented a silver cross and a silver cup—two of his trophies of the path—to Denmead Church. The cup is nearly twenty ounces in weight, and will be used as a chalice. The cross is two feet six inches high and will be used as an altar cross.

"Perseus" makes a suggestion in the last *Sporting Life* as follows: "Who will be the first to put a full nickeled safety on the market?" To which we would reply that a full nickeled Victor safety has been on exhibition for some time in Spalding's window. Come up, "Perseus," and win the 25-mile road race on Decoration Day if you would possess it.

In the contest at New Bedford last week, to decide who shall race twenty miles against a Taunton five, on Memorial Day, Hayland Smith was first in 1h. 13m., E. G. Rogers second, then A. M. Parlow, C. L. Dunham and Charles Chase. Dr. F. A. Wyman came in next to last man, in 1h. 20½m. It looks as if Taunton would be given a good tussle for the cup.

Messrs. E. F. Rogers, J. M. Weissman and T. Barron, of the Harvard Bicycle Club, have been suspended until June 1 by Chairman Davol, of the Racing Board, for "competing in a race at Harvard, on May 11, in which both ordinary and safety were ridden." This sentence is a mild one, but may be taken as an indication that the Racing Board and its Chairman are in earnest and mean to inforce the rules.

Bicycling News of May 11, under the heading "Cartoon No. 11," publishes an excellently printed sketch of the Manhattan Athletic Club House, on Fifth Avenue near Forty-fourth Street, as it will be some time in the future. With a Belgian block paving to ride over, we would criticise the number of wheels appearing in the foreground as a trifle questionable. Evidently Coventry printers do not know the New York pavement.

A grand union run of wheelmen of Boston and vicinity on May 19 was largely attended. At least 150 wheelmen, representing twelve different clubs, met at South Natick, the rallying point. After lunch at Bailey's the party was photographed by one of the Somerville Cycle Club. The Boston contingent started to return in a body, but scorching was indulged in, with the result that the party was widely divided on reaching the Reservoir.

A large bicycle club has been formed in Waco, Tex., and a track is to be built in the base-ball park. The club already numbers twenty-six, and the following officers have been chosen: President, C. H. Thacker; Vice-President, J. G. Slicer; Secretary-Treasurer, W. H. Corey; Captain, W. Parker; Lieutenant, E. S. Thorpe; Bugler, J. R. Davis. A constitution and by-laws will be drawn up and adopted, and the club shows every evidence of prosperity.

At the meeting of the Boston Press Cycle Club, Monday, three new members were admitted; a uniform of dark grey and colors of silver and pale blue were adopted. The membership is now 23. The first run will be to Wakefield, on Sunday, May 26, starting from Copley Square at 9:30 A. M. The executive committee, wishing to make this, the first run of the club, a success, earnestly request the co-operation and support of the members, and it is desired that all who possibly can will participate.

"The reports of our St. Louis and Chicago correspondents do not agree; one says the St. Louis entries have been withdrawn and the other announces the entries as having been accepted.—"[ED.] *Bicycling World of May 17.*

Entertaining "Jack," the Elwell tourists, *et al*, seems to be too much for the usually careful editors of our contemporary. Those left in doubt after comparing the St. Louis and Chicago letters can find the correct version in "Ithuriel's" letter in present issue of THE WHEEL.

George R. Bidwell has systematized his business so well that it is a pleasure to do business at his establishment. He has increased his force so that every attention is paid to visitors to his salesrooms. His storage customers find their wheels in excellent shape, and the lockers and bath rooms in excellent condition. The wheels which are specially used for renting are kept as well as any private wheel, and no accidents have been reported this season. Mr. Bidwell's tutors are teaching a number of ladies to ride, all safeties.

In the first of three races between Stone and Lumsden for championship of the West, Lumsden won in 3m. 45s., with twenty feet lead. For a mile, and at Cheltenham Beach track, this time is decidedly slow, and far below times made by novices on the same course, or at the Exposition Building the same day. Neither contestant could have exerted themselves much, and are probably waiting for the three and twenty-five mile races. The winner of one of the series is to receive a gold medal valued at $50, while he that wins two gets a medal worth $100.

A wheel at Mr. Bidwell's establishment which attracts much attention is Copeland's steam tricycle. The wheel is double seated, a square cushioned seat in front for a lady and a regular saddle seat just behind for the gentleman, who regulates the supply of power and steers. The engine is behind both riders; the fuel is oil, and eighty pounds of steam can be developed. The engine is neat; the steam is exhausted, and there is no puffing; in fact, the wheel glides along gently and attracts but little attention. A number of capitalists are being interested, and a stock company will probably be formed.

The annual meeting of the Eastern Road Club for the election of officers for the ensuing year and the transaction of other important business will be held on Monday, May 27, at 7:30 o'clock P. M., at the office of Dr. Kendall, 176 Tremont Street, Boston. At this meeting the subject of the further continuance of the club will be brought up. The executive committee deemed it advisable last year not to levy the annual assessment of $10; if the club is to continue, the assessment can no longer be deferred. Secretaries of clubs belonging to this organization are requested to see that their club is represented by at least two qualified members.

The White Cycle Co., of Westboro, Mass., take exception to "Jack's" statement that *Frank* White is the inventor of the White Flier Safety Bicycle. F-r-e-d-e-r-i-c-k White is the man, the same gentleman who was presented with a medal by the Boston Bicycle Club in 1885, for climbing Corey Hill on a tricycle of his own invention and construction, which weighed a cool hundred pounds. Mr. Frederick White though he did not weigh much more than the tricycle, and was not bigger than a New Jersey mosquito, rode the hill in six minutes and eleven seconds, while Williams, the coon-promateur, (who weighed about 170 and rode a tricycle weighing about 65 pounds) had to be almost lifted off his machine at the top of the hill.

At a recent meeting of Park Commissioners held in Chicago, it was decided that bicycle riding should be allowed on the Lake Shore Drive and Fullerton Avenue, in Lincoln Park, after 8 P. M., subject, of course, to the usual rules restricting use of bicycles and tricycles in the Park. Credit for obtaining this permission is largely due to Messrs Gerould and Whitney, of the Lincoln Cycling Club. For the benefit of possible visitors to Chicago we reproduce the regular rules in reference to use of wheels in Lincoln Park.

"Riders shall not be permitted to pass along the drives in a body; not more than two abreast.

No riding shall be permitted at a rate faster than six (6) miles per hour.

No bicycle will be allowed in the Park after 8 P. M. without a lantern."

(Does this mean a *lighted* one? Ed.)

RIVERSIDE NOTES.

The Menge brothers, of the Riverside Wheelmen, will ride a tandem safety this season, and as both are strong riders, they may be heard from later.

The R. W.'s will have a run to Fort Schuyler May 26, starting from the club-house, 158 W. 104th Street, at 8.30 sharp. An all-day run is called for Decoration Day through the Oranges, first taking in the road race at Irvington.

At the next regular meeting a second lieutenant will be elected. Three candidates are in the field.

Mr. J. W. Judge will represent the R. W. on the path this season.

E. A. POWERS, Captain.

New York State Division L.A.W.

OFFICIAL ORGAN.

OFFICERS FOR 1889.

Chief Consul, W. S. BULL, 754 Main Street, Buffalo, N. Y. Vice-Consul, M. L. BRIDGMAN, 1255 Bedford Avenue, Brooklyn, N. Y. Secretary-Treasurer, GEO. M. NISBETT, 50 Wall Street, New York City. Executive and Finance Committee, W. S. BULL, M. H. BRIDGMAN, DR. GEORGE E. BLACKHAM, Dunkirk, N. Y.

IMMEDIATE ATTENTION!!

To the Consuls, Bicycle Dealers, Clubs and Membership at large of the New York State Division:

I call your attention to the following rule which was adopted at a meeting of the Passenger Agents of the Trunk Lines held in New York City on May 9:

"For the transportation of bicycles twenty-five cents for each 100 miles or fractional part thereof."

This is a matter which calls for *immediate attention* on our part, and as the best means of reaching the heart of the trouble I would advise that letters from the officers of your local clubs and others be sent *at once* to the General Passenger Agents of the line you patronize.

Showing by facts and figures the loss of local traffic that will result if this rule is enforced. That by preventing runs, interfering with race meets, local excursions of wheelmen, etc., they are doing an injustice to a large body of men who travel frequently during the summer time, and at the same time depriving the roads of a source of revenue. Yours respectfully,

W. S. BULL, Chief Consul.

Buffalo, N. Y., May 18, 1889.

TO THE MEMBERS OF THE NEW YORK STATE DIVISION:

The 3-mile New York State Division bicycle championship is hereby assigned to the Kings County Wheelmen, of Brooklyn, to be run at their race meet, June 28 and 29.

W. S. BULL,
BUFFALO, May 8, 1889. Chief Consul.

THE "OLD HOSS" OF CYCLING.

As an instance of the harm a wheelman can do himself, by overdoing cycling, we have a very good instance in G. P. Mills, the erstwhile crack, who did so much fast long-distance pedaling some three seasons ago. Never again will G. P. be the strong chap he once was, never again will he be a crack among cracks on the road. If I am not mistaken it is nothing more than the long and killing rides he has taken that is responsible for his present wretched form. A man has only got so many years allotted him, in my way of thinking, and if he lives at too great a pace or tries to live twenty-four calendar months in the year, he will be likely to shorten his days considerably. "It is the pace that kills." "You cannot eat your cake and have it," no matter how you figure, and the gain of a few paltry miles on a previous record may mean the loss of a few valuable years of a man's life-work.

Not as "the candle brightens toward the close" may a man be said to brighten, for as a rule he attains the maximum of his greatness, like the sun at midday, (in middle age), and then descends the heavens to the glowing west of forgetfulness. Taken in a calm, dispassionate manner, what is so much tinsel and glitter with a number of miles and the magic word "record" thereon, but so much over-estimated mineral that has cost expenditure of precious nervous force to attain? Little mannikins on this earth "with insecure enough adhesion," straining muscles and nerves to their utmost that the crowd may cheer and then forget them. Have you never seen a sadness in it all? Have you never turned your head tearfully away as you saw the champion of the year win the applause of the multitude? Had they not cheered *you* in like manner a few seasons before, when you were strong of wind and limb as any latter-day flier? The cycling favorite of a brief season, the duffer of a couple and the prematurely old man at thirty. That is the average *record* of the "racing man." The public do not remember your old three-minute mile, when handle-bars were short and high and wheels heavy. They do not remember the cries that rose from your comrades' throats as they carried you into the dressing-tent, when you won the State championship in the "phenomenal time of 2.59." To-day when you venture on the track they only see a man who was said to be a good one *once*, trying in vain to do better than Sanders Seller's famous 2:39, and not able to do it. You have had *your* day. Others are having theirs. You are no longer an amateur "drawing card," and had better, far as cycling is concerned, keep between the hedges where the birds sing and the flowers nod in the wind.

You burnt the candle at both ends in your youth, and consequently find it shorter to-day than if you had been less wasteful in its use. But say boys, *think of the fun we had*, and if we could live those days over again, we'd live them differently. *Would we?* No, I think not. We'd just do the same over again. The memory does us good. We can still hear the shout of that crowd of old-time wheelmen, in the days when every wheelman was a gentleman, and our blood tingles as it did then. It is all very well to settle down and harp about the follies of youth when our faculties have become impaired and our eye dim and step less elastic, when the warm, impulsive blood of frolicsome youth no longer makes it a pleasure to live, but when we *were* buoyant and young we thought differently, and our lives were comparatively harmless and enjoyable. We paid for what damage we did to ourselves and others, in many ways, and the few financial "scorches" we got made us better men by their chastening. Oh, yes, old age and discretion and sluggish faculties—and "youth—youth and folly," and scenes in the long ago which you will remember as long as your heart throbs. I think I have a hankering after the latter with its attendant awakenings in St. John's Wood or Pimlico, and the drive home in mid-day with a dress suit and a soiled collar scarce hidden by the lapel of an Inverness cape.

I think I like the honest bent of youthful inclination better than the cant of cold-blooded old age, but *chacun a son gout.*

"JACK."

A SELECTED LIST OF PATENTS.

[Reported especially for THE WHEEL AND CYCLING TRADE REVIEW by C. A. Snow & Co., patent attorneys, Washington, D. C.]

W. R. Smith, Beloit, Wis., wrench.

B. D. Stevens, Burlington, Vt., Lamp extinguisher.

J. B. Glover, Dubuque, Iowa, lubricating device.

All bearing date of May 21, 1889.

AN INFLATED SADDLE FOR BICYCLES.

My invention relates to saddles, such as are used on bicycles, tricycles, velocipedes and the like. Hitherto these saddles have been mostly made of leather, and they have been supported by springs of various sorts.

The use of bicycles on rough roads and pavements necessitates a saddle which shall have a maximum elasticity and which shall prevent, so far as possible, the chafing of the inside of the leg, which is common in riding long distances.

I accomplish this by means of a saddle made of an inflated rubber bag, preferably covered with leather or other strong material and having a longitudinal aperture along its centre, by means of which it is thoroughly ventilated, being suspended from the perch of the bicycle by two rear straps and a single forward strap attached to the leather covering. The many advantages of my saddle are evident from its construction. It is very elastic and readily conforms to all the motions of the body, thus avoiding all chafing and friction. It is cooling, by reason of the confined air within the saddle and the means of ventilating pointed out. By its use long distances can be ridden without the strain on the back and loins frequently caused by such riding.

CHAS. F. SWETT,
Patentee.

ODDS AND ENDS.

May 14, the Trinity College A. A.'s 2-mile bicycle race at Charter Oak Park, was won by E. K. Hubbard, '92, in 6m. 43s.

L. L. Clarke, of Berkley School, won the 1-mile bicycle race at the Inter-Scholastic A. A.'s Sports, May 18, in 3m. 22s.

The Manhattan Club has a new member seven days old. The boys have made up a purse to buy the little chap some "fixins."

Arrangements are all made for the Florida Division L. A. W. Meet, and names are rapidly pouring in on the managers.

It is a close race between the St. Augustine and Jacksonville clubs for lead in membership, the latter being only three ahead.

A. B. Rich, of the Staten Island A. C., will be under the care of W. J. Corcoran, the well-known bicycle trainer, this present season.

Brother Fourdrinier, of the *Bicycling World*, is to be congratulated on his election to the Presidency of the Boston Press Cycling Club.

Philadelphia's associated cycling clubs are petitioning for free carriage of bicycles by the Pennsylvania R. R., when accompanied by owners.

Wheelmen that have spent the past winter in Florida speak favorably of the fine riding surfaces the hard beaches furnish, much superior to the Florida roads.

In the Episcopal Academy A. A.'s Field Sports at Philadelphia, May 16, the 1-mile bicycle race was won by F. Archer, '90, in 3m. 34 1-4s; A. G. Coolidge, '92, second.

A 1½-mile bicycle handicap is among the events at the Manhattan Athletic Club's Spring games, June 1. Their grounds are located at 86 St. and Eighth Avenue, New York City.

The 2-mile Eastern championship bicycle race on Saturday, June 1, at the Berkeley Oval, promises to be very interesting. Gold, silver and bronze medals will be given to the winners.

Wheelmen in Boston and vicinity will do well to call on Harry D. Hedger, at 473 Tremont Street, with any kind of cycle repairs. Mr. Hedger possesses that most important qualification in this line, experience.

Howard A. Smith & Co., of Newark, N. J., have probably the largest stock of sundries of any dealers in this part of the country. Any of our readers needing extras in that line can not do better than give them a call.

The St. Louis Bicycle Track Association, is the name of a new organization at the Mound City, the officers of which are: President, George McAndrews; Vice-President, R. W. Sanders; Secretary and Traesurer, W. M. Brewster.

The marriage of Mr. Gerry Jones and Miss Emilie P. Isham is announced to take place June 6th, at Dunkirk, New York. A reception follows at the house of the bride's parents, 401 Central Avenue. Our very best congratulations are respectfully tendered.

Mr. Wm. J. Corcoran, bicycle trainer, wishes the public to know that after May 30, he is at liberty to accept a position with riders desiring first-class training. Mr. Corcoran can refer to many successful wheelmen that have been under his care. Letters addressed to him, care of this office will be forwarded.

Columbia's Champions, a new Athletic Weekly published at Boston, and making its best bow this present week, has a short but well-edited column on cycling. "Leh Sharty"—whatever that may mean—is responsible for it. Under the heading "Round the Sporting Hub," the Editors ring in quite an amount of clever advertising. In their own classic language, "there are no flies on them."

We have received two splendid photos of Willie Windle one showing a "bust" picture and another the American champion standing by his wheel. Willie writes as follows: "I am not riding as yet, though your newspaper men have me so. My father has built me one of the finest tracks I have ever ridden on. It is five laps to the mile. I shall be in New York on the 15th of June, to compete at the New York Athletic Club games at Travers Island."

HERE'S A CHANCE.

The one-day record for Ceylon appears to be an insignificant one, as R. Skeen, by riding ninety miles, has secured it. It is considered good for the warm lower part of the island, although bicycle riding in the tropics is not as bad as it looks, the pace travelled creating a current of air. A twelve hours' night ride should result in 120 miles or so being covered.—*Land and Water.*

GREAT CENTURY RUN.

There will probably be about 125 starters. Two tandem bicycles will be in the party. Names should be sent to L. A. Clarke, 25 Broad Street, by June 1. The following is a probable list of starters: Citizens, 5; Harlem Wheelmen, 5; Riverside, 10; Long Island Wheelmen, 10; Kings Co. Wheelmen, 10; Brooklyn B. C., 10; Mercury W. C., 4; Huntington, 5; Plainfield, 6; Bloomfield, 8; New Brunswick, 1; Orange, 15; Trenton, 10. Ten clubs are yet to be heard from.

Louis Hill, the favorite member of the Pennsylvania Club, is 23 years of age, 5 feet 8 inches in height, and has ridden four years previous to this. His racing experience covers three seasons, and with J. G. Fuller, of the same club, he holds the world's amateur tandem bicycle records for five and ten miles. These gentlemen also hold the tandem records on the Lancaster pike from Ardmore to 52d street toll gate, and from Bryn Mawr to same place.

On the tandem bicycle Mr. Hill, last season, won four firsts and one second, the latter starting from scratch in a handicap. His best track records are: quarter-mile in 53s., half-mile in 1m. 26s., and mile in 2m. 46s. This coming season will doubtless see him again on the track. Mr. Hill reciprocates the pride that Pennsylvania takes in him.

MR. CHARLES L. SEAVEY, of Portland, Me., will send THE WHEEL special letters describing the Elwell European Tour. A. J. Wilson ("Faed"), one of the cleverest writers of the English cycling press, will act as guide to the tourists in England and Ireland, and will write THE WHEEL some interesting sketches.

KINDLY APPRECIATION.

Editor Prial, of THE WHEEL, knows the demands of reading cyclists, and caters to them with success. Wheelmen who desire to keep posted on the latest cycle news will always find it recorded in THE WHEEL.—*Nashville American.*

WESTBORO, Mass., May, 17, 1889.

EDITOR WHEEL:

Dear Sir—Inclosed please find subscription for one year for your paper. We wish you all manner of success, and hope it may always be as bright and newsy and as free from prejudice and favoritism as it now is.

We are, sir, very faithfully,
THE WHITE CYCLE Co.

"WHEELING" AND "THE WHEEL" AGAIN UNANIMOUS.

We congratulate the *Cyclist* on its new American correspondent. The reading public will appreciate the information derived from the source which was responsible for the mammoth swindle of the Temple *versus* Rowe matches. So we read the signature, "Senator."—*Wheeling.*

To THE EDITOR OF THE WHEEL:

The following are the officers and Chairmen of Committees in connection with the Tenth Annual Meet L. A. W. at Hagerstown, Md., July 2, 3 and 4, 1881. All communications relating to the meet should be addressed to the chairman of the committee, as indicated by their subjects.

ALBERT MOTT, C. C., G. W. H. CARR, Sec'y-Treas., 201 Lennox Street, Baltimore. P. O. Box 693, Baltimore.

TRANSPORTATION.
W. M. Brewster, National, Olive Street, St. Louis, Mo.
JOS. T. Chism, Md. Div., 10 East Lombard Street, Balt., Md.
Samuel C. Miller, Local, Hagerstown, Md.

RECEPTION AND HOTELS.
N. B. Scott, Jr., Hagerstown, Md.

ENTERTAINMENTS.
E. B. MacD. Baechtel, Hagerstown, Md.

PARADE.
George F. Updegraff (Vice Consul), Hagerstown, Md.

TOURS AND RUNS.
R. B. Emmert, Hagerstown, Md.

INVITATION.
V. M. Cushwa, Hagerstown, Md.

RACES.
H. B. Irvin, Hagerstown, Md.

FINANCE.
Frank S. Heard, Hagerstown, Md.

PROGRAMME.
John S. Bridges, Hagerstown, Md.

PRESS.
L. R. Mobley, Hagerstown, Md.
Respectfully and truly yours,
ALBERT MOTT,
C. C. Md. Div.

Baltimore Md., May 18, 1889.

IRVINGTON-MILBURN ROAD RACES.

W. Van Wagoner, Newport, R. I.; G. W. Kohney, Talcotville, Ct.; O. C. Boegler, N. Y. C., and T. W. Bearsley, K. C. W., are to be added to the list of entries for this race, published in THE WHEEL of May 17. Fifty entries promise to make this one of the most important coming events. It is rumored that a sprained ankle will compel the withdrawal of L. W. Beazeley, Jr., but we trust this is only a rumor. Still, Kings Co., will be fairly well represented. F. H. Hesse is claimed by some wheel scribes to be the "dark horse" in this race.

The Huntington, L. I., Bicycle Club is expected to attend this race in a body, and be the guests of the Brooklyn Bicycle Club.

WHEEL GOSSIP.

The Riverside Wheelmen are holding their house-warming this evening.

The Atlanta Wheelmen held a reception at their new club rooms, in Newark, on Tuesday evening.

The Maine Central Railroad carries wheelmen to the Maine Division Meet at Biddeford at half rates.

Route Wanted—From Great Bend, Pa., to Hagerstown, Md. August Kinne, Richfield Springs, New York.

One of the clubs of Baltimore is making arrangements to camp out at Hagerstown from June 29 to the night of July 4.

The petition for reinstatement as an amateur made by F. F. Ives has been practically refused by the L. A. W. Board.

Mr. A. B. Rich will train this year. Mr. Rich is now a member of C. G. Obrig & Co., a new wheel agency and banking firm, and will have plenty of time to train.

C. B. Keen, Ex. and M. O. Register, '91, will represent Pennsylvania University in the 2-mile bicycle race run at the intercollegiate games at Mott Haven next Saturday.

Howard A. Smith & Co., Newark, N. J., keep a line of Columbias, Victors, Stars, G. & J.'s and Warwicks in stock, and can fit out their customers without delay.

The race between Schaeffer and Bailey has been definitely arranged. It will be one mile, and will be run off the end of this month, probably on the Y. M. C. A. grounds in West Philadelphia.

Strong and Green, of Philadelphia, are endeavoring to make fashionable regular wicker-work cycling helmets, something after the order of the headgear the ancient Britons wore.

The Camden Wheelmen are to run off their five-mile road race on June 25, on the Haddonfield pike. Mr. J. H. Crossley has presented a gold medal for this race, and there will be other prizes.

Philadelphia, May 1, 1889.

MORE KIND WORDS.

The *Wheel*, of New York, shows a marked improvement. It is now one of our most welcome visitors among cycling periodicals.—*Philadelphia Sunday Times.*

Harvard has entered these representatives for the 2-mile bicycle race at the Mott Haven Inter-Collegiate Track and Field Sports this year: R. H. Davis, '91; E. A. Bailey, '91; W. B. Greenleaf, '92; Kenneth Brown, '91.

In the two-mile bicycle race, May 18, Register and Keen, of Pennsylvania University, and Heulings, of Swarthmore, competed. Keen took the lead at starting and kept it to the finish, making 6m. 13 1-5s. Heulings was second in 6m. 17 3-5s.

Amherst will be represented at the N. E. Inter-Collegiate A. A. in Worcester, on May 23, by eighteen men, of whom these three, T. G. Dunham, P. A. Delabarre and B. H. Dingley, will enter the 2-mile bicycle race; L. H. Harriman, of Worcester, being the only other contestant.

E. Irving Halsted, of the Harlem Wheelmen, and popular with every man who knows him, has taken a position with a corporation just started at Tacoma, W. T., for the manufacture of a plaster called "adamant." The new concern starts out with bright prospects, and we hope "Irv." will be as successful in his Eastern friends wish him.

Safety bicycles are barred from competing in races to be run at the New Jersey A. A.'s Decoration Day Games at Bergen Point. Bar them from running in the same races with ordinaries, if you will, but why not have a separate event, open to safeties only? This season, at least, the safety is the favorite, and people like to see what time can be made on it.

Bicycle races will be held at Huntington, L. I., on Wednesday, June 12, 1889. The following events will be decided: Half-mile Dash, scratch; gold medal, silver medal; One-mile Handicap, gold medal, silver medal; Two-mile Handicap, gold medal, silver medal; One-mile Scratch, gold medal, silver medal. Entrance free. All entries must be addressed to S. C. Esbess, Huntington, L. I., on or before June 8.

A union run will be taken by the Lynn Cycle Club about June 1 to some point ten or twelve miles out. All riders in that city are invited to participate, and a caterer with full supplies of eatables and drinkables will meet the tired and hungry crowd at the close of this exhausting tour. The cost of refreshments will be moderate, and no after-dinner speeches permitted. President Sherman has the management of all details, and their completeness is thus assured. As the pace will not exceed five or six miles an hour, "union half," would seem a more appropriate title than "union run."

PROMISED HELP.

To Pennsylvania Division, L. A. W.: The committee on Rights and Privileges will assist *gratis* in any case of oppression or trespass upon wheel privileges—especially in those where the road hog may be the defendant. Address the nearest member. In addition, the Chairman offers his legal services, free, wherever possible.

SAMUEL A. BOYLE,
Chairman, Ass't District Attorney, Phila.
JOHN J. VAN NORT,
312 Lackawana Street, Scranton, Pa.
D. K. TRIMMER,
York, Pa.

THE WHEEL

—AND—

CYCLING TRADE REVIEW.

Published every Friday morning.

Entered at the Post Office at second class rates.

Subscription Price,   -   -   - $1.00 a year.
Foreign Subscriptions,   -   -   - 6s. a year.
Single Copies,   -   -   -   -   - 5 Cents.

Newsdealers may order through AM. NEWS Co.

All copy should be received by Monday.
Telegraphic news received till Wednesday noon.

Advertising rates on Application.

F. P. PRIAL, Editor and Proprietor
23 Park Row,

P. O. Box 444,   New York.

Persons receiving sample copies of this paper are respectfully requested to examine its contents and give us their patronage, and as far as is convenient, aid in circulating the journal, and extend its influence in the cause which it so faithfully serves. Subscription price, $1 per year.

AT a meeting of the Eastern Trunk Line Association, held on Tuesday, the resolution fixing a tariff on transportation of wheels was rescinded and a resolution was passed leaving the matter of transportation charges on wheels entirely in the hands of the roads. The measure was helped through by Mr. Scull, G. P. A. of the Baltimore & Ohio R. R., and Mr. Eckerson, Asst. G. P. A. of the West Shore Road. The Association were induced to reconsider the resolution by the efforts of these two gentlemen, and with the indirect help of Chief Consul Bull, of New York State, Mr. Geo. R. Bidwell, Transportation Committee, Chas. A. Shechan, Manhattan B. C., whose connections with the West Shore people were of great assistance, and F. P. Prial, New York Bicycle Club. The importance of the new resolution cannot be estimated. The railroads are not compelled to charge transportation rates, but may fix them at their will, and as two of the most prominent roads have carried wheels free, it is probable that other roads will follow suit.

MR. ALBERT MOTT, Chief Consul of Maryland, has put his shoulder to the wheel of preparation for the League meet, and that the wheel will revolve more quickly for this addition to the force of pushers, no one who knows the Chief Consul will doubt. We have given the Chief Consul several columns of this week's issue, on which he spreads an admirable sketch of the possibilities of the '89 meet. Mr. Mott, who is an old newspaper man, enlisted his sympathies as well as his ability to do justice to Hagerstown and its ridable neighborhood, and those who read cannot resist the temptation to go South in July. We can add nothing to the Chief Consul's story. The city is there and it will belong to us, for a week at least. The people are there, Bombarger, Updegraff and all the rest of them. They are waiting for us and will work body and soul to give us a good time. Can we resist such a hearty invitation to join the festive crowd ?

"BICYCLING WORLD" very properly suggests that the League should aid the early closing Saturday half-holiday scheme.

The Saturday half-holiday is a boon. The struggle for existence is carried on too fiercely in this country, and we are going to the dogs body and soul as a consequence. We should all hold up every Saturday afternoon ; none would then be the loser. We believe contending armies have resorted to armistices with benefit to both sides.

AT the intercollegiate games, held last Saturday at New York, Davis, of Harvard, on a safety, collided with Clark, of Yale, on an ordinary. We trust that the Racing Board will at once subject all the riders in this event to the penalty of temporary suspension from the track for this violation of the racing rules. We believe all the contestants were gentlemen ; we are particularly interested in Davis, one of the best fellows on the path to-day, but the powers that are must assert themselves. The matter of infringement was fully discussed ; the contestants felt themselves morally bound to represent their colleges in this event, no matter what the result might be, but the collegiate officials were divided between open defiance of the Racing Board and the opinion that that body wouldn't "dare do anything." We advise the Board to assert itself. The rules were deliberately broken. We are sorry for the college boys, but there must be a Racing Court and the rulings of that court must be observed.

If the signs of the times amount to anything, road racing in the East has about seen its best days, and there is a strong tide of sentiment among wheelmen, in some sections where road racing has been most popular, that the time is about ripe to pull out.

The probable action of the Eastern Road Club, of Massachusetts, and the evident opposition to road racing which exists in New Jersey, where once the wheelmen were unanimous in favor of road racing, are all indications going to show the trend of growing sentiment against this branch of the sport.

We ourselves have promoted road races, but we have always held that, where we discerned an indication of opposition by the public or wheelmen, we should use our influence to carry it out.

The question is now, has the time come to take such a stand ?   We think it has.—*Bicycling World.*

Our contemporary reads the signs of the times not aright.   There is no strong tide of sentiment against road racing among wheelmen, and if there is a weak rivulet of sentiment, it has found but weak expression.   Road racing takes its proper place just like path racing.   It is one of the side issues of the sport.   Might as well claim that scorching has seen its best days.   In discussing any phase of cycling, it is best to look out and beyond one's own little local circle. This is a big country and so much given to booms that while parading is effete in the East, it may simply sizzle at white heat in the West ; that while road racing is dead in the North, it may be excessively active in the South.   We cannot work up very much of a road race craze in Boston, because Boston is very dead to cycling crazes just now ; same with New York, which could not be very much excited over anything just at this time.   Both are in a sort of *blasé* state, cyclingly speaking.   There is no well developed opposition to road racing in New Jersey that we can discover ; some things are best seen from a distance, however.   At the race held yesterday all the local clubs were present, and the representative men of these clubs acted as officials.   We shall probably have a New Jersey and Long Island road racing association this Fall.   When the sport is new then will road racing flourish.   While there are new riders road racing will be indulged in, and as new men come up every year this branch of cycle racing will be kept alive.   We hope no one will take a "stand," whatever that is.   We

trust the League will take no "stand ;" that would be very unfortunate.   We do not encourage men to race on the road ; they have no legal right to do so, and few of them can stand the strain of a hot race.   But if the men will race let us take hold and manage the thing as well as possible.

RACING cyclists should recollect that men who ride in any event not handicapped by the League handicapper, or who compete in safety races on ordinaries, or who compete in ordinary races on safeties, or who ride against a suspended man, will be suspended from the racing path for such a time as the Racing Board may decide.   The sport is now in a healthy state ; there are no half-breeds on the path, and there is a man at the head who intends to keep it so.   If we have an amateur rule, let us live up to it in the strictest sense.

IN response to a letter from the Road Race Committee, the Eastern Department of the Trunk Line Association decided to waive charges on transporting wheels between New York and Orange on May 30.   We are sure all wheelmen appreciated the kindness of the Association.

GREAT CENTURY RUN OF 1889—OPEN TO ALL CYCLISTS.

FINAL NOTICE.

Rendezvous, Mountain House, Mountain Station, D. L. & W. R. R. (Barclay and Christopher Street ferries, New York City ; trains frequent in afternoon, hourly in evening) ; supper, lodging and breakfast, $2; lodging and breakfast, $1.25; accommodations very good and others, Schedule : Routed out at 3 A. M.; breakfast, 3.30 A. M.; start, 4 A. M.; Newark, Elizabeth, Westfield, Plainfield (23 miles, rest), New Brunswick, Kingston, Princeton (55 miles, rest), Trenton (65 miles; dinner, 75 cents; arrive 1:30; leave 2:30) ; Bristol, Holmesburg, Frankford, Philadelphia (100 miles; arrive 7 P.M.); Continental Hotel, supper, lodging and breakfast, $2, or, with dinner on 9th, $2.50

Roads good to fine ; average pace, about 7½ miles per hour.

On the 9th, Sunday morning, parties will be arranged to visit several of the celebrated resorts which abound in the suburbs, where fine dinners may be had (75 cents and $1), and special cars are hoped for for the return to New York in the afternoon.   The cost of the trip will be within $10 per head.

A party of ladies will leave New York on one of the noon trains to meet the run in Philadelphia on its arrival, under the charge of Mrs. L. A. Newcomb, Harlem Wheelmen, Sixth Avenue and 124th Street, New York City, with whom all intending lady participants are requested to correspond immediately.

All those who join the run along its route will report to Captain J. V. L. Pierson, of the Committee, for number and badge, having their names written on a slip of paper ready to hand to Mr. P.

If intending participants will take the advice of one who has "been thar" several times, they will wear full length tights, flannel shirts and helmets and each carry a sponge as large as their individual two fists suspended from their handle-bars.   They should send their valises on to the Continental with the usual necessaries and some unnecessaries, and wear nothing on the run that they can do without.

The pace will be set by the committee, no scorching will be allowed, and we guarantee to take all who stick by the schedule through to Philadelphia on what will prove to have been the biggest thing of its kind ever gotten up.

L. A. Clarke, Chairman, Committee of Arrangements, 25 Broad Street, New York City.

New York State Division L.A.W.

OFFICIAL ORGAN.

OFFICERS FOR 1889.

Chief Consul, W. S. BULL, 754 Main Street, Buffalo, N. Y. Vice-Consul, M. L. BRIDGMAN, 1255 Bedford Avenue, Brooklyn, N Y Secretary-Treasurer, GEO. M. NISBETT, 50 Wall Street, New York City. Executive and Finance Committee, W. S. BULL, M. H. BRIDGMAN, DR. GEORGE E. BLACKHAM, Dunkirk, N. Y.

NEW YORK NOMINATIONS.

G. M. Nisbett, Sec'y-Treas. N. Y. State Div., L. A. W.:

DEAR SIR,—At the meeting of the Nominating Committee, held May 22d, 1889, at 47 and 49 West 14th Street, the following gentlemen were present: Geo. Dakin, of Buffalo, N. Y., by proxy; H. E. Raymond, of Brooklyn, N. Y. and W. H. De Graaf, of New York City.

The meeting was called to order at 10:30 A.M., and the following gentlemen were unanimously nominated for the offices of the New York State Division, L. A. W., for the ensuing year: W. S. Bull, of Buffalo, for Chief Consul; M. L. Bridgman, of Brooklyn, for Vice-Consul; Geo. M. Nisbett, of New York, for Sec'y-Treasurer.

Yours fraternally,

[Signed.] W. H. DE GRAAF,
Chairman Nominating Committee.

N. Y., May 23d, 1889.

To the Members of the New York State Division:

I hereby appoint Mr. H E. Raymond a member of the Division Nominating Committee, vice Mr. H. C. Spaulding, Jr., deceased.

W. S. BULL,
Buffalo, May 16th, 1889. Chief Consul.

APPOINTMENTS OF DISTRICT COMMITTEES.

To the Members of the New York State Division:

In accordance with Article 5, Section 4, New York State Division By-Laws, I hereby appoint the following committees:

FIRST DISTRICT.

J. M. Warwick, 30 Broad Street, New York City; E. J. Shriver, Metal Exchange, New York City; Jas. L. Miller, 158 West 105th St., New York City.

SECOND DISTRICT.

G. W. Mable, 50 Putnam Avenue, Brooklyn, N. Y.; James Fox, Temple Court, New York City; M. L. Bridgman, 1255 Bedford Avenue, Brooklyn, N. Y.

THIRD DISTRICT.

Joshua Reynolds, Stockport, N. Y.; R. D. Cook, 14 Wathyne Blk., Troy, N. Y.; Jas. C. McClelland, 455 Madison Avenue, Albany, N. Y.

FOURTH DISTRICT.

L. S. Wilson, c. o. *Journal* Office, Syracuse, N. Y.; A. B. Gardner, 11 Broad Street, Utica, N. Y.; Jas. L. Hickok, National Bank, Auburn, N. Y.

FIFTH DISTRICT.

H. W. Bullard, 374 Maine St., Poughkeepsie, N.Y.; E. H. Towle, Binghamton, N. Y.; Otis Dockstrader, 118 Lake Street, Elmira, N. Y.

SIXTH DISTRICT.

R. C. Chapin, White Building, Buffalo, N. Y.; Louis Burch, 82 East Tupper Street, Buffalo, N.Y.; Robert Thomson, 90 South St. Paul Street, Rochester, N. Y.

The duties of the committees and the boundaries of the districts are defined in Article 5, Sections 1, 2 and 4 as follows:

Section 1.—For the purpose of electing general representatives the Division shall be divided into districts as follows:

First District—New York, Richmond and Westchester Counties.

Second District—Kings, Queens and Suffolk Counties.

Third District—Columbia, Green, Rensselaer, Albany, Saratoga, Washington, Warren, Hamilton, Essex, Franklin, Clinton, Schenectady, Schoharie, Montgomery and Fulton Counties.

Fourth District—Wayne, Oswego, Cayuga, Jefferson, St. Lawrence, Lewis, Herkimer, Oneida, Madison, Onondaga, Seneca, Yates, Ontario, Steuben, and Schuyler Counties.

Fifth District—Chemung, Broome, Chenango, Otsego, Delaware, Sullivan, Ulster, Dutchess, Orange, Putnam, Rockland, Cortland, Tompkins and Tioga Counties.

Sixth District—Niagara, Orleans, Genesee, Wyoming, Erie, Livingston, Cattaraugus, Chatauqua, Monroe and Alleghany Counties.

Section 2.—Each district shall be entitled to one representative for each one hundred members of the Division residing therein on the first day of July in each year.

Section 4.—On or before the first day of June in each year the Chief Consul shall appoint a committee of three in each election district, whose duty shall be to recommend suitable nominations for general representatives from their respective districts; such nominations to be sent to the Secretary-Treasurer of the Division on or before the 1st day of July. In event of the failure on the part of these committees to perform this duty, the Chief Consul, and Secretary-Treasurer shall nominate All nominations shall be published in the Official Organ on or before July 1.

W. S. BULL,
Buffalo, N. Y., May 23. Chief Consul.

A SCRANTON BANK FAILURE—GEO. A JESSUP INVOLVED.

The lay press has been publishing, at great length, reports of the collapse of the City Bank of Scranton, Pa., of which Col. George A. Jessup, of the Scranton Bicycle Club and Chief Consul of the Pennsylvania Division, is cashier. Many cyclists have read these statements, many of which are exaggerated or misleading, and it is only fair to suspend judgment until the real facts of the case are made public. From private advices we learn that Mr. Jessup was a large stockholder in the bank, cashier and director. We are informed on excellent authority that Mr. Jessup was permitted to conduct all the affairs of the bank, without oversight on the board of directors. It seems very clear that Mr. Jessup used the funds of the bank to carry on personal enterprise in the coal and mining regions, and that the shrinkage in values in his properties during the past winter caused him heavy losses. It is to be said in Mr. Jessup's favor that he is ready and claims to be able to make his shortage good, that he has enough property to make up all losses. It is also significant that his personal friends have perfect faith in his ability to satisfy all parties, and the president of the bank is doing all in his power to straighten things out. The question of Mr. Jessup's culpability in using the funds of the bank is not worth considering beside the broader question as to whether the entire banking system of the country has not been undermined, whether some means should not be devised by law to prevent the men who handle the moneys of banking institutions from using these moneys, with no dishonest intentions, perhaps, for their private ends. It is true that it is the duty of boards of directors and presidents to oversee, but they notoriously fail to discharge that duty conscientiously, and that failure should be a criminal offense.

BICYCLERS AS TARGETS.

GRIFFIN, GA., May 18.—Yesterday afternoon R. L. Brantly, Whitely Kincaid, Chas. Walcott, Louis Niles, Eli Brewer, Otis Crouch, bicyclists of this city, made a trip on their wheels to Orchard Hill, about six miles south of this city.

As they were returning they passed a house where a crowd were congregated, and without any provocation were set upon by a pack of hounds and fired at five times by the crowd. The wheelmen not being armed, were forced to rely on their mounts for protection. but it is likely that proceedings will be instituted against the roughs who made the unwarranted attack. —*Savannah paper.*

Advices from our Columbus correspondent state that this seeming outrage may, on investigation, prove to be nothing but a rough joke (?) with a view to seeing how fast a bicycle could be ridden. We think the Griffin wheelmen may be relied on after this to either drag a Gatling gun after them when touring or take along an escort of mounted policemen. If they carry "guns," the use of the cycle in war may be demonstrated here at home long before our English brethren are done manœuvring and wheeling and counter-wheeling to settle the point.

THE LEAGUE WILL STAND BY HIM.

Official notice was sent from New Bedford May 27 to Chief Consul W. H. Emery, Massachusetts Division L. A. W., in regard to the suit brought by J. A. Beauvais against J. B. Bradford for taking a header from his bicycle and scaring Mr. Beauvais' horse. Word was received to-day by Consul Frank L. Wing that the League would take Bradford's case up and fight it to the end. The jury, it will be remembered, disagreed at this term of the court.

LAST OF THE EASTERN ROAD CLUB.

Ever since the fatal accident to Robert S. McCombie, while racing for the Eastern road cup early last season, there has been talk of disbanding this organization, as road racing in this vicinity had received a black eye by the unfortunate occurrence. Last evening, May 27, representatives of the Massachusetts, Boston, Cambridgeport, Chelsea and Dorchester bicycle clubs, five of the original eight, gathered, in answer to the call of the president of the Eastern Road Club, at the office of Dr. W. G. Kendall, 176 Tremont Street, and the affairs and prospects of the club for the coming season were informally discussed, and when the meeting came to order it was unanimously voted to disband the Eastern Road Club, which was organized in 1887 to promote interest in road racing hereabouts. It was further decided that the silver cup of the club, for which many a hard battle was fought, and which was twice won by the Dorchester Club, be given to that organization, as it is the only club willing to enter a team to defend it.—*Boston Herald.*

PSYCHE'S NOTES.

I see that both your columns and those of the *Bi. World* last week gave up most of the space devoted to wheelwomen's use to the various opinions of different riders on the subject of dress.

I have already aired my views, but if you don't mind will give a rebash of them, for I think I have struck the *ne plus ultra* of comfort, etc., in my present costume.

A skirt two yards in width of corduroy, gored in front, faced high as the knee, all the fullness in the back, a close-fitting body of flannel, same color, knickerbockers of silesia same color as dress and stockings and low shoes. My hat is a toque, being the most becoming shape I can wear.

I want to register a protest against wheelwomen of all sizes and ages getting themselves into blouse waists immediately they begin riding a bicycle. There is no more excuse for them for this exercise than there would be if one were on horseback, and the average woman looks remarkably like a pudding tied in the middle when gotten into one of these loose waists. Of course there are some, a good many, who have pretty, slight figures and would look well in this get-up, but the great majority certainly do not.

Among Helen Gray's correspondents is one who advocates the weighting of the riding skirt with shot. I think the rider will bitterly regret ever doing such a thing, for it would be simply suicidal. The weighted edge would catch in the spokes infallibly, and probably mean a bad fall for the rider, as well as utter destruction of the dress if the wheel was going at any rate of speed.

I don't believe in white for wheeling, for it is apt to get soiled, and unless one is a millionairess and prepared for unlimited washing and an irate washerwoman, I would not advise it.

Again, I don't believe in too wide skirts. They catch the wind, and a rider from the rear is apt to look like a twin balloon. They don't conceal the knee motion a bit more than the narrower skirt, and show the ankle more, for they fly a great deal and give a chance for the wind to get under and blow them about.

Mrs. B., from Boston, writes to Miss Grey that she wears divided skirts. I have never seen them, and don't want to be narrow-minded, but it seems to me they are "neither fish, flesh, fowl, nor good red herring." I don't see any reason for wearing them for wheeling. If there is one will somebody please tell me it? PSYCHE.

CYCLING MATTERS IN PROVIDENCE.

The *Providence Journal* of Sunday last devoted over three columns to a well-written article on "The Season of Cycling," which in correctness of statements and accuracy of illustrations is far ahead of the usual lay article on this subject. Evidently, it is the work of a wheelman or a writer that had read up for his subject most thoroughly. One illustration represents Mr. John W. Arnold, who commenced cycling at the youthful age of seventy-five, and is now in his seventy-eighth year. The *Journal* claims him as "the oldest cycler in the U. S." Without data at hand to disprove it, we will not contradict them, but still have the impression there are one or two other wheelmen in the country fully as old. Another *rara avis* among cyclers, and of which, we think, Providence has the monopoly, is a Chinese laundryman that takes his exercise on a bicycle—no safety either, but the good old ordinary. Who says the Chinese must go? When a Mongolian grasps the English language, attends the American Church and rides the bicycle, what's the matter with him as a citizen?

Among riders of the safety in Providence may be counted a dozen or so of leading teachers and professors, one or two ministers, and some half-dozen lady riders. For a city in a State not noted for the best of roads, Providence would appear to take a remarkable interest in cycling.

THE LEAGUE MEET, HAGERSTOWN, JULY 2, 3 and 4.

DEAR EVERYBODY:

I want to have a little confidential chat with you about the tenth annual Meet at Hagerstown—just as we would talk it over if we met upon the road, and you asked for information. That way is best for a clear understanding, and there is no fear of misapprehension when we take into consideration the freemasonry existing between us when a-wheel. It might be put up in the highest style of dude literature and be clear as Omaha mud in consequence, but it is certain you would not wish that.

To a Baltimore or Washington wheelman the mere mention of something going on at Hagerstown has always been enough to make a scramble to that city, for the people up there between the mountains —cyclers and citizens—make "a go" of anything they undertake in the curriculum of cycledom.

Eight superb limestone pikes radiate from Hagerstown, which is the hub of the Shenandoah Valley, while intersecting pikes and cross-roads form a network of thoroughfares for wheelmen that realizes the stereotyped phrase of cycler's paradise. These pikes are of that smooth, sand-papered kind that entrance the wheelman, while his surroundings of scenery and sweet odors from Nature's garden make his runs veritable trips through fairy land.

A wheelman can do almost anything he chooses in Hagerstown, and his uniform is considered a sort of badge—a metaphorical snuff-box or keys of the city—entitling him to the freedom of the town. "Oh, he's all right," is the verdict of the guardian of the peace as he leniently views the little fun scrapes of the cycler. At the hotels it is the same. The soiled traveler a-wheel is a thing of beauty to the affable host and the special pet of the head waiter, while he far outrivals the gigantic sparkling gem gracing the bosom of the clerk and flashing defiance to dignity. Oh, the wheelmen have great times in Hagerstown.

Scotty Bomberger lives in Hagerstown. You might think he has something to do with the artillery, "but he hasn't" (as Ned Hayden's song puts it), though he is very quick on the trigger, and can get a wheelman *half*-shot in the shortest time on record. Geo. Updegraff also entertains the cycling tourist at Hagerstown, and is aided and abetted by Cushwa, Irvin, Miller and a host of other good fellows. All the tourists from Maine to California know them by those familiar names. When you first get to town it is Mr. So-and-so, but in ten minutes you will be putting in Scotty and George as pat as any of us. You would be amused at a recital of all the funny business that has occurred there, but, you know, it wouldn't do to chronicle it here. Outlines of some of the incidents are: A weary and sleepless wheelman, exasperated to frenzy by insomnia in a neighboring mocking-bird—appearance of the cycler at the hotel office, to say the least *not* in uniform—accommodating clerk with shot-gun—bang—midnight stillness on outside—aroused fellow cyclers appearing *en dishabille* in the hotel corridor—climbing pillars "for the beverages," in which the hotel clerk was the chief instigator and abbettor—somnolence induced by the combined influence of the nectar and the lightly-attired athletics—finale, oblivious sleep, nature's sweet restorer.

You see, some of the boys call this "fun." The term appears to have an elastic definition with wheelmen in Hagerstown. They call it "fun," too, to shoot the tail off a fellow cycler's coat with a roman candle, to assist at "a fire" by capturing the hose and turning the nozzle on perspiring chums, and all that sort of thing. "Secretary," an old timer of THE WHEEL—the one, you know, who wrote so charmingly—did that. See is a great boy. Well, of course, nothing of this kind will happen at the Meet. There will be no wild horse-play, but it all illustrates with what consideration for his "fun" a wheelman is treated in Hagerstown. We who don't approve may dismiss these amiable faults by calling the whole thing a delightful absence of conventionality or something of that sort. All down through "the Valley" the wheelman is king.

Of course, now and then, there is another experience, but it is never very disagreeable. A novelty surprises the natives into forgetting themselves for a moment occasionally, as, in some instances, recollected by the writer when on a tandem tour with Mrs. Chief Consul—or, to be more familiar with you—"old Jeeswax" when it is desired to stroke the fur with a pet wheeling name. She is "Birdie" at home, but she is "old jeeswax" on the road. Well, anyway, a horseman on a distant hill of the old National Pike was observed to dismount and watch the coming "cantankerous consarn" with considerable curiosity, and when we passed, remarked that "that ere pesky thing was enough to scare the devil." Jeeswax sympathized with him in the remark that she "saw it was." So, too, when a big man with a little horse showing a disposition to fly the fence at our uncommon appearance exclaimed, in an oratorical and sonorous voice, "t-a-k-e t-h-a-t *thing* o-f-f t-h-e public highway." Well, now, the tandem pair are exceedingly even tempered, especially "Old Jerry," but when our pretty tandem was denominated a "thing," why, a few well chosen remarks in polite nomenclature flowed from the tongue nimbled by rage that perfectly paralyzed the denizen of the mountain, and when finally he was told that all he needed was a cat-gut string and an antiquated appearance to be a third-class lyre, even the frisky quadruped hung his head in horsensical shame.

Great place that Shenandoah Valley. Forty odd members of the Marylands, on a club run, were each supplied with a fragrant Havana as a result of Sam Clark's shocking prodigality in handing a boy 25 cents and telling him to "bring some cigars" and even then Sam had a pocket full left. It reminds one of the five loaves and three little fishes and the seven baskets left over. Fact, as sure as you live. But say, see here, we can't go on in this way or the editor will fire this out. [No, No. We will give you a page if you can prove Sam Clark guilty of prodigality.—ED.]

Hagerstown, a city of about 20,000 population, is situated in the midst of the great and fertile valley, lying at the foot of the Allegheny mountains, and extending from the Susquehanna river at Harrisburg, Pa., to the northern limits of Alabama. This valley is known in Pennsylvania and Maryland, as the Cumberland Valley, and in Virginia as the Valley of the Shenandoah. But it is one continuous and homogeneous valley well watered by numerous and beautiful streams fed by great springs which gush out of the limestone rocks.

The surface of the valley is beautifully undulating, presenting a varied scene of hill, dale and plain, with the Blue Mountains limiting the view to the east and west. Of this great, fertile and beautiful valley Hagerstown is the queen city. Its location is 560 feet above tide-water. The climate is pleasant, cool and healthful, and every circumstance contributes to make it a most agreeable place for the meet. In fact, from the wheelman's standpoint, no fitter place in these whole United States could be found for a meeting of cyclers.

Hagerstown is built upon a solid foundation of blue limestone rock. In the centre is a square, through which the two principal business streets of the city pass. One of the streets, Potomac, running to the north, after it passes through the business section, widens out into a beautiful avenue, on the west side of which is an eminence or ridge from 100 to 200 feet back from the street. This ridge is crowned with villas which would do credit to the largest cities. Running down the broad street are the well-kept lawns, and from the front porches is a view, of the mountain and the intervening valley, of striking beauty. Washington Street, which passes through the square at right angles with Potomac, continues to the west along the old national pike, and at the western suburbs reaches a high and beautiful elevation. At right angles with this street Prospect Street extends to the south. It is on the summit of a high ridge, and the houses on this street are of great beauty and surrounded by charming gardens.

The streets, where not a natural bed of rock, are made of limestone, which is broken and laid down to a great depth, and topped with stone crushed very fine, and then rolled with a heavy iron road-roller weighing thirty tons, which packs the streets into a solid and smooth mass of stone, very durable and smooth as asphaltum, making road-beds of a very superior character, and for wheeling even surpassing those of Washington.

To illustrate its commercial importance, it may be mentioned that fifty-three passenger trains arrive or depart from Hagerstown every day. The streets are almost perfectly illuminated by electricity, making night riding quite as safe and much more exhilarating than in the day.

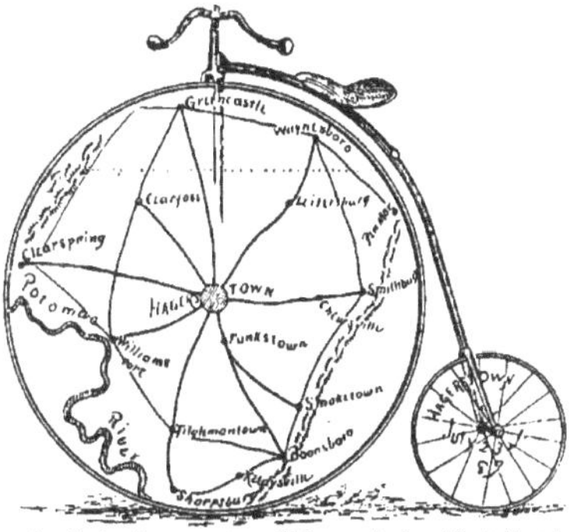

A few miles from Hagerstown, situated high up on the slope of South Mountain, is the Blue Mountain House with its pretty station, one of the most attractive summer resorts and best kept hotels in the country. It is admirable in all its details and commands from its piazzas and windows a magnificent view of the great valley at the foot of the mountain. But this view can be enjoyed to the utmost from the Pen-Mar Observatory (to which place a run will be made), a mile from the hotel, and far as natural scenery is concerned, there are few places in the Eastern States of America better worth seeing. There is spread at the feet of the spectator a magnificent panorama of valley and mountain scenery, extending into four States and dotted with the towns, villages and farmhouses of a teeming population. Higher up, on the extreme summit, there is a high tower, named Mount Quirauk, approached by a fine road, from which the view is extended to the other side of the mountain, and from which can be seen Westminster, Emmittsburg, Hanover, Gettysburg and numerous other towns and villages, together with a great expanse of rich and picturesque country, from beyond the Potomac river on the south to beyond the Susquehanna on the north, and to Parr's Ridge on the east.

Near Monterey a most surprising freak of nature appears hid away in the midst of the woods, the Devil's Race Course. It is a rugged expense of broken mountain rock spreading over a mile in length, and believed to be the result of the tremendous forces of the glacial period. Across the line dividing Pennsylvania and Maryland, to the north and south, lies Pen-Mar, mentioned above, with this name derived from its location between the two States. On a rocky spur, 2,000 feet above the sea, towers High Rock Observatory from which magnificent views are obtained over the Cumberland and Shenandoah Valleys. As far as the eye can reach from the Susquehanna river southward to the Massanutton mountains, miles beyond the Potomac, stretches the Valley, studded with towns, villages, hamlets and farmhouses. The towns of Chambersburg, Hagerstown, Greencastle, Smithsburg, Leitersburg, Waynesboro, and interspersing settlements are taken in at almost one sweep of the eye. The road continues from High Rock upwards to the picturesque points of Brinkwood and Ragged Edge, and to the summit of Mount Quirauk, with the iron observatory affording one of the grandest of views.

If all the points about Hagerstown, interesting to cyclers, were described it would fill a volume. They follow each other in quick succession. The wheelman going south sees on his right, a few miles after leaving Hagerstown, the College of St. James and the old Ringgold Manorial seat. A few miles further he enters upon the historic field of Antietam (to which place a run will be made) and gets a glimpse of the splendid statue or monument in the National Cemetery at Sharpsburg keeping sentinel over the "bivouac of the dead." Crossing the historic Potomac, at the very spot where James Ramsey launched his little steamer in 1787, he lands in West Virginia upon the high rocky precipice over which 2000 Federal troops were driven by Stonewall Jackson.

On the road from Hagerstown is the wonderful Luray Cave and the Natural Bridge of Virginia. All along are points of historic interest, such as the estates of Lord Fairfax and his residence, the old Greenaway Court, while innumerable summer resorts, with their fine hotels, dot the valley and mountains.

For many years it has been the habit of people of sea-side cities to spend some of the summer months in the mountain city of Hagerstown. As a summer resort it possesses many attractions. Its hotels and boarding houses are well kept and moderate in their charges. The climate is cool and agreeable as that of many of the more widely known fashionable resorts. As has been intimated before, Hagerstown is peculiarly situated as regards points of scenic and historic interest. Next to the old battle field at Antietam, with the old Tunker church and the Bloody Lane, both so famous in history, come Lee's headquarters in Sharpsburg, which looks today precisely as it did in September, 1862.

The ruins of old Fort Frederick are interesting relics of pre-Revolutionary times. It was erected by the Colonial Legislature of Maryland about 1755, during the panic which ensued upon the defeat of General Braddock on his Fort Du Quesne Expedition.

In the city there are five large and well-equipped hotels that would do credit to Baltimore, and numerous smaller ones, besides excellent boarding houses. Many families receive private boarders, so there is ample accommodations for all who come. The prices are, of course, very much less than the same accommodations would cost in the larger cities.

Owing to the beauty of the surroundings of the city, some clubs acquainted with the locality propose to form a wheelman's camp, and have already engaged tents and the

proper paraphernalia. This will be a delightful feature, and one hardly possible for a wheelman's meet in New York, Boston, Baltimore or other larger cities.

What wheelman has not heard of the Shenandoah Valley riding district, a region superior for cyclers, in many respects, to the Oranges or Boston. Certainly the members in Pennsylvania, New Jersey, Maryland and the District of Columbia are familiar with it, for their annual tours are nearly always turned in that direction. We quote from the Road Book of the above Divisions: "From Reading westward, the delightful Lebanon Valley offers fair grades to Harrisburg, beyond which point the Cumberland leads past Carlisle and Chambersburg to Hagerstown, and thence as the Shenandoah Valley—that wheelman's paradise—to Staunton, Va. *No finer straightway exists in the Eastern States than that from Reading to the last-named town*, a distance of 264 miles." Wheelmen coming to the Meet from the West via the Baltimore and Ohio Railroad can experience a delightful variety by leaving the train at Martinsburg, W. Va., and riding a-wheel down the Valley to Hagerstown, a distance which cyclometers twenty and one-half miles. Leave the pike and cross the Potomac on the ferry at Falling Waters, and take the smooth-piked towpath to Williamsport, when you will have the entrancing scenery and the novelty of riding with the clear waters of the river and canal on either side, while the hills and mountains tower above. It is more than grand, it is awe-inspiring.

As to the season of the year for holding the Meet, July 2, 3 and 4, it is a comparatively cool and pleasant time in those mountainous regions. My touring has consisted of two weeks in each year spent in the valley, and preferably a little later in July. The upon which a fair margin would be left. Accordingly, the invitation was given and the meet held, and the Division came out of it with a legitimate profit of some $1,201 after entertaining the guests generously. My dear sir, there was no tax on anybody, nobody suffered and everybody was pleased. Baltimoreans are usually generous, but they are practical too. Business men seldom give money without an equivalent. The money gotten for the entertainment of the League was mostly from a business investment of business men who received and expected to receive quid pro quo. The money was derived from hotels which made a profit from the guests even while giving them reduced rates—from cycling firms who made a profit on the sale of machines to the increased membership induced by the increased interest—from merchants who derived a profit from increased sales to an increased floating population—from profits on the official programme, from profits on a sort of a church fair affair, a raffle, whatever one chooses to call it, whereby wheelmen all over the country purchased chances in a lot of cycles and which netted something like $1,500, from profits on the races, from the sale of tickets to the entertainments, from *taxes on the pockets of local cyclers*, (oh ye gods!) to the extent in my own case of $5, and I will risk my reputation for veracity by affirming that the whole amount raised from taxes on the pockets of local cyclers, outside of those engaged in the cycling business, would not average twenty-five cents for each wheelman of the State. I farther affirm that I, myself, without assistance, could with the exception of the official programme, duplicate the preliminaries and arrangements of the Baltimore meet, by two week's personal attention to the matter, and without seriously affecting my private business. We had a committee of fifteen to arrange for that one, and the personal expenses

contrast in getting away from a hot city to the cool mountains and springs of that country is not the least of its merits.

There has been a great deal of cant and misrepresentation concerning League Meets, and no doubt the impression has gone forth to some that the Maryland Division is inviting members of the League to "pay their own way," and that hospitality ceases with the Baltimore Meet. Perhaps there is no better way to counteract such a false impression than to publish the following letter to President Luscomb, which is frank enough to explain itself. It was written from one business man to another and not intended for publication, but perhaps it will enlighten some divisions without experience who fear the "burden and expense." Men of the L. A. W., you will honor us by accepting our hospitality. We know how to entertain you without assuming any unjust burden or expense. We are not aiming to make money, but shall keep inside our income, and if a surplus is left, as in the case of the Baltimore and St. Louis Meets, why so much the better. The whole thing in a nutshell is simply this: When preparing for a League Meet, *provision* is necessarily made to entertain the greatest number that could by any possibility be expected. Naturally the number attending the meet falls short of this extreme limit, and expenses are just so much less and leave a surplus.

"Maryland is a loyal, noble, generous, hospitable Division, and I love her. She is my pride, and none the less because with all her generous chivalry, she is at the same time a good, practical business Division. She generously entertains guests, but at the same time she does not lose sight of a good business investment. Before the Baltimore meet, this Division was in debt, but a practical mind in the person of then Chief Consul J. Kemp Bartlett, Jr., saw the opportunity of increasing interest in cycling in the State—increasing membership and thus enhancing revenues, and a good business scheme of a League meet of the committee were paid so far as known, certainly mine were, and I know others were and should be. There is of course some little personal "time and attention to the reception and care of the visitors," but so there is my dear Mr. Luscomb in social every-day life, and it is considered a pleasure and a privilege by every refined or generous nature.

"But enough of that. I simply want to assure you that the privilege of entertaining the League is not a burden but a pleasure. Let each Division decide for itself what the word entertainment shall imply. As for Maryland we would be glad to "point a moral" for other divisions, but we cannot do it at the cost of our reputation for hospitality, especially when that reputation is so cheaply acquired. I can assure you, however, that we are plain business men and will not involve the Division financially, or sacrifice the pleasure of any local cyclist. We hope to depart from the usual rut of entertaiment, and produce unique features at less cost that will be enjoyed much more. Trust us, and you will not regret it. We have the success of the administration of the League at heart, whoever sways the gentle sceptre."

So no one need hesitate about coming on account of the burden and expense to the Maryland Division. From indications in my correspondence, and the reports brought by members on their travels, the Meet at Hagerstown promises to be the largest in attendance of any yet, and it can be safely promised that the enjoyment will be the greatest; for if a place for a wheelman's meet were to be made to order it could not much surpass Hagerstown, and, therefore, the entertainment part is quite simple.

Respectfully and truly yours,
ALBERT MOTT,
C. C. Md. Div.

WHEEL GOSSIP.

The Hartford Wheel Club recently opened its new club rooms.

A ladies' bicycle club is about to be organized at Boston Highlands.

F. L. Olmstead, of Brookline wants to wheel from Boston to the meet at Hagerstown, and is desirous of finding a companion.

Arrangements are being made for a party of Massachusetts wheelmen to go to Baltimore by water to attend the League meet.

Chief Consul Davol, of Rhode Island, has appointed George Lewis Cooke, of Providence, Vice-Consul, to fill the vacancy caused by the resignation of Mr. H. L. Perkins.

Rochester, N. Y., has started a young ladies' tricycle club: Julia Langie, President; Rebecca Linder, Vice-President; Clara Bier, Treasurer, and Mazie Gardon, Secretary.

Chief Consul Emery will deliver a lecture on "Constitution and by-laws, the scope and development of the L. A. W., and the advantages of League clubs" at the Hagerstown meet.

PROSPECT WHEELMEN.

At a meeting of the Prospect Wheelmen, on Thursday, May 23, C. Newbourg was elected Captain, vice H. Newman resigned, and R. Wulff, Secretary, vice C. Newbourg.

MILWAUKEE'S HANDICAP ROAD RACE.

The Milwaukee Wheelmen's handicap road race will take place June 29, over the Wauwatosa course. Besides the usual number of prizes a valuable medal will be awarded for the best time made. Entries close June 24.

Mr. H. C. Stratton, the well-known bicycle rider and polo player, is in hard luck. Some miscreant stole his newly purchased New Mail bicycle, 53-inch, numbered 5586, from his residence, 63 Hawthorne Street, Chelsea, Mass., recently.

The South End Wheelmen, Philadelphia, are arranging for a summer's outing by the club this season, which is to take the shape of a tour to the Delaware Water Gap, Dingman's Ferry and Pike county. They expect to make it a great success.

The Bacheller Bros., well known grocery dealers at Lynn, are achieving a local notoriety as trick bicycle riders. Upper Broad Street is the scene of action, and some entirely novel dismounts are mentioned. A public exhibition may be given by them June 17.

Lynn wheelmen had hoped for an appropriation of $25,000 for paving, but the order authorizing that amount failed to pass, and one for the reduced sum of $10,000 went through. That amount, though hardly what a city like Lynn should expend, will do much good if judiciously laid out.

The Washington Park track, on which the K. C. W. meet will be held in June, will be in very good shape for fast time. The track is four laps to the mile, with very easy corners. Jack McMasters, the ground man, will have the corners raised, and will roll the surface smooth and hard.

Circulars have been issued by the Board of Directors of the Pennsylvania Bicycle Club asking for subscriptions to an additional issue of the club bonds for the purpose of erecting an extension to the wheel room. The bonds will bear interest at five per cent., and will be secured by a mortgage on the building.

The proposed reception which was to have been given by the Camden wheelmen in their new club house in Camden, on Thursday evening, has been postponed until June 7th. The house, which is the one formerly occupied by the Young Men's Republican Club, has been entirely refitted and is handsomely arranged for the purpose intended.

ABOUT CORRECT.

Editor Prial of THE WHEEL AND CYCLING TRADE REVIEW is determined that his publication shall maintain its place at the head of the cycling press. He is continually perfecting plans by which he is enabled to get all of the latest and best cycling news in the world.—*Brooklyn Press.*

Mr. Gething, of the Buffalo Club, has for some time been engaged on a map of that city, which is now completed, and will prove of incalculable value to cyclists. It is a complete street map on which is marked every roadway in the city, with special indications as to what streets are paved or likely to be paved with asphalt. One of the maps will be hung in the club room.

President Luscomb will be chief marshal of the parade at the L. A. W. meet, and his staff will be as follows: Albert Mott, adjutant and chief of staff; George S. Atwater, Wallace Merrihew, William M. Brewster, C. E. Lemmon, M. L. Bridgman, H. H. Hodgson, George R. Bidwell, William J. Gilhllian, Charles S. Davol, William H. Emery, Charles S. Butler, Sanford Lawton and James R. Dunn.

The careless practice of reckless riding would seem to have received a set-back the other day in Cupar, Scotland, when a verdict of £10 19s. and costs, amounting to about $75.00 in all, was given against James Wallace, a cyclist of Leven. This suit was brought by Andrew Tod, of Pittenween, he claiming that his horse was knocked down and seriously injured by the wheelman's colliding with him. They must either ride heavy wheels in Scotland, or go at a tremendous pace. Fancy an American wheelman knocking down a horse and cart in event of a collision!

Messrs. W. D. Allen & Co., Chicago, who represent the NEW YORK BELTING AND PACKING COMPANY, New York, in that city, have just issued a new and attractive catalogue, containing full description of their large line of vulcanized rubber goods. The cover, which is of a good quality of paper, is of a buff tint and printed in red and bronze; a view of the company's warehouse and salesrooms, 151 Lake Street, being shown on the back. It is a pamphlet of forty pages, profusely illustrated, typographically correct in every particular, and great care and much labor has evidently been bestowed in its preparation and production. Its perusal cannot fail to be of benefit to those interested in the line of goods which Messrs. W. D. Allen & Co. handle.

THE GREAT ROAD RACE.

"And there was mounting in hot haste
And hurrying to and fro."

W. F. Murphy, K. C. W., wins first prize.
John Bensinger, K. C. W., wins the time cup.
Rain in morning, sunshine in afternoon; big attendance.

Course kept very clear; race won in good time, and everybody satisfied.

Such is the history of the first twenty-five mile handicap road race.

The night before the race all was expectancy. Barkman went home with the knowledge that the mine was all prepared, and all that was needed was the magic click of his pistol to explode it. I went up to Bidwell's place and found him in a state of certainty that it would rain, though the stars were winking and twinkling with promise. At the Manhattan Club the crowd had gone home for a good night's rest, after getting their wheels into prime condition for the morning's ride. The New York's was deserted, save for a select coterie, De Goicouria twangetwanging the bango, "Pit," the "Vet.," pirouetting to the dulcet strains, and McFadden, big with the importance of his duties of the 30th. For was he not to lead the New Yorks, Manhattans, Riversides and Harlems down Fifth Avenue on the way to the depot?

In the morning I drew aside the curtain of expectancy and saw without the weather of disagreeability. It was 6 A. M., unearthly hour for me to leave the couch of indolence. But that Barkman was, I always claimed, something of a military man, for was it not a soldierly trick to rout us all out at six "all of a bright May morning," as the children sang; but this May morning was not bright, it was leadeny, drizzly, sticky, chilly, quite English.

After the inevitable coffee and roll, (in novels they never breakfast on anything more substantial) I searched the newspapers for consolation, but unearthed only an army of croakers. It was going to rain; the rain will become heavier as the day lengthens. Bright prospect. I threw dice to decide whether I should go out in mackintosh and goloshes, or risk pneumonia and influenza by donning the scant habiliments of cycling. Fate smiled on me; I donned my best cycling rig, my giddiest shirt and very smartest tie, and the weather cleared up at eleven; the sun shone out of a clear blue sky all the afternoon, with a few brief exceptions, when old Jup. Pluvius tried hard to turn on the shower bath, but old Sol., who is a stayer, knocked him out in good shape, and Jupe returned to his lair; all wicked people have lairs.

At 8.30 we sailed from New York aboard the good old tub Communipaw, manned by a goodly crew and a boot-black. After a sail across the stormy Hudson, we put in at Hoboken—from Ho, last, bo, place, ken, made. (I always was good on etomology). On the train I found some good company; as Referee Bidwell, in overcoat and rubbers—he suffered later in the day; R. F. Hibson, in mackintosh and comfortable—he threw them away at noon; Judge Furst, Clerk of Course Crichton, Judge Bridgman, Scorcher Putney, Captain Powers, and a lot of others. I almost forgot McFadden. He sat sadly in a corner, drawing extract of umbrella from the handle of his parachute. I asked him where were his "four hundred." "In the vanilla," he replied, airily.

After an eight-mile scorch from Newark, I landed at the Hilton Hotel. First man I saw was Barkman, pale and resolute, like a man at a marriage ceremony. He was looking for Prial. I pointed out the Chief Scorer to him, as I saw them intimately, and a very fine fellow I think him. I mean that he thinks nothing too good for me. At the hotel many wheelmen had gathered, mostly without wheels. The crowd was reinforced by natives and the small boy, with a sprinkling of hossy men, who discussed bicycles in the carriage yards. The bar was being worked double time, lemonade—a glass of dirty water with a lemon drop in it—being in demand. Upstairs the competitors were being rubbed down; downstairs sandwiches and pie were being dealt out at five cents the piece.

At eleven a move was made from the hotel to the starting point, a five-eighth mile level stretch southwest of the Hilton Hotel. The Clerk of Course worked a few moments, Starter Barkman raised his weapon on high, blazed away, and the first batch went sent off, quickly disappearing amid huzzas, and so each successive

batch was started until all were gone; then came a transformation. You all know Marion of the Kings County Wheelmen. He is short and stocky, looks as if he might hit hard, don't talk much, means what he says. Marion was armed with a golden badge, legended "Marshal," and a large club. The badge galvanized the club repelled; a sort of a positive and negative movement, you see. Up and down the course he flew and before him the crowd fell away, even as the pancake disappears from the boarding-school breakfast table. He was ably assisted by his aides and the course was kept in splendid condition. His chief assistant was Mr. Miles, of the K. C. W., a tall youth with auburn hair. We kept a record of how many times he took a judge or a scorer by the nape of the neck and fired him back into the crowd.

For two hours the men kept passing and repassing, the crowd being kept at fever heat. At an early stage of the game Dauchy loomed up as favorite, but later on the house of Murphy asserted itself and William, of that ilk, was picked out as a winner, so strong was he riding. The scratch men were rather disappointing to the crowd, who could not understand why they did not run down the men as wheat falls before the scythe-wielder. Fact was, they were sadly out of condition and nowhere near their best form. As the men reached the finish they were heartily cheered. Not a soul knew, until the official record was announced, that John Bensinger, K. C. W., had made the fastest time of the day, and that "Charl" Murphy was but six seconds behind him.

The table given above contains all details of the race as to positions and times at the important stages of the race.

The fastest five miles was ridden by Taxis, 17.04. Three other men rode the first five miles in 17.15.

TABLE OF NET TIMES.

	5 Miles.	10 Miles.	15 Miles.	20 Miles.	25 Miles.
1. Bensinger	17 32	35 34	55 01	1 12 44	1 31 41
2. C. Murphy	17 30	35 33	54 03	1 12 59	1 31 49
3. W. Murphy	17 19	34 55	53 41	1 12 13	1 32 13
4. Hesse	17 19	35 45	55 45	1 13 40	1 32 47
5. Hall	17 49	36 02	54 30	1 13 32	1 33 04
6. Class	17 19	35 52	54 40	1 13 13	1 33 38
7. H. J. Hall	17 39	35 37	55 50	1 14 13	1 33 43
8. Van Wagoner	17 51	35 50	54 59	1 14 15	1 33 53
9. Conighey	17 23	36 07	55 27	1 14 32	1 33 55
10. Dappman	18 04	36 42	56 10	1 14 48	1 34 40
11. Borland	17 15	35 52	54 54	1 14 32	1 34 31
12. McDaniels	17 33	35 50	56 00	1 14 45	1 34 52
13. Elliott	17 33	37 08	56 00	1 14 25	1 35 17
14. Stevens	18 09	36 59	56 72	1 16 95	1 36 44
15. Miller	18 35	38 56	58 06	1 17 14	1 37 13
16. Putney	18 35	38 18	59 03	1 18 49	1 38 57
17. Merribew	17 33	36 58	57 05	1 18 28	1 40 54
18. Watson	17 33	38 49	1 12 21	1 18 49	1 43 53
19. F. Elliot	17 52	38 10	55 41	1 16 15	1 45 52
20. Van Wagoner	17 33	38 58	57 50	1 16 35	1 47 09
21. Leflaud	19 48	41 54	61 07	1 24 54	1 48 07
22. Robertson	23 36	46 26	66 34	1 17 10	1 48 09
23. Lincoln	18 00	38 02	56 01	1 15 81	
24. Dauchy	18 09	36 57	55 18	1 16 00	
25. Matthews	19 31	40 08	60 20	1 23 33	
26. Quortropp	17 07	36 37	64 49	1 18 15	
27. Taxis	17 04	35 23	54 99	1 15 20	
28. Gregg	19 04	39 33	60 45		
29. Nisbett	18 39	39 51	60 72		
30. W. Van Wagoner	18 04	37 00			
31. Gobelman	21 28	43 33	70 56		
32. Wilhelm	17 51	35 56			
33. Bate	21 18				

The fastest ten miles were ridden by W. Murphy, 34.55, and the fastest fifteen miles are credited to W. Murphy, 53 41.

Robertson started 5 minutes 20 seconds behind his time. Deduct this from his net time, and he would have 19th position. He would have occupied 17th instead of 22d position at the finish.   TITNAN.

PULLMAN ROAD HANDICAP, MAY 30.

(Telegram to THE WHEEL.)

It rained hard to-day in Chicago, and the course was simply horrible. Out of 123 entries but 68 starters faced the mud and rain. The nine men lucky enough to win prizes finished in the following order:

1. L. Bodach, Illinois D. C., 11m. handicap. Time, 1h. 13s.
2. F. L. Dale, Illinois C. C., 10m. 30s. handicap. Time, 1h. 1m. 58s.
3. Geo. H. Pratt, Lincoln C. C., 11m. handicap. Time, 1h. 3m. 17.
4. H. W. Harland, Lincoln C. C., 12m. handicap. Time, 1h. 4m. 28s.
5. W. P. Hassard, Englewood, 11m. 45s. handicap. Time, 1h. 5m. 58s.
6. J. Guthrie, Alpha C. C., 7m. handicap. Time, 1h. 2m. 33s.
7. O. Wimmerstedt, Lincoln C. C., 4m. handicap. Time, 1h. 1m. 30s.
8. Frank Raabe, Eolus C. C., 10m. 30s. handicap. Time, 1h. 3m. 30s.
9. Geo. W. Starrett, Illinois C. C., 11m. 30s. handicap. Time, 1h. 5m. 36s.

A. E. Lumsden, Chicago Scratch, wins the time medal in 56m. 48s., good enough for a rainy day and wet track. Prizes given in this race aggregated over $1,000 in value, and included choice of Light Roadster Safeties or

Ordinaries from these houses: Henry Graham Gun Co. (New Mail); Spalding Bros. (Victor); Western Arms Co. (New Rapid); Pope Manufacturing Co. (Columbia); Chas. F. Stokes (Springfield Roadster). Other houses gave fine gold medals, among whom were Gormully and Jeffery and John Wilkinson Co., while still others contributed sundries. With good weather to help, the present record would have materially lowered.

FIXTURES.

June 1, 1889.—Manhattan Athletic Club 1½-mile Handicap. Entries closed May 25, with C. C. Hughes, 524 Fifth Avenue, N. Y. City.

June 4, 5, 6, 1889.—Kansas Division Meet at Forest Park, Ottawa, Kansas.

June 6, 1889.—Five-mile Bicycle Race at Seymour, Ind. Entries to be made to John A. Ross, Seymour, Ind.

June 8, 1889.—Century Run, Orange, N. J., to Philadelphia. Chairman, L. A. Clarke, 25 Broad Street, New York.

June 8, 1889.—Two-mile Bicycle Handicap at Schuylkill Navy A. C., Univ. of Penn. Grounds, Phila. Entries close June 1, with W. T. Wallace, 123 North 7th Street, Phila., Pa.

June 9, 1889.—Cyclists' Union Meet at Clarksvill, Mo.

June 10, 1889.—Regular Annual Meeting of Kentucky Division, L. A. W., at Danville, Kentucky.

June 12, 1889.—Bicycle Race at Huntington, L. I. Entries close with S. C. Ebbetts, Huntington, June 8.

June 13, 1889.—Two-mile Bicycle Race at Berkeley Oval—Eastern championship, A. A. A. Entries close May 25, with W. Janssen, P. O. Box 125, N. Y. City.

June 15, 1889.—L. I. W. Race Meet at Brooklyn Athletic Grounds. Entries close June 8 with L. H. Wise, 1,281 Bedford Ave., Brooklyn.

June 15, 1889.—Two-mile Bicycle Handicap at New York Athletic Club Grounds, Travers Island.

June 17, 1889.—Annual Meet of Massachusetts Division, L. A. W., at Squamtum, Mass.

June 18, 1889.—Third Annual Meet of Tennessee Division, L. A. W., at Nashville, Tenn.

June 22, 1889.—New Orleans Bicycle Club's Race for the Hill Cup.

June 28, 29, 1889.—Kings County Wheelmen's Annual Meet at Washington Park, Brooklyn. Address W. C. Nellis, 1,255 Bedford Avenue.

June 29, 1889.—Handicap Road Race of Milwaukee Wheelmen, over Wauwetosa course. Entries close June 24.

July 1, 2, 1889.—C. W. A. Annual Meet at St. Catharines, Ontario.

July 2, 3, 4, 1889.—League Meet at Hagerstown, Md.

July 3, 1889.—L. A. W. Race Meet, at Hagerstown, Md. Entries close June 20, with Harry B. Irwin, 34 West Franklin Street, Hagerstown, Md.

July 4, 1889.—Race Meet at Brownsville, Pa

July 4, 1889.—Illinois Division, L. A. W. Meet, at Ottawa.

July 4, 1889.—Tournament held by Lancaster (Pa.) Bicycle Club.

July 4, 1889.—Fort Schuyler Wheelmen, Utica, N. Y., 50-mile Road Race

July 20, 1889.—One-mile and 25-mile Bicycle and 5-mile Tricycle N. C. U. championships at Paddington, Eng., track.

July 27, 1889.—One-mile and 25-mile Tricycle and 5-mile Bicycle N. C. U. Championships at Paddington, Eng., track.

October 23-29, 1889.—Race Meet at Macon, Ga.

EUROPEAN CYCLING FIXTURES.

Austro-Hungary.—Graz, June 9 and 10; Pilsen, June 9 and 10; Prague (Smichow) June 29 and 30. Germany.—Berlin, June 16 and 17, July 21, September 15; Hanover, June 23, September 8; Cologne, June 2 and 30, August 12; Chemnitz, September 8; Frankfort-on-the-Maine, September 1; Mannheim, September 8; Crefeld, September 8. Hamburg.—Altona, September 22; Bochum, August 25; Soram, June 9; Coburg, June 9; Magdeburg, June 30, September 8. Denmark.—Copenhagen International Meeting, August 18.

National Cyclists' Union.—Championship Fixtures—At Paddington, August 24, 50-mile Bicycle and 1-mile Dwarf.

RACES AT WOODSTOCK, CANADA.

As befitted the day, the Queen's Birthday was favored with good weather at Woodstock, and that pretty city crowded with visitors. All available bunting was spread, and the local press explain that if decorations of an elaborate character were wanting, it was due to a lack of bunting.

The Woodstock Minstrel Company paraded at 10:30 A. M., headed by the St. Thomas Band. Base ball matches filled in the remaining part of the forenoon.

At 1:30 P. M. the parade was formed, numbering about 180, with representatives from the Forest City, Toronto, Woodstock, St. Catharines, Brantford and other clubs. Among the Forest City representatives were seven ladies on safeties and tricycles. In competition for the club prize the Torontos won, having thirty-one in line, but the audience thought the London club, with only twenty-eight members, better entitled to it. Following is a summary of races and winners:

TWO-MILE BICYCLE, NOVICE.—A. F. Edwards, Woodstock, 1st; E. W. Walbourn, Woodstock, 2d. Time, 7m. 43 2-5s. The last quarter was made in 43s., good against a high wind.

ONE-MILE BICYCLE, OPEN.—E. O. Rassicoe, Woodstock, 1st; Campbell, of Niagara Falls, 2d. Time, 2m. 59s. Rassicoe took the lead and was never headed, being 20 yards ahead of Campbell at the finish. The first quarter was made in 49s., the half in 1m. 36s.

HALF-MILE HANDICAP, OPEN.—Rassicoe again won in 1m. 22 4-5s., with a lead of fifteen yards. McCune, of Boston, came second, with Campbell third. This race was very close from start to finish, and at the last quarter it was thought to be Campbell's race. Both Campbell and Rassicoe were at scratch, and it is plain the others were not placed far enough ahead.

ONE-MILE HANDICAP.—Six entries started in this race, and Rassicoe again captured first prize in 2m. 54 3-5s., leading Carman, of Toronto, by twenty yards. The handicapping seems to have been poor in this race also.

TWO-MILE COUNTY CHAMPIONSHIP.—This had but two entries, and was easily won by E. W. Walbourn, of Woodstock, in 7m. 10s.

HALF-MILE HANDICAP, SECOND HEAT.—Rassicoe won as he liked in 1m. 27 2-5s., with Carman his only competitor.

FIVE-MILE HANDICAP.—Rassicoe's lucky star seems to have been in the ascendant, for this race was also his, in 15m. 53 4-5s., with a lead of seventy-five yards.

In all handicap races the scratch men seem to have been wrongly placed. Carman, 150 yards, came in second, and at the thirteenth lap was well in the lead.

ONE-MILE SAFETY.—McCune took this in 3m. 4 2-5s., with Doll, of London, second and Carman third.

Both McCune and Carman rode Springfield racers, and Doll an Extraordinary Challenge. McCune had an easy victory, with seventy-five yards lead.

ONE-MILE CONSOLATION.—Iven of Rochester, N. Y., who is said to have ridden a wheel two inches too large for him, won with thirty yards lead. Time not given.

Various athletic events were interspersed among the bicycle races, to give the wheelmen a chance to recover themselves. The Woodstock A. A. cannot at the most clear over $250, and stood a good show in the event of unfavorable weather of loosing over $1,000. Prizes given were more valuable than any yet offered this side of the line.

Rassicoe would seem to be the best man in all Canada, barring Foster, and the only man that can push him to his utmost is Windle. We hope to see the two meet before long. Rassicoe is only twenty years old, and has been riding but two years. Of quiet and unassuming manners, dark eyes and hair, he is popular with all who know him. He is in good training, and in the Woodstock races won two watches, a diamond ring, and a photographic outfit.

FOREIGN RACING MATTERS AND FACTS OF INTEREST.

We fancy our safety men are inclined to run to extremes in the matter of gearing and crank-length. How often do we see a short-legged competitor laboring along on a fairly fast track with 7-inch cranks and 60-inch gear, doing something over 3:20 to the mile. Surely, when ordinary racers here can get under 3 minutes on 56 and 57 inch wheels, with 5 or 5½ inch cranks, there must be something astray with this gaping after the 2:58 pace of our English riders. High gears and long cranks won't make a man a flyer if he is not suited to them. We know a few who have lowered the one or shortened the other with beneficial results.—*Scottish Cyclist.*

At the Glasgow University sports May 11, the one-mile handicap was won by A. J. Young, 95 yds., in 2m. 56 1-5s., good time on a wet track. R. A. Vogt, scratch, won the three-mile handicap in 9m. 32 1-5s. This race had seven starters, four falling out before the finish. Vogt led by 10 yds. in winning, with Torrance second, and Young a close third. In the two-mile safety handicap, J. E. Young, 25 yds., won in 6m. 17s. Four men fell among eleven starters, evidencing the uncertainty in steering safeties at a high rate of speed.

The Perth Amateurs also held a race-meeting on May 11, with favorable weather and good attendance, but time made was slow. In the one-mile handicap, run in four heats, the best time made was the final mile in 3m. 1 1-5s., by M. Bruce, of Edinburgh. The final heat of the one-mile roadster safety handicap was also the best, D. McArthur, of Perth, winning in 3m. 4 3-5s. C. Elsworth, with 50 yds. handicap, won the two-mile safety in 6m. 26 4-5s., with twenty yards lead at the finish. Bruce, who would seem to be a "coming man," also won the three-mile bicycle handicap, by fifteen yards lead, in time of 9m. 33 1-5s. Bruce started from scratch, with eight ahead, handicaps varying from 100 to 240 yds. Good things may be looked for this season from both Vogt and Bruce.

The Whitsuntide tournament, inaugurated by *Sport and Play*, which takes place June 10 and 11, sees the opening of the new cycling track at Ashton, Eng. This track is a four-lap, straightaway, 110 yds each, curved ends each exactly the same curve, and banked all round to no less than four feet. It is largely modeled on the Coventry track, and predicted to be one of the fastest in the Kingdom.

Rain from one end to the other of the races at Leyton, Eng., May 11, had a most discouraging effect on times made, such speed as 4m. 3 5-8s. and 4m. 8 1-5s. in the novice's one-mile handicap and one-mile safety handicap, being common things. Entries for the one-mile novice's handicap (mixed classes of machines), numbered 110 (!)—liable to be record for some time to come—but of these 110 forty decided the weather and wet track were too much for them. Safeties were in the background, the ordinary proving the superior in such a slushy state. The amateur champion of Holland, Scheltema Bevrin, made his appearance, but had no show against Osmond, who won in 3m. 47 3-5s. In spite of the weather some 2,000 spectators turned out, and the meeting is claimed not to be a financial loss. Keen was to have ridden an exhibition mile but declined to start.

Fred Lees and Harry Roberts are riding a tandem safety bicycle geared up to 72, weighing 33 lbs. This wheel is turned out by Humber & Co., and is well spoken of by the riders.

Verdicts respectively of £16 and £13, have been given in favor of cyclists against a 'bus driver and the owner of a runaway horse. In both cases the machines were total wrecks, but the riders escaped with slight injuries.

Harrington & Co., whose name is familiar to all cyclists through connection with their cradle springs and combination saddles, have disposed of the entire business to W. Middlemore, of Birmingham, Eng., an extensive maker of saddles of various kinds. Mr. Middlemore is to carry on the manufacture at the present place of business, Mr. Harrington devoting his whole time to the patent tube chime business.

RACES AT OTTAWA, CANADA.

Two thousand people witnessed the bicycle races on the Metropolitan Athletic grounds, Ottawa, May 24th. The track was in fine condition. Results:

ONE MILE (Green Club)—H. W. Skinner, 1, time 3.32; H. F. Hardy, 2; W. Parr, 3.

ONE MILE (district championship)—W. H. Sproule, 1, time 3.30 1-8; D. F. Blythe, 2.

ONE MILE (open)—J. H. Robertson, Montreal, 1, time 3.15 3-5; F. J. Whatmough, Toronto, 2.

TWO MILE HANDICAP (club)—H. F. Hardy, 1, time 7.02 4-5; W. Parr, 2.

HALF-MILE (without hands)—M. F. Johnson, 1, time 1.44 4-5; T. Hawey, St. Jerome, 2.

ONE MILE.—W. H. C. Mussen, Montreal, 1, time 3.21 3-5; F. D. Scott, Montreal, 2.

FIVE MILE OPEN (bicycle)—J. H. Robertson, Montreal, 1, time 18 54 1-5.; Gerry, Toronto, 2.

ONE MILE HANDICAP—G. Morgan, Ottawa, 1, time 3.18 1-5; R. Penistone (Wanderers), Toronto, 2.

TWO MILE LAP RACE (open)—Scott, Montreal, 1, time 7.25; Gerry (Wanderers), Toronto, 2.

THREE MILE HANDICAP (road machine)—W. H. C. Mussen, Montreal, 1, time 10.23; H. F. Hardy, Ottawa, 2.

HALF-MILE HURDLE (bicycle) open—W. Odell, Ottawa, 1; F. S. King, Ottawa, 2.

Two mile bicycle race at N. Y. State Intercollegiate A. A. May 18: H. D. Kittenger, H., first, in 7m. 37s.; C. W. Hills, U., second, by ten feet.

Eight members of the Hope Bicycle Club were entered in a five hours' race at the London Theatre, Pittsburgh, Pa., May 25. Score: Snodgrass, 75 miles 14 laps; Lawton, 28.1; Bahl, 18.1.

Two mile bicycle race at Staten Island A. C.'s games May 18: F. G. Brown, New Jersey A. C., 155 yards start, first, in 5m. 46 2-5s.; S. B. Bowman, New Jersey A. C., 160 yards, second; D. Oakes, Bloomfield Cyclers, 225 yards, third.

The Queens Bicycle Club 1-mile championship came off May 30 at Queens, L. I., resulting as follows: Geo. Boyce, first; R. A. Kissam, second; Len. R. Roughty, Jr., third. Time made, 3m. 45s. A heavy headwind accounts for the slow time made. Real racing did not commence till the last lap.

Five men started in the annual 5-mile road race of the Indianapolis Bicycle Club, held on May 26, on the old National road, near Greenfield. Edward Eads looked like a winner a mile from the finish, but a severe header put him out of the race, which was won by Charles McKeen in 17m. 20s.; Arthur Johns second, in 17m. 32s., with Charles Vantilburgh a close third.

ONE AND A HALF-MILE M. A. C. HANDICAP.

To be decided Saturday, June 1st, at the M. A. C. games: Brown, Schoefer, scratch; Bowman, 15; Schumacher, 25; Steves, 30; R. L. Jones, 45; Rollins, 50; Marshall, H. L. Powers, Wieners and W. F. and C. Murphy, 60; Class, 70; Hinds, 80; Worden, 80; Burgess, 80; Pelin, 80; Quortropp, 80; Sanford, 90; Findlay, 90; Bensinger, 85; Hanson, 65.

TWO MILE INTERCOLLEGIATE CHAMPIONSHIP.

This event was decided at Berkeley Oval last Saturday: 2-mile bicycle race: first round: first two in each heat to ride in final.—First [illegible]; H. Davis, '91, H., 6m. 4-5s; F. A. Clark, '91, S., Y. [illegible], a wheel; E. Bailey, '91, H., 3, by 2 feet; A. F. Koomize, '91, S., Y., 0; F. A. Delabarre, '90, A., 0. Davis and Bailey rode safety machines, in violation of the rules of the League of American Wheelmen, and were protested by all the other competitors, but under the Intercollegiate rules they could not be debarred. Second heat, W. B. Greenleaf, '92, H., 6m. 14 1-5s.; W. W. Weare, '90, S., Y., 2; C. B. Keen, '89, U. of P., 0; H. V. Register, '92, U. of P., 0; F. Gubelman, '89, Stevens Institute, 0. Final heat, at first turn of third lap Davis, riding wide, ran into Clark's wheel, knocking out several spokes and upsetting the rider. Continuing, Davis finished first, Greenleaf second, and Weare third. Davis was disqualified, Weare awarded third place, and Greenleaf and Clark ordered to ride again May 27, at 3 P. M. This second trial was ridden in a rain storm, on a muddy path, and Clark, trailing until the last lap, won easily by 20 yards, in 6m. 48 2-5s., as many had foretold from a study of the trial heats, in which Clark rode 13 2-5s. faster than Greenleaf.

LEAGUE MEET RACES AT HAGERSTOWN, MD., JULY 4, 1889.

To racing men in particular the tenth annual meet will prove interesting. The three principal L. A. W. national championships have been located here and the winners of these races can deservedly feel proud of holding League championships. From the present indications the victors will earn their spoils.

The track is elliptical in shape with easy turns and very fast.

There will be handsome gold prizes for all firsts and valuable second prizes, except in the team race; for this the prize will be a fine silk banner. Send in your entries early as possible and save the committee a rush of work for the few last days.

Mr. W. J. Corcoran, a trainer comparatively new to New York wheelmen, but with experience, that best of recommendations, will be disengaged after May 30. At present Mr. Corcoran has charge of the Yale racing men, and in the space of six weeks has brought F. A. Clark rapidly to the front. Among riders that Mr. C. has had charge of are the following amateurs: Fred Foster, of Toronto, amateur Canadian Champion, '86, '87 and '88; Howard Hart, of New Britain, Conn., prominent in '86 and '87; A. B. Rich, who needs no introduction to New Yorkers; E. O. Roscoe, novice of Woodstock, Canada, who won three out of the four races he entered in, and H. R. Arnold, of New Britain, Conn., with a record of nine races out of a possible fourteen.

Since penning our editorial on the break of the Racing Rules which occurred at the intercollegiate races, we have reason to believe that the following men will be temporarily suspended from the path: R. S. Davis, Harvard; F. A. Clark, Yale; E. Bailey, Harvard; A. F. Koomtze, Yale; F. A. Delabarre, Amherst; W. B. Greenleaf, Harvard; W. W. Weare, Yale; C. B. Keen, Univ. of Pa.; H. V. Register, Univ. of Pa.; F. Gubelman, Stevens Institute. Davis and Bailey rode safeties.

The one-mile bicycle race at the spring meeting of the Wm. Penn Charter School A. A., last Saturday, was won by Woolman in 3m. 18 1-5s., breaking the former school record. There were four entries, Logan coming in second.

F. A. Delabarre, of Amherst, took the two-mile bicycle race in the time of 7m. 33 3-5s. at the games of N. E. Intercollegiate A. A. May 23, at Worcester, Mass. Harriman, of Worcester, came in second.

THE SAFETY BICYCLE.

"Talk about fads," said a well-posted man-about town yesterday, "but the craze for safety bicycles beats them all. So long as 'biking' was solely a masculine privilege its popularity was limited, but now that it has become possible for women to take a skim on a two-wheeled machine and sit astride just like a man there is a pell-mell rush for bicycles being made by young ladies. This makes victims of a horde of young men, who are forced to become 'bikers' or lose their girls. I tell you the mania promises to infect society through and through and to bankrupt whole lots of fond papas and low-salaried clerks. From a close observation of women I have come to the conclusion that whenever they see an opportunity of taking up in strict propriety some particularly mannish sport or habit they are mighty glad to do it. I haven't a doubt that dead loads of women have had a consuming desire to ride one of the big wheels, but, of course, they couldn't do this and wear skirts, and, as propriety forbade them donning pantaloons, they had to snub this yearning. Now, however, the difficulty is obviated. Some genius invented a new kind of 'bike,' which is not only suitable for a woman to ride, attired in an ordinary street dress, but which the majority of men prefer also. And there you have it. The boulevards of evenings are plentifully used by young couples on their bicycles and it looks very nice to see a young man and his best girl spinning along side by side. The girls seem to take an almost wild delight in it and now and then a strong-limbed young woman will run away from her escort. The safety 'bike' opens up a field to women for healthful exercise and enjoyment as necessary as it has been long delayed. A funny thing about this style of bicycle is that though there are half a dozen different firms manufacturing it, they have formed a pool right at the start off, destroyed competition, and put the prices about $40 higher on each machine than they have any license to do."—*Chicago Mail.*

THE PENN'S HOUSE WARMING.

The Penn Wheelmen had a royal time at their house warming in the Hagenman building, Court St., Phila., the other evening. The elegantly furnished apartments, redolent with perfume of flowers; the banqueting table loaded with tempting viands; the animated conversations of wheelmen and their lady guests; and the Germania Orchestra's music, all combined to make the evening one to be remembered. About thirty ladies of Philadelphia were present, besides the Reading Bicycle Club and their ladies. The club now numbers thirty-six, and prospects for a rapid increase in membership are [illegible]. Present officers are as follows: President, Frank N. [illegible], Vice-President, J. Ed. Wanner; Recording Secretary, [illegible]vin T. Reiter; Financial Secretary, Frank James.

BICYCLING BOOMING IN WACO, TEXAS.

The Waco Cyclers will hold a meeting this week. Will some bicycle club be kind enough to send the Waco Cyclers a copy of their constitution and by-laws. J. C. Stephenson has sent orders for fifteen wheels. They are expected this week. The club will start out with twenty wheels on the road. Waco has the largest bicycle club in the State. Chas. R. Turner is the pluckiest beginner we have, only fifty headers last week. Lewis Crow and Arthur King ride sixty inch wheels. W. Parker is the finest bicycle rider in the South. He was a pupil of Prince Wells. T. N. Parker will be the winner at the Dallas races this fall.

"VERNON," in *Spirit of the South*, May 19, 1889.

CHICAGO LETTER.

RULINGS OF THE JUDGE.

I have never witnessed quite so much excitement over the wheel in this city as that which has surrounded us on all sides during the past month. Chicago itself affords glorious facilities for cycling, her boulevards and parks, bordering as they do the beautiful city, render it almost a paradise to the wheelman. One can start in the morning and ride straightaway for forty miles over the most delightful sand-papered roads and through the parks. Just think of it, forty miles and always in sight of the city! Is it any wonder that Chicago dealers have experienced the most marvelous demand for wheels? I remember the time in this city when cycling was indulged in by but a few, and all this in the latter part of the '70's, when cycling was considered by nearly everybody a sport which should be relegated to small boys, and imagined in the clouded condition of their minds that a ride on a wheel was as much out of place for a young man as would be a game of marbles in some back alley.

The safety bicycle in this city has developed an altogether different class of riders from that of the ordinary. Some of Chicago's most respected business men use the wheel as a mode of conveyance for themselves between their homes and places of business. It is nothing unusual to see a stout, pompous gentleman rushing down the road mounted upon his Volante safety, and bowing right and left to the wheelmen he meets. This individual can sign his check for over a million dollars. I might mention the names of a great many gentlemen over fifty years of age who are the most ardent and enthusiastic devotees of the wheel. Surely, with such indorsement as this, it can hardly be wondered that the dealers of this city have experienced so much difficulty in getting from the manufacturers enough wheels to meet the demand.

The Chicago Cycling Exhibit and Tournament, held during the middle part of this month in the great Exposition Building, has also served to boom an already well-boomed sport, and now, as I write, I hear nothing from the boys but "Pullman Handicap Road Race." The Pullman road race of '87 and that of '88 were gigantic affairs, and provoked the amazement of the entire country by their magnitude. The race of '89 will unquestionably be the greatest road race ever run in this country. A great deal of credit is due to Mr. R. D. Garden for the excellent judgment exercised in completing arrangements for this event. Over one hundred and thirty of Chicago's fleetest wheelmen have entered, and over one hundred will undoubtedly start.

The course is between fourteen and fifteen miles in length, and if the day is fine the winner will have to ride it in less than fifty-four minutes. The racers will leave the front of the Leland Hotel, which is situated at the north end of Michigan Boulevard, and will run directly south over Grand Boulevard, through South Park and over the famous Stony Island Road, over the far-famed, heavy-hearted sand hill into that beautiful little hamlet that George built, finishing directly in front of Hotel Florence.

The race will undoubtedly be won by some dark horse. Heaven only knows how many there are among the starters. A special train has been chartered that will carry the hundreds, possibly thousands, of spectators from the starting point directly to the finish, and, providing no accidents occur to stop the train, those who go on it can see both the start and arrive in Pullman in good time to see the finish.

The prizes offered amount in number to nearly 90, and in value over $1,000, consisting of high grade bicycles, watches and various other little nick-nacks. Will wire you the names of the first 10 men in, giving you at the same time the exact time made by each man.

Considerable comment has been excited by the failure of the Western Arms and Cartridge Company. This concern, during the first part of the year, opened a bicycle department and placed the festive Tom Roe at its head. Thomas turned out to be a pretty good manager, and I, for one, am inclined to think that if every department had proved as profitable as Tom's, the concern would not have been closed by a relentless, stony-hearted Sheriff. I understand that poor Temple, Heaven soothe his heart, seeing an opportunity, as he thought, for a good investment, invested a few thousand dollars of his hard earned currency in the purchase of a few shares of stock in this concern. Possibly Ralph would have done better had he remained in Galesburg and embarked in the hat business there, although slower, it would certainly have been surer.

The Chicago boys were considerably put out by the failure to run the Stone-Lumsden Race last Saturday in St. Louis. I am told, however, by one who was there that the track was in a beastly condition, and, to use my friend's own words, it was nothing more or less than a 10-acre lot with a little of the turf pulled off rendering it impossible to ride over it, especially as the rain of the day before made it soft and muddy. I am surprised that a city like St. Louis should have such poor accommodations for racing. It has been concluded to postpone the race for one week; Lumsden, in the meantime, has returned to Chicago and will ride in the great Decoration Day Pullman Road Race.

The Chicagos had quite a gay time last Monday evening. Owing to Pres. Shinkle's removal from the city his resignation was accepted, and the popular Will Thorn unanimously elected for the office. I was somewhat surprised to hear that Seig resigned the Secretaryship, but then Seig is in the bicycle business and seems to think that he has not sufficient time to devote to the club. A. G. Wainwright has been elected to fill his vacant chair. Thos. Roe got the fever and resigned the Captaincy, and old war-horse Van Sicklen was elected to fill that office. For such a steady old club as this I was greatly surprised at all these resignations, but understand it is simply a coincidence that the 3 most important offices should be vacated the same evening.

My writings are not strange to the readers of THE WHEEL, although, for reasons best known to myself, I shall have to introduce myself by a new name. I trust that my notes, which, by the way, I shall endeavor to make as interesting as possible will afford my readers as much pleasure in reading as they do me to write them.

Chicago, May 29th, 1889. THE JUDGE.

The party of American cyclists who went to Europe with Mr. Elwell, of Maine, arrived at Queenstown, Ireland, May 27, on the steamer Cephalonia, from Boston. Delegates from different Irish clubs met them in the harbor and tendered them a hearty Celtic welcome, afterward escorting them to Cork, where they were to be banqueted. Thence they are to go to Youghal, where they are to board the Duke of Devonshire's steam launch and be taken to Blackwater, also visiting Mount Melleray. They will ride to Dungarvan, Waterford and other places of interest, arriving in Dublin on Saturday, where they are to be feasted at the Shelburne Hotel, leaving the following day for England.

TACOMA, WASHINGTON TERRITORY.

This morning ten of the boys start for Victoria, B. C., on the five o'clock boat and expect to remain in that quiet old city until Saturday evening. The Secretary of the Victoria Club sent us a very cordial invitation and assured us of a most enjoyable time. The celebration of the Queen's birthday is the Britishers' "Fourth of July." The Tacoma and Seattle boys are to be represented in the parade and also in the races, and I think Tacoma will hold her own. At present we do not know the exact order of the programme, but a knowledge of the hospitality shown to all visitors to Victoria is sufficient guarantee that we will return amply repaid. The following compose the Tacoma contingent: Messrs. Karl Thompson, E. S. Barlow, Hays, Weiler, McCoy, Clarke, Manning, Benj. Thompson, H. Huggins, Prince Wells, S. E. Rainey and Bast.

We are pleased to announce the arrival of Mr. Reynolds and wheel, and happy to know he intends locating permanently in Tacoma. The wheelmen of Washington, D. C., lost a good man when Mr. Reynolds left that city for the new State.

At last Culver is satisfied that life is worth living. His fair protege has finally gained complete mastery over the safety and now rides like a fairy. I overheard a remark of one lady to another, as Miss Metzler passed, to the effect that she had no idea a lady could ride a bicycle so gracefully. Tacoma will soon be able to boast of at least half a dozen lady riders.

Since the road race many opinions have been expressed regarding the final spurt, and it has been said that Karl Thompson slipped his pedal purposely so Halsted could win. It is a fact that Halsted coached Thompson throughout the twenty miles, or, rather, within 1½ miles of the finish, and Halsted claims that at that point Thompson was to ride his own race and use his own judgment. Many of the boys think that the latter could have outspurted Halsted, and naturally they want to witness a fair trial of speed between these two riders. We now look forward to some interesting developments.

Ben Thompson is seen riding his father's safety each afternoon and has "caught on" in great shape. Will Ben soon get a lady's safety of his own?

Tacoma is built upon the side of a hill, and at first sight a wheelman thinks a bicycle useless for riding around the city. Although the streets from the water front to the top of the hill are almost insurmountable, nevertheless we are favored with two "diagonal" streets on which we can ride from the bottom and by an easy grade reach the top of the hill, either end of the town, so that it will be seen we can ride from any part of the city to another without a dismount and without tugging up grades of one foot in four.

Ed. McCoy has invited the cyclists of Tacoma to go with him to his ranch next Sunday and help pick strawberries. This means a hearty luncheon of strawberries and cream, a picnic that all the boys enjoy.

Rainey, McCoy, and others of racing propensities, will soon begin to practice for the Fourth of July race. The programme will include ¼-mile and ½-mile dashes, 1, 3 and 5 mile races, one of which will probably be a handicap. If the road is in good condition Prince Wells will try to lower the 10-mile unicycle record, which now stands at 59m. and some odd seconds.

We are all watching with interest the accounts relative to the great 25-mile road race to take place on the Irvington-Milburn course, 30th inst. Halsted, who knows many of those who have signified their intentions to compete, eagerly scans each issue of THE WHEEL and tells us it will be a grand sight at the finish.

Prince Wells gave the Victoria people an exhibition of his fancy riding on the 24th and surely opened the eyes of some of the Britishers.

SNOHOMISH.

May 25, 1889.

ST. LOUIS.

As I wrote you in my last letter, the races announced for Saturday were postponed until Monday on account of rain. On Sunday night the rain fell in torrents; the storm seemed to concentrate right over the track, and on Monday morning it was a sea of mud. Every one who saw it up to 11 o'clock in the morning agreed that no racing could be done on it that day, and postponement was again resorted to. By 2 o'clock, however, it began to look as if the track would be all right in an hour or two, and it was decided to go ahead with the programme. In the meantime, Lumsden, supposing that the races were off, had made other arrangements for the afternoon and could not be found. Not wishing to disappoint the crowd that had gathered the other events were run off, and the Stone-Lumsden race postponed until June 5.

The half-mile scratch and the one-mile and two-mile handicaps were won very handily by Frank Mehlig. Alex. Lewis captured the mile novice, and Ed Cunningham won the one-mile handicap for rear-driving safeties, starting from the seventy-five yard mark. The races were all closely contested and the crowd was enthusiastic. Being a clay track it suffers from wet weather, but it dries rapidly and two hours sunshine is sufficient to put it in good shape. Had we known this on Monday the Lumsden-Stone affair might have been decided and much disappointment averted. It will surely be run off next Wednesday, and I will wire you the result.

Bob Garden was here from Saturday morning until Monday night, and made hosts of friends. He will always find a hearty welcome awaiting him whenever he chooses to visit us; likewise Mr. Livingston who accompanied him. The big crowd that was coming down loaded with stuff to bet on their favorite, failed to materialize, and the gallons of strawberries and cream prepared for their delectation at Ballwin had to be otherwise disposed of, *i. e.*, thrown away.

The annual meeting of the Missouri Division will be held at Sedalia, July 3 and 4. The arrangements are in the hands of Consul Joe H. Kelly and the Sedalia cyclers. I have seen no announcement of the programme as yet, but it will no doubt be forthcoming in a few days. At any rate Mr. Kelly and his associates can be depended on to furnish something attractive.

On Tuesday President W. G. Sherk, of the Buffalo Zigzags, met with a rather severe accident on Richmond Avenue, and is now in bed suffering from the effects of the fall—which are somewhat serious.

Wheelmen should not forget the division meet at Danville, Ky., on June 10th. The Louisville cyclers will leave on the morning of the 8th and wheel to Bardstown that day, thence to Danville via Lebanon, Mitchellsburg and Parksville. This route is over the best roads in the State and through a pretty country. The division tour will be on Tuesday, the 11th, to Crab Orchard Springs, Ky.

Miss Hilda Kempton, who is in her tenth year and rides a 22-inch safety bicycle, accompanied the C. R. C. on their run to Delhi, Ky., on the first Sunday in May. The round trip was twenty-two miles, and two-thirds the distance was ridden on narrow and tortuous side-paths. Those who saw Miss Hilda leading the procession were so surprised that they regarded her with silent and open-mouthed wonder. She did not seem to feel the effects of the ride at all.

A number of ladies have signified their intention of participating in the union run of the Lynn, Mass., Cycle Club to Humphrey's Pond, Lynnfield, Sunday, June 2d., where a bountiful lunch is to be served. The hour for starting from the club room has been changed from 9 to 10 o'clock A. M. The ladies to wheel into line in Market Square, West Lynn. It should be remembered that all wheelmen in the city are invited. Any balance remaining after the caterer's bill is paid will be devoted to reducing the cost of the next run of a similar kind.

It seems that the Seventh Street Bridge Company, of Pittsburgh, had much to do in causing several important clauses in the Pennsylvania Wheelmen's Liberty Bill to be stricken out. This is news, but 'tis none the less true, and had the local cyclists paid attention to the bill it would undoubtedly have gone through entire. Mr. C. W. Robinson, a local member of the recent legislature, is authority for the statement that the bill was not rushed at all by the Philadelphia members, and had nothing to do therewith; that it would have passed without much debate. As it was, the bridge company interested itself enough to have the clause, which gave wheelmen the right to ride across their bridge, stricken out. The end is not yet, however, and if the officials refuse to permit wheelmen the same rights as vehicles, it is probable that a test suit will be the result. Hugh Fleming, Jr., is much interested in the matter, and is strongly in favor of making the test. An amicable arrangement will be entered into if possible failing in which the law will be appealed to. As the matter now stands wheelmen are compelled to dismount and walk across the bridge,

Arthur Couillard, alias George Welch, lately purloined a tricycle from a friend at Newburyport, and, after a severe struggle, reached Lynn Tuesday, and was at once arrested for the Newburyport officers. The young man was taken in charge by the Deputy Marshal of Newburyport, and at 3:47 that afternoon the return trip was started by rail.

All cyclers and travelers in general will do well to avoid the towns of Norwood and Walpole, on account of the disgraceful condition of the highways. A delegation from the Massachusetts Club rode to Walpole last Sunday week, returning across country via Milton, and found the roads unridable and almost impassable for man or beast between Dedham and Walpole, and between Walpole and Canton. The authorities have covered the road with broken stone, sand and gravel, and left them unrolled.

Capt. Paul L. Hassenforder, of the Belmont wheelmen, has invited the clubs of Boston attending the anniversary celebration in Belmont, Mass., June 4 and 5, to make use of the club rooms in the Crocker Building on City Square.

The property owners residing in the neighborhood of School Lane, west of Wissahickon Avenue, German own, Pa., have raised $12,500 to repair that well-known thoroughfare.

It is proposed to throw a bridge across the River Schuylkill at a point where City Line Avenue strikes the river. When this is done and City Line Avenue cut through, and the necessary and proposed improvements made from the other side of the river to Germantown, the public will have splendid riding and driving facilities between West Philadelphia and Germantown.

President Luscomb and a number of Brooklyn wheelmen will arrive in Hagerstown on Monday, the day before the meet proper. He will be met by the Hagerstown authorities, who will present him, as representing the League, with the freedom of the city.

The round trip rate from New York to the meet, over the Baltimore & Ohio and Pennsylvania roads, will be $10.

The streets of Hagerstown are macadamized, and one can ride all over the city. The principal hotel is the Hamilton, the League hotel.

Two distinguished Bostonians were in town last week, "Doc" Emery, down on League uniform business, and with a large club for the editor of this paper, who, fortunately, was out of town, and Editor Fourdrinier, down on some official organ business, we believe,

J. R. Dunn, of Massillon, Ohio, has been confined to his house for some weeks with a severe illness. We are glad to hear that Mr. Dunn is convalescent.

General Passenger Agent Farmer, of the New York and Greenwood Lake Railroad, has a long head; so long that he placed several special cars at the disposal of the clubs on Decoration Day, and scooped a great deal of business as the result of his enterprise.

H. M. Sabin, formerly manager of the Rudge Agency, and late head salesman for the Pope Mfg. Co., has gone into partnership with A. Sidwell, and will continue the business recently started by Mr. Sidwell, at 131 Congress Street, under the firm name of Sidwell & Sabin. They will handle new and second-hand wheels of reliable makers, beside doing a general repair business. Mr. Sidwell sailed for England on Saturday, May 18, from New York. He will be gone about six weeks, on business for the firm.

The Scranton Bicycle Club is booming this year. Considerable riding is being done, and their club-house and grounds present an attractive appearance. Flowers ornament the lawn, and the janitor keeps the lawn-mower's bearings well oiled, for fear of a "hot box." Last Sunday a party of Wilkes-Barre wheelmen were up at Scranton, and took dinner at the latter's club-house. The Scranton boys have a weakness that may be kindly forgiven. It is fondness for a good dinner, and their club-house allows them to indulge their liking. "Meals at all hours" should be on the Scranton banner.

The doors of the Western Arms and Cartridge Company, Chicago, have been closed by one of the Chicago banks on a judgment note for $69,000. This company was located on State Street, appeared to be doing a good business, and this spring added a wheel department. First Tom Roe had charge of it, then Temple and Munger increased the staff in that department, and things appeared to be rushing. Just how heavily the firm is involved is not known, but a meeting of the creditors will be held so look over the state of affairs. The company themselves claim a speedy resumption of business.

We are in receipt of a new composition entitled "Wheelmen's Waltz," composed by John Young, published by Wm. Adrian Smith, New York. The conventional bow-legged wheelman riding a wheel with steering-head ten inches high, helps ornament the title page. In grade this piece may be classed as 3, and should prove useful to teachers. Keys of C and F, without octaves. As the melody is pleasing, it seems well adapted for dancing purposes.

Number		Holder		Letter No.

APPLICATION FOR MEMBERSHIP IN THE L. A. W.

ABBOT BASSETT, Secretary, Box 5267, Boston, Mass.—Enclosed you will find $............for initiation fee and dues in the League of American Wheelmen to April 30 next ensuing.   I hereby certify that I am over 18 years of age, and that I am an amateur within the meaning of the definition printed herewith.   I refer to the persons named below.

Date,   18   Name,..

Club..   St. and Number, or Box,..........................

References:..   City,..

                                               State,..

(Each Applicant must give as references the names of two L. A. W. members or three reputable citizens.)

BROOKLYN NEWS.

The first game of base ball between the Kings County Wheelmen and Brooklyn Bicycle Club was played at the parade grounds last Saturday, resulting in a score of 15 to 13 in favor of the K. C. W. nine. Considering the small amount of practice done by the two nines the score was a fair one, and some respectable playing was done on both sides. The Brooklyn's battery was Mathews, pitcher, and Hardie, catcher, the two men changing places for the final innings, to which the B. B. C. nine attribute the loss of the game. A return game will be played shortly, when they can try it again, if Hardie's hands are a little less tender by that time.

I saw in the Brooklyn papers a short time ago an advertisement for bids on the repairing of Cobblestone Hill, or, at least that part of Bedford Avenue which includes the much-talked-of terror to wheelmen, so I suppose we may reasonably expect some improvements to be made in that direction during the present riding season by the city authorities—of course, excepting the "many a slip," etc., which seems to especially appertain to the Brooklyn Street Commissioners. The Cyclists' Union has twice hired men to remove the loose stones from the hill, which made a slight improvement, although temporary on account of other stones working through. This action was duly appreciated by the many riders who are obliged to use that thoroughfare.

The Thirteenth Regiment had an all-night bivouac at Richmond Hill last Saturday and induced some wheelmen to assist in the ceremonies, as an experiment to ascertain to what uses bicycles might be put as advance guards or scouts and night patrols, etc. I have not heard what the official report of the subject was, but will try and obtain it for next week's letter.

L. H. Wise, L. I. W., is still disabled from riding by the results of the fall he took some time ago. It has proved more serious than at first supposed, and it will be some time yet before he will be seen awheel. He is greatly put out by it, as the other men in the club are getting a big lead on the mileage records.

The list of club runs and informal Sunday runs just issued by Captain Meeteer for the Brooklyn Club for the month of June is quite comprehensive, and the boys who participate in them all will cover quite a number of miles. It reads as follows: Saturday, June 1, "Around the Block;" Sunday, June 2, Roslyn, L. I; Saturday, June 8, Park for base ball game and Century run to Philadelphia; Sunday, June 9, Gravesend Bay for fish dinner, sail, etc.; Saturday, June 15, L. I. W. race meet; Sunday, June 16, Long Branch, Seabright and Red Bank; Saturday, June 22, Poughkeepsie and Ramapo Valley; Saturday, June 29, K. C. W. race meet; Sunday, June 30, Massapequa Hotel, South Oyster Bay, for dinner. The last run will probably be one of the largest in point of numbers, as it was a very favorite one of the Brooklyn boys last summer, if I remember rightly, the principal feature being the dinner, for wheelmen certainly enjoy a good meal a little better than any one else.

Query—Does "Miles" Murphy ever ride without scorching? I think I never saw him riding in an upright position.

ATOL.

BROOKLYN, May 28, 1889.

PHILADELPHIA.

Quite a large delegation of Philadelphia wheelmen were present to witness the annual 5-mile road race of the Camden, N. J., Wheelmen, which took place last Saturday afternoon, on the Haddonfield Pike. As the hour for the race drew near there were fully two hundred people congregated about the finishing point, each one eagerly awaiting the outcome. After several false alarms the racers hove in sight, and when they got near enough to be recognized it was seen that Buzby (who had the benefit of a 55-second handicap) was in the van, crossing the tape in 19m. 35s., followed by Eyre (90-seconds handicap) in 20m. 10s., while the third man in was Browning, in 20m. 35s. Then came Jessup, and finally the two scratch men, Green and Weaver. After the race all the wheelmen repaired to the handsome house now occupied by the local wheelmen and partook of some light refreshment, then, mounting their wheels, were soon aboard the ferry crossing the noble Delaware. Arriving on the Philadelphia shore, much to the amusement of a large crowd of spectators, an impromptu hill-climbing contest was started, a goodly number succeeding in surmounting the roughly-paved hill leading down to the river. The time made in the 5-mile race may seem slow, but considering the condition of the road, it being very sandy, the time was not so bad, and I would predict that those same riders would make some of the hustlers on this side of the river look to their laurels.

No one doubts for a minute W. G. Spiers' ability as a trick rider, and often he has varied the monotony of a club run by little exhibitions of fancy Star riding on the road, but alas! all is over; no more shall we see Willie doing his acts, to the unbounded delight of the countryman and the terror of those unlucky enough to be riding near him. The sad, sad tale is this: Several Sundays ago, while he was taking out the boys, they espied a charming lady on a bicycle. When she had almost reached them our gallant lieutenant wanted to ride on one wheel, but losing his balance, fell off backwards. A safety rider right behind him could not stop in time, and in a few seconds two bicyclists and a safety wheel were pretty well tangled up. Finally they were extricated none the worse for their mishap. It has been whispered that when Spiers saw how nicely the lady looked on her wheel his conscience smote him for voting against admission of lady members, and he was so overcome that he nearly fainted, hence the accident.

The Bailey-Schaefler race comes off May 30, at 4 P. M. on the University Track, not on Y. M. C. A. grounds. The Pennsylvania Division L. A. W. is in hard luck with her officials. First the Aaron case, and now the affair in Scranton implicating Mr. Jessup. We hope the report has been exaggerated; no doubt it has. Notwithstanding the cloudy weather the S. E. W.'s had six men out and up to Fort Washington. Well done! I beg leave to blend my gentle voice with the sweet tenor (I think it is a tenor) of "Ariel" and ask "Where, oh where" is that road book?

May 27, '89. ARGUS.

Send to HOWARD A. SMITH & CO., Newark, N. J., for your bicycle supplies or call at Oraton Hall and learn to ride. Open evenings.***

MINNEAPOLIS.

If the wheeling season of 1888 may be considered as having closed at all in this portion of the country, that of 1889 opened remarkably early.

Usually wheels are stored away for the winter early in November, but last year November furnished twenty-five good riding days and December twenty. As for 1889, one wheelman of my acquaintance rode on twenty-six days in January. February was our only real winter month and wheeling was rendered impracticable by cold weather and snow. By March the snow was nearly gone and by the 5th, wheeling was again good and the month presented us with thirteen suitable days for riding. April had twenty-three pleasant days. May so far has been very favorable, the writer having used his wheel twenty-one out of twenty four days.

The early opening of the riding season produced an early demand for wheels, and our dealers found themselves in the midst of a rushing business season a month earlier than they anticipated, and considerable trouble has been experienced in procuring wheels fast enough. More safeties than ordinaries have been sold here, though the ordinary has by no means lost all its friends. I do not know of any rider who has changed his mount, the safeties all having been purchased by new riders. I notice quite a number of elderly gentlemen that have been induced to enjoy the pleasures of cycling by the advent of the low wheels, and this is the class of men to whom in my opinion, safeties properly belong.

The Minneapolis Bicycle Club commenced in February to "hustle" for new members and the result is quite gratifying. They weeded out the most undesirable of their old membership which reduced their number to sixteen, to which they have added twenty-six or eight new members, all good and enthusiastic riders. They have fitted up two good sized rooms in a very cosy and comfortable manner, one being nicely carpeted and furnished with a table and chairs for a meeting and reading-room. The other contains the billiard table and adjoining are coat and wash rooms, closet, etc.

This is a long step forward in the way of cycling club rooms for this city and they were formally opened and dedicated on the evening of April 27. The ceremonies included instrumental and vocal music, recitations, an original poetical essay on wheeling by one of the members, remarks from several local wheelmen and an adjournment for light refreshments to the rooms of a caterer next door. Quite a delegation from St. Paul were present. The event was thoroughly enjoyed and considered a grand success.

Three club runs to St. Paul and one to Anoka, twenty miles distant, have been held and were participated in by large delegations. Not long since five of the club's long-distance members planned a ride to Mankato, distant ninety-one miles. They went as far as Excelsior, nineteen miles, one evening, intending by an early start to ride the remaining seventy-two miles in time for dinner. However, with the coming of dawn came also a strong wind directly against them. Unwilling to give up the trip they started and all day did valiant pushing and walking against that wind arriving at their destination at 9 P. M. One of the participants in relating their experience stated that on the prairie where the road was straight and smooth for two or three miles they had to walk, as *riding* against the wind was impossible. Two Star riders in the party could not keep the small wheels of their machines on the ground owing to the force of the gale.

The managers of our baseball club are going to build a cinder path on their grounds. It will be about a six-lap track and good as it is possible to make. This will furnish an opportunity for several race meets and it is proposed to wind up the season with a district meet to include the States of Wisconsin, Iowa and Minnesota, to be held early in September, when our Exposition is in full blast and the State Fair in progress at St. Paul. Both these will furnish additional inducements for wheelmen to visit us and insure a good attendance at the races. With races on two afternoons, mornings spent in visiting points of interest in and about the city, and the Exposition in the evening it is thought we can hold a very enjoyable and successful three days' meet.

DOBSON.

May 20, 1889.

BUFFALO.

The Wanderers' Bicycle Club is the name of the newly organized wheel club on the East Side. It starts in with a small membership; but, as it is the only club on the East Side, its success is assured beyond doubt. This organization is the fifth one devoted to cycling in this city. The clubs and memberships are as follows: Buffalo Bicycle Club, 136; Ramblers, 123; Zig-Zags, 46; Women's Wheel Club, 28; Wanderers, 15. Buffalo claims 2,000 wheelmen. Out of the entire number but 348 belong to clubs. Surely this percentage of non-members will not be allowed to stand any very great length of time.

The Zig-Zags go to Niagara Falls on Decoration Day instead of Batavia as previously announced. The donation party and reception of the club will be held June 6th. Many hardy road-riders belong to this club, and they will heard from before the season is over.

The first out-of-town run of the Women's Wheel Club will take place on Decoration Day. Whither they go and where they will stop are matters of mere conjecture. The dear creatures will take their luncheon, and picnic in some grove where fancy and the condition of the roads dictate.

The gentler sex are becoming rabid exponents of the wheel, and it seems as though all, at least a good portion, of the ladies are learning to ride the two-wheeler. They have got the craze, and got it badly, too. Many expert lady riders are now to be seen, and the number is steadily growing. Our asphalt pavements afford excellent places for beginners to learn on. The other night I counted no less than eight ladies being initiated into the art.

The Ramblers have received their life-size crayon of the dog "Rambler," the former Mascot of the club, but now a resident of Boston, where his owner, Otto Schmidt, an honorary member, now lives. The dog accompanied the club on many of their runs last year; among them being the fast 100-mile ride from Erie on June 17th. The run was done in 15 hours, 5 minutes; actual riding time 9 hours, 5 minutes.

ZO.

Send to HOWARD A. SMITH & CO., Newark, N. J., and get stocking supporters, tire cement, belts, bundle carriers for all machines, tire tape, etc.***

ST. LOUIS.

The result of the first race between Stone and Lumsden caused a feeling of disappointment hereabouts, though it was not entirely unexpected. The time made, 3m. 4s., shows it to be a loafing race with all the sprinting done at the finish. Stone made the pace until the homestretch was reached, when Lumsden forged ahead and won, apparently with the greatest ease, by twenty feet. In a short sprint Lumsden seems to be superior to Stone, whether he is better in a bruising race remains to be seen. In the second of the series, which occurs to-morrow afternoon, Lumsden declares that he will set the pace and will make it as hot as he can for the entire distance in order to demonstrate, if possible, that he is better than Stone at either kind of race. He has been here all this week and has made quite a favorable impression. He wants to see the giving of medals abolished, substituting therefor useful prizes, or if there is objection to this latter arrangement, then let the races be run for a ribbon, a laurel wreath, or something of that sort. He modestly observes that he has no desire to wear his medals in the first place, and even if he were disposed to wear them, he could not do it without exciting unfavorable comment and being accused of having enlargement of the cranium. In this view of the case he differs materially from some other Chicago riders, as visitors to Baltimore last year will cheerfully testify. Speaking of Van Sicklen, he must feel pretty sore over his defeat in the team race last Saturday by the novice Tuttle.

If the weather continues favorable the new track will be in fine shape for the race Saturday afternoon. There will be six events besides the match race, and as the interest is running very high, a large audience will no doubt be present. I will endeavor to send you the results in this letter. A special prize is to be offered for a 5-mile contest between Bob Garden and Ned Oliver, with a time limit of one hour. If this arrangement is made there will be a race worth going miles to see, as both of these doughty champions have a large number of partisans who are anxious to see the question of superiority settled. If it should be determined that they can not ride five miles the distance will be shortened. It is exceedingly fitting that this contest should be decided on neutral ground, for the feeling runs so high in Chicago, it is doubtful if a fair race could be held there.

A very pleasant entertainment was given Friday night at the Missouri club-house, comprising musical and athletic features. With the exception of club swinging by Prof. Newton, the athletic exercises consisted entirely of exhibitions of what Mr. Morris called the "Delsartian system," or in plain, every-day English, sparring matches.

The entertainment was given in response to a very general request that the lady attendants at the club might have a chance to see what boxing matches were like. Their ideas of boxing are generally supposed to be associated with bloody noses, broken ribs, black eyes, etc., and it was the purpose of the exhibition to disabuse their minds of these impressions, and to show them that there is nothing safer than prize boxing.

Messrs. Newton and Parsons, Morris and Victor, and Applegate and A. L. Newton, represented the light, middle and heavy weights, respectively. Refreshments followed and then dancing.

May 24, 1889.

LATER.

The weather has given the Track Association its first black eye and put an effectual veto on the races advertised for this (Saturday) afternoon. It rained more or less all day yesterday, cleared up at night, and then promptly started in again this morning. This is exceedingly unfortunate, for if the weather had remained pleasant the races would have attracted a large crowd, and enough money would have been made to put the track in first-class condition. As it is, the only thing that could be done was to postpone the races until Monday afternoon.

ITHURIEL.

May 25, 1889.

NEW ORLEANS.

The New Orleans Bi. Club held its first "stag sociable" in its new quarters on Friday evening last, 17th inst. Everything was "bang up," and everyone had a good time.

The Louisiana Cycling Club holds its third race for the Baison trophy on the 26th. Distance, 25 miles over an asphalted course. Experiment of sealed handicaps will be tried on this occasion for the first time in the South.

The New Orleans Bi. Club's opening race for the Hill cup, which was fixed for the 18th, failed to fill, and the contest consequently did not take place.

The L. C. C. "excursions" to Hammond, La., on June 2, and on the 15th and 16th of the same month holds its annual moonlight century run. Silver souvenirs of the latter event are to be given all who finish.

Mrs. Ed A. Shields, wife of the club's President, who takes a lively interest in the club affairs, has presented the N. O. B. C. with a very beautiful tablecover, made entirely from the castoff neckties of the members.

The five-mile national bicycle championship has been located with this Division, and will be contested at our September meet. It is a long pull and a hard pull on a horse track, but I reckon we can stand it.

The ladies' bicycle, with a New Orleans lady for a rider, is at last a reality in this city. Miss Belle Fairchild, a sister of our own Charley—himself a pioneer on the "gentlemen's bike"—is the lady, and she rides, too.

The Louisiana's club house project is progressing nicely, and has now reached the "sticking point"—the selection of a site.

Hodgson's idea of holding the '91 meet in this city has not aroused any great amount of enthusiasm among the boys, but the few with whom I have spoken seem inclined favorably toward it, and if the League cares to hold an annual powwow as early as February or March—around Carnival time—I think New Orleans could stand it and furnish a howling good time to boot.

BI.

Write to HOWARD A. SMITH & CO., Newark, N. J., for their illustrated catalogue and second-hand list of bargains. Complete repair shop.***

K. C. W. NOTES.

Esteemed by all for his many manly qualities, the sudden death of our club-mate, Mr. Eugene D. Skidmore, was a sad surprise to his many friends in the K. C. W. His relatives and friends have our most heartfelt sympathy in this, their hour of affliction.

By the time these notes reach the light the greatest road race to date will be among the events of the past. Who will win? is the question everyone asks, and since the publication of the handicaps the solution of the problem seems to be more difficult than ever. That none of the scratch men will be near the front is the opinion of the majority. The very much improved form of the other riders gives rise to this supposition. Still all are loud in the praise of the good work done by the handicappers. But the race is won and lost ere this, and all have my most hearty congratulations—the winners for their success, the losers for their grand efforts to win and the cheerful way in which they met defeat and last, but by no means least, the promoters, who have brought forth the grandest road race on record. The next thing on the programme is the century run.

The following events will be contested at the K. C. W. race Meet to be held at Washington Park on June 28 and 29:

FRIDAY, JUNE 28.

1. 1-mile, novice, K. C. W.; wheels 35 lbs. or over.
2. 1½ miles, "ride and run;" open.
3. 1-mile, boys under 16; open.
4. 2-mile, handicap; open.
5. 1-mile, handicap; open.
6. 2-mile, Rover type, handicap; open.
7. 5-mile, championship; K. C. W. members.
8. Triangular race; bicycle, runner and walker.

SATURDAY, JUNE 29.

1. 2-mile, Rover type, handicap; open.
2. 3-mile, N. Y. State championship; L. A. W.
3. 1-mile, novice; wheels not under 35 lbs.; open.
4. 1-mile, handicap; open.
5. 1 mile team race (teams of four men).
6. 2-mile, Tandem bicycle, handicap; open.
7. 2-mile bicycle, handicap; open.
8. Brooklyn Bicycle Club 1-mile, handicap.

F. P. Prial handicapper of cycle events.

By the above dates the Union Elevated will be running direct to the grounds, and so the transportation facilities will be far in advance of previous years. The events will be run off with the usual K. C. W. promptness, and all who are *so fortunate* as to attend will find no dreary waits, but three hours of continuous and exhilarating excitement.

BROOKLYN, May 29. RAM LAL.

WASHINGTON, D. C.

The Washington wheelmen are beginning to think they will have to seek some other place for bicycling, as the weather for the past month has been anything but favorable to that invigorating exercise. Last Sunday the Cycle Club had as its guest Capt. Hilderbrand, of the Mo. Bi. Club, of St. Louis, who is on his way home from his European tour. He was very much pleased with our streets, and especially with the roads and scenery of the Soldiers' Home. In the afternoon a club run was called for Cabin John's Bridge. Although it is what the boys term a "chestnut," there is no run which embraces such beautiful scenery and good roads. The L. A. W. meet at Hagerstown will be well attended by Washington wheelmen, and especially by the Cycle Club, as it is the only League club in the city. Their membership has already begun to increase, and they have a number of applications to act on at their next meeting.

At their annual election recently held, the following officers were elected: President, Geo. S. Atwater; Vice-President, J. C. V. Smith; Treasurer, Dr. J. H. DeMeritt; Secretary, Geo. R. Ide; Captain, E. E. Curry; First Lieutenant, W. C. Babcock; Second Lieutenant, W. G. Wilmarth.

MARYLAND.

The new club-house of the Chesapeake Club was opened last week. Wheelmen of different clubs visited the handsome club-house, which is situated at the corner of Fulton and Lafayette Avenues. It was purchased and fitted up at a cost of $6,000, and is considered one of the best in the city. Mayor Latrobe and his secretary, Col. W. H. Love, were present, and the Mayor added much to the entertainment of the evening by some recitations, delivered in his best style. Ex-President Abbott and President Reed made neat speeches. The interior of the building was appropriately decorated with flowers and potted plants, which added much to its attraction. The basement is devoted to the locker and wheel-room; also a capacious bathing room. On the first floor the parlor and reading rooms are situated, and are handsomely furnished. On the second floor are the executive, billiard and toilet rooms, and on the third the gymnasium and janit r's apartment. The club organized about one year ago and at present has sixty active members.

BAY RIDGE.

NEWARK.

A meeting of the New Jersey Team Road Racing Association was called for May 24, at the Atalanta Wheelmen's house, on Clark Street. Only delegates from Hudson Co. Wheelmen and Atalanta were present, so no meeting was held. Captain Day, H. C. W., read several communications from the different New Jersey clubs, and the scheme of road racing as presented to them, did not meet, judging from what was read, with anything like popular favor. The meeting, if it may be called such, adjourned *sine die* at an early hour. We think this *proposed* association must have joined hands with the A. B. C. Association and gone under.

The Atalantas have ten names now of members for the "century" on the 8th of June.

During May the Atalantas have had five club runs with an average attendance of fifteen (15) members at each run. The mileage will be at least five times as much as April.

"SPARK."

HART CYCLE COMPANY, PHILADELPHIA.

This enterprising firm comes to the front again with a well arranged and neatly garbed catalogue for 1889 of all the wheels they represent. The cover is ornamented by a unique design of an old-style—as befits a pioneer house—guide-post, with all its arms pointing the way to 811 Arch Street, Philadelphia, that he who rides may read. Against it leans a bicycle. The company, as of old, make the Columbia their leading wheel, carrying a full line of machines and parts, but do not confine themselves wholly to that line. We notice the Crescent, National, Singer, Psycho, Juno and Rambler among the single safety types, and the Singer Tandem for two riders. Prices of the singles vary from $60 to $140, and tandems high as $220.

A most bewildering variety of low-priced bicycles, children's tricycles and velocipedes, is shown, and, with prices ranging from $2.75 up to $55, there should be no difficulty in suiting the purse of any child's parents, rich or poor. The line of lanterns and sundries is complete, and covers all found desirable by riders. A specialty is made by this house of repairs that are satisfactory, and their facilities for enameling and nickel-plating are of the best. Mr. Hart was among the first dealers in the country to establish a riding-school, and this desirable feature is still retained. The location, at Belmont and Elm Avenues, being close to Fairmount Park, makes it a favorite among wheelmen, and a capital place to store wheels.

Renting of bicycles and tricycles, an indispensable part of the business, is well provided for.

A list of charges for storing wheels, prices for renting and a copy of the rules regulating cycle riding in Fairmount Park make the catalogue a handy book of reference for any wheelman visiting Philadelphia.

HARRY COREY WITH THE SPRINGFIELD BICYCLE CO.

Mr. H. D. Corey, one of the fastest men on the road and path of his day, at one time manager of Stoddard, Lovering & Co.'s bicycle department, and late with the Pope Mfg. Co., has come back to the cycling trade as Secretary of the Springfield Bicycle Mfg. Co. Mr. Corey left the Pope Company to settle up the affairs of his father's estate. He had determined to engage in no active business, but found idleness a sad way of taking pleasure, hence his return to the busy haunts of the cycle mart. In a general letter Mr. Corey explains himself as follows:

I wish to inform you that I have been elected Secretary of the Springfield Bicycle Mfg. Co. and shall take an active part in pushing and developing this business. As you know I was for five years connected with Messrs. Stoddard, Lovering & Co. in the capacity of Manager of their Rudge department, but have been out of the business for about six mo ths. Later I was with the Pope Co., until my private affairs demanded my attention, but upon investigating different makes of Machines and the positions they occupy in the trade, I believe for the following reasons that the Springfield Bicycle Mfg. Co. has a great future before it.

These machines, as you know, have been made now for some three years, and have been very favorably received by the Wheelmen. The Company had their Machines made in Worcester for the first two years, but with their increasing business they decided to become their own manufacturers, and accordingly have now at Highlandville, Mass., a large Factory equipped with the finest machinery that can be obtained. Some little difficulty has been experienced so far this year in filling orders, incident to the erection of new machinery and getting matters in shape, but now with a Factory which is second to none and employs on a average one hundred and twenty-five men, I feel that the Company is in as good a position to manufacture Bicycles as any Company in the country. We are catching up with orders, and shall soon be in good shape.

Very truly yours,
H. D. COREY.

A SELECTED LIST OF PATENTS.

[Reported especially for THE WHEEL AND CYCLING TRADE REVIEW by C. A. Snow & Co., patent attorneys, Washington, D. C.]

A. O. Brunne, Meriden, Conn., Lamp.

F. G. Johnson, New York, N. Y., Spring Washer.

G. J. Taylor, Salt Lake City, Utah Terr., Velocipede. A. Taplin, Forestville, Conn., Wick-Raiser for lamps.

H. D. Millett, Maywood, Ill., Machine for making Coiled Springs.

All bearing date of May 28, 1889.

A NEW BICYCLE TIRE.

A Mr. Thomas R. Weston, of Bristol, Eng., has invented a steel tire for bicycles and tricycles, for which the following are some of the principal advantages claimed:

"The use of india rubber for tires is rendered quite unnecessary, and entirely superseded by the adoption of Weston's tires.

"They run very smoothly and easily, and without the waste of power incident to the use of soft india rubber tires.

"These patent tires run on a much finer line than india rubber tires, in some sections the line of running being not more than ⅛ of an inch, thereby nearly nullifying all friction with the ground.

"Being firmly attached to the spokes of the wheels, they cannot come off, as the india rubber ones frequently do, often rendering the machine useless when the rider is miles away from home.

"They are much more durable, and at the same time much less expensive than india rubber tires.

"They are very light in weight, but of great strength, and are especially suitable for racer bicycles or semi-racers.

"They do not throw the mud, etc., like the india rubber ones, and they are therefore much cleaner in use."

We commend this to the attention of manufacturers who think the rubber tire can be improved upon. It would seem to us that hard and smooth roads would be a requisite for their success.

INFLUENCE OF MIND OVER BODY.

That the mind has an immense control over the body (especially in human beings who are several removes from the brute), has been long acknowledged. The same in one thing as in another. The marksman shooting at the target will assure you he can generally tell when his finger presses the trigger, whether the shot is going to be good or bad. If he goes out in the morning full of hope and is full of confidence at the time of shooting, history will tell you his score is almost invariably a fine one, depending of course upon his possibilities as a marksman. The same thing with bicycling. The mind exercises some wonderful effects over the body in this sport. Not long ago I heard of a man who was riding an "ordinary," and as he wended his way home, his machine kept up a continual squeaking. Runs hard, *thought* the rider as he got down, and oiled the bearings at all points. Then he mounted, but the squeaking continued just as before. The consequence was, that in riding home, he expended so much nervous force in *thinking* that squeak was caused by a tight bearing, that upon arriving at his destination, he was completely tired out. Next day upon giving the machine a through overhauling he discovered that the squeak was *in the saddle* and in no way affected the running of the machine, yet his *mind* had all the way home been busily occupied in *convincing the body* that the easily-running wheel was fatiguing him. This is the effect the mind has over the body. Give a man a bicycle or a gun which he does not *believe in*, and he will never amount to much as a rider or a shot. You may have noticed how a man brightens up in appearance, and how much stronger he rides when you tell him there are *only two laps more*, in a hundred-mile race. If he had not a mind to *control* the actions of the body, he would not be sensible of any difference in his physical feelings, but the mind "cheers him on" and says to the tired-out body, "Only two laps more, old fellow," and the body pulls itself together, and races in fresh as at the start. The *reaction* soon comes, though.

Men of high-strung temperaments should never strain themselves in cycle racing, as their intense natures are apt to over-estimate the strength of their bodies, and they urge the body to do more than it is really able to without experiencing injury. High-strung men are like Cremona violins tuned to "concert pitch." They are all right '*till s rings break*, and then—utter collapse.

That is why a man of a highly-strung temperament is so intemperate in his habits as a rule. He is intense, and can't do things by halves, and, careless of results, he pitches in "neck or nothing." The water jump looks too broad for cautious Farmer Dick, and he rides round it; but what cares young Sir John? He is "in for a penny, in for a pound," and if he is thrown and perhaps killed for his recklessness, we must still admire the fine dashing fellow, who was not going to back down in the face of danger, and who fell "in scarlet" on the hunting field. We must say that *we'd* rather die by a bullet from some Zulu's gun (or even be dispatched by his uncouth club) in fair man to man warfare, or get stretched out in a regular British way in a steeplechase, than die from some dyspeptic ailment caused by the deadly American biscuit. We would like to "die game," with unimpaired faculties, and not live to be a source of nuisance to ourselves and others. We do not happen to come of a contented kind, and are ambitious, and having sipped the nectar of youth, we do not care for a revolution of condition. Unlike Gurth, the swineherd, born-thrall of Cedric the Saxon, our neck is resting place for no man's foot, our mind gives lodgment to no churchman's views unless they be logical. We have no blind faith, but must have reasons, and failing these we sit in darkness. Better to grope in the darkness of honest disbelief than exult in the simple faith of the feeble-minded, ready to accept any theory which the brain of their poor minister may consider a panacea for the ills of his unquestioning flock. We are argumentative, and want reasons and "blue-prints," and a little "cause and effect" thrown in to assist digestion.

"JACK."

G. A. Litchhult, of 128th Street and Lenox Avenue, has one of the neatest cycle stores we ever set foot in. It is well stocked with Singer wheels, and there are a number of good renting bicycles, tricycles and tandems.

THE WHEEL

— AND —

CYCLING TRADE REVIEW.

Published every Friday morning.

Entered at the Post Office at second class rates.

Subscription Price, - - - $1.00 a year.
Foreign Subscriptions, - - - 6s. a year.
Single Copies, - - - - - 5 Cents.

Newsdealers may order through AM. NEWS CO.

All copy should be received by Monday.
Telegraphic news received till Wednesday noon.

Advertising rates on Application.

F. P. PRIAL, Editor and Proprietor
23 Park Row,

P. O. Box 444, *New York.*

Persons receiving sample copies of this paper are respectfully requested to examine its contents and give us their patronage, and as far as is convenient, aid in circulating the journal, and extend its influence in the cause which it so faithfully serves. Subscription price, $1 per year.

THE Racing Board has suspended R. H. Davis and E. A. Bailey, both of Harvard College, until August 1, for violation of the racing rules, both these riders having ridden safeties in a race for ordinaries, despite the protests of the other competitors. The other riders were not suspended because it was clearly proven that they had protested against Davis and Bailey. The wisdom of the Racing Board in separating safeties and ordinaries on the path has already been demonstrated. No man can control a safety wheel at top speed, and it is dangerous to permit both classes to compete together on the path. At the present time it is not likely that the rule will be changed. It is a good rule and ought to stay.

THERE is no reason why the utmost harmony should not prevail between the N. C. U. and the L. A. W. Racing Board. International competition is becoming more frequent from year to year, and as a matter of self-protection both bodies should act in harmony. We should think that the N. C. U. would recognize any distinction or ruling made by the L. A. W. Racing Board, and *vice versa*. If the Racing Board declared a man a suspend the English should recognize him as such, and bar him from their competitions. It is clearly the duty of the executives of both bodies to agree upon a treaty of some kind.

MR. DAVIS reports that he will go to England and race there. Unless the N. C. U. will recognize Mr. Davis as a suspend, he may compete at English meets, despite the fact that he has violated the rules which govern the American race path. We think the Racing Board can with good reason suspend any man who competes with Davis on either an American or English path. We have had too much vacillation in the League. Let it now return to methods of the Medes and Persians, whose laws were made to be obeyed.

THE New York State Division L. A. W. has a magnificent opportunity to distinguish itself. A few days ago Governor Hill signed a bill appropriating six millions of dollars to be spent on New York City pavements during the next three years. It is a matter of fact that beyond a general idea that the city could use some better pavement than Belgian block, the great daily papers have no definite suggestions to make, because they have no technical knowledge on roads and pavements. The city officials are in a still more benighted condition. Chief Consul Bull should at once set the State machinery in operation to see that some part of this six millions is spent properly.

NEW YORK Wheelmen have no favorite run, no favorite rendezvous. The Londoners take the Ripley Road, and on Sundays all the world on wheels glides to Dan Albone's hostelry. In Gotham a man rushes past you on the Drive, or in the Park, or you may see him near the Casino or at Mount St. Vincent's. As half the pleasure of an out is seeing or being seen, we would suggest that the "Circle," in the upper part of the Park, be the recognized rendezvous of wheelmen. It is on high ground, splendidly shaded, with seats and a fine view. It would be a pretty thing if wheelmen would wheel up there every Sunday afternoon between three and six.

THE Pennsylvania Railroad has issued general orders to carry all cycles free when accompanied by owner. The Associated Cycle Clubs of Philadelphia have worked hard to secure this result, and no doubt the step was largely the result of their influence, though the question of policy no doubt finally decided the matter.

MILLIONS FOR NEW YORK'S PAVEMENTS.

Now that Governor Hill has signed the Ives Bill, six million dollars will be spent on New York's pavements within the next three years. The distribution of this money rests with the Board of Estimates and Apportionment, who shall determine when, where and how much money will be spent. The Board consists of Mayor Grant, Comptroller Myers, President Arnold, of the Board of Aldermen, and President Coleman, of the Department of Taxes and Assessments. Acting under direction of the above Board, Commissioner Gilroy, of the Department of Public Works, controls the direct expenditure of the money.

Mr. Gilroy has not yet decided on any definite plan, neither has Mayor Grant, who states that he will have some suggestions to make at the proper time. Mayor Grant's last message to the Board of Aldermen contained this reference to pavements:

The granite-block pavement appears to be the one best adapted to our climate and soil, though recent experiments on Madison Avenue seem to show that in certain localities an asphalt pavement might meet the public requirements. The cost of both pavements being about equal, the selection might be determined by the character of the thoroughfare to be paved and the amount of traffic which it would be compelled to bear. It will, however, be impossible to maintain our thoroughfares in a proper condition so long as the power is given by law to private corporations to disturb the pavements whenever they think proper to do so for the purpose of laying pipes and mains. At the present time the city is helpless to prevent the disturbance of our streets by certain corporations, and I would suggest that the Consolidation Act be so amended that the local authorities shall have the right to determine when excavations may be made in the time and manner in which such an ervatings may be prosecuted. And the city should be armed with this power of self-protection before any substantial sums of money be expended on the streets.

Commissioner Gilroy makes the following statement:

"We have a more difficult problem in the street pavement question," he said, "than has the Government of any big European city. The peculiar shape of the city concentrates a great deal of heavy traffic on a few thoroughfares, and the wear and tear upon our business streets is, I am pretty sure, greater than upon the streets of London or Paris. Our climate also is destructive. Stone disintegrates here in our atmosphere more rapidly than it does abroad. Our horse car tracks help spoil a pavement. But worst of all is the nuisance of the gas, steam, water and sewer excavations. You no sooner get a street well paved than along comes some corporation ripping up the stones or asphalt and ruining the pavement. No matter what this department tries to do, it seems almost impossible for it to secure the relaying of the disturbed pavement in as good condition as it was at the beginning."

Ex-Commissioner-General Newton favors granite laid on a bed of concrete with a smooth, noiseless pavement for the uptown avenues. "What we ought to have," he said, "is granite laid on a bed of concrete. The concrete is absolutely necessary, and the granite blocks must all be of certain dimensions. The substantial stone pavements I would place in the down-town business parts and on the principal up-town avenues, where there is heavy traffic. Then, as fast as possible, I would lay in the residence streets a noiseless pavement. Let it be wood or asphalt as is deemed best. I favor asphalt. Objections are made that such smooth surfaces are dangerous because they get slippery. But they are not slippery when they are clean, and we must have some system of keeping decent pavements clean or they will not remain descent. It ought to be made obligatory upon the owners or occupants of houses in the streets paved with asphalt or wood to keep them absolutely clean. The cost would be slight. It would merely amount to taking care of a good thing. It is what is done in foreign cities."

The New York *Times* published an intelligent editorial on the subject of the new pavements, and suggests that the Commission employ experts that the best results may be obtained.

NEW ROADS FOR UNION COUNTY, N. J.

The Union County, N. J., Board of Freeholders has voted to raise $150,000 for the improvement of the four principal roads in the county. The roads to be repaired are the one from Rahway to Elizabeth, the one from Elizabeth to New Providence, passing through Summit, Springfield and Union; the one from Plainfield to Elizabeth, passing through Union, Cranford, Westfield and Elmora, and the one from Rahway to Westfield, running through Clark township. The county will issue bonds to defray the cost, bearing four and a half per cent. interest, and the work will be completed within a year.

MARGUERITE'S LETTER.

Though our Decoration Day picnic run was not attended by the best of weather, it turned out a grand success. Lynnfield Grove surrounding Lake Suntaug, more commonly called Humphrey's Pond, was chosen for our stopping place, and is one of the prettiest picnic grounds imaginable—by that I don't mean excelling in the seashore resort style—rather the opposite. A good time was to be the order of the day, and club friends, recipients of special invitations, were cordially welcomed. Judging from the turnout the Middlesex Cycle Club has many friends—more than it deserves. Neither the Captain nor Lieutenant were able to be present, so we followed our own sweet wills in regard to pace, and considering the number of different style machines in the party we did remarkably well. The sole drawback was the weather, and to say the least we have been very badly treated lately in this respect. The Saturday morning was evidently too fair to last, as about x s ... just when we were engaged in making necessary preparations, great dark clouds loomed up, completely covering the sky. We were not to be frightened, however, so our contingent of five started from Maplewood, reaching the first meeting-place, Oak Grove Depot, in good season. After a ten-minute wait we were joined by our enthusiastic Everett friends. Surprise was easily to be seen written on their countenances when they rode up, and I don't wonder at it, for it is very seldom I keep great enough time to be first at the fray. After a solemn consultation in regard to the weather (decidedly dark at this time), we descended to start for rendezvous No. 2, Melrose Depot, where we found a goodly number variously grouped, discussing the all-important topics—weather, route and course. Others kept arriving, and on departing for "Meet" No. 3, Wakefield Town Hall, we numbered twenty-five or thirty, on wheels with a conveyance in due time for friends and two conveyances. I have already explained how the club members cover many districts, and that we either have to select a central meeting-place or pick them up as we go along. The latter was the mode of procedure upon this occasion. The younger members having sampled soda and "Tutti Frutti" at the neighboring drug store, a final start was made and the entire route now lay through the woods. 'Tis an

ill wind that blows nobody good;" the over-abundance of rain had certainly done much to help nature, and had the sun been shining we would have found her dressed in her best. It was nice and cool riding through the narrow roadways, and striking a nice easy pace our cup of joy was full. One or two short stretches of sand prevented the cup from overflowing, but these were easily tided over and we were soon at our destination.

We found swings, games and boats at our disposal, and the former two were speedily brought into requisition. A game of baseball was first on the tapis, the ladies joining. Two acknowledged leaders in baseball chose sides, and the game commenced with no prelimary practice. The greatest game of baseball that I ever remember seeing was the consequence, but the fun—don't mention it. At a most interesting point in the game the rain came down "helter skelter," and a grand rush was made the ladies for the cottage where dinner was to be supplied, and the gentlemen to secure proper shelter for the wheels.

The dinner had been most invitingly set out under the trees, but the Fates forbade, and everything had to be re-spread in the cottage, which was none too roomy. Of course, you all know what I am now coming to, but it is a solemn fact that soon as everything had been shifted it *stopped raining*. Thirty-eight sat down to dinner, seventeen of whom were ladies. The noticeable features of the hour were the absence of talk at the first half, and the increase of joking during the latter half.

After dinner the boats were freely used, the pond being one of the most beautiful for woodland scenery within many miles of Boston. Our crack amateur photographer was on hand, and negatives flew thick and fast. The President also had a convenient Kodak, and one picture he "tooked" I would greatly like to see. On his asking the youngest member of the club to look pretty for the camera's benefit, she replied by "making a face" at him. He got it, sure enough, although she didn't think so at the time, and it remains to be seen if it is an exact reproduction.

The home run was rather divided, part going via Wakefield, taking in a *bona fide* ball game on the way, and others taking a short cut.

May we have another picnic run soon is the wish of

Marguerite.

THE PULLMAN ROAD RACE.

Despite the northeaster and a cold rain, the Pullman road race was held yesterday and was a success in every way, though not as pleasant as it might have been had the weather been more favorable. But, notwithstanding all this and extremely poor roads, good time was made, Lumsden, one of last year's winners, covering the sixteen-odd miles in 56m. 45s., with Van Sicklen at his heels in 57m. 48s., and Terry Andrae in 57m. 49. Notwithstanding this good time Bodach carries off the first prize, as he was the first to cross the finishing line, amid the cheers of some five hundred ladies and gentlemen who had gathered at the Hotel Florence to see the finish.

Of the 123 men entered only seventy started in the race, though some followed over the course down Michigan Avenue for a short distance while others took the train to Pullman to see the finish. The boys were prompt in getting their positions in front of the Leland Hotel—the rain would not permit of their loafing much. The limit men started at exactly eighteen minutes after ten, so that Starter Conkling had just time to catch the train for Pullman. The boys started out with a spurt, and in a short time were separated to a remakable degree. Down the boulevards, with the wind at their back, they made great time. The roads were good here, though fearfully muddy. When the Stony Island Road was reached the time began to be slower, and when opposite the Nickel Plate shops every rider had to dismount. The rains had softened the pure blue clay so much that the wheels sank into it six inches, and the safeties became so clogged that it was almost impossible to move them. The larger wheels stood the best show. Many had no trouble in riding over the "sand hill," though some preferred to push their machines over it. When the foundry, at 114th Street, was reached some took to the sidewalk, and, as a result, protests were entered against them. The train which left at the same time as did the wheelmen only passed the boys at Grand Crossing, showing that the poor time was made in the bad places spoken of.

It was just 11:19:13 when Bodach, of the Æolus Club, whizzed past the crowd at the hotel. He was wet, spattered with mud and tired, having covered the distance in 1h. 13s. Two minutes later Dole and Pratt came in, and then others came thick and fast. It did not take long for the boys to change their clothes. They were prepared for a change, friends having carried out their dry clothes. When Lumsden and Van Sicklen crossed the line they were greeted with rounds of cheers. Lumsden looked as fresh as though he had just started, but Van seemed a little fatigued.

Lumsden, Van Sicklen and Andrae were scratch men, and so showed their powers on the wheel by the time made. The finish was made in the order of the names, the actual time being also given in the following:

F. Bodach, 1h. 13s.; F. L. Dole, 1h. 1m. 58s.; G. P. Pratt, 1h. 3m. 17s.; H. W. Harland, 1h. 4m. 28s.; W. B. Hassard, 1h. 15m. 58s.; A. Gutherie, 1h. 2m. 33s.; R. Kinsley, 1h. 3m. 30s.; Frank Robbe, 1m. 5m. 37s.; George M. Skeer, 1h. 6m. 37s.; Irving Otis, 1h. 7m. 45s.; F. H. Tuttle, 1h. 1m. 13s.; J. S. Corey, 1h. 4m. 12s.; Frank Riggs, 1h. 2m. 18s.; F. L. Chase, 1h. 6m. 22s.; William Rennaker, 1h. 8m. 24s.; George Kurtz, 1h. 2m. 18s.; A. E. Lumsden, 56m. 15s.; George A. Thorne, 1h. 15m. 15s.; Albert Kuehne, 1h. 3m. 25s.; G. S. Haskell, 1h. 6m. 5s.; W. P. Ulrich, 1h. 5m. 6s.; N. H. Van Sicklen, 57m. 49s.; A. W. Harris, 1h. 3m., 28s.; C. H. Tobey, 1h. 6m. 29s.; Rome O'Connell, 1h. 7m. 45s.; E. C. Bode, 1h. 5m. 47s; J. W. Thorne, 1h. 5m. 34s.; G. H. Sage, 1h. 7m. 28s; C. F. Sage, 1h. 7m. 28s.; Charles Brignon, 1h. 7m. 17s.; J. Gutherie, 1h. 7m. 14s.; H. E. Sauer, 1h. 2m. 22s.; C. A. Patterson, 1h. 12m. 26s.; John Errickson, 1h. 12m. 26s.; F. E. Spooner, 1h. 2m. 37s.; George K. Barrett, 1h. 10m. 41s.; H. E. Loveday, 1h. 3m. 10s.; M. J. Andrews, 1h. 8m.; S. H. Farnham, 1h. 8m. 5s.; G. P. Washburn, 1h. 8m. 36s.; C. A. Stokes, 1h. 10m. 51s.; W. P. Robertson, 1h. 13m. 13s.; A. S. Bradley, 1h. 9m. 24s.; J. M. Irwing, 1h. 8m. 25s.; C. C. Mead, 1h. 9m.; J. C. Harrington, 1h. 8m. 38s.; A. J. Street, 1h. 7m. 41s.; A. M. Luce, 1h. 6m. 36s.

Lumsden will receive the special time prize, while Bodach will have first choice of a large list of prizes, consisting of bicycles, medals, cyclometers and other sporting goods. He has been riding only about two years, although, in that time, he has made some good records. At the Exposition tournament he carried away one or two small prizes, and his riding of yesterday rather surprised wheelmen. The time of Lumsden is not considered particularly good, for the distance over the same road was made a few days ago in 54m., although in more favorable weather. Had the roads not been so soft, this time would undoubtedly have been beaten. Lumsden says he can beat that record, and that he ought to have done so yesterday.—*Chicago Herald.*

ECHOES OF THE ROAD RACE.

The winner of the road race, W. Murphy, owed a great deal to his wheel, which was a 27 lb. Victor Road Racer. He finished strongly, and thinks he could have knocked a minute off his record.

Miller, of the Riversides, proved somewhat of a surprise. He rode a Columbia Light Roadster. He rode through to Philadelphia on the Century Run of last year, though he had been riding only a few months at the time.

Class rode a 27 lb. Victor and made the very creditable record of 1.33.38.

Bensinger, the winner of the fastest time prize, was a complete surprise. He rode a Light Champion. No one noticed the pace at which he was riding, and some even doubted that the time credited to him was correct, but the scoring was so carefully done that no such mistake could have occurred.

Chas. Murphy, who was mounted on a New Mail ordinary, rode but six seconds slower than Bensinger. His record is remarkable for so young a rider. Had he ridden a light wheel he might have won.

Coningsby did the best work of any man in the race. He rode a 47 lb. Victor safety, a wheel 20 pounds heavier than W. Murphy's, Class', or Borland's mounts, yet he finished only 52 seconds behind the winner. A header, also, lost him some time.

Borland showed marked improvement over his previous form. He took two very severe headers, spraining his wrist and badly bruising himself. He was badly used up after the race, but under the good care of "A. B.," his mentor, he pulled out all right three days after the race. He should keep out of such hard races, as he rides on nervous force.

Hesse, the Kings County's "dark horse," justified all the good things predicted of him, riding the course in 1.32.47, the fourth fastest time. He rode a Columbia.

Putney, of the Manhattans, showed unexpected good form.

Tom Hall bettered his record over the course, but expected to do better.

The three Wilmington cracks, Merrihew, McDaniels and Dampman, were disappointments, and could not go the pace with our boys.

The scratch men did not do so well as was expected. Harry Hall had only trained a few weeks, Wilhelm had only trained a few days, and Baggott was way out of form.

Nisbett, who rode a 25 lb. Demon, geared to 64 inches, with eight inch cranks, pulled off his handle-bar at the eighteenth mile.

In future contests of this kind a new rule should be made to limit the weight of wheels. The men who rode racers had a great advantage; not an unfair advantage, because no restrictions had been made.

The record over the course is: C. E. Kluge's, 1h. 30m., made May 30, 1888. In that race 4 men rode the first five miles under 17m., and 12 men rode it under 18m. In the last race no man beat 17m. for the first five miles, but 19 men rode inside of 18m., a big improvement in the average form.

In the '88 race, Kluge, Baggot and Bradley rode the first ten miles in 34m. 5s., 6 men rode within 35m., and 11 men within 36m. In the '89 race, the fastest time at ten miles was W. Murphy's, 34m. 53s.; only 1 man rode inside 35m., and 9 men rode inside 36m.

At fifteen miles, Kluge, Baggot and Bradley led in 53m. 20s., while 6 men rode inside 54m., and 7 men rode inside 55m. In the '89 race, W. Murphy led at fifteen miles in 53m. 41s., while 2 men beat 54m., and 10 men rode inside 55m.

At 20 miles Kluge, Bradley and Baggot led in 71m. 32s., while 3 men beat 72m., 4 men beat 72m. 30s., 6 men beat 73m. and 6 men beat 74m. In the '89 race the best time at 20 miles was W. Murphy's, 72m. 13s., while 4 men beat 73m. and 7 men beat 74m.

At 25 miles the times of both races compared as follows: '88, 3 men beat 1h. 31m.; '89, no man beat 1h. 31m.; '88, 4 men beat 1h. 32m.; '89, 2 men beat 1h. 32m.; '88, 5 men beat 1h. 33m.; '89, 4 men beat 1h. 33m.; '88, 5 men beat 1h. 34m.; '89, 9 men beat 1h. 34m.; '88, 8 men beat 1h. 35m.; '89, 11 men beat 1h. 35m.

Hensinger rode the last 15 miles in 56m. 9s.; C. Murphy, 56m.; 16s.; W. Murphy, 57m. 20s.; Hesse, 57m. 4s.; T. J. Hall, 57m. 2s.

Hensinger rode the last 10 miles in 36m. 42s.; C. Murphy, 37m. 46s.; Coningsby, 38m. 30s.; W. Murphy, 38m. 32s.

The times of the leaders for each five miles were:

Bensinger.	C. Murphy.	W. Murphy.	Hesse.
m. s.	m. s.	m. s.	m. s.
17.32	17.30	17.19	17.26
18.04	18.03	17.34	18.19
19.27	18.30	18.52	18.11
17.43	18.27	17.52	18.44
18.50	19.19	20.00	20.07

Murphy started 16th and finished 1st, gaining 16 places; Bensinger jumped from 18th to 4th; Hesse, from 23d to 9th; T. Hall, from 28th to 11th; Harry Hall, from 34th to 17th; Baggot, from 32d to 18th.

The handicapping must be judged creditable. The difference between the first 17 men at the start was 15m.; at the finish, 9m. 38s. The difference between the five leaders at the start was 6m.; at the finish, 44s. Six men finished within a minute; 10 men finished inside of three minutes. Of the first 22 men 19 advanced in position from 1 to 17 points.

A SELECTED LIST OF PATENTS.

[Reported especially for The Wheel and Cycling Trade Review by C. A. Snow & Co., patent attorneys, Washington, D. C.]

J. F. Breux, Vineland, N. J., Bicycle.
S. D. Reynolds, Nevada, Mo., Bicycle.
A. Easthope, Wolverhampton, Eng., Velocipede.
H. A. King, Springfield, Mass., Velocipede.
E. S. Boynton, New York, N. Y., Wrench.
J. L. Sanford, Albany, N. Y., Wick Trimmer.
All bearing date of June 4, 1889.

FIXTURES.

June 8, 1889.—Century Run, Orange, N. J., to Philadelphia. Chairman, L. A. Clarke, 25 Broad Street, New York.

June 8, 1889.—Two-mile Bicycle Handicap at Schuylkill Navy A. C., Univ. of Penn. Grounds, Phila. Entries close June 1, with W. T. Wallace, 123 North 7th Street, Phila., Pa.

June 9, 1889.—Three-mile Race of Louisiana Cycling Club, New Orleans, La.

June 9, 1889.—Cyclists' Union Meet at Clarksville, Mo.

June 10, 1889.—Regular Annual Meeting of Kentucky Division, L. A. W., at Danville, Kentucky.

June 12, 1889.—Bicycle Race at Huntington, L. I. Entries close with S. C. Ebbetts, Huntington, June 8.

June 13, 1889.—Two-mile Bicycle Race at Berkeley Oval—Eastern championship, A. A. A. Entries close May 25, with W. Janssen, P. O. Box 125, N. Y. City.

June 15, 1889.—L. I. W. Race Meet at Brooklyn Athletic Grounds. Entries close June 8 with L. H. Wise, 1,281 Bedford Ave., Brooklyn.

June 15, 1889.—Two-mile Bicycle Handicap at New York Athletic Club Grounds, Travers Island. Entries will close June 5, with Frank D. Sturges, Secretary N. Y. A. C., 104 West Fifty-fifth Street, N. Y.

June 17, 1889.—Annual Meet of Massachusetts Division, L. A. W., at Squantum, Mass.

June 18, 1889.—Third Annual Meet of Tennessee Division, L. A. W., at Nashville, Tenn.

June 21, 1889.—House-warming of the Brooklyn Bicycle Club. Tenth anniversary.

June 22, 1889.—New Orleans Bicycle Club's Race for the Hill Cup.

June 28, 29, 1889.—Kings County Wheelmen's Annual Meet at Washington Park, Brooklyn. Address Wm. F. Murphy, 1,255 Bedford Avenue.

June 29, 1889.—Handicap Road Race of Milwaukee Wheelmen, over Wauwatosa course. Entries close June 24.

July 1, 2, 1889.—C. W. A. Annual Meet at St. Catharines, Ontario.

July 2, 3, 4, 1889.—League Meet at Hagerstown, Md.

July 3, 1889.—L. A. W. Race Meet, at Hagerstown, Md. Entries close June 26, with Harry B. Irwin, 34 West Franklin Street, Hagerstown, Md.

July 4, 1889.—Two-mile Bicycle Handicap at Washington Park, Fifth Avenue, Brooklyn. Entries close June 26, with F. G. Webb, Treasurer. Prospect Harriers' Race, run under L. A. W. rules.

July 4, 1889.—Race Meet at Brownsville, Pa.

July 4, 1889.—Illinois Division, L. A. W. Meet, at Ottawa.

July 4, 1889.—Tournament held by Laccaster (Pa.) Bicycle Club.

July 4, 1889.—Fort Schuyler Wheelmen, Utica, N. Y., 50-mile Road Race.

July 20, 1889.—One-mile and 25-mile Bicycle and 5-mile Tricycle N. C. U. championships at Paddington, Eng., track.

July 27, 1889.—One-mile and 25-mile Tricycle and 5-mile Bicycle N. C. U. Championships at Paddington, Eng., track.

October 23-29, 1889.—Race Meet at Macon, Ga.

EUROPEAN CYCLING FIXTURES.

Austro-Hungary.—Graz, June 9 and 10; Pilsen, June 9 and 10; Prague (Smichow) June 29 and 30. Germany.—Berlin, June 16 and 17, July 21, September 15; Hanover, June 23, September 8; Cologne, June 30, August 12; Chemnitz, September 8; Frankfort-on-the-Maine, September 1; Mannheim, September 8; Crefeld, September 8. Hamburg.—Altona, September 22; Bochum, August 25; Soram, June 9; Coburg, June 9; Magdeburg, June 30, September 8. Denmark.—Copenhagen International Meeting, August 18.

National Cyclists' Union.—Championship Fixtures—At Paddington, August 24, 50-mile Bicycle and 1-mile Dwarf.

NEW HAVEN RACES.

The New Haven Bicycle Club held its annual 5-mile handicap race at the Elm City Driving Park, Thursday, May 30 (Decoration Day), at 3 P. M. A 1-mile safety race and a 2-mile (open) were also run, but none competed but club members. Officers of the day: Club Handicapper—Frank Thompson; Referee—E. C. Bennett; Starter—Capt. W. F. Perkins; Judges—Palmer Field, C. H. Voorhes, and F. C. Kinney; Timers—J. A. Dockendorff, A. N. Welton, Frank Thompson and E. J. Perkins.

FIVE-MILE HANDICAP—H. C. Backus (scratch), 17m. 30s., fourth; F. E. Weaver (scratch), 17m. 25s., third; T. J. O'Tell (1m.), 18m., sixth; G. H. Parkington (2m.), 18m. 50s., first; C. T. Bartlet (2m.), 19m. 10s., second; J. M. Verhoeff (scratch), 17m. 35s., fifth.

This was very good, considering the heavy track and strong head wind on the home stretch. It was a close race between the scratch men. They kept together till the last mile, when Weaver spurted and gradually left the others. The race was won by Parkington, a "dark horse," who got too big a handicap. All our handicap races are won by "dark horses." Backus is our fastest man, but he did not do so well this time, as he has been riding the Star and has changed to the Eagle. He is not used to it yet.

ONE-MILE SAFETY—C. E. Laum, 3m. 10 1-5s., second; A. N. Welter and F. E. Welter (tandem), 3m. 9½s., first; H. C. Backus, 3m. 14½s., third.

This was a fine race from start to finish. Laum started on a spurt and held it for the mile, with the tandem right after him. They tried to pass him four or five times, but could not do it till they got on the home stretch. The tandem spurted for all they were worth, and passed Laum, beating him by about a foot. It was hardly a fair race, as two men were racing against one. Laum rode finely, and should have won the race.

TWO-MILE OPEN—J. M. Verhoeff, 6m. 50s., first; F. E. Weaver, 6m. 52s., second; H. C. Backus, 7m. 3¼s., third.

This race was a hot one between Weaver and Verhoeff for first place. Verhoeff had the pole, and kept the lead to the finish, though Weaver was right behind him, and tried repeatedly to pass but could not as the track was rough outside the pole. Weaver was tired, having ridden every race.

The races were the best the club has had for years, and showed us we had lots of good racing material we did not know of. If Meriden still thinks she is the hub of cycling in this state and can get away with us, just let her put an amateur team on the road and we will show the Silver City how we can ride. If she thinks we cannot entertain just ask the four Meriden Club boys that came down to see us on Decoration Day how they enjoyed the hospitality of the N. H. Bi. Club.

Mr. Verhoeff showed lots of pluck in the race. He rode a new wheel, and every time he pedaled his ankle hit the hub and tore the skin, covering his wheel with blood, but he was game to the end.

We had a "smoker" in the evening. A very enjoyable time, though rather an impromptu affair. John Verhoeff gave some fine recitations. Mr. Lehent and Mr. Larom rendered some good vocal selections, Mr. Bartlett did some fine balancing, and Mr. Fields some fancy business on the wheel, while Mr. Rowe did some high kicking.

Mr. G. A. Pickett entered the Providence races, and brought home a Kodak Camera and a revolver.

Yours truly,

ELM CITY.

New Haven, Conn., June 3.

ANNUAL RACES OF WEST END BICYCLE CLUB, ROCHESTER, N. Y.

The Wheelmen at Rochester appear to have been the only ones not flooded out by the rain on Memorial Day. Though the track was in good condition, the wind made its presence felt, and prevented good time being made, while the 1,500 spectators sat and shivered patiently through the entire events. Some two hundred wheelmen, headed by the Fifty-fourth Regiment band, gave a parade highly spoken of, the West End Club leading. The tournament was not only a success in furnishing good amusement for the spectators, but in adding dollars to that most vital part, the treasury. Following is the result of the races:

Half-mile handicap: E. O. Rassicoe, Woodstock (scratch), first; W. S. Campbell, Niagara Falls (scratch), second. Time, 1m. 21s.

Safety novice race: W. F. Gassler, Niagara Falls, first; Frank Chamberlain, Rochester, second. Time, 3m. 22s.

One-mile Monroe County Championship: J. A. Heusner, first; C. J. Iven, second. Time, 3m. 2s.

Novice race, road wheels: E. A. Folsom, Rochester, first; W. H. Whitbeck, second. Time, 3m. 8s.

One-mile open handicap: E. O. Rassicoe (scratch), first; Campbell (scratch), second. Time, 2m. 50s.

100-yard slow race: Won by L. G. Mabbett, Rochester.

Five-mile open handicap: Rassicoe, first; Pratt, Rochester, second. Time, 17m. 58s.

Quarter-mile dash: Rassicoe, first, in 39s.; Campbell, second.

Two-mile State: E. P. Cochrane, first, prize, diamond badge; C. J. Iven, second, prize Kodak camera. Time, 6m. 47s.

One and one-half-mile handicap: Rassicoe (scratch), first; G. F. Kohler, Millersville, Pa. (60 yards), second. Time, 4m. 53½s.

One-mile safety race: G. F. Kohler, first; Gassler, second. Time, 3m. 53¼s.

One-mile tandem: Chamberlain and Heusner, first; Campbell and Gassler, second. Time, 3m. 5s.

One-mile consolation: Connolly, first; Patchen, second. Time, 3m. 40s.

The visiting wheelmen were given a reception in the evening at the club rooms. Rassicoe, of Woodstock, won five first prizes, and his pretty riding and modest ways made him many friends.

PROVIDENCE, R. I., TOURNAMENT.

Rain the morning of May 30 spoiled the track at Narragansett Park, and it was in wretched condition when the events in the bicycle and athletic tournament of the Rhode Island wheelmen were called at 2 o'clock. Some 2,000 spectators were present, however. R. H. Davis and E. A. Bailey, the Harvard Club safety cracks, were on hand, but were barred from racing, the Chairman of the L. A. W. Racing Board having suspended them from the race track until August 1, for contesting on safeties with ordinaries in the intercollegiate games at Berkeley Oval on the 11th inst.

The one-mile novice race was won by G. A. Armstrong, of Boston; L. L. Clark, New York, second; W. C. Miller, East Greenwich, third. Time, 3m. 36⅘s.

The two-mile national L. A. W. championship was contested by J. P. Clark, of Dorchester; Mont Scott, of Providence; A. C. Banker, of New York; Ludwig Forster, of Hartford; G. M. Worden, of Boston, and W. E. McCune, of Highlanddale, Mass. Worden and McCune dropped out, and the others finished in the order above given—Clark first. Time, 6m. 58 3-5s.

G. A. Pickett, of New Haven, was given the two-mile safety, Davis and Bailey, his only competitors, being under suspension.

Scott won the three-mile State championship. Time, 11m. 24s.

Ludwig Forster, of Hartford, won the one-mile bicycle open; J. W. Schoefer, of New York, second. Time, 3m. 31 1-5s.

W. S. Doane won the one-mile safety handicap; Pickett second. Time, 3m. 23s.

Scott won the one-mile State safety championship. Time, 3m. 53s.

The one-mile handicap was won by G. A. Armstrong, of Boston, 200 yards; Clark, of New York, 175 yards, second; Worden, of Boston, 150 yards, third. Time, 3m.

In the mile tandem safety handicap Clark and Benson, of Dorchester, won. Time, 3m. 18¼s.

Doane and E. W. Bailey won the tandem safety open. Time, 3m. 34 1-5s.

The team race was won by the Dorchester team—Clark, Benson and Armstrong—with 18 points; Hartford Wheel Club, 14 points; Berkeley Athletic Club, 13 points.

BICYCLE RACES AT NORTH ADAMS MASS., MAY 30.

In the 1-mile there were three entries, Grant, French and McLaren; Grant won in 3m. 32¼s. ½-mile dash; McLaren and Card; McLaren won in 1m. 45s. 1-mile handicap; three entries—McKee, Lassor and Shields; McKee won in 3m. 46¼s. Club championship, 1-mile; French, 1; Pierce, 2; McLaren, 3; time, 4m. 7s. In the novice Lassor won in 4m. 13s.

3-mile, County championship; five entries—McKee, Grant and Brady, of Pittsfield; McLaren and French; French, first; time, 11m. 45s.

ANNUAL TWENTY MILE CYCLE RACE BETWEEN NEW BEDFORD AND TAUNTON WHEELMEN.

The challenge cup annually raced for by New Bedford and Taunton bicyclists was raced for May 30, on French Avenue, distance twenty miles. Five members of each club contested, and ten points were given for the first man, nine for the second and so on. The score is as follows: Anthony of Taunton, 10, time 70m. 6s.; Hyland Smith of New Bedford, 9, time, 1h. 10m. 7s.; Rogers of Taunton, 8; Robinson of Taunton, 7; Dunham of New Bedford, 6; Chase of New Bedford, 5; Parlow of New Bedford, 4; C. G. Rogers of New Bedford, 3; Bolton of Taunton, 2; Hardy of Taunton, 1. Total, Taunton, 28; New Bedford, 27.

ENGLISH RACE PATH NOTES.

THREE NEW AMATEUR RECORDS.

At the Catford Meet, held May 18, some rare sport was seen. The novice mile attracted 142 entries, and was won by a 200-yard man in 2m. 38s. The half-mile open was won by A. R. Salsbury, 80 yards, in 1m. 13 2-5s. In the first heat of this race, W. C. Jones rode a quarter mile in 37 3-5s. and the half mile in 1m. 16 1-5s., supplanting the previous safety records of 39 3-5s. and 1m. 17 1-5. The heats of the open quarter-mile scratch race produced three fast times: Heat 1, Mayes, 38 2-5s.; heat 2, E. Osmond, 39 2-5s.; heat 3, Adcock, 39 3-5s.; heat 4, F. J. Osmond, 37 3-5s. In the final heat Osmond made a great race, winning in 37s., record for the standing quarter; Mayes second by seven yards.

TWO-MILE ORDINARY BICYCLE RECORD.

On May 21, on the Coventry track, W. A. Illston made a successful attempt to lower the two-mile amateur record for an ordinary bicycle. The times made were: Quarter-mile, 40 1-5s.; half-mile, 1m. 18s.; three-quarters of a mile, 1m. 57 3-5s.; one mile, 2m. 34 3-5s.; one mile and a quarter, 3m. 14 2-5s.; one mile and a half, 3m. 53 1-5s.; one mile and three-quarters, 4m. 33 1-5s.; two miles, 5m. 12 1-5s. This is ten seconds faster than F. J. Osmond's record, made at the Crystal Palace, September 25, 1887. Timekeepers: H. Sturmey, S. Golder and E. H. Godbold. The pacemakers were F. W. Allard and G. R. Adcock. Rowe's record is 5m. 11s.

"BICYCLING NEWS" CACKLE.

From the American papers we learn that William Windle, "the Wonder," (that's what they call him) the youth who is "second only to Cortis," etc., etc., etc., and who has *actually* ridden a mile in 2m. 45s., or, was it 2m. 43s.? IS going to race this year, and this statement has been made and denied any number of times. Since "Ducker's Buffalo post" of last autumn we wait for further developments. Why not send Windle over to England to convince us? Perhaps Rowe's experiences are not encouraging to "the Wonder." By the way, we note that our own Richard—Howell is the other name, you know—is quite ready to "do up" any visitors. Now, then! You on the other side! Haven't you a professional "Wonder" who is good for 2m. 40s. or so, *with lots of shekels?*—this is a *sine qua non.* If so, start him along, and don't keep Dickon waiting.

Yes, we do call Windle a "Wonder"—that is, the backwoods papers do. On the other side they don't call Osmond a wonder, they call him "Hillier's man," "Hillier's pet," etc. Windle's speed *is* 2m. 43s., and there is nothing very wonderful about it either. We hope that the N. Y. A. C. will send Windle over, but not to convince you. If Windle waited to convince you—of what, we know not—he might never return. Took us nearly two years to convince you about the Rowe records, besides Windle will not bother with you. You would find him a large-sized, fresh-faced, firm-lipped nineteen-year-old boy, rather shrewd, and singularly free from flies and fads.

INDORSEMENT OF THE RACING BOARD'S CHAIRMAN.

The following, from the columns of the *Providence Sunday Journal*, may be looked upon as voicing the sentiment of representative Rhode Island wheelmen concerning the Chief Consul's action at Providence, May 30. If any paper in Providence knows whereof it speaks it is the *Journal*, with thirteen cyclists on its staff and all departments, from business manager to office boy, represented. This paper took a personal interest in the success of the tournament at Narragansett Park, and the wheelmen there are to be congratulated on so enterprising an assistant:

"Rhode Island's Chief Consul, Charles S. Davol, showed himself the right man in the right place as Chairman of the National Racing Board, when he announced the suspension of Davis and Bailey, of Harvard, Memorial Day. The suspension of the two men before the tournament began killed one event and took much of the interest from two others, but the Racing Board's Chairman was plucky enough to sink his sympathies with the tournament and his own club and go ahead and take the only square step that was left to him, which was to suspend the men without waiting to give them a chance for the sake of the tournament to race. The Racing Board has more backbone and purpose to it this season than it has shown since Mr. Bassett had the helm, and nothing has more clearly demonstrated its honesty and lack of prejudice or personal interest than this episode at the Park. Some of the boys kick because the races were hurt, and avow, with charming ignorance of the plain duty in the case, to say nothing of the fitness of things, that the suspension might just as well have been made at the close of the tournament. But the Chief Consul is all right in his position with thinking wheelmen, and a little growling at home can be better stood than to have had the whole country sit down upon him, to say nothing of the injury to its integrity that the Racing Board would have suffered."

YORK CO. MEET AT BIDDEFORD, ME.

On May 30 bicyclists from different parts of the Pine Tree State arrived in the city to take part in the annual York County Meet. One hundred and fifty wheelmen took part in the parade. After Biddeford and Saco's principal streets had been traversed the cyclists made a run to Old Orchard, where a sumptuous repast was spread. They then returned to Saco and betook themselves to the trotting park.

At 2.45 o'clock the rain poured down in sheets, but the bicycle races commenced in the presence of over a thousand spectators. The first race called was the club race, open to York County wheelmen, one mile, best two out of three heats. Prizes, championship cup, Kirkpatrick saddle, pair of bicycle shoes. The participants were R. A. Fairfield, of Saco; Walter L. Ayer, George M. Leavitt and Nathaniel Adams, of Biddeford. In the first heat Leavitt led in time of 4m. 12s.; Ayer at the start fell from his bicycle, but came in second, Adams third. The second heat was won by Leavitt in 4m. 8s. In the final heat Leavitt also won. The safety race proved interesting. This was open to all safety riders in the State, half-mile, best two in three heats. Prizes, pin, silk umbrella, box of Havanas. At the start Cobb fell from his machine, but, regardless of the starter's signal, the boys went the half-mile. This was not scored, so the first heat had to be started over again. West, of Portland, made an easy win, coming in first in 2m. 2⅗s; Cobb, of Biddeford, second, and Alexander, of Portland, third. The next half-mile safety heat was again easily won by West in 1m. 58s. Cobb and Alexander again mounted, and had one of the prettiest runs of the afternoon, Cobb winning in 2m. 45⅗s.

The State race was next called. This was one mile, open to all amateur riders in Maine, best two in three heats. Prizes, Victor cyclometer, Bower's bicycle lantern, traveling bag. Participants: A. Fairfield, Saco; C. S. Wyer, Fairfield; Edward Stetson, Lewiston; Nathaniel Milliken, Biddeford; John Lawrence, Biddeford; F. M. Brown, Portland; Nathaniel Adams, Biddeford. Wyer came first over the tape in 4m. 13s., Lawrence, second and Nat Milliken third. There were seven entries for the first heat and three for the second. Lawrence took a tumble when near the quarter-mile mark, and many thought that Dwyer ran him down. Lawrence did the distance in 4m. 31s., with Milliken second. This made a tie between Lawrence and Milliken for the second prize, which was run off. Lawrence beat the record of the afternoon by making the mile in 4m. 2s.

The mile race for Pope cup, open to all, was won by C. S. Wyer, of Fairfield, the only contestant, who made a record of 4m. 6s.

Chief Consul G. E. Dow, of Portland, was referee.

The games of the Manhattan A. C., which were to have been run June 1, are postponed to June 8.

N. Y. State Intercollegiate A. A., at Albany, May 24—Two-mile bicycle race, won by H. D. Kittenger, Hamilton, in 7m. 37s.; C. W. Hills, Union, second.

De La Salle Institute, on grounds of M. A. C., N. Y., May 31—One-mile bicycle, won by S. Campbell, in 4m. 2-5s. Half-mile bicycle race, won by J. R. T. Ryan, in 1m. 57s.

St. Paul's School A. A., at Concord, N. H., May 28–29—Juniors 1-mile bicycle, won by H. D. Kountze, in 3m. 36s. Seniors 2-mile bicycle, won by C. C. Goodrich, in 8m. 33-5s.

John M. Draper, of the Pennsylvania Bicycle Club, starting from scratch, took the 1-mile bicycle handicap at the Y. M. C. A. Sports, at Philadelphia, May 30. Time made, 5m. 53⅗s., which would indicate a very slow track. E. Woolman, 40 yards, second.

TIMES MADE AT SCHOOL SPORTS.

N. E. Interscholastic Association, at Cambridge, Mass., May 30—One-mile bicycle, won by F. L. Olmsted, Roxbury Latin, in 3m. 16 1-5s.; Fred. Johnson, Worcester Academy, second.

A. A. U. CHAMPIONSHIP ENTRIES REOPENED.

The 2-mile A. A. U. Championship will be run next Wednesday, at the N. J. A. C. Grounds, at Bergen Point. Entries close Saturday with F. W. Janssen, P. O. Box 125, New York City.

At the spring meeting of the Pullman A. C., held at Pullman, Ill., June 1, the 1-mile bicycle was won by Fred. Nelson in 3m. 2 4-5s., F. Griggs, second. A 3-mile bicycle race had been put down to take place, but not enough contestants (three being needed) were entered to run it off.

The 1-mile bicycle race between M. J. Bailey, of the Century Wheelmen, and Theodore A. Schaeffer, of the Pennsylvania Bicycle Club, came off May 30, on the University Athletic Grounds, Philadelphia, and was won by Bailey in 3m. 12 4-5s. There was a stiff breeze blowing. It was a closely contested race and Bailey only won by a few inches.

The Amateur Athletic Union championships, postponed from Saturday last, will be held Wednesday, June 12, at the N. J. A. C. grounds, at Bergen Point. The entries for the 2-mile bicycle race are: W. E. Crist, Columbia A. C., Washington, D. C.; A. C. Banker, Berkeley A. A.; L. L. Clarke, Berkeley A. A.; W. W. Windle, N. Y. A. C.; A. B. Rich, S. I. A. C.; F. G. Brown, N. J. A. C.; E. P. Baggot, N. J. A. C.; C. E. Kluge, N. J. A. C.

AT SPORTS OF N. J. A. C. HELD AT BERGEN POINT, N. J., ON MAY 30

One and one-half mile bicycle race—Won by A. A. Zimmerman, Freehold, N. J., 200 yards, in 4m. 25 4-5s.; S. B. Bowman, N. J. A. C., 120 yards, second; W. Schumacher, L. I. W., 115 yards, third.

Three-mile bicycle race—W. Schumacher, 180 yards, first, in 9m. 33 2-5s.; A. A. Zimmerman, 300 yards, second; F. G. Brown, New Jersey A. C., 130 yards, third.

HUNTINGTON, L. I. RACES, JUNE 12.

The bicycle races to be held at Huntington, L. I., on June 12, are deserving of the attendance of wheelmen in this city and vicinity. They will be started punctually at 1:30 P. M., giving plenty of time to take the 4.30 train back to New York. Some fifteen of our best-known wheelmen, among whom are Bowman, L. L. Clarke, Wise, Miller, Schoefer, Brown, Class, Murphy, Baggot and others, are entered up to date, and good sport is promised. The Huntington boys claim one of the best tracks in the State. Entries close with S. C. Ebbetts, Huntington, June 8.

MINNEAPOLIS WHEELMEN ANXIOUS TO RUN A RACE FOR THE STATE CHAMPIONSHIP.

The following challenge explains itself and puts the St. Paul wheelmen in a position where they must race or yield without a struggle:

To the Sporting Editor of the *Tribune*:

There has been a great deal of talk one way and the other, and numerous squibs and defies published in the papers as to which of the twin cities have the fastest bicycle riders. To settle all speculations, we hereby challenge any amateur team in this State, St. Paul preferred, to run us a race any distance, on road or path, for the championship of Minnesota. The losing team to furnish a cup or trophy, the value of which shall be mutually agreed upon, as shall also the time, place, distance and judges.

J. R. STOCKDALE,
COLIE BELL,
E. J. HALE,
Minneapolis Bicycle Club Racing Team.
—*Minneapolis Tribune.*

THE WINSTED WHEEL CLUB'S LITTLE UNPLEASANTNESS.

From all accounts, the ambition of one man in the Winsted Wheel Club to, *Pooh-Bah*-like, fill all offices, and be accountable to no one, resulted in their proposed Meet Decoration Day being declared off. It is not necessary to mention this particular member's name, suffice it to say that he is a well-known racing man, and was quite conspicuous at the Hartford Meet last September. At his own request he was appointed Finance Committee, but failed to render an account of funds collected. Not satisfied with this achievement, he also took the business of the Press and Race Committees in his own hands. At this point the Club "kicked." A meeting was held and the coming Meet given up. The over-ambitious member is left in the cold by all other members, and there is even talk of expelling him. We are sorry the Club was obliged to abandon the races, but experience is always valuable, even at a high price.

THE RAMBLERS' CENTURY.

Captain Dietzer, of the Buffalo Ramblers, issues the following notice:

The annual century run of the Ramblers will be made on Sunday, June 9. Will leave Buffalo by Lake Superior Transit Co's. steamer; meet at foot of Main Street, at 6.15 prompt. I have decided to go by above route, principally for reasons of economy, as it is impossible to get a reduced rate by rail. Fare will be $2.50, including berth and breakfast. Breakfast will be served previous to our arrival at Erie, which will be about 3 A. M. One hour will be given at Erie to "stretch." Start for Buffalo at 4 A. M. First stop will be made for second breakfast at 8 A. M. Leave Westfield at 8.30. Next stop will be made at Angola at 1 P. M. A short time will be given the members at Silver Creek Hill to recuperate, and ponder upon the possibilities of winning the medal I have offered to the world renowned "scorcher." One and a half hours will be given for dinner at Angola. The route from Bay View will be via Limestone Hill, Smith Street, Filmore Avenue, Utica Street, to Main Street, arriving at club rooms at 6.30 P.M., thus finishing a run that any one can look back upon with pride.

NOTES FROM THE CITY OF BROTHERLY LOVE.

Well, on Decoration Day Philadelphia had the much-talked-of interclub run, held under the auspices of the Associated Cycling Clubs. This run has been talked and planned for some time, but it was not until about ten days ago the committee fully decided to proceed with the venture.

The day opened raw and disagreeable, but by ten o'clock, the time set for the start, old Sol had dispelled the ominous-looking clouds, and the day promised to be all one could ask. Shortly before 10 the Mt. Vernons made their appearance at the Pennsylvania Club House, shortly followed by Philadelphia South End, Century and Tioga. At 10:30 all started off under command of Mr. P. S. Collins, Vice-President of the A. C. C., Captain W. C. Smith, of the Philadelphia Club, following with 10 men; the Pennsylvania Club, with 29 men, under command of Captain William D. Supplee; Century Club, Captain E. G. Carter, with 22 men; Tioga Cycling Club, Lieutenant Winfield Van Dusen, with 5 men; South End Wheelmen, Captain C. A. Dimon, with 17 men, and the Mt. Vernon Wheelmen, Captain Scott, with 11 men, order mentioned being order of the organization of the different clubs. The route lay through the Park, Montgomery Avenue and Lancaster Pike to Devon, where, at Devon Inn, a most sumptuous repast had been provided. After the enjoyment of that, the start was made for home. The run was pronounced a decided success, and I think it an advisable scheme to follow the custom at least once a year.

By the way, I understand the Century Club are to lose their Captain. This move is taken as Captain Carter intends spending most of his time away this summer, and does not feel justified in holding the position. Much regret is expressed, as under the command of the present genial Captain club runs had been on the boom.

The Pennsylvania Club have announced the following club runs for the balance of this month:

June 8—100-mile run from Orange to Philadelphia; on the afternoon of the same day those unable to get off for the run will assemble at headquarters and ride to meet the party.

Sunday, June 9—No regular run has been announced as yet, the day being reserved for the entertainment of the visiting wheelmen.

Thursday, June 13—Moonlight run to Wayne.
Sunday, June 16—Ambler.
Sunday, June 23—Phœnixville.
Sunday, June 30—Downingtown.

For the 100-mile run some ten or twelve men have signified their intention of participating, the party to leave Philadelphia on the midnight train, reaching Newark shortly after 3 A. M. I hope they will not be too tired to make the start at 4 A. M.

The League Meet promises to draw quite a number of wheelmen from Philadelphia. The Century Club anticipate taking some forty men, while Pennsylvania will probably be not far behind. The other clubs will no doubt all turn out fair delegations, so I would not be surprised to see 200 men from our city on hand.

On Sunday, June 2, the Pennsylvania Bicycle Club with twenty-three men ran to Chester, where dinner was served at the Cambridge Hotel. Some fifteen of the Wilmington men also made headquarters at the same place, and as Captain S. Wallis Merrihew, B. Frank McDaniels, Charles and Fred Elliott were among the Wilmington men, we heard much news concerning the great 25-mile road race. Oh! the "ifs" and "whys" were thick. To tell the truth we were surprised at the result, as some of these men were looked to as ones likely to be in the first batch; well, better luck next time.

To our agreeable surprise the Pennsylvania railroad has issued orders that hereafter all bicycles, tricycles and tandems, be carried free when accompanied by owners. This is certainly a feather in the caps of the Associated Cycling Clubs, who have worked hard and faithfully to secure this, their aim. Especial thanks I feel are due President W. R. Tucker, and Secretary-Treasurer J. R. Lincoln Edwards, for their untiring efforts, which have succeeded so well.

"Penosy" is still heard from in the *Athlete*, but still persists in treading on the boys' toes. Look out, young man, or you will be 'sot on' some time and rather hard, too, I fear.

On Thursday evening the Pennsylvania club hold their regular monthly meeting, when the revised by-laws come up for action. As a number of changes are proposed, a good attendance should be assured.

On Friday evening the Century Club also hold their monthly meeting, when the question of lady membership will be brought forward again. Since the club have now admirable facilities for the fair sex, it seems a shame the motion should not pass, and I trust this time the kickers will be overcome.

On Decoration day, the great Bailey-Schaeffer race came off at the University grounds, Bailey winning by some four yards. On the same day, Draper, Pennsylvania Bi. Club, won the 1-mile open at the Y. M. C. A. games held on their grounds, 44th Street and Elm Avenue.

Oh, My! I would like to see Thompson and Halstead have a go at *any* distance. I have not had the pleasure of meeting Mr. Thompson or seeing him ride, but I have a little to wager on the boy from the East.

Well, wishing that my time would allow of my participating in the 100-mile run (but unfortunately it will not), I must rest content with the anticipation of riding out on Saturday afternoon to meet the party. Wish them good weather, roads and a clear sky.

WESTFIELD.

PHILADELPHIA.

What was without doubt the largest body of local wheelmen ever seen in Philadelphia, participated in the inter-club run to Devon, on May 30th. The scene around the Pennsylvania club-house in the morning was exceedingly lively, and many were the compliments passed on them by the jolly crowds bound for a day's pleasure in our grand park. When shortly after ten o'clock Vice-President Collins of the A. A. C.'s gave the signal to mount, and fully a hundred wheelmen were under way, a hearty burst of applause spread along the line of admiring spectators, and as they passed through our great pleasure ground, looking neat and trim, no doubt many a manly breast was filled with a feeling of envy, or a longing to be with such a jolly looking lot of fellows, and many a fair maid turned from her less fortunate escort to wave a dainty 'kerchief at the fast receding line of wheelmen. After a very pleasant ride of nineteen miles they arrived at Devon Inn shortly after twelve o'clock, where, after a "wash up" and a little rest, they sat down to a truly sumptuous repast. At three o'clock they all started homeward, all the way on the pike picking up some club man or other, so when they reached the city the line had swollen to a pretty large turnout, almost 150 men being in line. After leaving the Pennsylvania and Philadelphia boys the remaining cyclists met the Century crack, Bailey, and much to the surprise of the pedestrians, gave him a rattling hurrah in honor of his victory in the morning. Every one present voted the thing a big success and all hoped for a repetition in the near future.

The long talked of Bailey-Schaeffer race came off on May 30, at 10.30, on the Univ. of Pa. track; both men seemed to be in first-class condition, though it was noticed that the Pennsylvania man was nervous at the start, while Bailey, the Centurion's hope, was as cool as a "vet." When Mr. Perret, the well-known sprinter, sent the racers off, it was soon evident that neither wanted to make the running and, as expected, it turned out to be a waiting race until the decisive lap. The first quarter was finished with Bailey slightly in the lead in 51s.; the second in 1m. 40s.; the three-quarters in 2m. 32s. and then the real racing began. Schaeffer quickly shot to the front and soon led by two laps. This order was kept up for about an eighth of a mile, when Bailey made *his* effort; inch by inch he crawled up to his opponent, finally passing him and when they came into the straight it was seen that Bailey had the race well in hand, finally coming in four lengths ahead in 3m. 11 4-5s. A telegram was sent out to Devon to his club mates notifying them of the result, and was read out while at dinner amid much applause.

Whitesides' mileage for May is 530 miles, and so far this year he has ridden over 1,200 miles.

Louis Kolb is seen out riding frequently on a tandem bicycle, with a very charming young lady occupying the front seat. My! how the boys envy him.

Philadelphia, June 4, 1889.

ARGUS.

K. C. W. NOTES.

Were we there? *Well, rather. Where!* Why, at the great twenty-five mile handicap road race. And what a time! It seemed as if none but Kings County men *could* cross *that* tape, and how the boys did shout! Just look at the list below, and judge whether the K. C. W. boys know how to ride, and four of their best men, Wilson, Beazeley, King and Morehouse absent.

Mr. Ammerman copied the following list and times from the New York *Herald*. Consider the race a team-race from scratch, then the rider with the fastest time is first, and scores his points in accordance:

Pos.	Names.	H.	M.	S.	Points.
1.	J. Bensinger, K. C. W.	1	31	43	20
2.	C. Murphy, K. C. W.	1	31	49	19
3.	Wm. Murphy, K. C. W.	1	32	05	18
4.	F. B. Hesse, K. C. W.	1	32	47	17
5.	T. J. Hall, Jr., K. C. W.	1	33	04	16
6.	W. G. Class, B. B. C.	1	33	38	15
7.	H. J. Hall, Jr., K. C. W.	1	33	53	14
8.	E. P. Baggot, H. C. W.	1	33	56	13
9.	F. Coningsby, B. B. C.	1	33	57	12
10.	F. M. Dampman, Wilmington.	1	34	40	11
11.	J. F. Borland, B. B. C.	1	34	51	10
12.	B. F. McDaniels, Wilmington.	1	36	07	9
13.	C. A. Elliott, Wilmington.	1	36	17	8
14.	R. W. Steves, K. C. W.	1	36	44	7
15.	F. R. Miller, R. W.	1	37	13	6
16.	S. W. Merrihew, Wilmington.	1	38	54	5
17.	W. H. Putney, M. B. C.	1	40	04	4
18.	N. F. Waters, B. B. C.	1	41	39	3
19.	F. B. Elliott, Wilmington.	1	43	49	2
20.	E. Van Wagoner, Newport.	1	47	52	1

Take the total of the K. C. W. men as a team of seven and the total of the seven highest not Kings County, and compare.

Seven Kings County total.......... 111
Seven next highest, without regard to club.......... 78

How is that for a team in an *open* race, and, as I said before, four of our best men absent?

The riders say that the road was in the best condition they have ever seen it, and so the committee of arrangements deserve the thanks of all.

WHAT THE BOYS SAY.

Bensinger (truly modest)—"I am glad I rode so well, and you are all pleased. The cup is a dandy. That Light Champion was a great help."

Chas. Murphy—"Only six seconds, but I could not quite do it. Glad it was Ben."

W. F. Murphy (the winner)—"Wish the wheel-room was larger. Will have to give my safety away. That New Mail was a Victor."

F. B. Hesse—"Wish the handicappers had not used me quite so hard, but it is all right. Our boys got about all there was."

T. J. Hall, Jr.—"I thought the Penn. boys would ride better, so let them cut the pace. Shall know better next time."

W. G. Class—"That is a beautiful clock. Had my eye on it all along."

H. J. Hall, Jr.—"In no condition. Rode better than I expected. You should see that *Jersey*."

R. W. Steves—"Who wants to buy a lamp?"

What we all say is that the race was the greatest on record, the result all we hoped for; and we all hope the promoters are as well pleased with their work as we are.

I understand that T. J. Hall, Jr., has challenged Harry Hall to a road race over the Irvington-Millburn course. If Harry gets into his old form by the time the race comes off there will be some fun. If not, Tom will have it all alone. Anyway, I shall be on hand to shout for the victor.

Among the prizes for the K. C. W. races are gold and silver watches to first and second in the handicaps, medals and useful articles in the other events. Many of the fastest men in the country have already sent in their entries, but this need not keep younger riders from trying for racing honors. Many of the events are handicaps, and in these all are on an equal footing. The track is four laps to the mile, and of clay surface. We fully expect to see the Brooklyn record of 2.37 broken.

A. B. Rich will again appear on the path, and has selected the meet of his old club, the K. C. W., as the one to be first honored. His old competitor, E. Valentine, will also try once more on the same dates. This return to the path of two such riders shows that time does not dull the taste for competition.

RAM LAL.

BROOKLYN, June 5, 1889.

BROOKLYN NEWS.

The great twenty-five mile road race is an event of the past, and Brooklyn scooped in a very fair percentage of the prizes, consequently Brooklyn wheelmen are beginning to think they have about as good racing material as the average riding district of its size can show up. The prizes were very handsome, and the winners of them may well feel satisfied. Borland of the B. B. C., is perhaps the only man who is not satisfied, as he took a bad header in the early part of the race, which resulted in several contusions on the shoulder and hands, and a slight dislocation of the wrist. Notwithstanding his injuries, he rode to a finish, and a very good one at that, considering the difficulties of riding, after such a fall.

Fuller, Allen, Raymond and Cole, B. B. C., enjoyed a run in the Oranges on Sunday, and reported on their return that the Pennsylvania R. R. has issued a new rule, following the lead of the D. L. and W. and other roads, and removed the charges for carrying wheels, when accompanied by a rider. This will be heartily welcomed by a great many Brooklyn men who frequent the Oranges, and who find the Pennsylvania road more convenient on account of the Annex, and the frequency of trains. However, the boys should remember that the D. L. and W. and Erie roads have favored them in the past, when the Pennsylvania strictly enforced its charges. I believe in returning favors, when it is in one's power to do so.

I have been unable to obtain the official military report of the experiment with bicycles at the 13th Regiment bivouac, held at Richmond Hill last week. I had hoped to obtain the full report for this week's letter, but can only inform you that the innovation was considered very favorably.

The next cycling affair of interest on the *tapis* is the great Century run at Philadelphia. The arrangements are all perfected and the only thing needed to bring it to a successful finish is a good day. The writer met Clarke the other day, and he is wearing away his usually prominent *embonpoint*, in worrying about the weather. Let us all hope that the point in question may be favorably decided, for we shall want him again next year to manage the Century run of 1890.

Another topic of conversation is the race meetings of the K. C. W. and L. I. W., which are to be held on June 15 and 29 respectively. Nearly all the Brooklyn crack riders are entered in more or less of the events, and some fine races are expected. The Prospect Harriers are to hold their games on July 4, and a bicycle race is included in the programme. Entries should be sent to F. G. Webb, Treasurer, No. 736a Union Street, Brooklyn. Prizes will be silver watches to first and second, and a third prize not yet decided upon.

The K. C. W. and B. B. C. baseball nines will play a second game at the Parade Grounds on Saturday, June 8, at 4 P. M.

ATOL.

Brooklyn, June 6, 1889.

BIRMINGHAM, ALABAMA.

EDITOR OF THE WHEEL:

When I was at the University of Virginia, I belonged to a Greek letter fraternity, and far be it from me to say aught against the brotherhood, the remembrance of which is among the happiest of my college days. But I could not help being struck with a little incident recently. About a month ago, I had occasion to write to a member of my fraternity in a neighboring city. I had never met him, but presuming on belonging to the same club, I asked a favor of him. By the same mail I also wrote to a wheelman, whom I did not know, asking him for some information about the roads in his vicinity. The wheelman wrote me a four-page letter and told me all I wanted to know. I have never yet heard from my fraternity man, though if he had not gotten my letter it would have been returned to me. Wherefore I am lead to believe that the fraternal spirit among wheelmen is certainly very strong, and somewhat akin to Freemasonry.

Did you ever notice the expression of the driver of a watering cart, as he goes along and covers the face of the earth with mud? Specially when he encounters a wheelman, he puts on a look of fiendish delight. There is one consolation, however, that bicyclers can have about the water-cart man, and that is that there is only one place such a devilish expression can take a fellow when he goes hence.

The average rainfall of Alabama is 56 inches, which makes it one of the rainiest States in the Union. I do not know at all accurately, but since January 1 the rainfall cannot have much exceeded 6 or 8 inches. So in the next seven months we may look for a flood. The dust now is so deep, and has been for several weeks, that there is no pleasure riding.

The party of Georgia tourists will arrive here the morning of June 5, unless some unforeseen accident happens. Mr. Ingram, the pilot of the party, is an old and experienced rider, and if anybody can he will bring them through all right.

Will some rider of a safety kindly say what is the effect of riding a low wheel in windy weather as compared with an ordinary? I ride a forty-eight inch wheel, and I find it very disagreeable to ride in a wind. Possibly the wind does not have so much effect on a safety.

May 29, 1889.

L. D. A.

CYCLING IN WAPPINGERS FALLS.

Decoration Day was a gala day for the wheelmen of Wappingers Falls, N. Y. In the morning at 9:30 there was held a bicycle parade through the principal streets, with fifty-four wheels in line, including fifteen members of the Wappingers Wheel Club. The afternoon was devoted to viewing the road race starting from Poughkeepsie to turn at Wappingers Falls and return to Poughkeepsie, a distance of sixteen miles. The following started at 3:17 P. M.: D. L. Walker, Ed Cashin, V. T. Woodfield, C. Hurley, M. Farrell and I. Halliwell, of Wappingers Falls; T. W. Roberts and H. Von der Linden, of Poughkeepsie, and E. Van Benschoten and Jno. Van Benschoten, of Freedom Plains. Woodfield held the lead the first three miles. After that the Van Benschoten Brothers led to the finish. The order at the finish and time made was as follows: J. Van Benschoten, first, in 1hr. 2m. 11s.; E. Van Benschoten, second, in 1hr. 2m. 14 3-5s.; E. Cashin, third, in 1hr. 3m. 4s.; I. Halliwell, fourth, time not taken.

The surprise of the day was the place taken by E. Cashin, who has ridden but three months. His mount is a Victor safety, and on that he captured a fine gold medal and the championship of Wappingers Falls.

BOSTON WHEELMEN'S DAY OUT.

Not enough rain fell Decoration Day to prevent the thousands of Boston cyclers from carrying out their plans for a day's outing on the wheel. The roads were thronged with the pedal-pushing fraternity throughout the day. Eight hundred and thirty-two were counted wheeling through the main entrance of Chestnut Hill reservoir before 3 P. M. Other favorite resorts were as liberally patronized, and it would be safe to believe that only a very few of the estimated 15,000 wheelmen in Boston remained at home.

The majority wheeled to places distant from twenty-five to fifty miles from the city, and, of course, they all got more or less of a ducking. During the afternoon cycles seemed as numerous on the Mile ground and Beacon Street as were carriages. The good roads through Brookline, Longwood and the Newtons were sped over by hundreds of flyers. The sandpapered roads near Milton were also seemingly in much favor, and it would be difficult to estimate the number of riders on the smooth highways of the suburbs north of the city. More than 200 dined at one hotel in Salem, and the proprietors of hostelries in Lynn, Marblehead, Gloucester and other towns had all they could attend to. The host of the hotel at South Natick was visited by more cyclers in quest of dinner than his big dining hall could contain, and the same was true of the hotels at Sharon.

About 100 Boston wheelmen attended the races at Providence. Several clubs, including the Rovers, of Charlestown, and the Brooklines, rode to Providence on their wheels. The others went by train. A few Boston men went on to New York to attend the road race, and some went to the Meet at Biddeford, Me.

The Boston Bicycle Club has had an outing Memorial Day annually for the past ten years. The excursion yesterday was to North Weymouth, and a very enjoyable trip it proved. The run was made jointly with members of the Town Club, and it was at the fishing box of President Everett, of the latter club, that all were entertained. Captain Kendall and a number of the bicyclers rode there on their wheels, and the Town Club men reached their destination on a four-horse drag and on several yachts. The latter battled with contrary winds and failed to appear until late in the afternoon. The few hours passed in the enjoyment of Mr. Everett's hospitality were most pleasant.

A pleasant feature of the day was the picnic of the Middlesex Cycling Club at Lynnfield. About half a hundred lady and gentlemen cyclists gathered there and had a merry outing. A band of Somerville clubmen had a hard ride over muddy roads to Downer Landing, but the fun on arriving there fully repaid them for all their labor. The Dorchester, Hyde Park, Milton, Roxbury, Maverick, Jamaica Plain, Medford and Cambridge clubs all had well-attended runs to various resorts.—*Boston Herald.*

CINCINNATI.

For the last two Sundays the wheelmen of this city have been disappointed by cold and rainy weather regarding the road race from Ivorydale to Glendale and return. The race is a handicap with some of our best riders entered, and is now set for June 9. Indications point to B. Burroughs and F. Koppes winning first and second places respectively. Prizes offered are handsome gold and silver medals.

The Championship Club race of the Cincinnati's comes off June 16, and there is much rivalry among the boys. Harry Buckles is developing an alarming muscle by daily riding over granite sets, and may prove to be a "dark horse" in this race. Previous records will surely be broken.

Nothing is more popular among the boys than meeting at Bennett's store Sunday afternoons and taking a short run into the country. The run most frequented has the most places of refreshment on it, and is called Clinton Avenue. While refreshing our thirsty selves a few Sundays since, the following fairy tale was sprung on us by Will Krienan: "Once upon a time a rider was coming down Race Street, when riding at a lively gait he collided with a passer-by. Both men stopped abruptly and after the mutual surprise was over and they had been dug out from the wheel, each stared solemnly at the other. The pedestrian first broke the silence, "I was in the wrong," said he, "I did not see you coming, accept my apologies." They were accepted, and both men went on their way, sadder but wiser." No, we were not taking anything but ginger ale.

Mr. Will Kappes met with a severe accident last week, coming near losing his fore-finger. When he is well again the dogs will once more seek the seclusion that the barns and piazzas grant.

Chas. Colling can be daily seen looking at his wheel and pondering new inventions. He has some good ideas, but perhaps he had better take Hatfield's advice and try a flying machine for plenty of fresh air.

More news in my next. SAFETY.

CINCINNATI, June 1.

DECORATION DAY AT LANCASTER, PA.

Well, here we are, down to date; and a day that will wipe from the cycling slate a goodly dozen of "fixtures." Quite an extensive slate, too, with events from Maine to California. Thanks to the benignant weather bureau, that so considerately parcels out a variety on the same day, some points in the great kingdom of wheeldom will have more favorable allotments fall to them than we are having; a consummation devoutly to be wished for the sake of the boys engaged in the tug and tussle of friendly rivalry, as well as for the sake of the thousands of those who assemble to see the "wheels go round."

Fortunately for the riders in this vicinity there is no "fixture" for them at this date. Unfortunately for the boys-in-blue, marching from cemetery to cemetery to decorate the graves of departed comrades, the intervals between showers are short; but the hardy veterans who have marched through storms of shot and shell, are not to be deterred by the harmless spite of his Jovian highness, the clerk of the weather. The strains of martial music come to us, through the open window, in chunks, as they are borne along by the moisture-laden wind. It is not, I must confess, a very inspiring sound. A wheelman might find the familiar head-wind coming from any point of the compass, but he will wisely refrain from going in search of it.

Yesterday we had quite a different kind of weather, and last evening was a delightful one for a run. Your correspondent and his chum were out, of course, and we rode over what is our most popular route—a seven-mile run, over good macadam, to Robinstown and return.

Unlike any other pleasant evening, we found the road almost deserted by wheelmen, which somewhat rare condition will be explained by what follows. It seems that a delegation of riders from York, Pa., was expected, and in due time they put in an appearance. There were ten members of the York Bicycle Club under command of Capt. Swartz, on their way to Philadelphia. They were met at the Three-Mile Tavern, on the Columbia Pike, by fifteen members of the Lancaster Bicycle Club, Capt. J. B. Miller, and were escorted to the Cooper House, this city, where a reception was tendered them by the Lancaster boys. The red and white roses blended beautifully, and it seems superfluous to say that they had a "right elegant" time. Wheelmen always do have. The York boys did the handsome thing by presenting to the Lancaster Bicycle Club a valuable gold medal, to be contested for at the coming races in this city, on July 4. At 5 A. M. (this morning) the visitors left by train for Paoli, where they will resume their wheels and ride to Philadelphia.

Capt. Miller, of the Lancaster Bicycle Club, is a live man and an ardent wheelman. He has the good of his club very much at heart. He proposes, in the near future, to stimulate the boys to increased proficiency, by offering a silver medal to the one who shall win in a race *up* Potts' hill. The hill is tough, because it is a long one; but it has a good surface, and will afford a fine test of wind and muscle. May the best man win, and we shall, waiting, listen to hear

"A voice sing out, far up the height,
Excelsior!"

Lancaster, Pa., May 30. TENTOONE.

TACOMA, WASHINGTON.

The celebration of the Queen's birthday at Victoria, B. C., on the 24th and 25th of May, goes down in the annals of history as one of the most successful festivals ever held in that part of the country. The city was dressed in holiday attire, and presented a cheerful appearance. Everybody, men, women and children, were happy, and intent upon making visitors feel at home. Tacoma sent a large delegation, including thirteen of the bicycle club members, as follows: Messrs Karl R. Thompson, Will Ramey, Barlow, Bast, Prince Wells, Ben Thompson, H. Huggins, Hays, Manning, McCoy, Weiler, Cochrane and Nichols.

The wheelmen of Victoria did everything in their power to make our boys enjoy themselves, and their efforts were crowned with success. Mayor Grant extended unbounded courtesies, and everywhere the citizens were most cordial to us. During the morning, the base-ball game was played, and the 2-mile bicycle championship of British Columbia contested for, which resulted in the victory of Karl Thompson, time, 7m. 26s.; Edgar A. McCoy, second, and W. H. H. Kean, third. The road was in poor shape, which accounts for the slow time. The road on which the race was run is called the Beacon Hill Course and is not a regular track. Taking this fact into consideration, Prince Wells signified his intention to enter the contest, knowing he would not jeopardize the amateur standing of his competitors, as the course was not a track but a road. However, some of those intending to compete objected to Wells' entry, and refused to ride if he did. After a short discussion Wells withdrew, and the race resulted as above. In the afternoon the aquatic sports were enjoyed by many thousand people, who swarmed thick as bees on the sides of the Gorge. Special mention should be made of the Indian canoe race, in which there were ten entries, with thirteen Indians in each canoe. They worked with the zest of an O'Connor or Hanlan, but using paddles instead of oars, and were cheered vociferously. After the sports the cyclists were banquetted, and later in the evening "shown about town." Everybody was thoroughly satisfied with the day's program.

On the following morning the committee called upon our boys and wanted them to give an exhibition or parade. Accordingly Captain Prince Wells arranged for a club drill and a lantern parade in the evening. Everyone was enthusiastic in praises for the excellence of the evolutions gone through with. The fancy trick riding by Prince Wells needs no comment. Although he had to ride on the turf, which was very uneven and full of holes, he did himself great credit. The lantern parade was a great success, all the wheels carrying from seven to sixteen lights.

Lack of space and time prevent my going more into details. Suffice it to say, we all returned to Tacoma delighted with the warm reception accorded us, and sincerely hope we may sometime enjoy the privilege of showing a more substantial appreciation. To one and all of Victoria's citizens we extend our heartfelt thanks for the manly and friendly spirit that prevailed in our favor.

SNOHOMISH.

May 29, 1889.

A. B. Barkman recommends a mixture of ammonia, sweet oil and laudanum for sprains. If well rubbed on it will take out the soreness in a very short time.

BUFFALO.

Decoration Day proved a sore disappointment to local wheelmen, the weather making sad havoc with the runs which had been so carefully planned. The most noteworthy cycling event of the day was the 100-mile ride from Erie made by the "Spartan eight" of the Buffalos. At 6:30 P.M. on the eve of Decoration Day, twenty-four members of the Buffalos made their appearance at the dock of the Lake Superior Transit Company to take the boat for Erie. About 4:45 the next morning the desired haven was reached in the midst of a rain storm. A council of war was held at the Reed House, and the rain subsiding, a party was sent ahead to reconnoiter. Three miles were covered and found to be in ridable condition, and Capt. Donaldson returned to report. He had but made his statement when it commenced to rain again. The reconnoitering party, after waiting forty minutes for the return of the Captain, became impatient, and decided to go on. North East was the first stopping place. Shortly after crossing the State line James Hedge and C. F. Hotchkiss hove in sight, having scorched it from Erie to catch up. They brought the news that the balance of the party, with the exception of Kingston, who was following behind, had decided to return to Buffalo by train. At Westfield the next stop was made, and here Kingston joined the party and Thompson and Courter dropped out, completely gone. Brocton, ten miles on, was the next resting place. Just before reaching the village Lewis took a severe header, rendering his right arm useless, but he pluckily stuck to his wheel and came in with the rest of the boys. Fredonia, Silver Creek, Angola and Bay View were stopped at in the order named, and the club rooms, on College Street, reached at about 9:30 P. M. It was one of the toughest rides ever attempted, and the names of the "Spartan eight" follow: C. N. Adams, John Jewett, C. F. Hotchkiss, D. H. Lewis, James Hedge, W. G. Brogan, J. E. White and William Kingston.

The Zig-Zags also had a tough experience on their trip to the Falls, and but four succeeded in riding the entire distance by wheel, the others taking the train.

The Ramblers abandoned their trip to Batavia, the roads being terrible. Next Sunday they will make the run from Erie. ZO.

NEWARK.

In response to the call of Captain Drabble, for a run Decoration Day, twenty men of the Atalantas were present at the road race, Irvington. After the race several of the members started, with other wheelmen, for Morristown. At Summit they were caught in a heavy rain-storm, which lasted several hours, and in consequence they did not reach their destination, but got home just as tired "all the samee."

Mr. Eichborn, the *trick* rider of the Atalantas, has sold his wheel, a handsome Harvard.

Mr. Edwin Dauchy, of Wilmington was the guest of the Atalanta wheelmen on the evening of Decoration Day. He was counted on as a sure winner in the afternoon, but owing to stomach trouble, while riding his twentieth mile was obliged to give up.

The club runs of the A. W. for this month are:

June 8, Saturday—From Club-house at 5 P. M. Route, Milburn. June 11, Tuesday—From Club-house at 7 P. M. Route, Caldwell (Moonlight). June 13, Thursday—From Military Park, 7 P. M. Route, Jersey City (Moonlight). June 19, Wednesday—From Club-house, 5.30 P. M. Route, South Orange. June 22, Saturday—From Club-house, 3 P. M. Route, Short Hills. June 28, Friday—From Club-house, 5.30 P. M. Route, Upper Montclair. The Captain will probably call an all-day run some time during the month.

Mr. Keer, of the H. C. W., is to be congratulated as Captain of the Triton Boat Club. Arthur Snow, of the Atalanta's, with Mr. Keer, was of the Triton's triumphant six in the Passaic Regatta.

Jersey wheelmen can *row* as well as *wheel*.

Mr. E. M Halsey has the best mileage record for May of the Atalantas, having ridden 607 miles. "Go it, Eddie, you'll be a stone crusher if you keep on."

Nine applications for membership were received this month. SPARK.

The Pittsburg *Bulletin* heads its column of cycling comment with a cut depicting a bicyclist taking a distinctively vile header. The cut is of unpleasant suggestion to non-cyclists, and the good that might be accomplished by the column is offset by the illustration. Change it, Br'er Seidell.

NEW YORK TO THE WEST VIA B. & O. R. R.

The B. & O. R. R. Co. now operates a complete service of fast express trains direct from New York to Chicago, St. Louis and Cincinnati. Pullman Sleepers are run through from New York to the three cities named, without change or transfer.

The fastest trains in America run via B. & O. R. R. between New York, Philadelphia, Baltimore and Washington, and all the trains are equipped with Pullman Buffet Parlor and Sleeping Cars.

Great improvements have been made in the roadway and equipment of the B. & O. in the last two years and its present train service is equal to any in the land. In addition to its attractions in the way of superb scenery and historic interest, all B. & O. trains between the east and west run via Washington.

The principal offices in New York are at 415 and 1140 Broadway, and Station at foot of Liberty Street. ***

COMPLIMENTARY BANQUET.

On May 29 the Peoria Bicycle Club, of Peoria, Ill., tendered a complimentary banquet to Mr. Hert Myers, as a recognition of the splendid work done by him in the recent tournament at Chicago. Freidrich's Hotel was the scene of the spread, and three spacious tables were required to seat all the club members and invited guests. At each plate was a handsome *boutonnière* and a *menu* card that is a work of art. The first page is inscribed, "Our honored guest; champion unicycle rider of the world, and holder of world's amateur twenty-four hour record." Below is a list of the victories won at Chicago, both in the Exposition building and at Cheltenham Beach. Seven firsts, two seconds and one third make a fine showing.

The *menu* that follows simply makes one's mouth water to glance over it, and we refrain from tantalizing our readers by giving it in detail. At one end of the largest table were two decorated bicycles, one of them almost hidden in a profusion of flowers. This was the machine ridden by Myers at Chicago. The other wheel was trimmed with club colors, each guest being presented with generous slips. At the conclusion of the banquet the usual amount of speech-making and congratulation were indulged in, and the members separated with the most kindly feelings for the recipient of the banquet and each other.

A MEADVILLE OUTING.

I am sorry to say our Decoration Day tour was finally spoiled by mud and rain, but not till after thirty-three miles, of excellent roads had been covered. The night before the 30th looked discouraging, but to our surprise the roads were found in excellent shape the next morning. Our party consisted of five, of whom my wife made one (by the way she is the only lady bicyclist in M., and has chosen a Rambler as her mount). Our dog Towser, little wotting of the trip he was to take, insisted on following us.

We started at 5 A. M., our route lying through Kentown, where my wife returned home, to Evensburg, nine miles, where our first stop was made. At this point Conneaut Lake is situated. This is the largest body of water in Penna., a favorite summer resort, and noted for its great depth. In some places the bottom has never been touched. From Evensburg we pushed on to Harmonsburg, five miles away at the other end of the lake. Breakfast was taken at a private house called "hotel," and as fine a meal as could be wished for. "How much," said we: "Twenty-five cents," said the landlord. We dove into our pockets, extracted *thirty-five* cents each and thanked him for his courtesy. The next place was Dicksonburg, but no stop was made. Further on we had a chance to dispose of Towser in trade. While riding along at a brisk pace, a voice was heard saying, "I wish I had that dog." "All right," said I, "have you got any butter milk?" "Of course," said he. "Bring out three glasses and you can have him." But on inquiring, the voice's owner found the milk was all fed out. "Never mind," said I, "you can have the dog any way, get a rope to tie him up with." He departed for the rope and *we* departed for Conneautville, dog and all. Probably the farmer is "waiting, waiting still." The net cash sales of the storekeeper at Conneautville were increased by our buying ginger ale and bannanas. After this light repast, we rode on to Shadeland, Powell Bros.' great stock farm, passing through Springboro on our way. Shadeland may be called a village of barns. The residence of Powell Bros. on one side, and a W. U. T. office on the other, are the only other dwellings. Barns for horses, ponies, cattle, sheep, and all domestic animals are everywhere to be seen scattered over the farm, which covers thousands of acres. Visitors to this farm are treated very kindly, guides taking you wherever you wish to go, and pointing out places of interest, no charge being made. After leaving Shadeland we had our first trouble with rain and mud, but managed to wheel on to Albion, four miles further, through mud five inches deep. Here we took train for home, well pleased with the day on the whole. On a pleasant day this trip might be lengthened and varied by visiting the State Normal School at Edenboro, and the Mineral Springs at Cambridge, Seagretown, and Ponce de Leon, all of them quite noted. For variety of scenery and good roads there seems no county in Penna. more favored than Crawford. Meadville itself is a noted pleasure resort, situated in the centre of the county, and pleasant runs can be taken in all directions. With more favorable weather, I hope to send you more accounts of tours taken.

Very truly, H. S. R.

RUTHERFORD WHEELMEN'S FIVE-MILE CHAMPIONSHIP.

The race for this was run off Decoration Day, on the Washington Boulevard, in the presence of a large crowd of wheelmen and passing picnickers. There were but two contestants, A. P. Jackson and F. W. Van Sicklen. The medal, which is of great beauty, a ½ carat diamond set in intricate gold work and known as the Hancock Medal, had previously been twice won by Jackson. The medal must be won three consecutive times to be the winner's property. On July 7, 1888, Jackson had defeated Van Sicklen in a contest for this same medal. At that time Van Sicklen entered with a badly sprained arm, and re-sprained it in the race by a bad fall. The second time the medal was raced for, Jackson had a walk-over with no competitors.

Under these circumstances the interest felt was great, Van Sicklen being the favorite.

The first mile was loafed over in 4m. 4cs., the second in 4m. 10s., and then Van Sicklen set a better pace for the third mile, that being done in 3m. 1s. At this point Jackson fell away, and Van Sicklen covered the fourth mile in 3m. 2s. The fifth mile was made in 2m. 58s., making Van Sicklen a winner by 27s., and the last three miles run in the good time of 9m. 1s. The good Jerseyites, who hardly knew what Van Sicklen could do, were slightly surprised.

RUTHERFORD.

THE LOUISIANA'S NEWDEPARTURE.

On Sunday, May 26, the Louisiana Cycling Club inaugurated long-distance contests and sealed handicaps in New Orleans, and bolstered up effectually their claim of "leading, not following." The course was laid out on the asphalt of St. Charles Avenue, in five laps of 4 70-100 miles each, with an additional mile and a half to complete the twenty-five miles. Of six "sure" starters but three came to the mark, Messrs. L. J. Frederic, Jr., Malcolm S. Graham and Bert M. Sprigg.

The word was given at 7.40 A. M., and a sharp pace set, Sprigg leading. Following are positions and total times for each lap respectively: First lap: Sprigg, 16m.; Graham, 16m. 5s.; Frederic, 17m. 10s. Second lap: Sprigg, 33m. 15s.; Graham, 33m. 15s.; Frederic, 35m. 25s. At this point Frederic changed to a lighter wheel, and an improvement in form was plainly seen. Third lap: Sprigg, 51m. 4s.; Graham, 52m. 45s.; Frederic, 54m. 40s. Graham complained of cramps when the post was reached, and gave up the struggle, leaving Sprigg and Frederic to fight it out between them. Fourth lap (18 miles): Frederic, 1h. 12m. 33s.; Sprigg, 1h. 22m. 33s.

This sudden change was explained by Sprigg's saddle worrying him, and a severe pain in the hips compelling him to dismount on the nineteenth mile. Changing wheels enabled him to finish this lap, but from that time on he was practically out of the race. Frederic made the fifth lap (23 50 100 miles) in 1h. 33m., and the whole twenty-five miles in 1h. 39m. 13s. The sealed handicaps were made public after the race, but its outcome had rendered them valueless. Those that entered and failed to start then realized what might have been, as their allowances were read out.

Immediately after Frederic's victory, one of these same non-starters challenged him to another twenty-five-mile race; but Frederic refused, on the ground that the challenger had had an excellent chance to meet him that very day and refused it. The club unanimously sustains this view of it.

Another race will be held June 9, but for the shorter distance of three miles. A large number of entries are expected.

THE LEAGUE HOTEL SYSTEM.

EDITOR OF THE WHEEL:

In your issue of May 24 you reprint a communication of "Verax" to the *American Athlete* upon the subject of the League hotel, and in connection with it you make some very pertinent comments. In connection with this matter I desire to call your attention to the form of contract in the N. Y. State Division which landlords are required to sign in order to secure the appointment of their hotel as a League hotel. The salient features of this contract are published in the *Bulletin* for May 17, over the signature of Chief Consul Bull.

There is no doubt of the fact that in the past many landlords have been perfectly willing to reap all the advantages of such appointment while they have been very slow to accord to wheelmen the privileges which they are entitled to by virtue of such appointment. You suggest that in consideration of a small sum, to be paid annually by the landlord, the Chief Consul of each Division agree "to use all practicable influence for the hotel, recommending all League tourists to stop there, and assuring them of good accommodation and courteous treatment, at regular rates." This contract secures the same and, by providing that the landlord shall furnish, at the rates specified, accommodations equal in all respects to those furnished regular guests. This contract is a new one, only issued this year, and, in securing from landlords a contract which shall be of some practical benefit to L. A. W. tourists, Chief Consul Bull, to whose efforts it is due, is deserving of the thanks of all members of our organization. Even with this new contract there may be occasional cases where tourists will be denied their rights, and in all such cases the aggrieved wheelman should immediately write to the Chief Consul, stating the facts fully, and if, upon investigation, it is found that any landlord is not keeping his part of the contract, such steps will undoubtedly be taken as will prevent a repetition of the offense at that hotel.

No. 11,893.

L. A. W. TRANSPORTATION COMMITTEE REPORT.

NEW YORK, May 31, 1889.

EDITOR OF THE WHEEL:

Dear Sir—Referring to the matter of charges for the transportation of bicycles, I am pleased to state that the recent resolution of the Trunk Line Association has been modified to the extent that at the last meeting of the Association a resolution was offered and adopted allowing the lines who desired to do so to make no charge for the carriage of a bicycle when accompanied by a passenger with a first-class ticket. I would state that this practically places the transportation matter in the same position as occupied for the last seven years, far as the Trunk Line Association is concerned.

I do not wish to infer by sending you this letter that I have in any way secured the friendly legislation, as the resolution above quoted originated in the Association, as did the original resolution placing a tariff on wheels. As I understand it, it is merely a reconsideration of the entire question by the Association.

Yours respectfully,
GEO. R. BIDWELL,
East. Rep. L. A. W.
TRANSPORTATION COM.

HOTEL RATES AT HAGERSTOWN, JULY 2, 3 AND 4.

The following are the hotels at Hagerstown, Md., with the rates fixed for wheelmen attending the L. A. W. meet:

Name.	Accommodate.	Reduction Rate.
Hamilton	250	$2.00 and 2.50
Baldwin	250	2.00 " 2.50
City	150	1.50
Franklin	200	1.50
Seminary	150	2.00

The other hotels, which are on the American plan, are:

Name.	Accommodate.	Reduction Rate.
American House	30 to 50	$1.00
Central House	75	1.00
Mansion House	75	1.00
Valley House	30	1.00
Beeler House	30	1.00
Allegheny House	30	1.00
Hoover House	30	1.00

Twelve hotels is a pretty fair showing for the so-called "hamlet."

MARYLAND.

The Potomac Wheelmen, of Cumberland, Md., gave a lantern parade on Baltimore Street, that city, recently. It was visited by hundreds of people. The wheels were trimmed with bright colored bunting, Chinese and bicycle lanterns of all sizes and colors, and presented a fine appearance as they went through their drill. The cyclers, twenty in number, were under command of Captain A. C. Willison. After the parade the club in a body spent the rest of the evening at the lemon compression party held at the residence of Captain R. A. French, on Williams Street.

The hotels at Hagerstown are rapidly filling up. The Baldwin and the Hamilton's parlors have already been engaged, and many others. It is probable that this will be the largest Meet in the history of the L. A. W.

Hagerstown lawyers and business men have formed committees among themselves, and are preparing to give President Luscomb a splendid reception when he arrives July 1.

About three hundred entry blanks for the races were mailed last week. The work on the track was begun this week.

BAY RIDGE.

STONE-LUMSDEN RACE.

(Telegram to THE WHEEL.)

Lumsden wins the three-mile race against Stone by five feet lead. Time made, 9m. 44s.

St. Louis, Mo. [illegible]

DeGraaf, of the Harlem (N. Y.) Wheelmen, has earned by the number and costliness of his mounts the title of "the Bonner of bicycling."

Mr. W. F. Bartlett, of the Harlem Bicycle Company, has been ill for three weeks but is now about again. Mr. Wood reports excellent business in renting and repairing. The company are agents for several lines of high grade wheels.

WHEEL GOSSIP.

The Manhattan club's uniform is the best we have seen.

The Riversides will have a team entered in the K.C.W.'s team race.

Karl Kron took his first ride and his first fall ten years ago May 29.

J. W. Bate & Co. opened their new cycle depot in Brooklyn on Tuesday last.

The New York Club has three new Psychos in its wheel-room, one a ladies' wheel.

Bowman and Schoefer are entered in the Schuylkill Navy games to be run at Philadelphia on Saturday.

Wappingers Falls, N. Y., with 6,000 inhabitants, has seventy-five wheelmen and a prosperous club.

Charlie Schwalbach publishes a neat advertising card on which are printed the riding rules in Prospect Park.

Col. George A. Jessup has turned over deeds of property valued at $200,000, to make good his shortage of $135,000.

Mr. Jas. Miller, President of the Riverside Wheelmen, is a recent addition to the League Committee for N. Y. City.

The next regular meeting of the Riversides has been postponed from Friday to Monday, on account of the Century run.

A bicycle has recently been stolen from F. I. Hughes, Rochester, N. Y., while stored in the building of the Young Men's Catholic Associa ion

One of our esteemed cycling contemporaries published a table of the road race. The times of the first thirteen were correct - with seven exceptions.

Mr. William Sutton, formerly of Messrs. Starley & Sutton, the English makers, died on May 22, from injuries received in a fall from his carriage.

Florida, the sandy road State, has but fifty wheelmen in the State. St. Augustine, with its asphalt streets, has twenty riders with a rapid increase in the ranks.

I like THE WHEEL better than any cycling paper that is published, and always like to get subscribers for it.

CHARLES J. SCHERER, Memphis, Tenn.

The Menge Brothers, Riverside Wheelmen; the Sheehan Brothers, Manhattan B. C., and Messrs. Harrison and Hubbard, New York Club, ride tandem bicycles.

Captain A. P. Benson, of the Dorchester Bicycle Club, has invited the Press Cycling Club to stop and examine its club-rooms on the way to Squantum, June 17.

The New York Division, L. A. W., received 1,698 members in 1888. This year they have 1,035 to date, and it is expected that last year's figures will be wiped out.

The officials of Brooklyn have advertised for bids for the paving of Cobblestone Hill. After the hill is repaired, Brooklyn cyclists may allow their life insurance policies to expire.

Fred Owen, of the Capital Cycle Club, has designed a new style of centreboard for yachts. The New York *Herald* recently devoted three columns to Mr. Owen's device.

The English have already inaugurated the record-breaking campaign. On May 18 Osmond broke the quarter-mile bicycle record and Jones the quarter and half mile safety records.

Captain A. Fraleigh and eight members of the Poughkeepsie Bicycle Club took a run to Fishkill and return on May 19, making seventeen miles in two hours. Dinner was taken at Newburg.

Coming meets reported, for amateurs only, are one of two days by the Hartford Wheel Club early in September, and one by the New Haven Bicycle Club, the last week in August, for one day.

The Bridgeport (Ct.) wheelmen would like to have the next State meet held in that city. It is one of the most enthusiastic wheel cities in New England, and would, doubtless, give riders a great time.

Mr. F. de C. Davies, President of the St. Augustine Wheelmen, is in town for a few days. He will tour to Canada, where his home is, and spend three months wheeling about the Canadian roads.

Col George A. Jessup has tendered his resignation as C. C of Pennsylvania Division L. A. W., on account of his business troubles. Mr. Jessup evidently wishes to save his Division as much as possible.

T. J. Hall, Jr., has challenged H. J. Hall, Jr., to a 25-mile race over the Irvington-Milburn course. The race will take place some Saturday in June, and with favorable conditions the record will be broken.

The proposed road racing association of New Jersey bicycle clubs has fallen through for the present, the handicap race, which promises to become a permanent fixture, being regarded as supplying all wants in this direction.

Brown, Baggot and Bowman, of the N. J. A. C., will make the circuit of all the bicycle races given in this vicinity this season They have an active campaign before them, as there will be an average of almost two races a week.

The New York *Press* had the best report of the Decoration Day road race, giving the handicap and net times in table form Brother W. I. Harris, well known in the wheel world, is responsible for the space the *Press* gives up to cycling.

IMPORTANT RAILROAD ACTION.

At a meeting of the Eastern Trunk Line Association, held last Tuesday, all railroads belonging to the Association were instructed to carry cycles free of charge when accompanied by owners.

Send to HOWARD A. SMITH & CO., Newark, N. J., for your bicycle supplies or call at Oraton Hall and learn to ride. Open evenings.***

We republish from the *Bicycling News* an article from the pen of the experienced Lacy Hillier entitled, "Position—Are We Not Overdoing It?" It contains a volume of suggestion, and we commend a careful perusal of it to new riders.

We have been trying a 38-pound Psycho, geared to 60 inches. The wheel is a beauty to look at, and "runs like oil." It is very fast on the level, the long cranks on the level making propulsion easy; it is easy on hills and coasts fast as any wheel of its weight.

There was a young man named David,
Who said I will make Davis crawl.
His actions at college
Have come to my knowledge,
And d——n it he shan't race at all.
—Abbot Bassett, *Poet-Laureate.*

One Hundred and Tenth Street is yet unrideable. A favorite way to reach the Park from the upper end of the drive is to cross 122d Street, up Boulevard to 125th Street, across 125th Street to St. Nicholas, down St. Nicholas to 123d Street, across 123d Street to Sixth Avenue and down to the Park.

Three safeties have been stolen at Rochester, N. Y., within the last thirty days One is a Victor, No. 2,800, one an American Rambler, and one a Singer. Wheelmen should take the number of their wheels as certainly as that of a valuable watch. It may some day lead to recovery of stolen goods.

Some few months since the *Bicycling World* announced that it was going to take charge of all road racing records, to supervise, accept or reject, as it might see fit. We felt very sad that we were shut out of all this, but now, alas! the *Bi. World* bubble has collapsed, for they tell us that road racing is dead.

The New York *Sun* of Sunday last published a three-column article on cycling, full of information for new people, fairly correct, but rather guide-booky. The writer made two gross mistakes in decrying cycling for ladies and in stating that but four per cent. of the wheelmen of New York City rode safeties.

"G. AND J." TO THE FRONT.

The Gormully & Jeffery Mfg. Co. are more than pleased over the results of the Pullman Road Race and the Orange Road Race. In the former, the first prize was won by Frank Hodach, on a Light Champion, and in the latter, John Bensinger made the fastest time on a Light Champion.

At a game of base ball played Saturday, May 25th, between the K. C. W.'s and Brooklyn B. C., the score resulted in favor of the former, as follows:

	1	2	3	4	5	6	
K. C. W	2	0	0	4	8	2	—16
B. B. C	4	3	1	3	3	0	—14

Courtney and Wheeler acted as battery for the K. C. W.'s and Matthews and Hardie for the Brooklyns.

Messrs. Ward and Bonner, of the K. C. W.'s, made the round trip from Brooklyn to Oakdale, on Sunday, May 5. Dinner was had at Babylon, where a number of Huntington wheelmen were met. Unless some wheelmen had made the same distance previous to this date, the first century run of the season in New York certainly belongs to these gentlemen, and Messrs. Scudder and Gruman, of the Huntingtons, will have to yield in their favor. Next.

The Hyde Park (Mass.) cyclists, Jenkins and Rhodes, who started for Portland on the morning of Decoration Day in an attempt to make the distance in fifteen hours, arrived home yesterday. Captain Jenkins states that they made Biddeford, Me., distance 140 miles, in eighteen hours. They had to face a strong wind and mist the latter part of the distance, and were disappointed in not meeting "pacers." Jenkins had cramps, which delayed them two hours on the road.

Watch G. A. Armstrong, of Boston, Mass. He won the novice race at Narragansett Park Thursday, won the mile handicap with 200 yards start, and took a position in the team race that his place at finish, seventh, doesn't indicate, because eight out of the nine men in crossed the tape in a bunch, and Armstrong was there with such men as Clark, Foster, Benson, Schoefer and Banker. He is a well-built fellow, and ought to show up well if he goes into racing this season.

While coasting on a tandem tricycle near the Charles gate, West, Back Bay Park, Boston, May 31, a wheel caught in the electric conduit on Beacon Street, and one of the riders, Miss Alice A. Adams, residing at 180 West Canton Street, was thrown from the tricycle to the ground, striking on her head. She was sent to her residence in a carriage by the park police. A physician who was called said there were internal injuries.

The New York Club is ever ready to second any movement to help wheeling. The asphalt pavement on West End Avenue is paid for by the property owners. When it was proposed to lay asphalt from Seventy-second to Sixty-eighth all the property owners consented to the assessment except the owner of the building occupied by the New York Club. Rather than have the project of repaving the avenue fall through, the club stepped forward and paid an assessment of $265.

The Kentucky Division League meet, at Danville, June 10, promises to be the best one ever held in the State. A fight will be made to transfer the headquarters to Louisville from Covington. A large party of Louisville wheelmen will leave Saturday morning. They will go by slow stages, traveling forty-two miles the first day and forty-seven the second. Among those who will make the run are Messrs. Lucas, Lamb, Gunther, Phil Allison, Bresee, Kneller, Johnston, Simpson and Johnson.

The Aberdeen Wheelmen is the title of a new club organized recently in Aberdeen, South Dakota, with the following officers: President, H. M. Marples; Vice-President, C. M. Coe; Secretary, G. Jewell, Treasurer, O. K. Pellman; Executive Committee, R. D. Bentley, C. B. Thompson, W. P. Butler; Captain, W. H. Wendell; Lieut., C. L. Brockway. The Captain, Mr. Wendell, is a recent accession from Albany, and would seem destined to infuse new life in cycling matters at Aberdeen.

Send to HOWARD A. SMITH & CO., Newark, N. J., and get stocking supporters, tire cement, belts, bundle carriers for all machines, tire tape, etc.***

Coincident with the laying of asphalt pavement in the city of Chattanooga, Tenn., a bicycle club was formed in that city. This was only a year ago. To-day the club numbers forty-five, and is composed of the best young men in the city. A tournament is spoken of for Fourth of July, and clubs from Rome, Ga., Murfreesboro, Tenn., Clarksville, Tenn., Knoxville, Tenn., and Gadsden, Ala., will be invited to take part. The election of officers for the ensuing year takes place the first part of June.

The Eagle Bicycle Co. have just published a second edition of their catalogue. The principal feature of the new catalogue is the number of testimonials it contains W. C. Marion, Jr., Captain of the K. C. W., speaks of the easy-running and hill-climbing qualities of the Eagle. Mr. Eldridge, of the Hudson County Wheelmen, says the wheel is equal to the best in finish and workmanship. We saw Pendleton, of the New Yorks, out on an Eagle last Sunday. He mounts the wheel gracefully and rides easily.

The New York club held its regular monthly meeting on Wednesday evening. The feature of the meeting was a debate over a sundry expense item of $30 for clean towels. The members thought this a large price for cleanliness and upon investigation it was proven that there were $2 worth of lemons and sundry other items mixed up and lumped with the wash bill. After considerable discussion the men were very hazy as to whether they dried themselves with lemons or towels; a motion for adjournment prevented several cases of insanity.

LOCKPORT DOINGS.

E. E. Pool, J. E. Broadbent, A. M. Montgomery, A. L. Cook and A. Gross, all of Lockport, N. Y., rode to Lewiston, on Decoration Day, on their wheels in three hours and twenty minutes. After dinner two contests were had. One was for the slowest down-hill race for 300 yards. This was very exciting, and was finally won by J. E. Broadbent by about a foot in 6m 50s. The other contest was the hill climbing one, also for 300 yards. This was won by A. L. Cook in 1m. 14s. The prizes were gold medals and donated by Elmer E. Pool. The boys came home on the cars, owing to the rain, which had begun to fall, and the terrible condition of the roads.

That Massachusetts party that went down to the Memorial Day tournament at Providence took about everything worth taking away with them. Boston captured the novice first prize and the mile handicap first and third, while those Dorchester men walked off with the two-mile national championship, the mile safety handicap first, and with Somerville took first and second in the mile tandem safety handicap, first in the tandem safety scratch, and the Dorchester Club three captured the team race. That was a pretty good haul out of eight open events, one of which no Massachusetts man started in. However, there are no fellows anywhere that the Rhode Island cyclers would be more pleased to give their medals to than Chief Consul Emery's boys.

THE COMING MEET.

The tenth annual meet of the L. A. W. promises to be the "red letter" one in the history of that organization. Maryland hospitality will be dispensed in the most liberal style, and Hagerstown will do all in her power to entertain the visiting wheelmen. President Luscomb will arrive on the evening of the 1st, and will be received at the train by a committee of prominent citizens, escorted to the Hamilton and there tendered a reception.

The business meeting, runs over Washington County's superb roads, an evening ride of six miles to the beautiful and historic Potomac, where everybody will indulge in a swim and witness a display of fireworks by the citizens of Williamsport, will occupy the time of the visitors on the 2d. On the morning of the 3d an opportunity will be given those who wish to visit the battlefields to do so. A run will start about 9 A. M., taking in the battlefield of Antietam, the National Cemetery at Sharpsburg, and the South Mountain battlefield, returning in time to take train for Pen Mar.

A special train will leave for that famous resort of the Blue Ridge Mountains, where a magnificent view can be had of twenty-five miles up and down the beautiful and fertile Cumberland Valley.

Supper will be taken there, returning in time to enjoy a fine pyrotechnic display.

The parade on the 4th will occupy about thirty minutes, which will fully satisfy the average wheelman's desire to exhibit his "calves" to an admiring multitude. Refreshments will be served after the parade, and the photo. taken by the club photographer, who made a special trip to Baltimore to secure a camera guaranteed not to break.

The races will take place on the Fair Grounds on the afternoon of the 4th, and give promise of some very exciting sport.

The finale will consist of a grand open air "smoker" and concert by a military band.

A few "kickers" have objected to the Meet coming here—as they say—on account of inferior hotel accommodations. I wish to contradict that statement, as Hagerstown is justly termed "the city of hotels," and has ample room within her gates for all who will come.

HAGERSTOWN.

WANTED.—A 50-inch Springfield Roadster. Address P. O. Box 2225, N. Y. tfc

FOR SALE.—A 53-inch Columbia Light Roadster, in best of shape; ridden part of two seasons; price $75, without cyclometer. G., care this paper.

FOR SALE.—Rudge Light Roadster, 54-inch, enameled and nickle finish; ball bearing; ball pedals; spade handles; lantern, stand, etc.; in perfect condition; $90. R. W. Muns, 41 Water Street, N. Y. City. 6-14

Write to HOWARD A. SMITH & CO., Newark, N. J., for their illustrated catalogue and second-hand list of bargains. Complete repair shop.***

KARL KRON AND "234."

MEMORIAL LETTER ON THE TENTH ANNIVERSARY OF HIS FIRST RIDE.

TO THE EDITOR OF THE WHEEL:

The first blood spilled by me in behalf of bicycling, and for the glory of Washington Square, was spilled ten years ago this day, when I first mounted the saddle of No. 234, and when my brief ride of twenty feet ended with a dislocated left elbow, at 3.45 P. M. The tragedy was commemorated by the following parody in the New York *World* of June 9:

> Said the Bicycler to the Cobblestone,
> As he mounted with careless glee,
> "Flattest of all the things I've known,
> Do you think you can injure me?"
>
> Said the Cobblestone to the Bicycler,
> As it fractured his elbow joint,
> "You'll find, however flat I may be,
> I always carry my point."

At last, after a decade of writing, the affair is to be further celebrated by a Memorial Arch, for whose erection a committee of thirty-four citizens are trying to raise $100,000 by popular subscriptions. As the arch is nominally in honor of Washington, I have felt no hesitation in urging the public to subscribe; and I have been spurred onward with something of the same enthusiasm as that which once possessed me to rake the world fore and aft to win supporters for building a monument to bicycling.

In every day's issue of the *Commercial Advertiser* since that of May 13, I have printed a letter of half a column or more, ringing the changes in support of the theory that, as Washington Square is "the real centre of the world," patriotic people ought gladly to help pay for building the arch there. I know none of the men connected with that paper, and I never before wrote a line for it; but, as it welcomes all contributions favorable to the arch, I shall probably keep printing a daily appeal in its columns until I reach the "record" of twenty or more. If any former supporter of mine will send $2 for the arch to the Treasurer of the Committee, W. R. Stewart, at 54 William Street, he will please me almost as much as if he paid me for another copy of "X. M. Miles."

As a matter of strictly personal news, you may as well announce that I am now selling a new $2 book descriptive of American touring routes, entitled "Ten Thousand Miles on a Bicycle." It is so large a book ("equivalent to nine octavo volumes of 300 pages each") that I've been obliged to print a 150-page book of "press notices and specimen pages" in order to advertise it properly. These smaller books cost me ten cents each to manufacture (edition, 5,000), but I mail them to all applicants "for nothin'," in the hope that a perusal thereof may awaken sluggish consciences to the propriety of paying $2 for the big book, which represents an investment of $13,000 "in behalf of American roads."

KARL KRON.

THE UNIVERSITY BUILDING,
Washington Square, N. Y., May 29, 1889.

A GOOD STORY CAN NOT BE TOLD TOO OFTEN.

The editor of the *Crosby County News* published in Estacado, Texas, thus indorses the advice of a contemporary regarding giving weak and sickly boys bicycles to ride:—

"There is nothing that a father or mother can do that will do more to save a weak and sickly boy than to put him on a bicycle and let him ride whenever he can find time. Such exercise will benefit him greatly in his physical development, and be equally efficacious in moral growth."

In giving space to the foregoing paragraph, we are sensible of the fact that many people look upon bicycling as an expensive and unremunerative sport. But those who killed the early astronomers for teaching that the earth is round and that it revolves around the sun every year, were not more mistaken, than they. Bicycling, or cycling, has been widely and thoroughly tested all over the world by men of science and culture, and their verdict is that it is the most healthful exercise known to man, that it is of especial benefit to persons over forty years of age, to those who lead sedentary lives, and to those unhappy people who are afflicted with constipation, disease of the kidneys and liver, and weakness in bone and muscle of back and limbs. In our experience we can testify that we have entirely ceased being bothered with neuralgia, while before we learned to ride a "spell" was expected at least once a week, and a recurrence thereof at every damp season and east wind. Now we are not troubled at all with neuralgia, which redemption we attribute jointly to cycling and the purity of our atmosphere.

West End Avenue, which has been asphalted from Seventy-second Street to Seventy-ninth Street, is now being repaved with asphalt from Seventy-second street down to 68th Street. This will enable the Manhattan men, whose club is in Seventieth Street, to gain the drive without walking their wheels from Seventieth to Seventy-Second Street.

HOW TO TOUR.

There is no doubt about it, that touring is the nicest part of cycling, though it does not make nearly the stir that racing or road "record smashing" does. So uncertain are the ways and tempers of touring companions, that were a man certain of pleasant company at his inn at the end of each day's journey, we should almost recommend touring alone. Certainly we have carried out several tours alone, with perfect satisfaction to ourselves. On the other hand, the addition of a companion does add to any pleasure; and touring with a companion is no exception to this rule. One great mistake in touring is to try and do too much distance in the day. We do not believe, even if a man's muscles can enjoy a seventy or eighty miles ride in the day, that his mind can do so. For a really enjoyable tour, taking the rough with the smooth, we should place as a maximum forty miles a day. It would frequently be only thirty, but good roads and a favoring wind on off days would keep up the average. Another point is feeding. Whilst cycling eventually improves bad digestions and strengthens still further good ones, to a beginner at long distance riding, the act of feeding requires attention. Cycling increases the appetite enormously, but the muscles naturally draw away the blood from the digestive organs, and if time be not allowed between a ride and a meal—thirty minutes should elapse—or too many "square meals" be taken, disastrous results may occur. We will give a novice's experience in this line. It was in August, 1874, and he started from London on a 44-inch Ariel ordinary bicycle to ride to Harwich. Laying in a good breakfast beforehand and sundry drinks *en route* he reached Colchester about 1:30, and had dinner at the ordinary, a very good one, and started for Harwich, which he eventually reached, and at the Great Eastern Hotel ordered chops and tea, subsequently retiring to a bed in a room next door to the works of the big clock in the front of the house, and speedily dropped into a deep slumber. After two hours or so of sleep he gradually began to awake, and thought he heard his heart beating (a delusion helped by the ticking of the clock next door), and eventually did awake choking and with strong palpation. Seeking the night porter he informed him quietly that he believed he was dying and asked him to bring a doctor. The porter showed far more excitement than the cyclist, who simply sat on the bottom stairs of the grand staircase in his vest and trousers and pressed his heart. Presently appeared the Irish "understudy"—*locum tenens* we believe the faculty call them—of the local medical man. "Ye have indigestion," he said promptly. "I thought from the signs the porter told me ye had *angina pectoris*." "You are sure it is not that, doctor?" "Oh, no! if ye had ye would be 'rowling' about the 'fleur' with pain," was the prompt reply. The cyclist parted his half-guinea and learnt a life-long lesson as regards the uses and misuses of the body.

Our advice to the tourer is take a good breakfast at starting, lunch on eggs and bread and butter, finish by daylight, and have as good a dinner as the hotel and your means allow, and if not a teetotaler and the funds allow put a bottle of Burgundy under your belt, and after a stroll through the place retire to rest, eating nothing more; and drinking as little more as your strength of mind will allow. In this way it will be found that a man grows stronger each day; but neglect to take proper food at proper times and touring becomes an injury, not a health giver or restorer.

Clothing on tours should be well thought out. Our advice is ride in flannels, and when stopping for the day change into dry flannels and a suit of the very thinnest blue serge made. This occupies little room, and enables a man of any position in the world to associate with his equals in the coffee-room without feeling like a pariah. Square the chambermaid immediately on arriving, and then have your working dress thoroughly dried and ready for you with the matutinal knock and "Hot water, sir."—*Wheeling.*

The Pope Manufacturing Company, through its courteous representative, Mr. N. C. Fowler, Jr., has presented to the Boston Press Cycling Club, an elegant light blue silk banner, trimmed with silver braid and fringe. In the field, in letters of gold with dark blue shading, are the words, "Boston Press." At the end of the pole is an eagle. The company has also presented the club with printed copies of the constitution and by-laws, neatly printed and bound.

SOME TIMELY TOPICS.

CUSSED AND DISCUSSED by CHARLES ALEX. PERSONS.

Of *all* the *fool* statements that I have ever seen in print, the greatest recently appeared. It read thus: "Show me a rider of the bicycle, and I will show you a case of spinal complaint, says Dr. Agnew." I'll bet two to one, that if I could have America's 75,000 wheelmen examined, and let Dr. Agnew pick out 75,000 *other* men, he would find more diseases among the latter than the former, especially the trouble mentioned. May be Dr. Agnew meant he would show *us* the spinal complaint in some man other than the bicyclist, but if such was the case, the newspaper man should have taken care to so express himself.—Ain't that so, "Jack?"

In a recently written letter, Mr. W. L. Welch says "Does it not come within the province of the League to devise some scheme by which tourists may safely arrange for the transmission of their neccessary funds to poin's en-route? In common with other tourists, the writer has felt the need of some scheme that will obviate the necessity for carrying a comparatively large sum of money through a strange country and into many wild and deserted places. My tours are generally taken in company with my sister and we are compelled to have, easily accessible, from $50 to $100. Post office money orders are not reliable owing to the undue caution exercised by the provincial P. M. A request from a stranger for cash for a draft or check naturally causes him to be looked upon with suspicion. Cannot the League devise some scheme to overcome this difficulty.

Yours, L. A. W. No. 19308, W. L. WELCH."

This is an important matter and should receive attention. The transmission of funds is something that should interest every one, and no one more than the touring wheelmen. European tourists are splendidly provided for in this way, by having their letters of credit, Bank of England cheque-books, etc., but the tourist here at home is either compelled to run the risk of carrying his cash with him, or be put to inconvenience by P. O. money orders and registered letters. The sooner something is gotten up, the sooner will a great want be filled.

Please allow me to pause; put my left hand on my heart, remove my derby, and bow a low and respectful bow to Mr. Albert Mott, Chief Consul Maryland Division, whose letter in THE WHEEL of recent date is enough to make various parties of various places feel like running into a stone wall at full speed. As to Hagerstown, it stands as monumental evidence of all that has been claimed for it.

After reading THE WHEEL of May 24, I counted the amount of matter in its make-up, and found that, all told, there were *two hundred and forty-one* distinct articles, and that was counting the letters as *one* each. When a paper appears that will beat THE WHEEL please drop me a line, some of you, and if I don't get it I'll subscribe.

[Spare our blushes.—ED.]

The vision of a wheelman coasting down Cotton Avenue, a few days since, with one leg crossed over the other, eye-glass on, holding up an open umbrella with one hand and a copy of THE WHEEL in the other, which he was intently reading, was a rather new one in these parts.

No section will outdo this one, when it comes to tournaments, between now and Christmas. T. L. Ingraham, of Columbus, Ga., writes me that the Montgomery Exposition Co. will hold one in November next, at which the value of prizes will exceed a thousand dollars. Atlanta will "blow in" a thousand the same way; Augusta and Macon six or eight hundred, and possibly Columbus also. I am getting down in *fine* condition, can now do a mile in 4.23, and *nine* of them in an hour. *Look out for me.*

Griffin, Ga., is a new cycling centre, where wheeling has taken quite a hold. "Bob" Brantley, who has taken the road for the G. and J.'s, has placed fifteen new wheels there, about ten of which are Ramblers. I passed through there recently, on my way to Atlanta (awheel), and was highly pleased with the roads thereabouts.

Georgia's "Road Congress" is now a thing of the past. For two days representatives of each county were in Atlanta (at the State's expense) discussing the whys and wherefores of our having better roads and pikes, and having them *at once*. The advantages, pro and con, of the advisability of the use of the State's guests (in stripes) on the highways was an important topic. Papers on "Practical Road Building," "Scientific Road Building," "Good Roads the Better Economy," and others of as interesting a nature were read by men of learning. Resolutions pertaining to the work were drawn, and will be submitted to the Legislature at its next meeting, and many practical improvements are looked for as a result.

It is now after midnight, and I've got to do *something* to keep awake until 3.25, to catch an early morning train. It's all about that Southeastern cycle tour, you remember, and I hope to soon be on my way to Columbus, where we expect to start. When I gave the route in my last letter I mentioned "Bgham" as the first stopping place outside of Columbus. Well, that was Ingram's fault. *He* wrote it "Bgham," so I did, too, but since then he writes that "we will roll into Birmingham for breakfast next Wednesday morning," and now that place is over here in Alabama. "I'm sorter disappointed." In another letter he writes: "Now don't you go an' try an' look *nice*. By the time we turn the top of Red Mountain, we'll look like a pack of tramps, and if the police don't get us, the only reason will be that we can outrun them."

MACON, GA.

SEVEN STAYERS OF THE BUFFALOS.

Hedge, Adams, Jewett, Fenton, Russel Bros. and Nicholas, all of the Buffalo Bicycle Club, wheeled to Springville and back on Sunday, a distance of seventy miles, the round trip. Russel reports the roads in excellent condition, and claims it to be the prettiest ride out of the city.

THE BUFFALO ZIGZAGS' UNLUCKY NUMBER.

Thirteen of the boys recently wheeled out to the park to have their photos taken on their wheels. When they were all in line some one tried to dismount, resulting in a general mixture of wheels and boys. The Captain's new wheel was badly buckled, also some others, but not quite so badly. Although the boys are not in the least superstitious, it seems very strange that thirteen have never been together on any run, without ending in some kind of a "scrape." This seems to be the club's unlucky number. It will be remembered that thirteen started out the night Mr. Sherk took his severe header on Richmond Avenue, and also when so many wheels were broken on Elmwood Avenue, besides other instances too numerous to mention.

THE WHEEL

—AND—

CYCLING TRADE REVIEW,

Published every Friday morning.

Entered at the Post Office at second class rates.

Subscription Price,   -   -   - $1.00 a year.
Foreign Subscriptions.   -   -   -   8s. a year.
Single Copies,   -   -   -   -   -   5 Cents.

Newsdealers may order through AM. NEWS Co.

All copy should be received by Monday.
Telegraphic news received till Wednesday noon.

Advertising rates on Application.

F. P. PRIAL, Editor and Proprietor
23 Park Row,

P. O. Box 444,   Now York.

Persons receiving sample copies of this paper are respectfully requested to examine its contents and give us their patronage, and as far as is convenient, aid in circulating the journal, and extend its influence in the cause which it so faithfully serves. Subscription price, $1 per year.

IT is a fact well recognized in newspaperdom that most writers are only at their best when making the retort, courteous or discourteous, as the case may be : the latter nine times out of ten. It is characteristic of human nature, and of animal nature for that matter, that small men and small animals are always most ready to make the retort uncourteous. They are continually expecting and making ready to be jumped upon by their larger and more powerful fellows, and consequently they are always in a state of armed neutrality, ready for active warfare at the slightest provocation. The newspaper world has its small and its large men, and should the big fellow overlook the small one, or consciously or unconsciously slight him or his, forthwith he betakes himself to his slimy inkpot and lays about him in great fashion. Our own little cycling world has seen too much of this petty warfare. We do not refer to legitimate criticism or correction, for of that we cannot have too much ; but to the descent into nasty personality, personality not supported by a scintilla of fact or even probability, but based on the excited individual's unbridled imaginings. The lesson to be learned by all cyclists is, that when A attacks B you are not qualified to judge of the merits of the case unless you have read B's story and learned the cause of the attack. If you cannot read B's story you may safely conclude that B has embedded an arrow in a particularly sensitive spot in A's makeup.

The case in point is an article in the *Sporting Life* signed by "Perseus," entitled by the editor "An Unwarranted Attack Sharply and Ably Answered." Our readers will recollect an editorial discussion on the question of patents in which we made use of the *Sporting Life* to illustrate a point, and for this presumption "Perseus" indulges himself in a paroxysm of insinuation and belittlement, and then admits that THE WHEEL is the "most readable cycling paper in the country, and that he is in perfect accord with our opinion," as per the following : * * * "For, like Mr. Prial, he believes that the true inwardness of the patent rights and ownership can be determined only in the courts.

For that reason he has refrained from making any comment one way or the other, and has simply presented the facts as they are."

A BRIGHT day is dawning for Wheelmen in New York. The press is thoroughly aroused to the necessity of smooth pavements. The majority of the great dailies advocate the use of asphalt for the residence streets, which would include all New York above Fourteenth Street, with the exception of such heavily travelled streets as Ninth, Eighth, Sixth, Third and such Avenues. Some even go further and approve of smooth pavements for the down-town streets. The Chamber of Commerce is alive to the situation and has put itself on record, by formal resolution, in favor of asphalt pavements up-town, and the smoothest possible pavements that will stand heavy traffic. It is not ready to accept the vague hints about smooth pavements not being able to stand our climate ; they want the authorities to experiment, that the best possible results may be obtained. At any rate, the result of the agitation is that the area of asphalt pavements in Gotham will grow from this time, and the ending—no man knoweth.

WHEELMEN have much to be thankful for in this, the "Month of Roses." The railroads have decided to transport wheels free to all parts of the country, and the wave of good roads Improvements is crystalizing.

The resolution, reprinted in another column, came up before the Railroad Association for discussion. It was passed as an experiment. One of the most prominent officials of the Trunk Line Association, in discussing the resolution, made a statement to the effect that wheelmen individually were gentlemen, but as a crowd they were —— fools. This railroad official forgot that all crowds are more or less " fresh," whether they be boys on the way to a baseball match or statesmen en route to a political convention. At any rate it behooves cyclists to use some discretion when traveling. They should not monopolize the train, cause the officials any trouble, or annoy other passengers. We wish to impress upon cyclists the fact that should any misbehaviour on their part ever be reported to the railroads, the resolution just passed will be rescinded, and it will be many a day before the Trunk Line Association will ever consent to reconsider the question if they ever decide to fix a tariff.

LOOK AT THE NUMBER.

It has been brought to our attention recently that many second-hand wheels bought and sold have either had the number effaced or tampered with. Anything of that sort pre-supposes something crooked, and riders, new or old, should, as much as possible, beware of dealers or authorized agents, to avoid possible difficulties. Of course, where the seller and wheel sold have been known to the purchaser any length of time, there is little danger of fraud, but readers of cycling papers cannot fail to note the rapid increase of late in the number of stolen wheels. It is only fair to presume that the thief does not want a wheel for his own use, but will sell it at whatever price is obtainable. Removing or changing the number destroys all identity so far as tracing stolen property is concerned. For that reason it has always seemed to us that *each detachable part* of a wheel should have its number deeply and plainly stamped upon it by the makers. When that is done, the difficulty of removing it is increased. Let the wheelman make record of the number, as he would that of a hundred and twenty-five dollar watch, and when lost or

stolen, he has something besides the general appearance to go by. Riders may say that they would know their own wheel among a thousand others. Perhaps they would, but this country is a large one and the means of transit rapid. The unlucky owner may never have a chance to compare it with others. We venture to say that not five out of every ten stolen wheels are ever recovered.

KEEP YOUR BUSINESS EYE OPEN.

The *Press* is glad to see that the Chamber of Commerce has taken ground in favor of the idea advocated in these columns—that while heavy stone pavements should be laid in the business part of the city, a clean and noiseless asphalt pavement should be put on the streets mostly used for residence. General John Newton advocated this adaptation of pavements to the nature of the streets, while Commissioner of Public Works, in a valuable report full of information as to the estimated cost of these improvements per square yard ; but until the Legislature that recently adjourned had authorized the expenditure of $1,500,000 a year for this purpose it was lawful to spend only $500,000 a year therefor. The interest taken in the subject by the Chamber of Commerce should not be fitful. Let its committeemen, Messrs. F. B. Thurber, Cornelius Vanderbilt, J. B. Crane, J. Claflin, J. H. Seymour and Henry C. Meyer, provide themselves with copies of General Newton's report and keep a close watch on the expenditure of the increased appropriation available, so that the city may get its money's worth as estimated by expert authority. Few people stop to consider what a valuable impetus would be given to New York's trade by making it, say, ten per cent. easier to drive a wagon load of goods one mile. Time is money, and the Chamber of Commerce is the very body that ought to keep an eye on the improvements of the streets.—*New York Press.*

TRY ASPHALT.

The voice of the Chamber of Commerce, to this effect, should be heeded by those who have the spending of the city's millions. The great merchants urge that in the residence portions, and where the business traffic is not heavy, asphalt pavements be given a thorough trial. The suggestion is eminently wise and should be carried out. The harshness of our climate, the volume and weight of trucking, and the perpetual digging in our highways are the chief excuses that the city can offer for the horrible condition of its streets. But they will not be accepted as adequate, in so far, certainly, as they relate to the quieter districts. In those sections, at least, we might luxuriate in civilized pavements. Here asphalt can do valuable pioneer and missionary work. For revolutions never go backward, and once let this style of pavement, judiciously and honestly laid, be extended over a considerable area, and it is bound to spread over the city except where the granite block may be required by the conditions of our heavy down-town traffic.—*New York Sun.*

A GENEROUS ACTION.

At the regular meeting of the West End Bicycle Club, Rochester, N. Y., on June 7, it was voted to contribute $25 from the club treasury toward relief of the Johnstown sufferers. Other clubs with a full treasury can not do better than follow in the Rochester club's footsteps. At such a time of need and suffering, all thought of club junketings, improvement of roads, etc., must step aside and give way to all necessity and want.

Looking at the matter from the more selfish point of "good policy," the action would still be creditable. It can do no harm to wheelmen all over this broad land to be known and—well, advertised, if you put it so—as generous men and women. When cyclists in England purchased and presented to the Life Saving Service a staunch and serviceable life boat, no one sneered at the widespread publicity the generous act brought upon them. All honor to such actions, say we !

WHEEL GOSSIP.

The annual outing of the Springfield Bicycle Club will be held on June 25.

"Tandem" will kindly note that we have several letters for him at this office.

Eleven New Bedford bicyclists made the trip to Providence and back on June 9.

Class, Schoefer and Clarke, will be trained by W. B. Troy, at the Berkeley track, this season.

The Brooklyn Bicycle Club will start on a pleasant trip to Poughkeepsie and Ramapo Valley on June 22.

The Louisville Cycle Club, 100 strong, is announced to head the Masonic parade in that city on St. John's Day, June 24.

The Lynn Cycle Club contemplates holding a race meet at Glenmere Park, July 4, if there be no celebration of the day by the city.

The race for the championship of the Cincinnati Bicycle Club will be from Chester Park to the Hamilton toll gate, a distance of 17½ miles.

Herbert Doughty, 55 Chatham Street, Lynn, reports to the police that some one on Saturday last stole his bicycle from in rear of his shop.

At least half a dozen bicycles are ordered by different members of the Women's Wheel and Athletic Club, and tricycles are selling at a discount.

T. A. Carroll, of Lynn, will devote his time principally to the cycle business for the present, having resigned the secretaryship of the Heelers' Union.

Our old friend "Free Lance," steals into the Crystal Palace grounds on a summer evening, and shows us the fliers at work, Hillier, Osmond and the rest of them.

F. E. Olds, of the Los Angeles Wheelmen, has himself constructed a Rover type safety, and it made its appearance for the first time at the Los Angeles Meet, May 30.

Irish inventions seem to be coming to the front with a vengeance lately, as witness Keating's patent spring fork and luggage carrier and Dunlop's Pneumatic Safety.

The captain of the Roxbury Bicycle Club has called the following runs for this month: June 16, Waltham, via Dedham; 17, Squantum; 23, Cobb's Tavern; 30, Nahant.

Twenty-two wheelmen of the Louisville Cycle Club took a most enjoyable run from that city to Shephardsville and return, on June 2. On June 9 a well-attended run was also taken to Greenville, Ind., and return.

Charles E. Thomas, the new General Secretary of the Y. M. C. A., at Nashville, Tenn., is a believer in muscular Christianity, as evidenced by the fact that he rides a safety machine despite his 225 pounds avoirdupois.

Charles Schwalbach has offered a handsome silver cup to be competed for in the five-mile club championship of the Kings County Wheelmen, and another to be competed for by teams from the Brooklyn wheel clubs only.

Mr. W. G. Shack, of Buffalo, N. Y., is one of the most enterprising wheelmen in that city. Located at 110 Laurel Street, he has chosen two good wheels to handle, the New Rapid and Quadrant, and has no cause to complain of trade.

RIGHT YOU ARE.

I take the paper because it is the best cycling paper published.

F. W. Kitching, New York Bicycle Club.

Wheelmen that intend having anything done in the line of re-enameling, re-nickeling, or repairs, can not do better than read the advertisement of Geo R. Bidwell & Co., 313 West 58th Street, in this issue, and then talk with Mr. Bidwell on prices.

The Milwaukee Bicycle Club has called runs as follows: June 16, Oak Creek and New Coeln; 23, Racine; 30, Butler Post Office; July 7, Pewaukee and Waukesha; 10, Silver Springs, moonlight; 14, Menomonee Falls; 21, Whitefish Bay; 28, Waukesha.

Capt. Newman of the Cambridge Club, Capt. Robinson of the Charlestown Rovers, Messrs C. S. Clarke, Burns and Haley of the Cambridge club, and Messrs. Robinson and Libby of the Rovers, are the acknowledged best safety riders in Eastern Massachusetts.

Miss Mabel Beers of the Middlesex cycle Club, rode from Everett to Newburyport, June 1, a distance of forty-two miles, making but one dismount in twenty-five miles. She rode back the following day as far as Ipswich, where the rain forced her to take the train.

In The Wheel of May 31, the opening of the Penn Wheelmen's new club-rooms was erroneously located in Philadelphia, instead of Reading, Pa. We can only lay the blame on the broad shoulders of the printers, and the club will please accept our apologies.

James Lynch, residing at No. 16 Sachem Avenue, Lynn, while riding on a bicycle through Nahant Street, June 7, came into collision with a team driven by Frank Foss and sustained a very serious injury to the hip. His injuries will necessitate confinement for several weeks.

Mr. T. A. Carroll, the former president of the Lynn Cycle Track Association, has just completed arrangements whereby he will be able to hold either a two or three days' bicycle tournament at the Lynn track some time during September. He promises it will eclipse all previous tournaments held on this famous track.

If any intending cyclist of either sex is deterred from first attempts by fear of publicity, they should remember that Geo. R. Bidwell & Co., have a large and commodious riding hall near their place of business, where every aid is given to beginners. Rates are moderate, and special hours can be secured by appointment.

Probably the largest number of applications for membership in a bicycling club received and acted upon at one meeting, was received by the Ramblers' Bicycle Club of Buffalo during the month of May, and acted upon at the meeting held on the 4th inst., when twenty-three of the applications were favorably received.

The celebration at Highlandville, Mass., July 4, will include a bicycle race, twenty-five miles handicap, for three prizes. In the afternoon there will be a mile novice bicycle race; mile scratch race; three-mile bicycle, handicap, open; five-mile bicycle, handicap, open; mile bicycle consolation. Entries close June 30, with W. E. McCune, Secretary.

HONOR WHERE IT IS DUE.

We note the *L. A. W. Pointer* of May 15 clips freely from current number of The Wheel, but omits to mention the source. We know that wheel news is scarce in the West, but, Brother Hinman, do you not think the mill that does the grinding should have credit for the grist?

Enoch Townsend, of Saco, Me., has announced his intention of trying to wheel from Boston to Portland between sunrise and sunset. The distance by road is 116 miles, and over some very rough stretches. Townsend is considered among the most hardy of New England road riders. Last year, in the course of his duties as electric lineman, he cycled 3,500 miles.

A woman's bicycle club has been organized at the Boston Highlands. There are at present nineteen members, and the captain is one of the recognized leaders of Boston society. They have runs once or twice every week, and as all are uniformly attired in neat riding habits of dark blue, they present a charming appearance wheeling over the smooth roads of the suburbs.

C. H. Smith, of Detroit, Mich., comes to the front with a luggage carrier that will fit any safety bicycle. The clamps are adjustable and fit any size steering rod, from ¾ in. to 1⅝ in. When not needed it can be readily carried in the pocket, being neat and light. Finish is nickeled metal parts, with glazed straps. For price and general appearance see our advertising columns.

JACK'S FRENCH CRITICISED.

Purvis-Bruce is communicating a blood-curdling "Tale of a Skull" to the *Bicycling World*. We have under its nervous influence thrown the office paste-pot at an old gentleman who called to ask about differential gearing, and we hereby offer him our sincere apologies. We wish Bruce would print an "r" in "quartier" though.—*Wheeling*.

In a comprehensive letter in last *Bicycling World*, Chief Consul Emery, of Massachussetts, refers to the uniform committee as a "so-called" committee. The committee was never discharged, and we think the Doctor slightly presumptuous in applying this adjective to it. It is scarcely good policy to quibble in the official organ. It is for the executive committee to decide whether the committee is "so-called" or *bona fide*.

W. Van Wagoner, of Newport, challenges any amateur wheelmen of New Bedford to a ten mile race, to be ridden in Newport; a twenty-five mile race, to be ridden at New Bedford, and a fifty mile race, to be ridden in the town where the winner of the twenty-five mile race resides. All of the races to be ridden on the public road, and with road wheels not weighing less than thirty-eight pounds.

We beg to call the attention of the editor of the *Bicycling World* to one important correction. In issue of June 7, it is editorially stated that "*all* the competitors in the inter-collegiate race were suspended." This is not true, as only Bailey and Davis were suspended. In the official department of the same issue, appears Chairman Davol's official notice of suspension. Can it be that the editor of our esteemed contemporary does not read his own paper?

GRAND BOULEVARD FROM BERGEN POINT TO FORT LEE.

The Hudson County Board of Freeholders will issue $1,000,000 bonds within a month to build a new county road from Bergen Point to Fort Lee. The work will be at once commenced. The distance between these two points is about twenty miles, and no doubt the road which will be of macadam, will be one of the favorite stamping grounds for New York wheelmen.

DEATH OF MR. H. F. GRIFFIN, LONDON.

We regret to learn that Mr. H. F. Griffin, the founder of Goy, Ltd., is dead. Mr. Griffin, who was well known in London cycling circles, was connected with the sport from its earliest days. He was President of the Stanley Dramatic Society, and interested in several other clubs. He was also the first to deal in machines on what was for a long while termed Goy's New Plan.

OUR UNGALLANT CONTEMPORARY.

The following lines are scrawled on an inn window in Shropshire:

"Dust is lighter than a feather,
Wind much lighter is than either;
But alas! frail womankind
Is far lighter than the wind."

It is stated that the man who wrote this never took his girl out on a tandem.—*Bicycling News*

Wheeling, in a recent issue, succinctly "sizes up" and comments on Whittaker's interview, as published at length in various American papers, both lay and cycling:

"Stillman G. Whittaker interviewed says that you can do no good on the English professional path unless you are with the gang. Which gang? Morgan's? He (Whittaker) has done with professional racing, and is going in for reinstatement as an amateur. We are tired of being a journalist, and are in strict training for a dukedom."

LADY CYCLISTS AT BUFFALO.

The Women's Wheel Club held a regular monthly meeting at the club-house of the Buffalo Bicycle Club the evening of June 3. The by-laws of the club were amended so as to include the Pedestrian Club recently formed. In consequence of this amendment the name of the club hereafter will be the Women's Wheel and Athletic Club, under which name the ladies will lend their influence to promoting physical culture of all kinds among the women. Five new names were added to the membership list. The Wheel-club uniform as finally decided upon is of dark-green cloth plainly made and having a soft hat made of the same material.

ELWELL'S PARTY ARRIVE IN LONDON.

The party of thirty American cyclists who landed at Cork May 27, arrived in London to-day from Oxford. They will be quartered at the cosey Hotel Bloomsbury. They report a most cordial reception along the line. At Birmingham a delegation of sixty local cyclists met them outside the city, and the Mayor ordered the streets cleared of traffic to facilitate their triumphal progress into the town. At Oxford the whole party was entertained sumptuously by the undergraduates. They remain here a week, during which time they will every day be engaged upon some entertainment with the local cycling clubs.—European edition *N. Y. Herald* of June 10.

In a recent number of The Wheel, we wrote some interesting paragraphs about English racing men. Both *Wheeling* and the *Cyclist* object to two statements, viz.: That Furnivall will compete this year, and that some of the crack amateurs are in the employ of makers on weekly salaries. We had no desire to misrepresent things English. The information on which the paragraphs were based was received direct, by word of mouth, from an American professional lately returned from England. We believe that he had many friends among the English racing men, and we are not yet ready to believe that he deliberately misrepresented his friends. If so, we should be glad to know it and will publish any explicit denial which *Wheeling* or the *Cyclist* may make.

The Gormully and Jeffery Manufacturing Company furnish employment to about 300 men at their factory in Chicago. They have been running over-time the entire season, and are still far behind their orders. Unlike most American manufacturers they have found a lively demand for their ordinaries. This is perhaps due for the most part to their widely scattered clientage, which is by no means confined to the cities where the safety craze is in vogue. Decoration Day was a gala one for the Light Champion. Under Frank Bodach it won the Pullman race in the best time of the day, bar the time of the three scratch men. Bodach chose an American Rambler as first prize. The Light Champion under John Bensinger took the time cup in the great Irvington-Milburn road race also.

STEAM TRICYCLES IN FRANCE.

A race interesting as a novelty recently took place in France on steam cycles, all built by the same firm, Dixon, Bouton & Trepardaux. The machines resembled miniature locomotives, and were ridden by each of the three partners of the firm. The course was from Neuilly to Versailles and back, a distance of 19¾ miles. The road was hilly and in rather bad condition, but the winner covered it in 1 h. 28m. 6s. This mode of travel does not seem to be an unmixed pleasure, for the riders are spoken of as covered with dust from head to foot, and with eyes bloodshot by road and coal dust blown in their faces during the rapid passage. It must be something like riding on the ordinary locomotive with no cab for shelter.

An unfortunate accident at Newport, England, which resulted in the death of an old man named James Jones, aged 78, who was struck on the right hip by the handle of a safety, whose rider was traveling at a slow rate along the Commercial Road, has caused quite a scare in that place. On Monday morning, May 20, before business commenced at the Borough Police Court, the Mayor said he should like to draw the attention of the head constable to the reckless way in which bicycles were driven through the streets of the town. He said that a poor man was knocked down near Commercial Road on Tuesday last by a bicycle and was now lying dead. Six miles an hour should be the maximum rate at which they ought to travel through the public thoroughfares. He hoped the head-constable would impress it upon his subordinates to stop bicyclists at all hazards in the same way as they would stop a runaway horse. The Head-constable said the matter would be attended to.

PROGRAMME OF CAMBRIDGE (MASS.) CYCLERS.

Captain W. J. Newton has issued the following circular to Cambridge Club men:

The following runs are called for June:

Sunday, 16.—Providence. Two-day's run. Start from club-house at 6 A. M. sharp, ride to Walpole or Cobb's for breakfast, then to Providence for dinner, and in the afternoon take the steamer to Rocky Point, returning to Providence at night. Next morning take the train for Boston in time to arrive at Copley Square and join the Massachusetts L. A. W. Division Spring Meet at Squantum; returning from Squantum Monday evening by wheel. Those who cannot go to Providence will meet the club in Copley Square, Monday morning at 10 o'clock, when they start for Squantum.

Sunday, 23.—Lynnfield, via Wakefield. Arrangements will be made for dinner and boating on the pond.

Sunday, 30.—Union run to Massapoag Lake, Sharon.

The ease with which the common every day reporter gets swamped in touching on any unfamiliar specialty, is obvious in the *Evening Telegram's* mention of the Century Run to Philadelphia last Saturday. After perusing it, the reader is left in doubt whether a road race or tour took place, or if a free advertisement of one of the L. I. W. is not intended. This scribe speaks of "Young Parker" as a "wonder on the wheel," and his performance last Saturday as something "phenomenal." He further misleads the reader by speaking of Parker's being *fouled* by Beazely, of the K. C. W.'s, in his thirty-fifth mile. We had the impression that an average pace of less than eight miles per hour was to be taken. Of course collisions and accidents might occur, but *fouls*—well, scarcely. One more slight correction and we are done; Instead of only *thirty-seven* making the entire run, *forty-six*, including one lady on a tandem, rode through to Philadelphia. Without wishing to detract from any particular man's fame, it seems to us that the performance of the whole party was equally well worth mention. A more complete account may be found elsewhere in our columns.

Columbia's Champions, a bright athletic weekly, published at Boston, and presumably never read in the New England College world, makes unfair and misleading comments on Chairman Davol's suspension of Davis and Bailey. Notwithstanding "Leh Sharty's" assertion that he has a "pretty shrewd idea of what justice is," we beg to assure him that his shrewdness is ignorance in this case. Other papers are not "silent on the subject of Chairman Davol's suspensions." It has been commended on all sides and by many influential papers. *Columbia's Champions* is the only paper which has failed to commend Chairman Davol's action. The decision is not "extraordinary," and "Leh Sharty" has not looked at the matter from every point of view. Referee Curtis had no power to prevent Davis and Bailey from riding in the Intercollegiate race. The duties of a Referee extend only to that which happen while a contest is going on, such as fouls, etc. In matters of this kind his decision is final. Upon the question as to a man's eligibility to ride, the Referee has no power to pass. He simply receives protests and orders the prizes to be withheld until the status of the man is decided. This question of status or violation of laws can only be decided by the body governing the branch of sport to which the contest belongs. In the case of Davis and Bailey, Chairman Davol, representing the Racing Board, had full authority to suspend the men.

THE GREAT CENTURY RUN '89.

LIST OF STARTERS.

1 (88) L. A. Clarke, Citizens B. C., Chairman Com.
3**. W. E. Fuller, Brooklyn B. C., Committee.
5**. J. V. L. Pierson, Capt. Bloomfield Cy., Committee.
6. W. B. Krug, Captain Citizens B. C.
7. C. L. Smith, Citizens B. C.
8*. J. V. Hoffman, Citizens B. C.
9. N. H. Weed, Brooklyn B. C.
10. B. M. Cole, Brooklyn B. C.
11*. W. H. Meeter, Captain, Brooklyn B. C.
12*. C. Quimby, Brooklyn B. C.
13*. H. G. Fay, Brooklyn B. C.
62**. G. L. Warner, Brooklyn B. C.
14*. F. V. Oakes, Bloomfield Cyclers.
15. T. C. Van Auken, Bloomfield Cyclers.
16*. J. L. Miller, President Riverside Wheelmen.
17**. F. R. Miller, Riverside Wheelmen.
18. F. M. Cossitt (80 mi.), Riverside Wheelmen.
19. Mrs. F. M. Cossitt, Riverside Wheelmen.
20. Dr. A. C. Griffen, New York.
21. W. F. Pendleton, New York B. C.
22. W. H. Putney, Manhattan B. C.
23. J. Post, Jr., Manhattan B. C.
24. J. W. Sheehan, President Manhattan B. C.
25. C. C. Clements, Manhattan B. C.
26. C. G. Thomas, Harlem Wheelmen.
27. P. C. Shaeffer, Harlem Wheelmen.
28. E. C. Locke, Harlem Wheelmen.
29*. W. H. DeGraaf, Harlem Wheelmen.
30. L. W. Beazeley, K. C. W.
31*. W. F. Murphy, K. C. W.
32. W. Newman, K. C. W.
33. R. Starrett, K. C. W.
34. C. M. Isbell, K. C. W.
35*. M. L. Bridgman, President K. C. W.
36*. W. Bonner, K. C. W.
37*. A. L. Ward, K. C. W.
38*. G. G. Teller, L. I. W.
39*. O. E. Parker, L. I. W.
40**. J. L. Bromley, Century Wheelmen, Philadelphia.
41**. W. G. Speier, Century Wheelmen, Philadelphia.
42*. W. L. Degn, Century Wheelmen, Philadelphia.
43*. C. W. Dalsen, Century Wheelmen, Philadelphia.
44*. C. A. Dimon, Captain S. C. W., Philadelphia.
45. Frank Becraft, Tuxedo, New York.
46. A. B. Taylor, Sloatsburg, N. Y.
47**. A. W. W. Evans, Captain New Brunswick B. C.
48*. H. E. Krober, Yonkers B. C.
49**. H. M. White, Trenton, N. J.
50. C. M. Perrine, Trenton, N. J.
51*. W. G. Hilyard, Rosemont, Pa.
52*. H. Grant Cline, Bryn Mawr, Pa.
53*. Warren L. Welch, Wissahickon Wheelmen, Phila.
54*. Miss Kate W. Welch, Wissahickon Wheel'n, Phila.
55*. C. B. Scudder, Capt. Huntington B. C., New York.
56*. C. C. Grumman, Huntington B. C., New York.
57. C. F. Johnson, New York.
58. H. T. Jacoby, Brooklyn.
59. H. L. Biel, Brooklyn.
60. W. W. Slack, Trenton.
61. H. S. Josephs, Harlem Wheelmen.

ORANGE.

64*. C. A. Lindsay, Captain Orange Wheelmen.
65*. F. P. Jewett, Orange W.
66*. C. W. Freeman, Orange W.
67. C. F. Foiles, Orange W.
68. Everitt Townsend, Orange W.
69. H. W. Hampden, Orange W.
70. Mr. Noyes, Orange W.
72*. John Long, Orange W.
73*. F. H. Amerman, Orange W.

NEWARK.

4*. F. W. Keer, H. C. W., Committee.
74*. H. Russell, Essex B. C.
76*. A. F. Rummell, Essex B. C.
77*. A. H. Scudder, Essex B. C.
79*. C. H. Edge, Essex B. C.
80*. E. C. Harris, Essex B. C.
85*. W. Garrabaut, Essex B. C.
84*. C. S. Swain, Essex B. C.
86*. W. C. Swain, Essex B. C.
82*. R. L. Prindle, Essex B. C.
83*. J. T. Logan, Essex B. C.
— Mr. Uhl, Essex B. C.

CRANFORD.

81*. R. F. Hibson, K. C. W.

PLAINFIELD.

? 75. F. L. C. Martin, Capt. Plainfield B. C., Committee.
78 75. W. T. Milliken, Plainfield B. C.
100. C. Newbourg, Prospect W., Brooklyn.
101. H. Newman, Prospect W., Brooklyn.
R. V. Whitehead, Trenton Wheelmen.
F. L. Wallington, Trenton Wheelmen.
C. T. Aronson, Trenton Wheelmen.
H. M. Nichols, Trenton.
Daniel Hickey, Trenton.
Edward Smith, Trenton.
Walter Apgar, Trenton.
William Howard, Trenton.
Frederick Duncan, Trenton.
Thomas Sebold, Trenton.

PHILADELPHIA.

C. A. Sheehan, Man. B. C., N. Y.
L. A. Newcombe, Harlem Wheelmen, N. Y.
Mrs. L. A. Newcombe, Harlem Wheelmen.
Miss Maude Eisinger, Harlem Wheelmen.
Miss Adelaide Raisbeck.
Mr. Raisbeck.

Names of Century makers marked thus *.

Century makers should mark their badges SURVIVOR, and put them away for next year. Survivors of both runs are designated by **.

Following reached Trenton and registered: 1, 2, 3, 4, 5, 6, 7, 8, 11, 12, 13, 16, 17, 18, 20, 21, 22, 23, 30, 31, 36, 37, 38, 39, 40, 41, 42, 43, 44, 47, 48, 49, 51, 52, 53, 54, 55, 56, 57, 62, 64, 65, 66, 68, 76, 77, 78, 79, 80, 81, 82.

THE GREAT CENTURY RUN OF 1889.

I think I may be pardoned a little pride in the success of the "great century run, 1889." With a total of about ninety starters forty-six finished in good shape, and nobody badly hurt, with perhaps the exception of Mr. Gessleman, of Germantown, who took a severe fall in Orange, Friday, the 7th, breaking the backbone of his wheel and shaking him up so badly that he immediately took train for home.

The weather was propitious and the light showers were just heavy enough to lay the dust and make no mud. Everything worked smoothly, and, with the exception of the troubles arising from lack of system at the Mountain House, no set-backs were experienced.

At the Mountain House they are obviously not used to crowds and did not appreciate the necessity of punctuality, the clerk going to sleep and not waking us up on schedule time, 3 A. M., so that we were half an hour late in leaving.

Captain Pierson, acting as aide, left fifteen minutes in advance, supplying badges to and collecting the assessments from those who joined the run at Orange and Newark and later at Plainfield and Trenton. Start, 4:30 A. M.; Newark, 5; Elizabeth, 5:30; Westfield, 6:20; Plainfield, 7, on time, having gained half an hour in twenty-three miles without scorching. This was made possible by the excellent character of the road, where, last year, we were forced to walk a large part of the way.

We stopped at Dr. Kinch's, in Westfield, to sample the water in his old-fashioned well. The Doc. was away on a professional visit, but had left the road into and out of town carefully marked out by pointed bright red signs which we immediately proceeded to disregard—of course, by accident—striking the Scotch Plains Road about a mile further up than he intended. We were fully recompensed by the beautiful surface of this road which many said they had never seen equalled.

Captain Martin, of the committee, met the run just out of Plainfield and led the way to the Plainfield Bicycle Club's house, where plenty of rich milk and sandwiches were awaiting us.

From Plainfield we continued down Front Street to New Market where a turn to the left was made, and on time we reached New Brunswick after an extremely rough stretch of thirteen miles. Here a short stop was made on the campus of Rutgers College. A strong head wind had been coming up from the south meanwhile, and the next stretch, to Kingston, was a terror, although but few fell out. About an eighth of a mile from the hotel I loosened my rear tire for nearly two-thirds of its length and was forced to fall out in company with Messrs Beazeley and Isbell, of the K. C. W. The former was suffering from a sprained ankle and the latter had broken his handle-bar in a fall and had ridden nearly ten miles with one handle. Getting a stop over at Trenton, I found on arriving at the hotel that there were a number of others there waiting for the run, ready to start for Philadelphia. At 1:40, ten minutes late, the first bunch came in, reporting the last ten miles to be in bad condition, followed very shortly by the stragglers.

The dinner at the Trenton House was a good one, and as soon as everybody was ready a break was made for the front of the State Capitol, on West State Street, when two photographers got five shots at us, in all. The Trentonians derived about as much fun as we did from it. The "Man in the Window," got a dandy negative, he developed it immediately, and, aside from the fact that some of those on the extreme ends may have been left out, the picture is a good one.

No time was lost in getting away from Trenton, Bristol was reached but little behind schedule, and Philadelphia at last, about 7.30, the sand below Frankford being exceptionally bad.

At Philadelphia the run was met by representatives from the clubs in the A. C. C., and a party of ladies from the Harlem Wheelmen accompanied by several ladies from the Philadelphia Bi. Club, under the guidance of Mr. Jos. R. L. Edwards.

The survivors, some forty-five in number, were taken to the Century Wheelmen's house, and thence after brushing up, to the Continental for supper.

On Sunday, the 9th, a run was taken through Fairmount Park to the Philadelphia Bi. Club's house, thence to Strawberry Hill for a little blow off, and thence to the Columbia Avenue Station, P. & R. R. R., when the wheels were placed on board the special baggage car provided for our use. Dinner was partaken of at 1.30 at the Continental, and at 3.30 we left for home on the P. & R. with a special car all to ourselves. New York, 7 P. M.

Miss Kate W. Welch, Wissahicon Wheelmen, Germantown, accompanied by her brother, Mr. Warren L. Welch, on a tandem, made the entire distance. They were everywhere well up, and Miss W. was as fresh as any of the party at the end.

Mrs. Cossitt, the other lady entry, attempted the run on her single, but the stiff head wind at New Brunswick made it extremely hard for her on the narrow tracks and she wisely gave it up at that point, taking train to Philadelphia.

The thanks of the "great century" runners are due to Dr. Kinch, Westfield; R. V. Whitehead, Trenton; J. R. L. Edwards, Mr. Andrews (P. & R. R. R.), the A. C. C. and a host of others in Philadelphia, for our splendid reception at all points.

At Frankford, Trenton, Plainfield and Philadelphia thousands were out to see the run go by.

R. F. Hibsen, K. C. W., joining at Cranford, broke a handle-bar before reaching Westfield, went back to New York, bought a new one and reached Trenton by train in time to join the run. Messrs. Sheehan and Clements, M. B. C., riding tandem, broke the neck of the machine while going at speed, and, as it was described to me, turned a double somersault, which, of course, ended their riding.

Miss Raisbeck rode the new "Castor" wheel safety, which is ridden as easily as an ordinary, hands off, at Philadelphia.

President Miller had a funny experience. He lay down on the bank near Princeton and unintentionally fell asleep, and might have been there yet but for the kindly offices of a passing farmer.

Warner, on the mouth-organ, and Fuller and Evans, on bugles, were as entertaining as usual, and Wm. DeG.'s patented, duplex, elastic dog-scarer was a screaming success.

The total cyclometer measurement varied from 95 to 101 miles, and but few took the trouble to complete the century, but among those who did were Miss and Mr. Welch, of Germantown, and E. C. Harris, Newark.

It was well that Jay-Purist B—ce wasn't along. There were several immodest young men in the ranks who didn't have their vests and high collars on.

The Trenton photographs can be obtained by sending fifty-four cents, which includes postage, to L. Holdridge, 4 South Green Street, or to D. S. Crystal & Co., 208 Broad Street, Trenton, N. J. The former is the one taken from the window, the latter from the street; both are very good and well finished.

All actual starters in the run are eligible to purchase a memento pin, which will be supplied at the exact cost on receipt of application and one dollar by L. A. C., 25 Broad Street, N. Y. City.

After paying all expenses there will remain a balance of some five dollars, an account of the disposition of which will be published next week.

TRANSPORTATION FROM NEW YORK AND VICINITY TO BALTIMORE.

Mr. C. Newbourg, Captain of the Prospect Wheelmen, of Brooklyn, N. Y., who is employed by the Baltimore and Ohio Railroad, is arranging to run special cars through from New York to Hagerstown, Md., for those desiring to attend the tenth annual Meet of the L. A. W. The Baltimore and Ohio Railroad, noted for its picturesque scenery, equipment, service and fast time, and particularly so for its friendly feelings toward wheelmen, has given Mr. Newbourg charge of the transportation of wheelmen from this section, and we can assure a pleasant trip to those who go via the B. & O. It may be of interest to know that all trains of the B. & O. R. R. pass through the cities of Philadelphia, Baltimore, and within one block of the Capitol at Washington. Any communications addressed to Mr. C. Newbourg, at 415 Broadway, New York, will receive prompt attention. If you intend to go to Hagerstown confer with Mr. Newbourg and he will arrange everything regarding transportation, tickets, certificates, etc.

Elwell's European Tourists.

THE TRIP IN THE CEPHALONIA.

EDITOR OF THE WHEEL:

Since the advent of cycling, there have been tours and touring parties without number, but never before, I venture to assert, have so large a number of wheelmen undertaken as much as the European Cycling Party, which boarded the Cunard steamship Cephalonia on the morning of May 18. The party has been very quietly worked up during the last six months by Mr. Frank Elwell, of Portland, Me., whose name is familiar to every wheelman who ever made any very extended tour. He arranged and conducted the "Down East," Bar Harbor, Quebec, "Blue Nose," two Bermuda tours and many others, but this year's effort on his part is by far the largest ever attempted by Mr. Elwell or

MR. F. A. ELWELL, MANAGER.

any other tour-master. Wheelmen on "the other side" are making quite an international affair of it, and many a taste of foreign hospitality will these fortunate individuals be treated to before their return.

The party, thirty strong, met the night before we sailed at the Tremont House, Boston, and were entertained in the evening by the Boston Athletic and Town clubs. The morning saw us clambering up the ship's gangway, laden with gripsacks, steamer-chairs, ulsters and all the usual paraphernalia of an ocean voyager—some of them old veterans of three or four trips, others on their maiden cruise and asking all sorts of crazy questions. What a jolly mixture of all trades and professions we represent! It reminds one of our childish rosary of "Rich man, poor man," etc. I shall have to draw the line on "beggar man" and "thief," but I am pretty sure the rest of the category are all here. (I can personally answer for one "poor man"). Of ages varying from sixteen to forty-nine, of opinions widely different on political, moral and all other subjects, of exactly opposite tastes in many matters, and each with strong likes and dislikes ; still a feeling of perfect harmony and loyalty prevails. We are bound together by that strongest of ties—we are fellow-wheelmen. We have our dude, but who ever heard of a tour without a dude? We have our kicker, but how lonesome we should feel without him ! Everybody is pleased, and nothing is seen but smiling faces.

Our staterooms were allotted us on coming aboard, and in half a day we were all settled down and feeling as much at home as though we had resided there since infancy. The bedroom steward had a particular veneration and respect for No. 32 (a double room occupied by three companions and myself), it being the room once occupied by the quondam pugilistic champion, John L. Sullivan, on his voyage across. While chaffing the steward the other day he told me that I must not think myself a fine gentleman because I slept in Sullivan's bunk !

Much as we regret the absence of John L. we are not without some few lesser lights on board. That contented and peaceful-looking individual

whom you see in the chair by the door is James Russell Lowell who, as one of our members puts it, "rather 'put his foot in it' with the Queen." He is a man of short stature, with a full beard of white, incessantly smoking and somewhat resembling the familiar pictures of the poet Longfellow. He is an easy conversationalist and a very pleasant story-teller. That dignified, quiet man promenading with his wife up and down under the huge awnings is Dr. M. M. Bigelow, Professor of Law at Harvard College, author of numerous standard law books and a contributor to various scientific magazines. Accompanying our party is Mr. H. G. Priest, of Birmingham, Eng., who has lately visited the States on a business trip in the interests of the Quadrant Tricycle Co. He is a typical Englishman, not at all reserved but full of life and fun and a great "bluffer." The one-mile road record on the tricycle (2m. 36s.) made by Mr. Priest in 1885 stands to-day unbroken. Not the least among the celebrities, from a wheelman's point of view, is our own Elwell. "Papa" Elwell, who, if not actually celebrated, is beyond a doubt one of the most widely known cyclists and one who has done as much, if not more, for real outdoor cycling than any other man.

The dining-saloon is a very popular room and full of "surprises," the first one being the chair you sit in. You find yourself seated about three inches too far away from the table, and reach down both hands to give it a slight hitch forward, but, like the policemen in "The Pirates of Penzance," it "don't go," and your hands slip off and strike the edge of the table with force enough to bring tears to your eyes. But you smile sweetly, for the lady opposite you has been over four or five times and knows just how you did it. This operation you repeat in periods of absent-mindedness during the entire meal. The different tables (there are five on our boat) are presided over by the ship's officers, the seats of honor being at the "Captain's table," presided over by that worthy in a dress suit.

The next surprise is the bill of fare, which is surprisingly good, and the manner in which it is served, which is surprisingly bad. Everything is brought on in gigantic "soup plates." Not a saucer, sauce dish, salt-cellar, or butter dish have we seen since we left America ! One plate, slightly smaller than the other, is known as the "bread-and-butter plate," and sets diagonally in front of your other plate. On the edge of this you roost a piece of unsalted butter, and in it, if you wish to be in "good form," you never put anything but a piece of bread. Everything else is brought in these enormous, deep, dinner plates. Imagine a dab of ice-cream, the size of a silver dollar, a single tart, or your morning oatmeal being served in one of them ! The knives and forks are immense, the soup spoons, monuments of metal—but the food is unexcelled.

I have said the dining saloon was a popular room, because four meals are served there each day, and various games and all our

MR. H. S. HIGGINS. TREASURER.

writing done there in the evening. As we are generally doing one of these, we spend a great deal of time there. Next in popularity is the smoking room, where you can always find at any time of day or night a dozen or more enthusiastic pedal-pushers, scraping over the virtues and vices of the various makes, or swapping stories of century runs and hill

climbing, that stretch your belief in the possibilities of muscle and steel to the utmost.

Here you find that prince of good fellows, "Milord," (Priest) relating stories of English racing and racers, to a knot of "scorchers" whose eyes are bulging out like pegs on a hat tree. Here practical jokes are concocted, and schemes are laid for the downfall of the unwary, and here many a rubber of whist and struggle at six-handed euchre is pulled off. Choruses are shouted and tales invented "while you wait."

The music room is probably the pleasantest room on the ship. It is similar in shape to the letter D, and around the curve reaches a line of port holes to the number of twenty or more, the view from which is singularly fascinating. Nothing to be seen but the ever-changing sea, to be sure, but that is a host in itself—a kaleidoscope whose vastness and variety hold one than that of a huge ship, with every stitch of canvas set, careening forward and backward on the long, heavy swells some half mile distant, the whole surrounded by these circular frames of polished brass.

In this room we have our songs and musicals, and here we retire for a quiet stretch of reading or writing when the breeze is too strong for comfort on deck. We have not picked out our glee club or baseball team yet, but there is plenty of good material for both.

The weather during the voyage has been exceptionally good, the elements having allowed free use of the decks at any and all times, a privilege for which we have given thanks to Father Neptune daily. The convention il caper is a brisk walk up and down the deck on the windward side, which is usually free from chairs and obstructions, before breakfast (if we got to bed before the lights were out the night before), after which we have a go at shuffle-board or ring-toss. Shuffle-board is a game marked out upon the deck and played with long cues and flat discs—half hop-scotch and half billiards. It is quite interesting, and serves to while away many an hour.

The infantile game of ring-toss suddenly acquires renewed interest, and portly grey-beards and stately dames alike may be seen throwing the rings with a battle-of-Waterloo expression on their physiognomies, and making the most horrible faces if they fail. Then a file of fifteen or twenty cyclists pass by, in the regulation lock-step, chanting some melody (?) indicating their belief that wheelmen are the best, most courageous and handsomest men in existence. Woe unto the unfortunate man who falls asleep in his chair! Just as he gets comfortably off into dreamland, and firmly believes he is witnessing some grand pageant in Paris or wonderful scene from the tops of the Jura, a dozen men tip-toe up to him, and, after silently beating one measure, simultaneously yell "Great Scott!" with a snap and vehemence that bring the sleeper back to mid-ocean with a leap. One unfortunate who fell asleep in the smoking room was relieved of his shoes and stockings, and quietly awakened by the breezes toying with his "tootsies." One of our party wears a cap similar to those worn by the officers of the ship, and has been asked various official questions by timorous ladies, one of whom offered him her ticket. An antique dame with corkscrew curls, in search of the mate accosted the cook and inquired if he was that individual. "No, mum," replied he, in an elegant brogue, "I do be the man wot cooks the mate"

Cabin passengers are allowed almost unlimited liberty of the ship, and we have been all over her. I was enlightened on sailors' habits, the third day out, by going down through the intermediate and out in the stern on the lower deck, where the donkey engine which dues the steering, and the complete steering-gear may be seen. A jolly tar in a blue guernsey explained it all, and I was congratulating myself that I was "pulling his leg," when he suddenly reached down, and with a lump of chalk, drew a cross on the toe of my shoe.

I gazed at him in amazement. He grinned like a fiend and said:

"You're 'chalked,' sir."

"Chalked ?" I repeated blankly.

"Yes, sir," you must 'pay the footing," said he. "And what is the 'footing ?'"

"The price of half a dozen bottles of beer," with another grin. I tossed him "two-and-six," with a mental resolve to ask no more questions of anyone, but was twice more "chalked" on

382 [VOL. III., No. 16.

the voyage, and when we left the steamer, more flunkies, waiters, stewards, etc., than I had any idea were on the ship, stood by and insisted on carrying my coat, grip, books and wishing me "God speed," with a look on their faces that would admit of but one translation. I had, by good fortune, only about five dollars in money about me, and it all went. One of the boys expressed a belief that if he met the Prince of Wales, and tossed him a shilling, he would pocket it with a nod.

The steerage passengers are by no means such an unhappy and much abused lot as I have always imagined they were. They have enough to eat, plenty of room, and a clean place to sleep. They all seem happy and perfectly contented. They sing, dance, read, play games and bask in the sun. This is all greatly due, no doubt, to the unusually pleasant weather, and I am told that coming back they carry three times as many as we have at present. A curious sight in the steerage, was an old crone, clad in a dingy, ragged calico dress, a shawl over her head, fast asleep in the sun and tightly clasping to her aged bosom a copy of "Robert Ellsmere." In the intermediate are some very comfortable looking people, and two fine looking young fellows, whom we have decided are on a "lark."

Something that seldom, if ever happened before, is the birth of a child and a death on a single voyage. On the Queen's Birthday (May 24) it was whispered that a new passenger had boarded the Cephalonia during the night, and it was then and there decided that his future cognomen should be "Victor Cephalonia," in honor of the day and the ship, and a collection taken up for his benefit. The following day a poor little steerage soul, of only eleven months, went to its Maker, and the dismal sight of a burial in the ocean dampened our spirits for some hours.

One day is much like another on shipboard, and I am aware that this letter is of but little interest, but in my next, Mr. Editor, I shall address you from the road and not from the ship, and hope to have something of interest to tell my brother wheelmen.

TAM O'SHANTER.

THE EUROPEAN TOURISTS ARRIVE OFF QUEENSTOWN.

[From our Special Correspondent.]

The Cephalonia arrived off Queenstown this midday, and the party of tourists organized by Mr. Elwell were taken off by the tender, on which were a number of Irish cyclists as well as Messrs. J. Pennell and A J. Wilson ("Faed"), from London, a hearty welcome being accorded our countrymen. The only absentee was Mr. Krumm, of Columbus, Ohio, who is to join the tour at London. The arrival being a day later than had been expected, the rail was taken for Youghal so as to keep engagements.

Cork, Ireland, May 27.

THE EUROPEAN TOURISTS.

[From our special correspondent.]

The wisdom of taking train to Youghal was manifest upon preparations being made over night, several hours having to be devoted to adjusting luggage on the bicycles. Heavy rain during the night rendered the roads very sticky, but when, at 9 A. M., on Tuesday, May 28, a start was made there was very little of the anticipated awkwardness in managing the new mounts. A long climb up the mountains, however, was tiring, the only rider who kept his saddle the whole way up being "Faed." The weather was fine and hot during the morning, but after noon a series of sharp showers came on. From Cappoquin a detour was made to the monastery on Mount Melleray, where the good-natured monks entertained the tourists at a first-rate lunch and escorted them over the premises, the quaint and curious arrangements of the priests and brethren exciting the utmost wonderment. Wheels were then mounted for Dungarvan, upon nearing which town it was found that the entire population was expectantly awaiting the advent of the Americans, numerous displays of bunting, principally the Stars and Stripes, affording visible signs of the welcome which also vented itself in lusty cheers as the tourists entered the town, which is a poor but clean place, principally supported by fishing. After ablutions the tourists adjourned to the residence of Mr. R. E. Brenan, the C. T. C. Chief Consul, who entertained them at dinner and kept open house the whole evening, songs and merry speeches making the time pass pleasantly.

A fine, bright morning, May 29, gave promise of a pleasant and an easy ride to Waterford, but soon after leaving Dungarvan a succession of heavy showers came on, although a strong wind behind helped the cyclists along over the excellent road. Luncheon was taken at Kilmacthomas and the main body of riders was met a few miles out by the Waterford Bicycle Club, who escorted them into their ancient city, the entry to which was decked with flags. In the evening the local club entertained the tourists to a smoking concert, Dr. Mackay (President of the W. B. C.) and Captain O'Toole (Mayor of Waterford) presiding.

Another promising morning gave false hopes of a fine day, heavy showers again marring the ride and upon reaching New Ross it was found that nothing was to be obtained at the primitive hotel owing to its being a Fast Day—"Ascension Thursday." Fortunately "Faed," as usual, had friends at the Post Office, who, although taken by surprise, contrived to provide a little refreshment. A dozen of the tourists then determined to take train to Enniscorthy, thus escaping further drenchings; and the bold spirits who kept to the road had a hard ride over the hills, but arrived in good time to visit the local sights; and in the evening the Enniscorthy Bicycle Club entertained the visitors at supper.

A beautiful morning, May 31, and splendidly smooth and dry roads, aided in making the run to Gorey a memorable one, and although the inevitable showers after lunch somewhat damped the spirits of a few, there was none of the steady downpour of rain previously experienced, and the glories of the Vale of Avoca were keenly enjoyed, the intensely emerald verdure being typical of Ireland at its best. A pause was made at the Meeting of the Waters, and then, in company with Mr. and Mrs. R. J. Mecredy, of Dublin, on a tandem, a visit was paid to the residence of Mr. Parnell, the famous Member of Parliament, and Rathdrum was reached in good time, "early to bed" being the order in view of the hard day's riding on the morrow.

FAED.

THE BOSTON PRESS CYCLING CLUB'S FIRST RUN.

The long planned and often postponed run of the above organization to Wakefield was taken last Sunday. The weather clerk, who doubtless bore in mind the many jests and gibes hurled at him in times gone by, did not dish out an attractive state of things that morning, and instead of the expected thirteen only some half a dozen materialized. The start was made at Copley Square, and a large number of people gathered to see how a pen-pusher looked when wielding the handle-bar and tempting Providence in such a lofty position. The struggle between the riders and thick mud began at the outset and was continued until Melrose was reached. From there to Wakefield things were little better, and the mud determinedly climbed up tires and impartially bestowed itself on the persons of the wheelmen. As they rode up to the Wakefield Bicycle Club rooms every man presented an unattractive appearance, being coated with the stickiest and most disagreeable sort of mud. After taking dinner with Capt. Robinson and a few of his men an invitation to sail on the lake was accepted. Previous to the start for home the party was joined by Captain Cubberly and a few of the Somerville riders. Together they made a creditable showing and were photographed by Mr. A. H. Binders, of the Middlesex Club. As slight compensation for this ordeal, he afterwards spread before the appreciative crowd a light lunch. From that point the run to the city was uneventful and made with less weariness of mind and body than the morning's trip. The Press Cycling Club had as its guests E. B. Pillsbury, First Lieutenant Sprague and Secretary Ryder, of the Massachusetts.

ST. LOUIS.

The Missouri Bicycle Club had its regular monthly meeting last Tuesday night, and, like all the recent meetings of that organization, it was interesting. In point of attendance it was one of the largest in the history of the club, and the cause of it was the announcement of the reopening of the Sunday question. I fear your readers are getting tired of this question; so are we, and it is with much satisfaction that I am able to state that nothing more will be heard of it. It received a "swipe" that effectually disposed of it, and the champions of the repeal will have to hunt up some other issue. This is how it was done: The two members of the House Committee who were present saw the handwriting on the wall soon after they arrived; the "tureen" was evidently yawning wide for them, and after a hasty consultation with the President and others, a plan was evolved which it was hoped would save them from the apparently inevitable immersion. When the President called for "new business" there was any amount of silence, and receiving no immediate response he passed to the Treasurer's report. It then became apparent that the House Committee did not intend to bring the matter up and seeing that they were likely to be cheated of their prey, and fearing some ulterior motive for the change of front, the friends of the rule called a halt, and directing attention to the notice of the Committee, asked that the question be put and decided. The President ruled the motion out of order on the ground that the meeting had passed that order of business. A motion was then made to revert to that order, and the President having inquired if this could be done legally, and being informed that it certainly could, it was so ordered. Mr. Brewster then called up the matter of change in rule 8, and the President responded by reading the by-law defining the duties of the House Committee. When he had finished, the proposed amendment was offered, and the President again read the by-law, ruling the motion out of order on the ground that matters relating to the house rules could only emanate from the House Committee. It only took a few words from Mr. Will Chauvenet to lay bare the sophistry of this position, and the President said; "Since you are the first person who has presented this matter to me in a gentlemanly manner, I must acknowledge that you are right." Inasmuch as no one had said a word on the subject, either in a gentlemanly or ungentlemanly manner, this remark of the President was decidedly unique. He then put the question, and the few friends of the repeal stood up to be counted. They looked so lonesome scattered around the room, even reinforced as they were by some of the associate members (who had no more right to vote, Mr. Editor, than you have) that it seemed a pity to jump on them; but it had to be done, and the "dull thud" quickly followed. That there may be no misapprehension as to the motives that influenced so many to take a stand in favor of this rule, it should be stated that the moral or religious feature of the case was not allowed to enter at all; they simply did not think it was politic or expedient, or for the best interests of the club, the circumstances and surroundings considered, to repeal the rule, and there will be no compromise on that question.

There was one incident of the meeting that I have saved for the last, though it did not follow in that order. I have hesitated about writing of it because I hate to be a bearer of bad news, and unless you are fortified to face dire calamity you had better stop right here, for when you read on and learn of the adversity that has overtaken you, and realize its extent and enormity, you will need all your courage to bear up under the blow. I want to break it to you gently, and so I will simply state that the Missouri Bicycle Club has stopped taking your paper!!! If you want the particulars we will have to revert to "new business" again. When this point was first reached, the President turned to Willie Brown, who was seated on his left, and in a voice trembling with suppressed emotion asked him if he was ready. Mr Brown, the pallor of his face contrasting strongly with the inky blackness of his whiskers, admitted that he was. The President touched the button, there was a deep reverberation from a cannon placed in front of the house, rockets were exploded, chains began to rattle, the gas went out, the "guyascutis" howled and the "whangdoodle" mourned. Surrounded by almost impenetrable gloom, relieved only by the ghastly hues that came from the different colored fires that were burning, and accompanied by the dismal wailing of the "swinette," Mr. Brown read the following resolution and moved its adoption: "*Resolved*, That the Treasurer be instructed to stop the club's subscription to THE WHEEL on account of the false and scurrilous statements of its St. Louis correspondent, and that the Secretary be instructed to write a letter 'roasting' the editor." That may not be just exactly the phraseology of the resolution, but that was its tenor. The first part of it seems to refer indirectly to me, the latter to you. You seem to be getting the worst of it all around; to get even with *me* they stop taking *your* paper, and then they propose to "roast" you besides. This is hard lines for you, but I warned you that something dreadful had happened, or would happen, and if you are not prepared it is your own fault. Seriously, could there be anything more childish—nay, babyish. It was an action fit only for the nursery, and having a natural and, heretofore, pardonable pride in the club, I regret that it has made itself so ridiculous. True, the action taken did not represent the sentiment of the club, for out of nearly fifty in attendance only about thirty voted, including the two or three associates, and the majority, as announced by the Secretary, was only three. The rest were either paralyzed by the dramatic features of the situation, or considered the whole affair a farce in which they did not care to participate.

It is the letter of May 17 to which exceptions were taken; the others are apparently all right. Now, there is not a line in that letter that is not strictly true. Of course, we all know that the truth, plainly spoken, is not always agreeable, but I can't help that. I frankly admit that the term "bow-legged" should not have been used, not because it was untrue, but because it was unnecessary. I did not, however, intend the term to be taken in its offensive sense; it was merely used to help out a faithful description, and if it has been misconstrued I am very sorry, and beg to offer my apologies. Just the same, all that I said was true. There was considerable surprise expressed that a man of age, experience and education, such as Mr. Brown is (I am told he is also a lawyer), could be induced to present the resolution. I would like to tell you the language used by some of these people in describing those who voted against them, but it is unfit for publication.

If my space was not already more than filled, I would tell you about the second race between Lumsden and Stone, but really there is little to tell. Percy did his best, but Lumsden used his head as well as his legs, and the race was little more than a romp for him. He is a good 'un and no mistake.

ITHURIEL.

A feature of the Harogate camp this year will be the presence of Singer's Apollo Band, which will be attached to the camp from Saturday, 3d August, till the Tuesday morning following.

THE NEW YORK-PHILADELPHIA CENTURY RUN AT PHILADELPHIA.

To merely say the great New York Century run was a success at this end of the route would be doing it a rank injustice. It was more than a success—it was a veritable triumph for that plucky band of wheelmen who had ridden from the Oranges to this city. Very few local bicyclers had the least idea that forty-six would finish the hundred miles (remembering last year's run, when seven out of sixty-five finished). Oh, ye Western "toughs!" paste this in your hats. Show us a time when you can get up a club run of a hundred miles, with forty-six participants, and *one a woman*, who finished as fresh as anyone in the party.

On Saturday, June 8, a large crowd of wheelmen assembled at the Century Wheelmen's new house, in response to a call to meet the run, and at 4:00 about seventy knickerbocker-clad chaps started for Holmesburg, where they were to wait for the New York party. After a tough ride along some very bad roads they reached Holmesburg about 6 o'clock, and, stopping at the hotel, then awaited the run, with ill-concealed impatience. Being anxious to get a sight of the party as soon as possible, your correspondent, in company with a couple of others, decided to push on a little further. After about three miles we came in sight of the party, and a pretty sight it was, all riding a narrow side path in single file, and going at a lively pace, the long line of glittering wheels stretching down the road, looking, in the dying sunlight, like some monstrous serpent gliding along. Seeing some acquaintance among the riders, we quickly turned, and were soon asking and answering questions in regard to the distance to be yet traveled and the condition of the road. By this time we had reached the hotel at Holmesburg, where the waiting wheelmen were assembled, and when the first of the "hundred milers" arrived there cheer after cheer was given with a will, and when Miss Welch and her brother Warren arrived on their tandem bicycle, a spontaneous "hurrah" burst from every throat, a compliment that the plucky little Germantown lady richly deserved, and which she acknowledged with a graceful nod and a sweet smile.

At 6:30 Lieutenant Spier, of the Century Wheelmen, gave the order to start, and amid the musical "tootings" of bugles and the plaudits of the spectators, the calvacade of wheelmen started for the city proper. On going through Frankford and Rising Sun they attracted large crowds of admiring spectators, who lined the streets through which they had to pass, and finally arriving on Broad Street they were joined by an additional crowd of cyclers; so when they at last rode down the smooth asphalt-paved street they numbered fully two hundred men and women, engaging the attention of the large crowd of promenaders who congregate on this beautiful street. On arriving at the Century's house the wheels were checked and stored away, and the visitors taken down to the Continental Hotel where an informal but bountiful supper was spread, to which they did ample justice.

On Sunday, at 10:30, the entire party, reinforced by many local riders, in all about 150 wheels, took a spin through the Park, winding up with some light refreshments at Strawberry Mansion; and, as they had to go home on the 3:30 train, they were escorted to the depot where the wheels were put in a baggage car and adieus said, all regretting that the stay could not be prolonged.

There were two disappointments in store for the Centurions which in a way threw a wet blanket over the spirits of the boys. One was that they could not have these two New York clubs as private guests, Mr. Clark saying that it was desirable to keep the party together; and the other was the refusal of the Mayor to let them shoot off fireworks, they having made elaborate arrangements for a grand pyrotechnic display Saturday night on arrival of the strangers.

As usual the Centurions do not belie their name "Century," as they had the largest delegation of our local clubs in the run. They were Messrs. Bromley, Spier, Degn and Dalson; the former two having ridden over on their wheels on Thursday and Friday and back again on Saturday.

Mr. Welch and his sister, who rode the 100 miles so well, are members of the Wissahickon Wheelmen of Philadelphia.

Philadelphia, June 11. "ARGUS."

MARYLAND.

The Crescent Club gave a "smoker" at their clubhouse, 401 North Avenue, last week. The other clubs were invited, and each was well represented. The house was decorated with leaf tobacco, covering the walls in every room and hanging from the ceiling in great quantities, making a typical "smoker" house. The entertainment consisted of speech-making and singing.

The Clark Cycle Company, N. Charles Street, Baltimore, has sent to each member of the Hagerstown Club a neat gold pin made of wire and twisted into the word "Hagerstown," as souvenirs of the approaching meet. The Hagerstown Club last week elected four active members.

Applications for hotel accommodations are constantly coming in and the hostelries are rapidly filling up. In two mails, last week, 105 applications for rooms were received. This was owing to Hagerstown being cut off several days on account of the flood. A list of boarding houses has been prepared, from which accommodations can be secured by all to whom hotel rates are out of reach. A committee has been named which will show visitors to their abiding places on arrival. Mr. H. McStouffer is Chairman of the Committee on Hotel Arrangements, and persons seeking accommodations, by addressing letters to him, will receive immediate attention. Letters addressed to Hagerstown will reach him.

A hearty reception will be given Mr. Luscomb on his arrival at Hagerstown by the lawyers and business men.

Joel Gutman & Co., on North Eutaw Street, have their large window now devoted to sporting. The background is given to tennis, archery, etc., but the central figures in front are a little girl lost in admiration of a Victor tricycle, a lady in the act of mounting a Swift safety, and a youngster spinning along on a Victor spring-fork safety. The display is attracting a great deal of attention.

Ten members were elected at the regular meeting of the Maryland Club last week. The club has issued circulars intended to test the sentiments of the members on the subject of camping out at Hagerstown during the Meet.

The project of a united club run, which was inaugurated by members of the Crescent Club, is being discussed with much interest. BAY RIDGE.

TACOMA, W. T.

If the excellent beginning of the Race Committee's work is any criterion we may expect some exciting contests on July 3. The reasons for not holding the meet on the "Fourth" are many, but principally because on that day six of the wheelmen are ordered to Olympia with their regiment to pay their respects to his royal highness Governor Moore, and because the fire department claims the personal attention of six others the same day. The Committee in charge are Messrs. E. A. McCoy, Chairman, Barlow, Clarke, Halstead, Howell and Brockett, and all of them are bound to make a signal success of this tournament, although they labor under many disadvantages, especially a poor trotting track that requires much attention to make fit for racing.

The Committee have carefully figured up the expense of this undertaking, and find that $500 is necessary to insure a successful and creditable race meet. But they look to the open-hearted people of Tacoma to make sufficient subscriptions, either in cash or prizes, to fill the bill.

The following programme has been decided upon: One-mile novice, quarter-mile heats, best two in three; one-mile race for visiting wheelmen, half-mile without hands; quarter-mile boys' race (under 15), one-mile championship Washington; half-mile novice; one-mile safety; half-mile dash and one-mile consolation.

I think the idea of the committee is to have exciting short races, and do away with monotonous five-mile "processions." They should be congratulated for showing such excellent judgment.

Alas! amid our many successes I am called upon to record doings of the Tacoma Bicycle Club that cast discredit upon her fair name. On Saturday last the members of the Rod and Gun Club showed the wheelmen how to play baseball, and, while the game was close and very exciting, nevertheless the T. Bi. C. got left. At the end of the fourth inning the scores were 5 to 4 in favor of the cyclists, but somehow or other we got "all broke up" at the same time, and were badly rattled. Ed Rainey and Cromwell made an excellent battery, and Barlow, Halstead and Bill Rainey guarded the "boys" in creditable style. The fielders (especial mention being made of Prince Wells, who had an old hoopskirt over his head as substitute for a parasol) were very slow to field the out-flies. However, another game will soon be arranged, and although the Gun boys beat us 8 to 4, they will do well to get even four runs next time. After the game a keg of sarsparilla (Hood's?) was brought from the wagon, and a general quenching of thirst indulged in. To the members of the Rod and Gun Club we extend our hearty thanks for their courteous treatment, and hope some day to be able to repay them for the pleasure given our boys.

Mr. E. W. Johnson, champion all-round athlete, is in town, and very desirous of having a good athletic track somewhere in the suburbs of the city and near the motor line. Mr. Johnson is well-known to the members of all the Eastern athletic clubs as just the man to take charge of such a project, as he has a practical knowledge of general athletics. Both Halsted and Prince Wells have interviewed him, and urged the necessity of a track that will also prove good for cycling, and I am sure that whoever builds a track will keep the wheelmen in mind, especially as public interest is in their favor.

Both Prince Wells and Karl Thompson made many friends in Victoria, B. C., during the celebration of the Queen's birthday. All of the Victoria papers speak in very flattering terms of Wells' exhibition of fancy riding and Thompson's winning of the handsome championship trophy in the 2-mile race. The several accounts were unanimous in the opinion that the Tacoma Bicycle Club members' drill and parade was a great success, and an important part of the programme, and our boys were congratulated many times for the fine display, especially as it was of an impromptu nature. I hope the Victoria wheelmen who favor us by a visit on the "Fourth" (or rather 3d of July) will be able to return home with as many pleasant memories as our boys can readily recall of the good times enjoyed in British Columbia.

JUNE 5, 1889. SNOHOMISH.

WASHINGTON, D. C.

About twenty-five wheelmen from the Baltimore Cycle Club visited Washington, and were guests of the Washington Cycle Club on Sunday, June 1. A run was taken to Cabin John Bridge, where dinner was had. In the afternoon the return was made and the remainder of the day spent in visiting the scenes of high water along Pennsylvania Avenue and the Potomac front. Captain Curry, reported at the last meeting that Washington had never entertained a more orderly and gentlemanly set of wheelmen, and, he says: "Come again, gentlemen, we have other beautiful roads to show you."

The Capital club intend to give a moonlight excursion down the Potomac to Marshall Hall, a place notable from the fact of its being the former residence of friends of the immortal George, whose home, Mt. Vernon, is just across the river.

A new club of about fifteen members has been organized in Washington under the name of "Columbia."

L. A. W. renewals and applications are not fast forthcoming from the District of Columbia.

An L. A. W. run to Cabin John Bridge is announced for the near future. If the boys turn out in round numbers and show themselves, it will help the District Division a great deal in obtaining new members.

MADISON AVENUE TO BE ASPHALTED.

Madison Avenue, which is already paved with asphalt from 23d to 32d Street, will be laid with asphalt to 59th Street. Madison Avenue runs from 23d Street to the Harlem River. It is one short block east of Fifth Avenue, and will be used in preference to Fifth Avenue by all wheelmen who wish to gain the Park from down-town. It will enable Brooklyn wheelmen to visit the New York riding district with very little uncomfortable riding and *vice versa*. On the Brooklyn ride, there are but three blocks of pavement before one reaches the asphalt which will bring him down Bedford Avenue, to the Park and the Coney Island Boulevard. On the New York side, the route is a half mile of trap-block pavement in 23d Street, from the ferry to Madison Avenue, up Madison Avenue to 59th Street and across to the Park. Madison Avenue is lined from 59th Street up with the houses of some of New York's most prominent citizens, and it is only a question of a short time when the street will be asphalted all the way up-town.

LANCASTER, PA.

East of our city, in a straightaway course of a mile, flows southward our beautiful little river, the Conestoga. The Philadelphia pike passes over it, on a stone bridge of seven arches, built in 1799 by a man whose name it bears, and to whose memory it stands an enduring monument. A tablet in the parapet wall gives its history as follows:

"Erected by Abraham Witmer, 1799-1800. A law of an enlightened Commonwealth, passed April 4, 1798, Thomas Mifflin, Governor, sanctioned this monument of the public spirit of an individual. Mr. Witmer was remunerated by tolls, and some person or persons still continue to reap the harvest of his investment. Such a work at an early day was indeed an enterprise of which the State might have been proud, much more so an individual."

This is true, for in those days this road was the great thoroughfare between Philadelphia and Pittsburg, and the then famous Conestoga wagons were of as much importance as are the great ocean steamers that now plow the main between the two hemispheres.

Half a mile north of this bridge the Pennsylvania Railroad crosses the stream by a most substantial stone bridge, such as the wise managers of that great corporation are now substituting for those built of other material. The original Big Bridge, as it was called, was destroyed by fire. They then wanted something that would not burn, and tried iron and steel for a time. Soon they found that they needed something that could not be weakened by rust, and that heat could not expand nor cold contract; and now they will build of stone, solid stone. So they builded over the Conemaugh at Johnstown, and the rains descended and the floods came and beat upon that bridge, and it fell not; neither could fire consume it, for it was rock. A most complimentary indorsement of the wisdom of the man who lived and builded almost a century ago, Abraham Witmer.

At the eastern end of Witmer's Bridge stands the toll-gate before alluded to. This relic of the dark ages should be done away with, having served its day and purpose. All public roads should be free. However, the toll gate has no terrors for the cycler. He passes through with all the nonchalance of a legislator on a railroad train with a free pass in his pocket.

At the western end of the bridge is Potts' Landing, named after the proprietor of Potts' Tavern. I like that term. Hotel would be utterly out of keeping. Sam Potts knows how to run the place, and has stored in his numerous boathouses from seventy-five to eighty pleasure boats, about one-third of which he owns and has for hire. It is a beautiful sight on a summer evening to see the fleet dotting the water. The bright colors of the caps and suits of the rowers, and the flowers and ribbons worn by their lady companions, make a brilliant show upon the fair bosom of the quiet stream, to say nothing of the other fair bosoms whereon the ribbons and flowers are wont to nestle themselves.

I spoke in a former letter of a hill-climbing contest that was to come off shortly. It took place the evening of Thursday, June 6. The open space in front of Pott's tavern was the starting point. A large concourse of people was present to see the fun, and also numerous wheelmen, but only five entries for the contest. Miller and Kohler rode Star machines, Griel and Reist, ordinaries, and Rose, "the indomintable," his rear-driving safety. All good men and true and strong riders. Dave Rose would ride through a stone wall if he thought it desirable to get to the other side by that route. I mentioned that it was an uphill piece of business, and the length of the course is 1,660 feet, and pretty steep. What the rise is I have not been informed. The whole race could not be witnessed from either end. The route is a pretty one, the road on either side being lined with handsome cottages, with front yards filled with blooming rose bushes, and, on this occasion, with blooming maidens, also. We chose to see the finish, which was made in 1m. 45s., the crank ordinaries in the lead. Reist won the prize, a silver medal, with Griel a close second. Both were nearly exhausted when they crossed the tape. It was a tough run and shook the boys up pretty lively. Another race for a gold prize is promised to take place soon, possibly over the same course.

An exciting incident occurred previous to the race. A well-built young rider on a 50 or 52 inch ordinary came down the hill at a rapid rate, and as he was probably not familiar with the course his wheel got the upper hand of and ran away from him. He was game though and stuck to his wheel manfully. It was a thrilling sight to see him jump the "breaks" in the road, his little wheel in the air. The gamey fellow slipped on to the backbone of the machine but kept a guiding grip upon the handles. This and the velocity with which he was moving kept him from taking a header. He got down safely, and when he struck the level he jumped but still held one handle. He did this so expertly that neither he nor his machine got a fall. His feet struck the ground with a slap and he got off with a sprained ankle from what might have been broken bones if not something worse. I pitied him as he limped to a chair, but I admired his pluck and skill.

The tournament of the Lancaster Bicycle Club, July 4, promises to be an interesting affair and the boys are hard at work with a view to making it such. All are invited. Come and receive a good, old Pennsylvania Dutch welcome. YAH! TENTOONS.

June 11, 1889.

NEWARK.

Nine members of the Atalanta Wheelmen were participants in the "G. C. R.," under command of Lieutenant Rummell. The treatment the boys received while in Philadelphia was of the best, and the trip to all was a most enjoyable one. Several visitors accompanied the A. W.'s.

Eight (8) new members were elected at the last meeting of the club, and five more applications held over until the next meeting. The Atalantas have never been in as prosperous a condition as at the present time. The club-house is being fixed up, and with Captain Drabble to take care of the racing men—well? they will show for themselves what they can do at the K. C. W. meet.

We sadly miss our esteemed friend's (Coaster) notes from that beautiful hamlet, Jersey City, the home of the H. C. W. Is he sick or making new rules for a bowling league?

Last Tuesday night (11th) was the date for a "moonlight" to Caldwell, but a heavy thunder shower frightened away most of those who were going. Four went, however, with Captain Drabble, and had a glorious time. It seems we are fated to have *black* moonlight nights. The rain coming home was rather wet, and so were we when we got home. SPARK.

FIXTURES.

June 15, 1889.—L. I. W. Race Meet at Brooklyn Athletic Grounds. Entries close June 8 with L. B. Wise, 1,281 Bedford Ave., Brooklyn.

June 15, 1889.—Two-mile Bicycle Handicap at New York Athletic Club Grounds, Travers Island. Entries will close June 5, with Frank D. Sturges, Secretary N. Y. A. C., 104 West Fifty-fifth Street, N. Y.

June 17, 1889.—Annual Meet of Massachusetts Division, L. A. W., at Squantum, Mass.

June 18, 1889.—Third Annual Meet of Tennessee Division, L. A. W., at Nashville, Tenn.

June 21, 1889.—House-warming of the Brooklyn Bicycle Club. Tenth anniversary.

June 22, 1889.—New Orleans Bicycle Club's Race for the Hill Cup.

June 28, 29, 1889.—Kings County Wheelmen's Annual Meet at Washington Park, Brooklyn. Entries close June 21. Address Wm. F. Murphy, 1,255 Bedford Avenue.

June 29, 1889.—Handicap Road Race of Milwaukee Wheelmen, over Wauwatosa course. Entries close June 24.

June 29, 1889.—One Mile Bicycle Handicap at Field Meeting of Pittsburgh Cricket Club, Brushton Station. Entries close June 26, with A. MacPherson, 61 Fourth Avenue, Pittsburgh, Pa.

June 30, 1889.—Massachusetts Union Run to Massapoag House, Sharon. Address Capt. A. W. Robinson, 33 Winter Street, Boston.

July 1, 2, 1889.—C. W. A. Annual Meet at St. Catharines, Ontario.

July 2, 3, 4, 1889.—League Meet at Hagerstown, Md.

July 3 and 4, 1889.—Missouri Division L. A. W. Meet at Sedalia, Mo. Races on second day. Entries for handicaps close June 25; for open events June 27. Both to be made to Fred. E. Hoffman, Sedalia, Mo. No entry fee.

July 4, 1889.—L. A. W. Race Meet, at Hagerstown, Md. Entries close June 26, with Harry B. Irwin, 34 West Franklin Street, Hagerstown, Md.

July 4, 1889.—Two-mile Bicycle Handicap at Washington Park, Fifth Avenue, Brooklyn. Entries close June 26, with F. G. Webb, Treasurer. Prospect Harriers' Race, run under L. A. W. rules.

July 4, 1889.—Race Meet at Brownsville, Pa.

July 4, 1889.—Illinois Division, L. A. W. Meet, at Ottawa.

July 4, 1889.—Tournament held by Lancaster (Pa.) Bicycle Club.

July 4, 1889.—Fort Schuyler Wheelmen, Utica, N. Y., 50-mile Road Race.

July 20, 1889.—One-mile and 25-mile Bicycle and 5-mile Tricycle N. C. U. championships at Paddington, Eng., track.

July 27, 1889.—One-mile and 25-mile Tricycle and 5-mile Bicycle N. C. U. Championships at Paddington, Eng., track.

September 4-5, 1889.—Amateur Race Meet of the Hartford Wheel Club, at Hartford, Conn. Entries to be made with W. M. Francis, Secretary, P. O. Box 745.

October 23-29, 1889.—Race Meet at Macon, Ga.

EUROPEAN CYCLING FIXTURES.

Austro-Hungary.—Prague (Smichow) June 29 and 30. Germany.—Berlin, June 16 and 17, July 21, September 15; Hanover, June 23, September 8; Cologne, June 30, August 12; Chemnitz, September 8; Frankfort-on-the-Maine, September 1; Mannheim, September 8; Crefeld, September 8. Hamburg.—Altona, September 22; Bochum, August 25; Soram, June 9; Coburg, June 9; Magdeburg, June 30, September 8. Denmark.—Copenhagen International Meeting, August 18.

National Cyclists' Union.—Championship Fixtures—At Paddington, August 24, 50-mile Bicycle and 1-mile Dwarf.

STATE RECORDS BROKEN AT LOS ANGELES, CAL.

California may be congratulated on having more favorable weather for her race meet, May 30, than most Eastern States experienced. Buildings in the beautiful city of Los Angeles were elaborately decorated with bunting in honor of the guests, and the headquarters at Panorama Building, on Main Street, was a brilliant sight.

At 11:30 A. M. the command to roll into line was obeyed by 200 wheelmen, and the procession slid along over the asphalt streets, around the Plaza, then up Spring Street to Ninth, and back by Main to headquarters.

After breaking ranks a lunch was served at the Westminster, after which the races took place at Agricultural Park. A good crowd attended, and the principal features were the lowering of three State records, though the track was somewhat heavy, and the winning of all the prizes by the Los Angeles boys. If they had foreseen this result, even more decorations would have been lavished on the town—red paint, in fact.

Following is a summary in regular order of events contested:

One-mile, Novice.—J. R. Tufts, Los Angeles. Time, 2m. 54s.

One-mile, State Championship (best previous time, 2m. 48⅘s.)—Won by W. S. Wing, Los Angeles; J. Phil Percival, second. Time, 2m. 47s.

Quarter-mile Dash, Open (race against time).—Percival, Los Angeles, won in 43s.

Half-mile Dash, Open.—Burke, Los Angeles. Time, 1m. 26⅕m.

One-mile Safety Race.—J. R. Tufts, Los Angeles, first in 3m. 4⅘s.; 6s. better than the State record.

One-mile, 3:15 class.—J. R. Tufts, Los Angeles. Time, 2m. 57s.

Half-mile, boys.—Will Tufts, Los Angeles. Time, 1m. 37s.

Quarter-mile, Open.—Burke, Los Angeles. Time, 52¼s.

Three-mile Championsip.—Won by J. Phil Percival in 9m. 48⅗s. This was such a lagging performance that the judges fixed for the big event of the day (the five-mile open) a time limit of sixteen minutes. W. S. Wing, of Los Angeles, won it in 15m. 40s., beating State record by 9s. The track was in poor condition—particularly heavy on the backstretch—and the performances were looked on as wonderful.

PROGRAMME FOR MASSACHUSETTS SPRING MEET AT SQUANTUM.

Chief Consul Dr. W. H. Emery, for the Committee on the Spring Meet, reports the following entertainment for those who will attend on June 17 at Squantum: There will be three handicaps for ordinary bicycles, safeties and tandem bicycles, two medals for each race. The committee will also furnish a medal for every club which desires to establish a club championship, the medal for each club to be competed for by the members of that club. At least three men must start in every race. Entries 50 cents, to be made prior to June 15, to Dr. W. G. Kendall, 176 Tremont Street, Boston. Races will occur at 3 o'clock.

In accordance with the idea of making this Meet a picnic, the committee has decided to allow each wheelman to furnish his own lunch, and to avoid bother a wagon will be furnished, which will leave Copley Square after the wheelmen. Each man can deliver his lunch, with his name written plainly in ink on the covering, at this wagon, and obtain it after arriving at Squantum.

Captains of clubs are requested to notify Dr. Kendall how many members will be likely to attend.

ENGLISH RACING NOTES AND FACTS OF INTEREST.

If the number of events to be contested on June 10, 11 and 12, at the Molineux grounds, Wolverhampton, Eng., and the list of entries is any criterion, there will be excellent sport.

Fred Wood, late of Leicester, now at South Shields, was to make his first public appearance this season on Saturday, June 8, in a ten-mile match against his old opponent Dick Howell for a trophy value £25 to be selected by the victor. The event was to take place at the new Cycling Grounds, Sunderland, where a splendid cinder track has been laid, four laps to the mile.

We understand that Illston, who is in grand form just now, intends, after the Whitsuntide meetings are over, having a fair shot at all the bicycle path records, and will do his best to lower them all round. Given a good day and efficient pacemaking, we opine he will succeed

A Brighton correspondent of the *Cyclist* thus writes of a miniature cycle constructed by a Mr. Loosley, of the same city: "Mr. Loosley's bicycle, which weighs only two ounces, is in perfect working order, every spoke being screwed into hub and is fitted with cone bearings and adjustable Stanley head. He has also a tricycle of "Salvo" pattern, which has Starley's patent balance gears, tubular frame, Arab cradle spring, 60 spokes to each wheel, each one screwed into hub, rubber pedals, 6-inch wheels, complete chain composed of 500 pieces alone, and which, with all the accessories, weighs under six ounces These models were exhibited at the Stanley Show." These must be marvels in the way of delicate workmanship.

On May 22, a destructive fire did much damage to the premises and stock of a Mr. Hale, cycle agent, on Terminus Road in Littlehampton. The total loss is estimated at £1,200, only partially insured. Among the wheels destroyed were £200 worth of new machines just received. All that was saved comprised a couple of dozen bicycles and tricycles.

W. C. Thompson, of Jarrow, has developed into a grand safety rider, and on Saturday did a capital performance at North Shields, where he won the mile handicap from the 40 yards mark in 2m. 38 3-5s.

SOUTHERN SCORCHERS.

The first of a series of races at New Orleans for medals given for competition between local riders by that veteran wheelman, A. M. Hill, was contested June 2 over a one-mile asphalt course, and won by B. M. Sprigg, by some 15 or 20 yards, in 3m. 58s.; H. L. Carey, second; A. M. Hill, third by some inches; George A. Solomon, a bad fourth. It looked like a playing match. Sprigg moved with greatest possible ease, while Hill, who is certainly a match for him, contented himself with holding on to position three, doing outside of four minutes. There are to be six races—three of one mile each for a silver medal and three of five miles for a gold one, best two in each series to win.

W. A. Illston is said to have ridden a mile in 2m. 28s. at a recent trial at Coventry, England.

C. W. A. MEET AT ST. CATHARINES, JULY 1 AND 2.

A dispatch from St. Catharines says: Mr. Hal. B. Donelly, the C. W. A. Secretary, will send all members of the association a programme of the races, etc., to be held on July 1 and 2. The hill-climbing contest will be quite a feature, as there are two or three very steep hills here. The Rochester, N. Y., drill corps have entered the drill competition, for which a handsome trophy is offered. They have eight men who will ride Pony Stars. The West End, Rochester, N. Y., Club say they will send thirty men. Fairvale Park, which has a very fine track, has been secured for the races. The evening's entertainment will be at the Palace Rink, which can hold 5,000 people and is one of the largest rinks in Ontario. The drill corps will have a clear space of 150 feet by 65. Everything indicates a very large Meet.

A MINNEAPOLIS RACING MAN.

Colie Bell, who has been representing the Minneapolis Bicycle Club at the L. A. W. meet at Ottawa, Kan., is doing some fine riding and upholding the name of the club. The track at Ottawa is in poor shape and Bell has had a hard time of it. The local handicapper seemed to think Colie was much better than local talent and handicapped him heavily, but he managed to show the other wheelmen how to ride, after all. He succeeded in winning the half-mile L. A. W. championship race in 1m. 20 1-5s.; also the one-mile handicap in 2m. 54⅕s. The members of the club are jubilant over the showing of Captain Colie, and when he returns he will be given a hearty welcome by all local wheelmen.—*Minneapolis Tribune.*

SPORT AT THE MANHATTAN GAMES.

The 1½ mile bicycle handicap, decided at the Manhattan grounds last Saturday, would have produced one of the most notable finishes of the season, but for an accident on the last lap. In the final heat, the six men who were fortunate enough to get into the final had come together and a warm last lap was anticipated. Rounding the sharp turn for the last quarter, one of the wheels swerved a few inches out of the course, its rider going over and bringing three others with him. Schoefer who was but a few lengths behind the field, steered quickly to the outside but cropppered over the fallen men, shooting through the wooden paling, which broke as easily as chips.

Schoefer was carried off and Class led away. Bensinger re-mounted, but H. L. Powers and C. M. Murphy were a hundred yards ahead, and he made no impression on them. Summary: Heat 1, John Bensinger, K. C. W., 85 yards, first; H. L. Powers, New York City, 60 yards, second; time, 5m. 24 2-5s. Heat 2, S. B. Bowman, N. J. A. C., 15 yards, first; J. W. Schoefer, B. B. C., scratch, second; time, 5m. 38 4-5s. Heat 3, C. M. Murphy, K. C. W., 60 yards, first; W. G. Class, B. B. C., 70 yards, second; F. G. Brown, K. C. W. scratch, third; time, 4m. 39 2-5s. Final Heat, Murphy, first; Powers, second, by a length; time, 4m. 35 1-5s. Murphy out-spurted Powers down the home-stretch. Schoefer rode the first mile in 3m., the fastest time ever made on the track, and the fifth quarter in 42s. He would have won, with Bowman second, had not the accident occured.

Trainer W. J. Corcoran has been visiting his many friends in Boston. He handled Clark, of Yale, in the inter-collegiate race, and is naturally elated over the result of his labors. He trained E. O. Rassicoe, of Woodstock, who won four firsts there on the Queen's birthday. This rider will probably take part in all the tournaments in the fall. Mr. Corcoran thinks that the outlook for amateur racing was never brighter, but that professional racing is a thing of the past.

Young F. A. Clark, the bicycle rider, who won the intercollegiate two-mile race on the Berkeley oval, thereby bringing the cup to Yale and giving Harvard a most unpleasant surprise, is only eighteen years old, and his home is in Plantsville, Ct. He weighs 140 pounds, and is five feet eight inches in height. He has been riding two years, and first raced in a boys' race two years ago. He rides a 54-inch wheel. He is a member of the Sheffield Scientific school, '91.

The Berkshire County Wheelmen have arranged for a field day on July 4, at the Pittsfield Agricultural Grounds. There will be bicycle races and other athletic sports.

East Hartford wheelmen will have a race meeting on July 4.

At Schuylkill Navy Games, June 8: Two-mile bicycle (handicap), won by W. W. Taxis, G. M. Gregg, second; time, 6m. 55⅘s. One mile bicycle race (match for special medal), J. J. Bradley, South End Wheelmen; John H. Draper, Penn. Bicycle Club; won by Bradley; time, 3m. 7 4-5s.

Bowman, of the N. J. A. C., won the two-mile bicycle at the Actor's Amateur A. A. sports June 11. Time made was 6m. 49 2-5s, and the Powers brothers his only competitors.

In the Athletic Games at Oakland, Cal., May 30, the half-mile bicycle was won by C. Harner, B. C. W., in 1m. 32 2-5s; C. E. Townsend, second. In the one-mile handicap, C. N. Langden, 75 yards, won; Lakeman, second; time, not taken.

The L. A. W. Racing Board has declared the amateur status of Arnold Heilborn of Providence, forfeited for competing with a professional swimmer.

New York State Division L.A.W.

OFFICIAL ORGAN.

OFFICERS FOR 1889.

Chief Consul, W. S. Bull, 754 Main Street, Buffalo, N. Y.; Vice-Consul, M. L. Bridgman, 1755 Bedford Avenue, Brooklyn, N. Y.; Secretary-Treasurer, Geo. M. Nisbett, 20 Wall Street, New York City. Executive and Finance Committee, W. S. Bull, M. H. Bridgman, Dr. George E. Blackham, Dunkirk, N. Y.

SHOW YOUR LEAGUE TICKET!!

To the MEMBERS OF THE NEW YORK STATE DIVISION:

Your attention is called to the following circular letter to hotel keepers.

All violations of the agreement on the part of hotels should be at once reported to this office:

"*Dear Sir*—I desire to again call your attention to the following extracts from the agreement with this Division signed by you:

"That I will, during the continuance of this agreement, furnish to any member of the L. A. W. *producing his Membership Ticket for the current year*, accommodations equal in all respects to those furnished regular guests, at the following rates.

"That I *will not* accord any privileges, reductions, use or inspection of the "Record Book," or other benefits derivable under this agreement to any wheelmen except *members of the L. A. W., who shall produce their individual Tickets as Members only for the current year*."

"To aid you in carrying out these provisions, which were inserted in the agreement in order to protect both the hotels and the L. A. W. from imposition by wheelmen not members of the organization, I inclose a fac-simile of the Membership Ticket for the current year, which please preserve for comparison.

"Yours respectfully,
"W. S. Bull, Chief Consul."

TARIFF ON BICYCLES.

To the Members of the New York State Division:

At a meeting of the Trunk Line Passenger Committee, held at the office of the Trunk Line Association, 346 Broadway, New York City, Tuesday, June 4, 1889, it was

"*Resolved*, That bicycles, when accompanied by their owners, be carried free of charge over ALL LINES IN THE TRUNK LINE ASSOCIATIONS; this action to be in effect immediately."

TRUNK LINE ASSOCIATION.

Allegheny Valley R. R.
Baltimore & Ohio R. R.
Boston & Albany R. R.
Boston, Hoosac Tunnel & West. Ry.
Buffalo, Rochester & Pittsburg Ry.
Cairo, Vincennes & Chicago Line.
Central Vermont R. R.
Chicago & Alton R. R.
Chicago & Atlantic Ry.
Chicago, Burlington & Quincy R. R.
Chicago & Grand Trunk Ry.
Chicago, Rock Island & Pacific Ry.
Chicago & St. Louis Ry.
Chicago & West Michigan Ry.
Cincinnati, Hamilton & Dayton R. R.
Cincinnati, Indianapolis, St. Louis & Chicago R. R.
Cincinnati, Jackson & Mackinaw R. R.
Cincinnati & Muskingum Valley Ry.
Cincinnati, Wabash & Michigan Ry.
Cincinnati, Washington & Baltimore R. R.
Cleveland, Akron & Columbus Ry.
Cleveland, Columbus, Cincinnati & Ind. Ry.
Cleveland & Marietta Ry.
Cleveland & Pittsburg R. R.
Columbus & Cincinnati Midland R. R.
Columbus, Hocking Valley & Toledo Ry.
Dayton & Ironton R. R.
Delaware, Lackawanna & Western R. R.
Detroit, Grand Haven & Milwaukee Ry.
Detroit, Lansing & Northern R. R.
Evansville & Terre Haute R. R.
Fitchburg R. R.
Fort Wayne, Cincinnati & Louisville R. R.
Grand Rapids & Indiana R. R.

Grand Trunk Ry.
Indiana, Bloomington & Western Ry.
Indianapolis, Decatur & Western Ry.
Indianapolis & St. Louis Ry.
Indianapolis & Vincennes R. R.
Jefferson, Madison & Ind. R. R.
Kanawha & Ohio Ry.
Lake Erie & Western Ry.
Lake Shore & Michigan Southern Ry.
Lehigh Valley R. R.
Louisville, Evansville & St. Louis R. R.
Louisville & Nashville R. R.
Louisville, New Albany & Chicago Ry.
Michigan Central R. R.
New York Central & Hudson River R. R.
New York, Chicago & St. Louis Ry.
New York, Lake Erie & Western R. R.
New York, New Haven & Hartford R. R.
New York & New England R. R.
New York, Ontario & Western Ry.
New York, Pennsylvania & Ohio R. R.
Ohio & Mississippi Ry.
Ohio & Northwestern R. R.
Ohio River R. R.
Pennsylvania Company.
Pennsylvania R. R.
Peoria, Decatur & Evansville Ry.
Philadelphia & Reading R. R.
Pittsburg, Fort Wayne & Chicago Ry.
Pittsburg, Cincinnati & St. Louis Ry.
Pittsburg & Lake Erie R. R.
Pittsburg & Western R. R.
Saginaw Valley & St. Louis R. R.
Scioto Valley Ry.
Terre Haute & Peoria R. R.
Toledo, Ann Arbor & No. Michigan Ry.
Toledo & Ohio Central R. R.
Toledo & Ohio Central R. R.
Toledo, Peoria & Western R. R.
Valley Ry.
Vandalia Line.
Wabash Ry.
West Shore R. R.
Western New York & Pennsylvania R. R.
Wheeling & Lake Erie Ry.

Yours fraternally,
W. S. Bull, Chief Consul.

NEW YORK STATE DIVISION—CONSULS AND HOTELS.

LIST NO. 2.

To the MEMBERS OF THE NEW YORK STATE DIVISION:

All appointments of consuls and hotels not issued by W. S. Bull, Chief Consul, are hereby revoked.

All regular appointments will appear in these lists.

Members are urged to patronize "League hotels" solely, as only by concentration of patronage will we be enabled to perfect our hotel system.

Look for the Hotel Certificate and ask for the "Record Book."

PLACE.	CONSUL.	HOTEL.
Angola		Angola Hotel.
Auburn		New Nat. Hotel.
Batavia		Hotel Richmond.
Bath Beach, L. I.		Avon Beach Hotel
Binghamton		Hotel Bennett.
Cambridge		Union House.
Canandaigua	Wm. H. Welch.	
Cayuga		Titus House.
Chatham		Chatham House
Cincinnatus	W. B. Holmes.	Cincinnatus House
Coeymans		
Corymans Junction		Pulver House.
Cooperstown		Warner House.
Coopertown		Hotel Fenimore
Downsville		Downs House.
Dryden		Dryden Hotel.
Elbridge		Monroe House.
Franklinville		Globe Hotel.
Geneva		The Kirkwood.
Gloversville		Alvord House.
Hamburg	P. M. Thorn.	Kopp's Hotel.
Hillsdale		Mt. Wash'n Hotel.
Holley		Mansion House.
Hornellsville	C. H. Baldwin	Page House.
Jamestown	Allen Falconer.	Sherman House
Little Falls		Metrapof'n Hotel
Marathon	L. T. Wilcox	Marathon House.
Mechanicville	A. B. Orcutt.	
Montgomery		Palace Hotel.
Mt. Vernon	F. T. Davis.	
New Brighton, S. I.		Pavilion Hotel.
New York City	W. E. Findley, N.Y.H.C.	
Nyack	Wm. Gray, Jr.	St. George.
Ossining	M. R. Potter.	Windsor
Owasco		Johnson House.
Port Byron		Howard House
Rochester	Clias. J. Iven, W.E.H.C.	
Rome	J. H. Putnam.	
Rushville		Park House.
Salem		Mason House.
Schuyler's Lake		Bulli n House.
Scott		Scott Hotel.
Sherburne		Dean House
Sinclairville		Sylvester House
Tunawanda		American.
Troy		Mansion House.
Walton		St. Nicholas.
Whitehall		Hall House.

Yours fraternally,
W. S. Bull, Chief Consul.

WINDLE DECLARED A PROFESSIONAL.

Willie Windle, the fastest amateur of last year, has been declared a professional by the League Racing Board. The charge on which Windle is professionalized is that his cousin and trainer, Asa Windle, received $100 from a bicycle concern last year, which was used for traveling expenses. The chairman of the Racing Board had a personal interview with Windle, who at once admitted that the money had been taken for expenses, and on this ground he was declared a professional.

It is rumored that other charges could have been made against Windle, but it is fair to presume that Chairman Davol based his charge on information received from one of the firms who paid Windle last year.

From a private letter we cull the following: "As he admitted the first charge, further trouble was unnecessary. He received punishment for what he did, and could have done a great deal worse and not received any worse penalty. He says he will not race as a professional. He is a very gentlemanly, nice, quiet chap. Makes no "kick;" says he deserved it, and took it like a man."

In a private letter to us Windle writes: "My father received $125 in all from the one firm last year. I never received a cent directly or indirectly from any company more than the amount referred to above. I suppose I have always raced illegally, as I was not of age to belong to the League, in any race I have run. My father wishes me to never ride again, and I don't think I will, as I never should want to run in a professional race. It seems rather hard to look out of one's window and see a beautiful track going to waste, though."

HARTFORD'S RACE MEET SEPTEMBER 4 AND 5.

At a meeting of the Hartford Wheel Club, held June 11, it was voted to give a race meeting Wednesday and Thursday, September 4 and 5. In consequence of the professional exhibitions given by professionals in late years, it was decided to make this tournament strictly an amateur affair; the public preferring good honest racing to being obliged to witness the loafing contests of the professional stars.

The club has appointed the following committee to manage the tournament:

L. A. Tracy, Chairman.
W. M. Francis, Sec., P. O. Box 745.
Joseph Goodman,
E. A. DeBlois,
H. N. Wilcox.

The Connecticut League of American Wheelmen have accepted an invitation to hold a meet in Hartford during the tournament, and at a meeting of the division board of officers a large appropriation was voted for the entertainment of League members at that time. In order to avail themselves of these privileges the Connecticut wheelmen should join the League American Wheelmen without delay.

A CORRECTION IN L. A. W. RACING RULES.

The attention of racing men and race officials is clearly called by Chairman Davol of the Racing Board to Rule 26.

In the correct version it should read:

"The officers of a race meeting shall not be permitted to compete in any race *at a race meeting* with which they are officially connected."

Ignorance of this rule will not be deemed sufficient excuse for breaking it.

The Racing Board has also decided that the word "bicycle," when used in defining a race, shall be construed as referring to the "ordinary" bicycle: a one-mile bicycle race is for "ordinaries" only, and "safeties" *cannot* compete.

If race-meet promoters wish to hold races for safeties, they must be plainly classified as such. For example again: One-mile *safety*, Five-mile *safety* Handicap, etc.

The prompt action of the Racing Board thus far must have convinced wheelmen that no "monkeying" with the rules will be allowed. Racing men "will take due notice and govern themselves accordingly."

TENNESSEE'S COMING L. A. W. MEET.

There is now no doubt of the complete success of the coming meet of the Tennessee Division of the L. A. W. in Nashville the 18th inst. The committees appointed at the mass meeting, June 6, to take charge of the arrangements, have gone to work with a will, and the result of their efforts will be seen in the gathering crowds of wheelmen early next week. A full attendance of all the committees was had at the club-rooms June 8, to agree finally upon the various programmes to be carried out. The General Committee reported gratifying progress in the work of the other committees, and Mr. J. C. Combs was added to the committee and made Chairman.

The committee will issue a circular letter early this week to all wheelmen in Nashville whose names can be ascertained, inviting them to join in the parade. This will also be sent to out-of-town cyclists. The circular will recommend the following dress in order that the line may present as near a uniform appearance as possible: Blue or dark knee pants and stockings, white flannel shirt, ordinary straight rim straw hat, no coat.

The Committee on Parade has reported the following line of march: Start from club-rooms at 3 P. M. promptly. From club-rooms to Summer, Summer to Union, Union to College, College to Square, around the Square to Market, down Market to Broad, out Broad to Vanderbilt Avenue, through Vanderbilt Avenue to Hayes, Hayes to Belmont Avenue, through Belmont Avenue to Demonbreun, down Demonbreun to McNairy, McNairy back into Broad, Broad to Vauxhall, Vauxhall to Demonbreun, Demonbreun to Vine, Vine to Church, Church to club-rooms.

Committee on Runs and Tour reported the following route for the four days' League tour: First day, June 19—Leave club-rooms at 7 A. M. for Shelbyville via Nolensville and Eagleville; take dinner at Eagleville, distance 28 miles. Leave Eagleville at 1:30 P. M. for Shelbyville, distance 26 miles; stay in Shelbyville that night. Second day, June 20—Leave hotel after early breakfast for Fayetteville, distance 26 miles; dinner in Fayetteville; start for Shelbyville via Lynchburg at 1 P. M., distance 32 miles; supper in Shelbyville. Third day, June 21—Leave Shelbyville at 7 A. M. for Murfreesboro; leave Murfreesboro at 2 P. M. for Lebanon, distance 26 miles. Fourth day, June 22—Leave Lebanon for Nashville at 8 A. M., distance 31 miles. This route shows the following distances: First day, 54 miles; second day, 58 miles; third day, 52 miles; fourth day, 37 miles; total, 201 miles.

MISSOURI'S MEET AT SEDALIA, JULY 3 AND 4.

The city chosen as the scene of the gathering of Missouri's wheelmen, known as the "Queen City of the Prairie," has macadamized streets, and the prairie roads (given dry weather) are good for miles in all directions. The Sedalia cyclers have taken hold of the enterprise with commendable push, and expect to entertain over 200 visitors. All the railroad lines in the State make a rate of one fare for the round trip to Sedalia and tickets are good from July 2 up to July 5.

The committee of arrangements submit the following programme:

First day, July 3—Reception and escort of wheelmen to hotels; at 9 A. M. run to McAllister Springs for dinner; 6:30 P. M. return to Sedalia, either awheel or on special train; 8 P. M. a "smoker" concert.

Second day, July 4—Parade at 9 A. M.; Division meeting, at 11; dinner, at 12; races at 2:30 P. M. These comprise nine events, as follows: One-mile bicycle, open; half-mile bicycle, Missouri Division championship, L. A. W. members only; one mile handicap; two-mile open, Missouri Division championship, L. A. W. members only; one-mile safety handicap; team race, open, three men from one club in each team; one-mile novice; two-mile handicap; one-mile consolation.

In addition to the above a hill-climbing contest will probably be arranged for. A grand banquet at Sicklen's Hotel on night of July 4 winds up the meet.

L. A. W. RACING BOARD SUSPENSIONS.

The following are suspended till July 1, 1889:

For violating Clause 3 of Rule F, at New Haven, May 30: Messrs. G. H. Parkington, C. L. Bartlett, F. E. Weaver, H. C. Backus, T. J. O'Tell, J. M. Verhoeff. For same offence, at Rochester, May 30: Messrs. E. O. Rassicoe, W. S. Campbell, G. F. Kahler. For same offence, at North Adams, May 30: Messrs. Chas. Lassor, McKee and Shields.

B. R. Millison and H. H. Everest, of Wichita, Kansas, are suspended till August 1, 1859, pending investigation as to amateur standing.

W. A. Turpin, of Rochester, N. Y., is reinstated.

HAVE YOU ENGAGED YOUR ROOM AT HAGERSTOWN?

Though accommodations at Hagerstown are not limited, as perusal of the hotel list will show, yet there are rooms *and* rooms, and the early cycler gets the largest amount of sleeping space. Among the larger hotels are the Hamilton, with room for 250; the Baldwin, same number; City, 200; Franklin, 200; Seminary, 150. These numbers are allotting one man to a room, but by doubling up, twice that number can be accommodated. In addition to these, there are seven smaller hotels that hold from 30 to 75 each, with numberless first-class boarding houses. To the man that wishes to get a moderate amount of sleep nights, the quiet of a boarding house will prove attractive. The Hotel Committee is well organized and will see that all attending are made comfortable if they will leave the whole matter to them. The estimated number that will attend varies all the way from 1,500 to 2,500. Chief Consul Mott puts it at between 1,800 and 2,000.

The Pope Mfg. Co., Overman Wheel Co., and Clark Cycle Co., have already taken time by the forelock, and engaged rooms for their displays. The "Official Programme" will be issued about June 15, giving full details. It is doubtful if as much enthusiasm outside wheeling circles has ever before been shown at places selected for League Meets.

HAGERSTOWN NOTES.

It is exceedingly gratifying to note the progress toward making the tenth annual Meet a "howling success." On entering the club-house one has the stereotyped question fired at him, "anything new?" when, of course, he has to relate everything he knows.

Applications for quarters continue to come in at a lively rate, there being no less than 105 last Friday.

General Agent Hickok, of the Pope Mfg. Co., arrived in town last Thursday from Pittsburg, having left the ill-fated Johnstown the day before the catastrophe. He is devoutly thankful for his escape

The Pope Mfg. Co. will be quartered at the Baldwin, with a full line of wheels, where all visitors will be received and made welcome.

The Overman Wheel Co. have engaged a parlor at the Hamilton, where they will have an exhibit of Victors of every description and entertain their friends.

Genial Sam Clark, with his affable assistant, Ned Le Cato, will also be on hand, with New Rapids and Quadrants in endless variety, also a full line of sundries. The Clark Cycle Co have distributed a very neat badge to the members of the Hagerstown Club, and the boys have expressed themselves as being highly delighted with it.

A party from New Haven, in charge of Chief Consul C. E. Larom, will take train to Baltimore, on Sunday, June 30, and wheel from there to Hagerstown, arriving Monday, July 1.

HAGERSTOWN.

A PLEASANT TOUR.

Messrs. E. S. Brown, Capt. W. H. Bradford and Secretary-Treasurer George B. Woodruff, all of the Winsted (Ct.) Wheel Club, start July 1 to wheel from Winsted to Niagara Falls via Albany and Buffalo. There they cross over to Hamilton, Ont., then go to Toronto and Oshawa. At the latter place they take boat down Lake Ontario, passing through the Thousand Islands and over the Lachine Rapids to Montreal. From that picturesque city the trip home is made awheel, touching at Lakes Champlain and George, not forgetting Saratoga Springs. The route outlined is a most attractive one, and we think any intending tourist cannot do better than join them if the ranks are not already full.

TRANSPORTATION TO THE HAGERSTOWN MEET.

To secure cheap transportation and good accomodation en route to the meet. When ticket is purchased have Ticket agent furnish a certificate that full fare has been paid through to Hagerstown. Upon presentation of this certificate at League Headquarters in Hagerstown, it will be endorsed by Samuel C. Miller, which will entitle the holder to a one-third rate returning to starting-point.

From points in New England and Eastern States, blanks for the above certificates must be obtained through W. S. Bull, Buffalo, N. Y., or C. Newbourg, 415 Broadway, New York, who will also furnish any information desired relative to transportation from these points.

From points between the Mississippi and Ohio Rivers, apply to W. M. Brewster, National Transportation Committee, 309 Olive Street, St. Louis.

From prominent points the following are defined as the best routes, especial attention being called to the position the B. & O. R. R. has always occupied in regard to the free transportation of wheels, and the committee request that all who can will patronize that road, and prove their appreciation of the favors extended us

Western Maryland Railroad.—Trains leave Hillen Station, Baltimore, through to Hagerstown without change, 4.10 and 8.05 A. M., 3.25 and 4.00 P. M. Special excursion ticket at two cents per mile for the round trip from any point on this road or its branches from June 29 to July 4. To secure special rates you must procure an order which will be furnished upon application to Samuel C. Miller, Hagerstown; Clark Cycle Co., 340 North Charles Street, Baltimore; Eisenbrandt Bros., 424 East Baltimore Street, Baltimore; Cline Bros., 304 West Baltimore Street, Baltimore. This route offers especial attractions to parties from points convenient to Baltimore, as it passes through a country noted for beautiful mountain scenery.

Special train service will be arranged from New York. Full information can be obtained from C. Newbourg, 415 Broadway.

From New York and Eastern points to Hagerstown.—Leave New York (foot of Liberty Street, Central R. R. of N. J.), 11.00 A. M., 12.00 night; Newark, N. J., 11.05 A. M., 11.25 P. M.; Elizabeth, N. J., 11.30 A. M., 12.33 A. M.; Trenton, N. J. (P. & R. R. R.), 12.00 noon, 2.10 A. M.; Philadelphia, B. & O. R. R.), 1.35 P. M., 4.10 A. M.; Chester, Pa., 1.51 P. M., 4.28 A. M.; Wilmington, Del., 2.08 P. M., 4.50 A. M.; Newark, Del., 2.24 P. M., 5.10 A. M.; Arr. Baltimore, 4.00 P. M., 7.00 A. M.; Leave Baltimore, 4.15 P. M., 9.15 A. M.; Washington, 5.30 P. M., 10.15 A. M.; Arr. Hagerstown, 8.30 P. M., 1.30 P. M.

From Chicago and points West.—Leave Chicago Central time, 10.10 A. M., 2.55 P. M.; Garrett, 1.52, 6.54 P. M.; Defiance, 3.05, 7.55 P. M.; Fostoria, 9.18 P. M.; Tiffin, 4.41, 9.38 P. M.; Sandusky, 3.20, 6.25 P. M.; Monroeville, 3.45, 7.15 P. M.; Mansfield, 6.07, 11.05 P. M.; Mt. Vernon, 7.04 P. M., 12.04 A. M.; Columbus, 6.50, 11.05 P. M.; Newark, 7.45 P. M., 12.47 A. M.; Zanesville, 8.45 P. M., 1.38 A. M.; Bellaire, 11.06 P. M., 3.54 A. M.; Wheeling, Eastern time, 11.50 P. M., 4.35 A. M.; arrive at Hagerstown, 1.30 and 8.30 P. M.

From St. Louis, Cincinnati, etc.—Leave St. Louis (via O. & M. Ry.), Central time, 8.10 A. M.; Vincennes, Ind., 12.26 P. M.; Louisville, Ky., 3.40 P. M.; Cincinnati (via C. W. & B. R. R.), 7.30 P. M.; Chillicothe, Ohio, 10.47 P. M.; Athens, Ohio, 12.34 A. M.; Parkersburg (via B. & O. R. R.), Eastern time, 2.50 A. M.; Grafton, 6.00 A. M.; arrive at Hagerstown, 1.30 A. M.

From Washington.—Purchase tickets by B. & O. Full information can be obtained from ticket agents. For the benefit of those who desire to visit Washington, special rates will be made from Hagerstown.

Cumberland Valley Railroad.—Leave Harrisburg 4.35 A. M. and 12.20 P. M., daily; 7.45 A. M. and 3.45 P. M., daily except Sunday. Special excursion rates on main line and branches.

K. C. W. NOTES.

Some weeks ago, it was loudly proclaimed by the cycling press that that particular member of the genus road-hog which lives on, and therefore thinks it owns the Bath road, had been compelled by the authorities (through the exertions of the Cyclist's Union of Long Island), to remove the iron posts that for some time have graced the pathway adjacent to the said road—hog's abode. If the authorities did compel the removal of the obnoxious posts, they (the posts) have once more put in an appearance, and endanger the safety of any who may chance to be riding on the path. Though I do not approve of path riding, I still think that if the powers that be, permit the use of this path by cyclists, the road-hog in question should be made to remove these obstructions.

Chas. Murphy won the bicycle race at the games of the Manhattan A. C. and now sports two fine watches. This is the fourth handicap this spring that has fallen to the K. C. W.'s. Some of our boys are path as well as road riders.

Brown and the Bros. Murphy will represent Kings Co. in the relay race of the L. I. W. They will have all their work cut out to win from the Berkeley team, but never say die, boys, you are all riding in good form and I hope to see that water set come up to 1,255 Bedford Avenue.

Those who went on the "century run," report an excellent time. Five of the Brooklyns and four of Kings Co. finished, Bridgman, Murphy, Bonner and Ward were the K. C. W. fortunates. At New Brunswick Beaseley had a very severe fall, but pluckily kept on to Kingston, 49 miles, where his sprained ankle became so painful that he had to take train to Philadelphia, which all found to be indeed "The City of Brotherly Love."

The Captains of the following clubs will call runs to attend the Kings Co. races on the second day, Saturday, June 20. Hudson Co. Wheelmen, Harlem Wheelmen, Riverside Wheelmen, Manhattan Bicycle Club, and Brooklyn Bicycle Club. A section of the grand stand will be reserved for our wheeling friends, and all that we can do to make the afternoon a memorable one, will be done.

Brooklyn, June 13, 1889. RAM LAL.

The Omaha Wheel Club has called the following runs for the month of June. Seventy-two miles, the distance laid out for June 30, would seem quite far enough for the average club member. June 14, Moonlight run to Manawa, 15 miles; June 16, Springfield, 40 miles; June 23, A. M., Papillion, 22 miles; P. M., Manawa, 15 miles; June 25, Florence, 14 miles; June 30, Fremont, 72 miles.

PSYCHE'S LETTER.

I hear on all sides remarks as to the difficulty of mounting, and wonder if it is practicable to give any real help by advice through "our columns. I have described in a former letter as minutely as I can the way I do it, and since writing you I have been struggling with a new mount myself, and will give the benefit of my experience to any one who wants it.

It is a pedal mount while the machine is in motion, and I learned it on principle; for, though it is effective, it is not as pretty as the pedal mount while the machine is at rest.

To do it I stand with my machine held by the two handles, then begin to walk, take two or three steps, place the left foot on the pedal as it begins to go up, giving a little spring simultaneously with the other foot, swing the right foot past the left through the space, and as I rise on the pedal, seat myself on the saddle. The machine should be inclined very decidedly *from* the person mounting. This looks very easy and effective.

While we were out the other day it was brought very forcibly to my attention how important it is that a lady should be experienced in the use of the brake. It ought to be instinctive with her to put it on, for its instant application at a critical moment may be the means of saving her from a very bad fall. I was riding a borrowed wheel, one that had no dress guard whatever, and my skirt caught in the chain. I was going down hill, though not coasting, as it was a stony grade. As I felt the pull my hand instinctively reached for the brake, and before I was really conscious of what had happened I was standing beside the machine, with a few gathers pulled out, but otherwise intact.

I think this also shows conclusively the importance of having a strong and simple brake, one that can be relied upon not to get out of order, and from my experience I should say that the place for the brake was on the front wheel. Many of my gentleman friends have machines with the rear brake, and are unable to descend several of our steepest hills, owing to the fact that a rear-wheel brake will not hold their wheels.

The front-wheel brake has fewer parts, and although some riders consider it too powerful, yet a little experience teaches one how to use it, and in cases of great emergency when the brake is most needed you are sure to stop.

PSYCHE.

POSITION — ARE WE NOT OVERDOING IT?

In asking this question we are not addressing the racing division, but the average tourist and road-rider, the "non-scorching" section, if we may be permitted to use the phrase. Strange as it may seem, the speedy man on road or path is not necessarily tremendously powerful; he usually strikes the happy medium, and combines sufficient power with remarkable rapidity and dexterity. This combination is undoubtedly seen at its best when the rider sits a certain distance behind the vertical line drawn through the crank-axle; then a good rider, road or path, can use his ankles and keep his mount swinging along at a steady pace, and though he may at first find his climbing something more of a task than hitherto, yet in the whole he will find himself speedier, and, as was the case with Mr. Wilson, decidedly more able to spurt.

The steady road-rider, especially when "somewhat fat and scant of breath," is to be advised not to go in for too much sitting back on any form of cycle, bar *the* bicycle. Such a rider would find the position irksome and unsatisfactory, for he does not want to hurry on the level, and he does want to go easy uphill. For a rider who does not "grasshopper" over his handles, but who sits fairly upright, a position approaching the vertical is both easy and comfortable. It would not be so to our youthful road scorcher, but to the sturdy rider of tricycle or safety it is simply a question of use and the proper placing of saddle and handles. We of course do not mean that the rider should rush to the other extreme and place himself *in front* of the crank axle, *à la* Buckingham, but we do mean that if a heavy rider who goes in for comfort places himself well over his pedals, he will find that, while

Send to Howard A. Smith & Co., Newark, N. J., for your bicycle supplies or call at Orange Hall and learn to ride. Open evenings.*₊*

---

out any skill in ankle-work, he can go a fair pace on the level, and climb hills with conspicuous comfort by comparison. If anyone not a "scorcher" doubts this assertion, let him repair to the foot of some hill, and make two fair attempts to ride up it—one with the saddle back, the other with it well over the work. The result will not be doubtful. As the rider becomes more expert, he may, if he sees fit, get behind his work, but go per cent. of the people to whom these remarks are addressed will find that they ride with greater ease, and tackle the steadygoer's *bête noir*—hills—with greater success, when they are placed in a position which calls for no special skill, and enables them to use the weight of the body in a perfectly effective and simple manner. The racing man we do not address—he is quite right to go back—but we think it in the interests of a large section of our readers to emphasise our question once again.

Are we not overdoing the sitting-back business?—*Bicycling News.*

AN UPTOWN HOUSE.

While taking a spin the other day on our new mount—which shall be nameless for the nonce—a rider on a new type of safety rushed past us. Thinking it might be the Star Safety, of which we had heard much and seen little, we followed at a respectful distance. When he struck the rough pavement near Central Park we caught up a little, and located him at No. 4 East 60th Street. Recognizing that as the new location of the N. Y. BICYCLE CO., we dismounted for a needed rest, and were cordially received. "How do you find trade?" we asked Manager Irving.

"Never better," said he. "Things are just booming with us." "Does your new up-town location have anything to do with that state of things?" asked we. "Both that and the line of goods we handle," said Irving. "We have an enamel, which we call our 'special brew' that gives satisfaction, oils for lubricating and lighting purposes, and everything in parts and sundries that is called for." "Any repairing to do?" said we. "Well, I should say so," and a bland smile overspread Irving's face, while the clerks grinned appreciatively. "For got facilities for doing anything in that line, from re-building a Star to tiring the wheel of an ordinary. If there *is* anything the other houses give up, all we want is for them to let us have a try at it." "By the way," said he, "did you notice how the Victors came out in the Decoration Day race: ten firsts isn't bad, is it?" "You're correct there," said we, "but now we've got cooled off a little, other engagements at 72d Street," and we thoughtfully jolted our way to the Boulevard.

A SELECTED LIST OF PATENTS.

[Reported especially for THE WHEEL AND CYCLING TRADE REVIEW by C. A. Snow & Co., patent attorneys. Washington, D. C.]

W. Goulden, Clapton, London, Eng., Velocipede, which consists in the combination of a cylinder with a stuffing-box attached at either or each end, the cylinder being dust-proof, and a long coiled spring or springs with piston rod working through the centre of coil spring or springs, and stuffing-box or boxes extending through the box or boxes, any convenient distance each way for the purpose of attachment at each or either end.

Dated June 11, 1889.

The Goat Cycle Club has been organized in Boston with William J. Shannon President and O. H. Graves Secretary. Its object is to provide social rest at no expense to members. The club having no rent to pay for rooms, any rider of a safety, "a goat," can become a member. The club meets every Sunday at 9 A. M. at Cottage Farm bridge and thence any one to fall in. The club will go to Bath, Me., for three days June 15, to Walpole June 23 and to Gloucester June 30, leaving Gloucester at 6 A. M.

Hal Greenwood, of St. Louis, issues a challenge for a hill-climbing contest, to take place within four months, anywhere in the United States, to any amateur in America, for the $50 or $100 medal, best two out of three climbs, and the loser to pay all travelling and training expenses of the winner.

Road races of the Manhattan Bicycle Club will be held June 16 over the Irvington-Milburn course.

THE WHEEL

— AND —

CYCLING TRADE REVIEW,

Published every Friday morning.

Entered at the Post Office at second class rates.

Subscription Price,   -   -   - $1.00 a year.
Foreign Subscriptions,   -   -   -   6s. a year.
Single Copies,   -   -   -   -   -   5 Cents.

Newsdealers may order through Am. News Co.

All copy should be received by Monday.
Telegraphic news received till Wednesday noon.

Advertising rates on Application.

F. P. PRIAL, Editor and Proprietor
        23 Park Row,
P. O. Box 444,   *New York.*

Persons receiving sample copies of this paper are respectfully requested to examine its contents and give us their patronage, and as far as is convenient, aid in circulating the journal, and extend its influence in the cause which it so faithfully serves. Subscription price, $1 per year.

ONCE A SICKLY SHEET.

IT NOW CONTAINS MORE READABLE NEWS AND COVERS MORE TERRITORY THAN ALL THE OTHER CYCLING JOURNALS.

Advertisers and readers will note the following paragraph, which is doubly valuable because published in the leading paper in New Jersey and because unsolicited.

Three years ago THE WHEEL was a rather sickly sheet of from eight to twelve pages per week printed in long primer type, but under the live management of Frank P. Prial it has increased in the number of its pages from twenty-four to twenty-eight and is now printed in solid brevier and nonpareil. It contains more readable news and covers more territory than all the other cycling journals. The last issue contained special correspondence from twenty-two different sections, reaching as far as California and Tacoma, W.—*Newark Sunday Call.*

TO BE READ BY ALL NON-SUBSCRIBERS.

THE WHEEL—Such is the name of a weekly bicycle newspaper published at 23 Park Row, New York City, box 444, by F. P. Prial, for the very low price of $1 per year. Every edition is full of interesting contributions from the best of writers describing journeys a-wheel in our own and foreign lands, and on all other subjects pertaining to the bicycle. Also the advertising columns obtain advertisements of manufacturers of and dealers in bicycles, tricycles, safeties and all that belong to them, and also of those who deal in second-hand and shop-worn bargains. To the beginner or learner of cycling, THE WHEEL is a great help. Bicycle exercise is healthful and respectable. The most respectable ladies and gentlemen in the United States ride bicycles, and Mrs. Grover Cleveland heads the list of recent converts in New York City. Our plains country is much better for the sport than the hilly and rocky states and the time will come when they will be in general use here. Meantime send Mr. Prial a dollar for THE WHEEL and post yourself on the subject.—*Crosby County News,* Estacado, Texas.

AT the Hagerstown Meet, two important questions will be discussed by the Chief Consuls of the League, who have been called to attend a special meeting for the purpose. The first is on the question of State official organs. The second on the question of League uniforms.

The first question has been raised by the *Bicycling World* Company, who claim that, under the publishing contract they hold with the League, all official League matter is to be published exclusively in their paper. The *B. W.* Company have never objected to State official organs until THE WHEEL was appointed the New York State official organ L. A. W., by Chief Consul Bull, although Pennsylvania, Illinois, Minnesota, Wisconsin and other States have had official

organs for some time. Let it be noted in passing that none of these organs were influential or important enough to threaten the *Bicycling World's* alleged supremacy. At this meeting of Chief Consuls, we hope that some of the following points will be borne in mind before the question is decided. And in making them, let it be thoroughly understood that we write without prejudice, for we consider that, in the case of THE WHEEL, the advantage is all on the League's side, that the official news crowds out more general matter and that we will cheerfully give up our organship at any time. The point on which the Chief Consuls must decide is whether the League is benefited by State official organs or not. It is obvious that the *Bicycling World* is of no use as a proselytizing medium, while non-League members who read State organs cannot help having their attention called to the official notices published in them. The Chief Consul of a State can do more good work through a State organ, first, because he has more space than the *Bicycling World* can afford to place at his disposal, and second, because League news has a larger circulation among local non-League men, who are the people to whom he wishes to address himself. The only argument that can be advanced against the appointment of State organs, is that the *Bicycling World* has a contract with the League and that the publication of League news in State organs weakens its influence with the trade, and this is simply a question as to whether the growth and development of the League is to be sacrificed to the business interests of the *Bicycling World* Company. We are simply trying to discuss the merits of the case, without wishing to make any issue between ourselves and the *Bicycling World* Company, since we don't concede that there is any rivalry or any confliction of interests between the two papers.

The other question to be discussed by the Chief Consuls is whether the League should, after the present fashion, have one style of official uniform for the entire *United States* League memberships, or whether each State should adopt its own style, make and price. This question has been raised by the Chief Consul of Massachusetts, whose attempt to appoint an official tailor for Massachusetts was very properly frustrated by the Uniform Committee, which action caused the Massachusetts Division to adopt a resolution, in substance directing a committee to confer with the Uniform Committee with a view to having its action reconsidered, and in the event of a failure, to make provisions for a new Massachusetts uniform for members of the Massachusetts Division. In discussing this question the Chief Consuls should keep in mind the many excellent points made in the preamble of the resolution adopted by the Massachusetts State Board. In this preamble it appears that the Massachusetts Division members can obtain the League uniforms much cheaper through a Massachusetts tailoring concern than through the League's official tailor ; that they can not only save money but that the League may make a profit on the cloth sold ; and finally that more wheelmen will wear the uniform if made in Boston than if made in New York. The arguments made in this preamble may be applied to any State in the Union ; that is, if there are League tailors in each State, more uniforms will be worn than at present ; they can be procured more quickly and perhaps cheaper, as the cost of production, including rent and labor, is smaller in some places than in others. These facts being well established, it comes within hailing distance of authorized robbery to compel a man to buy goods at one place

when he can get them cheaper elsewhere. If the Chief Consuls decide on branch League tailoring establishments, all the States will doubtless use the League uniform as adopted by the National Committee. If they decide to leave the matter as it stands at present, many States will adopt their own uniforms and unity and community of interests are lost, and these are the vital elements of League development.

THE American tourists spent a week in Ireland—May 26 to June 2—riding 192 miles. All honor to "Jack" White, of Youghal, who stuck to the party all through the Emerald Isle and simply exhausted himself in attention and courtesy. From Youghal, where the cornerstone of Ireland's greatness was laid, the first potato having been planted there, the party rode to Mount Melleray, where the monks of the monastery prepared such a dinner as never was. At Dungarvan a prince of good fellows was met in H. E. Brennan. At Waterford a great reception was held, the mayor of the city presiding. The tourists stopped at Enniscorthy, Rathdrum and at Dublin, at which latter place two hundred wheelmen received them. At Dublin Mr. and Mrs. R. J. Mecredy, the former editor of the *Irish Cycling and Athletic News,* entertained the tourists at their home, and a public dinner was given at the Shelbourne. The "poor, distressed country" has done herself proud. Her cyclists exhausted all the resources of heart-whole hospitality, and have given us a notable lesson in international courtesy. "Ours is a poor country," they said, "but we are rich in gratitude to the nation which has given us substantial aid in time of need." There was enough golden-tongued ability among the tourists to assure the Irishmen of their sincere appreciation of the kindnesses showered upon them ; but a tribute to this country was embodied in the general welcome, and we want to assure our Irish friends that many American cyclists will, in spirit, re-echo the feelings of the Elwell party.

NEW YORK Wheelmen will permit us to call attention to the fact, that while they seldom have an opportunity to attend race meets in New York, they do not properly support the meets given by Brooklyn Clubs. The Long Island and Kings County Wheelmen's meets now draw a corporal's guard from Gotham, yet the grounds at which they are held are less than half an hour from the New York end of the Bridge. Let us have a big turnout for the K. C. W. meet, which will be held at Washington Park, next Friday and Saturday.

FREE TRANSPORTATION OF WHEELS.

The Philadelphia and Reading Railroad Company has issued a circular to station agents and train baggage masters, bearing date of June 10, as follows :

"Bicycles, velocipedes and tricycles will hereafter be checked and carried free of charge, at owner's risk, to points on lines of this Company, Atlantic City R. R., Central Railroad of N. J. and Lehigh Valley R. R., and passengers must be notified.

"When Philadelphia transfer is necessary, 25 cents will be charged for each transfer, otherwise wheels to be checked to Philadelphia only.

"Release forms should be taken in each instance, and if not given regular rate for 100 lbs. excess baggage will be charged for each.

"Circulars and local baggage excess tariff of former dates are hereby amended accordingly.

"H. W. SQUIERS,
"General Baggage Agent."

"C. G. HANCOCK,
"General Pass. Agent."

WHEEL GOSSIP.

The length of the Washington Bridge is 2,380 feet.

Entries for King's County Wheelmen's race meet close to-day.

The Cambridgeport Club will have a tally-ho coach ride on July 4.

Sixth Avenue, Brooklyn, at one time one of the worst paved streets in the city, is now nicely laid with asphalt.

The annual Meet of the Massachusetts Division, L.A.W., at Cottage City, will probably be held August 8, 9 and 10.

The Lancaster Bicycle Club need the services of a fancy rider for July 4. Address President D. F. Grove, Lancaster, Pa.

The wheeling clubs of Taunton, Fall River, North Easton and Whitman will make a union run to Nantasket, on July 23.

The Racing Board of the Rhode Island Division L. A. W. has decided to hold the annual 25-mile race in September instead of in June, as in past years.

WARWICK AND NATIONAL SAFETIES READY FOR DELIVERY.

Messrs. William Halpin & Co advise us that they are now ready to fill all orders for Warwick and National safeties.

Several members of the Pennsylvania Bicycle Club will make a tour on their bicycles to Boston and the Eastern riding district this Summer, spending a fortnight on the trip.

Dr. A. C. Griffin, of New York, writes us saying that he was one of those finishing in the Century run to Philadelphia, but failing to attend the dinner at the Continental did not get counted.

We shall publish in the next issue of The Wheel an article on training, from the pen of George Hendee. George is clever with his pen, and has put down a number of valuable ideas.

At Inter-academic A. A.'s Spring Sports at University Grounds, Philadelphia, June 3: One-mile bicycle race, E. Rodgers, R., first, in 3m. 18 2-5s.; E. Woolman, C., second; R. Elliot, G. A., third.

The Wheel simply slithers the *Cyclist* correspondent who lately had his little say on the Bown patents as affecting American trade, and the article is one of Mr. Prial's best efforts.—*Wheeling.*

Mont. Scott of Providence, has accepted the challenge of Wm. Van Wagoner of Newport, to ride a fifty-mile race for a $50 medal. The Roger Williams Park track is selected, and the 4th of July is the date.

The Warsaw, N. Y., Bicycle Club has elected the following officers: President, C. E. Ketchum; Vice-President, F. A. Owen; Captain, B. P. Gage; First Lieutenant, W. E. Miller; Secretary and Treasurer, E. J. Abner.

MASSACHUSETTS' SPRING MEET POSTPONED.

The spring Meet of the Massachusetts League of American Wheelmen, which was to have taken place at Squantum, June 17, was postponed on account of the rain.

Elie Millett, of Holbrook, Mass., was severely injured while riding a bicycle June 13, by collision with a Randolph coach driven by J. E. Blanche. The machine was demolished and young Millett seriously injured about the legs and back.

A Brooklyn correspondent inquires if something cannot be done to reduce the charge the Long Island R. R. makes for carrying wheels. We would reply that Consul Geo. Teller has the matter now in hand and hopes to be able to secure some concessions from the company.

A 1½-mile bicycle handicap will be decided at the Y. M. C. A. games, to be held this Saturday afternoon, on the club grounds, 150th Street and Harlem River, at 3.30 P. M. Harry Powers is at scratch, with Hanson, 20 yards, Parker, 35 yards, and several runners, 50 yards.

It looks as though the Washington, Pa., races, to be held in the latter part of this month, would be exceedingly interesting, as quite a number of Pittsburg wheelmen will be entered. Gloninger, Davis, W. D. Banker, George Banker, L. E. Shoup and quite a number of others have signified their intention of entering.

The second annual bicycle tournament of the Fort Dayton wheelmen will be held at the Driving Park in Herkimer, N. Y., on July 4. Prizes to the value of $300 are offered, and the best half-mile track in New York State is claimed by the Fort Daytons. Entries should be made with C. F. Giesey, Secretary.

The Springfield Rovers have organized with Wilbur N. Winans as Secretary and Treasurer. The club has a charter membership of ten and will be a strictly cycling club. F. A. Nickerson is the promoter of the organization and other members are A. C. Patterson, W. N. Winans, City Treasurer Tifft and F. A. Eldred.

During a twenty-three days' trip to the Yosemite Valley and the big trees, Messrs. Richard J. Mier and William S. Moore, of San Francisco, encountered very severe weather, and at one point near the summit at Wawona they were obliged to trundle their wheels up the grade through seven miles of snow averaging two feet in depth, and in the face of a heavy snowstorm.

Miss Fredericka Cooke, sister of Vice-Consul George L. Cooke, is one of the most industrious of the ladies who bicycle in Rhode Island. On her safety, accompanied by the Vice-Consul, she recently rode the long way round from Providence to Taunton, 27¾ miles, covering the distance in four hours, including all stops. That evening she rode 13 miles more on the club run.

CENTURY RUN CORRECTIONS.

In addition to the list of men published in last week's Wheel the following men finished the run: Dr. A. C. Griffin, N. Y.; W. F. Pendleton, N. Y. B. C.; C. F. Johnson, N. Y.; W. H. Putney, M. B. C., and J. Post, Jr., M. B. C. Our special correspondent failed to meet the men, hence these corrections.

Messrs. Jo Weakley and Thornwell Shipp, of Nashville, Tenn., left June 8 for New York. There they took steamer for Liverpool. On arriving in the latter place they will each purchase an English safety and tour through England, Ireland and Scotland; then to France and the Paris Exposition, through Germany and along the Rhine. They will return to Nashville in September.

Toil and be strong.
By toil the flaccid nerves grow firm
And gain a more compacted tone.
Go climb the mountain:
From the ethereal source imbibe the recent gale.
The cheerful morn beams o'er the hills.
Go mount the exulting steed.

—*John Armstrong.*

Tom Roe, of Chicago; H. L. Kingsland, of Baltimore, and Percy Harris, formerly of New York, and now of Bridgeport, flocked into the sanctum on Saturday last. Roe is no longer with the Western Arms and Cartridge Company, but may resume the bicycle business at another stand if proper arrangements can be made. Kingsland is now with the Clark Cycle Company, in Baltimore. He will train on the Arlington track for the Hagerstown races.

At the Massachusetts Board meet, held June 8, a committee was created to confer with the Uniform Committee to arrange for securing League uniforms through a Massachusetts tailor, or, failing in that, to report plans for adopting a State Division uniform. That we were right in stating that Chief Consul Emery was mistaken in denying the existence of a Uniform Committee is now proven by the fact that the Massachusetts Board recognizes such a committee.

The big dailies are doing splendid work for the cause of good pavements in New York when they oppose the constant tearing up of the pavements which is now the custom. It is of no use to put down new pavements if they are to be constantly torn up by corporations. Last year $1,105,675 was spent by the Commissioners of Public Works. Over 350 permits were issued for re-opening streets and 13,334 square yards of pavement were disturbed, much of which was not properly replaced.

There never were so many mishaps on any run as in the century run from New York to Philadelphia on June 8. Few wheelmen escaped without headers, and many machines received hard usage. Omaha seems to have had the same experience in a 100-mile run. Seventeen men started and but four finished. It was the toughest run ever taken out of Omaha. The exact distance was 118 miles, 70 miles over hills and part of the last 23 miles was covered in the rain. This is overdoing things.

THE OWNER IN LUCK.

A man whose appearance created considerable suspicion in the mind of the police was seen traveling up Niagara Street Saturday evening, having in tow a bicycle. Superintendent Cusack and Detective Kilroy arrested the individual and took him to Station 10. It was learned later that the bicycle was the property of C. H. Smith, of 15 Fargo Avenue, and had been stolen from in front of Hudson's clothing store on Main Street. The prisoner gave his name as Thomas Danton.—*Buffalo Sunday Times.*

Mr. W. F. Bartlett, formerly of Bartlett and MacDonald, and late associated with John Wood in the Harlem Bicycle Company, died last Sunday, after a lingering illness. Mr. Bartlett was quite old and has been ailing a long time. While in business with MacDonald, he failed, owing to the peculation of his partner, but he settled on the most honorable basis possible. Mr. John Wood has bought out Mr. Bartlett's interest and will continue the business of the Harlem Bicycle Company, as sole proprietor. This same MacDonald is still about town. He is oily, insinuating and dishonest, and cyclists who may run across him will profit by letting him severely alone.

Sports Afield, the bright paper published at Denver, Colorado, has a speaking likeness in a recent number of Robert Gerwing, the Denver Rambler's best man, and appends a short summary of his cycling life. In the recent road race between the Denver Ramblers and the Social Wheel Club for a challenge cup, Robert Gerwing easily took first place, and was never headed. Previous to this race, his own time of 2h. 18m., over a road none too smooth, and a distance of 33⅓ miles, had stood as record. The cup must be won twice out of three times for a club to retain it permanently, and *Sports Afield* remarks prophetically that the second race, to be held in June, 1890, will be witnessed by at least 2,000 people.

RUMORED ARREST OF DE CIVRY, THE FRENCH PROFESSIONAL.

The Paris correspondent of *Bicycling News* writes as follows: "I learn on reliable authority that De Civry was arrested on Saturday, 25th ult., outside the Rudge depot, and given into custody by Mr. George Woodcock, the cash accounts having been tampered with. De Civry has been brought before the Juge d'Instruction for examination, and has now been transferred to the Paris prison Mazas, awaiting his trial. This terrible downfall is understood to be the result of gambling at the tables at Monaco last winter, poker at the Grand Café, Paris, as well as a deal of money lost at baccarat in one of the betting clubs of the capital. I will send a full report of the trial."

THE MONMOUTH COUNTY BOULEVARD.

Present indications point to an appeal from the act passed ordering the proposed Boulevard in Monmouth County, N. J., in order to leave no doubts of its legality. As matters at present stand, the construction of the road would be in the hands of the Board of Chosen Freeholders; but a bill will most likely be introduced at the Legislature next session giving control to the present Park Commissioners. A million dollars seems a large amount to be allotted for road building, but when the purchases of land and buildings standing in the way are taken into account, that sum even may not suffice. For that very reason control of the expenditure should be vested in the hands of those best qualified.

A FRENCH ACTRESS ON AMERICAN ROADS.

Mme. Jane Hading, the French actress, sends two columns of "views" to the *New York World*. Like all visitors to this country, Jane Hading objects to our dirt and disease-breeding pavements: "I don't like the street pavements, however, nor the telegraph poles. The Americans are very peculiar in some things. They have everything—churches, schools, libraries, museums, theatres, gas, water, electricity, telephones, railways, and any amount of money for each and all of these—and yet they seem to have no spare cash for decent roads and streets. It is inconceivable that a public spirit so active and energetic should stop at the highways. They seem to be utterly indifferent as to the condition of the city streets."

To those of our New Jersey readers with children to send to school, especially those blessed with daughters, we would recommend the Home School at Plainfield, advertised in another column. The ladies in charge of this school have had years of successful experience in the art of teaching, and particularly so with girls and young ladies. To New Jersey people familiar with Plainfield it is unnecessary to say anything in praise of its beauty. To those unfamiliar, we would recommend it as a city possessing rare natural advantages, largely made up of residences, and with all city comforts and conveniences. The climate is very healthful, and the inhabitants never molested by that bird of prey, the New Jersey mosquito. Can aught more be said in regard to its superiority?

A gentleman with a sympathetic heart writes: "A little Johnstown eight year old cries about losing his bicycle and fears he may never be able to get another. Will enough wheelmen who read this give dimes or other amounts to make the boy a happy owner of a new bicycle." We are not in sympathy with the scheme. While we are aware that children's troubles, whether real or imaginary, cause them acute pain, we think the parents of this eight-year-old have a splendid opportunity to point out a simple little lesson of thanksgiving which even the brain of an eight-year old could comprehend. We see no reason why thirty dollars should be spent to make this discontented child happy, when the same amount, invested in bread, would feed five hundred starvelings for a day.

At the annual meeting of the Meriden Wheel Club, last Wednesday, Frank F. Ives was elected an active member of the club, having been reinstated as an amateur. He was at once elected representative of the Meriden Club to the meeting of the League of American Wheelmen, to occur in Hagerstown, Md. The boys were very enthusiastic over the subject of having a new bicycle track at the fair grounds, and the president was empowered to appoint a committee to pursue the matter, and, if the proper arrangements can be made, to solicit subscriptions. The officers-elect are as follows: President, W. Collins; secretary, E. A. Hall; treasurer, J. E. Brainard; captain, F. F. Ives; first lieutenant, F. T. Grant; second lieutenant, E. W. Hall; color bearer, H. J. Rolfe; bugler, W. H. Carter; executive committee, President Collins, Secretary Hall, Treasurer Brainard, Captain Ives, Dr. T. S. Rust, L. A. Miller, F. A. Stevens.

BICYCLE RACES AT HUNTINGTON, L. I., JUNE 19.

The events run off were four in number, and in the following order: Half-mile dash, won by F. G. Brown, N. J. A. C., in 1m. 34s.; Wm. Murphy, K. C. W., second. Brown also took the 1-mile handicap which followed with six starters, in 3m. 8⅘s.; Chas. Murphy, second, and Wm. Murphy, third. In the 2-mile handicap, Wm. Murphy moved forward two places, and captured first prize, in 6m. 4/5s.; F. R. Miller being second. The 1-mile open, was won by F. G. Brown, who would appear to have had a "picnic," in 3m. 20s., with Wm. Murphy a close second. The following gentlemen officiated: E. R. Aitken, H. B. C., Thos. Lloyd, Queens A. A. C., and C. B. Scudder, H. B. C., judges; A. C. Ebbetts, H. B. C., clerk of course; H. P. Rogers, H. B. C., starter; E. C. Gruman and C. P. Rogers, H. B. C., scorers.

It is whispered that several clubs in New Jersey have organized a Road Racing Association, that they may hold a road race this fall and will surely hold one next spring. From a Jersey City cyclist we learned that a man in Freehold, N. J., is President of the Association, that it is to run a nice quiet road race and that everything is to be kept dark. All this secrecy seems extremely absurd. The principal glory of racing is a wide publication of results. If Mrs. Pigsticker has a million dollar diamond, her greatest pleasure is in showing it to Mrs. Porkpacker, Mrs. Oilwell and the rest of her set. What good does it do Johnny Scratchman to ride a mile in 2m. 30s. on a dark night? It is only when he downs the other fellow in the broad daylight, to the applause of the multitude, that he gets any return for his work. We are all more or less working for this applause, this appreciation by our fellows. One man secures it by muscle, another by money and still another by brains. A road race conceived in the shade and run off in the dark is not a paying investment.

HOW IT STRIKES THEM.

We have come across the waters,
Paddyland, Paddyland!
To inspect your sons and daughters,
Paddyland!
To admire your lovely scen'ry,
Paddyland, Paddyland!
Your mountains and your green'ry,
Paddyland!
But your Clerk of Irish Weather,
Paddyland, Paddyland!
Does not please us altogether,
Paddyland!
Yes, the circumstance is paining,
Little pleasure are we gaining,
For *incessantly 'tis raining*,
Paddyland!

Poet Laureate in *Bicycling News*.

A NOTEWORTHY CENTURY.

On Sunday the 16th, W. S. Doane, of Dorchester, started out about five o'clock A. M., and not having any special place to go, rode toward Providence, about forty-five miles from Dorchester, over some of the worst roads in Massachusetts. He arrived there at 9:05, having been obliged to walk two miles through deep sand, and rode a mile through the grass on the road-side. He rested about an hour and a half, and started on the return trip, taking dinner at Foxboro, and arriving home at 4:10 P. M., with ninety-four miles to his credit. He then went over to Franklin Park and finished the hundred miles in the presence of twenty-five or thirty wheelmen. After resting a short time, he rode home by a roundabout way, seven miles, arriving there at 6:20 P. M., making 107 miles in the total time of thirteen hours and twenty minutes, his actual riding time being 8h. 55s. Doane road a "57" gear Royal Singer Safety, weighing 40 lb., and he reports that the machine stood the run in magnificent shape, nothing breaking but one spoke. The weather was very warm and he was badly burned about the head and neck. As Doane was leaving Providence, he again climbed College Hill. He has often taken a century run on his ordinary, and claims to have felt better at the end of this ride than ever before.

THE AMERICAN TOURISTS.

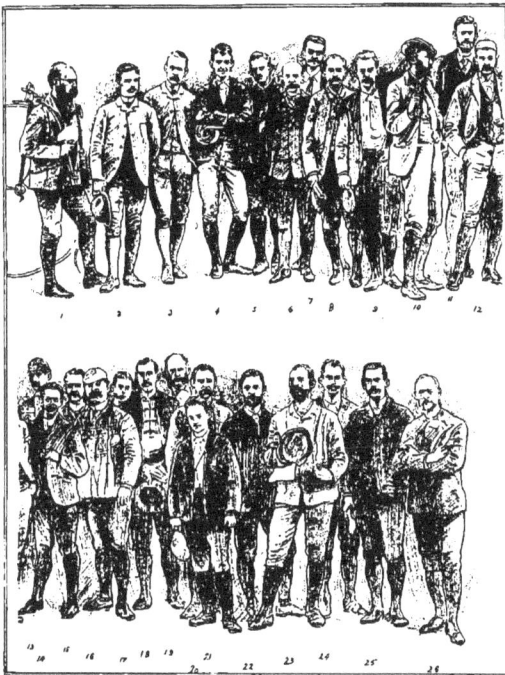

1, W. C. Rosebroom, Cherry Valley, N. Y.; 2, S. L. Breed, Lynn, Mass.; 3, S. H. Phillips, Portland, Me.; 4, T. C. Brimsmade, Cleveland, O.; 5, W. H. Bennett, Chicago, Ill.; 6, W. J Penrose Newark, N. J.; 7, A. J. Wilson (special representative of *Bicycling News*); 8, A. C. Buttolf, Chicago, Ill.; 9, H. Wentworth, Skowhegan, Me.; 10, J. Pennell, Philadelphia, Pa.; 11, A. McAlpine, Bradford, Pa; 12, J. White, Dublin, Ireland; 13, A. G. Collins, Boston,

Mass.; 14, F. A. Elwell, Portland, Me.; 15, R. B. White, Quincy, Ill.; 16, P. H. Reilly, Hartford, Conn.; 17, Clark Cooper, Trenton, N. J.; 18, H. R. Wilson, Clarion, Pa.; 19, W. W. Eastabrook, Elmira, N. Y.; 20, D. W. Levy, Quincy, Ill.; 21, W. H. Kirk, Philadelphia, Pa.; 22, Chas. Seavey, Portland, Me.; 23, J. E. Beal, Ann Arbor, Mich.; 24, F. H. Palmer, Portland, Me.; 25, H. S. Higgins, Portland, Me.; 26, J. Newton Smith, Philadelphia, Pa.

ELWELL'S EUROPEAN TOURISTS.

To the Editor of the Wheel :

Our journey in Ireland, to everyone's regret, is now a thing of the past. We are to-day (Sunday) very comfortably quartered at the Wicklow Hotel, Dublin, ready to leave Kingston to-morrow for Holyhead, England. Some of our members are a little "knocked out," but one and all have had a week of rare sport and have nothing but enthusiastic praise and warm gratitude for the Irish wheelmen and the nation generally. We have had everything, barring the weather, our own way, and our visit to the land of hospitality, potatoes, evictions and brogue will be remembered for months to come, be what there may in store for us. We expected a quiet trip through the country, with perhaps a little guidance and attention from cyclists; we found instead the most lavish hospitality, the heartiest of welcomes and the greatest excitement everywhere. We have been heralded, welcomed, cheered, banqueted and feted until

we all feel like Jim Blaines just before election, or a baseball team touring around the world. There could not have be more enthusiasm and excitement had we all been Presidents of the United States come over to see about "annexing" the nation. We have ridden nearly the entire distance from Cork to Dublin between lines of cheering and excited natives, who yelled themselves hoarse with "Welcome to Ireland," and "Three cheers for the Yankee byes." Americans are very apt to look down on the Irish, to think they are an ignorant, slothful and unprincipled people, but could they see them as we have seen them and meet them as we have met them they would know why it is that an Irishman clings to his brogue and boasts of the fact that he was born on the "ould sod." There is not, I am sure, a more generous, free-hearted, open-handed race on the earth than the Irish.

Perhaps the one man to whom more thanks are due than any other for the success of our trip so far, is "Jack" White, of Dublin, Chief Consul of the C. T. C., for Ireland. He met us when we left the ship and has been with us eversince. He has figured, telegraphed, written, palavered and worked incessantly and untiringly for us. "Jack" was telling the other day

how he and a number of other Irish boys were awaiting our arrival in Queenstown. The vessel was expected Sunday, but did not arrive until Monday noon. Sunday night they sat up nearly all night, feeling nervous and anxious. "And oh," says Jack, in his excitable hurried manner, "if I had died that night you would have found 'Cephalonia' written on me heart." And I verily believe we would. On the tug which took us off when we finally did arrive were Day, Hanrahan and Hallinan (President, Secretary and Treasurer of the Munster Safety Club, of Cork), Jack White(Secretary of the Irish Cyclists' Association) Colie O'Connell, C. L. Jamison and other big cyclists who have accompanied us the entire distance to Dublin. At Cork the American party was increased by two very valuable additions. Mr. Jo. Pennell, of the *Century* magazine, whose pictures (cycling and otherwise) have made his name familiar to every wheelman in America, has become a member. Mr. Pennell has ridden all over England and the Continent, and is to have charge of the party while we are in France. The other member is A. J. Wilson, of London, who, under the pseudonym of "Faed," is familiar to every cyclist who reads *Wheeling* and *Bicycling News*, or, indeed, any journal devoted to the sport. He is considered one of the best, if not the very best, road rider in the United Kingdom and is a very fast man on the track. We have also been accompanied by Brennan, of Dungarvan, A. B. Allport, of Cork, a "scorcher." W. Tyner, and Macredy, editor of the *Irish Cyclist*. Thus made up we have come from Cork to Dublin under one solitary difficulty—the weather.

As we were eating our last lunch aboard the Cephalonia, word was brought down that the tug from Queenstown was alongside and we scrambled up the stairway at a lively pace. About a hundred feet away was a small tug and in her bow dancing up and down with excitement were half a dozen Irish lads. They were acting in a manner to justify the adjective "wild," as frequently applied to them. They shouted and yelled and waved their caps frantically calling for "Reilly!" and "Elwell! Which is Elwell? Hold him up!" I can't begin to tell how glad we were to get ashore once more and to meet with such a jolly crowd of fellows. Our vessel being one day late we were obliged to skip our visit to Cork and merely stopped to get our wheels of Allport the bicycle agent. It was a great day for Mr. A. and the crowds flooded his store and obstructed the sidewalk, as we pulled our Quadrants out and looked them over. The Quadrant is not at all a handsome machine, but it is a great one on the road. The front wheel is 26 inches, and the driver 30 inches. Over the front wheel is a luggage carrier, substantial and roomy enough to carry, it is claimed, seventy-five lbs. of baggage. However this may be, we find twenty-five lbs. all we care to push up these Irish hills, many of which are over a mile in length.

We boarded the train and reached Youghal in time for a good six o'clock dinner from the wheelmen of that ancient town. Our Cork friends were bitterly disappointed at this, but it was not a matter of choice, for we were obliged to catch up with scheduled time cost what it might. So great was their desire that we should taste their hospitality that they even whispered amongst themselves as to the advisability of purloining each and every saddle from our machines and hiding them, but when they realized that it was an absolute necessity for us to "move on" they relinquished the scheme.

After a jolly evening in the town where the first potato was planted in Ireland (Youghal), we retired early for a good start in the morning. The day's run was to Dungarvan by the way of Cappoquin and Mt. Melleray, a distance of thirty-eight miles. Oh that ride ! If I live to be a thousand years old I shall never forget that ride ! Ride, did I say? Excuse me—I mean walk. These Irish hills are very gradual in ascent and so picturesquely winding that you cannot see the top. Consequently you start up bravely, thinking forsooth the top is just around yonder bend. That bend reached, surely it must be just around the next Ye gods ! Another up-hill stretch ! And so on until with panting lungs and aching knees you dismount in disgust and push machine and baggage anywhere from a quarter of a mile to a mile and a half. It rained steadily during the night, and looked bad when we left Youghal. A mile out and the gentle dew descended in a quantity

sufficient to hold us up for over an hour—Another mile and we struck our first hill. Why continue the agony? It rained once an hour on an average, and the roads were of the consistency of Le Page's glue. Let the rain which fell hide from your view those twenty-seven tired wheelmen, unacquainted with their wheels, unused to the roads, and just through with a nine days voyage across the Atlantic—each with from ten to thirty pounds of luggage strapped on his machine. We staggered into Cappoquin where we divided into three parties—one to take train for Dungarvan without more ado, one to rush into the hotel and demand of the landlady the best she had, and the last to take a jaunting-car for Mt. Melleray, where the monks in the monastery had prepared a most excellent spread for us. The joys of that dinner will remain a green spot in our memories when the good monks have made their final reckoning. In Dungarvan we were received by no less than a thousand of the inhabitants assembled in the public square, who cheered us and shouted as only honest Irishmen can shout on their native heath. We were in this place the guest of Mr. H. E. Brennan, the "Knight of Dungarvan," around whose well-spread mahogany we recounted the events of the day—the hills, the dales, the miles that we had walked. We toasted the Green and they toasted the Stars and Stripes. Mr. B. was tireless in his efforts on our behalf, and was constantly trotting from room to room to ask "and are ye all right? have ye cigars enough?" We had speeches from Elwell, Brennan and Jack White, and retired delighted with everything but the weather. It has rained constantly since we first set foot in the country, and aside from its taking up much of our time it has put the roads, which otherwise have been far better than those we are accustomed to at home, in a very bad condition.

I am glad to say, however, that after the first day we picked up wonderfully in our riding and manage to do our distances quite handily. On Wednesday we rode to Waterford, a good sized place where we were met by seventy wheelmen who insisted on our parading the city in the ever-present rain, and in the evening tendered us a smoking concert which was an exceptionally enjoyable occasion. They had some magnificent voices among them and we readily fell into the choruses of "Father O'Flynn," "Killaloo," "Soldier Boy," etc. The Mayor of the burg presided and we had the usual exchange of courtesies and compliments. On Thursday we made forty miles to Enniscorthy. More rain, more mud, and more entertainment. The Enniscorthy boys had a "ladies' night" and a spread for us and we made our bow to Erin's daughters, whom we found fully as hospitable and interesting as her sons, and perhaps, a little handsomer. Certainly a true Irish girl is a very attractive creature, with her blue eyes, rètroussè nose, and exceptionally clear complexion. She is not to be chaffed, either, and is fully able to hold her own at repartee. We soon enough discovered the susceptible hearts in our party. Apropos of the ladies we are all charmed at the manner in which Mrs. Macredy rides the wheel. In company with her husband on a tandem she made forty-one miles yesterday in a way which put many of our boys to blush. She was apparently as fresh at the finish as at the start, and I don't think they walked a step. She pedals along at a good gait, with ease and grace which show that she is thoroughly "in touch" with the machine and has caught the knack of it.

Leaving Enniscorthy we rode on Friday to Rathdrum with our rubber capes on all the way, and on arriving, for the first evening since our visit commenced, had nothing to do but go to bed. We all seized the opportunity of making up back arrears of correspondence. Truly the amount expended in postage stamps must have been a great help to the British revenue. Saturday we took our last day's ride on the Emerald Isle, from Rathdrum to Dublin. Had it been pleasant it would have been a most delightful run—through the Seven Churches, the Scalp, the Dargle and a five o'clock tea, tendered us by Mr. and Mrs. Macredy, at their residence, a short distance out of Dublin. We were met at the Scalp by over two hundred Dublin wheel men, and everything they have done for us has been on the same scale. We were escorted to the Wicklow, and in the evening they gave us a dinner at the Shelbourne, at which we sat down at a quarter of eight and arose at a quarter past twelve.

Our riding throughout has been through scenery so fine that it is hard to believe that it can anywhere be surpassed. Ruins of castles and fortresses of great antiquity are to be seen on every hand, and we are very loath to leave a country where there is so much of interest to be seen and so much courtesy extended. At Dungarvan we were in the midst of the eviction district, and, although we saw none going on, we saw the somewhat exciting scene of a jaunting-car containing three or four political men endeavoring to address the people, closely pursued by two more cars of police ready to arrest them the moment they commenced. The politicians were about twenty yards in advance, and all three cars on the dead gallop. At the Waterford smoking concert a young fellow sang "Wearing of the Green" with a great deal of feeling, and on inquiring about him his fellow-townsmen informed us that his brother had recently been put in jail for life as a political offender.

We also discovered, much to our amazement, flaring posters in many of the towns announcing the arrival of a party of American bicyclists and calling on all cyclists to extend the right hand of fellowship. It ended by saying: "Ours is a poor country, but we are rich in gratitude to the nation that has given such substantial aid in our time of need," and to what extent we found them so it is needless for me to tell. We have had constant kindness and attention from beginning to end.

Our Irish friends ride the wheels like fiends, and we felt all the worse at our poor showing on account of the fact that they expected to find in us a team of regular racing men. They labored under the impression that we were an organized team of "scorchers," whereas in reality we have amongst us several men who had not been on a wheel for three or four years and quite a number who had never been on any style of safety machine whatever. Settled weather and dry roads are all that is necessary, however, and we anticipate no trouble in England. Kirk, of Philadelphia, Collins, of Boston, Cooper, Coke and many others are already riding splendidly.

Our route for next week is from Chester to Oxford via Birmingham, Warwick, Kenilworth and Stratford-on-Avon—a most interesting week. TAM O'SHANTER.

THE EUROPEAN TOURISTS.

(From our Special Correspondent.)

It was a dismal prospect that greeted the tourists upon awaking this Saturday morning, vast sheets of rain descending pitilessly, propelled obliquely by a strong gale of wind. Would-be early risers therefore, were fain to turn over in bed for another nap; and when breakfast was over the rainy outlook impelled nearly half the party to decide upon taking the train to Dublin. About 9 o'clock, however, there was but a drizzle, and the hardy ones forthwith sallied out and tackled the muddy roads. Luckily the wind was again favorable, and the nine miles up and down hill to Glendalough were covered in fair time, waterproofs being, however, in continual requisition owing to the frequent showers. Wheels were stabled at the hotel, and a couple of hours spent in a stroll through the Glen, inspecting the "seven churches" and round tower, admiring the cascades, and gazing with delight upon the grandeur of the lakes and surrounding mountains. Cycles being remounted, a lot of up-hill work ensued to Roundwood, where the second "snack" of the morning was enjoyed, and whence more hills were tackled until the summit of the plateau was reached, whereupon a series of magnificent "coasts" down capital roads, winding around the mountain sides, with grand scenery all around, brought the riders to "Pluck's," at which inn a gentleman from Dublin had provided tiffin for the party. Here also were a few Dublin cyclists, and from this spot right away to Dublin the tourists' escort was continually augmented by Irish cyclists joining the line, until there must have been some 500 wheelmen in the procession as it entered the Irish capital. At the Scalp, seven or eight miles out, a group photo of the tourists was taken; and at Dundrum a brief stoppage was made to take five o'clock tea at the residence of Mr and Mrs. R J. Mecredy; the city being reached before six o'clock, after a most enjoyable, although damp, day's ride. In the evening a grand banquet was given to the visitors at the Shelbourne Hotel, by a committee of representative Dublin cyclists, the toast-list being as follows: "The Queen," proposed by the chairman, C. J. Thompson, Esq., and drunk with musical honors, Irish and Americans joining heartily in "God Save the Queen;" "The President of the United States," responded to very eloquently by Mr. J. E. Beal, of Ann Arbor, Mich.; "Our Visitors," proposed by Mr. C. Z. Jameson, of Dublin, and responded to by Mr. Elwell; "Cycling in Ireland," by Mr. P. Harvard Reilly, of Hartford, Conn., and acknowledged by Messrs. W. Tyner and H. A. Quinton; "The Cycling Press," from the chair, responded to by F. Percy Low, of *Wheeling*, A. J. Wilson, representing *The Cyclist and Bicycling News*, and representatives of the Dublin press; "The Chairman," was toasted by Mr J. Baynham, and in replying Mr. Thompson appropriately suggested an extra toast, that of Jack White, the Dublin Chief Consul of the C T. C., who had won all hearts by his thorough-going endeavors to further the success of the tour; the toast was drunk with musical honors, cheers and a "tiger," and White modestly replied. "Auld Lang Syne," sung by the entire company in traditional fashion, brought the proceedings to a happy conclusion on the stroke of midnight.

The tourists are all well. Two or three have been a little "queer," and some who are accustomed to early hours have been complaining of want of sleep, but the two days rest in Dublin will doubtless set them up ready for the conquest of England. There have been no accidents whatever. All the bicycles go well, and seem in perfect order.

Dublin, Ireland, June 1, 1889. "FARD."

(From our Special Correspondent.)

CHESTER, ENGLAND.

The sights of Dublin monopolized the whole of Sunday and Monday, Phœnix Park being particularly admired; and on Monday parties of the tourists were conducted over the various places of interest, including the Bank of Ireland, Guinness's brewery, the Castle the Museum, the Masonic Hall, etc. At 7 P. M. the steamer was boarded for Liverpool, a very rough passage being experienced, no less than fifteen of the tourists being seasick. Liverpool was reached at 8:30 A. M. on Tuesday, and after ferrying across the Mersey an easy ride was effected to Chester, the weather being delightfully sunny and mild; and the remainder of the day was spent in visiting the objects of interest in and around this fine old town.

A wagonette was chartered in which the majority drove while a few cycled to Hawarden Castle, the seat of the Rt. Hon. W. E. Gladstone, M.P., and thence to Eaton Hall, the seat of the Duke of Westminster—the richest man in England—a thorough inspection of the interior making the tourists feel a trifle envious. Boating on the river Dee occupied the evening, and the following day's ride to Nantwich and Stafford was accomplished without accident, in charming weather.

From Chester to Stafford there was very little in the way of scenery or sight seeing, the chief feature of the day being the exquisite state of the weather and the abominable paving of the small towns—Tarporley and Nantwich—en route, giving us a foretaste of the sort of "*pavé*" we may expect in France. Stafford was reached early, and here we found ourselves lodged at one of the snuggest hotels yet met with, the people being most agreeable. From Stafford on Thursday, another splendid run took us to Litchfield, where an hour was spent at the Cathedral, which is a most marvellously beautiful and impressive pile. After lunching, wheels were remounted in company with some wheelmen of Birmingham, who piloted the tourists to Sutton-in-Coldfield, where a large number of Birmingham cyclists joined the ranks, and escorted the visitors to Aston Hall, whose curious antiquities were especially shown. Thence into Birmingham it was a tortuous ride along busy streets effected without accident, and at the Colonnade Hotel the Birchfield Wheeling Club entertained us at collation, at which over a hundred local riders were present, and their president made sundry post-prandial speeches, presenting Mr. Elwell with a handsomely illuminated address of welcome. Free seats were offered the tourists at the Theatre Royal, and a few of the livelier men visited the Music Hall, several carriages conveyed others out to the select suburbs of Birmingham, and many of the tourists were taken to inspect a monster bicycle, having a driving-wheel 96 inches in diameter, upon which Albin used to give trick-riding performances.

Friday morning dawned fine, and over a magnificent road fast time was made to Stonebridge, where a number of Coventry cyclists were met. The majority of the tourists went to Coventry, inspecting Singer's and Rudge's factories, a few going direct to Kenilworth Castle, where the whole party met later on. The fine old ruins having been explored to hearts' content, wheels were mounted for Warwick, whose castle afforded more food for interest. Thence the final run was made to Stratford-on-Avon, over a superbly smooth road. "FARD."

June 8, 1889.

ELWELL'S PARTY DINED BY THE STANLEY CLUB.

The Stanley Cycling Club gave a dinner to the visiting American cyclists at the Inn's Court Hotel last evening, which was attended by nearly all the visiting wheelmen as well as by about sixty other advocates of rotary locomotion.

Toasts were drunk, speeches were made and songs were sung without number, and indeed everybody spent a most enjoyable evening and laid plans for the cycling excursion to Ripley to-morrow, when the American guests will be entertained by the Ripley Club.—*European Edition N. Y. Herald, June 15.*

CYCLISTS' MAPS.

Among the many things to be enumerated under the head of "long-felt wants," maps of any state in the U. S. (outside of those in the few road books), of convenient size and reasonable price, take a leading position. They do these things better in England. Philips' Cyclists' Maps of Counties of England, showing the main roads distinctly colored, marking dangerous grades and hills, giving locations of repair shops and residences of C. T. C. Consuls, are invaluable to touring wheelmen in that country. They cost but one shilling each are easily carried and inspected, and are *forty-three* in number, speaking of counties only. Wales has two to itself, and the Isles of Wight and Man one each. Supplementary maps of Lancashire, Yorkshire, and the country round about London are also to be had at slightly larger prices. Inside the cover of each map is a list of recommended hotels for guidance of the wayfarer. Any map publishers in this country that are enterprising enough to follow this lead and sell at low prices, will, we are sure, reap a bonanza from the venture.

FIXTURES.

June 21, 1889.—House-warming of the Brooklyn Bicycle Club. Tenth anniversary.
June 22, 1889.—New Orleans Bicycle Club's Race for the Hill Cup.
June 28, 29, 1889.—Kings County Wheelmen's Annual Meet at Washington Park, Brooklyn. Entries close June 21. Address Wm. F. Murphy, 1,255 Bedford Avenue.
June 29, 1889.—Handicap Road Race of Milwaukee Wheelmen, over Wauwatosa course. Entries close June 24.
June 29, 1889.—One Mile Bicycle Handicap at Field Meeting of Pittsburgh Cricket Club, Brushton Station. Entries close June 26, with A. MacPherson, 61 Fourth Avenue, Pittsburgh, Pa.
June 30, 1889.—Massachusetts Union Run to Massapoag House, Sharon. Address Capt A. W. Robinson, 33 Winter Street, Boston.
July 1, 2, 1889.—C. W. A. Annual Meet at St. Catharines, Ontario.
July 2, 3, 4, 1889.—League Meet at Hagerstown, Md.
July 3 and 4, 1889.—Missouri Division L. A. W. Meet at Sedalia, Mo. Races on second day. Entries for handicaps close June 25; for open events June 27. Both to be made to Fred E. Hoffman, Sedalia, Mo. No entry fee.
July 4, 1889.—L. A. W. Race Meet, at Hagerstown, Md. Entries close June 26, with Harry B. Irwin, 34 West Franklin Street, Hagerstown, Md.
July 4, 1889.—Two-mile Bicycle Handicap at Washington Park, Fifth Avenue, Brooklyn. Entries close June 26, with F. G. Webb, Treasurer. Prospect Harriers' Race, run under L. A. W. rules.
July 4, 1889.—Race Meet at Brownsville, Pa.
July 4, 1889.—Illinois Division, L. A. W. Meet, at Ottawa.
July 4, 1889.—Tournament held by Lancaster (Pa.) Bicycle Club. Entries close July 1 with H. F. Griel, Lancaster.
July 4, 1889.—Fort Schuyler Wheelmen, Utica, N. Y., 50-mile Road Race.
July 4, 1889.—Second Annual Tournament of Fort Dayton Wheelmen, at Herkimer, N. Y. Entries to be made with C. F. Giesey, Secretary.
July 4, 1889.—Fifth Annual Tournament of Berkshire Co. Wheelmen, at Pittsfield, Mass.
July 8, 1889.—Connecticut Division L. A. W. Meet at Bridgeport, Conn.
July 20, 1889.—One-mile and 25-mile Bicycle and 5-mile Tricycle N. C. U. championships at Paddington, Eng., track.
July 27, 1889.—One-mile and 25-mile Tricycle and 5-mile Bicycle N. C. U. Championships at Paddington, Eng., track.
August 24, 1889.—Fifty-mile Bicycle and 1-mile Dwarf N. C. U. Championships at Paddington, Eng.
September 4-5, 1889.—Amateur Race Meet of the Hartford Wheel Club, at Hartford, Conn. Entries to be made with W. M. Francis, Secretary, P. O. Box 745.
October 23-29, 1889.—Race Meet at Macon, Ga.

EUROPEAN CYCLING FIXTURES.

Austro-Hungary.—Prague (Smichow) June 29 and 30. Germany.—Berlin, June 16 and 17, July 21, September 15; Hanover, June 23, September 8; Cologne, June 30, August 12; Chemnitz, September 8; Frankfort-on-the-Maine, September 1; Mannheim, September 8; Crefeld, September 8. Hamburg.—Altona, September 22; Bochum, August 25; Soram, June 9; Coburg, June 9; Magdeburg, June 30, September 8. Denmark.—Copenhagen International Meeting, August 18.

LONG ISLAND WHEELMEN'S MEET.

The elements conspired to drown out the Long Island Wheelmen's race meet, held at the Brooklyn Athletic Club grounds on Saturday afternoon last. They, the elements, outlined a neat programme and carried it out to the letter. They decided to flirt with the race meet committee so that the meet would not be postponed. At ten the day was gloriously fine; at two the clouds assembled as per order and cast shadows over the scene; at 3:30 the great shower bath was turned on and it looked like a postponement. Then the shower-bath let up, the clouds parted and it was decided to run the races. When things had got fairly started the clouds closed up, the shower was turned on full force and it poured all the afternoon, slowing up at short intervals, during which hopes of a clear-up were raised, only to be dashed to the ground by a heavier deluge than the preceding one. A few thunderbolts were let off at intervals to add to the general disgruntlement. The whole would have furnished a splendid theme for Wagner, only that no stage manager could have reproduced the celestial reverberations.

The track, a five-lap cinder path, carefully prepared for the occasion, was muddy, and in many places covered with water. The races were started at four and were run off with but few waits and these were due to the general demoralization caused by the rain. The result of each event was announced to the spectators. The officials discharged their duties acceptably, and there was neither hitch nor accident. The features of the day were, the remarkable success of the Kings County Wheelmen, whose men carried off almost all the prizes, and the good form shown by F. B. Hesse, a new man, who won three prizes. The grand stand was fairly well filled, and but for the weather the meet would would have been one of the most successful ever held in Brooklyn. The various events resulted as follows:

Committee of Arrangements.—G. G. Teller, L. H. Wise, Geo. M. Halsey, Carl C. Alden and Geo. W. Mabie.

Field Officers.—Referee: C. H. Luscomb, President L. A. W.: Judges: M. L. Bridgman, K. C. W.; Elliott Mason, Citizens B. C., and W. H. Meeteer, Brooklyn B. C. Umpires: W. C. Marion, K. C. W.; H. J. Hall, Jr., K. C. W.; Jos. M. McFadden, New York B. C., and H. E. Raymond, B. B. C. Timekeepers: C. A. Sheehan, Manhattan B. C.; T. C. Crichton, K. C. W., and F. P. Prial, New York B. C. Scorers: F. H. Douglas, K. C. W., and W. H. Warner, L. I. W. Clerk of Course: Geo. G. Teller, L. I. W.; Assistants: A. P. Topping and J. H. Bagg, L. I. W. Starter: Robert Evans, L. I. W.

ONE-MILE NOVICE.—Heat 1: F. B. Hesse, K. C. W., 3m. 31 2-5s.; A. S. Farmer, K. C. W., 3m. 31 3-5s.; J. H. McCue, Brooklyn A. A., distanced. Heat 2: A. H. Miles, K. C. W., 3m. 41 3-5s.; H. A. Ostermayer, K. C. W., 3m. 42 1-5s. Final Heat: Hesse 4m.; Farmer, second by several lengths. The others were not in it.

TWO-MILE L. I. W. CLUB HANDICAP.—W. Schumacher, 50 yards, 6m. 55 3-5s.; L. H. Wise, 50 yards, 7m. 28 1-5s.; Geo. W. Kreger, scratch, third. Schumacher had some trouble with Wise for the first mile and after that was never headed. Wise led at the first mile in 3m. 18s. Kreger, who has not ridden much nor trained any this year, rode the first lap in 36s. and then slowed up, riding the remainder of the distance leisurely.

ONE-MILE HANDICAP, ROVER TYPE WHEELS.—W. F. Murphy, K. C. W., 70 yards, 3m. 35 3-5s.; W. G. Class, B. B. C., 80 yards, 3m. 42 3-5s.; J. F. Borland, B. B. O., 80 yards, third. Murphy rode away on the last half, and riding in good form won easily.

ONE-MILE BICYCLE HANDICAP.—Heat 1: F. B. Hesse, K. C. W., 80 yards, 3m. 18s.; L. L. Clarke, Berkeley A. A., 75 yards, 3m. 19 3-5s.; F. N. Burgess, Rutherford, N. J., 70 yards, third by twenty yards; R. W. Steves, K. C. W., 50 yards, 0; J. H. Hanson, N. Y. B. C., 65 yards, 0; A. C. Banker, Berkeley A. A., scratch, 0. Heat 2: F. G. Brown, K. C. W., 25 yards, 3m. 25 3-5s.; C. M. Murphy, K. C. W., 55 yards, second; R. L. Jones, K. C. W., 60 yards, third; J. W. Schoefer, Berkeley A. A., 10 yards, did not finish; L. H. Wise, L. I. W., 45 yards, did not finish; H. P. Matthews, B. B. C., 70 yards, did not finish; H. O. King, K. C. W., 65 yards, did not finish. Final Heat: Hesse, 3m. 30 2-5s.; C. M. Murphy, 3m. 33 3-5s.; Burgess, third; Clarke did not finish.

ONE-MILE NOVICES, BROOKLYN CLUB MEMBERS.—W. E. Stuffield, 3m. 55 3-5s.; W. J. Masterson, 3m. 56 3-5s.; N. A. Robertson and C. L. Snedeker did not finish.

RELAY RACE, ONE AND FOUR-FIFTHS MILE.—Kings County Wheelmen, first; Berkeley Club, second; Long Island Wheelmen, third; time, 6m. 19 4-5s. Each club entered three men, each of whom rode three laps and was then relieved by a club mate. The men entered were: K. C. W., Hesse, Brown and W. F. Murphy; Berkeley A. A., Banker, Schoefer and Clarke; L. I. W., Schumacher, Morrell and Wise.

ONE-MILE RIDE AND RUN.—R. W. Steves, K. C. W., 4m. 54s.; E. P. Baggot, N. J. A. C.; 5m. 20m.; R. N. Burgess, Rutherford, N. J., did not finish. Steves made big headway on the runs and mounts.

THREE-MILE BICYCLE HANDICAP.—W. H. Schumacher, L. I. W., 100 yards, 12m. 24 1-5s.; W. F. Murphy, K. C. W., 175 yards, second by a few lengths; A. C. Banker, scratch, 0; F. G. Brown, 80 yards, 0.

ONE-MILE CONSOLATION.—King, 4m. 1-5s.; Hanson, second; Brown, third; Morrell, fourth; Brown, who was leg-weary with much riding, fell off his wheel at the finish of the race.

At Spring Games of Montreal A. A., Cote St. Antoine Grounds, June 1: One-mile bicycle handicap, W. H. C. Mussen, Montreal Bicycle Club, 10 seconds, first, in 3m 22 3-5s.; J. H. Robertson, Montreal B. C., scratch, second. Three-mile bicycle handicap, J. H. Robertson, Montreal Bicycle Club, scratch, first, in 9m. 56s.; W. H. C. Mussen, Montreal B. C., 25 seconds, second.

RACES AT LANCASTER, PA., JULY 4th.

The Bicycle Club of Lancaster, Pa., issue an attractive programme of races to be run off at McGrann's Park, July 4. Entries close July 1 at 12 M., with H. M. Griel, Lancaster. Everything has been well arranged for comfort and convenience of racing men and the track put in good shape. Reduced rates have been secured at the American, Stevens and Lancaster hotels, and railroads carry wheelmen at special figures. Following is a list of events to be contested. Wheelmen will note that two State championships have been allotted Lancaster instead of one, as at first announced.

MORNING RACES, 10 O'CLOCK SHARP:

Half-mile Boys' Safety.—Boys under 15 years.
One-mile—Novice.—Open.
Two-mile Safety.—Open.
One-mile Ordinary.—Open to boys under 16 years.
One-mile.—Open. State L. A. W. Championship.

FANCY RIDING.

Two-mile Lancaster County Championship.—Open to all amateur wheelmen in the County.
One-mile Club Safety. Open to Club Members only.

AFTERNOON RACES, 2.30 SHARP.

One-mile—Flying Start.—Open.
Half-mile Dash.—Open. L. A. W. Championship event
Two-mile Club Handicap.—(Safeties barred.) Open to Club Members only.
One-mile Tandem Safety.—Open.
Half-mile Club—Novice.—Open to Club Members only.
Two-mile.—Open.

FANCY RIDING.

Half-mile "Hands-Off."—Open.
Three-mile Lap Race.—Open.
One-mile—"Consolation."

EUROPEAN RACING NOTES.

At the North of Ireland Cycling Club's sports on June 1 the 5-mile bicycle championship of Ireland was won by Arthur Du Cros, in the time of 20m. 13 2-5s.

At the Bath (England) Road Club's 25-mile race, June 1, the winner, P. T. Pyne, 5m handicap, covered the distance in 1h. 27m. 23s., on a "Farringdon" ordinary. The rider placed at scratch, P. C. Wilson, bestrode a "Premier" safety, and covered the distance in h. 23m. 41s. The road was in excellent condition, but a strong headwind prevented faster time being made. Seven safeties competed against two ordinaries and one tricycle.

West, the one-legged champion, won the mile professional handicap at Coventry June 1 from the 295-yard mark in the brilliant time of 2m. 33 1-5s.

RECORD BREAKING IN SCOTLAND.

On May 30, at the meet of the Bellahouston and Cathkin Cycling Clubs, Mr. J. E. Young established the Scotch safety records for the distances of quarter, half, three-quarters and whole mile, as well as two and three miles. Following are the times: Quarter-mile, 41 2-5s.; half-mile, 1m. 22 2-5s.; three-quarters, 2m. 7s; one-mile, 2m. 51 2-5s., three miles, 9m. 17s. In the half-mile ordinary handicap, M. Bruce made a new record for that distance, and established a record for the starting quarter in the final of the half-mile after having made a record for the flying quarter in his heat. The Scotch ordinary records now read: Standing: quarter-mile, 39 4-5s.; half-mile, 1m. 30 3-5s. Flying: quarter, 30 3-5s. As the track was not in first-class condition and Bruce rode a strange machine, much better things may be expected from him in future. A praiseworthy feature of this meet was the fact that it was concluded within five minutes of the time allotted. We fancy that fact alone would give a claim for "record." An attendance of some 2,000 gladdened the hearts of the managers.

At athletic games of the Schuylkill Navy, June 8: Two-mile bicycle handicap, W. W. Taxis, Philadelphia, 150 yards, first, in 5m. 55⅗s.; G. M. Gregg, W. A. C., 200 yards, second. One-mile bicycle match, J. J. Bradley, South End W., first, in 3m. 17 4-5s; J. H. Draper, Penn. B. C., second, by 15 yards.

Fifth Annual Games of Adelphi Academy, Brooklyn, L. I., June 7: One-mile bicycle handicap, H. L. Pratt, '93, 60 yards, first, in 3m. 38s.; F. M. Helden, 150 yards, second, in 3m. 38 1-3s.

The Buffalo police are anxiously looking for a quartette of girls who rented two tricycles of the Misses Ducker, of Niagara Street, the morning of June 10. The girls have not yet brought them back.

At the inter-scholastic tournament between Philips, Exeter and Andover Academies, June 12, one of the six out of nine events won by Andover was the 1-mile bicycle. Hallock took that in the time of 3m. 18⅖s.

The 1-mile bicycle race at Macalester College Sports, June 10, in Macalester, Minn., was won by W. P. Kirkwood, in 3m. 43s.

In the Manual Training School sports held at the University Grounds, June 4, the 1-mile bicycle was won by W. A. Scott, in 3m. 34s.

"SURVIVOR" ON THE GREAT CENTURY RUN.

Was there much fun in the G. C. R.? Well, I should smile. From the time the first man touched off De Graff's ear-splitting dog scarer in the wheel room of the Mountain House, on Friday evening, until the last man housed his wheel at the Century Club in Philadelphia, there was fun all the time. Some of the boys in "41" kept things moving from midnight until after 2 A. M., then shortly after 3, our bugler sounded the *reveille*, and the day commenced. Breakfast, then the start at 4.30 with a good pace through Newark and Elizabeth, and on to Plainfield, DeGraff scoring a point on a dog near Newark with that screamer of his, and our bugler making the dull morning resound with merry calls, assisted by the "silent" rachet on a Star.

We made Plainfield, after a run of a few miles over a road, the superb surface of which gave opportunity to those in the rear to enjoy a scorch, the only chance of the day.

From Plainfield to New Brunswick there was a tough road, and the rising wind in our faces, made the going slow, and the arrival at Rutgers College, straggling.

From New Brunswick on to Philadelphia we practically rode sidepaths, the ordinary wheels here showing their superiority over the safeties for work in narrow sandy paths. The Tandem Safety with its light weight team, being handicapped by side slipping and the difficulty of managing so long a wheel in narrow paths.

The sight was strange as well as beautiful, the line stretching out in single file until each end was lost in a turn of the road, it seemed a huge snake, ever writhing and twisting, and ever moving onward. On and on to Trenton, the distance from Princeton to Trenton being over a very poor road that caused the line to break and most of us to enter a go-as-you-please, that brought us to Trenton with an interval of about half an hour between the leaders and the stragglers.

A fine dinner at Trenton put new life into the tired muscles of those who, taking the trip without sufficient training, felt in their triceps the rebellion of tired nature.

Here, after dinner, the party adjourned to the Court House, with which building as a background our party was photographed, thus perpetuating our impressions of the faces of the participants.

Now let my little growl be heard. How much better as a souvenir it would have been if only the Century Run men had been in the photo instead of including the Trenton men!

From Trenton to Holmesburg, more sidepaths and warmer weather. At Holmesburg the Philadelphia contingent gave us a rousing reception. Apropos of which, the attentions paid to the lady who came through, formed not the least pleasant feature of the run. Commencing at Kingston, repeated at Princeton, supplemented there by a rousing cheer from some college men, all former cheers paled in comparison with the one let loose at Trenton, as the tandem hove in sight at the Court House. Even the "Rah, Rah, Rah, Pennsylvania," at Holmesburg, must take a back seat to that Trenton howl.

It seems to the writer that the committee have not received sufficient praise for the magnificent way in which the run was planned and carried through. Boys, we owe 'em a debt of gratitude.

The Ramblers, of Buffalo, made a Century on Decoration Day, and speak of "the Spartan Eight" having made the run in the elapsed time of about fiteen hours thirty minutes, with a total riding time of between nine and ten hours, and consider it a scorch. The Orange Century was completed in fifteen hours fifteen minutes, elapsed time, at a steady pace all day, no extended rests except at dinner time, and I will wager that our forty-six who finished were more fresh than the eight of the Buffalo men.

For a long run a steady pace is better than a scorch and then a rest, indefinitely continued.

SURVIVOR.

GREAT CENTURY RUN NOTES.

Mr. Clarke writes us that Mr. R. F. Hibson, K. C. W. did not finish the run, but "trained" from Westfield to Trenton. Mr. Uhl, of Newark, finished the run. The small cash surplus left in the hands of the Committee of Arrangements has been expended for one of the memento pins of the run, done in gold, which is to be presented to Miss Welch, of Germantown, in appreciation of her plucky ride. Miss Maud Eisinger, credited to the Harlem Wheelmen, should be "unattached."

BUFFALO BICYCLE CLUB.

The regular monthly meeting of the Buffalo Bicycle Club was held at their club-houss on June 10. Seven application for membership were received and favorably acted upon.

The committee on ways and means presented a proposition giving a member six years' membership in the club upon payment of $50, which was adopted and a committee of three appointed to carry out the provisions of the same.

The club took a decided stand on the question of fast riding and coasting on the crowded asphalt streets, and defined its position by adopting the following preamble and resolution offered by W. S. Jenkins, chairman of the rights and privileges committee of the New York State Division L. A. W.:

Whereas, It is becoming a common practice for many wheelmen in this city, in utter disregard of the city ordinance to ride at a very rapid pace, much in excess of the rate of speed permitted by such ordinances, and to coast upon streets which are in constant use by other vehicles, and by pedestrians, to the great danger of life and limb; and

Whereas, Such practices should be discountenanced by all good citizens, and especially by wheelmen who have at heart the best interests of wheeling and do not desire to see it brought into disrepute; therefore

Resolved, That the Buffalo Bicycle Club express their thorough disapproval of such practices, whether upon the part of members or others.

The nomination of Mr. W. S. Bull of the club, for election as chief consul, New York State Division L. A. W. was, upon motion of Dr. C. S. Butler, L. A. W., representative, unanimously endorsed, and his election recommended to all wheelmen throughout the State. Mr. Bull is at present acting chief consul and doing yeoman service for the league.

A communication was received from the Pennsylvania Railway Company naming a rate of a fare and a third to Hagerstown, Md., on the occasion of the L. A. W. meet on July 2d-4th and offering Pullman accommodations if a party of 20 or more went, bicycles carried free.

CLUB DOINGS AT PITTSBURG, PA.

The East End Gymnastic Club met on last Monday evening and decided that they could not accept the proposition for amalgamation with the Keystone Club, as proposed. There was a stormy debate on the subject, and the failure of the scheme may properly be laid to internecine differences of the first mentioned organization. While the matter is one for regret by members of both clubs having the best interests of their organizations at heart, it may lead to good in the end—an organization of local wheel clubs that would of itself be strong enough to erect a club-house and attain a membership that would in a few years outrank many of those that have become famous in other cities. The Keystone Club should not be misunderstood in their action with a view toward uniting with the Gymnastic Club. The proposition came from officers of the latter club, and was repeatedly made during the past two years, and finally decided favorably upon by the Keystones. Then, in order to facilitate matters, a formal proposition was presented to the Gymnastic Club to join under certain conditions, which proposition was rejected at the last club meeting, owing to some of the conditions not meeting with their approval.

CONNECTICUT'S COMING MEET.

A joint meeting of the Bridgeport Wheel Club and the Rambler Wheelmen to make arrangements for the coming meet of the Connecticut Division, L. A. W., was held, June 14, at the rooms of the former club in the Studio Building. C. E. Moore, Consul of Bridgeport, presided, and W. Shelton Stevenson acted as secretary. It was decided that the meet should be held in Bridgeport, on Monday, July 8. The following were appointed a committee to receive subscriptions to defray the expense of the meeting: George Fryer, H. B. Morris and W. H. Horr, of the Bridgeport Wheel Club, and S. J. Wakelee, C. A. Read and F. Atwater, of the Rambling Wheelmen. The entertainment committee appointed were: William Healy and W. M. Richardson, of the Bridgeport Wheel Club, and Frank Goodsell and W. P. Hopkins, of the Rambling Wheelmen.

At Fourth Annual Spring Sports of Cathedral School of St. Paul's A. A., Garden City, L. I., the 1-mile bicycle was taken by O. Cohnfeld, in 3m. 33⅘s.; A. H. Cassebeer, second.

TROY BICYCLE CLUB'S EIGHTH ANNUAL PARADE.

The annual parade of the Troy Bicycle Club occurred June 6. The members, together with a delegation from the Albany Bicycle Club under Captain Simmons and one from the Albany Wheelmen under Captain Elmer Irving, left the club house and proceeded over the line of march published recently. After the parade, the club and its invited guests, numbering about 200, sat down to a spread which was furnished in elegant style by R. C. Kruger. Four large tables were loaded down with an endless supply of good things to which every one did ample justice.

Orange S. Ingram acted as master of ceremonies and made the address of welcome. Joseph C. McClellan, President of the Albany Wheelmen, responded on behalf of his club and Dr. Adams on behalf of the Albany Bicycle Club. Dr. Marsh made a happy and clever response to the toast "The ladies." Tobias S. Heister rendered a tenor solo in a pleasing manner. Captain Hanley and Louis Herman gave an exhibition of fencing. The R. P. I. Banjo Club was heard with pleasure in several selections as was also the T. B. C. glee club.

Captain P. F. Hanley was chairman of the committee of arrangements. The affair passed off very pleasantly and everybody was well pleased. The Albany boys took the 11 o'clock local for home, being escorted to the depot by the Trojans.

ORNII OBA.

HARVARD'S HANDICAP ROAD RACE.

The handicap race of the Harvard Bicycle Club six times around Chestnut Hill reservoir, distance seven miles, was run off June 15. Soon after the men were started it was evident that the scratch men had been too heavily handicapped. Although they rode very fast they were three-quarters of a mile behind the winner at the finish. On the third lap Greenleaf, entirely through his own carelessness, fell over Davis' little wheel, but was on his machine again instantly. Davis dismounted and waited until Greenleaf remounted, not wishing to take advantage of Greenleaf's carelessness. Seven men started and six finished in the following order:

Position.	Handicap.	Actual time. M. S.
1. Barron, '91	1¾m.	23 51
2. Holmes, '92	3½m.	24 17⅕
3. Spencer, '90	5m.	26 19⅘
4. Rodeman	5m.	27 16
5. Greenleaf, '92	Scratch	28 03⅘
6. Davis, '91	Scratch	28 13

The race between Greenleaf and Davis was very interesting. Davis began to increase his speed on the backstretch, but Greenleaf stuck to him, and a third of a mile from home put on a tremendous spurt, and finished a hundred yards ahead.

Barron is a remarkably good man. His time was not much slower than Greenleaf's although he rode a heavy Expert an inch too large for him. K. Brown, '91, refereed the race.

ROAD RACING AT NEW ORLEANS.

Only Frederic, Sprigg, Harris and Grevot contested in the race for the Batson medal, June 9.

The road was in poor condition, being several inches deep in dust, and fast time was out of question. W. C. Grevot, with a start of fifty seconds, did some good riding and finished first, doing the three miles in 13m. 25s.; B. M. Sprigg, scratch, second, in 12m. 55s.; A. B. Harris, 2m. 20s., third; L. J. Frederic, 30s., took a tumble, and was buried out of sight in the dust.

ANSWERS TO CORRESPONDENCE.

H. M. G.—Don't know address of Barber, fancy rider. Will some one please send it?

S. B. S.—Write F. L. Olmstead personally.

W. L. R.—Yes. Eagle is a high grade wheel; easy on hills, fast on level; very safe.

J. G. B.—The winner of the road race rode a Victor. The fastest time was made on a Champion. Of the first ten wheels home six were Victors.

E. L.—Julius Wilcox, 33 Murray Street, New York City.

On June 6, at the University of Vermont A. A.'s games in Burlington, Vt., the quarter-mile bicycle was won by V. O. Whitcomb, in 59⅘s.

New York State Division L.A.W.

OFFICIAL ORGAN.

NEW YORK STATE DIVISION—CONSULS AND HOTELS.

LIST No. 3.

PLACE.	CONSULS.	HOTELS.
Albany		Globe Hotel.
Caledonia		Annin's Trout Ponds
Lewiston		Waggoner Hotel.
Rossburgh	J. Willis Stockwell.	
Salamanca		Dudley House.
Schenectady	Ed. L. Davis.	Carley House.
Upper Red Hook		Park Hotel.
Yonkers		Getty House.

W. S. BULL, *Chief Consul.*

BUFFALO, N. Y., June 15, 1889.

KINGS COUNTY WHEELMEN'S LANTERN PARADE.

TO THE EDITOR OF THE WHEEL:
The Annual Lantern Parade of the King's County Wheelmen will take place Thursday evening, June 27. Assemble at Bedford Avenue and Brevoort Place, opposite the clubhouse, at 8:15, start at 9 o'clock sharp. Route, Bedford Avenue to fountain at lower end of avenue and counter-march to clubhouse, where refreshments and a little musical and literary entertainment will be given. All the local clubs will be invited, and through your paper we wish to extend an invitation to the "unattached." We want them all to join in and help to make this the largest parade ever held. Very truly yours,
W. C. MARION, Jr., Capt.
In case of rain the parade will take place the following night.

GOOD ADVICE TO MONMOUTH CO.

The new road law which permits the county freeholders to improve highways should be utilized by the county of Monmouth for a boulevard from Red Bank to the Manasquan River bridge by way of Sea Bright and the coast. A portion of the present road is in excellent condition, but there are long stretches that should be improved into thorough condition. The vast increase in the valuations of this part of Monmouth County by the erection of cottages, hotels and stores, designed almost exclusively for summer residents, would warrant the expenditure of the money necessary for the high way, and it would prove an unqualified blessing to all affected. The resorts need this bond to achieve the perfect prosperity which their advantages merit.—*Newark Sunday Call.*

THANKS TO ALDERMAN STORM.

F. P. PRIAL:
In reply to yours of June 8 : After a long fight I am glad to say that I have at last succeeded in my endeavors to have Madison Avenue paved with asphalt. It takes in all of Madison Avenue from Thirty-second Street to Fifty-eighth Street, and through Fifty-eighth street to Fifth Avenue; with the exception of the two hills on Madison Avenue—viz., from Thirty-third Street to Thirty-sixth Street, and from Forty-first Street to Forty-second Street. I am, however trying to arrange for a noiseless pavement which will be practical on those hills. The resolution providing for the foregoing work passed the Board of Aldermen June 4, and was signed by the Mayor June 11, so that I trust the work will be done this summer.
WALTON STORM.

GOOD WORK IN UNION CO., N. J.

At a meeting of the Board of Freeholders, held May 29, in Elizabeth, it was resolved that the County road leading from the junction of Morris turnpike and Springfield Avenue through Summit and New Providence townships to South Street in New Providence, should be graded and paved with either Telford or Macadam. This resolution was unanimously passed by the board and a vote taken to increase the width to sixteen feet in all practicable places. Committees of five on each of the roads between Elizabeth and Rahway, and Elizabeth and New Providence were appointed, and a committee of six on the road between Elizabeth and Plainfield. The duties of these committees are to act in co operation with the engineers in laying out and improving these roads under the County law act.

At a later meeting on June 6, it was resolved and unanimously adopted, that all roads heretofore known as County roads be graded and paved with Telford or Macadam, the width to be increased to sixteen feet wherever possible. On these actions, which will have the hearty commendation of all using the highways and wishing for good roads, the *Westfield Standard* comments as follows :

"The most important step ever yet taken by the progressive citizens of Union County is that of securing good county roads. The Board of Freeholders are at work in good earnest, getting ready to make the roads. The body moves slowly, some think, but large bodies are proverbial in slow locomotion. Especially is it true when the enterprise is great. We want the roads to use and we want them right off. As things look now, we are to have them. It is the favorable season now to work and build roads. Twice or three times as much can be accomplished in the cool, moist weather of May and June as in the hot, dry months of July and August. On the score of economy as well as speed, we would speed the surveyor and the committee. The road from Westfield to Rahway could and ought to be half done by the 4th of July. What do you say, chosen freeholders of Rahway, of Union, of Westfield? Will you complete your county road from Westfield to Rahway and do it right off?"

With the press of the State alive to the needs and ready to urge on the good work, New Jersey should soon be famed as the small State with the best roads in the country.

BICYCLE RACES AT NEW ORLEANS IN SEPTEMBER.

Grand preparations are being made by the wheelmen of New Orleans for a grand race meet to be held some time in September. There will be some fifty or sixty entries and complimentary tickets will be issued to friends of the wheelmen. Among the great events will be the 5-mile L. A. W. championship of the United States, open to all riders in the United States who are members of the L. A. W., which organization now numbers over 12,000.

The programme is very interesting and consists of the following events :

Novice race for bicycles, 1-mile dash, open to L. A. W. members ; 5-mile championship of the United States, open to L. A. W. members ; half-mile dash, for boys sixteen years and under open to L. A. W. members ; 1-mile State championship of Louisiana (Louisiana members only); slow race, too yards (mixed), open to L. A. W. members; Louisiana Club championship, 1 mile dash; 1-mile dash, open for safeties only, to L. A. W. members; New Orleans Bicycle Club championship, 1-mile dash; run and ride race, half-mile (mixed race), L. A. W. members; lap race, 2½-mile (mixed race), open to L. A. W. members ; consolation race, 1-mile dash (mixed), open to riders who have not won at this meeting. These races will be run about the 14th of September and start at 2 P. M. Entries will be open with Ridgley P. Randall, Esq., on August 1. Fifty cents for each entry.

From the former race meets and the early work commenced by the energetic Racing Board there is every reason to believe that the meeting this year will be the grandest ever held here.

Particulars of the prizes and date of meeting will be announced.

Charles Schwalbach, the well-known bicyclist and dealer, has secured the spacious Fifth Avenue Casino building and will open a wheeling school. Competent instruction will be given in both tricycling and bicycling. This place will be the largest of its kind in the world, and will be opened on Monday at 1 P.M. until 5 P.M. The regular hours after Monday will be 9 to 12 M., 1 to 5 P. M. and 7 to 9 P. M. Sundays except 9! Next Saturday he will give a series of races by the members of the different clubs of Brooklyn. A band of music will also be in attendance.

PIONEER'S PENCILINGS.

Please allow me to say a few words in your interesting ladies' column about a trip which I enjoyed on Sunday, June 1, in company with a gentleman friend.

It was a beautiful morning and the sun shone brightly while a lovely blue sky looked down upon us in smile that seemed to say, "Another sunny day has greeted thee, where is thy nature's helpmate." Said I to my companion, " Let us take our latest and dearest friends, our safeties, and have a country run," and he quickly responded, "Yes."

Part of our trip was very romantic, on account of the hills we climbed and the incidents that happened, while during the other portion of the trip we witnessed very deplorable sights. Our trip was to Cabin John Bridge, taking the way of Chain Bridge Road, this being more desirable on account of the flood which had taken place, and which we wished to see. We had not gone a great distance when the Potomac River came in view, and in such a furious state that it was indescribable. From Little Falls to Chain Bridge the river presented a picture of wild devastation, while at the bridge it looked like Niagara Whirlpool. Here we spent some time. Before our departure I counted eighteen wheelmen who had come the same way to see the destruction the mighty waters had wrought.

This Chain Bridge Road which we had selected was extraordinarily rough, and several forced dismounts were taken. One wheelman, on an upright, had a queer fall, though he quickly p cked himself up, and only laughed at the peculiar manner in which he dismounted, his foot catching between the handle-bar and the brake lever. After spending some time at this place, we concluded it not best to tarry longer, for we had yet four miles before reaching our destination. We had not gone far when we discovered that the road that leads to Cabin John Bridge had been destroyed by the flood, and a moment later, a number with a husky voice shouted out, " You can't go any further that way !" So what were we to do? Well, the only resource we had was to climb a cliff a hundred feet high. It was some time before I could get courage enough to do this ; but I could not contemplate the idea of going back to where we had started from, so finally decided I would attempt it. We had some wading to do before we could get to this massive rock, but it seemed only a short time when we were half way up. Here we encountered a ravine, the only way across which was by means of a plank, consequently we had to carry our bicycles across. Lucky for us they were not tricycles, and before we could realize it we were on the mountain top. I assure you, reader, this was adventuresome but romantic.

We soon found a spring and quickly refreshed ourselves with its cooling waters. "Is there a cup here?" asked I of a lady who was stooping over, evidently trying to get a drink. "No," was her quick reply, "No silver cups on this occasion."

In half an hour we once more found ourselves gliding swiftly along on beautiful roads, and soon made the balance of the way. We met twenty-six Baltimoreans, accompanied by eleven members of the W. C. C. of our city and many more wheelmen. I presume we met upwards of a hundred before returning home.

When we reached our destination, as our appetites had increased rapidly, we felt it a necessity to partake of a lunch. On this, like all other occasions when out with my bicycle, I never fail to have a good appetite, and never have to go far behind when I am ready for lunch. Oh ! why are the ladies so long making up their minds to bicycle riders, and at this late day too? Since we can take the two-wheeler, we need not wait for a companion to have some one to assist us up the hills, as in former years when we poor mortals had to propel a tricycle twice our weight. When I think it over, I wonder we have so many tricycle riders as we do, for I have often heard ladies say: " I should like to go much oftener, only it is mortifying to ask your escort to do all the wor . when ascending a hill, you know a girl don't like to acknowledge she is tired. While, on the other hand, the boys will complain to their sisters when they come in from a long tricycle ride that they had to do all the work, and say, "Oh ! that we had so much help in climbing hills, and you know how heavy Miss So-and-So is."

I understand it all, I have had the same experience.

Well, as I said before, we satisfied our appetites and were ready for the return home, which was made in a short time.

On reaching Pennsylvania Avenue, we thought we would go to the Capitol to see what harm the flood had done, and, in order to do this, had to ride through four inches of water at one place. I believe I am the first lady rider that ventured to do that. We also saw people boating on the avenue, which was a novel sight.

At 9:15 P. M. we arrived home, and I assure you were glad of it, for we had experienced quite an exciting, yet interesting day.

I am waiting most anxiously to see the ladies take to two-wheelers, and, if they will, they cannot help enjoying themselves as I do

I trust the future will be a splendid field for the ladies' safeties, and our health and happiness will increase.

Fraternally yours,

PIONEER, 18,123.

Washington, D. C., June 1, 1889.

PSYCHE'S ADVICE.

DEAR EDITOR:

I have been long wanting to give my fellow riders a little piece of advice, and hope they will take it in good part. I notice so many wheelwomen who would look incomparably better on their wheels, and gain in power and ease too, if they would turn their toes in more, their heels out, and keep their knees together.

It gives one a very bow-legged feeling at first, but you get accustomed to it very soon and wonder that you ever rode in any other position. I don't mean to really assume a pigeon-toed position. Everyone as a child is taught to turn their toes out, and instead of presenting our feet straight as Indians and all people in a natural state do, we civilized people walk along with our feet broadside on, more or less. In wheeling get back to a state of nature in that respect, and you will save the leather of your shoes if they are high and the skin of your ankles if they are low many a tear-compelling rub.

There would be many more graceful riders if more attention was paid to ankle motion. So many ride with rigid ankles This, of course, makes the knee motion very apparent and the rider very unsightly.

Another point. Why not use short cranks for city and easy riding?

They do away with much of the unsightly knee motion, and short cranks are very nearly as easy to ride with unless you have some hard work to do.

One more thing· have your machine perfectly adjusted to your personal and individual needs. Never ride with your handle-bar so high as to make you take the position of looking over a fence, nor so low as to pull you forward and make you round shouldered. The proper position is so that your arms are naturally before you, a little extended. No two persons that I ever saw or heard of could fit the same machine, and I think it a perfectly safe thing to say that no two persons can ever ride one machine with an equal degree of comfort. The bicyclist has not tasted the complete joy of his or her wheel till it has become a complimental part of its rider.

One more "don't." *Don't* ride with your elbows out. It looks ungraceful, narrows your chest, partially destroying the benefit you ought to derive from your exercise in the fresh air.

To avoid this don't ride a machine whose construction is such that the handle-bar's position makes you reach *out* in front instead of *down*.

PSYCHE.

THE "VICTOR" IN SCOTLAND.

We had a call on Monday last from Mr. Otto C. Nussle, of Walnut, Ill., U.S.A. This gentleman is one of the American cycle tourists at present in England. He followed by a later steamer, and shows his good sense by deciding to see at least a portion of "Caledonia stern and wild" ere he returns home. He intends visiting the Trossachs via Loch Lomond, then Stirling and Edinburgh, and, if time permits, Yarrowdale, joining his compatriots in London. His mount is a "Victor" safety, made by the Overman Wheel Co., Boston, with anti-vibrating front forks, 30-inch tangent wheels, curved diamond frame, spade handles, ball-socket steering, back-wheel brake and enamelled dull black. As is usual with all American goods, there are a number of intricacies which are absent from our own makes, but it looks and feels a good, strong machine, though a trifle weighty for its breadth of tire.—*Scottish Cyclist* of June 5.

Bert Owen, of the Capitol Cycle Co., was in town on Sunday, leaving in the evening for Boston. His Psychos are going well all over the country, especially in the metropolitan district.

K. C. W. NOTES.

The Kings Co. Wheelmen "racing team" is made up of some of the most forward young men of my acquaintance; they are continually pushing themselves to the front much to the annoyance of their more modest competitors. On Wednesday the 12th inst., F. G. Brown finished first in the two-mile A. A. U championship, defeating the champion W. E. Crist. Not satisfied with this, he goes to Huntington, L. I., on the 13th, and there takes three firsts, while his clubmates, W. F. and Chas. Murphy, win one first, two seconds and one second respectively. Then came the L. I. W. meet, on the 15th: here the Kings County won six firsts and three seconds out of a possible seven firsts and six seconds. Last week's score for the boys of the Kings County stands: Eleven firsts out of a possible twelve and six seconds out of eleven, and in two of these races but *one* K. C. W. man started.

The weather clerk did his best to spoil the Long Island games, but Te ler refused to be subdued, and at 4 o'clock the first race on the programme—the 1-mile novice, open—was started. Ferd Hesse in this race showed, to the observing ones, what might be expected from him, for he had more of the style of a "vet" than a novice, and future events showed his ability equal to his style. As the regular correspondent of THE WHEEL was at the games I will not go into detail, but cannot pass by that relay race. The Brooklyn's team was under the colors of Berkeley, so but three teams came to the scratch: L. I. W., Berkeley and K. C. W Kings County rode with a vim that set their friends wild, and Brown won with a grand spurt. For a few minutes after the finish pandemonium reigned, the Brooklyn's and Kings County striving to out-do each other in cheers for the victors. Wm. Murphy's last lap on the safety was well worth seeing. A seventy-five inch gear sounds high, but William arrived there with it. Schumacher was just a shade too rapid for Miles in the 3-mile, but it was a good race, and the only open event we did not win.

The Long Island's programme was one of the neatest I have yet seen. One can look over it with pleasure, the sketches being far more attractive to the eye than the monotonous "ads." that usually surround the list of events.

That water set is quite an addition to our "club trophies," which I think, rival in number and value, those of any other club in the country.

Brown's striving to ride in every event on the card proved too much for him and his final collapse will, we all hope, prove a good lesson. A man who admits he has no staying power, and who has only lately tried to develop a spurt should know that several hard races through the mud and rain would prove more than he could stand. If Mr. B. will read "Hints on Cycling" by A. B. Barkman, he will there find excellent advice, which, if followed, will put him in far better condition that he now is.

If the boys do half as well at their own Meet on the 28th and 29th, we will be satisfied. There is one event they are bound to win, *i. e.*, the "club championship." Who will be the victor is the question, but if I may be permitted I should like to predict a surprise.

It seems an odd idea to have to win a championship trophy twice in succession, but that is the case with the five-mile championship of K. C. W. for the "Advertisement Cup."

Everyone is looking forward to a fine time on Sunday next, when the club has what is termed a picnic run to "Lake Success." The memory of the last event is still fresh in the minds of those so fortunate as to attend, and the outlook for a large attendance is very promising. The man with the white horse has promised *not* to be present, so no accidents need be feared.

'Gene Valentine won the cycle event at "Traver's Island" on the 15th, adding one more to our score.

RAM LAL.

Brooklyn, N. Y., June 20, 1889.

ST. LOUIS.

"One woe doth tread upon another's heels, so fast they follow." No sooner is the Rule 8 matter disposed of than the announcement is made by one of the members of the House Committee that, in consequence of the action taken by the club on that question, he has declared a boycott on the billiard tables, and henceforth neither he nor his partisans will patronize the club tables. It is also rumored that he will resign his place on the House Committee, and, as if that were not enough, he will withdraw his support from the club entirely, resign his membership and join the Pastime Athletic Club. If there is anything else that he is going to do I have not heard of it. He says that since the club will not permit him to play billiards when he wants to play, he will not play when the club wants him to. This is undoubtedly his right, and no one will question it for a moment, but thinking members will ask how he can with decency hold an office in the club, charged with carrying out part of its management, and at the same time defiantly work against its interests. It is necessary to state that he was not elected to the office which he holds; he was appointed, and the President has the remedy in his hands, if he cares to do his plain duty in the premises. If he finds that he is not *en rapport* with the club in his conduct of the committee (and he ought to realize that fact by this time), he ought, in all fairness, make room for some one not built on so narrow a gauge. If it is his intention to coerce the club into his way of doing things, I feel perfectly safe in assuring him that he is doomed to failure. It is only just to say that the other members of the committee do not approve of his action; they say that it is foolish and prejudicial to the interests of the club, and this view of the case is shared by all true friends of the organization. Fortunately his influence in the club is *nil*, and the balls continue to click merrily notwithstanding his pompous proclamation.

There is considerable dissatisfaction with the management of the new Track Association, and a meeting of the stockholders is to be held next Monday night to straighten matters out. There does not appear to be any system in the conduct of its affairs, and an effort will be made to locate the difficulty and if possible remedy it. The association can easily be made remunerative, but it will require careful, business-like management, something it has not heretofore had.

Brother Miles, in the last issue of the *Referee*, charges your correspondent with saying that the Chicago riders were afraid of the St. Louis men and refused on that account to let them in the Pullman race. "This is untrue." *Your* correspondent said nothing of the sort as Mr. Miles can easily ascertain by a reference to his files He has evidently got me mixed up with the *Bulletin* correspondent. The latter did say that one of our riders had told him that the Chicago men were afraid, but this was promptly denied by Captain Sanders himself, and by both "Stroller" and "Linneus." Then Mr. Miles goes on and gives what he calls a true history of the case The only *true* history of the Pullman race, so far as St. Louis' connection with it is concerned, has been published in THE WHEEL. You will find that none of the others have the name blown in the bottle; they are spurious articles and the public is warned against them.

Great preparations are being made by the Sedalia wheelmen for the entertainment of the State Meet July 3 and 4. A rate of one fare for the round trip from all points in Missouri has been obtained, and the indications now point to a large attendance The races will be interesting, judging from the number of entries that have been made, and there will be a big delegation from here.

Jno. Greathouse will not steal any more bicycles for awhile. He filched one from S. C. Cabanne and got a sentence of three years in the penitentiary. A few convictions of that sort will soon stop bicycle thieving.

ITHURIEL.

MARYLAND.

A bicycle club has been formed at Relay Station with fifteen members.

About twenty members spent last Saturday at their ducking shore at Middle River, several visitors from out of town accompanying them.

LEAGUE MEET NOTES.

The *Sunday Herald*, of the 16th inst. says that "there are very pronounced indications of a big kick about the mailing list, and indeed there would seem to be no good reason why this Division should be made or even asked to pay $100 for such a thing. It is necessary that a copy of the official programme be sent to each member of the League, and to do this a list of the names and addresses of such members is, of course, necessary. Such a list must in the nature of things be in the possession of the publishers of the *Bulletin*, as it is the official organ of the League and goes to all the members; but as that paper is really a private enterprise, its publishers, perhaps, have a right to charge for a mailing list if they see fit. They must get their list, however, from Secretary-Editor Bassett, who is paid, and well paid, too, for performing his duties. It is argued that one of these duties should be to furnish a list of the members of the League to the Division, which, in such a case as the present, offers to entertain them all if they will come to the Meet, and which wants to send each one an invitation anyhow. By what authority he makes it necessary for such a Division to pay a comparative outsider a round sum for such a necessity is an interesting question which is likely to be inquired into. [The authority Secretary-Editor Bassett acts under is that of the Executive Committee of the L. A. W., it being embodied in the bylaws, and he himself is unable to change the rule.—ED. THE WHEEL.] As the case now stands, it seems that the contract with the *Bulletin* to furnish the list was made by the old officers of the League, and that President Luscomb, feeling his hands tied, has done the best he could by himself paying the money, which the Division is to return if there are any funds left after the expenses of the Meet are paid."

The race-course on the Fair Grounds received last week the first touches of preparation for the festivities of the Fourth of July. The grand stand at the track seats 2,200 comfortably, and more stands are to be erected.

The Hagerstown Club are very proud of the triple-plated rolled gold pins presented to them by the Clark Cycle Co., of Baltimore.

The ladies of St. Paul's M. E. Church will serve refreshments in the old Post-Office room during the Meet.

The Hagerstown Club are drilling regularly every Monday and Friday evenings for the parade during the Meet.

BAY RIDGE.

ERIE, PA.

The meets and runs this season have been few and far between on account of the abominable weather. There are no better roads in the country than in and about Erie, but even here they have been in a state of chronic mush a greater share of the time. If the damp weather ever does let up, there will be a general rejoicing in the ranks of wheelmen and wheelwomen of Erie. Yes, the ladies are getting the craze, too. Some four of them already have wheels and are doing credit to their sex, beside having lots of fun and exercise. One of them remarked to the writer recently that she had been both surprised and delighted at the general good-fellowship shown her by the wheelmen of Erie. She had been expecting ridicule at the very least, but the only dampers she had yet received had been from women and dogs. This was putting it a little strong, but I have no doubt she was in the main correct. Whether the cutting remarks that are showered upon Erie's pioneer wheelwomen by others of their own sex, are engendered by jealousy or whether they are the result of a disordered stomach, I am not prepared to say. I only know they are not in good taste.

Probably the great number of wheels in Erie is due to a considerable extent to the untiring zeal of Frank Fairbairn, the agent for this territory. He is not only a good salesman and a first-class judge of wheels, but he is a jolly fellow all around and a general favorite wherever known. To Mrs. Fairbairn belongs the honor of being the first lady bicyclist in the vicinity, and she rides, as she does everything else, gracefully and well.

Crawford finds his wheel quite indispensable to news-gathering, and manages to be in more places at once than any reporter ever did before, and that's saying considerable. But for thorough enjoyment I recommend you to McGill. "Don" can do anything but grow thin. May his shadow never grow less.

N.

Erie, Pa., June 17, 1889.

MAPS OF THE ORANGES.

We have several fine maps of the Orange riding district, compiled by Mr. Mead, of Newark. Distances, condition of roads, and points of interest are well defined on the maps. Price fifty cents.

FRESH SUBJECTS FOR "COPY" AND "PARS."

The hearts of our English and Irish contemporaries must indeed be glad within them at the advent of Elwell's tourists. Not alone at the prospect of a chance to do them kindly courtesies, but at the thought that column after column of new "matter" can be furnished their hungry readers. In fact, they naively admit as much, as witness the frank confession of Mr. Baynham, of the cycling press, at the dinner tendered the "Yanks" in Dublin June 1:

Mr. Baynham said: Mr. Chairman and Gentlemen—After the very able and eloquent remarks of my friend Mr. Low, I am afraid very little is left for me to say on this important subject (laughter). It is not every day that we have the opportunity of listening to an Englishman gifted with that natural eloquence which we think one of the characteristics of our own country. Therefore, I think that our worthy Chairman's exhortation to be brief will be accomplished by me. It was very good of you to honor us press men in this way. We are accustomed to this sort of thing, and it is no use. What we want is something to write about. We don't care what it is, but we want something. Your little peccadilloes, if you have any, are what we like. It's all very well to talk about virtues, but virtues make bad paragraphs. We like to get at your big sins; to catch you when you are not doing what is right; when you take the train at a time you ought to ride. Virtue is all very well in its way, but give me vice (oh)—good, hard vice. One cannot make more than a stickful out of virtue, but one can make a whole column out of vice. I do do not think I need keep you any longer talking about the press. We want something to write about, and if you supply it we shall be most happy to receive it.—*Little Blue 'Un.*

If we were to give space to all the good things said at that dinner, both by our representatives and their entertainers, there would either be room for nothing else, or we should have to emulate the New York dailies and publish a "European edition." Suffice it to say that when it comes to speech-making, Messrs. Beale Elwell, Reilly and others have shown they are fully able to sustain our reputation in that line.

It is a close race between *Bicycling News* and the *Irish Athletic and Cycling News* as to which shall furnish the most complete and original account of the tourists' doings. While on its native peat we think the latter paper leads, but when the Englishmen get our boys down on the Ripley Road, and give all their press men, ably aided by the pencil of Geo. Moore, a good chance, the result will be plainly seen. What the tourists think of their entertainers is shown in the letters from our two special correspondents, but how the visitors strike the wheelmen abroad the following clipping from "Scorcher's" writings in the *Little Blue 'Un* will show. It is of interest to all of us at home that know the tourists:

Such of the Yanks as I have met personally I found to be awfully decent and nice fellows. Beale is one of the right sort. He comes from Michigan, and tours till November, being only stopped from going on till December by the fact that there will be no place for him to go to. He takes in Russia and Siberia, and talks of returning through Ireland. He looks a likely man to find Stanley, has an eye for a pretty lass, keeps a real good weed and enjoys the distinction of being the youngest presidential elector in the States. P. Harvard Reilly I regard as a brother. He did not tell me why he dropped the "O," but this is his tenth visit to Ireland, and he is full of the most generous feelings and good wishes for our country and her people. Is the best-looking man in the crowd, in appearance more English than American, being quite as stout and comfortable-looking as Low himself. Makes a rattling speech, and is not above perpetrating a bull. Collins is an artist, and friend to Quinton, paragraphs concerning whom he carried about for years in his pocketbook. He showed me some of my Quintonian "pars," not knowing at the time that I was the distinguished author. Collins is a quiet, steady goer, and never keeps on eating prawns when he knows he has had enough. Low to took possession of Elwell that I could not get at him; however, I observed that he is a calm, placid man, with a great deal of go and energy hidden under an outer coating of undisturbable imperturbability never leaps until he has looked, and never looks except through spectacles. Has a fund of quiet humor, and can orate some very pretty compliments. From the little I saw of Higgins (the man who carries the till) I thought he was a jolly little divil. Palmer is a very quiet fellow, but another young fellow—a mere boy. Is quite Irish, you know, in everything but his guesses and calculations. A chaplain travels with the party, but while in Ireland he enjoyed a sinecure. "Faed," who is not proud of the cycling press, "did" Cork to Dublin for a couple of Saxon prints. Mr. Pennell, who indignantly denies that he belongs to the cycling press, travels for, I presume, *The Christian Herald*. He has been specially appointed to get the men to bed early, but up to Sunday morning had been a dismal failure in the office. Does not talk of resigning, but keeps on appealing to his constituents; looks clever—is clever; a capital artist, with all the outer peculiarities of his tribe; wears whiskers which are a long way senior to his beard; also sports an unusually tight-fitting skin. The whole party are secretly bound to express astonishment at nothing. Amongst those who rode from Cork was Allport, who came as understudy to the chaplain by special invitation, his fame for administering spiritual comforts having long since penetrated to the States.

One more quotation from the same writer, who was present at the dinner and took a prominent part, and we are done:

I don't know whether the quantity we ate or what we drank or the amount we talked was the cause of it, but certain it is that there never was such a case of *tempus fugitting* as there was at the dinner. Just fancy a dinner in Dublin with only one song! And yet it was half past twelve when we broke up. Beale, Reilly and Elwell made excellent speeches, as did Jameson, Tyner and Quinton for the other side. When I read the Centennial efforts of Chauncey M. Depew and Bishop Potter I knew that American orators still live to sway the world at their will, but I was not prepared to find that every American is an orator. They all are. Everyone of them that spoke on Saturday night scored any amount of runs off his own bat, and clean ran the Irishmen out. Let us hear no more blither about Irish eloquence.

We have a secret suspicion that the men who could have gone and didn't will go out and club themselves when they read of the good time these wheelmen have. Talk of triumphal processions! Barnum himself, in all his glory, simply "wouldn't be in it" with the American tourists.

"JACK" FAVORABLY "SIZED UP."

If Purvis Bruce were not such a hardened dyed-in-the-wool newspaper man as to be beyond blushing, we feel sure the following paragraph, extracted from *Wheeling*, would cause a roseate flush to mantle that noble brow:

"*Pen and Pencil* has been giving Purvis Bruce some pleasant words and likens him to Byron in appearance. Curiously enough, when Bruce first came here he wore a flowing garment which W. McC. christened his "Childe Harold Cloak," and the chaff drove Bruce to divest himself of the cloak though we could never get his hair off. Here is what *Pen and Pencil* says of him: "Of rather a sarcastic turn of mind, and fond of sitting on the world's balcony and secretly laughing at the antics of the fools who pass below, he possesses at once a musical and a bitter pen—'bitter-sweet' in his nature with a dash of the Byronic disposition (which is strongly shown in his features, resembling Watteau's picture of the poet very strongly), he has a touch of velvet and iron in his writings, a dash of the man-of-the-world, of the free-thinker who must have proofs for belief, and yet a softness of heart almost approaching womanliness. An odd, likeable mixture of contradictions is J. Purvis Bruce. Mr. Purvis Bruce, besides being one of the acknowledged authorities on the cycle and its mechanism and purpose, is a facile writer on other subjects—especially those relating to life out of doors. Angling and shooting are subjects which under his treatment are well known to readers of papers devoted to these subjects."

STILL IN BUSINESS AT THE OLD STAND.

ST. LOUIS, June 15, 1889.

MR. F. P. PRIAL, EDITOR THE WHEEL:

Dear Sir—At the last meeting of the Missouri Bicycle Club, held June 4, a resolution was passed that, owing to an article which appeared in THE WHEEL under date of June 17, written by "Ithuriel," your St. Louis correspondent, making several uncalled-for remarks about members of this club, the subscription of this club to your paper be discontinued.

Therefore, please discontinue same, and oblige

Yours truly,
J. B. S. LYNCH,
Secretary.

[The "remarks" referred to appeared in the May 17th, not the June 17th, issue of THE WHEEL. Our correspondent described the May meeting of the Missouri Club, at which the question of Sunday billiard-playing was excitedly discussed. Our correspondent, being a man of discernment, naturally wished to know whether the club was going to be "run" by the House Committee or *vice versa*. When it was decided that billiards should not be toyed with on Sunday, one excited individual vowed that he *would* play, rule or no rule, and this vastly amused our correspondent, who, like a true journalist, put his amusement into print. The only uncalled-for remark we note is that the descriptive adjective "bow-legged" is applied to the excitable individual mentioned above. While we are willing to confess that the spectacle of any man shouting defiance to the club law is always amusing, it is doubly so when the defiance comes from a fellow who is both little and bow-legged; yet the adjective should not have been applied, because the curvature of one's bones is a thing quite beyond one's control.—ED.]

WATCHING THE LIONS AT THE CRYSTAL PALACE TRACK.

The world-famed Crystal Palace track is within an arrow's flight of my castle, and when the jigger is at the hospital, or my b——s want patching, or any other such obstacle deprives me of my usual evening ride, I just give orders to the watch to lower the drawbridge, and stroll across to have a look at the lions training.

The track is pretty nearly a perfect circle, three and a half laps to the mile; the surface is always kept in first-class order, and dries fairly quickly after rain. There is a well-appointed pavilion for the boys, and machines are also stored there, and the grand stand is well built and roofed. The greater part of the centre of the track is taken up by an ornamental piece of water, where ducks disport themselves, varying their aquatic exercise at times by a military march across the track at imminent risk of their lives. Over this water has been erected a large model of the new bridge now being built over the Thames, a pretty enough object in itself, but vexatiously situated, as it is impossible now to obtain a view of the whole track from any one point. The general surroundings (save for two modern absurdities, a couple of hideous toboggan slides) are pleasing in the extreme. Grassy banks slope down in all directions, on which the public congregate, and under the misapprehension that a race is going forward, encourage a safety rider with shouts of "Go it, little 'un," and bluntly inform another man, who is doing an "easy" after some fast laps, that in their opinion "he ain't no good." Trees meet the eye at every point, and on the evening breeze come scent of flowers and sound of music from the rosery. It is a beautiful track, in a beautiful garden.

Having thus briefly described the cage, I will venture on a few personal, but, I trust not rude, remarks about the lions themselves.

Only one lady trains on the C. P. path, Mrs. Smith, who rides a tandem tricycle with her husband. She is a slightly built, small-featured, healthy and wiry-looking little woman, with a very quiet manner. Her speed and staying power, for a lady, is very remarkable, and she gets through a rare lot of work on path and road every season. Her worthy lord is also lightly built, and has a rather over-trained look about him; his crop of curly hair is particularly fine and large.

Adams is a man who is doing a rare lot of pedaling every evening. He rides an ordinary built by his own firm, and is a well-set, fair-complexioned man, with a merry face; when riding he crouches down to his work, and gives one the idea of being a stayer. Another hard worker is Adcock, a very powerful-looking fellow—in fact, he looks too heavy for path racing, and would, I should say, do better in a good, steady plug than a sprint. He is now (May) riding an ordinary. Few riders are more generally popular than Bramson, "Lord Bram," as the gang call him. To see the elegantly attired "Lord Bram," with his shining silk hat knowingly tilted over his right eye, lounging about the Crystal Palace with an air of "never exerted myself in my life, *deah bhoy*," and then to see him on his ordinary, straining every muscle of his long body, his parchment-like skin wrinkling on his thin face with determination, and sprinting with the best of the string, is a revelation, and a lesson not to judge by appearances.

The Dutchman, Scheltema-Bedoin, is a new comer; he has been training on a tricycle, but when I last saw him was mounted on an ordinary, in which elevated position he did not seem quite happy. He is strongly built, of medium height and has a great deal too much fat on him. He trains in gorgeous habiliments, bares his arms to the shoulders, and rides best on a heavy track. Of safety riders at the C. P., Edge, the Anerley B. C. man, is decidedly the best. He is a dark, good-looking young fellow, full of life, animation, light hearted and gay, has good broad shoulders but is very slight in the waist. He does not believe in killing himself whilst training; when racing, however, will use up his last ounce of strength if required, and rides with a good deal of judgment, and a pretty style, sitting far back and using his ankles a lot. To see him watching an opponent with side-long looks, of not exactly love, is a study. He is a first-class man on the tricycle. A brother of Edge's is a promising young lion in the tricycle way; he has come on the track this season and after

two evenings of watching him I will venture a prophecy that he will be heard of later on. Annison is a curious-looking fellow on a safety; he is tall and has long legs—of course he wobbles horribly, and the whole show being top-heavy, his "croppers" are frequent.

Lacy Hillier, the old lion, is on the ground nearly every evening, timing and training the boys; he also trots out his ordinary at times to have a turn with the "young uns," riding with a good, steady swing, and holding his handles underneath, the palms of the hands being turned upwards. He is a big, athletic-looking man, makes himself very pleasant to the boys, and springs back after saying "go" to a flying start as if he had just escaped treading on a cobra.

But "the best of them all, the pick of the lot," is the clipper that rejoices in the name of Osmond. A very long, thin man, clad in tight-fitting chocolate-colored garments, a small, clean-shaved, delicate-looking face, a quiet, subdued voice, a rather serious expression and a manner utterly destitute of the slightest suspicion of bounce; in short, a gentleman, such is Osmond, the best man in a handicap in the world. To see him ride is grand. He crouches on his long ordinary, his long back arched up, his head low, bow knitted, mouth slightly open, his thin face cutting the air like a greyhound. The machine is forced shrieking along by his great powerful legs, the backbone bends backwards and forwards with the strain, on he flies resistless, an eagle swoops down on his prey. Osmond, like Edge, has brought a brother out this year; the youngster has a good deal of his brother's style; whether he has his powers, judgment and heart remains to be proven. This concludes the list of old and young lions at the C. P. track, but mention should be made of their keeper, Charlie Wilson, the ground man. Charlie in the season lives on the track—it is his world. He has a secret belief that no other track could ever hope to rival it, and he tends it with a patience and care begotten of his great love. The boys have just a little fear of him but are on the best of terms with him, and well they may be, for a more obliging, better-tempered man it would be difficult to find. It is: "Charlie, put my pedals on, please," "I say, Charlie, old man, bring us a towel," and so on all the evening. "They are just like a lot of children," says Charlie, trying vainly to disguise his sun-burnt face, brimming over with good humor, in an affected frown.

And so every evening the lions wander round and round. Whether the result is worth all this labor and self-denial I suppose they know best, but for me the road, the open common and the changing scene.   FREE LANCE.

A SAN FRANCISCO HOUSE.

Mr. Edwin Mohrig of San Francisco, Cal., not content with acting as Chief Consul of that large division, also shows enterprise as a business man by issuing a small but attractive catalogue of goods handled. Among them we note the New Mail Ordinary and Safety (a favorite wheel on the Pacific Coast); Rudge Light Roadster; National, both Safety and Ordinary; the Electric Juvenile Safety and Juvenile Apollo; and lastly but not least in importance, a full line of Psychos. Mr. Mohrig explains that each and every article catalogued is carried in stock, and unnecessary delays thus avoided.

Only the best and most useful lines of sundries are handled, and a specialty of repairs of the most difficult nature is made. Second-hand wheels are bought and sold, the poor but honest cyclist is allowed to purchase on installments, and we cannot see but the California rider has every advantage his Eastern brother possesses.

In addition to other duties, Mr. Mohrig finds time to issue stirring circulars to wheelmen to be won into the Division fold, and has done much toward the success of the race meet just held at Los Angeles, Cal. We congratulate the California Division on their Chief Consul.

THE PARADE AT HAGERSTOWN.

I would have sent you details of parade sooner but plans were not consummated. The officials have already been stated. The parade will be assembled at 9 A.M. July 4, by ringing of all the church and fire bells. Line of march will move from club house prompty at 10:30. Each division will be located by a large painted sign. Then will avoid confusion of marching. The route will be over the finest portion of the town, but not a lengthy one, forty minutes will see us through. At dismission liquid refreshments will be served, and the customary photograph taken. The whole agony will be over by 12:30 at the outside, giving ample time for dinner and a rest before the races.

The race-course is but six blocks from the Hamilton House over fine streets, and eight minutes is sufficient time to get there. The grounds are in the corporate limits. The grand stand seats 2,500 people and a special stand adjoining the judge's stand will be erected exclusively for the press. The club house is right in the centre of the city and only a block and a half away from the hotels. Open house will be kept day and night and plenty of ice cold lemonade on draught. We are going to do the right thing and hope to see you all there.   HAGERSTOWN.

June 18, 1889.

CINCINNATI.

Here we are in a pleasant fix. Rain, rain, rain! It seems as though the boys would have to add fins to their wheels and swim out into the country. Just think of it. Forty days, and I don't know how many nights. Both the road race and the Cincinnati Club race have been postponed to June 16, when we hope for better weather. I hear that work on the new Athletic Grounds of the Cincinnati Gymnasium is to be soon begun, and that a good cycle track will be one of the features. This will give much pleasure to wheelmen here. At a recent conversation with the Alderman responsible for the city ordinance regarding sprinkling of streets, he said there had been so much rain lately, and prospects were good for so much more, that he intended to introduce an ordinance leaving the sprinkling entirely to nature. I hope he succeeds, and know the good wishes of every wheelman in the city will go with him in this event. Frank A. Koppes has a new wheel, and is as proud of it as a boy with his first pair of pants. Some of the boys have wondered at dogs giving Chas. Colling so wide a berth, but they knew the reason now. He was riding up Race Street last Sunday evening at a lively gait on his Safety, when a new dog that had not had the pleasure of an introduction met him. The dog was struck broadside by the Safety and both wheels passed over his body which, on turning a spoke. The dog wended his way home, a sadder and wiser animal. A most amusing sight was witnessed by two or three hundred people in front of the Post Office the other evening. Mr. Hatfield got hold of a Safety without a saddle, and a gallant attempt was made to master it. Before he had gone far, the front wheel went under, Mr. Hatfield followed suit, and the balance of the machine climbed up on his neck. After violent efforts by the delighted crowd, he was pulled out of this perilous position. Another attempt, and the cheers of the crowd, was more successful.

Messrs. Miller, Bennet, Koppes, Dubbe and Orr gave a fine exhibition recently of fancy riding that was worth miles to witness. It being hot weather, I'll let you off easy this time.

Yours truly,
SAFETY.

ST. AUGUSTINE, FLA.

No doubt our brother wheelmen in the Northern States think it impossible for bicyclists to ride during the summer months in Florida and the South, but if they would only pay a visit they would at once see we have very pleasant weather for that sport in the "hot" season. The evenings, after 5 o'clock, are delightfully cool, and when offices and stores begin to close you can see numbers of wheelmen gliding over the smooth asphalt streets enjoying themselves. I have been here four years, and have seldom seen the thermometer register high as 95°.

We miss our club president very much, as he was the life of the club, and it was from his enthusiasm in bicycle matters that the club was formed. We hope to see him return soon as possible, but know his health will be greatly improved by the trip to Canada. (N. B.—He was not connected with any bank.)

The Athletic Association of this city in connection with their annual games, on the 18th, will include two medals as first prize for a 1-mile bicycle race. They have invited any amateur wheelman in the State to participate. Jacksonville will be well represented, and the Alcazar B. C. will enter three men. The time promises to be fast, as we have a splendid track, two laps to the mile.

Mr. H. M. Flagler, the owner of the three magnificent hotels in this city, will put a baseball ground after the plan of the New York Association's, and will probably lay a bicycle track in the same enclosure. We will then expect to see some of the fast riders from the North down here during the winter to practise for summer races.

We receive your paper regularly and look forward to its coming with a great deal of pleasure. There have been seven applications to join the L. A. W. sent from here lately, and we expect more.

FRANK. J. HOWATT.

THE WATER BICYCLE IN MINNESOTA.

Despite the inclemency of the weather, quite a large number of people congregated at Lake Harriet, June 8, to witness the performance of "Prof." Alphonse King, who was advertised to walk and ride a bicycle on water. At 4:30 P.M. the professor, clad in gaudy-looking tights, appeared with his mechanical contrivances, which resembled miniature pontoon bridges. He launched his shoes and walked about 200 yards out into the lake, and rode in on the bicycle, which had been towed out by several men in a boat.

The shoes are of tin, 32 inches long, 9 inches high and 8 inches wide. On the bottom are small tin fins which open and shut, giving material aid in propelling the wearer forward. The bicycle consists of: two light tin cylinders about five feet in length, pointed at each end and far enough apart to admit of the free working of the wheel. These cylinders are almost totally submerged during the use of the wheel, giving the rider the appearance of being sustained by the wheel alone. The wheel is of iron, about three feet in diameter and provided with small iron paddles, and surmounted by an ordinary bicycle saddle. The steering is done by an apparatus consisting of four handles aided by cords attached to a rudder.—*Minneapolis Tribune.*

Chas. Garfield, of Holly, N. Y., writes: "The Springfield Roadster which I have received is a beauty, and 'way ahead of your last year's pattern. I have ridden over one hundred miles, and everything runs finely."

HAGERSTOWN, 1889.

Vol. III.—No. 18.]   NEW YORK, JUNE 28, 1889.   [Whole Number, 70.

There has been a good deal said about

THE IRVINGTON-MILLBURN ROAD RACE.

We haven't said much, didn't know we had a wheel in it, in fact.

We understand there were a good many specially constructed and very light bicycles in the race, but it remained for one of our ordinary

LIGHT CHAMPIONS,

under Bensinger, to win the

TIME CUP.

The only other wheel of our make in the competition finished second.

Funny how things turn out, isn't it?

Decoration Day was certainly our plum. We took first place in the Pullman race, you know, with seventy starters.

Don't you want our catalogue? We like to mail it.

GORMULLY & JEFFERY MFG. CO.

CHICAGO, ILL.

Largest American Manufacturers.

MERWIN, HULBERT & CO., New York Agents.

Not so Bad for the Star.

Can any Machine beat this Record for 1889?

Three-Mile L. A. W. Championship, May 30th,

J. PHIL. PERCIVAL, Los Angeles, Cal.

One-Mile State Championship, May 30th,

W. S. WING, Los Angeles, Cal.

Five-Mile State Championship, May 30th,

W. S. WING, Los Angeles, Cal.

The Star holds the Records, on the Pacific Coast, from one mile to five miles.

Half-Mile L. A. W. Championship, June 4th,

COLIE BELL, Ottawa, Kan.

Ten-Mile L. A. W. Championship, June 4th,

COLIE BELL, Ottawa, Kan.

The NEW "39" and "24" STAR.

THE WHEEL

—AND—

CYCLING TRADE REVIEW.

Published every Friday morning.

Entered at the Post Office at second class rates.

Subscription Price, - - - $1.00 a year.
Foreign Subscriptions, - - - 6s. a year.
Single Copies, - - - - - 5 Cents.

Newsdealers may order through AM. NEWS Co.

All copy should be received by Monday.
Telegraphic news received till Wednesday noon.

Advertising rates on Application.

F. P. PRIAL, *Editor and Proprietor*
23 Park Row,
P. O. Box 444,   *New York.*

Persons receiving sample copies of this paper are respectfully requested to examine its contents and give us their patronage, and as far as is convenient, aid in circulating the journal, and extend its influence in the cause which it so faithfully serves. Subscription price, $1 per year.

The editor desires to say that all historical material, that is, matters of record used in this paper, were compiled so hastily that inaccuracies will probably be noted. The material here published is taken from some notes which the editor is making for the compilation of a handbook of the sport, to be published in the near future.

THE development of the cycle is an interesting study; we say "development," for it was a growth rather than a discovery, though most cyclists invest Lallement with an inventive genius he did not possess. The first form of cycle or aid to locomotion was due to the characteristic indolence of a G_rman, Baron Von Drais landscape gardener to the Duke of Baden. The Baron invented the "Draisine" or "Dandy Horse," in 1816, at Manheim on-the-Rhine. On this wheel he made his rounds in the discharge of his official duties. It supported the weight of the body, the rider's feet touching the ground. Having been conceived in Germany, it took three other nations to develop the cycle — England, France and America. The Baron showed his "Draisine" at Paris in 1816, but no patents were obtained until 1828. For nearly forty years no advance was made, but important improvements were made in 1865 by Mareschal, Woirin and Leconde, who applied foot-cranks to three-wheeled velocipedes. In the same year Lallement, who had seen the crank applied to the three-wheeler, applied it to the two-wheeler, and thus laid the foundation of the modern bicycle. Thus the credit given to Lallement has four other claimants.

Lallement was an employee of Michaux & Co., Parisian manufacturers, and this firm made the "bone-shakers" and supplied the French craze, which lasted until 1869, when it died the death. In England the history of the sport commences with an exhibition of the "Draisine" in 1816, followed by an improvement by Johnson —1818—and another improvement by Gompertz —1821. There the march to perfection rested until Lallement's "bone-shaker" appeared. The English being more mechanical than the French, went to work on Lallement's type and

built up the trade from 1870 to the present day, starting with a "bone-shaker" and ending with the modern bicycle.

In America the sport commences with an exhibition of the "Draisine" in 1819, and a patent for an improvement in the same year by W. K. Clarkson, record of which is lost. The wheel is heard of no more until Lallement arrives at New Haven in 1866, makes a couple of bone-shakers and exhibits them. The "bone-shaker" craze lasted through '68 and '69, being as brief as it was violent. Then for almost a decade the cycle is lost sight of until 1876, when David Stanton, an English racing man, brought over an English bicycle. This bicycle was a growth of Lallement's bone-shaker, which had been vastly improved in '68—a large front wheel and small rear wheel by L. F. A. Riviere, of England; a rubber tire by C. K. Bradford, of America and anti-friction bearings by E. A. Gilman, of England. In 1877, Mr. Alfred D. Chandler, of Boston, imported and rode, and induced Messrs. Weston, Cunningham, Heath, Dalton and others to ride. Then the sport went rapidly ahead. In this one year two firms commenced to import —Cunningham & Co. and the Pope Manufacturing Company. The Cunningham Company were intimates of the first riders and imported to supply their trade. The Pope Company came to import through Mr. John Harrington, who had a wheel made and taught Colonel Pope to ride. In the same year a bicycling paper was established. In the next year clubs were formed and manufacturers turned out American wheels. In 1880 the formation of a League was possible ; then the sport advanced in leaps and bounds.

THE *Journal of Commerce* of Monday last devotes a column to street pavements under the title of "More Job Pavements." Mr. Stone is evidently on strange ground. His screed against the introduction of asphalt pavements in New York is churlishness itself ; it is merely assertive, and possibly libelous, as may be gleaned from its heading, which is at once a trial and conviction of the Commissioners of Public Works.

Mr. Stone arrays abuse against expert testimony, denouncing as bribe-takers the scientists who have given opinions in favor of asphalt, accuses the New York dailies of wanting to put up jobs, and reflects on the integrity of the city officials. As a species of wind-up, Mr. Stone accuses Professor Newbury, who recently published an opinion on pavements, as being "young," always the cry of the pessimistical fossil.

A NUMBER of wheelmen at Hagerstown will see THE WHEEL for the first time. We only ask them to look carefully over the paper, feeling assured that they can best determine whether it is worth a dollar a year. We want you all to subscribe. We think we are publishing the best wheeling paper in the country, and every time we get a subscription we know that some wheelman or some wheelwoman thinks the same thing. There is matter in its columns for all—the tourist, the racing man and the members of the trade. Agents should keep the paper on file, and know what is going on about them. We cover all fields, from Maine to California ; we have space enough to devote a line to Tommy's investment of his surplus in a receptacle for oil, because we know that Bobby and Bobby want to know what Tommy is doing ; we have also space enough to devote several pages to show the Hagerstown Meet.

PICKINGS FROM THE LEAGUE PROGRAMME.

GOOD THINGS IN STORE.

The tenth annual Meet of the L. A. W., as has repeatedly been stated in THE WHEEL, will be held in Hagerstown, Md., on the 2d, 3d and 4th of July.

The official programme, a very handsomely printed thirty-six page pamphlet, has been issued and distributed among the fifteen thousand or more League members in the U. S. Following are interesting extracts from its contents:

THE CURTAIN RISES.

"Blue mountains east and west enfold
A vale of waving green and gold,"

and midway between, where the foot of the beautiful Cumberland Valley rests upon the head of the famous Shenandoah, nestling like a gem on the fair bosom of a courtly stream, lies Hagerstown—the queenly mountain city, swaying her sceptre over hundreds of miles of the finest wheeling district the sun ever kissed. Southward a few miles, like a blue ribbon dividing the North and the South, flows the historic Potomac ; eastward are the famed South Mountains, and westward the beautiful Blue Ridge. Within easy wheeling distances are the battlefields of Antietam and South Mountain, and Pen-Mar, the picturesque. Six miles north to the Pennsylvania line, and six miles south to the valley of Virginia. With over twenty miles roller-made streets and eight "sand-papered" pikes, this is verily the cycler's "Land of Promise," and "Canaan's Land" looked no fairer to eager Israelitish hearts than does this to the weary wheelmen. Turn hither, touring ones, and abide with us, if but for a little while, that we may rejoice together and make merry with many wheels. The keys of the city will dangle from your belts and walls await their coloring of crimson. We propose to make this, the Tenth Annual Meet of the L. A. W., "a thing of beauty-and a joy—" till the next one. Welcome to the tribes of the wheel—the Safety-ite, the Crank-ite, the Lever-ite. Come hither and we will "take you in."

RECEPTION.

Visitors coming by rail or road will be met at the various depots and at designated points and escorted to headquarters.

Wheels will be received and stored by the Committee. The Hotel Hamilton will be the headquarters, where guests should report immediately upon arrival, register and receive badge admitting them to entertainments and general fellowship.

Hagerstown may be justly termed the "City of Hotels." The Hamilton, Baldwin City and Franklin are hostelries that would honor and ornament any city. In addition, the Hagerstown Female Seminary will be open as a Summer Hotel, and will offer elegant accommodations.

ENTERTAINMENT.

Tuesday, July 2.—The forenoon will be devoted to receiving guests, business meeting, and "go-as-you-please" riding. In the evening a run will be made to Williamsport, where the time will be spent in sight-seeing, on the Potomac, etc. Huge bonfires on the banks of the river will add to a unique scene. Distance, six miles.

Wednesday, July 3.—Runs to Pen-Mar, Antietam, National Cemetery, South Mountain, etc. An excursion train will leave Hagerstown in the afternoon for Pen-Mar and Blue Mountain House, returning at night with those who went by wheel. This magnificent summer resort, on the topmost peak of the picturesque "Blue Ridge," is too widely celebrated to require a description here. Elegant orchestra and dancing.

Thursday, July 4.—Formal reception and address of welcome at 9:30 A. M. Immediately after the parade refreshments will be served and the usual photograph taken. Races at 2.30 P. M. In the evening a grand pyrotechnic display, national open-air smoker and military band concert will be given in a beautiful suburban grove.

Further entertainment will be bulletined at League headquarters, Hotel Hamilton, other hotels and club-house.

PARADE.

Parade will form at South Potomac Street and start from the club-house at 10 o'clock

A. M., Thursday, July 4. Captains of clubs and unattached wheelmen will report to headquarters at 8.30 and be assigned position in line.

RACES.

With a fine half-mile track, especially prepared for fast time, together with a most attractive list of events, an occasion not to be surpassed this season will be presented to the racing fraternity. The following L. A. W. National Championships have been located here, *i. e.*, one-mile ordinary, one-mile safety, one-mile tricycle. These will be run off in connection with a number of interesting events, all amateur. Entries closed June 25.

BAY RIDGE.

AT HAGERSTOWN.

HOTELS.—Hamilton (Headquarters), $2; Baldwin, $2; City, $1.50; Franklin, $1.25 per day.

Report at Hamilton at committee headquarters, register and receive badges, etc.

PROGRAMME, JULY 2.

3 P. M. Run to Williamsport, 6 miles; bath in Potomac.

JULY 3.

9 A. M. Run to Antietam, National Cemetery. 3 P. M. Excursion train to Pen-Mar.

3 P. M. Run to Waynesboro, to Pen-Mar, and return by excursion train.

JULY 4.

10 A. M. Parade.
2:30 P. M. Races.

TABLE OF DISTANCES.

Hagerstown to Sharpsburg	Miles,	14
Sharpsburg to Boonsboro	"	6
Boonsboro to Hagerstown	"	11
Hagerstown to Williamsport	"	6
Williamsport to Cearfoss	"	7
Hagerstown to Cearfoss	"	4½
Cearfoss to Greencastle	"	6½
Greencastle to Waynesboro	"	9
Waynesboro to Hagerstown	"	11½
Waynesboro to Pen-Mar	"	4
Hagerstown to Smithsburg	"	8
Hagerstown to Leitersburg	"	6
Leitersburg to Waynesboro	"	5½
Hagerstown to Clearspring	"	11
Hagerstown to Smoketown	"	6
Hagerstown to Middleburg	"	5

A FEW DONT'S.

Don't stay up all night.
Don't try to be in several places at once.
Don't fail to be "chummy" with every one after introduction.
Don't fail to make yourself known to every good fellow you meet.
Don't fail to look your best on parade.

We are all here; the same old people—that is, almost the same. We all fought at the battle of Bay Ridge—the assault on the grubbery—last June, and we were in line at the attack on that St. Louis brewery.

In the evening, after supper, you will find the crowd in the vestibule of the League Hotel. They have ridden all day, washed up, eaten heartily and feel chatty. There is the League "gang," the "trade" gang, the "press" gang, the Washington "crowd," the Baltimore "crowd," the Philadelphia "crowd" and the Boston "crowd."

YOU WILL KNOW THEM WHEN YOU SEE THEM.

Luscomb: Sharp-featured, swarthy, medium-sized, deep-voiced, full of the dignity of office. He will tell you a story.

Mott: Nice little man, hair slightly grayish, kindly-natured, bright, brainy and busy; is a grand-pa.

Brewster: Neat, sharp-faced, gold-spectacled, cynical, witty, adept at repartee; no flies on Brewster. He looks toward you and he likewise bows.

Bidwell: Medium-sized, light-haired, freshly-complexioned, humorous, quiet, smokes much, thinks more, talks little. Has been dodging "Doc" Emery.

Emery: Well-knit in figure, earnest-faced, eloquent, silver-toned, emphatic and dogmatic. Has been chasing Bidwell with an axe and Prial with a club. First question he asked was, "Have you seen 'Mike' Atwater?" Look out for his speech on League uniforms.

Bassett: Massive-featured beetle-browed, self-contained, not to be hurried, full of statistics; takes pepper and salt in his coffee—sometimes.

Clark: "Sam" Clark—little, but oh, my!—long head, sees much; Lord High Jinks of the P. W. and B.

Le Cato: "Ned"—right near Clark—quiet, brainy, pillar in Maryland Club; to know him is to love him; thoughtful, never makes positive assertions—simply talks, and you always agree with him; chief usher in P. W. and B.

Atwater: Solidly built, fresh-faced, clear-headed; old townsman of "Jim" Dunn, of Massillon.

Oliver: Tall, well proportioned, talks better than well, sings well, bugles well, High Muck-a-Muck-a-Muck in P. W. and B.

Howard: Belongs to the Boston "gang," represents Boston *Globe*, writes much, small, pale, nervous, moustache twister, always going somewhere to regain his health.

Brown: "Doc" Brown, small, gray uniform, quiet, effective, great roads improvement fiend and one of New Jersey's favorite wheelmen.

Butler: "Doc," of Buffalo, professional looking, Sunday school superintendent, though you wouldn't guess it, may have a very fine and large beard and may not, as he is a lightning-change tonsorial artist, pulls with the "gang" is up in codes and laws and talks to the point in executive session. Ask him if he knows a man named Bull.

De Graaf: One of the best fellows in town; he is liable to appear clean-shaved as a clergyman, though he sometimes disguises himself in a flowing, auburn beard; hard-headed, large-hearted, live-and-let-live sort of man, business man, likes a good time and had it at Baltimore. That young lady he had on the tandem bike is Miss De Graaf; sister, oh, no, daughter.

Kirkpatrick: "Kirk," smiling, shelved but still in the swim, quiet, like a man who has held high office should be, big business man, one of the brightest men in the League.

Dunn: "Jim" Dunn, big man in Massilon in business and politics, tall, blonde moustached, serious faced, reserved, remarkable judgment; is one of the statesmen of the League, a wise counsellor, above slates and jobs; should be next President L. A. W.

Van Nort: Of Pennsylvania, sharp, auburn-haired, chipper, eye-glassed; the kind of man one doesn't want to jump on.

Gormully: Strong-featured, furtive-eyed; drops leading questions, listens much, thinks more; rich, enterprising, public-spirited; up in music and art; odd in some things; generous, if you know the combination. Mr Gormully will smoke good cigars, talk to all the agents, listen to all the inventors and retire bored at the funny things he hears and sees. Near him may be Mr. Jeffery, inventor, soberly clad and not so well known to wheelmen as his partner.

Overman: "C. R.," always on the road; small, but far bigger than his size; neat, the pink of courtesy; talks wheel in the finest language one ever heard. His parlor will be decorated with flowers, and you will find it the prettiest place in Hagerstown.

Purvis-Bruce: Small, curly-haired; Scotch-English accent; full of White Flyer, Ripley Road, Scotch Highlands; clever with the tongue, more clever with the pen.

No dirty linen to wash, no slate to make, no midnight sessions.

Don't try to own the town; if you must raise Cain, don't publish it from the house-tops.

HAGERSTOWN NOTES.

A few more d ys and the Meet of '89 will be in full blast with a gathering of cyclers larger than ever before known in the history of the League, and as the intervening time grows short, the prospects of a thorough success become more and more assured.

Chief Consul Mott has designated Messrs. C. E. and F. S. Heard and John Bauer, of the Hagerstown Club, as the official buglers

Entries continue to come at a lively rate, there being ten received in one mail on Saturday.

The track has been put in first-class condition, under the efficient superintendency of Vice-Consul Updegraff.

The club championship has been declared off and a tandem safety race substituted, to meet the demand for a race of that class. The entries number over sixty, including all the crack flyers of the country. Gormully & Jeffery have engaged rooms at the Hamilton.

Eisenbrandt Bros. will be quartered in a large room on Potomac Street, with a full line of Columbias, and also sundries of all kinds

Billy West, of the Clark Cycle Co., is here arranging a very attractive display for his house.

Among the latest to secure quarters are thirty of the Century Wheelmen of Philadelphia

Pennsylvania will send her "clans" to the number of 700, with the prospect of more.

The Germantown, Pa., Wheel Club will tour the entire distance, arriving here Monday, July 1.

Come one, come all, and Maryland shall once more take pleasure in extending the right hand of fellowship to her guests, The League of American Wheelmen.

HAGERSTOWN.

SPECIAL TRAIN SERVICE TO THE L. A. W. MEET AT HAGERSTOWN, MD., VIA B. & O. R. R.

The Baltimore & Ohio Railroad will provide special cars, which leave New York at 11 A. M. Monday, July 1, arriving at Hagerstown, Md., 8:30 P. M. same day. This train will pass through the cities of Philadelphia, Baltimore and Washington to Hagerstown without change. The fare going will be $7.75, and, to those who provide themselves with a certificate, the return fare will be $2 59, or $10.34 for the round trip. When purchasing your ticket at the depot foot of Liberty Street, New York, or at the company's office, 415 Broadway, New York, request the ticket agent to give you a properly filled up certificate; this certificate and $2 59 presented to the ticket agent at Hagerstown will entitle you to return ticket.

If you intend to go to the tenth annual meet of the L. A. W. make your arrangements at once with Charles Newbourg, 415 Broadway, New York, who has tickets, certificates and all information relative to the trip; he will also arrange for any parties who would like to see the cities of Washington, Baltimore or Philadelphia, returning. If it is not convenient to go on the special train, take the 12 o'clock midnight train Monday, arriving at Hagerstown next day noon.

The Century Wheelmen, of Philadelphia, are experiencing a lot of trouble from the actions of a maliciously inclined person, who makes a practice of borrowing the property of members without permission, and sometimes returning it in a damaged condition, at other times not returning it at all. The latest to suffer at this vandal's hands is Philip Roserau, who has had a new and valuable machine badly injured. It is rumored that extraordinary means are to be taken to find out who did the injury, and if he be a member of the club his resignation will be requested.

WHEEL GOSSIP.

"You publish the best paper I know of." L. D. Aylett, Birmingham, Ala.

Mr. Chas. F. Stevens, cycle agent, of Elmira, N. Y., was in town on Monday.

Willie Walcott, of the Orange Wanderers, climbed Corry Hill on a Star, last Sunday.

A new Victor Safety has just been delivered to Mr. J. W. Spalding, who is about to take up wheeling.

The Kings County Wheelmen are running their race meet to-day and to-morrow at Washington Park. Be sure you attend.

Mr. Lynch, representing the Lynch Mfg. Co., of Madison, Wisconsin, was in town last Tuesday. This company manufactures a bicycle lock.

New men should not fail to examine the New Mail Safeties and Ordinaries before making a selection. The New Mails are of the highest grade.

The present six-days' race in England between cyclists and Wallace Ross and George Bubear, on road-sculling machines, was easily won by the oarsmen.

We see by a recent issue of the *Coventry Journal* that the Psycho Safety captured all first prizes, and two second prizes, at the meet during which the West of France Championship race was run.

Don't humiliate me by printing my batch in that darn pee-wee type, that reminds one of the Lord's Prayer on a three-cent piece. Give us the old original pica, as most of our boys use glasses. COASTER.

A party will leave the Century Wheelmen's house at Philadelphia, June 30, with the intention of riding to Hagerstown via Gettysburg. The distance is 155 miles, and roads are said to be very good.

D. H. Lewis, one of the pluckiest riders in Buffalo, and one who wheeled from Erie to Buffalo on Decoration Day, took a bad fall on the Utica Street Hill last Sunday. His face was badly cut up and wrists sprained, and for ten minutes he was senseless.

The Bishop of Chester, England, is as ardent a cyclist as a theologian, and while presiding at a meeting of English wheelmen recently, declared that nothing in the shape of exercise had ever been introduced that approached wheeling in its benefits to the masses.

A slight fire Thursday evening in the show-window of Chas. Sewalbach's store in Brooklyn scorched a few goods, and the remainder were well wet down by the contents of an ice-water tank. A Babcock Extinguisher was sent around, but its services were not needed.

W. G. Schack, W. G. Brogan and C. W. Holland, of Buffalo, accomplished a difficult feat last week. They climbed Lewiston Hill from the hotel to the Rome, Watertown and Ogdensburg road. This is the first time on record that this hill has been climbed, it is said.

Mr. F. R. Birdsall, of the Nashville (Tenn.) *American*, is doing all in his power to advance the interests of cycling in that State, and his efforts should meet with appreciation by the wheelmen there. The recent Tennessee L. A. W. meet and tour so successfully carried out is earnest of the work done by the promoters. Tennessee is not blessed with the most smooth or level of roads, and touring awheel in that State means plenty of muscular exertion.

A MARVEL OF BEAUTY AND SWIFT AS A BIRD.

The Warwick Perfection Safety Bicycle has arrived, and is now on exhibition in the window of Humphrey's dry goods store, Wall Street, Kingston. Mr. Louis Hoysradt, one of the best bicycle riders in this city, having given the wheel a thorough trial, has this to say of it: "It is the best and handsomest machine I have ever ridden." All who who have seen it pronounce it the handsomest wheel in the market. It can be ridden by either lady or gentleman.—Kingston *Daily Freeman*.

Several members of the Lynn Cycle Club made a run to Concord, June 23, and partook of a "biled dinner" in that historic old town. J. Harry Shunman ate so heartily of the famous New England dish that his machine broke down. The boys were disappointed at not meeting the Portland Wheelmen, whom they rode out there to see. A number of the members of the Portland Bicycle Club were the guests of the Massachusetts and Somerville Clubs, and a run to Concord was arranged. Through some misunderstanding the Massachusetts Wheelmen took the visitors to Natick and dined at Bailey's Hotel. The Somerville Club went to Concord, and thus the two clubs failed to connect. A dinner had been ordered for the party at a restaurant, and when the hungry wheelmen sat down to the table the menu spread before them contained but one course—a fragrant boiled dinner, with heaps of cabbage.

TENNESSEE'S "TOUR."

The "four-days' tour" was completed in twelve hours. But of an entry of nearly a dozen, only seven faced the starter Wednesday morning. These moved off from the club-rooms, however, hopeful that Jupiter Pluvius had about exhausted his water supply, and that the wet spell of a week or more had been finally broken. Their hopes, however (and their clothes as well) were greatly dampened when they reached Nolansville, where they had to seek shelter from a heavy rain-storm. After the rain subsided they resumed their journey to Eagleville, but the road was so muddy and some portions of it so bad on account of having been recently laid with rock, that a council of war was held, and it was decided to abandon the idea of attempting to continue the journey. After dinner all of the party except J. C. Combs, Norman Smith and Frank Newson returned by the same route, while the gentlemen named wheeled from there to Murfreesboro, where they arrived just in time to catch the train for home, arriving here about 6 P. M., an hour after the others. They made the eighteen miles, from Eagleville to Murfreesboro, in an hour and three-quarters, all mounted on safeties. Jesse Sparks, Jr., of Murfreesboro, wheeled to Shelbyville to join the party there, but on account of the unavoidable change in the programme he missed them, and had the pleasure of his own company there and back.—Nashville *American*.

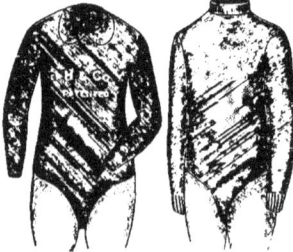

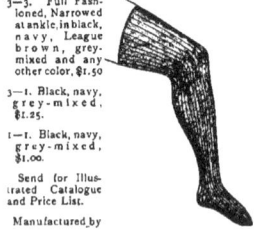

FIXTURES.

June 28, 29, 1889.—Kings County Wheelmen's Annual Meet at Washington Park, Brooklyn. Entries close June 21. Address Wm. F. Murphy, 1,235 Bedford Avenue.

June 29, 1889.—Handicap Road Race of Milwaukee Wheelmen, over Wauwatosa course. Entries close June 24.

June 29, 1889.—One Mile Bicycle Handicap at Field Meeting of Pittsburgh Cricket Club, Brushton Station. Entries close June 26, with A. MacPherson, 61 Fourth Avenue, Pittsburgh, Pa.

June 30, 1889.—Massachusetts Union Run to Massapoag House, Sharon. Address Capt. A. W. Robinson, 33 Winter Street, Boston.

July 1, 2, 1889.—C. W. A. Annual Meet at St. Catharines, Ontario.

July 2, 3, 4, 1889.—League Meet at Hagerstown, Md.

July 3 and 4, 1889.—Missouri Division L. A. W. Meet at Sedalia, Mo. Races on second day. Entries for handicaps close June 25; for open events June 27. Both to be made to Fred. E. Hoffman, Sedalia, Mo. No entry fee.

July 4, 1889.—L. A. W. Race Meet, at Hagerstown, Md. Entries close June 26, with Harry B. Irwin, 34 West Franklin Street, Hagerstown, Md.

July 4, 1889.—Two-mile Bicycle Handicap at Washington Park, Fifth Avenue, Brooklyn. Entries close June 26, with F. G. Webb, Treasurer. Prospect Harriers' Race, run under L. A. W. rules.

July 4, 1889.—Race Meet at Brownsville, Pa.

July 4, 1889.—Illinois Division, L. A. W. Meet, at Ottawa.

July 4, 1889.—Tournament held by Lancaster (Pa.) Bicycle Club. Entries close July 1 with H. F. Griel, Lancaster.

July 4, 1889.—Fort Schuyler Wheelmen, Utica, N. Y., 50-mile Road Race.

July 4, 1889.—Second Annual Tournament of Fort Dayton Wheelmen, at Herkimer, N. Y. Entries to be made with C. F. Giesey, Secretary.

July 4, 1889.—Fifth Annual Tournament of Berkshire Co. Wheelmen, at Pittsfield, Mass.

July 4, 1889.—One-mile Club Championship Race of N. J. A. C., at Athletic Grounds, N. J.

July 8, 1889.—Connecticut Division L. A. W. Meet at Bridgeport, Conn.

July 17, 1889.—Two-mile Bicycle Race at Caledonian Games, Minneapolis, Minn.

July 20, 1889.—One-mile and 25-mile Bicycle and 5-mile Tricycle N. C. U. championships at Paddington, Eng., track.

July 25, 1889.—At Minneapolis, Twenty-five Mile Road Race for Championship of Minnesota. Entries close July 20 with Will. Monarch, Secretary-Treasurer, Minneapolis Bicycle Club. Entry fee, $1.

July 27, 1889.—One-mile and 25-mile Tricycle and 5-mile Bicycle N. C. U. Championships at Paddington, Eng., track.

August 24, 1889.—Fifty-mile Bicycle and 1-mile Dwarf N. C. U. Championships at Paddington, Eng.

September 4-5, 1889.—Amateur Race Meet of the Hartford Wheel Club, at Hartford, Conn. Entries to be made with W. M. Francis, Secretary, P. O. Box 745.

October 23-29, 1889.—Race Meet at Macon, Ga.

EUROPEAN CYCLING FIXTURES.

Austro-Hungary.—Prague (Smichow) June 29 and 30. Germany.—Berlin, July 21, September 15; Hanover, September 8; Cologne, June 30, August 12; Chemnitz, September 8; Frankfort-on-the-Maine, September 1; Mannheim, September 8; Crefeld, September 8. Hamburg.—Altona, September 22; Bochum, August 25; Magdeburg, June 30, September 8. Denmark.—Copenhagen International Meeting, August 18.

RACES ON JULY 4 AT HERKIMER, N.Y.

We acknowledge the receipt of an oddly-designed yet attractive programme gotten out by the Fort Dayton Wheelmen and announcing the list of events to be run off, on July 4, at Herkimer, N. Y. Both the cover and the "greeting" inside are unique. On the former two lavender-plumaged and wide-awake looking owls stare at the spectator and perch on a limb so lofty that it cuts athwart the crescent moon. We would gladly reprint the "greeting" in full did space permit, but must content ourselves with two short paragraphs:

"Come and we will try to please you. If we fail we will never ask you more. Come early. Stay as long as you please. Win all the prizes you can, and go home when you choose. Only come!"

"An answer will tickle us to death."

Local wheelmen had better risk this sad calamity. Cast an eye over the valuable prizes and have a "go" for them. Medals and badges have been discarded and articles of real value and merit chosen in their stead. Following is a list of events, in regular order:

Road race, seven miles; half-mile novice, '89 riders; half-mile club race; one-mile handicap, open; one-mile tandem bicycle; one-mile, Herkimer Co.; one-mile team race, three in each team; half-mile Safety, Rover type; one-mile club handicap; fancy riding competition, ten minutes limit; three-mile lap race, six laps; half-mile unicycle; one-mile time limit; half-mile consolation.

Entries close at 12 M. on July 2, with Geo. W. Nellis, Jr., Herkimer, N. Y. An illuminated parade is to be held on evening of July 3. To quote once more from the greeting: "The road race is remarkable for the fact that it stretches over just seven miles, has seven hills (vouched for by seven liars), seven turns, seven incidents, takes thirty-seven minutes to run it and calls for seven prizes." S-eventually we will print the result.

In the account in The Wheel of June 21 of the Harvard Handicap Road Race, ridden June 15, Greenleaf's and Davis' times were made to read 28m. 3⅘s. and 28m. 13s. This should have been five minutes faster, or 23m. 3⅘s. and 23m. 13s. This correction makes a little better showing for the scratch men, and they will please excuse us for the unintentional error.

LOUISIANA CLUB'S ROAD RACE.

The Louisiana Cycling Club decided its fifth contest for the Hatson trophy June 23. The distance was twenty miles, and the starters L. J. Frederic, M. C. Grevot, M. S. Graham, R. G. Betts, F. B. Walshe and B. W. Cason, Jr. The twenty miles were made up of one short lap of 1.20 miles and four others of 4.70 miles each. The course was of asphalt, and the weather decidedly sultry. Sealed handicaps were also tried on this occasion.

The following table gives the race in detail:

	1.20. M. S.	5.90. M. S.	10.60 M. S.	15.30. M. S.	20. H. M. S.
Graham	4-4 04	1-20 59	2-38 45 1-5	1-56 22	1-1 15 27
Betts	2-4 01	2-20 59	1-38 45	2-56 22 3-5	2-1 15 27 1-5
Frederic	5-4 06	4-21 48	4-39 50	3-58 33	3-1 19 07
Grevot	3-4 02	3-21 37	3-39 46	Withdrawn.	
Walshe	6-4 34	6-23 50	5-45 00	Withdrawn.	
Cason	1-4 00	5-21 48 1-5	Withdrawn.		

Officers of contest—C. M. Fairchild, H. C. Christy, E. M. Graham.

The race between Graham and Betts was very close, not over a yard separating them at any time, and their finishing spurt was hot and exciting, and though Graham got his wheel across the line a scant foot to the good, he failed to make up but a fraction of a second of the handicap allowed Betts; consequently the race and medal go to the latter.

When the envelope containing the handicaps was opened it showed the following allowances: Graham, scratch; Frederic, 1m. 15s.; Betts and Grevot, 3m. 15s.; Walshe and Cason, 7m. 15s.

A QUICK RUN TO CABIN JOHN.

Yesterday William T. Robertson, on his Eagle bicycle, lowered the record of forty-three minutes made on July 4, 1887, by Percy Seyfferle, starting from Ninth and G Streets and ending at Cabin John, making the distance ten miles. Robertson started at 11:21 A. M., reaching Cabin John thirty-eight minutes after, beating the record by five minutes. Timers, Messrs. Smiley and Sickle. He now holds the record both to and from Cabin John, making the latter trip in forty-two minutes in 1884.

Borland made his last appearance on the path at the K. C. W. Meet.

The Allegheny Cyclers, Pittsburg, have secured accommodations for sixteen at the Baldwin House, Hagerstown.

Rich and Schumacher have joined the Berkeley Club. Rich has settled in New York as a permanent residence place.

R. J. McCreedy broke the mile tricycle record of Ireland at the recent championship meeting in Dublin. His time was 2m. 44 2-5s.

A. G. Buchanan won the amateur 25-mile championship of New Zealand recently. His time, 1h. 35m. 17s., is the best on record for that country.

Hempstead, L. I., June 22, one-mile handicap on grass course: N. F. Waters, scratch, 5m. 10s.; W. Hamlet, Hempstead A. C., 75 yds, 2d; A. L. Stoutenburgh, Queens B. C., 90, 3d.

At Amateur A. U. sports, June 15, at Detroit, Mich.: Two-mile bicycle race—A. E. Lumsden, U. A. C., first, in 6m. 14s.; G. E. Lane, D. A. C., second, by a quarter mile; J. D. Lamont, Detroit B. C., third.

At a meeting of the Commissioners of Public Works, held at the Mayor's office last Thursday, it was decided to pave all residence streets of New York with asphalt and the heavily-traveled streets with Belgian block.

It is expected that fully fifteen members of the Pittsburg Cyclers will attend the League Meet. This is of the club membership proper, and does not include a number of unattached that have expressed a wish to join the club in their excursion.

Y. M. C. A. Race—One and a half-mile handicap, decided at Y. M. C. A. Grounds, Mott Haven, N. Y. City, June 22. Howard P. Wier, 50 yards, 5m. 27 4-5s.; J. H. Hanson 20 yards, second, by several lengths; H. L. Powers, scratch, third, by a few inches. Wier is but sixteen years of age.

RACING BOARD SUSPENSIONS.

For violating clause 3 of Rule F, at Rome, N. Y., on May 30, the following are suspended till July 12, viz: A. H. Dobson, Harold Marguisee and John C. Robins, of Utica; R. S. Judd, J. P. Becker and T. C. Yehle, of Syracuse.

Chas. S. Davol,
Chairman Racing Board, L. A. W.

Following is the programme for the Brownsville races, which take place Thursday, July 4, under the auspices of the Brownsville (Pa.) Cycle Club. Entries close with E. S. Michener on July 2. Races to commence at 2:30 o'clock: Half-mile novice; 1-mile open; ½-mile, 1:35 class; 1-mile lap race; ½-mile handicap, for boys under fifteen years; 2-mile L. A. W. State Champion; 1-mile, 3:20 class; 1-mile handicap; ½-mile, horse vs. bicycle.

KINGS COUNTY WHEELMEN RACE MEET.

The K. C. W. lantern parade, Thursday night, was a great success. The first day of the Race Meet, Friday, was favored with good weather. The attendance was very small. Summary of events: One-mile races, K. C. W.—Bensinger 1, Stevens 2; 3m. 16 3-5s. One-mile handicap—Hesse, 55 yds, 1st; W. F. Murphy, 45, 2d; Clarke, 65, 3d; 3m. 1 1-5s. Two-mile handicap—Zimmerman, 105 yds, 1st; C. M. Murphy, 95, 2d; Bensinger, 125, 3d; 6m. 17 2-5s. Two-mile safety handicap—W. Murphy, 70 yds, 1st; W. Newman, 150, 2d; 7m. 21s. Five-mile K. C. W. championship—W. F. Murphy, 17m. 29 1-5s.; Jones 2d, Steves 3d. Complete report in next issue.

K. C. W. NOTES.

The tenth anniversary of the Brooklyn Bicycle Club and the formal opening of their new house took place on Friday evening, the 21st. By nine o'clock the club parlors were filled to overflowing, and then the usual programme for such occasions was gone through with. After the guests had been most heartily welcomed, and the more prominent visitors had expressed the feelings of all in their praise of the new home of their hosts, and their gratification at being able to be present on such an occasion, Mr. Torrey (you know Torrey) told us, in the musical metre of Hiawatha, of "Merry Men Who Ride a Cycle." This mirth-provoking effort was received with hearty and well deserved applause. Later, refreshments were served in the lower part of the house, and then the party broke up into groups, listened to the orchestra and chatted about coming events in general, and the L. A. W. meet in particular. Everyone was there, from the executive officers of the League and Union to the limit men in the local handicaps, and all had a word of praise for the new home of their entertainers. One feels more at home in 62 Hanson Place than in the more commodious quarters of the boys in gray and brown on Bedford Avenue. This is partly due to the style of the house, but in far greater part to the fact that every B. Bi. C. man appears to be a PERFECT HOST. Truly the Brooklyns are the premier entertainers, as well as cyclers, of this, the "City of Churches, Clubhouses and Cobbles."

The Kings County race meet is now the topic. The largest and best list of entries ever received. In the flat races, such men as Dohm, Downs, Skillman and Barr will be on hand, and those interested in running will be entertained by the best exponents of the (art?) in the country.

The conditions of the race for the "Schwalbach cup" have been changed. The man who wins on Friday will hold the cup permanently. This is much better, and is very much approved of by the winner, Mr. ———.

The Pope Mfg. Co. have presented a cup for the 2-mile handicap to be run on Saturday. The winner of this event will have a prize worth showing.

Among the gentlemen who will attract considerable attention at the K. C. W. meet will be Mr. F. W. Loucks, our ex-President. Mr. Loucks has been some months in California in the search for health, and judging from appearances he did not look in vain. He will be gladly welcomed home by his many friends among the wheelmen.

The wind prevented the attempt of the two Halls to do record over the Millburn course on Saturday. Wait till an open race, boys, and then have a go. These records made on the quiet never receive much credence. The public like to see performances, not hear about them.

Brown, Hess, Murphy and Steves will represent the King's Counties in the team race. All are training hard for the event, and show marked improvement in form. If they do not win they will at least give a good account of themselves.

Bensinger is booked for the club novice race, and I think should win.

The K. C. W. lantern parade will start, weather permitting, at 9 o'clock sharp on Thursday evening, from the club-house, Bedford Avenue and Brevoort Place. Preparations have been made to accommodate more wheelmen than ever before. One of the features of the evening will be the appearance of the Long Island Wheelmen in line. This will be the first *parade* ever attended by the L. I. W. On the return from the fountain the musical and literary talent of the club will furnish entertainment in the parlors, after which refreshments will be served, and those who so desire can attend the *promenade concert* on the "Brevoort Estate." Wheelmen in uniform admitted free after 10 P. M. "Music by Twenty-third Regiment Band."

The picnic run was a great success. What with boating, swimming, etc., the time passed so quickly that the call to mount and start for Brooklyn was received with regret by all. The general demand is another, and that at an early date. Mr. Marion brought back a plough as a souvenir of the trip. When appropriately embelished it will decorate the billiard-room.

Guess again Reitsnyder. Ram Lal.

Brooklyn, June 27, 1889.

SAN FRANCISCO.

The Bay City Wheelmen-Oak Leaf Wheelmen Race Meet, to be held at Stockton on July 4, gives promise of much sport and some new coast records. No claim has as yet been made for the records made at the League Meet at Los Angeles on May 30.

The semi-annual election of officers of the Bay City Wheelmen resulted as follows: President, R. M. Thompson; Vice-President, F. W. Pierson; Treasurer, W. D. Sheldon; Secretary, A. D. Allen; Captain, J. G. Cox; First Lieutenant, F. E. Richardson; Second Lieutenant, L. G. Hodgkins.

George Nash, the trick rider, has been exhibiting here for some time. The riders are divided in their opinions as to whether he or Maltby is the better performer.

There has been more touring out here this year than any previous year. Some of the riders have gone over nearly every road within a hundred miles of this city.

While on a visit recently to a country town near here, I had an opportunity of studying cycling in perhaps its best guise, that of utility. The country rider apparently does not think it necessary to dress for the occasion, but rides in whatever apparel he finds himself. His trips to the post-office, express office and to the beach for a swim are all of such short distances that he does not feel cumbered with clothes that a city rider would think it a hardship to ride in. Even the assistant minister, a manly gentleman, may frequently be seen on his 54-inch Victor, taking a quiet ride through town, clothed in the sober black cloth of his calling.

One gentleman of 65 summers seems to extract much pleasure from his tricycle, and he may often be seen explaining the mechanism to some elderly friend. He usually leaves him mystified by lifting the wheels and sending them spinning in opposite directions.

The pleasantest evening of my visit was spent as the guest of the —— Social Club, composed of ten young men. The meeting was held two miles from town, and as the majority of the members were bicycle riders, they went to the meeting on their wheels. The president was late, but the members lost no time and singing and music was soon commenced. After the lapse of some time a wheel was heard on the graveled drive and the president's arrival was noted. When he entered the room inquiries were at once made as to the cause of his tardiness. Between his efforts to regain his breath, he explained how a driver "took him on" for a sprint some distance up the road, and he had ridden a mile past the house before gaining a decisive victory. The fact was then developed that one of the unwritten laws of the club is that any driver challenging a member to a race must be accommodated and *beaten*. Later in the evening the president reclined on the sofa *a la* Little Lord Fauntleroy, and between songs quoted Shakespeare from a ponderous volume before him. The members are quite musical, playing among them the violin, mandolin, guitar, piano and flute. The ride home by moonlight was most enjoyable. The unwritten law of allowing no driver to pass them on the road was enforced on the return journey by the cycling members "taking on" their less favored friends in buggies and beating them. The only serious business of the meeting was the selection of the next meeting place, and knowing the excellent cake made by a certain kind lady, they did not hesitate to vote to hold the next singing festival at her house and honored me with an invitation to attend. Yours, CALIFORNIA.

San Francisco, June 19.

WASHINGTON, D. C.

About two weeks ago the members of the L. A. W. residing in the District of Columbia were awakened to knowledge of the existence of a Chief Consul and other League officers by receiving a notice to the effect that a League run had been called for Sunday, June 16. The run was called to start from Washington Circle at 9 A. M., which most of the boys took for granted to mean 10 o'clock. By quarter-past the party began to get restless, and numerous were the inquiries as to the whereabouts of our Chief Consul. After waiting in vain a while longer the boys got uneasy. Then it was learned that Vice-Consul Demaray was present, and he was urged to lead the procession. He chose Mr. Borden, of the Capital Club, to assist him, and they led the line. At first the pace was easy, but after a while it was increased, and a number, unable to keep up, withdrew. There was a charming lack of discipline or attempt to have an orderly appearance, and for half an hour after the first men reached the bridge the stragglers came rolling in. Dinner was had by a number of the boys, and they straggled back, with even less uniformity of pace than on the way out

It is hoped that another such run will be called, and that some one will be delegated to marshal the attendants.

But few club men were present, and a number of those who were in attendance were not L. A. W. members.

WASHINGTON.

RIVERSIDE NOTES.

The R. W's will be represented in the K. C. W team-race by Messrs. E. A. Powers, F. R. Miller, Jos. Judge and H. C. Bryant. Pres. Jas L. Miller, brother of Fred. R. Miller, is developing into quite a racer, and will ride his first race next Saturday. Messrs. F. R. Miller and Cossett rode to Peekskill on June 23 and visited friends at the State camp.

The runs for July are: July 4, Long Branch and vicinity; July 7, Yonkers; July 14, Englewood; July 21, South Oyster Bay; July 28, Tarrytown.

The R. W's had a very enjoyable run to Coney Island on June 16. Twenty-seven members took part, and enjoyed a refreshing bath at the beach. On the way down we met the H. C. W., who went to the same place.

The R. W's now have eighty members. Mr. F. Menge has ridden over 2,000 miles this year. The club have decided to adopt a new uniform, and will have same in about a month. E. A. P.

The Louisiana Cycling Club, ever active, has been at work for the past six weeks on a club-house project, and has at last about perfected plans that will locate them in a house of their own somewhere in the Garden District. This club's century run, which was to have started June 15, has been deferred until next month.

TACOMA, WASHINGTON.

For the past week cycling has been quiet, and consequently we of the far Northwest cannot contribute any very interesting items to the columns of your most excellent paper. It is indeed a "chestnut" to allude to the delightful weather we are now enjoying, and which will keep "steady company" with us for some time to come. Our evenings are especially adapted to cycling, as we suffer none of the many disadvantages experienced in the Eastern cities in connection with night-riding, principal mention being made of the cool evenings and the long twilight.

The lady contingent of cyclists are making rapid strides to the goal of perfection—in fact, some of them have already evinced a strong desire to accompany their escorts on a run outside the city limits, and more thoroughly enjoy riding over suburban roads.

We are all much surprised to hear of the suspension of Willie Windle, and hope he will soon be reinstated. I hope he will be exonerated and again eligible to represent America on the English path. We do not claim that he is invincible, but that he can make the best of them ride their prettiest to defeat him.

The committee in charge of the proposed race meet have done nothing the past week in the furtherance of this project, mostly on account of the great interest taken by all the business men in the Seattle sufferers. I hope, however, that satisfactory arrangements can be made and the first annual race meet be a grand success, as it surely would have been, without doubt, had not the Seattle conflagration absorbed so much of our attention.

At the annual picnic of the railroad employees a most interesting programme was run off. The games included flat races, hurdle races, jumping contests, races for girls and married women, and many other interesting features. The bicycle race was won by *Prince Wells*, with Burton Manning second, by two feet, and the third man distanced. The distance was about a quarter of a mile, over rough ground and turf full of holes, and the time was comparatively slow. As Wells approached the judge's stand and asked the time the referee and others showed considerable surprise, and said they were of the opinion that the riders were *simply practising*. However, the winner and second man received their respective prizes, and were duly applauded. The wheelmen then chose partners for the prize dance, and Mr. Manning again came to the front by his superiority in the "mazy" waltz.

Prince Wells won the hearts of several of the girls, "he is so cute, you know." Oh! that Prince would enlighten us poor mortals how he captivates so many fair ones.

The street pavement agitation has struck our "City of Destiny," and we are living in hope that our councilmen will take immediate action upon the matter. Cedar blocks and asphalt have the preference, and I hope the latter will be accepted, not only because it is better for cycling, but on account of its being the better pavement. For the steep hills, asphalt must take a back seat, as its smoothness precludes a good foothold for horses. For the avenues, all of which are perfectly level and wide, the cedar block will not prove as durable as asphalt, and will prove to be more expensive in the long run.

If the wheelmen of Tacoma and Seattle could exchange some of our best roads for the A 1 turnpikes of the Eastern cities we would like to enter a team of from six to ten men in the next handicap road race that takes place on the Irvington-Milburn course. In Tacoma we have some excellent stock, and, with a track or perfectly smooth road to practice spurts on, we could put our men in very fast form. We hear much of the Irvington road and the Lancaster pike in Philadelphia, and actually covet them. Probably "time will tell," and in the dim future we may claim, at least, a short stretch of road on which to make creditable performances, if but merely to show our Eastern cousins that we can ride a little bit.

June 19, 1889. SNOHOMISH.

NEWARK.

All the names, from Newark, of those who went on the "Century" were credited from the Essex Bi. Club. We just want to say that Messrs. Rummell, Russell, Scudder, C. S. and W. C. Swain were representatives of the Atalanta Wheelmen. F. L. Brock's name was omitted, though he was also a starter from the same club.

Mr. C. L. S. Walker, of the Atalanta Wheelmen, has ridden over 2,000 miles since January 1, 1889. He rides a 45-inch Pony Star, is out on all kinds of roads and in every kind of weather. Mr. Walker has just passed his 57th birthday, but acts just as young and jolly as any of the boys in the club.

Frank Brock is entered in the 1-mile handicap bicyle race and C. A. Woodruff in the 75-yard dash (running) of the K. C. W. meet.

John Herman, the well-known gent's furnisher on Market Street, is among the applicants for membership to the Atalanta Wheelmen.

President Miller of the Atalanta Wheelmen has just returned from a short vacation at Ocean Grove. His principal amusements while there were bathing and writing poetry.

Twenty-five men have been booked for the lantern parade, Thursday, 27th inst., at Brooklyn. Meeting at Military Park the route will be down Broad to Market, to Pennsylvania R. R. Depot to take 6:33 train.

"Doc" Crane has a new wheel. This time it is a Warwick Perfection. "Doc" was anxious to enter in the K. C. W. races, but thought it best not to show so early in the season what a racer he was.

Quite a number of the boys contemplate joining the H. C. W. on their run, Sunday (30th) to Pompton. We have been over that road, and know it is a good one "Good luck to you, boys." SPARK.

Newark, June 26, 1889.

The Indiana Bicycle Company have just placed on the market a $125 diamond-framed safety; weight, 50 lbs.; geared 51 to 64 inches.

A meeting of the League of the First and Second District Consuls will be held shortly after the League Meet, to discuss the feasibility of holding the New York State '89 Meet in New York and Brooklyn.

MARGUERITE'S LETTER.

A few weeks ago I noticed an inquiry from your Troy correspondent "Ornh Qba" relative to the superiority of the bicycle over the tricycle for the use of ladies on ordinary country roads. Now, as I have taken a long-talked-of and much-wished-for trip to Portsmouth, I am going to write how I found the roads with my safety. I mentioned in a previous letter how often I had desired to visit the above place, but was told by friends it was not to be "did" on a three-track machine

Truer words were never spoken, for the twenty-six miles between Newburyport, Mass., and Portsmouth, N. H., are not only ordinary country roads; they are *extra*-ordinary, as you will see later.

For two weeks previous to the 17th we had been talking up and planning this trip. The original itinerary was: Start 7 A. M. for Portsmouth on Saturday, the 15th; boating on the river Sunday, the 16th; return home Monday, the 17th. This was decidedly the best programme, and especially when Captain D. was to be the "commander-in-chief." We were sadly disappointed to miss part of it, owing to inability to start before Sunday. We decided to make the best of it, however, and the final arrangements were made, three friends, members of the M. C. C., including one lady on a safety tandem with her brother, starting on Saturday, as did also the Captain with two other riders. Time of departure in the two cases was different, but all joined in Newburyport for dinner, "Mac" and his wife with my brother and I to start Sunday morning at 4 A. M., reach Newburyport for breakfast and Portsmouth for dinner; return with others on Monday.

In consequence of our mother rising at 3 A. M. and routing us out, we were soon seated at the table, deep in the pleasant mysteries of a hot breakfast.

The morning was beautiful, not a cloud to be seen, and while at this time it was delightfully cool, the day gave promise of being a "roaster" later on.

We had packed and strapped on our bundles the night before, so 3.50 A. M. found us and our safeties all in readiness. Besides our bundles, my brother and I each had a large (*very* large) shade hat tied on the front handle-bar for future use. On reaching country districts we would doff our small caps and put on our "fly-aways." On previous tours, when wearing the small white cap, we have always returned with faces and necks "brown as berries," and while on the road would participate in the lively sensation of being slowly cremated. A large hat alone for summer riding does not find much favor in my eyes, for while I admire its sun-shielding qualities, should the wind rise suddenly, that settles it; no more comfort for the wearer during the ride.

The school clock in Maplewood struck four and we anxiously scanned the vicinity for a flying safety tandem. We waited and waited, but the "blue-suits" were still missing. Until 4:30 we did not complain, but after that time, seeing the best part of the day (for riding) slowly disappear and our sixty-four miles before dinner not started, we commenced to rain blessings (?) upon the "Mac's" devoted heads.

Again the chimes, this time for five o'clock, and we now decided to start, leaving "Mac" to catch up with us, if not on the road, at breakfast in Newburyport. It certainly was warmer than an hour previous, for before I had ridden three miles I packed a handkerchief inside my collar to try and preserve some part of the laundry finish, if only on the outer edges. The hour we had lost was worth two further on in the day, but no use "crying over spilt milk," and while enjoying every minute of the present with our machines gliding along in great shape, we felt that only the company of "Mac" and his wife were needed to complete our happiness.

Up the turnpike through Cliftondale and Saugus, straight through Lynn along Ocean Street, the prettiest avenue of all. Spectators were few and far between; here and there we would see a girl or boy accompanied by either the useful milk can or the festive jar of Boston baked beans. Reaching Salem we found the people all going to church, some of them gazing in holy horror at us, probably me in particular. Over Beverly Bridge and through North Beverly, in the latter place taking the sidewalks with perfect freedom, there being few early strollers and perfectly awful roads. In crossing a gutter the brazing of the attachment for holding the seat-post on my safety gave way, slightly tipping the saddle forward. This handicapped me greatly, as at every jolt I slipped forward on the saddle, subjecting my hands and arms to a constant strain. It felt like learning to ride all over again, and though riding over eighty miles with it in this condition, I rode no easier at the end than at the beginning. The mishap also made it a shorter reach for me, and since I ride with the post up the full extent no alteration could be made.

While we were intent on this examination the tardy T. B. rode up, having reached and left our house at 5:15. "Mac" will never dare to say a word for some time to come in regard to broken promises, and that hour and a quarter will cover a good many five and ten minute late-marks on our side. Before they joined us we had made several stoppages for water, etc. (no soda at this uncivilized time of day), but now we pushed right on through Wenham and Hamilton. Ipswich was reached, where I found that in my case every vestige of the hot breakfast was entirely exhausted. "Mac" was in the same box, but after a reviving drink (from a neighboring pump we flew on to Rowley—at the well) stopping for an impromptu lunch, which I had thoughtfully (from previous experience) tied inside "Will's" hat. Did ever anything taste so sweet? and with cool water, the only available lubricant, we felt very much refreshed.

Five miles more and we were in Newburyport, making a bee-line for the Wolfe Tavern, one of the nicest hotels on our list. A late breakfast, an hour's rest and 11:30 found us on our wheels bound for Portsmouth. After crossing the chain bridge outside Amesbury the roads were frightfully sandy, and six-inch side-paths were taken with gladness. At the top of a rocky hill the beating sun reminded us of our big hats, which we donned at once—after admiring their picturesque shapes and proportions. But who cared, so long as they shaded our aristocratic features? Certainly not we. The fun with the roads now commenced, at least convincing me that the tricycle has no home in that direction.

About this time we began to see our dinner vanishing in the distance, knowing that with these roads we could not reach our destination anywhere near 2 P. M. As it was Sunday no stores of any kind were open, and not even a tooth-pick could be bought for love or money. Plenty of water, but water without even the dry bread we voted as no good. The food question was the dark side of the picture, and as I had been almost starved once, cannot say

that I relished the thoughts of a similar visitation the same day. The bright side was riding—paths covered with grass we e all the same to us; we had only to glance at the roads to be satisfied. We hurried through Hampton, sampling the sidewalks, as usual, and left the people we met almost speechless with surprise. They had evidently never seen any lady cyclists before, and I am unable to state which created the most comment—the wheels, hats or wheelists, but it is safe to say that the total was sufficiently large. Some of the people we found very genial and home-like, especially at one house, where we had a large pitcher of milk, which they would not allow us to pay for. This was all the lunch we had from 10 A. M. to 6 P. M., with bad roads in the bargain.

We had two or three dog episodes, but nothing alarming, and at one place I took a charming tumble into a wayside brook. The road was all sand and had no hard side-paths whatever, while this particular spot was bounded by a two-foot banking. We all took the extreme edge, and the others who were in front came through all right, but my wheel swerved through the saddle-post's still further weakening, and over I went. Part of my dress, my foot with half my handle-bar and bundle (luckily the latter was covered with rubber) received the benefit of the spring-bath, but the warm weather soon dried the whole business and then I let my more fortunate but less sympathetic friends laugh as much as they pleased.

About 4 o'clock we reached the "Rockingham," one of the finest hotels this side of New York. We certainly made no record, only in the fun we had; after we found our dinner gone, we saw no necessity for haste. We found all our friends out, part having gone up the river and part on a wheel trip to Kittery, Me., just across the line.

Our rooms assigned, we departed, to be seen no more for awhile. The others soon returned and what incidents and experiences we each had to relate! I believe they had the most exciting, notwithstanding our lost dinner. About four miles from Portsmouth, on Saturday night, they had struck a full sized thunder-storm and were obliged to seek shelter in a farm-house near by. After the rain gave over they continued their trip, but three of the party, finding the roads in an almost impassable condition, gave it up as a bad job when two miles out. Hiring a team and a buggy, they completed the ride on four instead of two wheels. The rest of the party had to climb a stone-wall and carry their machines on the top at a particularly bad spot. We had noticed the place in our ride, and though it had dried considerably, the right-hand side still gave evidence, of the struggle.

We did not need to be asked twice in regard to supper, and oh! how we enjoyed it. After supper we took a four-mile ride around Portsmouth.

The next morning we awoke to find a well developed rain-storm in progress, and the roads in a very sticky condition. At 11 A. M. the down-pour stopped for the time being, so our contingent, with Captain D., decided to start for home and take the roads as we found them. Two of the party had started an hour previous in the rain, and the "four-wheel" party departed on the 11:05 train to Newburyport. The time flew on; bundles were not packed and all ready until 11:30. I shall not attempt to describe the roads, lest the air should turn "blue." At a small grocery-shop we refreshed on bottles of tonic and dozens of cream vanillas. We returned by a different route, which in dry weather must be vastly superior to our road of the previous day.

After again missing our dinner and being caught in two showers we reached Newburyport. We didn't mind the dinner *that* day; all the stores were open.

Stopping a minute at the hotel to hear how our friends had fared we pushed on again. When two and a half miles out, on reaching the top of a hill, the bolt in my machine broke, letting the whole saddle, seat-post, attachment and all drop with a thud. I felt thankful that it had not occurred when coasting, or the ending might have been different. There was no remedy but for me to walk back and "train" it home, my brother and Mr. D. doing the same, while "Mac" and his wife continued on their way. Leaving my safety to the tender mercies of the express, we left on the 5:40 train, reaching home in due time. The "Mac's" on their Columbia had an extra hard ride after leaving us, since twice the amount of rain had fallen nearer home, though really I envied them finishing the trip in true cycling style. They certainly deserve credit for pushing through the whole distance, while we viewed the muddy roads from a car window. To take the train on a cycling trip does not suit me, but in this case it was impossible to avoid it.

Nevertheless we had a grand, good time, and expect to make the trip again when we have another ladies' safety for my sister's use and the weather is more settled. My safety was repaired within three days, and is now much stronger (because improved) than when new. "MARGUERITE."

No one has done more for cycling than Charles E. Pratt, who was the literary cyclist of hi time, a man of splendid foresight, with a legal and practical mind. There may have been cyclists as well informed as "Charlie" Pratt, but certainly none had such command of the pen as he, and while they may have had much knowledge, he was enabled to spread h s. He conceived the League, and largely projected and directed its policy; his contributed papers on the sport were valuable to beginners, and to his persistence and legal abilities were largely due the early legal decisions classing the cycle as a vehicle. Mr. Pratt now occupies a spacious private desk at the Pope Mfg. Co.'s place at Boston. He is counsellor to the firm, as well as a large stockholder.

Ram Lal and Atol describe the Brooklyn's house-warming on Friday last. A house warm it was, Friday night being about the warmest of the year. The Brooklyn's fittingly celebrated their anniversary by moving to their new house, which will be the most comfortable wheel house in Brooklyn. The parlors were filled with cyclists in full evening dress; the halls were crowded, the stairs filled, while a number who found the lower part of the house too crowded, took a breath of air on the door-step, toyed with the billiard balls, or smoked in the reading-room. The entertainment was perfect. The speeches of Mr. Fox, Mr. Bridgman and Mr. Koop were bright and to the point; the supper was temptingly and prettily served, and conversation was facilitated by smoke and music. The mantel of the front parlor was handsomely decorated with a piece of cut flowers. Mr. Raymond very cleverly arranged a window in the basement, making it to look like a miniature conservatory. The hits of the evening were Sam Torrey's book, which cleverly hit off all the men in the club, giving their weak and their strong points, and the presentation to Mr. Raymond of a set of resolutions, engrossed, setting forth in well-deserved lines what he had done for the club. About two hundred cyclists were present.

A FEW BACK NUMBERS.

I hardly think the editor of THE WHEEL thoroughly appreciates the embarrassing position he places me in when he requests me to furnish him with some recollections of the earlier days of cycling. A few years ago I wouldn't so much have minded it, because then there were but very few ladies connected with the sport, and in consequence there were but few feminine readers of the wheel papers, while now, with the great number of fair wheelwomen interested in the wheel and its literature, it is an entirely different thing; and when I sit down here and write these reminiscences of long ago, and sign my name in full to them, I at once go on record, over my own signature, as being considerably older than I care about acknowledging before a jury of the fair readers of THE WHEEL. Not that I am afraid to plead guilty to being on the verge of becoming an antique, but—well, never mind why—but it don't improve my chances for getting married if I go on this way advertising in the public print what an old bachelor I really am.

It is always an "old timer's" privilege to declare that "things are not what they used to be," and I don't propose to sacrifice any of the privileges of my already confessed antiquity by declaring any different. It depends upon just how I feel whether I think the difference above noted, between the past and the present, is for the better or for the worse. At times I think they are an improvement and again I think they do not compare with the past, but the fact remains a certainty, however, that I personally had more fun in the bygone days of wheeling than I have now, though I guess what my friends tell me in explanation of this must be true, and that is that I was a great deal younger then than now, and it is I who have changed for the worse, not cycling. If I keep on this way, though, I won't begin my story till the space allotted me has been used in writing about myself, and that isn't what either the editor or I want, so here goes:

They talk about their bicycle clubs to-day, and say to me that we never had anything in the old days of cycling to compare with them, but they only make me laugh. It is true we didn't have magnificent club-houses of our own, nor clubs with one or two hundred members to inhabit them; there wasn't but one or two hundred of us all told, and we thought ourselves a pretty big club when we had six or seven members. But with all their boasted superiority of the clubs of to-day, I can show them one that existed in the earlier days of wheeling that for exclusiveness and unanimity of thought and action surpasses anything of the kind existing to-day. The club I speak of was the Lone Star Bicycle Club, and was organized, I think, along in '79 or '80. It was so deucedly exclusive and select that the entire membership and board of officers was condensed into one individual. How's that for an exclusive organization? This membership and board of officers had another peculiarity that has never been seen before or since, and that was that it was neither amateur nor was it professional. Now, this club owed its organization, exclusiveness and peculiar non-amateur and non-professional organization to an attempt to declare Will. R. Pitman, the then greatest rider of the wheel in America, a professional, but Willie wouldn't become a professional, and as the powers that were said he shouldn't be an amateur, he found himself placed in a position where he couldn't join any club, so he just organized the Lone Star Club, elected himself member and officer thereof, irrevocably closed the membership, and then went in to fight those who said he wasn't and shouldn't be an amateur. Well, the Lone Star Club flourished, it never became any smaller nor any larger, it remained always very select, never had any quarrels among its members or officers, and at last, when its most prominent member and officer, Mr. Will. R. Pittman, won his fight before the N. A. A. A., and was declared by them to have always been an amateur, it quietly ceased to exist, having performed its mission, and it now stands in cycling history as the most peculiar and select wheel club that has ever existed.

When I went through the wheelroom of one of our large clubs the other day and saw the handles upon the various wheels there my mind went back to the day when our cycling Solomons declared that the only proper handle for a bicycle-bar was a billiard ball, and forthwith most of us broke ourselves through buying ivory billiard balls and having them attached to our handle-bars for handles. We were strong believers in ball-bearings those days, and this just shows you how far we were ahead of to-day in those days. Where can you find me a wheel now that's got ball-bearing handle-bars? Saddles, too, have changed, but I don't know as I ride any more comfortably on these new-fangled super-spring affairs, with their bifurcation and suspensions, than I did on an old Lamplugh & Brown saddle, consisting only of an iron frame covered with pigskin, stuffed with a little hair—yes, with a very little hair at that. Seated in this same saddle, and swinging along on a Harrington cradle-spring, we "old-timers" had equally as much comfort then as we get now, and I don't believe that any modern saddle-spring is any more comfortable than this same cradle-spring was. Uniforms! Well, we were a little bit go-as-you-please, perhaps, in regard to them, with a slight tendency towards the fashion set by Joseph in his famous selection of the ulster of many colors, but then, you know, we used to think that when a man rode a wheel it was his duty to look as picturesque in his dress as possible, as he was so constantly being admired and envied by the onlookers. I guess most of us came up to the full requirements of the picturesque part of the performance, too. How the "old timer" would have looked down—of course, he couldn't have looked up—at the miserable little dwarf wheels of to-day. Why, in those days no man could you find who it would be possible for you to have convinced that he should ride a wheel smaller in size than a 54-inch. No, sir; we all wanted to ride just as big machines as it was possible for us to, by any means, propel, and to accomplish this, I have known cork soles of over an inch in thickness to be attached to the rider's shoes to enable him to reach the pedals at all. This was what might have been termed a sort of 'over-reaching ambition, as it were. Corduroy breeches, with chamois-skin seats, were thought to be just the proper thing for riding in, and if any of the readers of this don't think that we earned the pleasures of cycling those days by the sweat of our bodies just let them encase themselves in a corduroy riding suit, reinforced with leather, and then, in a brimless polo-cap, take a fifty or sixty mile run, mounted upon a machine weighing maybe sixty pounds and equipped with 12-inch handle-bars and cone bearings, and if they got back home outside of an ambulance I will be somewhat mistaken.

Every wheelman when he met another wheelman on the road was personally acquainted with him, or if he wasn't he was greatly astonished at not being so, and went at once to inquire who the new rider was. It's different, very different now; a man is lucky in the large clubs if he knows all of his own club mates, let alone the riders he meets upon the road. I can't say that I think this change is any pleasanter for me; it shows how the sport has grown perhaps, but it is not near so pleasant as the old state of affairs.

Did we race then? Well, I rather think we did. I won't soon forget the first time a mile was ridden on an out-door track in three minutes. Victor C. Place propelled a 54-inch Howard bicycle, weighing nearly fifty-six pounds, that distance within the time above mentioned at Buffalo, and the land at once resounded with his praise, and great was the wonder expressed at so marvelous a performance. Of course these figures don't compare with the present records, but let the riders, of to-day, without any knowledge of training and upon a soft trotting track, drive that same wheel a mile in three minutes, as Place did, and then let them laugh at the performance. If no one laughs till this is done, there won't be many wheelmen in America to-day who will be able to laugh, I tell you. About measuring race tracks for wheel races, now there was a question we just did let ourselves out on in the days gone by. Some argued that the same measurement that existed on a trotting track, *i. e.* thirty-six inches from the pole, should be the point at which the track should be measured, while others wanted the inner edge of the track or pole itself to be the line of measurement, claiming that that was the line on which a bicycle was ridden, and consequently its distance should be computed upon it. Finally after tons of paper and the Lord only knows how much oratory and argument had been wasted over the matter, eighteen inches from a fixed curb was accepted as standard. FRANK A. EGAN.

PATH RECORDS

FOR

Ordinaries, Safeties, Tandem Safeties and Tricyles.

AMERICAN AMATEUR.

ORDINARY.

Ms.	H.M.S.	Name.	Date.
¼	35 1-5	W. A. Rowe	Nov. 5, '85
½	1.12 4-5	"	Oct. 19, '85
¾	1.55 1-5	"	Oct. 26, '85
1	2.35 2-5	"	Oct. 23, '85
2	5.21 3-5	"	"
3	8.07 2-5	"	Oct. 19, '85
4	11.11 4-5	"	"
5	14.07 2-5	"	"
6	16.55 3-5	"	"
7	19.47 2-5	"	"
8	22.41 4-5	"	"
9	25.41 2-5	"	"
10	28.37 4-5	"	"
11	31.37 1-5	"	"
12	34.32 3-5	"	"
13	37.24 3-5	"	"
14	40.25	"	"
15	43.26 1-5	"	"
16	46.27 2-5	"	"
17	49.25	"	"
18	52.25 1-5	"	"
19	55.22 2-5	"	"
20	58.20	"	"
21	1.06.25 2-5	F. F. Ives	Oct. 9, '85
22	1.09.50	"	"
23	1.13.02	"	"
24	1.16.04 4-5	"	"
25	1.19.06 3-5	"	"

26–50 Miles—S. G. Whittaker, Nov. 26, '85.

M.	H.M.S.	M.	H.M.S.	M.	H.M.S.
26	1.24.55	34	1.53.30	42	2.23.54
27	1.28.30	35	1.57.19	43	2.27.49
28	1.31.57	36	2.01.00	44	2.31.35
29	1.35.26	37	2.04.45	45	2.35.26
30	1.39.00	38	2.08.22 2-5	46	2.37.01
31	1.42.29	39	2.12.08	47	2.41.31
32	1.46.05	40	2.16.04	48	2.47.45
33	1.49.45	41	2.19.59	49	2.51.50
		50	2.55.38 3-5		

51 to 62 Miles—F. F. Ives, Oct. 10, '85.

M.	H.M.S.	M.	H.M.S.	M.	H.M.S.
51	3.07.47 1-5	55	3.23.13 2-5	59	3.39.21 3-5
52	3.11.32 2-5	56	3.27.03 3-5	60	
53	3.15.26 2-5	57	3.31.22 1-5	61	
54	3.19.21	58	3.35.29	62	

63 to 92 Miles—Geo. Hendee, Nov. 11, '85.

M.	H.M.S.	M.	H.M.S.	M.	H.M.S.
63	3.56.32 1-5	73	4.38.01 1-5	83	5.16.45 1-5
64	4.02.59 3-5	74	4.41.35 3-5	84	5.20.45 2-5
65	4.06.28 3-5	75	4.45.07 4-5	85	5.24.41
66	4.09.58 3-5	76	4.48.48 1-5	86	5.28.23 1-5
67	4.13.32	77	4.52.31 1-5	87	5.32.01 3-5
68	4.17.12 3-5	78	4.56.11	88	5.35.50 1-5
69	4.21.26 3-5	79	5.00.05	89	5.39.55 2-5
70	4.27.27 1-5	80	5.04.17 2-5	90	5.43.57
71	4.31.03	81	5.08.25 3-5	91	5.47.58 2-5
72	4.34.30 3-5	82	5.12.33 2-5	92	5.52.24 3-5

93 to 100 Miles—F. F. Ives, Oct. 10, '85.

M.	H.M.S.	M.	H.M.S.	M.	H.M.S.
93	5.57.41 2-5	96	6.09.32 2-5	99	6.21.50
94	6.01.47 4-5	97	6.13.39 4-5	100	6.25.30
95	6.05.44 3-5	98	6.17.42 4-5		

SAFETY.

M.	H.M.S.	Name.	Date.
¼	0.41 4-5	A. P. Englehart	Sept. 9, '85
½	1.24 3-5	A. P. Englehart	Sept. 10, '85
¾	2.07	A. P. Englehart	
1	2.46	R. H. Davis	Sept. 14, '88
2	4.46 3-5	A. P. Englehart	Sept. 10, '85
3	8.35 4-5	A. P. Englehart	Sept. 10, '85
4	12.55	A. P. Englehart	Sept. 3, '85
5	16.04	A. P. Englehart	Sept. 3, '85

TANDEM SAFETY.

M.	H.M.S.	Name.	Date.
¼	45 1-5	C. H. Miller, F. R. Brown	Sept. 17, '84
½	1.32	C. H. Miller, F. R. Brown	Sept. 18, '86
¾	2.22 3-5	C. H. Miller, F. R. Brown	Sept. 18, '86
1	2.44 1-2	W. E. Crist, R. H. Davis	Sept. 14, '88
2	6.00 4-5	A. E. & F. M. Bailey	May 11, '89
3	10.14 1-5	C. H. Miller, F. R. Brown	Sept. 17, '84

TRICYCLE.

M.	H.M.S.	Name.	Date.
¼	42	G. M. Hendee	Nov. 4, '85
½	1.21 4-5	G. M. Hendee	Nov. 4, '85
¾	2.10 2-5	R. Cripps	Sept. 10, '85
1	2.53 4-5	R. Cripps	Sept. 10, '85
2	6.03 4-5	P. Furnival	Sept. 9, '85
3	9.08 2-5	"	"
4	12.15 1-5	"	"
5	15.18 3-5	"	"

6–10 Miles—A. G. Powell, Aug. 27, '85.

M.	H.M.S.	M.	H.M.S.	M.	H.M.S.
6	22.43	8	30.32 1-5	10	38.05 2-5
7	26.43	9	34.26 2-5		

ENGLISH AMATEUR.

ORDINARY.

Ms.	H.M.S.	Name.	Date.
¼	37	F. J. Osmond	May 18, '89
½	1.14	Osmond / Illston	Sept 12, '88 / July 9, '87
¾	1.53 4-5	F. J. Osmond	Sept. 12, '88
1	2.31 4-5	"	"
2	5.12 2-5	W. A. Illston	May 21, '89
3	8.14 2-5	F. J. Osmond	Sept. 8, '87
4	11.05 2-5	"	"
5	13.55	"	"
6	16.40 2-5	"	"
7	19.33 4-5	"	"
8	22.26 1-5	"	"
9	25.16 4-5	"	"
10	28.04 3-5	"	"
11	32.07 3-5	P. Furnival	Sept. 22, '87
12	35.04 2-5	"	"
13	38.02 4-5	"	"
14	41.03 1-5	"	"
15	43.59 2-5	"	"
16	46.55 1-5	"	"
17	49.55 1-5	"	"
18	52.53 2-5	M. V. Cassal	"
19	55.50 1-5	P. Furnival	"
20	58.56 2-5	"	"
21	1.01.59 1-5	"	"
22	1.04.51 1-5	"	"
23	1.07.51 2-5	"	"
24	1.10.52	"	"
25	1.13.49 3-5	"	"

26 to 36 Miles—J. H. Adams, Aug. 22, '88.

M.	H.M.S.	M.	H.M.S.	M.	H.M.S.
26	1.20.49 3-5	30	1.33.47 2-5	34	1.47.24 3-5
27	1.24.04 4-5	31	1.37.12 2-5	35	1.50.36 4-5
28	1.27.18 1-5	32	1.40.34	36	1.53.55 3-5
29	1.30.21 2-5	33	1.43.51		

37 to 50 Miles—Chas. Potter, Sept. 24, '87.

M.	H.M.S.	M.	H.M.S.	M.	H.M.S.
37	1.57.16	42	2.13.54 1-5	47	2.30.51 3-5
38	2.00.37 2-5	43	2.17.15 1-5	48	2.34.05 2-5
39	2.03.56 2-5	44	2.20.37 3-5	49	2.37.22 3-5
40	2.07.16 1-5	45	2.24.01	50	2.40.33 2-5
41	2.10.35 2-5	46	2.27.20 2-5		

51 to 55 Miles—J. H. Adams, Aug. 22, '88.

M.	H.M.S.	M.	H.M.S.	M.	H.M.S.
51	2.47.21 3-5	53	2.54.47	55	3.07.33 4-5
52	2.51.04 1-5	54	2.58.38 2-5		

56 to 100 Miles—F. R. Fry, July 27, '83.

M.	H.M.S.	M.	H.M.S.	M.	H.M.S.
56	3.14.30	71	4.06.51	86	5.00.49
57	3.18.03	72	4.10.21	87	5.04.28
58	3.21.32	73	4.13.54	88	5.08.10
59	3.25.01	74	4.17.31	89	5.11.34
60	3.28.30	75	4.21.12	90	5.15.02
61	3.34.07	76	4.24.45	91	5.19.37 1-2
62	3.35.35	77	4.28.10	92	5.22.03
63	3.39.01	78	4.31.38	93	5.25.21
64	3.42.28	79	4.35.03	94	5.26.47 2-5
65	3.45.55	80	4.38.[illegible]	95	5.32.28
66	3.49.20	81	4.42.04	96	5.36.11
67	3.52.45	82	4.45.35	97	5.40.23
68	3.56.12	83	4.49.02	98	5.43.21
69	3.59.50	84	4.52.30	99	5.47.00
70	4.03.17	85	4.56.31	100	5.50.05 2-5

SAFETY.

M.	H.M.S.	Name.	Date
¼	0.37 3-5	W. C. Jones	May 18, '89
½	1.16 1-5	W. C. Jones	May 18, '89
¾	1.53 4-5	F. J. Osmond	Sept. 19, '87
1	2.37	C. W. Schafer	Sept. 4, '89

2 to 21 Miles—H. E. Laurie, Aug. 31, '88.

M.	H.M.S.	M.	H.M.S.	M.	H.M.S.
2	5.31 3-5	9	25.21 1-5	16	45.37 2-5
3	8.20 2-5	10	28.11 1-5	17	48.28 2-5
4	11.08 3-5	11	31.04 1-5	18	51.25 1-5
5	13.58 4-5	12	33.59 1-5	19	54.10
6	16.48 3-5	13	36.52 4-5	20	56.58 2-5
7	19.42 2-5	14	39.49	21	59.41 4-5
8	22.32 1-5	15	42.42 2-5		

TRICYCLE.

M.	H.M.S.	Name.	Date.
¼	39 4-5	E. H. Sanson	Aug. 31, 1888
½	1.17 3-5	E. H. Sanson	Aug. 31, 1888
¾	2.02	G. Gatehouse	July 8, 1887
1	2.41 3-5	G. Gatehouse	July 8, 1887

2 to 8 Miles—G. Gatehouse, Aug. 26, '86.

M.	H.M.S.	M.	H.M.S.	M.	H.M.S.
2	5.37 2-5	4	11.26 4-5	6	17.25 3-5
3	8.30 4-5	5	14.27 3-5	7	20.16 4-5
		8	23.15 4-5		

9 to 19 Miles—J. B. King, June 13, '88.

M.	H.M.S.	M.	H.M.S.	M.	H.M.S.
9	26.16 3-5	13	38.07 2-5	17	50.15 2-5
10	29.10 2-5	14	41.09 1-5	18	53.16 1-5
11	32.09 2-5	15	44.17 1-5	19	56.14 4-5
12	35.06 2-5	16	47.15 2-5		

20 59.10 3-5 .. G. Gatehouse, Aug. 26, 1886.

21 to 25 Miles—S. F. Edge, June 18, '88.

M.	H.M.S.	M.	H.M.S.	M.	H.M.S.
21	1.03.14 4-5	23	1.09.28 4-5	25	1.15.44 3-5
22	1.06.21 2-5	24	1.12.38		

AMERICAN PROFESSIONAL

ORDINARY.

Ms.	H.M.S.	Name.	Date.
¼	36 2-5	G. M. Hendee	July 5, '86
½	1.13 2-5	"	"
¾	1.50 1-5	W. A. Rowe	Oct. 22, '86
1	2.29 4-5	"	"
2	5.11	"	Oct. 14, '86
3	7.48 4-5	"	"
4	10.41 2-5	"	Oct. 25, '86
5	13.23 4-5	"	"
6	16.12 3-5	"	"
7	18.59	"	"
8	21.41 2-5	"	"
9	24.26 2-5	"	"
10	27.07 1-5	"	"
11	29.51 3-5	"	"
12	32.35	"	"
13	35.18 2-5	"	"
14	38.01 2-5	"	"
15	40.41 2-5	"	"
16	43.26 4-5	"	"
17	46.14 4-5	"	"
18	48.58	"	"
19	51.40 1-5	"	"
20	54.25 2-5	"	"
21	57.07 3-5	"	"
22	59.46	"	"
23	1.08.22 3-5	W. M. Woodside	Nov. 5, '86
24	1.11.24 4-5	"	"
25	1.14.23 1-5	F. F. Ives	Oct. 9, '86

26–50 Miles—F. F. Ives, Oct. 9, '86.

M.	H.M.S.	M.	H.M.S.	M.	H.M.S.
26	1.17.27	34	1.41.00	42	2.06.48
27	1.20.16 1-5	35	1.44.05 4-5	43	2.10.04
28	1.23.13 1-5	36	1.47.18 1-5	44	2.13.25 4-5
29	1.26.11 3-5	37	1.50.34 4-5	45	2.16.42 2-5
30	1.29.07 4-5	38	1.53.47 2-5	46	2.19.56 1-5
31	1.32.05 3-5	39	1.57.01	47	2.23.23
32	1.35.03 2-5	40	2.00.17 2-5	48	2.26.44 2-5
33	1.38.01 1-5	41	2.03.30 3-5	49	2.30.14 4-5
		50	2.33.54		

51 Miles—F. E. Dingley, Sept. 27, '87.
S. P. Hollingsworth, Oct. 5, '87.

52–65 Miles—S. P. Hollingsworth, Oct. 5, '87.

M.	H.M.S.	M.	H.M.S.	M.	H.M.S.
52	2.47.03 4-5	57	3.05.05 4-5	62	3.23.00
53	2.50.50	58	3.08.34 1-5	63	3.26.36
54	2.54.27 3-5	59	3.12.09 1-5	64	3.30.24 1-5
55	2.57.59 2-5	60	3.15.54	65	3.34.11 1-5
56	3.01.32 4-5	61	3.19.27		

66–100 Miles—F. E. Dingley, Sept. 27, '87.

M.	H.M.S.	M.	H.M.S.	M.	H.M.S.
66	3.37.47	77	4.17.21	88	4.56.05
67	3.41.33 2-5	78	4.20.55 4-5	89	4.59.56
68	3.45.11 4-5	79	4.24.27 3-5	90	5.01.37 1-5
69	3.48.41 3-5	80	4.28.01 4-5	91	5.07.08 4-5
70	3.52.14	81	4.31.33 1-5	92	5.10.33 2-5
71	3.56.01	82	4.35.04 2-5	93	5.11.55 3-5
72	3.59.29 4-5	83	4.38.33	94	5.17.19 4-5
73	4.03.03 2-5	84	4.42.00 2-5	95	5.20.52 2-5
74	4.06.31 1-5	85	4.45.33 4-5	96	5.24.42 4-5
75	4.10.15 1-5	86	4.49.08 4-5	97	5.28.14 2-5
76	4.13.49 3-5	87	4.52.39	98	5.31.45 1-4
		99	5.35.20 4-5	100	5.38.41 1-5

SAFETY.

M.	H.M.S.	Name.	Date.
¼	43	R. Howell	Sept. 25, '85
½	1.22	"	"
¾	2.01 3-5	"	"
1	2.43	"	"
2	5.55 2-5	"	Sept. 8, '85
3	9.11	"	"
4	12.22	"	"
5	15.36 2-5	"	"

TRICYCLE.

M.	H.M.S.	Name.	Date.
¼	39	H. G. Crocker	Sept. 17, '86
½	1.22	H. G. Crocker	Sept. 17, '86
¾	2.07	R. Howell	Oct. 2, '85
1	2.49 2-5	R. Howell	Oct. 2, '85
2	5.53 4-5	H. G. Crocker	Oct. 2, '85
3	8.49 1-5	"	"
4	11.50	"	"
5	14.50 1-5	"	"

6–10 Miles—H. G. Crocker, Oct. 22, '86.

M.	H.M.S.	M.	H.M.S.	M.	H.M.S.
6	17.49 4-5	8	23.53 3-5	10	29.54 3-5
7	20.51	9	26.56		

11–25 Miles—T. W. Eck, Oct. 20, '86.

M.	H.M.S.	M.	H.M.S.	M.	H.M.S.
11	37.30 4-5	16	55.49 3-5	21	1.14.04
12	41.14 2-5	17	59.21 2-5	22	1.17.48 4-5
13	44.46	18	1.03.04 2-5	23	1.21.31 4-5
14	48.35 4-5	19	1.06.30 4-5	24	1.25.03 3-5
15	52.16	20	1.10.25 2-5	25	1.28.26 1-5

ENGLISH PROFESSIONAL.

ORDINARY.

Ms.	H.M.S.	Name.	Date.
¼	35 4-5	H. G. Crocker	Aug. 3, '88
½	1.17	R. Howell	—— '86
¾			
1	2.33 4-5	A. H. Robb	Sept. 12, '88
2	5.20 2-5	H. G. Crocker	Aug. 3, '88
3	7.59 1-5	"	"
4	10.42	"	"
5	13.27	"	"
6	16.09	"	"
7	18.57 2-5	"	"
8	21.41	"	"
9	24.24 2-5	"	"
10	27.08	"	"
11	30.55	Jules Dubois	"
12	33.41	"	"
13	36.32 2-5	"	"
14	39.24 4-5	"	"
15	42.20	"	"
16	45.10	"	"
17	48.03 3-5	"	"
18	50.52	"	"
19	53.40	"	"
20	56.28	"	"
21	59.15 2-5	"	"
22	1.02.01 2-5	"	"
23	1.04.58	"	"
24	1.07.48	"	"
25	1.10.34 4-5	"	"

26–50 Miles—W. F. Knapp, Aug. 16, '88.

M.	H.M.S.	M.	H.M.S.	M.	H.M.S.
26	1.16.34	34	1.41.18	42	2.05.20
27	1.19.35	35	1.44.25	43	2.08.20
28	1.22.39	36	1.47.21	44	2.11.26
29	1.25.43	37	1.50.17	45	2.14.31
30	1.28.49	38	1.53.13	46	2.17.27
31	1.31.48	39	1.56.19	47	2.20.36
32	1.34.46	40	1.59.20	48	2.23.31
33	1.37.58	41	2.02.23	49	2.26.43
		50	2.29.41		

51 to 100 Miles—W. F. Knapp, July 17, '88.

M.	H.M.S.	M.	H.M.S.	M.	H.M.S.
51	2.43.15	67	3.44.19	83	4.50.06
52	2.46.27	68	3.48.51	84	4.53.41
53	2.49.53	69	3.52.53	85	4.57.16
54	2.53.31	70	3.56.47	86	5.00.52
55	2.57.15	71	4.00.46	87	5.04.33
56	3.00.58	72	4.04.47	88	5.08.59
57	3.04.40	73	4.08.42	89	5.13.12
58	3.08.18	74	4.12.41	90	5.17.11
59	3.11.52	75	4.16.44	91	5.21.04
60	3.15.30	76	4.20.52	92	5.25.00
61	3.19.19	77	4.24.50	93	5.29.01
62	3.23.18	78	4.28.41	94	5.33.07
63	3.27.03	79	4.32.42	95	5.37.12
64	3.31.00	80	4.39.56	96	5.41.06
65	3.35.20	81	4.43.17	97	5.44.43
66	3.39.52	82	4.40.40	98	5.48.08
		99	5.52.14	100	5.55.21

SAFETY.

M.	H.M.S.	Name.	Date.
¼	36	S. G. Whittaker	Aug. 3, '88
½	1.18 1-5	A. P. Englehart	June 13, '88
¾	1.53 3-5	F. W. Allard	May 12, '88
1	2.31 4-5	S. G. Whittaker	Sept. 29, '88

2 to 11 Miles—S. Whittaker, Sept. 11, '88.

M.	H.M.S.	M.	H.M.S.	M.	H.M.S.
2	5.18 2-5	5	13.22 1-5	8	21.38
3	7.59	6	16.07	9	24.22 2-5
4	10.40 1-5	7	18.52 3-5	10	27.03 2-5
		11	29.50 2-5		

12 to 25 Miles—S. Whittaker, Sept. 29, '88.

M.	H.M.S.	M.	H.M.S.	M.	H.M.S.
12	33.26	17	47.48 1-5	22	1.02.21
13	36.18	18	50.41	23	1.05.18 3-5
14	39.14	19	53.37 1-5	24	1.08.11 1-5
15	42.03 2-5	20	56.32	25	1.11.05 1-5
16	44.56 2-5	21	59.26		

M.	H.M.S.	Name.	Date.
26	1.15.28 2-5	S. G. Whittaker	Oct. 15, '88
27	1.18.58 1-5	S. G. Whittaker	Oct. 15, '88
28	1.22.26 3-5	S. G. Whittaker	Oct. 15, '88
29	1.25.40 2-5	E. Oxborrow	Sept. 12, '88
30	1.28.29	E. Oxborrow	Sept. 12, '88

TANDEM SAFETY.

1–20 Miles—Dan Albone & E. E. Glover, Oct. 15, '88.

M.	H.M.S.	M.	H.M.S.	M.	H.M.S.
1	2.58	8	24.44	15	46.43
2	5.56	9	27.53	16	49.50
3	9.00	10	30.58 4-5	17	53.07
4	12.03	11	34.09	18	56.13
5	15.12	12	37.13	19	59.15
6	18.19	13	40.23	20	1.02.16 3-5
7	21.25	14	43.32		

TRICYCLE.

M.	H.M.S.	Name.	Date.
¼	40 3-5	F. W. Allard	July 13, 1887
½	1.20	"	"
¾	2.01 2-5	"	"
1	2.43 3-5	"	"

2 to 10 Miles—C. C. Taylor, Sept. 18, '88.

M.	H.M.S.	M.	H.M.S.	M.	H.M.S.
2	05.45 3-5	5	14.31 3-5	8	23.01
3	08.38 3-5	6	17.25	9	26.14
4	11.34 3-5	7	20.24 2-5	10	29.45 2-5

11 to 14 Miles—Fred Lees, Sept. 18, 1888.

M.	H.M.S.	M.	H.M.S.	M.	H.M.S.
11	32.33 1-5	12	36.01 2-5	13	39.06 2-5
		14	42.16 1-5		

15 to 25 Miles—F. W. Allard, Oct. 22, '87.

M.	H.M.S.	M.	H.M.S.	M.	H.M.S.
15	47.34	19	1.00.04	23	1.12.18
16	50.39	20	1.03.06	24	1.15.25
17	53.48	21	1.06.07	25	1.18.32
18	56.57	22	1.09.12		

SKIP THIS PAGE,

For you might learn something of interest to League members who will be having a **H. O.** Time at

HAGERSTOWN.

THAT'S WHAT THEY ARE GOING TO HAVE.

CHIEF CONSUL MOTT,

of Maryland, says so, and it *must* be true.   He has been trying to club this fact into your heads for a few months.   See our advertisements in the L. A. W. Meet programme, THE WHEEL, "The Bicycling World" and " The Wheelmen's Gazette"; also the "Cycler and Tourist," and read them.   (That's what we write them for).   Colonel Pope, and Colonel Overman, and Lieut.-Colonel Gormully, and Captain Jeffery are going to tell you their story, but we want you to read OURS.   Brigadier-General Aitch Dee Corey and the Right Hon'ble Algernon Kennedy-Childe will have their song and dance, and Sterling Elliot will talk about his Andrew Jackson wheel (Old Hickory, you know), but when it comes right down to the fine points of the case, what IS the matter with

"The White Flyer."

IT IS ALL RIGHT.

We have a catalogue printed in this number, so you had better sit down and read it in case you might not have another chance to do so, and thus be eternally left.   We do not believe in sensational advertising.   In our advertising we do nothing commonplace.   The papers in which we advertise reach the cream of buyers.   Who else do you care to reach?   "*Dagonet*," of the " Referee " (London, Eng.), writes :

"Having good wares and not advertising them is like winking at a pretty girl in the dark.   You know what you are doing but she does not."   (For "you" read "makers"; for the "pretty girl" read the "cycling public.")

The cycling public (judging by the basketful of letters received in this morning's mail) seems to be like certain pretty girls we have known (ahem !)—they are fast "catching on."

We do not intend to speak at length upon the merits of our " White Flyer" Safety Bicycle, but when we modestly claim that for the "scorcher" or the business rider (who potters down to his office in the morning and potters back in the evening) it has no equal.   There never was a bicycle, in this or any other country, finished in such exquisite style as the " White Flyer."   If you have not our catalogue

Why Don't You Send for it ?

It is mailed free to your address.

Agents wanted in every town in America.   Advertisement solicitors will please send rates that will bear comparison to J. PURVIS-BRUCE, White Cycle Co., Westboro, Mass.

N. B.—Advertisement solicitors who call and tell us of a "soft, soft thing" with ridiculously high rates need not tarry long.   It only takes us thirty seconds to put on our heavy boots.   They have four pounds and ten ounces of Scotch nails in the soles.   We yearn to try them on thin lavender pants.   Our bull-dog is working up a good appetite, and when he does get turned loose on the enemy he will eat cloth and all.

CYPHER CABLEGRAM AND TELEGRAM ADDRESS

"CYCLE" - WESTBORO, MASS.

THE WHITE FLYER CYCLES.

"The OUTSIDE of a BICYCLE is the best thing for the INSIDE of a MAN" (Do not take this statement for granted, but prove it for yourself.)

COMPILED BY "JACK."

If you are too well posted or to ignorant to learn, hand this catalogue (with our compliments) to some wide-awake fellow who knows a thing or two. He may profit by the perusal. Blessed is he who knows nothing, for he has nothing to learn.

Do not waste time in trying to solve "Pigs in Clover Puzzles."

You will spend fifteen minutes more profitably by reading this catalogue. Then hand it to your cycling friends.

"Time is money."

THE WHITE CYCLE CO.,

OF WESTBORO, MASSACHUSETTS.

U. S. A.

DIRECTIONS

TO BUYERS AND AGENTS

Terms, net cash with order. With EVERY ORDER give full shipping instructions. Freight or express charges always to be paid by the purchaser.

Correspondence must be sent plainly addressed to The White Cycle Company of Westboro, and not to individuals.

Our responsibility in the matter of delivery of goods ceases when the goods have been delivered at post-office, express offices, or freight depots. C. O. D. orders from outside of New England must be accompanied by money enough to pay express charges both ways, in case the goods are not accepted. Our stock in our Boston store is for local trade only. Orders from Agents will be shipped direct from our factory at Westboro, Mass., on the Boston & Albany Railroad. — thirty-two miles from Boston.

Our prices are invariable, and no discounts are allowed except to regular agents.

We warrant the White Cycles to be free from imperfections in material or manufacture, and agree to make good, at store or factory, at any time within a year, any *defects* in them not caused by use, misuse, or neglect. If such defects are found, all defective parts must be sent to us for examination before any claim is allowed. This warrant does not apply to nickel-plating, though no care or expense is spared to make it the best.

No goods should be shipped to us without first obtaining instructions from our office at Westboro, Mass.

The "White Flyer" Safety Bicycle.

Crated free on board the train at Westboro, Mass., with TOOL-BAG, WRENCH, SPRING-TOP OILER and SCREW-DRIVER. Weight, 50 pounds. Put it on the scales and test it.

$135.00.

AGENTS WANTED. WRITE FOR TERMS.

To the Cycling Public. Greeting:

The White Cycle Company, of Westboro, Mass., in making their initial bow to the practical wheeling public, do so with the comfortable consciousness that they have something which will amply reward the investigation of all in search of health upon wheels.

In presenting their catalogue of White Cycles to the public, it gives them great pleasure to say that the " White Flyer" Safety Bicycle is something new, and unlike many novelties in the cycling line (now either, or fast becoming, obsolete). The White Cycle Company, of Westboro, have received the endorsement of some of the most noted wheel mechanics and practical cycling authorities, when they say that they have got something *good*. That is what the practical road-riding American cycler has been crying for all along, and the White Cycle Company are now prepared to give it to him.

The White Cycle Company have noted the rise and fall of many poorly-made and unmechanical absurdities, and when they decided to embark in the cycle business, they did so in a calm spirit, assured of the superior nature of the machine which they intended to place upon the market. They did not go into the cycle business of high-grade cycle construction for " a year, or a day," but to " stay," and appreciated the necessity of doing so handicapped in no way, but fully equipped with the finest plant, the best material, and no lack of financial backing or skillful workmen. Everything is the best that mechanical experts, supplied with the necessary funds, could purchase in the market. They realized from the bitter experience of other manufacturers, that cheap rattle-trap machinery and poor material could result in but one thing,—cheap (?) rattle-trap cycles which would cost much money (in the long run), and would give abominable results, disastrous alike to manufacturer and purchaser.

They appreciated the fact that they had a class of gentlemen-sportsmen to deal with, who by reason of their " press " are constantly educated as to what is what, knowing that they have

WHITE ALL ORDERS PLAINLY.

WHITE CYCLE COMPANY, OF WESTBORO, MASS. 3

men of intelligence to deal with, they have started out to make the highest grade bicycle in any market, both as regards fit and finish of interiors and bearing surfaces, as well as an exterior of the *highest possible* finish, results which can only be accomplished by using the best of machinery, the best of material, and the most intelligent mechanical assistance on the part of the employés of the Company.

A visit to the model factory of the White Cycle Company, of Westboro, Mass., thirty-two miles (by road and rail) on the Boston & Albany Railroad, will convert the most jaundiced mind to the fact that we have got what we claim to have, and the visitor has only to use his eyes to corroborate our assertions and claims in every way.

"Honesty is the best policy"—in the beginning and in the end. In their perfectly lighted and ventilated factory, which, with the plant, was built for cycle construction at a very great cost, and occupied *solely* by the White Cycle Company, you will find all the material, machinery and mechanical skill essential to finely-fitted, honestly-constructed, accurate and *absolutely* interchangeable work. You will also find experts on hand super'sing the various processes of manufacture, who are responsible for the accuracy of *every* nut, screw, bearing, chain-link, etc., which leaves the workmen's hands.

The White Cycle Company have no enemies in the trade; they pay their bills and treat their employés and patrons squarely, yet they start with much opposition from older firms. Realizing this, they are confident that their keynote to *success* will be touched by *excelling* all competitors in material and workmanship, and by enabling riders to economically utilize such natural power as is possessed by the *average human being* in the propulsion of the cycle.

Try our machine (give it a fair trial), learn it (it is easier to learn than any other bicycle), and you will find that up and down grade, on the level, on a good surface, and on an indifferent one, the "White Flyer" is a "corker." Quality of work is our gauge of a mechanic's capability, not quantity; and to avoid "cheap and unsatisfactory" work, we avoid "cheap and inexperienced" workmen. You say that they have got something *new*. "Yes, they have, and it is going to make its mark in both the English and American markets. What was good enough for

TO ADVERTISING AGENTS:—SEND IN ADVERTISING

4 WHITE CYCLE COMPANY, OF WESTBORO, MASS.

the *old fogy* cycler is *not* good enough for you, in this age of improvement."

If you are too well posted to learn anything new which will be of benefit to you, you will please hand this catalogue to some wide-awake cycler, with our compliments,—to some nineteenth century chap, who has his eyes open to a good thing, and is not too proud to learn. If he (mounted on a "White Flyer") passes you on the road at a nice lively gait, while you are bent double over your "Crock," and panting like a young robin, do not blame us. We advised you, and you would not listen to us—you neglected to read our catalogue—that was all. This catalogue is compiled by a well-known cycler, who has spent much time and money on cycles, and has had all kinds of experience in riding them; embarking on them and falling "overboard" on all sorts of surfaces, and at all kinds of paces, from a scorch to a dignified ministerial gait. Sometimes this was done gracefully, sometimes upon all fours and both sides simultaneously.

The advantages we claim over other existing types of the cycle are set forth in the remarks which follow this preamble. Hoping that we may have the pleasure of suiting the rapidly-growing legion of American wheelmen with our "White Flyer," which never grows weary, we are, gentlemen,

Most respectfully,

THE WHITE CYCLE COMPANY,
OF WESTBORO, MASS.

RATES WHICH WILL BEAR COMPARISON

ADVANTAGES CLAIMED FOR THE WHITE FLYER SAFETY.

1st. Greater speed, with the same amount of muscular expenditure than can be attained by any system of crank or lever motive power on the cycling market of today.

2d. A motion more natural than a rotary motion.

3d. It is almost impossible to slip a pedal; and if this is done through awkwardness or carelessness, there is no dangerous result attending it.

4th. The motion is calculated to suit the majority of cyclers, and not the few, who on account of their peculiar "build" ride one kind of a machine much better than another.

5th. The motion may be learned by a novice much sooner than any other existing motion. This fact will be appreciated by those who anticipate great difficulty in learning to ride a crank wheel.

6th. It is more comfortable to "coast" on, and more easily steered on down grades than the ordinary rear driver (with foot-rests on the front fork), as the feet do not require to be removed from the pedals, but are stopped at will and used at foot-rests. Being connected with the driving-wheel, steering is rendered easy to the novice.

7th. It will out-coast any other machine. Try it. That's all we have to say on this question.

8th. It is better finished inside and outside than any wheel on any market.

9th. Less friction than a chain-driven, Rover type safety (there are no cogs on this safety), the chain passing over hardened steel pulleys.

10th. There are no "dead centres." Those who use this express sion in regard to crank bicycles, with imperfect understanding of its meaning, need do so no longer, if they will take a good look at the accompanying "cut."

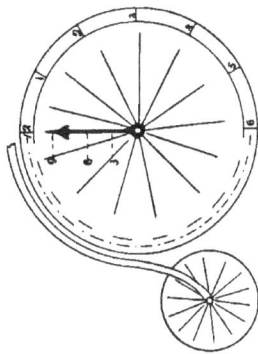

TO MR. J. PURVIS-BRUCE,

Take a good look at this. You know you have some time to spare. We shall suppose that we have before us an "ordinary" crank bicycle, and that (for ease of illustration) the front wheel has been marked off like the face of a clock, and the crank indicated by a clock-hand or indicator. Well, if you will but look, you will see what "dead centres" mean. When the hand (or crank) is at twelve o'clock, it is on "dead centre"; when it is at one o'clock, the dead centre has been overcome. When the crank is at three o'clock, the greatest amount of power or maximum of crank leverage is attained. When the crank is at six o'clock it is again on dead centre, and all the way from six o'clock to twelve, absolutely no power can possibly be utilized by the rider upon that pedal, unless his feet were in some way attached (à la Jack Keen) to the pedals, so that an upward pull might be effected. This would be dangerous, and a muscular effort of this nature would be very exhausting.

The figures 3, 6 and 9 are added to give a rider an idea of the leverage of cranks. Thus, a six-inch crank means three inches of leverage; a six-inch crank, six inches of leverage, and a nine-inch crank, nine inches of leverage.

This is as good an illustration as any of what we have had to content with in crank machines — dead centres.

WHITE CYCLE COMPANY, WESTBORO, MASS.

A BRIEF DESCRIPTION OF THE "WHITE FLYER."

This season we place upon the American market a safety bicycle, which, unlike the majority of alleged "safety" bicycles, is safe.

We do not make a cycle for ladies' use this season. We do not believe in machines adapted to both sexes, for, like most "general utility" tools, they are not very good for any one purpose. Our machine does one thing well — carries riders of the masculine persuasion fast and safely, and that's about as much as any one machine can be expected to do.

The WHEELS are each of thirty inches in diameter, and the rear driving wheel is geared to sixty inches. The RIMS are the "Warwick Perfection" (about which comment is superfluous), the front rim taking a tire of three-fourths of an inch, and the rear wheel a tire of seven-eighths of an inch.

The TIRES are the very finest of Para rubber. The SPOKES are tangential, of the finest obtainable material. The hubs are graceful in outline, and of the very best of steel.

The BEARINGS of the machine are ROLLERS, and the adjustment of the points so delicate that the bearings are positively dust-proof. The bearings will, without adjustment or touching (except, of course, occasional oiling), wear as long as the machine itself. Some people may say, "Why do you not put in ball-bearings?" Well, simply, my friends, because it is an absolute impossibility to make a perfectly accurate sphere of steel. There is not a ball-bearing in the market that has a roll of balls in its bearing-case with anything like uniformity. Micrometer and sensitive scale tests have proved this, and one ball in a bearing-case, varying the one-thousandth part of an inch from its fellows, will raise the devil with the running of the bearing. A roller-bearing can be turned with positive accuracy, so that variations of even the four-thousandth part of an inch would unseat it for the bearing cases which are placed on the White Flyer.

UNIQUE METHODS OF ADVERTISING

And why was the old roller-bearing discarded? Simply because it was an imperfect absurdity, which twisted and jammed, and was a source of annoyance and mistrust and danger to the rider of twelve years ago. As soon as the ball-bearing was invented, "the trade" discarded the then imperfect roller-bearing, and used the ball-bearing instead. But if you put properly hardened steel rollers in a case where there is no room to twist, they will "nut-coast old coaster himself." You can easily prove this on the road. We don't need to howl about a thing which we can prove.

The front wheel of a White Flyer fitted with their perfected (and perfect) roller-bearing, ran fourteen minutes and ten and two-fifths seconds — not by computation, but by the watch — and any one of them will do it, as the most perfect system of interchangeability is insisted upon by the White Cycle Company.

The TUBING is the finest obtainable Credenda steel tubing. We do away with brazings as much as possible, and gain strength thereby. The Mud-guard is put on "to stay" or to detach easily, and is not musical, there being no "rattling accompaniment." We believe that this is a luxury which most riders are willing to deny themselves, — a noisy mud-guard.

The SADDLE-POST is a hollow steel tube, and is light and strong, and adjustable to suit the requirements of a tall or short rider.

The SADDLE is the unexcelled "Keystone" saddle. The saddle-spring is sufficiently pliable for comfort on the roughest of roads, and admits of a proper spring, fore and aft. We do not believe in saddles such as are on the market, built on the mole-trap or mouse-trap plan, which are so springy that they absorb about half the power which should be transmitted direct to the point where the driving-wheel comes in contact with the ground. When you lay out muscular effort you like to feel the wheel move forward, not to feel the saddle-spring double up. In our machine you have an adequate return for all muscular expenditure.

When a ship is towed astern of a tug, they use a stiff hawser, not a flexible rubber rope, as they wish to pull that ship into port. We use a spring which does not absorb power, therefore we calculate to get there. We put no "spring arrangement" on our front fork, for we do not believe in such things; we have tried both, you know. We are not proud, and like to be able to steer our wheel to a hair's-breadth on the road, and keep our feet on the

SOLICITED, AND IF UTILIZED

pedals while running a down grade. You can do this with a rigid and stiff front fork. With a spring fork, never. The *Brake* is not put on for ornament, and though it is a marvel of elegance in the matter of outline and finish, still you can *actually stop your wheel with it*, and you do not (when you apply it) bend the brake-handle up to the handle-bar, either. It is fashioned after the plunger pattern. The *Steering-head* is of the good old reliable cone-bearing type improved by us, so that you can tighten it up so that there is no side play, and yet it moves with perfect freedom. We have tried ball-bearing heads and "tired" them. (They made us "so weary," you know.)

We are getting dreadfully practical and matter-of-fact in our old age. We used to experiment in ball-heads and spring forks, but our bill for repairs was excessive. We are not so extravagant as we used to be.

In our STEERING-HEAD we have got something undoubtedly fine. It has long been admitted that the cone-head was the finest steering-head for cycles, if it could be made so that when it was *sufficiently tight* it would not *bind*, and yet *sufficiently loose to move easily without rattling*. We have at last solved this issue of cone-bearing heads, by introducing an "*automatic adjustable*" cone-head. If you will ride your "crock" in a blistering *hot* day, you will find that the cone-head will *work loose*; if you take it out in a *cold* day, you will notice that the head works *tightly*. Why? Simply because the *heat expanded* the outer case of the head, while *cold* weather *contracted it*, and the inner neck-pin was comparatively unaffected by heat or cold.

We have met and answered this difficulty, and now have it under control, by introducing a rubber washer of such construction, that it is *unaffected by oil*, which allows the head to be screwed down tight, and yet to move easily, which allows the steering-head to move as easily on a cold day as on a warm one, and never to rattle, even under the influence of the blistering glare of an Arizona sun. This thing must be seen and used to be appreciated. One of the big American makers will recognize in this a thing which he tried to buy, but we managed to get there ahead of him.

The HANDLES are hard rubber and peculiarly cool and comfortable to the grip, and rather longer than the ordinary handle, permitting a greater variety of hand-position. The CHAIN is one of

our own design, and is neater and better finished than any other chain on the market. As there are no sprocket wheels to run over, it is made narrower than other chains, being thus, *lighter* and neater.

The SWING-FRAME is made of the very finest material, and as it folds back toward the rear wheel, it cannot be broken by a large stone on a rough road, as in the case of a rotary safety pedal. It does not hang so near *the road-surface* as does the pedal on rotary motion safety bicycles.

The FORKS and all the tubing are round in section, of the best Credenda steel. We make them round, as fittings can thus be made with greater accuracy than with oval or flat tubes, and better and stronger brazings can be effected. You can "turn" a round tube *more perfectly* than any other shape.

The PEDALS are so adjusted that they can be stopped in any position, and by equal pressure of both feet they become foot-rests. The length of the stroke can be varied; pushing one pedal down raises the other a corresponding distance. There are *no springs* used to draw the pedals back to the starting-point, the weight of the one pedal, when it is pressed down, raises the other one. A very good point in this machine is that any person affected by a *stiff knee, or one whose leg has been injured*, so as to make one *shorter than the other*, can, by adjusting the pedal and driving-chain, suit the peculiar conditions. The swing or guide frame hanging from the backbone, on which the pedals move up and down, can be thrust while the rider is in motion to almost any angle. Thus, *if he wishes a vertical tread*, the frame can be swung so that the pedals come well under the saddle. If, on the contrary, the rider wishes to change the position, and get *more of the thrust stroke* which uses the thigh muscles (as in a rotary motion crank safety), this can instantly be done by swinging the frame toward the front wheel. This ability to vary *the stroke* will rest the rider, who, if he rides an ordinary crank safety, may often weary of the monotony of a never-changing motion, and yet, by the peculiar construction of his machine, he is unable to change it. With the White Flyer this is different.

When the driving pedal is on top of the guide-frame, and in the beginning of a stroke, the construction is such that the rider has more leverage than at any other point in the whole stroke. The leverage lessens as the pedal moves down, and as the legs straighten

WHITE CYCLE COMPANY, OF WESTBORO, MASS.   11

out, thus equalizing the force to be exerted necessary to drive the machine.

It is the *business man's wheel par excellence*, and the "scorcher" will find in it a machine "after his own heart." As we desire to cater to the tastes of men who know, from actual experience, what looks best and is most serviceable in the way of enamel, we have decided to enamel the machine in such portions where nickel-plating has been found to be a failure. We put nickel on such portions of the White Flyer as will give it the most workmanlike and artistic finish and appearance.

Our cycle factory at Westboro, Mass., was built expressly for the construction of the highest possible grade of cycles, according to the instructions and plans of practical cycle manufacturing authorities. It is owned and occupied entirely by The White Cycle Company, and none but practical men who are authorities in their special line, are employed by the Company. We employ no professional riders to create records of more or less accuracy, and believe that the mission of the cycle is to be a fast and safe *vehicle*, rather than an acrobat's plaything. It is safe to say that there is no *cycle manufactory on earth* so well appointed, and none which has better facilities for making absolutely accurate work.

If you have time and inclination, drop down and see the factory. It is open to every one; you can be shown through and believe for yourself. We have nothing to hide, and nothing to be ashamed of. We have the *model factory of the world*, and we will gladly travel a long way to see a better one. We will always be pleased to inspect designs in relation to cycles, and should they prove good, practical ideas, we are prepared to pay well for the patent rights.

The White Cycle Company start out handicapped in no way. They have plenty of funds and everything requisite for the manufacture of high-grade cycles.

The cut is a fair representation of the machine. The motion is not awkward or ugly, as in the case of several of the unmechanical abortions which have been a waste of material and a hindrance to enjoyable cycling in this country.

Mr. Frederick White is the inventor of this machine, and has spent much time in perfecting it. He is the same gentleman who climbed Corey Hill on a tricycle weighing one hundred pounds, of his own construction, in '85, when that hill had been ridden but once

AND IF YOU WRITE A POOR HAND, PRINT IT.

12   WHITE CYCLE COMPANY, OF WESTBORO, MASS.

that year on a light tricycle. Much could be said for the machine, but the experience of actual riding this season will be better praise than all the newspaper advertising.

Mr. J. Purvis-Bruce, of the famous English "scorching" club, "The Ripley Road Club," is with the Company, and will go among the boys with the new "goat." He will meet his many old friends and make new ones. The White Cycle Company's factory is at Westboro, thirty-two miles from Boston, on the Boston and Albany road. The road from Boston to Westboro is very good. Those intending to visit the factory had better come by way of Boston Common, out Beacon Street to Newton Lower Falls, then by Wellesley, Natick and South Framingham. Here you can either take the *shortest* road by way of Framingham and Ashland to Westboro, or by way of Southboro to Westboro, which is two miles longer, but a better road. If you come out some Saturday, bring your pipe with you. You will find "Jack" there, unless he is in New Orleans, or Montana, or some other place. "Look out for the White cycles."

CORRESPONDENCE SOLICITED AND PROMPTLY ATTENDED TO.

THE STARS OF THE RACE PATH.

2.29 4-5—Rowe.
2.30* —Furnival, August 24, '86.

2.30¼ —Rowe, August 11, '87.
2.30 2-5—Busst, October 15, '88.

2.31 —Hendee, September 19, '86.
2.31 2-5—Howell, September 29, '85.
2.31 4-5—Osmond, September 12, '88.
" Whittaker, September 29, '88.

2.32 2-5—Synyer, May 21, '88.
2.32 2-5—Furnival, August 23, '86.
2.32 3-5—Wood, September 15, '86.

2.33 —Wood, September 9, '86.
2.33 —Engleheart, June 13, '88.
2.33 4-5—Robb, September 12, '88.
2.34 2-5—Osmond, May 21, '88.
2.34 2-5—Woodside, September 19, '86.

2.34 3-5—Illston, May 21, '89.
2.34 3-5—Crist, May 21, '88.
2.34 4-5—Speechley, July 3, '86.

2.35 —Hendee, September 15, '86.

2.35 1-5—Hendee, June 10, '87.
" Osmond, May 21, '88.
" Howell, June 20, '87.
2.35 2 5—Howell, September 23, '85.
2.35 2-5—Rowe, October 23, '85.
" Rowe, September 24, '86.
" Rowe, August 14, '86.
" Hendee, July 5, '86.
2.35 3-5—Wood, September 8, '85.
" Rowe, July 4, '87.

2.35 4 5—Furnival, August 21, '86.
" Hendee, September 24, '86.
2.36 —Rowe, August 12, '87.
2.36 —Woodside, September 15, '86.
2.36 2-5—Rowe, October 17, '85.
" Rhodes, August 27, '86.
2.36½ —Rowe, July 4, '87.
2.36 4-5—Osmond, May 21, '88.
" Osmond, August 12, '87.
2.37 —Woodside, September 24, '86.
2.37 1-5—Shaefer, May 4, '89.
2.37 1-5—Rowe, October 13, '86.
2.37 1-5—Schafer, May 4, '89.
2.37 2-5—Rowe, June 19, '86.
2.37 4-5—Laurie, August 31, '88.
2.37 4-5—Hendee, June 6, '85.

2.38 —Synyer, May 21, '88.
2.38 —Rowe, October 23, '85.
2.38 —Lees, July, '86.
2.38 —Rowe, September 14, '86.
2.38 2-5—Rhodes, August 23, '86.
2.38 2-5—Hendee, September 25, '86.
2.38 2-5—Dwyer, '86.
2.38 2-5—Rowe, September 25, '86.
2.38 2-5—Brewerton, May 21, '88.
2.38 2-5—Frazier, October 19, '86.
2.38 2-5—Duncan, June 7, '87.
2.38 3-5—W. C. Thompson, May 17, '89.
2.38¼ —Hendee, September 8, '86.
2.38 4-5—Osmond, August 12, '87.
2.39 —Sellers, September 9, '84.

2.39 —Prince, September 17, '84.
2.39 —J. Illston, May 21, '88.
2.39 —Engleheart, June 23, '87.
2.39 2-5—James, September 25, '86.
" Oxborrow, September 12, '86.
2.39 2-5—Howell, July 7, '86.
2.39 2-5—Medinger, August 25, '87.
2.39 2-5—Webber, July 9, '85.
2.39 3-5—M. Webber, July 9, '85.
2.39 4-5—Hendee, June 8, '85.
2.39 4-5—Mayes, July, '86.
2.40 —Foster, August 10, '87.
" De Blois, August 24, '87.
" Engleheart, July 19, '87.
" Woodside, September 26, '86.
" Woodside, August 27, '86.
" Rowe, June 19, '86.

2.40 2-5—Rich, September 30, '86.
" Rowe, October 12, '86.

2.40 3-5 —Howell, August 18 '83.

2.40 4-5—Kluge, September 14, '86.
" Howell, July 7, '86.
2.41 —Woodside, September 15, 86.
" Wood, October 1, '85.
" Dolph, September 9, '84.
" Rowe, September 10, '85.
2.41 1-5—Whittaker, September 11, '88.
" Crocker, September 25, '86.
" Rowe, September 10, '85.

2.41¼ —Ives, September 9, '86.
2.41 2-5—Laurie, August 31, '88.
" Hendee, September 26, '81.
" Kluge, September 8, '85.
" Wood, September 26, '86.
2.41½ —Percy Stone, September 9, '86.

2.41 3-5—Ives, September 26, '86.
" Cortis, June 7, '82.

2.41 4-5—Whittaker, August 20, '87.
" Crist, May 21, '88.

2.42 —English, September 10, '84.
" Rich, September 30, '86.
" Rowe, August 13, '87.
" Rhodes, September 15, '86.
" Engleheart, August 21, '86.
" Woodside, August 27, '86.
" Adams, September 8, '85.
2.42 1-5—Foster, May 24, '87.
" Knapp, September 8, '85.

2.42 2-5—De Blois, August 25, '87.

2.42½ —De Blois, September 9, '86.
2.42½ —Rich, August 11, '87.
2.42 3-5—Robinson, May 21, '88.
2.42 4-5—Rowe, September 10, '85.

2.43 —Illston, July, '86.
" Weber, June 19, '86.
" Osmond, July 4, '87.
" Howell, June 17, '87.
" Kluge, September 23, '85.
" Windle, June 19, '88.
" Howell, September 25, '85.
2.43 1-5—Woodside, September 26, '86.
" Rowe, September 26, '86.

2.43 2-5—Furnival, June 27, '86.
" Osmond, June 23, '87.
" Whittaker, September 29, '88.
2.43½ —Foster, June 19, '88.

2.43 4-5—Rhodes, September 26, '86.

2.44 —Hendee, July 3, '85.
" Rowe, July 4, '86.
" Illston, June 27, '86.
" Hendee, September 15, '86
" Wilhelm, July 2, '85.
2.44 1-5—Illston, May 1, '86.
" Ives, August 27, '86.
" Prince, September 15, '86.
" Wood, September 16, '86.
" Temple, May 23, '88.
" Temple, August 9, '87.
2.44 2-5—Weber, July 3, '85.
" Crocker, September 15, '86.
" Neilson, September 16, '86.
" Rich, July 3, '85.
2.44½ —English, September 3, '85.
" Neilson, October 16, '85.
" Prince, October, 16, '85.

2.44 3-5—Illston, July 4, '85.

2.44 4-5—Rowe, October 9, '85.
2.45 —Moore, June 15, '82.
" Engleheart, June 29, '86.

2.45 1-5—Furnival, September 9, '85.

2.45 3-5—Hendee, September 18, '84.
" W. A. Illston, June 13, '85.
" Woodside, October 23, '85.
" Webber, July 4, '85.
" F. Wood, August 4, '84.
" Hendee, September 18, '84.
" Hamilton, June 6, '85.
" Sellers, June 14, 84.

2.45½ —Crist, June 19, '87.
" Rowe, May 30, '87.

2.45 4-5—Frazier, October 19, '86.
" Wood, September 30, '86.
" Illston, May 30, '87.
" Illston, May 2, '86.
" Webber July 2, '85.
" Renton, September 8, '85.
" Burnham, September 3, '85.

2.46 —Davis, September 14, '88.
" Speechley, June 14, '84.
" Howell, August 6, '85.
" Hendee, June 11, '86.
" Furnival, June 27, '86.
" Woodside, September 17, '86.
" Weber, September 17, '84.
" Brooks, September 18, '84.
" Hersey, September 8, '85.

2 46 1-5—Furnival, September 10, '85.

2.46 2-5—Neilson, August 28, '86.
" Woodside, October 2, '86.

2.46½ —Rich, September 9, '86.
" Neilson, September 17, '85.

2.46 3-5—Keith-Falconer, May 26, '80.

2.46 4-5—Lamb, June 13, '84.
" Speechley, June 27, '86.
" Neilson, September 17, '86.
" Stenken, July 4, '87.
" De Blois, August 5, '87.
" Garnett, May 21, '88.

2.47 —Rowe, September 3, '85.
" Illston, September 9, '85.
" Kluge, September 8, '85.
" Rowe, May 31, '86.
" Gatehouse, August 21, '86.
" Allard, May 23, '88.
" Howell, May 30, '87.
" Wing, May 30, '89.

2.47 1-5—Furnival, June 27, '86.
" Rich, August 13, '87.
" Rowe, September 3, '85.
" Mecredy, July, '86.

2.47¼ —Lamb, July 4, '87.

2.47 2-5—Fenlon, June 27, '86.
" Moore, June 15, '86.

2.47½ —Kavanaugh, August 27, '86.

2.47 3-5—Hendee, October 1, '86.
2.47 4-5—Rowe, September 15, '86.
" Rich, September 25, '86.

2.48 —Harding, June 27, '86.
" Davies, September 4, '86.
" Rich, August 28, '86.
" Howell, June 12, '87.
2.48 1-5—Illston, June 11, '87.
" Illston, September 10, '85.
" Furnival, September 8, '85.
" Hollingsworth, September 4, '86.
" Hendee, October 2, '86.
2.48¼ —De Blois, July 8, '87
2.48 2-5—Rich, September 24, '86.
" Rowe, October 2, '86.
" Hillier, September 25, '84.

2.48 3-5—Foster, September 24, '86.

2.49 —Barber, September 10, '85.

2.49 1-5—Kluge, August 27, '86.

2.49¼ —Parsons, September 9, '84.

2.49 2-5—Howell, September 9, '85
" Mayes, May, '86.
" Howell, October 1, '85.
" Howell, October 2, '85.
2.49½ —Howell, October 1, '85.
2.49 3-5—Kavanaugh, August 28, '86.
" Gaskell, September 15, '86.
" Crist, September 24, '86.
" Stenken, August 20, '87.
2.49 4-5—Illston, June 27, '86.
" G. Illston, June 8, '85.
" Wood, September 9, '85.
" Cook, September 10, '85.

* Not accepted by Records Committee, on account of a technicality.

"FIRSTS."

The first bicycle rider in this country was Alfred D. Chandler, now an eminent Boston lawyer, July, 1877.

The first bicycle made in this country—1877—cost $313, and weighed anywhere between a hundred-weight and a ton.

The first racing wheel owned in the country was an Eclipse racer, 27 lbs., sold by John Keen to C. K. Billings, of New Haven.

The League was organized at Newport, May 31, 1880. The idea of a League was conceived by Charles E. Pratt and the call for the meeting was issued by C. K. Munroe, then Captain of the New York Bicycle Club.

The first remarkable ride was W. R. Pitman's tour from Boston to Haverhill, 42 2-3 miles, in 5h. 40m.

The first amateur race was run at Lynn, Mass., July 4, 1878, and was won by W. R. Pitman.

A. T. Lane, of Montreal, brought the first bicycle into Canada, 1874.

The first Brooklyn rider was Mr. H. Koop, Jr., now deceased. The second was W. F. Gullen, now a member of the Brooklyn Bicycle Club. The wheel is still in existence.

The first decision on the status of a cycle was given March 25, 1879, in England.

Central Park, New York, was first invaded against the law July 1, 1881, by S. Conant Foster, W. M. Wright and H. H. Walker.

The League gained its first legal victory, 1880.

The first American decision defining the cycle as a carriage was given May 20, 1877.

The first wheels imported were "Harvards," by Cunningham & Co., November, 1877.

The Pope Manufacturing Company's first shipment of wheels were "Duplex Excelsiors," January, 1878.

The first number of an American cycle journal was published December 22, 1877.

The Boston Club was the first wheel organization, February, 1878.

The first bicycle made, a "boneshaker," was exhibited at the Paris Exposition, 1865. Lallement exhibited wheel of same type at New Haven, 1866.

AN OSCILLATING SINGLE BALL-BEARING PEDAL.

It may be noticed that the pedal as now used by our many riders has received little or no attention in the way of improvements as compared to other members of the world-wide cycle. The saddle has had many fluctuations in the way of improvements, as well as the wheel and its many parts. The bearing also comes in for its share in the study. In this, however, as in an old saying, which applies very well, "that the first shall be last and the last first," the Æolus bearing is one of the first improvements in that line, and has not only held its own over other bearings now upon the market, but is to-day the most universally adopted and used.

The rubbers also may be mentioned as coming in for a share of attention, but these members remain about the same, except perhaps that which is used for the pedal. This last member has been made in many forms and much study put upon it. First came the round exterior with cone bearings. Then one with a square cone or exterior, to prevent turning over. Then Hancock's patent corrugated rubber was put upon the market with most deserved success. This make, owing to the hardness of the rubber, was found to possess one or two features which remained to be improved upon. Hence the patent square exterior, and some with concave sides. All of these, it may be remarked, would wear flat and smooth by the rider's foot, caused for the most part by the shoe oscillating horizontally as the rider works his limp pedal and machine. It has been thought that this might be improved and render the pedalling of the rider more easy and natural. It will be readily seen by a moment's study that the three joints in a person's limb do not work in the same vertical plane, but more in accord with a warped service. The lateral motion of the knee when in action causes the foot to move about one-eighth to three-eighths of an inch horizontally on the pedal rubbers during one revolution of the pedal, causing an unsteady footing and a wear. Although a very small feature, yet for a perfect machine and pedal this point may possibly be improved so as to give better results, especially in racing. Mr. Fred. D. Owen, of Washington, D C., Capital Bicycle Club, has invented and perfected an oscillating pedal which will give the desired results, and save a few pounds of weight to the machine.

This pedal is constructed upon a conical shaft (which is attached to the crank) and a one ball-bearing box, together with a band of thin elastic steel securely fastened to the bearing, and serrated at the fore and aft edges to engage the rider's foot.

By its construction, it will be seen from the cut above that any tendency of the foot to oscillate sideways is at once met and governed by the elastic steel frame, and brought back instantly to its normal condition as soon as the twist is removed, and *vice versa*. This oscillation of the foot and pedal is uniform and regular with each stroke of the lines and cranks, and always around the bearing box as a centre. Still one more feature will be seen in the above design. This elasticity in the steel strap, formed as it is like a figure 8, projects out beyond the ridged part of the bearing, so that, should the machine fall over upon the ground or have a collision of any kind, the axle or crank, or both, are shielded, as it were, by this elastic member and spared much unnecessary damage, a feature which may be as desirable as the other when the cost of repairs is considered. This feature is specially desirable in racing, where the regular rat-trap is used, as it possesses all the desirable qualities of the older forms, and is somewhat lighter in weight, making, it is claimed by experienced riders, sufficient reason for its favorable consideration and notice.

Enoch Townsend, of Saco, accomplished the feat on Sunday last of riding from Boston to Portland on a bicycle in a single day. He started seven miles west of Boston at 5 A. M. and arrived in Portland at 8 o'clock that night. He rode on horseback from Portland to Saco, experienced no mishap on the way, and was in good condition when he arrived at his destination.

The Massachusetts Division of the L. A. W., augmented by the Providence Bicycle Club, will hold its annual meet at Cottage City August 6, 9 and 10. There will be races and excursions. The Martha's Vineyard Association will tender the visitors many courtesies. Three hundred men are expected.

A SELECTED LIST OF PATENTS.

[Reported especially for THE WHEEL AND CYCLING TRADE REVIEW by C. A. Snow & Co., patent attorneys. Washington, D. C.]

L. J. Atwood, Waterbury, Conn.; Lamp holder.

W. H. Kitto, Plymouth, England; Velocipede.

H. S. Henry, Stonington, Conn.; Wrench. All bearing date of June 18, 1889.

J. Davidson, Guelph, Canada; Safety lamp.

J. Knous, Hartford, Conn.; Velocipede saddle and supporting device.

W. H. Bevinger, Middletown, Ohio; Hip belt. All bearing date of June 25, 1889.

A very pretty wedding occurred at Christ Church, Cambridge, Thursday evening, the contracting parties being Mr. A. Douglass Salfield, of the Massachusetts Bicycle Club, and Miss Winnifred W. Cobb. Among the numerous gifts was a handsome piano lamp from friends of the Massachusetts Club.

Mrs M. E Seals recently issued invitations to the marriage of her daughter, Miss Iola B. Seales, to Mr. Percy Stone, all of St. Louis. The ceremony was performed at Christ Church Cathedral, on Tuesday evening, June 25.

George W. Childs says that the Telford roads around Wootton, Pa., were laid at the instance of Gen. U. S. Grant, who thought the bad roads the only drawback to the place.

Three New York men rode to Peekskill on Sunday to visit the Seventh Regiment in camp. They returned by train and reported the roads as very bad from Tarrytown up. Three other members of the club rode to Coney Island.

A party of "Brooklyn" will go down to the Massapequa House, on Long Island, on Sunday.

Mr. Darkman and eleven other members of the Brooklyn Club had a delightful trip last Saturday and Sunday. Leaving on the 2.30 P. M. boat Mary Powell, they spent the night at Poughkeepsie In the morning they rode down to Fishkill Landing, crossed over to Newburg and rode to Highland Mills, taking train from latter place for home. At Mr. Franklin Harper's house, near Newburg, they were hospitably treated by the Messrs. Harper, and at Highland Mills, Mr. Henry Hall, Jr., gave them such a good time that they remained at his house all the afternoon.

St. Nicholas Avenue, from 125th to 155th Street, is as smooth as a race path.

It is rumored that three large Western agents will combine forces and manufacture for next year's trade.

The Pope Mfg. Co. issue a neat little pamphlet, vest-pocket size, containing many flattering testimonials of the worth of the World Typewriter. It is gotten up in scrap-book style, after the idea of the collection of favorable testimonials concerning the Columbia wheels, issued some time since. The idea shows much originality in the advertising department of the Pope Co.

SOLD HIS WHEEL AT ONCE.

The following letter fully explains itself. In the elastic language of the English cycling press, "Comment is needless":

"EDITOR THE WHEEL:

"Do please stop my ad. Wheel was sold right away, and I can't sell it again. No question as to THE WHEEL being a good advertising medium. L. P. THAYER. "West Randolph, Vt., June 24"

"Jack" Prince, Manhattan B. C., is a "sight," the result of a bad header.

The Des Moines Wheel Club has a membership of twenty. A movement is on foot among the members to hold a bicycle race on the Fourth of July.

The New York house, and Messrs. Pattison and Hickok, of the Pope Mfg. Co., will be at the League Meet.

A two-mile bicycle handicap will be held at Washington Park on July 4 at the Prospect Harriers' games.

The number of lady bicyclists in Buffalo has reached nearly sixty. Many of them are fast becoming experts.

President Bates was the first cyclist who wrote on roads improvement.

C. E. Whitten, dealer at Lynn, Mass., had a Columbia two-track tricycle stolen on Tuesday last.

SPALDING'S NEW YORK HOUSE.

Mr. Walter Spalding will sail for Europe on July 14 for a well earned rest. Mr. Spalding personally superintends the New York house, which we believe now surpasses the parent house at Chicago in income. The New York house, originally occupying the ground floor of 241 Broadway, has extended up two stories and grown down into the basement and cellar. Even this was not enough space, and the enormous stock the firm carries has overflowed into the cellars and sub-cellars of the adjoining buildings. We recently made a trip through the building holdings, accompanied by A. B. Barkman and a tallow candle. Had the "dip" gone out we should doubtless be still prowling about the subterranean alleyways between cases of sporting goods. Besides the New York plant there are suggestions of lumber yards and base-ball bat factories, where any number of bats a minute are turned out. And there is still another addition to be noted, for the Spaldings buy up many specialties and practically control manufacturing plant from Maine to California. The manager of this plant is a splendidly-proportioned man, over six feet tall, whose voice harmonizes with the man, deep and reverberating, but slightly harsh, or husky, as if the air passages had felt the all-destroying New York climate. The protruding forehead and sharp, impatient eye-glance bespeak the qualities of the successful man of affairs. The watchful man of the concern, and a member of the firm, we believe, is Mr. Curtis, a massive, clean-shaven, alert, actor-looking number of bars a minute are turned out. An important man in the concern is Mr. Frank White, a slightish blonde man, full of oil and honey and the milk of human kindness. He is the complement of Messrs. Spalding and Curtis; they think, he acts. If they decide to buy up a forest and turn it into base-ball bats, Mr. White is on the spot instanter and does the buying. The business is subdivided into departments and the heads of each are held responsible.

Elwell's European Tourists.

FROM DUBLIN TO OXFORD.

EDITOR OF THE WHEEL:

"Awful" is a much-abused adjective. It is tossed about on every lip, applied to this and that, good, bad and indifferent. It seldom finds its right place, but I put it there when I use it to describe that trip across the Irish Sea. It was purely and simply awful. Such pitching and tos ing about I never would have believed possible—no, nor such convulsions of the human anatomy, either. The wretched little tub in which we crossed from Dublin to Liverpool (the Longford) was as much at the mercy of the wind and sea as a chip would have been, and our only wonder was that she held together during that memorable night.

WASHED WITH SALT WATER.

Our machines were stored on deck, and the breaking waves dashed completely over the whole business. Quadrants, Singers, Victors, Columbias and all The flimsy tarpaulin with which they were covered proved but little protection. Two of our number, and two only, were able to sit down to a lunch of cold meat, bread and coffee at nine o'clock, and while we were stowed away four in a room they "laughed in ghoulish glee" and inquired if we would partake of their fat ham. One youth, in the midst of his agony, wanted to know "why Elwell couldn't have taken us by train instead of on this miserable boat" When morning broke a wan, emaciated, limp and lifeless-looking crowd of men might be seen on deck scrubbing up machines with a remarkable lack of energy.

Ye gods! Can these be Elwell's sturdy cyclists, who crossed the "briny" without missing a meal? The same! But how they are fallen!

FIRST IMPRESSIONS OF ENGLAND.

Arriving at Liverpool we took the ferry for Birkenhead, which, on the way there, took us past a fast fading monument of American enterprise and energy. The Great Eastern, high and dry upon the flats at Birkenhead, is being fast pulled to pieces for old junk. She is not so far gone, however, as to prevent our getting a good idea of her once immense strength and size. The "camera fiends" (of which there are some twelve or thirteen in the party) took a shot at her from all points, probably the last time the good old ship will ever be photographed.

The contrast between Ireland's rainy days and heavy roads and England's sunny skies and perfect highways was certainly delightful, and despite the fact that we had "passed a wretched night," we did the fifteen miles between our landing place and the ancient town of Chester in considerably less than an hour and a half. England's roads certainly justify all that has been said in their praise, and we cannot but appear doubtful when we are assured of "much finer ones in France." We certainly ask no better. For miles and miles we roll over perfect roads without meeting with any grade that can be dignified by the name of a hill. On either side are well-trimmed holly hedges or smooth stone walls with moss-covered tops, between which we simply *glide*, without any exertion whatever.

LIGHTNESS OF ENGLISH MACHINES.

Small wonder that English makers build rigid machines and do away with all sorts of anti-vibration springs, for they have no need nor use for them. It's easy to see why a machine weighing forty pounds or over is looked askance at, and called an "express wagou" or a "mail-coach." Our English cousins sail along on safeties weighing from twenty-five to thirty-thre pounds, and I myself had the pleasure of riding a five-mile stretch to-day on a safety scaling just nineteen and three-quarter pounds the tires being scarcely the size of a lead-pencil.

FINE RESIDENCES AT CHESTER.

At Chester we found much of interest, including a visit, just outside the city, to the residences of Gladstone (Hawarden Castle) and a person whom the natives call the "Juke" of Westminster (Eaton Hall). There is certainly enough of interest in Chester to keep one very busy for a week or more, but at that rate our trip would last us the rest of our natural lives, and as we have undertaken seeing a great deal in a short space of time we have to be content with a glance and a mental resolution to come again "when our boys get over the falls," and do the place more thoroughly. Our next day's run was to Stafford, fifty miles distant, by the way of Nantwich, where we lunched. We all start in the morning saying, "We will ride together and ride slow, and stop when we please." Do we do it? Yes, for a mile. After that we keep increasing our speed imperceptibly and unconsciously until it gets to ten or eleven miles an hour, when the more moderate ones drop back, and a dozen or so, known as the "Mac Scorchers," and led by "the O'Faed" (A. J. Wilson), on a racing trike, put it through in short order. However, our party is of such dimensions that one can always find plenty of jovial companions at any pace, however fast or slow.

PIG VS. BICYCLE.

On the road to Stafford occurred the amusing episode of a race between a cyclist and a pig. The pig is usually accounted an animal very slow of locomotion, but I can bring e idence to prove that this particular pig was built for speed. He was taking a stroll on the Queen's highway, on this particular afternoon, and was just in search of a good opening in the hedge to crawl through, when up behind him came several cyclists at a fairly good gait. The opening in the hedge did not materialize, and the pig started ahead at a lively gallop, while one of the wheelmen endeavored to pass ahead of him in order not to cause him unnecessary fatigue. The pig thereupon let himself out to full speed, and I am certain that a good half mile of ground was gone over before the cyclist (encouraged meanwhile by laughter and cries of "five to three on the pig") was able to pass his opponent.

PENNELL ON CATHEDRALS.

We lunched at Nantwich, and visited an interesting cathedral of the twelfth century. Cathedrals, however, are much alike, and about the only man in the party who knows enough about them to be able to tell if they are good or bad, is Mr. Joseph Pennell, who, it is alleged, will dismount and enter one, look about a bit and then "Oh, gammon! there's nothing here," and despite the explanation of a curate with a six-pence eye, will mount his machine in disgust. Just outside Stafford we passed the estate of one of the Meakin brothers, the great crockery-ware manufacturers. Stafford is a manufacturing place whose interesting (?) feature is the bells on the steep e of St. Mary's, which play an air every hour, and run scales on the quarters. The first time it is heard it is amusing, the second time you listen indifferently, the third time it's a bore, and by the time you are trying to compose your nerves to rest, they fairly drive you frantic. We have not been so well pleased for a long while as when we were out of hearing of Stafford's everlasting bells. Birmingham, or "Brum.," was our next sleeping place, via Lichfield. At the latter place we had more cathedrals, but this time well worth seeing, as the outside of the Lichfield Cathedral is by far the most elaborate of any of the old cathedrals in England. Here we were met by the two Priest boys, sons of the "Quadrant" manufacturer, and several other Birmingham wheelmen, who informed us that a large body of cyclists were to meet us at Sutton, and escort us to our hotel in "Brum."

MET BY THE BIRMINGHAM BOYS.

We found the Birchfield and several other clubs, to the number of two hundred or more, and in addition four photographers, with their cameras all focused and seats arranged. This was a little more than we had bargained for, as the boys had each and every one, when they saw that diabolical cut of "The American Tourists" in the *Bicycling News* (the result of a photograph of the party in Dublin), registered a solemn vow that not another camera should be pointed at them until they requested it. After being assured that it was not for any newspaper and teasing the operators until their hair turned gray, we were once more permitted to "pursue the even tenor of our way." It is no small task to pilot over two hundred wheelmen through three miles of crowded streets, but it was done at last in safety. The dinner given us here by the Birchfield Wheel Club was one of the most thoroughly enjoyable affairs we have yet had It was done on a large scale, but was perfectly informal, and the laughter and clatter of tongues that went on must of itself have been sufficient guarantee to the Birchfield boys that we were thoro ghly enjoying ourselves. The affair was ended at 8:30 by the presentation to us of a very elaborate, illuminated address of welcome by the club. The boys then adjourned, and have since said that they "looked about the town."

MACHINES OVERHAULED.

The Quadrant machines were thoroughly overhauled and fixed up, by men sent by the Quadrant Tricycle Co., whose factory is situated here, and some of the boys availed themselves of the offer Mr. Priest very kindly made, to exchange for another style of machine if they desired. We left Birmingham with a warm feeling of fellowship for the men who had used us in such a hospitable manner, and started on what was to most of us the most interesting day we have yet had. The journey was through Coventry, Kenilworth, Warwick, Stoneleigh, stopping over night in Stratford-on-Avon.

INTERESTING SCENES

A more intensely interesting day's journey could hardly be imagined. We are in the very centre of England, and of the most celebrated district of it. We are seeing the very same quaint and charming scenery which Stoddard so vividly portrays in his lectures on "Old England," which no one can attend without mentally resolving to "go there some day." We are on the very stage of the theatre where so much of England's history has been played, and I think it quite needless, as well as useless, to try to convey to you any accurate idea of what a grand time we are having.

MONEY WELL INVESTED.

A young friend I left at home would not accompany us on this trip because he could not afford it, but was on the lookout for "a good investment for five or six hundred dollars" at the same time. I told him then that a trip to Europe would yield twenty per cent. interest, but now I want to make it one hundred per cent. There is not a man in the party but what has had his money's worth already, and we have not yet reached London. If anyone is contemplating a trip abroad I want to tell them just here that the way to take it is on a cycle of some sort, if they want to see a nation as it is and the people as they are. By doing so they will travel when and where, and as rapidly or slowly, as they desire. They will have everything their own way, and enjoy better health than they ever did before. Excuse me; I'm getting enthusiastic.

COVENTRY CYCLISTS.

At Stonebridge, seven miles from Coventry, we were met by a crowd of wheelmen on all sorts and conditions of wheels (for Coventry is the wheelman's Mecca), amongst them being a Victoria, from the Singer factory, with seats for eight. Of course, we all had to have a ride on this machine, and I assure you the sport was great. The sight of seven sturdy backs bending in unison in front of you would put strength into the weakest legs, and we bowled into C. at a good jog, passing on the way the stone which marks the centre of England. We are traveling in distinguished company.

STURMEY'S OPINION OF US.

At Stonebridge we were met by no less a person than Henry Sturmey, who, in company with a friend, was riding a Rudge quadricycle. As we were coming up to this place some one said to him, "Here comes the Americans; what do you think of them?" "Well," said H. S., "they look as tho' they ought to be comfortable, at all events." He alluded to our cycling dress, or rather undress. Hardly a man rides with a coat on, and the majority steam along with sleeves rolled up, and pants unbuttoned at the knee, in striking contrast with our English cousins, who, however hot the day, preserve a neat appearance, their caps nicely adjusted, coats buttoned, shoes shiny, and many with a pair of gloves or a handkerchief in their hand. At Coventry many of the boys went through the Rudge factory, the largest in the world, and very interesting indeed. The boys who are riding Singers either had their machines overhauled at the Singer factory, or exchanged for new wheels of a different style.

ROMANCE AMONG RUINS.

From here we journeyed to Kenilworth and inspected the grand old ruins of Kenilworth Castle, whose every stone conjures up recollections of Queen Elizabeth and her times. After an hour's admiration and romance, we once more pulled our wits together and started for Warwick, where we lunched at the "Warwick Arms," and again got romantic over Warwick, the best preserved castle in England. The camera fiends suffered here. Their Kodak's were rudely snatched from them at the entrance, and on no account would they be allowed to take them within the castle walls. They were forced to be content with taking anew the old picture in the history book of "Warwick Castle from the Bridge." The ride from here on to Stratford-on-Avon is one of the prettiest and most interesting stretches in the day. At Stratford we could not be accommodated at the famous "Red Horse," and had to content ourselves at the Golden Lion, directly opposite.

SHAKESPEARE'S HOME.

Stratford is exceptionally pretty and quaint, and one could linger here a month without suffering from ennui.

We saw the usual lions, and in the afternoon did the thirty-eight miles to Oxford quite easily. At Woodstock, seven miles from Oxford, we were met and paraded into Oxford by over one hundred wheelmen, representing the University and Oxonian Clubs. We were by them shown over Blenheim Castle, the residence of the Duke of Marlborough, who recently married an American lady. I am happy to say that we don't suffer as badly at the hands of the English newspapers as His Grace did at ours, or I am afraid we should be discouraged. The men who met us were most all students at Oxford, and we felt greatly complimented that they should show so much interest in us.

DINED BY OXONIANS.

They also gave us a dinner in their own quarters to-day, which was cosy, informal and extremely palatable If our wits went wool gathering at Kenilworth and Warwick I can't tell what they did in this grand old place—I won't try. We were called upon in Oxford by another "big gun" amongst cyclists. Mr. G. Lacy Hillier, editor of the *Bicycling News*, dropped in to ask after our health and be introduced. To-morrow night we land in Hampton Court, and the following day in London.

CURIOUS WAYS TO AMERICAN EYES.

Our British cousins are curious chaps. They send you to bed with a candle simply that they may charge you for it. They shave you for three or four cents and black your shoes for nothing, but if you want a cup of coffee with your meals you must pay twelve cents for it They turn to the right when walking but to the left when driving. They call candy "sweets," pies "tarts," grip-sacks "portmanteaus," horse-cars "trams" and carriages "traps." Funny old England!

TAM O'SHANTER.

CRUSHED AGAIN.

We are not often given to complaint, but have to endure troubles, great and small, with that equanimity so much admired by our friends. There are times, though, when even the trodden worm must turn and feebly attempt to give a reason for presuming to exist. This wail of woe is called forth by the editors of our trans-Atlantic contemporary, *Bicycling News*, delegating the easy task of cutting-up this young and struggling sheet to one "Violet Lorne." This is the way she does it:

"Great indeed is local fame in the eyes, at least, of the local THE WHEEL has risen up in a burst of virtuous indignation at the crass ignorance displayed by this journal in regard to a certain Amelie Rives, whose somewhat startling remarks upon cycling subjects were commented on not long since. That *Bicycling News* should confess to never having heard of Amelie Rives seems to THE WHEEL a thing incredible. 'We wonder,' it says, with a scathing irony which ought to cut the staff of this paper to the soul, 'if the *Bicycling News* people have ever heard of a woman who called herself George Eliot?' Ah, yes! and they have also heard of the people of Slocum Podger, who confidently expect that young Bl bkins, who writes 'such lovely poetry' for the Poet's Corner of the *Slocum Podger Market Gazette* will succeed Lord Tennyson as Laureate, if the jealousy of the rest of the nation permits!"

If it is any satisfaction to you, "Violet," you may look upon us with the eye of imagination as clothed in sackcloth and ashes and cowering in the darkest corner of the sanctum sanctorum. Seriously, we think it a little unkind of the editors of the *B. N.* to turn us loose in the arena before "Violet," as it were. We cannot courteously quarrel with a lady, and, although we would cheerfully turn the matter over to our lady contributors, "Marguerite" and "Psyche," we fear they lack the lengthy experience of our fair enemy in England. It *may* be, and we hope is, that "Violet" merely hits us on general principles, or for lack of other and more valuable material to make "copy" from. But that is mere conjecture. We can only ask to be excused for living and breathing, and hope for more merciful treatment in future.

A party of wheelmen will leave Boston about July 1 for a trip to Halifax by boat and thence to Annapolis by wheel. There is to be a carnival of outdoor sports at Halifax between July 5 and 10, and the tourists mean to be present. The regular fare to Halifax and return is about $10, and it is hoped to secure a rebate on these prices. Those who desire information about the trip can address Messrs. W. T. Roop, 557 Main Street, or R. H. McLean, 407 Main Street, Cambridgeport.

Two excitingly interesting races were decided at New Orleans on Sunday last. The first, a 1-mile straightaway over St. Charles Avenue, asphalt, had seven starters, and was won by B. M. Sprigg, with H. L. Cary, second, and H. C. Rae, third. There were no timers, no judges, "no nothin'," and wheelmen there rather laughed when the local press announced the time as 2m. 54s., breaking previous local records by 16s.

All they had to go by was the record of a stop-watch carried by one of the contestants in his pocket (?), and guessed at when he finished; 3m 10s is apt to stand for some time yet as local record.

The second race was the N. O. Bi Club's first handicap contest for the A. M. Hill cup, and had four starters. B. M. Sprigg and H. L. Cary were placed at scratch, and J. W. Dodge and C. H. Fenner given twenty-five seconds start Distance 2½-miles. Dodge took the lead at once and was never headed, winning in 7m. 17s.; Sprigg, second, in 7m. 27s.

HENDEE ON TRAINING.

Cycling has opened up a new branch of athletics which is becoming more and more popular each year, and the questions are often asked, who is the champion and what is the record? That "record," which has steadily been battled with from the early days of cycling until the present time, is a marvelous piece of human endurance and pluck. Each year some one from out the host of cyclers has been fleeter of foot than his predecessors and has hammered the record lower and lower, until now the rate of speed attained seems almost incredible.

This has not been achieved all at once, however, but has been reached, not only by the manufacturers' building lighter and better wheels, and the construction of better tracks, but by study and careful training on the part of the riders themselves.

"CONDITION" THE IMPORTANT THING.

Whenever a great feat has been accomplished, not only in cycling but in all athletic sports, "condition" was the starting point. Little does one think while watching a race, of the many weary hours that have been spent and the self-denial gone through to bring the man into the perfect shape in which we see him.

Training for cycle racing has most certainly opened a new branch of the art, and although no two men can be trained alike, still there are many fundamental rules which can be followed with the best of results.

DISTANCE TO BE RIDDEN.

One of the leading points to be considered is the distance to be raced. Many athletes claim to be good at any and all distances, and, to a certain extent, this is true; but at some point they excel; so in entering upon a course of training lay out your work, and leave no stone unturned to get yourself in the best condition possible.

We train to bring ourselves into that condition from which we can obtain the greatest amount of speed from the least exertion.

WEIGHT TO BE REDUCED.

To gain that end all unnecessary flesh must be removed and the muscles left to act freely and easily. The flesh can be removed in many different ways; most common of which are the shower-bath and the use of a "sweater."

Some persons cannot stand the rigor of the former, and many find the "sweater" a very uncomfortable thing to wear.

Therefore some experimental work must be done. The "sweater" is most generally used, however. The reducing of the flesh should be conducted slowly, as there are chances of weakness following a too sudden falling away of superfluous flesh. Your weight may not decrease, however, in pursuing a course of training, and strange as it may seem, some increase in weight. The flesh that is displaced is more than equalled by the muscle developed.

This does not apply except in rare cases, and many reduce themselves several pounds. The writer has found that one of the best ways to begin a course of training is by taking a good dose of physic and following it up, in the course of a day or two, with another. This gets your system into good working order for the hard work of actual training to follow.

DEVELOP THE CHEST AND ARMS.

There is one point that has been sadly overlooked thus far in the preparation for racing, and that is the development of the upper body. There is no reason why the arms should not be as well developed as the legs.

True, the legs are really the motive power, but the arms and chest impart their share of the power through the means of the handle-bar.

Many times the writer has been questioned regarding training for cycle racing, and when discussing the really small amount of work actually done in comparison with the tremendous preparation of the college student for foot races and other college sports, many have remarked that there was not enough work done. Certainly the cyclist undergoes an entirely different method, as far as exercise is concerned, from any other branch of athletics, the idea being not simply to obtain the greatest amount of strength and endurance, but to combine with these the elasticity and ease of action of the muscles in the quick pedaling necessary to rapid riding. The muscles have to be brought into that state which is at one moment hard as iron and the next soft and pliable. This action has to take place very rapidly when traveling at a high speed. For example, a man with short and knotty muscles, either above or below the knee, never makes a fast rider, simply because his muscles are not capable of the rapid relaxation necessary.

KNACK OF SPURTING.

The art of spurting is a study in itself, and much might be written which would be of practical use to the beginner, but space forbids. A few points alone can be mentioned. The body should be held as still as possible, thus enabling the rider to hold his wheel steady. If this point could be practiced, many a bad spill could be avoided and a greater rate of speed attained. The daily routine of training ought to be such that no fatigue should be felt and you should feel at all times ambitious and confident that you are capable of doing a little more than you ever have done; ambitious to such an extent that when walking quietly along you feel like breaking into a run. This is the point to which training is supposed to bring one. From all facts gathered it is certainly ill-advised to take any other exercise than riding. For example, walking or running to any extent tends to make one "slow." Exercise in the shape of dumb-bells or Indian clubs is certainly a splendid thing before breakfast, but the *track* should be the main point of preparation. The spins should be taken regularly and vary according to the distance in view. For short distance riding, say from one to five miles, the spins should vary from one to three miles, with short sprints now and then. The full distance never should be run but once a week. This should be in the shape of a trial. Thus from week to week you can see the results of your training. It would be wise to keep a complete list of the miles run in practice; this might be valuable for reference.

HOW TO AVOID "STALENESS."

Practicing riding at full speed each time you mount will soon bring you into that condition called "stale." This is a point to be avoided by all means. Once "stale," training might as well be given up for a month and you should confine yourself to road riding. Care and judgment should be used at each mount, considering at each time the weather, condition of the track, and rider. Should the wind be high it would be policy simply to confine yourself to spurting with the wind, thus becoming accustomed to quick peddling. At each regular spin it would be well to finish strongly, each time increasing the length of the spurt until you have reached your limit. By the limit is meant the exact point from which you can hold your spurt to the very end. This you will find to be of great benefit and it will give you confidence, when, without knowing, you might become hopeless of holding out to the finish.

Human endurance has a limit, but many and many a race has been won by the sheer grit and determination of the rider.

UNADVISABLE TO CHANGE ROUTINE.

The daily routine of the athlete while in training must necessarily be about the same from day to day. His hours must be regular, not only in his exercise but in his hours of repose. Let us suppose, for instance, one is training for short-distance work. He rises at six, has a dry rub-down, a short walk and is ready for breakfast, which might consist of soft boiled eggs, a couple of good wholesome mutton-chops, and dry toast. After breakfast he is at his leisure until the hour of exercise, which may vary from ten until half-past.

He now has another rub-down and dons his practice suit. The spin consists this morning of three miles at a good swinging gait with a rapid finish, which starts the blood into good circulation. Now comes the hard and laborious rub-down.

This is accomplished with a rough towel, which is freely used until the flesh is brought to a rosy tint and all the pores are wide open.

Following this comes the manipulation of the muscles and the application of witch hazel, alcohol, or other like substances, which prevents the muscles from becoming stiff.

POINTS ON DIET.

When the rub-down is completed it is nearly dinner-time. This meal may consist of a great variety of foods, as the old idea of beef and mutton alone has long since been dropped. However, there is nothing better than good mutton, especially if the wind needs improving. In following a diet, simply drop all food that is fattening or does not agree with you. The writer would suggest for dinner light soup, beef or mutton, very little vegetables and a small amount of pudding. A cup of weak tea for breakfast and supper would do no harm, but for dinner it should be dropped. The afternoon exercise should be confined to spurting different distances, increasing to a run of two miles or so, if you are in need of more exercise. This is followed by a rub-down similar to that of the morning. The supper should consist of cold meats, dropped eggs, etc. The evening should be passed quietly, and the rider be in bed by ten or half past.

Many rules might be written, but one of the best guidances is good common sense, and with a little judgment and experimental work, together with observance of all the regular rules of training, one ought to soon discover the best method to obtain the best results.

"G. H"

TENNESSEE DIVISION MEET.

June 18 was a red-letter day for Tennessee wheelmen. Rain in the morning threatened to spoil the parade, but the clouds were soon dispelled, and the streets rapidly dried up by the sun's heat.

The parade was formed at 3 P. M., and when in motion, covered fully a half mile; the route taken being the same as previously mentioned in our columns.

At the Custom-house a dismount was made and the customary photo. taken.

After the parade, a large party took an enjoyable run to Bosley Springs.

Much credit for the success of the parade is due to Chief Consul Wilson, Representative Combs, who had general charge of the Meet, and the Committee on Parade, especially its chairman, Mr. Ed. Palmer, who left nothing undone to make the parade a complete success.

At 7:30 P. M. the State Board of officers of the Division met and conducted routine business, after which the regular annual meeting of the Division was called to order by Chief Consul Wilson. The Chief Consul read his report, which showed a gratifying condition of League matters. The report stated that local consuls had been appointed in every Tennessee town where there were members, including Bristol, Clarksville, Chattanooga, Franklin, Knoxville, Memphis, Murfreesboro, Union City and Nashville, most of whom had done good work in securing renewals and soliciting applications for membership. The Chief Consul emphasized the importance of every member going to work to secure recruits, declaring that upon the work of the members now depends the future success of the Division.

The report of the Secretary-Treasurer was next read, showing a healthful financial condition. The number of league members in the Division was shown to be 120, distributed as follows: Nashville, 41; Memphis, 27; Chattanooga, 17; Clarksville, 16; Knoxville, 13; Franklin, 2; Bristol, 2; Murfreesboro, 1; Union City, 1.

Chief Consul Wilson and Secretary-Treasurer Patch were re-nominated without opposition, although the nominations will not close until July, allowing towns not represented in the meeting last night to make additional nominations.

The question of a road book and map for the State was next brought up and discussed, and the chairman of the committee which already has the matter in hand was urged to give the matter his earliest possible attention. Much data and valuable information is now in possession of this committee, and there is no doubt the book will be published in time for use early next season, at furthest.

On Wednesday morning, the 19th, a party of ten wheelmen, including two Georgia visitors, started on a four days' tour, following the schedule outlined in WHEEL of June 14. They will traverse much country new to wheelmen, and the sight of so many riders at once will be a novel one to people along the road.

A dispatch from St. Catharines, Ont., says: "Mr. Hal. Donly, the Association Secretary, has posted programmes to all members of the Association, and Mr. John Corbin, the Meet Secretary, has posted them to all the United States clubs that are at all likely to be here on July 9. Mr Corbin is in receipt of quite a number of entries for the races, and all racers should secure an entry blank, fill it out and return as soon as possible, as the time for entering is growing very short. The Rochesters, thirty in number, will arrive here on Sunday, June 30. Several of our riders will meet them at the Falls. The prizes are very handsome, and without doubt the finest ever offered at a C. W. A Meet."

CYCLISTS AND SOME OF THEIR WAYS—SOME OF THEIR FOLLIES AND FALLACIES—BY "JACK."

THE CRANK WHO TALKS NOTHING BUT "BICYCLE"—THE SIDEWALK CRANK—THE LEAGUE MEMBER CRANK—THE FULL-NICKELED CRANK.

"Joe Howard," of the Boston *Globe*, was about right when he said, "Those bicycle fellows don't care '*nothing for nobody*.'" They don't—worse luck. Now, the little chat I am going to have with you is about a fellow whom we all know—the "bicycle crank."

Probably crankiness never takes a more harmless form than this. The bicycle crank, as a rule, is a man who was born with a strawberry mark of a bicycle on his brain; for morning, noon and night the topic is "bicycle." His room is a study for a caricaturist. The walls are covered with "celebrities" Jack Prince and Cortis are slapped up next to one another, and Louise Armaindo is assigned a place next to gentlemanly M. V. J. Webber. He knows they are celebrities—that's *all* he knows.

Guiteau was a man who would have made a splendid "bicycle crank." He was just the proper sort of ass to shine in that capacity. I am really tired of this man, who is forever talking bicycle. His mind has got into a *rut*, and his thinking power is concentrated on a practical recreation which should be treated *as* a practical recreation only. The man who lays awake nights thinking out "Sun and Planet" ideas for cycles should be shut up where he can't do us any harm. There is the cyclist who rides in a full suit of tights on the road (when not engaged in a race); he is generally a proper "cad," and does not know the meaning of the word indecency. "Jay Purist Bruce" was what a talented contributor to this paper termed me.

Now that is only half the truth, for if there is anything which delights my mischievous soul it is to "sneak in" a carefully veiled *double-entendre* in my "copy" to be passed upon by the sleepy editor, whose blue pencil has worn so short that marking is difficult and sharpening it is a bore. (When the editor gets his paper out, and sees the passages I have introduced in a very innocent way, he has been known to declare that I was a regular "mine of phosphates.") I am young, you know, and life is sweet. [The editor takes care not to read Jack's letters. He turns them over to the assistant editor as a mild penance.—ED.] I like a little *fun* to take off the sharp corners off the prose of this life, but I am anything but a purist.

There is the "sidewalk crank" who comes rushing down the pavement like a Juggernaut of old, on his 56-inch roadster, sweeping past the terrified nurse-maid with her precious little charge, sleeping soundly in its nest of wool and lace. He says this is a free country, and doubtless understands by that that he is free to endanger the lives and militate against the happiness of other people, that he may gratify his own selfish whim. The sidewalk crank is found as a rule in towns of from 3 to 15,000 inhabitants. He generally wears a corduroy coat and elastic-side congress gaiters, and shows you his League number without a word of warning. There is the *League number crank* who speaks of the "free masonry of the wheel," and tells you "I am number 590,743,298 L. A. W." We always feel that that man is a kind of a microbe anyway, when he numbers himself like a convict or a lunatic. The League number was given as a means of facilitating League work, not as an adjunct to the member's name.

There is the "pace crank" who thinks that when he is riding at ten miles an hour that ground is being covered at the rate of three minutes to the mile, up hill and down dale. He is a harmless kind of fellow and makes a nice pace for a warm day. There is the soda-water crank who tries to make me believe that soda is better to ride on than light ale. Self-esteem oozes out of every pore of this man's body, and you had better leave him alone. He says: "You will go down the mouth of the fathomless pit if you undo the top of a Jake Worth or Pilsener." There is the egg-shake crank who beats an egg until it leaks in a tumbler of milk and acid phosphate, and behaves altogether like a Mormon elder in the busy season. He is a nuisance. About the most tiresome crank is the cyclometer crank, who gets off every block to read the measurement on the dial. The full-nickeled crank is an ornamental sort of organism, who does not know that nickel is porous and therefore does not keep out "wet" like enamel. He is never slothful but carries all kinds of pigments and polishing pastes in his saddle-bags. There is the crank that rides right over his pedals and *believes* that his wheel goes easier than when sitting well back. In a safety bicycle the line of the front fork and the line of pedaling should be parallel. In other words, the line of the front fork and the line from the riders' hip joint to the centre of his "foot-travel," which, with a six-inch crank, is over twelve inches in diameter, or about a yard in circumference. There is the "cad crank," who kisses his hand to chambermaids and pretty girls along his line of wheel. He should be "jumped on" with spiked shoes. The disrespectful crank, who shouts in at the open door of the meeting-house on a Sabbath morn, showing his asinine and puerile contempt for Sabbath observers. He is a bigot and a swelled head of the worst description. There is the other crank who goes to the other extreme.

There are all these and many other cranks more or less obnoxious, but we will not mention them all. There is the "coasting crank," the whistle crank, the bugle crank (—— him), the military uniform crank—but, hold on. In the words of the prophet, Jeremiah, when he went over to Hoboken to teach the natives how to hack wood, "The woods are full of 'em." The man who really enjoys cycling is the moderate man, who is not a crank and who does not sleep with his bicycle. He is a man who attends to business and uses the cycle as a means of lengthening his days and eking out his boyhood. He is not a man who annoys his friends with bicycle—bicycle—bicycle.

JACK.

Another union run is on the carpet for June 30. The Massachusetts Wheelmen go to dinner at the Massapog House, and the Rhode Islanders will ride to Sharon and join their Bay State brethren. The party from the vicinity of Providence will leave the Rhode Island Wheelmen's quarters, 70 South Main Street, at 7:30 A. M. A glorious outing is assured if the weather is good, and the occasion will be a grand opportunity to give the few Rhode Islanders who haven't experienced it a chance to learn how Massachusetts hospitality is dispensed at Massachusetts hostelries when two or three hundred hungry wheelmen assemble at the dinner call.

JERSEY CITY.

Here we are again. My absence from your columns was not caused by lack of news in the H. C. W. ranks, for on the contrary there has been plenty. Neither have I been "doing a term" on the Island; but my voluminous duties in my endeavor to earn bread and butter for a lot of poor relations caused me to drop the cycling journalistic pen temporarily.

I notice that my friend "Westfield" is also out of sight, crawled back into his shell, so to speak; but I understand he has purchased a tandem bike with a *dress shield* over the front chain, and as he usually sits on the rear seat his time is doubtless well occupied.

Well, Billy, you have my best wishes, for "I've oft been there before many a time"—no, only once.

At the last regular meeting of the H. C. W., Mayor Cleveland, of Jersey City, was elected an honorary member of the club. The Mayor is a very popular club man in this borough, and as a long programme is being made up in connection with the repaving of our streets, a twenty-mile country road and several other like prizes, it is valuable to the wheelmen to have the Mayor in the ranks.

I accordingly notified the Mayor (on our fancy note paper) of his election to the honorary position and received an autograph reply, from which (without his permission) I quote the following:

"I am under obligations to the Hudson County Wheelmen for their kindness and thoughtfulness, and accept the honor as entirely unmerited on my part. What have I ever done that you should grant me the privilege, without payment of dues, of taking a 'header' from one of your 'wheels?' I am puzzled to know how a wheelman can balance himself after getting his mind confused and his eyes turned in or out by the study of the hieroglyphics at the upper left-hand corner of your envelopes and at the top of your note paper.

"Of course, I know that to be a wheelman one must keep perfectly sober, else the wheel will cast him, and it may be that those Greek letters are intended as a gauge or standard, so that if a member has his head clear enough to read them he is all right for a bicycle spin.

"However that may be, if it is understood that no member shall laugh at the comic sight of *two hundred and fifteen pounds* taking a header, nor look pleased while I am puzzling over those Cinglese-Russian-Greek characters, I will try to become such a member of the club that nobody shall be able to charge that I am either *useful* or *ornamental*.

Yours truly,

(Signed) "ORESTES CLEVELAND."

Thus are we enabled to shake hands with Brooklyn in having our Mayor "one of the boys."

I have it on good authority that Dr. H. A. Benedict, of the H. C. W., will be nominated for the office of Vice-Consul of this State. It was announced some time ago that Dr. Carlton Brown and Mr. George C. Pennell, of the Elizabeth Wheelmen, would doubtless be slated for Chief Consul and Secretary-Treasurer, respectively. With three such men to run New Jersey's League affairs I feel safe in predicting that our League membership will soon reach its old notch of 1885–6. When Drs. Brown and Benedict begin their tour how "the teeth will fly." Pennell, you have my sympathy.

Speaking on League affairs, there is lots of missionary work to do in New Jersey, and the officers elected will find that much of their time will have to be sacrificed in order to make a good showing. League hotels will take up fully one-fourth of their time, while the condition of roads and L. A. W. road signs should also have much of their attention. With the appointment of good, live local consuls, however, this labor would be considerably lightened. Something is certainly necessary to be done here to convince non-L. A. W.'s that members of the national organization are enjoying special privileges in this State that wheelmen not of the League are forfeiting. I think Chief Consul Bull, of New York, has struck the key note in his hotel agreement system.

The county road law passed at the last session of our Legislature is already bearing fruit. Union County is ready to spend her $150,000, while Hudson and Monmouth Counties are considering the route their new country roads will take. With the advent of new boulevards and improved streets will come converts to the wheel, especially in this part of the State. It is therefore necessary that some valuable inducements should be held out to these new men in order that the power of the League shall be felt in New Jersey.

The H. C. W. intend giving an excursion to Boynton Beach (near Woodbridge, N. J.) some time during July. This is principally for the benefit of ladies who have taken a very lively interest in the club affairs during the winter months and assisted the boys greatly with their smokers. A boat has been secured for their exclusive use, and all we want now to make the affair a success is a clear day and a big crowd.

Messrs. W. E. Eldridge and H. F. Morse started on Saturday last on a tour to Massachusetts and up through the Berkshire Hills to Rutland, Vt.

Dr. H. A. Benedict has resigned the office of First Lieutenant and Captain Day has appointed J. L. Robertson to fill the vacancy. G. E. McLaughlin is Second Lieutenant.

I understand that an invitation is to be extended to the Elizabeth (N. J.) Wheelmen and the Atalanta Wheelmen of Newark, to spend an evening with us in the near future.

I am given to understand that the authorities having the matter in charge will send out the "Pa., N. J. and Md. Road Book" as soon as Tommy Stevens arrives at Zanzibar with Explorer Stanley. As this is the first reliable date we have had we should all be truly thankful.

On July 4 Captain Day will take the H. C. W. to Long Branch via the famous Rumsen Neck Road.

CUARTER.

An earnest effort is at last being made toward improving North Broad street in Philadelphia, and the right sort of men have taken hold of the movement to make it a success. An improved pavement, connecting Germantown Road with the end of the present asphalt, will bring Germantown and Chestnut Hill a half hour nearer to wheelmen and give a bigger boom to wheeling in that vicinity. The outcome of this agitation is sure to be the paving of Broad Street throughout its entire length with improved pavement.

ST. LOUIS.

The Track Association held a meeting on Monday evening, and at one time the proceedings promised to be lively. It appears that there was a meeting of the Board of Directors on Saturday night previous to the second race meeting, at which arrangements were made for the tickets, prizes, etc. The only members present were Brown, Smith and President Andrews—all Missouri club-men. None of the Cycle club-men were notified, and on the face of things it looked as if they were being ignored. Such, however, was not the case. There was a good deal of carelessness displayed in neglecting to have the notices sent, but it was simply oversight and not intentional. An effort was made to explain the matter, but really there was no explanation to make, and the only thing that could be done was to disavow any intention of overlooking the Cycle Club delegates. President Andrews undoubtedly thought that the secretary had received instructions to call the meeting, but the latter insists that he received no such instructions and did not know that the meeting was to be held. At this meeting it was decided to issue a lot of complimentaries to be distributed at the Exchanges, the City Hall and other places. These were not to be given out until late in the afternoon, so as not to interfere with the sale of the regular tickets. The original idea was to distribute these free tickets among the prominent merchants, city officials, etc., and by getting them there once create an interest that would bear fruit at subsequent meetings; but this arrangement was misunderstood, and the tickets were given out indiscriminately. The result was that few of the regular tickets were sold. The majority of the members of the Association doubted the wisdom of this complimentary ticket proceeding. It looked like double dealing to *sell* one man a ticket and *give* one or a dozen to his neighbor, and it was finally agreed, under the circumstances, to allow the treasurer to use his discretion in settling with those who had taken tickets to sell.

Mr. Lucas offered a resolution that a manager be elected, who was to have entire charge of the track and the races run thereon, under the supervision of the Board of Directors, and that no orders relating to the track or races be given except through him. This provoked a lively discussion. Mr. Brown insisted that under the articles of incorporation no officers could be elected except those named in the charter—*i. e.*, the five directors. Mr. Lucas and his friends insisted that they *could* elect, and the proposition that the board appoint the manager was rejected. They wanted the officer elected by the Association and they carried their point, Mr. Brown finally admitting that the officer could be elected if he was called superintendent instead of manager. This was rather a small hole to get out of, but it answered the purpose. Professor Stone was thereupon elected superintendent, and a better choice could not have been made. One interesting fact developed during the meeting was the information that the organization was not incorporated as a stock concern, but merely as an association, and those who subscribed more than $5, in the belief that they had extra shares of stock, find that they are mistaken and that they have no more voice in the management of affairs than the party with one share, unless they transfer their memberships to persons whose votes they can control. This change was made without any notice to the secretary-treasurer, and he has been giving receipts right along for stock. This is a state of affairs that is liable to cause trouble hereafter, unless the members of the Association are advised of the situation and some concession made to those who have made overpayments. Mr. Brewster resigned as secretary-treasurer and Mr. Child was elected his successor. It was decided to give a tournament some time during August or early in September.

Hal Greenwood has received an acceptance to his challenge for a hill-climbing contest from H. A. Wilson, of Chicago. A thunderbolt out of a clear sky could not have occasioned more surprise than this letter. Chicago is the last place in the world to look for a hill-climbing champion and the letter looks like a "fake." The party, in accepting the challenge, writes that he will ride at any time, at any place and on any kind of a wheel that will be satisfactory to Greenwood. This chap seems to be more easily suited than the average Chicagoan, and this creates additional suspicion as to the genuineness of the letter. However, the opportunity of "getting a fall" out of a Chicago man in a contest on the hills, after our recent disastrous experience on the track, would be hailed with delight in this section, and we are all praying that Mr. Wilson will stiffen his vertebræ and toe the scratch. Possibly we can then recover that dollar that Ingalls won on Lumsden. By the way, Professor Stone tells me that Lumsden has asked for a diamond ring—to be suitably inscribed—in lieu of the three medals that he won, and Stone has agreed to that disposition of the matter. A two-hundred-dollar ring ought to be something quite swell.

"Linneus," in the current issue of the *Bulletin*, charges your correspondent with "boasting that he had an understanding with the editor of the old *Bulletin* to cut out all matter criticising the Missouri Club." In the first place, I have not criticised the Missouri Club; in the second place, I never had any such understanding with the editor of the *Bulletin;* and in the third place, I never said anything of the kind. I entirely agree with him when he says that this State ought to have an Emery or a Bull for Chief Consul. If it had, the first thing they would do would be to summarily stop "Linneus'" officious and offensive interference in the affairs of their office. When he says that Jordan, Greenwood and "myself" are the only ones who are doing any recruiting he is romancing again.

We are going to have a fine time at Sedalia. The boys up there have developed into a lot of hustlers, and all they want is a crowd to entertain. The St. Louis, Kansas City and St. Joseph wheelmen ought to be largely represented, and the indications are that they will be. It has always been a difficult problem to get anything like a large attendance at meetings of this Division, but this one promises to be an exception.

ITHURIEL.

WOMAN AND THE BICYCLE.

The plucky woman is ahead in the bicycle race. When she entered the lists the men good-naturedly said: "Oh, she'll get tired of this. Bicycling isn't for women and it won't take long for them to find it out." The men started in to call all the women's attempts at a simple and suitable costume "mannish," but how times have changed. Now in all the cities and villages a woman whirls down the street and no attention is given her, while if a man comes riding by on a "U-frame" bicycle everybody hollers: "See the man on his sister's wheel!"—*Des Moines Graphic.*

BROOKLYN NEWS.

The B. B. C. house-warming, which has been much talked of and the invitations for which have been much sought after, was held last Friday night, and voted a glorious success by the three hundred or more cyclists who were present. The handsome new club house was beautifully decorated throughout, and the entertainment in its entirety was carried out to a most successful ending in the wee small hours of Saturday morning. As I saw "Titnam" present, I will not enlarge on the details, as I know they are in good hands, but must congratulate the house committee, Messrs. Raymond, Fuller and Snedeker, on the successful finale with which their untiring efforts were crowned.

The K. C. W. lantern parade will take place before this goes to press, and will probably be a great success, as usual. Almost every wheelman is intending to participate. On the same night there is to be held a promenade concert in the grounds which are almost opposite the K. C. W. club house, and between the lantern parade and the concert it is an open question which will draw the largest crowd on that section of Bedford Avenue.

The B. B. C. sent out two informal runs for last Sunday, which were both quite replete with interesting incidents. One party, composed of Captain Meeteer, Fay, Pouch, Barkman, Borland, Cole, Lewis, Mead, Allen, Quinby, Rogers and Ackerson, left New York on the Mary Powell Saturday afternoon, spending the night in Poughkeepsie, leaving there Sunday morning and riding via Fishkill, Newburgh and Vail's Gate to Highland Mills, where they had dinner. They then spent the afternoon at the handsome country residence of Mr. Hall, who entertained the boys royally during their stay. The party returned to the city by the evening train on the Erie road, and were very enthusiastic in their tales of the good times enjoyed. The other run was composed of five members of the Brooklyn Club, and is well worth recounting, inasmuch as the day was one of accidents and adventures. The start was made from the club house at 8.15 Sunday morning, all five on hand. Just before mounting Masterson, in attempting to tighten a nut, broke the axle pin of his rear wheel. Nothing daunted, he started for the repair shop, while the rest of the party rode on. Weehawken was safely made, the long hill slowly and perspiringly climbed, when *snap!* another cripple—backbone this time—and Corby turned his face homeward. On the remaining three pressed until within a mile of Hackensack, when Miller, who had been lagging behind, reported ball-bearings broken, and wheel otherwise out of order. This last unfortunate was laid off at Hackensack. The party had been re-enforced in the meantime by two "native" wheelmen, one of whom had been a member of the B. B. C. in days past. Under their guidance the two survivors pedaled on with fear in their hearts, wondering who would break down next. But joy! Englewood, the objective point, was reached without further mishap. There Masterson was found awaiting them, having ridden from Brooklyn after having his wheel repaired, and by taking a direct route, reaching there in advance. Just as they were about to have dinner the Hackensack unfortunate arrived, having dissected his wheel with beneficial results. After dinner a start was made for home, and all would have gone well, but this unlucky party espied the glistening cheeks of the rosy cherry peeping from between the leaves of a tree upon the roadside—evidently public property. A dismount was the result, and four of the wheelmen climbed the tree and proceeded to enjoy the fruit. Directly on a line with the tree, in front of a house, a party of Germans were enjoying their Sunday by picnicking under the trees, and one of their number, who claimed to own the cherry tree, went to his house and, without warning of any kind, returned with a shotgun and deliberately fired upon the men in the tree, drawing blood from Fuller and stinging the remainder of the party. It is needless to state that this outrage will not go unpunished, as steps are now being taken to have the man arrested. Messrs. Fuller, Miller, Corby, Masterson and Raymond, who composed the party, agree that it was the most eventful day in their wheeling career.

At all the large gatherings of wheelmen in Brooklyn lately, considerable comment has been caused by the call given by the Kings County Wheelmen, part of which has been copied from the club call of the Brooklyn Bicycle Club boys. Members of the B. B. C. think the plagiarism rather rough, inasmuch as they are the undoubted originators of the use of the word or syllables "Um-pi-ah" in a club call.

AROL.

Brooklyn, June 25, 1889.

MINNEAPOLIS, MINN.

Since May 20 it has not rained in the day-time to interfere with wheeling, although we have had showers in the night the past two nights. Twenty-nine consecutive days of good wheeling weather is a pretty good record for this section. The roads were beginning to get somewhat dusty, but the rains we have just had will put them in excellent condition again.

Three or four years ago, there was an attempt made at interesting the ladies here in cycling, but owing to the fact that the roads were not at that time in very good condition for tricycles and the tricycles not very well adapted for ladies' use, but little was accomplished. The ladies who tried soon became tired and gave it up. This spring there is something of a revival. One lady has been riding a safety for several weeks, and on Tuesday last another made her debut on the street after a week's practice in seclusion. Starting from the centre of the city she rode to her home, a distance of nearly three miles, with only two mishaps. This lady was quite an accomplished tricyclist, and with a little more out-door experience will undoubtedly become an expert on the two-wheeler. About three weeks ago the first tandem bicycle came to the city. It is the property of a young married gentleman and is ridden by himself and wife. The wife takes very naturally to the wheel, and already they have no trouble in going anywhere about the city. The husband accompanied me last Sunday morning on a ride on bicycles, around lake Harriet, a run of 17½ miles, and next Sunday morning the wife is to be one of the party, going with her husband on the tandem. This is quite a beginning in cycling among the ladies, and I hope others will follow the example.

Tom Eck has been here several days endeavoring to make arrangements for his combination of female and male cycling celebrities, to ride a six-day race, but I learned to-day, did not succeed; I hope he did not, for this city has had a surfeit of cycling fakes, and an exhibition of this kind would certainly do the sport more harm than good.

June 21, 1889.

DOBSON.

CINCINNATI.

As I promised to write a letter every week, and am still on the other side of the fence from the bull, I'll try it again.

Some interest has been created among THE WHEEL'S readers in this city, and I have heard some threats. Of course, if the bull gets through the fence, I shall have to get up and go. I am glad to read that New York City is to have better pavements, and hope they will stick to asphalt for a material.

Nothing can be meaner to ride on than granite. Here we have some eight miles of asphalt and twenty or more of granite. Outside the city we have beautiful roads and fine scenery for the cycler to feast his eyes on. If you will allow me, I wish to give friend Hatfield a small ad., by saying that he has opened fine dining rooms on Sixth Street, to be styled the "L. A. W." When any League man strikes this city, he will surely visit Hatfield's. Just ask him to give you, with the other good things, the story of what the bears did at the "Zoo." It's good enough to tell here, but I won't infringe on Hatfield's copyright.

The Cincinnati Club race comes off June 22, and I'll send you full details next week. Weather has been fine lately, and if it stays so to-morrow, every wheelman in the city will be out on the road.

The Athletic Cycle Club will soon have a road race, and I can come to no other conclusion than that Walter Wise and Will Strauss will give the others a hard tussle for the medal. (They are now riding *five miles per hour*.)

Bert Levi had his wheel *clean* the other day, much to the surprise of his young friends. Frank Rappes goes to Brookville, Ind., the 22d, with the Crescents. Mr Bennett has a new Columbia Tandem on exhibition, and many are the looks of envy cast on it by the boys. Wait a little while, boys, and you may get a chance to try the machine, as I hear that Chas Colling is going to buy it.

I was going to tell you how some of the wheelmen climb hills, but this letter is getting long already. All I will say to-day is that most of the climbing is done on the inclined railway and in the club-rooms. More news next week, but for Heaven's sake don't let Hatfield know these letters are written by

SAFETY.

June 21, 1889.

NEW ORLEANS.

LOUISIANA CYCLING CLUB NOTES.

We had a whopping big meeting on Thursday last, and when it was over it looked like the club-house matter was settled. But it wasn't, and now a special meeting is fixed for Saturday night to wrestle with it again.

At Thursday's meeting we took four new ones into the fold, among them Walter Frank, who is "some" at running and jumping and looks like he has in him the making of a medal winner in the bicycle line as well. We also elected to honorary membership New Orleans' first bicyclenne, Miss Bell Fairchild and so soon as their numbers warrant (and I don't think it is very far off, either), I have no doubt that the L. C. Club will welcome the ladies to the active list. A feeling letter of acceptance from our first and oldest honorary, Mr. G. W. Christy, was read, and the well wishes from one who had already rounded out the allotted cycle of life to those but little more than "buckling" to its varied tangents sunk deep, provoking applause and a bright remark from Harris.

Next we had a lively little tilt over the question of dues, which was finally settled by the withdrawal of the provoking motion. While the tilt lasted, however, it was right interesting, and President Renaud for the first time had occasion to display his parliamentary ability and get rattled.

A most unpleasant feature of the evening was the expelling of one whom I least expected would display such a petty spirit regarding the payment of his arrears. I would like to give his name, but he was one of the original eleven and for the sake of old times I suppress it. But unless I miss my guess he and all future "delinquents" who think so lightly of an expulsion will have occasion to rue it. Secretary Graham will furnish the names of all such to the secretaries of the other clubs and ask for an exchange, and if the clubs co-operate as they should, we can from this time on make these fellows swallow a pretty big pill of regret, should they ever wish to try to re-enter the ranks again. A nicely printed list, too, trimmed with deep black ribbon has also been provided, and our "friend's" name gives it a start, and when added to it will prove a right neat parlor ornament.

BI.

June 16, 1889.

MARYLAND.

At the regular meeting of the Division board of officers, held on Wednesday, June 19, the election of officers, which, by the new constitution must take place July 15 and August 15, was discussed. It was resolved that nominations be made by a committee as follows: Each club made up or partly composed of League members is to choose one representative on this committee with one additional representative for each twenty-five additional members. These selections must be made known to the Chief Consul not later than July 20. The unattached League members are to be represented on a basis of one committeeman to each twenty-five, such representatives to be designated by the board of officers. The committee so made up must meet and make nominations not later than July 25 (proxies being allowable), and report to the Chief Consul not later than July 25. The election will then follow by mail vote. Harry Patchett, of Easton, and Chas. K. Fink, of Westminster, have been appointed representatives of the unattached members.

LEAGUE MEET NOTES.

There are more than sixty entries for the races. The club championship race has been abandoned and an open mile tandem safety race substituted.

The Chief Consul has designated C. E. Heard, F. S. Heard and John Bauer, of the Hagerstown Bicycle Club, as the official buglers.

Last week Messrs. J. T. Chism, E. F. LeCato, Albert Mott and E. P. Hayden, of the board of officers, Maryland Division, L. A. W., arrived at Hagerstown from Baltimore in the evening and held a conference on the approaching Meet. The Chairmen of the various committees made favorable reports, and Chief Consul Mott complimented the boys on their work.

BAY RIDGE.

NOTES FROM THE CITY OF BROTHERLY LOVE.

Ho, for Hagerstown! This is now the club cry. All the club captains are working hard endeavoring to secure a good attendance, which promises to be certain. Century wheelmen claim they will have forty men on hand. Pennsylvania will in all likelihood put in an appearance with some thirty men, while Philadelphia, Tioga, South End and Mt. Vernon should all turn out with from ten to twenty men each. Two parties are being planned in the Pennsylvania Club. One, under command of the captain, will leave in special train on Monday, July 1, going right through to Hagerstown, while the other party, under command of Lieutenant Leisen, will in all likelihood start down on Friday evening via wheel, spend the 2d, 3d and 4th at Hagerstown and then go on down the Shenandoah Valley to Luray, returning via train. There is also some talk of a party riding home from Hagerstown, this for those who will be unable to start with the first party on June 28. Once more we find proof of the old adage, "Too many cooks spoil the broth." This time in connection with the 100-mile run to Philadelphia. Mr. Clarke endeavored to run things in Philadelphia, or, rather, I should say, made necessary arrangements for meals and accommodations. Besides this he had the A. C. C. working for him. One party would give one order while the other party would endeavor to give other orders. Consequently everything was mixed up and the big dinner arranged for at the Continental proved a decided fizzle. For Sunday following it was through some mistake understood that the Century wheelmen had charge of the run. The captain of the Pennsylvania Club called no run for this day, expecting to join the visitors and show them what runs were to be enjoyed in the vicinity of the city, but as no word was mentioned by those in charge of the entertainment no plans could be made and Pennsylvania was absent. Some comment, I understand, was made in regard to this, but as no slight was intended it is earnestly hoped the inattention will be pardoned.

The Pennsylvania mileage report to June 1 shows up quite well. With thirty-eight men who have reported they show a total of 25,292 3-5. Among the first are H. Frank McDaniels, 1,860; John H. Draper, 1,820; Fred Mears, 1,628½; S. Wallis Merrihew, 1,504; Chas. T. Harrey, 1,501; John B. Young, 1,227 2-5; Geo. D. Firmin, 1,089½; J. P. Simmons, 1,000. Pretty good for so early in the season.

The report was spread abroad on Sunday, the 23d, through the *Sunday Item*, that W. D. Supplee intended resigning his membership in the Pennsylvania Bicycle Club. This gentleman wishes me to most emphatically deny this statement, having no intention of doing so. The only way to account for such a report originating is that his resignation is already in for the captaincy, he finding that his time is too much occupied to allow him to attend to the duties as he feels they should be.

Sunday last all Phœnixville turned out to see the "bi-uy-sickels fellers," as one old coon termed them, nineteen men from the Pennsylvania Club having ridden from Philadelphia for dinner. The start was made at 8:40, and Phœnixville reached at 11:45, covering the distance, twenty-seven miles, in a little over three hours. Considering that it was mostly over side roads, I think this a pretty good record. The return home was also made in good time, but it would have been better had ginger-ale and ice-cream stands been passed by. I think this about club record for this section—nineteen men covering fifty-four miles in an ordinary day's run.

WESTFIELD.

PHILADELPHIA.

Hereafter when a bicyclist gets married, that can hardly do for an excuse to give up wheeling, taking for example a few cases of wheelmen with family responsibilities in Philadelphia. A well-known clergyman can be seen almost daily riding through the park on a tandem bicycle, on which he has had three extra seats arranged so as to comfortably accommodate his three children. Sometimes he is accompanied by his wife and the two youngest, while his first-born dutifully follows on a safety. Another Benedict, a well-known member of the Century wheelmen, is often seen airing his family in a truly novel manner; his better half rides a ladies' safety, he glides along on a Star wheel, while their "Pride" is carefully strapped in a wicker-work arrangement, attached to the steering-rod of "Papa's" Star bicycle. It looks decidedly shaky, but it seems to go.

The residents of North Broad Street have at last taken the matter into their own hands, and formed an association to see about paving that thoroughfare in a decent manner. No doubt something will be done toward bettering the condition of the street, as in its present condition it is a disgrace to the city.

The failure of Fred. Whitesides to show up in any kind of form at the Odd Fellows' races, a few weeks ago, was a bitter disappointment to his friends. To Whiteside's astonishment it was impossible for him to get up any kind of a spurt, and he could not for the world think what was making his wheel go so hard. For want of a better reason he blamed it on his imagination and the track (which was bad). When the boys got back to the club-house after the races he determined to examine his "bike," when on taking it apart, it was found that every ball on one side of one bearing was broken, naturally making the wheel run very hard. This was rather rough, as it was the first time he had attempted to do any racing on the path, but the wheel is all O. K. now, and those smart people who did all their laughing and blowing at his expense, had better laugh just once more and go around using the words "I" and "me" as long as they have a chance; for unless I am a false prophet, they won't have a chance after this plucky little rider gets through with them.

ARGUS.

June 25, 1889.

Hal Greenwood, of St. Louis, has received and accepted the following challenge: "In answer to your challenge in *Bi-World*, would say that I am willing to contest with you on any hill which you may name. I will also ride any machine which will be satisfactory to you, loser to pay all traveling expenses. In case you decide to accept my challenge my address is W. A. Wilson, No. 81 Bryant Avenue, Chicago. P. S.—Any date you name will be satisfactory.

The Racing Board guillotine is still at work. Every issue of the official paper announces suspensions nowadays, but the early harvest will doubtless make business light for the Board later on in the season, though how long it will take racing men to learn that the Board's battle flag, with "No Monkeying with the Rules" in gold letters on it, is nailed to the masthead is an open question.—*Providence Journal.*

BIRMINGHAM, ALABAMA.

The Birmingham Bicycle Club was ushered into existence on June 17, 1889, with the following officers: M. S. Cann, President; S. Caheen, Senior Captain; W. C. Swem, Junior Captain; Philip Muller, Secretary-Treasurer; Burr Ferguson, Bugler.

A standing committee was appointed, consisting of the above officers, and Messrs. George Warren, Clarence Jackson, A. R. Shaver, P. R. Gregory and Claude Allen. There are about twenty members already enrolled, and the club starts out under very favorable auspices. The majority of the members are enthusiastic wheelmen, and seem thoroughly imbued with the desire to do all that is possible to advance the cause of cycling. The roads around the city are being rapidly improved, and the club hopes to have a good quarter-mile asphalt track before long. Some of the boys will make fast time if they have a place to do any training, notably the bugler, who, though dubbed "the kid" by the Georgia tourists, is a good road-rider for his age, and can scorch with the best of them.

If the cyclers throughout the country could each one see THE WHEEL regularly and be impressed with the most important of all matters to wheelmen—the improvement of roads—and work together to accomplish that one object, it would bring about great results. You may have heard the expression, "in union is strength."

The Georgia tourists, Messrs. Ingram and Persons, passed through here early in the month, and were joined here by two Birmingham wheelmen, who accompanied them as far as Huntsville, Ala., 131 miles. Their route for about 65 miles took them up the valley, where they found good, fair country roads most of the way. The rest of the way was across country, up and down mountains, through a sparsely settled region, "where the whangdoodle mourneth," and the moonshine whiskey is made. At Gadsden, on their route, they were kindly entertained by the local bicyclers, Messrs. Tolson, Fulcher, Hart, Burger, and others. But they "do say" that at Guntersville the hotel keeper charged them so much for dinner, it amounted to highway robbery. It is the only chance the hotel man will ever have at a wheelman, so that is something to be thankful for. And they "do also say" that the next time they go to Huntsville on their wheels, they propose to employ a bodyguard to keep back the crowd of inquisitive, insolent creatures, who probably never saw a wheel before, and made them glad to leave on the first train. Huntsville has beautiful streets and roads, and the wonder is there are no bicycles there.

A man may be pretty good on geography, and not so good on arithmetic, but there is one hilarious party in New York who knows what ten per cent. of $1,500,000 is; that is, if we can take his word for it, and he has advertised the fact twice.

Who of us does not envy "Our Cyclers Abroad," as the New York *Herald* calls them, being entertained by the Ripley Road Club, and rolling over the gorgeous roads of the "tight little island?" Just out of curiosity, I would like to know the sensation of a man spinning over English roads, who has been accustomed all his bicycling days to the vile country roads we have to put up with in the South. If wheeling is exhilarating here, what can it be there?

AYLETT.

June 21, 1889.

THE BUFFALO RAMBLERS' 100-MILE RUN.

The great 100-mile club run of the Ramblers' Bicycle Club was made from Erie to Buffalo June 22, and the hustling Ramblers smashed all records by bringing in thirty-four out of thirty-five men and making the run in less time than ever made in a club run in this country before. The boys went to Erie on the steamer Idaho Saturday night, and an early breakfast was given the cyclists on board the boat at 3 o'clock A. M. The start was made from Erie at 4:30. Not a stop was made from Erie to Westfield, a distance of thirty-three miles. At the last-named place the second breakfast was taken, and after a short rest riding was resumed. Fredonia was made without a stop, and from Fredonia to Silver Creek, fourteen miles, not a rider dismounted.

Silver Creek Hill is one of the steepest in the country, and it is an exceedingly difficult task to climb it on a wheel. A number of the Ramblers attempted it, but only one succeeded, Charles E. Gates. Gates went up the hill faster than it was ever before mounted. Capt. E. H. Dietzer was next to Mr. Gates; he went to within fifteen feet of the top, but was forced to stop out of sheer exhaustion. Gates was not satisfied with making a hundred miles and after he finished went twelve miles more.

Twelve safeties started in the race and every one came through.

Two accidents marred the pleasure of the trip. One wheel became unmanageable and crashed into another. Before A. L. Georger, C. G. Koester and G. C. Kempke could stop they had taken headers. Georger sprained his wrist, but started again after bandaging it up. He rode from Westfield to this city by steering his wheel with one hand.

The actual riding time was ten hours and fifteen minutes, and the total time occupied in the trip fifteen hours and fifteen minutes. Every hill, except at State Line and Silver Creek, was climbed.

Those who came through were Capt. E. H. Dietzer, First-Lieut. George C. Laub, Second-Lieut. E. H. Dold, Third-Lieut. O. H. Sauerwein, T. J. Maytham, F. W. Heeman, E. R. and A. T. Flack, C. E. Gates, Charles Bamberg, A. F. Georger, George Hummel, H. W. Dawson, C. J. Ritter, Charles Bonney, G. C. Kempke, A. M. Vincent, W. O. Graham, H. J. Dunn, W. S. Clemens, U. Dietzer, A. P. French, G. J. Hager, A. C. Hager, E. A. Vogt, F. B. Klipfel, W. J. Lautz, W. H. Butler, W. G. Shack, S. P. Scheu, Louis Bruch, G. J. Buckheit, J. W. Van Velsor, B. C. Jewett.

The pacemakers were George C. Laub and G. H. Sauerwein. Capt. Dietzer has made the trip three times, W. O. Graham twice and George C. Laub thrice. Last year seven Ramblers made the run in nine hours and five minutes.—Buffalo *Morning News*.

At a recent meeting of the Harrisburg Wheel Club a cordial invitation was extended to all wheelmen passing through that city en route to the meet at Hagerstown, to pay them a visit at the club rooms, Third and Market Streets, if convenient to do so.

New York State Division L.A.W.

OFFICIAL ORGAN.

OFFICERS FOR 1889.

Chief Consul, W. S. BULL, 754 Main Street, Buffalo, N.Y.
Vice-Consul, M. L. BRIDGMAN, 1155 Bedford Avenue, Brooklyn, N Y. Secretary-Treasurer, GEO. M. NISBETT, 50 Wall Street, New York City. Executive and Finance Committee, W. S. BULL, M. H. BRIDGMAN, DR. GEORGE E. BLACKHAM, Dunkirk, N. Y.

NEW YORK STATE DIVISION—CONSULS AND HOTELS.

LIST No. 4.

PLACE,	CONSUL	HOTEL.
Albany	C. B. White	
Heekmanville		Beekman House
Gainsville		Gainsville
Rossburgh		Soule's House
Sing Sing	Dr. H. G. Marshall	Hotel Keenan
Waterloo		Towsley House
		W. S. BULL,
		Chief Consul.
BUFFALO, N. Y., June 22, 1889.

ANNUAL MEET OF THE CONNECTICUT DIVISION AT BRIDGEPORT, CONN., MONDAY, JULY 8.

The Division will be entertained by the members of the Bridgeport Wheel Club and the Rambling Wheelmen, who are all working to give the boys a fine time.

An ample store-room for wheels has been secured near the rooms of the Bridgeport Wheel Club and within a block of the depot.

The League hotel is "The Atlantic," opposite the depot, American plan ; L. A. W. rates, $9 and $2.50 per day.

The programme as far as completed is given below.

The runs will be over some of the finest roads in Connecticut.

PROCLAMATION—SATURDAY, July 6, 6.30 P. M., special concert at Seaside Park, by Wheeler and Wilson Band.

SUNDAY, July 7, 3 P. M., run to Samp Mortar Rock, leaving the rooms of the Rambling Wheelmen ; distance about seven miles, over a splendid road.

MONDAY, July 8, 9 A. M., a run will leave the rooms of the Bridgeport Wheel Club for Beardsley's Park, where refreshments will be served, returning by way of East Bridgeport, 10.30 A. M., business meeting of the Division, in the rooms of the Bridgeport Wheel Club. 11 A. M., another run to Beardsley's Park over the same route, starting from the rooms of the Bridgeport Wheel Club. 12 M., parade with mounted band forms on Broad Street, between State and Elm. 2.30 P. M., races at Seaside Park.

L. A. W. rules to govern, as follows : One mile ordinary, open ; one-half mile ordinary, open ; one mile safety, open ; three mile ordinary, open ; one mile tandem safety, open ; one mile ordinary, championship of Bridgeport ; hill-climbing contest at Greenfield Hill.

Two prizes will be offered for each event, some of which are very handsome. Entrance fee to each event fifty cents, returnable to starters. Entries close July 5, with P. M. Hartig, 18 Bishop Block, Bridgeport, Conn.

A run to Greenfield Hill, where the hill-climbing contest will take place, will start from the track immediately at the close of the races ; distance about six miles. On return from this run a stop will be made at the rooms of the Rambling Wheelmen, where a lunch will be served. In the evening a variety of entertainments will be provided.

C. E. MOORE, Chairman, Bridgeport, Conn.

MISSOURI'S COMING MEET AT SEDALIA, MO.

In a recent letter Mr. F. E. Hoffman, Jr., Secretary of the Sedalia Cyclers, briefly outlines some of the many pleasant features that visiting wheelmen may expect. To the list of events given in THE WHEEL of June 14, one more, a one-mile open, for wheelists, should be added :

DEAR SIR—Yours of the 19th inst. received. In reference to our Meet, July 3 and 4, we are making preparations for a grand thing, and you will notice by programme that on the 3d we intend to make a run to McAllister Springs, which is situated twenty-five miles north of this city. It is a famous summer resort and the proprietors have promised us everything in the way of accommodations and amusements. We return to the city by train or awheel, as the boys may desire, special train leaving Springs at 3.30 P. M. Then at 8.30 we give a "smoker" (programme not out). Grand banquet on the evening of the 4th, and fireworks by the celebrated Sedalia Flambeau Club.

As to our racing we expect, has pulled down nine of ten over the State, including Percy Stone, from St. Louis. You will notice our prizes are quite extensive and valuable and well worth racing for. We are going to give them a good time or know the reason why.

KENTUCKY'S ANNUAL L. A. W. MEET.

That most enjoyable affair is now a thing of the past, and those taking part have returned home. Louisville boys were heart-broken Saturday, the 15th, on account of the heavy rains, but a train at 3 A. M. Sunday took eleven of the faithful far as Bardstown, where no rain had fallen. From Bardstown to Springfield took five hours' time, and dinner was had at the latter place. The road from Springfield to Perryville is said to be the roughest in Christendom, and took till 4 P. M. to cover. Roads from there to Danville are splendid, and that place was reached at 6 o'clock. Twenty-eight League members answered to the roll-call, including representatives of Covington, Cincinnati, Nicholasville, Richmond, Springfield, Perryville, Danville, Louisville, and also G. C. Clark, Consul of Mississippi, and H. T. Kincaid, of Washington, D. C. The business meeting then followed, and by unanimous vote A. J. Lamb was elected Chief Consul, and G. E. Johns, Jr., Secretary-Treasurer, for the ensuing year, to enter upon the duties of office on September 1, 1889. It was decided to add needed information to the present road map. It was also decided to hold the next regular meet in the city of Louisville on June 23, 1890.

On account of heavy rain the meet broke up Tuesday morning, some riders returning directly by train, while others continued their tour through the State. That it was not all one long coast is evidenced by a startling telegram received from Lexington, which said : "Three dead and others expected to die ; roads rocky ; tough pull."

G. C. Clark, Chief Consul from Mississippi, came to Louisville especially to take part in this tour, and was a great and welcome acquisition to the party.

One of the youngest men in the crowd was Pap Ruff, of Richmond. Pap is sixty-four years of age, but he is one of the boys just the same. He rode sixty-eight miles, from Richmond to Danville, in eight hours, including stops, and was as fresh at the end of the trip as any one. When coasting down hill, his long, flowing white beard behind his head, gives him the appearance of Old Father Time on a bicycle.

BROOKLYN'S RIDING SCHOOL.

The mammoth building known as the Fifth Avenue Casino, situated at Fifth Avenue and Union Street, Brooklyn, has been secured by Charles Schwalbach, the well-known dealer, and has been converted into a riding academy and instruction rink. The floor has no posts, measures twelve taps to the mile, and is as smooth as well-laid asphalt, having been laid for roller skating. We believe this to be the largest riding school in the country.

It was formally opened Saturday evening, June 22. Exhibitions were given by Professor Snyder on the unicycle, the Star and the buggy wheel. Professor Louis Peoples (instructor) gave an amusing exhibition of how the beginner first mounts and rides. A half-mile bicycle race was contested by Messrs. Bolster, Miller and Evans, who finished in the order named ; time, 1m. 2s. Half-mile roller skating race—Dower, first ; Carter, second. Time, 58s. 4s.

BRING ON YOUR BICYCLE PRODIGIES.

Little Eddie Schwalbach (Charlie's oldest) gave an exhibition on the crank, safety and tricycle. This youngster's riding is phenomenal ; although only five years old he rides like an old stager. He has in den some sort of wheel ever since he could walk, and we think he is the youngest prodigy in the country, not excepting California, which claims precedence in bicycle prodigies as well as most of the other good things of this world.

The Casino is open daily from 9 to 10 mornings 1 to 5 afternoons, and 7 to 10 evenings. The morning session is devoted exclusively to instructing ladies, the afternoon and evening sessions being directed more to the sterner sex. Although the venture is new, a large clientele has already been secured. scores are being instructed, and cycling in Brooklyn has received a great boom from the enterprise, and a long-felt want is supplied. We wish the genial Charlie much success. [We are backing Mr. Schwalbach in the prodigy line against all comers.—ED.]

HARD CASH AT STAKE.

Either "Jack" or Van Wagoner is sure before long to lose the enormous sum of $10, as the former accepts the latter's offer to ride a mile on a safety inside of three minutes, with both hands tied behind him. Five yards are allowed to start in, that distance not to be included in timing. Course is to be kept clear of dogs, apple-women, policemen, and all other obstacles, and the funeral expenses, if any, are to be borne by Van Wagoner's friends. Of course these whimsical suggestions emanate from Purvis-Bruce, and their rather solemn final clause may cause "Jack" to refuse. We have Van Wagoner—is to be allowed three trials, to vary, in presence of at least five cycling witnesses, and no doubt that two weeks to elapse between the first and third trials. Not to subject the stake-holder's honesty to too great a test, what is the matter with depositing those amounts with some reliable Safe Deposit Company?

A "COPY" BEHEADED.

Constable Mott, of Cranston, who has for a season or more been the terror of wheelmen by reason of his extraordinary vigilance in pulling up cyclers who run on the sidepath bordering the road that bounds the city line on Broad Street, is no longer an officer of the law. The extraordinary vigilance with which he informed that one little section in the town ordinances finally killed him. Thoughtless blame may be charged somewhat to the wheelmen for the offender's pernicious activity, for there has been a little time of boyishness displayed in days past by young riders, who would rather take the sidepath than the road just for the fun of teasing Officer Mott, with the result that more conservative men were brought to earth by the officer's hooked stick and hauled up in the District Court which sheer necessity had compelled a walk or a ride in that usually deserted sidepath. The Court has always been, evidently enough, in sympathy with the wheelmen, but in the eyes of the law the path was a sidewalk, and so long as the proof of guilt was there and not denied the rider could pay so much attention to one of the town ordinances without slighting some of the others.—*Providence Journal.*

Mr. Charles D. Alexander and Mr. Warren West, both of Portland, Me., accomplished on Sunday last the feat of riding their bicycles from Portland to Boston, arriving in the latter city in the evening. They returned by rail and were at work as usual Monday.

Messrs. Merwin, Hulbert & Co. find the advantages of their line position increasing daily. This season their trade in bicycles, uniforms and general sporting goods has been larger than ever before.

Any of our Western Massachusetts readers in need of any part of gymnasium outfits and bicyclists' goods, such as full and knee tights, long sleeve and sleeveless Jerseys, shirts, shoes, gaiters and supporters, can do no better than call on S. B. Call, at 358 Main Street, Springfield, Mass.

At Y. M. C. A. Athletic Club Games in Philadelphia, June 91, the 1 mile bicycle race was taken, hands down, by W. W. Taxis, A. C. S. N., in 3m 45s.; Jones, Y. M. C. A., second.

A committee of the Lynn Cycle Club will be intrusted with the management of the bicycle races around Lynn Common, July 4.

Second-Hand Columbia Bicycles,
Second-Hand Star Bicycles.

Safeties, etc., cheap, all sizes.

Enamel, Cement, Sundries of all kinds. The enamel is the best and cheapest in the market.

W. I. WILHELM, Reading, Pa.

REGULAR COLUMBIAS.

A "Safety Year," certainly, inasmuch as more Safeties have been sold this season than during any other season; yet the regular bicycles hold the riding lead. All the wheelmen of America are not forsaking the standard machines. Take the Pope Mfg. Co.'s orders, for example, day by day, as the mail and telegraph bring them in — Safeties, many of them; regulars, on many days a great many more regulars.

Columbia Light Roadster.

The handsomest, strongest, most extensively used, and most generally satisfactory Light Roadster ever made. More good points than are to be found in any other single Bicycle. The lightest road machine. Compare its actual weight with that of any other brought into competition with it.
"The nearest to perfection of anything yet attained in wheel construction."

Volunteer Columbia.

The best wheel for the money ever seen. Made to ride, and guaranteed to wear. All steel, and no castings.
Why spend your dollars for a second-hand Bicycle when the same amount will buy a new Columbia?
The general construction of the Expert, with some of its least essential advantages modified. A saving of money without a loss of efficiency. Study it up in the Columbia catalogue, and examine the machine itself.

Expert Columbia.

Best known Bicycle in the world. The established favorite for long-distance touring, and all other uses where the highest possible qualities are requisite with durability pre-eminent.
The best made and equipped all-round Roadster; and note this point, it's just as light as most Light Roadsters.
Direct spokes for durability, elasticity, and ease of repair when necessary. All our latest improvements.

Columbia Semi-Roadster.

Give the boy a real Bicycle, and remember that the best is the cheapest, because it will last the longest, and has a market value when you are through with it.
Columbia Bicycles, like Brewster carriages, may cost a little more to begin with, but the value is there, and you can depend upon it.
The most durable, easiest running, and best equipped Boy's Bicycle yet built.

POPE MANUF'G CO., Boston, New York, Chicago, Hartford.

THE WHEEL

—AND—

CYCLING TRADE REVIEW,

Published every Friday morning.

Entered at the Post Office at second class rates.

Subscription Price, - - - $1.00 a year.
Foreign Subscriptions, - - - 6s. a year.
Single Copies, - - - - - 5 Cents.

Newsdealers may order through AM. NEWS Co.

All copy should be received by Monday.
Telegraphic news received till Wednesday noon.

Advertising rates on Application.

F. P. PRIAL, Editor and Proprietor
23 Park Row.
P. O. Box 444, New York.

Persons receiving sample copies of this paper are respectfully requested to examine its contents and give us their patronage, and as far as is convenient, aid in circulating the journal, and extend its influence in the cause which it so faithfully serves. Subscription price, $1 per year.

FIRST IN THE FIELD.

THE WHEEL, the N. Y. cycling paper and League organ for the State of N. Y., is the first to be on the scene of action of the coming meet in this city, its representative having arrived here Thursday evening. Arrangements have been made to place 2,000 copies of a special edition of this paper before the local and visiting wheelmen, and on and after Monday copies will be found at all the leading news stands. This particular paper, containing tables of racing, records of dates, a list of all importers and manufacturers in the trade, articles on training, and a complete calendar of the sport's progress from its earliest beginning up to now, will be specially valuable for references.—Hagerstown *Daily News.*

ON the last day of the League Meet we can only turn to stretch the general impression that it has been a big success. To be sure, the weather has behaved in beastly style, but the men have rose superior to this. The Hagerstown Club have done all that they have promised to do, and the Maryland Division has carried out its part of the programme in good style. There was a good deal of drinking done, but this is essentially the southern style of manifesting good fellowship, and once this fact is understood, all criticism vanishes.

AT the meeting of Chief Consuls the following business was transacted: It was recommended that no division appoint official tailors. It was decided that the League must abide by the present uniform contracts. League members may, however, purchase cloth through the League secretary and have it made up when they desire. On account of the small number of club consuls present, it was decided not to take action on the question of State official organs, and the matter slipped into innocuous desuetude. The Bicycling World Co. desired the League to prohibit chief consuls from supplying official news to any paper but the League organ, in order that its importance might be increased. We shall discuss the matter at length at some future time.

THE last issue of *Wheeling* states the American tourist was abroad. The failure of the American party seems to be, in the opinion of *Wheeling*, that they accept every courtesy shown them in a matter-of-course fashion. We cannot tell how much truth there is in this just at this time. We have had two private letters from England in which the writers agree with *Wheeling's* opinions. If true, 'tis sad.

IT must grieve all good Americans to know that Mr. Jo. Pennell, of Philadelphia, and resident in London for some time, sat down at the dinner given the American tourists, while the "Toast of the United States" was being given. Mr. Pennell attempted to sit down while the party sang "God Save the Queen," but was forcibly kept on his feet by two stalwart and patriotic Englishmen. This is a point where eccentricity becomes insult and impertinence. We have a kind of regard for those kind of men who wear long hair and have taken the vow against soap and water. They generally have talent of some order; but they have not tact. They are continually butting against custom to their own distraction; their mad desire to be odd causes them to be irregular, and mental irregularity is merely a mild form of insanity. It is not destructive; therefore we tolerate it, though it is continually violating the code in use among gentlemen. We desire to say to the great English public that the President of the United States has in no way been discommoded by Mr. Pennell's mark of signal disrespect.

WITHOUT wishing to boast or unnecessarily glorify ourselves, we think the report of the Tenth Annual League Meet, just over at Hagerstown, appearing in this week's issue of THE WHEEL, as complete as possible to make it. Two pairs of eyes are always better to see with than one, and we flatter ourselves ours were wide open. How well they were used, we leave our readers to decide for themselves.

THE ELWELL TOURISTS.

THE ARRIVAL AT LONDON.

We have arrived in London in tip-top shape, without injury to ourselves or the city either, except, perhaps, one certain spot in the Queen's highway where our heaviest member and several others came to earth a little unexpectedly. On coming in we found the banks and shops closed and the nation taking a general holiday, the occasion for which we endeavored to convince ourselves was the entrance within the city limits of the American tourists. The natives, however, preferred to call it Whit-Monday, and rather than quarrel with them we did not insist. The elements have precisely that same disregard for the public in England as in America, and the rain insists on coming down on legal holidays here in a way which reminds us strongly of home. To this may be attributed the fact of our arriving in two sections; one by train from Oxford under the guidance of "Pedals," the other sticking to scheduled dates and riding in the following day via Hampton Court, chaperoned by Joe Pennell. Owing to the rain our first impression of London was, I am afraid, rather poor, and London's first impression of us was, I am dead sure, a great deal worse. They think we are a rather disreputable-looking lot in good weather, but in bad we are beyond the pale of civilization!

We found Burr's Hotel to be a very respectable establishment in Bloomsbury, near the British Museum. The proprietor is something of a cyclist himself, and gave us a most cordial welcome. Our first afternoon was spent in settling down in our new quarters, a "seven night stand" being quite a luxury; and in cleaning up what was, I venture to say, the most disgraceful-looking lot of wheels seen in London for some time. Our transatlantic cousins have ideas of their own on this subject, and clean their wheels (or exchange them) just once a year, but we have plenty of necessary luggage without carrying about from place to place some ten or fifteen pounds of British soil as well. They also express mild surprise at seeing us down on our marrow-bones industriously digging away on the bicycles instead of hiring it done. Experience is a dear teacher and we did find it rather expensive business paying "Boots" a shilling for hammering the mud and enamel off with a wrench, and then having to do the job over again ourselves. Consequently, the majority of the party dispense with the former part of the programme and confine themselves assiduously to the latter.

We met with our trunks, which had been forwarded from Liverpool here, and with what we found in them and the aid of sundries bought in town the party came out the following day so entirely and completely changed that its own mother wouldn't know it. Our Adonis appeared on the scene gotten up quite regardless of all expense—tall collar, brown chimney-pot, walking-stick and a pair of shoes of which the word "startling" is a very weak description. Our wheels are safely packed out of sight and there seems to be a general determination to raise for the following week a citizen from the ashes of a cycler. Of London, from a wheelman's point of view, it would be sheer folly for me to attempt to give you the faintest idea. The city changes for nobody and we found it just as it has been found and described by hundreds of Americans who had time and ideas to devote to the subject. Of its vastness, variety and life; its nationalities and languages, its aristocracy and beggars, its joys and sorrows I can give you no conception. We simply keep "on the go" from morning until night, and it is always something new. I was surprised to find such an immense quantity of asphalt pavement in the city. I always had the notion that London thoroughfares were horrible, but I find that it is just the reverse except in wet weather. The asphalt is smooth as glass and kept as clean as a ball-room floor. When dry a finer ride is not to be had, but when wet it is "mind your eye." We have been very well met by the London boys and many of the big guns have called to bid us welcome. Of the Stanley Club's banquet and the Ripley Road Club's entertainment I shall write you later.

June 17. To confess ignorance of the Stanley Club of London, is to argue one's self a novice in the pleasures of cycling or unaware of the existence of newspapers devoted to it. In the way of advancing the best interests of the sport it has done far more than any other power of any kind. The annual Stanley Show is the most gigantic affair of this caliber that ever existed and is entirely the product of the energy and ability of this club. When I tell you that we were their guests on Friday evening it is sufficient guarantee that everything was done for our comfort and entertainment that possibly could be done. I don't wish to cast reflections on our past entertainers but this evening was enjoyed by the majority of the boys more than anything of the kind which we have yet had extended to us. We arrived at the Inns of Court Hotel in High Holborn (they call it "Eye Obun") at 6.30 and found the Stanley Club awaiting us attired in dress suits to a man. After being introduced by "Faed," we sat down to a royal repast amongst such high and mighty cycling lights as Col Saville, Geo. Lacy Hillier, Percy Low, M. A. Harpham, Harry Swindley, McCandlish and a host of others.

The toasts following the dinner, usually so dry and tiresome, were short, witty and interspered with songs, comic and otherwise, most excellently rendered by members of the club. In the absence of our leader, who was that evening quite seriously indisposed, Mr. J. E. Beal responded to the toast "Our American Guests," and made a very taking speech, keeping the hundred listeners in a continual roar. The comic songs to our surprise were actually comic, and we looked in vain for the "cold, reserved Londoners" whom we have read so much about. We certainly found nothing but the most hearty and open-handed good-fellowship amonst the Stanley boys. "What's the matter with the Stanley Club?" "They're all right," and our American cheers were answered by the "Stanley rocket," and "For they are jolly good fellows." The evening wound up by the singing of "Auld Lang Syne," the entire assemblage standing on their chairs, one foot on the table, and each crossing his arms and grasping his neighb r's hands The following afternoon a number of the boys, sated for the time being with London's wonderful sights and historic spots, started for the Paddington grounds to see the sports of the Kildare Athletic Club. We were occupying very modest seats in the one shilling stand when Hillier's eagle eye espied us, and straight we were ushered into the judges' stand. They don't do things by halves in London, as we soon found out.

The races were very interesting. In a two-mile handicap, W. C. Jones won from seventeen starters in 5.26, beating the amateur record. In a two-mile tricycle we had the pleasure of seeing a lady among the contestants, Mr. and Mrs. J. H. Smith, riding a tandem. It certainly is a pleasure to see this little lady push the pedals. She dismounted from her machine apparently as fresh as before the race, and on our congratulating her on her fine showing simply said that the track was a little heavy. Mrs. Smith is a slight, pretty brunette, and an ideal example of a lady rider. Could she but be seen in America, I am sure our ladies would take to the wheel by hundreds. Mr. and Mrs. Smith are no strangers to Americans, as they have been written up and pictured in many of the leading cycling journals, and incredible though it may seem, they have held at different times almost every long distance road record, and have been but once beaten on the road.

To those of the party who might be termed "enthusiasts," the Sunday spent in the hands of the Ripley Road Club was by far the most enjoyable day yet spent on the trip. Who rides a wheel and has not heard of Ripley and the road thereto? And "Ye Anchor Tavern," so dear to the heart of every London cycler? It was then with unbounded delight that we found ourselves fairly over Hammersmith Bridge and well along on this historic run. There may be prettier bits of road and scenery, but they are few. There may be snugger taverns than the Anchor, but we have not found them, and there certainly is not in all cycledom a road upon which so many celebrated knights of the wheel can be met in a single day as the Ripley Road on a pleasant Sunday. And they were all there to give us a cordial welcome to this, their inner sanctuary.

It would take quite a volume to contain the names of all the well-known men who rode out that day. There were racing-men, record-holders, notorious scorchers, cycling scribes, etc., by the dozen, mounted on every style and make of machine conceivable, from the lumbering trikes of '76 to the racing safeties of the present day. New recruits joined the party as we rode, and on finally reaching our destination there were all of seven hundred wheelmen collected in this one small town. Well, yes; the pace was rather faster than we usually ride. These Englishmen ride like fiends, and never feel better than when stretched out in some wayside tavern completely blown, having done their nineteen or twenty miles an hour. After a "sluice" at the pump, we sat down to tables bending beneath the weight of everything good to eat imaginable and pyramids of "sparkling champy." Dr. Turner, President of the Ripley Road Club, headed the table and the toasting, and was well seconded by Harry Swindley and Percy Low. After the usual toasts to the Queen and President (President Harrison would blush with modesty could he but hear some of the complimentary remarks in regard to himself), Mr. Beal, in the absence of Mr. Elwell, very neatly responded to the toast of "Our Guests," proposed by Major Knox-Holmes. About the latter I want to say a few words to those who never heard of him. Major Knox-Holmes is a typical old English gentleman of eighty-one years of age.

He has been connected with cycling since its infancy, and is able to-day to do a hundred miles in twelve hours. After he was seventy-five he beat Hillier in a 100-mile road race, and won the record for that distance. He rides a tandem, on the diminutive rear seat of which sits his little six-year-old granddaughter. He says he and she are anxious to race with any other tandem team whose ages differ, as theirs do, by seventy-five years!

After attending the special service held for cyclers in the little chapel at Ripley, we started for London, voting the day to have been an ideal one, and a Sabbath long to be remembered. Long live the Ripley Road Club! We leave for Brighton in the morning, to be in Paris on Friday. Our portmanteaus (that's English), which we leave here until our return, are stuffed to distortion with giddy suits, startling ulsters, nobby coats, hats, and in short everything that goes to clothe the man. The price of clothes in London would have tempted Adam much quicker than the proverbial apple, and to look into a tailor-shop window is to be lost. If any of the boys at home wish to secure our everlasting gratitude send us some American tobacco, and we will gladly pay the duty. As the roads get better the tobacco gets worse, and we are promised a still viler mixture in France.

In Birmingham we received an addition to the party in the person of Mr. O. C. Nussle, of Illinois, and in London were joined by Messrs. Dan and Willie Krumm, who were unable to sail when the party did. To offset this we have lost three. Mr. J. Newton Smith is called home by private matters, Dr. McAlpin was ill when he started, and has not picked up as he expected to, and Mr. Penrose is prevented from riding by a lame ankle, but will, I believe, take the train for Paris and be with us during our stay there. Otherwise than this the party's health is good, appetite enormous and personnel will probably be as we are now until August 1.

TAM O'SHANTER.

"COME AND SEE THE AMERICANS."

The Rue d'Alger was in a state of excitement yesterday morning at half-past seven. When the neat little *bonnes* went out for their bread and morning milk they made a long stay to see the American cyclists preparing to start after a substantial early breakfast. The boys came out and strapped their haversacks upon their steel steeds. During this operation a waiter from the hotel had been round to a newspaper kiosque for a large bundle of *Heralds*, which were rushed for by the cyclists.

At 8 A. M. Mr. Fluett called out the usual "Are you ready? Prepare to start!"

Mr. Higgins, with his musical voice, shouted, "Wait! I have a word to say. Boys, what's the matter with the Paris edition of the New York *Herald?*" "That's all right!" replied the boys in chorus, following their reply with hearty cheers.

When asked if they had enjoyed their stay in the French capital, the Americans, one and all, replied: "Yes. If a man cannot enjoy himself in Paris he is not fit to live." Many of them would fain have remained longer, but their itinerary is prepared, and all arrangements have been made in advance, so away they went, *en route* for Geneva. They breakfasted at Melun and arrived a little later at Fountainebleau, where they will rest for a day, visiting its wonderful forest and environs.—European edition of the N. Y. *Herald*, June 30.

AN IMPORTANT CHANGE OF BASE.

Cyclists that have carefully watched the rapid increase of business of the Overman Wheel Co. have often wondered that their home office and factory were so far apart. We are glad to be able to announce that about September 1 this will be remedied. The store in Boston will be continued as in the past, but larger and more commodious offices for transaction of business will be secured at Chicopee Falls, Mass., in their new factory.

Forty thousand square feet of floor room will thus be added to their present space, and every pains taken to provide for the various needs of a large cycle business. It is always pleasant to chronicle deserved success, and we congratulate the Overman Wheel Co. on the increase in business that requires this change. On July 27, Mr. A. H. Overman, President of the company, is to sail for Europe, accompanied by Mrs. Overman. May they have a safe and pleasant voyage.

NEWARK.

Ten Atalanta men attended the lantern parade of the K. C. W. and had a fine time. Capt. Drabble (A. W.) unfortunately had a severe header while in the parade, caused by running in a hole. All reached home early (in the morning) and safe.

Ten new members were elected into the ranks of the A. W., among them W. I. Wilhelm, of Reading, Pa.

A. T. Rummell has the highest mileage for June, 607 miles.

E. Halsey, A. T. Rummell, L. N. Thorne and C. L. S. Walker have received 1,000-mile badges.

Newark, July 3, 1889. SPARK.

WHEEL GOSSIP

NOTES OF THE ENGLISH PATH.

A two-days' professional tournament was held at Whitsuntide, June 11 and 12. On the 12th, 10,000 people were present. English won the five and Howell the one-mile championshib, both waiting races. In the mile professional handicap Robb got within twenty yards of 2m. 38 4-5s.

On June 15 H. Synyer cut the half-mile grass record; time, 1m. 20 4-5s.

TWO-MILES SAFETY RECORD.

At Paddington, on June 15, W. C. Jones beat the two-miles safety record, riding in 5m. 26 3-5s.; previous record, 5m. 31 2-5s. S. F. Edge and F. J. B. Archer also beat the flying quarter-mile tandem tricycle record, doing 35 4-5s. The one-mile handicap was captured by W. H. Bardsley, 80 yards; time, 2m. 37 1-5s.

Edward A. Brown, of Kansas City, Mo., is wheeling in Scotland.

The Nominating Committees of the New York State L. A. W. districts have been holding meetings, and the tickets for the entire State will shortly be published.

Jos. McFadden has resigned the captaincy of the New York Club, as his business will compel him to travel for some time to come. G. M. Nisbett will probably be elected to succeed him. Mac's declaration is very much regretted by his club-mates, as he was enthusiastic and popular.

The New York Club will run to Coney Island on Sunday.

The *Referee* republishes Free Lance's paper on the Crystal Palace track and does not credit, though it was special correspondence to this paper.

Ralph Temple sailed for England on Monday last. He stated that he went abroad to purchase $50,000 worth of goods for the Western Arms & Cartridge Company. He will probably ride and exhibit in England.

The Massachusetts and Rhode Island Divisions will hold a combined meet at Cottage City August 6, 7 and 8.

The *Referee* reports that St. Louis will hold a big race tournament in August.

The amount of space given to an report of the League Meet has crowded out a deal of matter and compelled us to condense many important items.

The *Omaha Republican* of June 23, 1889, publishes a cut of "Senator" Morgan's face. We have looked on the same several scores of times, and we grieve that this illustrated chestnut has again been resurrected.

The Louisiana Cycle Club, of New Orleans, are making a strong effort to get enough money subscribed to build a club-house.

C. A. Rice, of the South End Wheelmen, Philadelphia, has presented his club with a "Rogers" group of statuary.

Some time during Abram S. Hewitt's term as Mayor of New York, our engineer suggested that if "iron wheelways" were laid on the heavily-traveled streets of New York City, all streets could be paved smoothly and the pavement would not be destroyed by heavy traffic. The idea was abandoned, but there is a movement on foot to experiment with the proposed plan, and it is likely that $10,000 will be appropriated by the Board of Aldermen for the purpose. The "iron wheelways" consist of strips of iron, about a foot wide, set in the pavements.

The Brooklyn Club enjoyed a run to the Massapequa Hotel, on Long Island, on Sunday last. With the party were Mr. Henry Hall and son, of Hilghland Mills, N. Y.

ALFRED WAS A WHEELMAN.

Scene—Almost any parlor these evenings. Alfred (reading from the latest erto-romance)—"He seized her in his arms and kissed her ripe, red lips with frenetic abandon. She shivered and writhed in his close embrace. Her breath came in quick knickerbockers. Her eyes——"

Gladys—"Oh, Alfred, what nonsense are you reading? *Knickerbockers?*"

Alfred—"A little emendation of my own. The text says, 'Her breath came in quick, short pants.'"—*To-Day.*

The Riverside Wheelmen will have a run to Yonkers on Sunday next. This prosperous club now has a membership of eighty active wheelmen.

The Hudson County Wheelmen will give an excursion to Boynton Beach this month. The run has been gotten up especially for the benefit of the lady members of the club. A boat has been engaged for their exclusive use.

The Cyclist's Union Meet, formerly announced to take place at Clarksville, Mo., was not carried out.

Zimmerman, of the Freehold Cyclers, showed by his performances at the Kings County races, June 28-29, that he is a hard man to beat, and would undoubtedly have won more prizes at the second day's meet, but for the breaking of his machine early in the day.

James Roberison, of the Hudson County Wheelmen, was recently elected First Lieutenant on account of the resignation of H. Benedict, and G. McLoughlin to the office of Second Lieutenant.

Frank Borland, the Brooklyn's racer, made his last appearance on the path at the Kings County Meet. He retires after having a very successful racing career.

BUSINESS MEN ASKING FOR ASPHALT.

A committee of business men from Wall Street called on Mayor Grant and Public Works Commissioner Gilroy and requested them to approve the project to put an asphalt pavement in that street from Nassau to Front Street. Both promised to think over the matter, but they suggested to the committee that, as asphalt pavement cost more than granite block pavement, and is not so durable under stress of hard usage such as a pavement is subjected to in a street like Wall, it might be well for the business men who want it laid for their comfort to pay for it themselves.

In several down-town streets asphalt pavements have been paid for by business men, who have recognized the fact that the City should not be made to pay for special advantages to themselves. The trouble about the request of the Wall Street men seems to be that to grant it would interfere with the general scheme of paving, and give a color of right to the people who do business on other streets in which the traffic is great, and therefore noisy, to demand that asphalt be laid for them. The Stock Exchange has already asked that Broad Street be laid with asphalt. The traffic there is almost as great as in Wall Street, though of a somewhat different character. Asphalt would last there no longer than in Wall Street, and not nearly so long as granite. The City would therefore have to repave both streets again in a comparatively short time.

Public Works Commissioner Gilroy said yesterday that he had heretofore expressed the opinion that asphalt pavement was only suited to the residential streets, and he had seen no reason to revise that opinion. He intended, however, to propose that in streets containing schoolhouses and hospitals asphalt should be substituted for stone in front of those buildings. He had received many complaints that in warm weather, when schoolhouse windows are kept open, the noise of traffic over hard pavements prevents teachers and scholars from hearing one another, and that the rattle of wagons makes sick people irritable and injures them.—*N. Y. Times.*

CONGRATULATIONS IN ORDER.

A pleasant surprise was inflicted upon us to-day when Stillman G. Whittaker walked into the editorial sanctum bringing with him a pretty, quiet-mannered young lady whom he introduced to us as Mrs. Whittaker. In the course of conversation the fact leaked out that this visit to New York was in the nature of a honeymoon trip, he being married on the Glorious Fourth. While not necessarily looking unhappy, there is none of the wrapped-up-in-each-other, bride-and-groom look about them, and they will not furnish amusement for the lookers-on while on their travels. Mr. and Mrs. Whittaker will remain in the city for some two weeks. Our best wishes for prosperity and happiness attend them.

THEY PINE FOR IRELAND.

Some of the Americans, we understand, were so disappointed at the way Jupiter Pluvius treated them in the Emerald Isle that they intend returning there when the touring party breaks up after visiting France, Germany, Holland, etc. Scotland will also be visited by some who have heard the "Land 'o Cakes" eloquently described. It can safely be said that the limited insight our visitors had into Irish scenery and habits has *whetted* their appetites for more.—*Bicycling News.*

YACHTS AND BICYCLES TO BE TAXED.

After September 1, the Winthrop, Mass., Assessors will tax all yachts and bicycles in the town as personal property, as the residents of the Centre refuse to pay taxes on their carriages unless the yachts and bicycles are assessed.

The words "Bonnie Annie Laurie" will revive pleasant recollections in the mind of every man that attended the recent L. A. W. Meet at Hagerstown, and cause a smile to brighten his countenance. "Jack," the agent for the "White Flyer," well realizing this fact, has taken advantage of it to concoct a telling advertisement, which may be found on another page. By all means send for their catalogue or else a copy of THE WHEEL of June 28, and post yourself concerning the machine's merits.

COLLABORATION FROM COLORADO.

A valued correspondent writing us from Denver, Colo., under date of June 27, makes the following correction of a recent paragraph gleaned from the columns of *Sports Afield*, published in that city:

"In your issue of the 21st inst. you have the following in regard to Robt. Gerwing: 'Previous to this race, his own time of 2h. 18m., over a road *none too smooth*, and a distance of *thirty-three and a half* miles, had stood as record.' I beg you will pardon my correcting you, but the facts are these: Mr. Gerwing's time of 2h. 18m. was made from Denver to Platteville, *thirty-six* full miles, over the roads when they were in splendid shape. The *race* was over a course starting just outside of Denver and finishing at Platteville. This made the distance thirty-three and a half miles. The roads at the time of the race *were* 'none too smooth,' making Gerwing's time of 2h. 2⅓m. very creditable."

He further says: "In the same issue you ask for the address of Barber, the fancy rider. By the time you receive this his address will be care Thatcher, Primrose and West's Minstrels, San Francisco, Ca. During Mr. Barber's engagement here, he had the misfortune of a fall which resulted in a badly-sprained ankle. His injury compelled him to lay over a couple of weeks while his company went on. The Social Wheel Club on the evening before his departure tendered him a reception. Refreshments and good cheer were indulged in by some eighty members and visitors until an early hour in the morning. All that participated in the 'blow out' agreed in saying that it was an informal affair that would be an honor even to the base ball tourists. Among the many old acquaintances whom Barber met here, Chas. Ford and Fred J. Bailey, of Rochester, might be mentioned." NOVICE.

A SELECTED LIST OF PATENTS.

[Reported especially for THE WHEEL AND CYCLING TRADE REVIEW by C. A. Snow & Co., patent attorneys, Washington, D. C.]

J. R. Rullman, San Antonio, Texas; Velocipede which consists in an Improvement in Velocipeds, the combination with a rocking chair mounted on a platform of a vehicle and retained in position by the slotted curved guides and pins, rods pivoted to the rockers of said chair and to a cross-head moving in vertical guides, the rods connecting said cross-head with the crank-pin of a gear-wheel, the pinion and propelling-wheel, the steel band encircling three sides of the said frame and platform and extending in rear thereof to form the supports for the propelling wheel, the standard provided with a loop at its upper end and the sliding-handled lever.

Bearing date of July 2, 1889.

TENTH ANNUAL LEAGUE MEET.

This tenth League Meet is going to be a rip-roaring success. It can't help itself. The Hagerstown Club and the Maryland Division have done themselves proud; nothing has been left undone that will add to the pleasure of the guests. The meet will be small, as compared with the numbers who have attended previous League Meets, but what is lacking in numbers is made up in enthusiasm and good-fellowship. A splendid programme has been prepared, the roads being taken mostly into the account—and such roads! The peculiarity of the meet is that the people of Hagerstown have risen to the occasion, and will do more than their share to make the thing a great go. The houses and stores are decorated, and everybody here, from the Mayor to the dirtiest pickaninny in town, is interested.

SERMON PREACHED TO WHEELMEN AT HAGERSTOWN JUNE 30, 1889, BY REV E. H. DELK.

Sunday evening about seventy-five cyclists attended by invitation d'vine service in Trinity Lutheran Church. Assembling at Hotel Hamilton, they marched in a body, marshaled by Chief Consul Mott, of the Maryland Division. They were assigned to seats that were reserved for them, and gave close attention to the sermon, which all pronounced instructive, elevating and encouraging to the healthful pleasure of cycling. Rev. E. H. Delk, Jr., pastor, preached an able sermon, taking for his text; "Watch, ye; stand fast in the faith; quit ye like men; be strong."—1st Corinthians, 16th chapter, 13th verse.

His sermon was chiefly impromptu, and was delivered with deep feeling and impressiveness. He started with the fact that we were upon the eve of a great national event—great because it tends to the physical culture of the American people—physical, as the basis of all intellectual and moral work. In the course of his sermon he said the wheelmen had come to enjoy our beautiful valleys, to see our historical battle-fields, for the exchange of fraternal greeting and for physical betterment.

In the midst of these festivities, it would be well for all to remember the Apostle's command, "Watch ye!" or in the wheelman's language, "Look out for a fall!" This is a warning for every day of life, but doubly so now, for "men are merriest when away from home." Men do things in a crowd that they would never do at home. Our bars will be doubly manned, painted faces will be found upon our streets, and snares will be spread for the thoughtless. Watch, ye! Stand fast in the faith. Stick to your guide-book.

Most of our visitors come from Christian homes. Let us offer them the very best we can give—Christian example.

It is the element of faith which makes the great life. The great leaders of national development have been men of large faith—Gustavus Ado'phus, Gladstone, Bismarck.

The guide-book calls to a faith in an overruling Providence. It arouses the conviction of the final triumph of righteousness. It stimulates the magnificent hope for the redemption of humanity. Other roads will be recommended, but stick to the old guide-book—the Bible.

Quit you like men! This is the last word of the starter in the great race. In your sports let not trickery take the place of merit. Preserve the high tone of your League rules. Do not permit fun to degenerate into rowdyism. Be honorable gentlemen, upon the track as well as in the parlor.

Quit you like men in your life's work! Your wheel must not be your master. Cycling, as a means of physical betterment, is good. But it cannot take the place of enthusiastic work and thoroughness in your chosen calling. Fitting illustration on this point was cited in the building of the great St. Louis bridge.

Your life's work will fall short of its full force and value unless it forms a part of your Father's work. At times this high calling seems like an impossible climb, but as you quietly take the hill with quiet determination, you shall reach the brow of the mountain and enjoy the exhilaration which comes through loyal endeavor.

Be strong. This is the purpose of your exercise. Christianity calls us unto perfect manhood. It has been caricatured. It is not a religion for the dyspeptic, the invalid and tottering age, but it is a call to sturdy youth. It demands of us the best and strongest from a physical, mental and moral standpoint.

Paul draws his illustrations from the foot-race, from the boxing-match, from the battle-field. To what great uses can this God-given power be applied. You, that are strong, ought to bear the infirmities of the weak. In your grand procession of the coming Thursday, remember there are other eyes that look down upon you besides those that peer from window and balcony. The eye of God is upon you, the noblest of earth and of heaven, watching with deepening interest the trend of your life. Shall it not be said of you, he was strong and like unto the Son of God?

"A cloud of witnesses around
Hold thee in full survey;
Forget the steps already trod
And onward urge their way.

"Tis God's all-animating voice
That calls thee from on high;
'Tis His own hand presents the prize
To thine uplifted eye.

"The prize with peerless glories bright,
Which shall new lustre boast;
When victors' wreaths and monarchs' gems
Shall blend in common dust"

—Hagerstown *Daily Globe.*

"MEET-LETS."

Master Marshall Wilhelm, of Reading, Pa., who accompanies his father and mother, is only seven years old, but he rides his pretty little "grasshopper" with a skill, grace and determination that is quite taking.

A feature of the run to Sharpsburg on Wednesday will be a lunch, served in the woods at the famous Dunkard church on the battlefield. Supper a'd dancing wi'l be the special attractions of the excursion to Pen-Mar.

The route of the parade on Thursday has been changed and will be as follows: Form on South Potomac Street, with the head at Lee Street, to Washington, to High, to Franklin, to Jonathan, to Charles, to Potomac, to Washington, to Locust, to Franklin, to Mulberry, to Fair Grounds and dismiss The regular League photograph will be taken on the grand stand by Mr. William B. King.

In addition to the regular programme already announced there will be plenty of outside entertainment for the visitors. The City Band has been especially engaged to enliven things, and there will be a series of baseball matches between the local club and the Bright S ars, of Ba'timore, both strong teams.

A run was taken this morning (Monday) by a number of 'he visitors to Cearfoss under command of Chief Consul Albert Mott.

The roads are in excellent condition and there is much favorable comment upon them.

The majority of the visitors are expected to get in to-morrow.

At a very early hour this morning merchants and citizens began decorating their business houses and residences orange, garnet and blue (the club colors), and national bunting entering into the attractive trimmings. Decorators also went to work upon the arch of welcome. This arch was designed by Messrs. Joseph Hopkins and H. C. Koehler, engineered by Messrs. Koehler and A. P. Connor, constructed by Messrs. Danzer and Emmert and decorated by Mr. W. Brogunier.

The formal opening of the festivities will be made this evening in honor of the arrival of President Luscomb from New York. He will be met at the depot by local and visiting wheelmen awheel, the City Band and a four-horse landau. A procession will be formed, moving up Antietam Street to Potomac, to Washington, to Hotel Hamilton, where a formal reception will be held by the authorities and citizens. He will be received with other signs of hospitality and escorted to the hotel. The keys of the city will be presented to him in token of absolute surrender on the part of the citizens to their athletic guests.

Immediately upon their arrival visitors are taken in hand by members of the local club and assigned to quarters engaged for them, escorted to Hotel Hamilton, where their names are recorded in the League register and presented with badges. Fifty-five arrivals have thus far reported.

The Philadelphia cyclers will leave that city at five o'clock this (Monday) evening via B. & O. Railroad. A special train will be run for their accommodation, coming directly through to Hagerstown without change of cars.

A number of the Pennsylvania Club, of Philadelphia, will tour from Hagerstown after the League meet down the Shenandoah Valley to Staunton, Va., the Caverns of Luray and Natural Bridge. The party will be under the command of Lieutenant Joseph H. Lehman.

The Century Wheelmen, of Philadelphia, will send a large delegation here via Lancaster and Gettysburg, riding all the way.

Harrisburg will send forty men to the meet. The Germantown, Pa., club will arrive this evening by pike, after having wheeled a l the way.

The Chesapeake Wheelmen, of Baltimore, will be represented by from fifteen to twenty men, most of whom will stop at the Baldwin. The Centaurs will scatter thirty men about the town.

The Marylan'd Club, of Baltimore, will be found at the Hotel Hamilton, where about fifty have engaged rooms.

The Baltimore Club will have about fifty men in attendance.

To the visiting wheelmen who are not familiar with the Hagerstown cyclers, it may be said when you meet a man arrayed in navy blue Norfolk jacket and knee breeches, white shirt and with a white band around his cap you may take entire possession of him, feeling assured that he is ready to serve you in any way you may desire.

As the time approaches for the beginning of the festivities, wheelmen flock in from all directions. Prominent arrivals Saturday evening were Chief Consul Mott and Mrs. Mott, Mr. and Mrs. S. T. Clark, on tandems, and one or two Baltimore ladies on single safeties, while quite a large delegation of Baltimore men accompanied them. Others from Washington and Philadelphia were also made welcome, and to judge from the flood of melody that saturated the Hamilton to a late hour last evening, keeping would-be sleepers awake, they were enjoying themselves. The register was opened in due form this—Sunday—morning, and President Cushwa was kept busy for some time putting down names, addresses and all the details necessary to properly identify visitors.

Several wheelmen took a run to Williamsport this morning to view the damage done recently by the Potomac at high water, and one of the number was unlucky enough to have the back-bone of the wheel he bestrode break with him some six and a half miles from Hagerstown. Luckily it was a hired wheel with a known flaw, and nothing worse followed than a walk in the blazing sun to the nearest livery stable and a pleasant drive of six miles back to this city. I could inflict a long threnody on my readers concerning the pecu'iar ill-luck of some whee'men, but I forbear to-day. It's too hot, and the "special service for wheelmen" that Chief Consul Mott commands us to attend this evening at the Lutheran Church, ought to drive away all blue or gloomy feelings. Whether this service is in the nature of absolution for any pranks that may be played this coming week, or whether the Chief Consul feels the necessity of good behavior this evening after the pleasure jaunt he takes this afternoon, I cannot say.

The arrival of Wilhelm is announced this afternoon, and causes a thrill of expectancy to run along the racing men's nerves. Two sybarites from Baltimore rolled in on a tandem trike to-day shaded from the sun by a broad white canopy and further kept cool by large wicker-work hats. The arrangement *looks* cool, but must catch what little breeze there is. There's little show for any man to get into town without being met and greeted. Committees go to every train, while all the broad white "pikes" are as carefully guarded by scouts in blue wearing the golden word "Hagerstown," as even in war times past. It is the club's chief aim to see that no wheelman comes without being met and escorted to his hotel if he have one selected, and each man has constituted himself an entertainment committee.

By the way, when one looks round over the fields of wheat and clover already being harvested, it is hard to realize that twenty-seven years ago this was the fighting ground of two great armies, and that every eatable thing in the animal line was nearly exterminated. Williamsport, that at one time came near being the Capital of this broad country, was in those days a mere slaughter-house for wh ch ever army happened to hold it. As I was shown to-day the stump of the giant elm tree under which General Robert Lee and his officers one Sunday met and offered up devout prayer for the going down of the Potomac's waters that they might cross into West Virginia, and further on saw the "pike" down which a bold dash of 3,000 Union cavalrymen early one morning guided Longstreet's ammunition trains away from the rebel army, it was difficult to re-enact such scenes in the imagination. Poss'bly I should not have appreciated this bold feat so keenly if it had been the other side that performed it. But this is of the past, and if I have raked up the dead past it is because a blatant bugler is testing his lips' strength in the court-yard Such sounds make me feel war-l ke, and if I ask to be excused while I go down and slay him, I feel sure all lovers of peace and quiet will over-look the act.

FROM NEW YORK TO HAGERSTOWN.

I started to catch the B. & O. 11 A. M. of Monday. All the big guns were to be aboard, and I wanted to be with the crowd. I wanted to buzz Luscomb about the League uniform business, and I wanted Davol to decide some knotty points of racing etiquette. I started with "Jack" and two heavy bags. We arrived at the ferry in ample time, but waiting to gulp down a glass of soda, the gates were closed upon us, and we were left in outer darkness metaphorically, and in utter misery actually. A wee bit of lunch consoled us, and we at last got off on the 2:30.

The ride to Philadelphia is through flat and uninteresting country, and we were more than glad when a party of twenty-six Pennsylvania boys and one Century wheelman, headed by Captain Supplee, boarded our train at the Quaker city. At 7:30 we reached Baltimore and were transferred to a dining car, a palatial dining-room on wheels, secured by Mr. McCarty, of the Pennsylvania Club, who represented the B. & O., and facilitated our transit to Hagerstown

Rushing along between Baltimore and Washington we stilled the longings of the rapacious inner man, the dinner being above the average railroad service. We never knew what a good healthy appetite was until we had watched Lehman, of the Pennsylvanias, clear off the courses with lightning rapidity, open a few buttons, and sigh cadaverously and ravenously for more.

The ride from Washington to Hagerstown was decidedly unpleasant. It was raining hard—falling in torrents in fact—while we rushed on through the dark, seeing nothing and tired mentally and physically. The Pennsylvania men, among whom were some fair vocalists, whiled away a part of the weary stretches, but they wearied shortly, and for the last hour it was a choice between silent stupidity or listening to "Jack's" stories.

At last the cry of "Hagerstown" glads us, and all fatigue vanishes before the royal welcome we get. We simply fall into the lap of hospitality and in a jiffy we are at the bar and have smiled ten times within as many minutes. We smile with Sam Clark, De Graaf, Le Cato, McFadden, Semple, Dr. Hamilton, Shipsey and a host of others. We get a whole-souled P. W. and P. welcome from Haggerty of the Maryland club.

We are at the hotel Hamilton, and it is one a. m. Tuesday morning. The racing men have retired to get into condition for the morrow. Deacon Raisbeck walks the corridor pondering on that new safety of his. President Luscomb, on good terms with himself over the splendid reception

given him, wanders towards the bar with his friend Gilfillan. In the bar-room of the Hamilton, a number of the good fellows who have come for a good time are making merry and fluid hospitality is the watch-word. A negro amuses the crowd with dancing, singing and decidedly clever imitations. The New York Club, numbering twelve, are sharing a love-feast with the Maryland men, and they shout their club cries. The hotel is packed, many private houses are accommodating men, and a seminary near the hotel accommodates many lady cyclists and their escorts.

The Hotel Hamilton is decidedly not a good place to sleep in. In our room were four pressmen—Wills, of the Baltimore *Sun*, the irrepressible "Jack," Graves, of The Wheel, and yours truly. Sleep came not to this aggregation of journalistic intellect. The men in the bar-room continued to make merry; then they wandered to their rooms, still making merry; then they entered their rooms; more merriment. After we had stopped Jack in the middle of one of his Scotch ditties with a well-directed pillow, we dozed off as the church bell sounded three, to awake to the noise of a giant fire-cracker at 7 A. M. This was our first experience in Hagerstown.

PRESIDENT LUSCOMB'S RECEPTION.

As the evening of Monday drew near the threatening look of things increased, and the wind blew strongly from the southeast—a bad quarter here. At 7:30 rain commenced falling fast enough to cause the wheelmen already assembled to give up all ideas of wheeling to the B. & O. depot to meet President Luscomb. The interested populace and the City Band, which had been waiting patiently under shelter of awnings and trees for an hour or more, drew long breaths of relief when it was at last decided to "move on," and the wheelmen formed in line—Hagerstown Bicycle Club leading—and tramped down Jonathan Street, forming in line near the station.

Of course, the train was half an hour late, and when it finally rolled in the darkness was thick enough to cut. Wheelmen had to peer around among the new arrivals by the unsatisfactory light of lanterns and matches, and it was rather a wonder how President Luscomb was disentangled and seated in the four-horse barouche sent to meet him. The march back was around the Square and up Washington Street to Hotel Hamilton, where President Luscomb was welcomed in behalf of the Mayor and City Council in a neat but brief speech by Col. Buchanan Schley. In effect Col. Schley said that everything in Hagerstown was freely thrown open to the wheelmen, but he hoped that they would refrain from poaching on any preserves of hearts already posted by Hagerstown boys.

President Luscomb said in reply that such a reception far exceeded any expectations of his, and such treatment would go down in the League's history as a model for future entertainers. In regard to the timely caution of Col. Schley, he said it must be remembered that many of the wheelmen were already married men, but that he trusted all introductions would be in regular form and vouched for by Hagerstown boys. After the speeches a short reception was held in the rotunda, and many prominent citizens were presented to Mr. Luscomb.

When the Maryland Club marched musically up in lock-step and were formally introduced the spell seemed to be broken, and wheelmen proceeded to demonstrate that they considered the city theirs. Pandemonium reigned, to use a time-worn way of putting it. Tin-horn brigades were formed, and marched up and down the streets; local dealers in fire-works and fire-crackers drove a brisk trade; and even the buglers had to go off by themselves when they wished to test their dreadly instrument's lungs. Small but lively bodies of colored musicians gave short concerts at the street corners, not forgetting the necessary collection at the end. On the 11 o'clock train a large delegation was looked for, and to be in fashion that train was also late. About midnight it finally rolled in, and the weary but patient tin-horn brigade came once more to the front. Arrivals were at once taken in hand by expectant friends and rushed off to register at headquarters and then their respective hotels.

The register was finally closed at 12:30, but the fun did not let up till about 3 A. M.—only to begin again at an unearthly hour Tuesday morning.

TUESDAY, JULY 2—FIRST DAY.

Over 300 wheelmen are now registered, and the list embraces representatives from the following clubs: Maryland, Baltimore, Crescent, Centaur and Chesapeake Clubs, of Baltimore; Cycling Ramblers, of Westminster, Pa; Potomac Wheelmen, Cumberland; Patapsco Cycle Club, Ellicott City; Easton Bicycle Club, Pa.; Hudson County Wheelmen; Harlem Wheelmen; Dorchester Cycle Club, Mass.; New Bedford Club, Penn.; Massachusetts Club; Allegheny Cyclers, Pa.; Kittanning Cyclists, Pa.; Apollo Wheelmen, Allentown, Pa.; Chambersburg Wheel Club, Pa.; Prospect Harriers, N. Y.; Ravanna Wheelmen, Ohio; Winchester Cycle Club, Va.; Harrisburg Wheel Club, Pa.; Norfolk Cycle Club, Va; York Bicycle Club, Va.; Aurora Cycle Club, Ill.; Mt. Carmel Cycle Club, Pa.; Reading Wheelmen, Pa.; Berkeley Athletic Club; Columbia Cyclers; Washington Cyclers; Juniata Wheelmen, New Bloomfield, Pa; Blennerhasset Wheelmen, Parkersburg, W. Va.; Wissahickon Club, Germantown, Pa; Columbia Athletic Club, Washington; Boys' Cycle Club, Carlisle, Pa.; Wheeling (W. Va.) Wheelmen; Dayton Bicycle Club, Ohio; Chester Co. Wheelmen, West Chester, Pa.; Boston Bicycle Club; Milton Bicycle Club, Pa; New Haven Club; New York Bicycle Club; Hartford Wheel Club; New Orleans Bicycle Club; Springfield Bicycle Club; Northampton Wheel Club, Mass.; Ripley Road Club, London, Eng., and many unattached.

The lady members of the League are in greater force this year, and the admiration of all visiting wheelmen. Wherever they are, a surrounding circle of wheelmen soon forms, and a court in miniature is held. Some of them here now are Mrs. Albert Mott, Mrs. Sam'l T. Clark, Mrs. E. P. Hayden, Mrs. C. R. Eisenbrandt and Mrs. J. W. Cummings, all of Baltimore; Mrs. J. Martin, Philadelphia; Mrs. W. I. Wilhelm, Reading, Pa., and Mrs. A. W. Burkheim, Boston. The "Psycho," where ladies ride single safeties, seems to be the favorite mount. In a run of eighteen miles taken yesterday (Monday) to Cearfoss and Williamsport, Mrs. Mott demonstrated her ability to propel her share of the tandem ridden by her and Chief Consul Mott, and was as fresh at the finish as any taking part. Mr. Mott's daughter is said to be one of the coolest and strongest riders in the city of Baltimore, and when the whole stable of five wheels is on the road, about all left to take care of things at home is the house.

As the run to Williamsport, called for 3 o'clock, will not occupy the whole afternoon, and it will not do to let things languish, a lantern parade is called at 8.30 P. M., and the sight ought to do the heart of Hagerstown good.

The Overman Wheel Co. have a pretty parlor at the Hamilton, and the open door displays the word "Welcome." Owen, of Washington, has secured rooms close at hand, and in the rotunda there are exhibits of the "Dart" (Washington) and "Courier" (Chicago) Safeties. The H. B. Smith Machine Co. have a store here, in charge of the local Star agent, and a wheelman straying into any of the outfitters here would almost imagine himself in Perego's or Peck & Snyder's. Anything needed can be bought, and there is a large stock to select from.

Of course, all these local festivities call for expenditure of money, and citizens have not been backward in helping the boys. The gentlemen comprising the Citizens' Committee on Funds are Ex-Mayor Hahn, William S. Hammond, William McCardell, W. L. Keedy, State's Attorney J. A. Mason, and Thomas B. Louth, also of the legal fraternity. Perhaps a feeling of fellow-friendship toward President Luscomb, also a lawyer, may account for the interest lawyers here take. Of course, it goes without saying after Col. Schley's speech last evening, that the Mayor and City Council have abdicated until July 5.

Open house is being kept to-day by the Hagerstown Bicycle Club, in their cosy rooms in the Opera House's upper story, and the barrel of sugar contributed by a local merchant is finding its reason for being as a constituent of the barrel of lemonade kept on tap.

Newspaper men are fairly well established here. Howard, of the *Globe*; Wills, of the *Sun*, and Hull of the *American* (both Baltimore), besides the editor of The Wheel and Purvis-Bruce, of *Bicycle World*, have their eyes on most that is going on.

A component part of "Jack's" outfit is a heavy pewter tankard, bearing the inscription, "To Jack, from ye Anchor at Ripley, Surrey—1888." It has a suspicious, beery look, and, we fear, augurs ill for the ways contracted abroad by our festive contemporary. Not valuable enough for a racing cup, it is hardly needed to quaff the pure water brought to Hagerstown from the distant Blue Ridge.

THE INFORMAL AT-LARGE MEETING.

The Constitution has been so often changed that the annual business meetings lost their interest, but the President this year inaugurated the idea of an informal meeting for general discussion, and it proved a success.

The meeting was called to order at 10:30 by President Luscomb, at the Hose Opera House, some seventy men being present. The Hagerstown Club orchestra opened with music, after which President Luscomb made a brief speech explaining the object of the meeting, and calling for a free discussion of all subjects presented. The business presented was the various matters handled by League committees, and when members of the committees were not present a free expression of opinion was called for. The subjects presented were as follows:

Rights and Privileges of Wheelmen on the Road; not responded to.

Improvement of Highways; not responded to.

Racing and Its Rules; Mr. H. H. Hodgson, C. C. of Louisiana and member of the Racing Board, read the paper published below, pointing out the impossibility of having successful handicap races under present conditions.

CHIEF CONSUL HODGSON ON HANDICAPPING.

Brother Members of the League of American Wheelmen:

I have been selected to inflict you for a few minutes on the subject of racing and its rules. Knowing that you cannot well get out, and that to some extent curiosity detains you, I can refer to the audience as "large and attentive."

My career on the racing path has been long and varied, having been a wheelman for the past four years, and having entered a number of handicap races, yet am I eligible to enter a novice race because track rule No. 27 states that a novice race is open only to those who up to the date of the event have never won a prize. I am yet prizeless; have never been worse than the last man.

I have ridden against time and lowered my previous half-mile record of 2m. to 1m. 59 4-5s. I always take up the rear in all club runs and bring in the dead and wounded, hence my wheel is dubbed the "ambulance," from which it is to be inferred "better late than never;" "it is the pace that kills."

As for mileage, this season in six months I have ridden one thousand six hundred half miles, which is not bad for a novice.

I therefore think I am in a position to discuss racing and take for my subject "Handicaps."

My experience for the past four years as judge, referee, handicapper and timer, and a contestant in handicap races, has demonstrated the fact to me that handicaps are as imperfect to-day as they were four years ago.

A handicap race is intended for unequal contestants, where the slow men are given either time or distance handicaps to offset the speed of the faster men. The special inducements seem to be either a large field of starters or a large number of prizes, but I have yet to find a single instance where there was a close finish between a majority of the contestants, which should be the case. On the contrary, the finish is between not more than two or three men, and it is seldom that the slow men get anything; the majority of the contestants are strung all over the track, and if the handicappers had done their proper duty (which I contend cannot be done) all the entries would make a close finish.

I insist that handicaps cannot be made in such a manner that all are given an equal chance. It is all guess-work as far as the handicapper is concerned; he does his best (guessing), but is prevented from making a correct estimate of every man's time by the riders not giving their best time, or not giving it at all; then, here again, there will be guessing.

One rider may give his best time made on a sand-papered track, the other his best time on a track on which horses are exercised; the last man may be the best rider but the track on which he rides prevents better time being shown. But how is the handicapper to know this? Where is there a basis on which to calculate or guess?

Under the circumstances there is neither rule or reason to determine distance or time that should be given to entries in a handicap race, and I challenge any gentleman here to give me a basis or rule on which to work and show me it is otherwise than guess-work.

If there is a handicapper present he can certify as to the general dissatisfaction generally expressed with his work, as the contestants are never satisfied; and they have reason to kick, as the handicapper has been guessing, and guessing is chance.

There is only one mode of running races outside of scratch races, that is, class races. Even class races are not infallible, but a closer basis can be arrived at; then the 3m. man will not contest against the 3:40 man, and when a record is established it can be kept by the official handicapper on record for future reference, very much after the record kept of trotting horses.

The desire to have a large field of starters and a number of prizes is then the only inducement for a handicap race, but it is not, has never been and cannot be made a fair race, as the handicapper, with all his experience and knowledge of racing, cannot do justice to all, and if he fails in one case his work is incorrect, and until some basis can be arrived at on which to figure handicaps will be a matter of guessing, and guessing is not correct.

In a handicap race often the scratch man makes the best time for the distance, yet he is badly beaten by one of the men with a good handicap. If there was a proper basis the scratch man should be within a few yards of the winning man at the finish.

I have no doubt that handicap races will continue and that numerous prizes will be given, a large field of starters will participate, but the usual kicking will take place and the rank and unfair handicaps will be given, and the guessing continue, and all the figuring and estimating that can be done by the best mathematician cannot make them perfect, the basis will be as far off as ever, and the finish will find three or four men to the front and the remaining riders will be strung out over the track, one man pacing another and some few trying to get a pair of shoes or a bicycle whistle.

I am therefore against handicap races, they are unfair, and time or distance given is purely and simply guess-work.

Gentlemen, I thank you for your attention.

Being called upon by the Chairman, F. P. Prial, handicapper for New York and New Jersey, commented on Mr. Hodgson's paper. He stated that it had been a mistake to have only one handicapper for the entire country, and that had the system of handicappers in different sections been adopted long ago, the system of handicaps would have been more perfect by this time. Under the new system improvement had already been shown, and he referred to the Kings County Wheelmen's races, held June 28-29, as a sample of the improvement, the handicaps having produced some interesting sport. In his opinion, the system of handicapping could not be improved by rule; as race meets become more frequent and the handicapper gets better posted in his district, handicapping would improve. Mr. Prial referred to a new system just being introduced into bicycling, the system of athletic clubs holding out inducements to fast men and thus weakening bicycle clubs. The rich athletic clubs of New York, Brooklyn, Washington and other cities will induce cycle racing men to become members by waiving all dues and initiation fees, and by paying entrance fees and expenses to all the meets. The injurious effect of this system had already been felt on the bicycle clubs, many of which had lost their best men. Mr. Prial suggested that it would be well to settle the question one way or the other; it must be strict amateurism or none at all; no half way measures could be taken.

Mr. Scott, of the Hagerstown Club, responded to the question of "Transportation." In fluent and flowing language he gave the wheelmen welcome, and was rewarded with a three cheers from the Maryland Division, and a proper acknowledgment by President Luscomb.

The following gentlemen then ascended the platform and made a few "remarks." W. H. DeGraaf, of New York, denied that he was an orator, but he made a few points, favoring the League taking measures to prevent athletic clubs from paying the expenses of racing cyclists.

Mr Purvis-Bruce made a plea in favor of the professional. He didn't believe in class distinctions; he believed that the League of American Wheelmen should be in fact what it was in name, and protect all American wheelmen.

Mr. M. L. Bridgman, of Brooklyn, spoke in the same strain as Mr. DeGraaf, and took the same stand as that gentleman. He believed in a strict amateur code, the protection of bicycle clubs, favored the present system of handicapping, and referred to the excellent handicapping of the Kings County Wheelmen.

Mr. W. H. Morrow, a 54-year-old, gray-haired, one-armed wheelman of Ada, Ohio, spoke of his wheel experiences; he grew reminiscent, and his bronzed old face lighted up as he told how he beat that horse up the hill. Always be gentlemen, he concluded, with gentle simplicity; "I have always tried to live by that principle, boys, and I find that it pays."

Chief Consul Mott ascended the platform, was greeted with rounds of hearty applause, and gave a short talk. He was no orator, he said, and then he delivered a little gem of a speech. The meeting then adjourned.

THE MEETING OF CHIEF CONSULS.

At noon the Chief Consuls met in private session, there being present Mott, Maryland; Irvin, West Virginia; Lawton, representing Massachusetts; Hodgson, Louisiana; Bridgman, representing New York. After considerable discussion it was decided that the League uniform system, which was brought up by Massachusetts, who wished to establish her State official League tailor, should remain as in the past. The League had a contract with Browning, King & Co. which must be respected. According to the contract, however, League cloth could be ordered through the League Secretary and be made up wherever the purchaser desired. This decision is liable to cause much dissatisfaction in Massachusetts, but it is a wise disposition of the question. Chief Consuls of States can purchase quantities of cloth from the League Secretary and establish their own State tailoring establishments if they so desire. The point to be observed is that if the League is to have an official uniform, it should be adopted by all the States.

The question of State Official Organs was also discussed. The Bicycling World Company recently developed the idea that their influence with the trade was weakened on account of the publication of official League news in such papers as The Wheel, the *American Athlete* and other papers which publish official League departments. The *World* people at once demanded that the terms of their contract be lived up to in the strictest sense, and thus the question arose. The meeting was not representative or large enough, and it was decided to hold a further meeting before finally deciding the matter. It was practically decided, however, that chief consuls be requested to discontinue the publication of official notices in the cycling papers. The meeting then adjourned.

THE AFTERNOON RUN TO WILLIAMSPORT.

At 2:30, some 200 wheelmen had gathered in front of the Hagerstown Club-house, to start on the Williamsport run. Safeties were arranged on one side of the street, and ordinaries on the other. A number of ladies were also present. Just as the party was about to start, the clouds opened and let down a flood, accompanied with noise and fire. The crowd waited patiently, but it was fully three quarters of an hour before the downpour ceased.

After the shower, over 200 wheelmen, under command of President Luscomb and C. C. Mott, made the run of six miles in about thirty minutes. Even after so hard a shower the roads were in excellent shape, as the time made gives evidence. Swimming in the Potomac's shallow waters, riding across on the ferry and viewing the *débris* left at the canal locks and bridge by the high water, filled up the time of the stay there, and the whole crowd look much fresher for the jaunt.

In the evening there was an attempt at a lantern parade, but the effort fell flat on account of the poor condition of the streets. The men gathered in the hotel vestibules and discussed the features of the meet, or sat smoking on the veranda. In the bar-room a particularly festive crowd gathered and made Rome howl until the wee sma'.

Thus ends the first day, Hagerstown, July 2.

WEDNESDAY, JULY 3—SECOND DAY.

Wheelmen have been steadily coming in all day and yesterday, and there are now over six hundred registered at headquarters.

About fifty of the Baltimore and Centaur Clubs arrived to-night, and will materially aid in swelling the numbers in to-morrow's parade. Their plan had been to stop over night at the Blue Mountain House, have a dance there, and wheel in to-morrow morning, but rumors of no one being there and a rain that set in shortly after 6 o'clock put an end to any such ideas.

The weather has not been very favorable up to date. Last evening every indication was anxiously watched, and when the moon and stars consented to modestly appear at intervals, great was the joy of wheelmen, and the faces of the Hagerstown boys visibly broadened.

THE LANTERN PARADE.

Slight dashes of rain interfered with the proposed lantern parade, and only some twenty bolder spirits marched up and down with lighted torches and a large *cortége* of small boys in attendance. Fire crackers and other noise-producing machines were popular as ever, and the racket appeared to last till a late hour. For quiet-loving people that sort of thing soon loses its charm, and visitors rooming at the more distant Seminary must enjoy a much larger modicum of sleep.

THE RUN TO ANTIETAM.

The principal event to-day until the departure of the train for Pen-Mar, at 2:30 P. M., was the run to Antietam. The start was made from the club-house at 8 A. M., and from then till 8:30 stragglers came along after the main line. The particular pike selected can hardly be described as "sand-papered," for the surface was very rough and stony with new-laid metal. On the way over, about a mile and three-quarters this side of Antietam, R. O. Goodman, of West Hampton, L. I., took a very bad fall, breaking his arm a little above the wrist and badly cutting his face and hands. He was taken to the nearest house and attended by Dr. Griffiths, of Pittsburg.

On this run there was a painful lack of system in arrangements. When the party reached Sharpsburg, no one seemed to know where any point of interest was situated, and none of the promised guides materialized, any more than did the smooth roads.

The first and principal thing was a unanimous "stretch-out" on grass under the trees, for the pace set had been a hot one. When all the party had got along, thoughts of lunch became prominent in their minds, and regarding this there was the same charming uncertainty. Some thought that it would be held in the famous Dunkard Church, a mile and a half back toward Hagerstown, but it was finally discovered at the Antietam House, after some skirmishing around. This proved to be an L. A. W. hotel, and the visitors were evidently expected. Sixty-seven cyclists sat down to a bountiful, country-cooked dinner, and when through but few baskets of fragments could have been taken up. Among the party were three ladies, two *en tandem* and one safety rider, while President Luscomb and C. C. Mott were along to add dignity to the affair. Plenty of time for rest was taken, a return by way of Boonestown was decided on, and the party got as far as the National Cemetery that way. A thunderstorm in the distance, reported to be directly over Hagerstown (of course), rather dampened these plans, and it was finally decided to go down to the nearest station, a mile and a half away, and wait for the 3:44 train to Hagerstown. The road there is being newly macadamized, and the natural surface yet left is wet, clayey, very rough and rutty. Safety riders had much the best of it then, as also on the entire run, but many forced and sudden dismounts were in order. To add to the general pleasure a light shower set in, and made walking much more interesting. We finally captured and invaded the small station, and proceeded to kill time. To fill this particular want two small darkies appeared on the scene, both poor and willing to be more wealthy. One was dubbed "Edwin Booth," from his long mop of curls, and the other was nameless. A collection was immediately made, and those infant performers induced by hard cash to sing songs, dance, wrestle, run foot races over recently-shorn wheat fields and misconduct themselves in divers and various ways. The boys were evidently confederates, and acting with a view to to-morrow being the glorious Fourth. Even money so easily earned seemed, after a time, to pall on them, and it was in vain to try and stimulate the white boys present to bestir themselves in any way. A diversion was effected by a hack-load of girls and young ladies that drove up and were greeted with "When the band plays 'Annie Laurie,'" and the accompanying war-whoop." It was quite an ordeal for them to alight under the scrutiny of so many young men in flannel shirts and knickerbockers. One thing worthy of note is that Maryland's fair daughters seem not to have been at home this particular day on the Antietam pike, or if at home not visible. Not a pretty face was seen on the trip from Hagerstown to Antietam. After that—well, they were not so bad.

At length the train put in an appearance and took back a baggage-car crowded with wheels and a damp and tired crowd of cyclists. As we rolled into Hagerstown the words "Annie Laurie," with tin-horn obligato, apprised us of the departure of the Pen-Mar train.

If our customary shower holds off till the races to-morrow they—the Pen-Mar visitors—will simply have a great time. If wheelmen can be truly said to pray, they are doing that very thing for fair weather to-morrow. For two days now the racing men have been unable to use the track, and nothing but a warm and sunny morning will give them even a trial spin to-morrow. A cold wave is predicted by the New York *Herald* for the 4th, and no one is objecting to the prospect. If it proves rainy early departures will be made, and as Updegraff puts it, "We shall mortgage the club property—pool-tables and piano—and, levying another large assessment, start life afresh as a bicycle club."

An additional offer stimulating to fast time is that of the Clermont Knitting Co. of an iron-clad cycle suit to the man making the best time in the half-mile race to-morrow.

All the professions are well represented here, as well as all sections. Very few are fat men; many wear glasses; about one-half smoke, and nine-tenths lubricate their throats with various liquids when dry. "Open house" is kept by the Maryland and Baltimore clubs, and visitors to last year's meet know what that means. The press men from the large dailies who, with the exception of Charley Howard, of the Boston *Globe*, are not wheelmen, are at their wit's end to get "stuff" enough to make readable columns for their papers, as wheelmen spread out and cover so much space and territory that their movements are hard to trace. The local press, particularly the afternoon *Globe*, with four wheelmen on its staff, are covering affairs in fine shape, and doing work worthy of more widely-known papers.

To get rid of the annoyance of the wheels that the hotel rotunda fairly swarms with, and give other visitors a chance to sit down occasionally, the Hamilton has erected a shed near by, and their removal there is requested.

The parade is to be at 9:30 to-morrow morning, and wheelmen are all requested to be on hand and form divisions early as 8:30. Safeties are to be wisely given the lead in all divisions. After the customary photo., and a route covering some forty minutes, and previously outlined, the line will disband and return.

At date of writing a gentle rain that goes on as if "it might be for years or might be forever" is causing the hearts of wheelmen to sink within them. As President Luscomb graphically puts it, "Hagerstown, thy name is mud!"

PRESENTATION FROM NEW ORLEANS BICYCLE CLUB.

A pleasant surprise awaited the Hagerstown Bicycle Club when called to order by President Cushwa this evening. When drawn up in line, Chief Consul Harry Hodgson of Louisiana addressed the Hagerstown boys, speaking feelingly of the courtesies extended the New Orleans tourists, Messrs. Hill, Fairchild and Fairfax, when on their tour to the League Meet of 1887. He also alluded to further courtesies extended at Baltimore, and in token of the brotherly love and esteem between these widely separated clubs, presented the Hagerstowns with a beautifully embroidered silk banner of the club colors. President Cushwa responded in a neat little speech, saying that though not a member of the club at the time the New Orleans tourists were here, he had always heard them spoken of as perfect gentlemen, a fact plainly exemplified in C. C. Harry Hodgson. He called on President Luscumb for a speech, and a short response was made, followed by three hearty cheers for "the President of the L. A. W." The club's rules were temporarily suspended and the New Orleans Bicycle Club placed upon the honorary list. Ex-Chief Consul J. Kemp Bartlett was called for and responded briefly, C. C. Mott having escaped a similar call by timely absence. Captain Updegraff was next called for but pleaded his inability as a speech-maker and was let off easily.

The club rooms wore quite a gala appearance during the evening, most of the visiting lady cyclists being present and inspecting the banner.

THE EXCURSION TO PEN-MAR.

The event of Wednesday afternoon for those who did not go on the run to Antietam was the excursion to Pen-Mar. A special train of six cars left the Western Maryland Depot at 2:30, and climbed up the steep grades of the Blue Mountains until the destination was reached, some sixteen miles from Hagerstown. As the train drew above the sea level, magnificent views were disclosed, increasing in beauty and breadth every moment. Arrived at Pen-Mar the visitors took possession of the grounds. They were of the usual pic-nic order. There was the little open platform and the crude orchestra, which played queer tunes to still queerer dances. There was the photograph man, who arranged you in a group and shot you at a quarter the head. His work was villainous. Then there was the lung-testing man and the man who gave you poisonous cigars if you succeeded in hitting the nigger with the rubber ball. On the west of the bluff was an observatory, from which a magnificent view of the Cumberland Valley was obtained. It encompassed a stretch of sixty miles, the eye taking in many villages, with a back-ground of dark blue mountains.

A woodland path led along the bluff to the Blue Mountain House. To this point many people walked, while others drove over in carryalls. The party from Baltimore was particularly merry. Arrived at the hotel, a charming view was disclosed. The building is a fine piece of architecture of its style. It is nearly two hundred feet long, and overlooks the valley. The grounds are well trimmed and gardened, and it is as pretty a mountain resting spot as one could well find. Supper was served at Pen-Mar, and at dusk the wheelmen returned to Hagerstown, arriving in the midst of a driving rain.

This downpour was not of the usual splurge and dry-up variety. It had considerable staying power and it drizzled all the evening. The crowd, having nothing to do, went mischief making. Between 8 and 9 P. M. the band played "Annie Laurie" three hundred score of times, giant fire-crackers were exploded and the P. W. and B. held a midnight session to discuss an important point of its theology.

In the evening a large party of the Maryland Club arrived and spent most of the evening in their club parlors, taking "badges" in the one and singing and making merry in the other. The men got to bed in sections and quiet reigned when Tuesday had pretty well become Wednesday.

THIRD AND LAST DAY OF THE MEET.

THE PARADE.

If frequent discharges of gunpowder have anything to do with causing rain, the wheelmen at Hagerstown have only themselves to thank for wet weather. Since Monday night the firing of crackers and other explosives has been nearly incessant and a pall of gunpowder smoke has hung over the city. At breakfast-time this morning it was raining hard, and the contemplated parade was postponed till 12 o'clock. By that time rain had stopped and a favorable breeze was blowing. Roads were thick with mud in the centre of the city, but in spite of that, some 450 riders in all turned out to face the slippery ordeal of showing themselves.

The shrinking timidity of wheelmen has often been remarked upon, but it is never shown to better advantage than when a parade is proposed. The man who may be the boldest leader in any plan for general deviltry, or most successful in keeping people awake, dislikes making a "holy show" of himself on a wheel. The sidewalks were lined with people all along the route, and much envy and admiration was excited as casual wheelmen sped rapidly along the slippery streets to the starting point.

It was nearly 1 o'clock before the parade got under way, the line being formed on Potomac Street near the club-house. The string of glittering cycles and uniformed men extended for over a quarter of a mile. The oldest organizations were given the right of line, the New York Division, which was organized in 1876, being in the lead. Following the Empire State wheelmen were the men from Connecticut, Massachusetts, Maryland, Louisiana, the District of Columbia, Pennsylvania, West Virginia, Ohio, and Virginia. The unattached men, of whom there was quite a brigade, brought up the rear under charge of President Cushwa, of the Hagerstown Bicycle Club.

President Charles H. Luscomb was Grand Marshal, and Chief Consul Mott Adjutant and Chief of Staff. The aids who carried out their directions were M. L. Bridgman, S. Wallace Merrihew, H. H. Hodgson, C. E. Learom, Wm. J. Gilfillan and Sanford Lawton. The route was the same as that previously given, and included all sorts of streets and grades.

CLUBS IN LINE.

These clubs were represented in line, with the following captains: New York Bicycle Club, J. McFadden, captain; Waiontha Club, Richfield Springs, August Kinne; Mercury Wheel Club, Flushing, L. I., L. A. Clarke; Manhattan Bicycle Club, C. A. Sheehan; Northampton, Mass., Wheel Club, L. B. Graves, acting captain; Maryland Bicycle Club, Baltimore, E. F. LeCato; Baltimore Cycle Club, W. A. Black; Hagerstown Bicycle Club, George F. Updegraff; Crescent Cycle Club, W. S. Callaghan; Cycling Ramblers, Westminster, C. E. Fink; Centaur Cycle Club, Baltimore, Henry Ehrman; Chesapeake Bicycle Club, Baltimore, Wm. Holland; Potomac Wheelmen, Cumberland, A. C. Willison; New Orleans Bicycle Club, H. H. Hodgson; Washington Cycle Club, E. E. Curry; Columbia Cyclers, Washington, H. A. Lammond; Capital Club, Washington, H. N. Low; Mt. Vernon Wheelmen, Philadelphia, J. A. Scott; Columbia Cyclers, Philadelphia, H. E. Mole; Harrisburg (Pa.) Wheel Club, George Ives; Century Wheelmen, Philadelphia, W. G. Speier; Allegheny Cyclers, Pittsburg, C. C. Tagart; York (Pa.) Bicycle Club, W. P. Swartz; Pennsylvania Bicycle Club, Philadelphia, W. D. Supplee; Waynesboro (Pa.) Cyclers, E. D. Tanney; Milton (Pa.) Bicycle Club, B. Galbraith; Blennerhasset Wheelmen, Parkersburg, W. Va., E. Nelly; Winchester (Va.) Cycle Club, A. S. Allen; Norfolk (Va.) Cycle Club, W. J. Stanworthy. The unattached men represented clubs from nearly all over the Eastern and Central States. The Baltimore clubs showed up in fine style, and their riding was much admired. The Marylands had about 60 men in the parade, the Baltimores 50, Crescents 35, Chesapeakes 18 and Centaurs 15, with a total strength from that city of 178.

Among the lady cyclists in line were Mrs. Albert Mott, Mrs. Victor Emerson, Mrs. U. T. Slee, Mrs. E. P. Hayden, of Baltimore; Miss Mamie Mayberry, of Hagerstown; Miss Adelaide Raisbeck and Miss DeGraaf, of New York; Mrs. A. W. Burkholm, of Boston, and Miss Schaaf, of Chambersburg, Pa. Nearly every window along the route, from which a good view could be obtained, was crowded with spectators. W. H. Morrow, the one-armed cyclist from Ada, O., who left the best part of his upper left member upon the field of Chancellorsville, was the recipient of an ovation all along the line.

The following statistics regarding numbers of different types of wheels in line are interesting, as showing the steady growth in favor of the safeties: Stars, 20; Springfield Roadsters, 9; Tricycles, 9; Double or Tandem Tricycles, 9; Tandem Safeties, 6; Ordinary or Crank Wheels, 191; Safeties, 194, divided as follows: New Rapids, 20; Ramblers, 11; Victors, 45; Columbias, 60; Psychos, 23; miscellaneous, 24. Proportions on a larger scale are as follows: Uprights, Stars and Springfield Roadsters, 220; Safeties, all kinds, 194; Tricycles, 9; Double Machines, 15. Four hundred and thirty-eight machines were in the parade, carrying four hundred and fifty riders.

The parade wound up at the Fair Grounds, where W. B. King photographed the cyclists in a group with their wheels stacked in front of them. The grand stand served as a background. Photos were also taken of the Maryland Division and the Hagerstown Club. Lemonade in large quantities was rapidly disposed of, and the return made to town in a go-as-you-please sort of style by the hungry crowd. At the Hamilton the service was very slow during this last day, and many complaints were heard at the tables. Not enough boarding-houses seem to have been utilized, all visitors preferring to crowd into one hotel. They have been divided up in about these proportions: Hamilton, 100; Baldwin, 150; City, 75; Franklin, Mansion and Seminary, 50 to 60 each, the rest being with friends or at private boarding-houses.

The League photos are said to be very clear-cut and satisfactory, and orders will be filled fast as received by Mr. King. The price of the large size, 24 inches, is $1.25, 75 cents cheaper than usual; and the smaller ones, 11 inches, only 75 cents. We understand these prices include mailing.

RACES AT WASHINGTON COUNTY FAIR GROUNDS.

By four o'clock, the time finally set for the races to begin the sky was bright and clear, and a light south-west breeze was blowing. With the track a little dryer, conditions

would have been nearly ideal for fast time. The Blue Ridge, hazy with hot airs in the far distance, lent a charming prospective to the view from the well-filled grand stand. From all vantage points outside, spectators were taking in the races free of charge, and many carriages were drawn up among the lookers-on. The race officials were as follows: Referee, C. H. Luscomb; Judges, Albert Mott, Baltimore; Ed. Le Cato, Baltimore, and H. Hodgson, New Orleans, La.; timers, Will H. Dotter, Phila., W. H. De Graaf, N. Y., E. P. Hayden, Baltimore; starter, Sam'l T. Clark, Baltimore; clerks of course, Harry B. Irvin, Hagerstown, M. L. Bridgman, Philadelphia; scorers, Messrs. N. H. Carr, Balto., N. D. Schmidtt, Woodstock, Va., F. P. Prial, N. Y. Previous to the races beginning, which was not till fully five o'clock, many wheelmen rode around the track to help harden the surface, and numerous spurts between well-known men took place, encouraged by the wheelmen in the grand stand. A Kodak fiend in line with the starters occupied the quadrant trike that carried a small brass cannon, used as a signal for starting. For one thing a kind Providence be praised, the city band could *not* play "Annie Laurie," having left their music of that beautiful melody at home.

Following is a summary of events run off, in their regular order:

ONE-MILE NOVICE.

The push off was not very good in this. V. L. Emerson of Baltimore, led at the half mile by a long distance, with Ash, also of Baltimore, second; and Schmidtt a bad third. Emerson won with ease in 3m. 24s., with Ash second in 3m. 40 1-2s.; Schmidtt falling out.

ONE-MILE L. A. W. CHAMPIONSHIP.

Seven starters faced the tape in this. At the first quarter, W. H. Benton, of Washington, led in 48s., Isaac Hinds, of Baltimore, at the half in 1m. 40s., but A. B. Rich, of New York, went ahead at the three-quarter. He could not hold the place though, and A. C. Banker won easily in 3m. 8s.; W. E. Crist, second; Wilhelm, third; Rich, fourth, and Phil Brown, fifth.

ONE HUNDRED YARDS SLOW RACE.

Only three entered for this, all from Hagerstown. Messrs. Lechlider and Emmert fell off and out; and H. E. Dayhoff won in 2m. 36s., riding straight and steadily to the finish.

HALF-MILE DASH.

This was to have been in three heats but only six entries appearing, it was consolidated into one heat. Benton, Hinds, Wilhelm, Barber, Brown, and W. D. Banker entered. The race management must be criticised as being very slow, fifteen to twenty minutes elapsing between each race. Dressing-rooms were about an eighth of a mile way. Phil. Brown led at start and Banker went ahead at quarter, time 44s. Wilhelm won in 1m. 28 1-5s.; Phil Brown, second; L. J. Barber, third. Hinds claimed a foul from Brown, but the protest was not allowed.

FANCY RIDING BY THEO. FINLAY, OF SMITHVILLE, N. J.

This was well received, but a second exhibition, to have come off later, had to be declared "off" on account of lateness of the hour.

TWO-MILE HANDICAP L. A. W. CHAMPIONSHIP.

In this race it was noticeable that the Clerks of Course were remiss in duties, for too many people were on the track and in the way. Five men, Hinds (250 yds.); Ash (250 yds.); Barber (70 yds.); Killiner (250 yds.), and L. L. Clarke (145 yds.) entered, with none at scratch. With such a condition of things the 70 yds. man should have been placed at scratch, and the others moved back accordingly. Ash was first at the half, Killiner second, Hinds third and Clarke overhauling them rapidly. At the first mile they were in the same order, and at the mile and a half Ash led, with Hinds a close second. Here Hinds tried to pass on the *inside*, and ran into the picket fence, taking a bad fall and being practically out of all events after that. Evidently he was rattled by a narrow escape from a fall above the tape, where Clarke was fouled by Killiner and his racer spoiled. Clarke pluckily mounted another wheel and rode it out. His claim for a foul against Killiner was allowed, and he was given second place.

ONE-MILE TRICYCLE, L. A. W. CHAMPIONSHIP.

There were but two entries for this—Emerson on a Racing Quadrant, Brown on a Roadster of the same make. Emerson led from the start, making the half in 1m. 30s., the mile in 3m. 20 2-5s. Brown loafed down to the half, and was ordered off the track by the referee.

ONE-MILE SAFETY, L. A. W. CHAMPIONSHIP.

There were five starters in this. Larom, of New Haven, led. At the half Larom, Crist and Pickett were respectively first, second and third. W. E. Crist won, after a sharp struggle with Wilhelm, in 3m. 5 1-5s.; Wilhelm second, Pickett third, Larom fourth. This was a pretty race, and Pickett would have made a better showing but for slipping his pedals.

ONE-MILE TANDEM SAFETY.

Three tandems started, Crist and Brown on one, Banker Brothers on another and the third manned by Emmert and Dayhoff, both of Hagerstown. This latter pair should have received a liberal handicap. Banker Brothers took the lead and were never headed, making the half in 1m. 25s.—record on track in this country for that distance. Crist and Brown fell out at the half, and the Hagerstown boys rode to a finish, though standing no show. Winning time was 3m. 12 1-5s., and might have been better with a good team to push the Banker Brothers.

ONE-MILE TEAM RACE.

Teams of three men each entered from the following clubs: Penn Club, of Reading, Pa., and Berkeley Athletic Club, of New York; the Baltimore and Washington teams falling out. Berkeley led at both the half and mile with two men, Rich and Banker, and scored twenty-seven points against the Penn Club's fifteen. Time made, 3m. 2 2-5s.

If criticism is to be made, it is that things were a little slow and amateurish, and lacked the necessary "snap." Arrangements for the spectators and press were convenient. Lemonade flowed freely—as often as the juvenile son of Ham could be induced to bring a pailful—and hundreds of copies of the souvenir number of THE WHEEL lent a piquant touch of color to the ranks of spectators. It is pleasant to chronicle the fact that the Hagerstown Club will not loose money, even with all the bad weather experienced.

SCENES DURING THE EVENING OF JULY 4.

The proposed "smoker" was transferred from the Seminary Campus to the Hose Opera House, on account of dampness of the trees and grass at the Seminary grounds. A plentiful stock of clay pipes, tobacco and lemonade had been provided, and after several hundred dollars worth of fireworks had been let off at Market Square the wheelmen began to pour in from the crowded streets. The City Band soon filed in and took seats on the stage, and for an hour rendered popular overtures, polkas and waltzes, while the happy crowd danced up and down the open space. Many were arrayed in tennis caps and blazers loud enough to banish sleepiness from any one present. Impromptu accompaniments were executed on calliopes and vocaphones, and ladies and children peered in through the wire netting at the window to see the animals "perform" at a safe distance. The few lady cyclists that had wandered in soon withdrew to the more retired dress circle and private boxes, and were interested spectators of the frolics.

Dancing was carried out with much spirit, and all lacking was the presence of the fair sex for partners.

At about 10:30 President Cushwa called the crowd to order, and soon as that difficult feat had been accomplished stated that President Luscomb wished to say a few words to those present and briefly bid them good-by. Three cheers were given for Cushwa, and Mr. Luscomb ascended the stage. In his remarks he spoke of this Tenth Annual Meet being an absolute success, in spite of discouraging weather. To the unattached wheelmen present he said there could now be no doubt of the many advantages of belonging to the L. A. W. The spirit of brotherly friendship had never been more manifest than at this particular meet, and the boys had pulled together through everything. Over 200 new members was already one good result, and the cycling boom must not be permitted to languish in Maryland. What it needed, said he, was "whooping up," and to judge from what he had seen, no men in the world were better qualified to "whoop it up" than these same Maryland boys. He then said that he should go home with the most kindly feelings toward all present, and bade all a regretful good-by.

Three cheers were given for President Luscomb, the L. A. W., and Hagerstown generally.

A large body of cyclists left at midnight on the B. & O. special, some intending to stop off at Washington and ride out to Cabin John Bridge and take breakfast there. Many were left off at Baltimore, but a lively crowd of some twenty took care that no one should feel homesick for lack of fun in general all the way to N. Y. City. It was long after 1 A. M. before any one had much sleep, as figures in airy raiment flitted up and down the aisles, fired pillows at each other, and kept things well on the move till the lights were put out.

Through some unaccountable error the baggage car, containing the wheels was side-tracked at Wayne Junction the next morning, July 5, and great was their owners' disgust. Mr. Newbourg at once telegraphed to have them forwarded to New York, but a wait of some hours was necessitated before they were received.

KINGS COUNTY WHEELMEN'S RACE MEET.

The first day's races of the Kings Co. Wheelmen were run off Friday and Saturday, June 28 and 29, at Washington Park, Brooklyn. The track was in excellent condition, and some exciting races were run. The large audience usual at the K. C. W. races was absent on the first day. The second day was a big improvement on the one preceding; the audience being large and demonstrative, and the meet declared a success. Following is a list of the events run off on both days:

FIRST DAY, FRIDAY, JUNE 28.

One-mile Novice, for K. C. W. members.—J. Bensinger, first; J. P. Stevens, second. Time, 3m. 17 3-5s.

One-mile Handicap—First Heat—A. A. Zimmerman, Freehold, N. J., 70 yards, first; F. B. Hesse, K. C. W., 55 yards, second; H. O. King, K. C. W., 65 yards, third. Time, 2m. 57 1-5s. Second Heat—L. L. Clarke, Berkeley Athletic Club, 65 yards, first; C. M. Murphy, K. C. W., 55 yards, second; W. F. Murphy, K. C. W., 45 yards, third. Time, 3m. 0 1-5s. Final Heat—Hesse, first; W. F. Murphy, second; Clarke, third. Time, 3m. 1 1-5s.

One-and-a-quarter mile Ride and Run.—The men alternately rode and ran a lap, pushing their wheels with them. R. W. Steves, K. C. W., first; W. W. Taxis, Athletic Club, Schuylkill Navy, second; H. A. Kellum, Newark, third. Time, 5m. 23 1-5s.

Two-mile Handicap (twelve starters).—A. A. Zimmerman, Freehold, N. J., 205 yards, first; C. M. Murphy, K. C. W., 80 yards, second, and J. Bensinger, K. C. W., 125 yards, third. Time, 6m. 17 2-5s.

One-mile Boys' Race.—A. H. Feldmeier, Brooklyn, 4m. 44 1-5s.; C. Jackson, Brooklyn, second.

Two-mile Safety Handicap.—W. F. Murphy, K. C. W., 70 yards, first; W. Neuman, K. C. W., 150 yards, second; and W. G. Class, B. A. C., 110 yards, third. Time, 7m. 21s.

Five-mile K. C. W. Championship.—W. F. Murphy, first; R. L. Jones, second; and W. R. Steves, third. Time, 17m. 29 1-5s.

Match Race.—W. F. Murphy rode four, while P. D. Skillman ran three, and T. G. Sherman walked two miles. Murphy won easily in 14m. 9 4-5s. Skillman stopped at two miles, covering it in the fast time of 9m. 59s. Sherman stopped at a mile and a half.

SECOND DAY, SATURDAY, JUNE 29.

One-mile Novice.—J. Bensinger, K. C. W., first; R. Miller, Brooklyn, second; W. C. Heydecker, New York Bicycle Club, third. Time, 3m. 17s.

One-mile Handicap.—First Heat—F. B. Hesse, K. C. W., 55 yards, first; W. W. Taxis, Athletic Club, Schuylkill Navy, 35 yards, second; L. L. Clarke, Berkeley A. C., 65 yards, third. Time, 2m. 58 3-5s. Second Heat—C. M. Murphy, K. C. W., 55 yards, first; J. Bensinger, K. C. W., 70 yards, second; W. F. Murphy, K. C. W., 45 yards, third. Time, 3m. 3-5s. Final Heat—Taxis, first; Hesse, second; C. M. Murphy, K. C. W., third. Time, 2m. 59 4-5s.

Two-mile Handicap, Brooklyn Bicycle Club Members.—F. B. Hesse, K. C. W., 85 yards, first; R. L. Jones, K. C. W., 150 yards, second; W. Schumacher, L. I. W., 40 yards, third. Time, 6m. 14 4-5s. Second Heat—W. T. Murphy, K. C. W., 80 yards, first; C. M. Murphy, K. C. W., 95 yards, second; W. W. Taxis, Athletic Club, Schuylkill Navy, 50 yards, third. Time, 6m. 24 2-5s. Final Heat—W. F. Murphy, first; Taxis, second. Time, 6m. 22 1-5s.

Two-mile Safety Handicap—W. F. Murphy, K. C. W., 70 yards, first; W. F. Class, B. A. C., 110 yards, second; W. Neumann, K. C. W., 150 yards, third. Time, 6m. 49 1-5s.

Three-mile Team Race.—Each club entering four men. Berkeley Athletic Club, Messrs. Banker, Schaefer, Class and Clarke, 36 points; Kings County Wheelmen, Messrs. Brown, Murphy, Steves and Hesse, 30 points. Banker finished first in 9m. 50 4-5s.

Two-mile Tandem Handicap.—J. F. Borland and F. Coningsby, B. B. C., 175 yards, first; W. F. Murphy and C. M. Murphy, K. C. W., 125 yards, second. Time, 6m. 18 4-5s.

Three-mile New York State L. A. W. Championship.—A. C. Banker, Berkeley A. C., first; F. G. Brown, K. C. W., second. Time, 10m. 2-5s.

RACES AT EAST HARTFORD, CONN., JULY 20.

The eighth race meeting of the East Hartford Wheel Club will be held the 20th of July, at 3 P. M., on the East Hartford Bicycle Track. Programme as follows: One-mile, East Hartford, championship; half-mile, handicap, open, in heats; two-mile, handicap, open; half-mile, novice, open; one-mile, 3:20 class, open; one mile, open; one and a half-mile, lap, open; one-mile, 3:30 class, open; relay race, open to all clubs, teams of five men; one-mile consolation. Rules and regulations governing these races are as follows: All races are for amateurs only. No one will be allowed to use a wheel weighing less than thirty-five pounds. L. A. W. Rules to govern all bicycle races. Any competitor guilty of careless or reckless riding in a race will be disqualified in that race, and is liable to be for the following races. The arrangements of the heats in the handicap will depend upon the number of entries. Not more than five riders will be started in any scratch race at once. Should there be more than that number, trial heats of half a mile will be run. Time limits will be placed on all scratch races, and class races will have to be won in the class-time or better. The time limit will be governed by the state of track and weather. Club and East Hartford riders only will be allowed to compete for the East Hartford championship. Rover Type Safety machines will not be allowed in regular events. Handsome prizes will be given in every event. The Committee reserve the right to reject any or all entries. Entries close July 16th. No entry accepted without fee. Entrance fee for Relay Race, $1.00. All other races, 50 cents each.

Ralph Temple, the well known cycle rider, arrived in Boston from Chicago July 1. For the past six months he has been connected with the Western Arms Company. Temple goes to England on business connected with this firm. He intends to make a thorough study of cycle construction. While attending to this, he did not deny that he would engage in racing should an opportunity present itself. He is looking remarkably well, and has kept himself in condition by riding with the Chicago clubs on the roads about that city. He was to sail on the Adriatic from New York July 3, and expected to be away six months.

T. A. Carroll, ex-President of the Lynn Cycle Club, who has received an appointment as special expert on labor matters in the National Bureau of Statistics and was to report July 1, has had the date extended to July 6, and will remain in Lynn a few days longer.

ST. LOUIS.

The marriage of Percy Stone to Miss Iola Seales took place last Tuesday afternoon at 6 o'clock, at Christ Church Cathedral. The friends of both parties turned out in force, and the spacious edifice was well filled. Ab Lewis officiated as best man and escorted the bride, who looked charming, to the altar A reception, to which only the bridal party and relatives were invited, followed the ceremony. Percy is to be congratulated. His bride is pretty, amiable and sensible, and their many friends here and elsewhere all join in wishing them long life, happiness and prosperity.

Harry G. Stuart, for a long time L. A. W. representative for the Kansas City District, but now a resident of California, was married on Thursday last at Paris, Mo., to Miss Bina Pitts, of that city. They will reside in Los Angeles, and the best wishes of their friends go with them.

I would have liked to scare up a few more weddings and made this a matrimonial number, but though there are any number of eligibles, none of them, so far as I can learn, have had the luck—or nerve, maybe!—to catch on. I have my eye on two or three, however, who will surprise the boys before long, if there is any dependence to be placed on the usual signs.

As the date for the Division Meet approaches the crowd of promised attendants increases, and everything points to the most successful meeting the division has ever had. Consul Kelley has worked indefatigably, and deserves great credit for what he and his associates have accomplished. He reports all the arrangements completed, and the only thing now needed to insure success is for a generous weather clerk to give us fair skies. A dozen or more of our local riders are training every night on the new track, with the evident determination of scooping in all the prizes in the races, and if Lumsden only stops at home they may do so. It is expected, however, that be will be on hand, and we will welcome him, even if he does wipe up the ground with our fast men.

The *Post-Dispatch* had an announcement in its local columns Tuesday evening that an important meeting of the Track Association would be held that night to make all arrangements for the tournament to be given in August, but Secretary Child said he knew nothing of it, and none of the members had notice, so far as I could learn. Possibly the party who put the notice in the paper thought his presence there would be quite sufficient

As I intimated in my last letter, the challenge to Greenwood from the Chicago party turned out to be a "fake" pure and simple. The challenger never rode a bicycle, and, as Bob Garden writes, "he has lived in Chicago all his life, and, it is reasonable to assume, has never seen a hill." Some friend of his wrote the letter as a joke. So Ingalls will keep his dollar after all, and

"Prostrate lies the shattered ruin of our hopes."

ITHURIEL.

TACOMA, WASHINGTON.

I regret to announce that the committee in charge of the Fourth of July tournament, has finally decided to reconsider the subject, and accordingly have reported that no races would be run on that day.

The great conflagration in Seattle three weeks ago is the principal reason for this change of programme. Arrangements have been made to have a grand celebration both in Tacoma and Seattle on the Fourth, and liberal appropriations were apportioned for the cycling entertainment. But the Council voted to turn the entire appropriation over to the Seattle Relief Bureau, for the benefit of the sufferers.

However, we are not going to get left while we have strength enough to assert ourselves, and have therefore decided to carry out the following programme on the Glorious Fourth In the morning a run will take place, in which all visiting cyclists will participate. It has not yet been decided what point we will favor, but ample arrangements will be made in due time to secure sufficient refreshments for all. In the afternoon there will be a hill-climbing contest in the city, probably on Ninth Street, and an exciting climb will be the result, as all of the boys are good strong riders. At 8:30 P. M. a Japanese lantern parade will take place, and at 9 o'clock a bicycle entertainment will be given in the Opera House, the programme consisting of an exhibition of fancy and trick riding by Prince Wells, slow races, obstruction races, amateur fancy riding, club drill and other athletic performances, concluding with a dance.

Mr Dorsey, a Canadian wheelman, arrived in this city last week with his safety, having traveled from Victoria, B. C, on his wheel via Yale and Whatcom. He stopped in to see the boys at Prince Wells' agency, and told many interesting tales of his numerous experiences, some of which were very thrilling. One afternoon, while riding through a thickly wooded valley, Mr. Dorsey met a good size bear, which was off the road, a few feet from the side path, and naturally felt somewhat uncomfortable. Mr. D. stopped and dismounted, whereupon Mr. Bruin sat himself down and quietly took in the situation—possibly cogitating in his active mind upon the apparent advantages of the safety over the ordinary. But as Mr. D. started to take advantage of Bruin's recumbent attitude, the bear also rose, showing that if Dorsey was ready to start the hostilities, he could be accommodated. As the sun was fast setting, our hero felt somewhat uneasy, and finally decided to make a detour, which was done, successfully eluding the cause of detention. It was evident that the bear had recently feasted, for otherwise Dorsey would probably have suffered a similar fate to that experienced by some lumberman a short time since. His other adventures were not quite so interesting as the above, but still sufficient to make his hair stand on end and cause his heart to flutter.

Mr. Dorsey is now on his way to Portland, Oregon, where he will probably make a short visit, and then go further South and possibly into California.

Tacoma claims two more lady riders this week, both of whom are doing well in the management of the safety. There are several others who will join the ranks as soon as their wheels arrive.

For the past two weeks none of the boys have seen Ed. McCoy, and all have arrived at the conclusion that he is off somewhere, practising daily for the race, that were to have taken place or for the hill-climbing contest.

The other boys are all doing more or less riding, and will be in good shape for the contest on the Fourth. Prince Wells, Thompson, Halsted and Hays should make a good fight for the first prize—with Wells the favorite. Halsted has not decided whether to enter the contest on a "Star" or ordinary, but will decide in a few days.

"Pop" Cristie is now one of the boys and can stay with the crowd on any ordinary run.

A few days ago a bicycle was sold to an Indian, who lives on the Reservation, and he intends teaching several of his brother "bucks" to ride. The first thing we know, the Indians will challenge some of the club boys, and then look out for some fun.

SNOHOMISH.

LANCASTER, PA.

"There's a woman in it." That's it, exactly. The ladies' bicycle has come to Lancaster, and has come to stay, for there's a woman in the saddle. In other words, some of our most respectable ladies have determinedly taken hold of the frisky steed and have it under control, and now manage it to their own infinite delight and to the open-mouthed wonderment of the Van Winkles of either sex. The cycling fever is spreading amazingly, and it is astonishing how quickly the ladies learn to ride. And having learned, their enthusiastic expressions are limited only by the dearth of English adjectives. "Lovely," "Heavenly," —well, I will not attempt to repeat. The fact of the matter is that girls have long since realized the need of just such exercise and recreation as the wheel affords, and to which they are as justly entitled as are their big brothers or any other girl's brothers; but—and this was the sticking point—who should make the start?

After some experimental riding on the tricycle, tandem trike, and eventually on the bicycle, by the wives of some of the dealers, Miss E. was induced to go, just to see. She came, saw and was conquered. But she was soon herself a conqueror, and was able to spin around the floor of the riding school at a lively gait. Her friend Miss B. followed and was equally successful. Then came Mrs. G., who already rides splendidly. So there you are. The start is made. About fifteen others have the fever badly, and I shall not be surprised at an early formation of a lady bicycle club of Lancaster, Pa.

The first mentioned two ladies have already been out on the road, and are quite able to take care of themselves. But they don't propose to do so. Of course not. This requires no explanation in a locality where there are so many gallant wheel-*men*. I suppose the ladies will have to hear occasionally what Mrs. Grundy has to say, but they are away and above being affected by any invidious remarks, as these are well understood to be, in most cases, what are denominated "sour grapes." Be that as it may, the ladies have certainly taken a step in the right direction. Any respectable movement that tends to their physical development and the consequent improvement of their health is commendable and worthy of all encouragement. I notice that some of the ablest of our periodicals are seriously considering this matter. From a well-written editorial in the Lancaster *New Era* I quote:

ATHLETICS FOR WOMEN.

Why is it that as a rule athletic amusements are provided only for men? In these times every college and high school has its gymnasium where boys and young men may indulge in all manner of physical exercises And there is nothing to which the youthful male takes more kindly than to these games, sports and exercises intended to develop the body. But when we come down to girls and young women we find that very little has been done in this direction, and yet it is notorious that the average woman of to-day stands a good deal more in need of this kind of development than the opposite sex. A mere glance at the young women one encounters on the streets is sufficient to prove this. It is rarely that one sees that physical robustness noted in the women of England and the continent of Europe. Frail, pale and delicate is the style in which by far the great majority are found. Although on the street a good portion of the time, their feet are "cribbed, cabined and confined" in shoes not intended seemingly for wear outside the parlor. The English woman thinks nothing of walking her ten or fifteen miles daily, but she does it in strong, stout shoes, intended to protect the feet and do serviceable work. Of course, there are many young women who are the picture of health, robustness and endurance, but they are far fewer in number and furnish a striking contrast to their pale-faced sisters, who outnumber them ten to one.

And again from the *Business Women's Journal*:

MUST WOMEN BE INVALIDS?

RATIONAL DRESS AND PLENTY OF EXERCISE BETTER THAN MEDICINE.

It would surely be time well spent for such women to learn some of the laws of health and wisdom to obey them. The first requisite for this work is for them to disabuse their minds of the idea that women are by nature feeble, and that efforts to change the prevailing conditions are futile, because contrary to natural laws

It would seem to have been demonstrated times enough to satisfy any reasonable person that if women would treat themselves rationally, vigorous health would be easily within their reach; indeed, their present condition, notwithstanding the many ways in which they outrage their bodies, prove that they have great powers of endurance.

A HOPEFUL STATE OF THINGS.

There are, nowadays, many women who persist in believing that invalidism was not the original intention in their creation, and that their misfortunes are caused by art and not nature, their own mistakes and not the Creator's This is a hopeful state of things; for when we begin to look earnestly for causes, there is reason to believe that remedies, or, better still, preventives, will be forthcoming.

TROUBLE BEGINS IN GIRLHOOD.

It is beginning to be understood that the trouble commences far back in girlhood, when the child exchanges for indoor occupations rolling hoop and playing tag, and other amusements which exercise the muscles in the fresh air at the same time that they keep the mind pleasantly occupied. At this period the rational dress of childhood gives place to corsets and tight dresses, and instead of an abundance of exercise and air they too often sit in a heated room from morning until night, crocheting, sewing or reading, eating their meals irregularly during the day, and nibbling candy at convenient intervals. When they go out of doors it is for a short, slow walk, and their exercise consists in a dance, which perhaps lasts all night.

With no aim in life except to kill time and to amuse themselves, is it any wonder that their health fails?

These are serious subjects, well considered, and the remedy rests greatly with those most interested—the ladies Let them be up and doing, without regard, so long as they are doing right, to what this one or that may say.

All honor to those who know the right, and, knowing, dare to do.

TENTOONE.

July 1, 1889.

RACES AT BOSTON ON THE FOURTH.

The bicycle races at Franklin Park, July 4, proved an attractive feature of the day. The winners were as follows: One-mile Novice, A. K. Cressey, Newton; time 3m. 41s. One-fourth Mile, open, J. Berlo, South Boston, first, 34 4-5s.; J. Clark, Dorchester, second. One-quarter Mile for Safeties, Berlo, first, 37 2-5s.; A. P. Benson, Dorchester, second. One-mile Handicap. H. G. Andres, Hyde Park, 200 yards, 2m. 16⅝s.; B. R. Felton, Somerville, 200 yards, second. One-mile Safety Handicap, A. W. Porter. Newton, 75 yards, 2m. 25 2-5s.; G. West, Boston, 100 yards, second. Consolation Race, One-mile, E. J. Clark, Dorchester, 2m. 38 2-5s.

RECORD BREAKING IN ENGLAND.

W. C. Jones beat the two miles safety record on June 15, at the Kildare B. C. sports. Morris, who was on 40 yards, went easily until caught, and then pulled Jones along. The latter stayed behind Morris a bit too long, but when he did pull out in the fifth quarter he went along grandly. In the seventh quarter, coming up the straight, two men fell in front of him, and he had to ease, but happily he escaped a fall, and, coming inside the wreeks, went on and beat amateur record easily. Times : Quarter, 41s.; half, 1m. 19 3-5s. ; three-quarters, 2m. 4-5s.; one, 2m. 44s.; one and a quarter, 3m. 26 4-5s.; one and a half, 4m. 1-5s.; one and three-quarters, 4m. 45 1-5s. ; two, 5m. 26 3-5s. Previous record, Herbert E. Laurie, 5m. 31 3-5s. Professional record, S. G. Whittaker, 5m. 24 4-5s. S. F. Edge and F. J. B. Archer also beat the tandem flying quarter record on an "Olympia" tandem, covering that distance in 35 4-5s., the previous record being 38s., standing to the credit of Messrs. E. B. Turner and E. Kiderlen. Both records were timed by Mr. G. Pembroke Coleman, official timekeeper, N. C. U.—*Bicycling News.*

A THRENODY ON GEORGIAN ROADS.

Not smooth ! What can you want? A billiard table surface? Try a few miles of our sand or one of our fine "bumps" that we Georgians call HILLS, and go back to your *good* roads and easy grades and be happy forever after. Muscular exertion? Where does it come in on your roads? I had rather ride from Elkmont to Nashville, something over one hundred miles (as we did), after two weeks continual rain, and over three hours riding in the rain, when your riders tron unced the road in its worst condition, than ride fifty miles of Georgia road. "Mr. F. R. Birdsall, of (the Nashville (Tenn.) *American*, is doing all in his power to advance the interest s of cycling in that State, and his efforts should meet with appreciation by the wheelmen there. The recent Tennessee L. A. W. Meet and tour so successfully carried out in earnest of the work done by the promoters. *Tennessee is not blessed with the most smooth or level of roads, and touring awheel in that State means plenty of muscular exertion."*—THE WHEEL.

Ye Gods ! And are we to believe that the region around

Nashville is not blessed with good roads? What do the Nashville riders want ? Come to Columbus, go over our best road, take a hundred miles straightaway in any direction, and then you will be supremely happy to get on the Tennessee roads in their worst possible condition and in the worst weather. Hills? In over 300 miles touring in Tennessee and Kentucky I discovered *three* only, one out of Pulaski ; one going to ferry at High Bridge, on Kentucky Riv r ; and one after crossing the ferry, under the most favorable circumstances. *Don't ! Don't !* kick about your roads! Come down and see some poor roads and "hills" *for* a change. No one could be more delighted to pilot any of you around than Lewis. Columbus, Ga , July 1, 1889.

K. C. W. NOTES.

The "Kings County Wheelmen's Lantern Parade," on Thursday, the 27th, was a grand success—273 wheelmen in line, with wheels decorated at every possible point with Chinese lanterns is quite an unique sight, and the people of Brooklyn turned out by the thousand to see their cycle-loving fellow-citizens and friends. Bedford Avenue was lined from Hutton Street to the fountain with a mass of people who annually admire this event. On the return to 1355 the entertainment in the club parlors and refreshments in the wheel-room kept our guests pleasantly occupied for some little time. When the hour to adjourn arrived, all felt with best wishes for the success of our Race Meet, and declared that our next annual would see them on hand.

As Titman occupied a front seat on the grand stand I will have but little to say of our meet. Friday, of course, was rather dull, the crowd was conspicuous by its absence, and in consequence the riders put but little vim into their work. The features were: the fine riding done by W. F. Murphy and Hesse, and the delays caused by the lack of system in the work of the assistant to the Clerk of Course. Saturday everything went off with the usual K. C. W. promptitude. The audience, though, large, was lost in the vast grand stand. A large percentage was of the fair sex, and to their cries of encouragement the racers responded with a will. The racers were close and interesting throughout, out, and once more Murphy, "he of handle-bar fame," demonstrated his ability to stand any amount of hard work. The Berkeley team came over fully resolved to have revenge for their defeat at the Long Island Meet, and to accomplish this they remained in their dressing room till the ninth (9th) event (the team race) was called. This they won by six points from the K. C. W. team, who had ridden in almost every other race. Though we were fairly beaten and have no excuses to make, we would like to see a race the same teams when all the men are fresh. Still to would be a bett r test of their relative merits. The State championship (three miles) was won in hollow style by A. C. Banker half a lap ahead of the field. The time, ten minutes is slow (in the track, but the other contestants had had enough in the previous events, and could not stay at even a good gait. Brown's sprint at the finish caused his friends to think that he had not done his best to win, but had been satisfied from the start to play second fiddle to the boys from Berkeley

At the business meeting of the L. A. W. at Hagerstown, July 2, it was decided that no League news should be published in any cycling papers except the official organ. This will by no means please the New York State members. The good work of The Wheel in reporting all matters of interest to L. A. W. members of New York State has been greatly appreciated. The Wheel, as the "Division organ," has given us more information in one issue than we can glean from the *Bulletin* in four.

On the Fourth the following States will be represented by racers from the K. C. W.; New York, New Jersey, Pennsylvania and Maryland—pretty well scattered at the start, but we hope they finish together, i. e., in first place. Where is the "Division Meet" to be? Why not in Brooklyn? Three of the largest clubs in the country are here. True they are not League clubs, but the majority of their members are L. A. W. men, and having the meet here might be the cause of the clubs returning to the fold in a

body. Many reasons could be given why Brooklyn *should* be the place chosen, but let the following suffice for now. The division could make money by having races. The Washington Park track is not only good and fast, but within five minutes' ride of Prospect Park, so if a parade was given, and paraders and photographs *always* go with meets, the grounds could be reached with ease. Those who do not care for races but would rather tour, could also be well attended to, for some of the finest runs in the State are to be had right here on Long Island.

"Atol" thinks the Kings Counties are poaching on Brooklyn's preserves, when they use the syllables "Um-pi-ah" in their club call. We hope the Brooklyn boys will forgive us when they know "the wherefornes of the why." "Imitation," says the author of Lacon, "is the sincerest flattery," and we only wished to express, by this piracy, our sincere regard for the Brooklyns.
Brooklyn, N. Y., July 4, 1889. RAM LAL.

PROFESSIONALS AT FLOATING BRIDGE.

The professional bicycle race Tuesday evening, at Floating Bridge, Mass., between Jack Hunt and Carey Libby, 375 yards, $50 a side, resulted in favor of the former. J. H. Shurman acted as starter, Eugene Wiswall, referee, and W. H. Bingham, B. S. Curtis and S. R. Brown, as judges. The race was witnessed by nearly 200 spectators.

Laud and many are the complaints that are being made by San Francisco wheelmen against the managers of the Haight Street Grounds for their negligence in keeping the track in good condition. Several wheelmen say that if the track was kept in good, or even fair condition, they would be only too glad to pay a liberal fee to be allowed the privilege of training there.

G. R. Adcock, while doing a training spin on the new Torquay (Eng.) track on the 14th inst., decided to try for twenty miles within the hour. He succeeded in doing the distance, with several seconds to spare. This seems to show that the track will soon be one of the fastest in the kingdom. He was timed by several local gentlemen and was paced by M A. Trenchard and E. R. H. Masters. The last mile was done in 3m. 15s. dead.

Fred Wood's Australian ten-mile grass record of 31m 7 7-5s. was at Easter lowered by John Hogan, of Victoria, who covered the distance in 28m. 45 1-5s. Wood's time has stood since March 3, 1888.

"THE WHEEL." REPRESENTATIVE ON THE RIPLEY ROAD.
Mr. Seavey, who corresponds for the New York Wheel, refers to the trip to Ripley last Sunday very enthusiastically, asked point-blank by a reporter to state his impressions of the day, In a few words Mr. Seavey replied : "The day, which was spent on the road to and in the town of Ripley, was certainly one of the very pleasantest which I have passed on the trip. The day was fine, the road excellent, the scenery beautiful, and the hospitality of our hosts a credit to the nation. The memory of this day will be given in my mind when all the rest of our journey has faded from it."

At a recent meeting of the San Francisco Park Commissioners the offer of Superintendent Foley, of the House of Correction, agreeing to furnish fifty convicts for the completion of the park speed track and other improvements was accepted. July 1 the men were to begin work ; the Park Commissioners to pay the expenses of transportation to the park and the cost for five guards. This step marks a long advance in liberal ideas, and one often advocated by this paper. The 1889 Code of Cal., Section 5, chapter 135, expressly provides that prisoners sentenced to hard labor in any penal establishment, may, upon the request and requisition of the officers having charge of the work upon the parks and roads under their control. Not wishing to see a road that had already cost some $35,000 destroyed by the complaints through neglect, the President of the Board, Mr. P. Hammond, called the Superintendent's notice to this statute, and the suggestion was at once acted upon.

The Wheel and Cycling Trade Review.

F. P. PRIAL, Editor and Proprietor.

23 Park Row, New York. P. O. Box 444.

ONE DOLLAR PER YEAR.

Herewith I hand you $1.00 in payment for one year's

subscription, to begin with the issue of ....

Name

Address

Town or City

County   *State*

BROOKLYN NEWS.

During the coming year the city officials will have about two million dollars to expend on the paving of Brooklyn's streets, and the following year they will have nearly twice as much more, and they are now busy debating on the respective good qualities of cobblestones, Belgian block and asphalt pavements. The cobblestone pavement is the most inexpensive to lay down and the most expensive to keep in repair. The Belgian block paving seems to be considered in the most favorable light, on account of its durability, for it is claimed that asphalt pavements need almost constant repairing, and will not stand rough usage by heavy trucks and wagons passing over it. However, it is used in the most satisfactory way in a great many of the largest cities on the face of the globe, and if properly laid and looked after there is no reason why it should not be fully as serviceable and satisfactory in Brooklyn. The plan of the contractors who have laid down asphalt pavements in Brooklyn up to the present date has, in most cases, been to lay it on whatever foundations they happened to find in the streets, and the result has been that the principal part of Brooklyn's asphalt pavements have gone decidedly wrong after a comparatively short usage, for the want of a good foundation or a little extra care and attention. Flatbush Avenue, between Atlantic Avenue and Bergen Street, was repaved only about a year ago, and has already commenced to show very heavy depressions, and even holes, in its surface. The wheelmen of Brooklyn should all embody in their daily (or otherwise) prayers a devout hope that Mayor Chapin will not forget the promises and reasons for hope which he gave the boys at the "Pearl of Pekin" dinner the last winter at the Clarendon.

The number of lady riders of bicycles is quite on the increase in the city, and several are availing themselves of the excellent opportunity for learning to ride which is offered by Charlie Schwalbach's new riding school. He is booming his new venture very successfully, and is working hard to make it a popular resort in cycling circles.

The K. C. W. race meet was carried through in a most successful manner and shows some very good management. Murphy seemed to have a mortgage on the prizes though, and ought to be satisfied with his share of the spoils. Horland, of the Brooklyns, is said to have made his last appearance on the race track at the meet, where he and Coningsby won the tandem safety race.

The Brooklyns had a fine day for their run to Massapequa last Sunday, about twenty of the boys riding down Sunday morning and returning after a good dinner, for which the Massapequa Hotel is obtaining a large and well-earned reputation among the cyclists of this vicinity. Spelman, Mead, Raymond, Fuller, Cole and Snedeker were down their Saturday afternoon and spent the night in the usual "impromptu good time" style of the Brooklyns, and when their fellow-members arrived the next day in a dusty and perspiring condition they met them on the hotel veranda arrayed in conspicuously cool and summery clothing, which filled the tired riders' souls with a good-sized nugget of envy.

Keep and Horsboostel, B. B. C., had a little run to Huntington on their own hook on the same day.

Since the house-warming of the B. B. C. the applications for membership have been largely on the increase, and some of the K. C. W. and L. I. W. men are talking of joining the Brooklyns as associate members.

PHILADELPHIA.

The Pennsylvania Bicycle Club without a doubt on an average takes out one of the largest if not the largest weekly club runs of any club in the country. Any Sunday, rain or shine, warm or cold, you are sure to meet the Pennsylvanias on the road, generally with their genial captain in the van, and it must be admitted that they always present a splendid appearance. Of course they have lots of inducements in the shape of a good search, medals, etc., to urge the members to attend these weekly runs, but it is mostly through the efforts of its wonderful set of road officers, Messrs. Supplee, Leisen and Lehman, that has made the turnouts of the Pennsy boys an example for the local clubs to follow. And now for obvious reasons it is announced that their gallant captain is to resign. Ah, well! may a worthy successor be appointed, but no doubt they will miss the musical tootings on the "whistle," and the cheery voices from," while on the road, of the best of captains, W. D. Supplee.

It seems that Philadelphia is not to be outdone by Brooklyn and San Francisco in the "prodigy" line. Last Sunday our fellow pen-pusher "Ariel" was seen out on the road with his phenomena (league cap and all). Along comes a Century man on a staunch Star, and phenomena expresses a desire to ride one of these exchange, is helped to get on by C. M. and to papa's unalloyed delight glides gracefully along the road. Can it be possible that after taking that header he will forsake his beloved Victor and be forced to ride that delectable Star? Ahem! Say, "Argus," that was a pretty hard rap of "Jonah's," wasn't it? It seems that "Jack" does a little theorizing, on page six of his catalogue, that does not bear very close scrutiny. He has a wheel divided into sections like a clock the quarters, figure twelve on top, being divided into three, six, nine and twelve respectively, pursuing a long explanation, he furthermore says, that absolutely no power is obtained on that side from six to twelve, this it true, but does not say what the rider does on the other side to drive all this time. In the wheel that he advocates it is possible to push one single along the road, but after taking off the other in going down? Of course not, it remains the same as in a crank wheel, i.e., while one foot is pushing from twelve to six the other is going from six to twelve, and vice versa.
Philadelphia, July 2, 1889.
ARGUS.

REPAIRS OF ROADS.

I was amused the other day, as I sauntered along Morris Avenue, to see the street repairers undoing the thing they had done by clearing off the thick coating of mud which hid the light of the macadam under a bushel. No such coating is ever seen in the Essex turnpikes, for there the road makers have marked, learned and inwardly digested the main maxim of McAdam, that in the construction of highways after his pattern not a spadeful of loam should be mixed with the stone, that the essential drainage might not be interfered with. Let me here suggest that county engineers communicate with the Secretary of the American Association for the Improvement of Roads at Philadelphia, whose object is to furnish highway builders with all the literature on the subject compiled from the writings of the most famous road engineers.

Counting our chickens before they are hatched, let me urge the vital necessity of constant repair. Roads will not take care of themselves, but made very constant attention or they will soon go to rack and ruin. To build them and then let them alone is the falsest of false economy. At least twice a year, in addition to the filling of the holes and ruts as they occur, there should be a top dressing of fine stone put on. With these precautions observed, the road beds will become firmer and firmer each year, and the cost of maintenance in good condition will be reduced to the minimum.—The "Rambler" in Elizabeth Journal.

FIXTURES.

July 8, 1889.—Connecticut Division L. A. W. Meet at Bridgeport, Conn.
July 17, 1889.—Two-mile Bicycle Race at Caledonian Games, Minneapolis, Minn.
July 20, 1889.—Race Meeting of the East Hartford Wheel Club, at East Hartford, Conn. Entries close July 16, with Mr. E. E. Arnold, East Hartford.
July 20, 1889.—One-mile and 25-mile Bicycle and 5-mile Tricycle N. C. U. championships at Paddington, Eng., track.
July 25, 1889.—At Minneapolis, Twenty-five Mile Road Race for Championship of Minnesota. Entries close July 20 with Will. Monarch, Secretary-Treasurer, Minneapolis Bicycle Club. Entry fee, $1.
July 27, 1889.—One-mile and 25-mile Tricycle and 5-mile Bicycle N. C. U. Championships at Paddington, Eng., track.
August 8, 9, 10, 1889.—Annual Meet of Massachusetts Division L. A. W. at Cottage City.
August 24, 1889.—Fifty-mile Bicycle and 1-mile Dwarf N. C. U. Championships at Paddington, Eng.
September 4, 5, 1889.—Amateur Race Meet of the Hartford Race for Championship at Hartford, Conn. Entries to be made with W. M. Francis, Secretary, P. O. Box 74.
October 23-29, 1889.—Race Meet at Macon, Ga.

THE COVENTRY MACHINISTS' CO., Limited,

239 COLUMBUS AVE., BOSTON, MASS.

SWIFT BY NAME AND SWIFT BY NATURE.

The Buffalo Express, May 29, says:

"James S. Hedge of the Buffalo Bicycle Club made the first century run of the year on May 26th. Leaving the club house at 8 A. M., he rode via Seneca Street, Potter's Corners Road, Orchard Park, and Colden to Springville. Here a stop of two hours was made for dinner, and return was made via Boston and Hamburg to the club house, arriving at 6:45 P. M. Starting again at 7 P. M. he pushed on out to Bowmansville and return and rode three times around the meadow, arriving at the club house at 10:25 P. M. Hedge rode a Swift Safety, and considering the fact that he did not start out to make a 'century,' and did not think of it until he had ridden about seventy miles, made very good time, his riding time being ten hours and thirty minutes for 105 miles, or an average of ten miles an hour. Four hours and five minutes were used in stops. This is the first time a century run has been made by a rider in this city on a Safety, and it is also the first time a century has been made over this route, there being a great many short steep hills to climb."

THE SWIFT.

The most practical Lady's Wheel on the market.

"The Wheel's" lady correspondent, Marguerite, says: "A Swift is my choice, which for symmetry and easy running exceeds my expectations, and is a credit to the makers."

THE LADY'S SWIFT.

NEW YORK AGENTS:

WM. HALPIN & CO., No. 13 Murray Street.

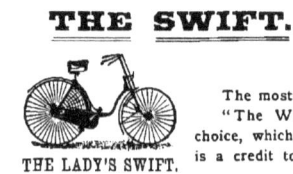

THE WHEEL

—AND—

CYCLING TRADE REVIEW,

Published every Friday morning.

Entered at the Post Office at second class rates.

Subscription Price,	- - -	$1.00 a year.
Foreign Subscriptions,	- - -	6s. a year.
Single Copies,	- - - -	5 Cents.

Newsdealers may order through AM. NEWS Co.

All copy should be received by Monday.
Telegraphic news received till Wednesday noon.

Advertising rates on Application.

F. P. PRIAL, Editor and Proprietor
23 Park Row,
P. O. Box 444, *New York.*

Persons receiving sample copies of this paper are respectfully requested to examine its contents and give us their patronage, and as far as is convenient, aid in circulating the journal, and extend its influence in the cause which it so faithfully serves. Subscription price, $1 per year.

KIND WORDS FROM VARIOUS SOURCES.

THE WHEEL has begun a series of cycling memoranda, which promise to be interesting and valuable as contributions to cycling history and for the use of the future historian of the wheel, which title Editor Prial proposes to lay claim to for himself in a handbook of the sport, from material for which the memoranda are made.—*Providence Sunday Journal.*

THE GREATEST AND ONLY.

THE WHEEL is the greatest and only bicycle paper published in America. It is to the wheelmen what the *Sporting Times* is to the ball players and athletes. Well, that's recommendation enough.—*N. Y. Sporting Times.*

TAKING LONG STEPS AHEAD.

The New York WHEEL, which has been making enormous strides of late in the field of cycling journalism, prints one of the best accounts issued of the doings of the European cycling tourists in England, and wheelmen wishing to keep track of the party cannot do better than patronize THE WHEEL.—*Philadelphia Item.*

BOUND TO LEAD THEM ALL.

THE WHEEL, which seems bound to lead the other cycling journals, published a full list of path records for ordinaries, safeties, tandem safeties and tricycles, in the issue of June 28. The list is very complete, giving English and American professional and amateur records to date.—*Newark Sunday Call.*

WE ARE GETTING ON.

"G. Hendee's article on training was well worth reading.
"Prial is a great handicapper of bicycle events.
"'Oh,' said the athletes, 'if Robertson and Carter could only handicap like Prial.'"—*Sporting Times.*

A NUMBER of racing men are much perturbed over the Windle case. Not a few have grown maudlin over the matter and pettishly pout over his reinstatement; others are much disturbed over the bare prospect of such an act and shout the good old cry of "once a pro. always a pro." We want to assure those sympathetic young persons who rail against the Racing Board, the Racing Rules and what not, that the half of the Windle story has never been told in print. They howl "injustice," but they don't know what they are talking about. Windle

was one of the cleverest fellows that ever came on the path, yet with all his cleverness, his intelligence, and with an abundance of private means, he accepts money from manufacturers to represent them on the path. He not only accepts expenses, but something more. Now, there is no harm in all that; Windle is neither whiter nor blacker for it. But he violated a principle; he rode under false pretenses and won prizes that should have been the property of other men. He took money and raced with Smith and Jones, who were not allowed to take money. No one understands the ethics of the question better than Windle. As a matter of opinion, he should have been suspended for a year, but having been expelled, reinstatement is impossible. There is too much "gray matter" distributed among the Racing Board. They are not the kind of people who wear fools' caps and do the clown act.

AT the Hagerstown race meet a Star rider, having but little experience on the path and absolutely no racing style or control over his wheel, drove his little wheel between two cranks and tumbled their riders to the dust. One of the riders was L. L. Clarke, whose club had sent him all the way from New York to compete, and who would have undoubtedly won the handicap had not this piece of stupidity deprived him of all chance. In addition to the loss of the race his beautiful racing wheel was wrecked. The case stands about as follows : A man trains carefully, leaves business, travels several hundred miles, loafs about town three days, starts in his event and is riding surely to victory, when some ninny rides up behind him, and lo ! the entire output of time, money and perseverance is lost. We have too much jayism on the path. Few of these novices know how to place their saddles, to adjust their wheels or to ride them on the path. They haven't even brains enough to remove the steps of their mounts, which become positively dangerous. The only way to raise the standard is to criticise, and writers for the cycling papers should not fail to show up all such violations of the rules of common sense and call attention to them, even though the perpetrators or their friends may object.

THE cycling trade are asked to note that at the Hagerstown Meet a boy handed to each person on the grand stand at the Hagerstown races a copy of THE WHEEL of June 28. As the people of Hagerstown were very much enthused over cycling, it is fair to presume that many of them looked for new mounts among the advertising pages of THE WHEEL.

WE publish a few items concerning our issue of June 28. We reproduce them, not for personal glorification, but to point out that THE WHEEL is rapidly striding away from all rivals in its special field.

AN Englishman has applied for patents on a device which he claims will enable him to instantly change the gear of a safety or other wheel. The advantage of a high-geared safety on the level is often discounted on the hill, especially when the rider is not over strong, the increased power necessary to drive the highly-geared wheel up the hill taking too much out of the rider. This English inventor claims that he can instantly lower the gear as soon as a hill is reached and raise it as soon as the hill is mounted. The advantage of such a device is obvious.

AN English tricyclist recently died suddenly on his wheel. He had suffered from heart disease for a long time and had been warned not to violently exert himself. This is a warning to those who have affections of the heart. They should take care never to ride beyond the point of pleasure. People with hereditary predisposition to heart disease should have the advice of a physician before they take up cycling.

WE desire to apologize for the typographical errors in last week's WHEEL. The printers did not attack the mass of copy sent them until Friday morning, yet the paper was mailed on Saturday at 6 P. M. We covered the entire League meet, scoring a "beat" over all other cycling papers.

COPIES of THE WHEEL of last week were mailed to every man who registered at Hagerstown. The names were obtained from the registry book, which was kindly loaned us by the Maryland Division.

WHEELMEN AND CITIZENS IN ACCORD IN BIRMINGHAM, ALA.

The Birmingham, Ala., Bicycle Club had another largely attended and enthusiastic meeting June 24, and business of importance was transacted. Committees were appointed to see at once to the incorporation of the club and to consider the question of the construction of an asphalt race track in the old base ball park that Dr. Caldwell has so generously devoted to the use of the new organization.

It has been determined to have a race meet in the fall, probably about the time that the State fair is in full blast, and all the clubs in the South will be invited to contest in the prize drills and races. The wheelmen's day will be a grand event, with a parade of the visiting clubs in the morning, the drills and races in the afternoon and a grand ball at night. It is estimated that from ten to fifteen clubs will be present and 200 or 300 wheelmen in line. The matter was referred to a special committee and the details will be announced in a few weeks.

One of the chief objects of the banded wheelmen is to secure the improvement of the county roads, and recognizing how great an improvement there has been in Jefferson County during the past two or three years, the club passed resolutions showing appreciation of that body. On motion of L. D. Aylett, seconded by W. C. Swem, the following preambles and resolutions were adopted :

Whereas, The County Commissioners have shown a broad-minded spirit of liberality and enterprise in having already built good roads in the neighborhood of the city of Birmingham ; and,

Whereas, The said Commissioners now propose to build a fine boulevard, fifty feet wide, from Elyton to the fair grounds, a distance of one and a half miles ; therefore, be it

Resolved, That the Birmingham Bicycle Club, one of whose main objects is the improvement of roads, tenders to the County Commissioners their heartfelt thanks for what they have already done, and wishes them god-speed in the good work which they propose to continue to do ;

Resolved further, That a copy of these resolutions be spread upon the minutes of the club, and that the Secretary be instructed to transmit a copy of them to the County Commissioners.—*Daily Age-Herald.*

A MOTION FOR INJUNCTION DENIED.

CHICAGO, Ill., July 8, 1889.

Before Judge Blodgett, U. S. Circuit Court, Northern District of Illinois, on Monday, July 1, a motion to enjoin the Gormully & Jeffery Mfg. Co. from using the Copeland patent was argued by the attorneys of the Pope Mfg. Co., Coburn & Thatcher; Offield & Towle appearing for the defense. The Court took the case under advisement, and on Monday, July 8, delivered his decision, denying the injunction. This case is the outcome or continuation of an interference case that was pending for some time in the Patent Office at Washington.

NEW CRANK WHEEL—THE SPEEDWELL.

[Special to THE WHEEL.]

In order to supply our agents who have a demand for a crank safety (as well as the lever motion) we have arranged the future construction of our Volant so that cranks can be attached as well as levers without altering many of its details, and we are now prepared to fill orders for the crank safety wheel, which we shall call the '' Speedwell.''

This machine is well and carefully made, being fitted with ball-bearings throughout, including ball-pedals, Fish's patent hammock saddle, which reduces the vibration to a minimum, and is not only neat in design, but simple in construction. Its price will be $115.

SPRINGFIELD BICYCLE MFG. CO.

BROOKLYN NEWS.

I have noticed that the majority of wheelmen are still using the outside path which enters Prospect Park at Third Street, and for their benefit would say that the newly macadamized road between the Plaza entrance and Third Street is now in good condition for riding, and far superior to the aforesaid path on the outside of the park.

It is quite a favorite ride now for Brooklyn wheelmen to go down to Brighton Beach in the early evening and listen to one of Seidl's magnificent concerts, returning home at about 11 P. M. To lovers of music it makes a most delightful way of spending an evening, especially when there is a good moonlight for the return ride. Now that the July full moon is near at hand all the clubs are organizing moonlight runs, and as the principal destination is Coney Island, I doubt not that the Brighton Music Pavilion will be well patronized by cyclers during that stage of the moon.

Next Saturday the L. I. W. will have a run to Roslyn; also the B. B. C. have booked a large party to go down awheel in the afternoon, returning from there by moonlight on the boat, which lands them at Peck Slip, which is easy of access to Fulton Ferry for the return to Brooklyn.

The Brooklyn clubs did not have a very extensive showing at the League Meet this year, and I hardly think any one club in the city sent down more than half a dozen men. President Bridgman, of the K. C. W.'s, spent the whole week in the vicinity of Hagerstown, touring beyond there to the Luray Caverns and other noted places. That was his programme when he left here, and if he followed it he must have had a most enjoyable week.

President Fox, of the B. B. C., departs this week for a six weeks' vacation trip on Long Island, making his headquarters at Westhampton.

The B. B. C. have adopted a new by-law, which empowers the treasurer to pay the entrance-fees of club members in any races held on Long Island, and which makes it an offense for its members to enter under any other club or association than the B. B. C. in any races held on Long Island.

A party of the Brooklyns, composed of Captain Meeter, Fuller, Lewis, Masterson, Fay, Cole, Raymond and Cooke, took the Long Branch boat, Sunday morning, arriving at Seabright in time for a bath in the surf before dinner, which was eaten at the Peninsula House. After dinner they did up the famous Rumson Road to Red Bank, returning to the Branch for the evening boat for the city.

Tales of disastrous Fourth of July trips fill the air, each party that undertook a run on that day having something amusing to relate. A party of five members of the Brooklyn Bicycle Club, under the guidance of Captain Meeter, rode to Huntington, and while on their way from the latter place to Roslyn were caught in the rain, and were forced to disrobe in the boiler-room of the Roslyn boat and wait until their clothes were dry enough to put on again before they could venture out.

Some fifteen members of the same club went to Bath in the morning and, as they expressed it, "had a bath all the way."

Probably the two who suffered most were Messrs. Masterson and Raymond, who were storm-bound in a country barn near Westfield, N. J., and had for company three dogs, one of which, they were pleasantly informed by the owner, "would bite if he got the chance." The mud bespattered cyclers kept a safe distance from the canines, and when the rain permitted continued their journey to Plainfield. The roads were so bad in places that they were forced to take to the railroad bed, and rode in ditches three inches deep in water to Fanwood, from which place it was all plain sailing. At the Plainfield Bicycle Club-house a hearty welcome awaited them, and after a wash and rest, supper was had at the home of Mr. Slavin, a member of the Plainfield Club. After that the fireworks at the Netherwood Hotel compensated in part for the hard ride, and a late train was taken for home. It is needless to add that the next day their wheels found their way to the repair-shop.

Ram Lal pays so graceful a compliment to the members of the Brooklyn Bicycle Club, in regard to the adoption of a portion of the Brooklyn's "club-call," that it would savor of unfriendliness to further insist that it would be better to have each "club-call" distinct from one another.

Brooklyn, July 9, 1889. ATOL.

CINCINNATI.

We have had a very quiet Fourth here, nothing being done in the cycling line. Last Sunday a jolly lot of wheelmen met at Bennett's and decided on a run into the country as far as Oakley, it being some nine miles by the route we took. A start was made for the Bellview incline, and we reached Mount Auburn in good shape. Streets there were badly torn up, but we managed to pull through to a road better than the rest, and on to Dutchman, or "Die Easy," as it is called.

From there we rode to Walnut Hills, taking the asphalt street and sprinkling it well with perspiration. When Madisonville pike was struck we had a delightful spin to Oakley, with the exception of a few hills to climb. Hills always delight Mr. Dubbe, who was of the party.

At Oakley some of the Athletic Club men were met, and after discussing refreshments we repaired to a fine race-track situated in that place.

The boys made ready, and it was a grand sight to see them struggle against the wind to be first in. Walter Wise was the winner, and as regards the time—I won't give away any of our racing men. Eleven minutes to the mile is near enough.

Our return to the city was made in the cool of the evening. One of our men that rides a very large wheel—64 inches, I think—had a fall while going home. Dropping from such a distance must have been like falling from a brick house.

The bootblacks on Fourth Street seem to think "Keggy" needs a shine, and even go so far as to thoughtfully lay their boxes under his wheel.

The Athletic Club's race is to come off the 7th at Oakley track, and I think fast time will be made. Mr. N. Perrin won a race at Maysville, Ky., recently, taking a handsome gold medal. Some of the Crescents were at Brookville, Ind., on the Fourth, but I've seen no medals yet.

Our City Council have passed an ordinance condemning Spring Grove Avenue, and if some workers among the wheelmen only take hold of the matter we can have it paved with asphalt. Actions of that kind would do more than anything else in this city to help cycling. Who will be the one to push the idea? SAFETY.

K. C. W. NOTES.

The "Glorious Fourth" was a day of disappointments to the local aspirants for racing honors. Murphy and Beazley, of "Ours," and Hoefer, of the Brooklyn's, journeyed to Lancaster, Pa., but in vain, for postponement was the verdict. Nearer home, Brown at Bergen Point and Charles Murphy and Hesse at Washington Park, received the same response. This only added to their ardor, and the way the boys are training shows that they intend to try hard for some of the many events to come off in the neighborhood of New York during the coming season, and if prizes from Hartford find their way to Brooklyn it will by no means surprise those who *think* they know.

Every evening after five o'clock the men may be seen at their work on the Brooklyn Athletic Club track. Miles Murphy, under the able care of Beazley, shows daily that his great staying qualities have by no means been overrated, and the improvement in his sprint is marked. That "rear numeral," Harry Hall, has charge of Brown and Hesse, and appears to derive as much pleasure from their good work as they do. Both are improved men, and we expect to see many a good race fall to the pair before the season closes.

The unwarranted and unkind remarks made in regard to that "team race" have caused the injured member to declare he will never again ride under the King's County colors. This is wrong. Through the *chatter* of a few men, who actually know nothing of what they are talking about, we lose a sterling good rider, who has not only brought credit to the club, but has himself lost chances for that purpose.

Cobblestone Hill, the terror of all tyros, will soon be in ridable shape. For the past two weeks work has been going on from Butler Street to the Sackett Street Boulevard, and the long-promised macadam will, at an early date, gladden the hearts of all wheelmen. How long it will then take the *scorchers* to go to the Island remains to be seen, but methinks the pace will not be slow.

What has become of the "Kings County Ball Team"? Since that memorable game with the Brooklyns, the opening game of the season, nothing has been heard from them. Have they met the enemy, and been vanquished, or has the "Unequaled Sport" taken them for a training trip to Bermuda? Come, boys, start the ball curving again.

Come, "Atol," that's too much. We have admitted the theft of "Um-pi-ah," and in every way possible acknowledged the greatness of the B. Bi. C., but when it comes to leaving the grand old club of Kings, we draw the line, and to join the B. Bi. C. as associate members would mean that our by-laws permit membership in no other cycle club in the city, and the prefix "associate" would not pass with the K. C. W. trustees.

Memories are all that remain of the L. A. W. Meet of 1889, and pleasant memories they must be, to judge by the smiles and winks that go round among the fortunates who were there, whenever "Meet" is mentioned.

Everything at Hagerstown was *wet*—in fact the only dry articles obtainable were a few remarks by "Jack."

Our worthy President was there, of course, and ever mindful of the welfare of the Division he so ably represents as Vice Consul. He, at the business meeting, took a decided stand in favor of retaining THE WHEEL as New York's "official organ." Though no definite arrangement was arrived at, the probabilities are that Chief Consuls will do as heretofore, *i. e.*, suit themselves, and we may hope for a continuance of the good work of THE WHEEL.

July 10, 1889. RAM LAL.

ERIE, PA.

Elwell's tourists have inspired a very un-Christianlike spirit in my breast. From the bottom of my heart I envy them. It is rather tantalizing to us poor stay-at-homes to hear what magnificent times the boys are having on the other side of the pond, and how they seem to be fairly pedaling themselves into glory everlasting. Queen Kap. in all her blackness failed to arouse such wide-spread enthusiasm among us Americans. But, then, we are usually termed a cold-blooded race, and the tax-paying portion more especially, seem to be very much opposed to public demonstrations. I wonder why?

In speaking of "cranks" Jack has omitted one species which I believe to be indigenous to small cities—say the size of Erie. This is the affectionate young bridegroom who takes his bride out for an evening's run. And verily it proves to be a "run" for her, for while "hubby" bowls along at a spanking pace on his wheel, with a good hard road bed under him, she takes to her heels—and the bricks—and makes such time as only a desperate woman can. And he, dear unselfish creature that he is, calls fondly back to her as he finally disappears in the distance, "are you tired, darling"? Probably "darling" isn't tired, but by this time I am. Still, mingled with my fatigue, is a feeling of devout thankfulness that I was not born a woman.

To offset this, Erie is blessed with a more practically considerate wheelman, who, though he hasn't yet provided his better half with any other means of locomotion than did her Creator, yet knows how to break up the monotony of a six-mile ride by "changing off." This certainly is an improvement over the tactics of the "affectionate" young man; but boys, why in blazes don't you get your wives some wheels of their own. It has been clearly demonstrated to us recently, that women can and do ride as well as men. The wheelwomen in Erie seem to have heaps of fun and it is only a question of time till every woman who can afford it will be riding a bicycle. It is certainly laughable, though, to follow along in the wake of the dear creatures as they roll through the aristocratic part of the city and note the diversity of opinion which prevails regarding the propriety or impropriety of a woman sitting a-straddle a wheel.

I understand that Dr. Drake is contemplating the purchase of a wheel. Whether as a matter of business or pleasure, I am not informed. One would suppose, however, in his profession the two might be easily combined.

What is the matter with Erie's Cycling Club? I haven't seen them out together this season. With such roads and such weather as we are enjoying at present, this is disgraceful. Let us hope the run that is now talked of will not fall through. N.

The attention of traveling cycle agents, desiring to handle a side line of goods, is called to the advertisement of one of the large German cycle spoke makers, appearing in another column. The work of this firm has a high reputation abroad.

BUFFALO.

The talk of a Fall tournament will be settled at the meeting of the Ramblers this week. From the present indications it is safe to say that a meet will be held in Buffalo this Fall that will be the biggest thing of the kind attempted since the palmy days of Springfield. The Ramblers have proved themselves to be hustlers of the most pronounced kind, and with a membership of 157, and Ducker at the helm, the most flattering aspects are presented for a successful meeting. An effort will probably be made to secure the State meet, and as Buffalo has proved herself a most generous hostess in the past, the invitation will be accepted without doubt.

The history of the Ramblers Club is an interesting one, and shows what pluck and persistency will do in cycledom. On the evening of January 26, 1885, a meeting was called by some wheelmen at No. 587 Main Street, when the organization known as the Buffalo Ramblers Bicycle Club was formed. This club began its existence with a total membership of twelve, and during the year 1885 the number was increased to thirty-three. During the first and second year the club had one continuous struggle for existence, and only for the persistent efforts of the members, such a club as the Buffalo Ramblers would not now be known.

During the first year meetings were held at No 587 Main Street, and in February of 1886 club-rooms were secured in the Armory Roller Rink. On the evening of February 16, the first meeting was held in the new club-rooms, and on the night of February 22, the Armory was destroyed by fire, entailing a considerable loss to the club and leaving it homeless. It was about this time that some members of a rival organization gave the Ramblers six months to live, but they were made of better stuff than credited with, as is shown by the flourishing condition of the club at the present day. The fire was quite a blow to the Ramblers, but they did not give up.

The former club-rooms, at No. 587 Main Street, were engaged and life begun anew, although with a considerably decreased membership. Another set-back to the club was had in 1886, when it held a tournament which was a failure financially. The year 1886 might well be called the Ramblers' "blue year." As 1887 progressed, the club began to take courage, and although fourteen resignations were handed in to the club, and accepted, the year was ended with a membership of twenty-eight.

The years '88 and '89 will be memorable in the life of this club. 1888 was ended with a membership of seventy-eight, showing an increase for the year of fifty members. A still better record has been made thus far this year, the club having increased its numbers to 157, which shows an increase in six months of seventy-nine, an average of over thirteen members each month.

Increase in membership means increase in accommodations, and the subject of a club-house is being frequently discussed. It is predicted that the Ramblers will have a club-house before another year. The walls of the club-rooms are decorated with a number of pictures which have been won at several contests in which the club has entered.

This club holds the best record for time from Erie to Buffalo, 100 miles, having made the run in nine hours and fifteen minutes, riding time, in the summer of '85. They also hold the record for bringing through the largest number at one run, thirty-four out of thirty-five members, on June 23 of this year, besides bringing four visitors at the same time, making a total of thirty-eight out a possible thirty-nine. The riding time was ten hours and fifteen minutes.

Miss Rummill and Miss Prince have accomplished a ride of which they may well be proud. One day last week they rode from Buffalo to the Falls and return, a distance of fifty miles, over roads that are anything but good. They made the run easily, and can now claim the longest record ride of the ladies. Thus far this season Miss Rummill has ridden 1,400 miles on her bicycle.

ZO.

CINCINNATI.

Although I had my bad luck with me last Sunday, and could not go to see the Cincinnati Club's race, I secured a fairly accurate description of it from a more fortunate friend. Here is what he says:

The club-house was left at 7 A. M. and Carthage, the starting-point, reached at 8:15. The racing men were sent off at 8:55. Nearly all the members entered, but only a few were "in it" from the start. Thos. Wayne, the winner, found the backbone of his own wheel was broken, but had pluck enough to borrow another wheel and go through.

Distance run was 14 miles and time 8m. Some of those entered say they were frequently compelled to slow up, for fear of interfering with the "racers." One of the club, who rides a wheel built in England after his own ideas (back wheel 22 inches and geared to 60), met with a mishap, his saddle spring breaking. But for that he would have stood a good chance of winning.

When riding back to Hamilton the club had formed in two lines. My informant was riding on the side-path, when he was ordered to fall in in the rear of the club if he wished to ride with them.

The "Duke" giving orders soon found he was talking to a free American citizen, that had no intention of obeying.

The man that took a header when tipping his hat to a pretty girl has my sympathy.

Some of the unattached riders in this vicinity are going to try and lobby a bill through the Legislature this fall giving legal possession of all roads to the Cincinnati Bicycle Club, and anyone then wishing to ride will have to obtain a permit. At the races this coming fall, the "Duke" may have a chance to see how much dust "Safety's" back wheel can kick up.

Will Strauss got lost in Hartwell, and after riding over a few telegraph poles his wheel got tired and kicked him in the mouth. He is not saying a word just now.

I met with a sight this morning that was new to me. While walking in Sycamore Street, which is paved with asphalt, I saw a safety rider pass at a 4-minute gate. Further down the street he took a fall, and I hurried to his assistance, thinking him hurt.

As he rose up from the mud he held out a $5 gold piece in his hand, saying: "I took some chances, but got there all the same." Any one doubting this can see the gold piece by asking Charlie ——

SAFETY.

A. C. Banker will try for the Irvington-Milburn course record after the racing season ends.

New York State Division L.A.W.

OFFICIAL ORGAN.

OFFICERS FOR 1889.

Chief Consul, W. S. BULL, 754 Main Street, Buffalo, N. Y. Vice-Consul, M. L. BRIDGMAN, 1255 Bedford Avenue, Brooklyn, N Y Secretary-Treasurer, GEO. M. NISBETT, 50 Wall Street, New York City. Executive and Finance Committee, W. S. BULL, M. H. BRIDGMAN, DR. GEORGE E. BLACKHAM, Dunkirk, N. Y.

NEW YORK STATE DIVISION NOMINATIONS—1889-1890.

For Chief Consul—W. S. BULL, Buffalo.
For Vice-Consul—M. L. BRIDGMAN, Brooklyn
For Secretary-Treasurer—GEORGE M. NISBETT, New York.
For Representatives, First District, comprising New York, Richmond and Westchester Counties:

J. C. GULICK, Citizens' B. C., - - New York.
W. H. DE GRAAF, Harlem W., - - do
J. L. MILLER, Riverside W., - - do
G. B. WATTS, JR., New York B. C., - do
J. A. CLAIRMONT, Manhattan B. C., do

For Representative, Second District, comprising Kings, Queens and Suffolk Counties:

CARL C. ALDEN, - - - Brooklyn.

For Representative, Third District, comprising Columbia, Greene, Rensselaer, Albany, Saratoga, Schoharie, Washington, Warren, Hamilton, Essex, Franklin, Clinton, Schenectady, Montgomery and Fulton Counties:

HENRY GALLIEN, - - - Albany.

For Representative, Fourth District, comprising Wayne, Oswego, Cayuga, Jefferson, St Lawrence, Lewis, Herkimer, Oneida, Madison, Onondago, Seneca, Yates, Ontario, Steuben and Schuyler Counties:

CHARLES W. WOOD, - - Syracuse.

For Representatives, Fifth District, comprising Chemung, Tioga, Broome, Tompkins, Chenango, Otsego, Cortland, Delaware, Sullivan, Ulster, Dutchess, Orange, Putnam and Rockland Counties:

CHAS. F. COSSUM, - - Poughkeepsie.
H. W. ARNOLD, - - Binghamton.

For Representatives, Sixth District, comprising Niagara, Orleans, Genesee, Wyoming, Erie, Livingston, Cattaraugus, Chautauqua and Monroe Counties:

WALTER S. JENKINS, - - - Buffalo.
WILL. G. SCHACK, - - - Buffalo.
ROBERT THOMSON, - - - Rochester.
DR. GEO. E. BLACKHAM, - - Dunkirk.

GEORGE M. NISBETT,
New York, July 8, 1889. Sec'y-Treas.

VOTING BLANK—1889-1890.

New York Division, League American Wheelmen.
MAIL VOTE.

For Chief Consul.....................................
For Vice-Consul......................................
For Secretary-Treasurer..............................
For Representatives:
..........................of..........................
..........................of..........................
..........................of..........................
..........................of..........................
..........................of..........................
Name...
Address..

N. B. Votes must be signed and returned to the Secretary-Treasurer on or before August 15, 1889.

Article IV., Sec. 2, L. A. W. Constitution—"Each Division shall elect a Chief Consul, Vice-Consul, Secretary-Treasurer and Representatives annually, between the 15th day of July and the 15th day of August, as follows:

"One Representative for each one hundred resident League members, also one Representative from each League club of not less than twenty members, and an additional Representative for each fifty additional members upon its roll on July 1. Club Representatives to be chosen each by the club of which he is a member. These shall constitute the Division Board of Officers."

Regular nominations as prescribed by the Division By-Laws can be found in the "L. A. W. Bulletin" for July 12, 1889. (See copy of nominations inclosed herewith).

Messrs. Strong and Green, of Philadelphia, are to make a change of location before long to the "Casino," where they will occupy two floors, the lower one to be used as a riding school. A large trade in Quadrant wheels is reported by this enterprising house.

The New York *World* of Sunday last published a dozen cycling paragraphs which simply bristled with errors of the most absurd kind. We even thought of reproducing it as a burlesque of facts. Our respect for the "great New York dailies" diminishes as we grow older. If the cycling column is absurd to cyclists, the athletic column amuses athletes. The only departments properly edited are those which are in the hands of experts.

ST. LOUIS—THE MISSOURI DIVISION MEET.

The Division meeting at Sedalia Wednesday and Thursday turned out to be even more enjoyable and successful in every way than the fondest hopes of the most enthusiastic had presaged, and the unfortunate ones who were not there missed a rare treat. In the first place, Sedalia possesses more advantages for entertaining a gathering of that kind than any other city in the State, and in the second place the wheelmen and citizens know just how to manage affairs of that nature. The first day's programme comprised a run to McAllister's Springs for the day and a "Smoker" in the evening. The hard rain of Tuesday night made the clay roads unfit for riding, and the boys only succeeded in getting five miles from town, two of which were made on foot. I have attended lots of "Smokers," but the one at Sedalia was incomparably the most enjoyable and best managed of them all. There were good cigars, tobacco, pipes, lemonade and claret-punch, all in abundance. The citizens turned out in force, and all vied in making the visitors welcome. Mayor Crawford, in a neat speech, extended the freedom of the city. He told the boys to go ahead and have a good time, and added, significantly, that if any of them got into trouble he knew the man who had the power to remit the fines. We immediately made him our next candidate for Governor.

The business meeting took place Thursday morning, and was conducted expeditiously and harmoniously. Mr. Brewster declined a re-election as Chief Consul and the choice fell on Robt. Holm. For the other officers the following gentlemen were chosen, viz: Vice-Consul, A. L. Jordan; Secretary-Treasurer, J. H. Kelley; Representatives, Walter Jaccard and Geo. A. Case; Chairman Racing Board, N. T. Haynes; Chairman Touring Board, C. B. Ellis. Mr. Brewster was chosen chairman of a committee to conduct the election and canvass the votes. Mr. Holm, who was chosen C. C., is a strong supporter of the League, and will put his whole heart into the work of his new office. Jordan will make a popular V.-C., and will prove a hard worker. There was no mistake made in selecting Joe Kelley as Sec.-Treas Jaccard, Haynes and Ellis, the Kansas City contingent, are all good men, and will make their influence felt in their district. Mr. Case can be depended on to keep the Southwest in line.

THE RACES.

The races were called at 2:30 P. M. Mr. Brewster was referee, Messrs. Ellis, Kelley and Child judges, Greenwood, Hoffman and Jaccard timers, and Holm clerk. The weather was perfect and the track in good condition, though slow. The Cycle Club men had trained hard for the events and presented a fine team. It was a veritable picnic for them, and the way they wiped up the ground with their adversaries was a caution. The Missouri Club only had four men entered, and of these only two, Hodgen and Ring, had done any training. Stone practiced the day before, and seemed to be riding strong, but he was run completely off his legs in the first race he entered, and finished last. He made no further attempts.

With the exception of Stone, the Missouri men rode ordinary road wheels, while the Cycle men had racers. This fact, however, did not affect the results. The Cycle men won on their merits: they were well coached, rode with intelligence and skill and deserved their success. They were "out for the stuff," and every first place but one fell into their hands. The one exception, appropriately enough, the consolation prize, went to the Missouri Club, but it was by the closest kind of a margin, Tivy only being beaten three inches He was ahead two yards from the tape, but Ring had a little spurt left, and lifted his wheel over the line just in time. In the team race Stone, Hodgen and Ring were named to represent the M. B. C., but Stone refused to ride, and as no substitute could be found the Cycle team, Barnard, Harding and Sanders, had the race to themselves. They went over the course in a hurry; in fact, they were feeling so gay that they ran away with themselves and could not be stopped until they had run an extra half mile, and even then they had to be pulled off.

The referee had a hard time of it; there were no less than five protests entered in the first four races, four for unfair starting and one against Barnard for foul riding. The protests against Pomerade, Mehlig and Barnard were overruled; the others were sustained. In the evening there was a grand display of fireworks by the Sedalia Flambeau Club, and afterward the banquet and presentation of prizes. Owing to the late hour of starting the banquet the toasts had to be dispensed with in order that the St. Louis men might reach the station in time for their train. Before the first course was brought on, however, Capt. L. L. Bridges, who could not remain to the banquet, made an address on the subject of "The bicycle as a vehicle in the eyes of law." This gentleman is a lawyer and speaker of national reputation, and his address was attentively listened to and enthusiastically applauded. He ventured the prediction that our old enemy Warner, of "Warner bill" fame, would be riding a bicycle inside of a year.

The toastmaster, Mr. Brewster, presented the prizes, and the proceedings closed with three rousing cheers for Sedalia, her wheelmen and her citizens.

The Cycle Club men had a great time on Thursday; it was clearly their day on. They landed on top in every event and kept registering all day long. They won over the dining-room girls, scooped the best things from the kitchen, took all the races and finally captured the girls from Jefferson City. Their pernicious activity caused many heartaches from the Missouri men and there were deep vows of future retribution. While the Cycle boys were justly jubilant and laughed with "ghoulish glee" whenever they accidentally poked a Missouri man out from under the bed or from behind a door, they were not offensive about it at all and no one begrudged them their good fortune.

Pomerade took pity on one forlorn M. B. C. man who was trying to hide behind a freight-car at the depot until his train arrived and offered to introduce him to the young lady from Jefferson City who hung confidingly on his arm, but the offer was declined. For fear that too much credit may be given Pomerade for this apparently generous act, it should be stated that the man he selected to bestow his favor upon was the only married man in the Missouri delegation and one who has a well-earned reputation for circumspect conduct when away from home. Is it not reasonable to suppose that Pomerade knew what he was about when he made the offer and had calculated the chances of its acceptance before he made it? Did he make any such offer to Alex. Lewis or Bob Holm? Not very much he didn't.

Dr. Henderson, of Kansas City, was there with his "sawed-off" bottle-green velvet coat, helmet, bugle and whiskers. The latter were carefully combed out at right angles with his face. This not only gave him a very distingue appearance but it also gave the wind a chance. The "ahs" and "ohs" as he passed in review before the grand stand must have been very gratifying even to him, modest and shrinking as he is known to be.

The Missouri men should remember that "sweet are the uses of adversity" if they will only take advantage of its teachings. They needed a little "swiping" of this kind to bring them to a realization of the situation, and the lesson will do them lots of good. Look out for them in August. As one man of the Cycle Club said with convincing emphasis but suspicious grammar, "We learned them a thing or two this time that they won't soon forget."

ITHURIEL.

A SELECTED LIST OF PATENTS.

[Reported especially for THE WHEEL AND CYCLING TRADE REVIEW by C. A. Snow & Co., patent attorneys, Washington, D. C.]

E. Mohrig, San Francisco, Cal. Bicycle.

F. J. Pratt, Jackson, Miss. Combination wrench.

O. Hanson, Worcester, Mass. Velocipede.

T. B. Jeffery, Ravenswood, Ill. Velocipede.

A. H. Overman, Newton, Mass. Brake for velocipedes.

All bearing date of July 9, 1889.

The party of American wheelmen reached Geneva July 7. All the party are in good health.

The Brooklyn Bicycle Club will have a run to Far Rockaway on Sunday next, leaving the club-house at 8:30 A. M.

W. D. Cruikshank, of Ovid, N. Y., sailed on Wednesday on the City of Paris. He will wheel through England and France.

The Cyclists' Union, of Long Island, was unsuccessful in its attempt to have bicycles admitted to Greenwood Cemetery.

A number of Eastern racing men will go on to the Lancaster, Pa., tournament, as the programme of events is very attractive to long-distance racers.

Darien, Conn., bicyclists organized a club on Wednesday evening. In the town there are said to be upward of fifty wheelmen and the number is increasing.

The rapid increase in membership of the Prospect Wheelmen, of Brooklyn, makes it necessary for the club to look for club quarters in the vicinity of Prospect Park.

The Hagerstown people were wondering where Secretary Bassett was. It seemed rather curious that the Secretary of the League should have absented himself from the meet.

Harry Hodgson loitered about Boston until Wednesday, spent Thursday in New York and left for New Orleans on Thursday evening. Harry will probably join the Maryland Bicycle Club.

Beginning on Thursday, August 1, it will be unlawful for bicyclists in Norwalk, Conn., to ride after dusk unless provided with a lamp and whistle, which must be blown at short intervals.

Psycho cycles are shipped the same day as ordered is the burden of the Capital Cycle Company's advertisement. Psychos showed up strong at Hagerstown, there being forty-one Psycho safeties all told.

M. L. Bridgman, President of the Kings County Wheelmen and the L. I. C. U., played the quiet, dignified gentleman at the League Meet, made a good speech and left an impression of worth and solidity. "Bridgy" is a man of destiny.

Mr. Coan, Superintendent of the Electric Light Co. in St. Catharines, Ont., met with a severe accident recently. He was riding a racing machine on Ontario Street, and ran into another bicycle and got a fall, cutting open his chin and spraining his arm.

"Bronson Hill," which was selected for the hill-climbing contest at the Bridgeport, Conn., meet of the L. A. W., is said never to have been climbed, save by two Bridgeporters, until Clark Barnum tried it. He succeeded, too, the first time, although the hill, which is a quarter of a mile long, tried him sorely.

Chairman A. W. Robinson and Capts. Cubberly, of Somerville, and Benson, of Dorchester, have called the next union run of Massachusetts wheelmen to Nantasket Beach for July 28. The headquarters will be at the Pacific House. Captains are requested to call their runs for that day in accordance with this notification, and to notify the committee before July 25 how many will attend.

SERIOUS LOSS BY FIRE.

The Pope Mfg. Co.'s stock at Boston was damaged to the extent of some three thousand dollars by fire and water last Tuesday evening. Prompt measures were taken to save as much as possible by covering with rubber blankets, the fire having caught on the roof, but the covering was not sufficient to protect against all damages. There will doubtless be some damaged Columbias for sale cheap.

The members of the New York Club deeply regret the sad death of their fellow-member, Mr. Frank C. Leeper. Mr. Leeper rode to Coney Island on Sunday last, and going in to bathe went beyond the life lines and was drowned. Mr. Leeper was a gook swimmer, and his death must have been caused by cramps. It was fully two hours after dinner before he entered the water, so that his death cannot be traced to lack of caution. At the June meeting of the club, held Wednesday evening, a committee was appointed to draft resolutions of sympathy.

RED HOT IN '90.

Trade for '90 promises to be red hot. The figures of the League parade, in which the "safes" actually outnumbered the "cranks," gauge the strength of the safety tide, and the waters seem to be rising still higher. Here are some of the trade rumors that float into this sanctum: That two New York gentlemen have organized a company; this is fact as well as rumor. That three large Western agents will manufacture or have wheels manufactured for them. That Rudge & Co. will be represented here, but that their product will not be named "Rudge."

PIONEER'S PENCILINGS.

I am so happy, and feel so grateful for the advantage that ladies now have with their safeties of enjoying themselves with their brother wheelmen that I cannot resist relating in your valuable columns, in as few words as possible, what a glorious time I had at the Tenth Annual Meet of the League of American Wheelmen.

Yes, I attended the meet, and I am sure that every one who did can only say that they had a most enjoyable time. Our Hagerstown boys certainly did everything to make each and every one happy.

There were nine in our party, and a jolly crowd were we: Deacon Raisbeck and Wm. De Graaf, accompanied by their charming daughters, Mr. and Mrs. Frisbie and the Messrs. Smith brothers and Mrs. Smith. We had such a jolly time in Hagerstown that after the meet we prolonged our pleasures by returning home via Washington.

Leaving Hagerstown on the midnight train of July 4, we reached our destination at 7 A. M. It took but a few moments to get our wheels out of the baggage car, and we were soon gliding swiftly along on the elegant streets. Of course, the usual question was not forgotten: "What did the band play?" * * * * This only increased our pleasure.

Well, we sought accommodations for the party only to rest their heads for a few hours.

Arrangements were made to meet at 10 o'clock A. M., and when I reached the hotel all were on hand. This day (Friday) we selected for sight-seeing. The Capitol was the first place, where we had every point of interest shown us. On leaving, the guide gave us permission to cut a chip of wood out of the Judge's desk in the House of Representatives.

Next was the Bureau of Engraving. We were the fourth bicycling party that had been shown through the building that day. Thence to the Smithsonian Institution and National Museum. Then another call, "What did the band play?" and in a few minutes we found ourselves looking out from the marble windows of the Washington National Monument. "Possibly as near heaven as we will ever get." Then followed eight minutes' coast in the elevator—not on wheels, but wire ropes.

The next important feature was to satisfy our appetites, and we soon had a delicious dinner before us. I am often ashamed of myself, for it seems since I have taken to the safety, I take these kind of runs so often, and my appetite grows so intense, that at home they declare they must increase my board bill.

After dinner, a run was made to the Soldiers' Home. This was most enjoyable on account of being taken in the cool moonlight. At 11:30 we returned home.

Saturday, the sixth day on the wheel, we arose early and took the road for a nine-mile run arriving at Cabin John Bridge at 8 o'clock with a most delightful appetite. We had ordered our breakfast by telephone; consequently it was awaiting us. We rested for a while in the sunny woods of Maryland, and then took our wheels for a hot, sunny ride back, via the National Arlington Cemetery. Here we had the pleasure of registering at the old homestead of Gen. Lee.

Another delightful day of pleasure nearly gone. Dinner was next on the programme, with a short city run; in the meantime we had our photographs taken.

I could hardly realize that train time was so fast approaching, and that we must part. We had experienced one continuous round of pleasure; and we hope not for years, nor forever, but until our next L. A. W. Meet.

At 10:30 the New York train took away our dear ones, and all that echoes back is "Annie Laurie."

I was pleased to see so many ladies attend the Meet, but hope to see more safety riders next year.

Such are the enjoyments on the two-wheeler. Can you blame me for persuading our fair sex to ride the safety?

PIONEER, 18173.

Washington, D. C., July 10.

RACES AT LANCASTER, PA.

Owing to unfavorable weather July 4 the Lancaster (Pa.) bicycle races were declared off for that date, and will be run on the afternoons of July 18 and 19.

The entries have been reopened and a club team race of three miles added. Teams to consist of three men.

Greater preparations than before are being made for this as a cycling event, and more prizes added.

Reduced rates at hotels have been secured, as follows: Americus, $1.75; Stevens, $2.00; Lancaster, European plan.

A special feature will be the lantern parade, to take place July 18, at 8:30 P. M. Capt. John B. Miller, of Lancaster, has charge of formation of line of parade.

Headquarters is at the Stevens House, where everybody will be made heartily welcome. With good weather, a large crowd should be present.

We append below a complete list of events for both days:

One-mile novice, open; 2-mile safety, open; 1-mile ordinary, open to boys under sixteen years; 1-mile Pennsylvania L. A. W. championship; 2-mile Lancaster Co. championship; 1-mile club safety; 3-mile club team—teams of three men; 1-mile "flying start," open; ½-mile Pennsylvania L. A. W. championship; 2-mile club handicap (safeties barred); 1-mile tandem bicycle, open; ½-mile club novice; 2-mile, open; ½-mile, "hands off," open; 3-mile lap race, open; 1-mile safety "consolation"; 1-mile ordinary "consolation."

PROGRAMME OF THE HARTFORD TOURNAMENT.

The Racing Committee of the Hartford Wheel Club are earnestly at work on the details of a cycling tournament, intended to be the greatest ever given in this country, and have decided upon the programme of races given below, subject to changes prior to August 1.

The club has also decided to give a 20-mile road race, to be run on the morning of the second day, open to any and all members of the League of American Wheelmen, the details of which will appear at a later date.

The committee on behalf of the Connecticut Division are hard at work arranging for the entertainment of League members who attend the meet. It is the intention of the committee to make this the largest and best entertainment ever given at any gathering of League men, and from both a racing and social standpoint the greatest event that has occurred in New England for years.

FIRST DAY, SEPTEMBER 4.

One-mile novice; one-mile novice, Rover type R. D. Safety (no wheel under 35 pounds); one-mile State L. A. W. championship; two-mile tandem safety National L. A. W. championship; one-mile Columbia Cycle Club handicap; one-mile open; three-mile National L. A. W. championship, Rover type R. D. Safety; two-mile handicap; one-mile open, Rover type R. D. Safety; one-mile, 3.00 class; one-mile team race (3 men), for Connecticut clubs only.

SECOND DAY, SEPTEMBER 5.

One-mile handicap (in heats), Rover type R. D. Safety; one-mile handicap (in heats); one-mile State L. A. W. championship, Rover type R. D. Safety; one mile Hartford Wheel handicap; one-mile, 3.20 class, Rover type R. D. Safety (no wheel under 35 pounds); five-mile lap; one-mile tandem safety handicap; one-mile, 2.50 class; one-mile consolation.

MISSOURI DIVISION RACES AT SEDALIA, JULY 4.

One-mile novice—J. R. Pomerade first, W. S. Snyder second. Time, 3.08 1-5.

Half-mile Missouri Division championship—E. Barnard first, J. M. Hodgen second. Time, 1.25 2-5.

One-mile safety handicap—R. Hurck first, G. E. Tivy second. Time, 3.22 2-5.

Two-mile bicycle handicap—E. N. Sanders first, A. M. Lewis second. Time, 6.10 3-5.

One-mile bicycle, open—A. G. Harding first, Jno. M. Hodgen second. Time, 3.03 4-5.

Two-mile championship, Missouri Division—E. Barnard first, E. N. Sanders second. Time, 6.35.

One-mile safety, open—R. Hurck first, Harry Gordon second. Time, 3.36 2-5.

One-mile team race, open—St. Louis Cycle Club, walk over.

One-mile bicycle handicap—A. G. Harding first, E. N. Sanders second. Time, 2.57 2-5.

One-mile consolation—V. P. Ring first, G. E. Tivy second. Time, 3.09 4-5.

GOOD TIME MADE ON THE ROAD AT PEORIA, ILL.

The 10-mile bicycle handicap between Peoria amateurs, which has been anxiously anticipated by lovers of the wheel and the public generally for some time, occurred yesterday afternoon on the Mount Holly road, and was witnessed by a crowd of 1,000 people, many ladies being among the number.

The road was in an exceedingly rough condition and covered in many places with loose gravel, making it especially hard on the wheelmen and very unfavorable for fast time. In the course selected there were fourteen hills to be climbed and descended, so the public can see at a glance what sort of an undertaking the ambitious aspirants had in hand. The start was made at thirteen minutes to five o'clock, in the following order:

	MINUTES.
George A. Monteith	12½
W. F. Harrah	12
Thomas Houghton	11½
L. H. Smith	10
Frank Lucas	9½
H. A. McGinnis	9
William Erler	8½
E. P. Blake	7½
C. R. Gibson	6½
Hiram Pierce	6
H. L. Pierce	5
F. F. Kneer	4½
Louis Finch	4
H. J. Smith	3
Bert Myers	Scratch

Long before Myers started many of the contestants were out of sight. He struck a terrific pace from the outset, and broke his previous record made on the same road two years ago (40m. 27s.), completing the distance, notwithstanding the rough road, in 37m. 10s., the fastest time of the race.

At Big Hollow, where the turn was made, the following was the order of the procession: Monteith, Harrah, Lucas, McGinnis, Erler, L. H. Smith, Vogelsang, Houghton, Kneer, H. L. Pierce, Blake and Downing, Hiram Pierce, H. J. Smith, Gibson, Schnebley, Misner, Finch and Myers, Hale.

The journey was continued and the finish was as follows:

	MINUTES.	SECONDS.
Geo. A. Monteith	47	15
W. F. Harrah	47	18
Frank Lucas	46	15
H. A. McGinnis	45	15
Wm. Erler	45	22
Bert Myers	37	10
F. F. Kneer	41	49
L. H. Smith	49	44
H. J. Smith	47	16
Hiram Pierce	45	30
H. L. Pierce	44	45
Thos. Houghton	52	30
E. P. Blake	49	27
Louis Finch	46	05
C. R. Gibson	50	33

Myers came in fresh and was greeted with a cheer, as was also Kneer, who made the next best time, 41m. 49s.

George A. Monteith, the winner of the race, is an employee of *The Transcript*, and, like Bert Myers, came from Toulon. W. F. Harrah, who came in second, is the son of the Rev. W. F. Harrah, pastor of Plymouth Congregational Church. Frank Lucas, third in the race, is a member of the Watch Factory Club, at which establishment he is employed.

The affair was under the management of the following gentlemen:

Referee, H. G. Rouse; judges, F. S. Reavis, H. H. Murray; timers, W. H. Smith, C. F. Vail, A. F. Westlake; checkers and scorers at the turn (Big Hollow), M. X. Chase, Jr., C. R. Beecher, J. E. Gilbert; checkers and scorers at finish (Jackson's Corners), W. H. McCulloch, F. D. Wolcott, B. L. Diefendorff; starter, C. F. Vail; official handicappers, W. H. Smith, President Watch Factory Bicycle Club; C. F. Vail, President Peoria Bicycle Club; A. F. Westlake.—*Peoria Transcript.*

A. H. Harkman spent three days of this week at the Victor factory.

J. K. Starley, of J. K. Starley & Co., is expected in this country shortly.

S. G. Whittaker and wife have left New York to spend a week at Washington.

Asphalt pavements are being laid on upper Broad and Clinton Streets, Newark.

A. E. Schaaf, of the Gormully & Jeffery Manufacturing Co., has been in Gotham. He will return within a week with Mrs. Schaaf and reside here during August.

George Updegraff was indefatigable. He placed an entire floor of his factory at the disposal of the press, but it was not used much. A newspaper man must be in the crowd.

C. E. Larom, of New Haven, finished first in the scorch from Hagerstown to Williamsport, on July 2. Purvis, Bruce, Shipsey, of the New York Club; Goodman, of the Hartford Club, were among the first six out of the fifty who started.

No man who attended the League Meet can forget Chief Consul Mott. Field-Marshal Mott was here, there and everywhere, yet bland and happy all the time. Mr. Mott was the "good, kind host" to perfection, and his efforts to oil the machinery of hospitality did not detract from the dignity of Maryland's Chief Consul. He is a truly great little man.

A. C. Banker rode in splendid form at Hagerstown, easily beating Wilhelm, Crist, Rich and Brown. Wilhelm was the fastest man at the meet bar Banker. Crist did not perform brilliantly and Brown was ill from the water. Rich was in poor shape and it will take him some time to get into form. Kingsland was ill and did not ride. Emmerson, who won the tricycle event in a canter, and romped home in the novices' race, is a new man, powerfully built, and should make a 2.35 man. We doubt if he will train for path racing, as he is married and could scarcely spare the time necessary to get fit.

THE PULLMAN COURSE.

The Pullman road race-course has never been accurately surveyed, but measures about 15⅛ miles by cyclometer. With the exception of the "sand hill," which is not much of a grade, and which is unridable for 75 yards, there are no hills worth mentioning. Eight miles of the course are perfectly smooth. The 9th and 10th miles are moderately good country road. The 11th, 12th, 13th and 14th miles are rough, uneven and hard to ride. The last mile is excellent, macadamized road, but with quite a number of right-angle turns in it. The best time over the course is 53m. 19 1-5s., by N. H. Van Sicklen.

EDITOR THE WHEEL:

Noticing the remarks of "Ram Lal" in "K. C. W. Notes" in your last issue, I would like to state that he misrepresents us in various ways. We did not keep our men inside the dressing-room until the team race was called, but, on the contrary, each one of us, with the exception of Banker, rode a hard race before this event was called.

In regard to the K. C. W. team having been tired out before the team race, I would say that we will accommodate them with another race if they desire to show what they can do when fresh. They can have the same men, the same distance and the same track, or may substitute other members of the team should they chose to do so. While we naturally feel elated over our success, we should like to meet the K. C. W. team again—for a suitable trophy—and then we should feel satisfied that the best team won.

I should like to hear from the K. C. W. in regard to this matter, and hope that they will consider this note simply an announcement that we wish to give all a fair show.

JOHN W. SCHORFER,
For the Berkeley Team.

[A match between the teams of the two clubs would make an interesting race. It is true, nevertheless, that the K. C. W. men had taken much out of themselves before the team race was ridden.—ED.]

ELWELL'S PARTY IN LA BELLE FRANCE.

GOOD-BY TO ENGLAND.

On Monday, June 17, we found ourselves, after the usual haps and mishaps incidental to packing a trunk, prepared to leave London and England. Guided by our landlord on a trike and accompanied by Dring, Philpot, and other metropolitan wheelmen, we slipped over Westminster Bridge and were successfully landed in the suburbs without mishap, although not without occasional attacks of the "shivers," for riding across this city at 9 o'clock in the morning can hardly be regarded as a pleasure trip.

ENTERTAINED BY FATHER OF FRANK WOOD.

Here we stopped for a few minutes to accept the hospitality of Mr. Wood, father of the great English amateur Frank Wood, and to say a final adieu to London, in which, despite the opinion to the contrary of *Wheeling*, we could not but feel that we had many very pleasant acquaintances. The run to Brighton, fifty miles distant, was an unusually pleasant day's work, including a view of the country from the top of the famous Reigate Hill, which was the finest seen on the trip through England. This hill will be remembered as being the one on which the first hill-climbing contest was ever ridden in England. Fortunately for some of us, we rode down instead of up this incline.

Brighton is a lively seaside resort on the south coast, and by the tales told of some of the boys who went "down on the beach to hear the band play," I guess we struck it "in the season."

FROM NEW HAVEN TO DIEPPE.

The Paris, a very comfortable side-wheeler, left New Haven for Dieppe at 10:15 Tuesday morning, and some of the unfortunates who were unable to obtain their "'am and heggs" on time were obliged to indulge in some lively sprinting to cover the intervening seventeen miles in the allotted time. At the steamer landing we all felt very sorry to have to say good-by to "Paed" Wilson, who has been with us since our landing at Queenstown, as a member of the party and as correspondent for two of the leading cycling journals in England. Although since his boyhood he has been afflicted with total deafness, he has achieved great success on the race track, and is known as the best road rider in England, and as a cycling scribe is possessed of talents second to none. Always cheerful and smiling under all circumstances, he was a most popular and valued member of the party, and his absence will be severely felt throughout the remainder of the tour.

THE CHANNEL SMOOTH FOR ONCE.

The trip across the English Channel was a decided improvement upon that across the Irish Sea, although the passengers, exclusive of our party, did not seem to think so. By dint of keeping our minds on subjects other than seasickness, the whole party (with one or two exceptions) managed to land at Dieppe accompanied by our breakfasts entire.

The customs officials were rather inclined to frown upon us, but either the simon pure accent or the " winning ways " (possibly the combination of the two) of our Joseph Pennell easily averted the threatened catastrophe, and we were allowed to proceed in peace to our hotel, the " Cellar Door " (Solieul D'Or).

DISTANCE FROM HOME NOW REALIZED.

The fact that we are over three thousand miles from home and in a foreign country struck us with full force for the first time, when we looked about at Dieppe and found ourselves unable to read the signs on the stores or understand what the people were talking about. Heretofore our travels have been in the United Kingdom, where we found friends on every side and all things, to a certain extent, just as they are at home ; and we did not fairly realize what a distance separates us from the home of Uncle Sam. Our five days in France, however, have brought us to a realizing sense of where we are, and some of our bluffs at the language are sufficient to bring tears of laughter to the eyes of a deaf and dumb Frenchman.

FINEST ROADS YET SEEN.

We had an idea that the roads in England were about as good as roads could possibly be

made, but we take it back now, for the thoroughfares here are far superior. I cannot give you any idea of what fine riding we have been enjoying. Not only are the surfaces as hard and smooth as time and money can make them, but every hill is graded and whittled down to such an extent that anything in the shape of an incline, if it be not more than half a mile long, is hardly noticeable. It is, in fact, a paradise for cycling, and the only wonder is that the sport is not more popular than it is.

THE FIRST RUN ON FRENCH SOIL.

The run from Dieppe to Rouen, of forty miles, which we had laid out as a day's work, was easily accomplished between eight o'clock and eleven or half past, and the following day we did the seventy-one miles to St. Germain very handily. As none of us are particularly strong riders and one of us at least a rather poor one, this speaks volumes for the roads. At the latter place we had a glimpse of Parisian life. The grand old forests are converted into a vast year, is thronged. We had our first glimpse of the celebrated Eiffel Tower from this place. The following morning we were met by twenty or so of French wheelmen to guide us into Paris.

CURIOUS WAYS OF FRENCH CYCLISTS.

French wheelmen are curious chaps. Their idea of entertaining us on the way seemed to consist of firing pistols, keeping up a continual blowing of bicycle horns, and photographing us once in every fifteen minutes. Having our pictures taken and never seeing even the proofs has long since gotten to be a "chestnut" of a wormy order. They also treated us to cold lemonade and allowed us to pay thirty cents a glass for it ! However, their intentions were good, and we sympathized with what grace we could muster. Our quarters in Paris we found to be very pleasant and centrally located, just off the Rue de Rivoli, opposite the Tuileries. The proprietor is a genial fellow, who speaks very good English, which I assure you is a great convenience.

HAVING A GREAT TIME IN PARIS.

In spite of the language and extremely primitive breakfasts, I am afraid it is going to be hard work for Mr. Elwell to persuade the boys to mount their wheels and leave Paris behind them on Saturday morning next. There is so much of interest to be seen in Paris, and so much to enjoy, that one and all will be very loth to leave the gay city.

Yesterday (Sunday) we were invited by the members of the *Circle de la Pedale* to take a run to Versailles, look about, and witness the junior races to be held there. Quite a large number of the boys availed themselves of the opportunity and enjoyed a treat, for Versailles is magnificent. We were well looked out for by Mr. H. O. Duncan and M. Louis Suerbie, of the above club.

THE WAY OUR FRENCH BRETHREN CONDUCT RACES.

French bicycle races are most peculiar. They have no tracks but stake off a half-mile or so of their magnificent road, plant a turning post at either end, and up and down this rather novel race-course they run all their races. The sight at either end, of a dozen racing men, attired in very giddy " togs," slowing up and turning one of these posts in a bunch borders on the ridiculous. They have some very good men, although as a class they are not nearly such strong riders as the English and Irish cyclers. The sport is comparatively young in France, but is growing rapidly.

COMPATRIOTS MET ABROAD.

We see a great deal of D. J. Canary, the trick rider, who is performing here, and also of Woodside, the English racer, who is on outing in Paris. Buffalo Bill has invited the party to attend the "Wild West" show, and on Wednesday evening we are to be entertained in the rooms of the Metropolitan Bi. Club. It is needless to say that we are having a grand time here, and enjoying ourselves as only Americans in Paris can.

TAM O'SHANTER.

Captain N. H. Van Sicklen, of the Chicago Cycling Club, has challenged the Illinois Cycle Club to a team race, three to five miles ; teams of three or more, the race to take place on Cheltenham Beach track, August 24

COURTESIES TO THE AMERICAN TOURISTS IN FRANCE.

The American cyclists were entertained last night by their French wheeling brethren at the Restaurant Dehouve, the spacious private hall of which had been specially engaged for the occasion.

The reception committee was composed of M. Grossen, President of the Societe Velocipedique Metropolitaine ; Dr. Minart, President of the Sport Velocipedique Parisien ; M. Duhayon, Vice-President of the Cercle de la Pedale ; M. Pradelles, Secretary of the " Veloce Sport Parisien," and M. de Baroncelli, Chief Consul of the C. T. C., and Consul of the " Union Velocipediquede Français."

WELCOME, AMERICANS.

A cordial welcome was given by the French cyclists to the Americans, who partook of coffee and cigars. Immediately afterward M. de Baroncelli made a telling speech in French, in which he expressed the great sympathy that the French velocipedists felt for their American brethren. M. de Baroncelli rendered all honor to the American wheelmen, who had accomplished a feat never before performed by any foreign cyclists.

CYCLING COURTESIES.

M. de Baroncelli then presented the Americans with a detailed itinerary of the roads to be followed from Paris to Geneva, and said that the Consuls of the C. T. C. in the different towns through which they had to pass had been informed of their arrival, and would be ready to meet them and render any assistance or give any information in their power.

M. Baroncelli's speech was translated by one of the Americans in a manner which elicited hearty applause.

AMERICAN THANKS.

Mr. Elwell, the manager of the American party, replied to the French toast in English, saying that, while expressing the thanks of all the party for the cordial reception that had been offered to them, he could only add that the more the Americans had seen of France, the more they appreciated it. There were bonds of sympathy between the two countries, which were the more appreciated as one learned to know and love France and the French.

Mr. Elwell proposed the health of the French cyclists, and specially thanked M. de Baroncelli and those English and American wheelmen who had gone out to meet them on their arrival in a foreign land.

AGREEABLE ENTERTAINMENT.

As soon as the toasts had been duly honored, several of the French cyclists gave proof of their capability to entertain their guests, both vocally and instrumentally, and in order not to be behindhand in contributing to the evening's enjoyment, several of the Americans gave some capitally rendered choruses in English.

Among the visitors invited to assist in welcoming the American tourists were M. Mousset, M. Porten, M. Frank Mennons, M. Colvin, the manager of Humber's ; M. Herelle, M. G. Austin Taylor, the C. T. C. Consul for Colombes ; M. Lenepveu, M. Renaud, M. Medinger, M. Pagis, M. Canary, the well-known trick rider ; and M. Jules Dubois, who gave a wonderful imitation of a pedantic lady singing Gounod's "Berceuse."

The Americans were thoroughly pleased with their reception, which, they said, was one more red mark in their diaries of the pleasant times they had spent in Paris.—European edition of *New York Herald*, June 27.

ELWELL'S PARTY RECEIVE A KIND INVITATION FROM MAYENCE, GER.

We have to ask of you a great favor. It is known here to the cycling clubs of this district that a party of American cyclists are now in Paris. The committee of the Frankfort-on-the-Main and Mayence bicycle clubs ask us to write to Paris and kindly invite the gentlemen to come to the Rhine. Their best route in via Strasburg, Heidelberg and Darmstadt, on to here. The clubs will meet them and accompany the gentlemen on their tours, so as to show them the beauties of the district. The committee here will furthermore arrange to have me

gentlemen met, when they leave, by the clubs of the next districts, and they authorize us to say that they will meet nowhere such a grand, handsome reception as awaits them here. We will shortly forward invitations from the clubs here to the American cyclists, and beg you in the meanwhile to make known the contents of this letter to those gentlemen, whose abode you will surely know. A reply would greatly oblige.

We can only repeat that a grand ovation awaits the cyclists.

Please let replies come to the *New York Herald* reading-room in Mayence. Trusting that you will have the kindness to make known the contents of this letter to the cyclists.

EDWARD SAARBACH & CO.

Mayence, June 24, 1889.

—European edition of *New York Herald*, June 27.

ELWELL'S PARTY AT THE "WILD WEST" SHOW.

In response to a kind invitation from Colonel Cody, the American cyclists now in Paris were present at the afternoon performance of Buffalo Bill's Wild West show yesterday afternoon.

The Americans started from their hotel at 2 P. M. Baron de Baroncelli, Chief Consul of the C. T. C., was, with his usual kindness, on hand to pilot them, and on their way they were joined by several American, English and French resident cyclists.

Upon arriving at the Wild West the horns "tootled," and in obedience to orders a private door opened. In went the cyclists, and spun once around the camp, to the great astonishment of the vastly increasing crowd of French spectators. Wheels were "stacked," and Colonel Cody, accompanied by Mr. Nate Salisbury and Major Burke, advanced to welcome the "boys" from across the sea.

A PRIVATE VIEW.

After a little friendly conversation with Colonel Cody, the American guests and their resident friends were conducted round the camp and the stables by Major Burke. Thence they were taken to the boxes reserved for them. Their entry was signaled by the playing of "Yankee Doodle" by the band.

When the performance began the horseman carrying the American flag was greeted with cheers of great enthusiasm by the American visitors. So also was Buffalo Bill, when he rode gracefully up and saluted them.

When the Deadwood coach started on its journey across the plains swarming with Indians, four of the American cyclists bravely took their places therein, taking with them Miss Agnes Taylor, one of the charming little daughters of the British Pro-Consul.

AMERICAN CHEERS FOR COLONEL CODY.

After the performance, which was greatly appreciated by the enormous house, and not less by the invited guests, the American cyclists proceeded to visit Colonel Cody in his tent, to thank him for his kind reception. As the Colonel appeared at the door to ask them in, the "boys" gave him a real American cheer.

"What is the matter with Colonel Cody?"

"He's all right!" in chorus, followed by the "Ou-Ouah" and the loud spelling of "A-m-e-r-i-c-a, U. S. A." The French spectators who had followed the little band so far were much interested, and when, after taking leave of Buffalo Bill, the American cyclists and their friends mounted to leave the camp, their departure in single file was witnessed by at least a thousand people, who cheered as they formed themselves into marching order outside the gate.

The visit of the Americans was a great success. They themselves were immensely pleased with the show, and Colonel Cody was not less gratified with the Americans' enthusiastic appreciation of it.—European edition of *N. Y. Herald*, June 28.

WHAT TO WEAR DURING THE SUMMER.

The underclothing should be of light-weight merino or balbriggan. This is preferable to any other material because it absorbs perspiration and does not retain or attract heat. The shirt should have long or at least half sleeves. The ends of the garments should be woven to fit snug. On very warm days, a flannel outside shirt and light colored and light weight trousers in addition to the merino underclothing outfit will make the best outfit obtainable. We have tried it and proven this theory of summer dress.

WHEEL GOSSIP

Wilhelm's racing safety is geared to "87."

Purvis-Bruce is importing a 27 lb. Referee.

The floating concert will be given by the Louisville, Ky., Cycle Club on the 17th.

Whittaker will go into training in August, and will try for path and road records this fall.

George Banker, the Banker Brothers' other brother, has just made his début on the path.

The sixth and final race for the Batson trophy will be run at New Orleans July 14. Course: St. Charles Avenue from Napoleon to Carrollton.

President Buckman, of the Minneapolis Bicycle Club, recently collided with a carriage on Fourth Street in that city, breaking his left arm at the elbow.

Genial J. Purvis-Bruce, well known as "Jack," is making a big reputation for himself in the cycling business as well as in the literary world.—*Philadelphia Item*.

New Bedford, Mass., has passed an ordinance prohibiting sidewalk riding; and also requires cyclists to carry lighted lamps after sunset. Both ideas are sensible ones.

Mr. H. Wade and daughter, of Newton Centre, Mass., are touring from North Adams to New York on bicycles, and were reported as in Great Barrington, Mass., June 29.

W. D. Banker, of Pittsburg, is the happy possessor of two beautiful Victor "safes," specially built, one a racer, under 30 lbs., the other a stiff-forked roadster, just over 30 lbs.

Mr. Birchfield, of the Louisiana Cycling Club, left Wednesday last for a three weeks' vacation, a good part of which will be spent awheel on the graveled pikes of Indiana and Kentucky.

Mr. William Brooks, of the firm of Morris & Lewis, Philadelphia, met with a painful accident on Oxford Street last week by taking a header from his bicycle. His face was badly cut and several teeth broken out.

West, of the Clark Cycle Company's Baltimore store, should show splendid form on the safety this fall. He is a medium-sized, heavy-built Englishman, and looks like a powerful rider. His new Rapid is geared to "75."

It is stated that Wm. Van Wagoner was to have made his first attempt to ride a safety a mile inside of three minutes, hands off, on the Roger Williams Park, Providence, R. I., about July 8. We await the result with interest.

Mr. J. M. Verhoff, of the New Haven Bicycle Club, in company with two wheelmen from Schenectady, N. Y., sailed for Europe July 1. The party will land at Glasgow, and ride through England, Ireland, Scotland, Germany and France on their machines.

The fastest records in the world should be made in Australia; the finest wheels should be built in America. By "finest" we mean not excellence of material, construction or finish, but this country, being essentially inventive, should produce some valuable ideas.

It is a singular fact that the first clergyman who has ridden down to Ripley in cycling uniform, and assisted in the service, is an American. The honor is held by the Rev. C. E. Fessenden, of Summit Hill, Pa., late rector of St. Phillip's Church, in the diocese of Central Pennsylvania.

Some time since one B. C. Leslie, claiming to hail from Indianapolis or Minneapolis, competed at San Francisco in a one-mile bicycle novices' race. The Racing Board desires better knowledge of this man's record, and would be glad of any information. Address Charles S. Davol, Warren, R. I.

The New York State Division nominations are published in another column. The men nominated are well known in their districts, with the single exception of C. B. Watts, New York Club. With so many prominent men in this club, one can hardly understand why a new and unknown member was selected.

The *Daily News* Paris correspondent says that the Minister of War has decided to create corps of cyclist messengers to be attached to the infantry. The officers are to ride tricycles constructed to carry a small case for plans and paper, a cartridge box, a rifle and some food. The soldiers are either to ride tandem bicycles or on ordinary machines.

The Stenton wheelmen organized at Wayne Station, Pa., last week. The following officers were elected to serve for one year: President, H. C. Remick; Secretary, Fred D. Jennings; Treasurer, Clarence Cowperthwaite; Captain, J. H. Weeks; First Lieutenant, J. H. Cowperthwaite; Second Lieutenant, Charles Wrigley; Bugler, Fay Donkelberger.

The officers and members of the Michigan L. A. W. Division will probably arrange for the business meeting at Ypsilanti, September 20, with the parade and races on the following day at Detroit. As the International Exposition will take place in Detroit, a large number of riders will be present, so that the event will be of a greater magnitude than any yet held.

Owing to the objections of local riders to making the 50-mile road race of the Springfield Bicycle Club an open-to-all race, it has been decided to have two events, a 50-mile open to all and a 50-mile open to local riders, to be run Friday, September 13, over the Springfield-Hartford course. It has been decided to reduce the entrance fee to $5, to be refunded to the first three men in. Entries will close September 1.

Mr. Bert McLean, of the Cambridgeport, Mass., Club is making arrangements for an excursion of a party to the summer carnival at Halifax, N. S., which begins August 5. It is expected that this party will leave Cambridge on August 3, attend the festivities of the carnival, which close upon the 10th, then wheel through to Annapolis, and, after resting for a brief period in that quaint old city by the sea, embark for home.

The regular monthly meeting of the Century Wheelmen, of Philadelphia, was held at the club-house on Friday night. The question of female membership was again brought up, but while the sentiment of the members is in favor of admitting ladies, it was decided that the club was not in position financially at present to incur the heavy expenditures which will be necessary to fit up quarters for their accommodation.

The bicycle club of Lansing, Mich., are to take a week's trip through Canada in August. The start will be made at Windsor, and the old "Talbot" road taken, via St. Thomas to London. There they will spend a day as guests of the Forest City Club. The return to Lansing will probably be made via Sarnia and Port Huron. Those of the Grand Rapids, St. John, East Saginaw and Bay City clubs that have accepted the invitation to join the Lansing boys will start August 18.

Wallace Ross and George Bubear, who have of late been road-sculling at Sale, have expressed a wish to ride against the best tricycle riders England possesses. They would be glad to take on any pedaler at from 25 to 100 miles on the path or on any fair road. This challenge has been taken up by Lee and Allard, who announce their readiness to pit tricycles against road-scullers. The rowers now express a desire that the cyclists shall ride machines equal in weight with their own.

At the annual meeting of the South End (Phila.) Wheelmen, held last week, the following officers were elected to serve for the ensuing year: Vice-president, J. J. Bradley; Secretary, T. W. McDougall; Assistant Secretary, Charles Hoffman; Treasurer, S. Young; Captain, C. A. Dimon; First Lieutenant, O. H. McCurdy; Second Lieutenant, H. M. Green; bugler, Charles W. Kolb. Mr. S. Jackson, Jr., was nominated for the presidency, but positively refused to serve; consequently that position is still vacant.

Some Englishmen are talking up the advisability of amalgamating the N. C. U. and the C. T. C. The N. C. U. legislates on all questions of the race-path, and is very much alive. The C. T. C. sells badges and coffee house lists, incidentally publishes a mummified monthly, and is very much dead. The C. T. C. membership was 21,000 in 1888, and now is 19,599, showing retrogression. Of its 21,000 members of 1888 over 5,000 failed to renew. There is little chance of the N. C. U.-C. T. C. amalgamation taking place.

While the Antique and Horrible procession was passing Mosely Block, Needham, Mass., July 4, a horse became frightened and sprang out to one side, upsetting and running over Mr. McCune, Superintendent of the Springfield Bicycle Company. Mr. McCune was considerably injured about the face and one ankle. The driver and owner of the horse, Mr. Bartlett, was thrown from the buggy when it came in collision with a team farther down the line, and was very badly injured by being run over. The horse was seriously injured.

The Pawtuxet, R. I., wheelmen have given up their club room, which they have occupied for about a year, and have had nicely fitted up. This has been brought about from several causes. The chief cause, however, is, that it had been practically of no use, as no meeting or club run had been held for some time, owing to the inability of a sufficient number to gather at the same time. The club, however, has by no means disbanded, and it is expected later on, when circumstances may be more auspicious, that it will again flourish.

The South End (Phila.) Wheelmen toured to Lancaster on July 3 to take part in the tournament given by the Lancaster Club on the Fourth. Rain prevented the races, for which Taxis, McDaniel and a number of Philadelphia flyers had entered, and they are postponed for a fortnight. The cyclers held their parade, headed by the Iroquois Band, and all the visitors were handsomely entertained by the Lancaster Bicycle Club. Representatives from the Williamsport, Wilmington, Reading, Kings County and other clubs were present in addition to the Philadelphia cyclers.

A KIND ACTION.

The following card of thanks from the Lynn *Daily Item* fully explains itself and shows that the world is not wholly devoid of thoughtfulness:

"I take this opportunity of thanking the teachers of the First Universalist Sunday School—Rev. N. R. Wright in particular—and others who have assisted in procuring a tricycle for my use, having been unable to walk for over two years on account of contraction of the cords caused by rheumatism. The "Silent Horse" at this time is indeed acceptable." A. BLAKELY.

The "American Team," under management of "Senator" Morgan, has again gone on the war-path, and this time is in pursuit of Australian scalps and shekels. They left Lincoln, Neb., July 4, for Salt Lake City, Utah, and go from there to Denver, Col. After filling a week's engagement there they go to San Francisco, sailing on Sept 1 for Australia. Morgan's backer, Mr. John J. Hardin, who accompanies the party, is rumored to be worth $100,000 in cash and Omaha real estate, and it is probable the party will neither have to walk home or trust to their bicycles to carry them back. Morgan says that all the stories regarding his marriage to Miss Oakes are false.

The following ticket for New Jersey L. A. W. officers has been proposed: Dr. G. Carleton Brown, of the E. W., Chief Consul; Dr. Benedict, of Jersey City, Vice Consul, and Mr. G. C. Pennell, of the E. W., Secretary-Treasurer. This is a strong ticket, and is supported by the large cycling clubs of the State and all of the prominent wheelmen. Dr. Brown's work while Chief Consul of New Jersey a few years ago is a guarantee of what he is able and willing to do. He built up the N. J. Division of the L. A. W. to be the third largest in the United States. Dr. Benedict is a popular member of the Hudson County Wheelmen, and an enthusiastic League member and worker. Mr. Pennell is President of the E. W., and his devotion in the cause is well known.

A PLEASANT TOUR.

Secretary C. F. Johnston, of the Louisville Cycle Club, returned from his tour on Thursday last, and reports a fine time. His route was as follows: By train to Frankfort, on account of bad weather, on Thursday; by wheel to Lexington via Versailles, thirty-three miles, time four hours, fine roads, Friday morning; the balance of the day was spent in visiting various places of interest, the principal one being the Chautauqua Assembly, a branch of the New York body. Wheel to Paris, Blue Lick, where a stop of two hours was made to visit the celebrated springs and enjoy the scenery. After dinner, wheel to Flemingsburg, Ky., over the finest pikes in the State—the day's run being fifty-eight and a half miles. The next two days were spent in riding to the small towns within a radius of fifteen miles of Flemingsburg. Fleming County is, no doubt, the banner county of Kentucky in the number of miles of pike. It has over 300 miles, and all in fine condition. The return trip was all by train, on account of very bad weather.

FIXTURES.

July 17, 1889.—Two-mile Bicycle Race at Caledonian Games, Minneapolis, Minn.

July 20, 1889.—Race Meeting of the East Hartford Wheel Club, at East Hartford, Conn. Entries close July 16, with Mr. E. E. Arnold, East Hartford.

July 20, 1889.—One-mile and 25-mile Bicycle and 5-mile Tricycle N. C. U. championships at Paddington, Eng., track.

July 25, 1889.—At Minneapolis, Twenty-five Mile Road Race for Championship of Minnesota. Entries close July 20 with Will. Monarch, Secretary-Treasurer, Minneapolis Bicycle Club. Entry fee, $1.

July 27, 1889.—One-mile and 25-mile Tricycle and 5-mile Bicycle N. C. U. Championships at Paddington, Eng., track.

August 8, 9, 10, 1889.—Annual Meet of Massachusetts Division L. A. W., at Cottage City.

August 24, 1889.—Fifty-mile Bicycle and 1-mile Dwarf N. C. U. Championships at Paddington, Eng.

September 4-5, 1889.—Amateur Race Meet of the Hartford Wheel Club, at Hartford, Conn. Entries to be made with W. M. Francis, Secretary, P. O. Box 745.

October 23-29, 1889.—Race Meet at Macon, Ga.

EUROPEAN CYCLING FIXTURES.

Germany.—Berlin, July 21, September 15; Hanover, September 8; Cologne, August 12; Chemnitz, September 8; Frankfort-on-the-Maine, September 1; Mannheim, September 8; Crefeld, September 8. Hamburg.—Altona, September 22; Bochum, August 25; Madgeburg, September 8. Denmark.—Copenhagen International Meeting, August 18

CONNECTICUT DIVISION L. A. W. MEET, AT BRIDGEPORT, CONN., JULY 8.

Everything seems to have favored the Bridgeport Wheel Club in the meet just held there, and the whole affair may be pronounced a success. Early arrivals Sunday evening painted the town a mild shade of crimson, as might be expected from the example just set at Hagerstown. Among prominent Connecticut wheelmen present we note Messrs. Grandler, "Joe" Goodman, E. De Blois, Chapman, J. F. Ives, L. B. Gaylor, of the Eagle Bicycle Company, P. M. Harris, C. E. Moore, Chief Consul C. K. Larom, and others too numerous to give at length. The day of the races was clear but warm, mercury stopping its flight upward at 88°. Some two hundred and fifty took part in the parade at 12, to the delight of a large audience.

The races were run off on the half-mile track (trotting) in Seaside Park. The track's condition was good, and the wind blew down the homestretch at the finish. No gate fee being charged, some 5,000 people witnessed the races, which were run off in the order given below, and commenced at 2:30:

One-mile ordinary—W. G. Class, Berkeley A. C., first; time, 3m.; Ludwig Foster, Elwood, Conn., second; time, 3m. 1 1-5s.; C. B. Fuller, Danbury, 0; C. A. Fox, Bridgeport, 0; Geo. Smart, Hartford, 0; E. Van Wagoner, Milford, 0; L. L. Clarke, Berkeley A. C., 0; J. W. Schoefer, Berkeley A. C., 0; F. T. Reid, Hartford, 0; W. F. Murphy, Brooklyn, 0.

One-half mile ordinary, open—J. W. Schoefer, Berkeley A. C., first; time, 1m. 25 3-5s.; Ludwig Foster, second, time, 1m. 27⅖s. C. B. Fuller, Danbury, 0; C. A. Fox, Bridgeport, 0; Geo. Smart, Hartford, 0; F. Lebing, Bridgeport 0; L. L. Clarke, Berkeley A. C., 0; F. T. Reid, Hartford, 0.

One-mile safety—C. A. Pickett, New Haven B. C., first; time, 3m. 3⅕s.; Wm. Harding, Hartford, second; time, 3m. 4⅗s.; C. E. Larom, New Haven B. C., third; F. R. Townsend, Bridgeport, 0; E. S. Raymond, Bridgeport, 0; H. Tyler, Bridgeport, 0; J. F. Ives, Meriden, 0; W. F. Murphy, Brooklyn, 0.

Three-mile ordinary—L. L. Clarke, Berkeley A. C., first; time, 10m. 17 4-5s.; W. F. Murphy, Brooklyn, second; time, 10m. 19 1-5s.; Ludwig Foster, third; L. Lebing, Bridgeport, 0; C. B. Fuller, Danbury, 0; Geo. Smart, Hartford, 0; W. G. Class, Berkeley A. C., 0; F. T. Reid, Hartford, 0.

One-mile tandem ordinary—J. W. Schoefer and W. G. Class, first; time, 3m. 8s.; A. N. Welton and C. E. Larom, New Haven B. C., second; time, 3m. 8 1-5s.; W. Harding, Hartford, and L. Foster, Elwood, third, 0; J. Wilkinson, Bridgeport, and W. Gould, 0.

One-mile Bridgeport championship—C. A. Fox, first; time, 3m. 21⅖s.; F. Lebing, second; time, 3m. 22 1-5s.; W. A. O'Neil, third; F. E. Soule, 0; H. Elliott, 0.

One-mile consolation, ordinary—Geo. Smart, first, 3m. 56s.; F. T. Reid, second, 3m. 56 1-5s. (Only competitors.)

Hill-climbing contest—Hill to be climbed was about a quarter of a mile high, and was surmounted by the best men in following order: W. B. Clough, Stamford, Conn. (Eagle), 1m. 10s.; G. A. Pickett, New Haven, B. C. (Rambler), 1m. 13 4-5s.; G. S. Hills, Bridgeport (Columbia Light Roadster), 1m. 15 2-5s.; H. J. Tyler (Columbia Light Roadster Safety), 1m. 21s.

The races and hill-climbing contest were in charge of the following gentlemen: Referee, C. E. Moore; Judges, R. B. Lacey, David Trubee, S. H. Jones, Geo. Prentice, D. S. Lacey; Timers, W. B. Middlebrok, Jas. H. Smith, C. F. Chew; Scorers, Wm. Richardson, Albert Bicks, H. J. Lebing, A. B. Post; Starter, P. M. Harris; Clerk of Course, C. A. Reed; Umpires, Geo. Fryer, Jas. Torry, F. M. Halligan, H. A. Morris.

The evening was closed with a performance at Wagner's Summer Garden, attended by about 150. The chief attraction of the evening and a genuine surprise for the boys was the appearance on the stage of Chief Consul C. E. Larom, in minstrel make-up. He gave an amusing speech à la Dockstader, and introduced many telling hits.

A 2-mile handicap will be decided at Cape May on Saturday. The entries are: F. S. Brown, scratch; W. W. Tasis, 15 yards; A. A. Zimmerman, 60 yards.

BICYCLE RACES AT ST. CATHARINES, ONT., JULY 2.

The postponed races of the bicycle tournament took place at Fairvale Driving Park, on July 2. Most of the wheelmen had departed for their homes, but all who had entered in the races remained. A petition, asking that the stores be closed, was handed around during the forenoon, and, in consequence, the majority of the business places were closed in the afternoon. About two o'clock the bicyclists, headed by the Nineteenth Reg't Band, took up the line of march for the course, where a goodly number had assembled. The weather was very warm, but it had the effect of placing the track in good condition, after the heavy shower of the day before. Everything went off smoothly, save a collision which occurred in the five-mile race between Messrs. Rassicoe, Connolly and Carman, in which the machines of those who collided were pretty well broken up, but no other injury followed. The following were the events:

Two-mile novice—First, W. B. Parr, Ottawa; second, G. S. Dunn, Hamilton; third, F. W. Hudson, Wanderers, Toronto. Time, 6m. 27 1-5s. Thirteen started. One-mile championship—First, E. O. Rassicoe, Woodstock; second, Bert Brown, Toronto. Time, 3m. 21s. Half-mile run and ride—First, W. A. Lingham, Belleville; second, D. F. Blythe, Ottawa; third, E. W. Walbourne, Woodstock. Time, 2m. 5⅕s. Six started. Smith, of Woodstock, led to the quarter-mile pole, but was passed after mounting his wheel. Three-mile lap race—First, W. S. Campbell, Niagara Falls, N. Y.; second, E. Folsom, Rochester, N. Y.; third, W. M. Carman, Mohawk. Time, 10m. 1s. Points, Campbell, 22; Folsom, 16. One-mile tricycle championship—First, J. H. Gerrie, Toronto; second, R. R. Fletcher, St. Catharines; third, W. S. Fletcher, same city. Time, 4m. 32 3-5s. One-mile, 3.20 class—First, C. J. Iven, Rochester, N. Y.; second, W. A. Lingham, Belleville; third, W. M. Carman, Mohawk. Time, 2m. 56 1-3s. Twelve started. Half-mile dash—First, W. S Campbell, Niagara Falls, N. Y.; second, W. H. C. Mussen, Montreal. Time, 1m. 31⅖s. Two started. This was a very fine race, the finish being particularly close. Five-mile championship—First, Bert Brown, Toronto; second, E. A. Rassicoe, Woodstock; third, J. H. Gerrie, Toronto. Time, 16m. 57⅖s. Three started. In this race Rassicoe and Gerrie collided after passing the tape at the end of the fourth mile. Rassicoe started again, but could not catch Brown. One-mile safety—First, C. J. Connolly, Rochester, N. Y.; second, R. S. Peniston, Toronto; third, W. J. Morgan, Ottawa. Time, 3m. 14⅗s. Six started. Half-mile without hands—First, J. H. Gerrie, Toronto; second, E. W. Walbourne, Woodstock; third, C. J. Lowes, Toronto. Time, 1m. 40s. Three-mile roadster—First, J. Gessler, Niagara Falls, N. Y.; second, W. A. Lingham, Belleville; third, C. J. Lowes, Toronto. Time, 11m. 36⅗s. Five started. Gessler, of Niagara Falls, rode a safety, and made a great finishing spurt with Lingham on the last lap. One-mile club championship—First, James Walker, St. Catharines; second, W. J. Bailey, St. Catharines; third, Ed. Everett, St. Catharines. Time, 3m. 17s. Five-mile, open—First, W. S. Campbell, Niagara Falls, N. Y.; second, W. H. Mussen, Montreal; third, Bert A. Pratt, Rochester, N. Y. Time, 17m. 57⅗s. Seven started. The men were all bunched together after passing the tape, after the fourth mile had been made, when some of the racers ran up against Rassicoe's little wheel, giving him a terrible header, and capsizing Carman and Connolly, whose machines were all pretty well broken up. Rassicoe has certainly had terribly hard luck. He states that he was well within himself, and with any amount of speed in reserve for the finish when the accident occurred.

The hill-climbing competition prize was won by Bert A. Pratt, of Rochester, N. Y.—*St. Catharines Journal.*

RACES AT THE KANSAS L. A. W. MEET, JULY 3 AND 4.

The races of the Kansas Division L. A. W., at Ottawa, Kansas, resulted as follows:

FIRST DAY.

Half-mile novice—W. H. Caniff, Topeka, first; W. A. Scheel, Emporia, second. Time, 1m. 35 2-5s.

One-mile Kansas City and Kansas—H. S. Hale, Junction City, first; W. A. Scheel, second. Time, 3m. 13 1-5s.

Half-mile handicap—W. C. Kerr (200 yards), Burlington, first; A. B. Mulvane (100 yards), Topeka, second; Colie Bell (scratch), Minneapolis, Minn., third. Time, 1m. 11 1-2s.

Five-mile Kansas championship—Won by Mulvane against A. J. Henley, Wichita. Time, 16m. 48 1-2s.

Half-mile L. A. W. championship—Colie Bell, first; Henley, second. Time, 1m. 20 1-2s. In this race a special prize of a $65 diamond shirt stud was to have been given if time equaled 1m. 19 1-5s., made by Windle in 1888.

Boys' race, half-mile—Geo. Hubbard, Olathe, first; Ollie Shiras, Ottawa, second. Time, 1m. 40s.

One-mile handicap—Colie Bell (scratch), first; H. S. Hale (200 yards), second. Time, 2m. 51 3-4s.

One-mile State championship—Henley first, Mulvane second. Time, 3m. 07 1-4s.

One-half mile, hands off—H. S. Hale, first; competitors Caniff and Scheel disqualified. Time, 1m. 43 3-4s.

Two-mile handicap—Henley (35 seconds), first; Scheel (40 seconds), second; Colie Bell (scratch), distanced. Time, 6m. 35s.

SECOND DAY.

Half-mile novice—J. H. Lane, Burlington, first; O. S. Townsend, Topeka, second; Lee Patrick, Ottawa, third. Time, 1m. 32s.

One-mile handicap—Hale (scratch), first; Kerr (8 seconds), second. Time, 3m. 12s.

Half-mile State championship—Henley first, Mulvane second. Time, 1m. 26s.

Ten-mile L. A. W. championship—Won by Colie Bell in 35m. 03 3-4s. Henley second.

Half-mile safety—T. E. Glavin, Kansas City, first; G. H. Smith, Kansas City, second. Time, 1m. 46s.

Half-mile handicap—Seven starters, Hale and Mulvane, scratch; Scheel and Lane, 75 feet; F. W. Metcalf, of Olathe, Patrick, and Hubbard, 150 feet. Hale won in 1m. 26s.; Hubbard second.

One-mile handicap—Henley (scratch), first; Mulvane (scratch), second; Kerr (100 feet), third. Time, 3m. 03s.

Half-mile consolation—J. M. Hill, Topeka, first; Metcalf, second. Time, 1m. 36s.

The closing event of the race programme was an effort on the part of Colie Bell to lower Windle's record. Though unsuccessful, the effort was highly creditable, considering the condition of the track and the strong wind. Time for half mile, 1m. 20 1-5s.

POOR HANDICAPPING AT BOSTON, JULY 4.

There was not the usual large attendance at the cycle races, which was due to the fact that they were held at Franklin Park instead of on Boston Common. There was little enthusiasm, and the races were never more dull or uninteresting. There was a great lack of proper police detail, and many people were allowed at the finish who had no business there. The crowd pressed into the track, and there was nobody to stop any one from crossing. Wheels were allowed on the track during the races. The officials were recognized wheelmen this year, but this did not prevent their work from being a flat failure. The races did not begin promptly, there were long waits, and it took over two hours to run the short programme. The handicapping was done by the League handicapper, and could not have been worse. There were three handicap events, and they were all robbed of any interest by the fact that the scratch men had no earthly show to win, and were out of the races before they began. The Clark brothers justly kicked against the severe handicap imposed upon them in the tandem race. The track was up-hill for 50 yards, and about 240 feet short of a mile. The scratch man, therefore, had to begin with an up-hill task, while the others were exempt from this additional handicap.

The events resulted as follows:

One-mile novice—A. K. Pressy, Newton, first; A. H. Rhodes, Hyde Park, second. Time, 2m. 41s. Won easily. Quarter-mile open, first two in each heat to ride in the final. First heat—P. J. Berlo, first; J. Clark, Dorchester, second. Time, 36 2-5s. Second heat—J. P. Clark, Dorchester, first; G. I. Whitehead, Everett, second. Time, 36 3-5s. Final heat—P. J. Berlo, first; J. P. Clark, second. Time, 34 4-5s. Quarter-mile open for safeties, first two in each heat to compete in final. First heat—A. P. Benson, Dorchester, first; W. S. Doane, Dorchester, second. Time, 38s. Second heat—P. J. Berlo, first; A. W. Scott, Hyde Park, second. Time, 37 2-5s. Final heat—P. J. Berlo, first; A. P. Benson, second. Time, 37 2-5s. One-mile bicycle handicap—H. G. Andrews, Hyde Park, 200 yards, first; C. R. Felton, Somerville, 200 yards, second. Time, 2m. 16 1-5s. J. P. Clark, the scratch man, covered the distance in 2m. 30⅘s., but the handicap was so great that he came in among the last. One-mile safety handicap—A. W. Porter, Newton, 75 yards, first; W. G. West, Boston, 100 yards, second. Time, 2m. 25 2-5s. W. S. Doane, scratch, made the distance in 2m. 36 2-5s., the fastest ever made by a safety on this track. One-mile tandem safety handicap—A. W. Porter and B. F. Leavitt, 150 yards, first. Time, 2m. 18⅘s. The Clark brothers made no effort to win on account of the overwhelming handicap. One-mile consolation—E. J. Clark, Dorchester, first; E. H. Galloupe, Hyde Park, second. Time, 2m. 38 2-5s.

Campbell & Co., of Providence, R. I., are pushing the Singer Safety for all it is worth, and have an advertisement in a recent Providence paper that fairly bristles with that make's good points.

RACES ON LYNN COMMON, JULY 4.

The starting point was at the upper end of the Common, and as there were five races the interest was in proportion to the size of the crowd. Races were called promptly at 8 A. M., an early hour. In the first contest, the one-mile handicap, there were eleven entries and starters. Morris Greenwood was declared winner; G. S. Buttrick, second; J. H. Shurman, third; time, 2m. 48s.

The one-mile novice handicap was won by C. H. Taylor; Harry Basset, second; time, 2m. 57 3-4s.

One-mile Safety.—Carey Libbey, first; Chas. Kelly, second; time, 3m.

Boys' mile race.—Harry Wilson, first; James Downs, second; time, 3m, 178.

The two-mile handicap was won by Greenwood; Taylor, second; Buttrick, third; time, 6m. 16 3-4s. This race would have been won by Taylor, but for an unfortunate "spill" from his bicycle at the finish. Instead of taking his wheel with him across the line, he left it lying in the street and ran across. Had he done as he ought the race would have been his, for he had a lead of 15 to 20 yards over the others. Starter and referee, J. H. Young; time-keeper, T. F. Carroll.

RACES AT BROWNSVILLE, PA., ON THE FOURTH.

They had a big time at Brownsville on the Fourth. The Pittsburg delegation scooped everything, and the results show that there are a couple of boys from that city that are apt to make good men on the path with proper training—George Banker and H. H. Willock. The former won everything in which he was entered and the latter also succeeded in getting two firsts. F. G. Lenz won the 2-mile State championship, and is happy. Following is a list of the events and results:

One-half mile, novice.—George Banker, Pittsburg, 1m. 54s.; George Lysle, McKeesport, 2m. 95s.
One-mile, open.—G. Lenz, Pittsburg, 3m. 15s.; J. H. Gloninger, 3m, 37s.
One-half mile, 1:35 class.—H. H. Willock, Pittsburg, 1m. 44s.; Lee Higbee, Pittsburg, 1m. 57s.
One-mile lap race.—J. H. Gloninger, Pittsburg, 12 points; F. G. Lenz, Pittsburg, 18 points.
One-half mile handicap, for boys.—George Banker, Pittsburg, 1m. 55s.; Willie Golhrens, Brownsville, 1m. 55 3⁄4s.
Two-mile State championship.—F. G. Lenz, Pittsburg, 7m. 47s.; J. H. Gloninger, 7m. 54s.
One-mile, 3:00 class.—H. H. Willock, Pittsburg, 3m. 37s.; H. A. Davis, Pittsburg, 3m. 40s.
One-mile handicap.—George Banker, 3m. 15s.; J. H. Gloninger, 3m. 01s.
One-half mile, horse and bicycle.—A. M. Thompson and horse, 1m. 42s.; Chas. J. Foster, 1m. 42⅗s.

A 1-mile handicap, open to riders of Queens and Suffolk Counties, will be decided July 20 at the Queens, L. I. track. Entries close July 15 with Thomas Lloyd, Queens, L. I. The prizes are medals, offered by Mr. Lloyd, who is an enthusiastic supporter of cycling and all out-door sports. Mr. Lloyd will present a medal to any man, mounted on an ordinary, who rides a mile on this track inside 3m. 50 4-5s. He will also present a medal for the fastest safety record made this year at the Queens track.

RECORD-BREAKING AT LEICESTER, ENGLAND.

R. BILLSON LOWERS THE FIFTY MILES AMATEUR RECORD.

Splendid weather prevailed on the evening of June 22, when R. Billson, of Leicester, essayed to lower the fifty miles record (2h. 40m. 33 2-5s., made by C. Potter, Surrey B C., at Surbiton, on September 24, 1887), on the Belgrave Road track, which was in capital condition. Billson began cutting record at eleven miles, registering twenty miles in the splendid time of 58m. 38s., and crowding in nearly twenty and a half miles inside the hour. This naturally took a lot of the go out of him, and from 23 miles to 25 miles he was outside the existing figures. From 26 miles to 40, however, he again reduced the record, and from 44 miles to the finish of the 50 He was much distressed at several periods of the trial and also at the finish. Appended are the records made, also previous records:

DURATION			PREVIOUS RECORDS.		
MILES.	H.	M. S.		H.	M. S.
12........		31 59........			39 7 3-5
13........		34 49........			35 2 2-5
14........		37 47........			38 2 2-5	P. Furnival, Surbiton,
15........		40 43........			41 3 1-5	Sep. 22, 1887.
16........		43 45........			43 50 3-5	
17........		46 46........			46 55 1-5	
		49 44........			49 55 1-5	M. V. Cassall, Sep. 22, 1887.
18........		52 45........			52 53 2-5	
19........		55 50 1-5				P.Furnival, Sep. 22, 1887.
20........		58 38			58 50 3-5	
21........	1	1 41........		1 1 50 1-5	
22........	1	4 44........		1 4 51 1-5	
23........	1	17 45........		1 20 49 3-5	
28........	1	21 25........		1 24 4 4-5	
29........	1	25 0		1 27 18 1-5	
30........	1	28 29........		1 30 31 2-5	J. H. Adams, Crystl Pal'ce, Aug. 22, 1888.
31........	1	31 58........		1 33 42 2-5	
32........	1	35 72........		1 37 12 2-5	
33........	1	38 50........		1 40 34	
34........	1	41 21........		1 43 51 1-5	
35........	1	45 55........		1 47 14 3-5	
36........	1	49 77........		1 50 36 4-5	C. Potter, Surbiton, Sep. 24, 1887.
37........	1	56 30........		1 57 18	
38........	2	0 10........	2	0 37 2-5	
39........	2	3 50........		2 3 56 3-5	
40........	2	7 16........		2 7 10 1-5	
45........	2	20 36........		2 20 37 3-5	
46........	2	23 33........		2 24 1	
47........	2	27 5........		2 27 20 3-5	C. Potter, Surbiton, Sep. 24, 1887.
48........	2	30 19........		2 30 51 3-5	
49........	2	33 33........		2 34 5 3-5	
50........	2	36 44........		2 37 22 2-5	
	2	39 45........		2 40 33 2-5	

Mr. A. Searson ("Cyclist") held the watch, and several others also clocked the performance, agreeing to a second.

At Summer Games of Pittsburg Cricket Club, Pittsburg, Pa., June 29: One-mile bicycle handicap—W. H Willock, Pittsburg, first. Time, 2m. 35½s. Handicap of 90 yards—W. D. Banker, at scratch, fell, but came in second.

There are twenty amateur races on the Hartford Wheel Club's Meet programme, September 4 and 5, which offers promise of genuine sport and fast time. Now, if the racing men will not indulge in too much "loafing" and the handicap men "go" all the way, the whole tournament will mark a decided advance in racing matters in America. The public, that pays to see these races, abominates "loafing" in cycle races as much as "scoring" in trotting matches.

THREE CHAMPIONSHIP RACES IN SCOTLAND.

The one-mile tricycle, five-mile ordinary and one-mile safety championships were run off in glorious weather on Saturday, June 22, resulting as follows:

ONE-MILE TRICYCLE.—John Carrick, Bellahouston B. C. (1); John E. Young, Western C. C. (2). Won by a foot; splendid finish. Time, 2m. 58 3-5s.—record for Scotland.

FIVE-MILE TRICYCLE.—Alex. Wills, Dundee Northern C. C. (1); M. Bruce, Edinburgh Eastern C. C. (2). Six riders started and for nineteen laps each rider took a turn at leading the procession. Time, 15m. 55 1-5s.

ONE-MILE SAFETY BICYCLE.—Chas. Ebsworth, Edinburgh Northern C. C. (1); John E. Young, Western C. C. (2); James Mark, Cathkin C. C. (3). The grandest race and most exciting finish of the day. Ebsworth made pace all the distance and certainly rode well, and deserved his win of four inches from Young, who made Mark by less than a foot. Time, 2m. 56 2-5s.—Bicycling News.

BICYCLE RACES AT HERKIMER, N. Y.

There was a fair attendance, but not what was anticipated, at the bicycle tournament, July 4, on the driving park. About forty wheelmen were in the parade, whereas two hundred were expected. The races were well contested, but lacked the excitement that the average Fourth of July celebrator demands, and as they have ceased to be a novelty, bicycle races fail to draw crowds. The Fort Dayton wheelmen are entitled to credit for their enterprise, and deserved better returns. The winners in the several contests were as follows:

Road race, seven miles—P. C. Hammes, Utica, 40m. 25s.
Half-mile novice—F W. Battles, Rome. Half-mile club—Joe Schermer, Herkimer. One-mile handicap—Wallace Roberts, Utica. One-mile tandem—E. H. Crosby, J. J. Saunders, Utica. One-mile, Herkimer County—G. W. Nellis, Herkimer. Mile team race—Crescent Cycling Club. Half-mile race—Rome. Half-mile, Rover Safety—G. H. Metz, Utica. Mile club handicap—E. W. Hartley, Herkimer. Three-mile lap—C. H. Metz, Utica. Half-mi'e unicycle—H. Nicholson, Utica. Half-mile consolation—L. B. Haynes, Rome.—Utica Herald.

DAVIS MAY NOT RACE ABROAD.

R. H. Davis, who, with a companion, has been suspended by the League of American Wheelmen for competing on ordinaries against safeties, contrary to law, announces his intention of coming to England to race here, as he can't get his wants gratified in his own country. He is very good. No one can fail to appreciate his kindness in thus honoring us, but perhaps he will be better off at home. The N C. U. has a way occasionally of suspending a man not too openly, but just effectually enough—and Mr Davis may find himself in the same position here as he is on the other side of the Atlantic.—Bicycling News.

[From the above, it would seem more than probable that the N. C. U. will co-operate with the L. A. W. Racing Board and recognize its suspension of Davis. The two organizations should work in harmony.—ED.]

SCHOVERLING, DALY & GALES,

302 Broadway, New York,

AGENTS FOR THE

NEW MAIL CYCLES.

THE NEW MAIL SAFETY A GREAT SUCCESS.

BEST HILL CLIMBER AND BEST COASTER.

DON'T BUY A SAFETY OR ORDINARY BEFORE SENDING FOR OUR CATALOGUE. FREE.

PSYCHO CYCLES

ARE SHIPPED

Same day order is received.

Capital Cycle Co.,

WASHINGTON, D. C.

A little higher in price but of unrivaled quality.

THE WHEEL

—AND—

CYCLING TRADE REVIEW.

Published every Friday morning.

Entered at the Post Office at second class rates.

Subscription Price,   -   -   - $1.00 a year.
Foreign Subscriptions,   -   -   -   6s. a year.
Single Copies,   -   -   -   -   -   5 Cents.

Newsdealers may order through AM. NEWS CO.

All copy should be received by Monday.
Telegraphic news received till Wednesday noon.

Advertising rates on Application.

F. P. PRIAL, Editor and Proprietor
23 Park Row,

P. O. Box 444,   New York.

Persons receiving sample copies of this paper are respectfully requested to examine its contents and give us their patronage, and as far as is convenient, aid in circulating the journal, and extend its influence in the cause which it so faithfully serves. Subscription price, $1 per year.

THE '88 and '89 League Meets have given a large number of League members abundant opportunity to gauge the calibre of Field Marshal Mott, who, by right of his office, was the most conspicuous figure on those occasions. We believe that those who have taken the trouble to observe will indorse our opinion that the Field Marshal is as fine a specimen of the gentleman cyclist as this country can present. The enthusiasm of the man has been manifested in the whole-souled invitation his Division has extended to the League on two occasions and in the perseverance and activity he has displayed in discharging his duties as host. But beyond the enthusiasm and the activity is ability of no mean order, coupled with conservatism and the air and manner which make the gentleman. We see in Mott the all-round man, not squeamish to the point of absurdity, not coarse to the point of disgust, but harmonious. Take it all in all, Mott should be the next President of the League. Let the "Maryland boys" arouse themselves and howl for Mott.

WE regret to say that the *Bicycling World's* report of the League Meet has caused a deal of unpleasant comment. We regret this all the more because we are sure that the *Bicycling World's* representative had no intention of doing aught but to report the meet as it appeared to him. We know that "Jack" would be the last man in the world to consent to our appearance as an apologist for him, but we will say that we know he appreciated the hospitality extended to him, that he had no intention to hurt the feelings of any one. The Maryland men are deeply offended, and this feeling is intensified by the *Bicycling World's* editorial on the meet.

AT Hagerstown there was a deal of fluid refreshment dispensed. The curious noises that proceeded from the bar-room of the Hamilton, which made the welkin ring until 2 P. X. and frightened off the god Somnus; the vain attempt to steal the Hagerstown fire department; the aggregate of noise sent up to the dome, and those other symptoms of "ilariousness" too numerous to catalogue, seem to have excited some fear that the Hagerstown meet was an orgy of the Shantytown variety; that cycling was being taken up by the "tough" element, and that the "League Meet" has seen its best days.

We do not wish to apologize for the Hagerstown boys; neither do we wish to gloss over the facts. The guest must, perforce, adopt the plan of his entertainer. If the host is horsey, he must be prepared to rave over the chestnut colt with the white star, stroke the gentle mare and admire the legs of a favorite beast. If the host is a yachtsman, he must be prepared to swear by a "wet sheet and a flowing sea," and listen to any number of sea-dog yarns.

So at Hagerstown, the Maryland people set the pace, and the course led many times past the bar, where short stops were made. We were informed by many Southern men that Southern hospitality is most expressed by the flowing bowl, and the larger the bowl and the oftener it flows the greater the hospitality. Now we are not going to quarrel with custom. It is useless. In the North they will still continue to extend the tips of the fingers in token of friendship, and in the South they will still clink the musical glasses, and an ocean of ink carefully distributed by the cleverest pens ever wielded will not change it all.

There was no drunkenness at Hagerstown; no brutishness. The weather was beastly, and the simplest vitality which might have been expended, with much pedal pushing, ran to firecrackers, vociferous club cries, and countless repetitions of that sweet tune so much affected by the band. Had the weather admitted of the programme being carried out to the letter, the noise and exuberance would have been reduced by half. As it was, it may have been annoying, but it was harmless. The Hagerstown people gave up the keys of the city, and when they were returned their city was still there. The public square was not carried off, and the post-office was left intact.

THE many rumors and published articles of trouble in the New York Bicycle Club are either gross exaggeration or stupid misrepresentation. It is true that Mr. Pitman criticised Mr. Shriver's actions as President, the same as many club members are continually criticising their officers. The Trustees of the club expelled Mr. Pitman, and the judgment of four trustees was afterwards reversed by the club, which, at the same time, assured Mr. Shriver of its esteem and respect. No one has left the club, which has 140 members and the finest club-house in this part of the country. The average reporter writes on space, and all is grist that comes to his mill. It is his duty to magnify, to stretch, to paint the shadows very dark and throw in strong, white light. It means so much per column to him.

A manufacturer's agent, who recently visited several of the club-houses in New York and Brooklyn, expressed some surprise at the number of light English wheels. We have noticed the growing disposition of wheelmen to privately import lighter wheels than are made in this country. Up to the present time the demand for light wheels has not been large enough to warrant the expense of the plant necessary to make them. But we believe that the opening of next season will witness a big demand for safeties weighing from thirty-five to forty pounds. We hope some of the leading makers will consider the advisability of turning out a medium-weight safety. The tendency is in favor of a medium or light safety, geared from 57 to 60, and even higher. The men who order these light wheels are, as a rule, experienced cyclists, and they buy with the full knowledge that they are sacrificing strength for lightness, but they argue that the increased pleasure, the additional speed and the decreased expenditure of power, more than repay them.

For the benefit of "Veras" and the ladies, we are pleased to say that the letters "H. O. T." recently used in a White Flyer ad. initialed, "High Old Time."

DR. J. W. BRANNON has compiled, and the Washington Life Insurance Company has issued, a volume of actuarial and medical statistics covering a period of twenty-six years, and based on 2,000 policies paid by the company. Merchants are reported as attaining the greatest average age, while the fact is emphasized that clerks live less years than almost any other class. The chief cause of the high death-rate among clerks is that one-third of them die of consumption. It is one of the most powerful arguments that can be made in favor of cycling, that it will cause a noticeable expansion of the chest even after a month's riding. In non-cycling mediums, we would suggest that the members of the trade use arguments of this kind in their advertisements. It will make many converts to the sport.

CYCLISTS whose wheels suddenly break off in a vital spot should learn that, no matter what precaution may be taken, and no matter how costly the material, it is impossible to secure absolutely flawless metal. If in working the metal into a part the flaw should come to the surface, any maker of repute is glad to cast the faulty part on the scrap heap, and thank the gods that it did not go out of the factory. When the back-bone of your wheel snaps, don't go about like a wild man condemning the maker on all sides. Look at the thing reasonably, and state your case to the man who sold you your wheel, and, if its maker has a good business head he will do the right thing. For, verily, one displeased man offsets the testimony of ninety-nine satisfied men.

MOTT.—As a man of fine feeling he appreciates the compliments of his friends in mentioning his name for the Presidency, and if those on whose advice he relies want him to run he will do so, and no man who might vote for him would ever have cause to regret it.

THE Cyclists' Union of Long Island works quietly but none the less effectively. Its semi-annual report, published in our news columns, shows a good balance on hand. At the annual business meeting the Executive Committee will report many little things undertaken and accomplished for the advancement of the sport.

"TAM O'SHANTER'S" reports of the Elwell tour are the best thing of the kind that have ever appeared in a cycling paper. They are being read extensively, usually excite the envy of the reader—a sure sign of their merit—and many copies of THE WHEEL are each week mailed to friends of cycling men, to show them what can be gotten out of wheeling. The publication of such reports as "Tam O'Shanter's" helps the sport.

THE cycling trade should aid L. D. Aylett, of Birmingham, Ala., in his work of roads improvement. Mr. Aylett is a man of ability, and devotes time, money and talent to the work of improving the roads. Mr. Aylett is the first man who has brought cyclists and horsemen together in a roads improvement convention. He and his co-operators have induced the County Commissioners to build a fine boulevard a mile and a half long.

THERE have never been so many good local men in training as this year. What we want is a meet, that they may show their powers. The Division Meet will probably be held here in September. The Berkeley Club should give us a meet in August, or some New Jersey club should hold a meet at Roseville during the droughty month.

NEW YORK'S CRYING WANT.

If the people and press of this city fully realized the comfort, convenience, efficiency and economy to city and citizens, directly and indirectly, which well-paved streets would establish, there would be less delay and neglect of our streets by Commissioner of Public Works Gilroy and Mayor Grant.

After a long struggle the needed money, an extra $1,000,000 a year for three years, beginning with last January, was added to the annual million to pave streets.

Then a general agitation took place. The kinds of pavements which well-equipped cities at home and abroad now use were described. The general conclusion was reached that a firm foundation of six-inch concrete made from cement, sand and broken stone must underlie all our principal streets.

Upon this should be placed either granite blocks or asphalt; granite blocks where the traffic is numerous and heavy, say about fifty-five hundred teams a day. Asphalt should be used where possible, especially where residences, hospitals, schools, public buildings, banks and other forms of severe brain work are involved. The protest made by all the property owners and others on Wall Street, from Pearl to Nassau Street, against stone, and their demand for a quiet street, is simply in keeping with the financial centres of the great marts of the world. Paris, London, Liverpool, Wien, Bruxelles, Marseilles, with whom we compete in finance, all have quiet asphalt pavement about their Exchanges.

There is but little traffic on Wall Street—less than one-third the traffic which our ashphalt streets now carry.

The unanimous passage by the Board of Aldermen, in response to the call from Wall Street for relief, is to be heartily approved. No doubt Mayor Grant will accede to the desires of the property owners and to the approval of the representatives of the people, and see that Wall Street is promptly paved with what is asked for—a noiseless asphalt on solid concrete.

The year is one-half past. The propitious time for general paving is at hand. Hundreds of pavers are idle. The law requires that each million be appropriated in its own year. Many people are away in summer, especially from the residence portion of the city.

The uncertainty as to what several street railroads will do makes it the plain duty of Commissioner Gilroy to arrange that streets without tracks be immediately repaved. The stone blocks take up so much room when piled along the streets that longer delay in beginning work will cause confusion and trouble of expense to all concerned. Work in the rainy and muddy autumn, and a failure to complete contracts before winter, leaves streets and sidewalks hampered and clogged with large piles of stones. Fifth Avenue was choked from end to end for more than two years. Proper inspection caused good work, and good work will be done on our new pavements. The Chamber of Commerce and the citizens are now informed as to what good pavements really are. Good work cannot be rushed quickly through. Our new pavements; the sooner begun, the sooner done.—*Mail and Express.*

The Brooklyn *Citizen* of Sunday last publishes an illustrated column on "Women on the Wheel," by Florence Finch Kelly. Miss Kelly has industriously rehashed the splendid article by Nelly Bly which recently appeared in the New York *World*. The illustrations used are: 1, cut showing fair maid clutching her wheel by the rear wheel mud-guard, and holding the wheel by that method, a cycling impossibility; cut 2, showing cut of woman alleged to be Miss Pauline Hall, mounted on a "safe," with arms in most ungraceful position (N. B.—Brake is half way down the tire of the front wheel, looking as if sun had melted brake-rod); cut 3, fairly good cut of *chic* young lady on Psycho, showing—well, look at it and see for yourself. The article helps the sport, no doubt, and attracts the attention of would-be cyclists to Mr. Bidwell's riding school, where we know they will be well taught and well treated by "Ike."

THE NEW JERSEY ROADS.

Engineer Dunham has just issued specifications of the contracts for new roads in Union County, upon which all bids must be based. A perusal of the specifications shows that Engineer Dunham has a perfect knowledge of road building, and if his plan is carried out the new system will be as fine as anything in the country.

The roadway is to be graded to such a depth that when properly shaped and rolled it shall be twelve inches below the surface of the broken stone when completed, irrespective of finishing material; all material that would allow shrinkage in the road-bed is to be removed; the road-bed must be rolled with not less than a five-ton roller to ultimate resistance. Even the foundation stone is to be of trap-rock (not field stone or any soft stone) and must be in pieces approximately eight inches deep, five inches in width and from eight to twelve inches long, and of such form as to properly join and wedge. This is to be laid by hand, to form a close pavement with broken joints, and after being set closely together they are to be firmly wedged by inserting and driving down with a bar in all possible places between them stones of the same quality until all are bound and clamped in position. This will certainly prevent any large stones working up to the surface and will make a most excellent foundation. Then will follow the bottom course of macadam stone, being broken stone of a practically uniform size to pass in any direction through a ring two and a half inches in diameter. This is to be two inches in depth. Then follows a third layer of broken stone, each piece an inch and a half in diameter and this is to be rolled down. The building material for the bottom course is to be trap-rock screenings, of the upper course half inch stone and clean, sharp gravel, practically free from dirt. In rolling the upper course of stone gravel is to be introduced dry and also with the assistance of water. This is a much more important point than usually believed, as it greatly helps to form a compact bed and to bind the road metal together. The surface is to be gravel, clean and sharp, practically free from dirt, and the rolling is to be continued until, by a sufficient use of water, a wave of gravel is produced before the wheel of the roller, and the rolling of the macadam and upper courses shall be with nothing less than a ten-ton roller. Throughout the whole specifications the engineer retains the right to decide every question without appeal. In other words, he takes the whole responsibility and manifests a determination to have the roads built strictly according to his ideas of proper road building.

GOOD ROADS AS AN INVESTMENT.

The city of Plainfied is estimated to have between forty and fifty miles of macadamized roads within its borders, thus making driving pleasant everywhere about the city. The natural advantages of the place are not equal to those of New Brunswick, and yet the former city's excellent roads have led to the settlement there of hundreds of wealthy families and the erection of many palatial mansions at an expense of millions of dollars. We believe our poor roads are the principal drawback to our city's more rapid growth. People will not erect houses on lands which are not accessible more than half of the year. There is a hint here also for Highland Park property owners.—*New Brunswick Times.*

Thus is the leaven of good roads working. It will spread—it is bound to spread—for every dollar put into good roads at proper cost is a dollar put out at a 100 per cent. interest. What good roads have done for Plainfield they will do for all of Union County, and the time is not far distant when "palatial mansions" and beautiful dwellings will dot all the beautiful sites along the hillsides of the county and will adorn the plains as flowers adorn a garden.—*Elizabeth Journal.*

DEFECTIVE LEAGUE HOTEL WORK.

EDITOR OF THE WHEEL:

My husband and self took a trip as far as Stamford on our wheels last Friday, and stopped at the Stamford House, it being a league hotel, where we found much to our surprise, there was no reduction in price to L. A. W. members. We have been traveling through the Eastern States this summer and we found this state of affairs at many of the so called L. A. W. hotels. This being the case, will you kindly inform me what particular benefit one derives from being a member of the L. A. W. In some instances we find we can make far better arrangements at houses that are not designated as League Hotels. PONY.

New York, July 15.

[The proprietor of the Stamford House should have been informed of his obligations by the Consul who made the appointment and placed the sign there. Doubtless the Chief Consul of Connecticut will look into the matter. The table at the Stamford House is excellent and wheelmen should patronize the hotel.—ED.]

A NEW HOTEL AND TOWER ON EAGLE ROCK.

Eagle Rock, one of the famous show places of the Oranges, is about to be brought still more prominently before the public. A number of Orange and South Orange men have formed a corporation to utilize the many advantages of the spot. It is proposed to build a large and well appointed hotel on the summit of the mountain near the rock and lay out the grounds about it as a summer park. A railroad is projected from the Washington Street station of the Erie Railroad to the foot of the rock itself. Here a tower, somewhat similar in design to the Eiffel tower in Paris, is to be built. It will be almost 400 feet high, and rise about 300 feet above the crest of the mountain. A commodious elevator will be maintained in it to convey passengers to the crest of the mountain as well as to the summit of the tower. It is proposed to make an arrangement with Edison to supply an enormous electric light for the summit of the tower, which will be visible far out at sea.—*Elizabeth Journal.*

PROSPECTUS OF SCRANTON BICYCLE CLUB'S TOUR.

Scranton, (club house). New Milford, 40 miles; dinner, Jay House. Binghamton, 22 miles; Hotel Bennett, night. Norwich, 42 miles; American House, night. Utica, 53 miles; St. Jame Hotel, night. Trenton Falls, 17 miles; Moore's Hotel, dinner. Train to Utica, 17 miles. Richfield Springs, 36 miles; Darrow Hotel, night. Cooperstown, 13 miles; Hotel Fenimore, dinner. Stamford, 40 miles; night. Catskills, 41 miles; Kaaterskill Hotel, night. Catskill-on-Hudson, 12 miles. Hudson, 7 miles; Worth Hotel, dinner. Great Barrington, 30 miles; Miller's Hotel, night. Springfield, 60 miles; Warwick Hotel, night. (Or Pittsfield, 25 miles; down Berkshire Valley; train, Springfield). Hartford, 30 miles; City Hotel. New Haven, 40 miles; Tremont Hotel, night. New York, 87 miles.

Or from Catskill-on-Hudson: Poughkeepsie, 38 miles; Morgan House. West Point, 27 miles; train Tarrytown, 25 miles; New York, 25 miles.

Or from Poughkeepsie: Newburg, 15 miles; Port Jervis, 50 miles; Delaware House, night. Water Gap, 37 miles

From New York: Train Newark, 8 miles; through Oranges; Morristown, 20 miles; Delaware Water Gap, 47 miles; train, Scranton.

The membership of the party will not be limited to members of the Scranton Bicycle Club, but any friends outside may join if congenial to the rest of the party. While no great reduction in rates is to be expected, the best accommodations will be looked after—at League hotels, etc.

In visiting such a list of places and famous summer resorts—Trenton Falls, Richfield Springs, Cooperstown, Catskill Mountains, Berkshire Hills, Hudson River points and the Oranges—it is proposed to ride only on good roads and train poor ones—a tour for pleasure and rest, not for hard work. We expect train service will be at 2c. per mile, wheels free. Parties desiring to join should decide as early as possible—not later than August 1—stating at what point they wish to join and what point leave the party.

B. P. CONNOLLY, Secretary.

A ROUTE THAT DESERVES TO BE KNOWN.

There is a beautiful ride quite near Elizabeth, N. J., which few wheelmen know about, and if better known it would be very popular. The run is first made to the stone bridge at Milburn. A turn is made here to the right over the tracks of the D. L. and W. R. R.; beyond the tracks the road forks. The right fork is taken and here the ride begins. The wheelman finds himself in the heart of the wildest part of the Orange Mountains. The road is fine, slightly sandy in hot weather, but always ridable. On the left, tower the mountains, and on the right the beautiful chain of mountain lakes which supply Elizabeth with water. The road is on the water's edge and shaded with trees the whole distance. During the greater part of the ride there is not a single house visible.

After having ridden about four miles the road over the mountains leading to Orange via South Orange Avenue is encountered. The hills are so long and steep here that one must dismount and walk. But once the summit is reached, a beautiful view compensates for the toil. The entire Orange valley, Elizabeth, Newark and all neighboring cities are spread out below like a map. The wheels are mounted, and after a wild, exhilarating coast of two miles down the side of the South Orange Mountains, one finds himself in the valley ready to try it again.

WHEELMEN AND HORSEMEN JOIN HANDS IN A GOOD CAUSE.

Wheelmen in Alabama are at last beginning to have some influence, particularly in the city of Birmingham. Two land companies there are competing to see which shall build them—the wheelmen—a track free, in order to have races held where their respective motor lines will carry the crowds. A most encouraging feature is the interest taken by horsemen in the wheelmen's agitation for better roads. Witness the following letter to the representative of THE WHEEL in Birmingham, Ala., from a prominent citizen there:

"Please accept my sincere thanks for the resolutions which you introduced and had adopted by the wheelmen of Birmingham. They have already had a good effect, and the Commissioners are being congratulated upon the popularity of their Boulevard project.

"Yours very truly,

"F. Y. ANDERSON."

Birmingham, Ala., June 28, 1889.

ABOUT ALUMINUM.

THE SECRET LOST. CLAIMS MADE BY AN INVENTOR.

The death of Fred J. Seymour, manager of the American Aluminum Co., of Findlay, Ohio, is reported. Aluminum possesses many of the qualities of steel, besides valuable properties not found in that metal. Its extreme lightness and beauty under certain processes would make it valuable for a multitude of purposes. It would be valuable for the construction of cycles, but it is impossible to either weld or solder it. Mr. Seymour invented the machinery for extracting aluminum from common clay by a cheaper method than any hitherto employed. The secret of extracting the precious metal died with Seymour, and the company will have to employ chemists to experiment in the hope of re-discovering Seymour's secret.

It is of interest to note that a Boston man named Washburn has been in New York for some time trying to interest capital in the production of aluminum. He claims that he can make it at a cost of less than five cents a pound and that he possesses the secret of both soldering and welding it. His claims are so extravagant, however, that he is regarded as a crank. Some of our cycle manufacturers should locate him and investigate.

BUSINESS MEETING AT BRIDGEPORT, CONN., JULY 8.

About 100 wheelmen were present at the annual business meeting in the Bridgeport Wheel Club rooms, the morning of July 8. Chief Consul Chas. E. Larom presided and read his annual report. Among other statements by the Chief Consul he said that the membership of the Connecticut Division is now 454, and the prospects favor a steady increase in their ranks. There are less men by nearly 100, who have dropped out of the Division this year, than last.

The most important business transacted at this meeting was the adoption of a by-law which provides for a Division lawyer, to look after all the legal business of the Connecticut Division. David J. Post, of Hartford, offered the resolution, which in substance was that the Division lawyer, who shall be a practicing attorney and also a wheelman, be appointed, the duties of whom shall be to collate all ordinances, laws and other information bearing upon the privileges and rights of wheelmen and place the same on record; also to record all decisions of the Court given in bicycle cases, and all accidents, and to defend wheelmen when so ordered by the Chief Consul. The records are to be open to the inspection of the Chief Consul Vice-Consul and Secretary and Treasurer. The Division lawyer's retainer was fixed at $100 per year, and the appointment was to be made for a term of five years, subject to removal by a two-thirds vote of the Board of Officers.

Mr. Post in explaining his motive for offering this resolution, stated that the bill passed by the lower branch of the Legislature and defeated in the Senate, which required that wheelmen should carry a lantern upon their wheels when riding after dark, or be liable to a fine of $7 and costs or imprisonment for thirty days, or both, was passed in the House before the Hartford wheelmen had any knowledge that such a measure had been presented. Mr. Post stated that the bill was defeated in the Senate owing to the work of Hartford wheelmen, and now it seemed advisable to have some one whose business it should be to look out for the interests of the Connecticut wheelmen. The by-law was unanimously adopted.

A by-law authorizing the Chief Consul to appoint a committee on transportation was also passed. Resolutions referring to the death of Stephen Terry of Hartford, one of the most active bicyclists in the State, were also adopted.

The Division Treasurer reported a balance on hand of $706.55. Officers were then nominated for the ensuing year. L. A. Miller nominated for Chief Consul David J. Post, of Hartford, and C. E. Moore, of Bridgeport, nominated Calhoun Latham, the latter being President of the Bridgeport Wheel Club. Mr. Moore stated that Hartford and New Haven had both had a Chief Consul, and Bridgeport ought to be favored this time. The only nomination for Vice-Consul was that of C. E. Moore, of Bridgeport.

Edward A. DuBlois, of Hartford, was renominated for Secretary and Treasurer. For Representatives to the National League the following were nominated: L. A. Miller, of Meriden; Joseph Gilman, of Hartford; F. W. Atwater, President of the Rambling Wheelmen of Bridgeport; and T. W. Gillette, of Danbury. The meeting then adjourned. —*Bridgeport Farmer*.

INDEPENDENT TICKET IN FIRST DISTRICT.

An independent ticket for at-large Representatives for the First District has been sent out, the change being the substitution of F. P. Prial, New York Club, for S. B. Watts, Jr., same club. Mr. Watts is a new member of the New York Club, and the general opinion seems to be that he is not entitled to the distinction, either by service or special ability, as he is new to cycling. An independent ticket, accompanied by the letter published below, has been sent out to all the voters in the district. If any person has already cast the regular ballot desires to vote the independent ticket he may do so by enclosing it, recalling his first vote. Mr. Prial is, of course, gratified at the action of his friends and he is working for election, not for the honor of office, but to show the absurdity of the position taken when his name was sent into the nominating committee, viz., that he was connected with cycling in a business way.

MEMBERS OF THE FIRST DISTRICT, NEW YORK STATE DIVISION, L. A. W.

GENTLEMEN—We beg to submit to you the enclosed list of candidates for Representatives from our district. This ticket differs from that issued by the Nominating Committee, in that we have substituted the name of F. P. Prial, New York Bicycle Club, and Editor of the "THE WHEEL," for that of Mr. G. B. Watts, Jr., New York Bicycle Club. We make the nomination with no ill-will toward Mr. Watts, but Mr. Prial has devoted some years to the advancement of the sport, is a persistent worker for improved roads, and we think he would be a valuable officer. Trusting that you will support our ticket, we remain,

Very respectfully yours,
William H. Krug, Citizens Bicycle Club.
W. H. DeGraaf, Harlem Wheelmen.
H. E. Voorhees, Riverside Wheelmen.
I. M. Shaw, New York Bicycle Club.
C. A. Sheehan, Manhattan Bicycle Club.

SAFETY—HANDS OFF—2.48.

Van Wagoner, of Newport, the champion long-distance bicycle rider of Rhode Island, performed a feat at Roger Williams Park Tuesday afternoon which places him as one of the fastest riders in the country. With his hands tied behind him he rode a mile on a Columbia safety in 2m. 48s. Messrs. Benjamin Smith, George P. McAuslan and George Ballou, of the Rhode Island Wheelmen, were the timers, and Mr. Thomas Lakey starter.—*Providence Journal*.

We should like to see affidavits of time and have measurement of course certified.

At Waltham, Mass., July 4: Ten miles, won by C. O. Adams in 32m. 15s.; 3-mile safety, won by C. F. Merrill in 8m. 47s.

NEW YORK STATE MEET, 1889.

A meeting of the officers of the first and second districts of the New York State Division was held at the Hotel Hamblin, in Chambers Street, last Friday night. The object of the meeting was to decide whether it would be advisable to invite the State Division to hold a meet in New York and Brooklyn this fall.

Vice-Consul Bridgman occupied the chair. F. P. Prial, New York Club, was elected temporary secretary. The other gentlemen present were: W. C. Marion, K. C. W.; Irving W. Shaw, N. Y. B. C.; W. H. DeGraaf, Harlem Wheelmen; C. A. Sheehan, M. B. C., and H. E. Voorhees, R. W.

The opinion of the men present was in favor of the meet being held, but no decided action was taken. In order to have the matter more fully discussed a meeting will be held July 22 at the Hamblin, at which all representatives of the first and second districts and all presidents and captains of the local clubs are invited to be present. A plan of entertainment was outlined which would surely make the meet a success. In case the meet is held the probable date will be September 12 and 13. New York will have the meet on Friday and Brooklyn on Saturday, with a race meet at Washington Park.

A "POINTER" FOR SAFETY MAKERS.

We have no doubt that all riders of safety machines, in common with ourselves, have been bothered with getting a proper adjustment of the seat-rod for height. Particularly is this the case with cyclists that have been riding the ordinary and come down to a more lowly position on the safety. All safeties that we have seen have a means of adjustment, but it is largely experimental at first. The rider takes his new mount trusting to the assurances of the dealer or renter that "that's about right for him," and goes out. For a mile or so on level, easy roads things may go well, or any awkwardness be laid to the newness and strangeness of the mount, but on a poor piece of road, or at the first hill a dismount and readjustment is necessary.

Not always does the rider have a wrench with him, and is fain to borrow or wait till he returns home. To some readers this may seem a small matter for consideration, but the comfort and convenience of cyclists is often dependent on just such small things.

What we would suggest is this: that manufacturers take measurements from the pedal at its lowest point to the top of saddle for all reaches, say from forty-six to sixty inch, and at the proper place on the seat-rod stamp the corresponding number. It is a simple thing and perhaps not a novel suggestion, but we feel sure its adoption would save wheelmen much annoyance and lessen one prolific cause of profanity. Who will be the one to adopt the idea?

A CHANGEABLE GEAR FOR SAFETIES.

S. J. Collier, cycle agent of West Cliffe and South Beach, Blackpool, England, has applied for patents on an important invention. Riders of the safety machines know that the small wheels can be geared up so as to obtain a greatly increased speed. This is all very well on the level, but when a hill has to be climbed the high gearing means that very much more power has to be put forward by the rider. Many attempts have been made to overcome this inconvenience, but so far all have been of too cumbersome and involved a character to recommend themselves either to the makers or riders of machines. Mr. Collier's invention, however, is extremely simple, and adds little additional weight to the machine. By the action of one pinion the gearing can be instantaneously reduced when extra power is required in riding up hill. For instance, if the wheel is geared up to 60 inches for riding on the level, the gearing can be lowered to 45 inches instantly whilst riding at full speed when a hill is reached. The advantages of this invention will be obvious to all who have had experience of the safety machines, and Mr. Collier ought to reap a substantial reward from his ingenious arrangement.—*Blackpool Gazette*.

The Hagerstown Club has passed a vote of thanks to the Baltimore *Herald* for the good work it did in spreading news of the meet. Very good; the *Herald* is no doubt proud. But the *Bicycling World* did, if we recollect correctly, publish a superb article on the meet, and THE WHEEL, if our recollection is not again at fault, published the Mott article in splendid style. We have a distinct recollection of drawing a pretty good sized check for a cycling paper's counting-room in payment for the cuts which accompanied that article. But no mattah.

K. C. W. NOTES.

On Saturday evening, the 13th inst., Messrs. Beasley and Wardell, of the Kings County Wheelmen, were on their way to Coney Island, and when about a mile from the park, on the "Ocean Parkway," they passed a member of the "mounted police," who appeared to be under the influence of liquor. Mr. Beasley noticed this, and turning to his companion, who was a few yards in the rear, mentioned in rather loud tones his suspicions as to the condition of the officer. His remarks were overheard by the man, who at once, in language not used in polite society, said he would show if he was drunk, and with that put spurs to his horse and endeavored to ride Mr. Beazley down. Unfortunately he was successful in his fiendish attempt, and the fact that assault in the first degree and not manslaughter is his crime is no fault of his, he did his best, but happily for all parties concerned some severe bruises and a wrecked wheel sum up the result. Beasley intends to push the matter to the utmost and will endeavor to make an example of this man. Here is a chance for the Cyclists' Union of Long Island to do some good work. What a condition of affairs where those men who are paid to protect the people deliberately ride them down on the public highway.

Safety wheels are all the go with the K. C. W. now. The New Mail appears to have the call, but we hear some talk of Psychos. The Park riders want the lightest to be had. Morehouse will be the first to decide whether lightness and strength go hand in hand on machines of the truss pattern; his decision will practically settle the style of safety Kings County men will want.

Frank Brown had a walk-over for the Cape May bicycle event, and in consequence adds a handsome silver cup to his already fine collection of trophies. Frank says a walk-over prize is of no account, but that this one commemorates a grand time, etc., etc.

I note Mr. Schoefer's remarks in the last number of THE WHEEL, and for his benefit would state that my notes are purely *personal* opinions, and therefore the K. C. W. as a club, or their team, are in no way responsible for what may appear in them. I thought, and still think, that the Kings County team were under a great disadvantage in their race with the Berkeley representatives, but still we were fairly defeated, and have accepted the defeat in a sportsmanlike manner, giving full praise to the victors, and having strong hopes that at some future time they, and not we, may be the vanquished. I sincerely hope that the two teams will have a chance to meet again at an early date, but let them be composed of the same men as on the 20th ult. Then, if Berkeley is the name to grace the winning pennant, none will give applause, where applause is due, with more vigor than yours truly.

Hesse is a member of the New Jersey A. C., still they go, the athletic clubs procure all the good men, and we poor cycle clubs have to see our best riders compete under other colors.

On Sunday next, the Kings County boys will leave headquarters at 7:45 A. M., for Pompton, N. J. Captain Marion promises a grand trip, and those who attend will long remember one of the finest rides in N. J.

T. J. Hall, Jr., on Sunday the 14th inst., made the run to Patchogue, 58½ miles, in four hours and fifty-five minutes. Leaving the club-house at 2:10 P. M., he was in Babylon, 8½ miles, at 5:10, and at Roe's Hotel, Patchogue, at 7:05. Mr. Hall reports the roads in excellent trim, and thinks he can do even better, but would like company.

Don't all speak at once.

RAM LAL.

Brooklyn, N. Y., July 18, 1889.

ERIE, PA.

At last it's come! The Sixth Street girls are awake to the fact that a bicycle is the proper caper. At least I judge this to be the case from what I saw one evening last week. It was somewhere in the neighborhood of 10 o'clock, and not having my wheel I was making tracks up a cross street for the car. Suddenly my attention was distracted by sounds of great hilarity. Evidently there was a woman in the case. There might have been twenty from the amount of noise. I of course dismissed "home, sweet home" from my mind and went in search of adventure. The circus had nearly exhausted itself when it came within the range of my vision, but even then it was highly entertaining and somewhat instructive. You have all seen the kids do the stomach act on their sleds in winter? Well, just imagine a girl of the period being trundled along in this position by a couple of her gentleman friends on one of their wheels! Verily, it was a sight for the blind.

About twenty of the boys took a run down to Dill's Park, a distance of some seventeen miles, last Sunday morning. Morning riding is hungry work even if you are fortified by a good, hearty breakfast and the prospect of a sixteen course dinner, but when you start out on a biscuit and a cup of coffee, ride this distance, and are then tantalized with a two-for-a-quarter dinner, it's enough to make Moses turn in his grave. Our boys are not as ethereal as they look, and it is altogether probable that some one besides Landlord Dill will make change for Erie wheelmen in future.

The club turned out fairly well for the run to the Head last Friday evening. Some of them, like your correspondent, failed to make the connection, but from what I hear the ones who did get there "cut a swell." Those who went up Monday evening of this week and forgot to take along any "filthy" were disappointed. Captain Boynton was advertised to be there, and as no statement had been made to the contrary, they expected to see him without money and without price. Some of them were in shape to meet the tax of 50 cents and some were not. Many who would willingly have paid double that amount came back without going in simply because they thought it a put up job. It was probably an oversight in the management, and one they should strive to avoid in future.

Perfect weather. Good roads. Not a thing to growl about this week.

N.

POINTS FOR AMERICAN CYCLISTS.

The criticism of an acute and fair observer is often valuable because the people who are the subject of his dissection may often get pointers by which they may improve the defects pointed out. A. J. Y., a Britisher, now resident in this country, sends some interesting notes to the *Scottish Cyclist*. On one point, however, A. J. Y. is entirely at sea. He says: "The general public decry anything which in any way brings them face to face with a country which they bitterly detest and fear. To such an extent does this exist that I have heard a British flag hissed at a popular theatre." Of course, this is too absurd to need comment.

Certain it is that the American club system is far and away ahead of anything in the old country. Every club has its club-house, and they are palaces compared with the average British hovel. In the big cities clubs average 200 members, generally all active, and the laws regarding subscription, arrears, the bane of club life, are very strict and rigidly enforced. With this membership, giving an average annual subscription of £3 15s. each, they have a splendid income to work on. Rent, servants' wages, etc., eat up a good proportion of this, but there is plenty left for entertainments, dances, picnics, racing prizes and the thousand-and-one items which go to make club life pleasant.

The subscription looks big, and certainly is compared with the 5s., 10s. or £1 subscription of your clubs. But money has a different value here, and the advantages are well worth the balance. With one-half this subscription and the same membership an old country club could certainly do as well, but it would be impossible to get 200 men together willing to pay even this. One or two of the London clubs are the nearest approach to the American standard, but even they have a good deal of leeway to make up. It is in the thorough understanding and working out of commercial laws that the American clubs lead you as they do.

Safeties have scarcely the popularity here which they have in the old country, but they are fast verging to it. Nor do they seem to be as well ridden—the style is wanting. Now and again a rider is to be seen who has the seat and style necessary to make the safety appear graceful, but the average rider cares not for this. His handles are away up chinward, his knees have an awkward wobble, his saddle isn't placed right, and no wonder he doesn't look happy. In striking contrast to this is the "ordinary" rider. He sits well back and gracefully, his handles are in the right place, and he looks a part of his machine. I believe it is the bad style of riding which accounts for the second-class position the safety holds here as a fast road machine. When this is improved the safety will stand first, as it does in the old country. One other peculiarity I would mention is the long crank used by the "ordinary" racing men. Six inches is too much, and a rider using this crank in a race is handicapping his sprinting powers to an extent he wots not of.

I am sorry I cannot speak in terms of the highest appreciation of the American-made safeties. It seems to be the aim of the manufacturers here to dazzle the senses of the would-be purchaser by a display of points and "fakes" which the machines would be far better without. As a consequence the machines are complicated, heavy, easy to get out of order and difficult to put in order. Americans are the most ingenious and inventive of any nation on the face of the earth, and why should not their cycle builders be able to invent ingenious points in their particular branch? One maker told me he had the best machine in the world; no other wheel embodied all the points his did; and I am certain he believed it was the truth.

The American manufacturers will soon learn that simplicity is a *sine qua non* in any cycle—in fact, a good many of them know it thoroughly already; but so long as the uneducated cycling public are ready to gape at every fresh fake and rush for that machine so long will the ridiculous price of American-made cycles be maintained, and so long will English makers hold a large part of the field. Ladies' safeties are in abundance, and the fair riders handle their wheels with a dexterity and grace which quite dissipated the prejudices I, from ignorance, had formed against them.

THE PAPER IS READ.

THE WHEEL of June 28 contained a well-written account on training for bicycle races by George Hendee, the ex-professional. The path records of b cycles were also printed.—*Buffalo Sunday Times.*

Fred. Coningsby has never received the gold medal he won in the Eagle Rock contest on September 2, 1868. This is not creditable with the people who projected the contest. They should at least explain to Coningsby why he has never received his prize.

The annual meet of the League of American Wheelmen will be held at Niagara Falls next year if the progressive citizens of that place, Henry E. Ducker and Buffalo wheelmen have anything to say about it. A meeting was held last week, and it was decided to invite the League to hold its meet at the Falls next year.

A meeting of the Bay City Wheelmen, San Francisco, was held on the evening of July 1 at their club-room on Van Ness Avenue. The following League officers were nominated: R. M Thompson, of San Francisco, for Chief Consul; J. Phil. Percival, of Los Angeles, for Vice-Consul; Walter D. Sheldon, of San Francisco, for Secretary and Treasurer; Representatives— C. C. Moore, of Stockton; Arthur C. McKenna, of San Jose, and John W. Gibson, of San Francisco. The election takes place between July 15 and August 15.

It is quite possible that Buffalo will have a bicycle tournament this fall. Henry E. Ducker, W. G. Schack and Captain Dietzer, of the Ramblers, have been appointed a committee by the club to consider the advisability of making efforts to have the New York Division Meet of the L. A. W. held in that city in the fall. The three gentlemen are boomers. There is no reason why Buffalo shouldn't have the fall meeting. With over 2,000 wheelmen there, splendid hotels and an excellent bicycle track, there is every reason for success

Send to HOWARD A. SMITH & CO., Newark, N. J., for your bicycle supplies or call at Oraton Hall and learn to ride. Open evenings *.*

CYCLING DOWN HILL.

The following leading editorial from *Wheeling* contains so many good ideas that we republish it for the benefit of our readers:

The fatal accident to a bicyclist at Purley Hill is happily one of those rare occurrences which are the exceptions to our golden rule that cycling is the safest of sports. Statistics prove it to be safer than the games of cricket and football, and it must be remembered that, included in these statistics, are the figures for path and road racing on the lightest of machines and frequently on the most unsuitable of tracks. The public is too apt, when some little accessory part of a cycle goes wrong, to forget how great a debt of gratitude is due to the trade for this splendid general result. The manufacturer who knowingly sends out an unsound bicycle is little better than the scoundrels who sent boots with paper soles to the Crimea, or those who to-day supply brittle swords to our cavalry. There comes a time in the experience of most men when the failure of a vital part of a bicycle means, under Providence, death to the rider, and that so few fatal cases occur is, as we have said, a tribute to the conscientious work of our manufacturers.

The poor fellow who has just passed to his rest was, according to the report, "coasting" down hill with his legs over the handles of a 52-inch "ordinary," and in many households there will be warnings addressed to cycling sons against this practice. It cannot, however, be too strongly insisted upon (and we speak feelingly, owing probably our life to it) that the safest way to "fly" a hill on an ordinary is with legs over handles. Sitting well back on the saddle, no ordinary obstacle will throw a man, and an extraordinary impediment would have the same effect were the feet on the pedals, or on the murderous side-clip rests once in vogue. In the case of these latter modes of down-hill traveling, a fall means the face and hands striking the ground first. In the case of "legs over handles" the feet strike first, and the rider, instead of having the handle bar across his legs, is free of the machine. Our opinion is that a skilled rider of an ordinary (and every man should become skilled as soon as he can) should be able to "back pedal" his machine down any rough-surfaced hill it is safe or advisable to ride with a brake, and that the machine should never be let go, or even trusted to the brake, unless the surface is known to be good. On an ordinary good country road, hills should be taken "legs over handles"; on a macadamized, stoned, or twisting hill the rider should trust to back-pedaling, assisted, if he chooses, by his front wheel clasp brake.

Of course, much of the foregoing will be mere leather and prunella to many of our readers, but we are anxious to deprecate any outcry against the "legs over the handles" position. We have practised it in every part of the country, from the Pass of Lennie and the Dumfriesshire Hills to Marlborough Hill and the Newlands Corner—Silent Pool declivity—and *we know* there is no safer mode of riding down any hill which a reasonable man will let his machine loose on.

A much more dangerous practice in connection with the riding of ordinaries is that pursued by novices to be seen Saturday after Saturday on the main roads out of the metropolis. They *will* ride machines too large for them. We will guarantee that if any of our readers will watch for this next Saturday or Sunday plenty of cases will present themselves. How these would-be cyclists can "kid to themselves" that they are cycling and enjoying themselves when their toes do not touch the pedals at the bottom of the stroke we cannot imagine, nor can we envy their feelings next day. The great beads of perspiration stand out upon their brows, and their legs and arms are all at work together, and yet the machine, comparatively speaking, "gets no forrader." Had these desperate strugglers, who groan at a railway bridge, invested in machines four inches or so smaller, life on a cycle would not have assumed so horrid a resemblance to death on a treadmill.

MARYLAND.

Prof. J. Emory Shaw recently left the city, on his bicycle, on a trip to points in the Cumberland Valley.

Albert Mott, Chief Consul Maryland Division L. A. W., was elected an active member of the Hagerstown, Md., Club, at their last meeting.

Edwin Doyle is an applicant for membership in the Chesapeake Club.

The Hagerstown Club people raised all the money spent on the meet except $300, which was subscribed by citizens, and $55 contributed by the Board of Trade. The money realized from the large attendance at the races enabled it to meet every liability and finish even.

Messrs Emmerson and Kingsland, of Baltimore; Wilhelm, of Reading, and Banker, of New York, remained at Hagerstown the day after the races and during the afternoon visited the Fair Grounds. Banker was timed by Wilhelm, Frank S. Heard and some others, and succeeded in breaking the American amateur half-mile record for safeties, making the distance in 1m. 12s. The visitors were loud in their praises of the track, and are anxious to have a series of races there in the fall, if the track could be secured.

Of the 200 new members whose applications were taken at Hagerstown, over 60 were Marylanders.

Isaac Hinds has not yet recovered from the fall he took at the races at Hagerstown, July 4. It is probable that it will be some time before he can get about on his wheel.

Harry Kingsland is credited with an intention to challenge Victor Emerson to a race on any sort of a machine, and an exciting contest may soon be expected to show the superiority between these two gentlemen. Victor Emerson was the victor of the 1-mile tricycle L. A. W. championship at the meet. Emerson now holds the championship won by Kingsland last year. Kingsland was entered in a number of events at the meet, but did not race because, as he claims, he was under the doctor's care, and the latter advised him not to work. He is anxious to race Emerson, and it is understood that the latter would like a go at Kingsland.

A. E. Wallis won the 1-mile bicycle race, making the distance in 3m. 5s., at the athletic sports, held at the Fair Grounds, Frederick, Md., under the auspices of the F. C. Y. M. C. A.

BAY RIDGE.

Send to HOWARD A. SMITH & CO., Newark, N. J., and get stocking supporters, tire cement, belts, bundle carriers for all machines, tire tape, etc. *.*

AN HONEST APPEAL.

We have the assurance of the best physicians in France and America that bicycling is the most healthful exercise persons above the age of 40 and those afflicted with liver or kidney diseases, constipation, indigestion, eczema, bad and sluggish blood, lassitude, no appetite, etc., can take. It is better than horseback exercise, or walking. Buggy riding is fit only for very weak convalescents, and it is not an exercise. Safety bicycles and tricycles are now made on which the most timid can ride with safety, comfort, and to their great benefit. But it is unfortunately often the case when one afflicted with some old chronic disease bicycle exercise will cure, has been convinced of its utility, and concludes to order a safety, along comes one of those people whose sole object in life seems to be to make as much unhappiness and misery as possible, and says, "My God! man, you goin' to git a bicycle! Why, the dad-gasted thing will kill you! Here, boys, come here. Don't yer never b'lieve me agin ef old man Blivins ain't goin' to get one uv them thar durned bicycles!" As every man in the crowd secretly fears his sharp tongue, they all join in the laugh, and as Blivins sneaks away from the cross-fire of ridicule he hears the chief critic and neighborhood monitor say: "Ef he does git one, boys, I hope every hoss I've got will git locoed ef I don't make it lively fur him! You hear me!" And poor, weakly, contemptible Blivins, what does he do? He continues to endure his chronic disease because he did not have the nerve to face down ridicule.

It is a fact, the world is full of Blivinses. Our advice is not for them. But to all middle-aged men, and all who are afflicted, and to all nervy, manly boys, we commend the counsel of the learned French and American physicians on the subject of cycling. And we know from experience that it is true.—*Crosby Co. News*, Estacado, Tex.

GAY SCENES AT ELDORADO SPRINGS, TENN., ON THE FOURTH.

The constant drizzling rain nearly all afternoon and night of the 3d prevented many cyclists from going to Eldorado Springs on the Fourth to attend the hop given in their honor by the hotel proprietor, Dr. J. C. Connell, but those who did go will ever cherish the memory of the occasion as one of the pleasantest in their experience. Ten gentlemen took their chances with muddy roads, and made their way to the Springs awheel. The party was not so large as had been expected, but what it lacked in numbers was made up in congeniality, and the run out was made one of social pleasure rather than speed. Arrived at the Springs, the cyclists were gratified and flattered to find that the young lady guests had profusely decorated the hallways in their honor, arches of evergreens, ferns, etc., being tastefully festooned over the main doorways of the halls.

Before the supper hour people began coming from all directions, and soon after the ball-room was opened it was filled by more than a hundred dancers and spectators. The ball-room at Eldorado Springs cannot be excelled anywhere. It is large enough to accommodate an immense throng, and the floor is as smooth as a piece of glass. The orchestra—a first-class one, too—soon struck up a lively waltz, and the room was a scene of splendor and gayety. Everyone present seemed to enjoy herself and himself, and never to tire of gliding over the polished floor to the strains of inspiring music.

After the last strains of the Home, Sweet Home waltz had died away it left time for the reflection that the occasion had been one of the most enjoyable and largely attended in the history of Eldorado. Dr. Connell has the combined and hearty thanks of the boys of the wheel for the ball in their honor, and for the systematic manner in which everything connected with it was conducted.—*Nashville American.*

G. M. Werden, of the John. P. Lovell Arms Co., of Boston, spent last week at his home in Hastings-on-the-Hudson. On Thursday, yesterday, he started to ride to Boston via Albany and through the Berkshire Hills.

Write to HOWARD A. SMITH & CO., Newark, N. J., for their illustrated catalogue and second-hand list of bargains. Complete repair shop. *.*

THE ELWELL TOURISTS IN FRANCE.

THEIR STRUGGLING WITH THE NATIVE TONGUE.

Life in Paris is beyond description. Artists have pictured it, lecturers have described it, authors have written of it and photographers have done their worst, but it is still a fact that a visit to the magic city is the only way in which a true idea of life here can be obtained. There is a certain all-prevading spirit about it which cannot be put on paper or canvas, try as you will. Monsieur Jacques declines to be delineated, and of our visit to Paris, I shall only attempt to jot down what we have done as cyclists, not as citizens.

Our struggles with the language are fearful and wonderful to hear, and it is hard to tell if our dense ignorance on this head is the most instrumental in detracting from, or adding to, our enjoyment. Certain it is that some side-splitting predicaments arise from it. Some four or five of the party are more or less conversant with it, and as long as we cling to them we are safe. In their absence, however, the boys are hardly to be considered accountable for what they say, and that they are always eager to "make a bluff of it" only makes a bad matter worse.

AMERICAN SLANG TAKES THE BAKERY.

Our Adonis was vainly endeavoring to make a petite and pretty waitress in a restaurant understand that he wanted some bread. He went through a series of gesticulations descriptive of breaking, buttering and eating the loaf, but without a sign of success. He twisted the word "bread" all out of shape, but to no avail, and giving up in disgust ejaculated in A 1 English, "Well, you give my neck a pain!" "*Oh, oui, oui, oui. Le pain, le pain!*" exclaims Phyllis, and tripping away she returns with the desired loaf. The look of blank amazement, surprise and idiocy which occupied the features of Adonis would have been a bonanza for a camera fiend. Such is the power of being obliged to do a thing, however, that by this time we can all of us find our way about and get enough to eat.

THE FRENCH BREAKFAST LIGHT—SO LIGHT!

French cooking is the best in the world, if you are not of an inquisitive turn of mind, but their meal which corresponds to our breakfast is a decidedly primitive one, and would never give a body indigestion. It consists of one cup of coffee, one roll and one grateful heart! I am not certain that we always have the latter; in fact I'm pretty sure we haven't. We tried riding forty miles one forenoon on this style of meal and before we had ridden twenty, the vigorous kicking of one and all resembled the roarings of the lion rampant in Barnum's circus. Papa Elwell has entered a protest, and we now get the addition of cold meats, liver, and bacon and eggs. The French breakfast (at twelve) and dinner (at six) are exactly alike, with the exception that soup is served at dinner.

I think I mentioned in my last that we see a great deal of D. J. Canary, the trick rider, and Woodside, the English racer. These two are thinking some, I believe, of starting for Australia, and thence around the world. We have also had several calls from W. E. Hicks, formerly of the Missouri Bi. Club, whom some of your Western readers will well remember. He is "on the Continent," perfecting himself in French and German, and rides a Springfield Roadster.

Our good times in Paris have been greatly added to by the efforts of the French cyclers in general, and M. de Baroncelli, Mr. G. Augustin Taylor, and Mr. Blackith, of the New York *Herald*, in particular. M. de Baroncelli is Chief Consul of the C. T. C., and Consul of the Union Velocipedique de France. (They don't pronounce this every time. They refer to it as the "U. V. F.") He rides a silver-plated ordinary with an air-cushion on the saddle in a somewhat erratic manner, but he is all right Mr Taylor is the British Pro-Consul. He was very kind indeed in regard to showing us about and interpreting the language at critical moments.

DINED BY THE METROPOLITAN BICYCLE CLUB.

On Wednesday evening, the 26th, we were entertained by a society the spelling of whose name would deplete the alphabet several times. In English it would be Metropolitan Bi. Club. They were assisted by members of several other clubs, whose names were not quite so bad. They gave us a very pleasant go-as-you-please evening, with speeches, songs, conversation, coffee and "champy." M. de Baroncelli made a very nice speech in French, which Mr. Blackith rehashed to us in English, and then Mr. Elwell made a very nice speech in English, which Mr. Blackith rehashed to them in French. We looked at the Frenchmen and the Frenchmen looked at us! They then sang songs and gave recitations in their native tongue for our amusement, and in return we sang some Johnny-get-your-gun choruses and gave them some cyclists' cheers. As Jo Pennell says, "they are really very decent sort of fellows," and we had an evening which everyone thoroughly enjoyed, even though we did have to do most of our conversing by signs.

AT THE WILD WEST SHOW.

Buffalo Bill is giving his Wild West Show here to crowded houses, and very kindly sent us an invitation for Thursday afternoon. The Wild West pleases the French immensely. There is just enough firing of guns and rescuing of pretty girls and riding of bronchos to make them long to be cowboys and look bad. When Mr. Cody does anything, he goes at it whole-hearted, as we soon found out, for we were shown all over the grounds and stables, were introduced to the celebrities by Maj. Burke, and finally planted in the best stalls in the place. On taking leave we attracted more attention than the show by telling Mr. Cody that he was all right and cheering him. It seems rather strange, "when you come to think of it," to see American buffalo running about, within a mile of the *Ecole d'Militaire*, and naked, yellow Indians prancing around within a stone's throw of the Champs Elysées!

Friday afternoon, through the kindness of somebody, I'm sure I don't know who, we attended a reproduction of the Bastile and an old street connected with it, which was, from a historical point of view, one of the most interesting sights we have seen, everything being reproduced life-size, exactly as it was before 1789.

Saturday, June 29, was the day which had been set for our departure from Paris, and Friday night we commenced the labor of packing up after an eight-day stand. It was with heavy heart, I assure you, that the work progressed, for Paris is to a young American a veritable Fairy Land. It's thousands of wonderful and historical sights, its Louvre and Luxembourg, its World's Exposition, its catacombs and sewers, its theatres and gardens, and all the rest form a combination which gets a tight grip on his affection, and he takes to his wheel in a very discontented frame of mind.

We have done fairly well at sight-seeing. At all events we have kept religiously on the go, and what one has not seen another has, and it may be said that as a party we have seen a great deal of Paris. As you can easily imagine we also "saw a great deal of Paris" from the famous Eiffel Tower, a journey to the top of which, owing to the awaiting crowds, occupies anywhere from three to seven hours! You wait patiently in line until the powers of endurance threaten to give way before the happy idea of beckoning to a waiter in a neighboring café strikes you. We find ourselves able to stand a great deal longer with a cup of coffee in one hand and a sandwich in the other.

OH, THESE FRENCH! THEY SMILE AND SMILE.

If we left Paris with heavy hearts I can assure you that our pocket-books were in no such desirable condition. Oh, these French! they smile and smile, and when you reach for your purse your money is almost gone and you don't know where it went to. The only remedy is to leave it, every cent, at home, for in a day you will surely spend all you have about you. Another week in Paris and one and all would have had to write certain letters home, the style of which would have been very similar. We may not have stayed as long as we desired, but we certainly stayed as long as was healthy for our wallets.

Apropos of packing up, have you ever seen the cyclist mend his stockings? He has a novel way of performing the ceremony. He lays a pair (in the toe of each being a hole the size of a half dollar) carefully on the chair and produces a "batchelor's button-box" or a "friend in need," which his best girl gave him just before he sailed. Can he darn stockings? Well, he should smile a smole of smothered ecstacy if he couldn't, and he settles down to it. Fifteen minutes elapse, occupied principally by exclamations expressive of disgust, which rapidly grow more and more vehement. Finally, with a big, big D, he gives up in disgust and running a stout piece of thread around the edges of the hole, he draws the ends up tight and ties a hard knot, effectually closing the gap "Women always make a mountain of a mole-hill,' says he. The trunks are finally packed and shipped back to London, whither most of us return on our way home, and we are once more upon the road.

I forgot to mention in my last that Papa Elwell met with somewhat of a loss at the hands of the French Government. His trunk was shipped direct from London to Paris. When it was inspected by the French custom-house officials, they saw fit to confiscate his maps and letters descriptive of the route from Paris to Geneva, as being dangerous manuscript. They seem to have the idea that he was contemplating marching an army across France and laying siege to Paris. M. de Baroncelli, at no little trouble to himself, has made the loss good, however, and given us a full description of the route.

Owing to pressure of business and slight indisposition, Mr. Jo. Pennell found himself unable to continue further with us, much to the regret of every member of the party. We had gotten into the habit of depending a great deal upon him, and the loss of his general knowledge and good company will be severely felt by all.

THE PARTY LEAVE PARIS.

We were accompanied out of Paris by several local cyclists, including M. Médinger, the champion rider of France, who rode with his wife on a swift tandem bike. Mr. and Mrs. Médinger are a French edition of Mr. and Mrs J. H. Smith, of London, and Mrs. M., accompanied by her husband, has often done over a hundred miles a day. In a little sprint of a mile or two just out of Melun, she showed up well to the front without, as a horse jockey would put it, "turning a hair."

AN IDEAL DAY'S TOUR.

The day's run was to Fontainebleau, whither they accompanied us, returning by train in the evening. The run to Fontainebleau, where we are spending the Sabbath, was an ideal day's touring—the weather and roads perfect, and everybody in good health and spirits. We rode leisurely to Melun before dinner, each at the pace which pleased him best, stopping every now and then in the shade of some huge tree, where the boys would stretch out at full length to smoke a pipe, read a book or fall asleep. Nobody feels hurried or worried and no heed is taken of the time. There's nothing to do but enjoy the very essence of touring as it should be done. After a hearty dinner at Melun everybody seeks a place for a comfortable nap, as we do not ride during the heat of the day. At four or half-past we journey slowly ownward toward Fontainebleau through the magnificent shady forest, stopping occasionally to dance a can-can on the old Druidical tables by the roadside, or give the photographers of the party a shot at us in some particularly pretty spot. We travel over nearly a mile of pavement laid by the Romans two thousand years ago. Is it any wonder, do you think, that everyone is enthusiastic and declares this to be the event of their lives? I don't.

The coming week we spend in traveling slowly through the south of France toward Geneva, arriving there on or about Monday, July 8. We shall be accompanied thus far by W. E. Hicks, before mentioned.

TAM O'SHANTER.

THE STREET PAVEMENTS OF LONDON.

There are three kinds of pavement in use in the London streets. The least used at present is that of stone. Where it does exist, however, it is much better than ours in New York. The stones are long and are set on end, the upper surface being much smaller than our Belgian blocks. Under these stones is a heavy bed of gravel and stone, the whole pavement being about eighteen inches in thickness. The wooden pavements are also formed of much smaller blocks than those tried in New York. But the most extensively used pavement in London is that of concrete. I saw one torn up for repairs a day or two ago, and had an opportunity to discover how it was built. First a foundation of stone is laid down in good substantial blocks. That is covered with tar and gravel, and upon this are set blocks of wood on end tightly pressed together. Over these, cementing them together, and when rolled smooth forming the surface of the street, is put on the concrete. The entire pavement is over two feet thick and is as solid as natural rock. It is as smooth as a billiard table, and over it the heavy vehicles of all kinds used in London roll smoothly and easily. One never sees a team of horses vainly struggling to pull a heavy load out of a hole in these streets. The stream of vehicles moves always smoothly and steadily onward, save when checked by the silent majesty of the inexorable English law, represented by the extended arms of an insignificant London "bobby."—*London Letter to New York Times.*

JERSEY CITY.

On Friday evening last the H. C. W. were visited by delegations from the Elizabeth (N. J.) Wheelmen and the Atalanta Wheelmen, of Newark. The Atalantas arrived about 8:15, but the Elizabeth boys were detained by "Eliza, Betsy and Bess" out on the Meadows, and did not show up until 9 o'clock.

In the way of entertainment the committee (consisting of Captain Day and Messrs. Griffiths and Merseles) had prepared a short programme. The Highland Orchestra, of Jersey City, rendered excellent music during the evening, one of the selections being "The Knights of the Wheel," dedicated to the H. C. W. Mr. George L. Bettcher favored us with several of his Dutch dialect recitations and "Our Only Will Lyle" followed in banjo solos and songs, and appeared "in black" later in the evening and told some side-splitting fables founded on fact. Our friends seemed to particularly enjoy Mr. Lyle. We were also visited during the evening by the "Little Flyer," Mr. S. G. Whittaker, who made a few remarks to the assembly. Elocution was also practised by Dr. G. Carlton Brown, of the E. W., President Miller, of the A. W., and Dr. Johnson, on the part of the hosts. The party broke up about 11 P. M. and were escorted as far as Newark by an H. C. W. body guard.

Messrs. Earl and Benedict have returned from a trip through the Shenandoah Valley, whither they wheeled after the League Meet at Hagerstown. Apparently both enjoyed the sunshine, and had basked in its rays considerably. Benedict's complexion has assumed a sort of black-and-tan color, and Earl's usually Pear's-soap hide resembles a peach-blow vase with whiskers on it.

Dr. Johnson, of the H. C. W., intends starting on the 26th inst. on his annual tour. This year he will wheel through the State of Maine. He has been very much exercised of late in deciding what route he will take and after corresponding with every local Consul in Massachusetts, Rhode Island and New Hampshire, he has decided to follow the T. P. (telegraph poles), "turning right at the cherry trees" and turning back at Seven-mile Hill. Every mail brings him a fresh batch of suggested routes. He was showing me his proposed route, as he had laid it out on the walls of his billiard parlor, which include maps, guides, histories etc. To make himself thoroughly acquainted with the route, he has driven a nail in the name of each town he intends stopping at. The following places he has nailed (or rather he will "nail" when he gets there): Providence, R. I.; Lebanon, Mass.; East Brattleboro, Mansfield, Cobbs Tavern, Boston, Medford, Lynn, Salem, Ipswich (Doc. can't say that name very plain yet), Newburyport, Amesborough, Portsmouth, Kennebunk, Biddeford, Saco, Portland, Brunswick, Lewiston, Augusta, Fairfield, Bangor, Bucksport *and* Bar Harbor. (If there's any places I've forgotten I'll advise you next week, as I haven't a very good memory for names.) He starts July 26, and we trust that wheelmen will take him in, dry him, feed him and bounce him (in the morning) with their blessing. For the benefit of cyclists not acquainted with him I will describe him for you. He will be known by an elephantine hat, which he calls a helmet, with the accent on the "met"; a morning glory mustache and limbs that woUld maKe A ChOruS GirL weeP witH eNvy. (After reading this he may change his personal appearance, but to overcome that I will add that if you see a fellow seated alongside the road, surrounded with 7 maps, 197 letters and 4 guides, with a big rock on each, serving as a paper-weight, you will know, without requesting his card, that he is Dr. Elliott Wheelman Johnson.)

Our friends, the Pennsylvania Bicycle Club, have again invited us to the Quaker City on August 3 and 4. I will say (simply to increase the agony of our Philadelphia friends), that there isn't the slightest doubt of the invitation being declined, and that we will come down with both feet. Under penalty of a heavy fine, no member of the H. C. W. intending to accept this invitation will be permitted to satisfy his appetite for the two days preceding the date of start, in order that we may do something in an *actual, positive* way, which will, on our departure from the gates of their city, convince the P. B. C's that we have been there, and that they "put their foot in it" by taking the risk of inviting us the second time down to their home. We feel doubly honored, as it seems this invitation is about the first act of their new Captain, Mr. C. L. Leisen. We hope he may have the success in his new office he deserves, and that he may prove as callous to all attempts to rattle him as did his popular predecessor, Mr. W. D. Supplee.

A few days ago fourteen of us Jerseymen reported at 5 A. M. at the club-house to start on the run called by the Captain to Long Branch. We rode direct to Perth Amboy, via Elizabeth and Rahway, where we took the train to Matawan, and thence to Red Bank and Long Branch, where we "filled in." The time from 2 o'clock until 6 was spent in strolling along the beach, and at 6:30 we took the boat for the city. Not the "slowest" part of the day, by any means, was the time spent on the boat on the way home. This run is an exceptionally fine one, and for a club run is certainly enjoyable. The following runs have also been called: July 20, for Staten Island; 21, Hackensack; 27, Rose Park; 28, Glen Island. COASTER.

SAN FRANCISCO.

Senator Morgan is on his way out here with a new American team. I have not heard who the riders are that compose it. They are to spend one week in Denver.

The Bay City Wheelmen are already in the field with their club ticket for League officers. They have nominated R. M. Thompson, of San Francisco, for Chief Consul; J. P. Percival, of Los Angeles, for Vice-Consul; W. D. Sheldon, of San Francisco Secretary-Treasurer; State Representatives, Dr. Gibson, of San Francisco, C. C. Moore, of Stockton, and A. E. McKenna, of San Jose. This ticket is a strong one, and there is not likely to be any organized opposition to it. It is a board that will undoubtedly accomplish much for the League. I understand that the Oak Leaf Wheelmen, of Stockton, and the Garden City Wheelmen, of San Jose, have endorsed it and will work for it.

H. G. Kennedy, one of Denver's most popular riders, is here on a visit. While here in 1886 he made many friends, who were glad to see him again. He is an excellent trick rider. We have had within a few months Maltby, Nash, Barber and now Kennedy, all great trick riders.

July 11, 1889. CALIFORNIA.

ST. LOUIS.

The members of the Cycle Club are enthusiastic over the fine showing made by their man, Barnard, in the races at Sedalia, and they are already talking about a meeting with Lumsden. I hardly think they are justified in the extravagant estimate they place on Barnard's abilities, notwithstanding the good showing he made at Sedalia, and the idea of matching him with Lumsden, before he has had a chance to demonstrate what he can do, seems a bit premature. He was not extended in any of his races at Sedalia, and as these events were the first in which he has ever contested, it is difficult to tell what he might do if pushed. He is a strong, lusty fellow, modest and unassuming, has fine action in the saddle, and, if properly taught and thoroughly trained, will undoubtedly develop into a fine rider, but it will take lots of experience and hard training to make him fit to race with Lumsden. The latter is probably the fastest amateur in America to-day, and the rider who beats him must get up a lively hustle He has had the benefit of the best training in Garden's hands, and being a man of good habits and thoroughly tractable, he is fit to race with the best of them. Garden evidently wants another St. Louis scalp, for he has already started inquiries about Barnard and the probabilities of getting on a match with Lumsden. He had so much fun (but so little profit) with us before that he wants to try it again. That is all right, Robert, but you will keep on fooling with these St. Louis riders until you get your leg pulled. Barnard may or may not do it, but if he don't we will find some one who will. Lumsden may get married himself one of these days, and then, verily! thy name shall be Dennis. We will swoop down on you like a wolf on the fold, and wipe up the earth with you (always assuming that Van don't go on the track again).

There is more trouble in sight for the Missouris, but its members have been kept in a ferment so long now with one thing after another that they are getting used to it, and the new turn affairs have taken does not create the consternation that it might have done a few months since. President Andrews gave notice at the last meeting that he would propose at the August meeting an amendment to the by-laws fixing the dues of both associate and active members at the same figure, say $1.50 per month, and extend the voting privilege to both classes. The effect of the adoption of this amendment will be to do away with the active list and transmogrify the club, so to speak, from a bicycle club into a social organization, with no distinctive features. True, it will for the present be called the Missouri Bicycle Club, but cycling will be an auxiliary—a side issue—and the change of name will soon follow, as a matter of course. The "milk in the cocoanut," as well as the "hair on the outside" of this new move, may be found in the action of the club on the Sunday issue. The proposed amendment is simply a transparent scheme to put the associate members (who do not ride and take no interest in cycling matters) on a voting basis, in the hope that enough assistance can be had from them to warrant another attack on the Sunday rule; but it won't work. The Missouri Club has always been a bicycle club, with all that the term implies, and it has a record as such that it may well be proud of. If the promoters of this latest scheme think they can succeed in their plans under the specious argument of a reduction in the dues of the active members they will fail, just as they failed in their other attempts to carry out features of what the *Spectator* alludes to as their "policy." One of the officers stated, just after the May meeting, that the action of the club at that time was a slap in the face of the new administration. Of course it was nothing of the sort, but if that is the view they take of the case they don't seem to mind slaps very much. They have had two or three hard raps since that time, but they are still working away at their "policy." If the club doesn't appreciate their efforts it isn't their fault.

The St. Louis Cycle Club is about to disband, and a new club called the Cycling Club will be organized in its stead. There are a good many undesirable men in the present club, and it is with a view of getting rid of this element that the reorganization is proposed. There are to be no deadheads in the new enterprise.

Captain W. A. Davis and E. J. Roberts, of the Illinois Cycling Club, were in the city Friday and Saturday. They made the usual trip—to the brewery—and hereafter will draw their matches from an Anheuser match box. Geo. Warwick, of Springfield, Mass., was here at the same time, and a couple of the bicycle agents undertook his entertainment. One of them succumbed at two o'clock; the other lasted until five, but the wreck was complete. When the Springfield man was last seen he was looking for more agents. Davis and Roberts expressed a desire on their arrival to take a ride over the famous—or infamous—De Soto road, and arrangements were at once made to gratify their wishes, but later in the day they concluded to go to Ballwin instead. Foiled again! ITHURIEL.

ELIZABETH.

So little has appeared in the cycling papers lately (THE WHEEL excepted) about the Elizabeth Wheelmen, that most people would suppose that they were out of existence. This is not the case, however, as the "E. W." are to-day stronger and more active, have more road riders, etc., than they have ever had before. The trouble is that there has been no one to gather the news for publication. Hereafter your readers will hear from us very frequently.

The debt of Elizabeth having been settled, and the city placed on a sound financial basis, the Board of Trade and the *Daily Journal* decided to get up a book setting forth the advantages of the place as a site for manufacturers, residences, etc. One of the first to apply for a place was the "E. W." The club was recently photographed in full uniform, and grouped in front of the house. They intend to have a large photo-engraving made, and inserted in the book, with a full history of the club, names of officers, members, etc. As the book will be sent to all parts of the country, it will be a good advertisement for the wheelmen.

The E. W. attended the smoker of the H. C. W., on Friday evening last, and were delighted with their reception; as you will probably get a full account from "Coaster," I will only say that the "E. W." think that it was a big success.

The "E. W." are talking of giving another lantern parade this fall, about the latter part of October.

Mr. N. H. White, our only Eagle rider, has just returned from an extended tour through Connecticut. He visited the Eagle people at Stamford, attended the meet of the Connecticut Division, and toured home via New London.

"COMET."

BROOKLYN NEWS.

THE ROAD-HOG IN UNIFORM.

The very latest tidbit of news which is now causing extended comment in the cycling clubs of this city is the unwarranted action of a mounted policeman of the Park force in riding down Beasley, of the Kings County Wheelmen. It seems that he and a club mate were returning to the city on the Ocean Parkway, and met this road-hog policeman in the vicinity of Parkville. The wheelmen decided that the officer was intoxicated, and Beasley remarked the fact to his fellow wheelmen, which, the officer overhearing, immediately rode at them and deliberately rode Beasley down, the horse's hoofs mangling the wheel in the most approved style and bruising Beasley somewhat, so that he and his wheel returned to the city in a four-wheeler. He has obtained a warrant against the officer for assault, and it is to be hoped that he will be dealt with in the most summary manner. There are a few others of the Park squad who should be put in a bunch with this man and all served in about the same manner. They are nearly all "from Cork," and take special delight in showing their authority not only on wheelmen, but on the many other frequenters of Prospect Park, and are at times very annoying, to express it mildly.

LET US HAVE A STATE MEET.

A meeting of prominent cyclists of New York and Brooklyn was held in New York on Friday evening, July 12, to discuss informally the subject of extending an invitation to the League to hold its State meet in this section of the country. Let us have the meet by all means! The hospitality shown our visitors will linger pleasantly in their minds for some time to come, I'll warrant.

A DELIGHTFUL RUN TO ROSLYN.

As early as half-past two on Saturday afternoon, July 13, Pettit's Hotel, at Jamaica, presented an animated appearance, this being the rendezvous of the Brooklyn Bicycle Club and the Long Island Wheelmen en route for Roslyn, L. I. Wheelmen kept arriving steadily, a number taking the train to Jamaica, arriving in advance of their more venturesome club mates who had elected to "ride through." At 3:30 P. M. First Lieut. Fay, accompanied by twenty-five members of the Brooklyn Club and ten members of the Bergen Point Wheelmen, from Hackensack, N. J., arrived, and the Brooklyn contingent started ahead, leaving the Long Island Wheelmen, some fifteen strong, to follow, under the guidance of Captain Teller.

It was a pleasant day for wheeling, the sky being overcast, but the doubt as to the appearance of the moon, which was counted on later to make the sail home by boat enjoyable, caused many to wish there were not so many clouds in sight. But wheelmen are naturally hopeful, and trusting that the "gods" would favor them and dispel the clouds before night, they continued on their way, only disturbed now and then by Bugler Fuller's attacks upon his horn.

All went well until the last five miles, when a nice, soft, sandy road was encountered, about which, by the way, nothing had been said in the flowery notices upon the club's bulletin boards.

Well, it was ridable and had nothing to do with Raymond's wheel breaking down about four miles from Roslyn and making him late for supper. However, he got there with a few of his club mates who had stopped to help him patch up, arriving just before the Long Islands.

The arrangements for supper should have been ample, notice having been given the proprietor in time, and it is to be regretted that several of the Long Islands were forced to procure supper on the boat, becoming disgusted with their treatment at the hotel.

But they should be charitable and remember that wheelmen are hungry mortals after a ride, and probably mine host of the Mansion House had never catered for so large a party before, and in consequence lost his head.

The ride home by boat is one of the features of this trip, and notwithstanding the fact that the moon would not be wooed from behind her fleecy veil until New York was almost reached, the trip was enlivened by song and merry jest. Not the least in causing merriment was an impromptu tug of war between the "Blue and Gray," the hawser of the boat serving as the rope. As there was no time limit and the Brooklyns had their end securely tied to an iron cleat, and the Long Islands anchor was braced round a post, they might be pulling yet, with no decision as to the winner.

Ah! it was a rare sight to see jovial Halsey, Dr. Wilder and genial Furst and other L. I. W.'s tug on that rope, typical of the new state of things among Brooklyn wheelmen. Let us have more of these pleasant trips, cementing good-fellowship and binding closer the sister clubs of our city.

I regret that "Ram Lal" has so misconstrued my well-meaning item in a previous letter. Far be it from my thoughts to even hint that a club member should *leave* his club and join another as associate member. On the contrary, the item was suggested by a conversation which was reported to me as having taken place between well-known members of the three clubs, to the effect that the fraternal and social side of cycling life might be materially augmented by the election of active members of various clubs to associate membership in other clubs, and naming a certain few of the up-town men who would probably join the B. B. C. for that reason, thus becoming members of both clubs without lessening their status in the original club. Sincerely thankful to "Ram Lal" as I am for his appreciation of the "greatness of the B. B. C.," it is a pleasure to afford this explanation. ATOL.

Brooklyn, July 15, 1889.

HARRISBURG, PA.

H. B. Gerhart, accompanied by Mr. Ed. Shoop, of this city, started Thursday morning for Martinsburg, W. Va., where they will be joined by Mr. Gerhardt's brother, and proceed from there, on their wheels, down the Winchester pike, en route to Luray and Natural Bridge, returning home via Richmond and Baltimore.

Everybody returned home from the Hagerstown Meet happy. The Harrisburg Club made an excellent appearance with thirty-five men in line. What did the band play?

Mr. L. R. Kelker has issued invitations to all of our wheelmen to attend a local meet to be held at his beautiful country residence on the banks of the Susquehanna, two and a half miles above the city. The boys anticipate a very "large" time, and I am sure they will not be disappointed. Thursday evening is the date upon which this august occasion takes place.

Mr. Hicock, of the Pope Manufacturing Company, spent several days with us, after a two days' sojourn at the meet.

Hagerstown girls are "just too sweet for anything." Our parade caps were objects of great admiration in their eyes, and as a consequence "Son" and I are conscious of several occult impressions made on them by their pretty lips. We should have preferred a closer contact, but publicity forbids. N. O. REMARKS.

July 10, 1889.

PHILADELPHIA.

RAIN—RAIN—RAIN.

This about describes the state of the weather for a week before the "Glorious Fourth," and to cap the climax at noon on that day it began to pour, a state of things which kept up for about three hours, when it cleared up, but too late, as every one's pleasure had already been spoilt. To make it all the more aggravating, the weather ever since has been delightful. Of course the Lancaster Club's tournament fell through, and the crowd of Philadelphia cyclers who expected to go were disappointed and staid at home. Notwithstanding the dubious aspect of the weather, eight members of the South End Wheelmen went thither and reported having a truly glorious time, and one and all voted the Lancaster Club a jolly set of boys.

Seven Philadelphia cyclers journeyed to Hagerstown on their wheels. They were: Draper, of the Pennsylvania's, Diamond, of the South Ends, and Wood, Fleming, McGlathery, Bromly and Spier, of the Century Wheelmen. The last four started on Saturday afternoon at 2:30 and reached Coatsville (42 miles) for supper. Starting at eight the next morning, they rode to Columbia for dinner, and Gettysburg (80 miles) for the night, arriving at Hagerstown at 3 o'clock on Monday afternoon; thus covering *one hundred and fifty-eight miles in two days*. The second days' ride of eighty miles is a great achievement, when one takes into consideration the bad condition of the road, a sandy one, as anyone who has ever been over it can testify. Of course the run was not without its accidents. Captain Scott, of the Mount Vernon wheelmen, who started with the party, rode a new wheel for the first time, and when about a mile from Coatsville broke the backbone off close to the little wheel. He turned back and went to the meet via train. Also Spier of the Centurions broke down on that beautiful Star no less than *five* times, but he got there all the same.

Every one that attended the League Meet reports a good time, and any one who wants to enjoy a good laugh is invited to have an hour's "chin" with A. G. McGlathery, or as he is called "Mack," about the time he had at Hagerstown. When he made that Fourth of July oration in the public square, the audience was so lost in emotions brought on by his fiery eloquence and patriotic language, that he in return completely lost his voice for the time being. When he returned to this city of Brotherly Love he could do naught but *whistle* the tune the band played.

The Century Base-ball Club on the 4th of July defeated the Newtown Club by the score of 17 to 1. "Kid" Allen, the phenomenal centre-fielder, wears crape around his hat because he made the error that let in that one run.

Messrs. Deitsch and Geyler, of the Century Wheelmen, expect before long to start on a tour to the northern part of the State via Delaware Water Gap, Dingmad's Ferry, etc.

July 8, 1889. "ARGUS."

ERIE, PA.

And still we labor under the depressing influence of much weather. What wheelmen will do if this state of affairs continues I cannot say, but it is fair to presume they will take flight to some other and drier world than this—the *Bicycling World*, perhaps. Who knows?

But little has been done among cyclists since my last letter. The heavy roads no doubt are largely to blame for such an unusual state of affairs at this season, but added to this, our wheelmen and wheelwomen have had large inroads made on their time by numerous festivals, receptions, etc. Everybody who can get out of the city will do so between now and the middle of July. This, of course, necessitates many farewell calls, and not until the superfluous portion of the community is safely packed off to Saratoga, Newport and Bar Harbor will we cyclists be able to fully realize on our investment. Intervening time will have to be bridged over somehow. After that you may look out for "fun on wheels" in Erie.

Some of the Buffalo riders came down on the night boat Saturday, reaching here about 3 A. M. Sunday, and starting back by wheel almost immediately. It was our intention to meet them here, show them what few courtesies we could in the limited time they were to stay, and then accompany them part or all of the way to Buffalo. However, when our first detachment struck the boat, they had been gone some two hours. Thus were all our hospitable intentions blasted.

We notice still more ladies on wheels this week. Miss Gunnison, who has had her "Psycho" for about four weeks, is riding very well indeed. Why is it so many of the old fogies dub the "bi" vulgar, and yet seem to consider the "tri" a regular Sunday-school machine? Possibly "Psyche" can tell me this. She seems to have a fund of information for her own sex.

You will hear from me again when the clouds roll by, if they ever do. P.

"BRAWN AND BRAIN."

A bright, seasonable volume that will interest a large number of people, entitled "Brawn and Brain, Considered by Two Noted Athletes and Thinkers," has just been issued. Twelve of the most popular sports are treated by a small army of champions, experts or specialists. Baseball is treated by a champion nine and an umpire; the elegant art of fencing by F. R. Coudert, the noted lawyer, and others; riding a horse by Buffalo Bill and others; canoeing by Charles Ledyard Norton, and tennis, polo, swimming, cycling, jumping, running and other sports by persons famous in those pastimes. Prof Laflin treats of health at home, and Wm. Wood and others of how to grow strong. The volume is a really notable addition to the literature of health and pleasure. John B. Alden, publisher, New York, Chicago and Atlanta.

WHEEL GOSSIP

Mott!

Maryland!

Mott! Mott!!

Mott! Mott!! Mott!!!

Mott is all right. This we guarantee.

Good old triple X Mott.

The *C. T. C. Gazette* for July is an arid waste.

"Ram Lal" and "Atol" should put on the gloves.

C. M. and W. F. Murphy will compete at the East Hartford races.

Joseph Boswell and W. B. Worrall are the oldest riders in Minneapolis.

Mr. George Warwick has just returned from an extended Western trip.

Messrs. E. W. Pope, C. F. Joy and H. A. Hickok spent July 5 at Antietam.

The Cyclist and Bicycling News have moved to new offices in London.

The Elwell tourists did themselves proud at the Buffalo Bill "Wild West Show" at Paris.

A. A. Taylor, one of the Pope Mfg. Co.'s travelers, has gone to Europe for a brief vacation.

The son of John I. Davenport, Supervisor of Elections of New York City, is a cyclist.

We should like to see an American who ever went abroad and did not come back a crank on light wheels.

Any club desiring a fancy rider should address W. H. Barber, 9 Merriman Street, Rochester, N. Y.

It is rumored that the New York Athletic Club is taking steps to form a strong bicycle team of racing men.

Minneapolis property owners are endeavoring to have Park Avenue, a fine residence street, paved with asphalt.

The Riverside Wheelmen have called runs to South Oyster Bay July 21 and to White Plains July 28.

The Wilkesbarre, Pa., Bicycle Club contributed $90 to the Johnstown relief fund, and the Scranton Club put in $60.

Two-mile handicap, decided at Cape May Athletic Club games on Monday last: F. G. Brown, K. C. W., walk over.

Albert A. Reed amusingly relates in the Boston *Globe*, of July 15, the first and last tandem outing of Mr. and Mrs. Spicer.

R. Howell has opened a public house. The English "pro." invariably finds his way behind the bar sooner or later.

The annual frolic, clambake and outing of the Mercury Wheel Club will be held August 10, probably at Willett's Point.

McCredy, editor of the *Irish Cycling and Athletic News*, will have a camping and touring party in Scotland, starting August 5.

Clemens, of the Manhattan Club, is riding a 42-lb. Swift, geared to "57." He intends to put on a higher gear and go on the race path.

A collie puppy, the title of a canine article, might be transposed into, a cool puppy, and applied to the road hog or the cycle thief.

The Long Island Cyclists' Union has reason to be proud of the most important work it has yet accomplished—viz., the paving of Cobblestone Hill.

W. E. Hicks, formerly of the St. Louis *Post-Dispatch*, accompanied the Elwell tourists from Paris to Geneva, spending a week with them.

Mr. C. A. Snow & Co. inform us that no patents pertaining to bicycles were filed at the patent office this week. This is a rare circumstance.

Mr. Arthur Burr will build a new track at Bellagio, Eng., which he will attempt to make the finest in the world. Five hundred men are employed on it.

L. A. Newcome, Harlem Wheelmen, has been having a pleasant time at Boston. Messrs. Stall and Ross kindly piloted the New Yorker over the roads.

The maker of the two-speed gear is Mr. Carter, Rueber Terrace, Bradford, Eng. There might be something in this for some of our American makers.

One of the charming sights of Gotham is Elliot Mason and his boy Hobart on a tandem bike. The two are great companions, and the boy does his share of the work.

Jacob W. Clute and J. T. Josline, two cyclists of Schenectady, N. Y., sailed for Europe this week. They will tour in England and Scotland and on the Continent.

The League had a membership of 10,272, July 19, of which Massachusetts had 1,386, being second to New York, which has 1,824. Pennsylvania is third with 1,250.

AMUSINGLY STUPID.—Every paper in London of Saturday last published this item: "Chauncey M. Depew and Ralph Temple, two American cyclists, arrived yesterday."

A. B. Barkman has a new patterned driving gear to his Victor Safety which is said to be remarkably easy-running. The Overman Wheel Company will use this new device in all '89 safeties.

The paragraph about the two girls who donned knickerbockers (alleged), mounted ordinaries (surmised), and rode on Bedford Avenue one dark night, is being copied all over the Union.

Many cyclists think that mud guards on safeties are made too long. When getting down off a curb they always strike, and often snap off. They are generally made longer than is necessary.

L. G. Spier, a cyclist of Coluna, Cal., has fallen heir to $500,000. The local paper devotes an editorial paragraph to it. Had Mr. Spier been found drowned a two-line local would have covered the case.

Henry E. Ducker's suit against the Buffalo International Fair Association for $1,114.15, salary claimed for running the bicycle meet, was dismissed on Friday last by the jury on the ground of no cause for action.

The Philadelphia *Press*, republishing our description of the Pen-Mar excursion, remarks on "the extremely full description of THE WHEEL." THE WHEEL did not get full at Hagerstown. We leave it to "Jack."

The Eagle is slowly but surely making a good name for itself. The Eagle Bicycle Co. publishes in our advertising pages a record of a century run over poor roads, which speaks well of the Eagle's qualities.

The Pennsylvania Bicycle Club will probably arrange their visit to the Hudson County Wheelmen for next autumn, and the Century propose a trip to the Kings County Wheelmen, of Brooklyn, N. Y., at the same time.

SILVER-PLATED AND AN AIR CUSHION.

Just think of this dilettanteism! M. de Baroncelli rides a silver-plated ordinary, with an air cushion on the saddle. "He rides erratic," says Tam O'Shanter, but "he's all right."

On Saturday evening last, W. T. Robertson rode from Hyattsville, Md. to Washington, five miles, in 19m. 2s. Returning, he covered the distance in 19m. 30s. His mount was an Eagle, and his time is record between the two cities.

Mr. Beasley should leave no stone unturned to jail the mounted park policeman who literally jumped on him. The road-hog is bad, but this brute, who is paid to stamp out brutalism, should be sent behind the prison bars to twirl his thumbs and moralize.

Referring to the Cottage City Meet, the Boston *Herald* publishes this note: "As twenty-five ladies are expected to be present, a contest for the fair sex will probably be one of the events." We hope not; if the sex is fair keep it so. The reporter of the *Herald* must be romancing.

ONE-MILE NOVICE'S SCRATCH RACE, OPEN.

At the Adelphia A. C. club games, to be held July 27, at the Manhattan A. C. grounds, Eighty-sixth Street and Eighth Avenue, New York City. Fee, 50 cents; entries close July 20 with T. P. Conneff, 347 West Forty-first Street, city.

The case of Mr. Beasley vs. the mounted Park policeman, who ran him down, was to have been heard this morning at the meeting of the Brooklyn Park Commissioners. After the Commissioners pass on the question, the case will be carried to the court. The case is in charge of Michael Furst.

Charley Sheehan, the indefatigable Secretary of the Manhattan Club, has advanced the suggestion that the '92 League Meet should be held in New York, when the International Exposition will be held here. It is looking a bit ahead, but it is a great scheme. We should get 5,000 wheelmen here.

On account of some of the objections made by several riders, the Springfield Bicycle Club have decided to have two events—a 50-mile race, open to all local riders, and a 50-mile race, open to all. The races will come off on September 13, over the Springfield-Hartford course. The entrance fee to the races is $5.

Good old A. J. Wilson, "Faed," clever writer, great on the road and great always, because though born deaf, he knows more than many two-eared, four-eyed men, caught the Elwell tourists on their arrival in Queenstown, and shadowed them until they left old England. Good old "Faed," we say.

To all men who cultivate adipose tissue, greeting: We are backing Mr. Henry Hall, of Highland Mills, New York, against any man over two hundred pounds for a race on the road, distance from one to fifty miles. Mr. Hall is 218 pounds, and rides a Victor safety geared up nobody knows how high.

Mr. J. D. Patterson, Captain of the Port Huron Bicycle Club, and several members, rode from Port Huron, Mich., to Buffalo, New York, *via* Woodstock, Bradford, Hamilton, St. Catharines and Niagara Falls, taking in the meet at St. Catharines. They report the roads (mostly gravel) in very fine condition all the way.

Brown-Sequard, the eminent French physician and hygienist, says that he has discovered the secret not only of immortal youth, but of rejuvenation. We have read, per cable, that the doctor extracts this wonderful fluid from the carcass of a "yaller dorg," but we believe it will finally come out that the doctor has taken up cycling.

The following advertisement appeared in the Belfast *News Letter*: "Bicyclette wanted by town missionary, for holidays; will some Christian of means offer one, and oblige?—Matt. vii., 7." The verse quoted by the "town missionary" says: "Ask and it shall be given you; seek and ye shall find; knock and it shall be opened."

RHODE ISLAND NOMINATIONS.

For Chief Consul, Charles S. Davol, of Warren; for Vice-Consul, George L. Cooke, of Providence; for Secretary-Treasurer, Nelson S. Gibbs, of Providence; for first representative, C. W. Greene, of Warren; for second representative, George C. Newell, of Pawtucket.

Our editorial statement in last week's WHEEL, that in our opinion Windle should have been suspended and not expelled, was no reflection on the ruling of the Racing Board, as they are obliged by the rule to expel. But we differ with the rules, and claim that it should be optional with the Board whether a man who accepts expenses should be expelled or suspended.

Tam O'Shanter is enthusiastic over French roads, which are smooth and with no heavy grades. The Parisian idea of entertainment is explosive and photographic at the same time. The Frenchmen blew horns, fired off pistols and had photographomania every ten minutes. They also fed the cyclists on lemonade and then charged them thirty cents per glass.

U. G. Edinger, of Kingston, N. Y., rides a Warwick Perfection Safety, and has this to say of it: "I have thoroughly tested the Warwick Safety, and am convinced that it is the best wheel on the market to-day. My wife learned to mount and ride it in three days, and is the first lady bicycle rider in this city. For path-riding, hill-climbing, speed, etc., it has no equal."

The 10,000 metre (6 miles, 380 yards) bicycle championship of Bohemia was decided at Prague on June 29. Warfel Kohout, of Prague, won in 20m. 10s. The tricycle championship, 5,000 metre (3 miles, 190 yards) was run on the following day, and was won by Arthur Keamer, Leipzig; time, 10m. 32 2-5s. The international mile bicycle race was won by Warfel Kohout, of Prague; time, 2m. 55 3-5s.

"Now, then, all together, where's the Deacon?" That is the favorite chorus of the Harlem Wheelmen, of which club the Deacon is a member. When the "Deke" goes about castle-building on that hands-off safety of his, the boys bring him back to earth with a lusty call. The Deacon also has an unhappy faculty of losing himself, and the general outcry generally results in his sudden appearance.

Mr. George K. Tapley, Treasurer of the Warwick Cycle Co., was in New York on Thursday. The company has its men working day and night, and the wheels are now being turned out in good quantity. Slight imperfections of the first wheels manufactured, and which must always be expected, have now been overcome, and the Warwicks are now giving satisfaction. The company will put in new machinery in the fall and increase its factory room.

Since his introduction into the office of Chief Consul, L. A. W., for Pennsylvania, J. J. Van Nort, of Scranton, has shown himself a pushing and energetic official, and worthy of a continuance of the honor conferred upon him by President Luscomb. Mr. Van Nort, through the columns of the League organ, issues a stirring appeal to members of the Pennsylvania Division to take an additional interest in official affairs, and adds that the long delayed Road Book will appear shortly.

What a funny scene that must have been at the dinner given the American tourists in Paris. M. de Baroncelli spoke a welcome in French, which was translated and re-spoken by one of the Americans. Then Elwell replied, and his speech had to be done over for the benefit of the Frenchmen. We are sure the Frenchmen had a cigar-store image, deadly, fixed grin while Elwell spoke, and that the Americans screwed up their features in mute appreciation of the Frenchman's "bong mots."

One of the quiet fellows who is known on every race track in the country, and is always at many State and all the national meets, is Joseph Goodman, of Hartford, publisher of many of the official score cards. Goodman is ruddy-complexioned, strong face and is a good rider. He has a habit of not worrying, has been known to imbibe to the point of jollity but never beyond the border of respectability, has tact, judgment, and therefore makes friends. Good, old Goodman, as the English say.

A trip to Maine has been planned by members of the New Bedford Bicycle Club. They will start for Portland July 20, and on the 21st to Prout's Neck, escorted by the Portland Wheel Club. On the 22d Old Orchard Beach, Saco and Biddeford will be visited. On the 23d the wheelmen will visit Deering and the islands in Casco Bay. On the 24th Poland Springs, Lewiston and Auburn will be visited, and on the 25th Gardiner, Augusta and Hallowell. The club will pay a visit to Onset to-day.

The most enjoyable ride we have ever taken was a stroll through the Park on Monday and Tuesday, starting at 12 Monday and ending at 2 A. M. on Tuesday. The thermometer had fallen to 65, and the night was clear and the air crisp. The moon threw leafy shadows on the white road with startling distinctness. The heavens were planet-laden and the greater stars seemed to beam with great intensity on the sleeping world. The morning star, which we have not seen for years, came up a magnificent globe of old gold.

The *Referee* ungenerously refers to two grammatical errors in our League Meet report, and causes a wrong impression among its readers. Our "fist" is not quite so clear as "type-writer" stuff; the copy was "tackled" on Friday morning, and the paper was mailed on Saturday night, leaving no time for the care and attention usually bestowed on the typography of the paper. We scored the greatest "beat" ever credited to a cycling journal, and we are well satisfied even if the compositors set "have rose" for "have risen."

SCOTCH ROAD RECORDS LOWERED.

The 50-mile Scotch road tricycle record was again lowered June 24, both A. Hutton and J. Steel beating M. Bruce's previous record by over two minutes. Hutton covered the distance in 3h. 50m. 10s., Steel being 120 yards behindhand, and finishing eighteen seconds slower. The first twenty-five miles took only 1h. 51m., and their chances then looked good for breaking the record, but an east wind that shortly after sprang up spoiled that. The road was in good condition, but the head-wind on the way back was keenly felt.

BICYCLE THIEF CAUGHT.

At ten o'clock last Saturday morning, Henry Gabel, a Buffalo cyclist, who has an office in the German Insurance Building, left his bicycle standing outside of the German Bank. It rested there only a short time when Claud Snyder came along. Claud says he is a laborer, but the police say he is simply a loafer. Snyder grabbed the bicycle, and, as he couldn't ride it, he rolled it down Main Street. Gabel missed the wheel a short time later, and reported the matter at once to the police. Snyder had got as far as Seneca Street when Specials Kief and Jordan observed him. They arrested him and locked him up on a charge of grand larceny.—*Buffalo News*.

AN OLD-TIME SPORTING MATCH.

The road from New York to Yonkers is very likely to be the scene of one of the most extraordinary contests ever known in the history of the sport. Mr. Heydecker, New York Club, and Mr. Thayer, Citizens' Club, are the high contending parties. Both have gone into strict training, and the match will be ridden when both are thoroughly wound up. Heydecker is in the hands of de Goicouria, who will act as his mentor, and until the day of the race he will not be permitted to make even a cigarette without the permission of his trainer, or to eat anything but raw beef mixed with sand, washed down by concentrated essence of Pilsner. It will be a great day. No news has been received from Thayer's training quarters up to the time of going to press, but he is reported as being hard as nails and moving in good form. The New York man is compelled, by the articles of agreement, to ride without the aid of a "lamp," and it is further stipulated that the race will be declared off if neither of the men finish the fifteen miles within eight hours.

New York State Division L.A.W.

OFFICIAL ORGAN.

OFFICERS FOR 1889.

Chief Consul, W. S. BULL, 754 Main Street, Buffalo, N. Y. Vice-Consul, M. L. BRIDGMAN, 1255 Bedford Avenue, Brooklyn, N Y Secretary-Treasurer, GEO. M. NISBETT, 50 Wall Street, New York City. Executive and Finance Committee, W. S. BULL, M. H. BRIDGMAN, DR. GEORGE E. BLACKHAM, Dunkirk, N. Y.

NEW YORK STATE DIVISION—CONSULS AND HOTELS.

LIST No. 5.

PLACE.	CONSUL	HOTEL.
Averill Park		Sand Lake Hotel.
Corning	F. C. Williams	
East Syracuse	F. A. Marshall	Baggs' Hotel.
Slingerlands Station		Home Lawn.
Syracuse		The Leland.

Mr. I. B. Knickerbocker has resigned as Local Consul for Cortland.

Mr. Fred. B. Corey has resigned as Local Consul for Homer.

W. S. BULL, *Chief Consul.*

STATE CHAMPIONSHIPS LOCATED.

To the Members of the New York State Division:

The half-mile New York State Division Bicycle Championship has been awarded to the Lockport wheelmen, to be contested for at their race meet August 15.

The two-mile New York State Division Bicycle Championship has been awarded to the Albany wheelmen, to be contested for at their September tournament.

W. S. BULL, *Chief Consul.*

NEW YORK STATE DIVISION NOMINATIONS—1889-1890.

For Chief Consul—W. S. BULL, Buffalo.

For Vice-Consul—M. L. BRIDGMAN, Brooklyn.

For Secretary-Treasurer—GEORGE M. NISBETT, New York.

For Representatives, First District, comprising New York, Richmond and Westchester Counties:

J. C. GULICK, Citizens' B. C., - - New York.
W. H. DE GRAAF, Harlem W., - - do
J. L. MILLER, Riverside W., - - do
G. B. WATTS JR., New York B. C., - do
J. A. CLAIRMONT, Manhattan B. C., do

For Representative, Second District, comprising Kings, Queens and Suffolk Counties:

CARL C. ALDEN, - - - Brooklyn.

For Representative, Third District, comprising Columbia, Greene, Rensselaer, Albany, Saratoga, Schoharie, Washington, Warren, Hamilton, Essex, Franklin, Clinton, Schenectady, Montgomery and Fulton Counties:

HENRY GALLIEN, - - - - Albany.

For Representative, Fourth District, comprising Wayne Oswego, Cayuga, Jefferson, St Lawrence, Lewis, Herkimer, Oneida, Madison, Onondago, Seneca, Yates, Ontario, Steuben and Schuyler Counties:

CHARLES W. WOOD, - - Syracuse.

For Representatives, Fifth District, comprising Chemung, Tioga, Broome, Tompkins, Chenango, Otsego, Cortland, Delaware, Sullivan, Ulster, Dutchess, Orange, Putnam and Rockland Counties:

CHAS. F. COSSUM, - - Poughkeepsie.
H. W. ARNOLD, - - Binghamton.

For Representatives, Sixth District, comprising Niagara, Orleans, Genesee, Wyoming, Erie, Livingston, Cattaraugus, Chautauqua and Monroe Counties:

WALTER S. JENKINS, - - - Buffalo.
WILL. G. SCHACK, - - - Buffalo.
ROBERT THOMSON, - - - Rochester.
DR. GEO. E. BLACKHAM, - - Dunkirk.

GEORGE M. NISBETT,
New York, July 8, 1889. Sec'y-Treas.

INDEPENDENT TICKET—FIRST DISTRICT.

J. C. GULICK, Citizens' B. C., - - New York.
W. H. DE GRAAF, Harlem Wheelmen, do
J. L. MILLER, Riverside Wheelmen, - do
F. P. PRIAL, New York B. C., - - - do
J. A. CLAIRMONT, Manhattan B. C., - do

VOTING BLANK—1889-1890.

New York Division, League American Wheelmen.

MAIL VOTE.

For Chief Consul..
For Vice-Consul..
For Secretary-Treasurer..
For Representatives:
..........................of..........................
..........................of..........................
..........................of..........................
..........................of..........................
..........................of..........................
Name..
Address..

N. B. Votes must be signed and returned to the Secretary-Treasurer on or before August 15, 1889. Address George M. Nisbett, 146 West End Avenue.

CYCLISTS' UNION OF LONG ISLAND.

SEMI-ANNUAL REPORT OF THE TREASURER.

1888.		1889.	
Dec. 17. To Balance (from E. K. Austin, Treasurer	$107 75	Feb. 2. By Printing.	$4 50
Dec 17. To Entertainment.	12 25	Mar. 4. " Postage.	4 77
1889.		Apr. 8. " Members tickets.	8 50
July 6. To Renewals.	95 00	" 23. " Printing.	7 00
" " New members	50 00	Mar. 11. " Type-writing.	1 00
" " Subscription	1 00	May 16. " Printing.	2 50
		" 27. " Postage.	1 63
		June 12. " "	3 41
		" " " Building of wooden bridge.	3 00
		July 1. By Balance.	$229 70
	$266 00		$266 00
July 1. To Balance.	$229 70		

In addition to the above, we have liabilities to the amount of about $75 for road improvements, the bills for which have not yet been rendered.

(Signed) W. J. FINN, Treasurer.

Brooklyn, July 1, 1889.

THE LEAGUE MEET PHOTOGRAPH.

A copy of this artistic souvenir faces us as we write, and contemplation of it revives many pleasant memories. The size is one of the largest obtainable by any lens the negative being 13½ by 22½ inches, and when mounted on cardboard the picture is 22½ by 28 inches. Appropriately framed, it will be an ornament to any club-room or private residence.

An excellent light was obtained by grouping the subjects under the grand stand, and but one small spot, a little to left of the centre, shows too strong a light. At the extreme right, as one faces the picture, and just where it was so difficult to get the cyclists to take positions, the focus is seen to have been the best.

Hagerstown boys, who are nearly all grouped there, have full benefit of this fact, and many pleasantly-remembered faces are plainly visible. Back of them are the Centaurs; to their left the Chesapeakes; while New York and Maryland, as befits such warm friends, and the home Division, take a central position. Chief Consul Mott has deserted his flock and stands among the Hagerstown boys. "Deacon" Raisbeck, Doctor Dillingham and veteran Morrow are among the best likenesses noted, though were we to enumerate all the good points a supplement to this paper would be necessary.

Baltimore, Harrisburg and the K. C W. are also conspicuous by their banners and a large and good-looking representation. The ladies are given good positions, and their likenesses only serve to add value to the picture as a souvenir. The foreground is full of picturesquely-grouped cycles of all styles and sizes, not forgetting the trike that bore the brass cannon, near which pensively leans young Wilhelm, with his tiny star not far off.

It is a pity that colors cannot be photographed in their original hues, for then this picture would be fairly tropical with many-hued badges But space forbids further mention. You will all want it, so send your little dollar seventy-five to W. H King, Hagerstown, Md. Be sure to order shipment by *express*. We assure you it's so natural that when from mere force of habit we asked, "W—t d—d t—e b—d p—y?" a murmur seemed to come from all the familiar features, and dimly, as in a dream, we heard the words "ANNIE LAURIE."

MASSACHUSETTS DIVISION, L. A. W., PREPARING FOR THE AUGUST MEET.

The Board of Officers of the Massachusetts Division, L. A. W., met at the Clarendon Hotel Saturday evening. The committee on rights and privileges were instructed to report to the Chief Consul in regard to the apportionment of representatives to the several districts, and it was voted to print 500 copies of the constitution and by-laws.

The committee on arranging a map reported it inexpedient. The uniform committee presented samples of cloth. The committee on programme for the annual meet at Cottage City, which is to occur early in August, announced the following events: Leaving Boston on August 7, the business meeting of the Division will take place on the 8th, at 10 A. M. A base-ball match will be the event of the afternoon, and in the evening an illumination and parade. On August 9, an excursion to Gay Head will be followed by a ball in the evening, and on the 10th, the last day, there will be a parade in the morning, and the afternoon will be given over to races.—*Boston Sunday Globe.*

S. G. Whittaker has been doing good work around New York for the Gormully & Jeffery Company. He has visited all the New York and Brooklyn clubs, and has been cordially received by the boys. On Saturday last he rode to Roslyn with the Long Island Wheelmen, and astonished the men by the pace he got out of a Rambler.

FIXTURES.

July 20, 1889.—Race Meeting of the East Hartford Wheel Club, at East Hartford, Conn. Entries close July 16, with Mr. E. E. Arnold, East Hartford.

July 20, 1889.—One-mile and 25-mile Bicycle and 5-mile Tricycle N. C. U. championships at Paddington, Eng., track.

July 25, 1889.—At Minneapolis, Twenty-five Mile Road Race for Championship of Minnesota. Entries close July 20 with Will. Monarch, Secretary-Treasurer, Minneapolis Bicycle Club. Entry fee, $1.

July 27, 1889.—One-mile and 25-mile Tricycle and 5-mile Bicycle N. C. U. Championships at Paddington, Eng., track.

August 5, 1889.—At Interstate Fair Grounds, Trenton, N. J.: 1-mile Bicycle Handicap and 2-mile Bicycle New Jersey State Championship. Entries close July 29th, with W. V. Blake, 146 Monmouth Street, Trenton, N. J. Entry fee, 50 cents.

August 8, 9, 10, 1889.—Annual Meet of Massachusetts Division L. A. W., at Cottage City.

August 24, 1889.—Fifty-mile Bicycle and 1-mile Dwarf N. C. U. Championships at Paddington, Eng.

September 4-5, 1889.—Amateur Race Meet of the Hartford Wheel Club, at Hartford, Conn. Entries to be made with W. M. Francis, Secretary, P. O. Box 745.

September 7, 1889.—A. A. U. Games at Brooklyn A. A. grounds; 1-mile Handicap. Entries close September 1, with James E. Sullivan, 73 Park Row, New York City. Fee, 50 cents.

September 7, 1889.—One-mile Bicycle A. A. U. Championship at Brooklyn Athletic Association Grounds. Entries close September 1 with J. E. Sullivan, 73 Park Row, New York City.

September 13, 1889.—At Springfield, 50-mile Road Race open to local riders only, and 50-mile Road Race, open Entry fee, $5, returnable to first, second and third men. Entries close September 1.

September 20, 1889.—Michigan Division L. A. W. Meet at Ypsilanti, Mich.

September 21, 1889.—Michigan Division Meet races at Detroit, Mich.

October 23-29, 1889.—Race Meet at Macon, Ga.

EUROPEAN CYCLING FIXTURES

Germany.—Berlin, July 21, September 15; Hanover, September 8; Cologne, August 12; Chemnitz, September 8; Frankfort-on-the-Maine, September 1; Mannheim, September 8; Crefeld, September 8. Hamburg.—Altona, September 22; Bochum, August 25; Madgeburg, September 8. Denmark.—Copenhagen International Meeting, August 18

ON THE ENGLISH PATH.

A race meet was held at North Shields on June 26, 27 and 28. The ½-mile youths' handicap was won by A. E. Revely in the remarkable time of 1m. 10 4-5s. A youth named Harris was at scratch. He tried all he knew how, but the time was a little fast. Half-mile bicycle handicap—J. C. Robson, 10 yards, 1m. 16 1-5s. Jack Lee won the 5-mile professional championship in 17m. 12 4-5s, doing the last "fifth" at a 2m. 23s pace.

The 5-mile safety championship of the North produced grand sport. The fastest heat was won by Isaac Carruthers; time, 14m. 49 2-5s; and the final was won by W. C. Thompson; time, 14m. 59 4-5s. Jack Lee, 15 yards, won the ½-mile handicap bicycle race in the splendid time of 1m. 15 4-5s.

The mile amateur handicap was won in the splendid time of 2m. 34s. by J. Johnstone, 145 yards.

Allard recently won the 25-mile professional bicycle championship, beating Robb, Howell and Lee. The time at ten miles was 30m. 52s; at twenty, 1h. 4m. 15s., and at twenty-five, 1h. 20m. 42s.

THE CATFORD CLUB'S 50-MILE ROAD HANDICAP.

This event, held June 29, attracted forty-six entries, with thirty starters. The course will be remeasured, as the fast times throw doubt on the correctness of the measurements. Of the first twelve men home nine rode safeties. K. E. Edge, 26 minutes start, won. His net time was 3h. 12m. 12s. The fastest net time was made by C. A. Smith, safety, viz., 2h. 59m. 50s. E. Dangerfield, safety, rode in 3h. 0m. 50s.; W. G. James' time was 3h. 5m. 38s. Smith rode the first thirty-five miles in 2h. 10m. 30s. net.

Ives will compete in the Fall tournaments.

J. K. Starley & Co. have opened an agency in Paris.

George M. Hendee will compete on a safety at the Hartford tournament.

The White Cycle Co. have issued a new catalogue with a catchily worded cover, compiled by "Jack."

A. S. Hill, of the Coventry Machinists' Co., was in town on Tuesday, leaving Wednesday for Philadelphia.

A good opportunity for novices is offered at the Adelphi A. C. games. Entries close July 22, with T. P. Conneff, 347 West Forty-first Street, New York City.

Mile handicap to be decided at Queens track, July 20. Waters, scratch; Quartropp, 15 yards; Boyce, 50 yards; Kissam, 60 yards; Doughty, 100 yards; Stoutenburgh, 100 yards, and Kimber, 125 yards.

A 2-mile bicycle race will be contested at the games of the Young Men's Christian Association on September 14 at the Mott Haven grounds. Entries close September 7 with G. Pool, 150th Street and Harlem River.

A three-mile bicycle handicap will be decided at the Y. M. C. A. games, to be held September 14, at Mott Haven, New York City. Fee, 50 cents; close September 7 with George Pool, 150th Street and Harlem River.

The Wheel

and

Cycling Trade Review

·P·O·Box·444·
·N·Y·

·23·Park·Row·
·N·Y·

Vol. III.—No 22.]   NEW YORK, JULY 26, 1889.   [Whole Number, 74.

ABOUT THE ONLY WAY THAT YOU CAN BREAK OUR WHEELS.

PROPRIETOR OF BICYCLE AGENCY (to newly engaged assistant): Great Heavens, Pat! What in the world are you trying to do?

PAT: Sure an' a long-ligged djude bees afther bringin' this machane in here an' sayin' as how he wants a break on it roight away, an' there was no wan here, so Oi was afther accommodatin' av him.

GORMULLY & JEFFERY MFG. CO.

CHICAGO, ILL.

80 PAGE CATALOGUE ON APPLICATION.

MERWIN, HULBERT & CO., New York Agents.

Some People think that THE EAGLE cannot climb a hill, but
The Eagle took First Prize at the Hill-climbing
Contest at the Meet of the L. A. W.,
Bridgeport, Conn., July 8.

SACRAMENTO, CAL., June 14, 1889.

THE EAGLE BICYCLE MFG. CO., Stamford, Conn.

GENTLEMEN :

I have been riding my Eagle now for a little over six weeks, and am better pleased with it every time I ride it. Those who were so loud at first in criticising the wheel, and who claimed that I would never be able to climb a hill with it, and that the wheel was not at all practical, have all had to "pull in their sails," as I have ridden through sand and up hills where a good many of our riders, both of ordinary and safeties, have had to dismount. I have also learned to ride one wheel for a distance of two hundred yards, and with only two days' practice, and I think that in the course of a week or so I will be able to ride one wheel any distance I wish on a good road.

To-morrow I expect to make the run from Sacramento to Stockton and return, a distance of 102 miles. This trip has only been made by three riders, though many have attempted it and failed ; and if I succeed, which I have no doubt I will, it will be a good advertisement for the Eagle.

Yours very truly,

H. G. TOLL.

SACRAMENTO, CAL., June 28, 1889.

THE EAGLE BICYCLE MFG. CO., Stamford, Conn.

GENTLEMEN :

I made the run of which I spoke without any trouble, and am more pleased with the Eagle than ever. My actual riding time was ten hours, which, taking the roads into consideration, was very good. I found the Eagle to be the easiest running wheel I ever rode. I was in no condition for the ride, having been ill and unable to ride my wheel until two days before I started ; and yet I made the trip without any difficulty, and my muscles did not bother me in the least, which is good proof to my mind that the motion of the legs, as used on the Eagle, is much less tiresome than that used on the ordinary.

Yours truly,

H. G. TOLL.

THE EAGLE BICYCLE MFG. CO.,

Stamford, Conn.

CATALOGUE FREE. APPLY FOR THE AGENCY.

THE WHEEL
—AND—
CYCLING TRADE REVIEW,

Published every Friday morning.

Entered at the Post Office at second class rates.

Subscription Price, - - - $1.00 a year.
Foreign Subscriptions, - - - 6s. a year.
Single Copies, - - - - - 5 Cents.

Newsdealers may order through AM. NEWS CO.

All copy should be received by Monday.
Telegraphic news received till Wednesday noon.

Advertising rates on Application.

F. P. PRIAL, Editor and Proprietor
23 Park Row,
P. O. Box 444, *New York.*

Persons receiving sample copies of this paper are respectfully requested to examine its contents and give us their patronage, and as far as is convenient, aid in circulating the journal, and extend its influence in the cause which it so faithfully serves. Subscription price, $1 per year.

"THE WHEEL," ONCE A MOUTHFUL, NOW A MEAL.

That is the terse verdict of a prominent wheelman.

Brother Prial, of that able cycling paper THE WHEEL, usually so correct in his published facts on cycling subjects, etc.—*Nashville American.*

COULD NOT AFFORD TO MISS IT.

"Could not afford to miss the paper that gives the best and latest wheel news."—Elbert Von Wagoner, Guilford, Conn.

NOTHING, IF NOT ENTERPRISING.

THE WHEEL is nothing if not enterprising. A full report of the Hagerstown Meet appeared in its columns a week in advance of any other wheel paper, and it reached its subscribers only a day behind its regular time.—*Nashville American.*

THE case of ex-Officer Kelly, who, while intoxicated, deliberately drove his horse upon Mr. Beasly, will no doubt be of considerable benefit to the cause of cycling. The escape of the cyclist was almost miraculous, and at the moment of his rage there is no doubt that the officer had every intention of killing him. The lesson of the past has been that you cannot convince the various forms of road-hog by logic that the cyclist has some rights which he is bound to respect. You have to convince him through his pocket, or with a club or a jail. It is a matter of congratulation that Mr. Beasly understands his duty to cycling, and that he has the intelligence and the will to push his case and make an example of this newest form of road-hog. The man was paid to protect the people. He was utterly incompetent, could scarcely write, was entirely lacking in judgment and, worst of all, was one of those importations who have "got the pull," and are ready to become Aldermen, before their ship gets half way across the pond. *Wheeling* recently pointed out that there was as much intolerance of cyclists to-day as ever there was, and we can indorse the statement from the American standpoint. In fact, there is scarcely a cyclist living in a large city who has not suffered at the hands of the hod-carrier, the tough, the drunk and the fat-witted human hogs who go out on the roads in vehicles. Often it is a sneer, and again it is a deliberate attempt to annihilate. And to reply is profitless. It is impossible to get the best of a man whose mind is too dull to grasp whatever hot-shot you may send back at him, and all one can do is to "boil within." An appeal to the police is as fruitless. The average policeman is himself a fair specimen of the tough, and his sympathies are with the louts who insult one, and appeal to him is received with lofty disdain or ill-concealed sneer. Here now is a case which may be made to serve to good purpose. It will be conducted in good fashion and sentiment will be out of the question If it is possible to jail the man, he will be jailed, as an example to people of his class Cyclists all over the country will appreciate Mr. Beasly's expense of time and money to protect the sport he loves.

THE invitation to hold the '89 meet of the N. Y. State Division, L. A. W. in New York and Brooklyn, is quite the proper thing. New York cyclists have been charged with a lack of enthusiasm and public spirit, and the charge is just in appearance if not in fact. The New York clubs have continued to increase in membership and to add to their club-house facilities, yet their club life has never been shown to the world. New York cyclists attend other meets and are the recipients of courtesy and hospitality which they never have an opportunity to repay. But the Fall meet, if the invitation is accepted, will give us an excellent chance to pay off old scores and to show the cyclists of the State and country that there is nothing rotten in Denmark.

AND THEREBY HANGS A TALE.

THE WHEEL, whenever it wants an illustration, has a reproduction made from the English papers, and very poor ones they are at that. As long as this paper has been established it has never published an original illustration in its reading columns.—*Wheelmen's Gazette.*

This is a sample of the petty lies which are constantly being published in the *Wheelmen's Gazette*, which neither deserves nor commands success. In THE WHEEL of August 30, 1887, we published a portrait of Edwin Oliver. The cut was sent to Mr. Oliver, and is resurrected as "original" in the *Wheelmen's Gazette* for May, 1889, page 66. In the *Wheelmen's Gazette* for July, page 103, appears cuts of a Milwaukee bicycle agency and its enterprising proprietor. These cuts were offered to us sometime ago, but we quoted the usual advertising rates, and they turn up in the July *Gazette* as original. In the July *Gazette*, page 105, appears a cut of a racing man on an ordinary labeled "A. C. Banker," but it is not a picture of Banker. On the same page appears a cut labeled "On the Home-stretch, Half-mile Dash." Four men are shown on ordinaries. Now, on the home-stretch Wilhelm led on a Star, and besides there is no grand stand at the curve on the Hagerstown grounds, so that we can only presume that the drawing was made in Indianapolis, not at Hagerstown. This *is* original. On page 106 is a cut labeled "One-mile L. A. W. Championship," showing the start. Six men are shown on ordinaries. As a matter of fact there were seven starters. The small stand shown in the picture does not exist, and was put in to "fill." More originality. Facts and mule-kicks are stubborn things.

NEW YORK STATE DIVISION MEET.

A second meeting was held at the Hotel Hamblin, on Monday evening, to further discuss the advisability of inviting the State Division to hold its annual meet in New York and Brooklyn. The men present were: M. L. Bridgman, K. C. W.; A. B. Barkman, B. B. C.; C. A. Sheehan, M. B. C.; J. R. Miller, R. W.; C. W. Newbourg, P. W.; J. S. Voorhees, R. W.; W. B. King, C. B. C.; J. W. Shaw and F. B. Prial, N. Y. B. C.

Mr. Bridgman occupied the chair, Mr. Prial acted as temporary secretary. The minutes of the previous meeting and several communications received by the secretary were read. Messrs. Furst and Alden, of the L. I. W., wrote strongly in favor of holding the meet, as did J. W. Sheehan, Manhattan B. C.

It was unanimously decided to invite the Division to hold the Fall Meet here on Sept. 13 and 14.

The following programme, presented by Mr. Prial, will probably be carried out if the invite is accepted:

FRIDAY.

Morning.—Reception of visitors.
Afternoon.—Runs, Park, Yonkers, etc.
Night.—Theatre party, New York City.

SATURDAY.

Morning.—Parade in Central Park.
Afternoon.—Run to Brooklyn and Prospect Park.
" —Run to Coney Island.
" —Supper at Coney Island.
" —Concert at Gilmore's Amphitheatre.

SUNDAY.

Informal runs to Yonkers, Tarrytown, The Oranges and points on Long Island.

The following Committee were elected to manage the meet: M. L. Bridgman, Chairman; A. B. Barkman, I. W. Shaw, J. C. Gulick and W. H. De Graaf.

MARYLAND DIVISION NOMINATIONS.

A VOTE OF CENSURE ON THE "BICYCLING WORLD."

At a meeting of the Nominating Committee of the Maryland Division L. A. W. held to-night the nominations were as follows: Chief Consul, Albert Mott, Baltimore; Vice-Consul, Geo. F. Updegraff, Hagerstown; Secretary-Treasurer, G. W. H. Carr, Baltimore; four representatives, R. P. Hayden, Baltimore; C. L. Mitchell, Baltimore; C. E. Fink, Westminster; J. H. Covington, Easton; all unanimous.

The meeting then adjourned as a Nominating Committee and re-assembled to pass the following resolution:

"Resolved, That the account of the tenth annual meet of the L. A. W. published in the *Bicycling World* of July 12, 1889, is untruthful and a scandelous libel on the members attending that gathering, and calculated to do the organization harm in giving a false impression of the membership at large.

"It is also resolved that we call upon President Luscomb and the Executive Committee to terminate the contract with the *Bicycling World* as the 'official organ' of an organization it appears to be doing its utmost to disrupt."

At this meeting there were present delegates from all city clubs except one, also from Hagerstown; and it is safe to say that every club in the State will take similar action at the next, or special, meeting.

2641.

KELLY INDICTED.

Officer Kelly, who drove his horse over Lester W. Beasly, has been indicted and will be tried before the Grand Jury in September. The hearing was held at Fort Hamilton on Monday evening at 7:30. Mr. Michael Furst represented Mr. Beasly. The officer was taken from the Raymond Street Jail, where he has been confined since the accident, being unable to obtain bail, to the court room. After hearing the case the Judge indicted him to appear before the Grand Jury in September, and he was released under bond. He has been suspended by the Park Commissioners pending the issue of the trial

The case against the officer is a strong one. Several people who witnessed his assault kindly gave their names to Mr Beasly. Mr. Cooper, a real estate agent of Brooklyn, who, with his wife, witnessed the accident, delayed his vacation in order to be present at the hearing. At the trial an attempt will be made to show that the officer was too drunk to control his horse, that he was drunk when he reported at the station, and that the written charge he presented was the work of a man in a maudlin condition.

A VALUABLE INVENTION.

PRINCIPALLY DESIGNED FOR THE LADIES.

A vast assistance to feminine safety riding should be the automatic standing gear, patented by Mr. Watkins, which altogether does away with the present difficulties of mounting and dismounting, of which many women complain as the hardest part of learning to ride a bicycle. This invention consists of two metal rods, which, projecting from the axle of the front wheel, support the machine in an upright position, enabling the rider to mount without the usual effort and exertion. Once comfortably and leisurely seated—an important point where feminine draperies have to be humored—the brake handle is pulled up, and immediately let go, with the effect of raising the support from the ground, the machine being, at the same time, started in the usual manner. When a halt is called, the machine is slowed up as much as possible, and the supports pressed down with the foot. As the wheels stop, a slight backward jerk of the handles secures the support in its position, and the rider is enabled to dismount with that unhurried ease and grace which should be the true aim of all womanly riding. This simple and ingenious invention seems most decidedly the right thing in the right place, and though my own experience of it is at present confined to a sketch which lies before me as I write, I am assured of its advantages by a valued correspondent, who has given it an exhaustive trial, and who speaks in high terms of its merits. It will be of especial value to women who are just learning to ride the safety, and who object strongly, as a rule, to the feeling of insecurity attending their first attempt at mounting. Dismounting, as I have always remarked is an affair characterized with the most absolute simplicity.—Violet Lorne, in *Bicycling News.*

The following programme will be run off at Schwalbach's entertainment at the Brooklyn Casino on August 13: One-mile bicycle, scratch; one-mile handicap; half-mile race, and a short race; exhibition of fancy bicycle riding by Eddie Schwalbach, and a drill team of eight men.

Two interesting races came off on the grounds of the Montreal Amateur Athletic Association, Cote St. Antoine, near Montreal, Can., July 18. They were weekly handicaps, and resulted as follows: Half-mile—W. H. C. Mussen, scratch, first, in 1m. 20s.; R. Pickard, 15s. start, second, in 1m. 20⅖s.; A. B. Kingan, 10s., third, in 1m. 27s. One mile—W. H. C. Mussen, scratch, first, in 3m. 5s.; A. B. Kingan, 15s., second, 3m. 20s.; E. Adams, 13s., third, 3m. 21s.

FIXTURES.

July 27, 1889.—One-mile and 25-mile Tricycle and 5-mile Bicycle N. C. U. Championships at Paddington, Eng., track.

August 3, 1889.—Queens Athletic Club Grounds, at 4:30 P. M., 1-mile Handicap. Entries close, July 31, with Thos. Lloyd, Queens, N. Y.

August 5, 1889.—At Interstate Fair Grounds, Trenton, N. J.: 2-mile Bicycle Handicap and 2-mile Bicycle New Jersey State Championship. Entries close July 29th, with W. V. Blake, 146 Monmouth Street, Trenton, N. J. Entry fee, 50 cents.

August 8, 9, 10, 1889.—Annual Meet of Massachusetts Division L. A. W., at Cottage City.

August 10, 1889.—Races at Cottage City. Entries close August 8, with C. S. Davol Hotel Naumkeag, Cottage City.

August 10, 1889.—Bicycle Races of Massachusetts Division L. A. W. at Cottage City, Martha's Vineyard.

August 10, 1889.—Mercury Wheel Club's Outing, at Flushing, L. I.

August 14, 1889.—Walontha Wheelmen's Race Meet and Road Race, at Richfield Springs, N. Y. Entries close with Fred Bronner.

August 15, 1889.—Race Meet of Lockport, N. Y., Wheelmen.

August 24, 1889.—Fifty-mile Bicycle and 1-mile Dwarf N. C. U. Championships at Paddington, Eng.

August, 1889.—Scranton Club's Tour, Scranton, Pa., to Utica, Springfield, New York, Catskills, Delaware Water Gap. Address, B. P. Connolly, Secretary.

August 31, 1889.—Monster Run of Brooklyn Wheelmen to Hotel Massapequa.

September 2, 1889.—Albany Wheelmen's Tournament.

September 2-3, 1889.—Amateur Race Meet of the Hartford Wheel Club, at Hartford, Conn. Entries to be made with W. M. Francis, Secretary, P. O. Box 745.

September 3, 1889.—Hartford Wheel Club's 20-mile Road Race.

September 7, 1889.—A. A. U. Games at Brooklyn A. A. grounds; 1-mile Handicap. Entries close September 1, with James E. Sullivan, 73 Park Row, New York City. Fee, 50 cents.

September 7, 1889.—One-mile Bicycle A. A. U. Championship at Brooklyn Athletic Association Grounds. Entries close September 1 with J. E. Sullivan, 73 Park Row, New York City.

September 13, 1889.—Springfield Bicycle Club's 50-mile Local Road Race and 20-mile Open Road Race, over the Springfield-Hartford course.

September 13, 1889.—At Springfield, 50-mile Road Race, open to local riders only, and 50-mile Road Race, open. Entry fee, $5, returnable to first, second and third men. Entries close September 1.

September 14, 1889.—Y. M. C. A. Games; 3-mile Handicap. Fee, 50 cents. Entries close September 7, with George Pool, 150th Street, Harlem River.

September 20, 1889.—Michigan Division L. A. W. Meet at Ypsilanti, Mich.

September 21, 1889.—Michigan Division Meet races at Detroit, Mich.

October 23-29, 1889.—Race Meet at Macon, Ga.

EUROPEAN CYCLING FIXTURES.

Germany.—September 15; Hanover, September 8; Cologne, August 12; Chemnitz, September 8; Frankfort-on-the-Main, September 1; Mannheim, September 8; Crefeld, September 8. Hamburg.—Altona, September 22; Bochum, August 25; Madgeburg, September 8. Denmark.—Copenhagen International Meeting, August 18

EAST HARTFORD RACE MEET.

The annual meet of this club was held on Monday at the club's quarter-mile track. The original date of the meet was Saturday last, but it rained until almost noon, compelling a postponement. The two Murphy boys of the K. C. W. were quite successful. They went up on Saturday and remained until Monday as a guest of Mr. H. E. Bidwell. F. P. Prial also came up from New York to referee the races, but was unable to remain until Monday. The crowd was only fairly large. Music was furnished by the East Hartford Brass Band

The officers of the races were: Referee, Joseph Goodman; Judges, C. B. Riply, W. M. Francis and R. P. Groesbeck; Umpires, Morgan Johnson and Robert E. Olmstead; Starter, E. O. Goodwin; Scorers, J. O. Goodwin and H. D. Olmstead; Timers, L. S. Forbes and A. G. Greundler; Clerk of Course, George B. Forbes.

One-half mile novice.—H. G. Cornell, Hartford, 1st; T. W. Laiman, Hartford, 2d; time, 2.48⅘.

One-mile East Hartford championship.—W. L. James, 1st; C. L. Snow, distanced; time, 3.21¼.

One-half mile handicap—Heat 1.—F. A. Bearse, Springfield, 15 yds., 1st; time, 1.33. Heat 2—H. G. Cornell, Hartford, 10 yds., 1st; time, 1.30. Heat 3—C. M. Murphy, K. C. W., 5 yds., 1st; time, 1.31½; F. T. Reid, Hartford, 2d. Heat 4—W. F. Murphy, scratch, 1st; time, 1.27. Final Heat—Cornell, 1st; W. F. Murphy, 2d; C. M. Murphy, 3d; time, 1.30½.

Two-mile handicap.—C. M. Murphy, 12 yds., 1st; W. F. Murphy, 10 yds., 2d; Culver and Wakefield, Springfield, 0; Foster and Smart, Hartford, 0; Dauchy, West Winsted, 0.

One-mile, 3.20 class.—C. M. Murphy, 1st; H. C. Wakefield, 2d; time, 3.16.

One-mile open scratch race, time limit, 3.15.—Ludwig Foster, 1st; W. F. Murphy, 0; George Smart, 0. The men loafed; did not equal the time limit, and the referee decided no race.

One-mile, 3.30 class.—Cornell, 3.27; Culver, 2d; Bearse, 0; Wilkinson, 0; Millett, 0.

One and one-half mile lap race.—W. F. Murphy, 1st; Foster, 2d; Wakefield, 3d; time, 4.54⅘. Wakefield led at the mile in 3.15.

Relay race, two and a half miles.—Three clubs participated as follows: Hartford Wheel Club, represented by Foster, Reid, Cudworth, Laiman and Cornell. East Hartford Wheel Club, represented by Terrill, Snow, James, Richmond and Bidwell. Springfield Athletic Association, represented by Culver, Grimes, Bearse, Wilkinson and Wakefield. The Hartford Wheel Club won in 8.30, with Springfield second and East Hartford about a yard behind Springfield.

One-mile consolation—Smart, of Hartford, 3.28.

THE LANCASTER CLUB'S MEET.

In running their annual meet the Lancaster Club had much to battle with. They were compelled to postpone twice, and on the last day the weather was so bad that but a handful of spectators were present. Yet the club had the finest races ever held in Lancaster, and it is to be hoped that they will not be discouraged, but give another first class meet in the fall.

Officers:—Referee, C. H. Obrieter, Philadelphia; Judges, Dr. J. M. Yeagley, Samuel B. Downey and John A. Burger; Timers, Dr. Walter Boardman, Dr. T. H. Nathorst and John E. Snyder, Clerk of Course, D. F. Grove; Scorer, H. M. Griel; Starter, H. M. Eichley; Umpires, George U. Best, M. B. Hirsh, John Traggresser and Grabill Shaeffer.

FIRST DAY, JULY 18.

The weather was warm, with a fair breeze. The attendance numbered about 800, not so many as was expected. Wilhelm did excellent work, winning three races. The competitors found excellent accommodations in two tents erected near the starting point. Music was furnished by the Iroquois band.

ONE-HALF MILE CLUB, NOVICES.—Alvin Reist, first; J. S. Musser, second; J. F Griel, third. Time, 1m. 29½s.

ONE-MILE NOVICES, OPEN.—Z. Loffland, Wilmington, first; J. S. Musser, Columbia, Pa., second; W. H. Reifsnyder, Pottstown, third; Samuel Musser, Reading, 0; Alvin Reist, Lancaster, 0; S. Breneman, Lancaster, 0. Time, 3m. 9s.

ONE-MILE, BOYS UNDER SIXTEEN.—Dawson Fornivalt, Columbia, first; Chas. Kuhl, Lancaster, second; A. B. Groff, East Petersburg, third; C. Malone, Lancaster, 0. Time, 3m. 35½s.

TWO-MILE BICYLE, LANCASTER COUNTY CHAMPIONSHIP.—George F. Kohler, Millersville, first; D. H. Miller, Lancaster, second; S. E. Arnold, Columbia, third; E. R. Griel and Alvin Reist, Lancaster, 0; W. S. Oberlin and J. J. McLaughlin, 0; time, 6m. 39¾s.

ONE-MILE BICYCLE, FLYING START.—The race was run in half-mile beats and the heat was a mile race. First heat: W. F. Class, New York, first; J. W. Schoefer, New York, second, W. W. Taxis, Philadelphia, third; Geo. M. Gregg, Wilmington, 0; S. Mosser, Reading, 0; time, 1m. 24½s. Second heat: W. I. Wilhelm, Reading, first; M. Kilmer, Reading, second; B. F. McDaniel, Wilmington, third; R. J. Powell, Burlington, N. J., 0; time, 1m. 25s. Final heat: Wilhelm, first; Schoefer, second; Taxis, third; time, 3m. 4s.

TWO-MILE SAFETY BICYCLE.—W. I. Wilhelm, first; W. W. Taxis, second; W. B. Riegel, Reading, third; J. A. Allgaier, Reading, 0; W. J. Grubb, Pottstown, 0; B. F. McDaniel, Wilmington, 0; H. D. Lembach, Denver, 0; time, 6m. 33½s.

THREE-MILE LAP RACE.—J. W. Schoefer, 19 points; Geo. F. Kohler, Millersville, 10 points; George M. Gregg, 5 points; R. J. Powell, 0; B. F. McDaniel, 0; S. Mosser, 0; Taxis, 0; Kilmer, 0; time, 10m. 5½s.

ONE-HALF MILE BICYCLE, STATE CHAMPIONSHIP.—W. I. Wilhelm, first; W. W. Taxis, second; D. H. Miller, third; J. S. Mosser, 0; W. J. Grubb, 0; A. Reist, 0; G. F. Kohler, 0; time, 1m. 23s.

THE PARADE.

In the evening the wheelmen's parade took place. About seventy-five riders were in line, captained by John Miller. The pace makers were George Walton and Harry Eichler. Almost all the wheelmen carried lanterns and were cheered all along the route. Fireworks were exploded at the American Hotel and at the *Intelligencer* office.

SECOND DAY, JULY 19.

The weather on Friday was beastly and only a few hundred people were present, making the meet a financial failure despite the fine fields of starters, and the general excellent arrangements. The events resulted as follows:

ONE-HALF MILE BICYCLE, HANDS OFF.—W. W. Taxis, first; Z. Lofland, second; J. W. Schoefer, third; B. F. McDaniel, fourth. Time, 1m. 35s.

TWO-MILE BICYCLE CLUB HANDICAP.—Geo. F. Kohler, 100 yards, first; Alvin Reist, 130 yards, second; Jacob F. Griel, 180 yards, third. Time, 6m. 22 1-2s.

ONE-MILE BICYCLE L. A. W. STATE CHAMPIONSHIP.—W. I. Wilhelm, first; W. W. Taxis, second; Geo. F. Kohler, third; Alvin Reist, 0; John J. McLaughlin, Columbia, 0; D. F. Miller, 0. Time, 2m. 58 1-4s.

ONE-MILE SAFETY BICYCLE CLUB CHAMPIONSHIP.—Edward R. Griel, first; D. R. Rose, second; D. H. Miller, third. Time, 3m. 20 1-4s.

THREE-MILE CLUB TEAM RACE.—Berkeley Athletic, A. B. Rich, J. W. Schoefer and W. F. Class, 89 points, first; Warren Athletic Club, Frank Dampman, B. F. McDaniel and Z. Lofland, 71 points, second; Pennsylvania Wheel Club, M. Killmer, 2 points, third. Time, 9m. 45 1-4s.

ONE-MILE TANDEM BICYCLE.—J. W. Schoefer and W. F Class, first; D. R. Rose and J. Rudy, second; Frank Dampman and B. F. McDaniel did not finish. Time, 3m. 1 1-4s.

ONE-MILE SAFETY CONSOLATION.—B. F. McDaniel, first; Jos. A. Allgaier, second. Time, 3m. 16 1-2s. This race was for those who contested in former safety races and failed to win a prize.

TWO-MILE BICYCLE, OPEN.—A. B. Rich, first; W. W. Taxis, second; S. Wallis Merrihew, third. Time, 6m. 10s.

ONE-MILE BICYCLE CONSOLATION.—M. Killmer, Reading, first; Samuel Breneman, Lancaster, second. Time, 3m. 38s.

THE COTTAGE CITY MEET.

The dates of the meet are August 8, 9 and 10, but a majority of those who attend the reunion will add a couple of days to their stay at the ocean city. They will leave Boston the afternoon previous to the meet and return the following Monday morning. An excellent programme has been arranged by the committee in charge. All the members of the committee have had experience in the management of affairs of this kind, and it is assured that nothing will be neglected which will add to the comfort or pleasure of the wheelmen attending. A pleasant feature is that the Rhode Island Division of the L. A. W. will hold its annual meet at the same time; in fact, the gathering at Cottage City will be a joint meet of the two divisions. It would be difficult to prophesy how many will attend, but the indications are that the attendance will greatly exceed that of former years, when it has varied from 300 to 500.

Members of the committee met at the office of the League Secretary yesterday afternoon, and made up the programme. Messrs. Davol and Howland were present as representatives of the Rhode Island Division, and the others attending were Chief Consul Emery, Dr. W. G. Kendall, Abbott Bassett and C. S. Howard. Following is a summary of their work:

THE PROGRAMME.

August 8—10 A. M., annual business meeting of the Massachusetts Division, L. A. W., in the Town Hall; 3 P. M., exhibition of fancy riding by Willie Windle; 8 P. M., Japanese lantern parade; committee in charge, C. S. Howard and W. W. Stall

August 9—9 A. M., excursion to Nantucket, returning at 3 P. M.; committee, W. H. Emery and C. E. Wing; 4 P. M., exhibitions of fancy riding and a run to East Chop and New York landing; 8 P. M., band concert and "bluffing."

August 10—10 A. M., annual parade of the divisions; 2 P. M., races about the circle. The events will consist of 1-mile ordinary bicycle race, 1-mile safety bicycle race, ½-mile bicycle race, ½-mile boys' velocipede race, and 1-mile ordinary bicycle race for the championship of the meet. The three first-named events will be open to all members of the L. A. W. The championship race will be limited to members of the Massachusetts and Rhode Island Divisions. Gold and silver medals will be awarded in each event. Entrance fee, 50 cents for each event, except boys' race, for which no charge will be made. Entries close August 8, with C. S. Davol, Hotel Naumkeag, Cottage City. Committee, C. S. Davol, W. G. Kendall and Abbott Bassett; 4 P. M., bass-ball game between crack cycling players and local talent.

Division headquarters will be at the Sea View Annex, which will be devoted wholly to the wheelmen. League members will register there on their arrival, and receive a badge which will entitle them to all the privileges of the meet. It is intended that this meet shall be exclusively for the benefit of League members. There are certain cyclists who endeavor to enjoy the advantages of League membership without paying for it. Such parsimonious individuals are to be severely excluded on this occasion. Special rates will be made by the Old Colony Railroad, and liberal reductions from regular prices have been secured from all the principal hotels on the island.

The Martha's Vineyard Club will contribute to the entertainment of the visiting wheelmen, but for various reasons it has been decided not to give the usual ball this year. The lantern parade will prove a unique feature, and to stimulate friendly rivalry, suitable prizes will be awarded those who make the most effective display.

Special cars for the free transportation of wheels will be attached to the train leaving Boston at 4 P. M., August 7, and also on the train which connects with the 6:30 A. M. boat from Cottage City the following Monday morning.—*Boston Herald*.

·VICTOR·

B·I·C·Y·C·L·E·S

THE ELWELL TOURISTS IN FRANCE.

Somebody—I have forgotten who (was it Thomas Hood?) once wrote:

"Never go to France
Unless you know the lingo;
For if you do, like me,
You will repent, by jingo!"

Had he been one of a party of thirty young and frisky Americans during his sojourn in this land of sweet simplicity and smiles, those lines of very poor advice would surely never have dropped from his pen. Far from being an inconvenience, ignorance of the language proves a never-ending source of fun and laughter. Enough French can be picked up in two or three days to inquire the way about and produce a good meal, and this is all that is absolutely necessary. The rest is all play, and it is wonderful how fast one learns. The idea of being kept out of France and apart from its joys, its scenery, its cathedrals, its blue sky and its Paris because you do not "parlez Français" is preposterous.

There is enough pleasure to be had in a single day in almost any part of France to make up for a year of "guessing" at the language. You may be sure that what little the party has learned has been attended by some curious situations. One of our members—from the City of Big-footed Girls—had the laugh turned on him a day or two ago. Two Frenchmen rode with us from Fontainebleau to Sens to show us the way and point out places of interest. They went back on the following morning, and the Chicago member managed to make them understand that they had been very kind and that he had enjoyed their company. Elated at his success so far, he extended his hand for a parting shake, and instead of "Bon jour," he exclaimed heartily, "Combien"? (how much.) Our Adonis also found himself "dans la potage."

We had scarcely been two days in France when we hauled up one dusty morning at a café in a wayside village. Adonis seated himself at a table with three others, and they decided, after mature deliberation, to have some sandwiches. Of this they notified the waiter. "Oui," said that worthy, counting up the party, "quatre sandweeche?" "Cat sandwiches be ——," roared Adonis, his mind full of fried frogs' legs, eels, horse-steaks, etc. "Come on out, fellers; I believe we'll get poisoned before we get through this blooming country, anyway!"

The only "Hig." was very much taken with a porcelain menu at lunch one noon, and resolved to ask the table-maid for it. He talked to her for half an hour in Portland High School French, at the end of which time she said she understood him perfectly, and, disappearing, she returned and presented him with a raw onion on a plate!

I remember, too, when we rode into Rouen a comical situation. Jack and I were some little way ahead of the others. We were getting pretty well into the city, and not seeing our hotel anywhere we dismounted to hold council. A bright-looking Frenchman stood beside us, waiting for a tram, and I advised Jack to ask him the direction we should take, and added a few remarks in regard to the gentleman's whiskers. Jack said the man did not look as though he knew enough to ache when he was in pain, but guessed he would ask him. "Monsieur, pardonnez moi," began Jack; "ou est la—ou est le—la Hotel Dauphin?" Imagine our chagrin when he calmly returned, in excellent English, "My friend, if you will tell me in English what you want I'll try to help you!"

It seems hardly possible that the party has drawn a line with their rubber tires across the entire republic of France, but such is the case, for to-morrow we cross the line and ride into Geneva, or Genève as it is called here. If anyone cares to see just how it has been done let him draw a line on the map of France running through the following places and he will have our route complete: Dieppe, Rouen, St. Germain, Paris (stick a pin here), Fontainebleau, Sens, Tonnerre, Montbard, Dijon, Dole, Poligny, Morez and Geneva. These are the places in which we stayed one night or more. Our journey in France has been as much of a success as were our tours in Ireland and England, although in an entirely different way. There has been a great deal less of cannon-firing, hand-shaking and banqueting than in the former countries, but it was not because we were any the less welcome. There are but few clubs in France, no large ones, excepting the U. V. F., and none at all so wealthy but what the entertainment of thirty hungry and thirsty Americans would have wrecked its coffers.

The French are not particularly fond of physical exercise, or the sport would certainly grow a great deal faster than it does, for never was a country so exactly fitted to the wants of cyclers as is this one. The road surfaces are perfect throughout, the weather mild and steady, the girls are pretty and the scenery (especially in the west and south) exceptionally fine. Needs a cycler much else? I trow not. The French cyclers will not, at all events, lodge against us, as an Irish paper did, the imbecile complaint that we "are not fast on the road," for we have "killed and buried" all the cyclers who have volunteered to act as guides since we have been in the country. At Sens the "guides," accompanied by one or two of the party, who waited for them out of courtesy, rolled into town three hours later than the main body, completely fagged by the gigantic mileage of the day—forty-six miles.

I have not worked off one-half of my enthusiasm over these roads! It is not simply in and about the cities, but go where you will! In the country anywhere—in the meanest, most poverty-stricken little village—the surface is as hard and smooth as a billiard table, and kept as neatly cleaned and repaired as a ball-room floor. If there is one person upon whose ashes we have called down all the blessings of Heaven, it is Napoleon, who made these marvelous highways. Away up here in the heart of the Jura Mountains (where these lines are being written), the road surface is equal to any in the world. If anyone can imagine fifty or sixty miles of Pennsylvania Avenue, taken out of Washington and twisted two or three times around Pike's Peak, they would have some idea of what a day's run in the Juras must be. The ascent is nowhere so steep as to be unridable, and the scenery just beggars description. The wooded ravines, gorges and valleys are magnificent, and now and then may be caught a glimpse of the surrounding country, which almost forces you to believe you are looking down upon a chart, so plainly can be seen the rivers and white roads, twisting here and there for miles.

The hundred-mile fever has raged amongst the boys ever since landing at Dieppe, and last week broke out on six of the party, past all cure. The day's run on Wednesday was from Sens to Tonnerre, a distance of fifty-four miles, with lunch at Joigny, twenty miles from Sens, at 11 o'clock. The morning run had been what the boys call a "joke"—they got there before they knew it—and lunch was no sooner over than some one suggested going back to Sens and starting over again, making ninety-four for the day. Some looked doubtfully at the hot sun, and others spoke discouragingly of a head-wind which had started, but nothing daunted, six of the party started out at this late hour (11:45). By 3:30 they were at Joigny again, having added forty more to their first twenty miles, and at 8:15 they rode up to the hotel at Tonnerre, with thirty-four more to their credit. The total now being but ninety-four, they mounted again, rode six miles back and returned, making a total of 106 miles at 10:30. They were lustily cheered, and carried into the smoking-room on the shoulders of those who afterward "wished they had started with them." The "centurians" are Messrs. Kirk, White, Shannon, Brinsmade, Schneider and Levy. They took the journey easily, and were no more fatigued than if they had been only half the distance.

On Thursday we listened intently, and imagined we heard from our native shores the various sounds relative to the proper celebration of "the glorious Fourth"—the snapping of the infantile torpedoes and paper-cap pistols, the explosion of the toy cannon and subsequent cry of "Ma-a-a-ma, Boo-hoo"; the mixing of "red lemo.," and the hard breathing of cyclers sweltering up a long hill on some club run. We saw, in imagination, the gayly-dressed crowds at the beaches, the picnics in the woods, the military parades and the country cousin come to town to spend the day. This and much more we heard and saw, and we—did we?—yes, we did—we wished that for that single day alone, and no more, we might be transported each to his own home, to celebrate the day in good old American style. This being impossible, we made what we could out of it over here in France. We bought red, white and blue sashes and wore them at our waists; we decorated our machines with our native colors, and with the stars and stripes flying from the head of the machine we surprised ("surprised" is mild) the natives between Montbard and Dijon not a little. To better fix the day in their memory, two members indulged in a spill while coasting at full speed. Fortunately they bear no worse memento of the day than a lame arm and a bruised chin, respectively. Much impromptu fun was had at dinner in the evening at Dijon. The "management" set up two delicacies, purely American, which we have not tasted since leaving England, namely, ice cream and lemonade, and the "Ohs" and "Ahs" heard when these were produced testified to the grip which they have upon the heart (or rather stomach) of every good citizen of the United States, be he from the North or South, Yankee or cowboy. Papa declared the lemonade to be punch, but if so, it was very much of the "shadow soup" order. Following this were speeches by different members. Beal gave a short review of the history of France and her famous generals, from Cæsar to Napoleon, and then proceeded to show how infinitesimal were their works compared with those of the great Gen. Elwell, who is now pushing his troops through France, a-wheel. The remainder of the night and part of the next morning were made hideous with national and college songs.

On Saturday we ran to Poligny. Poligny sounds first-rate. We all thought we had heard of Poligny, and had our minds made up that it was quite a large pleasure resort, and that we should have lots of sport there. Imagine, then, our disgust at finding it to be a veritable hamlet of scarce two thousand inhabitants, and our accommodations the worst without exception that we have had on the trip. Our dinner was horrible, and I can assure you we passed a wretched night. My very pen runs red ink as I write of the horrors of it, for on retiring we made a discovery causing "each particular hair to stand on end," etc. Our beautiful downy corn-husk mattresses and luxurious brown cotton sheets were just swarming with—with—yes, it is a historical fact and I *will* record it—with the celebrated American bedbug! Great, large, hungry fellows and each provided with a lantern and pair of shears! We looked at each other. "How far is it to the next stopping place?" asked Hig, dolefully. "Thirty-three miles, and it's a dark night." To make a long story short, we slept that night with our boots on. Jack reposed gracefully in a chair, woke up a hundred times, and got a stiff neck. Of the rest of us each carefully shook a blanket, spread it on the floor, and, with our baggage for a pillow, endeavored to fall into the arms of Morpheus. As usual, the writer of these lines was in hard luck. I think the insects must have been "stuck on my shape." At all events, when morning broke it was discovered that I had borne the brunt of the enemy's attack. I am happy to say that this was our first, and probably our last, real hand-to-hand conflict with this species of vermin.

At the hotel at Dole, when we arrived, we found the proprietor of a rival establishment awaiting the arrival of Papa Elwell with a very red face. In his hand he held a bill, and in his wake stood a lawyer, two constables and four gens d'armes. It seems that through somebody's mistake, meals and lodging for our party had been engaged at two different hotels, the proprietors of which, owing to this cause, were about to do mortal combat. It cost our management 100 francs to preserve peace in the village.

The boys are all strong and hearty, and are going well. They are one and all as brown as a nut. Next to getting well tanned, the most popular fad is to raise a beard of some description, and many a shadowy pair of "galways," "chinks" and "muzzles" can be seen, with here and there a promise of what will eventually be a full beard. The appearance of the party on the road is striking but not handsome. They wear just what they please and not any too much of it. Their stockings are continually coming down, and they wear anything on their heads, from a grape-box to a bird-cage. Our British cousins with their immaculate suits would surely cut us dead, but we are as jolly, happy, careless a lot of fellows as you will often see. Our last week in France has been full of enjoyment and a great success, and it is not without a feeling of regret that we shall to-morrow run into Switzerland, and leave behind a country that has given us so much to see and so much to enjoy.

TAM O'SHANTER.

The New York daily papers of last week report a serious accident to a carriage driven in Central Park, the horse having been frightened by a baby carriage. So it appears that the cycle and the horse have now struck up a friendship and that it is these bold, bad baby carriages that frighten the festive equine. We would respectfully call the attention of ex-Commissioner Crimmins to this fact. A bill for the "abolishment of baby carriages" would not be a bad go at Albany this fall.

COASTING EIGHT MILES.

THE SENSATION OF FALLING DOWN A DEEP, DARK HOLE—TWO ROVERS BOLT A CLUB RUN AND GO OFF WITH THE ENEMY—WHO WOULDN'T BE A WHEELMAN?

Tradition has it that late in the fall of 1887, after the season was over with Landlord Seymour of the Summit House, Greylock Mountain, Mass., two Star riders toiled laboriously up the hillside, raised a memorial karn on the roof of A. W. Locke's log house, and made the descent before the twilight shadows fell. In substantiation of this story strangers are shown the men and the mountain. It was left to the North Adams Wanderers, however, to make the first club run to the spot.

The sun was one hour past the meridian when we started. It was a perfect day for a ride, cool and cloudy, with but slight indications of rain. We make the first two miles with scarcely a dismount. Then the grade increases and we are obliged to walk and push our wheels. The roadside is lined with raspberries, and very soon so are the wheelmen. We meet berry pickers of all kinds and descriptions with pails filled with the luscious fruit; parties of campers who have spent the night on the mountain and pleasure seekers in carriages who have been contented with an hour or so. The road becomes steeper and the view more entrancing, and our wheels never seemed so heavy before. It is a steady uphill push now, with only an occasional quarter of a mile of riding, and the condition of the roads is somewhat startling. The unusually frequent rains of early summer have washed the loose mountain earth from the road-bed, leaving the broken rock exposed. The water bars were seemingly never before so ugly looking, while the springs which necessitate their existence have worn soggy gulleys of mud above them. We are certain that we could not coast such a place in the dark. But you don't know what you can do till you try.

The summit gained, and Mrs. Seymour's excellent meal disposed of, we drink in the beauty of the scene from the tower. It is a new experience for one member of the party, and doubly enjoyable to the rest on that account. But the scene has been so often and ably pictured that we pass it here.

The sun goes under a cloud, and the wind whistling through a flannel shirt is an uncomfortable reminder of the altitude we have reached, so we prepare for the descent. Brakes are examined, pedals are raised and everything made secure. The clock in Drury's tower is striking seven and we are off—the American Rambler, New Mail and Pony Star. Down the hillside with the speed of the wind; stumps of trees and rocks fly behind us in one unbroken, indistinguishable line! Now we pass the one-mile post and the water tank, bump a water bar, lickety-bang whizzle over rocks and gulleys, mud, roots and gravel; now we are on hard ground and sliding like fiends through the twilight! It is the very ecstasy of excitement. A broken brake would hurl us down a sheer descent of 2,000 feet. Down through mud and over jounces till *crash!* the leader strikes a villainous water bar near the three-mile post. A second of tremulous uncertainty and the wheel clears it, to be brought to a sudden halt on a slight up-grade two hundred feet away. The rider dismounts to see how the rest take it. Down the hill comes Patton like an avenging demon. He sees the danger and circles round it, though not without receiving a terrible jar. Affhouser is close behind, and, ignorant of his danger, strikes the obstruction fairly in the centre. Wheel and rider are hurled into air as though sprung from a catapult, and land together in a bed of soft mud. By actual measurement they have traveled twenty-three feet without touching the ground. It is a miracle that Tony's bones are not broken. As for his wheel, curvature of the spine doesn't begin to express the condition of its "front bone." What is to be done? We have covered three miles and consumed eight minutes, but are six miles from home, with a busted wheel. Close beside the wreck two birch trees have been growing together for years for this very occasion. The bone is disconnected and, after considerable effort, jammed back into shape. But it has grown as dark as Egypt. It is no longer possible to pick out a passageway between rocks and roots. We must trust to our brakes and luck to carry us in safety. The trees close around us and shut out all light. There is no longer any sensation of grades. It is like falling down a deep, dark hole and striking the sides as you go down. Patton has the lead. "Look out, Mabbett!" he shouts, and the next instant two wheels and a water bar are in collision and two riders are sprawling on opposite sides of the road. Out through the toll-gate and down toward Braytonville! We have harder roads again, but they are treacherous in the extreme. Not till we reach the old sawmill near the foot of the hill do we dare relinquish entirely our hold on the brakes, which are by this time smoking hot.

The descent was made in less time than it takes to tell it, but it was an experience of a lifetime, to say nothing of a victory for the safety type of wheel. And yet there are gillies who believe that an ordinary can be driven where a rear driver will go. L. A. W. 22,664.

—*North Adams Express.*

NEW ORLEANS.

The sixth and final race of the Louisiana Cycling Club's series for the Batson medal was decided on Sunday, July 14, over a 2½-mile course, and resulted in an easy win for R. G. Betts, his only competitor, L. J. Frederic, riding a safety, with which he was too unfamiliar to make much of a showing. No time taken.

The first race for the Hill 5-mile medal was also contested on the same date, and H. L. Cary scored a signal victory over A. M. Hill and H. C. Christy, the latter not finishing. Time, 16m. 34s.

The medal becomes the permanent property of Frederic, he being the only entry to ride in every race of the series and scoring the greatest number of points.

The La. Div. L. A. W. holds meeting July 23. Chief Consul and Secretary-Treasurer will be elected. Hodgson for the former and Geo. Russ for the latter position will probably be the nominees, though there are others to hear from.

N. C. Fowler, Jr., who gets up all the Pope Mfg. Co's ingenious advertising schemes, is vacating at Pittsfield, Mass.

WHEEL GOSSIP

There will be a race meet at Reading to-morrow.

W. M. Brewster will attend the Cottage City Meet.

The Reading Bicycle Club will hold its race meet to-morrow

Mr. Michael Furst has gone to Saratoga for a two weeks' vacation.

Bicycle makers will use the new Thompson electric welding process.

McCredy's tour through Scotland will last from August 8th to the 20th.

Chief Consul Mott is whooping up improved street pavements in Baltimore.

The Pennsylvania Club is arranging for a trip to Dingman's Ferry in August.

W. D Banker is teaching three ladies to ride safeties at Old City Hall Riding School.

The South End Wheelmen, of Philadelphia, will hold a ten-mile road race August 17.

Some of the English makers should sell the Shah of Persia a score of ladies' bicycles.

Messrs. Hesse, Brown and Hall will reside at Bergen Point this summer and train at the N. J. A. C. track.

Mr. E. B. Curry, Captain Washington Cycle Club, has been in town a few days on a pleasure trip.

The Rutherford Wheelmen, who reorganized in April, now have twenty-five members.

O. F. Woodruff, of the Louisville Cycle Club, set up a supper for his club-mates after the July meeting.

A number of wheelmen in New York and Brooklyn are anxious to have a road race held on Election Day.

The title of a late novel is "A Ride on a Cyclone." Cyclone would be an excellent name for a rakish "safe."

KENTUCKY NOMINATIONS.

Chief Consul, A. J. Lamb; Secretary-Treasurer, S. E. Johnson, both of Louisville.

While at Washington we saw a Psycho reposing its graceful lines against the wall of the White House. Great is Owen.

Fred. Merrill, the dealer at Portland, Oregon, believes that the tricycle he longs for was stolen by a woman. This is refreshing.

The Harrogate Meet, the great annual gathering of cyclists in England, will extend from August 2 to 7. There will be races on two days

"Bluffing" is one of the features of the Cottage City Meet. Abbott Bassett is said to be the greatest bluffer of them all. Guess what it is.

The Overman Wheel Company has donated a Victor bicycle as a prize for the winner of the fifty-mile road race at Springfield in September.

The Pennsylvania Club will hold its annual five-mile road race on Lancaster Pike August 3. Draper and Hill will be prominent among the contestants.

Miss Rummill, of Buffalo, has ridden 1,500 miles this year. Recently, in company with Miss Prince, she rode to Niagara Falls and back, a distance of fifty miles.

A contemporary writes of "female bicycle racing and masculine bicycle racing." We are left to conjecture whether our e. c. refers to men and women or codfish.

The *Boston Herald* of Sunday, July 21, illustrates the quarries of Cohasset, Mass., from which is obtained fine crushed stone specially advantageous in building roads.

We are wondering why any note of Ralph Temple's should be given space in a cycling paper. He and his confreres gave the sport a hard blow and are entitled to no recognition whatever.

The Hagerstown *Globe* compliments THE WHEEL on its report of the League meet, mentioning its interesting style and accuracy. The *Globe* republishes a column of THE WHEEL's report.

Chas. S. Luscomb is no longer Brooklyn Park Commissioner. During his term of office he was of much service to wheelmen, and it is hoped that they will again have a representative in the Park Board.

Editor Prial is running on an independent ticket for New York representative of the League. He should be elected, for few are so well equipped to satisfactorily fill such a position.—*Boston Herald*.

The Scranton Bicycle Club's tour, outlined in THE WHEEL of July 19, should be a great success, so excellent is the route chosen. Those who wish to join the Scranton party should address B. P. Connolly, Secretary.

HARRY HODGSON RE-ELECTED.

The Louisiana Division L. A. W. have re-elected Harry Hodgson as Chief Consul. John Dodge has been elected Secretary-Treasurer of the Division. We congratulate Harry, who is the best man the Division could select.

When Osmond went ahead in the ten-mile race for the Brixton cup, *Wheeling* says he just "snorked" past Illston, etc. In this country we say "shot," "stole" or "sneaked," but "snorked" is a very good word—a sort of Rivesish word.

F. C. Frese and C. S. Merrill, of Waltham, Mass., had a 12½ mile run on bicycles Monday evening, over the course through West Newton, for the Y. M. C. A. silver cup. Frese came in the victor in 48m. 5s. This is the second time that he has won the cup, the first time being on July 4.

HESSE BREAKS THE QUEENS BICYCLE TRACK RECORD.

On Saturday last, F. B. Hesse, K. C. W., reduced the Queen's track record to 2m. 57 3-5s. The previous record was 2m. 59 4-5s., held by E. P. Haggott. Hesse rode a 35 lb. wheel. The half was covered in 1m 26s.; F. G. Brown afterwards made a trial in 3m. 2 4-5s.

A WORD TO THE WISE.

There is one point on which we would warn too fond parents who are in the habit of carrying very young children strapped on their cycles, and that is that the cerebral excitement thereby set up is injurious in case of extreme youth.—*Wheeling*.

CALIFORNIA NOMINATIONS.

Chief Consul, R. M. Thompson, San Francisco; Vice-Consul, J. Phil. Percival, Los Angeles; Sec.-Treas., W. D. Sheldon, San Francisco; Representatives, C. C. Moore, Stockton, Dr. J. W. Gibson, San Francisco, Cal., and A. C. McKenney.

RUTHERFORD, N. J., NOTES.

F. N. Burgess, Captain of the Rutherford Wheelmen, left here at 10 A. M. Friday, to ride to Newburgh by way of Tuxedo. He arrived in Newburgh at 6 P. M., in time to catch the train for New York. His total riding distance was about sixty miles.

The *Wheelmen's Gazette* attempts to make game of the fact that we recently sent a copy of THE WHEEL to every student in Vassar College. Unfortunately the *Gazette* spells Vassar "Vasser," converting its attempt at wit into stupidity. And, by the way, the *Gazette* in our opinion, is not clean enough to be admitted to Vassar.

THE ORIGINALITY OF "THE WHEELMEN'S GAZETTE."

Say, by the way, did you see my beautiful picture in *Wheelmen's Gazette*, that picture of the winner of half-mile dash? They even raised a moustache for me and put me on a crank wheel. I guess the artist had too much of "Annie's" juice on board.

Yours truly,
W. J. WILHELM.

R. R. Leeds, of Rutherford, N. J., a member of the Rutherford Wheelmen, rode from that place to Yonkers Wednesday morning, to visit relatives on Prospect Street; distance by cycle, twenty-five miles. In the evening he was the welcome guest of the Yonkers Bicycle Club, at their house, 24 Hawthorne Avenue, seven members being on hand to entertain him.

CYCLISTS CELEBRATE AT LAPEER, MICH.

One of the features of Lapeer's "Fourth" was the bicycle riders. They had a position in the parade and attracted much attention. In the afternoon, races were held. Among the cyclists of Lapeer are Elmer Decker, A. Walterhouse, A. Yorker, F. Yorker, Chas. Smith, P. Marfilieus, Bert Giles and S. Marfilieus

Mr. J. W. Jenks, of the American Economic Association, has advanced an important point in favor of good roads. He asserts that in the Western wheat countries, where wheat is hauled eighteen and twenty miles, the cost of carriage eats up the profit. Mr. Jenks asserts that in the land west of Lake Michigan it does not pay to grow wheat at any distance greater than twenty miles from rail or water.

A CONTINUAL RISE.

First Bicycler—Did you ever ride through the State of Vermont?

Second Bicycler—Yes; went through there last season.

First Bicycler—How was it? Did you find much rising ground?

Second Bicycler—Yes, lots of it. It came up and struck me about six hundred times.—*Lawrence American*.

It is interesting to note that in the Bath Road Club 25-mile handicap, decided July 3, six men beat 1h. 34m., and four men beat 1h. 30m. The three fastest times were: 1h. 27m. 12s.; 1h. 27m. 14s. and 1h. 29m. 20s. These times surpass anything ever accomplished over the Irvington-Milburn course, but we think that on a course equal to the Bath Road, the men who beat 1h. 34m. over the New Jersey course could, if mounted on racing safeties, equal the work of the Englishmen.

The annual event of Singer & Co.'s Coventry employees is the annual picnic, the third of which was held July 6. At two, the party, numbering 350 cyclists, started for headquarters, paraded the principal streets, rode to Deer Park, were photographed, and then rode to Stoneleigh Park. There were twenty lady riders, one of them, Miss Starley, being mounted on a Psycho safety. Arrived at Stoneleigh, the party lunched *à la picnic*, listened to the music of the band, danced, enjoyed athletic games and then had a lantern parade home.

The independent ticket which has been sent out by the representatives of the L. A. W., with the name of F. P. Prial as the representative of the New York Bicycle Club, instead of S. B. Watts, Jr., of the same club, has met with the approval of all the League members, and there is not the slightest doubt about his election. It is rather odd that Mr. Watts' name was put on the list, as he has only recently taken up wheeling, and knows almost nothing in regard to League affairs, so that it is thought that the choice of Frank Prial was an excellent one.—*The Sun*.

On Saturday, July 20, at 3 P. M., Westervelt Haywood and Ed. Hutton, members of the Rutherford Wheelmen (Hutton is also a member of the K. C. W.), started from here to ride to Trenton. They stopped at Metuchen over night, after Hutton had taken a bad fall and discovered that he had lost his pocket-book, containing about thirty dollars and his commutation ticket. Leaving Metuchen the next morning, they arrived in Trenton about noon, when their cyclometer registered about sixty-five miles. Leaving there by the afternoon train, they arrived in New York about 6 P. M.

Tam O'Shanter winds up the Elwell tourists' ride through France in his letter to THE WHEEL. The boys no doubt had a great time in France, notwithstanding their ignorance of the native tongue. "Tam" simply raves over the roads and rightly points out that it is a pity that Frenchmen do not care more for physical exercise. The Elwell party celebrated the "Fourth" in humble but patriotic fashion, had a midnight scuffle with the great American bed-bug, assisted at the making of a "Century," paid 100 francs to keep out of jail, and at last accounts were running largely to beards.

T. I. Wilson states that aluminum can now be made for $6 per pound. The price of steel is 18 cents per pound. Aluminum is one-third the weight of steel, and an aluminum cycle would weigh twelve pounds. This would make the cost of the raw material about $1.00. The difficulty at the present time is to work the material. A number of milling concerns are experimenting, but none will guarantee to work the material into shape. The process of getting it is gradually lessening the cost of production and in time it will no doubt be used in part in the construction of cycles.

At the Hagerstown race meet a telegram was received from the Reading Bicycle Club protesting W. J. Wilhelm, and claiming that he was not an amateur. The telegram was sent with the evident intention of annoying Wilhelm, it being supposed that the race meet committee would debar him from the meet. No attention was paid to the telegram, however. We have written the president of the Reading Bicycle Club, giving him ample opportunity to place the responsibility of the telegram where it belongs, but he has not replied, and the thing goes on record as the dirtiest piece of business ever credited to a bicycle club. Wilhelm is one of the most gentlemanly fellows on the path, and an ornament to it, by the way.

POINTS OF INTEREST IN NEW JERSEY.

The cyclers in the vicinity of Sea Girt, Manasquan, Brielle, Union and Point Pleasant are particularly well blessed in the way of good riding, providing the weather is tolerably dry. In case of a big rain, however, the red clay rolls up on the tires in a beautiful quantity, and makes riding anything but a delight. The roads for the most part are of hard dirt, the major part of which is red clay. The side-paths are fine, as good and as frequently met with, in fact, as in any part of Jersey. One may ride for twenty-four hours at a stretch without being compelled to leave the saddle and trundle his wheel on account of poor riding. And the scenery in this part of the country is well worth viewing.

NEW CLUB AT WOONSOCKET, R. I.

For some time it has been felt by a large number of bicycle riders in the new city of Woonsocket that an association could be formed whereby meets could be planned and runs set going, to the advancement of the wheel riders hereabouts. To this end a meeting was held Thursday evening, and an association formed with twenty-five members, to be called the Woonsocket Wheelmen Association. The following officers were chosen: President, Fred L. Cleveland; Vice-President, Edmund R. Darling; Secretary, George F. Higgins; Treasurer, Eugene Getchell; Captain, Granville S. Conant; First Lieutenant, William Miller; Second Lieutenant, Francello Jillson; Bugler, Benjamin W. Washburn.

HOW TO SHUT OFF THE PESTS.

An Elmira cycle repairer, who also is interested in the wheel trade, has a repairer who has been pestered more or less with certain ones who frequent the shop, asking all sorts of questions about wheels that may be in for repairs or adjustment, and to answer these inquiries in as easy a manner as possible, and also to get some amusement out of it, gently touches the inquirer on the arm or shoulder and points up on the wall, where may be seen the following:

Whose machine is that?
What is it here for?
What is the matter with it?
How did he do it?
Did he take a header?
Did it hurt him much?
Where was he?
How did he get home?

Then the fellow tumbles and turns red in the face or else acknowledges it *good*.

DR. JOHNSON'S TOUR.

"Doc" Johnson, of the Hudson County Wheelmen, is going to take a month's enjoyment. The Doc says he is tired of putting off enjoyment until that time when he can float aimlessly along on the top of the gentle zephyr. He can't spare a month from business, but he is going to take it all the same. The Doc. is truly a philosopher. He will leave this evening (Friday) on the Fall River Line and commence his ride at Newport on Saturday morning. His route will be as follows: Newport to Providence, Boston, Malden, Lynn, Salem, Newburyport, Portsmouth, Biddeford. From Biddeford he expects to visit some of the beaches, as York, Old Orchard, etc., which give splendid riding at low tide. The route leads from Old Orchard beach to Portland, Lewiston, Augusta, Fairfield, Waterville, Pittsfield, Bangor, Bucksport, Ellsworth and to Bar Harbor, near which the Doctor has a cottage, at which his family are at present. One of the features of the trip will be a yachting and fishing excursion.

Last Monday evening, while riding with his wife along the concourse towards Belmont Avenue, in the West Park, Mr. Charles Harvey, of the Pennsylvania Bicycle Club was run down and injured by a horse and buggy. His machine was very much damaged, but Mr. Harvey, fortunately, escaped with slight injuries to one foot and one arm. Both Mr. and Mrs. Harvey were mounted on safety bicycles, and Mrs. Harvey was riding some little distance ahead of her husband, when a colt, driven by Mr. Smith Rogers, of 1200 North Forty first street, came up behind them, and, frightening at a bicycler coming from the opposite direction, the animal shied over on to Mr. Harvey, throwing him to the ground and trampling both him and his machine under his feet. After a few seconds of extreme danger the unlucky wheelman was extricated. He escaped material injury, but his machine was made a wreck, the frightened equine having trampled both wheels and drawn one wheel of the buggy across them. The affair was purely an accident, and Mr. Harvey states there was no malice on the part of the driver of the vehicle.—*Philadelphia Sunday Item*

THE DUPLEX MULTIPLICATION CRANK.

Did you ever meet the mechanical crank, who is going to revolutionize cycling with his invention of a four-hundred pound tricycle, with wheels as high as John Wanamaker's ambition, and as big as the public debt! It (the tricycle, not the crank) is usually driven by hand, and is going to travel thirty miles an hour, nevertheless. Has he ever built one? Oh, no! It is not necessary to build the machine in order to test its value; any one can see from the drawings that it will work, and, besides, he is a "first-class mechanic," and knows more about cycling to begin with than you will to end with. The machine is bound to go; all you have to do is to move that lever by a slight pressure of the hand and the wheels will make one hundred and sixty revolutions a minute. Has he ever ridden a bicycle? No, and never expects to. There is where you show your ignorance by supposing that it is necessary to ride in order to learn anything about the art. He has looked at a bicycle and has several young friends who ride them, and it is his opinion that the only thing necessary to make cycling as common as swearing is for him to lend it the help of his mighty intellect. This crank is becoming a very common bird just now, and something should be done to suppress him. What's the League good for, anyhow?—*Philadelphia Item*.

CONNECTICUTINGS.

The majority of Stamford wheelmen feel like keeping their hats in the air most of the time, now, and shouting "Hooray!!!" with a good many exclamation points thrown in among their Juicet (?) notes, for an Avling & Porter fifteen-ton steam road roller is actually here on a two weeks' trial trip, and will be fired up this week, we expect. If any really energetic and well-meaning roller ever had its hands full—that is, had an opportunity to show its metal—this one has, for there are just acres of unclaimed land on our streets that is only a weariness and a vexation of spirit.

The town is building a new jail, which we hope will be used as a cooler for all who oppose the much-needed street making. This last word is well put, as we have none worth the name, and some will have to be "made."

The Wheel's late item in reference to Darien wheelmen was a little oversketched, as we have heard of no club there, and there are nearer five than fifteen cyclers. Darien is one of the sleepy hamlets that we usually pass through the edge of, so as not to disturb its quiet; even the bees drone more softly within its gates, and the feathered songsters pipe in more subdued strains inside its borders.

In proof that every one is disgusted and wrought up to desperation at the condition of our streets (we will put it that way anyhow), Cycler Lewis, the druggist, has recently lost a couple of hundred dollars from the eccentricity (?) of a clerk. The latter is in durance, however, and will no doubt have a warm weather hair cut and a new suit of clothes.

We trained across the Jersey flats to "Brimville," one day last week, and saw Editor Wells among other great and good men. They gave it out that cycling there was three times as booming as it was last season, and that they were happy in consequence. *Vive la* the good cause!

Mr. President Mable, of the Long Island Wheelmen, is spending July at the historic "Old Oak," Coscob, four miles west of Stamford, and it has been our pleasure to ride with him occasionally while the days have been going by. We wheeled to Bridgeport and return with him on the occasion of the Division Meet. That word "return" means considerable when roads are in such a state as we found them, and under a July sun that was very much in evidence. We were the only ones from this section who did not return by rail.

It should be noted that the N. Y., N. H. & H. road does *not* carry cycles free of charge, as some of the papers said, but the same old story holds good—50 cents for each fifty miles or less.

Stamson.

MARYLAND.

The Chief Consul has notified the presidents of the Baltimore, Maryland and Crescent Clubs to hold elections for delegations to the Division Board of Officers by or before August 15. These clubs are entitled to one delegate for the first twenty League members, and one for each additional fifty League members on the rolls on July 1, 1889. The names and addresses of those elected should be forwarded to the Chief Consul promptly.

A letter from President Luscomb has been received here which contains some severe strictures on J. Purvis-Bruce, "Jack," and his recent publication in the *Bulletin*, and intimates that the matter will be laid before the Executive Committee of the League.

The Crescent Club will have an excursion to Tolchester on Friday, July 26. A number of races will add interest to the occasion.

The Chief Consul has sent the following letter to Mayor Latrobe in regard to the bad condition of the Pimlico Road:

Dear Sir—The Park Heights, or Pimlico Road, is in an extremely bad condition. The road-bed is now little more than a series of gutters, and the inequalities of the surface and the presence of large boulders make riding on it, especially at night, a real danger to life, limb and property. This has long been a favorite road for pleasure riding, besides accommodating a large business traffic. Cannot something be done in the way of repairing it? At least 5,000 cyclers and perhaps as many more drivers are interested in this road, and I have received many solicitations to call your attention to it. A rough estimate makes the cost of thorough repairs to be not over $3,000. It is urged by many that in the September festivities in this city, this road will be used more than any other in the vicinity, and that early action in the matter is desirable for that reason. Very respectfully, your obedient servant,

Albert Mott.

NEWARK.

On Thursday, 18th inst., thirty-one Atalanta Wheelmen and guests started for Bergen Point to enjoy the elegant supper and clam bake that had been prepared for them. From report we should judge that these gallant thirty-one did full justice to the bountiful spread. All reached home safely, no headers (until next A. M.) by any. Oh, yes, we almost forgot to say that the one on that thirty-one stands for S. G. Whittaker.

Our visit to the H. C. W. is one long to be remembered, and we can say heartily we all had a "bang-up time," reaching home safely and seasonably.

The house committee have been doing wonders in the way of furnishing the A. W. house. This can only be seen to be appreciated. Come and see us, boys.

Frank Brock, of the Atalantas while going at a three-minute gait around the park on his new Psycho safety, had a drunken man step in front of him. Both took glorious tumbles, the "drunk" getting the worst of it. Almost immediately the cry was to put the bicycles out of the park. We saw the whole affair and can swear that Brock tried to get out of the way and avoid a collision.

The safety craze has just commenced in the A. W's. We have seven low wheels now.

The question has been asked by several, "What prevents the Atalantas having a race meet?" That's just what we want to know.

A lantern parade, under the management of the Atalantas, is to take place next month. Captain Drabble is busy perfecting the arrangements.

Spark.

Newark, N. J., July 24, 1889.

BUFFALO.

It is a fact to be regretted that Buffalo, with about fifty lady riders, can claim but four members who belong to the L. A. W. Surely the fair sex should realize that the League will extend to them the benefits which are accorded their lords (?) or future masters (?) perhaps.

It is amusing to hear some of the stories told about the persistency with which the average woman objects to the wheel. It is also amusing to hear of the manner in which they often change their minds and become ardent devotees of the silent steed. A friend of mine related an incident to me the other day which illustrates the point very finely. He has been keeping company with a young lady for several years. Not long since she accepted a position in a downtown business house as a copyist. The indoor work severely told upon her. The young man tried by every possible means to persuade her to take a tandem ride but she refused. One evening a party of young friends stopped at her home, all being out for a ride on tandems. There was also a vacant seat for her, and, after a great deal of urging, she decided to try it. The next day she saw the young man and declared to him that it was the "loveliest" and most delightful ride she had ever taken, and that when she reached home after the ride she was not one bit tired and felt like a new person. She has almost decided to purchase a lady's bicycle.

Buffalo now has nine wheeling clubs and about 2,500 wheelmen. The clubs are as follows, and were formed in the order given: Buffalos, Zigzags, Women's Wheel Club, Mystics, Wanderers, Ladies' Bicycle Club, Columbias and Konxes.

Since the State Division Meet will not be held here the local wheelmen are very enthusiastic over securing the meet for Niagara Falls. This place would be a splendid locality—plenty of attractions, a good track, an excellent hill for a climbing contest, and Buffalo but twenty miles away. It is proposed to have the meet the first week in September, and then the wheelmen could visit the International Fair here, which commences on September 3 and continues for ten days.

The Ramblers are arranging an illuminated parade for the first week in August. All wheelmen will be invited to take part, and it will be the cycling event of the season. The Ramblers have definitely decided that they will hold no tournament this year, but expect to come to the front with something great for 1890.

It is to be hoped that a race will be arranged over the fine 100-mile course from Buffalo to Erie. Karl Kron and Thomas Stevens pronounced this course to be the finest straightaway for that distance in this country.

A one-mile safety, one-mile ordinary, and one mile for road wheels are the races arranged for Saturday in connection with the Scottish games.

E. N. Bowen has eleven hickory wheels, which he uses for renting purposes.

The *Courier* has commenced to devote considerable attention to cycling.

Zo.

ELIZABETH.

Club matters are rather quiet at present, owing to the fact that most of our members are out of town on vacations, and those who remain prefer to sit under their "vine and fig tree" and keep cool.

There are several important questions on hand which club members are beginning to discuss—viz., the land question and the enlargement of our present club-house. The land on which the club-house stands is leased by the club, and although the lease has several years to run, yet the members think that they might better settle the question now, as property is increasing in value every day. The club will have to pay more for the land if the question is put off much longer.

The other question—viz., the enlarging of the house, will come up for consideration this winter. The conservative element object to increasing the debt; the other members claim that if we had a gymnasium, bowling alleys, etc., that a large associate membership could be obtained, on the plan of the K. C. W. Something will be done, you may rest assured, as the present officers are pushers and are bent on making the E. W. the leading club in the State.

Since President Pennell has taken the Columbia agency for Elizabeth the other manufacturers seem to have aroused themselves. We now have Springfield Roadster, Eagle and Premier agents here, and are threatened with more.

We are having a large increase in the number of new riders here, but unfortunately they are of the "long pants, derby hat" contingent, and are not, as a rule, desirable for club members.

A word about the new road law is not out of place here. It shows the skeptical what the L. A. W., backed by the large cycling clubs of the State, can do. The new road bill recently passed by the Legislature was framed by a prominent L. A. W. member living near Elizabeth, introduced by Senator Miller, who is a firm friend of the wheelmen, and was actively supported by the State representatives in our vicinity. The *Elizabeth Journal* was one of the most active supporters of the bill. Mr. Aug Crane, its business manager, is a prominent member of the E. W.

The E. W. will pay a visit to Coney Island this Saturday without wheels or uniforms. They will take the P. R. R. to New York, and the Iron Steamboats from Pier 1, returning home at an early (?) hour. The treasurer has invested the contents of the club treasury in red paint and brushes, and the boys anticipate a jolly time.

Our friend "Coaster" has evidently not recovered from the stroke of paralysis which struck him when we let off our new club yell at the H. C. W. entertainment, as he has mixed the cause of our lateness up with something else.

Connt.

ON THE ENGLISH PATH.

At Crystal Palace July 6 some excellent work was done. The mile safety handicap was won by Burns, 130 yards, in 2m. 35 3-5s. The mile ordinary was won by Weatherley, 130 yards; time, 2m. 34 4-5s. Weatherley won easily. Burns also won the 2-mile safety scratch race; time, 5m. 48 1-5s. The 20-mile scratch bicycle race for the Buxton Cup was a grand contest, F. J. Osmond defeating F. P. Wood and W. Illston; time, 31m. 7s. The cup, which is valued at fifty guineas, is now Osmond's property.

At Leicester July 6 A. H. Robb, scratch, won the professional mile handicap in 2m. 36 4-5s.; Jack Lee, 35 yards, second; Howell, scratch, fourth.

ST. LOUIS.

LUMSDEN VS. BARNARD.

Bob Garden has issued a formal challenge to Barnard for a race with Lumsden on the track, distance one-half mile to ten miles, for a trophy valued at not less than $100. Although there has been a good deal of ill-advised boasting concerning Barnard's abilities, it was not thought that it would be heard as far away as Chicago, and the challenge was entirely unexpected. Opinion is divided as to the advisability of accepting it. The more conservative argue that Barnard has not had enough experience on the track to warrant him in trying conclusions with a thoroughly seasoned racer like Lumsden, and they favor waiting until next year, or until such time as they can ascertain just how much speed and endurance Barnard has. The other side, and they are by far the more numerous, say that he has already demonstrated, in his practice and in the races at Sedalia, that he has both speed and endurance in sufficient quantities to enable him to give any amateur in the country a good race, and, furthermore, that a race with Lumsden, even though the latter should win, would do more toward bringing him out as a racer and equipping him with the experience he needs than a year's racing with local riders would do. The races of the track association take place in August, and if the match is made it will be run off at that meeting. As an attraction, it will eclipse the Stone match. If no match is made Lumsden will doubtless enter the open events. He seems bound to have some fun with this new candidate for racing honors and he won't be denied. Good judges are of opinion that he can give Barnard twenty-five yards in a mile and a beating.

The bicycle championships of the Western Amateur Athletic Association will be run off at our meeting, and an effort is being made to get a League championship for the same time. The directors held a meeting last week and perfected the preliminary arrangements. Liberal prizes will be hung up, and every inducement offered for the racing men throughout the country to compete. Here is a golden opportunity for Banker, Crist, Rich, Lumsden and others to meet on neutral ground and settle this question of amateur supremacy. The track will be in good condition, and the weather here is always delightful at that time of the year.

The following item, clipped from one of the local dailies last week, will be read with interest by the many friends of the quondam cycling scribe of the *Post-Dispatch*:

"W. E. Hicks' name appears in the report of the Paris conference of single tax men as American secretary. Mr. Hicks has been active in the movement which brought about the conference, and his St. Louis friends are congratulating themselves with the thought that this city has furnished the cause so brilliant and enthusiastic a representative. On his return to America and St. Louis the Single Tax League will give him a most hearty welcome."

The conduct of some selfish, irresponsible wheelmen in riding the side paths in Forest Park has caused complaints to be filed with the Park Commissioner, and that functionary has served notice on the police to arrest any rider using the walks. To this extent he is all right, and will have the cordial support of all law-abiding wheelmen, but he is all wrong when he goes on to declare that if he hears of any more cases of horses frightening at bicycles he will rule them (the bicycles) out of the park altogether. If we are to consider as a precedent the experience of the New York wheelmen in fighting similar regulations made by the Central Park Commissioners, he has a perfect legal right to enforce just such a rule, but it is not at all likely that he will proceed to such extreme measures unless forced to it by the aggravating conduct of the riders themselves. That there is a class of wheelmen who abuse the privileges of the park is too apparent to admit of any denial, and if the League officials here would only take the bull by the horns, or, to speak more explicitly, the bull-headed riders by the neck, and do a little prosecuting on their own account, it would soon put a stop to the lawlessness complained of, and put the respectable, law-abiding wheelmen on a solid basis with the municipal authorities, as well as the citizens generally. We have never had our rights abridged in St. Louis in any way, and if we wish this state of affairs to continue we must be careful to confine ourselves to our *rights*, and pattern our conduct with due regard to the rights of others. If we undertake to assume privileges to which we are not entitled, in defiance of the regulations, we will soon be brought up with a suddenness that will be surprising—to a few, at any rate. Forest Park is purely a driving park; there are not half a dozen walks altogether in it, and the surface of these is generally not as good as the roads. Their use, therefore, by wheelmen can only be attributed to stubborn selfishness, and when one is found so utterly unreasonable as to use them, in violation of the park rules, it ought to be considered the bounden duty of every frequenter of the park, whether a wheelman or otherwise, to turn the offender over to the police and see to it that he is punished. It would not take more than one or two convictions to correct that trouble.

The reorganization of the Cycle Club is progressing favorably and will soon be completed. There were about a dozen to twenty members of the old club who did not bring it any credit, and these will have to walk the plank. Lucas will be the president of the new club.

Ithuriel.

RACE MEET AND ROAD RACE AT RICHFIELD SPRINGS.

The first annual meet and tournament of the Waiontha Club, of Richfield Springs, was held in August, 1888. It was a success, and conspicuous for the elegance of the prizes given. Richfield is a noted summer resort, and her hotel proprietors generously donated several of the more costly prizes, notably the Earlington and Spring House cups, and the Darrow House set.

Somewhat gratified with last year's success, the members will hold a meet on Wednesday, August 14, and committees have been nominated.

Among the events will be a fifty or hundred mile road-race, on a course leading around Lake Canadarago; the distance is twelve miles, and the finish, in either instance, will be made on the track where the tournament occurs. The course is a noted one for smoothness and level grade. At the time of the year chosen the course is in its best condition, and when so, it cannot be equaled in this country.

Further particulars will be given by the Secretary, Fred. Bronner, Richfield Spa, N. Y.

SAN FRANCISCO.

The joint meet of the Bay City Wheelmen of this city and the Oak Leaf Wheelmen of Stockton, which took place at the latter city on the 4th was an unqualified success. A large party of the Bay City Wheelmen left this city on the afternoon of the 3d and they soon owned the train. A number of them rode in the engine while more went out on top of the baggage car. If their enjoyment was measured by the soot and dust they accumulated then they must have had a good time. Some of the boys produced their cameras and took flash-light pictures of the riders on the train. Stockton was reached at dusk and the railway platform was crowded with riders, a number having gone up some days before, and there being a large party of local riders there. After a wash and supper the boys made their appearance on the street and found many acquaintances of former meets. As the night was very warm they did not go far from the hotel. The morning of the 4th was ushered in by the usual firing of cannon and ringing of bells, and the streets were filled with riders quite early.

The boat from San Francisco brought up a number who could not get away on the train. The wheelmen formed for the parade in front of the Stockton boys' club-house, and rode to the street where the military was making ready to march. There were nearly 200 wheelmen in line and they made a fine appearance, adding much to the parade. The boys regretted that there was not a slow race on the programme for the afternoon, as the practice they secured in the morning would have made such an event interesting and there would surely have been a record entry.

A visit to and a spin on the track in the morning showed it to be in perfect condition. It is a quarter-mile, shaped like the letter "D," and the corners are so well shaped and banked that they are not noticed at all; the only fault to be found is that the finishing straight is not quite long enough, being only 75 yards.

As early as one o'clock people began to arrive at the track, and when the first race was called the grounds presented an animated appearance. A large proportion of the audience was composed of ladies, and they made the grand stand bright with their light summer dresses.

The officers of the day were: Referee, R. M. Welch; Judges, Dr. Curragh, C. C. Moore, F. E. Richardson; Timers, E. Mohrig, W. M. McKee, Ed. Adams; Umpires, Edw. Tole, Burt Moore; Clerks of the Course, F. W. Pierson, B. Bartholomew; Scorers, C. A. Elliott, Dan Weaver; Starter, W. E. Thompson.

When racing commenced the day was very warm, the thermometer showing 95° in the shade.

The one-mile novice was won by T. H. Doane, B. C. W., Al. Col, G. C. W., 2d; time, 3 minutes. Also started S. E. Mastick, Oberlin (Ohio) B. C., W. R. Sipsett, G. C. W., W. H. T. Durant, unattached. Mastick led at a good pace for two and a half laps, when Doane took the lead and was never headed, winning by several yards, Col a good second.

The second race was a quarter-mile dash, and was won by J. E. Hickinbotham, O. L. W., C. W. Hammer, B. C. W., 2d; time, 41 2-5 seconds. Also started T. W. Gilmore, B. C. W., and F. E. Southworth, O. L. W. Gilmore drew the pole, but Hammer had secured it before a hundred yards was ridden and led until the straight for the tape was reached, when Hickinbotham drew up and passed him, winning by a yard.

The two-mile State championship was won by W. G. Davis, S. F. B. C., F. E. Southworth, 2d; time, 6.48. Also started R. W. Turner, B. C. W. Turner set a hot pace in the first lap, but as he was not in condition he let up after that and rode second. Neither Davis nor Southworth would make the pace fast, which accounts for the slow time. At the bell Davis drew out, and going on won easily.

The one-mile safety State championship was the best race of the day, and was won by W. A. Shockley, Bay City Wheelmen, S. Plummer, B. C. W., 2d; time, 2.50 1-5, a new coast record. Also started A. L. Wulff, O. L. W., C. B. Lakeman, U. of C., C. P. Fonda, S. F. B. C., C. N. Sangton, B. C. W. The riders were in a bunch for two laps, when Lakeman and Fonda collided and fell, bringing Langton over with them. Shockley took the lead a lap from home, and although Plummer made a great effort he lacked finish, and was beaten by two yards. Shockley's riding was a surprise to everybody, as on April 30 he had no speed at all, and although his practice was closely watched he did not seem to be improving very much. He was formerly a member of the Mass. Bi. C. His win was a popular one.

The only fall of the day was in the safety (?) race.

The ½-mile handicap was won by Al Col, G. C. W., 75 yards; C. W. Hammer, B. C. W., 40 yards, second. Time, 1m. 20 3-5s. Also started, W. G. Davis, scratch; J. E. Hickinbotham, 25 yards; T. W. Gilmore, 50 yards; W. H. T. Durant, 70 yards; S. C. Bloch, 75 yards. The scratch man was getting up rapidly, but stopped at 300 yards and went into the dressing-room and fainted from the effects of the heat. Hickinbotham was riding strongly and might have won, when he quit—a bad habit he has. The finish was close.

The 3-mile handicap was won by F. E. Southworth, G. C. W., scratch; L. G. Hodgkins, B. C. W., second. Time, 9m. 29s. Also started, T. H. Doane, 150 yards; W. R. Lipset, 200 yards, and S. C. Mastich, 200 yards. Lipset's saddle worked loose and he had to retire; Doane quit at two miles, and Mastich was lapped.

The 2-mile safety handicap was spoiled by the unexpected form displayed by Shockley, as he had been allowed a handicap in this race based on his previous performances. Wulff, one of the scratch men, refused to ride even after Shockley had signified his intention of going back to scratch. Langton, who had 100 yards, had been shaken up in the championship and did not ride. Consequently Shockley and C. B. Lakeman started from scratch. The promise of an extra medal for record did not induce them to ride fast, and the first mile took nearly 3m. 27s.; after this Shockley took the lead, and, riding very strongly, won in 6m. 25s., which is another coast record.

The last race of the day was the 1-mile scratch, and was won by W. G. Davis; J. E. Hickinbotham, second. Time, 3m. 11s. Also started, C. W. Hammer. Had Hammer and Hickinbotham made the pace severe they might have used Davis up, but as it was they let him set an easy pace until the last lap, when Hickinbotham took the lead and nearly won, Davis passing him just before the tape.

The races all through furnished good sport, and more records would have been beaten if some of the riders could have been induced to make the pace fast when they had no chance to win.

In the evening the wheelmen had an exhibition and dance at the pavilion. The Bay City Wheelmen drill corps of twelve members gave a splendid drill, doing all the difficult stands and intricate movements without a break. E. W. Adams, of the Bay City Wheelmen, gave an acceptable exhibition of fancy riding, and was followed by eight members of the Oak Leaf Wheelmen in a demon drill. The electric lights were put out, and the riders, clad in red, with horns, etc., went through many movements, the hall being illuminated with red fire and the band playing wierd music. Dancing was indulged in until an early hour in the morning. The return trip in the train was as enjoyable as the journey up to Stockton. All sorts of jokes were played on the persons who wanted a few hours' sleep. The meet just filled the vacancy caused by the League meeting being held at Los Angeles, and gave many an opportunity to see friends who only attend the large meets.

July 6. CALIFORNIA.

[This letter was crowded out of last week's WHEEL.—ED.]

CHICAGO.

The subject now uppermost in wheelmen's minds is the proposed lantern and bell ordinance which will very likely be passed at the next meeting of the council. The general opinion is expressed in two words—a shame—and I understand if passed the boys will make life miserable for residents along the boulevards until it is repealed. Numerous headlights, gigantic gong bells and other instruments of torture are now in process of construction in the various club house repair shops, to be sprung on the unsuspecting public as soon as the ordinance is passed.

I was handed a petition yesterday, which I very gladly signed, for the reinstatement of L. D. (Birdie) Munger. It will without any question receive the support of 95 out of every 100 Chicago wheelmen, who earnestly hope to see the racing board take favorable action. Birdie had the honor of being one of the first to introduce ladies' bicycles in Chicago, and now claims that we have very close to five hundred lady-riders. I think that is putting the figure a little high, and that three hundred would come somewhat nearer the mark.

Speaking of lady riders reminds me that there is a prospect of several accompanying the Chicago Club tour from Indianapolis to Cincinnati during the latter part of August.

The C. C. C. are again building castles in the air—excuse me, boys, I mean a club house at Jackson Park. The scheme is a good one, and if carried through would surely double the membership in a very short time, as the location is first class for the numerous boulevard riders and upper twelve picnics. How it will suit the newly-organized N. T.'s is an open question. Being a member of both organizations I will state that the objects of the N. T. Club are somewhat similar to the famous P. W. Bs.

The Lincolns are in camp at Powers Lake, and two members of the club who returned last evening, report a (as Jack says) H. O. T. It is rumored that Harvey (Oakes) Pounds, the heavy weight champion rider and fisherman of the party, on Sunday last (it may have been Saturday) caught 203 perch, some of which measured at least three inches.

The Illinois have rented a cottage at Geneva Lake and are as usual having a good time, at least when they can keep their minds off of the sad fact that Bob Ehlert (amateur (?)) has joined the Æolas.

Munger has discovered another lady flyer, who at a private trial last week rode a quarter in 42 1-5 seconds on a fifty-four pound machine, and who swears by her Rambler that she will be the first lady to ride inside of three minutes, but for speed I will for a time at least pin my faith on Miss Grace Lloyd, as I have on several occasions had plenty to do to keep in the dust from her rear wheel for a short distance.

The Illinois have accepted the Chicago's challenge for a team race, calling for five men and a distance of five miles, but object to the Cheltenham track, as the Chicago team sleep there. From the names in the C. C. C. team, Lumsden, Van Sicklen, Winship, Greenlief and Geo. Thorne, I am of the opinion that they mean business and will be found *not sleeping* on any track that is selected. What's the matter with making it a five mile road race?

Will say for our flyer, Lumsden, that he stands ready and willing to meet any of the Eastern or St. Louis sprinters at any time. NOVICE.

BROOKLYN NEWS.

Many and various were the runs taken by members of the B. B. C. last Sunday. Bradley and Sheffield rode through to Babylon and back, and Fuller and Cole to Massapequa and return, and all reported the Long Island roads in fine condition all the way.

Hornbostel and E. Koop took in the Roslyn run, while the Sunday morning run to Bath, which is becoming a stereotyped weekly run for the Brooklyns, was largely attended.

Melvin, Knowles and Sackett rode from Newark to Plainfield and were not over pleased with the condition of those Jersey roads.

Cobblestone Hill is scarcely recognizable now, as it is completely torn up, and loads of stone and other material are piled along its heretofore weary length. The Cyclists' Union deserve considerable credit for the influence which they have brought to bear on the repairing of that famous hill.

Several members of the Long Islands made century runs on the Island last Sunday.

The case of Beasly against the Park policeman has been set down for the September Court Calendar, when the policeman will be brought before the Grand Jury, indicted for assault in the first degree. The policeman has been liberated under one thousand dollars bail. It is to be hoped that a fitting example will be made of this species of the road-hog, and that our parks will be more free in future from this lately developed antipathy toward wheelmen by the Park police force.

W. G. Class, B. B. C., while competing in a race at Lancaster, Pa., last week, was thrown violently from his wheel by a collision with a dog that ran across the track. No bones were broken, but he received a severe shaking up, the effects of which still cling to him.

Warner, of the same club, also had an accident last Sunday in South Orange, taking a header and striking his hand on a sharp stone with such force as to cut a bad gash in his hand, which had to be sewn up by a surgeon.

A monster combination run to Massapequa, L. I., composed of members of the Kings Co. Wheelmen and the Brooklyn Bicycle Club, will take place on Saturday, August 31. Captain Marion of the K. C. W. and Captain Meeteer, B. B. C., are making arrangements to assure those participating an unusually pleasant time. It is proposed to arrive in time for supper Saturday night, attend a specially arranged hop in the evening, remain over night, and on Sunday morning take a sail and a swim, returning after dinner on their wheels to Brooklyn.

Brooklyn, July 23, 1889. ATOL.

K. C. W. NOTES.

Messrs. Marion and Bensinger intend taking a vacation trip through a part of the country, that for beauty and variety of scenery, is not to be surpassed. Wheeling from New York to Lake George, and Lake Champlain, via Albany, they will then journey on through Vermont and New Hampshire to the "White Mountains," a distance of more than 450 miles. Then changing their mode of travel, they will go down the St. Lawrence to Ogdensburg and the "Thousand Islands," here a few days will be spent in sight seeing, etc., and when the wheels are again mounted, the boys will be fresh for the trip to Buffalo and the Falls. Here the train will be taken later for home, and one of the finest outings on record will draw to a close.

Bridgman is once more with us, and looks much improved by his trip, and more anxious than ever to work.

On Sunday, the 21st inst., F. F. Brown, F. B. Hesse and H. J. Hall, Jr., New Jersey Athletic Club, F. F. Storm, Jr., Kings Co., and myself, journeyed to Queens to see what could be done with the one mile record of the local track.

We took train to Jamaica, and a pleasant drive of a half hour brought us to what is possibly the finest little six-lap track in the State. The cordial reception we received from Mr. Lloyd, the proprietor of the track, made us at once feel at home. F. B. Hesse was chosen to try and lower E. P. Baggott's time of 2m. 50 4-5s. Brown acted as starter, while Mr Lloyd and Harry Hall held the watches. At the crack of the pistol "Ferd" was off—29s. for the first lap, and riding easy, 29s. for the next and 30s. for the third, or 1m. 28s. for the half mile; still he goes easy, though a little slower, doing but 31s and 31⅘s. for the fourth and fifth; but then the whistle goes, and the boys shout, and—well, Ferd responded to the tune of 27s. for his last lap, and so finished in 2m. 57⅘s. Mr. Lloyd's watch read 2m. 57 3-5s., and as that was the slowest time, it was decided on as official. So the Queens' Amateur Athletic Club's track record for the mile stands to the credit of F. B. Hesse, N. J. A. C. Time, 2m. 57 3-5s.

Brown then borrowed Hesse's wheel and clothes, and ran the mile off in 3m. 2 3-5s., another good performance for a strange wheel and strange shoes.

The Murphy boys are ever at it. Two firsts and a second for Chas., and four seconds for "Miles," is the result of the trip to East Hartford.

Brown leaves on Friday for Cape May, where he intends to pass the next two weeks. As a racer will constitute part of his baggage, it is fair to presume that the natives, and fish, will be treated to some phenomenal spurts, when the ebb tide will permit of wheeling on the beach.

I am sorry that "Atol" and I should continually be at "cross purposes," but the suggestion of the editor, "of gloves, etc.," is too heroic. I am no student of the "manly art." The Kings Co. Wheelmen have in their constitution a by-law that states, "that a member of K. C. W. cannot at the same time be a member of any other cycle club in the city of B." The fact that if a K. C. W. member joined the Brooklyns as an ASSOCIATE, it would not pass muster with the Kings Co. board, is my opinion, hence my par——

Brooklyn, N. Y., July 25, 1889. RAM LAL.

LANCASTER, PA.

Variety is toothsome to our gross natural appetites, and is said to be the spice of life. Admitting that this is true, it accounts for our soon wearying of sameness, and we sigh for fresh fields and pastures new. And the cycler also acknowledges that he desires by-and-by, to travel over new routes and to explore hitherto untried pathways. Be the riding ever so good, he becomes familiar with every hill and hollow, and he knows what is before him, and pretty nearly what he may expect to see.

"The Two" had concluded that their evening ride should be over our best known and oftenest tried seven-mile-run, just because it is the best; but a notion that a change would be preferable led us to take a different course, one a few miles south-easterly, to the banks of the Conestoga. Good macadam with a fair surface, after getting beyond the city limits. In due time we struck the inevitable toll-gate.

Although the sun was still well up in the heavens, the churlish keeper had the bars down. To a polite request to please open and allow us to pass, he replied, "I got noting tu du mit yu." (No toll to collect.) The spunky member of the cycling firm said, "Nevertheless you might be a little accommodating." "I don't kommodate, nobody kommodates me." "Well, the reason for that is easily understood, you're too much of a chucklehead." The cyclers allowed themselves to pass through and rolled speedily away without waiting to hear the tirade of "dutchiness" that came spluttering after them.

We soon reached and crossed the bridge over the winding Conestoga, and turning to the right followed the wagon track until we reached Rockford. Dismounting we leaned our trusty wheels against the nicely white-washed stone wall that encloses the grounds, and stretched ourselves upon the green sward that slopes down to the water's edge. Behind us stands Rockford Hall, and from an abundant spring of pure water flows the brook whose voice is heard rippling and gurgling over the stones into the Conestoga, then to the Susquehanna to Chesapeake Bay to the ocean. What a picture of human life! The spring ushers into existence from the brooklet of childhood, to the stream of youth with its pleasures and aspirations, to the larger river of manhood with its cares, struggles and responsibilities, to the bay of rest and retirement in old age, and then into the ocean of eternity. We listened to the singing of the waters, and although this did not happen to be the Tennysonian brooklet, yet the music and the sentiment were the same.

The Pope Manufacturing Co. have issued one of the cleverest advertising devices of the season, in the shape of a base-ball book, compiled by Jacob C. Morse, of the Boston *Herald*. The book contains enough base-ball information to satiate the biggest crank on record.

New York State Division L.A.W.

OFFICIAL ORGAN.

OFFICERS FOR 1889.

Chief Consul, W. S. Bull, 754 Main Street, Buffalo, N. Y. Vice-Consul, M. L. Bridgman, 1255 Bedford Avenue, Brooklyn, N. Y. Secretary-Treasurer, Geo. M. Nisbett, 30 Wall Street, New York City. Executive and Finance Committee, W. S. Bull, M. H. Bridgman, Dr. George R. Blackham, Dunkirk, N. Y.

CORRECTED LIST OF LINES THAT CARRY WHEELS FREE.

To the Members of the New York State Divison:

In the issue of The Wheel for June 14, 1889, there was published a list of railroads as being those governed by the resolution published at the same time regarding the free transportation of bicycles. That list was furnished by prominent railroad officials in Buffalo as being a correct list of the roads affected by the resolution. Since the list was published, however, further investigation has revealed the fact that the Trunk Line Association and the Trunk Line Passenger Committee are different organizations and that such resolution was adopted by the latter. I have secured a list of the roads comprising the Trunk Line Passenger Committee, and by direct correspondence with those roads I am able now to say positively that all those roads are now carrying bicycles free when accompanied by owners. The following is a list of said roads:

Grand Trunk Railway.
New York Central and Hudson River Railroad.
West Shore Railroad.
New York, Ontario and Western Railway.
New York, Lake Erie and Western Railroad.
Delaware, Lackawanna and Western Railroad.
Lehigh Valley Railroad.
Central Railroad of New Jersey.
Philadelphia and Reading Railroad.
Pennsylvania Railroad.
Baltimore and Ohio Railroad.

W. S. Bull, Chief Consul.

Buffalo, July 20, 1889.

HARTFORD WHEEL CLUB'S TOURNAMENT.

CHANGE OF DATES.

September 4 and 5 were the dates assigned for this year's bicycling tournament, at Charter Oak Park, at Hartford. The dates have now been changed to Monday and Tuesday, September 2 and 3. Monday will be Labor Day and a legal holiday. This change will add greatly to the convenience of many who would find it inconvenient to attend the races on a regular working day and will afford out-of-town cycling clubs which had planned to wheel to Hartford on the first day of the meet and attend the races on the second day, the opportunity to make the cycling trips on Sunday and devote the two days following to the festivities.

From all indications the September event will be the most elaborate affair of the kind ever seen in New England. The Connecticut Division of the League will make the tournament the occasion of its annual meet, which will add greatly to its special interest to cyclists.

A programme of the combined features of the tournament will be issued soon and mailed to wheelmen throughout the State.

The handicap races at the Hartford tournament next September promise to be worthy of their name. Official Handicapper Burnham will be present throughout the meet, and instead of handicapping the racers on their past records, he will handicap them on what he considers their ability on the day of the race. One of the principal events will be a one-mile handicap race run in heats. The starters in the final heat will be re-handicapped and given positions according to their records in the preliminary heats.

RACES AT QUEENS.

A one-mile handicap was decided Saturday afternoon last with the following result: First Heat—R. A. Kissam, 60 yards, 3m. 7 4-5s.; George Boyce, 50 yards, 3m. 6s.; R. B. Kimber, 125 yards, third. Second Heat—L. A. Doughty, 100 yards, 3m. 30s.; N. F. Waters, scratch, 3m. 36s. Final Heat—Kissam, 3m. 6 1-2s; Doughty, 3m. 6 4 5s.; Boyce, close up; N. F. Waters, fourth; won by four feet. Waters rode inside 3m. 9s. The medal was presented by Mr. Lloyd.

VAN WAGONER'S HANDS-OFF MILE.

From information received, we are glad to be able to credit Van Wagoner with a mile in 2m. 48s., on a safety, with hands off. Van Wagoner's hands were tied behind his back. The starter was T. Lahey and the timers B. Smith, G. R. McAuslin, and M. L. Ballou. The track was the Roger Williams horse track.

Howard A. Smith & Co., Newark, N. J., report an unprecedented demand for their safety bundle carriers, both for handle bar and mud guard. *,*

ALBANY WHEELMEN'S TOURNAMENT.

On Monday (Labor Day), September 2, 1889, the Albany (N. Y.) Wheelmen will hold their third outdoor tournament and race meet. The attention of the readers of his paper is therefore called to the Wheelmen's ad., particularly the racing men. The Albany Wheelmen are noted, not only for their hospitality extended visiting cyclists, but for the facilities afforded and the prizes and medals awarded at their race meets.

With a track equal to any of the very best tracks in America, and in many respects their superior, no rider has the advantage of any of his competitors by reason of any fault of the track whatsoever. The track at Ridgefield, where the races are to take place, is indeed a famous one. It was on this path that Burdick, Crist, Stenken, Hall, Edmans and such men, particularly distinguished themselves, in that a majority of them beat their former records.

One of the events especially worthy of mention is the New York State Division 2-mile L. A. W. Championship, the winner of which secures a valuable diamond medal. There are several open events, as a glance at the ad. will show, backed by costly prizes and valuable and elegant medals.

Taking place, as it does, on September 2, just two days previous to the day appointed for the Hartford (Conn.) meet, it will give those *en route* for Hartford an opportunity of stopping over at the capital city of the Empire State, and not only enable them to view its many beautiful edifices, but will also afford them a chance of competing for some of the costliest prizes and medals ever offered at a race meet, and on a cinder path that has few if any equals. Thus the Albany Wheelmen will by this, their third meet, attempt to eclipse all former race meets held in that vicinity.

NEW HAVEN.

The New Haven Bicycle Club contingent at the Hagerstown Meet enjoyed themselves very much. They fell in with a very pleasant crowd of fellows, and they do not get tired of recalling reminiscences of the meet and of asking "What did the band play?"

This call was also adopted at the Connecticut Division Meet at Bridgeport, July 8, which was the most successful meet ever held in Connecticut. The Bridgeport Club entertained nicely. A large crowd was present. The races were exciting, and our man, Picket, won the one-mile safety race.

Last Sunday the club wheeled down to Merwin's Point, a very pleasant shore resort, which is quite popular with the boys here, and where we can get a good shore dinner. We go to Stony Creek next Sunday, another pleasant resort near here

We have several lady riders here, but they do not show themselves on the street much.

One of our members, John Verhoef, is touring in Europe on his wheel, in company with Mr. Parmalee, of New Haven, and two Schenectady, N. Y., gentlemen. Mr. Verhoef's home is in Louisville, Ky. He is attending Yale College here.

Elm City.

THE VALUE OF WAGON ROADS.

It is but natural that the subject of transportation should be considered one of paramount importance by the constitution builders of the four Northwestern commonwealths. The progress and development of the four States depend in a large measure upon the character and completeness of the means of transportation, and indications are that the four conventions will have the courage to adopt a common-sense policy in dealing with common carriers. But the constitution builders seem to be entirely oblivious of the fact that the railway is not the only means of transportation. It is true that since the introduction of railways the old time country roads have fallen into innocuous desuetude in this country. Few States have made any adequate provisions for the construction and management of such roads, and the Federal Government never took any active interest in the matter, at least not since 1830, when the railroad era began. Yet the value of good wagon roads is a potent factor in the economic life of a people, especially in a country where the cost of transportation is a matter of vital importance. In a paper appearing in the publications of the American Economic Association, Mr. Jeremiah W. Jenks discusses the subject of wagon roads as an element in the problem of transportation. He asserts that if wheat, in most of the Western wheat States, has to be hauled more than 18 or 20 miles to reach the railroad or water, this land carriage in ordinary years eats up the profit of culture. The assertion may be too sweeping and general, but it contains a great deal of truth. Under the census of 1880 the estimates of the average cost of hauling grain from the farm to the railway stations varied from twenty cents to $1 for 100 bushels one mile, and it is believed that the average cost was not less than sixty cents per mile. This is an important item in the cost of production and forcibly suggests the economic necessity of a complete system of good wagon roads in districts the chief industry of which is the production of cereals for export. "According to the estimates received"—Mr. Jenks says—"it costs the ordinary farmer more to carry each bushel of wheat a mile than it does the ordinary railroad to carry a ton, and consequently, when we get west of Lake Michigan, it rarely pays to grow wheat more than twenty miles from rail or water." The proposition is too general; but it touches a vital point in the economy of Western wheat producers and is entitled to serious consideration. The constitution builders of the Dakotas, Montana and Washington should not fail to give the subject due attention. It may not be deemed expedient or necessary to insert in the constitutions a clause making detailed provisions for a system of public roads, constructed and managed by the counties with or without the aid and supervision of the State. But the conventions are laying the foundations of the respective commonwealths, and their work will exert a decisive influence on the future development of the States in general. All important matters of public policy naturally receive more or less attention at the hands of the constitution builders, and the subject of wagon roads certainly is of sufficient importance to be entitled to consideration.—*Minneapolis Tribune.*

Howard A. Smith & Co., Newark, N. J., are teaching more persons how to ride the bicycle at Oraton Hall than ever before at this season of the year. Hall open evenings. *,*

TACOMA, WASHINGTON.

For the past ten days the weather has been simply perfect and most of the boys have accepted the unusually good opportunities presented. Each afternoon some of the wheelmen sought the seclusion of Lake Steilacoom, and although the temperature in the city was above 80° only one day, still the cool breezes of the lake and the refreshing bathing was sufficient to coax the boys in that direction. This beautiful sheet of water is about 8½ miles south of Tacoma, and just far enough away to make a comfortable run to after business hours and return by 8:30 or later if the moon favors the riders. Another point of interest to the riders is Puyallup, a small place, nine miles from Tacoma. The road is good most of the distance and winds its way through the Indian Reservation for several miles. Until recently the boys objected to riding to Puyallup on account of the two-mile stretch of sand. But a few weeks ago, Charlie Cromwell (direct descendent of Oliver Cromwell), and Harley Hays—the "obstruction fiend"—found a new road, and reported same A 1. On their recommendation, four of the wheelmen made arrangements for a moonlight run on Friday last (by arrangements, I mean took out accident insurance policies).

The quartette was composed of Mr. Ernest G. Rognon, Captain of the Jeffersonville (Ind.) Bi. Club; Prince Wells, Ed M McCoy and R. I. Halsted, and a jolly crowd they are. The road to Puyallup is A 1 for day riding, as a fellow can dodge the stones, roots, stumps, etc., etc. But by *night* I think the same road would be quoted about "Q eleventeen." As usual, McCoy wanted to kill someone and accordingly made the pace, and how those four ever pulled through without a scratch is more than I can explain. Before reaching Puyallup, a most beautiful sight presented itself, and the people in this vicinity say they never before saw the like of it. To the people of Tacoma and Puyallup the sun had long ago said "good night;" but to the grand old Mt. Tacoma, towering 14,444 feet above us—yet sixty-five miles away—the monarch of the day was just making his adieux, and the summit seemed bathed in sunlight. To make the effect still more gorgeous, the base of the mount was wrapped in heavy clouds, which gave the summit an appearance as if floating. As the thousands of people were gazing intently upon this beautiful scene, the moon gradually rose behind the tip-top of the mount, and in an incredible short space of time appeared as if resting upon the top of the gilded sentinel of the Cascade Mountains. This sight lasted only for a few moments, but it was indelibly printed in the memories of those who saw it, never to be forgotten. To return to our quartette, they reached their destination safely and after doing the town started for home at 10 o'clock. Strange to relate no bad headers were indulged in, although Halsted dropped in a sand hole and *got off* to see what he had struck, while McCoy tried hard to ride off the side of a bridge and saved his neck by a miracle. Mr. Rognon made many friends while here and his departure was regretted by all who had met him, as he is a jolly good fellow and "every inch a man," not to speak of his ability as a cycler. The Jeffersonville Bi. Club should be proud of their captain.

On Sunday (15 inst.), Halsted and Prince Wells went to Seattle, and with Dick Agassiz rode through the burnt district, and although six weeks have elapsed since the fire and much clearing up done, nevertheless the work of the flames can be seen in every direction. Large and small tents now stand where large stores, hotels and banks stood only a few weeks since. In going through the ruins, several remains of bicycles were seen twisted and warped to almost unrecognizable shapes. But the indomitable spirit shown by her people will soon put Seattle in shape again, and on a much stronger footing than before. Streets will be made wider and of better surface, and cycling consequently benefited.

Snohomish.

July 16, 1889.

SENSIBLE VIEWS OF TACOMA (W. T.) AUTHORITIES.

There is some talk of stopping bicycle riding on the sidewalks in Tacoma. This will deprive the young men of the city of the use of the upper streets. Many of the wheelmen use their bicycles as a means of conveyance to and from business and in traveling about town in pursuit of their various vocations. To be deprived of the use of the sidewalks would be the death-knell to cycling, they say, for the streets are too dirty or otherwise unfit for riding. Taking these facts into consideration, Chief Chesney will probably not enforce such a strict law unless it may be on C, Railroad Street, and Pacific Avenue, where bicycling should be prohibited on sidewalks.

"When this subject was brought before ex-Chief Thompson," said a wheelman, "he refused to take action, saying that the upper streets presented almost suicidal conditions, for the dust completely envelopes occupants of carriages and those on horseback and is sufficient to suffocate people. Of course wheelmen must exercise great care when using the walks, particularly when passing pedestrians, and if this is done, what objections can be raised? With the poor street-car system we have to contend with, the young man should be accorded a few privileges, one of which is the use of his bicycle as a means of conveyance."—*Tacoma Globe.*

The Connecticut Division adopted resolutions expressive of their regard for the late Stephen Terry. Resolutions of the same tenor should have been passed at Hagerstown. The suggestion was made there, once to President Luscomb and again to a Vice Consul.

Howard A. Smith & Co., Newark, N. J., have improved their Graphite for lubricating chains and bearings of bicycles and safeties, until it seems to be perfect. All riders should have a bottle. *,*

THE NEW PATENT "POMROI" BEARINGS.

Our readers will have often been noted in our columns an allusion to these bearings, and the more inquisitive will are this have visited the patent offices in Chancery Lane and inspected the models shown there. A safety bicycle has been fitted with these patent bearings, and from a recent visit to the inventor we glean the following :

As yet this invention has not been put upon the market, nor is there even any engraving extant ; but we will endeavor to give a description.

Taking first a *fixed* axle on which the wheel runs loose, as in a safety bicycle, we find that the axle at its point of contact with the inner part of the wheel hub is grooved at regular intervals, and in each groove is a steel roller, which rollers take the whole of the weight and friction. Not only are the points of friction kept to the edges of these rollers, but the grooves in which the rollers run act as oil receptacles ; and no matter how long a Pomroi bearing may lie idle, it has only to be used for the rollers to revolve, and thus release for general use the lubricating fluid. The rollers cannot by any possibility lock or jamb against any one wheel, and whilst with no weight on the wheel they remain quiescent, they are ready the moment weight and friction come to revolve and give ease to the propelling power, be that man, steam or horse.

The basis of Mr. Pomroi's invention is the ordinary parallel axle bearing, which touches the journal or bearing ca e all round. This parallel bearing he reduces the friction of to a minimum by his system of rollers. Even if these rollers remain quiescent they still lessen friction as compared with the plain bearing, whilst when they do revolve, which they do when the weight is on them, they still more reduce friction.

Our scope is, of course, to deal with the bearing as regards its applicability to cycles alone ; but Mr. Pomroi is so confident of the advantages of his bearing that he looks forward to the time when not only carts, carriages, omnibuses, street cars and other vehicles will be fitted with it, but when it will be found on locomotives, engines of all kinds and shafting, for the grooves and rollers can not only be fitted on axles which are rigid, but also *inside* a fixed bearing, through which, as in the case of an ordinary bicycle, a plain axle can run, touching only at its points of friction the aforesaid rollers.

We await the future of the " Pomroi " bearing with interest. Mr. Pomroi is an inventor who has done much, from humane motives, to lessen labor, and we feel sure that in the result of his present invention he looks forward as much to a moral as to a financial reward.

— *Wheeling.*

A SELECTED LIST OF PATENTS.

[Reported especially for THE WHEEL AND CYCLING TRADE REVIEW by C. A. Snow & Co., patent attorneys, Washington, D. C.]

H. Lucas, Birmingham, England ; lamp for velocipedes.

H. B. Morrison, Britt, Iowa ; wrench.

S. J. Talbott, Milford, N. H.; velocipede sled. All bearing date of July 23, 1889.

Lyman Jenkins, a cyclist of Newark, has had his designs accepted for a new church at Irvington.

Dr. E. Bogman, of Providence, R I., will be in New York for several weeks. Doctor Bogman will tour to various points of interest around New York.

A 1-mile scratch club race was decided at the N. J. A. C. games, held at Bergen Point on Saturday last. F. G. Brown won in 3m. 7 1-5s ; S. B. Bowman, second.

A Hartford physician states that the " curative emanations from asphaltum are quite similar to the beneficial influences of pine forest, and are of benefit to consumptives."

A 5-mile handicap will be decided at Trenton, N. J., August 5. There will also be a 2-mile scratch race, open to New Jersey wheelmen. Entries close July 20, with W. V. Blake, 146 Monmouth Street, Trenton, N. J.

T. L. Wilson, of the Kin s County Wheelmen, obtained an impr tant patent on July 17 f r a dynamo electric machine. The new machine will develop heat, light or power. It is very compact, and can be built at fifty or sixty per cent of the price now paid for constructing dynamos. A company is about to be organized to put Mr. Wilson's machine on the market. He has been working 14 years to perfect his machine.

A SEVEN-FOOT WHEEL.

The Bangor correspondent of the Brooklyn *Citizen* announces a find in the line of bicycle novelties, as below. We think the claim of its being the largest in the world is a little unfounded, for, if we remember rightly, a wheel of similar build was ridden on the track at Springfield during one of the tournaments there, and that wheel was said to be nine feet high. At any rate, the man perched upon the lofty saddle looked as though on an elephant, and climbing the backbone was like going up a ladder. Excuse us from such heights.

"Jack Simpson, who runs a lodging house and res aur ant in that delectable quarter of Bangor known as ' The Devil's Half-acre,' owns a bicycle which he declares is the largest in the world. This wheel is eighty-six inches in diameter, and, leaning against the wall, it occupies nearly the entire space on one side of the little dining room. Simp on as an Englishman, and for many years traveled with circuses and other shows, having been one of the three ' Dacoma Brothers,' famous several years ago for their aerial bicycle performances. They gave exhibitions at the Crystal Palace London, at the Cirque Fernando, Paris, and at other amusement centres in Europe and the United States. The big wheel, which has been a round the world was built at Birmingham, Eng., at a cost of $150, and, although its diameter is so great, a double system of pedal cranks enables a common cyclist to ride it."

The Pennsylvania Road Book will not be issued for several months, owing to a delay in completing the maps.

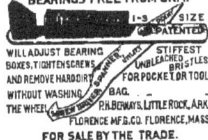

THE WHEEL

—AND—

CYCLING TRADE REVIEW,

Published every Friday morning.

Entered at the Post Office at second class rates.

Subscription Price, - - -	$1.00 a year.
Foreign Subscriptions, - - -	6s. a year.
Single Copies, - - - - -	5 Cents.

Newsdealers may order through AM. NEWS CO.

All copy should be received by Monday.
Telegraphic news received till Wednesday noon.

Advertising rates on Application.

F. P. PRIAL, Editor and Proprietor
23 Park Row,
P. O. Box 444, New York.

Persons receiving sample copies of this paper are respectfully requested to examine its contents and give us their patronage, and as far as is convenient, aid in circulating the journal, and extend its influence in the cause which it so faithfully serves. Subscription price, $1 per year.

I want to thank you for the great standard taken by THE WHEEL. It is the best cycling paper I have seen on this side of the Atlantic.—Mr. W. J. RICHARDSON, Berlin & Jones Envelope Co., N. Y.

THE *Bicycling World* having discovered, without any aid from us, that our effort to shield "Jack" from the imputation of improper motives was sincere, will come out man-fashion and do the right thing. We cannot but be pleased at this, because there are some men, not readers of the WHEEL, who might believe us guilty of the hypocrisy charged by the *Bicycling World*. We have before been accused of insincerity and have invariably believed our accusers hypocrites, for the dissembler cuts every one's character according to his cloth. It is impossible for him to conceive a disinterested motive or credit a disinterested action. In this case, however, we do not conceive the *Bicycling World* to be hypocritical. Its editor simply made the mistake of rushing into print with a baseless charge and further committed the absurdity of being unable to distinguish between our friends and his correspondents. The "white dove" will please flap its wings.

ECHOES OF THE HAGERSTOWN MEET.

MY DEAR MR PRIAL—You may say for the Maryland Division, in reply to the editorial of the *Bi World*: Yes, the "Marylanders" *are* "pleased" with the editorial in THE WHEEL of July 19, concerning the Tenth Annual Meet. The editorial of THE WHEEL is fair and truthful, and that is just what Maryland wants. It don't want any facts suppressed, nor anything glossed over, and it certainly will not tamely submit to be lied about, and any public print indulging in the latter and not afterward frankly retracting, and making a full and complete apology, will find in due time that Maryland can defend itself, and make its traducers feel it, too. The words in THE WHEEL editorial "that Southern hospitality" is *most* expressed by the flowing "bowl," were used on the statement of an informant (the editorial reads), but that informant, while no doubt meaning well, is mistaken. In the words quoted, for "most," substitute "*sometimes*," and the exact state of the case will be given. However, that is a small matter, and Maryland is perfectly satisfied that THE WHEEL, while confining itself to the truth, is the true friend of the wheelman, and not an enemy cloaked in an "official" garb. THE WHEEL is dependent on a *paid* circulation for its life, and therefore must be truthful and contain meritorious matter in order to succeed. It would be much to the advantage of the L. A W. if it had an "official organ" that was bound by the same ironclad rule, instead of being forced upon the membership whether members will it or not. To charge the Tenth Annual Meet with being a "bacchanalian orgie" of three days, and "mourning for the tender feelings of the ladies present" as the *Bi. World* did; and to "doubt very much the value of the compliment in mentioning them (the ladies) as visitors to the League meet of 1889," is a brutal insult to the ladies and to their escorts, whether husbands, brothers or fathers. To then, after all, publish their names, as did the *Bi. World*, is adding an injury to insult that appears to be too nice a point and too fine a distinction for the *refined* (?) people of the *Bi. World* (good *honest* old souls), to comprehend. And yet these whining hypocrites prate about distinguishing between gentlemen and hoodlums. Yes, with all these blunted perceptions, they claim to be critics on refinement. With most of the ladies but a few hours distance from home, the *Bi. World* charges them (in effect), with remaining *from choice*, at a three days' "bacchanalian orgie," and charges their husbands, brothers and fathers with permitting them to remain to witness the debauching scenes pertaining to a "bacchanalian orgie," and to hear the coarse, obscene and brutal conversation which is always understood to be a concomitant. These people claim to be refined, and yet publish such charges against the gentle sex without sufficient proof, or even evidence to justify them in publishing an ordinary political campaign yarn. And yet they set themselves up as critics on refinement, as judges in the supreme court of gentility. They even have no proof or even evidence of a "bacchanalian orgie" of three days, and Maryland defies them to produce in public the names of the people they say they rely upon for this evidence, and true evidence (not garbled) itself. The Maryland Division already knows the names, and the evidence on which they (the *Bi. World* people) rely, and it is a fact that it is no evidence of the charges they publish, nor was not intended as such. Some gentlemen merely told the story of the meet, giving a true and fair account, and Maryland would not be unwilling to have it published just as it was told. But the *Bi. World* distorts, misconstrues, misrepresents—and, yes, actually lies, for what purpose is unknown, and when called to account by the President of the League and the Executive Committee, refuses to retract and apologize, and *assumes* to believe the account true. Does it so believe? Does it believe that Mr. Mott, Mr. Clark, Mr. Hayden, Mr. Harvey, Mr. Taylor, Mr. Slee, Mr. Martin, Mr. Emmerson, Mr. Strahn, Mr. DeGraaf, Mr. Raisheck, Mr. Menizel, Mr. Burkholm, Mr. Smith and many others, retained their wives, daughters and sisters at "a bacchanalia orgie" for "three days"? Does it believe the ladies remained at "a bacchanalian orgie" for "three days" of their own free will, or otherwise? There was no "bacchanalian orgies" at Hagerstown. There were no inebriates there among the cyclers. The wheelmen drank moderately for the occasion, as gentlemen usually do drink on such occasions. Even the vintages indulged in were unusually innocent, consisting in great part of claret punch—but, of course, there were some beverages, tho' in greatly less quanties, of the nectar that cheers. But there was no more of it, if as much, than at Boston or New York, at any similar gathering. There was the noise of fire works, club songs, club calls, and general merriment, and that was anticipated and provided for, and nearly every one expressed themselves as having had a good time, notwithstanding the disobliging weather.

Baltimore, July 31, 1889. MARYLAND.

THE BICYCLE NUISANCE AND PERIL.

LET THE NERVES AND LIMBS OF THE PEOPLE BE PROTECTED.

"Our ancient rights," says the Springfield *Republican*, "have been in suspension quite long enough." The particular ancient right which the *Republican* now calls upon the people of Springfield to assert and defend is that of not being ridden down by bicyclists, who, it seems, in the city by the Connecticut have become utterly regardless of people on foot, and any number of narrow escapes and many accidents are the consequence. We have heard of no serious accidents here, but the wheelmen seem to be sometimes less careful of others' rights and safety than they should be. The rights of wheelmen are now pretty well established. Nobody disputes their claim to the use of the highways, but when that use implies special dangers the public are entitled to demand special precautions. A more liberal use of the gong or whistle in much frequented thoroughfares is one. In the evening and in shaded parts of city streets, as well as at all cross-walks, it is especially necessary. Aside from the danger of collision, it is trying to the nerves of some people to have one of these swift and noiseless riders rush by in the darkness without warning, and when the shrill sound of whistle or bell comes, as it sometimes does, just as the rider, until then unobserved, is passing, the sudden and sharp assault upon the organs of both sight and hearing is even more disagreeable and confusing to the pedestrian. The *Republican's* suggestion is not amiss: "The least that should be asked is that the riders be compelled to toot their whistles vigorously before passing the cross-walks."—*Worcester Spy*.

Exactly so. And when the nurse girl halts her baby-carriage while you pass, when the timid old lady, the gruff old gentleman, or the aggressive tough stands on the curb until you pass the cross-walk, always say "Thank you." If you do you have made a friend of the sport.

THE NEW YORK STATE DIVISION HANDBOOK.

The handbook just issued by Chief Consul Bull cannot fail to increase the Division's membership, as 6,000 of them have been issued, and many will, no doubt, fall into the hands of cyclists who were not aware of the League's existence.

The book is a seventy-six page pamphlet, pocket size. It contains a preface by Chief Consul Bull explaining the advantages of League membership, the L. A. W. constitution, list of officers of the L. A. W., N. Y. State Division constitution and by-laws, lists of N. Y. State officers, Consuls and League hotels, an article on touring, by Fred. J. Shepard, Buffalo B. C.; "Remedies to be Used in Cycling Accidents," by Dr. L. A. Bull, of Buffalo; "Practical Hints on Temporary Repairs," by E. N. Bowen; "The Law of Cycling," by Isaac B. Potter, and an article on "Roads Improvement."

The trade made the publication of the book possible, and are to be thanked for their liberality. It is their way of helping the sport. The firms represented in the book are: Pope Mfg Co., Overman Wheel Co., Clark Cycle Co., Geo. R. Bidwell, A. G. Spalding & Bros., Browning, King & Co., William Halpin & Co., Erie Knitting Co., Merwin, Hulbert & Co, and the Coventry Machinists' Co., Limited.

WESTCHESTER COUNTY WHEELMEN.

A meeting of cyclists interested in forming a club in Westchester was held July 15 at the residence of Eugene Valentine, of Locust Avenue. The meeting was called to order by H. F. Fuller.

The club was formally organized with fourteen charter members. Its officers are:

President, H. F. Fuller; Vice-President, Frederick Jenkins; Secretary and Treasurer, E. H. Sturges; Captain, Eugene Valentine; First Lieutenant, H. C. Perley; Color Bearer, S. D. Hoyt; Surgeon, N. P. Tyler, M. D., and Member of the Executive Committee at large, Frank R. Taylor, Mount Vernon. The other members are: C. K. Alley, S. C. Abramson, W. Depierris, B. C. Fuller, Oscar Le Count and Howard Safford.

No bicycle club ever organized in this country had so many "old timers" as the Westchester County Wheelmen. Mr. Fuller was an old member of the Chicago Bicycle Club, and was on the '84 Big Four tour. Mr. Jenkins is one of the oldest riders in the country, has organized clubs, founded the old WHEEL, was Secretary of the League, and has had his share of honor. "Gene" Valentine is the old K. C. W. man, member of the N. Y. A. C., one-time racing man and now on the N. Y. A. C. rowing "eight." Dr. Tyler was an old member of the New Haven Bi. C., and was Official Handicapper of the League. C. K. Alley was a member of the Buffalo Club, and is at present a member of the "Cits." Mr. Alley has been Secretary-Treasurer of the N. Y. State Division. The club has adopted a dark blue uniform. Its headquarters will be at the "Castle Inn," New Rochelle.

THE TRUE ELIXIR OF LIFE.

But there is an elixir of life which, while it will not give man earthly immortality, nor produce the magical results dreamed of by De Soto, will yet measurably renew the youth, improve the health and prolong the life of man. That elixir of life is simply a rigorous and intelligent observance of the laws of health. The secret is known to all. There is no mystery about it. It is not concocted by elaborate and expensive means from rare and costly ingredients. There is no patent upon it. The true elixir of life is simply fresh air, sunlight, exercise and temperance. This is the combination that constitutes the precious elixir. Temperance, mind you, in all things; not in drinking alone, but in eating, in devotion to business, in work of any kind, in the use of tobacco, in your emotions, your passions, in everything. Abandon all those furious consumers of your nervous and physical energies for a single month, and get out into the air and sunshine, with plenty of exercise, and you won't know yourself when the month closes.

This is the true elixir of life. It is easy and pleasant to take. Nature offers the ingredients, already mixed in perfection, in lavish abundance, free for everybody's use. Do not waste your time in the vain search of some mysterious decoction or compound that will magically repair the abused and dilapidated old system, restore the health and renew one's youth, because you will not find it, and old age, disease and death will surprise you in the search. Look at and seize upon the elixir that is under your nose, that is all around you, that nature proffers with both hands.—*Trenton State Gazette.*

DECIDEDLY INTERESTING.

Here are some statistics which cyclists may use to good purpose. They may be fired at the non-cyclist who ought to be a cyclist or they may be waved defiantly at road-hogs, at the person who "thinks it very dangerous," at Park Commissioners, stupid Aldermen and fat-witted backwoods legislators:

ACCIDENTAL DEATHS IN NEW YORK, 1888.

Tobogganing	1
Falls of heavy bodies	46
Railways	13
Kick of horses	6
Horse-cars	6
Drowning	173
Hatchways and elevator shafts	31
Runaway wagons	2
Fell from carts and wagons	8
Careless use of kerosene	17
Suffocated by illuminating gas	14
Poisoned by opium	12
Poisoned by gas	18
Killed by wagons in the street	55
Runaway horse-cars	14
Miscellaneous	
Grand total	1,258

Of the 1,258 people who met death accidentally, two were engaging in sport, one tobogganing and one roller-skating. It would seem that thirty-one fell through hatchways and elevator shafts, so that the cyclist is really safer on the road than when going about his business down-town. No one objects to the fire being lit, yet careless use of kerosene wafted seventeen souls aloft, and illuminating gas caused the death of thirty-two people. This agent in taking life is only surpassed by the danger of railways, which killed sixty-five people, by heavy bodies which fell upon and killed forty-six people, and by vehicles in the street which killed sixty-four. No one describes the horse as a dangerous animal, though six people died from the kick of the four-legged beasts; in fact, people will call him domestic and gentle, and characterize a wheel as a dangerous thing. One would scarcely think of considering a horse-car as dangerous, yet twenty-two people have met death through them. On the whole, a man is never safer than when on his wheel.

Tact is a superior kind of common sense, a peculiar hereditary instinct, which may be cultivated up to the point of clairvoyance, almost, in very fine natures. In woman it is called intuition; in man, perceptiveness. It enables one to do the right thing at the right time, securing admiration, confidence and success, and prevents one from doing the wrong thing at any time, avoiding condemnation, distrust and failure.—Referred to *Bicycling World* for meditation.

THE ELWELL TOURISTS IN GERMANY AND SWITZERLAND.

Three weeks from to-day the Elwell touring party will be a thing of the past, and its members scattered to the four winds, some to go north to Sweden and Norway, some to go south to Italy and Rome, some back to London and Paris, and some to answer the demands of business and start for home instanter. Already there is much moaning and groaning among its members, as they count the hours to elapse before that swiftly-approaching day, and not a man but what says: "Oh, won't I miss the gang after we break up!" And they will. Aside from the natural ties which bind all wheelmen together, being so far from home, in the midst of strange scenes, strange customs and strange languages, has created a fellowship the breaking of which will be severely felt by all. London will not be the same London nor Paris the same Paris when the good-natured, sun-browned faces of our thirty companions of the wheel are no longer to be seen about the hotel and at the places of interest, and the homeward trip across the water will contain for us but little of the everlasting jollity and continual laughter which marked our outward voyage. It is also much to be feared that the exceptional weather which we then enjoyed will be reversed. It would be trespassing on the good nature of the Clerk of the Weather to request a continuance of such a quantity of sunshine and blue sky as we have enjoyed since leaving Paddyland. It is raining to-day (July 15) for the first time since we left Oxford, England, June 11, an uninterrupted stretch of over a month of atmospherical pie. Add to this that we have been traveling on the finest roads in the world, amidst the grandest scenery and the most magnificent examples of architecture, art and amusement, and who can gainsay that our trip has been a most complete success from beginning to end?

THROUGH THE JURA MOUNTAINS—A NINE-MILE COAST.

On the day following that on which I last wrote you we finished our trip through the Juras, and rode into Geneva at noon. The last nine miles of the mountain were covered without touching a foot to the pedals—a steady downward coast. It was a severe trial on the brakes, and more than once the odor of red-hot rubber compelled us to dismount and allow the break and tire to cool.

It was here that "Rosey" came to the fore. You miss a treat if you don't know "Rosey." His slightly bald head is as full of original ideas as a mule is full of wickedness. "Life is too short to dismount every three minutes," said he to himself, coming down the mountain side, and, getting off beside a heap of brushwood, he attached about half of it to the step of his machine with a three-foot string. With this impediment trailing along on the ground behind him he came down without touching the brake, a cloud of dust following him like Banquo's ghost. "Ought to have seen the natives stare," said Rosey. "Guess they thought the mountain was afire."

THE BEAUTIFUL VALLEY.

The view of the valley between the Juras and Swiss Alps, with Lake Léman, Geneva and a hundred roads and rivers stretched out, map-like, four thousand feet below us, will never be forgotten by any of the party. Unmindful of the rays of old Sol, we sat and gazed until our eyes ached, and, seized with inspiration, our perpetual scribes brought out book and pencil and went to work.

The romance was knocked out of it all, an hour later, by a set-to with the Swiss custom-house officers, whom we imagined ourselves safely past. Riding along within three miles of Geneva, we suddenly beheld an officer with upraised finger in the middle of the road. We dismounted with very bad grace, and made the startling discovery that none of the officials knew a word of English, and of the four of us who happened to be together, no one knew a word of French! After much palaver and gesticulation we were forced to go down into our pockets for twenty francs, duty on our bicycles, which is refunded when we leave Switzerland and go into Germany. Our temper was not bettered by finding, on arriving in Geneva, that quite a number of the boys had escaped scot-free. Some of them had heard shouting behind them, and, not knowing the cause, had "done a little sprint," and escaped. Others were entirely unmolested, and the unfortunates were loud in their condemnation of the inconsistency of the Swiss Government.

At Geneva we put up at the Hotel de la Poste—the hundred and fortieth of that name at which we have stopped since leaving Paris. In Ireland the hotels were all the "Three Castles," in England the "Golden Lion," or "Queen's Arms," and in France and Switzerland the "Hotel de la Poste." The attractions at Geneva are the scenery and the prices of watches. The former is free and the latter the next thing to it. Six or seven dollars buys a very good timekeeper, and twenty-five dollars will put the town clock in your pocket. The town is a regular stamping-ground for rich English and American tourists, and the shopkeepers have a very convenient sliding scale of prices. The minute that an American with a striped shirt and enormous diamond stud enters, the prices fly up to the top notch with the rapidity of forked lightning. Aside from this little eccentricity on the part of the tradesmen, Geneva is a delightful place to do shopping. Everything you see is just what you want, and you want everything you see.

During our two days' stay there the boys were obliged to leave their pocket-books with the hotel proprietor. 'Twas here, also, that we sighted the first pretty girls—Americans, by the way. Since then we have found quite a number, but basing our conclusions on the entire trip, we are more than ever convinced that America is preëminently the land of pretty girls—and noisy boys. The Swiss costume is very fetching, but as far as can be ascertained is limited to the table girls in high-priced Alpine hotels.

A TRIP ON LAKE GENEVA.

On Wednesday, the 10th, we took the steamer from Geneva to Chillon. The two places are situated at either end of Lake Léman (or Lake Genève), and the sail is a wonderful one. On one side the Juras and on the other the huge Alps, and, as a noble *piece de resistance*, Mt. Blanc towers up grim and white in the background. The lake is some fifty-four miles in length, and ample time was afforded for writing letters. Dating letters from out-of-the-way places has become quite a fad amongst the party, starting, I believe, from seeing it done at the top of the Eiffel Tower. For my own part, I am ashamed to confess that my attention was in part wooed from the grand scenery by the fascinating pages of Stockton, whose "Lady of the Aroostook" fell into my hands at Geneva, the first book other than Badacker or Cook that I have looked into since leaving America.

The inspection of the old Chateau, or Castle, of Chillon, where the Duke of Savoy's arrangements for carrying on murder by the wholesale are yet to be seen, was full of interest. In the underground prison, made famous by Byron's poem "The Prisoner of Chillon," can be seen the excavation in the solid rock floor worn by the feet of Bonnivard, who was chained for seven years to one post. We also saw, in their own chirography, the autographs of George Sand, Eugene Sue, Lord Byron, Alex Dumas, Victor Hugo and other noted characters. On the way from Chillon to Aigle, where we spend the night, we pass through Villeneuve, where W. D. Howells passed an entire winter, although what could have attracted him there is hard to say.

ONE RODE UP THE ALPS.

Leaving Aigle, we start to climb the Alps in good earnest. We *rode* up the Juras, but I assure you we *walked* the Alps. One exception must be made to that "we," however. Bob White, of Quincy, proved himself *the* hill-climber par excellence of the party, by riding the entire distance of twenty-two miles, that hot and dusty Thursday, while everybody else walked. Twenty-two miles is not exactly what would be called a hard day's work under ordinary circumstances, but when you are going up the mountains it is an entirely different matter. During the morning we walked up fast enough to get all tired out, and accomplished the wonderful average of two miles an hour. We dined at Canbaliay, which, the hotel proprietor informed us thirty times an hour, is "5,000 feet above the level of the sea." His prices for everything were correspondingly high, and in addition to charging five francs for a two-franc dinner, he extorted a half franc each from those who washed their faces and hands!! We had no scruples about expectorating on his parlor carpet after that!

A MORNING IN FRANCE; AN AFTERNOON IN GERMANY.

From this point we gradually descended to Thun, where we arrived Friday noon, passing, on the way, from the French district of Switzerland into the German district as if by magic. We had a French morning and a German afternoon. Thun is an old place, with but little of interest to see. It is in the centre of the wood-carving and Swiss beer district, and very good work is done in both lines. The temptation to spend a lot of money in the beautifully carved articles of all descriptions is very great, and the range of prices for the same article simply wonderful! The road from Thun to Interlaken is called the best stretch of highway in Switzerland. It certainly is a very interesting ride. The road is built on the edge of the Thoner See, at the top of which is Thun and at the bottom Interlaken. The road takes you through tunnel after tunnel, hewn out of the solid cliffs, by cascades of water of indescribable beauty, and affords at all times a splendid view of the body of water which it skirts, and the noble Jungfrau, the principal mountain of the range of Swiss Alps. Like Mt. Blanc, it wears the year around a snowy cap of white.

Interlaken, "the Paris of Switzerland," was reached at 5 o'clock. It is just what its nick-name implies, a gay little place built of hotels and cafés, and full to the brim with tourists. It lives for and by tourists alone. As its real name implies, it is situated just between the two lakes, in a very convenient situation, and is surrounded on all sides by magnificent scenery. Our hotel, the Jungfrau—one of the best—is an enormous pile, facing the mountain of that name and surrounded by a tropical garden. It is crowded with guests of all nationalities, who seem to regard the party as a troupe of wild Indians. We left our baggage here, and on Saturday morning rode to Lauterbrunnen, with the intention of walking from there to Mürren, a little place half-way up the Jungfrau, where we were to spend Sunday, returning to Interlaken on Monday. At Lauterbrunnen we saw the famous falls, the Staubbach, and Trümmelbach, the latter being a truly wonderful example of nature's forces. After dinner we invested in alpenstocks marked with "Lauterbrunnen," and started upwards. They told us it was "three hours up." They have an odd way of reckoning distance by the hour, instead of kilometers, as heretofore, calling three miles and a half an hour's journey on the ordinary roads.

Did you ever climb a mountain? If not, you don't know what an elegant chance to lose your breath, patience and temper you have missed. We clambered and climbed, enjoying the grand scenery at first, but as we neared Mürren our appetites began to occupy our minds to the exclusion of everything else. To add to our sorrows a heavy mountain shower sprang up, or rather down, and we were obliged to seek the seclusion of a deserted saw-mill. It rained and hailed for all the world like a Kansas blizzard.

When this was over we soon reached Mürren and from there we looked about, and for half an hour forgot our aching backs and tired legs. Up above the snow-line we were looking down upon the clouds, and around us on every side could be seen the peaks of the Vetterhorn, the Schilthorn, the Matterhorn and forty other horns and stücks. No one regretted the arduous climb; no one could regret it. We retired with our heads full of ideas of a glorious Sabbath, but "man proposes," etc.

Sunday morning broke cloudy and rainy, and continued so all day. The coming week we visit the Brunig Pass, ascend the Rigi, visit Lucerne, Zug Zurich, and run in to Germany, spending next Sunday at Friburg.

TAM O'SHANTER.

MURPHY ACCEPTS VAN WAGONER'S CHALLENGE.

BROOKLYN, N. Y., July 29, 1889.

MR. WM. VAN WAGONER, Newport, R. I.

Dear Sir—Replying to your challenge to me, published in the L. A. W. *Bulletin* of July 26, I desire to say that, individually, I never remember having made the remarks which you credit me with in your challenge. I am not in the habit of doing my racing either by word of mouth or upon paper, and therefore accept your challenge without hesitation. I will race you twenty-five miles over the Irvington-Milburn course at any time you see fit. As to the prize, I am not in the gun business, nor have I any particular use for one; however, if you prefer to race for a gun I will race you for one, or for a $50 medal, or I will race you just for the fun of it. I desire to make the following change in the terms of your challenge: I will not restrict myself or you to any weight of wheel; either man may ride a wheel of any weight he chooses. As to the date, I should prefer to race on September 7, or later, as my time is occupied until then.

Very truly, W. F. MURPHY, K. C. W.

ELECTRIC LAND AND MARINE CARRIAGE INVENTED BY A WOMAN.

A combination electric land and marine carriage is the invention of Mrs. Angie Truax, who, with her husband, resides in "Intercarden," Saratoga.

Mrs. Truax is about 35 years old, of medium height, and an exceedingly bright and pleasant spoken woman. She is of New York birth, and traveled extensively in her theatrical profession previous to her retirement from the stage a few years ago. It was from a love of travel that she conceived the idea of her invention, which resembles a two-seated side-bar Surrey wagon, with top, and of about the same length and truck. The wheels are like those of a bicycle, but heavier. The steering apparatus is placed in front, and connects with the front axle by a gearing segment. The propelling power is connected with and turns the hind axle by a system of gears.

The electric motor in this invention is the important feature, and it is with the greatest pride that the inventor speaks of it. It is placed in the centre and on the bottom of the carriage, and takes up but little room. It has a "vibrating" armature instead of a rotary; and this is where the little woman inventor looks for the greatest results in her electric motor, claiming that more power can be obtained than from any other form of rotary motor, and that the horse power can be increased without the necessity of constructing a larger motor, by simply using more battery. With an eight-volt battery a constant current can be kept up for three hours, and this, too, at a test speed of fifteen miles an hour. A dry primary battery is to be used.

Underneath the carriage are air-tight metal tubes, cigar-shaped, of suitable size to buoy up the carriage and its load while crossing deep streams, and to the spokes of the hind wheels are ingeniously secured little brass paddles to propel the carriage through the water, and so nicely arranged that they are in no way liable to injury, nor do they interfere with road travel.

The carriage has many novel features, such as electric lights, tent, an electric stove for cooking and heating, and is altogether a wonderful affair. A speed of fifteen miles an hour is now easily obtained, and the fair inventor is confident of being able to increase it to thirty.

NEW STEEL PROCESS.

The Redemann-Tilford steel process is understood to consist of a bath with glycerine as the basis. This bath changes the whole structure of the metal submitted to it, and increases its ductile and tensile strength far beyond any record that has yet been established by either private or governmental test.

When it is stated that the very finest and strongest grade of steel, much better than any now in use, can be made by this process at little more than the cost of crude Bessemer steel, the value of the discovery may be understood. Thus far, in making experiments, every character of tool and steel goods has been worked with, and the process has been successfully used upon all.—*Manufacturers' Record.*

ABOUT HALF HOLIDAYS.

"Five days to labor, one day for recreation, one day for God,' is an ancient Scottish maxim. The modern business world is hardly ready to accept the full measure of this saying, but it began long ago to split the difference, until to-day the greater part of business stands still from about Saturday noon until Monday morning, and the professional, business and working man or woman enjoys a week-day half holiday. That the privilege of weekly opportunity for recreation, with family or friend, during at least a quarter of the year, is of benefit to every man or woman, has passed from a question to an axiom; and trade, in losing a few hours, gains the strengthened vigorous work of its workers, who, after relaxation, are able to give more and better results. With this end in view, the Pope Mfg. Co., of Boston, Mass., has published a beautifully colored lithograph of unique and artistic design, suitable to display in door, window, office or elevator, announcing the hours of closing for Saturdays and also for other days. By an arrangement of stickers any hour can be posted. These cards are sent free upon receipt of stamp. Address Typewriter Department, Pope Mfg. Co., 77 Franklin Street, Boston, Mass.

One of the features of the Drive on Sunday last was "little Tommy Miller," son of Mr. Thomas Miller, New York Club. Tommy is a six-and-a-half year old blonde, and rides his little "safe" like a "vet," not dismounting even at "Corkscrew" Hill. All the ladies look at him with open-eyed astonishment, and as for children, they half die with envy as the cute little fellow rides by.

A NEW BOY'S BICYCLE.

Messrs. H. A. Lozier & Co., of Cleveland, are selling a boy's safety called "The Superior" to the trade. The wheel can be ridden by boys of from eight to fifteen years of age. The wheels are twenty-four inches, with three-quarter rubber tires, best steel spokes, enlarged at both ends. The bearings are cone, of new style, and claimed to be very effective. The frame is well bound. The wheel is enameled, small parts finished. Price, $40.

NEW ORLEANS.

The Louisiana Division, L. A. W., held its annual meeting on Tuesday evening last (July 23), at the office of the Chief Consul. Chief Consul Harry H. Hodgson presided, with Secretary-Treasurer Fairfax at his post. Some twenty odd members were present.

Messrs. Frederic and O'Reardon were appointed a committee on credentials, and admitted all the proxies presented.

Chief Consul Hodgson made his annual report. He stated that 1887 was the banner year, the Division having seventy-two members. In 1888 the membership fell off to fifty-seven. This year the list shows sixty-eight members, with three applications, and 1889 is therefore expected to break the record. He urged the members to use their efforts to secure new members, and detailed his own recent experiences in attending the League meeting at Hagerstown, to show that it meant something to be a member of the organization.

He touched on the fat condition of the Division treasury, and likewise on the fall tournament, mentioning incidentally, that as a result of his visit to Hagerstown, the extreme probability of the attendance of the Berkeley team, A. C. and W. D. Banker, and J. W. Schoefer, and of Messrs. A. B. Rich, W. I. Wilhelm and V. L. Emerson.

Continuing, Mr. Hodgson remarked that he had about abandoned all idea of holding a League meet in this city, but that he had broached the subject to quite a number on his recent visit North, and felt that the annual election and meeting of the Board of Officers in February would in all likelihood be held here about carnival time, and that he would expect the wheelmen of the city to cut the proper caper in such an event.

In conclusion the Chief Consul said: "I desire to have a large run some time during the coming month, and will appoint a committee to arrange for a run some time early in August, to which all wheelmen in the city will be invited, and to start from an appointed place and run to West End. This will infuse new life into our Division, and will give us something to think about."

The Secretary-Treasurer's report was next read and approved, and showed a balance of $125.27, more than ever before.

The committee on the proposed summer encampment was *non est*, and it is evident that such an event is for the great dim future to deal with. It isn't wanted just now.

The Racing Board, through Mr. B. A. Shields, reported verbally. The September meet was the main topic, although, by way of side show, Mr. Shields pleasantly and very effectually stuck a pin into the balloon set adrift by the presiding officer—"that the Board had positively refused to listen to suggestions." The Chief Consul explained and the love feast was complete.

Local Consul B. C. Rea, in chair, declared the election of officers in order. A vote of thanks was first tendered to the retiring officers.

Chief Consul H. H. Hodgson was nominated for re-election, and the choice was made with enthusiastic unanimity.

Messrs. J. C. O'Reardon and J. W. Dodge were nominated for Secretary-Treasurer, but the former declined and seconded the nomination of Dodge, which then went through by acclamation.

Messrs. Shields and Renaud were appointed a committee to install the newly elected officers, and did so becomingly, Hodgson's bread-basket cutting a prominent part as he daintily leaned on the arms of his escorting "lightweights."

In accordance with the Chief Consul's suggestion for a League run, Messrs. Shields, Renaud, Frederic and Rea were appointed a committee to arrange the preliminaries, and on motion of A. M. Hill, the "run" was voted a monthly fixture.

The meeting then adjourned for a visit to the League caterer, where most of the boys made merry over a keg of mineral water, and Hodgson told 'em what the band played, and it is not to be wondered that Hodgson and his stomach proved more than a match for J. Purvis and his "pewter cup," "when last they met in Maryland."

BI.

BROOKLYN NEWS.

It is an accomplished fact that we are to have the annual meet of the New York State Division of the L. A. W. held in New York and Brooklyn. A most comprehensive programme has been drawn up by the committee in charge, and numerous side entertainments, runs, etc., are to be indulged in by the different New York and Brooklyn clubs and their individual members. The regular programme includes runs to Yonkers and Coney Island, with refreshments at the Bedford Avenue club-houses on the latter run; also a parade in Brooklyn, which will create some competition among the Brooklyn Clubs, as a banner will go to the club turning out the largest number of men. The meeting for the transaction of business will be held at the B. B. C. club-house. In addition to all this, one of the most enjoyable features will be an enormous theatre party at some one of the New York play-houses, where the knights of the wheel will undoubtedly own the house for the time being. Some performance will be selected which is of a light nature, and which admits of the interpolation of plenty of "gags." The committee in charge of the theatre party is headed by W. H. DeGraaf, of New York, assisted by W. C. Marion, K. C. W., and Bert Cole, B. B. C., who were managers of the very successful "Pearl of Pekin" party in Brooklyn last March. It is a most competent committee, and can be relied upon for the best results in that line.

Treasurer Raymond and Lawyer Potter, B. B. C., will spend the principal part of August camping in the Adirondacks, and are preparing to slay unlimited quantities of game and fish. Secretary Cole, of the same club, leaves this week for camp life on the shores of Cayuga Lake. He will take his tandem "bike" with him, with the intention of doing some touring with his sister in Central New York.

A small party of Brooklyns, comprising Fuller, Barkman, Horland, Hibert and Starr, took in the Oranges Sunday, taking dinner at Caldwell, where they received a very good meal. It is a place seldom patronized by wheelmen, and a memorandum of a good quiet dinner at Caldwell may be of service to Brooklyn cyclists, hence this item. They were so fortunate as to entirely escape rain throughout the day, while their club-mates who feared the threatening weather and rode through the Park, etc., got drenched and muddy to the last degree.

Brooklyn, July 30, 1889. ATOI.

JERSEY CITY.

"The bicycle men are mad, it is reported, because they *can't do as they please*. It seems that a little law is to be applied to them—as follows—under general orders: 'To carry a lighted lantern after dark, and when going over crossings to ring a bell; to take the right side of the street, keep off the sidewalks, and when motioned to by drivers of vehicles to dismount.' To this some of the wheelmen object but this is not likely to help the case very much. The bicycle is a jolly thing to ride on but it has a sneak-along-lively way with it which makes it somewhat of a menace to public comfort and safety, particularly at night, and needs a little law to hold it in check. There is really no grounds for complaint at the above rules. They are reasonable, and simply voice what should be the sentiment of every gentleman who rides the whirring wheel."

The above appeared in a recent issue of the Jersey City *Evening Journal*. It refers particularly to the Hudson County Wheelmen, and it is, I suppose quite unnecessary for me to say that the first sentence of the article is founded entirely upon fiction. On the contrary, all the privileges we are now enjoying in this city were secured mainly through our own efforts, and we know only too well the prejudice with which cyclists here are looked upon to jeopardize our own interests in defying the city ordinance.

I know positively that in a number of cases where "unattached" wheelmen have been seen riding their wheels on the sidewalks within the city limits, members of the H. C. W. have spoken to the law-breakers, and told them how they were injuring the interests of wheelmen in general by continuing to disobey the city laws. A second offense has been followed by a request to arrest the offender.

We have shown such a disposition to please the City Fathers and at the same time "holding our own," that we have won the good graces of the Police Department generally.

Only a few weeks ago, at the request of Captain Day, of the H. C. W., the Chief of Police issued instructions to the effect that wheelmen thereafter should be allowed to ride their wheels on the sidewalks of certain streets where there is but very little pedestrian travel, and the roadways are in XXX vile condition (if you know how bad that means).

Gentlemanly conduct on the part of the H. C. W.'s has also won the esteem of our Mayor, who, as you know, recently accepted an honorary membership in the club.

I do not mean to imply by what I have written that all we need is a pair of wings and a harp to make us angels on earth, but I do mean to explode the "truth" of the *Journal's* statement.

The ticket has been sent to all L. A. W. members in this State announcing the following nominations of officers of New Jersey Division: Chief Consul, Dr. G. Carlton Brown, E. W.; Vice-Consul, Dr. H. A. Benedict, H. C. W.; Secretary-Treasurer, Geo. C. Pennell, E. W.; Representatives, Dr. F. A. Kinch, Jr., Westfield; J. B. Lunger, Newark; G. H. Cain, Trenton; A. T. Dodd, E. Orange; E. F. Burns, Smithville. I do not think there is any doubt of the ticket going through all right "by an overwhelming majority," and judging from the number of "doctors," the N. J. Division should be in a very "healthy" condition next year.

Dr. Benedict has pledged himself if elected to see that we have a road book before the expiration of his term of office. Good.

The Jersey City Board of Works are to try an experiment in the way of repairing streets, by placing a top dressing of soft stone on the stone pavement of City Hall Place, which has been in bad shape for some time. I believe this is the practice in Trenton, N. J., where they have several miles of macadamized roads with a good sound foundation in the way of ordinary stone pavement. Thus do we see that the road makers are gradually waking up to what the wheeling press has been preaching for some time—that in good, hard, smooth roads a general benefit is derived, by less wear and tear on horses and trucks. For a "living example," stand at the corner of Broadway and Chambers street in New York City and watch a team, drawing a heavily loaded truck from the direction of the Bridge. Chambers Street east of Broadway is blessed with asphalt pavement, and the horses pull the heavily laden truck without a great deal of exertion apparently, but the instant they strike the belgian blocks of Broadway, presto! change!! Fire flies from the horses iron-clad hoofs, the drivers lose their tempers, and in a number of ways you are impressed with the idea that the weight of a second truck has suddenly been put on the same team; in other words, that the same horses were using twice the amount of strength they were when hauling the truck on the asphalt pavement. Selah!

COASTER.

BRIDGEPORT.

The members of the Bridgeport Wheel Club enjoyed a shore dinner at the "George Hotel," Black Rock, on the 23d. They left the club-rooms about 7 o'clock P. M., intending to have a run through the principal streets of the city, but on account of the mud they went direct to Black Rock. About forty members sat down to the dinner. Mr Calhoun Latham, President of the club, occupied the head of the table. After the dinner, the boys adjourned to the dancing pavilion, where two local wheelmen gave an interesting riding exhibition. Then dancing was indulged in by the young lady guests of the hotel and the wheelmen, until a very late hour. The boys returned, all voting to go again later in the season.

Considerable indignation is being expressed by the Bridgeport members, Connecticut Division, L. A. W., over the way Hartford has treated them. At the recent meeting of the Connecticut Division, at Bridgeport, on the 8th, three Bridgeport men were put on the ticket, Calhoun Latham, as Chief Consul; C. E. Moore, Vice-Consul, and Fred Atwater, Representative. The Hartford L. A. W. members have substituted a new ticket, leaving the Bridgeport boys out entirely. The Bridgeport boys feel that they have not been treated fairly, but what will be done remains to be seen. Probably a meeting of the L. A. W. members will be called.

The Rambling Wheelmen, at their last meeting, appointed a committee to find suitable rooms in a more central portion of the city. They have now decided to take the rooms over Clark & Nichols, on Main Street. The rooms are to be fitted up in fine style, and the Ramblers say the rooms will be inferior to none in the State. The location is certainly the best that could be desired. The only objection to their old quarters on State Street was that they were too far away. "PARK CITY."

ST. LOUIS.

"Destroy his fib, his sophistry, in vain.
The creature's at his dirty work again."

The present administration of the Missouri Club has done some queer things in the six months it has had charge, but the latest exploit caps the climax and comes nearer the outrageous than any other of its many high handed acts. The Secretary has sent out a circular on the subject of the change in dues and the abolition of the active list. Inclosed is a postal-card for a mail vote. Of course a mail vote is entirely unauthorized and illegal, but a little matter like that don't worry these people any. Instead of merely stating the proposition and leaving the members to judge for themselves as to its merits, he presents a long screed in favor of the change, preserving a most careful silence, however, touching the other side of the question. There can be no defense of this misuse of authority and the funds of the club in sending out this one-sided paper. However, the blame should not attach to the Secretary. He never wrote a line of the circular, except possibly the signature. The "fine, Italian hand" of the President can be seen in every line, and for rank sophistry it discounts his previous efforts, which is saying a good deal. If the proposition fails, and it undoubtedly will, it ought to convince the President that he is not in line with the club, that it does not approve of his methods, and that it would only be fair for him to retire as gracefully and quickly as possible from an office which he seems entirely too narrow to fill.

There was a meeting of the stockholders of the Track Association held at the Missouri club-house last night, and it was largely attended. As it seemed impossible to get any action whatever from the board of directors, the stockholders determined to take the matter in their own hands. The officer whose duty it was to convene the board persistently refused to do so, though frequently urged, and it became apparent that one of two things had to be done: the tournament must be abandoned or else the stockholders must take charge of the arrangements. The latter course was adopted.

The date was fixed for Saturday, August 31, and the following committees were appointed, viz: Press: Lucas, Mockler, Holm and Brewster. Prizes: Child, Stone and Wilder. Advertising and Tickets: Smith. Programme: Pogue. Superintendent Stone can be depended on to see that the track is in good order and that the ground arrangements are attended to. The monthly dues were fixed at 50 cents for the months of July, August and September, and 25 cents per month thereafter. Previous to the meeting there was a good deal of harsh criticism of the dilatory, not to say obstructive, conduct of the President and his obstinacy in refusing to convene the meeting. A majority of the members were in favor of calling on him for his resignation, and if such a resolution had been offered it would have been carried, but as he was present and seemed inclined to do his duty in the premises, the counsels of the more conservative prevailed and the resolution was not offered. One thing, however, can be depended on: if the executive officers of the Association do not show more zeal and activity in conducting its affairs, they will find themselves replaced by others who will. The members are in earnest now, and they will expect their officers to attend to the duties of their respective offices or else make room for others.

The W. A. A. A. have withdrawn their proposition to have their bicycle championships run off at our meeting, and the reason they give is the apathy of the wheelmen, but that is not the true reason. With the exception of Geo. Rhodes, the members of the athletic associations do not take kindly to the introduction of cycle racing, and they will not introduce it into their meetings until they are compelled to. Miles, of Chicago, who is one of the officials of the W. A. A. A., wrote down from Chicago objecting to the giving of prizes for bicycle races, and characterized the spending of money for prizes for bicycle championships as a waste of good money. With all due respect to Miles, who is a thoroughly good fellow, I submit that a remark of that kind comes from him with very bad grace. Nevertheless, I must admit that he is consistent; he certainly did not "waste any good money" on prizes at the last tournament he gave.

The Missouri's run to Collinsville last Sunday was fairly well attended, and was enjoyable notwithstanding the execrable roads. Under the guidance of Mr. Stockett and the Superintendent, the mines of the Consolidated Coal Co. were thoroughly inspected, and as few of the boys had ever been "down in a coal mine" it was an interesting experience. Capt. Hildebrand is doing his best to keep the Missouri Club in the front as a road-riding club, and he deserves more encouragement than he is receiving. He is one of the best riders that the city affords, is patient and amiable, and his runs are generally selected with good taste and with a view to variety. He never permits scorching, and the veriest tenderfoot can always keep in the front rank whenever he has charge of the run. In Lewis and Peckham he has two excellent lieutenants, and they are quite in touch with his views on the subject of club runs. Under these circumstances, the club is sure to keep up its good record on the road, even though it does seem sometimes as if the efforts of its road officers were not fully appreciated. Next month's runs are to Fenton, De Soto, Musick's Ferry, and one more to be chosen later. On Sept. 1 we hope to have some visitors from Chicago, who have promised to come down for the sole purpose of going over the De Soto road. If they come, we will promise them a good time, a safe ride over the road and an experience in the way of cycling which they have never had before. The terrors of this road have been greatly exaggerated. It is true that the hills are something tremendous, but the surface of the road is generally good and the scenery is simply magnificent. When taken as an all-day ride—the distance is forty-six miles—it is one of the pleasantest runs in this vicinity, and once taken is never forgotten.

The Cycle Club went to Ballwin last Sunday. This being the third consecutive run they have taken to this point, people are wondering what the attraction can be that takes this club of hard riders so often on so soft a run. Sanders will have to take his boys in hand or they will get away from him.

THURIEL.

The Hartford Wheel Club has closed a contract by cable with D. J. Canary for an exhibition of fancy riding on each day of the Hartford tournament. For Mr. Canary's appearance, his first in this country for four years, the club is giving the largest price ever paid to a fancy rider for a similar exhibition. Mr. Canary sails for this country August 7.

CHICAGO.

All Chicago—I should say the cycling population of the windy city—seem to have the training fever, and may be found any pleasant Sunday afternoon in large numbers at the Cheltenham track, doing quarters, halves and miles against the watch, though, with the exception of Lumsden, Van Sicklen and perhaps George Thorne, the times made have not as yet caused any hard feeling on the part of the watch.

While resting on top of a twelve-foot fence, over which we have to climb and lug our wheels to get to the track, I took the following census of the sprinters on the track: Lumsden, H. H. Van Sicklen, Fred. Van Sicklen, the big four Thornes (W. C., C. H., George A. and Jimmie), Hosford, Black, and last, but not least, Miss Potter, our new lady flyer, while the grand stand was filled with members of the Chicagos, Kenwoods, Illinois and Lincoln clubs. On pain of instant death, I am prevented from giving you the times made.

From an interview with the dealers and prominent riders, published in yesterday's *Herald*, I see that Charlie Sieg is the only one in the trade who expresses himself in favor of the bell-and-lantern law. Going up Michigan Boulevard, a few evenings since, I met Tom Roe doing his best to live up to the wishes of the city fathers with two automatic, never-silent bells, a hub and head lamp, when, as he passed, I discovered a third red light on the backbone. It is needless to say he got the whole street, as everybody thought the fire department was loose, and drew up to the curb, giving him full swing. Munger, with great respect (?) for the law, immediately put on a 20-inch gong, and on his first trip across town rung it for the benefit of a farmer with a hay wagon. The farmer, thinking the police patrol was after him, stopped short, while Birdie proceeded to dismount among the rear wheels of the wagon. He says the bicycle is at least worth thirty cents, but in future he will depend on his musical voice to clear the way.

I wondered, when I read the article in the *Wheelman's Gazette* on "Illustrated Journalism," if it would be more than a week before somebody jumped on friend Darrow's neck, as, novice though I am, I recognized the original (?) cuts in the same issue, as did Sam Miles, of the *Referee*, who, on behalf of that paper, will, I understand, read the *Wheelman's Gazette* a few lines.

Opinion seems to be divided in St. Louis as to the advisability of Lumsden's challenge to Barnard. Fred Ingalls says he hopes, in case of a race being made, that St. Louis' opinion will at least be worth more than a dollar on Barnard. He still has the one lonely dollar won at St. Louis on the second Lumsden-Stone race, and is patiently waiting for a chance to double or lose his all.

I agree with The Wheel in wondering why any space in cycling papers is given to notes from R. Temple—Friedburg. Besides giving the sport a hard blow on the path, he also tried his best to ruin the trade here in Chicago, as he rarely sold a wheel at list price if the customer could be prevailed upon to accept a discount. Of all the contemptible, back-biting bicyclists it has been the writer's pleasure to meet, he certainly took the medal.

Genial, visionary Fred Van Sicklen is with us, at present engaged in reporting sporting events for the *Herald*. I met him this morning with most of his good points considerably damaged, the result of a header taken in a friendly three-mile race with Geo. Thorne at Cheltenham yesterday.

John Bogue, who recently had his wheel stolen, yesterday purchased a new one, and last night at the club-house seemed to be greatly disturbed as to what disposition to make of it over night. He finally decided to leave the front wheel at the club, sleep with the backbone, while Belden (who, by the way, wishes to know if Charlie Sieg has any connection with the Chicago Liar) kindly consented to sit up with the handle-bar. Honestly though, boys, the new wheel is a beauty.

Will some one kindly inform us who the Chicago Club ladies are who, as per the *Referee*, are spending a few weeks in the woods at Benton Harbor. I was not aware that we had any female membership, but if the club is to be run, as at present, solely for the benefit of the upper twelve, I would advise taking them in and letting them contribute their little $1 50 per month. What are we getting for our one fifty is a question generally asked, but as yet not satisfactorily answered by either board of directors or house committee.

Novice.

TACOMA.

On Sunday last a party of eight or ten rode out to the old and forsaken Woolen Mill to spend the day. Each rider carried his own luncheon, and one of the boys carried ground coffee, sugar, etc. At noontime Chef Prince Wells started a fire and soon had a pot of delicious coffee before the hungry and dry crowd, which, though small in point of numbers, made sad havoc with the contents of the several baskets.

During the afternoon Wells and his satellite, Dexter, ventured forth with fish-lines and "wurms" with which to entice the unsophisticated little brook trout. Success seemed to have crowned their efforts, for they landed sixteen "bouncers" in a comparatively short space of time.

While the fishermen were deftly "casting the fly," Pop Cristie and his followers, Brackett and Dougan, disported themselves in a deep pool at one side of the brook, while only a hundred feet from them lay the apparently lifeless forms of Foote and Halsted; and were it not for an occasional snore or grunt that emanated from that direction, serious apprehension would have been felt for their health. And so the day passed—a model "day of rest."

While many clubs take delight in promulgating the fact that "on Sunday last we turned out forty-five members for the *run* to Squedunkville," nevertheless, I am quite safe in saying that those same members would occasionally like to go off on a quiet little Sunday run with a party of six or ten, and find refuge in some unfrequented spot, there to pass the mid-day hours. Of course, all clubs are anxious to make as large and brilliant a showing as possible, and will always vie with sister organizations to show supremacy, especially in point of numbers. If, however, they fail to make a better appearance in quantity, they will endeavor to do so in *quality*, and to that end send forth their "scorchers" to do up their adversaries. A good many will say, "'Tis not so"; but I know better, for "I've been there myself."

For several days last week Mr. Ed. H. Newmeyer, of the Indianapolis Bicycle and Athletic Club, was a visitor in our city, and his departure was deeply regretted by one and all. Mr. N. proved himself a staunch friend of cycling, and spoke in unqualified terms of our wheelmen.

Strangers coming to our city, either to locate or to visit, and especially those who are wheelmen, invariably express themselves as greatly surprised by the manner in which the majority of our riders, the "kids" included, handle their bicycles. I suppose it is emulation that spurs them on to try the pedal mount almost before they can ride a "chalk line"; and, as a matter of fact, about 90 per cent. of the wheels in Tacoma are without steps, the pedal being used instead. Fully 75 per cent. of the riders can do the "stand still," and also many of the fancy mounts; and what makes this all a source of wonderment is the fact that there was but one bicycle in Tacoma the first part of 1888.

July 24, 1889. Snohomish.

LANCASTER, PA.

"I chatter, chatter as I flow
To join the rippling river,
For men may come and men may go,
But I go on forever."

An idea paralleled by one who wrote on this very shore:

"The red man has gone forever,
But the stream runs on as before
Over the rocks, and the rushing sound
Is heard from either shore.

* * * * * * * *

"The poor red squaw and the courtly dame
Alike have passed and gone;
But the bold rock stands, and the old Conestoga,
Ever, like time, flows on."

That is sentiment; but if you want the poetry knocked out of you most effectually, just lie on the grassy bank of a stream about sunset on a hot summer day until you feel the midges crawling over your benign countenance and hear the buzzing wings of a few well-developed mosquitoes, and find that they have alighted from the tips of your ears or the back of your neck, and you will feel like doing as we did—reaching for your handle-bars and putting the cranks in motion. We slowly wended our way homeward over the route by which we came, and we crossed by the bridge and we climbed up the hill, at whose foot stand the walls of the ruined old mill. The mill was destroyed by fire years ago, and was never rebuilt. It has since become the property of the city, and was purchased as an experiment intended to relieve the pressure of back-water at the water-works in time of flood by the cutting of the dam at this point. It may be considered a dam poor investment, being useless and yielding no revenue. We expected another squabble at the toll-gate, and had a layout prepared for our antagonist, but did not have to put it into effect, for when we drew near the toll-gate opened as if by magic. The magician was a woman, probably the wife, who may have overheard the previous altercation. The "spunky member" thanked the woman and said to the man, who sat upon the porch: "I'll not report you this time, but don't try that on again." The "chucklehead" stared at us, and did not betray his close relationship to the animal once the property of Mr. Balaam, for he opened not his mouth and spoke never a word. I trust he may never see this, or he might consider it personal and resign, as did another great man quite recently.

Hadji Hassein Ghooly Khan.
Allah! have pity upon the man—
Fetch the camphor! Get a fan!
Hadji Hassein Ghooly Khan;
Good-by, Ghooly. Shah! let us have peace.

Safely past the bars and the ogre, we pushed ahead until we reached the suburbs, and then took the near cut to the Philadelphia (Lancaster) Pike, out which we ran to Knapp's Villa, a pretty, secluded spot. The house (with a license) stands in from the road on a lawn filled with trees and shrubbery. Rustic summer houses, benches, etc., are scattered around, where one may sit and sip his ambrosia (?), whatever other name or taste it may assume, or he may puff his fragrant Lancaster County Havana, as may suit his fancy. We sat outside, but we did not sip, neither did we squander of our wealth in the purchase of a fragrant "two-for." Nevertheless, we had our refreshment, and we refreshed until

"We quit, and that from sheer satiety—
Who says we did not have *variety*?

As this was a special occasion, an orchestra enlivened the scene, and we sat and listened to the music, under the able leadership and accompaniment of Prof. Haas. We got here in the early twilight, and as the shadows deepened the veranda and grounds were illuminated by numerous Japanese lanterns, and it was a pretty sight. But we had to tear ourselves away, and a pleasant run home by moonlight brought our ride, as it will this letter, to an end.

July 15, 1889. Tentoone.

ELIZABETH.

The rainy weather has somewhat hindered the riding, but still the records are coming in quite heavy.

Messrs. McNiece, A. L. Calkins and N. H. White intend to try for the century medals offered by the club some time this week, probably on Friday. They will be paced by Captain Gilbert and Lieutenant Caldwell for the first fifty miles, the second fifty they will ride alone. The cyclometer readings will be taken at the start and finish by the captain. In order to have the records officially accepted, they will present with their claim certificates from people living on the route, giving time and cyclometer reading.

Captain Gilbert, Lieutenant Caldwell and Mr. A. L. Calkins made a trip to Coney Island on Saturday last, returning via train late in the evening. Owing to the threatening weather, the crowd at the Island was small, but the boys enjoyed themselves just the same.

The club run cards for August are out, and have been mailed to the different members. If the attendance on club runs continues to increase as it has of late, the officers in charge of that department will have to be congratulated.

Messrs. G. Carleton Brown and A. S. Brown started out the other day for a run to Summit. On the way home Mr. A. S. Brown took a header and broke one of the handle bars on his wheel. He was compelled to ride to Elizabeth (twenty-eight miles) with one hand. Mr. D. B. Bonnett, the club veteran, is rolling up his record rapidly. The grand total now foots up to 15,000 miles.

Tanglefoot.

K. C. W. NOTES.

Have you seen that picture of Beasley and the "mounted minion of the law" in the *Illustrated News?* It decorates the bulletin board at the club-house, and Lester goes about armed with an S. & W. It will be a day in mid-winter for that artist (?) if by chance he crosses the path of L. W. B. Speaking of Beasley, he is to go into hard training for the Kings County team, and from his past work I should say he will make a good one. For a half mile he is the best man in the club, and his work in the road races proves him a stayer. With good training he will develop speed that will rather bother the best.

I understand that (Walter) is to be entered in free-for-all novice races. With a little more practice on that safety he will be a flyer.

For some weeks we have been looking forward to the joint run and sail promised by our Captain, but, *alas!* the boat is sold, and the pilgrimage to Canarsie will not take place. This was about the last hope for a club run, for they (the club runs) have not been very successful since the hot weather set in.

So "Miles" Murphy is to race Van Wagoner, he of the mile on safety without hands in 2m. 49s. fame. The course to be Irvington-Millburn, and distance anything from twenty-five yards to seventeen hundred miles in thirty days. Whatever the distance, we shall be on hand, and if Miles does not cross the tape first it will not be because our lungs are weak.

That pitcher won at the L. I. W. race meet has yet to be engraved, also the "Alphabetical Association" cup. What has happened the House Committee? Strayed, lost or stolen?

Hesse and Hall are reported as working on the Jersey track every afternoon, but judging from the weather during the past week, they must have taken to boating, and two more lovers of the "silent steed," will soon be talking of nothing but shells, regattas, etc.

Those new cards of Lloyd's are great. It is seldom that Kings County gets left, and when Mr. Lloyd sent round cards with Hesse's record of 2m. 37 3-5s. on, and the letters N. J. A. C. only, following, the boys of Kings rose up in their might, and the result is that K. C. W. has now such a large place on the new cards, that one has to use glasses to discover the poor offending characters, N. J. A. C. Bah—rah—ah— — — —, etc.—we are the people.

Well it is settled. We are to have the "State Meet" in New York and Brooklyn, but the absence of races will cause no little dissatisfaction, and many think the committee made a grave error when the racing events were scratched. If Washington Park track was not to be had, that of the B. A. A. is still at its old stand, and the annual in 1885 was held there. The races were good, and paid State championships should be run at the "Annual Meet." Such events were run at the K. C. W. meet and at Rochester. Local men won, and at the Albany meet to come, it is quite probable the same thing will occur. If races were run where all are attracted, the results *might* be the same, but it would be very satisfactory to the winner to know that he had met all the acknowledged fast men and had come out the victor.

Ram Lal.

Brooklyn, August 1, 1889.

THE COTTAGE CITY MEET.

The meet of the Rhode Island and Massachusetts Divisions will be held at Cottage City next week (August 8, 9 and 10).

The three days' visit to the charming island city promises great enjoyment to the wheelmen. Martha's Vineyard people are famous for the especial hospitality they have for the brotherhood of the wheel. Cottage City is a paradise for the cycles; everybody rides there, and every man who has a League ticket to show will find himself possessed of the freedom of the city. The committee's programme is not an elaborate one, but the three days are laid out with a nucleus of fixtures between and beyond which the individual wheelmen or the parties of them may seek their own amusement—which is to be found at Cottage City without going far. The chief feature of Thursday, the first day, is the illuminated parade in the evening, and, of course, every rider will drop all other considerations that night to swell the parade of lanterns and make it a success. Friday is devoted principally to an excursion, with a run around the Great Circle on return, just to stretch the legs after the sea voyage. The Great Circle is about four miles around, and will take the party to East Chop and the New York landing. Saturday morning there will be a parade of the two Divisions and races in the afternoon. Some time during the three days a baseball game may be sandwiched in, so the programme promises plenty of pleasure and glory for the individual and the Divisions as a whole; but as a matter of fact the trip to Cottage City would be well worth taking if there were no programme at all.

BUFFALO.

The Zigzags have decided to limit their membership to 100. The Buffalos have drawn the line at 150 active members, and the Ramblers talk of making their desired number 175 at the next meeting.

A new wheeling organization, the Y. M. C. A. Bicycle Club, has been formed, thus making ten clubs in the city. Another one also will be given life this week, and several more are projected. With 2,500 riders, there is room for many more to follow.

The Zigzags will have their century run from Erie on August 11. The Ramblers have one booked for some time in September, and the Buffalos will also have one.

The Buffalos have discontinued their Friday night club runs. Is the premier club going backwards?

Zo.

A SELECTED LIST OF PATENTS.

[Reported especially for The Wheel and Cycling Trade Review by C. A. Snow & Co., patent attorneys, Washington, D. C.]

L. A. Hill, Philadelphia, Pa.; bicycle.
T. B. Jeffery, Ravenswood, Ill.; velocipede.
J. E. Robinson, Oil City, Pa; ice velocipede.
All bearing date of July 30, 1889.

PARIS AND ITS EXHIBITION.

TIPS FOR VISITING CYCLISTS.

We would advise taking a machine, as it is to the benefit of the wandering pedal-pusher to ride the best part of the way between London and Paris, which is very enjoyable and scenery beautiful, but we will not detail the towns and villages that may be passed through, and only advise that the "silvery streak" should be crossed by way of Newhaven and Dieppe, if they want to find good roads between London and Newhaven and Dieppe to Paris, and not be bothered with the Custom House.

On arriving at Dieppe the cycle must be passed through the Customs, and it is best to tip one of the porters. Be careful you state you are going to the Exhibition, and that you return with your machine to England. Then see that you get a document, on which should be specified the maker's name, number and other such features, so as to get it easily identified when it is examined on the return journey. The duty will thus be avoided, and you can get on the road without delay; but should the officials oblige you to pay, the tariff is 1 franc 20 centimes the kilo (two pounds weight), which is returned—less cost of stamps, paper and other fees—when *la belle France* is left behind to gain the good old shores of Albion. The roads from Dieppe, by Rouen, to Paris are excellent.

When the capital is reached the first thing is to secure a bedroom in some comfortabele hotel, but as every man has his own taste we will only give a few valuable hints as to the "secret" of getting a good *chambre*, allowing the visitors the choice of hotels in whichever neighborhood that pleases best. It is well to keep far and wide from the Exhibition surroundings, and get for preference near Neuilly in the Avenue de la Grand Armée, or away either side of the principal Boulevards from the Madeleine to the Fouboug Montmartre, where excellent hotels are numerous, and nice rooms may be obtained from three to five francs, according to the floors and position. A very reasonable neighborhood is within a few minutes' walk around the Gare St. Lazare, the terminus station of the Western line on arriving by train from Dieppe. Before taking a *chambre* it is highly important to arrange the price per night, with *bougie* (candle) and attendance included, in all hotels, so as to avoid unpleasant surprises in the bills. Only use the bedroom to sleep in, and do not "worry the waiter," otherwise *pourboires* will become a necessity to keep him in good temper, as Frenchmen must not be overworked at the best of times. A very comfortable bedroom should be had for about five francs, everything included, such as candles and attendance; but, of course, "boots are tipped for" when leaving.

Having got fixed up with the sleeping part of the programme, the next important item is the food, and we should advise some restaurant in the above-mentioned neighborhoods, where one can get splendid breakfasts at about 2 francs 50 centimes, and dinners at 3 francs, wine included; attendance extra. This is at *prix fixe* (fixed prices). On the Boulevards the most moderate restaurants are Duval's or the Bouillons Parisians, and at either establishment—there are dozens about the city belonging to the same company—one can eat very well indeed, according to taste, appetite and pocket. In the morning and evening *café au lait* (coffee and milk) or tea may be had at any *café*, in any part, and the prices are reasonable and marked plainly on the saucers, so that one and all can easily manage this part of the business.

We now consider our visitor sufficiently well informed on the preliminary, financial and personal necessities, so we will now seek for the "fresh fields and pastures new." Undoubtedly a safety or tricycle will be the cyclist's friend in Paris, as it is difficult, not counting the expense, bother, time and trouble, getting to and from the Exhibition in train or cab. The roads leading to the many entries are more or less good, and there are plenty of places in which to store away the machine, up to 11 P. M., close to the principal gates, and a "tip" or a very small sum is asked for stabling. We now get into the Exhibition, after buying a few tickets, which now cost about fourpence each.

The history and description of the Eiffel Tower, 300 mètres high in the clear blue sky, the Central Dome, Palais des Machines, Rue de Caire and other such wonders, are more than this humble pen could well scribe, so that visitors must see for themselves—then believe. All we can say is, one must follow the saying relating to Rome, "See the Paris Universal Exhibition of 1889, then die in peace!" —(of course, when the time arrives). We do not believe every evening will be spent at the Exhibition, as the principal sections are closed at 6 o'clock; then there are the gardens and hundreds of peculiar things to pass away hours, days, weeks; but cyclists are good at sight-seeing, generally, so we expect them to get about the Boulevards, and to some of the most magnificent places of amusement under the sun. The Nouveau Cirque is a wonderful place, and a model of a circus. In place of the horrible sawdust, which used to blind the persons in the front row, a splendid cocoanut mat is laid down, upon which a really first class performance by the best clowns, horses and other novelties is given; then—as if by magic—the cocoanut mat is taken up, and the floor descends, and beautiful clear water rises, leaving a lovely swimming bath, in which a comic pantomine is given. The whole building is well lighted with electric light, and so is nicely cooled. The other places should be seen; for instance, the Hippodrome, Folies Bèrgere, and last, but not least, the Eden Theatre—a really magnificent "palace-sort-of-theatre" and a building which, with the Opéra, Paris can well be proud of.

Getting across our "steel steeds," a ride up the wood paving of the Champs Elysées, a glance at the Arc de Triomphe may be indulged in one fine morning, then a run down the right-hand side of the Avenue de la Grande Armée (asphalte), where the many cycling depôts are to be seen, and close to the Port Maillot, on the left side, is the celebrated Brasserie de l'Esperance, where Parisian cyclists flock every evening and on all cycling occasions—in fact, it is the wheelmen's rendezvous. A spin through the lovely Bois de Boulogne is a luxury not to be missed under any circumstances, as the roads are splendid, and the green foliage that covers the cool, shady avenues is a delightful change after the "buzz" of fashionable Paris. The lakes and other pieces of water, surrounded by pretty trees of every hue, among which can be found first-class restaurants, where a thoroughly Parisian breakfast can be had, served outside in some shady nook. The pleasures to be had out of a cycle around this wood are better realized than written, so we advise all to see if our words are true by bringing their cycle to Paris or riding same across the roads according to the route we have pointed out. In an early number we will endeavor to give a detailed account of the machines exhibited by the several manufacturers in the English and French sections of the Exhibition, which we think will prove of general interest, as there are several novelties, especially in the French division.—H. O. Duncan, in *Bicycling News*.

PHILADELPHIA.

The rain last Sunday spoiled what would probably have been the largest club run of the Century Wheelmen this season. Arrangements had been made for the club to go to Willow Grove, and as dinner had to be ordered beforehand, it was necessary that those who intended going should sign a slip, so that the officers would know exactly how many were going by Thursday night. There were thirty-four names down, a pretty good showing for this time of the year, when so many of the boys are out of town, and to make the run all the more interesting, Mr. Chas. Feurer intended to take a number of large photographs of the party. But, alas! it rained.

Next Sunday a "picnic run and swim" is on the card. The start will be made from the club-house at 8:30 sharp, the destination being "Cans Dam." There being no hotels near, and the distance not being great, each one will take his lunch along and put in a day in the woods picnic fashion, returning by the way of the romantic Wissahickon Drive and Fairmount Park.

The following runs have been called by Captain Spirer: for August 4th, Cans Dam; 11th, Paoli; 17th (Saturday and Sunday), Point Pleasant, going on Saturday and returning on Sunday; 24th, Willow Grove; 31st, Norristown.

On account of the large outlay of money, occasioned by purchasing the new house furnishings, etc., the Century Wheelmen have not offered any prizes whatever for mileage this year, notwithstanding which the boys have already rolled up a goodly amount of miles.

Almost every club in the vicinity boasts a baseball nine. What is the matter with arranging a couple of matches between the several organizations of this city, and the Camden wheelmen could, of course, be included?

W. T. Fleming, having been unable to get a companion for his Western trip, has been spending his summer at Island Heights, N. J.

Rather a lame excuse about the Pennsylvania Road Book, wasn't it? After promising it for two years, in fact it was *always* just ready for the press or binder, we are shoved off with the sickly plea that the map makers were unable to get the maps out in time. Fine management that.

Mr. Geo. Gossler, of the Centurions, who has just returned from a tour down the Shenandoah Valley, has kindly made the club a present of a number of specimens from Weyers Cave in Virginia.

A 10-mile handicap road race, for members of the Century Wheelmen, is on the tapis, and I would venture that there will be several surprise parties present. The hardest task would be the handicapping, there being a number of members who are excellent riders, and no one knows what they could do until hard pushed in just such a race.

"Argus."

"LOVE WILL SHOW THE WAY."

"Whither thou goest I will go and thy sports shall be my sports and thy muscles my muscles," is the dismaying proposal of the modern young woman to her cavalier and, willy-nilly, he takes her with him on the bicycle as well as the three-wheeler. Before joining him in the park or on the road she takes a few lessons in private in the halls which are beginning to be opened for that purpose. She submits to the indignity of a strap about her waist and to having her machine guided by an attentive but statuesque masculine person. She disburses $5 for five half-hour lessons, and then usually she goes back and pays $5 for five lessons more. She cannot learn as easily as a child, who has an instinctive notion of balancing, and she pays her teacher a higher rate than he charges a man, to sugar which pill he assures her that women learn more rapidly than their brothers, because they are more docile and painstaking. When she has caught the secret of the motion she takes a spin in the park some bright afternoon, and on Sunday her cavalier, instead of inviting her to a buggy ride on the Riverside Drive or along the Boulevard to Coney Island, mounts her on the tandem two-wheeler in front of him and the novelty of bicycling adds to the pleasure. The bicycle and tricycle will shortly be the summer afternoon vehicles for love-making.

Bertha von Hillern, the pedestrian, took a bicycle to Virginia with her, but prefers walking. Mrs. Josephine Redding, the editor of two well-known art periodicals, attributes to the bicycle her recovery from overwork and nervous prostration. Mrs. Florence Finch-Kelly, the lately risen novelist, is another of the Central Park devotees of the wheel.—*Mail and Express.*

NEW YORK STATE MEET.

NEW YORK AND BROOKLYN, SEPTEMBER 13 AND 14.

The General Committee met at the Grand Union Hotel, last Thursday night, and adopted as printed in last week's Wheel.

Messrs. W. H. DeGraaf and Bert Cole have been appointed to arrange the theatre party. Mr. C. A. Sheehan has been appointed Chairman of the Programme Committee, and Mr. George Bidwell, Chairman of the Transportation Committee.

The Committee will hold a second meeting this evening, at the Grand Union Hotel.

PROGRAMME COTTAGE CITY MEET, AUGUST 8, 9, 10.

MASSACHUSETTS AND RHODE ISLAND DIVISIONS.

Official programme of the annual meet of the Massachusetts and Rhode Island Divisions L. A. W., Cottage City, August 8, 9, 10, 1889.

AUGUST 8.

10 A. M. Business meeting of Massachusetts Division, Town Hall.

3 P. M. Fancy riding by W. W. Windle. Courtesy of Lincoln Holland, Esq., of Worcester.

8 P. M. Illuminated parade. Committee, C. S. Howard and W. W. Stall. Lanterns can be purchased of dealers at Cottage City.

AUGUST 9.

Excursion to Nantucket, giving members a chance to view this quaint old town.

4 P. M. Run around circle to East Chop and N. Y. landing.

AUGUST 10.

10 A. M. Parade. Committee, W. H. Emery and C. S. Davol.

2 P. M. Races. Committee, C. S. Davol, W. G. Kendall, A. Bassett. Open to any L. A. W. member. Course, twice around circle, 15-16 of a mile, except one half-mile and boys' velocipede races, which will be but once around circle. 1, one-mile ordinary; 2, one-mile safety; 3, one-half-mile ordinary; 4, boys' velocipede race, for boys under 12 years of age; 5, one-mile ordinary, open to Massachusetts and Rhode Island members only, for championship of meet.

Entries must be made to C. S. Davol, Hotel Naumkeag, to close August 8. Entrance fee, 50 cents. No entrance fee for boys' race.

HOTEL RATES.

Special rates will be given L. A. W. members as follows:

Sea View House, $2.50 per day.

Pawnee, $2.00 per day.

Hotel Naumkeag, $2.00 per day.

Island House, $2.00 per day.

Members should engage their rooms as early as possible, communicating direct with hotel.

TRANSPORTATION.

Old Colony Railroad express trains leave Boston 9 A. M., 1.00, 4.05 P. M. (via Wood's Holl), week days; 8.15 A. M. (via Wood's Holl) Sundays; connecting with steamers Martha's Vineyard, River Queen, Nantucket or Island Home, and due at Cottage City at 12.30, 4.00 and 7.15 P. M. week days and 12.20 P. M. Sundays. Returning, leave Cottage City 6.15, 9.30 A. M., 3.00 P. M. (via Wood's Holl) 1. P. M. (via New Bedford) week days; 4.45 P. M. (via Wood's Holl) Sundays, due at Boston 9.50 A. M., 1.10, 5.40 and 7.10 P. M. week days; 8.30 P. M. Sundays.

Trains leave Fitchburg 9.00 A. M. 12.13 P. M.; leave Lowell at 7.40 A. M. 12.45 P. M.

South Framingham 10.30 A. M. 1.55 P. M.; Walpole 7.12, 11.03 A. M. and 2.23 P. M.

Members from central and western part of the State can connect with Old Colony Railroad at Fitchburg and South Framingham.

Special rates of fare allowed *only* on presentation of League tickets by members.

Boston to Cottage City and return $2.50.

Lowell to Cottage City and return $2.50.

Fitchburg to Cottage City and return $2.50.

South Framingham to Cottage City and return $2.50.

Walpole to Cottage City and return $2.30.

Attleboro to Cottage City and return $2.00.

Bicycles will be transported free during the meet.

Tricycles will be taken only on the trains leaving Boston at 4.05 P. M. August 7, and Cottage City at 6.15 A. M. August 12. Those intending to send bicycles or tricycles on the 4.05 P. M. train August 7 will notify Chief Consul W. H. Emery, 109 Warwick Street, Boston, at earliest moment possible.

From Providence, a special car will transport bicycles and tricycles on 2 P. M. train August 7. Bicycles will also be carried free on Warren and Bristol Division to and from Providence to connect with the meet. Fare, Providence to Cottage City and return, $2.50.

The general party will leave Boston (Kneeland Street Station) at 4.05 P. M. and Providence at 2 P. M. August 7.

STAMFORD.

AFTER THE BRITISH AT ROUND HILL.

A delegation of Stamford cyclers, with sketch and note books, went after the enemy in the vicinity of Glenville and Round Hill on Tuesday, who they had heard were about to attack the Continental soldiers. Our reporter was uncertain whether they were acting under orders from General Putnam or from Editor Prial, of The Wheel, the leading cycling paper, of New York. The delegation was made up of President Mabie, of the L. I. W., Brooklyn, "Stamson" and Mr. Thos. Cumming, of Stamford.

The scribe of the repelling force promises Wheel readers some account of their adventures with the red-coats and Indians (?), with sketches of wayside scenery in that unfrequented-by-cyclers region of Connecticut and York State.

There is an excellent road system in and about Tivoli, N. Y.

The Binghamton Club will hold a race meet September 10 and 11. The track is a half-mile, of clay. Twelve events will be run each day.

D.—Any first-class safety will do. The spring fork safeties have many advantages and thousands of riders will use no other. You will have to experiment a bit before you are thoroughly satisfied or as satisfied as a cyclist can be; for satisfaction is a matter of fancy, and fancy like fortune is a fickle jade.

The Harlem Wheelmen will be consolidated with the Citizens' Club within a few days. The Citizens are conducting the matter in the quiet business like way in which they do everything, and it is impossible to obtain many admissions, but that negotiations have been held looking towards the consolidation is a fact.

A PHYSICIAN'S OPINION REGARDING CYCLING.

PARTICULARLY ADAPTED TO LADIES.

A Harvard graduate, Dr. Edward G. Bogman, '76, thus speaks of cycling:

The first claim of cycling is that it can be enjoyed by all constitutions, ages and by both sexes; by the weak and strong, "grind" and athlete; by the fleshy and thin, "class infant" and "class giant;" by the old and young, professor and student; by both sexes, the fair daughter of Vassar and the son of "fair Harvard."

Cycling, with the caution of moderation, is healthful. The question of perineal pressure has passed with the growth in the perfection of the saddle. The question of the heart is answered by moderation. "Scorching" on the wheel, as surely as excessive pedestrianism, base running, fast rowing, or prolonged tennis playing, will produce irritability and over action of this organ. Cycling in moderation is one of the best forms of exercise by which to overcome this too common result of excessive exercise in youth.

One of the best claims of cycling as a sport is, the constant change of scene and variety of adventure which it furnishes. Not limited to a prepared field or lawn, it carries its votary along the boulevards and turnpikes, from village street to country road, mid field and wood, over hill and dale, skirting pond and river, varied by the cautious riding in city streets, by a brush with a companion or trotter on the macadam, by a lazy run along the patch made shady by forest arches, by an exciting coast down some steep hill, by the cheering salutation of some passing wheelman, the quaint remarks of some farmer jogging on his way, or by the bright jibes of some street gamin.

Probably no sport is more fascinating than cycling. It would be hard to find a person who has followed it in moderation to whom this fascination has not increased with each succeeding year.

Cycling does not limit the follower to its pursuits alone, but may be combined with other sports and even turned to practical ends. While enjoyed as a recreation, it can at the same time be used as a means of transportation. The larger number of students in a college live within a radius of a score or two of miles. A large number of these return to their homes at least once a week. No better means of transportation and exercise combined can a student have at the close of his week's work than the afternoon ride home and the return ride to college. The student, collecting and arranging his thoughts for some intended essay or oration, will find them to come more readily and clearly while riding along some quiet road than in the closeness of his study.

It seems like stating an axiom to say that cycling is an economical sport. The first cost of a wheel may seem large, but when one considers the fineness of its finish, the warranty of strength and wear, the perfection of its running, the results seem greater than its cost. The repairs upon a wheel of reliable make are practically nothing.

In conclusion, let it be understood that all that has been stated above applies as fully to the fair student of the "Annex" as to the stronger undergraduate.—*Boston Herald.*

Trenton handicap, to be run August 5: Hine, 70; N. J. Hall, 30; Brown, 25; Bowman, 30; Shinn, 125; Lamb, 35; A. Rogers, 125; C. Rogers, 125; Sutherly, 100; Southgate, 125; Finlay, 60; Ash, 125; Clarke, 30; Zimmerman, 25.

NOT KILLMER'S FAULT.

EDITOR OF THE WHEEL:

Your article in a late number of THE WHEEL in regard to the smash on the track at Hagerstown, was an uncalled for attack on one whose fault it was not. The boy, Killmer, on the Star, did not cause the smash-up, as any one at that other end of the stand can say. It was this way: Hinds, in passing Killmer, struck his front wheel. Killmer, of course, slacked up to prevent going into Hinds. Clark and Parber being close to Killmer, of course when he slacked they run alongside of him, and as Hinds had knocked his small wheel all out, he could not help the other two going into him. There is no better or careful rider than Killmer is. I have known him for years, and he is the only one I had enough confidence in to loan any racing machine to that is one of my own.

W. J. WILHELM.

[The fault seemed to us to lay with Killmer, but we are glad to publish Mr. Wilhelm's statement. It was no attack, however; simply a caution to ride more carefully that life and wheels may not be endangered. ED.]

TURN THEM OUT, BOYS.

The executive officers of the Missouri Bicycle Club are evidently determined to keep up the excitement in that organization regardless of the consequences. At the last meeting President Andrews gave notice of his intention at the next meeting to offer an amendment to the by-laws fixing the dues of associate and active members at the same figure, $1.50 per month. This means that the active list is to be wiped out and all members placed on an equal footing so far as the management of the club is concerned.

Turning the club over to the management of the associate members, who do not ride and who take no interest whatever in cycling, may be a good way to secure those objects, but the average cycling member will hardly think so, and unless they are prepared to see the club go out of existence as a cycling club they will be on hand at the next meeting to defeat the proposed measure. The history of the club for the past three and a half years has been one of uninterrupted prosperity, and as there has been no call for any changes in that matter of dues common business policy would seem to dictate that well enough be let alone. The explanation of the move may be found in the recent action of the club on the Sunday question. The proposed amendment is simply a thinly disguised method of reopening that matter, the idea being to put the associates on a voting basis and then get the assistance of enough of them to carry the project through. One cannot help admiring the tenacity of these fellows, though condemning their reprehensible methods. One of the executive officers of the club is reported to have said that he did not propose to let the opposition dictate his policy to him! In plain English, this paragon of executive ability, this would-be oracle, proposes (always supposing that he is correctly reported) to exercise his own sweet will in the management of the club without regard to the wishes of the members. While freely conceding the ability of the present officials to properly conduct the affairs of the club, would it not be better for all concerned if they would confine themselves to enforcing the laws as they find them and not spend so much time defining a "policy"? The club has been kept in a constant state of turmoil for the last four months, the members not knowing in what new spot the "policy" of the officers was going to break out, and a continuation of this state of affairs must result in irreparable injury to the organization.

These facts should be borne in mind: The club was organized as a bicycle club by bicycle riders; its house was built and the lease guaranteed by the cycling members, and, until that lease expires, eighteen months hence, they will retain control of affairs. The dues may be lowered or they may be raised, but the associate members will not be given the power to vote without a hard struggle.—*St. Louis Spectator.*

J. Purvis-Bruce has a delightful sketch of a fishing jaunt in the July 25 number of *Shooting and Fishing*, a Boston paper.

The Boston *Herald* of August 1 publishes a column editorial calling attention to the poor condition of Boston's streets.

We have often stated that racing is not to be made or unmade by legislation, though legislation is conducive to fair and square questions. Racing is in a very healthy condition this year. It is the outcome of the healthy condition of the sport.

RACES AT FLINT, MICH., JULY 20.

One-mile heats.—First heat: Floyd Simpson, 3m. 09⅘s.; B. Kellerman, second; Bridgman, third. Second heat: Simpson, 3m. 14⅘s.; Kellerman, second. The prize was the Willet trophy, a fine engraved water pitcher and cup, valued at $75.

AS OTHERS SEE HER.

THE SWEET GIRL 'CYCLER.

The person who says that a girl does not look perfectly proper, modest and sweet as she glides along on her low-wheeled bicycle, ought to take a hand-glass and look on his back for moss; the chances are that he will find some. A girl can ride a bicycle—those low ones built especially for their use—with just as much propriety and a great deal less danger than she can ride a horse.

The position on a bicycle is more graceful than the one she occupies perched upon a horse, supported by one foot in the stirrup and hanging on by one knee while she tries to sit square with the horse. There is not a moment of the time that a girl is on a horse's back that she is not in danger; the most trusty horse is uncertain, and so is the saddle-girth. The bicycle can always be depended upon. It never kicks or shies sideways, and the saddle-girth never breaks. Propelling it is not as tiresome as walking nor as tedious as sitting still.

There is something delightfully independent and charming about a girl on a bicycle. She guides the machine along with such an air of confidence and self-possession. Her cheeks are red, her eyes shine and her whole appearance is of health and pleasure. You will find no foolish notions about the girl cycler; she has good common-sense; she is practical, and, withal, as gentle and charming as she can be. One longs to squeeze the plump gloved hand.

It has a good effect on her brothers and gentlemen acquaintances to have her go out riding with them. They are quiet and gentlemanly in her presence; they select the best part of the road for her to ride over; they do not shout back and forth at each other or at boorish drivers who run them off the good road. The rankest road-hog in the country will turn out for the sweet girl 'cycler and give her the right of way.

The girl who can skillfully guide a bicycle is just the one who will skillfully guide the destinies of a home. She will be able to take an obstreperous youngster by the coat collar and straighten out the little kinks, or bind up the bruised finger or soothe the aching head. Her tender solicitude and loving kindness will make a man's life worth living.

Gentlemen, lift your hats to the sweet girl 'cycler. The fact that she rides a wheel proves her worthy of your esteem.—*Texas Siftings.*

A number of men started August 1 to roll up mileage for the Adams medals for the highest month's mileage.

Races will be held at Spring Valley September 24, 25, 26 and 27, in connection with a fair. The details of the events will be in the hands of the Hudson County Wheelmen, and will be announced later.

Your editorial on the meet is most excellent and truthful, and I shall endeavor to have all our people subscribe for the paper that is our friend—wise and discreet—but not at the expense of truth.

Sincerely yours, ALBERT MOTT.

Queen's handicap, one mile, Saturday, August 3: Denner, 100; Burgess, 55; Zimmerman, 45; C. M. Murphy, 30; R. A. Kissam, 90; W. F. Murphy, 25; Doughty, 125; Class, 20; Schaefer, 20; Rich, 10; Clarke, 40; Schumacher, 30; Banker, scratch; Brown, 30; Boyce, 100; Waters, 60; Stoutenburgh, 100; Hesse, 20; H. J. Hall, 35; T. J. Hall, 60.

MILEAGE PENNSYLVANIA BICYCLE CLUB.

John H. Draper	2461	C. L. Leisen	1274
Fred. K. Mears	2401	J. P. Simmons	1257
B. F. McDaniel	2254	P. Sharples Hall	1220
Chas. T. Harvey	2137	H. B. Mingus	1139
Jno. B. Young	1980	Frank Deinler	1116
S. W. Merrihew	1849	Wm. P. Street, Jr.	1053
Geo. D. Firmin	1303	Geo. Truman Laing	1000
W. J. Mingus	1347		

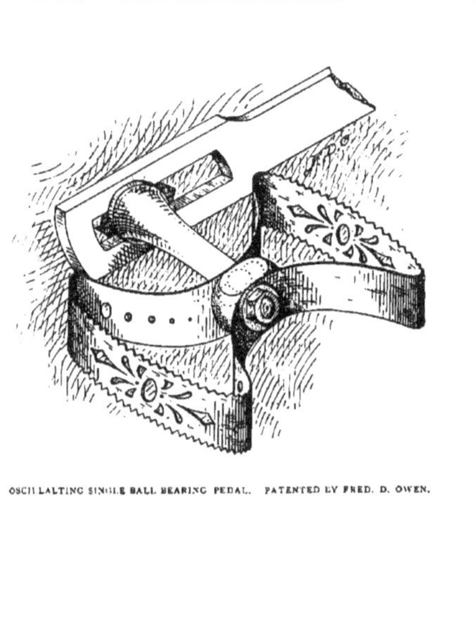

OSCILLATING SINGLE BALL BEARING PEDAL. PATENTED BY FRED. D. OWEN.

FIXTURES.

August 3, 1889.—Queens Athletic Club Grounds, at 4:30 P. M., 1-mile Handicap. Entries close, July 31, with Thos. Lloyd, Queens, N. Y.

August 5, 1889.—At Interstate Fair Grounds, Trenton, N. J.: 2-mile Bicycle Handicap and 2-mile Bicycle New Jersey State Championship. Entries close July 29th, with W. V. Blake, 146 Monmouth Street, Trenton, N. J. Entry fee, 50 cents.

August 8, 9, 10, 1889.—Annual Meet of Massachusetts Division L. A. W., at Cottage City.

August 10, 1889.—Races at Cottage City. Entries close August 8, with C. S. Davol Hotel Naumkeag, Cottage City.

August 10, 1889.—Bicycle Races of Massachusetts Division L. A. W. at Cottage City, Martha's Vineyard.

August 10, 1889.—Mercury Wheel Club's Outing, at Flushing, L. I.

August 14, 1889.—Waiontha Wheelmen's Race Meet and Road Race, at Richfield Springs, N. Y. Entries close with Fred Bronner.

August 15, 1889.—Race Meet of Lockport, N. Y., Wheelmen.

August 22, 1889.—East Greenwich, Conn., Handicap Road Race.

August 24, 1889.—Fifty-mile Bicycle and 1-mile Dwarf N. C. U. Championships at Paddington, Eng.

August, 1889.—Scranton Club's Tour, Scranton, Pa., to Utica, Springfield, New York, Catskills, Delaware Water Gap. Address, B. F. Connolly, Secretary.

August 31, 1889.—Monster Run of Brooklyn Wheelmen to Hotel Massapequa.

August 31, 1889.—Albany Wheelmen's Tournament. Entries close August 24, with W. B. Phipps, 51 Howard Street, Albany, N. Y.

September 2-3, 1889.—Amateur Race Meet of the Hartford Wheel Club, at Hartford, Conn. Entries to be made with W. M. Francis, Secretary, P. O. Box 745.

September 3, 1889.—Hartford Wheel Club's 20-mile Road Race.

September 7, 1889.—Berkeley Athletic Club's Race Meet at Berkeley Oval, Morris Dock, New York City.

September 7, 1889.—A. A. U. Games at Brooklyn A. A. grounds; 1-mile Handicap. Entries close August 29, with James E. Sullivan, P. O. Box 611, New York City. Fee, 50 cents.

September 7, 1889.—One-mile Bicycle A. A. U. Championship at Brooklyn Athletic Association Grounds. Entries close September 1 with J. E. Sullivan, 73 Park Row, New York City.

September 10-11, 1889.—Binghamton Race Meet. Address E. H. Towle, Binghamton, N. Y.

September 13, 1889.—Springfield Bicycle Club's 50-mile Local Road Race and 50-mile Open Road Race, over the Springfield-Hartford course.

September 13, 1889.—At Springfield, 50-mile Road Race, open to local riders only, and 50-mile Road Race, open. Entry fee, $5, returnable to first, second and third men. Entries close September 1.

September 1?-14, 1889.—New York State Division Meet at New York and Brooklyn.

September 14, 1889.—Y. M. C. A. Games; 3-mile Handicap. Fee, 50 cents. Entries close September 7, with George Pool, 150th Street, Harlem River.

September 20, 1889.—Michigan Division L. A. W. Meet at Ypsilanti, Mich.

September 21, 1889.—Michigan Division Meet races at Detroit, Mich.

October 4-5, 1889.—Peoria Bicycle Club's Tournament, Peoria, Ills.

October 8-9, 1889.—Races at Carlisle, Pa. Address John B. Steel, Carlisle, Pa.

October 23-29, 1889.—Race Meet at Macon, Ga.

EUROPEAN CYCLING FIXTURES.

Germany.—September 15; Hanover, September 8; Cologne, August 12; Chemnitz, September 8; Frankfort-on-the-Main, September 1; Mannheim, September 8; Crefeld, September 8. Hamburg.—Altona, September 22; Bochum, August 25; Madgeburg, September 8. Denmark.—Copenhagen International Meeting, August 18.

THE HARTFORD TOURNAMENT.

EVENTS, PRIZES AND SPECIAL CONDITIONS.

The Hartford tournament of September 2 and 3 will be the cycling event of the year. No other meeting after the old-time Hartford tournaments has been announced, and it is not probable that any such can be successfully conducted outside of Hartford. The great Hartford Meets originated in 1884, and have been continued without interruption by the Connecticut Bicycle Club and Hartford Wheel Club. The meet has increased each year in interest and importance, and this year's event promises to eclipse the greatest of its predecessors.

Most of the many details incident to the great race meeting have already been completed. A conspicuous feature of the tournament will be the absence of the professional. Last year's professional performances so disgusted the Hartford boys that it was resolved to have all future races strictly amateur in name and fact, and this seems bound to increase rather than decrease the general interest in the meeting.

The number of amateurs who have expressed their intention of racing at Hartford is so large that an entry list for three days' racing could readily be filled.

SPECIAL CONDITIONS OF HANDICAP RACES.

The following special conditions will govern the handicap races:

If, in any handicap race, the scratch man fails to start, the men with handicaps will be placed back at a corresponding distance, so that a scratch man will appear in all races.

The one mile ordinary and safety handicap races will be run in heats, according to the number of entries, as will be announced on the official programme of the day. All starters in final handicaps will be rehandicapped by the official handicapper. The new handicaps to be announced by the referee before the race.

Special attention is called to the following racing rules, which will be strictly enforced:

No. 24. The referee may place a time limit on any race. The time limit shall not be announced to the contestants until their arrival at the tape preparatory to the start of the race. If the competitors finish within the limit, they shall receive the prizes; if they fail to so finish, and the referee is convinced by their riding, and the time made, that they endeavored to reach the limit, he may award the prizes. It shall be his privilege to withhold any prize if, in his opinion, the competitor did not try to win the race.

No. 28. A class race is open only to those who up to date of the closing of entries have not won one of the first three positions in a public event in the same or better time than the class under consideration.

Entrance fee, $2 for one event and $1 for each additional event.

Entries close August 26; L. A. W. rules to govern. The right to reject any or all entries is reserved. W. M. Francis, P. O. Box 745, Hartford, will furnish all necessary information, entry blanks, etc., on application.

EVENTS FIRST DAY—MONDAY, SEPT. 2, 1889.

ONE-MILE NOVICE—First prize, gold medal; second prize, silver medal.

ONE-MILE NOVICE, ROVER TYPE R. D. SAFETY (No wheel under 35 pounds)—First prize, gold medal; second prize, silver medal.

ONE-MILE STATE L. A. W. CHAMPIONSHIP—First prize, gold medal; second prize, silver medal.

TWO-MILE TANDEM SAFETY, NATIONAL L. A. W. CHAMPIONSHIP—First prize, two gold medals.

ONE-MILE COLUMBIA CYCLE CLUB SAFETY HANDICAP—First prize, Pope cup; second prize, pair gold sleeve buttons; third prize, rug.

ONE-MILE OPEN—First prize, gold watch; second prize, Kodak camera; third prize, pearl opera glasses. Prizes added for fast time as follows: To man leading at first quarter in 40s. or better; half-mile in 1m. 20s. or better; three-quarters in 2m. or better; mile in 2m. 40s. or better.

THREE-MILE NATIONAL L. A. W. CHAMPIONSHIP, ROVER TYPE R. D. SAFETY—First prize, gold medal; second prize, silver medal.

TWO-MILE HANDICAP—First prize, Colt's rifle; second prize, fishing set; third prize, engraving.

ONE-MILE OPEN, ROVER TYPE R. D. SAFETY—First prize, diamond scarf pin; second prize, Smith & Wesson revolver; third prize, toilet set. Prizes added for fast time as follows: To man leading at first quarter in 42s or better; half mile in 1m. 22s. or better; three-quarters in 2m 03s. or better; mile in 2m. 45s. or better.

ONE-MILE 3:00 CLASS—First prize, smoking set; second prize, plaque clock.

ONE-MILE TEAM RACE (three men) FOR CONNECTICUT CLUBS ONLY—First prize, French clock; second prize, engraving.

EVENTS SECOND DAY—TUESDAY, SEPT. 3, 1889.

ONE-MILE HANDICAP (HEATS) ROVER TYPE R. D. SAFETY—First prize, silver watch; second prize, field glasses; third prize, brass umbrella stand.

ONE-MILE HANDICAP (HEATS)—First prize, Columbia light roadster, presented by Weed Sewing Machine Co; second prize, piano lamp; third prize, etching; fourth prize, Smyrna rug; fifth prize, shaving set.

ONE-MILE STATE L. A. W. CHAMPIONSHIP, ROVER TYPE R. D. SAFETY—First prize, gold medal; second prize, silver medal.

ONE-MILE HARTFORD WHEEL CLUB HANDICAP—First prize, brass table; second prize, seal ring; third prize, silk umbrella.

ONE-MILE 3:00 CLASS, ROVER TYPE R. D. SAFETY (No wheel under 35 pounds)—First prize, Pope cup; second prize, sofa pillow.

FIVE-MILE LAP—First prize, water set; second prize, diamond and sapphire serpent ring; third prize, sconce.

ONE-MILE TANDEM SAFETY HANDICAP—First prize, two gold-headed canes; second prize, two silk umbrellas.

ONE-MILE 2:50 CLASS—First prize, alligator traveling bag (furnished); second prize, pair Arab musicians (Bisque ware); third prize, wall cabinet.

ONE-MILE CONSOLATION.—First prize, oak card table; second prize, walking stick; third prize, brass mirror.

The Berkeley Athletic Club will hold a race meet September 7.

The Fort Schuyler Wheelmen will hold a race meet at Utica this fall.

The Pennsylvania Bicycle Club's tournament will be held October 4 and 5.

W. C. Jones, the English crack, recently rode the last quarter of a mile race in 35 4-5s.

At the Bristol sports the members' mile handicap was won by W. A. Daniells, scratch, safety; time, 2m. 46 4-5s.

At the Bristol sports held July 10, W. A. Daniells, 40 yards, won the two-mile safety handicap in 5m. 30 4-5s.

The one-mile tricycle championship of Ireland was decided at Dublin, July 15, A. Du Cros winning in 2m. 58 2-5s.; K. N. Stadnicki, second, by 20 yards.

R. H. Davis created a good impression at the Paddington Meet. Won "golden opinions," so says *The Cyclist*. Davis is a fine type of the gentlemanly amateur.

The Albany wheelmen have arranged an attractive programme for their fall race meet. Entries close August 24, with W. B. Phipps, 51 Howard Street, Albany, N. Y.

The Cumberland County Agricultural Society will hold races at Carlisle, Pa., Tuesday and Wednesday, October 8 and 9. For full particulars address John B. Steel, Carlisle, Pa.

A number of German cracks are at present in England to compete at the important events. The German representatives are: Louis Stein, August Lehr, champion of Europe, and Joseph Goebel.

Says *The Cyclist*: "Yet we do maintain that the N. C. U. championships are to all intents and purposes the championships of the world. We base this claim on the fact that the English championships are the only ones open in the world." The American Amateur Athletic Championship, to be held this fall, is open to the world. Send over your men, good *Cyclist*.

Several bicycle events were decided at the St. Andrew Society Games, held at the Buffalo Fair Grounds on Saturday last. The events resulted as follows: One-mile bicycle, scratch—W. Campbell, 1st; C. J. Connolley, 2d; W. B. Milley, 3d. Time, 3m. 10s. One-mile tandem—F. M. Brinker and John Milley. Time, 3m. 15s. One-mile safety—Gesler, of Niagara Falls, 1st; W. G. Schack, 2d; Stacy, Buffalo, 3d. Time, 3m. 23⅗s.

LOCKPORT WHEELMEN'S RACE MEET.

This meet will be held at Lockport, N. Y., August 15. The events are: 1-mile novice, amateur open, wheels not under 35 pounds; 1-mile club championship, wheels not less than 35 pounds; 2-mile lap, open; ½-mile boys' race, amateur, limited to boys who have not passed their 16th birthday; 1-mile race, amateur open, 3:20 class; 100-yard slow race, open; ½-mile club safety; ½-mile State championship, L. A. W.; ½-mile hands-off, open; ½-mile club tandem bicycle; 1-mile team race, three from each club; tourney with lance and rings, open; -mile handicap, open; 1-mile championship of city; ½-mile, open; 1-mile consolation. Entrance fee, 50 cents for each event; close with A. S. Cook, on or before August 8, 1889.

THE ENGLISH PATH—THE QUARTER-MILE TRICYCLE RECORD BEATEN.

On July 16, Louis Stein, of the Frankfurter Rad Verin Club, riding at Paddington Grounds, reduced the record for a quarter-mile tricycle, flying start. This distance was covered by Stein in 37 1-5s., thus beating the previous record made by H. H. Sansom, at Long Eaton, of 37 4-5s., by 3-5s. Timekeeper, G. P. Coleman, N. C. U.

The *Bicycling News* fails to note that when Windle rode at Buffalo in 2m. 50s., he was allowing from 70 to 100 yards to men capable of doing from 2m. 40s. to 2m. 45s. If *Bicycling News* will refer to THE WHEEL of October 19, 1888, it will find no statement to the effect that Windle had equaled the achievements of Curtis or Furnival, but it will find it stated that Windle had achieved an eminence equal to that of those other grand figures of the racing world. We simply reported that in the eyes of American people Windle was held in wonderful repute, whether worthily or not we did not state. Will the *Bicycling News* please try to understand it right this time and stop ranting?

Some rare sport was witnessed at Paddington July 13. Some 8,000 people were present. The one-mile bicycle member's handicap fell to F. H. Mason, 50 yards; time, 2m. 36 4-5s. The half-mile ordinary handicap was won by H. H. Harris, 80 yards; time, 1m. 14s. F. J. Osmond, scratch, 1m. 14 4-5s. or 4-5 seconds behind record; G. E. Osmond, 40 yards, close up. One-half-mile bicycle scratch race: F. J. Osmond won easily in 1m. 15s.; J. H. Adams, second. One-mile safety scratch race: F. C. Jones, 3m. 05 4-5s. One-mile safety handicap: G. Mordon, 170 yards, 2m. 32 2-5s. R. H. Davis, Harvard College, 50 yards handicap, rode a length behind, 2m. 35 3-5s., in the winner's heat.

R. H. Davis, the Harvard crack, made his first appearance on the English path on July 13. Davis was allowed 50 yards in the mile handicap and was beaten a length in 2m. 35 3-5s., equal to 2m. 40s. for the full mile.

A GLANCE AT "THE CYCLIST'S" ADVERTISING PAGES.

Hillman, Herbert & Cooper occupy the front page. Bown advertises his bearings, the "Keen" pedal and his "Rob Roy" lamp. The Quadrant and Coventry companies occupy half pages, as do Humber & Co. James Renouf & Cie., of Paris, devote a half page to "French Cycle Trumpets," of which they say: "Their rich sound calls immediate attention. Our trumpets are only dumb to the deaf. Used on Paris tramways, omnibuses and by wheelmen throughout France." Warman & Hayward, manufacturers of "Rivals," advertise a telegram calling for "more." In England they make the most out of firsts, and most of the manufacturers advertise their success on the path and on the road. On this side the firms get up something unique, or talk logic. Thomas Warwick & Sons advertise, "manufacturers of cycle materials of every description." They will supply you with all the parts of a wheel, and you assemble them and name the result to suit your fancy. The nearest approach to this system we have in this country is the method of having wheels made by contract by large milling firms, as the Ames Plow Co. and others. Thomas Warwick & Son's plan, however, is quite common in England, and it must obtain in this country some time in the future. J. Lucas & Sons devote a page to what they term "Cyclealities," meaning cycling accessories. The Centaur Cycle Co. devote a half page to a neat lined safety, and The Ivel Cycle Co. give a half page to Ivels.

Cooper, Kitchen & Co. advertise the "Collina Toe Clip" at 2s. per pair. They are a great advantage to racing cyclists, and are neither made nor imported into this country, though the New Rapid people (Clark Cycle Co., United States agents) make a fine toe clip. Henry Matthews is the Howard Smith of England, dealing in luggage-carriers, cement and things of that kind. A number of large milling concerns advertise balls weldless tubing, etc., etc. The Rudge Bicyclette and the "Rover" safety occupy half pages. The "Rovers" are being imported largely into this country through the enterprise of J. K. Starley & Co.

The St. George's Engineering Co. devote a splendid page to their New Rapids. G. L. Morris advertises a fine looking safety, "The Referee." In the line of odd advertisements we get Van Houten's pure soluble cocoa, and "Henderson's Perfect Food Biscuits," of which "*The Queen* says they are undoubtedly pleasant to eat." *The Queen* is a newspaper.

The cyclometer advertised is Downes' "patent crank log." A novelty in locks is "Mills' patent padlocks." Messrs. Ed. Carey & Co. tell us in a quarter page that they will sell every Friday and Tuesday evening, at 7 sharp, the following machines," etc. Messrs. Currie, Thompson & Co. advertise "pocket water-proof capes and jackets," an article not used in this country, but which might meet with a limited sale if Jos. J. Byers, the great rubber cape manufacturer, would make them. Lamplugh & Brown advertise their famous carrier, while an American concern shows the "Demon Detective Camera." A novelty is the horse-skin cycling shoe. The Bell-Rock safety lamp, handled by the Capital Cycle Co. in this country, is well advertised. An Irish firm advertises Belfast linen handkerchiefs. The Clayton Liniment is recommended as a panacea for all cycling ills. A. Paine spreads himself on his "Demon" safeties, which have been imported into this country and given satisfaction.

WHEEL GOSSIP.

W. J. Grandin, of Tidioute, Pa., rode 1,078 miles in June.

Springfield, Mass., has a Y. M. C. A. B. C., a new organization.

George C. Teller, Captain L. I. W., is summering at Asbury Park.

Messrs. Barkman and Borland have moved to Montclair for the summer.

The Pennsylvania Club holds its 10-mile race on Lancaster Pike to-morrow.

S. G. Whittaker is now with the Strong & Green Cycle Co., of Philadelphia.

Remember the date for closing of entries for the Hartford Meet, August 26.

E. J. Shipsey, N. Y. B. C., has started in for a big month's mileage for August.

The cycling trade should be, and no doubt will be, represented at the '92 World's Fair.

Each postmaster appointed by the new Administration has received a copy of The Wheel.

Woodside and Dan Canary sail for America on August 7. Both are at present in England.

The horsemen are organizing a movement to prevent a cable road being built on Jerome Avenue.

The Keystone Club, of Pittsburg, is considering the plan of holding a grand athletic meet in September.

"Dave" Moorehouse, K. C. W., has a record of 3m. 11s. on the N. J. A. C. track. He will compete this Fall.

The *Referee* says that "Morgan has set his face toward Australia." We are hoping that he will keep it set that way.

Clubs projecting road races will find an excellent set of rules governing such contests in The Wheel of May 10, 1889.

The Maryland people think that a "James" of the cycling press is a man who has never been there, yet knows it all.

The lady who steals out on the Riverside Drive just at dusk, her face heavily veiled, is Nelly Bly. She is a splendid rider.

John C. Wetmore, "Jonah," is editing the Elizabeth *Daily Journal* in the absence of the editor, who is on a vacation.

The Paterson *Press* wants all guide-boards at the intersection of roads renovated, corrected and maintained in good condition.

The Eagle Bicycle Manufacturing Co. are sending out a 6½x8½ photo, showing W. T. Robertson riding an Eagle down the Capitol steps.

W. I. Harris and wife were out on the Drive on Sunday on a tandem tricycle. Harris is a very hard worker, and finds cycling an antidote.

At the Cottage City Meet a number of League notables will be present, and many important points will be discussed and virtually settled.

One good country road from one town to another is worth more than the lives of twenty professional politicians.—*New Orleans Picayune.*

Probably the finest set of prizes ever awarded in a single race are the trophies for the 1-mile handicap at Hartford. Their combined value is over $300.

A correspondent writes us that a "James" of the cycling press is a Petulant Penman who Projects Peevish Paragraphs at the heads of other Prosperous Penmen.

Club life ebbs and flows. The Lynn Cycle Club, once so prominent, still has a large membership, but no club activity, and the members are seeking cheaper quarters.

The American "pros," Morgan, Knapp & Co., are "faking" at Denver. The Denver *Republican* recently published a cut of Rowe with a biography of Wilbur Knapp.

The road race announced for the second day of the Hartford Meet has been given up, on account of its conflict with laws regulating the speed of vehicles on public highway.

A road race from Tarrytown to New York will take place August 10 between B. L. Heydecker, N. Y. B. C., and Francis Thayer, Citizens' B. C. The race will start at 4 o'clock.

"Charley" Howard will probably be elected Secretary-Treasurer of the Massachusetts. No asinine "kick" against Howard because he is a member of an honorable profession.

Bicycling News speaks of "a person who has taken to peddling wheels in America, etc." Peddling is pretty good for an obscure stockbroker and floater of companies—small companies.

W. I. Harris and wife start on August 6 for a tandem tricycle tour to the Berkshires. Mrs. Harris was induced to take up cycling to benefit her health, and has been much benefitted by the exercise.

Frank P. Prial, who has made The Wheel the leader of cycling news in this country, has been nominated for representative of the New York Bicycle Club to the L. A. W.—*Sporting Times.*

A complete list of the events to be run at Hartford September 2 and 3 is published in another column. The prizes are valuable, and are trophies both for use and ornament. The road race has been abandoned.

In laying asphalt pavement in Paris the concrete foundation is required to extend under the curbstone, and four inches behind its rear face. This is obviously a wise precaution that ought to be adopted here.

Howard A. Smith & Co., Newark, N. J., report an unprecedented demand for their safety bundle carriers, both for handle bar and mud guard. ***

Messrs. Terry, Bogart and Miller, of the N. Y. B. C., ride safeties hands-off. Mr. Terry even prefers to ride in that manner, and coasts, changes from pedals to foot-rests and back again without touching the handles.

The Louisiana L. A. W. Division membership is 68; last year it was but 57. Chief Consul Hodgson is one of the most enthusiastic workers of the wheel world, and expends time and money to build up the sport in his state.

One of the most expert lady riders in New York City, is a young lady residing on West End Avenue, between Seventy and Seventy-first Streets. To see her manage her safety is a liberal education in the art of bicycling.

A rider with a sleeveless jersey and no coat was seen on Riverside Drive on Sunday afternoon. He should not repeat this performance. He casts discredit on his club and upon cycling. This kind of thing develops road-hogism.

Yes, *Bi. World* put on heavy boots and jumped on us. But we turn to letters from James R. Dunn, Albert Mott, Edwin F. LeCato, W. H. Butler and a thousand others which testify to *their* belief to our honesty, tact and energy.

We call it a breach of friendship and confidence when a newspaper makes public use of a private and confidential talk between man and man. What does our e. B. c. think of it? A certain Southern gentleman thinks as we do. This we guarantee.

G. J.—No, we don't know what a "James" of the cycling press is. But when you beat the other fellow out you must expect him to call you names. When you can't stop a fellow logically, you throw mud at him. That is the privilege of the foolish.

Mr. C. H. Luscomb has sent in his resignation to the Long Island Wheelmen, claiming that the club did not support him properly as President of the League. The Long Islands, we are informed, has more League members than any other Brooklyn club.

A. E. S.—No, dear boy, we violated no code of courtesy, as *Bicycling World* states. From Wheel sent you, you may glean that we simply apologized for "Jack," fearing he might be misunderstood. The *B. W.* is sliding so far to the rear that an exhibition of childish temper may be expected and pardoned.

Messrs. Schoverling, Daly & Gales report themselves as more than pleased over the business done in their bicycle department this year. The firm is an old one, but only took up cycling this year, devoting a floor of their mammoth store on Broadway to the department. They are pushing New Mails and Quadrants.

E. Berry Wall, who has been called King of the Dudes, and who has been teaching the young idea how to shoot in the way of the proper capah in clothes, states that "knee-breeches are beautiful and serviceable." Mr. Wall thinks the trousers has too strong a grip, however, and that it cannot be replaced by knee-pants.

Miss Eva Chase, of Buffalo, received a letter from the Toronto Bicycle Club this morning asking how many lady bicyclists would attend the Toronto bicycle meet August 12. The Toronto wheelmen are anxious to show Canadians how graceful ladies look on bicycles, and have extended to Buffalo ladies an invitation to attend the meet.

The boasted freemasonry of the wheel often extends to business. Away up in Temple Court three cyclists have pitched their tents in pleasantly-connecting offices, in which they expound the law. They are James Fox, President of the Brooklyn Club, H. S. Stallknecht, of the Brooklyn Club, and E. L. Heydecker, of the New York Club.

A ROAD RACE IN THE NUTMEG STATE.

The cyclists of East Greenwich, Conn., have decided to hold a handicap road race on August 22, at 5 P. M., the course being from East Greenwich to Silver Hook and return; distance not stated. There will be two prizes. Secretary V. J. Briggs, East Greenwich, Conn., receives all entries.

NEW CLUB IN BOSTON.

At a meeting of wheelmen, recently held at the Quincy House, it was decided to organize a club, to be known as the North End Cycle Club. The following officers were elected: President and Secretary, Dr. H. C. Macdonald; Treasurer, J. F. McGreeney; Captain, T. J. Kenney; Lieutenant, D. J. Breivogel.

A special meeting of the Board of Freeholders of Elizabeth County was held July 29 to open bids for the macadamizing of St. George's Avenue, connecting Rahway and Elizabeth. The bids ran all the way from thirty-six to fifty-five thousand, and no award was made. The appropriation will admit of the macadamizing of the roads connecting Elizabeth with Rahway, Plainfield and New Providence.

The men who are opposed to asphalt pavement very often point their argument by pointing out the poor service given by some pavements. The pavements which fail to give the proper service are generally put down by dishonest contractors, and the authorities whose duty it is to see that the contracts are filled to the letter are either too stupid to note violation of the contract, or are paid not to notice such violation.

W. F. Murphy comes out with a sportsmanlike reply to W. Van Wagoner's rather blatant challenge, published in the *Bicycling World* of July 26. Van Wagoner may have a wonderful backwoods record, but over the Irvington-Milburn course he showed poor form on Decoration Day. He covered fifteen miles in 60m. 41s., and then dropped out. W. F. Murphy covered the same distance in seven minutes faster time, and finished the twenty-five miles.

THE JACK-KNIFE BICYCLIST.

No, dear reader, not every bicyclist you see riding about town, affecting the "bent over" style of professionals, is a racer. Make no mistake. Professional cyclists, when jogging around for pleasure, have no affectations of that kind to "astonish" the sidewalk committee; they sit upright in the saddle, as is proper. The bent-over tribe are generally n. g.—*Lynn Item.*

Howard A. Smith & Co., Newark, N. J., are teaching more persons how to ride the bicycle at Oraton Hall than ever before at this season of the year. Hall open evenings. ***

The rumor published in the *Sun* that there was "trouble" in the L. I. W. is entirely without foundation. Every man knows that club men become absorbed in business or domestic life, sooner or later, and drop out one by one. At the last meeting of the L. I. W. six of the "old-timers" dropped out, and that is the only foundation for the rumor. It is true that the question of reducing the "age limit" is exciting some discussion, but that is an annual chestnut, revived principally to enliven the club meetings.

The New Haven *Paladium* says that there are 1,400 machines in that city. This list includes all sorts and styles of machines now on the market. It is no exaggeration to say that there are 500 safeties now in use. The local dealers have sold 200 this season. Who are the people who ride these bicycles? All classes are represented. The barefooted urchin may mount his wheel and ride past the bank president, or the clerk may start off for the evening spin, with a cigar in his mouth, and encounter the minister ere he has gone far.

Ernest C. Rowe, the well-known Fair Haven merchant, and an enthusiastic wheelman, has just returned from one of the most extensive trips ever made by a local bicycle expert. He has been away about a fortnight, and scored 548 miles on his wheel. In fact, with the exception of a three-mile space where the roads were too sandy, his entire journey, out and back, was made on his wheel. Running to Springfield, Mass., Mr. Rowe struck across the country due west, making a halt at Albany, Troy, Glen Falls and Lake George. On the days that Mr. Rowe rode he made an average of fifty-five miles per day.—*Boston Herald.*

TEMPLE'S VANITY CRUSHED.

When the Adriatic was approaching Queenstown, Temple was afraid to go to bed for fear he should miss the London newspaper men whom he expected would come down to meet him. He was much surprised to find no one there but the *World's* Queenstown correspondent, who had gone on board to see what had become of Mr. Depew *en voyage*. When the Adriatic got to Queenstown the passengers went to the purser and asked him for some penny English stamps. "I have not one left," said the purser, "Mr. Temple took every one I had." This was explained later. Every telegram in this country requires a stamp. Temple had sent ashore a stack of telegrams notifying numerous editors, "I am coming!"—*New York World.*

One of the favorite down-down lunching places for cyclists is Mouquin's, running from Ann to Fulton Streets, just east of Broadway. Between 12 and 1 a number of cyclists satisfy the inner man there, and many a good story and bright thought is inspired by the coffee and cigar or cigarette. One of the prominent groups to be seen there daily is composed of John C. Gulick, W. F. Miller and three friends, who linger long at their special table. Newcome, of the Harlems, Halpin, of the Manhattans, and Prial, of the New Yorks, may be found there almost any day. Newcome entertains with incidents of his career as a detective. Among the men who have dined there with the writer, or *vice versa*, are Messrs. Gormully, Clark, Whittaker, Hill, Schaaf, Atwater, Owen, Sheehan, Morgan, Barkman, and a host of others well-known in the cycling world.

THE LADY BICYCLIST.

The lady bicyclist is with us, and she has evidently come to stay. She occupies her seat too securely to be shaken from it. She appears upon her "machine" not in bifurcated skirts, but in her ordinary garb, for they have ingeniously invented something to meet the exigencies of her style of dress, and, quick to recognize when she is safe, she is at home and daring. She makes a graceful spectacle as she glides along, and she knows it. It is a good thing that the lady bicyclist has appeared. She would have done so long ago had she been given half a chance, for she is not averse to companionship with the monster, man, but for a long time they neglected to supply her with what she required. She could not be immodest nor ungraceful. Now she has no stress in the matter. She can go out with brother or sweetheart and ride beside him on a conveyance practically a duplicate of his and feel no apprehension. She is his equal.—*St. Louis Spectator.*

BICYCLE THIEF CAPTURED.

The man who stole the Warwick Perfection Safety from John Berry's place some weeks ago was arrested on Friday last. His name is Howard D. Elliott, of 300 Quincy Street, Brooklyn. He was taken to the Ludlow Street Jail, where he remained until Monday, when he was released on bail, pending the trial. Elliott is about 5 feet 6 inches tall, light complexion, and gave his age as seventeen. He wears glasses, and has the appearance of a student. Elliott stole the key of Mr. Berry's store, and, entering late at night, took a Warwick Safety. The next day he sold the machine to the New York Bicycle Company, who, learning that the wheel had been stolen, stopped payment on the check given to Elliott and returned the wheel to the owner. Elliott gave a false name to the New York people, and had the check mailed to the General Post-Office at Orange, where he called and received it. He is a clever thief, and therefore dangerous. It is to be regretted that he is of good family.

Howard A. Smith & Co., Newark, N. J., have improved their Graphite for lubricating chains and bearings of bicycles and safeties, until it seems to be perfect. All riders should have a bottle. ***

WE WILL EXCHANGE

any of the following wheels for Safeties of any good make, and pay the difference in CASH:

1	50-inch	Expert Columbia, price	....	$45
1	52 "	Victor	....	70
1	52 "	"	....	75
1	52 "	Expert Columbia	....	60
1	54 "	" "	....	65
1	55 "	Budge Light Roadster	....	70
1	58 "	Columbia Light Roadster	....	90

Remember, the above machines are NOT "wrecks," but are all full ball-bearing machines and in FIRST-CLASS CONDITION.

GEO. S. ATWATER & CO.,
1230 Pennsylvania Ave., Washington, D. C.

THE WHEEL

—AND—

CYCLING TRADE REVIEW,

Published every Friday morning.

Entered at the Post Office at second class rates.

Subscription Price, - - - $1.00 a year.
Foreign Subscriptions, - - - 6s. a year.
Single Copies, - - - - 5 Cents.

Newsdealers may order through AM. NEWS CO.

All copy should be received by Monday.
Telegraphic news received till Wednesday noon.

Advertising rates on Application.

F. P. PRIAL, Editor and Proprietor
23 Park Row,
P. O. Box 444, New York.

Persons receiving sample copies of this paper are respectfully requested to examine its contents and give us their patronage, and as far as is convenient, aid in circulating the journal, and extend its influence in the cause which it so faithfully serves. Subscription price, $1 per year.

I made up my mind some time ago that I would not take your paper any longer; but I know of no other paper where you can get so much for the money and which will keep one so well posted. Inclosed please find my subscription for another year.

Respectfully,
ANDREW A. PEABODY,
Brooklyn, E. D., N. Y.

"WHEELING" meanders into a high-sounding and meaningless tirade against "loafing" and "headwork" in races, pointing out the recent one-mile championship race as an example of the fallacy of the headwork system. *Wheeling* thinks that the German's win in the mile should "bring the flush of shame to the cheek of all those who have the honor of British athletics." This is all poppycock, and the great class of British sportsmen alluded to may spare their blushes. Osmond and Synyer used no brains whatever in the mile championship. Had they done any real "headwork," the German would not have won. They stupidly watched each other; the German used his head and backed it with his legs, pedaling the last quarter in 34 1-5s. On the day of the championship event Lehr was the best combination of brain and muscle competing, and therefore won. The "headwork" system is not wrong, good *Wheeling*. Osmond and Synyer are simply poor exponents of that system. *Wheeling's* cry is sent up to gain the favor of English cycling dealers, who should readily see through the game. *Wheeling* states that the English trade on the Continent has received a heavy blow because of Lehr's win on a German machine. *Wheeling* takes such pains to tell us how poor Lehr's wheel was that it quite forgot that his victory on such an old crock is proof positive that the rider had something to do with a victory; that it is not the machine, but the man.

THE advertising patrons of the *Bicycling News* are indeed dull-witted or lacking in self-respect if they do not take as a personal insult that paper's recent reference to Mr. James Purvis-Bruce as "a person who is peddling wheels in America"—accent on the "person" and "peddling." This is a direct slur upon every person engaged in selling bicycles, and the people who advertise in the *Bicycling News* must realize that if it were not for the good pounds, shillings and pence they pay into the *Bicycling News'* coffers, they would be jeered and jibed in the same manner. The man Hillier is vituperative, and should be shut off. Among the last things that Purvis-Bruce ever set eyes on was the *Bicycling News'* snobbish paragraph, and we know that it wounded him deeply.

IT is pleasing to note that the ladies who attended the League meet have repudiated the *Bicycling World's* charge that they were subject to insult and enforced spectators of loaferish conduct at Hagerstown. They are all ladies of social standing, and it must have been some sacrifice to them to invite the publicity their resolution will call forth; but their testimony is the more valuable. Chief Consul Mott also sends a pertinent communication, inviting investigation and calling for proofs which the *Bicycling World* claims to possess.

THE LADIES' OPINIONS OF THE LEAGUE MEET.

MARYLAND COURTS INVESTIGATION.

AUGUST 6, 1889.

TO THE EDITOR OF THE WHEEL:

It would be gratifying to Maryland if you would kindly publish the following document, "contradicting" the unsavory story published by the *Bi. World*. From the editorial in the *Bi. World* of August 2, the following juicy morsel is extracted: "When the League's "officials, acting within the scope of their "authority, calls us to account there will be "time enough to prove our report to be correct "or otherwise." The League's officials have already done this very thing, and the Maryland Division, in addition, now accepts the gage of battle thrown down and calls upon the *Bi. World* to "prove the report correct or otherwise." The Maryland Division will energetically and thoroughly attend to the "otherwise." Allow, please, the correction of the *Bi. World* in another assumption in the same editorial. "Marylanders" have sufficient "discern"-ment to comprehend all the praise as well as the abuse the Division has received at the hands of the *Bi. World*. Our hospitality has been praised surely, but one of the first duties of a host is to defend the guests that are untruthfully assailed because of the acceptance of an invitation. But the *Bi. World* untruthfully attacked host and guests. It set up a straw man full of "booze" to enable itself to hold up its hands in assumed virtue and holy horror, and then knock it down. Our guests were extremely considerate and were very far from abusing our hospitality. We enjoyed their merriment and were pleased that they were unrestrainedly happy.

Maryland is now prepared to meet the issue and courts the "proof" insinuated by the *Bi. World*. It must be fair and ungarbled evidence, and by responsible parties whose names should be given. All "reformers" will no doubt be justly proud of the opportunity, and Maryland and its guests are quite ready to be reformed.

This "proof or otherwise" is demanded in the interest of the L. A. W. Maryland is hampered, as no doubt other divisions are, by the charge in the "official organ," that the membership at large, who were fairly represented at Hagerstown, were susceptible of engaging in a "three days' bacchanalian orgy." Naturally, respectable cyclers, if they believe the charge has the *least* foundation in truth, would not join an organization of such decidedly brutal instincts, and the growth of the body is retarded. Therefore, in the name of fairness, equity, and all the many virtues possessed by the *Bi. World*, submit the "proof" insinuated and allow wheelmen and others to judge of its merits and the character of the men who furnish the evidence, and we will see whether their own personal habits are such as to admit of their casting the first stone and to admit of their being credible witnesses.

Very truly yours,
ALBERT MOTT.

TO PRESIDENT LUSCOMB, L. A. W.:

We, the undersigned ladies who attended the Tenth Annual Meet of the L. A. W. at Hagerstown, Md., hereby tender our thanks for the many courtesies there proffered by the wheelmen and received by us, and for the consideration with which we were at all times treated. Recognizing the fact that in an assembly of perhaps a thousand cyclers, or any other gentlemen, there is a certain freedom from the restraints of drawing-room manners, we were prepared to look with leniency upon effervescences which were innocent in themselves, but which are usually warped by morbid imaginations. It is with real pleasure, then, that we use the privilege of our sex and "contradict" the statement of the *Bi. World*, that "Never have we had such a hideous nightmare, such a bacchanalian orgie, than we have had for the last three days," . . . and, "We mourn for the tender feelings of the ladies present." We recognize the fact that in a large assembly of the most refined gentlemen who should be so unfortunate as to be cooped (excuse the expressive word) up from the rain, and dependent upon themselves for amusement, that there might be much to condemn; but these cyclers were *gentlemen*, and we saw nothing of impropriety, if any was committed, which we doubt very much. It pains us to read that the "official organ" of the League should deal the organization such an unmerited death-blow, and send forth the false impression to the fourteen thousand members that were not present that the ladies who were had cause to blush. Such was not the case, but, on the other hand, a most enjoyable time was had, which we would gladly see repeated.

(Signed) MRS. CLARENCE H. PLUMB.
" FRANK MCGLATHERY.
" N. E. SMITH.
" CHAS. T. STRAN.
" ALBERT MOTT.
" S. T. CLARK.
" E. P. HAYDEN.
" VICTOR EMMERSON.
MISS LIBBIE THOMAS MENTZEL.

Copies are in hands of the other ladies, after assurances that they will gladly thank us for the privilege of protesting.

THE STUPIDITY OF SOME CYCLISTS.

TWO INDIANA JUDGES RUN DOWN.

The Supreme Court of Indiana was recently called upon to review a non-suit in an action to recover damages for being struck down on the sidewalk by a bicycle rider. The trial court had held that bicycling was a form of pedestrianating, and that the bicyclers had as much right on the sidewalk as any pedestrian. The appeal from the non-suit was argued in the forenoon. When the court adjourned for dinner Judges Coffey and Berkshire started to walk to their hotel, and as they were passing out of the capitol grounds a clumsy bicycle rider ran into them, knocking both down, and badly bruising the former. This practical argument had such a convincing effect on the minds of the learned judges that they immediately overruled their unrendered decision, and filed an opinion setting forth that a person who "rudely and recklessly" rides a bicycle against a man standing on a sidewalk is responsible for damages for assault and battery.

After quoting an Indiana law forbidding persons from riding or driving on the sidewalks, the court says: "If sidewalks are exclusively for the use of footmen, then bicycles, if they are vehicles, must not be ridden along them, since to affirm that sidewalks are exclusively for the use of footmen necessarily implies that they cannot be traveled by bicycles. It would be a palpable contradiction to affirm that footmen have the exclusive right to use the sidewalks and yet concede that persons not traveling as pedestrians may also rightfully use them. We think, however, that a bicycle must be regarded as a vehicle within the meaning of the law."—*Exchange*.

[Cyclists have, of course, no right to the use of sidewalks. They are there on sufferance, and should not abuse the privilege.—ED.]

CHICAGO HAS ANOTHER CLUB.

A number of young wheelmen on the West Side have formed an organization known as the Washington Cycling Club of Chicago. It is the intention to make the club one that shall be strictly first-class in every particular, and handsome quarters have been secured at 653 West Adams Street, corner of Wood, which are now being elegantly fitted up, and will be thrown open about August 15. The club has been organized for the benefit of cyclers in particular, and for the promotion in general of social intercourse between the members, and it is confidently expected that the Washington Club will afford thorough enjoyment to its members and their friends through both the summer and the winter months. Although particular care is being exercised in the *personnel* of the club, the membership is rapidly increasing, and the outlook is particularly favorable. The following are the officers for the ensuing year: President, George D. Chisholm; Vice-President, W. M. Davidson; Secretary and Treasurer, Frank Barrow; Captain, B. F. White; Lieutenant, W. L. Whitson; Color-Bearer, E. A. Chisholm, Jr.; Bugler, H. N. White. Any information can be obtained of the Secretary and Treasurer, at 848 Fulton Street.

THE ADAMS MEDALS FOR HIGHEST MONTH'S MILEAGE.

A number of men who have started in for the Adams medals have written us, inquiring the conditions, and we republish them below.

"Messrs. Adams & Sons offer two gold medals, valued at $100 and $50, the first of which will be presented to the American wheelman who reports the highest one month's record between the first day of May, 1889, and the first day of November, 1889. The fifty-dollar medal will be presented to the wheelman making the second highest record. The first medal will be more costly and valuable than the first prize presented at the Pullman Road Race of last May.

"The conditions are as follows: All records must be submitted to C. W. Fourdrinier, of the *Bicycling World*, or F. P. Prial, of THE WHEEL. Records must be accompanied by sworn affidavits of the rider and Captain of the club to which he belongs. The affidavit must state distance ridden each day and cyclometer must be inspected before and after the trial. The cyclometer used must be tested before final awards are made."

THE ELWELL TOURISTS IN SWITZERLAND.

It is with vigorous grunts of discontent that the party are spending their last day in Switzerland. Our sister republic has a thousand charms, for which the bolognas and beer of Germany will be small compensation. In their letters home the boys have quite exhausted their descriptive powers, and first on the list of tabooed chestnuts are the seven adjectives—"beautiful," "charming," "superb," "wonderful," "grand," "magnificent" and "picturesque." From the beginning of the trip each country we have entered has been more and more interesting, and each large city more fascinating than the last, until Switzerland was reached, when all agreed that this little paradise is a fitting climax of the whole—the very pinnacle of perfection in roads, scenery and hospitality, and it only remains for us to make our descent to the base with what grace we may. We would be very grateful to Dame Nature, however, if she would let us down easy. The Valley of Hell (Black Forest) through which we ride to-morrow (our first day in Germany) will do very well for a starter.

IT IS COMING DOWN THAT KILLS.

The constituents of what I heard Cooper call "Elwell's European Road Race" may be in good condition for riding bicycles, but as mountain climbers they would be a complete failure. They kicked vigorously at climbing *up* to Mürren a week ago to-day, but they lived long enough to discover that it is coming *down* that kills. An hour and a half of slipping and sliding and continual what, on a bicycle, would be back-pedaling, landed us, with trembling knees and sore heels, at Lauterbrunnen in a state bordering upon nervous prostration. The gingerly leg-movements and looks of anguish on the faces of the party for the next three or four days proclaimed louder than words that the "Charley-horse" had seized one and all for its victims.

At Lauterbrunnen, where our wheels had remained during the sojourn on the mountain, we made the interesting discovery that the guests of the hotel had been so pleased with the idea of traveling about on cycles that they had evidently borrowed the machines and gone on a little excursion of their own. Various broken luggage-racks and bent pedal-pins gave evidence that there must have been quite a circus while it lasted. An indignant protest to the hotel proprietor only produced the non-committal reply, "Eet vas not my employees."

Leaving here we were at Interlaken and seated at dinner at the Jungfrau in an hour. It was here that we began to get beyond the reach of the French dinners The two heartiest meals of the French people are the breakfast, or "dejeuner" at midday, and the "diner" at six or seven in the evening. These two meals are exactly alike, with the exception of the fact that soup is not served at the former. The menu, in plain English, reads:

Fish.
Beef and Potatoes.
String-beans.
Mutton and Peas.
Chicken-wings and Salad.
Dessert.
Cheese and Butter.

There is no fault to be found with this until you have had it served up twice each day for four weeks. Then the monotony of the same old dishes begins to wear upon you, till one of J. Fennimore Cooper's "frugal repasts" would be a most welcome sight. The fish is usually eels; the rest is good until you come to "poullet," or chicken, the only part of which skinny fowl is served is a muscular, sinewy wing. A platter full of wings is presented before you, and your eyes wander about in vain for a wishbone or drumstick. It is "wing or nothing." What becomes of the rest of the bird is a deep, dark mystery. It is never served or seen in any form, and the question arises in your mind: Whence come the myriads of fowl necessary to produce all these wings on every *table d'hôte* twice each day? The question is never answered, but crows are awful thick in France.

From Interlaken the party rode (?) to the top of the Brunig Pass, where they spent the night, and by half-past ten on Tuesday were in Lucerne.

AT LUCERNE.

Lucerne is almost as gay as Interlaken, and, like it, is kept alive by tourists. Its Schweizerhof is the largest hotel we have seen since leaving Paris. It is full of old, quaint, Swiss architecture and interesting sights, and marks the centre of a most important district in the history of the republic. The principal point of interest is the famous "Lion of Lake Lucerne," by Thorwaldsen. We had imagined it as being sculptured out of some wild, barren cliff arising abruptly from the lake, and surmounted at the top by trees and brushwood, and at some distance from the haunts of civilization. Imagine then, our surprise on turning a corner in the heart of the city to find it staring us in the face! Cut out of the cliff, to be sure, but hardly within half a mile of the lake, and surrounded, instead of by wild scenery and beetling cliffs, by beer gardens, art galleries, knick-knack shops and panoramas. The lion itself, however, is grand and awe-inspiring enough to put to shame its tame and hackneyed surroundings. It is twenty-eight feet long, and being situated not more than twenty feet from the ground, its grand proportions strike the beholder with great force. It was some time before we could make up our minds to leave this celebrated monument to courage and bravery.

Another interesting sight in Lucerne is the old wooden bridge of the fifteenth century, which so inspired the poet Longfellow. It is a covered bridge, in the top of which, and supported by its roof-beams, are a series of flat triangular blocks of wood, on which are painted different scenes, biblical, historical, etc. They are fifteenth century art, and are very curious.

THE ASCENT OF THE RIGI-KULM.

At two in the afternoon we took steamer for a sail on the placid Lake Lucerne to Vitznau, from which point the party made the much-looked-forward-to ascent of the Rigi-Kulm. The lake, with its twists and turns, long arms and islands, is the most picturesque in Switzerland, and the sail along the base of the Rigi is enchanting.

If you close your eyes to the surroundings of Vitznau, it is very easy to imagine yourself in some small seaside resort in the vicinity of New York or Boston. Crowds of gayly dressed English, Americans, and a few people of other nationalities are hustling up and down the pier to the boat, and crowding each other for a place at railroad ticket office, hurrying, shouting and laughing. The cars are crowded, and you are uncomfortably jammed into a corner in true American style. The whistle whistles, the locomotive locomotes, and off you go at an angle of forty-five degrees, the engine puffing and the cog-wheels clicking. "It's the first time I have ascended the Rigi with a bicycle without uncomfortable exertion," says Beal. This is true, for his machine and "Bob" White's are in the baggage compartment, they having decided to stay at the top over night in order to witness the sunrise in the morning. They were obliged to take their machines along, as they are to make the descent on a different railroad on the following day, getting off at Arth, and overtaking us on the road to Zurich Theirs are the first bicycles of any description which have been to the Rigi-Kulm.

The ascent of 5,905 feet occupied an hour and ten minutes, including stops at several stations by the way. Arriving at the top, we found two grand hotels and plenty of "brass band, peanuts and lemonade." The view looking down justifies all that has ever been said about it, but around us on all sides were clouds and vapor. We were unfortunate in not having a clear day at the summit. It was windy, cloudy, cold and dismal. Not a man in our party, however, is disposed to kick at any sort of weather, owing to past favors in this direction. Our view, although not the best, was a grand one, and well worth the ascent. We learned a lesson in regard to mountain tops, and in the hereafter when we ascend, each will be accompanied by a heavy ulster.

While descending, an unfortunate young party, the brilliancy of whose diamonds was only equaled by the dirtiness of his nails, fell fast asleep. A number of our party in his immediate vicinity regarded him longingly for some time. Finally they could endure the temptation no longer, and leaning toward him they yelled in unison, "Great Scott!!!" The companion of Morpheus awoke with a leap that nearly took him out of the car, only to find his neighbors on either side gazing intently out at the land scape.

We arrived at Vitznau blue with cold. The ride to Gersau was only "a little one for a centime," and we put it through lively. There is nothing like a five-mile spurt to improve the circulation. On Wednesday we rode to Zurich, stopping for dinner at Zug, where Beal and White overtook us. They pronounced the sunrise from Rigi-Kulm wonderful. Zug is celebrated for its antiquity and the fact that, periodically, half of the town falls into the lake. The water undermines the buildings, and without warning they simply "slump"! We saw the place where a large slice fell in last year. It was once the residence of the versatile Göethe, and in the hotel where we dined the landlord (whose ancestors have been proprietors of the place for 400 years) pointed out with pride the bed-chamber formerly occupied by the poet philosopher.

A ONE-DAY STAND AT ZURICH.

Arriving at the Bellevue in Zurich, we unstrapped our luggage for a "one-day stand" Zurich is in every sense an elegant city. Its broad, well-shaded streets and bridges, its magnificent buildings, and the snap and "hustle" of its inhabitants make the place just what it shoud be—a model city under a republican government. No traveler in Switzerland should miss Zurich.

Two of the party got into a rather peculiar situation here. Their machines having got slightly out of repair, they hunted up a cycle agency to have the matter righted. The proprietor, it seems, is in the habit of sending his repairing to the prison to be done, as there are some skillful mechanics there. Being unable to go over with the boys, he sent his youngster to tell the workmen in the prison what was to be done. After the youngster had started back, our "Dave" and "Wilkie" (the long and short of the party) strolled leisurely out, looking about them as they went. Finally they wandered up a corridor and found themselves securely locked in, with no possible means of exit, and no knowledge of the language. Dave, it is true, knows a few words, but the situation frightened him to such an extent that he forgot them all, and a lot more besides. In spite of their expostulations, these two "bold bicyclers" were obliged to languish for over an hour in "durance vile," pondering on their past sins. The return of the infant cycle tinker brought them a chance to break jail, but they did not draw a comfortable breath until safely back at the hotel. Mr. Catlin, the U. S. Consul at Zurich, was kindness personified, and took a great interest in the party during our stay there. Through his influence some of the city fathers, when we departed on Friday, tendered us a dinner at the "Waid," a hotel some three or four miles out of town.

Not at all the smallest feature of the meal was the fact that it was eaten on a terrace from which we had an unequaled view of Zurich and its surroundings. Here over the well-spread board the two republics—"the small one over here and the great one over there"—toasted each other and clasped hands for freedom and friendship. Dinner over and our hosts bidden farewell, we started, with three of the Bicycle Club Zurich on a Rudge triplet to guide us, for Neuhausen, thirty miles away. The Swiss boys are all right on a wheel, and if our intentions were to bury them they were not in it. At Neuhausen we sat down to dine in what is called the finest hotel in Switzerland, the Schweizerhof. This, by-the-way, is the national name for a hotel, corresponding to the "de la Postes" of France, and "Golden Lions" of England. Here we again dined on a terrace, this time facing the beautiful milk-white falls of the Rhine. 'Tis here that in times long gone the bewitching Lorelei charmed on to their destruction, with her songs, the boatmen of the Rhine. The rock on which she used to sit still projects skyward from the centre of the falls, but the Lorelei, fickle female that she is, has decamped. The boatmen, too, have grown more skillful, and for "zwei franc" will row you up to the enchanted spot, and you may sit on her very seat and watch the spray dash about you. With our legs stretched under the mahogany we listened in vain for the silvery voice so laden with death. The Lorelei evidently has no use for American cyclists. The view, however, fully atones for the absence of the phantom. As Pedals says, we had "a panorama of Zurich for dinner and the Falls of the Rhine for supper." To-morrow we cross the line and get back the twenty francs we had to give up for our machines on entering Switzerland.

TAM O'SHANTER.

RECKLESS PROVIDENCE CYCLISTS.

The reckless riding of certain bicycle riders in the thickly settled portions of the city has occasioned many complaints of late, and it is understood that, if these riders do not conduct themselves in a better manner, they will be cared for by the police A night or two since two of them dashed down Mill Street and across Thames at so high a rate of speed, that they would have been unable to stop if there had been anyone in the way, and they would have surely run them down. Then, in the quiet hours of night, Thames Street is sometimes used as a race track.—*Providence Journal.*

CUFF MEMS. AT THE ENGLISH CHAMPIONSHIPS.

Mem. the First.—Good lot of people here. Find it rather awkward to write, even on a cuff, when one has a wooden bar across his stomach and twenty people pressing in the rear. Judge, conspicuous in white hat, starts the heats on one side of the track, then rushes across to the finishing post on the other, followed by small crowd of satellites. This periodical stampede of officials much enjoyed by the crowd. A hush comes over the people, the band is silent; up by the competitors' room a group of young athletes look fixedly at the starting post, or talk in almost breathless tones one to another. Edge comes up, and with a most unusually serious face, remarks: "How on earth you can stand there, Free Lance, in that cold-blooded way, talking when a race like this is just off, I cannot think." Then bang goes the pistol, and the final start for the one-mile championship has been made.

The cry is for Osmond and Synyer. Not much thought is given to the young-looking German—he is but eighteen—on the small machine, but early in the last lap he shoots away, and Synyer and Osmond, busy watching each other, seem slow in grasping the situation. But anon they go for him, and in the home straight Osmond, riding like a demon, pluckily attempts the seeming hopeless task of overhauling him. Lehr is a good man, however, and the one-mile championship goes to Germany, lost by a yard.

There are some long faces now in the crowd, not the least so being that of the gentleman who declared that he did not care who won, as they were all riding their machines (Humber), except the German fellow, and of course he was out of it. But soon the boys recover sufficiently from the awful shock to give the "sausage," as they familiarly name the winner, a hearty reception.

We find that to obtain any refreshment at this Paddington grounds two virtues are necessary: patience and perseverance. You first, by a considerable exercise of both these, reach near enough to the counter to shout your order, when you are immediately borne away by the crush. Having been brought up to the scratch again by the kind attention of friends outside, you venture once more into the fray, and this time manage to throw the money at the eye of one of the distracted-looking females behind the counter. This helps to fix you in her mind, and when once more you are whirled past in the resistless stream of humanity you seize something from her hand, and retire limp, exhausted, but victorious.

Another German, Louis Stein, won a heat of the five-mile tricycle championship in such good style that some trembled at the possibility of yet another championship going out of the country. The day was full of surprises, but nothing was more astonishing than the way elderly-looking Dr. Turner in another heat of the tricycle event romped away from the favorite, S. F. Edge, after having made a good warm pace nearly all the way. Sansom had quite enough to do to throw the tough Doctor off his wheel in the final, and the German was not in it.

Seldom is such enthusiasm extracted from an English crowd as was called forth by the popular Dr. Turner on his winning his heat. They cheered him again and again. If he had won the final, I believe they would have all danced a breakdown or stood on their heads, or done something very much out of the way to relieve their feelings.

As the day grew older, the wind blowing against the riders down the finishing straight increased in force. Two or three times it made a dash on the reporters' table. Away went the telegraph papers down the track, with Percy Low, the massive, and Larrette, the wiry, in hot pursuit.

The twenty-five mile ordinary championship was a most monotonous affair till near the finish, although the pace was decidedly brisk. Osmond rode the last lap grandly; he led all the way up the finishing straight, and landed home first by yards, a most popular winner.

During the last lap an elderly gentleman, tall and thin, was observed in the inclosure standing alone and rubbing his hands together in a highly nervous manner. As the winner passed him he clapped vigorously, and beamed such a look of pleasure it was really quite contagious. It was Osmond's father.

The twenty-five-mile safety afforded much more sport to the onlookers. On the opposite straight to the finishing one the men had the strong wind with them, and here positions changed nearly every lap, men sprinting up from the rear to gain the position they fancied in front, generally to lose it again before another lap was ridden. W. C. Jones was particularly fond of sprinting with the wind. He certainly did it in fine style; he seemed to drop behind for the mere pleasure of coming to the front again with a big rush. Burns, the new safety wonder, was another rider with a strong tendency to bolt away from the field. He indulged in some rare spurts, quite leaving his men at times, but they always closed up again sooner or later. It was a pretty sight to see some fourteen first-class riders come round the corner in a bunch and dive into the wind at a rare pace, which they well sustained throughout, for when it is remembered that the evening was cold, the wind strong and that they finished almost in the dark, all will admit that th. 1h. 16m. 34 2-5s. for twenty-five miles is a good bit of work.

Toward the end of the race things freshened up a bit. Not that it ever lacked interest, but new life was put into the men by the magic word "records." "Go for the records!" shrieked Nix, as the men flew past. "Go for the records!" was passed along the line, and go they did, treating the spectators to one of the finest races ever seen, and perhaps never again will so many first-class men be found racing together for records and a championship. Records were established for the latter miles, and F. T. Fletcher won the championship.

FREE LANCE.

A series of races will be run at the Minneapolis Driving Park on September 11, 12 and 13.

The Passaic County Bicycling and Athletic Association of Passaic, N. J., will give a grand bicycle and athletic tournament at the Clifton (N. J.) race track, on Saturday, August 31. Beside a number of athletic events, there will be a 1-mile bicycle race for novices, ¼-mile bicycle handicap, 1-mile safety bicycle handicap, and a 2-mile team race, teams of three men. Prizes, gold medal to first, silver medal to second in each event except team race, in which each man in winning team receives a medal besides the team trophy. Entry fee, 50 cents for each event; team race, $1 per man. Entries close August 20, with Chas. Blizard, 318 Gregory Avenue, Passaic, N. J. Prizes on exhibition at Peck & Snyder's, 126 Nassau Street, New York City.

*Believe me to be
ever faithfully,
Jack*

JAMES CUNNINGHAM PURVIS-BRUCE.

Died at Welford, Mass., August 4, 1889.

JAMES CUNNINGHAM PURVIS-BRUCE.

DIED AT WESTBORO, MASS., AUGUST 4, 1889

In the pretty little cemetery at Westboro lies and will forever lie the body of "Jack." The good heart will never beat again; we shall hear the soft Scotch-English accent never more; the fluent tongue will never again voice the workings of a fine nature; he is still frozen, mute, useless. Humanity has lost a friend and helplessness a champion. The bright receptive eyes will never again rest on lake or valley or hill. On a beautiful August sabbath he grappled with the grim monster and was conquered. Into the bosom of the calm lake he sank, with no human hand stretched forth to save him, no voice of kith or kin to nerve him for the final plunge into utter darkness. The world he loved so well noted not his going. One last agonized cry and the waters closed over him, pellucid and implacable as ever. A tragedy had been enacted and the victim was a worthy sacrifice.

Would that the agony of those last few seconds had been spared him. He saw Juggernaut face to face. The boy knew his race was run, that Purvis-Bruce was already a memory. No doubt confused thoughts of father and sister, the Ripley Road and Old England flashed through the tortured brain, and as the gurgling water drowned out consciousness he breathed a prayer to the Inscrutable One, and with arms stretched out in utter helplessness to the mother who had gone before, a poet, a philosopher and a man passed.

The daily papers of Monday last contained an Associated Press dispatch announcing the death of Purvis-Bruce. He had been training for the past week; for what purpose it is not known. On Sunday he had been exercising all day, having run and walked nearly twenty miles. He ate a very hearty dinner and shortly after started to run to Chamcey Pond, about one and a half miles distant from his residence in Westboro. He took his boat, and, rowing out into the pond, kept swimming and diving about it for twenty minutes. A Mr. Dean was watching him from the bank, and he states that at about 3:30 he gave a cry and disappeared. He rose to the surface three times, but long before aid could reach him he was beyond human help. The alarm was at once given, but the most persistent efforts failed to discover the body. Mr. Reed, of the White Cycle Co., wired the Boston Chief of Police for a diver, who arrived at 6 A. M. Monday, and recovered the body at 10:30 A. M. Mr. Reed cabled "Jack's" father for instructions, offering to send the body to the other side or to have "Jack" buried in his family plot in Westboro'. Mr. Bruce decided on the latter course, and the funeral took place on Sunday afternoon. The services were simple and impressive, as the final parting with a good man always is. There was a simple prayer, the reading of a beautiful poem and "Jack" was laid at rest.

James Cunningham Purvis-Bruce was born at sea near Cape Horn, about twenty-four years ago, on board the ship Victoria, *en route* from New Zealand to England. Although of Scotch parentage, he was declared a British subject. At the age of 16 he was taken to Calcutta, but remained there but a short time. He went back to Scotland and was then sent to his father, who had left his native land and become a planter in Mississippi. The uncle referred to was James Purvis, and from him "Jack" took part of his name. His mother, who was a gentle-faced woman, died when "Jack" was a child. Her maiden name was Cunningham.

In Mississippi "Jack's" father had a large cotton plantation near Vicksburg, probably near Purvis, for there is a town of that name in Mississippi. For five years "Jack" led an out-door life and was a sort of supervisor over his father's hands, assisting an elder brother. From there he drifted into Minneapolis, being anxious to gain more experience than could be found on his father's plantation. His subsequent history is written above. He adopted the *nom de plume* of "Gentleman John," and subsequently changed it to "Jack." His father resembles the late William Cullen Bryant in appearance, having a massive head, piercing eyes and enormous perceptives. He recently rented his Southern estate and has been living in Scotland. He is an out-door man, is nearly 60, but ruddy and active. Jack's sister is a sweet-faced girl of 20, high-browed and intelligent. She recently graduated from a famous European school and has been recruiting in Switzerland. At the present time she is somewhere on the Continent.

The brother I have alluded to above was accidentally shot on the Mississippi estate. I believe another brother was accidentally drowned. I know that when Jack told me of these accidents I told him to beware; that it seemed a fatality.

To the thinking man, Purvis-Bruce was the most unique figure in the American cycling world. In this little world of our own, he would have gone down in history as "queer," "clever," "odd" and "eccentric." But he was more than that, and I conceive it to be my duty to reproduce the man as he was; to portray his character, not transfigured by our mutual friendship, but as I knew it to be.

I first heard from Purvis-Bruce nearly three years ago. I had written some sharp paragraphs about him, a thing to which I was probably too much given at that time. I quickly heard from him in the form of an angry letter, with an invitation to duel. Accompanying the letter was a tin-type photo. showing Bruce with a belt full of pistols and bowie knives slung round his waist. I, of course, decided not to run up against a human arsenal, so I simply endorsed his letter with four words in blue pencil and returned it to him. A month ago, when I accompanied him South, he told me that my indorsement had cut deep, and that he had resolved never to again address a man as he had me. Knowing him so well, as I afterwards did, the motives that actuated the letter are clear to me. At that time Purvis-Bruce's writings did not reveal the deeper streams of kindliness and thoughtfulness that ran in his nature. I had read him through his contributions to *Recreation* as a shallow man, and his sensitive nature recoiled at my mistaken impression. To his last day even, Purvis-Bruce's heart was not worn on his sleeve. It was too true and good to be kept on dress parade, and casual acquaintanceship would often cause misunderstanding.

To return to the tin-type. At the time Bruce was unmistakably a jay. He had come into Minneapolis dressed as a cow-boy, with long hair, leggins, sombrero and pistol belt. To obtain a position on the staff of the Minneapolis *Tribune*, he was forced to abandon the garb of the cattle-herder and don the garments of civilization.

Bruce was then about twenty-one years of age. He did society work for the *Tribune* and afterwards reported cycling and other sports for the same paper. As a society reporter, he did not shine. He was not a Peeping-Tom sort of man in ever so slight a degree. He had no talent for complicated designs in feminine gownery and couldn't tell machine lace from the priceless films woven in the middle ages. He suddenly determined to abandon his career as a society reporter, for one day the paper came out with the startling announcement that at the opera on the evening previous, Governor So-and-So's wife wore a *shirt* slit up the back. Bruce had described the lady's divided overskirt, but the compositor had bungled. Bruce told me he almost fainted when he saw it and humorously described how the Governor and editor "saw" each other.

During that year, 1887, Bruce kept up his work for the *Tribune* and contributed to *Recreation*, slowly making a name for himself in the literature of the cycling world. He had no maturity of either style or matter at the time, but here and there a bright thought, a clever idea or a particularly felicitous bit of word painting told of latent ability.

I think it must have been very early in 1888, that Bruce came into my office one day. We had previously "explained" and were not unfriendly, but had no particular love for each other. He was dressed jay fashion and attracted some attention as we passed along Park Row. He was conscious of the impression he made, for he asked me if I thought he looked a bit "jayish" and I candidly assented.

He told me he inherited a fortune, which I afterwards learned amounted to about thirty thousand dollars. He was on his way to Scotland to claim this fortune and he left New York in a few days.

At this point of his career Bruce's life broadened, and he made a distinct advance in knowledge of men and things. He spent some time in Scotland, and later in England. In Scotland he rode and fished and wrote letters, principally to *Wheeling* and the *Bicycling World*, with an occasional contribution to THE WHEEL. His literary work showed a decided improvement. Bruce lived like a prince and had plenty of fresh air and sunshine, and it toned him up, as prosperity and good living will improve any man.

In England he made many friends. He became intimate with McCandlish, editor of *Wheeling*, and moved in the Ripley Road "crowd," drifting between London and the Anchor at Ripley. At this time he went the pace, like many a good man has done before him.

In the height of his prosperity he received a heavy blow, which drove him from London back to Scotland, where he remained until last April, when he returned to this country. During the few months that Bruce spent in Scotland, he spent many a sad hour in bitter reflection, and he came through his ordeal a better man. Adversity and opportunity often make men; men of the right composition.

He spent a few weeks in New York and at this time our acquaintance was renewed. I have to thank "Fenton," who was largely the cause of our coming together again. While in England an impertinent reference to me was made in *Wheeling*. Upon inquiry as to its source *Wheeling's* editor shouldered it upon Bruce, who sent me a denial, or, at least, claimed to be misunderstood. He afterwards tried to induce *Wheeling* to apologize, but it was never done. While he was living in New York, "Fenton," in his column of "Fancies," made some reference to one of his *Bicycling World* articles and he wrote me a reply for publication. I asked him to call and see me and mutual explanations founded a friendship which had strengthened every day. Bruce finally settled down at Westboro, Mass., with the White Cycle Company as their manager and advertising agent. His recent history is familiar to the cycling public.

I had the pleasure of having him with me as a companion at the Hagerstown meet, and being constantly in his company I was able to accurately gauge the impression he had made through his letters to the *Bicycling World* and THE WHEEL. On the train at Philadelphia the Pennsylvania boys gave him a rousing cheer, while the boy beamed with pleasure at this unexpected token of appreciation and good fellowship. I am forced to confess that when he was fully dressed to go down to breakfast at the Hotel Hamilton I was surprised at the ludicrous figure he cut. His cycling suit was of light gray Scotch home-spun. His stockings contrasted unpleasantly with the shade of the coat and trousers. The head of curly hair was surmounted by a Scotch cap the like of which could only be bought in Scotland. On its side he had pinned a solid silver circlet nearly two inches in diameter on which stood in bold, raised letters the mottoe of his family, "Do Well, Doubt Nought." I candidly believed that no other man in Hagerstown could have worn that suit and lived. But his independence and his nature neutralized its effect. No one, cyclists or non-cyclists, ever spoke harshly of him in my hearing. Before himself the subject was never mentioned. Those who met him liked him notwithstanding his much-abused card.

At the meet he did but little work, being sick most of the time. Beyond the little run to Williamsport, in which he got the boys scorching and finished third, we had but little time for enjoyment. In the evening, when hard at work, the curly head often looked up from his work with many a funny comment on some incident of the day. Very often he would troll a bit of Scotch ditty, the words and air fairly odorous of the Scotch hills and folk-lore, and of the heart entanglements of Jock and Jean. I found that his judgment of men was very accurate; that his character-reading corresponded with estimates which I had been able to form from long personal acquaintance.

At the general meeting held in Hagerstown Bruce was called to the platform. He was haggard with sickness, and he walked heavily to the centre of the stage. His Byronic look was most marked. Here are a few last glimpses I had of him. On the last night of the meet we were hard at work in the room, when in came Harry Hodgson, Samuel Goodman and Charley Howard. The company was too good for Jack to neglect, and he threw up his work while the party talked until nearly twelve.

About midnight, one of the newspaper men who had occupied a cot in our room came home in a very bad way. He had sent the best report of the meet to his paper, and the week of hard work so wrecked his nervous system that he had determined to woo the beery god. He went out at eleven, with malice aforethought, and had made a clean job of it by twelve. In the semi-darkness of the room he staggered here and there, delivering one of the greatest speeches on the tariff it has ever been my misfortune to hear. Bruce and I, lying on our respective cots, had a great, good time, and were convulsed for an hour, after which the poor devil succumbed and rolled over on his cot.

I shall ever carry the following picture as a dear memory. At Washington I succumbed to the water, as I always do. We were at the Saint James. Bruce was engaged with a number of cyclists, one of whom, a modest country boy, took his card with a devoted "I'm glad I got that card," spoken in a whisper. Feeling very unwell, I left the party, went to my room, and was soon in a feverish sleep. I was awakened by a heavy voice, which I recognized as that of Mr. De Graaf's, saying "This is your room, Jack." Jack came and stood looking at me through the filmy curtains. The gas was turned low, and I shall never forget the pained look of his face, nor the deep distress with which he learned of my collapse. The thing seems to me now like a scene from a play—so indistinct and half real.

In Washington, next day, we visited Bert Owen's cycleries, and after spending a few hours there were whirled in Bert's cycling barouche to the train. The motive power was a young colored boy, and the novel turnout attracted much attention.

On the following Monday, July 10, he dined with Mr. Shaaf, Mr. Whitaker and myself, and when he left for the Fall River Line boat it was the last I ever saw of him. I learned of his death in an out-of-the-way town on Long Island. Had it been possible, I should have joined the sorrowing throng that followed his body to Westboro Cemetery. But I was there in thought.

I have for some time thought that it was not the absence of bad traits, but the o'ershadowing of bad qualities by good ones. Sometimes a man has but one redeeming trait, and this is so strongly manifest that he is not harshly judged. On the other hand, many men have a number of good qualities, which neutralize the bad ones and produce a good general average, making the character acceptable. In estimating men, one should always be humble and never forget that, after all, much of our make-up is due to things beyond our control.

It is from this standpoint that we analyze the character of James Purvis-Bruce. We find that the dominant and dominating element in his nature is love of originality. With him this was a passion, so great that he did things that most men could neither understand nor accept as the act of a shrewd man. His personal card used at Hagerstown is a sample of this. His clothes are another. He would be queer. The same trait extended to externals, and he loved "queer" looking houses, old ruins, old cups and odd club badges. It might be said that he loved all "old" things. The Scotch tweed he wore at Hagerstown, the old pipe and the old pewter tankard were his friends. He had had many a good time with them and he loved them.

Next to his oddity, and almost as powerful, was his kindness of heart. He once told me that he had never denied a beggar, and I had opportunity to see him prove his creed, for the South is noted for its colored mendicants, and they always sent Jack's hands into his pocket. This kindness is shown in the last *Bicycling World*, in which "Jack" vowed he would never bet on the accomplishment of any feat which might endanger the happiness of any human being. With kindness you will find generosity. He simply didn't care for money, and any true friend of his in need could control his purse-strings.

His hobbies were nature and manhood. He loved a woodland path better than the drawing-room. He hated the theatre and the opera. He frowned at society and would be no witness of its pranks and goings on. He liked men and was ever on the alert to discover a good trait in those he met. He had set up a gentlemanly code which few humans ever attain to. He wanted to be one of nature's noblemen, and after brief wanderings in by-paths he would have realized his ambition.

Among the minor faults of his nature was his lack of perseverance. I believe he would have drifted into literature in the end. He had no talent for trade, and I know that he did not like business. He had all the elements of an attractive writer, and with years of practice and cultivation, might have become an essayist of no mean order. He was already getting out of shallow water, and the literary world would have heard of him. To prove that this estimate is not extravagant, I have but to note that in two years he developed from the backwoodsman into a cosmopolite, a man of letters, with rare insight and a relishable style, fresh, crisp and individual.

When he liked a man he said he had the proper "ear-marks." He liked labor and respected the humblest delver as much as he did a prime minister. He hated insincerity and shallowness; pretentiousness grated on him. He was decidedly not egotistical. He had a deep love for the sport which should endear his memory to all cyclists.

He was highly sensitive, and a mean action caused him real sorrow. To those who came near him, especially those who might be considered inferior to himself, he was deference itself. I have seen waiters instinctively interest themselves, and his "That's a good fellow" assured them of his sympathy.

Jack was a trim, medium-sized figure, of about five foot six, and weighing nearly 140 pounds. The frank, boyish face shown on the preceding page was gone. Experience had entirely changed it, marked it. It was dark, well-shaped, with the features harmonious. The hair thick and curly, was brown-blackish; the forehead full, and more thoughtful than practical; the eyebrows dark, shaggy and pronounced. The eyes were bright, incisive, reading eyes, yet not curious or repellant. They reflected a fine imagination and a kind heart. The lips were full and prominent. The nose and lips were not strong, and it was here that the lack of preservance lay. The whole face was not beclouded by that peevish, self-satisfied or dominant look found in most bright men.

"Jack" would have gone to England on September 2. He had the ambition to make a competency, that he might one day live the life of a gentleman of leisure on the shores of the Devonshire coast. He had described its lonely grandeur, the swishing sound of the impatient waves and the strange noises of the wind-swept forest. He had planned it all, and I was one day to visit him there, but—it will be otherwise.

In regard to the curious coincidence which has been harped upon so much, it has been passed over to the Society of Psychical Research, of Boston. This society was organized for the purpose of advancing psychology and its object

is to collect accurate data for the purpose of determining whether there are such things as premonitions, transference of thought, etc. All we know is that it was reported in Minneapolis that Purvis-Bruce was dead. That he, characteristically, turned the thing into an advertisement. It seems like the vengeance of Fate that "Jack's" death should have followed so closely upon this incident. It is not generally known that he wrote his own obituary, which we shall attempt to discover and publish. Below is a letter which reached us on Monday morning, and which was among the last things that Jack ever wrote.

Westboro, Mass., August 2, 1889.

Dear Prial—Probably you have not heard that it was reported all over the West that I was *dead*. A newspaper man by the name of Bruce perished in some cañon in Canada, and some Minneapolis paper commented and said that there could be no doubt but that the luckless newspaper wight was Purvis-Bruce, who was once a *Tribuner*. I use facsimile of telegram in an advertisement, and work it into a means of enlightening the public. A copy of the offending paper will be sent to me. I sent them a funeral notice for the *Tribune*, this afternoon, and wonder if they will bite.

Ever faithfully yours,

Jack.

We publish below the last tribute to "Jack" which will appear in the *Bicycling World* of this week. Mr. Fourdrinier, who was a close friend of "Jack's," kindly places the matter in our hands, and we thank him for his graceful and courteous act. We wish to call special attention to the beautiful poem written by Doctor Corey.

"All evidence points to the theory that the cause of drowning was undoubtedly cramps. Beneath a thin crust of eccentricity glowed a heart as true and pure as gold, and that heart is now forever stilled and a life of bright promise has been brought to an untimely end. We have only personally known Mr. Bruce for about four months, but during that time we have had opportunities to know him as he was. We had grown to regard him for his real worth; we had been permitted to see him below the surface, and we saw revealed a character which was an honor to mankind. His enemies admired him, and his friends loved him; some of his acquaintances laughed at him. True, original, eccentric and frank. None can accuse Jack of insincerity. He was outspoken to all alike—he kept nothing back; perhaps too outspoken sometimes 'for policy's sake,' but he hated duplicity, he despised 'Uriah-Heepishness.' His greatest fault was his loyalty to his own ideas and principles, which were honorable, to a degree eccentric.

"Personally we shall miss him as though he were a brother, the press will miss him as a fearless writer who was full of vigor and wrote in vigorous language. He was not afraid to write or talk as he analyzed and saw matters; he was a character, not a colorless specimen of humanity. There were some who failed to delve below the outer crust and find the real man; they simply saw his oddities, but it was our privilege to discern beneath the cloak a germ of value, the thoughts and character of a true man. A most curious and painful incident is that of the telegram in last week's *World* from Minneapolis in which it is stated 'Jack's' death was rumored. The fact of Jack's death will reach Mr. Stockdale before the fac-simile which appears in the *World* reaches him.

"THE FUNERAL.

"Sitting here at 'Jack's' desk, on 'Jack's' chair, and looking out of the window in full view of his final resting place, we pen the last sad facts of this painful catastrophe.

"Mr. W. A. Reed, on Monday, cabled Jack's father for instructions, saying that the body would be preserved in such a way as to be capable of transporting across the water if wished, but, on the other hand, if Mr. Bruce preferred that Jack's body be buried in America, the use of Mr. Reed's family lot in the cemetery at Westboro being generously tendered. Mr. Bruce chose the latter course, and so at 4.30, August 6, surrounded by nearly a hundred sympathizing friends, Jack's body was laid at rest forever.

"All services were conducted at the graveside by the Rev. D. Augustine Newton, who used the Church of England burial service, read from a book of common prayer owned by Jack. A quartette, composed of the following men in the employ of the White Cycle Co., rendered a couple of beautiful selections: Geo. W. Toney, first tenor; H. W. Butler, second tenor; H. G. Barr, first basso; R. T. Vinal, second basso. The bearers were Allen W. Acorn, A. L. Whitney, J. S. Bradly and Harry Morgan.

"All the men in the employ of the White Cycle Co. were present at the services, as also were President White, Secretary Peck and all the directors except Dr. Corey, who was confined to his house by sickness.

"The casket was inclosed in a heavy pine box lined with zinc and hermetically sealed, in anticipation that the body would be sent abroad. The box itself was covered with flowers and ferns, which he loved so well.

"The services were simple and impressive, and there was scarcely a dry eye to be seen. It was an ideal summer day, just such a day as dear old Jack loved, and so amid the tears of those who had learned to love him, even though friends of recent date, the coffin was lowered and the solemn words, 'ashes to ashes,' closed the services. After securing a rose from a wreath and a pebble from the grave-side, we sadly and silently turned away.

"During the services the Rev. Mr. Newton read the following beautiful poem, written by Dr. Corey, one of the directors of the company:

"Far from his native land—the mighty deep,
A thousand leagues, its restless billows sweep
Betwixt his kindred, who in vain must wait
His form appearing at the homestead gate.
Loving to roam his daring spirit found
All men his kindred and with friendship bound,
The recent stranger by that chain unseen,
Which made all feel the friendship long had been.
He came among us as the opening flowers
Break from the bondage of grim winter's powers
And like a vine with many tendrils set,
Made fast some clinger to each man he met.
Now cold he lies each generous impulse hushed;
Each springing hope by death's dread pressure crushed;
Life hence has fled, this bruised and shattered bowl
Has lost its tenant, an IMMORTAL SOUL.
Upon this grave will fall no parent's tear,
The earth must close without a loved one near;
No brother's fondness, nor a sister's care
To the sad spot at evening shall repair;
He sleeps alone—yes so we all must sleep,
Though scores of mourners at our grave-side weep.
To-day is *ours*, we mingle with our kind,
And pressing duties in our pathway find;
Defer them not, for ere to-morrow's sun
His circuit makes, *our* journey may be done.
It matters not to us when comes that time,
If it be remote or in our native clime!
Each for himself the gloomy path must tread—
All men are *strangers* 'mong the silent dead

"'BORN ON THE WATER, DIED IN THE WATER.'

"The subject of this brief sketch, and whose sad death we announce editorially, familiarly known by readers of the cycling press as 'Gentleman John,' and later as 'Jack,' was born at sea off Cape Horn, about twenty-five years ago, on board the British ship Great Victoria *en route* from New Zealand to England. Of Scotch parentage, it was held that he was a British subject, and his loyalty to his mother country is well known to his friends. At the age of 16 he was taken by an uncle to Calcutta, where he staid for a short time; then back to Scotland, and from there he was sent by his Scotch guardian to his father, who was at that time a planter in Mississippi. From this point he wandered West for a few months, and then back to Edinburgh, where he staid a short time, and then off to Egypt; back to the United States from Egypt, and out to Montana and Dakota, then to Japan and back to Minnesota. At this time Mr. Bruce was about 21 years of age. The past four years have been spent in Minneapolis, Scotland, and lately in Westboro, Mass., in which place he was in the employ of the White Cycle Co. at the time of his untimely death.

"In appearance 'Jack' was about the medium height. His head was a mass of dark brown curls, the complexion dark. His eyes were wonderfully expressive, steel gray in color, full and piercing; eyes that looked *into* you, not *at* you. His hobby was 'Nature,' and he was never so happy as when, with rod or gun, he was sauntering along the bank of a stream suggestive of trout, or walking over moor and through woods with eye and ear alert for game. He had no love for the crowded city streets, and he disliked show and glitter with an honest dislike."—*Bicycling World*.

CHICAGO.

As the writer has been absent from the city for the past few days, the Chicago notes from a novice's standpoint will have to be few and far between this week. I can imagine I hear Bob Garden thank heaven for being spared at least a little bit, as I understand from "Black Venus" that he says the sooner the "Novice" throws up the sponge the better. I was not aware of having hit Bob on any soft spot, but if I have done anything I am sorry for I am glad of it.

It is, however, reported, and on good authority, that Garden was the only one so far approached who refused to sign Berdie Munger's petition for reinstatement. While it is doubtful as to the result of such a petition to the Racing Board, Munger will at least know that he has the good will of a large majority of Chicago wheelmen.

If all reports are to be believed, Mr. Temple was not received in England with brass bands and open arms. We all have to smile when we think of the stories of banquets, etc., we shall hear of on his return, while we ruin our eyesight gazing at the diamond rings and other bric-a-brac presented to him by the Prince of Wales and others of the Royal family.

Official acceptance has at last been received from the Illinois Cycling Club to Capt. Van Sicklen's challenge in behalf of the Chicagos, calling for five men and the Oak Park course. It seems to the writer that the Illinois exhibit *almost* as much nerve in naming that course as the Chicagos did in suggesting the Cheltenham track. They also say: "Of course we will pay $25 toward the purchase of a $50 cup." Van will without doubt, however, accept the terms except that he will say that the C. C. C. will not put up $25 to help buy a cup for themselves, but they will invest $50 in one for the West-Siders if they can win it.

Burley Ayres (he of the fine Italian hand) will be with us again for good in the course of the next month or six weeks. He has already very strongly identified himself with the new Washington Club, lately organized very close to the Illinois territory. To a blind man, it looks like cloudy weather on the West Side.

John Cory has returned from a two-weeks' "think" in Michigan, and says that he will hereafter eat crackers and cheese, wear a patch on his blazer, and be a millionaire. We wonder if his good intentions will last as long as they did after the last Presidential election, when Jack, if rumor is true, struck the ceiling with a dull, sickening thud.

Four of the Chicagos—Van Sicklen, Roe, Ingalls and Bogue—at last, after many trials, reached Blue Island Sunday, returning via Pullman for dinner. The roads to that point had been fairly good, though all the party had at some points of interest made very rapid dismounts. At Pullman they picked up four tenderfeet (three on safeties) who wished to be shown the way home by way of the celebrated Stony Island road. They were taken in tow by the ever-accommodating Van, and gently drawn on to Stony Island road, which for exactly three-quarters of a mile was covered with from ten to sixteen inches of very wet water. On arriving at Seventy-ninth Street one of the safety riders thanked Van very kindly for his attention, and remarked that he would like to see Van Wagoner ride that in three minutes with his hands tied behind him; also, that while a safety was a pretty good thing to have in the family, he should surely provide himself with a life-preserver and an ordinary the next time he sailed with any of the Chicago Blazers.

My remarks as to the return we were getting for our one-fifty per month seems to have struck the right chord with many of the boys, and if the management do not get on a three-minute gait pretty soon something is liable to drop, as there is a rumor afloat as to the formation of a new club in which there will be no occasion to "suspend the rules."

Already there has been much figuring as to my identity, Sieg, Randall, Roe and others being among the accused. Sieg, when interviewed, said if he could not write a better letter than the "Novice" he would throw up his job as correspondent for the *Bicycling World*. If the editor is of the same opinion kindly consign this epistle to the W. B., and I will be heard of no more.

Novice.

[Dear Novice. We know you not, but we want you, very much.—Ed.]

SAN FRANCISCO.

IMPROVED STREETS.

At last the daily papers have commenced a crusade against our abominable pavements. Editorials on the subject appear in the *Chronicle* and *Examiner* nearly every morning, and they agree that the street covering this city needs is bituminous rock. This material laid on a concrete foundation is a clean, noiseless and lasting pavement. The basalt blocks and cobblestones now in use on most of our streets are noisy, disagreeable to travel over, and the wear and tear on vehicles and horses is an item of cost which would not exist with a smooth surfaced street, such as is now being advocated. May we soon see our streets in such a condition that San Francisco may be proud of them, as is Buffalo and many other Eastern cities.

ASSOCIATE MEMBERSHIP.

Your St. Louis correspondent evidently knows whereof he speaks, when he says that associate members, with the power of voting, will change the complexion of a bicycle club to that of a social club, and in a very short time it will be a cycling club in name only. In my opinion a cycling club has no use for associate members. Take the two clubs of this city, for example. In one you must own a wheel and accompany your application for membership with the amount of the initiation fee. The result is that this club is an unqualified success. The members all being interested in the same subject, work together harmoniously and have no internal dissensions as to whom shall be on the top of the heap, the wheelmen or non-wheelmen. Turn to the other club, study the condition of their affairs; they have an associate membership. A member who does use the wheel calls at the club-rooms and the chances are he will find some of the social element playing billiards or cards, and talking on all topics but those most interesting to a cyclist. The cyclist naturally loses interest in the club and in the course of time resigns. That is what some of the members of this club are doing now. I understand that three resigned at the last meeting, and that more will follow in the near future. The dues have also been raised to meet the requirements of those members whose sole object in joining a club is to have a place to lounge in, instead of meeting there and enjoying each other's company and talking over trips in the country, welfare of the club and members, and other kindred subjects which will occur to a wheelman and in which only a wheelman cares anything for.

Members of clubs, think well on this subject; associate members without the power of voting are no useful addition to a bicycle club, but an associate membership with the same rights as the active members is a dangerous element and a menace to the success of the organization.

RACE-PROMOTING CLUBS.

"The Kings County Wheelmen are beyond doubt the greatest racing wheel club in this or any other country." So says "Hawkshaw," the lynx-eyed correspondent of the *Bicycling World*. Don't doubt it in the least; but that item reminded me that, as an enterprising club in the racing line, the Bay City Wheelmen are not far from the head of the procession. Look at their record for 1889 (that is up to date). Two race meets held in San Francisco—one January 1 and another April 30; then they go to Stockton, a hundred miles away, and, in conjunction with the Oak Leaf Wheelmen of that city, give a race meet and tournament on July 4. The three events were all successes from a racing point of view, and the balance on their race meet account is on the right side of the ledger, too. Strange—ain't it?

The prizes given at these tournaments were the most valuable given at any meeting held in this country this year (my authorities on prizes are the wheel papers). That is not a bad showing for what the Bay City's rivals (?) are pleased to term a lot of "kids." Pretty good business heads on those youngsters, anyhow.

SHOCKLEY'S RIDING.

At Stockton, July 4, W. A. Shockley won the safety championship in 2m. 59 1/5s. On April 30 he was badly beaten, coming in a poor third or fourth in a race which was won in 3m. 14s. He met his defeat cheerfully and said: "Better luck next time." So he trained faithfully for the July races, and the improvement was astonishing. He not only won the one-mile, but got first place in the two-mile handicap, starting scratch with Lakenau (he was allowed 150 yards handicap, but went back to scratch). I am pleased to note these successes, as he is a perfect gentleman, and well liked by the boys. He was formerly a member of the Massachusetts Bi. Club, but has settled here now. When he came here he looked around and joined the *live* club, and what was the Massachusetts Club's loss was the Bay City Wheelmen's gain.

A "water-melon" run to Lodi by the Oak Leaf Wheelmen, of Stockton, is the fixture for August 11. An invitation has been extended to the Bay City Wheelmen to attend, and no doubt many will accept. At any affair in which the Stockton boys have a hand a good time is assured. (Say, if the overland train can get here in time, come and get the cholera morbus with us.)

"Headers."

NEWARK.

The heavy rainfall of the past two weeks has made sad havoc of Essex County's Macadam roads. Several Atalanta Wheelmen have been out to see the damage done, and have returned in disgust. "What did you see?" was asked them. "Nothing but floods, or mud where floods had been," was the only answer.

It is gratifying to know that the mud-hole on Broad Street, from Belleville Avenue to Gouverneur Street, is to be paved with Telford. More of the streets are in need of some kind of repair, and now that the great water contract is settled why not give us a much-needed improvement in street pavements?

Frank Brock, of the Atalantas, made the attempt last Sunday to climb "Eagle Rock." He succeeded in going up twice. Time for first round trip, 13 3/5m; second, 14 4/5m.

Several communications have been received regarding the A. W.'s proposed race meet. We are always willing to receive suggestions, and the undersigned would be glad to hear from anyone. Address care of The Wheel.

The Atalantas would be pleased to hear from any local club in regard to a team race of, say, five or ten miles.

Newark, N. J., August 7, 1889. Spark.

NEW ORLEANS.

The Louisiana Cycling Club now has its building scheme well advanced, and before this will have seen the light the purchase of the ground will have been effected. The site selected is a convenient one, on Octavia Street, half a square from the St. Charles Avenue (asp' a't), and something less than half a mile from Audubon Park. It consists of two lots, 30x135 each, and is in the most pleasant part of the city, in the midst of handsome, tree-embowered, large-lawned residences. The purchase price, $900, is a bargain, and no mistake, and the club will certainly be a gainer by the transaction, as the property will double its present value (which is really worth $1,200) inside two years, or I miss my guess pretty badly. The plans of the house, too, have been received from the architect, and met the approval of the club, and bids are now coming in. The building will have a frontage of 28 feet and depth of 84 feet, and consists of one story and a basement. In the latter will be located the wheel, locker, bath and janitor's rooms, while upstairs are the parlor and the reception, reading and pool rooms. The parlor is a fine, large affair, 20x40 feet, and with the sliding doors between the reception room thrown open, a dancing space of 20x58 feet can be secured. A roomy, 8-foot gallery extends half way around the house, and with a well-kept lawn or tennis court taking up the other lot, and a garden and walk the 20-feet space between the house and the sidewalk, this big gallery will add mightily to its occupants' comfort, especially during the warmer months. The house will cost something under $1,500, and, while neither grand or pretentious, it will present a neat and comfortable appearance, and when completed will be an immense feather for cycling and the club. Give the boys a pat on the back, dear WHEEL. They are working hard and altogether, and deserve every encouragement. This less-than-$3,000 house may not seem much away from here, but to us it is something big. Whoop 'er up, boys. 'Rah! 'rah! 'rah! Siss! Boom! Ta-raa-ra! Bully for you!

The Louisianas, at their last meeting (3d), elected five new members, bringing the roll up to the half-hundred mark, and postponed the adoption of a uniform until a Baltimore bidder could be heard from further.

At the same meeting the resignation of R. G. Betts as captain was accepted, and Lieut. L. J. Frederic unanimously, and with a rush, promoted to that office. Betts, who leaves on the 15th to take a position in New York City, was elected Honorary Captain.

For the vacant lieutenancy W. C. Grivot, one of the hardest workers in the club, was deservedly selected over two competitors.

Things around the New Orleans Bi. Club are quite quiet. An impromptu sparring matinee between the members enlivened matters very considerably one evening last week, and what the bouts lacked in science was made up in spiritedness. One of the boxers, so I'm told, stopped a sockdolager with his proboscis that caused him to dance a h-y-, and made his head swim so badly that gloves went off and he wanted a go *à la* Sullivan-Kilrain—bare fists—before he could be calmed down.

The second of the Hill medal five-mile races takes place on the 4th. On the same date a one-mile match race between two glimmering glims of the Louisiana Club, A. B. Harris and C. M. Shute, will be decided. It has been brewing for some time, and a medal hung up by partisans of both riders hastened matters. There is just enough of delicious uncertainty as to the respective merits of the two as to make the match of interest and speculation.

BI.

ST. LOUIS.

Last Monday's issue of the *Globe-Democrat* contained an article detailing the alleged antics of some wheelmen in Forest Park the day before. They were represented as snatching hats from the heads of pedestrians and riding off with them; riding alongside carriages and striking the horses with whips, and a lot of other stuff. Of course, the article was pure fiction from beginning to end, without the slightest basis in fact. It all originated in the diseased imagination of an unprincipled reporter. Publications of this nature, when read by persons unfamiliar with the facts and by others who have a prejudice against bicycles, are calculated to do great harm to the cause, and steps should be taken to secure their prompt denial. The *Republic*, of the week previous, printed a telegram from Manchester giving an account of the accident to the "Manchester to Barrett's" stage on Sunday afternoon, alleging that the horses were run into by a man on a bicycle, thus causing them to frighten. The *facts* are that the stage was drawn up on the edge of the road and the driver was assisting some passengers to alight. The wheelman came along and passed on the proper side, as far away from the horses as the width of the road would allow. The horses whirled suddenly and tipped the stage over the bank, wrecking the vehicle and injuring, more or less, the fifteen passengers. They all exonerated the rider from any blame, and seemed to think that the fault lay with the driver in leaving his team. Accidents on the road are always to be regretted, especially when, as in this case, they happen in a locality where there is so much animosity to bicycles. But the newspapers should not encourage this feeling by printing garbled or unfair accounts of them.

Wheelmen throughout the country will be surprised to learn that cycling is no longer to be considered as a sport, recreation, means of exercise or health restorer. It is simply an improved means of walking!!! This remarkable declaration is made in the circular issued to the members of the Missouri Bicycle Club advocating the abolition of the active list and the transfer of the club to the associate or non-riding members. It is one of the arguments (?) advanced, and the others are quite as brilliant. It is not offered as an opinion or a suggestion—it is put to us as a matter of *fact*. The man who wrote that circular has missed his calling; he ought to set himself up as a professional humorist and get the ebullitions of his mighty intellect syndicated *à la* Bill Nye, and when he dies he ought to have a "monument of jackasses' skulls" as high as the court-house. The club will be remiss in its duty if it does not attend to this.

The committees are hard at work on the race meeting, and the programme will be duly announced in a few days. The list of prizes will be given at the same time, and the necessary information relative to entries, etc. Chairman Davol has not been heard from in the matter of the League championship, but if there are any left we are pretty sure to get one. The local men have already begun training, and the track is in fine condition.

ITHURIEL.

TACOMA, WASHINGTON.

The boys repeated last Sunday's run yesterday, and again went to the Woolen Mills, on Steilacoom Creek. The day could not have improved upon, although several portions of the road were quite sandy, and caused much anxiety to arise in the minds of the several novices who accompanied us. As before, the boys took ample luncheon, and had no reason to complain of bad appetites. After the noonday repast, some of the boys tried their luck at fishing for brook trout, with varying success; Prince Wells, however, showed his superiority (?) as a scientific fly-caster, and landed the majority of the speckled beauties.

Halsted and Prince Wells will make a three weeks' trip through Oregon, Washington and part of British Columbia, to start in about two weeks. Prince will give exhibitions of fancy riding in all the towns along their route, and will also make a match with any owner of a trotting horse for any distance over five miles. Halsted will ride in all amateur races, and in a few instances, has arranged to ride five mile races against three men—who can relieve each other at the end of every mile. At Portland, Oregan, and Victoria, British Columbia, special arrangements are being made to have a Japanese lantern parade, club drill and a few other attractions, in addition to races and the fancy riding of Wells.

While in Victoria on the Queen's recent birthday (May 24) Wells made many friends, one and all of whom want him to repeat his performance in their city as soon as he can conveniently go up there. On the 24th of May he gave his exhibition on the grass, and was much hamperrd by the very uneven condition of the turf. The next time his performance will be given in the Assembly Hall, where he will surely paralyze the people of that sleepy town—for the last time they plainly showed their utter amazement. Some of the Eastern boys will recall one of the first Springfield meets when Dan Canary opened the eyes of the visiting English racing men and their attendants, by his many tricks on one and two wheels. At that time, our cousins from across the great pond would not believe what they had read of American fancy riders, and even after seeing Dan ride they entertained serious doubts as to their mental conditions. Many of our British friends across the line had to see Wells ride to be fully convinced.

The Victoria boys are becoming greatly enthused over the idea of Halsted's proposition to ride five miles against three of their men—allowing them to relieve each other as before stated. Halsted will surely have his hands full to cross the tape first; but as the races are to be in the hall, the track will measure about fourteen laps to the mile, and as Halsted claims that he used to know how to climb around the corners, he stands a good chance of winning.

I hear with regret that Harley Hays and Bert Manning will leave Tacoma about the first of September to finish their college days. While sorry to lose them, even for a year, still the knowledge that they will return, having grown in both wisdom and physique—is sufficient to warrant our wishing them God speed and a quick return.

SNOHOMISH.

July 20, 1889.

BROOKLYN NOTES.

It has been widely reported that all the athletic clubs will have a bicycle team to represent them next season, which means that bicycle clubs in this vicinity must give up all their aspirations to shine upon the race path, save in the rare instance where the love of the sport prevents a man from identifying himself with these "semi-professionals," as it is an admitted fact that the ranks of the athletic clubs are recruited from amongst the fast riders of bicycle clubs, who have fostered the sport. Note that as soon as a man has become fast, and his club-mates have sung his praises, how the athletic club bobs up serenely, and by an offer of expenses paid scoops him in. Ah! what a multitude of things are covered by—"expenses paid." The young and enthusiastic racer who trains himself stands no chance with the skillfully trained representative of an athletic club. It is an unfair battle, and can only be equalized by classifying the racers of the future.

What a disappointment last week was to the eager seekers after club mileage medals. July rained itself out, leaving a large number many miles short of their expectations.

Captain Powers, of the Riverside Wheelmen, and a number of his club-mates, were met on Sunday last by Messrs. Hebert, Star, Moore and Raymond, of the B. B. C., and escorted to Bath, where a swim and dinner was had. Afterward the party, which had been increased by other members of the B. B. C., rode to the Brooklyn's club-house, and the visitors were entertained there until it was time to leave for home.

Mr. Frank Demarest, an ex-member of the B. B. C., has organized a club at Englewood, N. J., at which place he now resides. The name is to be the Englewood Bicycle Club. May they prosper beyond their most sanguine expectations.

ATOL.

BUFFALO.

Two of the Crescent Wheelmen, of Cincinnati, Messrs. Fred. Allsup and George Bauers, were in town Saturday. They started for home Sunday morning.

There have been but few tourists through Buffalo this year compared with the number who have visited here in years past. Perhaps many are holding back for the purpose of taking in the city during the International Fair. They may rest assured that they will be well provided for, though there will be no tournament this year. But just wait for next year! and Buffalo will show something unequaled in the history of the past.

The "illustrations" of the *Wheelmen's Gazette* for July have been the cause of many smiles. Perhaps the Star Company does not patronize the Indianapolis pamphlet as it should. The best Star rider on a crank, and with a moustache! It caused some of Wilhelm's old Buffalo friends to question the whyfore, but the next issue of THE WHEEL enlightened them.

Seventy starters are expected to commence the second century run of the Ramblers this year. It will occur on the 18th inst.

The Zigzags and Buffalos also have century runs announced for this month. The Buffalo-Erie course is an excellent one.

The Lockport Wheelmen have arranged an attractive programme for their fourth annual meet, which occurs on August 13. Many local men will compete and a large delegation will attend.

ZO.

MINNEAPOLIS.

The 25-mile State championship race, which was postponed July 25, occurred on Wednesday July 31st, on the boulevard around Lake Harriet. The distance around the lake is a little less than three miles, and nine laps were required to make twenty-five miles. The entries were as follows: J. L. Bird and E. F. Hertz, of St. Paul; W. L. Day, P. A. Meyers, E. J. Hale, Cohe Bell, J. R. Stockdale, E. B. Tunstead, James Gray, Alex. Graham, F. E. Stockdale and P. Walsh. E. F. Hertz did not start owing to illness. The start was made at 3:30 o'clock, Bird taking the lead, followed closely by Hale, Bell and Stockdale. About a quarter of a mile from the tape Graham and Gray collided, breaking some spokes from Graham's wheel. Graham walked back to scratch intending to give up the race, but was induced to take another wheel and go on. He lost six minutes in making the change of mind and wheel, but, encouraged by some of his friends, rode hard and gained fourth place, making the best time of any. During the first lap the riders were well bunched, but in the second began to scatter out, Bird and James Stockdale taking a lead of about a quarter of a mile, and remaining there until the sixth, when Bell began to close up on them and in the eighth lap gained the lead, Bird second, Stockdale third, Hale fourth, the others scattered around the course.

In the ninth lap Bell held the lead, Bird and Stockdale striving for second place. On the home stretch Bell was thirty feet in the lead of Bird, Stockdale ten feet behind Bird. When Bell crossed the tape Bird and Stockdale were even, when Stockdale spurted and crossed the tape five or six feet ahead of Bird, who, not knowing "Jimmy" was quite so near, had not put in his final spurt.

Bell's time was 1h. 38m. 45s.; Stockdale, 1h. 38m. 50s.; Bird, 1h. 38m. 50⅗s.; Graham, 1h. 4?m. 16s., including six minutes lost.

The time was not remarkable, but considering the state of the road and a strong wind was very good. I have been over the course since the race, and am surprised that the time was as good.

There are some whisperings that Bird will challenge Bell to ride the same distance again.

I hear that Bell is going to Oregon to engage in business. If he does it will give some of the other boys an opportunity to win a race, Bell having heretofore proved a little too much for any of them.

DOBSON.

August 5.

HARRISBURG.

PARADE AND BANQUET.

The Harrisburg Wheel Club celebrated its third anniversary Monday evening, August 5, in a most auspicious manner. A parade was the first feature of the programme, in which nearly all the members participated, making a grand success of it. It being the evening for our regular monthly meeting, we returned to the club-rooms and transacted the necessary business.

After adjournment we proceeded to the Bolton House, where an elegant banquet awaited us.

After the banquet cigars were passed around and the toasts began. The L. A. W. was responded to by Dr. G. N. Gorgas, who referred to the influence exerted and how much was gained by the concerted action of the League. "Our Highways" was responded to by H. B. Gerhart, who spoke of the bad condition of the majority of our highways, and closed with an original poem. "The Star" was responded to by H. W. Stone, who regretted that there were not more in use in our city. "The Safety" was responded to by J. C. Duke, who claimed that there never was a wheel put on the market that has won such universal popularity as this machine. "The Wheelmen's Wives and Wheelmen's Sweethearts" was responded to by Thos. S. Peters, who advised all wheelmen to join the benedicts. Chas. R. Kees answered to "Father Time," and rejoiced that none of our members had yet been run down by this ancient old man. "Our Associate Members" was responded to by H. A. Chayne in an appropriate style. President Lusk closed with a brief history of the club from its organization to the present time.

A more delightful occasion cannot be imagined, and at 2 o'clock A. M., after giving the "club yell" with great emphasis, we retired to our homes as happy a set of wheelmen as you ever saw.

N. O. REMARKS.

August 6, 1889.

ELIZABETH.

The regular monthly meeting of the E. W. was held at the club-house on Tuesday evening last, and a number of important subjects were discussed and disposed of. The committee appointed to find a suitable building lot reported progress. The President appointed the entertainment committee for the winter, and the road officers were authorized to get up a lantern parade to be held in the latter part of October.

Several bonds were drawn, paid and canceled, and the Treasurer reported a good balance.

Messrs. N. H. White and A. N. Calkens made a run to Long Branch on Sunday last, visiting Red Bank, Ocean Beach, etc. Dinner was taken at the Branch, and the return was made to Elizabeth via the 10.30 P. M. train. They enjoyed the trip thoroughly, but reported plenty of road hogs.

If the ticket which is before the Division at present is elected, it is the general opinion here that L. A. W. affairs in New Jersey will be boomed as they have never been boomed before.

The prospect of soon having our new roads is very encouraging. The contract for the new turnpike between Elizabeth and Rahway has been awarded, and the work will be finished by October. The contracts for the Plainfield and Morris Avenue turnpikes are still open for bids. With the increased facilities for wheeling that Elizabeth will have in the near future, it ought to become one of the cycling centres in the Union, and we believe that it will.

The sidewalk fiend has been getting in his baneful work in our fair city, and, as usual, the club gets the blame. The club has actually forbidden sidewalk riding in certain districts, and will aid in the arrest of any wheelman caught there.

"TANGLEFOOT."

Mr. Stevenson Towle, a member of Tammany, has been appointed consulting engineer to the Public Works Department, having special charge of street pavements. Mr. Towle was at one time a Park Commissioner.

FIXTURES.

August 5, 1889.—At Interstate Fair Grounds, Trenton, N. J.; 2-mile Bicycle Handicap and 2-mile Bicycle New Jersey State Championship. Entries close July 29th, with W. V. Blake, 146 Monmouth Street, Trenton, N. J. Entry fee, 50 cents.

August 8, 9, 10, 1889.—Annual Meet of Massachusetts Division L. A. W., at Cottage City.

August 10, 1889.—Races at Cottage City. Entries close August 8, with C. S. Davol, Hotel Naumkeag, Cottage City.

August 10, 1889.—Bicycle Races of Massachusetts Division L. A. W. at Cottage City, Martha's Vineyard.

August 10, 1889.—Mercury Wheel Club's Outing, at Flushing, L. I.

August 14, 1889.—Queens Athletic Club Grounds, at 4:30 P. M., 1-mile Handicap. Entries close, Aug. 17, with Thos. Lloyd, Queens, N. Y.

August 14, 1889.—Walontha Wheelmen's Race Meet and Road Race, at Richfield Springs, N. Y. Entries close with Fred. Bronner.

August 15, 1889.—Race Meet of Lockport, N. Y., Wheelmen.

August 17, 1889.—At Washington Park, Brooklyn, N. Y. Prospect Harriers Games. One and two mile Bicycle Handicap and Triangular Race.

August 17, 1889.—South End Wheelmen's, of Philadelphia, 10-mile Road Race over the Montgomery Course.

August 18, 1889.—Second Century Run of the Buffalo Ramblers, from Erie to Buffalo.

August 22, 1889.—East Greenwich, Conn., Handicap Road Race.

August 24, 1889.—Montreal Bicycle Club's Annual Race Meet on the M. A. A. A.'s new grounds.

August 24, 1889.—Fifty-mile Bicycle and 1-mile Dwarf N. C. U. Championships at Paddington, Eng.

August, 1889.—Scranton Club's Tour, Scranton, Pa., to Utica, Springfield, New York, Catskills, Delaware Water Gap. Address, B. P. Connolly, Secretary.

August 31, 1889.—Brooklyn Bicycle Club and Kings County Wheelmen's combined run to Massapequa, L. I.

August 31, 1889.—Monster Run of Brooklyn Wheelmen to Hotel Massapequa.

August 31, 1889.—Missouri Bicycle Club's Races, at St. Louis, Mo.

August 31, 1889.—Albany Wheelmen's Tournament. Entries close August 24, with W. B. Phipps, 51 Howard Street, Albany, N. Y.

August 31, 1889.—Passaic County Athletic Association's Bicycling Tournament at Clifton, N. J., Race Track. Entries close August 20, with Charles Blizard, 318 Gregory Street, Passaic N. J.

September 2, 1889.—Pennsylvania State Division L. A. W. Meet at York, Pa.

September 2, 1889.—Pennsylvania Division Meet at Reading, Pa.

September 2-3, 1889.—Amateur Race Meet of the Hartford Wheel Club, at Hartford, Conn. Entries to be made with W. M. Francis, Secretary, P. O. Box 745.

September 3, 1889.—Hartford Wheel Club's 20-mile Road Race.

September 7, 1889.—Berkeley Athletic Club's Race Meet at Berkeley Oval, Morris Dock, New York City.

September 7, 1889.—A. A. U. Games at Brooklyn A. A. grounds; 1-mile Handicap. Entries close August 29, with James E. Sullivan, P. O. Box 611, New York City. Fee, 50 cents.

September 7, 1889.—One-mile Bicycle A. A. U. Championship at Brooklyn Athletic Association Grounds. Entries close September 1 with J. E. Sullivan, P. O. Box 611, New York City.

September 10-11, 1889.—Binghamton Race Meet. Address E. H. Towle, Binghamton, N. Y.

September 13, 1889.—Springfield Bicycle Club's 50-mile Local Road Race and 50-mile Open Road Race, over the Springfield-Hartford course.

September 13, 1889.—At Springfield, 50-mile Road Race, open to local riders only, and 50-mile Road Race, open. Entry fee, $5, returnable to first, second and third men. Entries close September 1.

September 13-14, 1889.—New York State Division Meet at New York and Brooklyn.

September 14, 1889.—Y. M. C. A. Games; 3-mile Handicap. Fee, 50 cents. Entries close September 7, with George Pool, 150th Street, Harlem River.

September 20, 1889.—Michigan Division L. A. W. Meet at Ypsilanti, Mich.

September 21, 1889.—Michigan Division Meet races at Detroit, Mich.

September 24-27, 1889.—Hudson County Wheelmen's Races at Spring Valley Fair.

October 4-5, 1889.—Pennsylvania Bicycle Club's Tournament.

October 4-5, 1889.—Peoria Bicycle Club's Tournament, Peoria, Ills.

October 8-9, 1889.—Races at Carlisle, Pa. Address John E. Steel, Carlisle, Pa.

October 23-29, 1889.—Race Meet at Macon, Ga.

EUROPEAN CYCLING FIXTURES.

Germany.—September 15; Hanover, September 8; Cologne, August 12; Chemnitz, September 8; Frankfort-on-the-Main, September 1; Mannheim, September 8; Crefeld, September 8. Hamburg.—Altona, September 22; Bochum, August 25; Madgeburg, September 8. Denmark.—Copenhagen International Meeting, August 18

Chicago, August 7.—At 7 o'clock this morning, F. W. Van Sicklen, a bicyclist of Chicago, left this city on his wheel for Kansas City, which he expects to reach by Friday night. To do that he will have to ride 123 miles each day. Mr. Van Sicklen hopes to do this by steady, hard work.

SCRANTON BICYCLE CLUB.

ANNUAL TOUR, 1889.

Saturday, August 10.—*Leave Scranton 6 A. M. (club-house). Waverly, Harford, New Milford, 40 miles, dinner (Jay House). Great Bend, Kirkwood, Binghamton, 22 miles, night (Hotel Bennett).

†Sunday, August 11.—Leave Binghamton 6 A. M. Chenango Forks, Greene, 20 miles, dinner (Chenango House). Norwich, 22 miles, night (American Hotel).

Monday, August 12.—Leave Norwich 6 A. M. Sherburne, Earlville, Hamilton, 27 miles, dinner (Park Hotel). Utica, 29 miles, night (St. James Hotel)

Tuesday, August 13.—Leave Utica, train, 6:35 A. M. Trenton Falls, breakfast (Moore's Hotel). Utica, 17 miles, dinner (St. James Hotel). Richfield Springs, 36 miles (Darrow House).

Wednesday, August 14.—Leave Richfield Springs 9 A. M. Cooperstown, 13 miles, dinner (Hotel Fennimore). Stamford, 40 miles, night (Delaware House).

Thursday, August 15.—Leave Stamford 6 A. M. Prattsville, Hunters, Tannersville, 31 miles, dinner (—— Hotel). Haines' Falls, Kaaterskill Falls, night (Hotel Kaaterskill)

Friday, August 16.—Leave Kaaterskill Falls 6 A. M. Catskills, Hudson, 19 miles, dinner (Worth Hotel). Hillsdale, Great Barrington, 30 miles, night (Miller House.)

Saturday, August 17.—Leave Great Barrington 6 A. M. Stockbridge, Lennox, Pittsfield, 25 miles, dinner (Berkshire House). Lebanon Springs, 10 miles, night (Field's Hotel).

†Sunday, August 18.—Leave Lebanon Springs 9 A. M. Kinderhook, 20 miles, dinner (Kinderhook Hotel). Hudson, 15 miles, night (Worth Hotel).

Monday, August 19.—Leave Hudson 6 A. M. Rhinebeck, 26 miles, dinner (Rhinebeck House). Hyde Park, Poughkeepsie, 17 miles, night (Morgan House).

Tuesday, August 20.—Leave Poughkeepsie 6 A. M. Newburgh, West Point, 27 miles, dinner (West Point Hotel). Train to Tarrytown, Yonkers, Kings Bridge, New York, 25 miles, night (Grand Union Hotel).

Wednesday, August 21.—Leave New York 6 A. M. Brooklyn Riding District and Coney Island. Train to Newark, night (Continental Hotel).

Thursday, August 22.—Leave Newark 6 A. M. Orange, Milburn, Morristown, 20 miles, dinner (Park House). Dover, 12 miles, night (—— House).

Friday, August 23.—Leave Dover 6 A. M. Hopatcong, Dingmans, 34 miles, dinner (—— Hotel). Milford, 8 miles, night (Cressman House)

Saturday, August 24.—Leave Milford 6 A. M. Dingmans, Bushkill, Water Gap, 37 miles, dinner (Kittatiny House). Train to Scranton.

* While the start is made Saturday, some will join by train, Monday, at Norwich; Tuesday, at Utica, via D. L. & W.; Wednesday, at Cooperstown, via D. & H.

† Those who rest on Sunday, August 11, at Binghamton, leave Binghamton, D. L. & W. R. R., Monday, 4:30 A. M., overtaking party at Norwich. Those resting Sunday, August 18, at either Pittsfield or Lebanon Springs, take Boston & Albany Railroad and overtake party at Hudson or Rhinebeck.

THE HARTFORD TOURNAMENT.

The Wheel Club men have been very busy the last few weeks getting things in shape for the September races, and have already got a great amount of the detail work out of the way. Entry blanks have been in great demand among the racing men, and a host of new riders have been heard from, indicating that a larger field will strive for the honors. However, the local flyers don't intend to get left, and Wm. J. Corcoran, the crack Yale trainer, has been engaged for the Wheel Club team, and has already taken charge of his men. The Charter Oak Park track, a noted fast one, will be better than ever this year, and no pains will be spared to make its condition perfect.

The railroad facilities are excellent, and excursion rates from Meriden, New Haven, Springfield and other places will be very reasonable.

The meet of the Connecticut Division, L. A. W., to be held in Hartford at the time of the tournament, will add greatly to the wheelmen's enjoyment. On the morning of the first day, Monday, September 2, a parade will be given, in which four or five hundred men will appear. Three prizes, the first presented by the Hartford Wheel Club, and the others by the Connecticut Division, will be offered visiting clubs for largest number of men and for best appearance.

In the evening an elaborate entertainment will be given at Germania Hall, under the auspices of the Division. This will consist of refreshments, peculiar to the cyclists' taste and fancy, supplemented by a concert of Weed's full military band, exhibition of boxing, club swinging, Glee Club songs and other attractions.

On Tuesday morning a run will be made to Wethersfield, where a lunch will be served at the residence of the Division's Secretary-Treasurer.

CYCLISTS' MEET AT READING, PA.

READING, August 3, 1889.

The bicycle meet at the Yellow House to-day was attended by a large number of wheelmen and admirers of the sport, and a great deal of enthusiasm was manifested which was dampened, however, by the heavy rains, which compelled the postponement of some of the most interesting events.

The first race, novice, half-mile, was won by Dundore, of Reading, in 1m. 38½s. The 1-mile, three minute class, by Z. H. Miller, of Lancaster, with Kilmer, of Reading, a close second. Time, 3m. 23½s. The 1-mile safety race came next, but just as the start was about to be made it began to rain hard. After the shower was over the race was run, and was won by Taxis, of Philadelphia, in 3m. 55s. The 1-mile handicap was a very interesting event, Taxis, who started from scratch, winning in 3m. 21s. At this point the rain again began to pour, compelling a postponement of the other events.

Detroit A. A. games, held at Detroit August 3.—One-mile handicap: G. O. Lane, 100 yards, 3m. 27s.; G. W. Jones, scratch, second, by two lengths.

ENGLISH AMATEUR CHAMPIONSHIPS.

A GERMAN WINS THE ENGLISH BLUE RIBBON—RECORDS IN THE SAFETY RACE.

The one-mile bicycle and twenty-five mile safety English amateur championships were decided at Paddington Recreation Grounds on July 20. The German, Lehr, furnished a complete surprise by winning the one-mile event—the first time it has ever gone out of the country—beating Osmond, Synyer and other first-class men. The details of the race are as follows; Heat 1: H. Synyer, 2m. 48 1-5s.; F. J. Archer, 2d. Heat 2: F. J. Osmond, 2m. 51 2-5s; S. E. Williams, 2d. Heat 3: A. Lehr, Frankfort, Germany, 2m. 48 1-5s.; E. Osmond, 2d. Heat 4: W. A. Illston, 2m. 44s.; B. Hincliffe, 2d. Final Heat: Lehr, 1st; F. J. Osmond, 2d, by five yards; Synyer, 3d, by six yards; Illston, by twenty yards. Time, 3m. 09 4-5s.

The start was very slow, Synyer leading. When the bell rang Lehr rushed into the inside berth, and quickening his pace wonderfully, had a fifteen-yard lead entering the straight. Osmond made a great rush, passing Illston and challenging Synyer. Both traveled faster than Lehr, but he had had too much advantage, and they were unable to reach him, Osmond riding second by about five yards. Lehr's last quarter occupied 34 1-5s., and Osmond, with the wind against him, rode in about 33s. for that distance. Osmond and Synyer were intently watching each other, or they would not have allowed the German to get so far away. The English papers report that Lehr rode an inferior-looking German-made wheel, with the saddle far back and with 4½-inch crank throw.

PREVIOUS WINNERS.—PLACE.

1878. Hon. Ion Keith Falconer, Stamford Bridge.
1879. H. L. Cortis, Stamford Bridge.
1880. C. E. Liles, Stamford Bridge.
1881. G. L. Hillier, Belgrave Grounds.
1882. F. Moore, Aston Lower Grounds.
1883. H. W. Gaskell, Crystal Palace.
1884. H. A. Speechly, Lillie Bridge.
1885. S. Sellers, Aston Lower Grounds.
1886. P. Furnivall, Jarrow Track.
1887. W. A. Illston, Aston Lower Grounds.
1888. H. Synyer, Coventry Track.

OTHER CHAMPIONSHIP EVENTS.

Five-mile tricycle championship.—H. H. Sansom, Nottingham, 17m. 15 3-5s.; E. B. Turner, Ripley Road Club, and Scheltema, Beduin, dead heat for second place; Louis Stein, Frankfort, Germany, 4th. Last quarter, 37 1-5s. Two of the trial heats were run in 15m. 40 3-5s. and 15m. 24 3-5s.

Twenty-five mile bicycle championship.—F. J. Osmond, 1st; F. P. Wood, 2d; D. McRae, 3d; J. H. Adams, 4th. Time, 1h. 18m. 27 2-5s.

Twenty-five mile safety amateur championship.—F. J. Fletcher, 1st; Louis Shute, 2d; W. C. Jones, 3d. Time, 1h. 16m. 34 2-5s. Records made: 22 miles, C. W. Nettleton, 1h. 07m. 18 3-5s.; 23 miles, W. C. Jones, 1h. 10m. 33 2-5s.; 24 miles, R. Burns, 1h. 13m. 41 3-5s.; 25 miles, F. J. Fletcher, 1h. 16m. 34 2-5s.

EAST GREENWICH WHEELMEN'S HANDICAP ROAD RACE.

A meeting of East Greenwich bicyclists was held at the Updike House, last Monday evening, to consider the advisability of holding a handicap road race from Cundall's drug store, on Main Street, that village, to the blacksmith shop, near Silver Hook, and return. There was no adverse opinion advanced, and the meeting was called to order and Charles H. Weld elected Chairman. Other officers were chosen as follows: Secretary, V. J. Briggs; Treasurer, Thomas B. Boardman; Committee to appoint starter, timer, judges, etc., and to fix rules for the race, James E. McKenna, V. J. Briggs, Sandy Powers. The race will be ridden on Thursday, August 22, starting at 5 o'clock in the afternoon. There will be two prizes, the first of which will be valued at twice the second. It is not yet decided what the prizes will be. The Secretary received the names of nine riders who wish to enter the race, and of this number Charles H. Weld, Walter S. Weeden and Thomas B. Boardman were elected to choose a committee of three from the local riders to arrange the handicap. The next meeting will be held at 8:30 P. M., August 7, in Firemen's Hall.

RACES AT TRENTON, N. J., AUGUST 6.

Two events were decided at the Sir Charles Napie Lodge picnic August 6. Summary:

TWO-MILE BICYCLE HANDICAP, OPEN.—L. L. Clarke, B. A. C., 30 yards, time, 7m. 10s.; J. R. Hazleton, Smithville, 125 yards, second; J. R. Sutterley, Trenton, 100 yards, third. The other starters were: A. H. Rogers, Trenton, 125 yards; W. H. Ash, Ballwin, 125 yards; C. H. Rogers, Trenton, 125 yards; George A. Rogers, Trenton, 125 yards; A. A. Zimmerman, Freehold Cyclers, 25 yards; Z. R. Hinkle, 125 yards; A. W. Shinn, Mount Holly, 125 yards

TWO-MILE HANDICAP, OPEN TO NEW JERSEY CYCLISTS.—The entries were: William Lamb, Mount Holly, 35 yards; Z. R. Hinkle, Smithville, 125 yards; L. L. Clarke, N. J. S. L., 30 yards; A. A. Zimmerman, Freehold, 25 yards; J. R. Hazleton, Smithville, 125 yards; Job R. Sutterley, Trenton, 100 yards; C. H. Rogers, Trenton, 122 yards; A. W. Shinn, Mount Holly, 125 yards. Won by Hazleton in 7m. 22 4-5s.

BICYCLE RACE AT QUEENS.

Mr. Lloyd is indefatigable in his efforts to help wheeling. At his grounds on Saturday last a 1-mile handicap was run. Of twenty-two entries but nine starters appeared. Three showers in the early part of the day spoiled the track. Summary: First heat C. M. Murphy, K. C. W., 30 yards, time, 3m. 07¼s.; A. A. Zimmerman, F. C., 45 yards, time, 3m. 07 4-5s.; R. A. Kissam, Q. B. C., 90 yards; G. W. Donner, Q. C. W., 110 yards. Second heat—L. L. Clarke, B. A. C., 40 yards, time, 3m. 07s.; N. F. Waters, B. B. C., 60 yards, 3m. 07⅖s.; G. Boyce, Q. B. C., 100 yards; T. J. Hall, K. C. W., 60 yards; Lew. R. Doughty, Jr., Q. B. C., 125 yards. Final Heat—C. M. Murphy, 30 yards, first, time, 3m. 11s.; L. L. Clarke, 40 yards, second, time, 3m. 11 3-5s.; N. F. Waters, 60 yards, third; A. A. Zimmerman, 45 yards, fourth.

A 1-mile ordinary and a 2-mile safety handicap will be held at Oak Island Grove, Revere, Mass., August 13.

New York State Division L.A.W.

OFFICIAL ORGAN.

OFFICERS FOR 1889.

Chief Consul, W. S. BULL, 754 Main Street, Buffalo, N. Y. Vice-Consul, M. L. BRIDGMAN, 1255 Bedford Avenue, Brooklyn, N. Y. Secretary-Treasurer, GEO. M. NISBETT, 50 Wall Street, New York City. Executive and Finance Committee, W. S. BULL, M. H. BRIDGMAN, DR. GEORGE E. BLACKHAM, Dunkirk N. Y.

NEW YORK STATE DIVISION FALL MEET.

SEPTEMBER 13 AND 14, NEW YORK AND BROOKLYN.

EXECUTIVE COMMITTEE.

M. L. Bridgman, 1255 Bedford Avenue, Brooklyn, Chairman.

W. H. DeGraaf, 47 West Fourteenth Street, Treasurer.

J. M. Shaw, 19 West Fifty-third Street, New York City, Secretary.

A. B. Barkman, 241 Broadway, New York City.

J. C. Gulick, 28 West Sixtieth Street, New York City.

SUB-COMMITTEE CHOSEN.

Entertainment, W. H. DeGraaf, 47 West Fourteenth Street.

Transportation, G. R. Bidwell, 313 West Fifty-eighth Street.

Programme, C. A. Sheehan, 5 Vanderbilt Avenue.

Press, F. P. Prial, P. O. Box 444.

Reception, L. A. Clarke, 25 Broad Street.

Tours and Runs, A. B. Barkman, 241 Broadway.

Theatre Party, W. H. DeGraaf, 47 West Fourteenth Street; Bert Cole, 62 Hanson Place, Brooklyn.

PROGRAMME.

FRIDAY, SEPTEMBER 13.

Morning—Reception of visitors.
Afternoon—Runs, Park, Yonkers, etc.
Night—Theatre Party, New York City.

SATURDAY, SEPTEMBER 14.

Morning—Parade in Central Park.
Afternoon—Run to Brooklyn and Prospect Park.
" —Run to Coney Island.
" —Supper at Coney Island.
" —Concert at Gilmore's Amphitheatre.

SUNDAY, SEPTEMBER 15.

Informal runs to Yonkers, Tarrytown, The Oranges and points on Long Island.

The General Committee report that all arrangements are being perfected and that a first-class meet is assured. Wheelmen from all over the country are invited to attend.

BOARD OF OFFICERS' MEET.

BROOKLYN, N. Y., August 10, 1889.

Notice is hereby given that the Annual Meeting of the Board of Officers, New York State Division, will be held at the Grand Union Hotel, Friday, September 13, 1889, 6:30 P. M. This notice is given pursuant to Article 2, Section 1, of the Constitution.

M. L. BRIDGMAN, Vice-Consul.

To the Members of the New York State Division and to Proprietors of League Hotels:

At a considerable outlay of time and labor I have succeeded in securing an advantageous contract with the official hotels in this Division. Some complaints have been made that L. A. W. members have not, in some cases, been accorded that treatment at certain of such hotels to which they are entitled. I am in readiness at all times to investigate all such complaints, and do my best to remedy them.

On the other hand, complaints have also been made that L. A. W. members did not, in some cases, always conduct themselves with proper decorum. I am informed by a League member that recently, at Van Buren Point, one of the pleasantest and most popular summer resorts in Western New York, and one largely patronized by wheelmen, the conduct of some wheelmen was such that the proprietor took down his League certificate in disgust. On account of the conduct of some wheelmen at this same resort last year, it was with a good deal of hesitation, and only after considerable persuasion, that the proprietor of this place signed the contract for this year.

The large majority of our members are gentlemen who know how to conduct themselves, and have a proper regard for the rights of others; but, as in all other large organizations, there will occasionally creep in disturbing and undesirable elements. One rowdy can do more to injure the good name of the organization than a score of gentlemen can do to build it up, and it is certainly unjust that the conduct of the few should be taken as indicating the character of the majority of those composing the organization. In justice to the vast majority of the League members of this Division, I shall endeavor to take steps to avoid any such result, and, if necessary, shall take steps to secure the expulsion from the L. A. W. of members who, by their conduct at League hotels, disgrace themselves and bring reproach upon the organization.

I urgently request all proprietors of League hotels, and all members of the League who have the best interests of the organization at heart, to immediately report all such cases to me.

Very respectfully,
W. S. BULL,
Chief Consul.

THE ANNUAL STATE MEET.

To the Members of the New York State Division:

Pursuant to Section 1 of Article 2, New York State Division By-laws, the Executive Committee have decided to hold the annual meetings of the Division and of the Board of Officers in New York City and Brooklyn, Friday and Saturday, September 13 and 14, 1889.

Cordial invitations to entertain the Division were also received from Binghampton, Richfield Springs and Niagara Falls.

An efficient committee have the matter in charge and are preparing an enjoyable programme.

It is desired that every member that can do so will attend the meet, as matters of great importance will be considered at the meetings

THE DIVISION HAND-BOOK BOOM—THE MEMBERSHIP.

I have caused to be mailed to 6,000 wheelmen in this State "The Hand-book of the New York State Division," enclosing with each book an application blank and an addressed envelope to the Secretary of the League.

Having placed in the hands of these wheelmen this book, showing the objects and advantages of the organization, I call upon all officers and members to use a little personal effort to induce non-league wheelmen to join the L. A. W.

The membership roll of the Division shows the renewals this year to be 212 less than last year. In the Second District the loss was 233. It will be seen from this showing that while we have gained in other sections the loss in Brooklyn more than overbalanced the gains.

The officers and League workers in Brooklyn are urgently requested to put forth every effort to make up this loss.

CHIEF CONSUL'S CHANGE OF ADDRESS.

As I will be absent from Buffalo between the following dates, viz., August 8 to 25, all communications between those dates requiring immediate attention should be addressed to W. S. Bull, care of P. O. Box 353, Milwaukee, Wis.

FIVE-MILE BICYCLE STATE CHAMPIONSHIP.

The five-mile bicycle New York State Division championship is hereby assigned to the Waiontha Bicycle Club, of Richfield Springs, to be competed for at their race meet, August 14, 1889.

Yours fraternally,
W. S. BULL, Chief Consul.

WHEEL GOSSIP.

The Australian 100-mile bicycle road record has been lowered to 7h. 53m.

The Toronto Bicycle Club will hold its race meet at Rosedale on Friday next.

The Rambler Bicycle Club, of Buffalo, had a great lantern parade on Wednesday night.

Furnival, Gatehouse and Webber were interested spectators of the English championship races.

Buffalo will have another fine road out of the city on Seneca Street, which is being asphalted.

The New York Bicycle Co.'s "General Information" pamphlet is unique and of much value to wheelmen.

W. Price, fifty yards start, won a mile bicycle handicap at the Paddington track on July 18; time, 2m. 31 2-5s.

The Berkeley Club are making great efforts for the success of their tournament, to be held at Berkeley Oval on September 7.

The hotel at Freeport, L. I., is "Scott's," right near the shore. The landlady is polite, the dinner excellent, the price fifty cents.

The combined run of the K. C. W. and B. B. C. to the Massapequa on August 31 will be one of the pleasantest cycling events of the season.

The Press Cycling Club, of Boston, rode to Great Head, Winthrop, on Sunday. Edward F. Draper, of the Boston *Herald*, entertained the party at Ocean Spray.

W. I. Harris and Mrs. Harris and Dr. Wells, of the Citizens' Club, started on Sunday last for a trip to Williamstown, Mass. Mr. and Mrs. Harris are on a tandem.

Ralph Temple made his first appearance on the English path at Leicester, on August 3. Temple rode ten miles in 32m. 14s., beating Howell and others. The race was probably a "fake."

The entries for the Prospect Harriers' 2-mile handicap close August 10, with F. G. Webb, 736a Union Street, Brooklyn, N. Y. The race will be run at Washington Park on August 17.

The White Cycle Company no doubt found that "Jack" had endeared himself to them. Their conduct of the last rites was extremely creditable. They showed their kindness throughout.

Lehr, the English one-mile bicycle champion, is a pale, slight, stoop-shouldered fellow, about nineteen years of age. The wheel he rides is a combination of the Royal Mail, Club and Rudge.

Had "Jack" returned home on Sunday night, he would have written us an article advocating Chief Consul Mott for the Presidency of the L. A. W. He was enthusiastic over the little Field Marshal. He had the "ear-marks."

Among the wheelmen who were at the Casino in the Park on Sunday last was a thing in a tight-fitting jersey suit and blue plush trunks; no coat, no knee-pants. Such things should be shot on sight. Wheelmen should hoot jays of that sort.

BICYCLE STOLEN.

H. J. Paine, 327 Juneau Avenue, Milwaukee, Wis., reports the loss of a Victor Safety, No. 2269, style, 1889. The wheel disappeared August 5, at 8:30, from Jenning's Resort on the Whitefish Bay Road.

W. D. Supplee, ex-Captain of the Pennsylvania Club, has become a prominent member of the Supplee Hardware Company, a large Philadelphia concern. This engrossment in business was the principal cause of Mr. Supplee's retirement as Captain of the Pennsylvania Club.

In our advertising pages Messrs. Wm. Read & Sons announce that they will accept high grade wheels in exchange for new mail safeties, and that they have for sale a few second-hand safeties in good condition. A list of second-hand wheels wanted and for sale will be sent upon application.

A Hagerstown cyclist, riding on the sidewalk, ran into a citizen. The citizen believed that the accident was unintentional and refused to prosecute. There is no reason why any cyclist should ride on the Hagerstown sidewalks when the roads are so good. The cyclist should have been arrested.

LONG ISLAND WHEELMEN NOTES.

The club meeting was held Tuesday night. All was harmony. C. C. Alden has gone to Bangor, Me., for a short vacation. The highest one day's record for July is 130 miles, credited to W. Schmid. The total mileage reported for June is 11 652 miles.

The invitation to hold the New York State Division Meet at New York and Brooklyn this fall has shut out the Niagara Falls B. C. The wheelmen at the Falls were determined to have the meet, and had enough money pledged to make it a success, but the New York and Brooklyn people got their invitation in first.

You will find a complete list of names of the club members here, and I trust you will be able to send each one a copy of your paper. It is certainly the best paper of its kind that has ever found its way into Erie, and I think if the boys can only get aquainted with it, its popularity will increase rapidly. Very truly, Nette A. Preston, Erie, Pa.

Fred and Robert Coningsby leave Saturday evening on the Albany boat for a tour to the Thousand Islands. Their route lies from Albany to Schenectady, Utica, Syracuse, Watertown and Cape Vincent, N. Y. From Cape Vincent they take Boat to Kingston and to the Thousand Islands. They will return by the same route, and will be gone two weeks.

The following club runs have been called by the road officers of the Pennsylvania Bicycle Club for the balance of the month: August 4, King of Prussia via Gulf Mills, distance 28 miles; leave 10 o'clock. August 8, ladies' moonlight run out pike; leave 7:30 P. M. August 10 and 11, with Hudson County Wheelmen. August 18, Willow Grove; leave 9:30; distance 32 miles. August 25, Chester, leave 9:30; distance 28 miles.

TOURING COMPANION WANTED.

A. Nichols writes that he will tour in the Berkshire Hills and Vermont during the third or last week in August, and desires to hear from any wheelmen who would like to join him. The route will be from New York City to Hudson by steamer Saturday night, Aug. 17 or 24, as convenient, thence by wheel to Berkshire Hills and Vermont. Address 64 John Street, New York City.

The Pennsylvania Clubs' 5-mile road race for a challenge cup was run on the Lancaster pike last Saturday afternoon. The course was from General Wayne Hotel, on Bryn Mawr Avenue, to Ardmore, finishing at Overbrook. Messrs. Hill and Fuller objected to the course chosen and did not ride. S. Wallis Merrihew finished first in 16m. 30s.; B. Clarke, two minutes start, second; time, 18m. 45s.; B. F. McDaniels, scratch, 18m. 40s. Merrihew rode a light roadster, and McDaniels a safety.

George B. Hulberd, of the New York Social Club, and John B. Miley, of the Lambs' Club, on their way home from a spin up Riverside Drive Tuesday afternoon, ran into two bicycles and demolished them. The bicyclists were Isidore Lowenstein, of 122 East Fifty-ninth Street, and a young lady whose name could not be learned. Lowenstein's knee was slightly injured. The two club men were taken to the Arsenal, where Acting Captain Flock discharged them, as they promised to pay all the damages, and the bicyclists would make no charge.

The regular monthly meeting of the Board of Officers of the Massachusetts Division League of American Wheelmen was held August 3, at the Clarendon Hotel, Boston. Chief Consul Emery presided, and C. S. Howard served as Secretary pro tem. Among the representatives present were J. S. Dean, W. G. Kendall, C. G. Whitney and G. A. Perkins. The Chief Consul reported that the Division had a larger membership now than ever before. The nearest approach to the present membership was at the time of the L. A. W. meet in Boston, May, 1886. Messrs. Emery and Howard were appointed a committee to consider the advisability of publishing a hand book of the Division, which should include the constitution, by-laws, etc.—*Globe.*

WAIONTHAS BICYCLE CLUB'S RACE MEET.

The meet of this club will be held at Richfield Springs, N. Y., August 14. The following are the events:

Fifty-mile road race, half-mile club novice, one-mile novice, three-mile lap race, fancy riding, five-mile L. A. W. State championship, one-mile tandem safety bicycle, one-mile team, one-mile safety, one-mile dash (ordinaries), one hundred yards slow race, one-mile Herkimer and Otsego Counties championship, two-mile open, half-mile obstruction race, consolation race.

Howard A. Smith & Co., Newark, N. J., report an unprecedented demand for their safety bundle carriers, both for handle bar and mud guard. ***

Howard A. Smith & Co., Newark, N. J., are teaching more persons how to ride the bicycle at Oraton Hall than ever before at this season of the year. Hall open evenings. ***

Howard A. Smith & Co., Newark, N. J., have improved their Graphite for lubricating chains and bearings of bicycles and safeties, until it seems to be perfect. All riders should have a bottle. ***

W. G. Schack, of Buffalo, has an '80 mileage of 3,704.

The Pennsylvania State Division meet will be held September 9 at York, Pa.

Mr. and Mrs. W. I. Harris and Dr. Wells passed through Poughkeepsie on August 1.

The Binghamton Club will hold a meet September 10 and 11. Twelve events will be run each day.

Don't forget Schwalbach's entertainment at the Casino, 114 Fifth Avenue, Brooklyn, on Tuesday evening.

Messrs. Raymond and Potter, of the Brooklyn Bicycle Club, leave to-morrow for a tour in the Adirondacks.

John Van Benschoten, of Poughkeepsie, recently rode sixteen miles in 1h. 10m. 11s. Van Benschoten rides a 58-in. Expert.

There is talk at Poughkeepsie of holding a race meet this year, but there is so much moisture in the air that the chances are small.

Colie Bell, the Minneapolis racing man, has retired from the path, and has accepted a position with the Western Union Telegraph Co. at Olympia, Minn.

Your issue of June 28 was a great one. Let the good work go on! [Yes! Yes!—ED.]   TAM O'SHANTER.

Messrs. Schoverling, Daly & Gales report a continued demand for New Mail safeties. There are nine New Mail rear-drivers in the King's County Wheelmen's club-house.

The following members of the L. I. W. have made century runs during the year: Messrs. G. S. Teller, Wise, Alden, Parker, Schemacher, Schmid, Beecher, Ballard, Topping, Isaacsen and Cammini.

W. J. Newman, Captain of the Cambridge Club, secured a cottage for the club's use at Cottage City. Captain Newman had called the following runs: August 18, Marblehead and Neck; August 25, Great Head.

Messrs. William Halpin & Co. are now promptly filling orders for Warwick safeties and ordinaries. The Warwick Cycle Co. have two gangs of men working day and night, and are rapidly catching up with orders.

The Coventry Machinists' Co., Limited, write: "Orders are away ahead of us on Swift safeties and Ladies' Swifts there is an unusual demand for Marlboro tricycles this season. The demand for the best never ceases."

Mr. Frank Eveland and wife, of the Hudson County Wheelman, have been spending a short vacation at Hyde Park, N. Y. Both ride safeties, and are enthusiastic over the good roads about Hyde Park and Poughkeepsie.

The Montreal Bicycle Club will hold their annual race meet on Saturday, August 24, at the new Montreal A. A. A. grounds. The track is a third of a mile, and protected from the wind. Races can be held on it rain or shine.

I am sorry to see the announcement in to-day's paper of the drowning of J. Purvis-Bruce. The wheeling world loses an enthusiastic rider and writer, and literature a promising devotee.   THEODORE W. ROBERTS.
Poughkeepsie, N. Y.

Messrs. A. G. Spalding & Bros. have just delivered to Mr. J. D. Dell, of the Long Island Wheelmen, as fine a tricycle as we ever laid eyes on. It was built to Mr. Bell's order by the Overman Wheel Co. It is a three-track, with a special Victor spring fork, 30-inch wheels, geared to 42, and built very narrow. The wheel weighs but 56 pounds, and will be used by Mrs. Bell.

Messrs. Powell and Beady, K. C. W., spent Sunday and Monday at Patchogue. Beady fished all day Monday and caught a lone sea robin. While out boating with a party of young ladies, one of them upset the boat for pastime—to bear the others scream. Mr. Beady saved the lives of all the girls, and proved himself an expert and courageous swimmer. The water where the upset occurred was fully three feet, six inches deep.

G. M. Nisbett was elected captain of the New York Club on Wednesday evening, in place of J. M. McFadden, resigned. A new feature of the club-house is a choice collection of magazines, illustrated papers, etc. The club will turn out in force on Saturday afternoon to witness the race between W. C. Heydecker, N. Y. B. C., and Francis Thayer, Citizens' B. C. The start will be made from Tarrytown at 4 P. M., and the race will finish at 60th Street and Boulevard.

THE WHEEL

—AND—

CYCLING TRADE REVIEW,

Published every Friday morning.

Entered at the Post Office at second class rates.

Subscription Price, - - - $1.00 a year.
Foreign Subscriptions, - - - 6s. a year.
Single Copies, - - - - - 5 Cents.

Newsdealers may order through AM. NEWS CO.

All copy should be received by Monday.
Telegraphic news received till Wednesday noon.

Advertising rates on Application.

F. P. PRIAL, Editor and Proprietor
23 Park Row,
P. O. Box 444, New York.

Persons receiving sample copies of this paper are respectfully requested to examine its contents and give us their patronage, and as far as is convenient, aid in circulating the journal, and extend its influence in the cause which it so faithfully serves. Subscription price, $1 per year.

I consider THE WHEEL the most intelligently edited cycling paper published.
G. S. TELLER, Captain, L. I. W.

I consider THE WHEEL the best paper of the kind in this country.
FRANK H RICH,
Jackson, Mich.

TAM O'SHANTER sends us the last paper on the "Elwell Tour," which broke up at Cologne, the members of the party to travel to the four winds; some to hurry back to the grind of business, some to still further "do" Europe, others to rush back to dear "Paree." The tour has been the most successful ever organized, and Elwell has proven himself a general on the road. Some personal rivalry between the *Wheeling* "crowd" and the *Cyclist* "crowd" momentarily shadowed the pleasure of the tourists, but they swept on, all unmindful of and without entangling themselves with the local squabble. It remained for Jo. Pennell to assure us that Elwell was "all right." The reception given to the tourists from the time they set foot on the Emerald Isle until they disbanded was most flattering, not only to the tourists, but to all American cyclists. The party will return with new vigor and broader views of men, women and things.

IN the ranks of wheelmen are a very large number of men who have taken to the sport for health's sake. We know that many of them are interested in all matters relating to health and to the upbuilding of the physique. No doubt many of them have run across articles on the newly discovered "elixir of life," alleged. Out of the hundreds of papers which come into this office we have clipped everything we could find, and, after careful perusal, have come to these conclusions: Doctor Brown-Sequard, an eminent French physician of unimpeachable integrity and reputation, has been conducting experiments based on facts which could only be properly stated in the columns of a medical journal. Taking certain parts of young guinea pigs, dogs or lambs, he has pulverized them, and, with the addition of some water, has obtained a fluid which he injects hypermodically, about thirty drops at a time, on three or four consecutive days. This injection has practically the effect of a powerful stimulant. It has a general revivifying effect upon the system, and old people are practically rejuvenated, but as soon as the fluid injection is discontinued the subject returns to his former normal condition. The doctor has discovered, in effect, a powerful tonic, which might be used to tide over the crisis of a severe illness, or might be employed when the use of solid food would be advisable, or when the introduction of food into the stomach is impossible. It has yet to be decided whether, by a continued use of the stimulating injection infirm people can rebuild their system to the point when the injection would be no longer necessary. We agree with Doctor Brown-Sequard's conclusion that that is improbable, that all must obey the laws of nature, which demand disintegration.

WHEN the Elwell party were in England, some comment was made on the style, or rather lack of style, of their cycling garments. It is, therefore, amusing to learn that some smart Englishmen, not too provincial to fail to catch on to a good thing, are now riding without coats. Our correspondent, Free Lance, writes as follows:

"The English tourist a-wheel seem to have caught on to the free-and-easy style of their late visitors, the Elwell party, and many riders are now seen looking cool and happy in their shirts, who a short time ago would have thought it almost indecent to be met on the road without their heavy C. T. C. jackets on."

A RATE of a fare and a third for the round trip has been obtained for all wheelmen who attend the New York State Division Meet over the roads of the Eastern Association of Trunk Lines. It should be borne in mind by all wheelmen that no man should take advantage of this system unless he intends to return on his ticket. The Transportation Committee have agreed to redeem at the full rate all return tickets found in the hands of scalpers.

A NOTE OF WARNING.

DON'T LET THE BOYS RIDE TOO MUCH.

A little incident that occurred in this city recently is pertinent to the ever recurring discussion of the injurious results of bicycle riding. At the examination of candidates for Congressman Spooner's appointment of a cadet to the United States Naval Academy four candidates turned up, unusually small number, by the way, for this district. Three of the candidates were disqualified on their physical examination. They were young fellows 15 or 16 years old, and the trouble was varicocele. The examination disclosed that it was caused in each case by bicycle riding. The doctors are of the broadest minded of their profession, and to a member of the board of examination on the studies, himself a cycler, they gave it as their opinion that while bicycle riding was one of the most healthful of recreations it was not exempt from the rule of all athletes, that it must not be indulged too persistently by youthful and undeveloped lads. The incident is, of course, no more an argument for the injurious effects of the pastime than is the argument against rowing that it develops stoop shoulders, or any other similar claims that may be brought against any athletic sport, indoor or outdoor. At the same time it points the moral that care should be taken in the use of the wheel by young riders, as well as in the practice of any athletics by young riders. The modern system of gymnasium instruction recognizes this very principle of youthful exercise, but a great many little fellows are no doubt riding their bicycles immoderately, and parents should exercise discretion in permitting their little sons and daughters the use of the wheel.—*Providence Sunday Journal.*

TRIBUTE TO "JACK."

Sad news the above will be to all who knew Bruce personally, as well to the thousands that knew him by his brilliant writings. A sad and curious coincidence was the receipt of the telegram of inquiry from J. R. Stockdale, of Minneapolis, the previous week, where Bruce's death had been rumored (the one used in W. C. Co.'s advertisement in *Bicycling World*) Stockdale was an old chum of Bruce's when the latter lived in Minneapolis, and the poor fellow will be heartily mourned by all who knew him there. At such times it is that one feels an inability to say anything adequate to the occasion, and can only repeat the old and trite truth that the best are those chosen to go first. Perhaps, if Bruce's own views on the subject could be known, he would have preferred to die at the hands of one of the most cruel forces of that Nature he loved so well. Cycling and sporting journals will feel his loss keenly, for, like Fitz Greene Halleck, he filled a place peculiarly his own. Writers may come and go, but we shall never have another "Jack" to send in his jottings.

Sadly, L. B. G.

COTTAGE CITY MEET.

A large number of Boston cyclists left for Cottage City on the afternoon of the 7th. Chief Consul Emery and Abbott Bassett looked after the party, among whom were members of the Cambridge B. C., Somerville B. C. and Boston Club. A number of ladies were with the party. The meet was the annual gathering of the Providence and Massachusetts Divisions of the L. A. W.

MASSACHUSETTS BUSINESS MEET.

The Massachusetts Division held its annual business meet on the morning of the 6th, Chief Consul Emery presiding. Charles S. Howard, of Boston, was elected Secretary and Treasurer. The membership was reported as numbering 1,444.

THE LANTERN PARADE.

In the evening a lantern parade was held in which 900 wheelmen took part. The men formed at 8:30 at the Oak Bluff's club-house. The route was through the principal streets, which were lined with spectators. Many of the houses were illuminated in honor of the cyclists. Sterling Elliott, of Newton, received first prize for the most elaborate display, and Mr. Phillips, of Providence, second prize. On the whole, the Rhode Island Division outdid the Massachusetts boys C. H. Luscomb, President of the L. A. W., was Chief Marshal and Consul George W. Smith was Adjutant. George S. Perkins, of Cambridge, was Marshal of the Massachusetts Division and J. A. Youngman, of Providence, commanded the Rhode Island Division The judges were A. S. Mott, J. S. Dean and W. H. Emery.

A game of ball was played between a picked nine, composed of wheelmen and the Martha's Vineyard Heralds, resulting in a score of 12 to 2 in favor of the latter. The picked nine was captained by Mr. Bean, of Cambridge.

THE RACE MEET.

The races were held on the afternoon of the 10th, around Island Park, a path a trifle less than a mile around, with two sharp turns which prohibited fast work. A large number of people were present. The officials were: *Referee*, C. H Luscomb, President L. A. W; judges—J. R. Dunn, First Vice-President L. A. W.; Albert Mott, E. E. Dow; timers—C. S. Howard, Boston; G. C. Newell, Providence; W. W. Share, Brooklyn; starter—W. M. Francis, Hartford; clerk of the course—W. S. Doane, Dorchester. The events: One mile, open—First prize, gold medal; second prize, silver medal. Entries—F. A Delabarre, Conway; T. J. Kerr, Worcester; T. L. Connelly, Dorchester; B. T. Bruse, Providence. First, Delabarre, 3m.; second, Bruse, 3m. 45⅗s.

The events resulted as follows:

One mile Safety.—First prize, gold medal; second prize, silver medal. Entries—William Van Wagoner, Newport; F. L. Olmstead Jr, Brookline; W. E. McCune. First, Van Wagoner, 3m. 8 1-5s.; second, Olmstead, Jr., 3m. 13s.

Half mile, open.—First prize, gold medal; second prize, silver medal. Entries—T. L Connelly, Dorchester; E. I. Culver, Springfield; A. H. Morse, Hyde Park. First, Morse, 1m. 29 3-5s.; second, Culver, 1m. 33s.

Half mile, boy's race (boys under 12).—Entries—Frank Phillips, Albert Van Vleck. First, Phillips, 1m. 41 3-5s.; second, Van Vleck, 1m. 43s

One mile championship, Massachusetts and Rhode Island meet.—First prize, gold medal; second prize, silver medal. Entries—Van Wagoner, F. A. Delabarre, Conway; C. A. Culver, Springfield. First, F. A. Delabarre, 2m. 49 1-5s; Van Wagoner, second 2m. 50s.

Safety race.—Entries—Newman and Burns, Cambridge; Van Wagoner, Newport, and Lakey, Providence, R. I.; Jewett and Nash, Cambridge. First, Van Wagoner and Lakey, 3m. 3 3-5s.; second, Newman and Burns, 3m. 9s.

WASHINGTON PAVEMENT.

Asphalt was first laid in Washington on M Street, in 1873 at a cost of $3.50 per yard; present cost of asphalt, $2 to $2.25 per yard. An official report of Washington pavements contains the following interesting facts: Of the concrete pavement there are three kinds—the standard sheet asphalt, the coal-tar distillate and the asphalt blocks. Of the former, up to 1888, there are 31.8 miles. With this Pennsylvania Avenue, from the Capitol to the Treasury, is paved, and also Sixteenth Street. It costs about $2.25 per square yard. Owing to a recent act of Congress, however, prohibiting more than $2 per square yard to be paid for paving, the standard sheet has been compelled to give way to coal, distillate, which is somewhat cheaper. Of this there are 37½ miles, all of which have been put down in comparatively recent years. Coal-tar distillate costs $2 per square yard and is superior to the standard sheet asphalt as a paving material, in that the different layers of its composition adhere more closely, and render it less liable to wavy indentations than the latter. It is inferior, however, in being more liable to softening by a high temperature. Of asphalt blocks there are little more than five miles already laid, and what has been tried has developed remarkably good qualities, and much more will be laid in the future. In the last ten years over $3,500,000 has been expended for street improvements, and during the present year over $75,000 was appropriated for streets. Besides making the necessary repairs this will make about fourteen miles of additional streets to be constructed. The cobble-stone pavements, of which there are 12½ miles in the city, are being replaced by asphalt and granite as speedily as possible, and before very long will have entirely disappeared.

The death of few men connected with the cycle profession and sport to-day, would bring so closely a sense of personal loss to the cyclers of two nations as has the death of J. Purvis Bruce, who was drowned last Sunday. With an extraordinarily wide personal acquaintance for so young a man, thousands of cyclers who had never seen him had come to look upon "Jack" as an intimate friend, whom it would be queer if they did not recognize and greet on sight, just as queer if he should not return the greeting promptly and without surprise. Magnetic and charmingly fetching must have been the personality of this man, who could make thousands who knew him only in his free and hearty writings, with their inevitable germ of a liberal philosophy, feel a fondness for him. "Jack" was the kind of man that a work-a-day world can ill spare. He was eminently a young man, light-hearted, genial, active of body and mind, a gentleman by instincts and education, a man who must have been a delightful element in a social gathering; the kind of fellow one never thinks of as ever growing old—or dying.—*Providence Sunday Journal.*

NEW YORK STATE MEET.

New York State Division L.A.W.

OFFICIAL ORGAN.

OFFICERS FOR 1889.

Chief Consul, W. S. Bull, 754 Main Street, Buffalo, N.Y.
Vice-Consul, M. L. Bridgman, 1755 Bedford Avenue, Brooklyn, N.Y. Secretary-Treasurer, Geo. M. Ninnery, 10 Wall Street, New York City. Executive and Finance Committee, W. S. Bull, M. H. Raidgman, Dr. George E. Blackman, Dunkirk N.Y.

COMMITTEES.

EXECUTIVE COMMITTEE.
M. L. Bridgman, 1755 Bedford Avenue, Brooklyn, Chairman.
W. H. DeGraaf, 47 West Fourteenth Street, Treasurer.
I. M. Shaw, 19 West Fifty-third Street, New York City, Secretary.
A. B. Barkman, 241 Broadway, New York City.
C. C. Alden, 6 Wall Street, New York City.

SUB-COMMITTEES.
Entertainment, W. H. DeGraaf, 47 West Fourteenth Street.
Transportation, G. R. Bidwell, 313 West Fifty-eighth Street.
Programme, C. A. Sheehan, 5 Vanderbilt Avenue.
Press, F. P. Prial, P. O. Box 444.
Reception, L. A. Clarke, 25 Broad Street.
Tours and Runs. A. B. Barkman, 241 Broadway.
Theatre Party, W. H. DeGraaf, 47 West Fourteenth Street; Bert Cole, 69 Hanson Place, Brooklyn.

PROGRAMME.

FRIDAY, SEPTEMBER 13.
Morning—Reception of visitors.
Afternoon—Runs, Central Park, Yonkers, etc.
— Board of Officers meet, Grand Union Hotel.
8:30 P.M.
Night—Theatre Party, New York City.

SATURDAY, SEPTEMBER 14.
Morning—Parade in Central Park.
Afternoon—Run to Brooklyn.
— Board of Officers meet, Brooklyn Club House.
2:30 P.M.
" —Regular Division Meeting at Brooklyn Club House, 3 P.M.
" —Photograph at Prospect Park, 4 P.M.
" —Run to Coney Island.
" —Supper at Coney Island.
" —Concert at Gilmore's Amphitheatre.

SUNDAY, SEPTEMBER 15.
Informal runs to Yonkers, Tarrytown, The Oranges and points on Long Island.

TRANSPORTATION.

All members attending the Annual Meet of the New York State Division are entitled to transportation for round trip at the rate of a fare and one-third from points on the following railroads:
Baltimore & Ohio (Parkersburg, Bellaire and Wheeling, and east thereof).
Baltimore & Potomac (Parkersburg, Bellaire and Wheeling, and east thereof).
Bennington & Rutland.
Buffalo, Rochester & Pittsburg.
Camden & Atlantic.
Central of New Jersey.
Central Vermont.
Delaware & Hudson Canal Co.
Delaware, Lackawanna & Western.
Elmira, Cortland & Northern.
Fitchburg, Cortland & Northern.
Lehigh Valley.
New York Central & Hudson River.
New York, Lake Erie & Western.
New York, Ontario & Western.
Northern Central.
Pennsylvania (except locally between Philadelphia and New York).
Philadelphia and Erie.
Philadelphia & Reading (except locally between Philadelphia and New York).
Rome, Watertown & Ogdensburg (except on Phœnix Line stations between Syracuse and Oswego.
Shenandoah Valley.
Western New York & Pennsylvania.
West Jersey.
West Shore.
The tickets are to be purchased on the certificate plan, which is as follows: Each person desiring transportation at reduced rate will apply to the undersigned, who will issue a certificate, which the holder will present to the ticket agent in purchasing ticket. The ticket agent will indorse the certificate, certifying that the holder has purchased one full rate ticket to New York, and on arrival here, by presenting to the undersigned, the certificates will be duly indorsed, certifying that the holder has attended the meeting, and when presented to a ticket agent in New York for any of the above railroads will entitle him to transportation for the return trip at one-third fare.
In granting this concession, the Trunk Line Association do so on the condition that I will guarantee to redeem, at full fare, any tickets procured by persons attending our meeting that may be found in the hands of scalpers after adjournment. It is therefore necessary that the tickets issued on the certificates should be used only by our members attending the meeting and not sold to scalpers.
Yours respectfully, Geo. R. Bidwell, Com. Transportation, L. A. W.
313 West Fifty-eighth Street, New York City.

COMMITTEE MEETING AT GRAND UNION HOTEL, AUGUST 9.

An enthusiastic meeting was held at the Grand Union last Friday night. Besides the General Committee of Arrangements, a number of sub-committee men and prominent club men were present, as follows: Messrs. Bridgman (Chairman), Shaw, DeGraaf, Newborog, Miller, Powers, Newcome, Sheehan, Prial, Fuller, Clarke, Findlay, Nisbett and Shriver.
A letter of acceptance from Mr. Bull was received. L. A. Clarke, Citizens' Club, was appointed Chairman of the Reception Committee. Mr. John C. Gulick resigned from the General Committee, and at a subsequent meeting Mr. C. C. Alden, L. I. W., was elected to fill the vacancy.
A letter from G. R. Bidwell, Chairman of the Transportation Committee, was read. It contained the list of railroads which had agreed to allow a reduced rate of a fare and a third for round trip ticket to all wheelmen who attend the meet. The letter is published elsewhere in this paper.
It was decided to give two prizes for the best showing made in the parade, one for competition among the local clubs, and one for competition among the visiting clubs.
Slight alteration was made in the programme, which will be found above, as corrected and finally decided upon. An inquiry was received in regard to the race meet. The committee desire it to be generally known that it was impossible to hold a race meet on Friday with any hope of success, and that no grounds could be secured for Saturday. From the reports made by the various committee chairmen, it was seen that all the men are working earnestly, and that the meet cannot fail to be a success.

In accordance with the request of Chief Consul Bull we send copies of this week's WHEEL to all League members in the State, to inform them in brief of the programme which will be arranged for their entertainment on September 13 and 14. Later, about September 1, an official programme will be mailed to each member of the Division.
A glance over the programme printed above will show that a unique entertainment will be provided. During the month of September the weather in New York is superb, and a two days' outing in town will be a treat to any man. The committees are hard at work, and arrangements will be made for the reception and care of visitors, that confusion, rush and discomfort will be avoided.
The Reception Committee will have men stationed at all the principal railroad and steam-boat terminals for Thursday evening until all the visitors may be presumed to have arrived. They will be shown to the various hotels, and will not be discommoded by their wheels, which will be stored near the park, right at the commencement of our riding district.
On Friday afternoon informal runs will take place in the park and on the adjacent drives. The park on a September afternoon is a picture. It has very fine natural beauty, and this is enhanced by the stream of pleasure vehicles which glide along the main driveways from three until six o'clock. The roads are splendidly surfaced, with no mentionable grades. From the park one may ride without a dismount over the Riverside Drive, an avenue of much beauty, stretching three miles along the Hudson. On the one side are many residences of great architectural beauty, on the other as fine a view as can be shown in this country. At the end of the Drive is situated Grant's Tomb, which will interest all visitors.
On Friday evening a mammoth theatre party will be held, at what theatre it has not yet been decided. The entire house will be i ought up for the evening, and the show in the orchestra should rival the stage performance. The theatre party is a great institution, and no one should miss it. After the performance the local clubs will keep open house, and visitors will have an opportunity to inspect the club-houses and to make many friends among New York cyclists.
On Saturday morning the feature will be the parade, which will take place in the Park and in some of the principal uptown streets. The last parade held in New York was the greatest event of the kind ever held in this country, the appearance of the men and the uniformity of the club costumes making a splendid show. After the parade, the men will ride directly to the ferry, and will be landed in Brooklyn, where dinner will be served.
The business meeting will be held at the Brooklyn Club-house, followed by a photograph in Prospect Park and a run to Coney Island. We shall not attempt to describe the beauties of this resort here. The wheelmen will have dinner, will hear the concert at Gilmore's, and see the fireworks in Paine's inclosure. But there are a million more things to be seen at the Island, and this part of the entertainment cannot fail of being a grand success.
On Sunday a number of runs will be held. We want you, one and all, down here to the meet; not only cyclists of New York State, but from all parts of the country.

Canary sailed from England August 7.

Akron has nine lady safety riders—six unmarried, three married.

The New York Herald is agitating new pavements for the Boulevards.

Did you ever see such a column of fixtures? Who says that racing is on the decline.

A photograph of Lumsden, the Chicago crack, will be published in next week's WHEEL.

W. H. DeGraaf holds the record from Tarrytown to Yonkers, 11⅝ miles, in 50 minutes.

Candidly, did you ever see a cycling paper so crammed full of stuff? Worth a dollar a year, is it not?

The Prospect Harriers' games will be held at 2:30 P.M. to-morrow at Washington Park. A bicycle race is on the programme.

The Capital Cycle Co. have a lot of tall wheels which they are clearing out at low prices. A postal will secure a list of wheels, descriptions and prices.

Harper's Weekly of August 10 has a four-page illustrated supplement on "Roads and Road-making." It is nice, interesting and valuable to any man interested in roads.

The Board of Health of Memphis will report the cyclists of that city as public nuisances. They claim that the new club uniform is ruining the eyesight of the Memphis people. A number have already taken to blue glasses and green blinders.

In the August Century, Jo. and Mrs. Jo. Pennell have a delightful article on the Thames, "the stream of pleasure." Jo's sketches are wonderfully fine for black and white work, and Mrs. Pennell's letter-press is supple, clear and relishable, as usual.

As one of New York's lady bicycle riders was gliding along the Ocean Boulevard, at Coney Island the other day, a woman shouted out to her in a voice reeking with prudence, sanctimoniousness and shame for her sex: "Shame on you, woman!" Poor woman!

W. H. DeGraaf, L. A. Newcome and one or two other wheelmen will leave New York on Saturday morning, August 31, and ride to Canajoharie, about 100 miles. They expect to reach Canajoharie on Monday night. They will foward dispatches to the New York World from different points on the route.

Cleopatra, Queen of Sheba, Solomon in all his glory and the lily of the field are nowhere—for, list! A new club was organized at Memphis, July 21, with Julius Seelig, President; C. R. Scott, Vice-President, and R. N. Whitemore, Secretary-Treasurer. It was decided to get a club uniform of black velvet knee-pants with black silk hose, orange cap and belt, striped sack coat and patent leather lace shoes, cut low.

[VOL. III., No. 25.

W. F. MURPHY,

Kings County Wheelmen.

Winner of the Twenty-five Mile Road Race, May 30, 1889.

THE ELWELL TOURISTS IN GERMANY.

GERMAN ROADS MONOTONOUSLY FLAT.

EDITOR OF THE WHEEL:

The end of my last epistle, if I remember correctly, marked the beginning of the tour in Germany, and of the "descent on the other side" from the summit of a cycling paradise. Germany is all right, and there is no fault to be found with it, but if you are about to tour through Germany and Switzerland, be sure you take the countries in the order mentioned, or the former will have but a small place in your heart and memory when you have finished. As far as simple traveling on the road is concerned, Germany is fully equal to Switzerland, for the German roads, although not possessing as fine a surface, are as flat as a pancake from morning until night. They are monotonously flat! After a day or two of this sort of traveling, anything in the line of hills, from a covered ditch to an Eagle Rock, would be hailed with joy and ridden and re-ridden—encored, you know.

In point of grand scenery and pleasant surroundings, however, Germany is to Switzerland as a free lunch is to a Stanley Club dinner. By this it is not meant that the party found no pretty scenery nor interesting cities in Germany; far from it. But Switzerland just captured us by storm. It is not that we love Germany less, but Switzerland more.

The party has made better time and longer runs here than in any other country. At twelve minutes past ten on Sunday, July 21, the party (having collected their twenty francs at the Swiss custom house) crossed over a small stream and halted at the German station on the other side, nearly every one in Bismarck's territory for the first time in their lives. Up to this time there had during the morning been a great deal of talk and discussion as to what right the German or any other government had to tax our wheels. Some wanted to "bluff 'em"; some declared our safeties "vehicles," and "Henry George" talked a great deal about our being "free-born American citizens," all of which proved unnecessary, for the portly official, on our showing a willingness to be inspected and taxed, smiled blandly and signified that we might pass on. Giving three cheers for "his nobs," we did so in such haste that we got started on the wrong road, a fact which was discovered after we had been traveling nearly an hour, and produced a loud and general "cussing."

A GRAND FOURTEEN-MILE COAST.

Titisee was eventually reached and dinner eaten, after which we plunged into the heart of the Black Forest—the magnificent Höllenthal. For fourteen miles not a pedal was touched, and all the time we were coasting through scenery wild and grand enough to lead one to imagine himself in the middle of the Rocky Mountains and facing west. Coasting through these deep gorges and rocky cañons at a two-minute gait, expecting every minute to shoot off into nowhere, beats champagne for exhilaration every time.

THE GERMAN IDEA OF HOSPITALITY.

At Freiburg we pulled up for the night. Freiburg is an old and interesting German city, and contains quite a number of cyclists. We have since then made up our minds that it was very fortunate that these gentlemen did not know we were in town until the following morning, as they then told us that they would have gotten up some entertainment for us had they known we were there. The way Dutch cyclists get up "some entertainment" for visitors consists of taking them to their club room and placing before each of them on a table a huge mug (mug? yes, *tub!*) of German beer, which he is expected to drain every time any one says, "Your health," which is twice per minute on an average. Shades of Bacchus! The quantity of beer a German youth can get into his skin in one short hour is little less than a miracle. If a member of the party should be unfortunate enough to get entangled in one of these expressions of cordiality, he would not be able to ride for a week. The Frankfurt and Mayence boys both extended very cordial invitations to visit their cities, but the route-book says "No."

The ride from Freiburg to Strassburg, in striking contrast with the day before, was hot, dry and uninteresting until within the limits of the latter city. The entrance to Strassburg must be made with strict attention to your p's and q's. We thought we had seen soldiers in England and France, but the larger German cities are positively swarming with them. In riding in we passed over a pontoon bridge, and for half an hour steadily rode through fortification after fortification, and past file after file of the defenders of beer and pretzels. At a dozen different times we thought ourselves going wrong, but inquiry showed our path to be straight ahead up to some cannon's mouth. Uncle Sam had better keep his eyes open! These fellows seem just spoiling for a fight, and we did not feel safe until securely within the walls of our hotel.

AT STRASSBURG.

Strassburg is a very quaint old place, and brings up recollections of John L. Stoddard very clearly. It is very easy here to give credence to the pretty little legends of the storks which they used to tell us in our childhood, for the birds are to be seen here on every hand, walking about the alleyways and perched on one long leg on their nests high up on the chimney tops. It is really a wonderful sight. Looking down on the housetops from the top of the spire of the famous cathedral, a hundred of these odd-looking bipeds could be easily counted.

In the morning we shopped and saw the sights, including, of course, the famous clock, the *piece de resistance* of the city. Strassburg is one of those fine old places where you feel perfectly at home, and as though you would "like to stay a week."

After lunch we started for Baden Baden, or, as they call it here, simply Baden. It rained four times before we got there! Losing one's temper does not change the elements, and we were obliged to "do the way they do in Spain." We stood it the more good-naturedly as the visitations of *aqua pura* on our heads have been exceedingly few of late. During the first shower we sought refuge in a brewery and destroyed its net earnings for 1889. Baden, although excessively gay and popular, is not the naughty city it was in days gone by. The gaming tables, they say, are abolished, and we looked—with regretful faces, I'm afraid—about the garden and into the great hall where once the steady calls of "*rouge*" and "*noir*" held hundreds captive. We decided amongst ourselves that, judging from the looks of some of the characters to be seen about the place, it would not be so very hard to hunt up a "little game" even at this late day.

WHAT DID THE BAND PLAY?

The local cyclists exerted themselves quite a little on our behalf. At the grand concert in the evening the band played the "Star Spangled Banner" in our honor. We applauded vigorously and they played "Yankee Doodle," at which our delight found vent in cheers and yells. In the morning, accompanied by half a dozen of the Baden Club, we started out in the rain for Heidelberg, sixty miles distant. Old Sol bobbed up serenely at ten o'clock, and we had a fine run to the city of student duels (with mug as well as sword), whither we arrived about four.

Everyone was disappointed in Heidelberg. The castle is a very interesting old ruin, but otherwise the town was a complete failure. No students to be seen, no immense assortment of meerschaum pipes and loud neckties, no music, no life and no activity. We looked in vain for something of interest, and were not a bit sorry to mount the wheel for Wiesbaden at an early hour the next morning. The wind blew a gale, but was slightly in our favor, so no complaint was heard. We had worms for dinner. I mean we stopped for dinner at Worms. We sat over two hours and were only able to get our soup and two courses. We gave up in despair and took to the road.

ALONG THE RHINE.

At Mayence we commenced our run beside the Rhine, and have not been out of sight of it since. Wiesbaden is a fashionable resort, famous for its springs and baths, and is full of first-class hotels and elegant dwellings. Our hotel here was evidently not in the habit of accommodating American cyclists, and in sizing up our appetites they fell woefully short. An excellent sandwich dispensary opposite saved us from a cruel death. There is nothing of interest at Wiesbaden save its society, and we were soon on the way to Coblenz via Bingen. This day a young Dakota blizzard met us full in the face. Oh! my knees ache at the thoughts of that steady grind; six miles an hour about the best that could be done. We passed through Johanissberg and Reudesheim, celebrated for their fine wines. As we see their hillsides covered with green grapes we vow that the next time we travel through this district it shall be a month later in the season.

THE GRAPE-CLAD HILLS, BINGEN, "GERMANIA."

From the latter place we take the train up the hillside to the newly erected German monument, "Germania," erected in honor of the soldiers who died in '71. At Reudesheim we cross the Rhine to "Dear Bingen," familiar to the mind of every schoolboy. Our visit here was rather peculiar. We were all rather tired, owing to the wind, and as we sat at dinner a steamer headed for Coblenz came slowly down the river. Every one ate in silence, with his eye on that boat. She swung slowly up to the landing, and still they ate. She made fast, and the boys began to hitch away from the table. With one accord fifteen of them rose, grasped their wheels and made a rush for that steamer!

At Coblenz the principal excitement consisted of hunting up meerschaum pipes. The pipe-fever has broken out on the party in its most violent form. One and all are in search of meerschaums. Little crowds of three or four stroll up and down the streets and salute each other with: "Struck any pipes cheap?" "Jack" has got a dozen, "Pedals" has twenty or so, and the others from one to ten apiece. The aggregate assortment of the whole crowd would fit up a wholesale store in good style. They cost a little more than half of the American price for the same goods. In the beer-gardens and beer-halls most excellent music is discoursed free of charge. In Coblenz we listened the entire evening, gratis, to a Hungarian Gypsy Band that was far superior to a concert by a similar band of performers which I paid a dollar to hear, just before leaving my native heath.

The run to Cologne was to have been our last day together on the wheel, as the original idea was to take steamer from there to Rotterdam, where the trip was to end, and each go where fancy led him. Later on, "the management" decided to have the trip end at Cologne, as this point seemed better suited to the divers paths of the majority. The Saturday (the 27th) on which we were to ride from Coblenz to Cologne, however, proved a nasty day, and all but eight decided at once to go by steamer to the latter place.

"Kirk" is the hero of the party, having ridden his wheel every inch of the trip. Several others deserve honorable mention for the plucky manner in which they have stuck to the road, through all sorts of conditions of weather and going. Amongst these are White, Elwell, Schneider, Levy, Riley and Fessenden. The sail down the Rhine is truly charming even on a drizzly, windy day. We glide in and out amongst such well-known and legend-haunted spots as the Mouse Tower, Schomberg and Rhinefels Castles, the Lorelei rock and the Kirhenbreitstein fortifications. This trip, and indeed our whole tour, has been intimately associated with the charming (?) society of scores of newly married couples. We see them everywhere and meet them at every turn, Switzerland and the Rhine being especially adapted to their wants. We have seen them at all the various stages of their honeymoon, from the time when they can't and won't make any effort to conceal their mutual affection from the public gaze, to the time when they begin to want to act like old stagers, but can't. They made us blush at first, but we have now become inured to their billing and cooing and have come to regard them as one of "the customs of the country."

COLOGNE, THE END OF THE JOURNEY.

We arrived in Cologne (its name may be spelled in seven different ways, from Köln to Cologne) in rags and tatters—dead broke, but enthusiastic over the cause which has reduced us to this extremity—*i. e.*, cycling. Undergarments have gradually come to be looked upon as luxuries for the use of the nobility only, and a whole pair of shoes or stockings is not to be seen in the party. My necktie for the past week has been put to the vile use of a substitute for suspenders, and I think others have gone the same way. The only way we can change stockings is to change from one foot to the other, and our outside garments are in various stages of decay.

One and all received a new remittance at Cologne, and hastened to pay up their little account with Treasurer Higgins. In spite of all this, for the past two months a more happy and careless set of young fellows could not be found, and it is with feelings of more than regret that we heard Higgins announce at dinner to-day: "It's my painful duty to remind you that after this meal everyone is to pay his own bills. The tour, as far as we are concerned, is at an end." I do assure you that there is a set of very long faces in the smoking-room downstairs at this moment. At dinner, speeches were made by Elwell and Beal, after which it was voted to form into a permanent society, of which Mr. S. B. Phillips, of Portland, was elected Historian and Secretary, and a committee to devise a badge, consisting of Elwell, Collins and Beal, was appointed.

FINIS.

And thus the great Elwell European Touring Party, the greatest and grandest tour awheel ever devised, comes to an end, as all things must, and quietly sinks into its place in cycling history. That it has been a success in every particular, far beyond the most sanguine hopes of its participants and management, needs but a glance at the brown cheeks and clear eyes of the members to prove. Not a man but what will tell you that it is the event of his life, and that he is healthier, wealthier and wiser in an hundred-fold can be found; and this trip has demonstrated to a greater extent the possibilities of cycling and the pleasures of touring than any event since bicycling moved from theory into practice. A hasty canvass of the party shows the following to be the dates on which the various members turn their faces homeward:

August 3, on the Etruria—Estabrook, Wentworth and Phillips.

August 17, on the Umbria—Cake, Higgins, Palmer and Seavey.

August 21, on the Lahn—Bennett and Buttolph.

August 21, on the City of Paris—Brinsmade, Breed, Shannon, D. Krumm, W. Krumm and Reily.

August 24, on the Servia—White, Levy, Roseboom and Schneider.

September 18, on the City of Paris—Elwell, Beal and Wilson.

Undecided—Fessenden, Kirk, Nussle and Cooper.

To stay in Paris—Collins.

Selah!

TAM O'SHANTER.

FRAUD!

EDITOR OF THE WHEEL:

Your editorial in the issue of THE WHEEL of July 26, headed "And Thereby Hangs a Tale," would have been much more pointed if you told where the illustrations of the *Gazette* came from. The one marked "A. C. Banker" is the picture of J. H. Adams, of England, and appeared in the issue of *Bicycling News* September 8, 1888. "On the Home-stretch, Half-mile dash," appeared in *B. N.* November 10, 1888, and represented "Fred Wood, the professional, on his favorite track." The picture labeled "W. I. Wilhelm" appeared in *B. N.* September 15, 1888, and is a picture of W. F. Ball, of the Speedwell Club, England. The picture of the start of the one-mile L. A. W. championship appeared in *B. N.* September 29, 1888, and represented the start of a race at Copenhagen, on the Continent. In the original there is a safety man on the inside, which was cut out of the *Gazette* picture; in this picture Teddy Mayes is on the outside.

S.

San Francisco, August 2, 1889.

TWO MILES A MINUTE.

THE SPEED ATTAINED ON A CIRCULAR TRACK BY A THREE-TON ELECTRIC MOTOR.

BALTIMORE, August 6.—On a two-mile circular track the startling speed of two miles a minute was this morning maintained for about ten miles by the three-ton motor of the Electro-Automatic Transit Company, of Baltimore City, at their grounds at Laurel, Md. This speed equals three miles per minute on a straight track. David G. Weems, the inventor, conducted the experiments. The company will build at once a five-mile circular track on Long Island to demonstrate the practicability of the electric passenger system and also the automatic system which was tried to-day, and is intended only for light express packages, mail matters and newspapers.—*Baltimore Sun.*

BICYCLES AND TRICYCLES, 1889.

BY H. H. GRIFFIN.

H. H. Griffin has just issued his "Bicycles and Tricycles of the Year 1889." This is the twelfth year of the publication of the book. It is a well-bound, paper-covered book of about one hundred pages.

In the preface Mr. Griffin notes the decline of the ordinary and the increasing popularity of the rear-driving safety. He also reports a great trade increase, these being makers alone in the London district. No reference is made to ladies' bicycles.

From the introduction we learn that 90 per cent. of all bicycles now being manufactured are dwarfs, that the best frames in use, according to Mr. Griffin, are the braced diamond pattern and the triangular rear frame.

The author describes ninety-four different patterns of bicycles and fifty one tricycles, and yet these are merely "selected." Many of the descriptions are illustrated. Price, one shilling. L. Upcott Gill, 170 Strand, W. C., publisher.

W. F. MURPHY.

On the preceding page we publish a photograph of W. F. Murphy the prominent path and road racing man of the Kings County Wheelmen. Murphy began riding in 1884, during which year he rode 500 miles. In the early part of 1888 he made a month's record of 1,210 miles, and afterwards rode 1,440 miles in 22 days in July. In October he rode 1,700 miles in 27 days, or 170 hours' actual riding time, including five century runs.

Murphy is strongly built, about 5 feet 7 inches in height and weighs 150 pounds. Murphy has made good pace on the path, and now divides road with path racing. His principal race was on May 30, when he won first prize in the local 25-mile road race, finishing in 1h. 32m. 13s.

THE NEW YORK CITY PAVEMENTS.

Professor J. S. Newberry, of the Columbia College School of Mines, has been making a careful examination of the street pavement used in some of the principal European cities. The Professor's views on the cheapness, practicability and advantages of asphalt are given below:

"The result of the experience of the last ten years has clearly shown that the pavement made with Trinidad asphalt is equal to any in the world and superior to any other kind of pavement in use. Its excellences, cleanliness, silence and salubrity are so apparent that no argument is now needed to enforce them; to these may be added, and placed first in the list, *economy;* for it costs as little and lasts as long any other good pavement, and is much less trying to horses, vehicles and human nerves. It is rapidly growing in favor, and it is not too much to say that it is the pavement of the future, and is destined in most localities to supersede all other kinds.

"In a recent visit to Washington I found some of the streets in a bad condition. Even on Fourteenth Street, in front of the Treasury Building, the asphalt pavement is full of holes, and the condition of this great thoroughfare has led to an opinion which I found quite prevalent, that asphalt was only adapted to streets where the traffic was not great and the vehicles were light. This is a mistake, however. There is no street in America or elsewhere in the world that has as much traffic as Cheapside, London, and among the vehicles which pass through it are omnibusses, loaded with passengers inside and on top, carts of all descriptions, and, heaviest of all, the trucks of the great brewers, with their enormous horses and tons of ale and porter. And yet Cheapside is paved with asphalt, and is as smooth as a house floor. The secret of its perfection is the thorough manner in which the pavement is laid and the incessant care given to it. In nothing is the axiom truer than in the asphalt pavements, 'that a stitch in time saves nine.' The material has little hardness, and if from irregular settling of the roadbed or local violence a break occurs, the passing wheels rapidly shear off the sides of the hole and it soon assumes formidable dimensions. *In London this is prevented by constant watchfulness; persons are employed to traverse the streets with a light repairing outfit, and wherever a defect is observed this is patched at once, and so effectually that the spot cannot be distinguished.* The contractors who lay the pavements agree to keep them in order for fifteen years at a price which does not average more than a few cents a square yard.

"*Our people seem to think that no pavement is a good one unless when once laid it will forever take care of itself; but there is no such pavement.* Even our rough stone roadways would pay excellent interest on the expenditure necessary for constant inspection and repairs promptly made when needed.

"One great difficulty stands in the way of the improvement of the pavements in the City of New York, and that is the frequency with which they are torn up for the purpose of laying new lines of gas, water or steam pipes, or for the repair of such pipes when broken or frozen. The depth to which frost penetrates the ground in our severe winters seems to make it necessary that our pavements, as at present laid, should be frequently torn up, and until more care is given to the removal and replacement of the pavement it is impossible that we should have smooth roadways. This evil could have been in a large degree obviated by sinking the pipes beyond the reach of the frost, but from the connections already made this would now be a matter of extreme difficulty, and it is even probable that we can never have a satisfactory system of paving until commodious subways shall be constructed to receive all the pipes and where they may be accessible without tearing up the streets. In the new streets opened in our rapidly growing cities the construction of such subways is possible, and would prove not only a great convenience to the population, but a substantial economy. In the older streets the cost and inconvenience would be much greater, but the difficulty is not here insurmountable, and the benefits would far more than compensate for the cost."

INTERESTING FACTS AND FIGURES ABOUT NEW YORK'S PAVEMENTS.

If there is any city in the country which can afford to be well paved it is New York. The fact that our population is more condensed than any other is well known, but the extent of this condensation is not generally realized. Philadelphia, with a population little more than half that of New York, has a street mileage three times as great. Excluding the unpaved portions of both cities, which is greater in Philadelphia than in New York, her mileage of pavements is more than nine hundred; ours is less than four hundred. New York can afford asphalt better than Philadelphia can afford cobblestones.

In pleading for better pavements we have urged the examples of the smaller cities of Washington, Buffalo, Cincinnati and Columbus. Compare for a moment their wealth and total street mileage as given in the last census:

	Valuation.	Street mileage.	Valuation per mile.
Washington	$90,000,000	230	$430,000
Buffalo	83,000,000	330	250,000
Cincinnati	169,000,000	402	4[illegible]0,000
Columbus	27,000,000	141	120,000
New York	1,094,000,000	565	1,940,000

The wealth of New York per mile of streets is more than four times as great as any one of these cities, and sixteen times as great as that of one of them. The burden of taxation which asphalt pavements would impose upon New York would be at the worst but a small fraction of that which it imposes upon these smaller cities.

But the reality of the burden is not only to be doubted but to be absolutely denied. In Columbus the miles of asphalt pavements which it had in 1880 were all laid on the petition of the majority of the abutting land owners, though the entire cost of pavement was assessed against their land. They believed that the pavement added more than its cost to the value of their property. The asphalt was regarded not as a burden but as an investment.

If, then, the asphalt pavements can be looked upon as worth their entire cost to the abutting land owners, what must be said of their value as an investment to the city at large? In speaking of the street mileage of New York, we have included that of the annexed district. When we confine New York to Manhattan Island, where its population and wealth are practically confined, we find its mileage reduced to 384. Should asphalt cost $40,000 per mile, every street in our city, including the worst tenement-house section and the long stretch of shanty town, could be paved for $15,000,000. If, as Captain Green estimates, the annual saving in the cost of transportation should be $5,000,000, or should it be but $2,000,000, the investment would be one of the finest ever contemplated by any city.

This morning's papers tell of the sale of our three per cent. bonds at a premium. When we remember that our tax-rate is two per cent., it becomes evident how soon our city gets its return upon money put into street improvement, which increases the value of its land and leads to the increased building of costly residences. By all means let the $6,000,000 which we have for street improvement be put into asphalt.—*Evening Post.*

TO PAVE THE BOULEVARD WITH ASPHALT.

The good feeling is spreading, and it will not be long before all the fine residence streets of the city will be paved with the asphalt. The *Herald* and *World* have both called attention to the vile condition of the Boulevard, and as soon as the property owners agree this much-neglected drive will be properly surfaced. From the *World* we republish the following:

"Commissioner Gilroy has reported in favor of asphalt, only he does not wish to take upon himself the responsibility of having it laid until after this district is built up. But owners of property and their tenants ask for it this year, and the Board of Estimate and Apportionment will decide it at their next meeting. Asphalt was at one time in disfavor as a pavement, because so many mixtures of tar and sand had been laid down here which were fraudulent and worthless, but as now laid down by some of the contracting companies it is the model pavement."

"If the controversy goes on much longer it will be shown that granite blocks are the worst, instead of the most durable. Besides this, it is impossible to pave the Boulevard with granite. The grade of the Boulevard has been fixed by law, and cannot be altered. There is the foundation of stone and concrete, the best ever laid anywhere—twenty inches thick. Upon this they laid about two inches of gravel, which has been ground up and blown away, and the empty space—two to three inches—is just what is needed to be cleared out and filled up with asphalt. To lay granite blocks requires that one-half the present foundation should be cut away. This is almost impossible, as it has become cemented into a solid rock. The granite blocks cannot be laid on top of it. The foundation must be cut away to let them in, for the top of the blocks must not come above the established grade; besides, even if it were possible, it would necessitate the raising of the curb and all the sidewalks, which would interfere with stoops and areas already built. Now, who could, or even would, cut off or dig out this foundation? It cost $500,000 a mile, and is too solid to be disturbed. It is the most costly foundation ever laid in this city or in any city. Half a million dollars a mile for the curb and sidewalks on the Boulevard and the foundation only for a pavement. It is three or four times as much as was spent on the best pavement ever laid on Fifth Avenue or on Broadway. No one is going to destroy it. We have had the foundation and the promise of a pavement, and now we want the pavement itself. Look at the thousands of new houses. Ladies come up to buy or rent. They get to this Boulevard and turn around and go home again. They cannot get across. It is almost a quarter of a century since the work on the Grand Boulevard was begun, and over eighteen years since we were assessed for its paving. Thus far, for our money, we have got only a concrete foundation and a promise. Tenth and Ninth avenues were cut through ten years later, but they were paved and are now well built up, and their improvements bring the city of New York annually a handsome revenue in taxes, while the Grand Boulevard, this magnificent 150-foot avenue, which was laid out by widening the old Bloomingdale Road and Eleventh avenue at a first cost of $6,106,537.91, has remained neglected and hardly occupied, paying the city very little in taxes and to its owners bringing only new assessments. To-day its filthy, unkept condition is a ruin to itself and a barrier to the marvelous improvements westward of it. It looks just as the outskirts of old New York must have looked one hundred years ago, before the passage of the 'hog ordinance,' when our ancestors used to put their garbage and their pigs into the street together.

"'Here is a strip of land which for two hundred years has been known as the 'garden,' the 'tenderloin' of Manhattan Island—once the abode of the Livingstons, the Apthorps, the Van der Heuvels, the De Lanceys, the Clendennings and others. Through it ran the celebrated fourteen-mile drive to Claremont, over which Washington daily drove his coach-and-six while he lived here as President. It has had more money spent upon it, at the cost of the owners, than any other similar section of our city. It has the benefit of the high-water service and the finest sewerage system in any city; high, dry land, with parks on either side, no unhealthy manufactories, but the broad Hudson and the beautiful scenery beyond it. Its natural advantages, with the energy of a few builders, have increased its taxes more than 100 per cent. in the last ten years, and it is bound to be in the near future the great residence section of our city. The Twelfth, Nineteenth and Twenty-second wards now pay over 40 per cent. of all the taxes of New York City, and now out of this year's $1,000,000 appropriation we think the west side is entitled to its fair share. It will take something like $350,000 to pave the Boulevard, an avenue 150 feet wide and five miles long, with the best asphalt pavement, with a substantial guarantee to keep it in order five years. The city could make no better investment than to provide the citizens of the west side with a civilized pavement on this Boulevard, the leading artery of west side travel and progress.

"'Commissioner Gilroy recommends asphalt pavement in the future, but we want it now, right away, if it is to do any good by improving the streets and thereby improving the character of the new buildings. He is right as to an asphalt pavement, for it is the cheapest, best and, in fact, the only pavement that can be put upon the present foundation. It is smooth and pleasant to drive upon, easily kept clean and repaired; is a sanitary pavement, needs no watering, and its durability, when properly laid, under the heaviest truckage has been tested with the most satisfactory results. Any money spent in repairing the Boulevard with the old gravel surface would be money thrown away. If the Boulevard is not paved that section of the city will not be built up in thirty years. So, is it any wonder that we, who are now paying such a large proportion of the city's taxes, claim our fair share of this $1,000,000 appropriation? Will the money, spent as has been suggested on downtown streets, improve the character of the architecture of the buildings already up or their occupation, or increase the city's taxes? But if this same sum which it is proposed to spend on the downtown streets is laid out in paving the Boulevard and other leading uptown avenues, it will be a stimulus to an improvement in the style of the buildings (for the owners are waiting for the pavement), and the valuations will so increase that in a few years the Twelfth, Nineteenth and Twenty-second wards will be paying taxes on $1,000,000,000 valuation instead of $517,000,000 as now, and this is where the benefit comes to the downtown property-owners in relieving them from taxation.

"'This pavement will not, like the downtown streets, have to be taken up, for the sidewalks are twenty-five feet wide, and all the sewers and pipes are laid under them. When laid it will stay laid. If the Boulevard is paved it will tend to the carrying out its original design—that it should be an avenue of the finest private dwellings and public buildings. We want to save it from becoming a street of tenement houses. It can be made as grand and imposing a street as any of the boulevards in Paris, and that will make a great difference in the taxes it pays to the city. Twenty years ago property below Forty-second Street paid three-fourths of the taxes; now 60 per cent. is paid by property above Twenty-third Street.

"'Yet, what is all this about? Only getting a street paved! They are paving ordinary streets by the hundred every season, and we ask a pavement for the finest street in the city—the future pride of New York, now in such a pitiable condition—and that after the owners have paid for it!

"'Why should not the City set the example now of giving this great street the most perfect pavement, and start the builders in making the grandest improvements, so as to get a fine street lined with magnificent buildings before the World's Fair comes in 1892? A petition has been sent to the Board of Estimate and Apportionment from about three hundred owners and occupants of property on and near the Boulevard, all approving of asphalt pavement, and now I have before me a petition headed by the Livery Stable Keepers' Association and the various proprietors of livery and road stables and all the riding-school stables, petitioning for this same asphalt pavement, as they think the present condition of the Boulevard is dangerous and a continual expense to them in repairs to carriages.

"'From this you will see that this is not a question alone for us who are property owners on the West side, but it benefits the city at large and the next generation who will throng the West side for their residences."

THE PATENT SPRING WIRED TIRES.

HOOKHAM'S PATENT.

Messrs. Singer & Co., 6 and 8 Berkeley Street, Boston, Mass., have secured the right to manufacture and sell this new tire, and will apply it to their wheels. We give a technical description of the device.

The main advantages claimed are:

1st. The tire *cannot come off accidentally.*

2d. The tire is *compressed instead of stretched.*

3d. The tire is more elastic.

As this is an entire novelty, a somewhat full description of it will be necessary.

The wire is a special quality of spring wire of great strength and is of spiral form.

It is of sufficient length to lie in the *bottom* of the U felloe, and it is then passed through a small hole in the centre of the tire. The ends of the wire are joined by merely interlacing the corrugations, and this makes a joint which it is absolutely impossible to stretch or separate accidentally, and thus one great difficulty is overcome. The ends of the tire itself are joined by a solution which is perfectly reliable, but the tire being longer than the circumference of the felloe, the compression is really sufficient to keep the ends of the tire together.

As the wire is only of the length of the bottom of the U felloe, in order to get the tire into its place, the wire must be stretched over the edge of the felloe. This is done by means of a screw apparatus, which springs the corrugations of the wire, and when the tire is in its place, they spring back sharply to their original position. Owing to the corrugations firmly embedding themselves in the tire, another great difficulty is overcome - viz., the cutting of the tire, which proved unavoidable when a straight wire was used.

The tire is in a 30-inch wheel, about 4 inches longer than the circumference of the felloe, instead of being several inches shorter, as in the case of ordinary tires, which require to be *stretched* on. Hence the tire cannot easily cut, and any cut made will close up at once. It is claimed there is a marked difference in the elasticity of the tire, which is of great advantage. While the tire *cannot possibly come off accidentally*, the tension of the wire is so arranged that it allows the tire to be pushed aside sufficiently to enable a spoke to be put in when required, a point of some importance. No cement is required, except for the purpose of preventing the entrance of wet between the tire and the rim, and in order to move any part of the tire, a little heat will therefore be necessary.

TWO OF A KIND.

Ralph Temple is a nice young man for a small tea party. If Ralph comes as a trick rider or as a man of business, I daresay he will be tolerably well received by those with whom he may come in contact; but he must pardon us if we are a little shy of him as a racing man. He and Morgan have been as well treated in Ireland as was possible. They came as racing men, and, believing that they were genuine and straight, we welcomed them. But we did not know the inner Temple then. We know now that Temple and Morgan were parties to a racing swindle which was carried out in such a deliberate fashion and on so large a scale as to beat all records—at least all discovered records, for there may have been greater swindles of which we never heard. They say that Temple is going to race in England. Who will believe in such racing? I have often said what I thought about professional racing, and now I am more convinced than ever that it cannot be relied on or taken seriously. When the American tourists were here everybody remarked that they did not talk too much in a conversational way, but on one point they were eloquent enough, and that was the downfall of professional racing in America. They all agreed that Morgan had killed the game, and we must admit that it would be queer if it were otherwise.—*The Irish Athletic and Cycling News.*

DISTRICT OF COLUMBIA DIVISION RUN.

Takoma Park is a beautiful suburban village, situated six miles from Washington, and has long been a favorite "run" for Washington wheelmen, as the road, out Fourteenth Street, Whitney Avenue and Seventh Street, past the Soldiers' Home, is one of the best to be found about Washington. The village of Takoma, is one of the prettiest of the many suburban villages surrounding Washington, and the inhabitants are composed of some of the best business people in the city. They are noted for the splendid manner in which they entertain visitors, and the members of the D. C. Division of the League are willing to testify to the above.

At the annual meeting of the Division, held a few weeks since, the Chief Consul suggested the idea of having monthly "runs" during the summer, the idea being that it would not only prove pleasant to the members, but would induce other wheelmen to join the Division, and thus swell the membership. The first run was called for last Wednesday evening to Takoma Park. As soon as the citizens of the village learned that the Division would visit their city, they sent word that if we would postpone the trip until Thursday evening they would give us an ice-cream festival, or something of the sort. This invitation was accepted, and the "run" postponed. On Thursday evening the boys assembled at Iowa C rcle, and at seven o'clock started by twos, one hundred strong. A perfect line was maintained until we arrived at the outskirts of the village, where every man dismounted and lighted his lamp. We then wheeled into the village, with whistles blowing and bells ringing, but not a word was spoken, thus making a sort of respectable "racket."

The sight was a very pretty one, as the long line of lights, outlined by the woods, came winding down the hill into Takoma. We dismounted in front of the Union Chapel, a beautiful s ructure recently erected, and still unfinished, and were greeted by the ladies and gentlemen, who gave us a hearty welcome and invited us into the chapel. Not a man in the party had an idea of what was coming, and we only supposed that we were to be entertained with ice cream, cake and lemonade. We soon discovered that the Takomans are not built that way, bu: bad provided an entertainment that was decidedly novel to say the least. Judge of our surprise when they ushered us into the lower room of the chapel, seated us in uniform order, and called us to order by the sound of the gavel (a combination of fruit can and shot), in the hands of Mr. B. H. Warner, one of Washington's best known business men and a citizen of Takoma. He announced that we "Common Council" of the city of Takoma would now come to order. He immediately called for the report of the Committee on Ways and Means. The Chairman arose, and after making an elaborate report, said that the committee strongly recommended the formation of a militia for the protection of the city against the surrounding villages, and moved that such a militia be at once organized. This motion was unanimously carried amid great enthusiasm, and the name of General Kniffin was at once proposed for the office of Commander-in-Chief. The General was immediately elected unanimously. (It is a characteristic of the Takomans to be unanimous in everything). The General arose and thanked the members for the $5,000 salary connected with the office. He said he was especially pleased at securing such a remunerative office without being compelled to pass the civil service examination. About two dozen colonels were then elected, and some one proposed that all the wheelmen present be elected majors. This was carried without a dissenting voice. Mayor Heaton then presented the freedom of the city to Chief Consul Atwater in a magnificent crystal casket (a bottle of sand) beauti ully inscribed. The Chief Consul was not prepared for a speech, but managed to thank the Mayor and the citizens for the splendid hospitality we had received, and stated that every wheelman present would always have a warm spot in his heart for the citizens of Takoma.

Councilman Yeatman then presented the Chief Consul with a key to the gates of the city. Said key is a ponderous looking affair and is warranted to wind up any watch that it will fit. Consul Atwater replied to Councilman Yeatman and was immediately elected a colonel of the militia. The following is a copy of his commission:

"United States of America, City of Takoma, District of Columbia. Greeting: Know all men, that I, Chas. M. Heaton, Jr., Mayor of Takoma, reposing special trust and confidence in Geo. S. Atwater, and considering him the possessor of suitable qualifications for such office, do hereby appoint him as a colonel in the militia of Takoma, at an annual salary of $2,000, to be collected by himself from such citizens as may desire to contribute thereto. Done at Takoma, which is six miles from Washington, this 8th day of August, 1889. C. M. Heaton, Jr., Mayor. Approved, B. W. Warner Duke, of Shadyside, Chairman Common Council. P. S.—According to the laws of Takoma, the party hereby commissioned is required to put one dollar, or more if he desires, in the enclosed envelope and mail it for the benefit of the Union Chapel. This Chapel is for the use of all denominations."

All the above is printed on fine paper, handsomely decorated and surmounted with the great and only American eagle. A committee was then appointed to devise means to fill the ranks with privates, and a suggestion was made to use the wheels for privates, for the reason that every one present, and in fact every citizen of Takoma, had already been supplied with an office, and it was thought that the wheels were the only "things" present who would not object to filling such a position. After several speeches by the citizens and a few of the wheelmen, the meeting was adjourned. The fun was immense and beyond my power to describe. The manner in which the chair "put the question" was novel, and I think Cushing's manual could take points from Chairman Warner. All the speeches were full of humor and every one present was in a continual roar of laughter. Coming in the nature of a surprise, as it did, the whole proceedings were heartily enjoyed by all, and the occasion will long be remembered as the most enjoyable evening ever spent by the Washington wheelmen.

After the adj urnment the ice cream and cake was discussed, and the pretty girls of the village (and, by the way, there are plenty of them) took good care to see that our plates were well supplied, and made us all wish we were "dressed up" in our good clothes. Everything seemed to smile on us. The moon was beautiful, the roads magnificent, the reception hearty, and, in fact, everything was so enjoyable that the boys are ready to respond to Chairman Warner's kind invitation to make Takoma the next run. We left Takoma about eleven o'clock with bright memories of our visit, and with a hearty cheer for the Takomans and their beautiful village.

This run has done a great amount of good for the Division, and it has already caused a number of riders to send in their applications. Our Division is different from the others, in several respects. In the first place, it is purely local. That is, we have only one city where any wheeling is done, and, as the streets are so fine, the riders do not see the necessity for joining any organization, and, as a rule, they know very little about the League and care less. Now, if we can keep up this series of runs, and show ourselves occasionally, it will not be long before the riders begin to see that there is some good to be derived from League membership, and we will soon have a very large membership. Let the good work proceed

The new officers for the coming year are as follows: Chief Consul, Geo S. Atwater (re-elected); N. MacDaniels, Vice-Consul; Wm. H. Stearns, Secretary-Treasurer, and Chas. Neil, Representative. A good dead of work has been planned for the coming year, and I think it will not be long before the District will compare favorably with the others.

NATIONAL.

Washington, August 13, 1889.

OUR TAKOMA PARK RUN.

All day long the boys were talking, cleaning wheels and filling lamps, getting ready for the first moonlight run of the L. A. W. Division of the District of Columbia. Soon the hour arrives, and "Our Crowd" leave for the start, at Iowa Circle. We find about one hundred cyclists already assembled at the circle—a jolly crowd, but very orderly. No "Annie Laurie" or "He's all right" business. The ladies did not show up very heavy, as Mrs. Chas. Smith and Mrs. Frank McGlathery were the only representatives of the hundreds of lady cyclists in Washington. They were given places of honor at the lead.

Chief Consul Atwater and Secretary-Treasurer Sterns were very much inclined to be frisky. Atwater's perpetual smile was something wonderful, and Sterns just bubbled over with joy. The cause was a new tandem safety. The wheel has been on exhibition all season, but George had had it shaved and generally cleaned up. Mr. and Mrs. McGlathery were also on a tandem.

Mrs Charlie Smith was smiling on all. She is our favorite; always in for a run and always on time, her little 37-pound Dart looking as if Mr. Charlie had sat up all night to shine the nickel

Well, we got away, riding out 14th Street, up the long hill, then across country, arriving at Takoma amid a clatter of bells and screeching of whistles We were taken into the City Council as active members for the night, and all enjoyed an hour with Takoma's people, who, for large-heartedness and good nature, can give even St. Louis a tip.

After the meeting we were waited upon by the belles of the city with ice-cream and cake at fifteen cents per wail. The night was perfect, the moon glorious and, taken as a whole, the run was a grand success. The run was suggested by C. H. Plumb, who knows a thing or two about good times.

One thing I think very queer is the condition in which dealers let out renting wheels. One of the tandems had no brake. It ran away, coming home, on a steep hill, struck a large stone and threw both riders, Mr. McGlathery being knocked senseless, besides being badly cut; Mrs. McGlathery badly bruised on her arm and side.

Mr. W. H. Teller was a very prominent figure on the run. Teller rides a 63 Club, without a step, and when he does the pedal mount the way that 30-inch leg sails up through space is something awful. His partner, G. W. Kosacks, is always doing the shadow act on a 51-inch Mail. They are a great pair. B. H. Warner, chairman of the Council, is a daisy. Give him room and he will be President.

Messrs. J. B. Johnson, Irwin and Arthur Woods, the Illinois tourists, who arrived last Wednesday, were along. They have come from Jacksonville, Ill.

C. H.

TACOMA, WASHINGTON.

Bicycling is again forgotten and our thoughts are with the sufferers of Spokane Falls, for that thriving and beautiful city has been visited by a conflagration that is proportionately greater and more destructive than the fires that crippled Seattle and Vancouver. The city of Spokane Falls was a very lively place and cycling was on the boom among its residents. It is to be hoped the indefatigable Spokane people will assert themselves as did the residents of the other burned cities and build even a more substantial city than of old.

Among the new projects here is an athletic track, and I sincerely hope those directly interested will succeed in their endeavors. If the cyclers of Tacoma and Seattle had a good track to practice upon, and on which to hold competitions, I know well we would surpass some of our Eastern cousins. As road scorchers we can hold our own, as Halsted will affirm, having arrived at that conclusion by close observation and closer competition. Speaking of racing, I might allude to the fact that Halsted is trying to arrange a series of races between Portland and Tacoma teams, and his suggestions are to-day being considered by the Portland Club. Dr. Miller, Secretary of the Oregon Bicycle Club, of Portland, thought it would be an excellent idea to hold the entertaiment during the Industrial Fair week, to be held in that city during the latter part of September.

Next week Halsted and Prince Wells start on their trip through Washington and Oregon, which they expect will cover about two weeks, as they will stop at all of the towns on the railroad, big and small, to show the people what can be done on a bicycle. Besides the exhibitions of Wells, "Heller, Jr.," the magician, will accompany them to still further mystify the aborigines with his sleight-of-hand manœuvres. Halsted will act in the capacity of "fast" man of the crowd, and although only a few races have been booked so far, others will probably bob up.

On the 16th, 17th and 18th of September the firemen's tournament takes place, and in conjunction with the firemen's races a bicycle race will probably be arranged between Prince Wells and Halsted for quarter-mile heats. So much has been said in regard to the respective sporting abilities of these two riders, that this race will be watched with great interest, as each of them has many friends who will back them. While Prince is the favorite for a race of this distance, nevertheless the constituents of Halsted claim he usually gets there when called upon. On Sunday last Dave Huntington, Scott, Halsted and Wells rode to Puyallup, where they spent the afternoon—and all the money they had. Both Huntington and Scott showed remarkable improvement for such novices, and greatly surprised the older riders. They will jump to the front some of these days and prove themselves second "Windles."

August 6, 1889. SNOHOMISH.

LANCASTER, PA.

Already are we looking forward with interest to the big "meet" in New York in 1892, an event that will commemorate the completion of another great *cycle*, the fourth *century run* made notable by the genius of the illustrious Genoese. New York is *the* place beyond question. It is eminently fitting that the congress of nations should assemble in the metropolis of the country, where all who will may see "Liberty enlightening the world." No other city possesses like facilities for making the affair a great success. Besides, the honor cannot be given to St. Louis when Chicago wants it, and *vice versa*. So keep quiet, you two twin-sisters rival belles that you are, and let your big *Knickerbocker* brother manage the affair, and a share of the glory will be yours as well.

As the holding of the World's Fair is not yet very close at hand, great advances will probably be made in cycle construction. That the best efforts of the manufacturers will be put forth is quite certain, and that they will produce something wonderful seems almost as certain.

The Lancaster tournament is a thing of the past, and road-riding is now the hobby, and wheelmen may be met at almost every turn Right. May they increase and multiply until they become as numerous—I will not say as the leaves of the forest, for they pile into each other in the fall. I will be moderate and say, until tens become hundreds. It is a pleasure and a delight to see the wheels go round, no matter who makes or who sells them. Of course we all have our preferences, and mine is ——

I understand that the Lancaster boys are looking forward to a run to Mt. Gretna, a place where half a dozen pic-nics can be accommodated at one time without interfering with each other, or with the great military encampment now being held there. The place is fast becoming the most popular resort in Eastern Pennsylvania. Besides its great natural advantages, its popularity is greatly owing to the efforts of its big-hearted and liberal owner, Mr. Coleman, who spares no pains or expense in making it an honor to the State. The latest improvement is a N. G. R. R. to Gov. Dick, the highest point on the mountain. From the observatory the grandest views may be obtained. Please don't misinterpret the meaning of those initials and confound the first two with the n. g. usually applied to a low-grade bicycle, or a rider of the same degree

That veteran wheelman, Martin Rudy, his wife and three gentlemen friends took a run to Lititz this afternoon, where they had tea. Mr. John G. Zook kindly took the party in hand and chaperoned it about the village and over some of the best roads in the vicinity. The lady rode her bicycle the whole sixteen miles, and climbed all the hills, except the redoubtable Kissel hill. She is also a marvelous coaster, and on the level she made the slow ones of the party hustle to keep up. By-the-way, she is the first and only lady member of the L. A. W. in this city.

August 9, 1889. TENTOONE.

ERIE, PA.

Every one who has a wheel is pretty sure to use it now. We are having - to borrow from Tam O'Shanter—"an uninterrupted stretch of atmospherical pie." The streets are fairly alive with wheels, and one may stand on the corner of Eight and Sassafras any day, between the hours of 12 and 1, and count them by the dozen. Men, women and children! Bicycles, tricycles and tandems! All go. But the funniest of all is the boy with the veloci. ede. You run across him everywhere, and the gymnastic feats a No 10 boy will perform on a No. 2 velocipede, are something wonderful.

Last week a notice appeared in the *Herald*, to the effect that Saturday evening's issue would contain a history of bicycling in Erie, together with a list of riders and kind of wheel used by each. The article was crowded out of Saturday's paper and appeared Monday evening of this week, but I am informed by some of the boys who profess to know, that it was "mangled" beyond recognition.

As an act of justice and courtesy, the different agents here were asked to give to the writer of the article a list of the riders to whom they had sold wheels, with kind and style of wheel. It seems that after the article was sent to the *Herald*, it was discovered that the "Columbia" showed up altogether too often in the list, so the make was left out entirely, and only the words "safety" and "ordinary" used. The club boys, one and all, irrespective of the kind of machine they use, are "hot," and it will be a long time before the *Herald* has another such opportunity to make itself popular among the wheelmen of Erie. N.

August 7, 1889.

CINCINNATI.

I have just received a programme of the fall races of the Hamilton County Fair and send you a copy of same. All the entries are not in, but among those that are entered are Frank Kappes, Wise, Foddy, Burroughs Bros., Colling and J. H. Hatfield. The Athletic Club race comes off tomorrow at the Oakley full-mile track, and they are making it attractive by sending out cards to other riders to accompany them, as the track is about seven miles from the city, and all that go are assured of a good time.

Last Sunday I took a spin over some of the roads in Kentucky, just across the river from us, and must say if all the roads in other localities were as good as these roads, the bicycle manufacturers would have to increase their facilities. The Lexington Pike is finely macadamized and somewhat up hill for about fifteen miles, but after that it becomes level and smooth as any one could wish. It will well repay any one to take the trouble to climb the hills for the pleasure of the long coast back home again.

I wonder what has become of the Kentons from over the river. I never hear anything more of them. Wake up, boys, and make the woods howl.

We have at last a lady rider, and I can say it pleases the boys to see Mr. B. and wife spinning along on their Columbia tandem. Why don't Krienan do likewise? Here Levi has shaken his wheel and now does all his riding on foot.

SAFETY.

Cincinnati, August 10, 1889.

SAN FRANCISCO.

The racing season is about over in this part of the State. Sacramento will hold its annual meet on some morning during the State Fair, early in September, and it is expected that a large delegation of local riders will attend. Many riders are away touring, and some, including Captain Cox, C. A. Howard and W. A. Searles, are at a fashionable seaside resort.

The run of the Bay City Wheelmen on July 28 was a most enjoyable one, but it was eclipsed on the 5th inst by the picnic run, that, for variety, could hardly be equaled anywhere. The members of the club and four of the Oak Leaf Wheelmen, of Stockton, who were their guests, left this city at 8:30, and riding leisurely down the Bay road reached San Mateo (twenty miles) at 11:30. The run was met a short distance from town by S. H. Knapp, Jr., of the Commissary Department, and the usual refreshments in the shape of milk and crackers was dispensed. Wheels were again mounted, and the picnic grounds were soon reached. Here were found a number of the Garden City Wheelmen, of San Jose, who had ridden up thirty miles to attend the run. The lunch was soon attacked, and its disappearance was a matter of a very short time. The committee, with wise forethought, had provided an extra supply of everything, and this supply followed the course of the other edibles. After dinner the members and guests, numbering fifty-five, were photographed, the photographer finding great difficulty, as usual, in keeping his subjects still. After dinner the riders visited the great dam of the Spring Valley Water Works, and viewed it with much interest. This dam has been in course of construction for five years, and has had at times nearly one thousand men working on it. Over 200,000 barrels of the best Portland cement were used in it, and it is to cost about $4,000,000

Steve Knapp, as lecturer, was a huge success. After absorbing a great deal of information regarding dams, the boys started for the beach, and were soon swimming in the pleasantly warm waters of the Bay. On the road leading from the beach is the home of D. W. Donnelly, a member of the club. The riders were invited in and regaled with fruit and watermelons, freshly picked.

The riders started for home at 4 o'clock, and arrived in the city at 7 o'clock. The Stockton Club members were delighted with their outing, and invited the club to their city on the 11th to visit Lodi, the great watermelon district of the State. Dr. C. C. Moore, of Stockton, has promised to provide a sufficient quantity of his H. H. H. medicine, to cure any riders attacked by illness from eating too much melon.

On the 31st the Bay City Wheelmen celebrate their fifth anniversary in their usual manner.

August 6. CALIFORNIA.

STAMFORD.

Cycler Cumming, who does not happen to be one of the Toilers, has difficulty in finding any one to ride with him, but has secured the entire Solitary Club for a jaunt among the beauties of nature up about Pound Ridge, N. Y., for some day in the near future.

Many of our wheelmen are of the very-seldom-go-on-the-road sort, and whose experience on wheels has hardly taken them out of sight of town, and as they have learned to do the "stand-still act," are considered pretty well up. We who ride safeties get them for going ahead purposes, and not so much for stand-still business. We prefer to get out into the country, where daisies nod to buttercups in the upland breezes, where squirrels bark at us and dispute our way, while we listen to bird concerts and the music of the brooks. Your tourist seldom loiters about town, but takes the shortest cut out of it, and revels in the pure air of the roads and fields, and sees the brightest side of cycling, drinks to the fullest of its joys.

One of our new men, seeing a copy of THE WHEEL on my desk, said that it came nearest to filling the bill of any paper he had seen, and the inclosed subscription seconds his words.

As you saw by the Sunday *Herald*, we have had a murder up here, and the fact that considerable space on Main Street is being macadamized has doubtless "averted a good many more," as we, the people "were getting desperate," and the road-making came just in time. The steam roller has been purchased, and grand work is being done with it and broken stone.

The recent accident to a big politician indirectly prevented Assistant P. M. Jessup and "us" from taking an outing about and beyond the Hub, but we will eventually arrive there.

Many are the regrets here at the death of "Jack," for, from his pen work, we had all come to like him.

STAMSON.

NEW ORLEANS.

The one-mile match race on the 4th inst. between C. M. Shute and A. B. Harris, of the Louisiana Cycling Club, resulted in a pretty contest and a four or five yards' win for the latter in 3m. 10 1-2s.

The first of the Division runs is fixed for to-night (9th), but the storm clouds are gathering and it looks mighty like rain and no "run."

New wheels are cropping out quite lively for so late in the season. Chief Consul Hodgson has forsaken the trike for a New Rapid safety, Captain Frederic changes to a Victor, while Bob Nowland and Grivot have pinned their faith to Light Champions.

The Louisiana Club loses three good members next week. Frank Walshe, who goes to locate in Alabama, Betts, who goes to New York, and the third, Charlie Fairchild, well, he commits matrimony, and, hold on, we don't lose him either, for I heard him sighing and talking tandem bike like a good fellow, and that means another lady rider. Talking about tandem bikes reminds me that R. M. Hill has just received one—the first in the city. It's a dandy, and say, but isn't it, when in motion and with a lady on the front seat, one of the most graceful looking objects you've ever sot eyes on?

Burchfield has returned from his three weeks' vacation and is full of Indiana and its roads. He spent most of his time awheel in the very heart of the gravel pike country, and makes you feel envious to hear him talk. BI.

JERSEY CITY.

Did you hear anything drop in Philadelphia? No? Well you would, had you been there on Saturday and Sunday last, on the occasion of the annual visit of the Hudson County Wheelmen to the Pennsylvania Bicycle Club.

As per invitation, we went down Saturday afternoon, leaving Jersey City at 4:15 P. M., reaching the club-house of our friends at seven o'clock. After having the hose turned on us, we mounted our wheels and were taken through Fairmount Park up to Belmont Mansion, where we supped, laughed, speech-maked, etc., after which we returned to the P. B. C. headquarters, housed our wheels and were then shown around the city, each man carrying a small pot of red paint, presumably to decorate the town.

At 10:30 the next morning the start was made for Devon, about sixteen miles out on the Lancaster Pike. The ride was a delightful one, the roads being in excellent condition and the scenery unequaled. At about one o'clock we rolled into the grounds surrounding that mammouth hotel "Devon Inn," where we enjoyed ourselves in strolling about the grounds until 1:30, when we were piloted to the dining-room, which had been tastefully decorated, and at the announcement of the old minstrel cry of "Gentlemen, be seated," the sixty-two Starvation Army men prepared for action. On the table, in front of each man, was placed a very pretty souvenir in the shape of a ribbon pin-wheel, made up of the club colors of the hosts and the visitors, *i. e.*, blue and gold (P. B. C.), red and white (H. C. W.). This was fastened to the coat by a small pin, a fac simile of the P. B. C. pin—a silver keystone with the abbreviation "Pa." in the centre.

The dinner was immense, both in quality and quantity. Under penalty of death, no man was allowed to refuse anything; and I might say it was almost the same penalty to *comply* with the order.

Being unable to navigate properly, we were rolled out on the porch and placed about the stoop, told to "look pleasant" and have the camera shot at us for the annual photograph, which, I think, was spoiled by Mr. Feury being annoyed as he was—by having a mosquito taste him directly under the left nostril—just as the cap was removed from the camera. It was truly laughable to see "Nick" wiggle his nose, work his mouth (so to speak) and finally try to push the intruder off of himself with his tongue—in fact, everything in his honest desire to refrain from raising his hands, and thus spoil the picture. Just as the cap went on, the mosquito, finding that Nick's blood disagreed with him, withdrew.

At 4 o'clock we started on the return trip, and before we had gone a half mile it was very evident that we were suddenly holding the 15-mile road race for the championship of the Sicily Islands. Me and Hufty Lehman finished first, of course, with Whittaker and such, second; *Day*, the *night*-in-gale, third, and *Benedict*, the *bachelor*, and *Christian*, the *sinner*, tied for third place. The finishing point, as far as the road race was concerned, was a restaurant in Fairmount Park, and as it was our intention to return on the 8 o'clock train, we had less than an hour to reach Broad Street station; consequently the race was kept up through the supper—Capt. Leisen finishing first, by putting all his supper in his pocket, and Thomiar last, owing to his losing so much time in thinking. He had evidently more on his mind than he had on his stomach. We then hied to the P. B. C. club-house, and then continued the race to the Broad Street station, where good-nights were said and club calls were murmured.

Verily, verily, the Pennsys. are the champion entertainers. Ki Yippy!

We have invited the New Haven Bi. Club to visit us Sunday, August 18, and trust they will bring a jam. At their suggestion, the run will be taken through Prospect Park and down to Coney Island. With so many inducements in the way—drop-your-boodle-in-the-slot machines, living skeletons, dead fat women, etc.—we will endeavor to make them happy.

I notice in last week's WHEEL that Spark, of Newark, N. J., says that the Atalantas would be glad to hear from any local club relative to holding a team road race of five or ten miles. Spark, you know our address. Send us the particulars.

Say, Spark, will you please see the Secretary of the Wheelmen's Bowling League and respectfully suggest that some preparations be made for this season's tournament? Next month is September, you know, and we should be shaking a lively hoof in order to get things in shape and give your Okalina Band a chance to rehearse. By-laws, rules and regulations, applications for membership from other wheeling clubs around New York, etc., will have to be considered before the schedule can be made out. Already I can hear the monotonous sound of the umpire's voice shouting, "Strike, Atalantas; six, all, Hudson County."

COASTER.

BUFFALO.

THE ZIGZAG'S CENTURY RUN.

The Zigzag Bicycle Club has taken its turn at a century run, and has succeeded first rate. We took the 7 P. M. boat for Erie, Pa., August 10, at least all that intended going, but one, who reached the pier just as she left; and, oh! what wouldn't he have given to have been aboard? He says he "didn't want to go," but we think it is a case of "sour grapes." After a very pleasant evening we tried to "turn in," but some of the boys were in for mischief, and only a few got any rest at all, so they did not have to be "called" for breakfast, which was served at 4 A. M.

At 5:05 A. M. twenty wheelmen left Erie to ride their first century—to Buffalo. Some Buffalo Club records might have been beaten, but alas for that species of wheel called "goat!" They were continually breaking down, and before North East was reached, at 7:07, thirty-five minutes had been lost in repairing them.

Only a short stop was made here, and we again resumed our journey at 7:26, only to be delayed another twenty-five minutes by a loose tire coming off. Another accident occured in this location. One bicyclist broke the head of his wheel, and after putting it into a wagon started for the nearest station; but, sad to relate, he was not to get away so easily, as the horse ran away with both him and his wheel. He then decided to walk. Westfield was reached at 9:14, and we decided that it was time for another breakfast. Three more took the train here, not being able to ride further.

Leaving Westfield at 10:40, we arrived at Brocton at 11:40 without a stop. After a short rest we pushed on to Fredonia, reaching there at 12:35. Then we made a "break" for that far-famed and seldom-ridden Silver Creek Hill. Only one can claim the honor—for such it is—as only two "ordinaries" in Buffalo have climbed it so far, to my knowledge, but my knowledge may not cover a very great extent. The hero is Geo. H. Luetti, who rode a Light Champion. Forty-five minutes were lost here viewing the hill. Attempts were plentiful but climbers few. The boys wanted dinner here, but as arrangements had been made and dinner was waiting at Angola, they pushed on. Well, I for one will never try a ride of about fifteen miles on an empty stomach. We were all bent over our handle-bars, groaning, and thinking how long before we could fill up that vacancy.

Some tried green apples, but one, who was more *green* than the rest, was compelled to remain at Angola on account of them. We reached this burgh about 4:25, and after dinner were escorted home by Messrs. Valentine and Whitman, who rode out from Buffalo to meet us. We arrived at the end of our century at 9:10.

Riding time, 10 hours, 10 minutes. Twenty starters, fifteen stayers. This club has only been organized since April 10, '88, and has a membership of fifty-three. It will in all probabilities be limited to 100, and will join the League. Lieutenant Holden acted Captain in the absence of Captain Geo. Hearne, who could not attend. Captain Hearne's arrangements were perfect, and Lieutenant Holden "saw them through."

The finishers are: Lieutenant Holden, Warren G. Sherk, Jas. N. Weig, Geo. H. Luetti, Wm. Patton, Walter R. Hearne, Wm. A. L'Hommedieu, Al. Coates, Samuel Somerville, Arthur Strong, Chas. Couch, Otis Starkey, Austin Crooks, —— Peck, Gus C. Miller. "DOODLE."

ST. LOUIS.

ST. LOUIS, August 7, 1889.

The Track Association seem to be doing some work in arranging for their coming tournament, and have decided to run the following races: One-mile novice, half-mile dash, one-mile open, one-mile safety handicap, one mile L. A. W. championship (open to L. A. W. members only) two-mile lap, half-mile for boys under 14, three-mile match, Harding *vs.* Ring; three-mile championship L. A. W. (open to members of the L. A. W. only), one-mile handicap, one mile consolation. Considerable interest is taken in the match race, and as both men are doing hard work, some fast time may be looked for. The prize for this race is to be a valuable gold medal, and to be furnished by the club to which the losing man belongs. To guard against an emergency, the Missouri Bi. Club has already set a suitable sum aside.

The prize list is not as yet complete, but will consist of a high-grade bicycle, gold watches, valuable medals, etc.

Entry blanks can be had by application to Secretary J. Harold Child, 1012 Olive Street. Entries close August 28, 1889. Entry fee, 25 cents for each event.

The St. Louis Cycle Club, we are told, is now a thing of the past, the last meeting being held last night. As there were a good many objectionable members in this club, this was the method taken to get away from them.

We now have the Cycling Club, organized from the better part of the old club, and with Mr. Lucas for President, Mr. Todd Vice, and Mr. E. N. Sanders for Captain, the club ought to prosper. Success to the new club.

We also have another new one, the North St. Louis Bicycle Club. This is an organization composed of nearly all new riders. We have not as yet heard much of them in cycling circles, but when we do we shall be glad to extend to them the right hand of fellowship.

The Missouri Bicycle Club had its monthly meeting last night, and on account of the circular which had been mailed to its members, almost every man who rides a wheel was there, and ready to jump on any effort to place the associate and active members on the same footing.

Judging from the circular sent out, the administration was at one time in favor of the change, but last night it appeared to favor keeping the club still a bicycle club. Doubtless it is learning wisdom, but the lesson is hard.

Everything went well till unfinished business was called for, when this matter was brought up. The President rose and stated the object of sending out the circular and the Secretary counted his postal cards and found he had fifty-eight out of a total membership of nearly three hundred. It looked as if the matter was going to rest here, until Mr. Frost asked the President what we were to *infer* from this vote. The President explained that this method was taken to find out whether the associates would be willing to have their dues raised fifty per cent., and that it was like "leading the horse to water," etc. But the ball was started, and was not going to be stopped so easily. Mr. Holm stated that he, with other active members, had been made very uneasy by that circular, and wanted the matter settled definitely now, and would like to hear more on the subject. Mr. Stewart, the "Grand Old Man" of the Mo. Bi. Club, rose and very clearly and amid much applause laid the matter before the meeting, stating that he came there for the purpose of opposing any action that would put the associate members in power. "Why," he said, "when they chose, they could turn us out of that wheel-room. This club was founded by bicycle riders, fitted up by bicycle riders; this house was caused to be built by bicycle riders, and should be controlled by bicycle riders, and so far as the use of the bicycle was concerned, it might be governed as well by people who rode the bicycle as 'an improved means of locomotion' as when they rode it for pleasure or sport.' As Mr. Stewart sat down, amid much applause, Mr. Frost rose and said: "Mr. President, I think you might put Mr. Stewart's remarks in big quotation marks as the voice of this meeting." After other remarks of a similar tone, Mr. Holm made a motion that would keep the control of the club in the hands of the active members. A point of order was raised and overruled. When the question was put the "ayes" were very loud, and a solitary little "no" from the corner.

So ends this chapter. The demon has been crushed once more, and we are now on the watch to see in what new form and place it will again break out.

The captain's report showed that the club was not yet dead, and with a few more like Mr. George Peckham, with over 1,900 miles to his credit, would be one of the first. The famous De Soto run will be taken next Sunday, leaving here by train at 4:30 P. M. Saturday, and riding back the next day. An ambulance, with an efficient corps of surgeons, will be in attendance.

ITHURIEL.

Fred. B. King, of Pontiac, Mich., is in Gotham, and reports bicycling booming in Pontiac through the efforts of C. H. Smith, of Detroit, who recently opened a branch store in that town.

FIXTURES.

August 17, 1889.—Queens Athletic Club Grounds, at 4:30 P. M., 1-mile Handicap. Entries close, Aug. 14, with Thos. Lloyd, Queens, N.Y.

August 17, 1889.—At Washington Park, Brooklyn, N. Y. Prospect Harriers Games. One and two mile Bicycle Handicaps and Triangular Race.

August 17, 1889.—South End Wheelmen's, of Philadelphia, 10-mile Road Race over the Montgomery Course.

August 18, 1889.—Second Century Run of the Buffalo Ramblers, from Erie to Buffalo.

August 22, 1889.—East Greenwich, Conn., Handicap Road Race.

August 24, 1889.—Montreal Bicycle Club's Annual Race Meet on the M. A. A. A.'s new grounds.

August 24, 1889.—Fifty-mile Bicycle and 1-mile Dwarf N. C. U. Championships at Paddington, Eng.

August 26-27, 1889.—Virginia Division L. A. W. Meet at Norfolk, Va.

August, 1889.—Scranton Club's Tour, Scranton, Pa., to Utica, Springfield, New York, Catskills, Delaware Water Gap. Address, B. P. Connolly, Secretary.

August 31, 1889.—Brooklyn Bicycle Club and Kings County Wheelmen's combined run to Massapequa, L. I.

August 31, 1889.—Monster Run of Brooklyn Wheelmen to Hotel Massapequa.

August 31, 1889.—Missouri Bicycle Club's Races, at St Louis, Mo.

August 31, 1889.—Albany Wheelmen's Tournament. Entries close August 24, with W. B. Phipps, 51 Howard Street, Albany, N. Y

August 31, 1889.—Passaic County Athletic Association's Bicycling Tournament at Clifton, N. J., Race Track. Entries close August 20, with Charles Blizard, 318 Gregory Street, Passaic N. J.

September 2-3, 1889.—Pennsylvania State Division L. A. W. Meet at York, Pa.

September 2-3, 1889.—Amateur Race Meet of the Hartford Wheel Club, at Hartford, Conn. Entries to be made with W. M. Francis, Secretary, P. O. Box 745.

September 3, 1889.—Hartford Wheel Club's 20-mile Road Race.

September 3, 1889.—Handicap Road Race of Westchester County Wheelmen.

September 3-4-5, 1889.—Iowa Division L. A. W. Meet at Des Moines.

September 7, 1889.—Berkeley Athletic Club's Race Meet at Berkeley Oval, Morris Dock, New York City.

September 7, 1889.—A. A. U. Games at Brooklyn A. A. grounds; 1-mile Handicap. Entries close August 29, with James E. Sullivan, P. O. Box 611, New York City. Fee, 50 cents.

September 7, 1889.—One-mile Bicycle A. A. U. Championship at Brooklyn Athletic Association Grounds. Entries close September 1 with J. E. Sullivan, P. O. Box 611, New York City.

September 10-11, 1889.—Binghamton Race Meet. Address E. H. Towle, Binghamton, N. Y.

September 13, 1889.—Springfield Bicycle Club's 50-mile Local Road Race and 50-mile Open Road Race, over the Springfield-Hartford course.

September 13, 1889.—At Springfield, 50-mile Road Race, open to local riders only, and 50-mile Road Race, open. Entry fee, $5, returnable to first, second and third men. Entries close September 1.

September 13-14, 1889.—New York State Division Meet at New York and Brooklyn.

September 14, 1889.—Y. M. C. A. Games; 3 mile Handicap Fee, 50 cents. Entries close September 7, with George Pool, 150th Street, Harlem River.

September 14, 1889.—Two-Mile Championship of America, at Travers Island. Entries close September 7, with Secretary N. A. A. U., P. O. Box 611, New York City.

September 14, 1889.—Louisiana Division L. A. W. Meet at Audubon Driving Park, New Orleans, La. Entries close September 10, with R. P. Randall, 54 Baronne Street, New Orleans, La.

September 20, 1889.—Michigan Division L. A. W. Meet at Ypsilanti, Mich.

September 21, 1889.—Michigan Division Meet races at Detroit, Mich.

September 21, 1889.—One-and-a-half-mile Handicap, at the Manhattan A. C. Grounds, Eighty-sixth Street. Entries close September 14, with C. C. Hughes, 524 Fifth Avenue, New York City.

September 21, 1889.—At the Warren Athletic Club Games, Wilmington, Del., 2-mile Bicycle Handicap. Entries close September 16, with W. F. Kurtz.

September 24-27, 1889.—Hudson County Wheelmen's Races at Spring Valley Fair.

October 4-5, 1889.—Pennsylvania Bicycle Club's Tournament.

October 4-5, 1889.—Peoria Bicycle Club's Tournament, Peoria, Ills.

October 8-9, 1889.—Races at Carlisle, Pa. Address John E. Steel, Carlisle, Pa.

October 12, 1889.—Three-mile Bicycle Handicap, at Staten Island Athletic Club Grounds.

October 23-29, 1889.—Race Meet at Macon, Ga.

EUROPEAN CYCLING FIXTURES.

Germany.—September 15; Hanover, September 8; Cologne, August 12; Chemnitz, September 8; Frankfort-on-the-Main, September 1; Mannheim, September 8; Crefeld, September 8. Hamburg.—Altona, September 22; Bochum, August 25; Madgeburg, September 8. Denmark.—Copenhagen International Meeting, August 18

TORONTO BICYCLE CLUB'S TOURNAMENT.

The race meet of this prominent club, held at the Rosedale Grounds, on August 82, was the most successful meet ever held in Canada.

In the morning a parade was held, in which were 200 wheelmen, including representatives from Hamilton, Montreal, St. Catharines, London, Niagara Falls and Woodstock. E. A. Scott, First Lieutenant of the Toronto Club, commanded. At the meet in the afternoon, 3,000 people were present.

The officers of the day were: Referee, J. Theo. Gnaedinger, Montreal. Judges, E. W. Smith, St. Catharines; R. A. Robertson, Hamilton; W. J. Suckling, R. H. McBride and Ewing Buchan, Toronto. Time-keepers, H. P. Davies, Toronto; J. A. McFadden, Stratford; Mr. Francis, Woodstock. Clerks of Course, A. F. Brewster, F. J. Whatmough and W. H. Cox. Scorers, J. F. Lawson, W. J. Mitchell and H. C. Pease. Starter, Dr. P. E. Doolittle. Race Committee, Harry Ryrie, Chairman; F. F. Peard, Secretary; W. H. West, Treasurer; W. H. Cox, P. E. Doolittle, M.D., W. Robins, R. T. Blachford, C. J. W. Lowes, E. A. Scott, F. J. Whatmough, W. H. Chandler, W. J. McClelland, C. W. Hurndall, J. W. Stanbury, A. H. Gregg, W. H. Thomas, C. Langley, H. C. Pease, Alf. Bryant and John W. Kerr.

The various events resulted as follows: One-mile Bicycle Roadsters.—Bert Woods, Wanderers, 1; W. Dixon, Hamiltons, 2; F. W. Hudson, Wanderers, 3; A. J. Welch, Torontos, 0; George Holtly, Torontos, 0; G. S. Dunn, Hamiltons, 0; J. F. Gibson, Wanderers, 0; J. B. Price, Wanderers, 0. Time, 3m. 22s.

One Half-mile Scratch.—W. S. Campbell, Niagara Falls, 1; Bert Brown, Wanderers, 2; F. D. Scott, Montreals, 3. Time, 1m. 25s.

One-mile Safety, Scratch.—F. W. Doll, Wanderers, 1; P. Ross, Wanderers, 2; C. J. Connolly, Rochester, N. Y., 3; W. S. Hemphill, Torontos, 0. Time, 3m. 12 1/5s.

Two-mile Club Championship.—W. A. Lingham, first; W. M. Carman, second. Time, 7m. 21 4-5s.

Five-mile Scratch Race.—W. S. Campbell, Niagara Falls, 1; Bert Brown, Wanderers, 2; W. M. Carman, Torontos, 3; W. A. Langham, Torontos, 0; J. H. Gerrie, Wanderers, 0. Time, 16m. 15s.

Half-mile Obstacle Race.—C. W. Hurndall, Torontos, 1; W. Robins, Torontos, 2; M. F. Johnston, 3; W. H. West, 4.

Three-mile Safety Handicap.—P. Ross, Wanderers, 75 yards, 1; F. W. Doll, Wanderers, 25 yards, 2; C. J. Connolly, Rochester, scratch, 3; Bert Woods, Wanderers, scratch, 0; W. F. Grassler, Niagara Falls, scratch, 0. Time, 10m. 22s.

One-mile Handicap.—F. D. Scott, Montreals, 50 yards, 1; Wm. Howell, Woodstock, 100 yards, 2; Bert Brown, Wanderers, scratch, 3; G. S. Dunn, Hamiltons, 75 yards, 4; Wm. Carman, Torontos, scratch, 5; A. J. Welch, Torontos, 150 yards, 6; W. S. Campbell, Niagara Falls, scratch, 7; Bert Woods, Wanderers, 100 yards, 0. Time, 2m. 55s.

Two-mile, 3:20 Class.—W. F. Gassler, Niagara Falls, 1; W. M. Carman, Torontos, 2; Bert Woods, Wanderers, 3; J. Knowles, London, 4; F. D. Scott, Montreal, 0; W. Howell, Woodstock, 0; C. J. Connolly, Rochester, 0 Time, 4m. 41 1-3s.

During the afternoon, little Florence Creed rode an exhibition quarter-mile on her safety in 1m. 2s.

SPORT AT RICHFIELD SPRINGS, N. Y.

At the first Annual Field Day of the Retail Grocerymen of Utica, held at the Richfield Driving Park on Wednesday, August 7, the following events were decided:

ONE-MILE OPEN.—J. A. Fuller, Rome, first; John C. Robbins. Utica, second; H. Marquisee, Utica, third. Marquisee took a bad header within 100 feet of wire. Time, 3m 19 1/5s.

ONE-MILE ROVER SAFETY HANDICAP.—W. W. Roberts, 50 yards, first; E. H. Crosby, 125 yards, second; A. H. Dobson, 100 yards, third Time, 3m. 12s.

TWO-MILE LAP RACE.—J. C. Robbins, first; F. Bowen, second; F. A. Russell, third. Time, 7m. 25 1/5s.

HALF-MILE TANDEM BICYCLE.—Metz and Hammes, first; Crosby and Sanders, 2d. Time, 2m. 37s.

THREE-CORNERED RACE.—Wheels 1 mile, runners 1,000 yards, walkers 700 yards. G. E. Truman rode a mile in 3m. 12 1/5s. The runner won easily, with the wheelman second; walkers distanced.

HALF-MILE UNICYCLE.—W. S. Nicholson, first; John Robbins, second. Time, 3m. 16 1/5s.

TWO-MILE RELAY.—Crescent Cycling Club, of Utica, first; Fort Schuyler Wheelmen, second. Time, 6m. 36s.

W. S. Nicholson won the fancy riding contest; H. Marquisee, second.

HALF-MILE RIDE AND RUN.—J. C. Robbins, first; W. W. Roberts, second. Time, 2m. 26 1/5s.

ONEIDA COUNTY CHAMPIONSHIP, ONE MILE.—F. P. Hammes, first; A. J. Fuller, second. Time, 2m. 55 1/5s. Track was in very good condition.

VIC.

SCHWALBACH'S RECEPTION.

Charley Schwalbach is ever on the alert to boom wheeling in general and his own wheels in particular in the City of Churches. Some time since Charley got the idea of holding a grand opening at the Fifth Avenue Casino, where he has established a riding school. Invitations were scattered all over the city, and the Brooklynites took to the idea so favorably that on Tuesday evening some three thousand people thronged the Casino and enjoyed the unique entertainment their host had provided. This included sprint and long distance running, boxing, exhibitions on the bars and rings, music, refreshments, dancing and bicycle exhibits truly enough variety to satisfy the most exacting.

The cycling part of the programme consisted of races and exhibitions. The 1-mile bicycle race was won by W. Bohan, Prospect Wheelmen; J. Doyle, second. Time, 4m. 21 4-5s. Bohan also won the 50 yards slow race; W. L. Wult, P. W., second. Time, 1m. 07s.

Exhibitions were given by Messrs. Peoples and Snyder and by little Eddie Schwalbach, who pushed his little safety several times around the track, and was rewarded with a gold medal which had been presented to him by W. F. Murphy. Messrs. Peoples and Snyder gave an exhibition game of bicycle polo, and the latter gave an exhibition of fancy riding. The entertainment concluded about 12 o'clock.

ENGLISH AMATEUR CHAMPIONSHIPS.

ONE MILE TRICYCLE—FIVE MILE BICYCLE—TWENTY-FIVE MILE TRICYCLE.

These events were decided at Paddington July 27. Track in grand condition. In the mile event, Stein, the German rider, and Dr. Turner collided, the former being disabled. Some fast laps and flying quarters were done as follows:

Bicycle, last lap, 503 yards—H. Synyer, 39 2-5s., a 2:18 pace; ¼-mile bicycle, flying start—H. Synyer, 33 2-5s., record; same, F. J. Osmond, 33 4-5s, equaling the previous record. Synyer repeated a last quarter in 33 3-5s. Osmond rode a first quarter in 38 3-5s. H. H. Sansom made a ¼-mile tricycle record, flying start, in 36 2-5s. Results of the races:

1 MILE TRICYCLE CHAMPIONSHIP.

Heat 1—H. H. Sansom, 2m. 53 4-5s.; D. Albone, second; H. H. Spencer, third. Heat 2—W. G. H. Bramson, 2m. 40s; A. H. Tubbs, second; S. F. Edge, third. Heat 3—A. J. Watson, 2m. 53 1-5s; B. W. Crump, second. Heat 4—A. DuCros, 2m. 57 2-5s.; W. Ward, second. Heat 5—P. W. Scheltema-Beduin, 2m. 51 3-5s.; F. T. Bidlake, second. Heat 6—L. Stein, 2m. 55 2-5s.; K. N. Stadnicki, second.

SECOND TRIALS.—Heat 1—Bramson, 2m. 47 4-5s.; Watson, second. Heat 2—DuCros, 3m. 11 2-5s.; Tubbs, second

FINAL HEAT.—Sansom, 3m. 12s.; Bramson, second. The winner rode the last quarter in 36 2-5s., beating Stein's record of 37 1-5s.

5 MILE BICYCLE CHAMPIONSHIP.

Heat 1—C. W. Brown, 14m. 43s.; F. P. Wood, second; E. Osmond, third. Heat 2—H. Synyer, 14m. 34 3-5s., last quarter in 33 2-5s.; Josef Gobel, 14m. 36 3-5s.; S. E. Williams, 14m. 40 2-5s. Synyer rode the last two miles in 5m. 39 2-5s. Heat 3—F. J. Osmond, 14m. 33 1-5s.; J. H. Adams, second. Osmond rode the last lap at a 2:18 pace.

FINAL HEAT.—Synyer, 18m. 24 1-5s., last quarter 33 3-5s.; Osmond second by four feet. The homestretch struggle was a grand race between Synyer and Osmond.

THE 25 MILE TRICYCLE CHAMPIONSHIP.

H. H. Bramson, 1h 20m. 27 1-5s.; Syd. Lee, second; P. C. Wilson, third.

The English had rare sport at their last championship meeting such as we have not had in this country since the old Springfield days.

The English one-mile safety and fifty-mile ordinary bicycle championships will be decided at Paddington August 24.

WORLD'S RECORD FROM TWENTY-SIX TO THIRTY-SIX MILES.

July 30, at Paddington, Eng., J. E. L. Bates, mounted on a safety, started on a record-breaking expedition, and succeeded in doing a marvelous performance, beating the old records for a bicycle of any type from twenty-six to thirty-six miles, inclusive. The times that are marked * are records for any type of bicycle:

MILES.	H. M. S.	MILES.	H. M. S.
5	0 15 5	*29	1 27 15 4-5
10	0 29 53 2-5	*30	1 30 33
15	0 44 29 1-5	*31	1 33 57 2-5
20	0 59 35 3-5	*32	1 37 13 3-5
21	1 2 35	*33	1 39 53
22	1 5 30 3-5	*34	1 44 40
23	1 8 30 2-5	*35	1 47 57
24	1 11 31	*36	1 51 16 3-5
25	1 14 37 1-5	37	1 54 55
*26	1 17 39 4-5	38	1 58 51 2-5
*27	1 20 47 4-5	39	2 2 28
*28	1 23 58	40	2 5 56 4-5

Safeties have been barred from the Australian mile and ten-mile championships.

Within the past year Synyer has beaten Osmond three times in important scratch mile events. Osmond has also beaten Synyer the same number of times.

ENGLISH AMATEUR TRICYCLE RECORDS.

On July 23, at the Paddington track, E. P. Moorhouse, of the Stanley and North Road C.C.'s, rode thirty miles on a tricycle in 1h. 32m. 17 4-5s., beating the previous record (made by A. L. Bower, 1h. 40m. 51 2-5s.) by 8m. 33 3-5s. The records from twenty-six miles were also beaten, as follows: 26th, 1h. 19m. 55s.; 27th, 1h. 23m. 6 1-5s.; 28th, 1h. 26m. 14 2-5s.; 29th, 1h. 29m. 24s.; 30th, 1h. 32m. 17 4-5s. He rode 19 3-4 miles in the hour. The new record beats the tandem tricycle record for the distance by 1m. 3 4-5s.

NEW FIFTY MILES BICYCLE RECORD.

On July 25, J. H. Adams beat all ordinary bicycle records from 33 to 50 miles, beating the latter record by 6m. 7 2-5s.

MILES.	ADAM'S TIME. H. M. S.	PREVIOUS RECORDS. H. M. S.
5	0 15 26 4-5	
10	0 30 42	
15	0 46 13 1-5	
20	1 1 50 2-5	
25	1 17 7 1-5	
30	1 32 47 1-5	
*33	1 41 55 4-5	1 42 21
*34	1 44 57 2-5	1 45 55
*35	1 48 6 4-5	1 49 27
*36	1 51 16 4-5	1 52 58
*37	1 54 19 2-5	1 56 30
*38	1 57 24	2 0 10
*39	2 0 24 1-5	2 3 50
*40	2 3 21 1-5	2 7 16
*41	2 6 21 1-5	2 10 35 2-5
*42	2 9 21 4-5	2 13 54 1-5
*43	2 12 21 3-5	2 17 15 1-5
*44	2 15 24	2 20 30
*45	2 18 23 1-5	2 23 53
*46	2 21 24 3-5	2 27 5
*47	2 24 36	2 30 10
*48	2 27 41	2 33 33
*49	2 30 45 2-5	2 36 44
*50	2 33 37 2-5	2 39 45

19 miles 730 yards in hour.

* Record.

PROFESSIONAL RACING AT LEICESTER, JULY 27.

One-mile professional handicap.—F. Laurance, 105 yds., 2m. 42 4-5s.; J. Lee, 25 yds, second. Three-mile professional handicap, A. Robb, scratch, 8m 46 1-5s.; F. W. Allard, 40 yds., second.

FIVE MILES SCRATCH RACE.

R. Howell, 15m. 45 2-5s., last quarter, 35 4-5s.; A. H. Robb, second.

LOUISIANA DIVISION MEET, AUDUBON DRIVING PARK, SEPTEMBER 14.

The programme of events is as follows: One-mile bicycle race for novices, open to L. A. W. members only; five-mile bicycle, L. A. W. national championship; one-half mile mixed race, for boys under sixteen years of age; one-mile Rover-type safety, open to L. A. W. members only; one-mile bicycle, Louisiana State L. A. W. championship; one-mile ride and run, mixed race, open to L. A. W. members only; one-mile tandem tricycle, L. A. W. members only; one-mile Louisiana Cycling Club championship; one-mile New Orleans Bicycle Club championship; 1½-mile lap race, mixed race, open to L. A. W. members only; one-half mile consolation, mixed race.

The entrance fee for each race will be fifty cents, all entries to be made with Ridgley P. Randall, Chairman Racing Board, No. 54 Baronne Street, New Orleans, Louisiana.

Entries to close on Tuesday, September 10, at 5 P. M.

Six thousand invitations will be issued. A fine band of music in attendance. All riders in the United States are invited to be present, and members of the Division will use every effort to make visitors feel at home.

HARRY HODGSON, Chief Consul.

HARTFORD TOURNAMENT NOTES.

The Wheel Club team have now got down to hard work, and are training every day at Charter Oak Park from 4 to 7 o'clock P. M. The team is composed of Forster, Cornell, Dresser and Reid on ordinaries, and Harding and Shea on safeties. Corcoran, the trainer, is well pleased with their work, and says great things may be expected of them.

According to the report of the different committees connected with the race meet, indications point toward the most successful tournament ever held in New England.

Hundreds of wheelmen throughout Connecticut will give Canary a grand welcome at the Hartford tournament. This is Canary's first appearance in this country in four years.

H. G. Cornell, of the Hartford Wheel Club, is coming fast, and will surprise some of the good ones at the fall meets.

F. A. Clark, of Plantsville, Conn., Yale's crack rider, has his eye on the State championship, and Forster, Ives and Miller will have to hustle to beat him.

WHEEL GOSSIP.

Mr. and Mrs. Kennedy-Childe are at Ocean Grove.

A one-mile open handicap will be held at Queens, L. I., August 17, at 4:30 P. M.

A Columbia tandem safety will be offered as a prize at the Pennsylvania races.

Harry Hodgson has forsaken his "trike"—sacreligiously called "The Hearse"—for a "safe."

The Minneapolis Park Board have spent $200,000 this year improving Kenwood Boulevards.

IRISH CYCLISTS' TOURNAMENT, at Dublin, August 5—Half-mile bicycle championship: A. Du Cros, 1m. 20s.

In the 10-mile race in which Temple defeated the English professional cracks the last mile was ridden in 2m. 44s.

Messrs. Wm. Read & Sons have written Mayor Grant suggesting the appointment of Mr. G. R. Bidwell as manager of the bicycle exhibit.

The Waiontha Club's Race Meet, announced for Wednesday at Richfield Springs, N. Y., was postponed until Friday, on account of rain.

Several races will be held at Beacon Park, Boston, on Labor Day, at the tournament of field sports to be held in aid of the Working Boys' Home.

At the fast Paddington track, August 5, G. L. Morris, 30 yards, won the mile handicap in 2m. 40 3-5s., and the scratch safety race in 2m. 49 1-5s.

At the games of the Adelphi Athletic Club, to be held at the Manhattan A. C. grounds, on Tuesday, September 3, a two-mile bicycle handicap will be decided.

The Montreal Bicycle Club hold their annual race meet at the M. A. A. A. grounds on August 24. For particulars address R. F. Smith, P. O. Box 958, Montreal.

At the athletic games held at Oak Island, near Boston, Mass., August 13, the three-mile bicycle race was won by P. J. Berlo, E. J. Clark, second. Time, 11m. 50s.

The New York Club will take thirty men to Staten Island on August 25. The party will have a special boat to take them from an uptown pier direct to Staten Island.

At the Warren A. C. games, to be held at Wilmington, Del., September 21, a two-mile handicap will be decided. Entries close September 16, with W. F. Kenty, Wilmington, Del.

The Dorchester Bicycle Club is a flourishing institution, having forty members, rooms on Neponset Avenue, and a balance in the Treasurer's hands. The club will hold fall races and a yachting excursion.

Henry J. Gallien, Albany Wheelmen, C. A. Sheehan, Manhattan B. C., and F. P. Prial, N. Y. B. C., will attend the Albany tournament on August 31, and afterwards tour to Hartford to attend the tournament.

W. F. Murphy and C. M. Murphy returned to Richfield Springs on Thursday night to compete in the road race on Friday. Messrs Banker, Clarke and Class competed at the Lockport races on Thursday and at Richfield on Friday.

A 1½-mile handicap will be decided at the Manhattan A. C. grounds, Eighty-sixth Street and Eighth Avenue, New York City, on September 21. Entries close September 14, with C. C. Hughes, 524 Fifth Avenue, New York City.

Howard A. Smith & Co., Newark, N. J., report an unprecedented demand for their safety bundle carriers, both for handle bar and mud guard. ***

A two-mile bicycle race for the amateur championship of America will be held September 14, at Traver's Island, at the grounds of the New York Athletic Club. Entries close September 7, with Secretary N. A. A. U., P. O. Box 611, New York City.

Elliot Mason left on Wednesday night for a short vacation. He will take boat to Hudson, N. Y., where he will join Mrs. Mason. From Hudson they will ride tandem bicycle through to Pittsfield, Mass., where they will remain a short time, touring in the vicinity.

At some sports held at Coventry on August 5, 7,000 people present, F. J. Osmond, scratch, won the mile handicap in 2m. 36s. The half-mile safety handicap fell to J. P. Norton, 65 yards; time, 1m. 14s. E. H. Taylor, 90 yards, won the safety handicap in 2m. 35 4-5s.

The Manhattan Club have called a run to Coney Island on Sunday next, leaving the club house, 263 West 70th Street, at 9 A. M., sharp. All wheelmen are invited to join. The club have appointed a Committee on Club House, as the Manhattan's lease of their present quarters expires next May.

W. J. Penrose, known to his friends as "Rosie," has just returned to his home at Newark, N. J., from his tour with the Elwell party. He is full of yarns, some of them fishy, and expresses strong approval of the management of the party. He states that a wheelman can travel abroad on one dollar per day.

Fred. T. Merrill, the Victor agent at Portland, Oregon, has done much to boom cycling in the Northwest. He has recently issued two catalogues of his store. The photograph of the exterior shows an imposing looking structure of peculiar design. It is called "Cycle Castle." The outside is as quaint as the interior is beautiful.

AT CINCINNATI, AUGUST 20,

The following bicycle events will be decided: one-half, one, two, two and a half and three-mile scratch races. A win bars a man for subsequent events. Entries close at one o'clock Aug. 20th, at Fair Grounds, with A. A. Bennett, or address 6 E. 4th Street, Cincinnati, O.

SPEED TRIALS AT QUEENS.

QUEENS, L. I., Aug. 10.—One-mile against time: A. C. Banker, Berkeley A. C., 2m. 57s; previous track record, 2m. 57 3-5s. Three miles against time: A. C. Banker, 9m. 26s; five miles, 15m. 41 1-5s. L. L. Clarke, B. A. C., rode one lap, one-sixth of a mile, in 24s., and a quarter mile in 40 3-5s.

The race between Messrs. Heydecker, N. Y. B. C. and Thayer, Citizens B. C., which was to have taken place on Saturday last has been declared off and will not be run until September, probably on the 14th. Thayer caught a severe cold during the rainy weather of last week and was advised by his doctor not to start. He is not over-strong at best and his decision is to be commended, though it will cause some adverse comment.

Some good sport resulted at the Bristol, Eng., meet, held July 27. One-mile safety handicap.—W. A. Daniels, 20 yds., 2m. 37 2-5s. One-mile ordinary handicap.—W. Brooks, 65 yds., 2m. 38s. Half-mile handicap.—G. R. Adcock, scratch, 2m. 36s. One-mile tricycle handicap.—W. Whitter, 250 yds., 2m. 45 2-5s. Three-mile safety handicap.—W. A. Daniels, 50 yds., 8m. 31s. Three-mile ordinary handicap.—A. J. Hickery, 130 yds., 8m. 32 4-5s.

It is reported that Messrs. H. A. Lozier and W. L. Yost will shortly establish a factory at Toledo, Ohio. Mr. Lozier is a prominent Western cycle agent, located at Cleveland. Mr. Yost was formerly President of the Springfield Bicycle Mfg. Co., but resigned his office and sold out his stock in the company last year on account of poor health. He has been at Los Angeles, and was no doubt much improved by the fine climate there. The new company will manufacture straight ordinaries and safeties, retailing at about $75.00.

BUFFALO RAMBLERS' LANTERN PARADE.

The lantern parade of the Ramblers' Bicycle Club, held August 7, was the biggest kind of a success in every sense of the word. Nearly 200 wheelmen were in line. Their wheels were prettily decorated with Chinese lanterns and the sight was an imposing one. Line was formed 8:30 at the Circle. The parade moved out Richmond Avenue to Massachusetts Street, to West Avenue, North to Delaware, to Niagara Square, countermarching to Summer, to Main and the Circle. Hundreds of people lined the sidewalks to see the procession. The first five wheels were ridden by ladies.

PHILADELPHIA PICKINGS.

The Philadelphia Bicycle Club had a ladies' moonlight run last week.—Charles Frayne, of the Century Wheelmen, has gone to Brazil. He expects to do some riding while there.—Sam Crawford, one of the "Penny's" founders, was out on the road last week, to the astonishment of the boys. Crawford was a good man on the path.—A. E. Binns, of the Century Wheelmen, has returned from a trip through Europe awheel. His club mates gave him a warm reception.—The South End Wheelmen will hold a 10-mile club road race at the Philadelphia Driving Park on Saturday next.

THE SCRANTON TOURISTS.

The party of wheelmen who left Scranton on August 10 will arrive next Tuesday night at the Grand Union Hotel. The programme from New York to Scranton is as follows:

Wednesday, August 21.—Leave New York 6 A. M. Brooklyn Riding District and Coney Island. Train to Newark, night (Continental Hotel).

Thursday, August 22.—Leave Newark 6 A. M. Orange, Milburn, Morristown, 20 miles, dinner (Park House). Dover, 12 miles, night (—— House).

Friday, August 23.—Leave Dover 6 A. M. Hopatcong, Dingmans, 34 miles, dinner (—— Hotel). Milford, 8 miles, night (Cressman House).

Saturday, August 24.—Leave Milford 6 A. M. Dingmans, Bushkill, Water Gap, 32 miles, dinner (Kittatiny House). Train to Scranton.

The tourists will no doubt be glad to have wheelmen in the vicinity of Gotham join them on the runs to Coney Island and the Oranges.

Howard A. Smith & Co., Newark, N. J., are teaching more persons how to ride the bicycle at Oraton Hall than ever before at this season of the year. Hall open evenings. ***

BROOKLYN.

The constantly increasing number of unattached wheelmen in this city, has often been the cause of comment amongst club-men. The three clubs of this city should devise some scheme to place before these fantastically dressed pedalers, the benefits of club life, and try to draw them into either one of the large clubs. If a wheelman could only be made to realize how it concentrates power toward freedom of the sport, it seems to me it would be a long step forward.

Meeteer and Borland, of the B. B. C., will take a two week's tour during the latter part of September, through Vermont.

Hailey, of the B. B. C., has just returned from an outing at White Lake, and reports having had too much water, insomuch as it was not confined to the lake.

Wheelmen are trying to wear a dirt path at the edge of the stone walk leading down the boulevard. Aid in the good work brother wheelmen, by riding on the grass every time you go that way, and we shall soon be able to go to Bath without shaking our bones out of joint.

The amendment to reduce the age limit, from twenty-one years to eighteen years, was defeated at the last meeting of the Long Island Wheelmen. As a friend of the L. I. W.'s, I can't help but think it would have been better to have opened their doors wide and taken in the younger wheelmen. Both the K. C. W.'s and B. B. C. welcome amongst them wheelmen of tender age, and are undoubtedly benefited by the young blood.

C. F. Quimby and F. H. Pough, B. B. C., are staying at Montclair, N. J., for the summer, rolling up the miles on the good roads to be found in the vicinity.

Not long since I read an article in one of the daily papers which gleefully made known that a certain writer of interesting notes, under a high-sounding *nom de plume*, was none other than a Mr. So-and-so. Thinking of this, and how infallible the daily press have become, I fell asleep at my desk. While asleep a strange dream disturbed me. My volume of wheeling papers had taken unto itself legs and was dancing all over my desk, and, after rudely pushing my pen one side, halts with a low bow directly in front of me. Now its leaves begin to tremble and open one by one, seemingly inviting me to read. What can it mean! Have I been writing chestnuts? But no! Note how the mischievous spirit who is working this charm hesitates at each page of correspondence and points laughingly to the fictious names signed below.

Listen, he knows them all. "Independent," that was Hornbostel, and "H. G.," easy to guess, Greenman; again, pugnacious "Bon," who called everything by their right names, that's Barkman, and "Nyx," Alden, of the grays, and so on, all of the past. The pages turn rapidly now and stop at—yes, "Atol!" "Enough," I cry, and with that cry awake. My volume of wheeling papers is undisturbed—it was but the passing effects of a disordered fancy.

Ah, friend, "Ram Lal," our time will come and we shall be numbered with the known and forgotten. Even as I write a dread comes o'er me. Our incognito life is a short one; just as we have chronicled some dainty tid-bit of news, safe in our fancied security, lo! suspicion becomes a certainty and we are unmasked, lucky, indeed, if we escape having a back number thrust in our face and the maledictions of the victims of our pens heaped upon our heads. However, safe in the present, I shall take no heed for the future, thankful that I can still sign myself simply

ATOL.

AN EXPERT'S OPINION.

The writer's recent visit to your factory, and his examination of the Warwick safety, convinced him that the Warwick wheels were being built right, were right. There is not a particle of doubt in my mind but that the Warwick Perfect Safety is the handsomest, the most beautifully constructed, the most comfortable riding, the easiest running and the easiest steering crank safety that I have ever ridden or seen. They are made as carefully as a Jurgensen watch, and the method of their construction, together with the care that is exercised in making the various parts, would hardly result in turning out anything less than the best on earth. I do not think there is a particle of doubt but that this office can dispose of a great many more wheels than we have ordered already, although I can assure you that we have lost the sale of nearly fifty or a hundred by not having our samples before this. Still, I look forward to an extremely busy and profitable season with Warwick wheels.

C. H. S.

Bridgeport, Conn., has about 350 riders. Almost every man has an agency for some kind of wheel. As a matter of fact there are fifteen agencies in the town.

GOOD BICYCLE REPAIRER can find steady work at H. W. Higham's, 905 G Street, N. W., Washington, D. C. tf

WANTED—Wheelmen to send 50 cents and receive by return mail one pair Black Cotton Ribbed Bicycle Hose. Cool and nobby for summer wear. Welch & Rogers, Bainbridge, N. Y. tfc

FOR SALE—Two Experts; 56-inch, $70; 54-inch, $75; 54-inch National, $60; all in fine condition. Brown & Greenleaf, Cambridge, Mass. tfc

FOR SALE—A Springfield Roadster in A1 condition; ball bearings; has been used very little. Address John C. Robbins, Oneida Square, Utica, N. Y. tf

ZOOK, Lititz, Pa.

Takes Cycles in payment for books, stationery, organs, pianos and miscellaneous goods. List free. Rare bargains in second-hand Wheels. Will trade a Tandem for a Safety. Advertising taken from newspaper men who wish mounts. One Buggy to trade. 8–16c

Second-hand Machines, many like new, prices reasonable. Wheels to rent. Repairing and nickeling. Note our change of address.

NEW YORK BICYCLE CO.,

No. 4 East 60th Street, Fifth Avenue entrance to Central Park.

Howard A. Smith & Co., Newark, N. J., have improved their Graphite for lubricating chains and bearings of bicycles and safeties, until it seems to be perfect. All riders should have a bottle. ***

At a meeting of the Society of Cyclists, held at Lewes, July 16, Dr. B. W. Richardson opened with an inaugural address, which occupied half an hour, and proved very interesting. Reviewing the past year's work of the society, the Doctor passed to the changes in machine construction, the adoption of small wheels for tricycles, the decline of tricycling in the favor of ladies--ascribed to tennis--the special machines recently designed for military cycling purposes; the unsuccessful attempt to produce a good water-cycle; the advance towards overcoming secondary vibration made by the inventors of the "Golden Era" and "Fleetwing" cycles; and the commercial aspect of cycling, in turn are dealt with. "The superiority of English manufactured machines has been maintained," said the Doctor, "and although there are few additions to the existing patents of real novelty, every day sees the cycle's extension to fresh uses. Besides the post-office, the fire brigade, the police, news agents, the traders largely use cycles. At present a social lull prevails. The performances on the racing path, and touring, are no longer regarded as marvelous. Tennis and golf compete in attraction with cycling. There are indications, however, of a new development in the future, probably in the direction of (*n*) supplementary power either chemical or electrical, (*b*) steel traction on cycle principles, or (*c*) the combination of horse traction with the cycle, as for example in connection with 'Victorias' and Multicycles for military transport. Scientific progress must be keenly watched by the society." The learned Doctor concludes with allusions to the relation of cycling to hygiene, the beneficial effects of judicious cycling during youth, maturity, and old age, its importance to women, and the evils arising from excess.

Bicycling News would like to know what an "Oklahoma Boomer" is. An Oklahoma Boomer is a man who drops off a train on any spot on Oklahoma, the Land of Promise, and that spot becomes a town before sunrise of the next morning, with a bank, a jail, a church, a newspaper and a real estate office. If he is a real out-and-out Boomer, he collects his fees and perquisites as sheriff, deposits them in the bank of which he is president, and then goes round to his newspaper office and writes an editorial to boom his real estate. That's what an Oklahoma Boomer is, good *News*.

The Credenda Seamless Steel Tube Co., of Birmingham, which supplies many English and American makers with tubing, have recently extended their plant by purchasing the property of the Birmingham Plate Glass Co., which occupies seventeen acres. The main building of the new plant is 528×155 feet.

Two-Mile L. A. W. State Championship

WILL BE RUN AT

THIRD OUT-DOOR TOURNAMENT

OF THE

ALBANY WHEELMEN,

TO BE HELD AT

RIDGEFIELD ATHLETIC CLUB'S GROUND,

SATURDAY, AUGUST 31st, 1889.

1. One-mile Novice.
2. " Ordinary (open).
3. " Star (club).
4. Two-mile L.A.W. State Champ'nship
5. One-mile Team-race (open).
6. One-third-mile Safety (open).
7. One-mile Club Championship.
8. " Tandem (open).
9. Two-mile Handicap (open).
10. One-third-mile Consolation.

ELEGANT GOLD MEDALS AND COSTLY PRIZES.

Entrance fees, 50c. each to open events; State Championship, $1.

Entries close on Saturday, August 24, 1889. Address to

WM. B. PHIPPS, Sec. Com.,

51 Howard Street, Albany, N. Y.

THE CYCLING EVENT
OF THE YEAR.

Hartford Wheel Club Tournament,

CHARTER OAK PARK,

September 2 and 3, 1889.

GOOD TRACK.

FAST TIME.

EXCITING RACES.

COSTLY PRIZES.

Special Engagement of the Distinguished Fancy Rider,

D. J. CANARY.

Entries close August 26. Entry Blanks mailed on application.

W. M. FRANCIS, Sec'y,

Box 745, Hartford, Conn.

NOTICE.

TO MANUFACTURERS AND AGENTS.

LOUIS GLASEL & CO.,

COVENTRY, ENGLAND,

The Continental Cycles,

CHEAPEST AND BEST IN THE MARKET.

Safety No. 1, £9 - $45.

BALLS THROUGHOUT. BEST MATERIAL. WORKMANSHIP GUARANTEED.

L. GLASEL & CO.

All rough and finished parts also supplied at Bottom Prices.

Chains, Hubs, Pedals, Tires, Stampings, Lamps, Cement, Forks, Tubes, Rims, etc., all cheap for cash. List free to Manufacturers' Agents. Prompt and best attention guaranteed.

NO CHEAP TALK BUT PLAIN FACTS.

"I say there is no need of a Safety being any heavier than an Ordinary, if properly made."

$175 BUYS A PREMIER TANDEM SAFETY, ridden only a few times, acknowledged to be the best Tandem made. $105 buys the latest Safety imported; diamond frame; ball bearing all round; all steel; no casting; and if you are ready to pay $125 for a Safety, don't put it out for 50 or 58 lbs. of material, even if it is steel. Steel is cheap, but pay it for less weight, more skill, finer workmanship, less noise, less talk, and a machine, the moment you see it, you will join others, who know, in saying, well, we have struck perfection; and the machine is the "Catford Premier Safety, weighs 38 lbs., stronger than your 58 lb. machine and runs as easy again. Just call and see it. The Premier Cycles are sold by

W. J. NEWMAN,

Cycle dealer, Harvard Square, Cambridge, Mass.

Plenty of new and second-hand Safeties, Ordinaries and Tandems in stock. Call. Open evenings.

Second-Hand
BICYCLES and TRICYCLES.

New York Bicycle Co.,

Nos. 4 and 6 East 60th Street.

We make a specialty of taking old mounts to part payment for New Victors, Stars, Rapids, Eagles, Halls, and for cycles of all other good makes.

KEY TO DESCRIPTION.

FINISH.—"1" Full nickeled. "2" All nickeled except rims. "3" Wheels enameled, balance nickeled. "4" Enameled with nickel trimmings. "5" Enameled with polished parts. "6" Half bright and enameled or painted. "7" Spokes nickeled, balance enameled.

BEARINGS.—"1" Balls to both wheels and pedals. "2" Balls to both wheels and plain pedals. "3" Balls to rear, cone to front, cone to rear, plain pedals. "4" Plain to front, cone to rear, plain pedals. "5" Balls to front, cone to rear, ball pedals.

CONDITION.—"1" Very little used, fully as good as a new machine. "2" Tires show but very slight wear, finish and bearings as good as new. "3" Tires but little worn, finish only slightly marred, bearings A 1. "4" Finish, bearings and tires all in condition of uniform excellence. "5" Tires slightly worn, finish somewhat marred, bearings A 1. "6" Finish and bearings in first-rate shape, tires somewhat worn. "7" Has new tires, finish and bearings excellent. "8" Tires somewhat cut, finish somewhat marred, bearings in very good order. "9" Good, durable machine, considerably used, but in very fair condition.

No.	Size.	Name.	Cost.	Price.		
306	54	British Challenge.	140 00	50 00	7	2
513	—	Humber Tandem,	250 00	115 00	4	2
523	48	Columbia Mustang,	85 00	25 00	4	2
521	52	Dictator,	135 00	50 00	4	3
525	48	Special Star,	135 00	100 00	4	Ball
537	51	Rudge Lt. Roadster,	130 95	100 00	4	4
533	51	New Mail,	128 75	75 00	4	2
544	—	S. S. S. Tandem,	250 00	180 00	4	1
553	51	Singer Matchless,	130 00	65 00	4	3
558	—	Col. Lt. Rdstr. T'ke.,	160 00	75 00	4	1
567	52	Columbia Expert,	122 50	55 00	3	2
574	53	Columbia Tandem,	250 00	130 00	4	2
575	50	Columbia Expert,	130 00	60 00	3	3
576	54	Victor Roadster,	130 00	78 00	4	2
580	50	Columbia Expert,	115 00	60 00	4	2
581	52	N. R. Roadster,	139 50	115 00	4	5
586	53	Columbia Lt. Rdstr.	127 50	78 00	4	1
592	50	New Rapid Safety,	135 00	80 00	4	5
596	46	Victor Junior,	90 00	50 00	4	3
598	48	Otto Special,	80 00	50 00	4	3
598	52	Coumbia Expert,	135 00	65 00	3	3
601	54	Columbia Expert,	130 00	65 00	4	1
602	48	Special Star,	137 00	75 00	4	Ball
606	56	Columbia Expert,	130 00	50 00	7	2
613	56	Columbia Expert,	127 50	90 00	3	1
613	54	Premier,	135 00	55 00	4	1
615	48	Special Star,	125 00	70 00	3	Ball
616	51	Special Club,	125 00	45 00	4	6
619	54	Columbia Standard,	80 00	55 00	4	4
600	51	Semi Racer Star,	135 00	100 00	4	Ball
605	52	Otto	90 00	50 00	4	3
697	44	Columbia Standard,	80 00	55 00	4	2
698	50	British Challenge,	130 00	50 00	4	3
630	54	Premier Tandem Safety,	200 00	170 00	4	1
631	48	Columbia Semi-Rdstr,	75 00	45 00	4	2
632	50	Special Club,	135 00	67 00	3	2
633	50	Springfield Roadster,	75 00	45 00	4	Plain
635	48	Apollo Lt. Roadster,	115 00	75 00	3	1
637	54	New Rapid Safety,	135 00	80 00	4	5
639	54	English,	100 00	45 00	4	3
640	50	Columbia Veloce Safety,	135 00	105 00	4	1
640	54	American Rudge,	100 00	45 00	4	5
641	50	Springfield Roadster,	90 00	55 00	3	Plain
642	50	New Rapid Roadster,	150 00	85 00	4	5
643	54	American Sanspareil,	135 00	45 00	4	3
644	54	Columbia Expert,	130 00	95 00	3	1
645	52	Columbia Expert,	132 50	60 00	3	1
646	48	Special Star,	132 50	95 00	3	Ball
647	54	Columbia Lt. R'dster,	125 00	65 00	4	1
648	54	Columbia Expert,	125 00	85 00	3	1
648	52	Victor Lt. Roadster,	132 50	85 00	3	1
649	54	Columbia Expert,	125 00	100 00	4	1

Upon receipt of $5 any Bicycle on above list will be sent C. O. D. for balance, with privilege of examination. Correspondence invited.

Vol. III.—No 26.]   NEW YORK, AUGUST 23, 1889.   [Whole Number, 78.

THE AMERICAN IDEAL RAMBLER

has demonstrated its intrinsic worth this season, in that it is the only small

rear driver that keeps away from the repair shop.

It is mainly constructed of weldless steel tubing and sheet steel, and

has ball bearings to both wheels in the standard finish.

It has proven an excellent mount for ladies not weighing over 125 lbs.

Its price, $65.00, stamps it as the best value on the market.

Balls can be added to crank axle, pedals and head if desired.

We can now fill orders for this wheel with a reasonable degree

of promptness.

GORMULLY & JEFFERY MFG. CO.

CHICAGO, ILL.

80 PAGE CATALOGUE ON APPLICATION.

MERWIN, HULBERT & CO., New York Agents.

WARWICK PERFECTION SAFETY.

A large number of cyclists
who have seen it say it is
the finest Rear=Driver
ever shown in New
York City.

WEIGHT, 48 lbs.   PRICE, $135.

CALL AND SEE IT.

The National Safety.

Price, with Ball Bearings to Wheels, **$75**
  "   "   "   all round,   **90**

A First-Class Safety at a Reasonable Price. Rear wheel,
30 inches, geared to 54; 30 inch steering wheel; ⅞-inch
crescent steel rims and ⅞ inch best quality rubber tires;
direct spokes, of special drawn steel wire of best quality;
cranks adjustable from 5½ to 6½ inch throw; chains of
special patent; vulcanite handle-grips; wheels fitted with
ball bearings; adjustable suspension saddle, with coiled rear
and front springs. Spade handle if desired.

The National Ladies' Safety.

Price, with Ball Bearings to both Wheels, **$75**
  "   "   "   all over,   **90**

WILLIAM HALPIN & CO.,
No. 13 MURRAY STREET,
P. O. Box 2225.   NEW YORK.

Full Line of "Warwicks." Full Line of "Clubs." Large Stock of "American" Cycles.

Agents wanted in every City and Town in New York State.

SECOND·HAND WHEELS.

THE proof of the pudding is in the eating, and the proof of our claims for the **Eagle** is in the practical experience on the road of riders of our wheel.

We claim the **Eagle** to be the best all around machine in the market.

The lightest running, and the fastest and safest coasting.

A machine that can be ridden over every kind of road, good, bad and indifferent, through sand, and up and down hills, with the minimum amount of fatigue and the greatest comfort to the rider.

The following letter from one of the best known wheelmen of the country is a sample of our testimonials :

NEWPORT, R. I., July 7th, 1889.

EAGLE BICYCLE MFG. CO., STAMFORD, CONN.

DEAR SIRS:—I rode my EAGLE on Sunday, July 7th, to Fall River, then to New Bedford and returned the same way. On the way back I rode from Fall River to Newport, 18 miles, by moonlight, in 1 hour and 45 minutes. I only made one dismount in the 18 miles, and any one that has ridden over the road by daylight will know that the road is not one of the best. As it was a cloudy night, the moon did not do me very much good and I had to ride by guess. The best time I have heard of being made on this road before was 1 hour and 52 minutes. That was made by myself last fall, in daylight, on a 39-inch Star. The EAGLE is the only machine I have succeeded in riding over that road at night, as I have walked 10 out of the 18 miles twice with other machines, and one of them was a Safety.

Yours truly,   WM. VAN WAGONER, R. I. Champion.

SEND FOR CATALOGUE.   **AGENTS WANTED.**

THE EAGLE BICYCLE MFG. CO.,
Stamford, Conn.

THE WHEEL

—AND—

CYCLING TRADE REVIEW,

Published every Friday morning.

Entered at the Post Office at second class rates.

Subscription Price, - - - - $1.00 a year.
Foreign Subscriptions. - - - - 6s. a year.
Single Copies, - - - - - - 5 Cents.

Newsdealers may order through AM. NEWS CO.

All copy should be received by Monday.
Telegraphic news received till Wednesday noon.

Advertising rates on Application.

F. P. PRIAL, Editor and Proprietor
23 Park Row,
P. O. Box 444, *New York.*

Persons receiving sample copies of this paper are respectfully requested to examine its contents and give us their patronage, and as far as is convenient, aid in circulating the journal, and extend its influence in the cause which it so faithfully serves. Subscription price, $1 per year.

THE *Providence Journal* sensibly points out the advantages enjoyed by cyclists at Roger Williams Park, and draws attention to the fact that these privileges are jeopardized by the darn-fool wheelmen--the things in plush tights who ride on the walks, contrary to law, knocking down babies and frightening old ladies and nurse girls by seeing how near they can come without hitting them. Wheelmen should realize, and that very forcibly, that their worst enemies are to be found among their own ranks. It may be accepted as a fact that the deep-rooted feeling against wheeling, among educated people as well as among the uncultivated, is founded on something more than mere prejudice, though that is the basis of the anti-cycling feeling. We should despise and cut dead the fellow who rides up and down some popular drive in tights and sleeveless jerseys. There is also the smart Aleck on wheels who cuts across in front of horses' heads, to the discomfiture of horse and driver. Let us combine and jump upon the "jays" of the wheel world.

IN another column will be found an article taken from the *Cyclist*, in which the idea of holding international championships is advocated. Our Racing Board should consult with European authorities with a view to arranging international championship contests.

THE editor of this paper is decidedly pleased over his election as a Representative of the New York State Division, and he is grateful to the gentlemen who nominated him and to those who voted for him. For the office he cares not a whit, but for the principle, everything. He ran for office merely to show the astounding absurdity of the assertion, that the "trade" should have no part in cycling legislation. When Mr. Shriver raised that objection, he not only committed himself to snobbery, but he aimed at a fellow club-man, and at one who had always been his advocate and friend. The election of the writer was a triumph for independence, and he hopes it will serve as an example to other men who may become tired of dictation.

SOME three months since the New York daily papers detailed, at great length and with much vividness of portrayal, the sufferings of the convicts in Sing Sing, who have been idle for nearly two years. The effects of this idleness were carefully noted and recorded. It was shown that sickness was on the increase, that some of the men were in a state bordering on imbecility, and that almost all were in a sort of miserable stupor. We commented on and republished the various reports at the time. The three days' wonder passed, however, and the editors of the great dailies, busied with world's fairs, divorce, murder and sea-shore gossip, have found no time to discuss the problem of Convict Labor. It is a fruitful theme, and we hope the papers will take it up again until a solution is found. We believe that the convicts should be employed to build and repair the roads.

FROM all over the country come papers containing references to the late Purvis-Bruce. In addition to these tributes to dear, old "Jack," we have received many personal letters expressing deep regret at the untimely death of one who was liked and loved far better than he knew. If "Jack" could know what a kind impression he had made in our little cycling world, it would please him right well.

AT a meeting of the Board of Estimate and Apportionment of New York, held last Monday, it was settled that the Commissioner of Public Works is unquestionably in favor of the use of asphalt pavements wherever it is found practicable. The smooth pavement is favored, not only for residence streets, but also for the business portion of the city. The Grand Boulevard, the principal cycling artery of New York, will be paved with asphalt as an opening wedge, and several blocks of asphalt will be laid on Park Avenue over the present granite pavement. This is an experiment to discover whether the Belgian block pavement will make a good foundation for the asphalt, in which case it will be introduced as rapidly as the appropriation will permit. The opening wedge having been entered, the work may be expected to proceed rapidly. It was a hard battle, but the victory was correspondingly great.

WE wonder whether these "anti-trade" cyclists would not keep quiet if they knew that some four years ago, when the League had not enough money to pay for a postage-stamp, that it was saved from bankruptcy by Colonel Pope. W. V. Gilman was Treasurer at the time and Fred. Jenkins was Secretary. Frank Egan, seeing inevitable ruin for the League, had blanks printed—printed gratis by Fred. Jenkins, by the way. Jenkins and Egan each contributed $10, and among the New York State Board of Officers the magnificent sum of $30 was subscribed. Mr. Egan then called on Colonel Pope, and the Colonel at once gave him $50, and added that if he wanted more he need only name the amount. These same anti-trade cyclists are invited to peruse the official report of the Road's Improvement Committee, from which they will learn that Colonel Pope offered to pay the whole expense of issuing fifteen thousand roads improvement pamphlets, and finally paid $350 toward its publication, the Barber Asphalt Co. contributing $100 and the Baltimore International Pavement Co. $50.

IN reply to many inquiries we would say that a man may sell any prize won in a road race without violation of the Racing Rules. We have the endorsement of the Chairman of the Racing Board that this opinion is correct.

IF a man wins first place in an open contest he is no longer a novice. If the promoting club fails to deliver his prize, as was the case at a tournament held at Poughkeepsie last year, it does not affect the case.

TO TRY ASPHALT.

At a meeting of the Board of Estimate and Apportionment held at the City Hall last Monday, the question of pavements was discussed for two hours. A number of prominent real estate men, including Messrs Eno and Stokes, advocated a new pavement for the Boulevard.

It was finally decided to appropriate $224,000 to pave the Boulevard with asphalt.

Resolutions were also adopted to pave with asphalt on concrete foundation Lexington avenue, between Forty-second and Fifty-ninth streets, and Broad street, between Wall street and Exchange place.

The proposal to pave a number of streets with asphalt laid on the old pavement was regarded by President Coleman as somewhat in the nature of an experiment. Most of the list of these streets prepared by Commissioner Gilroy was laid over, but it was decided to try the experiment on Park avenue, from Thirty-fourth to Fortieth street.

The total cost of the paving ordered at the meeting will be $661,500, and the issue of $700,000 of bonds was authorized.

To superintend the expenditure of this money and the million dollars a year for three years authorized by the act, Commissioner Gilroy asked for the authority to pay some additional help out of the paving money. He asked for a force whose salaries would aggregate $23,000 a year, and a resolution was passed giving them to him. The force is to consist of a consulting engineer at $5,000, an assistant at $2,500, two transitmen at $1,500, two levelers at $1,200, four rodmen at $1,000, one draughtsman at $1,500, two skilled laborers at $2.50 a day, and four axemen at $2.50.

The Comptroller also asked to have the appointment of an engineer to inspect the work before making payments on the contracts. He got one, at $2,500 a year.

INTERNATIONAL CHAMPIONSHIPS.

From a report received this week from our Australian correspondent, we are notified that the N. C. U. has given its sanction to the Victorian Cyclists' Union to defray the expenses of a team of Australian amateur racing men to visit England and compete in our championships. This brings us to a subject which we mooted a year or two since, and to which we briefly referred to in a recent issue—that is, the official and proper organization of a series of international amateur championships. Now that riders in all the civilized countries of the earth are riding up to championship form, the time is undoubtedly ripe for the elaboration and completion of such a scheme. The fact that the Union has given its consent to the payment of expenses by another Union, shows that it is at least prepared to accept the principle which we proposed when first projecting the scheme. We now take the opportunity of again calling attention to it. We would have a special committee of the Union appointed to confer with the Unions of other countries, and arrange a series of international or world's championships, which should be run once a year in the different countries of the International Union, the order to be decided by lot, or otherwise, and the expenses of the visiting teams to be defrayed by the Unions of their respective countries. We would have either the whole of the proceeds and expenses of the meeting be taken and defrayed by the Union of the country in which the meetings of any one year were held, or else that the home Union take one-half the profits, whilst the remaining moiety be divided amongst the other countries. The meetings should be held at the close of the season, say in September, and each country would, of course, select its team by a careful series of test races, and would pay the expenses of a given and limited number of officials to represent it. By this means we should secure the meeting of the best riders of the world. The interest in the races would naturally be enormous, wherever held, and the test races (which may be the championships of the respective countries, or not, as determined,) would be full of interest and importance, as the successful competitors would not only defeat their opponents and win the championship of their own country, but would thereby secure the right of defending the honor of their nation in foreign lands. We think the difficulties attendant on the working out of such a scheme would not be great, though it would undoubtedly entail a considerable amount of work. We should like to see the Union of this country take the initiative, and we have little doubt but that the ruling associations of other lands would readily fall in with its suggestions.—*The Cyclist.*

CYCLISTS ON THE SIDEWALKS.

There is one gentleman who should be suppressed the sidewalk fiend. He is the one who is responsible to a great extent for what little prejudice exists against wheelmen. A bicycle has no right whatever on the sidewalk for the purpose of riding. Its place is the street. There it has in the eyes of the law the same right as other vehicles. In sparsely settled districts, and where it is impossible to ride on the streets there is some excuse for using the sidewalks, exercising great care while doing so to avoid accidents. Of course this exception only applies to the remote suburbs, where few people are to be met on the walks. But in the city it is a different thing, and the full penalty of the law ought to be imposed upon persons disobeying the law. The great body of cyclists are gentlemen and ladies, but unfortunately there are exceptions.—*Chicago Tribune.*

One of the sights of Springfield, Mass., is a little bit of pink and white humanity perched on the bundle-carrier of papa's safety bicycle.

WHEEL GOSSIP.

A. B. Rich will ride at Albany and Hartford.

The Bay State Club, of Worcester, will hold a meet late in the fall.

WANTED.—Route: New City to Utica. Address care of this office.

The Louisville Bicycle Club, only a year old, has fifty-three members.

Campbell, of Niagara Falls, has developed a remarkably fast last-lap spurt.

An Englishman recently advertised a plot in High Gate Cemetery in exchange for a wheel.

Messrs. Stephens and Bridgman recently took a moonlight ride from the K. C. W. club-house to Patchogue.

Ralph Temple is doing fancy riding in England. Man can't "fake" in fancy riding. Wonder why Temple ever took to it?

Entries close August 29 for the one-mile handicap to be decided at the Brooklyn A. A. grounds on September 7. See Fixtures.

The *Scottish Cyclist* is improving from week to week. Building up a paper is hard work but the Scotchmen are getting there.

The *Athlete* makes a strong editorial plea for the extermination of the road hog, both in vehicles and on cycles, from Prospect Park.

Mr. Garrison, of the Highland House, at Garrisons on the Hudson, is a cyclist. On the hotel paper a cyclist is shown riding in the hotel grounds.

Mr. Warren L. Welch and sister, who went through on a tandem on the Century run, arrived in Hagerstown on Saturday last. On Sunday they left for Luray.

A party of seven wheelmen were arrested at Bath Beach on Sunday last for riding on the foot-path. The Judge, grizzly, gruff, but kind, acquitted the boys with a reprimand.

The Wakefield Club will inaugurate the social season early. A ball is announced for October 11. The club will hold a 25-mile road race in September, and a 10-mile race in October.

Chicago has a "Bicycle Reservatory," where men who ride downtown to business can leave their wheels during the day. In the evening they find them cleaned, oiled and inspected.

The Boston *Herald* of Sunday last publishes two columns of observations on the disgraceful condition of Boston's street pavements, and suggests new and improved systems of pavements.

Twelve hours' bicycle road record.—On July 31, mounted on a "Geared Facile," F. W. Shorland, an English cyclist, rode 50 miles on the road in 2h. 39m. 54s., and completed 160½ miles in 12 hours.

It is pretty generally admitted that Van Wagoner, of Newport, is a good fellow and a true sportsman, and he will be treated all right when he comes down this way, whether he wins or loses.

The C. T. C. will have to settle a libel suit to the tune of £550. It was all because E. R. Shipton did not like one Ned Clarke, and penned that dislike in the dry-as-dust columns of the *C. T. C. Gazette*.

A large number of cyclists within easy reach of Albany will attend the tournament, and will ride over to Hartford on Sunday. The prizes are valuable, the track fast, and a large field of entries should be received.

W. T. Robertson rode from Cabin John Bridge to the Le Droit Building in Washington on August 11. The distance is ten miles, and the time of the ride was 30m., which is record for the course. Robertson rode an Eagle.

H. W. Booth and E. H. Boehner rode from Erie, Pa., to Boston, leaving Erie August 7 and arriving at Boston on the 16th. They averaged 85 miles a day, and on August 9 rode 125 miles, from Hornellsville, N. Y., to Ithaca.

Messrs. Potter and Raymond, Brooklyn B. C., have gone to the Adirondacks. Both are hard workers and need a rest. Mr. Raymond writes that Mr. Potter is such a good shot that he, Raymond, never expects to reach home alive.

THE VIRGINIA DIVISION L. A. W. MEET.—The meet of the Southern Division L. A. W. will be held at Norfolk, Va., August 26 and 27, under the auspices of the Norfolk Cycle Club. The roads in Norfolk and vicinity are fine shell turnpikes.

MAINE DIVISION OFFICERS ELECTED.

Chief Consul, Dr. George E. Dow, Portland; Vice-Consul, Cyrus D. Batchelder, Sanford; Representative, James O. Whittemore, Fairfield; Secretary and Treasurer, A. L. T. Cummings, Biddeford.

L. A. Hill and Dr. J. G. Fuller made a remarkable tandem bicycle record on August 9, riding from Bryn Mawr to the last toll gate on Lancaster Pike, distance five miles, in 14m. 47s. This is faster than any previous track or road record for the tandem safety.

At half past six every evening, the agents of Bridgeport, with two exceptions, come out of their offices, get their wheels and stand at the street corners, that those who pass may see. The principal wheels sold in Bridgeport this year are Columbias and Singers.

The Lynn *Daily Evening Item* of August 14 publishes three columns descriptive of the Thompson-Houston Electric Welding Company's plant, located in Lynn. As this new process of welding may be used in cycle construction the paper may interest the trade.

During a long jaunt on Sunday last, extending from Harlem Bridge to Pelham and back over by West Farms, not a touring cyclist was encountered. The Southern Boulevard and its various branch roads form a riding system which it would pay to patronize.

"Human Magnetism," by H. S. Drayton, M. D., is in press by Fowler & Wells Co., 775 Broadway, for early publication. It considers all the latest phases of the subject, including its nature, physiology and psychology with its uses as a remedial agent, in moral and intellectual improvement, etc. It is a work that is likely to attract a good deal of attention.

NERVE.

A London Missionary wants to borrow a safety to go holiday making. "Will some one please forward me one?" he whines. That is just the kind of minister the "little Johnstown boy" who cried for a wheel would make.

Jo. Pennell states that he sat down at the toasts of the "President of the United States" and "The Queen" merely as a joke. Glad to hear it. Pennell is eccentric, but is good to the right kind of Americans who go abroad. But why didn't Jo. label it a joke? No one could ever have known it without a placard.

Chief Consul Mott and Mrs. Mott are spending a few weeks at Hagerstown. The Chief Consul writes that the roads which were in such poor condition at the time of the League meet are now "finer than the Oranges." The Hagerstown Bicycle Club wants the fall meet of the Maryland Division held there.

J. W. Hare & Co., the Brooklyn bicycle dealers, are doing such a large and increasing business, that they were compelled to seek more commodious quarters, and have removed to 440 Flatbush Avenue. This is the site of the old "Ilderan" Bicycle Club, and is well known to Brooklyn wheelmen. In their new quarters they will do general repairing and storing, and have much better accommodations than formerly.

The people of Frankfort, Germany, gave Lehr, the English champion, an ovation on his return home. The train was awaited by a crowd and a band of music. Lehr walked alongside of his bicycle, followed by the bicycle clubs of the city and headed by a band of mounted police. Bouquets were showered on the champion. After he passed the crowd surged after him. It was a remarkable demonstration.

ANOTHER CYCLING PRODIGY.

Mr John Wood, of the Harlem Bicycle Co., is the proudest man on Lenox Avenue, and his right to be, nobody disputes, as he is the father of the youngest bicycle rider in the world. Robert is but twenty-two months old, and can ride as well as many that are as many years old. He can be seen on Lenox Avenue, between 125th and 126th Streets, almost daily taking his ride.—*Harlem Reporter*.

In England the employees of the large cycling companies hold picnics in summer. On August 3 the Coventry Company's employees had an outing, among the picnickers being good old Mr. Grinyer, who once astonished the people of Young's Hotel, at Boston, by leaving out a rubber shoe and a boot to be polished. Perhaps, under the circumstances, Mr. Grinyer's mistake was natural. Wonder if the Boston Club fellows can still brew the same old punch?

When a cycle is stolen in England a notice of this style is posted in all the station houses.

WANTED.

Charged with stealing a bicycle on the 15th inst.,

A YOUTH,

giving the name of "Humphrey;" age, about 18; height, about 5ft. 1in.; pale complexion, round face, small mouth, thick brown hair. Dressed in black coat and vest, dark gray trousers, shabby boots, light check cloth cap.

AMENDED DESCRIPTION OF BICYCLE FOLLOWS.

Wheeling and its correspondents continue to blackguard the Elwell tourists. Its Paris correspondent writes as follows of the Elwell party: "Individually they are bearably, collectively they are bears. They seem more disposed to grumble at being asked to halt while cool drinks and polite words were offered them than to render a gracious or even a civil reply. It is a pity a more representative set could not have been got together, but if one may judge by appearances the fault lies not with the men but with the mismanager of a rather cleverly got up financial speculation."

MORE PROOF OF THE FRAUD.

Some one has been having a lark with the *Wheelman's Gazette*. That readable paper publishes in its July number a picture entitled, "Start of the One-Mile L. A. W. Championship," but the artist has taken it bodily from a photograph of the start of the international race at Copenhagen last year. This picture, which is supposed to represent an American championship, contains portraits of Teddy Mayes, Professor Jimmy, Otto Benzon, Rennemoe Gulbrandsen, H. G. Kelly, F. Percy Low, Valdemar Hansen, and the Crown Prince of Denmark. More American enterprise.—*Wheeling*.

FURTHER CLAIMS FOR GREAT SPEED.

The new sliding railway at Paris, by which it is said to be demonstrated that, by a curious combination of compressed air and water at high pressure, will render it possible to drive a train on slides at 100 miles an hour at one-tenth the consumption of coal at present needed by locomotives. There is no smoke, no noise and next to no danger. The train can be pulled up in thirty yards, can climb up gradients of sixteen inches in the yard and run on curves of forty-four yards radius. There is almost no consciousness of motion; you simply enter the car, and in an hour you are 100 miles from where you started.

W. S. Grubb, of Pottstown, has invented a unique and valuable chain for driving cycles. The links are easily detached, are not riveted together and the bearings are extra large. It is self-lubricating and at the same time applies the lubricant to the sprocket wheels. The lubricant can be applied to the chain without removing it from the machine. Another valuable feature is the complete protection of each bearing from dust and dirt, as they are completely covered. It is cheap in construction. The links can be dropped out of sheet metal and all other work done on screw and milling machines. The bearings are hardened. The sprocket wheels for this chain can be cut on a drill press.—*Sporting Life*.

A writer in the *Pall Mall Gazette* says: "Now, when it is feared by the pessimistic that the higher education of women will interfere with their maternal functions, no kind of exercise can be as beneficial to them as cycling. My attention has been called to this fact by a letter I have just received from a woman doctor of New England, who has been practising medicine successfully for the last seventeen years, and can therefore speak from experience. She is an enthusiastic cyclist. She writes: 'So many of our women of to-day are complete failures in child-bearing, that in looking for a sound, natural reason I find it, or I think I do, in the fact that they take very little exercise which develops pelvic and thigh muscles. Women and girls are pushed into this quiet by dress.' Those who think all forms of sport unwomanly should lay this to heart. The fact is that women are physically in need of as good sound exercise as men, and it may be, by emancipating themselves from the old conventions and sharing manly sports as well as manly studies, they will do much to counteract the physical weakness which is their inheritance from their mothers and grandmothers, whose noblest ideal was to stay at home in ladylike repose of mind and body."

Messrs. Mott and Norris of the Maryland Club, spent Sunday and Monday in New York as the guests of President Luscomb, who was indefatigable in his efforts to entertain. Messrs. W. H. Starrett and W. W. Share, Long Island Wheelmen, also went the rounds with the visitors. The party visited Manhattan Beach on Monday and had a ride in the Oranges on Tuesday, taking the midnight train for Baltimore. Mr. Mott looked ruddy and well rested from his visit to Cottage City. Mr. Norris, who is President of the Maryland Club, is known all over the South as "Mose" Norris, and has more friends than he can count. Mr. Norris has a slightly clerical look and five pairs of spectacles, yet with these drawbacks he arrives there all the time.

Robert Wagner, of Detroit, aged 17, recently completed a bicycle ride from that city to Toronto. He made the run in a little more than 50 hours, averaging nearly ten miles an hour. Master Robbie has a high opinion of the hospitality of Western Ontario farmers, and also of the purity of their milk, but he would oppose the annexation of Canada unless they would consent to the abolition of their numerous collies, which tried to bite his legs as he rode past their respective habitations. The wheeling from Sarnia to London was good, but between the latter place and Hamilton the farmers were doing statute labor, and he found the roads rather rocky. This young cycler intends to join a club in this city in the fall and thinks his long ride will prove his eligibility. The trip cost him $2.92.—*Boston Herald*.

The touring committee of the Rhode Island Division, L. A. W., are planning the annual autumn run of the Division for the last week in August either Wednesday the 28th or Thursday the 29th. Newport will be the objective point. The programme in outline is to charter one of the river steamers—one of the lightning racers—and leave Providence in the morning at 7 or 8 o'clock, running up Warren River to take on board the large party from that vicinity that always cordially supports the Division runs by the presence of themselves and their wheels. On arrival at Newport, there will be a run to the beach, just to stretch their legs after the voyage, then dinner, and then the ten-mile drive. The boat will start for home before sunset, and there will be a collation on board. A large company on this little tour will make a very enjoyable trip of it at small individual expense.

The Harrogate Camp opened on August 2, and remained open until August 7. The "camp" is a favorite method of taking a holiday outing. Tents are erected, prettily decorated, there is a parade and races, and altogether some fun is to be had out of the thing. We note from *Wheeling* the following facts about Harrogate: "The camp consists of forty-eight tents, arranged in the shape of an egg. The President's tent is called the 'Black Diamond Palace,' and is close to 'Ye Coal Hole,' right by the 'coal hole.' The Bromley Butterflies were well represented. The 'Manningham Penfold' was occupied by the 'Five Blighted Muffins.' On Saturday, August 3, there were races, a parade, a dinner and a smoker. On Sunday the fun was fast and furious, tempered by divine service at 4 P. M. There were 500 men in the parade. Singer's bicycle band and the fog horn fiend kept things lively. Such is the Harrogate Camp."

The Cottage City meet was a big success, that is, it was quiet and restful. The excursion to Nantucket was a frost. The Oak Bluff's Club was very courteous, and the visitors who had secured the courtesy of its club house, through the kindness of Brother Bassett, were fortunate. A conference between the Executive Committee of the League and the editors of the *Bicycling World* was held relative to the report of the League meet which recently appeared in their paper. It was decided that they should make some kind of explanatory statement, which will shortly be published in the *World*. Chief Consul Mott ably presented his side of the case. It was also decided that the Executive Committee would not interfere with the publication of League news in State official organs. The band did not play "Annie Laurie," though three good men and true, who had been at Hagerstown, late one dark night stole around to the shadow side of the League hotel and with many a curious incantation sang, soft and low, that beautiful old lyric, "Annie Laurie," in memory of ye olden time. The names of these three men were—but let it pass. A number of good people, cycling celebrities, crowned heads, or whatever, were present.

A BRIGHT AMERICAN ABROAD.

W. E. Hicks, who is well known by St. Louis wheelmen, and who was such an enthusiast on any subject that he became interested in that most of those who knew him called him a crank, is now in Paris. He wrote the "Wheel Whims" and "Church Chat" for the *Post-Dispatch*, and probably used his wheel more in attending to his duties as a reporter than any one in this or any other country. He wore shorts constantly, and no amount of ridicule ever seemed to change him. He would ride to church in his knee breeches and frequently walk up the long aisle to the first or second seat from the front to report the sermon, totally oblivious of the curious glances shot at him. He was such an enthusiast that despite what those whom he raked over the coal may say about him, he did more to create an interest in cycling in St. Louis than any other ten men in the city. He had no bad or extravagant habits and saved up a couple of thousand dollars and went to Europe for a tour of the different countries on his wheel. Something he had been counting on for years. He traveled around a great deal, writing a number of interesting letters to THE WHEEL, of New York, and also to the *Standard*, Henry George's paper in New York. He was always an interested student of Henry George's theories and is now occupying the position of interpreter to Henry George in Paris, as well as holding the position of Secretary of the American Department at the Paris Exposition. *Vive la* Hicks.—St. Louis *Spectator*.

New York State Division L.A.W.

OFFICIAL ORGAN.

OFFICERS FOR 1889.

Chief Consul, W. S. BULL, 754 Main Street, Buffalo, N. Y. Vice-Consul, M. L. BRIDGMAN, 1255 Bedford Avenue, Brooklyn, N Y Secretary-Treasurer, GEO. M. NISBETT, 50 Wall Street, New York City. Executive and Finance Committee, W. S. BULL, M. H. BRIDGMAN, DR. GEORGE E. BLACKHAM, Dunkirk N. Y.

COMMITTEES.

EXECUTIVE COMMITTEE.

M. L. Bridgman, 1255 Bedford Avenue, Brooklyn, Chairman.

W. H. DeGraaf, 47 West Fourteenth Street, Treasurer.

I. M. Shaw, 19 West Fifty-third Street, New York City, Secretary.

A. B. Barkman, 241 Broadway, New York City.

C C. Alden, 6 Wall Street, New York City.

SUB-COMMITTEES.

Entertainment, W. H. DeGraaf, 47 West Fourteenth Street.

Transportation, G. R. Bidwell, 313 West Fifty-eighth Street

Programme, C. A. Sheehan, 5 Vanderbilt Avenue.

Press, F. P. Prial, P. O. Box 444.

Reception, L. A. Clarke, 25 Broad Street.

Tours and Runs, A. B. Barkman, 241 Broadway.

Theatre Party, W. H. DeGraaf, 47 West Fourteenth Street; Bert Cole, 62 Hanson Place, Brooklyn.

PROGRAMME.

FRIDAY, SEPTEMBER 13.

Morning—Reception of Visitors.
Afternoon—Runs, Central Park, Yonkers, etc.
" —Board of Officers meet, Grand Union Hotel, 5:30 P. M.
Night—Theatre Party, Broadway Theatre, New York City.
" —11 P. M., Supper.

SATURDAY, SEPTEMBER 14.

Morning—Parade in Central Park.
Afternoon—Run to Brooklyn.
" —Board of Officers meet, Brooklyn Club House, 2:30 P. M.
" —Regular Division Meeting at Brooklyn Club House, 3 P. M.
" —Photograph at Prospect Park, 4 P. M.
" —Run to Coney Island.
" —Supper at Coney Island.
" —Concert at Gilmore's Amphitheatre.

SUNDAY, SEPTEMBER 15.

Informal runs to Yonkers, Tarrytown, The Oranges and points on Long Island.

NEW YORK STATE DIVISION FALL MEET.

SEPTEMBER 13 AND 14, NEW YORK AND BROOKLYN.

The General Committee report that all arrangements are being perfected and that a first-class meet is assured. Wheelmen from all over the country are invited to attend.

BOARD OF OFFICERS' MEET.

BROOKLYN, N. Y., August 10, 1889.

Notice is hereby given that the Annual Meeting of the Board of Officers, New York State Division, will be held at the Grand Union Hotel, Friday, September 13, 1889, 6:30 P. M. This notice is given pursuant to Article 2, Section 1, of the Constitution.

M. L. BRIDGMAN, Vice-Consul.

NEW YORK STATE DIVISION L. A. W. ELECTION.

RESULT OF MAIL VOTE FOR DIVISION OFFICERS AND REPRESENTATIVES, SEASON OF 1889-90.

For Chief Consul	*W. S. Bull, Buffalo	493
	Scattering	2
For Vice-Consul	*M. L. Bridgman, Brooklyn	496
For Secretary-Treasurer	*Geo. M. Nisbett, New York	493

REPRESENTATIVES.

1st District	*J. C. Gulick, Citizens Bi. C., N. Y.	247
"	*W. H. De Graaf, Harlem W., N. Y.	246
"	*J. L. Miller, Riverside W., N. Y.	246
"	*J. A. Clairmont, Manhattan Bi. C., N. Y.	249
"	*F. P. Prial, N. Y. B. C., N. Y.	175
"	G. B. Watts, Jr., N. Y. Bi. C., N. Y.	121
2d District	*C. C. Alden, Brooklyn	36
3d District	*Hy. Gallien, Albany	29
	Scattering	2
4th District	C. W. Wood, Syracuse	33
5th District	*H. W. Arnold, Binghamton	48
"	*C. F. Cossum, Poughkeepsie	42
6th District	*W. S. Jenkins, Buffalo	78
"	*W. G. Schack, Buffalo	78
"	*Robt. Thomson, Rochester	78
"	*Dr. George E. Blackham, Dunkirk	80
	Scattering	7

* Elected.

I hereby certify that I opened and canvassed the vote, in the presence of the Rights and Privileges Committee, and that the above is a true and correct statement of the result.

GEO. M. NISBETT, Sec'y-Treas.

(Signed) WALTER S. JENKINS, by MICHAEL FURST, for Rights and Privileges Committee.

New York, August 19, 1889.

PROPOSED CHANGES IN NEW YORK STATE DIVISION BY-LAWS.

The Division By-Laws having been found in practica working to be deficient in certain respects, some of which involve serious discrepancies, the following amendments will be moved at the annual meeting of the Board of Officers, on behalf of the Rules and Regulations Committee.

First—An amendment to Sec. 4 of Art. 1, to allow of limited proxy voting at Board meetings, for the purpose of ensuring a quorum.

Second—An amendment to Sec. 6 of Art. 2, to allow of proxy voting at Division meetings, similar to that provided for in Art. 7 of the National Constitution of L. A. W.

Third—Amendments to Sec. 3 of Art. 3, Secs. 3 to 6 of Art 5, and addition of new sections to latter article; to modify the manner of voting in accordance with principle of Australian Ballot Reform, so as to permit of easy and inexpensive presentation of independent candidates, and also to provide for secret ballots when desired and practicable.

Fourth—Addition of new section to Art. 3, defining duties of Consuls.

Fifth—Amendment to Sec. of Art. 4, conforming description of League clubs to that in National Constitution of L. A. W.

Sixth—Further amendment to Sec. 1 of Art. 4, conferring upon League clubs right of voting by delegates at Division meetings.

Seventh—Amendment to Sec. 3 of Art. 6, conferring upon Executive Committee power to manage finances of the Division, and to designate the Official Organ, without expense to the Division.

Eighth—Amendment to Sec. 3 of Art. 6, describing specifically the duties of committees.

Ninth—Amendment to Art. 8, giving the right to Divisions to revise by-law amendments made by the Board of Officers.

The text of above proposed amendments to be published in full in next issue.

E. J. SHRIVER,
Chairman R. and R. Com.

BICYCLE CHAMPIONSHIPS.

TO THE MEMBERS OF THE NEW YORK STATE DIVISION:

The one-mile tandem safety bicycle L. A. W. championship awarded to this Division, and the one-mile bicycle New York State Division championship, are hereby assigned to the Binghamton Wheel Club, to be competed for at their race meet September 10th and 11th, 1889.

W. S. BULL, Chief Consul.

RECEPTION COMMITTEE.

L. A. Clarke, C. B. C., Chairman; F. R. Miller, R. W.; W. F. Pendleton, N. Y. B. C.; C. B. Clemens, M. B. C.; W. W. Braden, H. W.; F. W. Lincoln, M. W. C.; Geo. Sloane, C. B. C.; F. J. Menge, R. W. Headquarters, Grand Union Hotel and G. R. Bidwell's, 313 W. 58th St.; storeroom for wheels at 59th Street and Eighth Avenue, entrance to Central Park.

On receipt of timely notice from intending participants in the meet residing at a distance from the metropolis, they will be met on arrival and escorted to headquarters, while their wheels will be transported to the storeroom, near Central Park, free of charge. Send to L. A. Clarke, Chairman, 25 Broad Street, New York City, name, residence, line of travel, time of arrival in New York, style of wheel and hotel at which you prefer to stop.

The Committee recommends the Grand Union, opposite the Grand Central Depot, Forty-second Street and Fourth Avenue. Rooms, $1 per day and upward; meals *à la carte*.

L. A. CLARKE, Chairman.

BOSTON'S SAND-PAPERED ROADS.

EDITOR OF THE WHEEL:

Of late I have noticed several accounts of wheelmen making excellent time over roads leading into Boston. All this reads very nicely on paper, and I have no doubt that in all cases they have covered the ground in the time mentioned, and when I rode over some of the roads, this summer, the only thing which surprised me was that they did not make the runs mentioned in far less time. Take a good road and a good wheel, and you have very little trouble in covering ground, and you need not be a racer either to accomplish it.

Not long since, I was on my way to Boston over the B. & A. road. At Worcester the country roads looked so inviting to me, as I was cramped up in the hot cars, that I could not resist the temptation to try them. I accordingly proceeded to the baggage car, procured my wheel, and then, telegraphing to my friends at South Framingham that I would arrive some time during the evening—for I had never been over the road before—I left Worcester at 5:30 o'clock. Well, Mr. Editor, if you want to see roads and make good time this is the place for both. I ride a Columbia Safety, you know, and it was no trouble to take the hills. The coasting on the down grades we will say nothing about. I reached my friend's house in South Framingham at 7:05 P. M., covering a distance of twenty-three miles in one hour and thirty-five minutes. This with only one dismount. I would like some of those fast riders of the Eastern States to try our roads leading out of New York City. If they make the same fast time over these roads as at home, then I will take a back seat.

Yours truly,
"THE JUDGE."

ST. LOUIS.

I hope, Mr. Editor, that you will place our race meeting in your "fixtures" column without further delay. The date is August 31. I append a list of the events and the prizes that are to be hung up. You will notice that the list is a good one and the prizes valuable. The railroads have agreed to a rate of one and one-third fares for the round trip on the certificate plan, *i. e.*, the passenger pays one full fare to St. Louis, and on demand will receive from the selling agent a certificate which, when indorsed by the proper official here, will entitle the holder to a return ticket at one-third the regular fare. In addition to this, reduced rates will be obtained at the hotels. On Sunday, September 1, there will be a grand consolidated run to De Soto, and an opportunity thus given our visitors to see the finest scenery short of the Rocky Mountains. The Executive Committee are looking after matters closely, and are not allowing their efforts to be interfered with by dilatory officers. That is to say, they are going ahead regardless of what other officers may or may not do. This insures a successful meeting.

Another notice appeared in the *Globe-Democrat* yesterday, to the effect that W. D. Banker had accepted Greenwood's challenge for a contest at hill-climbing. These acceptances have been telegraphed periodically to the papers here from Pittsburg, but Greenwood has received no word from Banker on the subject, and it looks pretty much as if the latter was simply working up a little cheap notoriety without any intention of meeting Greenwood on the hills. At any rate, he is pursuing a very queer course, and Greenwood is determined to put matters in such shape that he will either have to accept or decline without any more foolishness.

The greatest interest in the coming tournament centres in the match races that are to be run off. Besides the ones between Harding and Ring, Tivy and Mehlig and others that I do not recall just now, there is one between Wrieden, of the Bank of Commerce, and Tyler, of the Continental National. Their respective backers have arranged for the prize, which in this case is a supper for eight. Ab. Lewis is handling Wrieden, and Sanders is looking after Tyler. Tyler is slightly the favorite in the betting, but Wrieden wears a determined, do-or-die look that bodes no good to Tyler's chances. The track just at present is not in very good shape, but Superintendent Stone has returned from Colorado and promises to get to work with the scraper, roller, sprinkler, etc., immediately and put matters in shape.

Bro. Miles denies that he advised the officers of the W. A. A. A. against putting up any money for prizes for bicycle championships. He says that he gave no such advice, and, so far as he knew, the matter had never been brought before the officers of the Western Association. In response to a letter from Mr. Rhodes, he informed that gentleman that the L. A. W. would not recognize any championships not run under its auspices, and he deprecated the idea of contributing "$75 worth of prizes to be ridden for at a meeting with which the Western Association had no conection, and where even the riders themselves would not consider the events as championships." I am very glad to make the correction.

ITHURIEL.

BROOKLYN NEWS.

At last New York City is to have decent and respectable pavements on her streets, and it is a most pleasing result of the long pro and con discussions on the subject which have taken place among the city officials. We Brooklyn wheelmen are gratified, because the lead taken by New York will probably be followed by Brooklyn, and, besides, the touring part of the cyclists of this city often have occasion to ride through New York streets, en route to our many and varied destinations, and we will therefore reap some benefit from the proposed good pavements in New York City. The material will probably be asphalt. Of course, we have some good riding surfaces in Brooklyn, but they are more or less disconnected, and a rider must needs take the bad with the good, if he travels much awheel through Brooklyn.

I understand that the Cyclists Union are endeavoring to have three rough blocks on Schermerhorn Street repaved. Those three long blocks are as much dreaded by riders as was Cobblestone Hill, I think. It is certainly a most remarkable sample of the peculiar (?) way in which Brooklyn's streets are paved. The street is only seven and a half blocks in length, and the asphalt pavement is at both ends of the street, leaving the three centre blocks with a rough and uneven Belgian block surface, which is but little better than cobblestones. Yet it is the best way we have of reaching the bridge and ferries.

A great many of the club members are out of town now, and so few are left that a club run is almost an impossibility.

Of the Brooklyns, Bancroft, Seixas, Spelman and Snedeker are at Massapequa, L. I. A letter is on the club bulletin board from Raymond and Potter, away up in the Adirondacks, descriptive of their first few experiences.

A large party of New Haven wheelmen and Hudson County wheelmen visited the B. B. C. Saturday, and were taken to the Island by Waldo Fuller, where they had dinner at the Brighton.

Geo. Corby took a severe header in the Park, Saturday, in consequence of a collision with a safety. His head and arms were badly bruised, so much so that he had to be dressed by his club-mates on his return, he being unable to lift his arms.

Wheelmen who are accustomed to ride down to Bath occasionally should beware of riding on the sidewalks, as they have been in the habit of doing, as a new law has gone into effect prohibiting it, and the constables and sheriffs, or whatever they are called in that township, are watching for chances to arrest wheelmen who violate the new law, and they mean business, as they have arrested several wheelmen already.

Brooklyn, August 19, 1889. ATOL.

Our Brooklyn correspondent warns wheelmen not to ride on the sidewalks of Bath, L. I., as it is contrary to law, and the Bath constables take delight in enforcing the law.

New York City management, is the funniest thing in the world, outside of comic opera. Commissioner Gilroy, who has $661,000 to spend on new pavements, has asked for an additional allowance of $25,030 for increased help. The County Democracy men say that it is simply a scheme for making soft berths for Tammany men.

The Brooklyn B. C. and Kings County Wheelmen combined run to the Massapequa, will be held August 31.

CYCLING AT KINGSTON, N. Y.

I read your paper religiously every week—advertisements and all—and derive great comfort, amusement and knowledge thereby. In passing, however, let me say that there is a dearth of wheeling news and comment from this section, and if you will allow me the privilege, I will, in my feeble way, try and supply the want.

Kingston is one of the oldest towns along the Hudson River, and is very conservative withal. Mrs. Grundy lives here—in fact, it is hinted that she originated here. Be that as it may, it is a fact that she is well represented, but, thank goodness, there is still a large majority of the inhabitants who believe that God made the air to breathe, and did not stipulate who should breathe it.

For a matter of ten years, all attempts at club organization here has met with failure. That is, all athletic sports were considered too boisterous by some, and too hard work by others. Of the former, little need be said; of the latter class there are many who have changed their opinions within the last two years. There have been clubs formed here, but they have been short lived. But now I am glad to be able to state that, so far as cycling is concerned, it is looked upon within increasing favor. Within one year the increase has been 100 per cent.

The greatest drawback is the abominable roads, not only in the country, but in the city as well. Union Avenue, for a distance of one and a half miles, is a disgrace to any city, the ruts in some places being from six to eight inches deep. But with all the drawbacks, this city may be said to have the bicycle craze bad.

A favorite place where wheelmen congregate is the Driving Park. On any pleasant day large numbers can be seen spinning around the half-mile track. The Park is situated about one mile from the city, and commands a view of the three leading hotels in the Catskill Mountains. Cool breezes, fresh from Rip Van Winkle's slumber land, can be enjoyed at any time. A good half-mile track affords ample opportunity for cyclers to test their speed, and it is taken advantage of to the fullest extent. Here the boys tell wonderful stories, and "talk up" tournaments.

There are a number of fast riders here, who have developed within the past year or so, notably, Messrs. Hoysradt, Hudler, Van Wagonen, Bruyn, Armitage, O'Neil, Longyear, Davis, Hasbrouck and others.

We have two lady riders who have defied Mrs. Grundy, and ride their wheels with grace. One rides a Warwick, and the other a Rambler, and the end is not yet.

Long runs are taken by the boys—to Hudson, Albany, Barrytown, Poughkeepsie, Newburg and other places

A tournament is talked of this fall, and next season there will no doubt be a strong club organized.

Safeties are in the majority here, but there are a number of ordinaries. One gentleman rides a 60-inch wheel.

Two lady cyclers made the trip to "Elerslie Park," in the town of Rhinebeck-on-the-Hudson, the residence of Vice-President Levi P. Morton, on Monday. They were given the freedom of the park by Mr. Morton, with whom they had a pleasant chat. Mr. Morton expressed the opinion that bicycling was one of the best modes of out-door exercise, and evinced curiosity about the wheels. It is needless to add that all his questions were answered by the ladies. They rode through the beautiful park, which contains 900 acres. The drives are the finest to be found in the State, and as for the flowers they are simply beyond description. The views are magnificent. Shady nooks and sparkling fountains are a continuous surprise to the visitor at almost every turn. They were shown every point of interest by the superintendent, and invited to call again. They also had the pleasure of meeting Mrs. Morton, whom they describe as a "charming lady," etc. They arrived home at 5:30 P. M., having had a most enjoyable trip. The distance covered, including the ride in the park, was about twelve miles.

Kingston, August 17, 1889. FLOYD.

BUFFALO.

Asphalt is slowly pushing itself into the business portion of the city. Main Street, between Swan and Seneca—right in the heart of the business portion—is being paved with asphalt. The street is already paved with asphalt from the city limits to Chippewa Street, and if this last block proves a success Main Street will be an unbroken line of asphalt from the city limits to the docks, a distance of three and a half miles, through the centre of the city.

Buffalo will have no tournament this fall, but the local wheelmen will endeavor to entertain the visiting wheelmen to the International Fair in good style, and all who come may count upon a pleasant time in the "Mecca of Cycledom." One of the wheel doings during the Fair will be the illuminated parade under the management of the Zigzags. This affair will not be confined to one club, but will compose all the wheelmen of the city, besides several out-of-town clubs, among them the Flower City Wheelmen and the West End Bicycle Club, of Rochester.

It was my good fortune to be sent to Lockport to do the tournament of the Lockport Wheelmen. The track was in excellent condition, there was a good attendance and the races were hotly contested. There was only one set-back, the wind being too strong. The surprise of the day was the entrance on the path of young Green, who is scarcely twenty years old. He went into the novice race, easily captured that and three other firsts. His mount was a light (?) Star Roadster, weighing three times as much as one of the racing wheels of his opponents. The interest was for the most part centered in the meeting of Campbell, the Falls man, and Banker, the Berkeley representative. Banker won the 2-mile lap race, but Campbell's little wheel gave way, though he pluckily kept on and got one of the laps.

The following is from a local paper, and before many weeks have passed it is likely that the Press Bicycling Club will be a fixture: "There is some talk in the city of starting a Press Bicycling Club. Quite a number of the members of the fourth estate ride the silent steed, and there is no reason why the local ink slingers should not emulate Boston in this respect. Buffalo is decidedly ahead of the Bean City in every other particular but this one. Now, suppose the two "Billies" put their heads together and see what can be done. There is fraternal spirit enough among the Buffalo press men to make the affair a complete success."

The ladies are very active in wheel matters these days. At the last meeting of the Women's Wheel Club five new members were admitted, and the club accepted an invitation to attend the Hamilton carnival and take part in the parade. After the meeting a run of five miles was indulged in by the members.

Another ladies' club has been formed, to be known as the Mohawk Bicycle Club, with headquarters on the street of the same name. It is an L. A. W. club.

Five ladies will make the century run with the Ramblers on September 1. ZO.

EAST HARTFORD.

Saturday, August 17, the East Hartford Wheel Club defeated the Wethersfield Wheel Club, in a league ball game, by the score of 15 to 7.

On the 24th, the Columbia Cycle Club play in East Hartford, and the Hartford Wheel Club in Wethersfield. The record of the baseball league: East Hartford, won 3, lost 1, per cent. 750; Columbia, won 1, lost 1, per cent. 500; Hartford, won 2, lost 2, per cent. 500; Wethersfield, won 2, lost 4, per cent 333.

Upon the occasion of freeing the toll bridge over the Connecticut, between Hartford and East Hartford, to happen about the 10th of September, the people of East Hartford are going to have a grand celebration. There will be a parade, of teams and bicycles, headed by a brass band in the morning, with bicycle races and one of the cycle league ball games in the afternoon, and fireworks in the evening.

A large sum of money is being raised, and generous appropriations will be made for the sports in the afternoon. The bicycle races, etc., will all be free to the public, and there will, no doubt, be a great concourse of people.

Bicycle races always have been popular, and this will tend to make them even more so. The races will probably be mostly for local riders.

The Wheel Club are taking an active part in the preparations, and will probably serve a dinner for all those who join in the parade on cycles.

HARRISBURG.

The boys took a run over to Camp Sheridan at Mt. Gretna Sunday before last, and spent a most enjoyable time, the Governor's troop, of this city, being encamped there.

On Saturday work was commenced on the Third Street pavement here. It will be of sheet asphalt, and will extend from Mulberry to Maclay Street, a distance of three miles. We who are old riders care little for an asphalt pavement, but the new man and the non-rider are carried away in anticipation of its completion. It is a very common expression: "Oh! I will have a wheel next season, you can bet; Third Street will be paved then." And I really think it will have a tendency to largely increase the number of riders.

"Son" and I expect to make a trip to Reading soon. Look out for a fractured record. We have decided upon riding as rapidly as we are capable of, and, barring mishaps to our wheels, will set a pace that will excite the local wheelmen to new endeavors. It sounds egotistical, but we don't want to exert ourselves and then have it said we did so by mere accident.

Messrs. Thos. S. Peters and H. W. Stone, both ex-Presidents of the Harrisburg Wheel Club, expect to sport in the "briny" at Atlantic City this week.

President Chas. P. Lusk will make a trip down the Shenandoah Valley next month. A more delightful spin is not to be had in this section of the country.

August 19, 1889. N. O. REMARKS.

ELIZABETH.

The road officers of the E. W. held a meeting on Wednesday evening to formulate plans for the lantern parade which the club intends to give this fall. The route chosen is about four and a half miles long, with nearly three miles of macadam. The only block pavement that will have to be ridden is that of Broad Street, which is very good of its kind. So the clubs that are invited need not fear our pavements.

If the present enlightened policy in regard to street paving continues to be pursued by our city council, riders having occasion to pass through Elizabeth will be able to go almost the entire distance over macadamized streets.

The club members are beginning to talk of the annual ten-mile handicap of the club, which is always run off on Election Day. The race is usually looked forward to as a means of settling the vexed question of superiority on the road. There will be a large list of entries this year, as we have quite a number of new members who are anxious to show what they can do. The President and Captain will be placed on the same handicap, by request, as the former is confident that he is the best man on a long distance, and the other knows that he isn't. Mr. White is anxious to show how superior the Eagle is to any wheel ever made before or since, and Mr. Caldwell will race on a safety for the first time.

Mr. L. K. Hazard, one of our charter members, has just returned from a nine months' trip around the globe. He has visited every civilized country except Japan. The trip was taken for his health. Mr. H. says that ordinaries in Europe and Australia are scarcer than hens' teeth—that almost everybody rides a safety of some kind.

"TANGLEFOOT."

MINNEAPOLIS ELECTIONS.

The election of officers in this Division resulted as follows:

Chief Consul, T. M. Slosson, Minneapolis	57
" " E. A. Savage, "	22
Vice-Consul, George Howard, St. Paul	76
" " C. A. Roach, St. Paul	3
Secretary-Treasurer, H. W. Laird, Winona	76
" " B. D. Hatcher, Winona	4
Representative, H. M. Welles, Redwood Falls	76
Scattering	2

All the old officers were re-elected with the exception of Mr. Roach, who was not a candidate for re-election, as he is not at present an active wheelman. The Division is apparently in a prosperous condition, having now attained the largest membership it ever had, 123, and has a respectable balance in the treasury, to be devoted to whatever will best advance the interests of wheelmen. I understand a meeting will be called in September for the purpose of considering what work it is best to take up.

August 19, 1889. DOBSON.

OFFICIAL VOTE OF THE CONNECTICUT DIVISION.

Below is the official announcement for the vote of the Connecticut Division L. A. W.:

FOR CHIEF CONSUL.

David J. Post, Hartford	249
Calhoun Latham, Bridgeport	37

FOR VICE-CONSUL.

L. A. Miller, Meriden	190
C. E. Moore, Bridgeport	88

FOR SECRETARY AND TREASURER.

E. A. DeBlois, Hartford	279

FOR REPRESENTATIVES.

Joseph Goodman, Hartford	275
F. W. Atwater, Bridgeport	264
T. W. Gillette, Danbury	273
A. G. Fisher, New Haven	200

—Hartford *Courant*, August 21, 1889.

Riverside Wheelmen's runs: August 23, moonlight run, 7:30 P. M.; August 25, Seacliff, start at 8:30 A. M.

Wm. Schmid, a Brooklyn wheelman, reached Rutland on Friday last, having ridden from Hoosick Falls.

Geo. M. Nesbitt and C. F. Cross, N. Y. B. C., will leave Sept. 1st for a two weeks' trip in the Berkshires.

The United States will be the League Headquarters at Hartford. A special rate of $2.00 per day will be made.

The Bay State Bicycle Club will hold a tournament at Worcester, September 14. There will be a bicycle parade in the forenoon.

E. R. Pidgeon, of Westport, Conn., and Grant Riley, of Medea, Pa., joined the Scranton tourists at Newburg and accompanied them to New York.

The Berkeley Athletic Club have arranged a splendid programme for September 7. It is probable that Willie Windle will give an exhibition of fancy riding.

It has been finally decided to run the K. C. W. 25-mile handicap road race, open to club members only, on Labor Day. An attempt will be made to beat the Irvington-Milburn record.

The Scranton tourists decided to wind up at New York. After spending Wednesday at Coney Island, all but two of the men took train for Scranton. They were wore out with sightseeing, riding and hospitality.

The Scranton tourists arrived in Newburg on Saturday last. The left Hudson Tuesday morning, dining at Rhinebeck. The following are the names of the tourists: J. J. Van Nort, J. W. Nyles, H. C. Wallace, B. P. Connolly, J. A. Spencer, C. W. Silkman, J. A. Fritz, J. B. Van Kluck and Ed. Pryor, all of Scranton.

MARYLAND'S BOARD OF OFFICERS.

The regular ticket was elected as follows:

For Chief Consul	Albert Mott
For Vice-Consul	Geo. F. Updegraff
For Secretary-Treasurer	G. W. H. Carr

For Representatives: J. Harry Covington, C. E. Fink, C. L. Mitchell, and E. P. Hayden.

A two-mile bicycle handicap was decided at Washington Park on Saturday, last week, with the following result: F. B. Hesse, N. J. A. C., 35 yards, 6m. 14 3-5s.; S. B. Bowman, N. J. A. C., 60 yards, second; C. M. Murphy, K. C. W., 45 yards, close up; W. W. Zimmerman, Freehold Cyclers, 60 yards, 0; J. W. Schoefer, B. A. C., 25 yards, 0; H. J. Hall, N. J. A. C., scratch 0.

An experienced correspondent writes: "I should advise for a lady riding a Safety to have the saddle pretty far forward, as the knee motion is less conspicuous, and with the saddle way back of the centre I have found although you can spurt a short distance better, still I do not think a rider can keep up the pace. However it is a question that every rider must decide for himself, and the position ought to be like an easy fitting shoe, neither too short, nor too long, but a perfect fit."

DELAWARE WATER GAP, Aug. 21.—Messrs. D. C. Newton, J. D. Connor, P. G. Keane, D. H. Thistle, and E. J. Keane of the Manhattan Bicycle Club rode to Cold Spring, N. Y., on Saturday, Aug. 10. They visited all the surrounding towns and places of interest, and on Aug. 17 they started to tour through Pennsylvania. They expect to do some touring through New York State, and then to return to business after a four weeks' vacation, complimenting themselves over the fact that they have covered about 4,700 miles this season.—*Sun*.

T. C. Johnson and H. S. Birdseye, of Birmingham, Conn., are making a week's tour through New York, Massachusetts and Connecticut. They left Birmingham Sunday night, going to New York by steamer. Monday morning they started on their wheels up the old "Post Road," spending last night at Fishkill. They passed through Poughkeepsie Tuesday morning, stopping at Smith Brothers' for breakfast. They took dinner Tuesday at Hudson, stopping Tuesday night at Albany. Continuing their trip, they will visit Williamstown and Pittsfield, Mass., passing through the Berkshire Hills and so on home.

INFORMATION FOR MR. SHRIVER.

The opposition to the nomination of Frank P. Prial, of THE WHEEL, for an L. A. W. position, is absurd. The only reason his opponents advance in justification of their action, is that Mr. Prial is "in trade." There are at least a dozen Consuls, Vice-Consuls and prominent officials of the premier wheeling body against whom the same objection could be brought—if such an objection was legitimate. But it is not. The trade comprises the back-bone and life of the cycling world. The object is made more ridiculous still, when it be remembered that Mr. Prial is no more "in trade," than is any other of the nominees. He is a professional gentleman—an editor—of excellent character, and one who has done as much to further the legitimate interest of wheeling, as any man in the States. If his nomination results in election, an end to factions may be expected in the circles where it is most rampant.—*Buffalo Sunday News*.

FIXTURES.

August 24, 1889.—Montreal Bicycle Club's Annual Race Meet on the M. A. A. A.'s new grounds.

August 24, 1889.—Fifty-mile Bicycle and 1-mile Dwarf N. C. U. Championships at Paddington, Eng.

August 26-27, 1889.—Virginia Division L. A. W. Meet at Norfolk, Va.

August, 1889.—Scranton Club's Tour, Scranton, Pa., to Utica, Springfield, New York, Catskills, Delaware Water Gap. Address, B. P. Connolly, Secretary.

August 31, 1889.—Brooklyn Bicycle Club and Kings County Wheelmen's combined run to Massapequa, L. I.

August 31, 1889.—Monster Run of Brooklyn Wheelmen to Hotel Massapequa.

August 31, 1889.—Missouri Bicycle Club's Races, at St. Louis, Mo.

August 31, 1889.—Albany Wheelmen's Tournament. Entries close August 24, with W. B. Phipps, 51 Howard Street, Albany, N. Y

August 31, 1889.—Passaic County Athletic Association's Bicycling Tournament at Clifton, N. J., Race Track. Entries close August 20, with Charles Blizard, 318 Gregory Street, Passaic N. J.

September 2-3, 1889.—Pennsylvania State Division L. A. W. Meet at York, Pa.

September 2-3, 1889.—Amateur Race Meet of the Hartford Wheel Club, at Hartford, Conn. Entries to be made with W. M. Francis, Secretary, P. O. Box 745.

September 3, 1889.—Handicap Road Race of Westchester County Wheelmen.

September 3, 1889.—Kings County Wheelmen's 25-mile Club Handicap Road Race.

September 3-4-5, 1889.—Iowa Division L. A. W. Meet at Des Moines.

September 7, 1889.—Berkeley Athletic Club's Race Meet at Berkeley Oval, Morris Dock, New York City.

September 7, 1889.—A. A. U. Games at Brooklyn A. A. grounds; 1-mile Handicap. Entries close August 29, with James E. Sullivan, P. O. Box 611, New York City. Fee, 50 cents.

September 7, 1889.—One-mile Bicycle A. A. U. Championship at Brooklyn Athletic Association Grounds. Entries close September 1 with J. E. Sullivan, P. O. Box 611, New York City.

September 10-11, 1889.—Binghamton Race Meet. Address E. H. Towle, Binghamton, N. Y.

September 11, 1889.—Eight-Day Tour of the Southern California Wheelmen.

September 11-12-13, 1889.—Bicycle Races of the Northwestern Tournament Association, at Minnehaha Driving Park, Minneapolis, Minn. L. H. Turner, Secretary, 315 Hennepin Avenue.

September 13, 1889.—Springfield Bicycle Club's 50-mile Local Road Race and 50-mile Open Road Race, over the Springfield-Hartford course.

September 13, 1889.—At Springfield, 50-mile Road Race, open to local riders only, and 50-mile Road Race, open. Entry fee, $5, returnable to first, second and third men. Entries close September 1.

September 13-14, 1889.—New York State Division Meet at New York and Brooklyn.

September 14, 1889.—Y. M. C. A. Games; 3-mile Handicap. Fee, 50 cents. Entries close September 7, with George Pool, 150th Street, Harlem River.

September 14, 1889.—Two-Mile Championship of America, at Travers Island. Entries close September 7, with Secretary N. A. A. U., P. O. Box 611, New York City.

September 14, 1889.—Louisiana Division L. A. W. Meet at Audubon Driving Park, New Orleans, La. Entries close September 10, with R. P. Randall, 54 Baronne Street, New Orleans, La.

September 14, 1889.—Bay State Bicycle Club's Tournament, at Worcester, Mass.

September 20, 1889.—Michigan Division L. A. W. Meet at Ypsilanti, Mich.

September 21, 1889.—Michigan Division Meet races at Detroit, Mich.

September 21, 1889.—One-and-a-half-mile Handicap, at the Manhattan A. C. Grounds, Eighty-sixth Street. Entries close September 14, with C. C. Hughes, 524 Fifth Avenue, New York City.

September 21, 1889.—At the Warren Athletic Club Games, Wilmington, Del., 2-mile Bicycle Handicap. Entries close September 16, with W. F. Kurtz.

September 24-27, 1889.—Hudson County Wheelmen's Races at Spring Valley Fair.

October 4-5, 1889.—Pennsylvania Bicycle Club's Tournament.

October 4-5, 1889.—Peoria Bicycle Club's Tournament, Peoria, Ills.

October 8-9, 1889.—Races at Carlisle, Pa. Address John E. Steel, Carlisle, Pa.

October 12, 1889.—Three-mile Bicycle Handicap, at Staten Island Athletic Club Grounds.

October 23-29, 1889.—Race Meet at Macon, Ga.

EUROPEAN CYCLING FIXTURES.

Germany.—September 15; Hanover, September 8; Chemnitz, September 8; Frankfort-on-the-Main, September 1; Mannheim, September 8; Crefeld, September 8, Hamburg.—Altona, September 22; Bochum, August 25; Magdeburg, September 8.

THE HARTFORD TOURNAMENT.

EXCURSION RATES TO HARTFORD.

The following schedule of reduced rates on the New York, New Haven and Hartford R. R. to the Hartford Tournament, September 2 and 3, will be of interest to wheelmen desirous of attending this truly interesting meet:

From Springfield, $1.45; Meriden, $1.00; New Haven, $1.50; Bridgeport, $2.00. These rates, of course, include admission to the races.

Parties from Norwalk and Stamford are advised to purchase excursion tickets at Bridgeport.

Mileage books are advisable for visitors from Providence and Boston.

NOTICE TO RACING MEN.

Owing to the track being engaged previous to the Hartford Tournament, it will be impossible to gain admission to the park until the Saturday before the meet. Wheelmen in training will please take notice.

THE PARADE.

The parade of the Connecticut Division at Hartford September 2 will be a competition of the various State clubs for valuable prizes offered by the Division for numbers, appearance, drill, etc.

The Charter Oak Park one-mile track at Hartford is, without doubt, one of the fastest cycling tracks in the world. The mile made by Fred. Wood on this track in 1886 in 2m. 33s. was the fastest mile ever made in an actual race. Last year Rowe, on the same track, sprinted the last quarter of the first mile in the lap race in 30s., undoubtedly the fastest quarter ever made on a cycle.

The Berkeley Athletic Club team will have an opportunity to meet the fastest amateurs in the country at the Hartford Meet. The Berkeleys propose to dispute the statement that F. F. Ives, the Meriden flyer, made at Bridgeport, to the effect that the New York boys were due to get badly left at the fall tournament.

Two editions of the Connecticut Road Book, by C. G. Huntington, have been issued and sold by the Connecticut Division of the L. A. W. The demand for the edition was unexpectedly large, and the work will be out of print until next spring, when a new and revised edition will be issued.

F. F. Ives, of Meriden, the former promateur racer, has been fully reinstated by the L. A. W., and will make some of the men hustle at the Hartford tournament.

The Bailey Brothers, of Boston, are anxious to meet the Banker Brothers, of Pittsburg, at Hartford in a race for the amateur tandem championship.

The Hartford Wheel Club men entered for the Hartford races are Forster, the State champion; Cornell, Reid, Dorsser and Harding.

The prizes for the one-mile open handicap race at Hartford aggregate $300 in value.

The Hartford tournament this year will be a strictly amateur affair, the professional jobbery at Charter Oak Park a year ago having thoroughly disgusted the management.

Every amateur flyer of note will compete at Hartford September 2 and 3.

Entries for the Hartford races close August 26 with W. M. Francis, Box 745.

Large parties are being organized in New York, Boston and Providence to attend the Hartford tournament.

D. J. Canary, the world-renowned fancy rider, will make his first appearance in this country in four years at Hartford, September 2-3.

OFFICERS OF THE DAY.

Referee—Charles S. Davol, Warren, R. I.

Judges—Charles S. Howard, Boston B. C.; George H. Hort, Connecticut B. C.; F. P. Prial, THE WHEEL, New York B. C. Timers—Charles T. Stuart, J. H. Parker and R. N. Seyms. Scorer—F. E. Eaton. Assistant Scorers—F. C. Burnham and T. W. Saunders. Starter—H. H. Chapman. Clerk of Course—A. G. Gruendler. Assistant Clerks of Course—G. L. Bacon and J. K. Leitz.

MEET OF THE CONNECTICUT DIVISION L. A. W. AT HARTFORD, SEPTEMBER 2-3, 1889.

TO THE MEMBERS OF THE CONNECTICUT DIVISION L. A. W.:

The Division Board of Officers decided to hold the meet at Hartford during the annual Hartford Tournament, as that event is invariably marked by a larger gathering of League members from throughout the State than could possibly be assembled at any other time or place in Connecticut.

Upon unity and fraternity depends in a great measure the success of the Division's work for the cause of cycling. This, together with the additional inducements we offer to secure a large attendance at this meet, should, we think, result in a notable assemblage of our members.

We shall endeavor to make the promotion of acquaintance and good-fellowship among our members a special feature of this occasion. Further, we shall hope to afford them a more widely extended knowledge of the privileges and benefits conferred by the League of American Wheelmen, and to greatly increase their appreciation of that organization.

In order to thoroughly insure the enjoyment of all who attend this meet, the Division has appropriated $200 for entertainment purposes, and a very considerable additional sum has been subscribed by Hartford members to make the entertainment more elaborate and complete.

All who make this meet an incentive to a two days' pleasure trip to Hartford will have future occasion to remember it as a season of personal enjoyment as individuals and profitable experience as League members. Come everybody and bring your wheels with you. Reception committees will await your arrival at every train on the morning of September 2. Should you come to town awheel, members of the committee will be found at the parlors of the Hartford Wheel Club to advise and direct you.

A storeroom will be furnished, with help in attendance, to check and care for wheels. L. A. W. headquarters will be at Room 7, United States Hotel, where you will be welcomed, and where, upon exhibition of your L. A. W. ticket, you will be furnished with a Division badge entitling you to participation in the run and entertainments hereinafter described.

Applications for membership in the L. A. W. will be received by Secretary-Treasurer De Blois, at headquarters, Room 7, United States Hotel, and any such applicant, properly recommended, upon payment of initiation fee and dues, will receive a Division badge.

You are guaranteed courtesy, hospitality and a good time.

DIVISION COMMITTEE.

EVENING ENTERTAINMENTS.

Promptly at 8 P. M. the evening festivities will begin at Germania Hall with a concert.

During the evening the following programme of music and athletic exhibition will be given. The numbers will be interspersed with speeches by prominent L. A. W. men, and refreshments will be bountifully served:

PROGRAMME.

Overture, "Fra Diavalo,".......................Auber
Chillan Dance.......................Missuo
Fencing.......................Waltz and Heuter
Cornet Solo.......................Chas. P. Hatch
Boxing.......................Elwood and Buckley
Mandolin and Guitar.......................Gruet and Babcock
Serenade, for flute and horn.......................Elwin and Schumann
Wrestling.......................Fahy and Watson

INTERMISSION.

Spanish Fandango.........Band.......................Binns
Xylophone Solo.......................Frank Paulisch
Turning—Instructor, J. Waltz.......Hartford Turnerbund
"Trovatore".............Band.......................Verdi
Boxing.......................Fahy and Watson
"Chink of Gold"..........Band.......................Rollinson

ALBANY WHEELMEN'S RACES.

All indications point forward to the most successful meeting held by this well-known wheeling organization, as the entries already received include the fastest riders of the day, owing to the valuable prizes given at previous race meets.

The committee include old workers, and is as follows: Wm. B. Phipps, Chairman; Henry Gallien, Treasurer; Jos. C. McClelland, Jos. L. Adrien and John B. Brown.

The prizes and medals represent a value of $300, and are given below: One-mile novice, gold medal; 1-mile ordinary, open, first, French marble clock; second, racing suit; 1-mile Star, club, first, traveling bag; second Tolman shoes; 2-mile L. A. W. State championship, $50 diamond medal; 1-mile team race, silk banner; 1-3-mile safety, open, first, silver cup; second, plush toilet set; 1-mile club championship, gold medal; 1-mile tandem bicycle, first, two gold-headed canes; second, two silver-handled umbrellas; 2-mile handicap, first, French bronze; second, tennis racket; 1-3-mile consolation, plush dressing case.

The entrance fee is fifty cents each to open events, and $1 to State championship and must be sent to Wm. B. Phipps, 51 Howard Street, Albany, N. Y. The closing of entries has been extended to Tuesday, August 27. F. P. Prial, editor THE WHEEL, will act as referee and handicapper; Judges, P. F. Hanley, Capt. Troy Bi. Club; Joshua Reynolds, Stockport, Rep. N. Y. State Div.; H. C. Foster, Albany Bi. Club; Timers, R. P. Thorn, E. D. Mix, Jos. C. McClelland; Umpires, G. E. Bailly, H. De Ronville; Clerk of Course, Henry Gallien; Starter, J. H. Rothman; Scorers, F. H. Clerishire, J. H. Groot.

The track is one-third mile, and is in prime condition. A mile has been made on it in 2m. 45s., by H. L. Burdick and it is now in better condition than when that time was made.

The run to Hartford is being arranged, and a suitable route has already been selected, which will bring the tourists to Hartford in time to ride in morning parade.

All intending to visit Albany are requested to inform the Chairman of Committee on what trains they will arrive, when they will be met by members of the club and escorted to hotels and racing track.

BINGHAMTON WHEEL CLUB'S TOURNAMENT.

The second annual meet of the club will be held September 10 and 11 at the Driving Park. The following programme has been arranged:

FIRST DAY.—9:30 A. M., concert from Hotel Bennett balcony by band; 10:30 A. M., parade, disbanding at Court House Square for photographs; 2:30 P. M., races at the Driving Park; evening, programme of entertainment at Opera House.

SECOND DAY.—8:30 A. M., club run from Hotel Bennett—beautiful view of Chenango and Susquehanna valleys; 2:30 P. M., races.

The track is a half-mile clay path. Entries for handicaps and class races close September 2; for other events, September 5. Fee, 50 cents for each event. Address E. H. Towle, Binghamton, N. Y.

PROGRAMME OF EVENTS.

FIRST DAY—SEPTEMBER 10.

One-mile novice; three heats; for wheels of 35 lbs. weight or over.
One-mile safety; novices; heats; wheels 35 lbs. or over.
Quarter-mile safety, boys under 12 years.
Three-mile bicycle lap race.
One-mile bicycle; Junior Wheel Club, of Binghamton.
One-mile safety; 3:15 class.
One-mile bicycle; scratch.
One mile bicycle novice; second heat.
One-mile tandem safety; National L. A. W. championship.
Two-mile bicycle; 6:10 class.
One-mile safety; scratch.
One-mile bicycle team race.

SECOND DAY—SEPTEMBER 11.

One-mile bicycle novice; third heat.
One-mile safety novice; second heat.
One-half mile bicycle, boys under 16 years.
One-mile bicycle handicap.
Two-mile safety lap race.
One-mile bicycle; New York State L. A. W. championship.
One-mile safety novice; third heat.
One-half mile bicycle.
One-mile bicycle; Binghamton Wheel Club.
Three-mile safety handicap.
One-mile bicycle consolation.
One-mile safety consolation.

RICHFIELD SPRINGS, N. Y., RACE MEET.

For a postponed meeting, the second annual race meet of the Waiontha Bicycle Club, held August 16, was a decided success. The day was a beautiful one. The road and track were somewhat soft, making the time slow in all the races. The Lockport races, the day before, knocked out several men who were to have been here, as they were laid out by the Berkeley Athletic Club boys. However, the following events were decided:

THE FIFTY MILE ROAD RACE WON BY W. F. MURPHY.

Of the thirteen entries in the 50-mile road race only four started, viz: Wm. and Chas. Murphy, of Brooklyn; W. D. Shoemaker, Richfield Springs, and W. A. Parker, Rome. The Murphy boys were considered likely winners. On the first round the riders came in in a bunch, Wm. Murphy leading, Shoemaker second, Chas. Murphy third, Parker fourth. The time of the twelve miles was 50 minutes. The second round was the same, only that Parker lost a nut off his wheel and had to stop. Shoemaker dropped out. From this time on the interest somewhat subsided. Wm. Murphy won the race in 4h. 31m.; Chas. Murphy second, in 4h. 55m. 30s.

THE RACES.

In the half-mile club novice there were three starters, Sam. Kinne, J. W. Gibbs and J. F. Miller, and they finished in the above order. Time, 1m. 44s.

The mile novice was a contest of speed between two Utica cyclists, H. C. Burnett and Frank Miller, the former winning in 3m. 33½s.

The 3-mile lap race was won by Schoffer; Fuller second. L. L. Clarke, Berkeley Athletic Club, would have won but for a bad header. Time, 12m. 03s.

W. S. Nicholson gave a beautiful exhibition of fancy riding and won first prize; W. C. Bliss second; W. Shoemaker third.

The 5-mile L. A. W. State championship contest awakened much interest. The two contestants, A. C. Banker and W. F. G. Class, of New York, were hardly ten feet apart at the finish, Banker winning in 19m. 00⅕s.

Banker and Class immediately started together on a tandem to beat G. H. Crosby and J. J. Sanders, of Utica. They let the Utica boys set the pace to the head of the stretch, when they shot past and won easily in 6m. 46s.

Not content with winning two races in succession, Banker, with Class and Schoffer, entered in the team race, with Robbins, Marquisee and Burnett representing the Crescents, of Utica. The former secured 23 points and the latter 18. In this race Banker made the fastest mile of the day—3m. 13s. Burnett got a severe fall in this race.

The 1-mile safety race was won by August Kinne, of Richfield Springs, in 3m. 45s.; Roberts second, by five feet; W. F. Class third.

One-mile bicycle scratch race.—J. W. Schoffer, N. Y., 3m. 16s.; Marquisee, Utica, second.

The contest between Shoemaker and Kinne for the championship of Otsego County was close until they reached the stretch, where Kinne's spurt won him the race in 3m. 27s.

The 2-mile open was one of the best races of the day. Marquisee again set the pace, with Banker trailing him and Burgess right behind Banker. Banker's spurt was once more too fast for his competitors, and he won the Earlington in 7m. 50s.

In the half-mile obstacle race two hurdles were placed across the track. The wheelmen had to dismount and climb over the hurdles and mount again. Robbins, of Utica, won; Nicholson second; Shoemaker third. Time, 2m. 06s.

The consolation race was won by Parker, of Rome; Burgess second.

T. R. Proctor, E. M. Earle and E. Cary were the judges, Frank Baird was starter, John H. Shulty, Jr., did the timing, Fred. Bronner was clerk of the course. C. E. Cromby was judge and timer of the road race. President Hinds was everywhere and everything needed to keep the ball rolling.

FIFTY MILES TRICYCLE RECORD.

At Paddington, August 1, Dr. E. B. Turner, Ripley Road Club, beat the amateur tricycle records from 22 to 50 miles, cutting the previous figures at the latter distance by eleven minutes. Dr. Turner rode 19 miles, 1,650 yards, in the first hour, and 38 miles, 690 yards, in two hours. The records made are as follows:

MILES.	H.	M.	S.	MILES.	H.	M.	S.
22	1	6	18 4-5	37	1	55	4
23	1	9	20 3-5	38	1	58	47 3-5
24	1	12	25 2-5	39	2	2	10 2-5
25	1	15	32 4-5	40	2	5	36 1-5
26	1	18	44 1-5	41	2	8	58 2-5
27	1	21	57 4-5	42	2	12	20 1-5
28	1	25	9 2-5	43	2	15	46 1-5
29	1	28	26 1-5	44	2	19	19 1-5
30	1	31	40 4-5	45	2	22	53 2-5
31	1	35	15 2-5	46	2	26	17 1-5
32	1	38	31 4-5	47	2	29	34 1-5
33	1	41	50	48	2	32	42 3-5
34	1	45	9 1-5	49	2	35	48 3-5
35	1	48	24 1-5	50	2	38	44 1-5
36	1	51	40 4-5				

PENNSYLVANIA DIVISION L. A. W. RACE MEET AT YORK.

FIRST DAY, SEPTEMBER 2.—One-mile novice, open; half-mile safety, R. D. boys' race, limited to boys not past their 16th birthday; half-mile tricycle, L. A. W. championship; one-mile tandem; fancy riding, ordinary; one-mile safety, L. A. W. championship; quarter-mile ordinary, L. A. W. championship; one-mile team race, three from each club; one-mile club championship, wheels not under 35 pounds (medal must be won three times to be retained); half-mile steeplechase.

SECOND DAY, SEPTEMBER 3.—One-mile race, open, 3:20 class; two-mile safety, R. D., open; one-mile Star, open; two-mile tandem, L. A. W. championship; fancy riding, Star; one-mile safety, R. D. club championship, wheels not under 35 pounds (medal must be won three times to be retained); 100 yards slow race; one-mile tricycle, L. A. W. championship; one-half mile, hands off; one-mile consolation.

Gold medals, first prizes; handsome and useful articles, second prizes. The club reserves the right to reject any or all entries. Entries should be sent to the Secretary, Ellis S. Lewis.

RACES AT PASSAIC, N. J.

At the games of the Passaic County Wheeling and Athletic Association, the following events will be decided: Two-mile team race, teams of three; one-mile safety handicap; one and one-half-mile club race, handicap; one-mile handicap and one-mile novice, scratch.

The track is three-quarters of a mile and will be put in good condition. Entrance fees, 50 cents for each event. $3 for team race; close August 23 with Charles Blizard, 318 Gregory Avenue, Passaic, N. J. Trains leave on Erie road, foot of Chambers Street, N. Y., at 1 and 1:50 P. M., reaching Clifton, where the track is situated, in forty-five minutes, returning at 5:33 and 6:12.

RACES AT HAMILTON, AUGUST 21.

SUMMARY.—Two-mile novice—O. S. Gibson, Hamilton, 7m. 8 3-5s. One-mile, Roadsters—G. S. Dunn, Hamilton, 3m. 18 2-5s. One mile—Wm. Carman, Toronto, 4m. 3½s. Half-mile ride and run—C. J. Connolly, Rochester, first; J. S. Lamont, Detroit, second. One-mile safety—W. F. Gessler, Niagara Falls, N. Y., 3m. 33 2-5s.; C. J. Connolly, Rochester, second.

BERKELEY ATHLETIC CLUB TOURNAMENT.

The second annual tournament of this club will be held at Berkeley Oval, Morris' Dock, September 7, 1889, at 2 P. M. The events are:

1. ½-mile Heat Race, open.
2. ½ " Dash, open.
3. 1 " open.
4. 1 " 3:10 class.
5. 1 " 3:00 class.
6. 1 " Safety, Rover type, open.
7. 2-mile Tandem, open.
8. 2 " Lap Race.
9. 2 " Handicap, open.
10. 3 " Team Race (three men).
11. 1 " Novice.

Entrance fee, $1 for one event; 50 cents for each additional event. Entries close September 3, with Dr. W. L. Savage, 10 W. Forty-fourth Street, New York City. Prizes on exhibition at Bidwell's and Spalding's.

RACES AT PHILADELPHIA.

The annual 10-mile race of the South End Wheelmen was held on Saturday last at the Philadelphia Driving Park. A number of shorter races were run, with the following results:

Quarter mile.—J. J. Bradley, 43s.; R. P. McCurdy, 43 1-5s.; F. Wheeler, 0; C. Wilson, 0; W. F. Stryon, 0.

One Mile.—P. Wilson, 3m. 16 3-5s.; O. McCurdy, 3m. 17s.; A. Manning, 0; T. McDougal, 0; H. Green, 0.

Half-Mile Handicap.—L. J. Kolb, 1m. 31s.; T. McDougal, 40 yards, 1m. 35s.; A. Manning, 40 yards, 0; T. R. Morrow, 30 yards, 0.

Quarter-Mile Exhibition.—S. G. Whittaker, 40s.

Ten-Mile Championship.—L. J. Kolb, 38m. 15s.; R. McCurdy, second.

The officers of the day were: Referee, G. Van Vliet; Judge, A. H. MacOwen; Timer, W. W. Randall, Starter, Louis Doster. Everything passed off in good form, and the meeting was an unqualified success.

RACES AT CARTHAGE, OHIO.

The following is the result of the events held at the Carthage Fair, on August 20:

Two-mile.—D. V. Knight, 6m. 33s; W. Foddy, 6m. 34s.; J. M. Rowe, 0; M. Fuller, 0. Rowe would have won but for a fall.

One-half-mile scratch.—R. C. Anderson, 1m. 22 4-5s.; L. Perrin, 1m. 23s.; R. Bakman, 1m. 30s.; F. J. Allsopp, 0.

One-mile scratch.—J. M. Holloway, 3m. 9 1-5s.; Charles Roth, 3m. 10s.; A. Hanauer, 3m. 15s.; F. Kappes, 3m. 20s.

Three miles.—V. Perrin, 10m. 7s.; L. Perrin, 10m. 8 1-5s.; A. M. Watcher, 10m. 9 2-5s.

One-half-mile, Rover type, Heats.—Heat 1—Theo. Klauss, 1m. 36s.; A. Arnott, 1m 37s. Heat 2—Klauss won this heat and the race in 1m. 37s.; Arnott, 2d. Time, 1m. 40s.

Quarter-mile boys' safety.—Five starters. S. Hooker won in 59 1-5s. Geo. Boutillion, 60s.

Judges, Messrs. Nash, Keck and Meyers. Timers, Green, Nelson and Hall. Clerk, A. A. Bennett. Starter, M. T. High. Scorers, Speth and Goodman.

The tournament at Carlisle, Pa., under the management of the bicycle club of that city, will be held during the fair of the Cumberland Agricultural Society, October 8 and 9. On the first day there will be eight events, viz.: One-mile novice, 1-mile open, 3-mile lap race, ½-mile hands off, (for Cumberland County wheelmen only), 2-mile, 6:20 class, 2-mile handicap, 1-mile safety tandem, and 2-mile club team race. On the second day the winners in the following will be determined: One-mile handicap, 2-mile open, 2-mile safety, 10-mile open, 2-mile (for Cumberland County wheelmen), ½-mile open, 2-mile tandem safety. The prizes will be chiefly gold and silver medals.

The Bay State Bicycle Club of Worcester will hold a tournament Sept. 14. There will be nine races, as follows: One-mile novice, ordinary wheel; one-mile novice, Safety; two-mile Worcester county championship race; two-mile team race (three men to each team, teams entered by clubs); one-mile Safety, handicap, open; one-mile ordinary, handicap, open; three-mile lap race, open; one-mile ordinary, open; one-mile safety, open.

ODDS AND ENDS.

A Y. M. C. A. cycling club was organized at Cleveland August 20.

The Delaware and Hudson Canal Co. R. R., Pennsylvania Division, will carry wheels free in the future.

A "tricycle-cab" is plying for hire in Berlin. It is propelled by two riders, and carries two passengers.

All racing men should enter the Berkeley Club's races. Their track is the fastest in the vicinity of New York.

The Long Island Cycle Co. have secured new quarters at 1774 Bedford Avenue, a much better location than their old stand.

The New York *Engineering and Building Record* is doing much good work in agitating the matter of improved pavements.

With the introduction of asphalt pavement, New York City will become the greatest cycling centre in this country, and in time, in the world.

The Philadelphia *Item* of Sunday last published a two-column obituary notice of "Jack," being material from THE WHEEL and *Bicycling World*.

The Scranton tourists arrived at Poughkeepsie on Tuesday, and were entertained by the Poughkeepsie Bicycle Club. They had a mileage of 487 miles.

Wm. Van Wagoner and Arthur Cummins are reported to have ridden the 7½-mile drive at Newport in 25m. 05s. on a tandem bicycle. The trial took place on Thursday.

At the parade held at Hamilton, Ont., on Wednesday the Niagara Falls Bicycle Club was presented with two prizes for having the largest number of uniformed men in line.

Thirty members of the N. Y. B. C. will go to Staten Island on Sunday by special tug boat. They will wheel over the roads of the Island, bathe, dine, and have a good time generally.

Tuttle, of the Illinois team has been exhibiting rare form of late, doing a practice mile last week in 2m. 40 1-5s., and the Illinois Club men do claim that he will show Lumsden his little wheel in Saturday's match.

C. M. Fairchild, of the Louisville Cycling Club, whose New Orleans to Boston trip of some years ago made him known considerably in the cycling world, has committed matrimony. Mrs. Alice Rice is the lady.

Negotiations are pending between a well-known Chicago wheelman and a large publishing concern for a trip of the Stevens order, in which both North and South America and all the countries of the other hemisphere will be thoroughly "done" and written up.

Chicago is considerably exercised over the five-mile team road race between the Chicago and Illinois Cycling Clubs, which is fixed for to-morrow. Lumsden, Winship, Van Sicklen, of the Chicagoes, and Tuttle, of the Illinois Club, the flower of the Breezy City's racing talent, will meet in the match, and the Chicago boys are on tiptoe over the great sport that is promised.

AT QUEENS, L. I., August 17.—On Lloyd's track: Open amateur one-mile handicap. First trial heat, L. R. Doughty, Jr., Queens B. C., 135 yards, 3m. 5s.; G. W. Donner, Q. C. W., 135 yards, second by two yards; H. Quartrup, Q. C. W., 100 yards, third; J. H. Hanson, N. Y. B. C., 70 yards, fourth. Second trial heat, W. C. Heydecker, N. Y. B. C., 100 yards, 2m. 59 4-5s.; W. Schumacher, Berkeley A. C., 25 yards, second by a foot; G. Boyce, Queens B. C., 115 yards, third. Final heat, Schumacher, 3m.; Heydecker, second by two yards; Doughty, third by three yards; Donner, fourth.

Last year gallons of milk were spilled over the Greenwood-Wells hill climbing contest, and few drops only were necessary to report the result. The same thing will happen this year over the Greenwood-Hanker contest. We will report the match when it is ridden. One contest more takes place in St. Louis and one in Pittsburg, with the decisive hill on neutral ground; loser to pay all railroad fares and hotel expenses of winner, and to purchase him a gold medal valued at $50. The men should race for a trophy, and should each pay their own railroad expenses, to a place mutually convenient. If they can't pay their own expenses they should stay home.

A CENTURY RUN.

Three members of the Missouri Bicycle Club, Lieut. G. F. Peckham, Jno. Hurck and C. H. Peck, succeeded in covering 100 miles on their bicycles Sunday. The start was made at 6 A. M., from the Missouri's club house, and the total time was twelve and one-half hours. Three hours were taken for dinner and various stops for resting, thus making the actual riding time nine and one-half hours, which is very good considering the condition of the road. The participants had prepared themselves for some time for the long ride, and as a consequence no ill effects were felt, and all of them were at their desks as usual the next morning. Oscar Williamson started out with the intention of covering the full distance, but gave out at sixty miles. The run is a very trying one, and proves that the Missouri Club boasts some of the best road riders in the city.

Chicago Cyclists are circulating a memorial among the brethren for signatures, which will be presented to Ald. Cullerton, the parent of the bell and lamp resolution. In the preamble it states among other things that cyclists while lawfully riding along the streets day and night are frequently attacked by vicious dogs and that the brutes are a constant menace to wheelmen; that they have caused a number of serious accidents to citizens and taxpayers and may cause many more. Therefore, the cyclists respectfully represent unto Ald. Cullerton that inasmuch as he, said Cullerton, has championed the interests of wheelmen and gained distinction thereby he will further distinguish himself by introducing a resolution in the city council providing that an ordinance be passed compelling owners to provide their dogs with an automatic bell by day and a lantern by night, to the end that wheelmen may know when his dogship is around in time to dismount and hide. This will be a reasonable limitation on the privileges of the dogs, and will serve to aid wheelmen in escaping headers and hydrophobia.—*Tribune.*

Howard A. Smith & Co., Newark, N. J., report an unprecedented demand for their safety bundle carriers, both for handle bar and mud guard. ***

Howard A. Smith & Co., Newark, N. J., are teaching more persons how to ride the bicycle at Oraton Hall than ever before at this season of the year. Hall open evenings. ***

Howard A. Smith & Co., Newark, N. J., have improved their Graphite for lubricating chains and bearings of bicycles and safeties, until it seems to be perfect. All riders should have a bottle. ***

ASPHALT AND GRANITE.

One of the most interesting paragraphs in Capt. Francis V. Greene's instructive article on "Roads and Road Making," in the current number of *Harper's Weekly*, is that which he devotes to the subject of ease of traction on city pavements. The results stated are derived from experiments made by several engineers to ascertain the force required to draw a given load upon various surfaces. It is found that to draw a load of one ton on iron rails laid upon a level ground a force of ten pounds was required. The force in pounds required to draw the same load upon level pavements of various kinds is thus stated by Capt. Greene: Asphalt, 13; wood, 21; best stone blocks, 32; inferior stone blocks, 50; average cobblestone, 90; macadam, 109; earth, 200.

This demonstration has a direct and important utility in determining what kind of pavement should be laid in the City of New York with the appropriation made by the Legislature. Capt. Greene makes the following comment:

"For instance, in the City of New York it is estimated that there are 12,000 trucks, carrying an average load of one and a half tons for twelve miles on each of 300 days in the year, at an average daily cost of $4 for each truck. The result is about 69,000,000 tons transported one mile in every year, at a total cost of $14,400,000, or at the rate of over twenty-two cents per ton mile. The excessive nature of this charge is seen when it is remembered that the same goods are now carried by rail at six-tenths of one cent per mile. On asphalt or wood pavements the same horses could transport a load three times as heavy as on the present rough stone pavements. If the saving in transportation is proportional to the load carried it would amount to nearly $10,000,000 per annum. It is safe to say that at least one-half of this amount would be saved by substituting smooth pavements for those now in use in New York.—New York *Times*.

NEW TRICYCLE DRESS.

Those who like exercise on a tricycle will be glad to hear of a new costume especially designed for this purpose. It is made of tweed or cloth, the model is of a grayish brown check, a very serviceable color as not showing dust, the plain skirt full at the back and plaited in front. The novelty of the costume lies in the fact that the foundation on which it is made can be let down longer when the wearer is on the machine and shortened again for walking, this being accomplished by a simple arrangement of buttons and cord; thus, when cycling, the skirt is let down and covers the feet, when on the ground raised again to walking length. The bodice is cut as an ordinary Norfolk jacket, with a belt securing the plaits, and is lined with sanitary cloth.—*London Telegraph*.

FINED FOR SIDEWALK RIDING.

Salem, Aug. 12, 1889.—The case of Dr. W. W. Eaton, of Danvers, for riding a tricycle on the sidewalk in violation of a town by-law, was called in the District Court this morning. This was brought as a test case as to the validity of the by-law. Dr. Eaton admitted riding on the sidewalk to visit a patient, but he did not think that the law was in force, although he afterward learned that it had been passed. He thought he had a right to use the sidewalk as long as he did not interfere with any one else. The Court held that the laws were made to protect pedestrians, for whom the sidewalks were built, and it was only necessary to show that the town had passed a by-law and that the Superior Court had approved it, and he therefore fined the defendant $1 and costs. Case appealed.

A road race was held at Providence on Thursday.

The K. C. W. will hold a club handicap road race on either Labor or Election Day. The race will be run at Irvington-Milburn.

The North Adams, Mass., Wheelmen, at their annual meeting, chose the following officers: President, Harry G. Pierce; Vice-President, Walter S. Evans, Secretary; John B. French, Treasurer, F. H. McKee; Captain, George E. Patton; First Lieutenant, Eugene Smith; Second Lieutenant, John Jones; bugler, R. W. McLaren.

Races will be held at Montreal to-morrow.

GOOD BICYCLE REPAIRER can find steady work at H. W. Higham's, 905 G Street, N. W., Washington, D.C.

WANTED—Wheelmen to send 30 cents and receive by return mail one pair Black Cotton Ribbed Bicycle Hose. Cool and nobby for summer wear. Welch & Rogers, Hunbridge, N. Y.

FOR SALE—Two Experts; $6-inch, $70; 54-inch, $75; Springfield National, $65; all in fine condition. Brown & Greenleaf, Cambridge, Mass.

FOR SALE—A Springfield Roadster in A1 condition; ball bearings; has been used very little. Address John C. Robbins, Oneida Square, Utica, N. Y.

Second-hand Machines, many like new, prices reasonable. Machines to rent. Repairing and nickeling. Note our change of address. NEW YORK BICYCLE CO., No. 4 East 60th Street, Fifth Avenue entrance to Central Park.

THE CYCLING EVENT OF THE YEAR.

Hartford Wheel Club Tournament,

CHARTER OAK PARK,

September 2 and 3, 1889.

GOOD TRACK.

FAST TIME.

EXCITING RACES.

COSTLY PRIZES.

Special Engagement of the Distinguished Fancy Rider,

D. J. CANARY.

Entries close August 26. Entry Blanks mailed on application.

W. M. FRANCIS, Sec'y,
Box 745, Hartford, Conn.

NOTICE.

NO CHEAP TALK BUT PLAIN FACTS.

SECOND ANNUAL
Race Meet

OF THE

BINGHAMTON WHEEL CLUB,

AT

BINGHAMTON, N. Y.

September 10 and 11, '89

TWELVE EVENTS EACH DAY,

INCLUDING

The One-mile Tandem Safety, National L. A. W Championship, the first day.

One-mile New York State L. A. W. Championship, on the last day.

Entries for handicaps and class races close September 2; all others September 6.

ENTRANCE FEE (for each event), 50 CENTS.

Address,

E. H. TOWLE,

Chairman Race Committee.

Two-Mile L. A. W. State Championship

WILL BE RUN AT

THIRD OUT-DOOR TOURNAMENT

OF THE

ALBANY WHEELMEN,

TO BE HELD AT

RIDGEFIELD ATHLETIC CLUB'S GROUND,

SATURDAY, AUGUST 31st, 1889.

1. One-mile Novice.
2. " Ordinary (open).
3. " Star (club).
4. Two-mile L. A. W. State Champ'nship
5. One-mile Team-race (open).
6. One-third-mile Safety (open).
7. One-mile Club Championship.
8. " Tandem (open).
9. Two-mile Handicap (open).
10. One-third-mile Consolation.

ELEGANT GOLD MEDALS AND COSTLY PRIZES.

Entrance fees, 50c. each to open events; State Championship, $1.

Entries close on Saturday, August 24, 1889. Address to

WM. B. PHIPPS, Sec. Com.,
51 Howard Street, Albany, N. Y.

[VOL. III., No. 26.

ONE OUT OF MANY GOOD POINTS.

Of the many good points in the Columbia Light Roadster Safety there is none receiving more recognition than the SPRING FORK, which contains just enough spring, and not too much, to make it in every respect fill the purpose it was intended for.

The Spring Fork is the only spring fork that can be ridden satisfactorily on rough roads; a strong statement to make, but a true one.

As a result, the Columbia Light Roadster Safety is the best machine for long distance touring, as proven by the many tourists who are using it in this and other countries.

The Spring Fork can be used as a continuous fork, if desired.

The steering is perfectly rigid.

The machine can be ridden without hands. It was ridden by Mr. William Van Wagoner, of Newport, at Providence, on July 16th, Mr. Van Wagoner having his hands tied behind him, and making the full mile in 2.48.

A better coaster has never been put upon the market.

The action of the springs does not change the wheel base nor does it affect the true steering, a point which adds 25 per cent. to the value and life of the machine.

POPE MFG. CO.,

BOSTON.   NEW YORK.   CHICAGO.

PRESS OF F. V. STRAUSS, 120-126 WALKER ST., NEW YORK.